T0235901

# Lecture Notes in Computer Science 11781

More information about this series at http://www.springer.com/series/7408

Yu-Fang Chen · Chih-Hong Cheng ·
Javier Esparza (Eds.)

# Automated Technology for Verification and Analysis

17th International Symposium, ATVA 2019
Taipei, Taiwan, October 28–31, 2019
Proceedings

*Editors*
Yu-Fang Chen
Institute of Information Science
Academia Sinica
Taipei, Taiwan

Chih-Hong Cheng
DENSO AUTOMOTIVE
Deutschland GmbH
Eching, Germany

Javier Esparza
Institute of Computer Science
TU München
Munich, Germany

ISSN 0302-9743 ISSN 1611-3349 (electronic)
Lecture Notes in Computer Science
ISBN 978-3-030-31783-6 ISBN 978-3-030-31784-3 (eBook)
https://doi.org/10.1007/978-3-030-31784-3

LNCS Sublibrary: SL2 – Programming and Software Engineering



This Springer imprint is published by the registered company Springer Nature Switzerland AG
The registered company address is: Gewerbestrasse 11, 6330 Cham, Switzerland

# Preface

This volume contains the papers presented at the 17th International Symposium on Automated Technology for Verification and Analysis (ATVA 2019), which was held October 28–31, 2019, in Taipei, Taiwan. The conference is dedicated to the promotion of research on theoretical and practical aspects of automated analysis, verification, and synthesis by providing a forum for interaction between local and international research communities and industry in the field.

ATVA 2019 received 65 high-quality paper submissions, each of which received three reviews on average. After careful review, the Program Committee accepted 24 regular papers and three tool papers. The evaluation and selection process involved thorough discussions among members of the Program Committee through the EasyChair conference management system, before reaching a consensus on the final decisions.

To complement the contributed papers, we included in the program four keynote talks and three tutorials given by Armin Biere (JKU, Austria), Patricia Bouyer-Decitre (LSV, France), Rupak Majumdar (MPI-SWS, Germany), and Joseph Sifakis (Verimag, France), resulting in an exceptionally strong technical program.

We wish to thank all the authors who submitted papers for consideration, the members of the Program Committee for their conscientious work, and all additional reviewers who assisted the Program Committee in the evaluation process. Finally, we thank the Ministry of Science and Technology (Taiwan), fortiss research institute (Germany), Academia Sinica (Taiwan), and Springer for sponsoring ATVA 2019.

August 2019

Yu-Fang Chen
Chih-Hong Cheng
Javier Esparza

# Organization

## Steering Committee

| | |
|---|---|
| E. Allen Emerson | University of Texas, Austin, USA |
| Teruo Higashino | Osaka University, Japan |
| Oscar H. Ibarra | University of California, Santa Barbara, USA |
| Insup Lee | University of Pennsylvania, USA |
| Doron A. Peled | Bar Ilan University, Israel |
| Farn Wang | National Taiwan University, Taiwan |
| Hsu-Chun Yen | National Taiwan University, Taiwan |

## Program Committee

| | |
|---|---|
| Erika Abraham | RWTH Aachen University, Germany |
| Mohamed Faouzi Atig | Uppsala University, Sweden |
| Christel Baier | TU Dresden, Germany |
| Saddek Bensalem | VERIMAG, France |
| Udi Boker | Interdisciplinary Center (IDC) Herzliya, Israel |
| Luca Bortolussi | University of Trieste, Italy |
| Franck Cassez | Macquarie University, Australia |
| Krishnendu Chatterjee | Institute of Science and Technology (IST), Austria |
| Yu-Fang Chen | Academia Sinica, Taiwan |
| Chih-Hong Cheng | DENSO AUTOMOTIVE Deutschland GmbH, Germany |
| Alessandro Cimatti | FBK-irst, Italy |
| Loris D'Antoni | University of Wisconsin-Madison, USA |
| Alexandre Duret-Lutz | LRDE/EPITA, France |
| Javier Esparza | Technical University of Munich, Germany |
| Bernd Finkbeiner | Saarland University, Germany |
| Pierre Ganty | IMDEA Software Institute, Spain |
| Keijo Heljanko | University of Helsinki, Finland |
| Stefan Katzenbeisser | University of Passau, Germany |
| Siau-Cheng Khoo | National University of Singapore, Singapore |
| Orna Kupferman | Hebrew University, Israel |
| Ondřej Lengál | Brno University of Technology, Czech Republic |
| Anthony Widjaja Lin | TU Kaiserslautern, Germany |
| Shang-Wei Lin | Nanyang Technological University, Singapore |
| Hakjoo Oh | Korea University, Korea |
| Doron Peled | Bar Ilan University, Israel |
| Pavithra Prabhakar | Kansas State University, USA |
| Indranil Saha | Indian Institute of Technology Kanpur, India |
| Sven Schewe | University of Liverpool, UK |

| | |
|---|---|
| Jun Sun | Singapore Management University, Singapore |
| Michael Tautschnig | Queen Mary University of London, UK |
| Tachio Terauchi | Waseda University, Japan |
| Ashish Tiwari | Microsoft, USA |
| Bow-Yaw Wang | Academia Sinica, Taiwan |
| Chao Wang | University of Southern California, USA |
| Farn Wang | National Taiwan University, Taiwan |
| Zhilin Wu | Institute of Software, Chinese Academy of Sciences, China |
| Lijun Zhang | Institute of Software, Chinese Academy of Sciences, China |

## Additional Reviewers

Abdulla, Parosh Aziz
André, Étienne
Bozzano, Marco
Ceska, Milan
Chen, Hongxu
Coenen, Norine
Costea, Andreea
Cyphert, John
Ferrere, Thomas
Freydenberger, Dominik D.
Frtunikj, Jelena
Funke, Florian
Gainer, Paul
Gavrilenko, Natalia
Genaim, Samir
Giacobbe, Mirco
Gopalakrishnan, Ganesh
Griggio, Alberto
Hague, Matthew
Hahn, Christopher
Hahn, Ernst Moritz
Hark, Marcel
Hashemi, Vahid
Havlena, Vojtěch
Hecking-Harbusch, Jesko
Hofmann, Jana
Jaffar, Joxan
Jansen, David N.
Jiang, Lingxiao
Kragl, Bernhard
Kretinski, Jan
Lal, Ratan
Laurenti, Luca
Li, Yuekang
Liu, Depeng
Magnagno, Enrico
Malik, Kaushik
Moerman, Joshua
Nenzi, Laura
Nouri, Ayoub
Parys, Paweł
Pommellet, Adrien
Poskitt, Chris
Rabe, Markus N.
Renault, Etienne
Reynolds, Andrew
Roveri, Marco
Sagonas, Kostis
Schumi, Richard
Silvetti, Simone
Sun, Xuechao
Ta, Quang Trung
Taghian Dinani, Soudabeh
Tentrup, Leander
Tian, Chun
Toman, Viktor
Totzke, Patrick
Vandin, Andrea
Weipeng, Cao
Zhou, Yuan
Zimmermann, Martin

# Contents

## Testing



## Program Analysis



## Automata

## Synthesis



## Stochastic Systems



## Model Checking

# Invited Papers

# A Note on Game Theory and Verification

Patricia Bouyer(✉)

LSV, CNRS, ENS Paris-Saclay, Université Paris-Saclay, Cachan, France
bouyer@lsv.fr

**Abstract.** We present some basics of game theory, focusing on matrix games. We then present the model of multiplayer stochastic concurrent games (with an underlying graph), which extends standard finite-state models used in verification in a multiplayer and concurrent setting; we explain why the basic theory cannot apply to that general model. We then focus on a very simple setting, and explain and give intuitions for the computation of Nash equilibria. We then give a number of undecidability results, giving limits to the approach. Finally we describe the suspect game construction, which (we believe) captures and explains well Nash equilibria and allow to compute them in many cases.

## 1 Introduction

Multiplayer concurrent games over graphs allow to model rich interactions between players. Those games are played as follows. In a state, each player chooses privately and independently an action, defining globally a move (one action per player); the next state of the game is then defined as the successor (on the graph) of the current state using that move; players continue playing from that new state, and form a(n infinite) play. Each player then gets a reward given by a payoff function (one function per player). In particular, objectives of the players may not be contradictory: those games are non-zero-sum games, contrary to two-player games used for controller or reactive synthesis [23,30].

Using solution concepts borrowed from game theory, one can describe the interactions between the players, and in particular describe their rational behaviours. One of the most basic solution concepts is that of Nash equilibria [26]. A Nash equilibrium is a strategy profile where no player can improve her payoff by unilaterally changing her strategy. The outcome of a Nash equilibrium can therefore be seen as a rational behaviour of the system. While very much studied by game theoretists (e.g. over matrix games), such a concept (and variants thereof) has been only rather recently studied over games on graphs. Probably the first works in that direction are [15,16,31,32].

Computing Nash equilibria requires to (i) find a good behaviour of the system; (ii) detect deviations from that behaviour, and identify deviating players (called deviators); (iii) punish them. Variants of Nash equilibria (like subgame-perfect equilibria, robust equilibria, *etc*) require slightly different ingredients, but they are mostly of a similar vein.

Work supported by ERC project EQualIS between 2013 and 2019.


Y.-F. Chen et al. (Eds.): ATVA 2019, LNCS 11781, pp. 3–22, 2019.
https://doi.org/10.1007/978-3-030-31784-3_1

In this note, we first recall some basics of game theory over matrix games. Those games are not sufficient in a verification context: indeed, explicit states are very useful when modelling systems or programs, but are missing in matrix games. However stability notions like Nash equilibria or other solution concepts borrowed from game theory, are very relevant. We thus present the model of concurrent multiplayer games (played on graphs), which extends in a natural way standard models used in verification with multiplayer interactions. We explain how Nash equilibria can be characterized and computed in such general games. The ambition of this note is not to be a full survey of existing results, but rather to give simple explanations and intuitions; it gives formal tools to characterize and compute them and should help understanding simple interactions like Nash equilibria in rich games played on graphs.

Related notes are [30], which discussed the use of two-player zero-sum games in verification, and [21], which discussed solution concepts in multiplayer turn-based games on graphs.

*Notations.* If $\Sigma$ is a finite alphabet, then $\Sigma^+$ (resp. $\Sigma^\omega$) denotes the non-empty finite words (resp. infinite words) over $\Sigma$. If $\Gamma$ is a finite set, then we note $\mathcal{D}(\Gamma)$ the set of probability distributions over $\Gamma$. We write $\mathbb{R}$ for the set of real numbers.

## 2 Basics of Game Theory

In this section we present basic notions from game theory, which will be useful for our purpose. We refer the interested reader to the textbook [25].

A *matrix game* (aka *game in strategic form*) is a tuple $\mathcal{G} = (\mathcal{P}, \Sigma, (\mathsf{payoff}_A)_{A \in \mathcal{P}})$ where $\mathcal{P} = \{A_1, \ldots, A_k\}$ is a finite set of players, $\Sigma$ is a finite set of actions, and for every $A \in \mathcal{P}$, $\mathsf{payoff}_A \colon \Sigma^{\mathcal{P}} \to \mathbb{R}$ is a *payoff* (or *utility*) function for player $A$. In a deterministic setting, such a game is played as followed: independently and simultaneously, each player selects an action, resulting in a *move* (an element of $\Sigma^{\mathcal{P}}$), and each player gets the payoff specified in the game for that move. In a stochastic setting, each player selects a distribution over the actions, resulting in a distribution over the set of moves and an expected value for the payoff.

A *pure strategy* for player $A \in \mathcal{P}$ is the choice of an action $\sigma_A \in \Sigma$, while a *mixed strategy* for player $A$ is a distribution $\sigma_A \in \mathcal{D}(\Sigma)$ over the set of possible actions. Obviously, a pure strategy is a specific case of a mixed strategy where only Dirac probability distributions can be used. We let $\sigma = (\sigma_A)_{A \in \mathcal{P}}$ be a (pure or mixed) *strategy profile* (that is, for every $A \in \mathcal{P}$, $\sigma_A$ is (pure or mixed) strategy for player $A$). The probability of a move $m = (a_A)_{A \in \mathcal{P}} \in \Sigma^{\mathcal{P}}$ is written $\sigma(m)$ and defined by:

$$\sigma(m) = \prod_{A \in \mathcal{P}} \sigma_A(a_A)$$

Then, given a player $B \in \mathcal{P}$, the payoff of player $B$ is given by the expected value of $\mathsf{payoff}_B$ under $\sigma$, that is:

$$\mathbb{E}^\sigma(\mathsf{payoff}_B) = \sum_{m \in \Sigma^{\mathcal{P}}} \sigma(m) \cdot \mathsf{payoff}_B(m)$$

*Example 1 (The prisoner's dilemna).* Two individuals have committed a crime and are apprehended. The prosecution lacks sufficient evidence to convict the two individuals on the principal charge, but they have enough to convict both on a lesser charge. The prosecutors offer each prisoner a bargain: without any communication between them, the two individuals are offered the opportunity to Betray the other by testifying that the other committed the crime and get (partly) immunity, or to stay Silent. The payoff of both players is summarized in the table below, where the higher is the payoff the shorter is the jail penalty:

| $A_1$ \ $A_2$ | S | B |
|---|---|---|
| S | 2, 2 | 0, 3 |
| B | 3, 0 | 1, 1 |

In each cell of the table, the pair '$\alpha_1, \alpha_2$' represents payoff $\alpha_1$ (resp. $\alpha_2$) for player $A_1$ (resp. $A_2$). The table can then be read as follows: if bother players stay Silent (resp. Betray), then they both get payoff 2 (resp. 1). If only one prisoner Betrays, then he gets payoff 3 while the other prisoner gets payoff 0.

*Example 2.* We consider the following game (taken from [25, Example 4.34]) with two players, where payoffs are given in the next table:

| $A_1$ \ $A_2$ | L | R |
|---|---|---|
| T | 0, 0 | 2, 1 |
| B | 3, 2 | 1, 2 |

Note that in this game (and in several examples in the note), for more readability, we take w.l.o.g. different alphabets for the players.

*Example 3 (Matching penny game).* The game is a two-player game, where each player has two actions, a and b. This is a zero-sum game (that is, the sum of the two payoffs in each situation is 0): the first player wins (payoff +1) if the two chosen actions are matching, whereas the second player wins if the two actions are different. The payoffs are summarized below:

| $A_1$ \ $A_2$ | a | b |
|---|---|---|
| a | +1, −1 | −1, +1 |
| b | −1, +1 | +1, −1 |

The study of multiplayer games is to understand the rational behaviours of the players, assumed to be selfish. For instance, if for a player $A$, one of her strategy $\sigma_A$ dominates another strategy $\sigma'_A$ (in the sense that for all strategies of the other players, the payoff is larger using $\sigma_A$ than using $\sigma'_A$), then there is no situation where player $A$ should play $\sigma'_A$.

This is for instance the case in the prisoner's dilemna (Example 1), where action B dominates action S. Hence, the only rational issue in this example is that both players play action B, yielding a payoff of 1 for each. One realizes however that it would be much better for them to both play S, but the threat that the other betrays (plays action B) makes that solution unsafe.

In the game of Example 2, action R (weakly) dominates action L for player $A_2$ (in the sense, it is better than or equally good), hence playing R for player $A_2$ is safe; knowing that, player $A_1$ will play action T; hence, *a priori*, the only rational issue of this game should be the profile $(\mathtt{T}, \mathtt{R})$ with payoff $(2, 1)$. However, one also realizes that the profile $(\mathtt{B}, \mathtt{L})$ would be much better for both players, so only looking at dominating strategies might be too restrictive.

Finally, there might be no dominating strategies in a game, like in the matching penny game (Example 3), so other solution concepts have to be considered.

One of the most famous solution concepts for rationality is that of *Nash equilibrium* [26]. Let $\sigma$ be a strategy profile. If $A \in \mathcal{P}$ is a player, and $\sigma'_A$ is a strategy for $A$ (called a *deviation*), then $\sigma[A/\sigma'_A]$ is the strategy profile such that $A$ plays according to $\sigma'_A$ and each other player $B \in \mathcal{P} \setminus \{A\}$ plays according to $\sigma_B$. Later, we write $(\!|-A|\!)$ for the coalition of all the players except player $A$, that is, $(\!|-A|\!) = \mathcal{P} \setminus \{A\}$.

A *mixed (resp. pure) Nash equilibrium* in game $\mathcal{G}$ is a mixed (resp. pure) strategy profile $\sigma^\star = (\sigma^\star_A)_{A \in \mathcal{P}}$ such that for every $A \in \mathcal{P}$, for every player-$A$ mixed (resp. pure) strategy $\sigma_A$,

$$\mathbb{E}^{\sigma^\star[A/\sigma_A]}(\mathsf{payoff}_A) \leq \mathbb{E}^{\sigma^\star}(\mathsf{payoff}_A)$$

Note that even for mixed profiles, it is sufficient to look for pure deviations (if a mixed deviation improves the payoff, then so will do a pure deviation). Let $\sigma^\star$ be a strategy profile and $\sigma_A$ be a deviation for player $A$ such that $\mathbb{E}^{\sigma^\star[A/\sigma_A]}(\mathsf{payoff}_A) > \mathbb{E}^{\sigma^\star}(\mathsf{payoff}_A)$, then it is a *profitable* deviation for player $A$ w.r.t. $\sigma^\star$. If such a profitable deviation exists, then the profile is not a Nash equilibrium.

Coming back to the prisoner's dilemna (Example 1), the pair of pure dominating strategies $(\mathtt{B}, \mathtt{B})$ is a pure Nash equilibria, whereas the pair $(\mathtt{S}, \mathtt{S})$, which would yield a better payoff for both players, is *not* a Nash equilibrium.

In the matching penny game (Example 3), it is not difficult to check that none of the pure strategy profiles can be a Nash equilibrium since in each case, one of the players would benefit from switching to the other action. Also, one can argue that there is a unique Nash equilibrium, where each player plays each action uniformly at random, yielding an expected payoff of 0 for both.

Finally in Example 2, the two profiles $(\mathtt{T}, \mathtt{R})$ and $(\mathtt{B}, \mathtt{L})$ are the two Nash equilibria of the game. So there might be several Nash equilibria in a game, yielding possibly different payoffs.

A Nash equilibrium expresses a notion of stability. Indeed, it can be seen that a Nash equilibrium $\sigma = (\sigma_A)_{A \in \mathcal{P}}$ is such that each strategy $\sigma_A$ is the *best-response* to the strategies $(\sigma_B)_{B \in (\!|-A|\!)}$ of her adversaries. Formally, let $\mathbb{S}$ (resp. $\mathbb{S}_A$, $\mathbb{S}_{(\!|-A|\!)}$) be the set of mixed strategy profiles (resp. strategies for player $A$, strategies for coalition $(\!|-A|\!)$). For every $\sigma \in \mathbb{S}$, let

$$\mathsf{BR}(\sigma) = \left\{\sigma' \in \mathbb{S} \mid \forall A \in \mathcal{P},\ \sigma'_A \in \operatorname{argmax}_{\sigma''_A \in \mathbb{S}_A} \mathbb{E}^{\sigma[A/\sigma''_A]}(\mathsf{payoff}_A)\right\}$$

be the set of best-response strategy profiles for $\sigma$. Then, $\sigma$ is a Nash equilibrium if and only if $\sigma \in \mathsf{BR}(\sigma)$.

We state now the famous Nash theorem [26], which is one of the important milestones in the game theory domain.

**Theorem 1 (Nash theorem).** *Every matrix game has a (Nash) equilibrium in mixed strategies.*

The original proof of Nash uses Brouwer's fixed point theorem (see below). However it can also be seen that it is a consequence of Kakutani's fixed point theorem (see below), by taking BR as function $f$ (since the set mixed strategy profiles can be seen as a convex subset of $[0,1]^{|\mathcal{P}|\cdot|\Sigma|}$).

**Theorem 2 (Brouwer's fixed point theorem).** *Let $X \subseteq \mathbb{R}^n$ be a convex, compact and nonempty set. Then every continuous function $f\colon X \to X$ has a fixed point.*

**Theorem 3 (Kakutani's fixed point theorem).** *Let $X$ be a non-empty, compact and convex subset of $\mathbb{R}^n$. Let $f\colon X \to 2^X$ be a set-valued function on $X$ with a closed graph and the property that $f(x)$ is non-empty and convex for all $x \in X$. Then $f$ has a fixed point.*

As a final remark, let us define the *minmax value* of player $A \in \mathcal{P}$ as

$$\overline{v}_A = \min_{(\sigma_B)_{B \in (\!|-A|\!)} \in \mathbb{S}_{(\!|-A|\!)}} \ \max_{\sigma_A \in \mathbb{S}_A} \mathbb{E}^{\sigma}(\mathsf{payoff}_A)$$

where $\sigma = (\sigma_B)_{B \in \mathcal{P}}$. This is the best player $A$ can achieve, when she does not know how the other players will play. We will not discuss the minmax value, the maxmin value and the value of a game, but we notice that for every Nash equilibrium $\sigma \in \mathbb{M}_{\mathcal{P}}$, $\mathbb{E}^{\sigma}(\mathsf{payoff}_A) \geq \underline{v}_A$ (since otherwise the strategy giving the minmax value will be a profitable deviation).

*Conclusion.* Game theory is a very rich field of research, of which we have only given few hints on the basic concepts, which will be relevant for the use in verification. We refer again to the textbook [25] for an entry point to this research domain.

Matrix games represent a "one-shot" interaction between the players. In system or program verification, players may represent components or controllers; it is usually useful to allow models with states for such systems, and to consider temporal behaviour of such systems. Hence the interaction is the result of a dynamic process, and not of a one-shot interaction like in matrix games. This is not specific to verification, and towards that goal, more complex interactions have been studied under the names of extensive-form games (games are then played on a tree), or repeated games (a given matrix games is a large number of times). There are many elegant results on these systems, but this note is not sufficient for this purpose.

## 3 Multiplayer Games on Graphs in Verification

Matrix games and extensions like repeated games are not adapted to study interaction between players in a verification context. Indeed, to represent systems or programs, it is very useful to have models with explicit states. We will therefore first present the model of games on graphs that we will consider, and then argue why those games cannot be solved using the standard well-understood theory that we have recalled. We will then give some results and ideas for the computation of Nash equilibria in such games.

### 3.1 Definition of the General Model and of the Problems of Interest

We consider the model of concurrent multi-player games, based on the two-player model of [1], and extended with probabilities. The deterministic version of this model was used for instance in [4].

**Definition 1.** *A* multiplayer stochastic concurrent game *is a tuple*

$$\mathcal{G} = (V, v_{\mathsf{init}}, \mathcal{P}, \Sigma, \delta, (\mathsf{payoff}_A)_{A \in \mathcal{P}})$$

*where $V$ is a finite set of vertices, $v_{\mathsf{init}} \in V$ is the initial vertex, $\mathcal{P}$ is a finite set of players, $\Sigma$ is a finite set of actions, $\delta\colon V \times \Sigma^{\mathcal{P}} \to \mathsf{Dist}(V)$ associates, with a given vertex and a given action tuple (called* move*) a distribution over the possible target vertices, and for every $A \in \mathcal{P}$, $\mathsf{payoff}_A\colon V^\omega \to \mathbb{R}$ is a payoff function.*

We later write $v \xrightarrow{m} v'$ whenever $\delta(v,m)(v') > 0$.

As before, we assume an explicit order on $\mathcal{P} = \{A_1, \dots, A_k\}$. Also, given a player $A \in \mathcal{P}$, we write $(\!|-A|\!)$ for the coalition $\mathcal{P} \setminus \{A\}$. An element $m = (m_A)_{A \in \mathcal{P}} \in \Sigma^{\mathcal{P}}$ is called a move, and we may write it as $(m_{A_1}, \dots, m_{A_k})$. If $m \in \Sigma^{\mathcal{P}}$ and $A \in \mathcal{P}$, we write $m(A)$ for the $A$-component of $m$ and $m(\!|-A|\!)$ for all but the $A$ components of $m$. In particular, we write $m(-A) = m'(-A)$ whenever $m(B) = m'(B)$ for every $B \in (\!|-A|\!)$. Also, if $m \in \Sigma^{\mathcal{P}}$, $B \in \mathcal{P}$ and $a \in \Sigma$, then $m[B/a]$ denotes the move $m'$ such that $m'(-B) = m(-B)$ and $m(B) = a$.

A *history* $\pi$ in $\mathcal{G}$ is a finite non-empty sequence $v_0 v_1 \dots v_h \in V^+$ such that for every $1 \le i \le h$, there is $m_i \in \Sigma^{\mathcal{P}}$ with $v_{i-1} \xrightarrow{m_i} v_i$. We write *last*$(\pi)$ for the last vertex of $\pi$ (i.e., $v_h$). If $i \le h$, we also write $\pi_{\le i}$ for the prefix $v_0 v_1 \dots v_i$. We write $\mathsf{Hist}(v_0)$ for the set of histories in $\mathcal{G}$ that start at $v_0$. Notice that histories do not record moves used along a history.

We extend above notions to infinite sequences in a straightforward way and to the notion of play. We write $\mathsf{Plays}(v_0)$ for the set of full plays that start at $v_0$.

Let $A \in \mathcal{P}$ be a player. A *randomized (or mixed) strategy*[1] for player $A$ from $v_0$ is a mapping $\sigma_A \colon \mathsf{Hist}(v_0) \to \mathsf{Dist}(\Sigma)$. An *outcome* of $\sigma_A$ is a(n infinite) play $\rho = v_0 v_1 \ldots$ such that for every $i \geq 0$, writing $m_i(A) = \sigma_A(\rho_{\leq i})$, $v_i \xrightarrow{m_i} v_{i+1}$. We write $\mathsf{out}(\sigma_A, v_0)$ for the set of outcomes of $\sigma_A$ from $v_0$. A *pure (or deterministic) strategy* for player $A$ is a mixed strategy $\sigma_A$ such that for every history $h$, $\sigma_A(h)$ is a Dirac probability measure (that is, it associates to some vertex $v$ a probability 1, and to other vertices a probability 0).

A *mixed (resp. pure) strategy profile* is a tuple $\sigma = (\sigma_A)_{A\in\mathcal{P}}$, where, for every player $A \in \mathcal{P}$, $\sigma_A$ is a mixed (resp. pure) strategy for player $A$. We write $\mathsf{out}(\sigma, v_0)$ for the set of plays from $v_0$, which are outcomes of all strategies part of $\sigma$. Note that if $\sigma$ is pure, then $\mathsf{out}(\sigma, v_0)$ has a single element, hence we may abusively speak of the outcome $\mathsf{out}(\sigma, v_0)$.

Note that strategies, as defined above, can only observe the sequence of visited states along the history, but they may not depend on the exact distributions chosen by the players along the history, nor on the actual sequence of actions played by the players. Notice that this model is more general than the model where actions are visible, which are sometimes considered in the literature—see for instance [32] and [3, Section 6] or [14] for discussions—and the results presented here are valid (though actually simpler) when considering visible actions.

When $\sigma$ is a strategy profile and $\sigma'_A$ a player-$A$ strategy, we write $\sigma[A/\sigma'_A]$ for the strategy profile where $A$ plays according to $\sigma'_A$, and each other player $B$ plays according to $\sigma_B$. The strategy $\sigma'_A$ is a *deviation* of player $A$, or an *A-deviation.*

Once a strategy profile $\sigma = (\sigma_A)_{A\in\mathcal{P}}$ is fixed, for every $v_0 \in V$ it standardly induces a probability measure $\mathbb{P}^{\sigma}_{v_0}$ over the set of plays from $v_0$ in the game $\mathcal{G}$, by defining probability of cylinders as described below, and by extending it in a unique way to the generated $\sigma$-algebra. For every history $\pi = v_0 v_1 \ldots v_h \in \mathsf{Hist}(v_0)$, we let $\mathit{Cyl}(\pi) = \{\rho \in \mathsf{Plays}(v_0) \mid \pi \text{ is a prefix of } \rho\}$ and we define $\mathbb{P}^{\sigma}_{v_0}\Big(\mathit{Cyl}(v_0)\Big) = 1$, and then inductively

$$\mathbb{P}^{\sigma}_{v_0}\Big(\mathit{Cyl}(\pi v_{h+1})\Big) = \mathbb{P}^{\sigma}_{v_0}\Big(\mathit{Cyl}(\pi)\Big) \cdot \left( \sum_{\substack{m \in \Sigma^{\mathcal{P}} \\ v_h \xrightarrow{m} v_{h+1}}} \sigma(\pi)(m) \cdot \delta(v_h, m)(v_{h+1}) \right)$$

where $\sigma(\pi)(m) = \prod_{A\in\mathcal{P}} \sigma_A(\pi)(m_A)$ is the probability that move $m$ is selected by strategy profile $\sigma$.

[1] This is the terminology used in the verification community, which might nevertheless be confusing with that used in the game theory community.

Let $f$ be a measurable function in the $\sigma$-algebra generated by the cylinders above. Then we define its expected value w.r.t. $\mathbb{P}^{\sigma}_{v_0}$ in a standard way, and denote it $\mathbb{E}^{\sigma}_{v_0}(f)$. We will therefore assume that payoff functions $\mathsf{payoff}_A$ ($A \in \mathcal{P}$) are all measurable!

The notion of Nash equilibrium that we have defined on matrix games extends naturally to games over graphs.

**Definition 2.** *A* Nash equilibrium *from* $v_{\mathsf{init}}$ *is a strategy profile* $\sigma^\star$ *such that for every* $A \in \mathcal{P}$*, for every player-A deviation* $\sigma_A$*,*

$$\mathbb{E}^{\sigma^\star[A/\sigma_A]}_{v_{\mathsf{init}}}(\mathsf{payoff}_A) \leq \mathbb{E}^{\sigma^\star}_{v_{\mathsf{init}}}(\mathsf{payoff}_A)$$

Note that if $\sigma$ is a pure profile, then $\mathbb{E}^{\sigma}_{v_{\mathsf{init}}}(\mathsf{payoff}_A) = \mathsf{payoff}_A(\mathsf{out}(\sigma, v_{\mathsf{init}}))$. Also in this case, $\mathsf{out}(\sigma, v_{\mathsf{init}})$ is called the *main outcome* of equilibrium defined by $\sigma$.

As in matrix games, given a profile $\sigma^\star$, a deviation $\sigma_A$ for player $A$ such that $\mathbb{E}^{\sigma^\star[A/\sigma_A]}_{v_{\mathsf{init}}}(\mathsf{payoff}_A) > \mathbb{E}^{\sigma^\star}_{v_{\mathsf{init}}}(\mathsf{payoff}_A)$ is called a *profitable* deviation for player $A$.

*Payoff Functions.* A property $\phi$ over $V^\omega$ is said *prefix-independent* whenever for every $\rho$, $\rho \models \phi$ if and only if for every suffix $\rho'$ of $\rho$, $\rho' \models \phi$.

We say that a payoff function $\mathsf{payoff}\colon V^\omega \to \mathbb{R}$ is given by a Boolean property $\phi$ over $V^\omega$ whenever $\mathsf{payoff}(\rho) = 1$ if $\rho \models \phi$, and $\mathsf{payoff}(\rho) = 0$ if $\rho \not\models \phi$. Usually, $\phi$ will be some specific types of properties, like reachability, safety. We then abusively say payoff is a reachability (resp. safety, ...) objective. In a stochastic game, the expected value of such a payoff function is the probability to satisfy the property $\phi$.

A payoff function payoff over $V^\omega$ is said *terminal-reward* if there is some designed subset $\widetilde{V} \subseteq V$ such that all vertices of $\widetilde{V}$ are sinks in the graph of the game, and a function $w\colon \widetilde{V} \to \mathbb{R}$ such that for every $\rho \in V^\omega$, $\mathsf{payoff}(\rho) = w(\widetilde{v})$ if $\rho$ visits vertex $\widetilde{v} \in \widetilde{V}$ (which is unique if it exists since it is a sink), and $\mathsf{payoff}(\rho) = 0$ otherwise. A particular case is when the image of $w$ is included in $\{0, 1\}$, in which case we speak of *terminal-reachability*.

*Subclasses of Games.* We use the following subclasses of games. Game $\mathcal{G}$ is said:

- *turn-based* whenever there is a function $J\colon V \to \mathcal{P}$ such that for every $v \in V$, for every $m, m' \in \Sigma^{\mathcal{P}}$, $m(J(v)) = m'(J(v))$ implies $\delta(v, m) = \delta(v, m')$;
- *deterministic* whenever for every $v \in V$ and $m \in \Sigma^{\mathcal{P}}$, $\delta(v, m)$ is a Dirac probability measure on some vertex.

*The existence and the constrained existence problems.* For verification purposes, even if the existence of a Nash equilibrium might be interesting (due to the link with a stability property), we will also be interested in the constrained existence problem, and in the computability of Nash equilibria when they exist.

The *constrained existence problem* asks, given a stochastic multiplayer concurrent game $\mathcal{G} = (V, v_{\mathsf{init}}, \mathcal{P}, \Sigma, \delta, (\mathsf{payoff}_A)_{A\in\mathcal{P}})$ and a predicate $P$ over $\mathbb{R}^{|\mathcal{P}|}$, whether there exists a Nash equilibrium $\sigma$ such that $\left(\mathbb{E}^{\sigma}_{v_0}(\mathsf{payoff}_A)\right)_{A\in\mathcal{P}} \in P$.

Of course, for computability matters, predicates should not be too complicated, but one might think of lower bounds on the expected payoffs, or constraints on the social welfare (that is, the sum of the payoffs of all the players), *etc.* The *existence problem* is just the same problem when the predicate is $\mathbb{R}^{\mathcal{P}}$.

We add "pure" to the name of the problem if we restrict to pure strategy profiles.

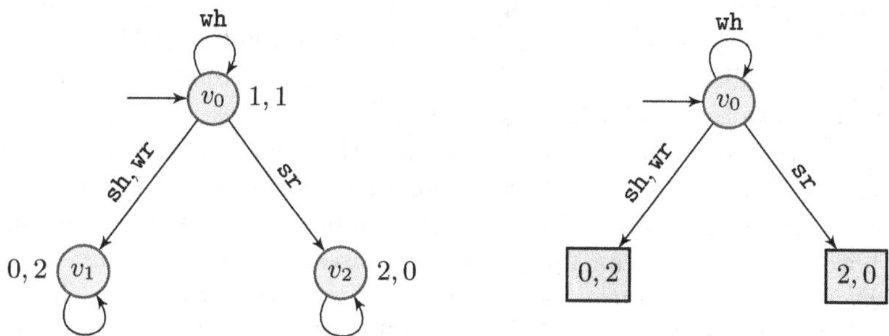


**Fig. 1.** Hide-or-run game, on the left; and one of its variants, on the right (black squared states indicate payoffs of the two players if the game ends there).

*Example 4 (Hide-or-run game).* We consider the hide-or-run game represented on Fig. 1 (left). There are three vertices and two players $A_1$ and $A_2$. The actions for player $A_1$ are `shoot` (the snowball) and `wait` while the actions for player $A_2$ are `hide` and `run`. Strings `sh`, `wr`, `wh` and `sr` represent all possible moves in the game. In vertex $v_0$, if player $A_1$ plays action `s` and player $A_2$ plays action `h`, then the game proceeds to vertex $v_1$. Actions from $v_1$ and $v_2$ are irrelevant hence omitted in the figure. Pairs of numbers close to each vertex represents a weight for each player. The payoff function for each player will be the mean-payoff along the play of all encountered weights.

In this game, player $A_1$ wants to hit player $A_2$ with a (single) snowball. Player $A_1$ can therefore either `shoot` the ball or `wait`, while Player $A_2$ can `hide` (in which case she is not hit by the snowball) or `run` (in which case she is hit by the snowball if it is shot at the same time. Payoffs are assigned according to the satisfaction of the two players (payoff 2 when the player is satisfied and 0 otherwise). Note that the pair `wh` forever is only half-satisfactory for both players, hence a payoff of $(1, 1)$.

One realizes that there is no Nash equilibrium in the hide-or-run game: indeed, if the probability of playing `wh` forever from $v_0$ (resp. of playing `sr` from $v_0$) is positive, then player $A_2$ can deviate and get a better payoff; conversely, if the probability of playing `wr` (resp. `sh`) from $v_0$ is positive, then player $A_1$ can deviate and get a better payoff.

The game of Fig. 1 (on the right) is a slight modification of the previous game, with a terminal-reachability payoff: if the game ends up in the bottom-left vertex (formerly $v_1$), then the payoff is $(0, 2)$, while it is $(2, 0)$ if the game ends up in the bottom-right vertex of the game (formerly $v_2$). It is very similar to the first game, the only difference is that playing wh forever yields a payoff of $(0, 0)$ instead of $(1, 1)$ previously. This slight modification yields a pure Nash equilibrium in the game, which is to play sh from $v_0$.

## 3.2 Why Does the Standard Theory Not Apply?

While matrix games are obviously special cases of our general model, one may nevertheless wonder why the standard theorems would not apply in this general model. We first realize that Nash theorem (stated as Theorem 1) does not apply: there are indeed potentially infinitely many pure strategies.

As we mentioned earlier, the proof of Nash theorem can be seen as a direct application of Kakutani's fixed point theorem (recalled as Theorem 3), which is in a much more general setting than its application to Nash theorem. We explain how this theorem can apply in some cases, but why it does not apply in our precise setting. A *stationary* strategy $\sigma$ is a mixed strategy such that for every $h, h' \in \mathsf{Hist}(v_0)$, $last(h) = last(h')$ implies $\sigma(h) = \sigma(h')$. Such a strategy can therefore be viewed as an element $\mathbb{R}^N$ for some integer $N$ (one value for each triple $(v, a, A_i) \in V \times \Sigma \times \mathcal{P}$). The subspace $X$ of $\mathbb{R}^N$ of stationary strategies satisfies the hypotheses of the theorem. As we have already discussed in matrix games, a Nash equilibrium $\sigma$ is such that each of its components is a best response to the other strategies. When restricted to stationary strategies, the *best-response function* can be defined as (we keep the same notations $\mathbb{S}$ and $\mathbb{S}_A$):

$$\mathsf{BR}(\sigma) = \left\{\sigma' \in \mathbb{S} \mid \forall A \in \mathcal{P},\ \sigma'_A \in \operatorname{argmax}_{\sigma''_A \in \mathbb{S}_A} \mathbb{E}_{v_0}^{\sigma[A/\sigma''_A]}(\mathsf{payoff}_A)\right\}$$

Nevertheless, over game graphs, continuity of this best-response function is not ensured (hence the graph of BR is not closed). Let us consider for example game of Fig. 2 (borrowed from [6]). It is assumed to be turn-based (vertex $v_i$ belongs to player $A_i$): from $v_i$, player $A_i$ can easer continue or leave the game. A stationary strategy profile $\sigma$ can be stored as a pair $(\sigma_{A_1}(v_1)(\mathtt{l}), \sigma_{A_2}(v_2)(\mathtt{l})) \in [0, 1]^2$, where the first (resp. second) element is the probability that player $A_1$ (resp. $A_2$) leaves the game from $v_1$ (resp. $v_2$). If one player decides to leave the game with some positive probability, the other player has all incentive to purely continue the game, until eventually reaching the terminal state (with probability 1). Hence $\mathsf{BR}((x, y)) = \{(0, 0)\}$ for every $x, y > 0$. However, if one player purely continues the game, the only way to win some positive payoff $\frac{1}{3}$ is to leave the game with positive probability. Hence $\mathsf{BR}((0, 0)) = \{(x, y) \mid x, y > 0\}$. We conclude that the graph is not closed, so Theorem 3 cannot be applied to the classical BR function. We finally notice that any profile $(x, 0)$ with $x > 0$, or $(0, y)$ with $y > 0$, is a Nash equilibrium.

Though this theorem does not apply in our general context, it can be used in others, for instance for stay-in-a-set games [28], for Nash equilibria with discounted payoffs or $\epsilon$-Nash equilibria [16].

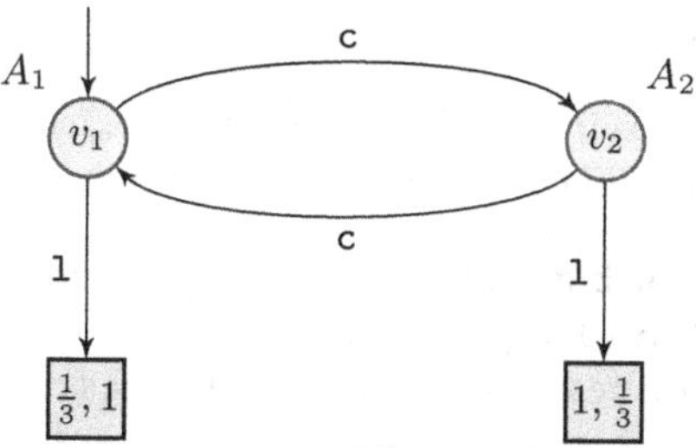


**Fig. 2.** Turn-based game with terminal rewards (black squared states indicate payoffs of the two players if the game ends there) showing the non-applicability of Kakutani's theorem; the first player who leaves the loop with some positive probability loses.

### 3.3 Discussion on a Simple Scenario

Let us focus on a simple scenario first. We fix for the rest of this subsection a game $\mathcal{G} = (V, v_{\mathsf{init}}, \mathcal{P}, \Sigma, \delta, (\mathsf{payoff}_A)_{A \in \mathcal{P}})$ which satisfies the following (restricting) assumptions:

- the game is turn-based and deterministic;
- for every $A \in \mathcal{P}$, the payoff function $\mathsf{payoff}_A$ is given by a Boolean prefix-independent objective $\phi_A$;

We note (†) the hypotheses of this simple scenario.

For every $A \in \mathcal{P}$, we let $\mathcal{G}[A]$ be the two-player zero-sum game built on the same arena as $\mathcal{G}$, where $A$ plays against coalition $(\!|-A|\!)$ (more precisely, all vertices which previously belang to some $B \in \mathcal{P} \setminus \{A\}$ now belongs to $(\!|-A|\!)$, and all vertices which previously belang to $A$ still belongs to $A$); the payoff function for $A$ is $\mathsf{payoff}_A$, while the payoff function for $(\!|-A|\!)$ is $-\mathsf{payoff}_A$ (here, in our simple setting, the objective of player $A$ is $\phi_A$ while the objective of $(\!|-A|\!)$ is $\neg\phi_A$). Let $W_{(\!|-A|\!)}$ (resp. $W_A$) be the set of winning states for coalition $(\!|-A|\!)$ (resp. player $A$) in this game. Since this game is turn-based and the objectives are prefix-independent, the game will be determined, that is, either $A$ has a winning strategy, or the coalition $(\!|-A|\!)$ has a winning strategy (that is, for every vertex $v \in V$, either $v \in W_A$ or $v \in W_{(\!|-A|\!)}$). Furthermore, for large classes of objectives, the set $W_{(\!|-A|\!)}$ (or $W_A$) can be computed. We report here to the whole literature on the subject, see [20] for an entry point.

One can then characterize pure Nash equilibria by the formula:

$$\Phi_{\mathsf{NE}} = \bigwedge_{A \in \mathcal{P}} \left( \neg\phi_A \Rightarrow \mathbf{G} W_{(\!|-A|\!)} \right)$$

borrowing notations from the syntax of LTL [27]: that is, $\Phi_{\mathsf{NE}}$ holds along a play $\rho$ whenever for every $A \in \mathcal{P}$, either $\phi_A$ holds along the outcome or $A$ cannot enforce winning anywhere along the play (or equivalently, $(\!|-A|\!)$ can enforce $\neg\phi_A$ in $\mathcal{G}[A]$). Note that the same formula can be used for reachability objectives but that a slightly different one has to be used for safety objectives.

One can show:

**Proposition 1.** *Assume setting (†). Let $\rho \in \mathsf{Plays}(v_{\mathsf{init}})$. Then, $\rho \models \Phi_{\mathsf{NE}}$ if and only if there is a Nash equilibrium $\sigma$ from $v_{\mathsf{init}}$ such that $\mathsf{out}(\sigma, v_{\mathsf{init}}) = \rho$.*

*Proof (Sketch).* Indeed, pick a play $\rho \in \mathsf{Plays}(v_{\mathsf{init}})$, and assume that $\rho \models \Phi_{\mathsf{NE}}$. Consider a player $A \in \mathcal{P}$. Such a player may have some interest in deviating only if her objective $\phi_A$ is not already satisfied by $\rho$. In that case, she has a profitable deviation after some prefix $\pi$ of $\rho$ if she is able to ensure winning after $\pi$. In particular, if no winning state of $A$ is visited along $\rho$, then $\rho$ can be completed into a Nash equilibrium as follows:

- all players play along $\rho$;
- as soon as a player deviates from $\rho$, then the coalition $(\!|-A|\!) = \mathcal{P} \setminus \{A\}$ starts playing a counter-strategy to $A$. Such a strategy is sometimes called a *threat* or a *trigger* strategy.

Conversely assume there is a Nash equilibrium $\sigma$ from $v_{\mathsf{init}}$ such that $\mathsf{out}(\sigma, v_{\mathsf{init}}) = \rho$. Pick a player $A \in \mathcal{P}$ such that $\rho \not\models \phi_A$. Then, since $\sigma$ is a Nash equilibrium, from every visited vertex $v$ along $\rho$, $A$ cannot enforce her objective $\phi_A$, which means that $v \notin W_A$, hence $v \in W_{(\!|-A|\!)}$. Hence $\rho \models \Phi_{\mathsf{NE}}$. □

The situation is illustrated on Fig. 3. Note that by determinacy, "Player $A_1$ should lose" can be replaced by "Coalition $\{A_2, A_3\}$ prevents $A_1$ from winning".

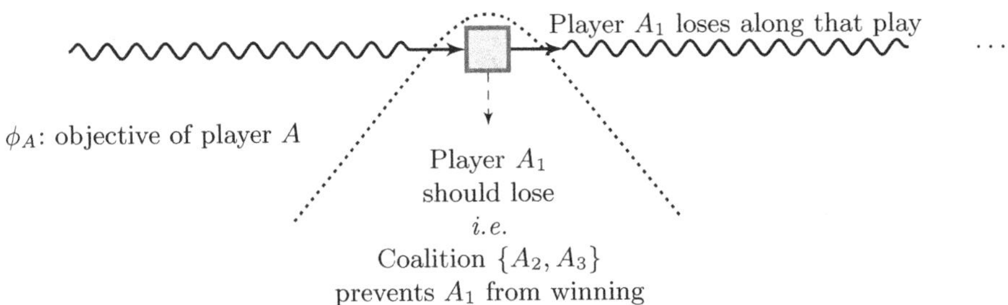
Player $A_1$ loses along that play
...
$\phi_A$: objective of player $A$
Player $A_1$
should lose
*i.e.*
Coalition $\{A_2, A_3\}$
prevents $A_1$ from winning

**Fig. 3.** General shape of a Nash equilibrium in the simple setting (example with three players).

In this simple setting we can also prove the following existence result:

**Proposition 2.** *Assume setting (†). There always exists a pure Nash equilibrium from $v_{\mathsf{init}}$.*

*Proof (Sketch).* In this simple setting, in two-player zero-sum games, there always exists strongly optimal strategies [19], that is, one strategy for each of the two players, say $\sigma$ and $\tau$, such that each of the two strategies is optimal (for the corresponding player) after any compatible prefix. For every $A \in \mathcal{P}$, we apply this result to each of the games $\mathcal{G}[A]$ from $v_{\mathsf{init}}$, and write $\sigma_A$ for the corresponding strongly optimal strategy for player $A$ in $\mathcal{G}[A]$.

We argue why the main outcome $\rho$ of $\sigma = (\sigma_A)_{A \in \mathcal{P}}$ satisfies formula $\Phi_{\mathsf{NE}}$. Assume that $\rho \not\models \phi_A$. Towards a contradiction assume that one of the visited vertices, say $v$ after prefix $\pi$, along $\rho$, does not belong to $W_{\langle\!\langle -A \rangle\!\rangle}$. By the strong determinacy result mentioned at the beginning of the proof, it implies that vertex $v$ belongs to $W_A$. Since $\sigma_A$ is strongly optimal, it is also optimal after prefix $\pi$: hence it is winning after prefix $\pi$. In particular, since $\phi_A$ is prefix-independent, $\rho$ should be winning as well. Contradiction: $\rho \models \Phi_{\mathsf{NE}}$. □

*Algorithmics Issues.* By combining the proof of Propositions 1 and 2, one can compute a pure Nash equilibrium from strongly optimal and trigger strategies.

Another solution consists in computing for every $A \in \mathcal{P}$ the set $W_{\langle\!\langle -A \rangle\!\rangle}$ (or equivalently $W_A$), and to compute an infinite path in the game which satisfies formula $\Phi_{\mathsf{NE}}$ (which can be done for instance by enumerating the possible set of losing players, and then finding an adequate ultimately periodic play). Obviously, for specific winning conditions, more efficient algorithms can be designed, but this is not the aim of this note. We report e.g. to [4, 33] for more algorithms.

### 3.4 Back to Stochastic Concurrent Games

By a non-trivial extension of the discussion of Subsect. 3.3 (see [35, Section 3] for details), one can show the following existence result:

**Theorem 4.** *There exists a pure Nash equilibrium in any multiplayer stochastic turn-based game with prefix-independent winning objectives (which we can compute). This also holds in the same setting for any $\omega$-regular objectives. [35, Section 3]*

This result in particular applies to mean-payoff objectives, which are prefix-independent.

Why are we not fully happy with such a result?

- one would like to go from turn-based to concurrent games;
- one would like more general payoff functions;
- one would like to solve the constrained existence problem.

It turns out that those extensions are very intricate, and that we can give a list of (related but incomparable) undecidability results.

**Theorem 5.** *The following problems are all undecidable:*

1. *the **constrained**[2] **existence problem** for stochastic multiplayer turn-based games with terminal-reachability objectives. This is true even if we restrict to **pure** strategy profiles* [35, Section 4].

[2] In the proof, we only impose that a player wins almost-surely.

2. *the* ***constrained existence*** *problem for* ***deterministic*** *multiplayer turn-based games with* ***terminal-reward payoffs*** [34, Section 7].
3. *the* ***constrained existence*** *problem for* ***deterministic three-player concurrent*** *games with* ***terminal-reachability payoffs***[3] [5].
4. *the* ***existence problem*** *for* ***deterministic three-player concurrent*** *games with* ***terminal-reward payoffs*** [5].
5. *the* ***constrained existence*** *problem for* ***deterministic three-player concurrent*** *games with* ***safety objectives***[4] [5].

### 3.5 The Suspect-Game Construction [4]

The setting we have chosen here assumes actions are invisible (since only visited vertices are visible along histories). Hence, a deviation from the main outcome can only be detected when the play goes out of the main outcome of the Nash equilibrium. However, even if a deviation occurs, there can be uncertainties for some of the players concerning the identity of the deviator.

Consider for instance the game in Fig. 4, with three players. Assume that the main outcome goes through $v_0 \xrightarrow{\mathsf{aaa}} v_1$.

- If the game proceeds to vertex $v_2$ instead of $v_1$, it means that either player $A_1$ deviated alone (playing $\mathsf{b}$ instead of $\mathsf{a}$), or both players $A_1$ and $A_2$ played $\mathsf{b}$ instead of $\mathsf{a}$; the second case cannot occur since Nash equilibria only care of single-player deviations; hence only player $A_1$ can be the deviator, and all players will therefore know the identity of the deviator.
- If the game proceeds to vertex $v_3$, then there are two possible suspects amongst the players: either $A_2$ or $A_3$ can be the deviator. In both cases, the two players $A_2$ and $A_3$ will know the identity of the deviator, while player $A_1$ will not know it.

This knowledge about the possible deviators is represented via a suspect function defined as follows:

- $\mathsf{susp}\big((v_0, v_2), \mathsf{aaa}\big) = \{A_1\}$
- $\mathsf{susp}\big((v_0, v_3), \mathsf{aaa}\big) = \{A_2, A_3\}$

with the meaning that, starting from $v_0$, if the game proceeds to $v_2$ (resp. $v_3$), then only $A_1$ (resp. $A_2$ and $A_3$) are suspect for the deviation.

More generally, we consider a game $\mathcal{G} = (V, v_{\mathsf{init}}, \mathcal{P}, \Sigma, \delta, (\mathsf{payoff}_A)_{A \in \mathcal{P}})$, and we define the function $\mathsf{susp}\colon V^2 \times \Sigma^{\mathcal{P}} \to 2^{\mathcal{P}}$ as follows:

$$\mathsf{susp}\big((v_0, v), m\big) = \{A \in \mathcal{P} \mid \exists b \in \Sigma \text{ s.t. } v_0 \xrightarrow{m[A/b]} v\}$$

[3] This holds even with a constraint on the social welfare. This result has therefore to be compared with the result of [18], which states that the existence problem is NP-complete in two-player games.

[4] This result has to be compared with the result of [28], which states that there always exists a Nash equilibrium in a safety game.

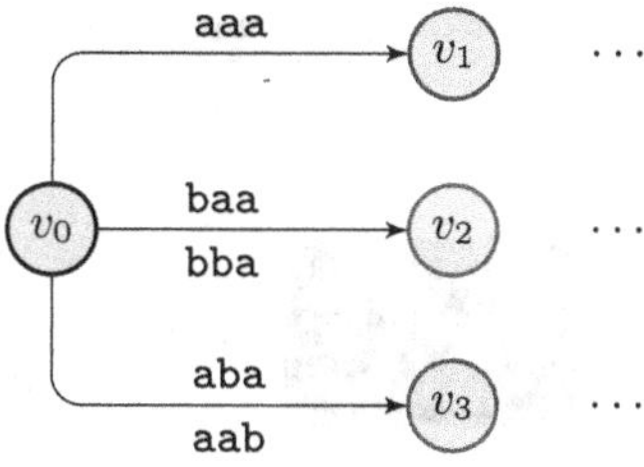


**Fig. 4.** Several suspect players.

Note that in the case no deviation occurred, that is if $v_0 \xrightarrow{m} v$, then the set of suspects is the set of all the players; this is because the set of suspect players becomes only relevant after a deviation has occurred.

The suspect game is now defined as the two-player[5] turn-based game $\mathcal{S}_\mathcal{G} = (S_{\mathsf{Eve}}, S_{\mathsf{Adam}}, s_{\mathsf{init}}, \Gamma, E, (\mathsf{payoff}'_A)_{A\in\mathcal{P}})$ where:

- $S_{\mathsf{Eve}} = V \times 2^{\mathcal{P}}$ is the set of states belonging to Eve;
- $S_{\mathsf{Adam}} = S_{\mathsf{Eve}} \times \Sigma^{\mathcal{P}}$ is the set of states belonging to Adam;
- $s_{\mathsf{init}} = (v_{\mathsf{init}}, \mathcal{P})$ is the initial state;
- $\Gamma = \Sigma^{\mathcal{P}} \cup V$ is the new alphabet;
- the set of edges is

$$E = \{(v, susp) \xrightarrow{m} ((v, susp), m) \mid v \in V,\ susp \subseteq \mathcal{P},\ m \in \Sigma^{\mathcal{P}}\} \cup$$
$$\{((v, susp), m) \xrightarrow{v'} (v', susp \cap \mathsf{susp}((v, v'), m)) \mid \exists A \in \mathcal{P}\ \exists b \in \Sigma \text{ s.t. } v \xrightarrow{m[A/b]} v'\};$$

- if $\rho = (v_0, susp_0)(v_0, susp_0, m_1)(v_1, susp_1)\ldots$, for every $A \in \mathcal{P}$, $\mathsf{payoff}'_A(\rho) = \mathsf{payoff}_A(v_0 v_1 \ldots)$.

Given a play $\rho = (v_0, susp_0)(v_0, susp_0, m_1)(v_1, susp_1)\ldots$, we define the set of suspect players for $\rho$ as $\mathsf{susp}(\rho) = \bigcap_{i\geq 0} susp_i$ (this limit is well-defined).

The winning condition for Eve is rather non-standard, since it is a condition on the set of outcomes of Eve, not on each outcome of the strategy individually. A strategy $\zeta$ for Eve in $\mathcal{S}_\mathcal{G}$ is winning for some $\alpha \in \mathbb{R}^{\mathcal{P}}$ if the unique outcome of $\zeta$ where Adam complies to Eve[6] has payoff $\alpha$, and for every other outcome $\rho$ of $\zeta$, for every $A \in \mathsf{susp}(\rho)$, $\mathsf{payoff}_A(\rho) \leq \alpha_A$.

*Example 5.* We consider again the small (part of) game depicted on Fig. 4 (all missing moves in the figure lead to $v_1$). The corresponding part of the suspect game is given in Fig. 5.

The role of Eve is to search for an equilibrium by suggesting moves to the players, and the role of Adam is to check whether there are possible profitable deviations. In particular, winning strategies of Eve in the suspect game will coincide with Nash equilibria in the original game:

---

[5] We call the two players Eve and Adam.

[6] That is, from $(v, susp, m)$, Adam chooses to go to $(v', susp)$ where $v \xrightarrow{m} v'$.

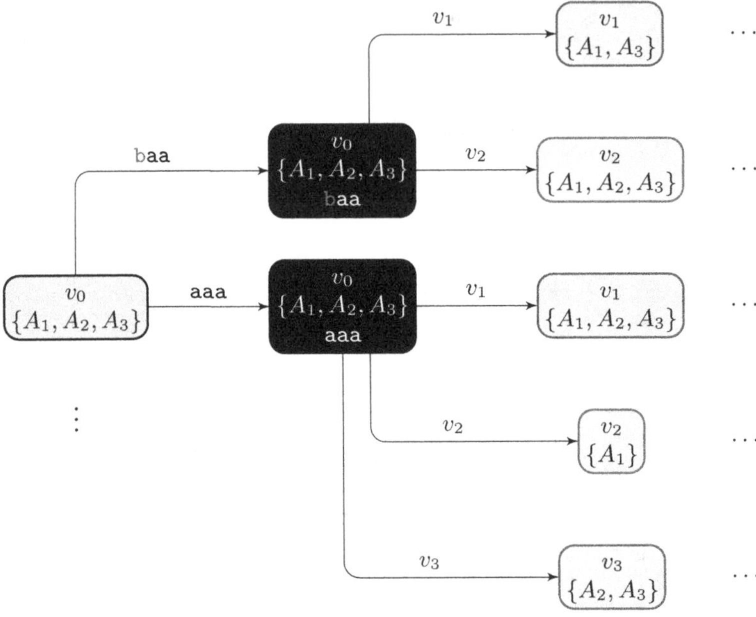


**Fig. 5.** Illustration of the suspect game construction (states in light colors are Eve's states while states in dark colors are Adam's states).

**Proposition 3 (Correctness).** *Let $\alpha \in \mathbb{R}^{\mathcal{P}}$. There is a Nash equilibrium in $\mathcal{G}$ with payoff $\alpha$ from $v_{\mathsf{init}}$ if and only if* Eve *has a winning strategy for $\alpha$ in $\mathcal{S}_{\mathcal{G}}$ from $s_{\mathsf{init}}$.*

*Remark 1.* Assume we start with a turn-based game. Then, since the arena of the game is known by the players, as soon as some deviation occurs, then all players will know which player is responsible for the deviation (since this is the player who controls the vertex at which the deviation occurred). In this case, the set of suspects will immediately be a singleton. The winning condition then ensures that, from a vertex controlled by player $A_i$, if a deviation occurs, then Eve plays an optimal strategy for the coalition $(\!|-A_i|\!) = \mathcal{P} \setminus \{A_i\}$. We somehow recover the intuitive explanation we gave in Subsect. 3.3.

Also, assume that actions are visible, then similarly, as soon as there is a deviation, the identity of the deviator is known by all the players.

*Algorithmics Issues.* Using the above construction, it is sufficient to solve the suspect game to compute Nash equilibria, since the equivalence of Proposition 3 is constructive. However, the winning condition is non-standard. In [4], many algorithms are designed for specific payoff functions. Complexities obviously depend on the (discrete) payoff functions which are used.

As an illustration, let us look at Fig. 6, where each player $A$ has a Boolean objective $\phi_A$. We assume players $A_1$ and $A_2$ are losing along a play. Then if this

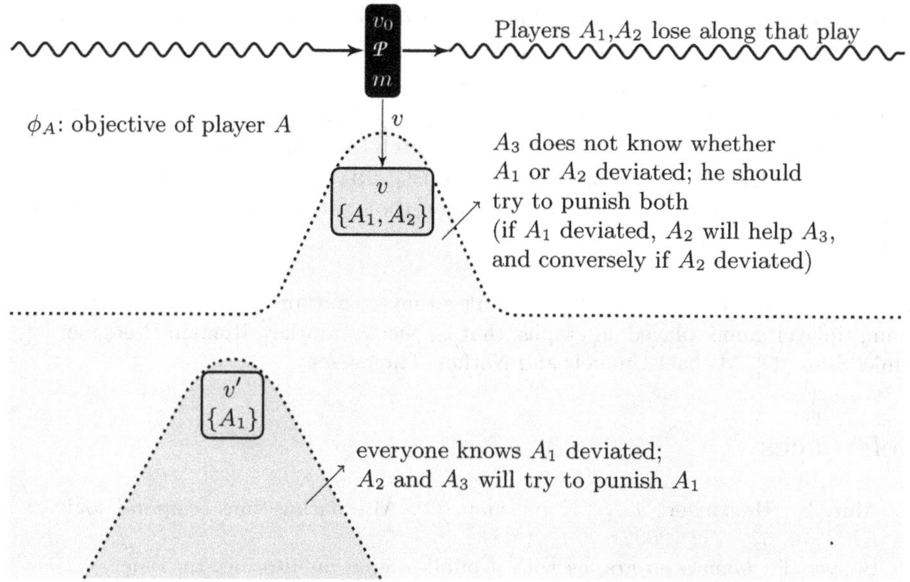


**Fig. 6.** Overview on the suspect-game construction.

play is the main outcome of a Nash equilibrium, it should be the case that from $v$, $A_3$ is able to punish both players (with the help of $A_1$ if $A_2$ is the deviator, and with the help of $A_2$ in case $A_1$ is the deviator); from $v'$, it is known by everyone that $A_1$ is the deviator, hence the coalition of both $A_2$ and $A_3$ should be able to punish $A_1$ from there. Algorithmically, it is therefore sufficient to compute states $(v, \{A_i\})$ which are winning for $\neg\phi_{A_i}$ for the coalition $(\!|-A_i|\!)$ (or equivalently Adam); and then (in a bottom-up manner) states $(v, \{A_i \mid i \in I\})$ which are winning for Adam for objective $\bigwedge_{i\in I} \big(A_i \text{ suspect at the limit} \Rightarrow \neg\phi_{A_i}\big)$.

In [34, Section 6], an algorithm for mean-payoff functions is designed (in a setting where actions are visible), which consists in computing values of the various two-player mean-payoff games ($A$ against $(\!|-A|\!)$) in each vertex, and then to find a lasso satisfying a given constraint on the payoff.

## 4 Discussion

In this note, we have presented some basics of game theory over matrix games, and discussed how concepts from game theory can be studied in the context of models used in verification. We have discussed in particular a general construction that can be made to compute Nash equilibria in games on graphs, and which gives some general understanding of how interaction between players can be understood. This construction has been refined in several respects (for other solution concepts [9,17], in some partial information contexts [2,7]), and might be useful in some more contexts.

Even though there are some known existence results (we have mentioned some of them in Subsect. 3.4), for simple payoff functions like terminal reachability payoffs. A related discussion can be found in [22].

In this note, we have not discussed temporal logics for multi-agent systems, even though this is a very rich domain of research (see [24] for some pointers). We have also not discussed domination and admissibility (see [10] among others), nor subgame-perfect equilibria, which have nevertheless been much studied (among others, see [11–13,33]).

**Acknowledgments.** I would like to thank all my co-authors since I started working on multiplayer games played on graphs, that is, Nicolas Markey, Romain Brenguier [8], Daniel Stan [29], Michael Ummels and Nathan Thomasset.

## References

1. Alur, R., Henzinger, T.A., Kupferman, O.: Alternating-time temporal logic. J. ACM **49**, 672–713 (2002)
2. Bouyer, P.: Games on graphs with a public signal monitoring. In: Baier, C., Dal Lago, U. (eds.) FoSSaCS 2018. LNCS, vol. 10803, pp. 530–547. Springer, Cham (2018). https://doi.org/10.1007/978-3-319-89366-2_29
3. Bouyer, P., Brenguier, R., Markey, N., Ummels, M.: Nash equilibria in concurrent games with Büchi objectives. In: Proceedings of the 30th Conference on Foundations of Software Technology and Theoretical Computer Science (FSTTCS 2011). LIPIcs, vol. 13, pp. 375–386. Leibniz-Zentrum für Informatik (2011)
4. Bouyer, P., Brenguier, R., Markey, N., Ummels, M.: Pure Nash equilibria in concurrent games. Logical Methods Comput. Sci. **11**(2), 9 (2015)
5. Bouyer, P., Markey, N., Stan, D.: Mixed Nash equilibria in concurrent games. In: Proceedings of the 33rd Conference on Foundations of Software Technology and Theoretical Computer Science (FSTTCS 2014). LIPIcs, vol. 29, pp. 351–363. Leibniz-Zentrum für Informatik (2014)
6. Bouyer, P., Markey, N., Stan, D.: Stochastic equilibria under imprecise deviations in terminal-reward concurrent games. In: Proceedings of the 7th International Symposium on Games, Automata, Logics and Formal Verification (GandALF 2016). Electronic Proceedings in Theoretical Computer Science, vol. 226, pp. 61–75 (2016)
7. Bouyer, P., Thomasset, N.: Nash equilibria in games over graphs equipped with a communication mechanism. In: Proceedings of the 44th International Symposium on Mathematical Foundations of Computer Science (MFCS 2019). LIPIcs, vol. 138. Leibniz-Zentrum für Informatik (2019, to appear)
8. Brenguier, R.: Nash equilibria in concurrent games - application to timed games. Ph.D. thesis, ENS Cachan, France (2012)
9. Brenguier, R.: Robust equilibria in mean-payoff games. In: Jacobs, B., Löding, C. (eds.) FoSSaCS 2016. LNCS, vol. 9634, pp. 217–233. Springer, Heidelberg (2016). https://doi.org/10.1007/978-3-662-49630-5_13
10. Brenguier, R., Pauly, A., Raskin, J.-F., Sankur, O.: Admissibility in games with imperfect information (invited talk). In: Proceedings of the 28th International Conference on Concurrency Theory (CONCUR 2017). LIPIcs, vol. 85, pp. 2:1–2:23. Leibniz-Zentrum für Informatik (2017)

11. Brihaye, T., Bruyère, V., Goeminne, A., Raskin, J.-F. Constrained existence problem for weak subgame perfect equilibria with $\omega$-regular boolean objectives. In: Proceedings of the 9th International Symposium on Games, Automata, Logics and Formal Verification (GandALF 2018). Electronic Proceedings in Theoretical Computer Science, vol. 277, pp. 16–29 (2018)
12. Brihaye, T., Bruyère, V., De Pril, J., Gimbert, H.: On subgame perfection in quantitative reachability games. Logical Methods Comput. Sci. **9**(1), 1–32 (2013)
13. Bruyère, V., Le Roux, S., Pauly, A., Raskin, J.-F.: On the existence of weak subgame perfect equilibria. In: Esparza, J., Murawski, A.S. (eds.) FoSSaCS 2017. LNCS, vol. 10203, pp. 145–161. Springer, Heidelberg (2017). https://doi.org/10.1007/978-3-662-54458-7_9
14. Chatterjee, K., Doyen, L.: Partial-observation stochastic games: how to win when belief fails. ACM Trans. Comput. Log. **15**(2), 16 (2014)
15. Chatterjee, K., Henzinger, T.A., Jurdziński, M.: Games with secure equilibria. Theor. Comput. Sci. **365**(1–2), 67–82 (2006)
16. Chatterjee, K., Majumdar, R., Jurdziński, M.: On Nash equilibria in stochastic games. In: Marcinkowski, J., Tarlecki, A. (eds.) CSL 2004. LNCS, vol. 3210, pp. 26–40. Springer, Heidelberg (2004). https://doi.org/10.1007/978-3-540-30124-0_6
17. Condurache, R., Oualhadj, Y., Troquard, N. The complexity of rational synthesis for concurrent games. In: Proceedings of the 29th International Conference on Concurrency Theory (CONCUR 2018), LIPIcs, pp. 38:1–38:15. Leibniz-Zentrum für Informatik (2018)
18. Conitzer, V., Sandholm, T.: New complexity results about Nash equilibria. Games Econ. Behav. **63**(2), 621–641 (2008)
19. Gimbert, H., Horn, F.: Solving simple stochastic tail games. In: Proceedings of the 21st Annual ACM-SIAM Symposium on Discrete Algorithms (SODA 2010), pp. 847–862. SIAM (2010)
20. Grädel, E., Thomas, W., Wilke, T. (eds.): Automata, Logics, and Infinite Games: A Guide to Current Research. LNCS, vol. 2500. Springer, Heidelberg (2002). https://doi.org/10.1007/3-540-36387-4
21. Grädel, E., Ummels, M.: Solution concepts and algorithms for infinite multiplayer games. In: New Perspectives on Games and Interaction. Texts in Logic and Games, vol. 4, pp. 151–178. Amsterdam University Press (2008)
22. Hansen, K.A., Raskin, M.: A stay-in-a-set game without a stationary equilibrium. In: Proceedings of the 10th International Symposium on Games, Automata, Logics and Formal Verification (GandALF 2019) (2019, to appear)
23. Henzinger, T.A.: Games in system design and verification. In: Proceedings of the 10th Conference on Theoretical Aspects of Rationality and Knowledge (TARK 2005), pp. 1–4 (2005)
24. Markey, N.: Temporal logics for multi-agent systems (invited talk). In: Proceedings of the 42nd International Symposium on Mathematical Foundations of Computer Science (MFCS 2017). LIPIcs, vol. 83, pp. 84:1–84:3. Leibniz-Zentrum für Informatik (2017)
25. Maschler, M., Solan, E., Zamir, S.: Game Theory. Cambridge University Press, Cambridge (2013)
26. Nash, J.F.: Equilibrium points in $n$-person games. Proc. Natl. Acad. Sci. U. S. A. **36**(1), 48–49 (1950)
27. Pnueli, A.: The temporal logic of programs. In: Proceedings of the 18th Annual Symposium on Foundations of Computer Science (FOCS 1977), pp. 46–57. IEEE Computer Society Press (1977)

28. Secchi, P., Sudderth, W.D.: Stay-in-a-set games. Int. J. Game Theory **30**, 479–490 (2001)
29. Stan, D.: Randomized strategies in concurrent games. Ph.D. thesis, Université Paris-Saclay, France (2017)
30. Thomas, W.: Infinite games and verification. In: Brinksma, E., Larsen, K.G. (eds.) CAV 2002. LNCS, vol. 2404, pp. 58–65. Springer, Heidelberg (2002). https://doi.org/10.1007/3-540-45657-0_5
31. Ummels, M.: Rational behaviour and strategy construction in infinite multiplayer games. In: Arun-Kumar, S., Garg, N. (eds.) FSTTCS 2006. LNCS, vol. 4337, pp. 212–223. Springer, Heidelberg (2006). https://doi.org/10.1007/11944836_21
32. Ummels, M.: The complexity of Nash equilibria in infinite multiplayer games. In: Amadio, R. (ed.) FoSSaCS 2008. LNCS, vol. 4962, pp. 20–34. Springer, Heidelberg (2008). https://doi.org/10.1007/978-3-540-78499-9_3
33. Ummels, M.: Stochastic multiplayer games - theory and algorithms. Ph.D. thesis, RWTH Aachen, Germany (2010)
34. Ummels, M., Wojtczak, D.: The complexity of Nash equilibria in limit-average games. In: Katoen, J.-P., König, B. (eds.) CONCUR 2011. LNCS, vol. 6901, pp. 482–496. Springer, Heidelberg (2011). https://doi.org/10.1007/978-3-642-23217-6_32
35. Ummels, M., Wojtczak, D.: The complexity of Nash equilibria in stochastic multiplayer games. Logical Methods Comput. Sci. **7**(3) (2011)

# Lazy Abstraction-Based Controller Synthesis

Kyle Hsu[1], Rupak Majumdar[2(✉)], Kaushik Mallik[2], and Anne-Kathrin Schmuck[2]

[1] University of Toronto, Toronto, Canada
kyle.hsu@mail.utoronto.ca
[2] MPI-SWS, Kaiserslautern, Germany
{rupak,kmallik,akschmuck}@mpi-sws.org

## 1 Introduction

Abstraction-based controller synthesis (ABCS) is a general procedure for automatic synthesis of controllers for continuous-time nonlinear dynamical systems against temporal specifications. ABCS works by first abstracting a time-sampled version of the continuous dynamics of the open-loop system by a symbolic finite state model. Then, it computes a finite-state controller for the symbolic model using algorithms from automata-theoretic reactive synthesis. When the time-sampled system and the symbolic model satisfy a certain refinement relation, the abstract controller can be refined to a controller for the original continuous-time system while guaranteeing its time-sampled behavior satisfies the temporal specification. Since its introduction about 15 years ago, much research has gone into better theoretical understanding of the basic method and extensions [11,18,29,33,35,39], into scalable tools [26,27,31,37], and into demonstrating its applicability to nontrivial control problems [1,5,32,38].

In its most common form, the abstraction of the continuous-time dynamical system is computed by fixing a parameter $\tau$ for the sampling time and a parameter $\eta$ for the state space, and then representing the abstract state space as a set of hypercubes, each of diameter $\eta$. The hypercubes partition the continuous concrete state space. The abstract transition relation adds a transition between two hypercubes if there exists some state in the first hypercube and some control input that can reach some state of the second by following the original dynamics for time $\tau$. The transition relation is nondeterministic due to (a) the possibility of having continuous transitions starting at two different points in one hypercube but ending in different hypercubes, and (b) the presence of external disturbances causing a deviation of the system trajectories from their nominal paths. When restricted to a compact region of interest, the resulting finite-state abstract system describes a two-player game between controller and disturbance, and reactive synthesis techniques are used to algorithmically compute a controller (or

This research was sponsored in part by the DFG project 389792660-TRR 248 and by the ERC Grant Agreement 610150 (ERC Synergy Grant ImPACT). Kyle Hsu was funded by a DAAD-RISE scholarship.


Y.-F. Chen et al. (Eds.): ATVA 2019, LNCS 11781, pp. 23–47, 2019.
https://doi.org/10.1007/978-3-030-31784-3_2

show that no such controller exists for the given abstraction) for members of a broad class of temporal specifications against the disturbance. One can show that the abstract transition system is in a *feedback refinement relation* (FRR) with the original dynamics [35]. This ensures that when the abstract controller is applied to the original system, the time-sampled behaviors satisfy the temporal specifications.

The success of ABCS depends on the choice of $\eta$ and $\tau$. Increasing $\eta$ (and $\tau$) results in a smaller state space and symbolic model, but more nondeterminism. Thus, there is a tradeoff between computational tractability and successful synthesis. We have recently shown that one can explore this space of tradeoffs by maintaining multiple abstraction layers of varying granularity (i.e., abstract models constructed from progressively larger $\eta$ and $\tau$) [25]. The multi-layered synthesis approach tries to find a controller for the coarsest abstraction whenever feasible, but adaptively considers finer abstractions when necessary. However, the bottleneck of our approach [25] is that the abstract transition system of every layer needs to be fully computed before synthesis begins. This is expensive and wasteful. The cost of abstraction grows as $O((\frac{1}{\eta})^n)$, where $n$ is the dimension, and much of the abstract state space may simply be irrelevant to ABCS, for example, if a controller was already found at a coarser level for a sub-region.

We apply the paradigm of *lazy abstraction* [21] to multi-layered synthesis for safety specifications in [23]. Lazy abstraction is a technique to systematically and efficiently explore large state spaces through abstraction and refinement, and is the basis for successful model checkers for software, hardware, and timed systems [3,4,22,40]. Instead of computing all the abstract transitions for the entire system in each layer, the algorithm selectively chooses which portions to compute transitions for, avoiding doing so for portions that have been already solved by synthesis. This co-dependence of the two major computational components of ABCS is both conceptually appealing and results in significant performance benefits.

This paper gives a concise presentation of the underlying principles of lazy ABCS enabling synthesis w.r.t. safety and reachability specifications. Notably, the extension from single-layered to multi-layered and lazy ABCS is somewhat nontrivial, for the following reasons.

**(I) Lack of FRR Between Abstractions.** An efficient multi-layered controller synthesis algorithm uses coarse grid cells almost everywhere in the state space and only resorts to finer grid cells where the trajectory needs to be precise. While this idea is conceptually simple, the implementation is challenging as the computation of such a multi-resolution controller domain via established abstraction-refinement techniques (as in, e.g., [12]), requires one to run the fixed-point algorithms of reactive synthesis over a common game graph representation connecting abstract states of different coarseness. However, to construct the latter, a simulation relation must exist between any two abstraction layers. Unfortunately, this is not the case in our setting: each layer uses a different sampling time and, while each layer is an abstraction (at a different time scale) of the original system, layers may not have any FRR between themselves. Therefore, we can only run iterations of fixed-points within a particular abstraction layer, but not for combinations of them.

We therefore introduce novel fixed-point algorithms for safety and reach-avoid specifications. Our algorithms save and re-load the results of one fixed-point iteration to and from the lowest (finest) abstraction layer, which we denote as layer 1. This enables arbitrary switching of layers between any two sequential iterations while reusing work from other layers. We use this mechanism to design efficient switching protocols which ensure that synthesis is done mostly over coarse abstractions while fine layers are only used if needed.

**(II) Forward Abstraction and Backward Synthesis.** One key principle of lazy abstraction is that the abstraction is computed in the direction of the search. However, in ABCS, the abstract transition relation can only be computed *forward*, since it involves simulating the ODE of the dynamical system forward up to the sampling time. While an ODE can also be solved backwards in time, backward computations of reachable sets using numerical methods may lead to high numerical errors [30, Remark 1]. Forward abstraction conflicts with symbolic reactive synthesis algorithms, which work *backward* by iterating controllable predecessor operators.[1] For reachability specifications, we solve this problem by keeping a set of *frontier* states, and proving that in the backward controllable predecessor computation, all transitions that need to be considered arise out of these frontier states. Thus, we can construct the abstract transitions lazily by computing the finer abstract transitions only for the frontier.

**(III) Proof of Soundness and Relative Completeness.** The proof of correctness for common lazy abstraction techniques uses the property that there is a simulation relation between any two abstraction layers [10,20]. As this property does not hold in our setting (see (I)), our proofs of soundness and completeness w.r.t. the finest layer only use (a) FRRs between any abstraction layer and the concrete system to argue about the correctness of a controller in a sub-space, and combines this with (b) an argument about the structure of ranking functions, which are obtained from fixed point iterations and combine the individual controllers.

**Related Work.** Our work is an extension and consolidation of several similar attempts at using multiple abstractions of varying granularity in the context of controller synthesis, including our own prior work [23,25]. Similar ideas were explored in the context of *linear* dynamical systems [2,15], which enabled the use of polytopic approximations. For *unperturbed* systems [2,8,16,19,34,36], one can implement an efficient forward search-based synthesis technique, thus easily enabling lazy abstraction (see (II) above). For nonlinear systems satisfying a stability property, [7,8,16] show a multi-resolution algorithm. It is implemented in the tool CoSyMA [31]. For *perturbed nonlinear systems*, [13,14] show

[1] One can design an enumerative forward algorithm for controller synthesis, essentially as a backtracking search of an AND-OR tree [9], but dynamical perturbations greatly increase the width of the tree. Experimentally, this leads to poor performance in control examples.

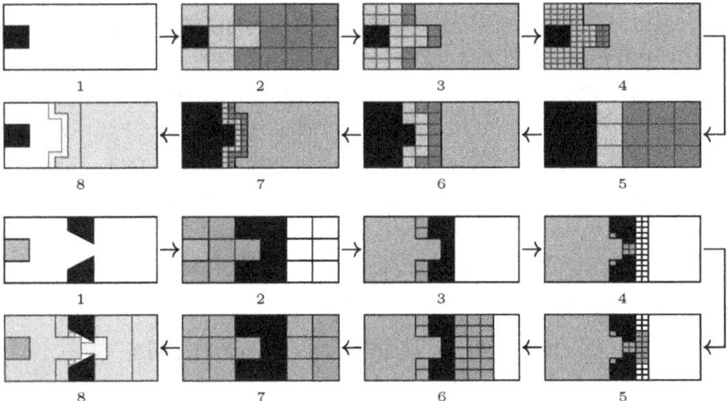


**Fig. 1.** An illustration of the lazy ABCS algorithms for safety (top) and reach-avoid (bottom) specifications. In both scenarios, the solid black regions are the unsafe states which need to be avoided. In the reach-avoid problem, the system has to additionally reach the target ($T$) red square at the left of Pic. 1. Both figures show the sequence of synthesis stages across three abstraction layers: $l = 1$ (Pics. 4, 7), $l = 2$ (Pics. 3, 6), and $l = 3$ (Pics. 2, 5) for safety; and $l = 1$ (Pics. 4, 5), $l = 2$ (Pics. 3, 6), and $l = 3$ (Pics. 2, 7) for reach-avoid. Both Pics. 8 indicate the domains of the resulting controllers with different granularity: $l = 1$ (yellow), $l = 2$ (green), and $l = 3$ (orange). The red regions represent winning states, and the blue regions represent states determined as winning in the present synthesis stage. Cyan regions represent "potentially losing" states in the safety synthesis. We set the parameter $m = 2$ for reach-avoid synthesis. The gridded regions in different layers represent the states where the transitions have been computed; large ungridded space in $l = 2$ and $l = 1$ signifies the computational savings of the lazy abstraction approach. (Color figure online)

a successive decomposition technique based on a linear approximation of given polynomial dynamics. Recently, Nilsson et al. [6,33] presented an abstraction-refinement technique for perturbed nonlinear systems which shares with our approach the idea of using particular candidate states for *local* refinement. However, the approaches differ by the way abstractions are constructed. The approach in [33] identifies all adjacent cells which are reachable using a particular input, splitting these cells for finer abstraction computation. This is analogous to established abstraction-refinement techniques for solving two-player games [12]. On the other hand, our method computes reachable sets for particular sampling times that vary across layers, resulting in a more delicate abstraction-refinement loop. Recently, Hussien and Tabuada [41] developed an orthogonal scalable abstraction method which explores the input space (instead of the state space) lazily.

**Informal Overview.** We illustrate our approach via solving a safety control problem and a reach-avoid control problem depicted in Fig. 1. In reactive synthesis, these problems are solved using a maximal and minimal fixed point computation, respectively [28]. Thus, for safety, one starts with the maximal set of safe states and iteratively shrinks the latter until the remaining set, called the winning state set, does not change. That is, for all states in the winning state set, there is a control action which ensures that the system remains within this set for one step. For reachability, one starts with the set of target states as the winning ones and iteratively enlarges this set by adding all states which allow the system to surely reach the current winning state set, until no more states can be added. These differences in the underlying characteristics of the fixed points require different switching protocols when multiple abstraction layers are used.

The purpose of Fig. 1 is only to convey the basic idea of our algorithms in a visual and lucid way, without paying attention to the details of the underlying dynamics of the system. In our example, we use three layers of abstraction $S_1$, $S_2$ and $S_3$ with the parameters $(\eta, \tau)$, $(2\eta, 2\tau)$ and $(4\eta, 4\tau)$. We refer to the steps of Fig. 1 as Pic. #.

For the *safety control problem* (the top figure in Fig. 1), we assume that a set of unsafe states are given (the black box in the left of Pic. 1). These need to be avoided by the system. For lazy ABCS, we first fully compute the abstract transition relation of the coarsest abstraction $S_3$, and find the states from where the unsafe states can be avoided for at least one time step of length $4\tau$ (blue region in Pic. 2). Normally for a single-layered algorithm, the complement of the blue states would immediately be discarded as losing states. However, in the multi-layered approach, we treat these states as *potentially losing* (cyan regions), and proceed to $S_2$ (Pic. 3) to determine if some of these potentially losing states can avoid the unsafe states with the help of a more fine-grained controller.

However, we cannot perform any safety analysis on $S_2$ yet as the abstract transitions of $S_2$ have not been computed. Instead of computing all of them, as in a non-lazy approach, we only locally explore the outgoing transitions of the potentially losing states in $S_2$. Then, we compute the subset of the potentially losing states in $S_2$ that can avoid the unsafe states for at least one time step (of length $2\tau$ in this case). These states are represented by the blue region in Pic. 3, which get saved from being discarded as losing states in this iteration. Then we move to $S_1$ with the rest of the potentially losing states and continue similarly. The remaining potentially losing states at the end of the computation in $S_1$ are surely losing—relative to the finest abstraction $S_1$—and are permanently discarded. This concludes one "round" of exploration.

We restart the process from $S_3$. This time, the goal is to avoid reaching the unsafe states for at least two time steps of available lengths. This is effectively done by inflating the unsafe region with the discarded states from previous stages (black regions in Pics. 5, 6, and 7). The procedure stops when the combined winning regions across all layers do not change for two successive iterations.

In the end, the multi-layered safety controller is obtained as a collection of the safety controllers synthesized in different abstraction layers in the last round of fixed-point computations. The resulting safety controller domain is depicted in Pic. 8.

Now consider the *reach-avoid control problem* in Fig. 1 (bottom). The target set is shown in red, and the states to be avoided in black. We start by computing the abstract transition system completely for the coarsest layer and solve the reachability fixed point at this layer until convergence using under-approximations of the target and of the safe states. The winning region is marked in blue (Pic. 2); note that the approximation of the bad states "cuts off" the possibility to reach the winning states from the states on the right. We store the representation of this winning region in the finest layer as the set $\Upsilon_1$.

Intuitively, we run the reachability fixed point until convergence to enlarge the winning state set as much as possible using large cells. This is in contrast to the previous algorithm for safety control in which we performed just one iteration at each level. For safety, each iteration of the fixed-point shrinks the winning state set. Hence, running Safe until convergence would only keep those coarse cells which form an invariant set by themselves. Running one iteration of Safe at a time instead has the effect that clusters of finer cells which can be controlled to be safe by a suitable controller in the corresponding layer are considered safe in the coarser layers in future iterations. This allows the use of coarser control actions in larger parts of the state space (see Fig. 1 in [23] for an illustrative example of this phenomenon).

To further extend the winning state set $\Upsilon_1$ for reach-avoid control, we proceed to the next finer layer $l = 2$ with the new target region (red) being the projection of $\Upsilon_1$ to $l = 2$. As in safety control, all the safe states in the complement of $\Upsilon_l$ are potentially within the winning state set. The abstract transitions at layer $l = 2$ have not been computed at this point. We only compute the abstract transitions for the *frontier* states: these are all the cells that might contain layer 2 cells that can reach the current winning region within $m$ steps (for some parameter $m$ chosen in the implementation). The frontier is indicated for layer 2 by the small gridded part in Pic. 3.

We continue the backward reachability algorithm on this partially computed transition system by running the fixed-point for $m$ steps. The projection of the resulting states to the finest layer is added to $\Upsilon_1$. In our example (Pic. 3), we reach a fixed-point just after 1 iteration implying that no more layer 2 (or layer 3) cells can be added to the winning region.

We now move to layer 1, compute a new frontier (the gridded part in Pic. 4), and run the reachability fixed point on $\Upsilon_1$ for $m$ steps. We add the resulting winning states to $\Upsilon_1$ (the blue region in Pic. 4). At this point, we could keep exploring and synthesizing in layer 1, but in the interest of efficiency we want to give the coarser layers a chance to progress. This is the reason to only compute $m$ steps of the reachability fixed point in any one iteration. Unfortunately, for our example, the attempt to go coarser fails as no new layer 2 cells can be added yet (see Pic. 3). We therefore fall back to layer 1 and make progress for $m$ more steps (Pic. 5). At this point, the attempt to go coarser is successful (Pic. 6) as the right side of the small passage was reached.

We continue this movement across layers until synthesis converges in the finest layer. In Pic. 8, the orange, green and yellow colored regions are the controller domains obtained using $l = 3$, $l = 2$ and $l = 1$, respectively. Observe that we avoid computing transitions for a significant portion of layers 1 and 2 (the ungridded space in Pics. 5, 6, respectively).

## 2 Control Systems and Multi-layered ABCS

We recall the theory of feedback refinement relations (FRR) [35] and multi-layered ABCS [25].

**Notation.** We use the symbols $\mathbb{N}$, $\mathbb{R}$, $\mathbb{R}_{>0}$, $\mathbb{Z}$, and $\mathbb{Z}_{>0}$ to denote the sets of natural numbers, reals, positive reals, integers, and positive integers, respectively. Given $a, b \in \mathbb{R}$ with $a \leq b$, we write $[a, b]$ for the closed interval $\{x \in \mathbb{R} \mid a \leq x \leq b\}$ and write $[a; b] = [a, b] \cap \mathbb{Z}$ as its discrete counterpart. Given a vector $a \in \mathbb{R}^n$, we denote by $a_i$ its $i$-th element, for $i \in [1; n]$. We write $[\![a, b]\!]$ for the closed hyper-interval $\mathbb{R}^n \cap ([a_1, b_1] \times \ldots \times [a_n, b_n])$. We define the relations $<, \leq, \geq, >$ on vectors in $\mathbb{R}^n$ component-wise. For a set $W$, we write $W^*$ and $W^\omega$ for the sets of finite and infinite sequences over $W$, respectively. We define $W^\infty = W^* \cup W^\omega$. We define $\mathrm{dom}(w) = \{0, \ldots, |w| - 1\}$ if $w \in W^*$, and $\mathrm{dom}(w) = \mathbb{N}$ if $w \in W^\omega$. For $k \in \mathrm{dom}(w)$ we write $w(k)$ for the $k$-th symbol of $w$.

### 2.1 Abstraction-Based Controller Synthesis

**Systems.** A *system* $S = (X, U, F)$ consists of a state space $X$, an input space $U$, and a transition function $F : X \times U \to 2^X$. A system $S$ is *finite* if $X$ and $U$ are finite. A trajectory $\xi \in X^\infty$ is a maximal sequence of states compatible with $F$: for all $1 \leq k < |\xi|$ there exists $u \in U$ s.t. $\xi(k) \in F(\xi(k-1), u)$ and if $|\xi| < \infty$ then $F(\xi(|\xi|), u) = \emptyset$ for all $u \in U$. For $D \subseteq X$, a $D$-trajectory is a trajectory $\xi$ with $\xi(0) \in D$. The *behavior* $\mathcal{B}(S, D)$ of a system $S = (X, U, F)$ w.r.t. $D \subseteq X$ consists of all $D$-trajectories; when $D = X$, we simply write $\mathcal{B}(S)$.

**Controllers and Closed Loop Systems.** A *controller* $C = (D, U, G)$ for a system $S = (X, U, F)$ consists of a controller *domain* $D \subseteq X$, a space of inputs $U$, and a control map $G : D \to 2^U \setminus \{\emptyset\}$ mapping states in its domain to non-empty sets of control inputs. The *closed loop system* formed by interconnecting $S$ and $C$ in *feedback* is defined by the system $S^{cl} = (X, U, F^{cl})$ with $F^{cl} : X \times U \to 2^X$ s.t. $x' \in F^{cl}(x, u)$ iff $x \in D$ and $u \in G(x)$ and $x' \in F(x, u)$, or $x \notin D$ and $x' \in F(x, u)$.

**Control Problem.** We consider specifications given as $\omega$-regular languages whose atomic predicates are interpreted as sets of states. Given a specification $\psi$, a system $S$, and an interpretation of the predicates as sets of states of $S$, we write $\langle\!|\psi|\!\rangle_S \subseteq \mathcal{B}(S)$ for the set of behaviors of $S$ satisfying $\psi$. The pair $(S, \psi)$ is called a *control problem* on $S$ for $\psi$. A controller $C = (D, U, G)$ for $S$ solves $(S, \psi)$ if $\mathcal{B}(S^{cl}, D) \subseteq \langle\!|\psi|\!\rangle_S$. The set of all controllers solving $(S, \psi)$ is denoted by $\mathcal{C}(S, \psi)$.

**Feedback Refinement Relations.** Let $S_i = (X_i, U_i, F_i)$, $i \in \{1, 2\}$ be two systems with $U_2 \subseteq U_1$. A *feedback refinement relation* (FRR) from $S_1$ to $S_2$ is a relation $Q \subseteq X_1 \times X_2$ s.t. for all $x_1 \in X_1$ there is some $x_2 \in X_2$ such that $Q(x_1, x_2)$ and for all $(x_1, x_2) \in Q$, we have (i) $U_{S_2}(x_2) \subseteq U_{S_1}(x_1)$, and (ii) $u \in U_{S_2}(x_2) \Rightarrow Q(F_1(x_1, u)) \subseteq F_2(x_2, u)$ where $U_{S_i}(x) := \{u \in U_i \mid F_i(x, u) \neq \emptyset\}$. We write $S_1 \preccurlyeq_Q S_2$ if $Q$ is an FRR from $S_1$ to $S_2$.

**Abstraction-Based Controller Synthesis (ABCS).** Consider two systems $S_1$ and $S_2$, with $S_1 \preccurlyeq_Q S_2$. Let $C = (D, U_2, G)$ be a controller for $S_2$. Then, as shown in [35], $C$ can be refined into a controller for $S_1$, defined by $C \circ Q = (\widetilde{D}, U_1, \widetilde{G})$ with $\widetilde{D} = Q^{-1}(D)$, and $\widetilde{G}(x_1) = \{u \in U_1 \mid \exists x_2 \in Q(x_1) \,.\, u \in G(x_2)\}$ for all $x_1 \in \widetilde{D}$. This implies soundness of ABCS.

**Proposition 1 ([35], Def. VI.2, Thm. VI.3).** *Let $S_1 \preccurlyeq_Q S_2$ and $C \in \mathcal{C}(S_2, \psi)$ for a specification $\psi$. If for all $\xi_1 \in \mathcal{B}(S_1)$ and $\xi_2 \in \mathcal{B}(S_2)$ with* $\mathrm{dom}(\xi_1) = \mathrm{dom}(\xi_2)$ *and $(\xi_1(k), \xi_2(k)) \in Q$ for all $k \in \mathrm{dom}(\xi_1)$ holds that $\xi_2 \in \langle\!\langle \psi \rangle\!\rangle_{S_2} \Rightarrow \xi_1 \in \langle\!\langle \psi \rangle\!\rangle_{S_1}$, then $C \circ Q \in \mathcal{C}(S_1, \psi)$.*

## 2.2 ABCS for Continuous Control Systems

We now recall how ABCS can be applied to continuous-time systems by delineating the abstraction procedure [35].

**Continuous-Time Control Systems.** A *control system* $\Sigma = (X, U, W, f)$ consists of a state space $X = \mathbb{R}^n$, a non-empty input space $U \subseteq \mathbb{R}^m$, a compact disturbance set $W \subset \mathbb{R}^n$ with $0 \in W$, and a function $f : X \times U \to X$ s.t. $f(\cdot, u)$ is locally Lipschitz for all $u \in U$. Given an initial state $x_0 \in X$, a positive parameter $\tau > 0$, and a constant input trajectory $\mu_u : [0, \tau] \to U$ which maps every $t \in [0, \tau]$ to the same $u \in U$, a *trajectory* of $\Sigma$ on $[0, \tau]$ is an absolutely continuous function $\xi : [0, \tau] \to X$ s.t. $\xi(0) = x_0$ and $\xi(\cdot)$ fulfills the following differential inclusion for almost every $t \in [0, \tau]$:

$$\dot{\xi} \in f(\xi(t), \mu_u(t)) + W = f(\xi(t), u) + W. \tag{1}$$

We collect all such solutions in the set $\mathrm{Sol}_f(x_0, \tau, u)$.

**Time-Sampled System.** Given a time sampling parameter $\tau > 0$, we define the *time-sampled system* $\overrightarrow{S}(\Sigma, \tau) = (X, U, \overrightarrow{F})$ associated with $\Sigma$, where $X$, $U$ are as in $\Sigma$, and the transition function $\overrightarrow{F} : X \times U \to 2^X$ is defined as follows. For all $x \in X$ and $u \in U$, we have $x' \in \overrightarrow{F}(x, u)$ iff there exists a solution $\xi \in \mathrm{Sol}_f(x, \tau, u)$ s.t. $\xi(\tau) = x'$.

**Covers.** A *cover* $\widehat{X}$ of the state space $X$ is a set of non-empty, closed hyper-intervals $[\![a, b]\!]$ with $a, b \in (\mathbb{R} \cup \{\pm\infty\})^n$ called *cells*, such that every $x \in X$ belongs to some cell in $\widehat{X}$. Given a grid parameter $\eta \in \mathbb{R}^n_{>0}$, we say that a point $c \in Y$ is *$\eta$-grid-aligned* if there is $k \in \mathbb{Z}^n$ s.t. for each $i \in \{1, \ldots, n\}$, $c_i = \alpha_i + k_i \eta_i - \frac{\eta_i}{2}$. Further, a cell $[\![a, b]\!]$ is *$\eta$-grid-aligned* if there is a $\eta$-grid-aligned point $c$ s.t. $a = c - \frac{\eta}{2}$ and $b = c + \frac{\eta}{2}$; such cells define sets of diameter $\eta$ whose center-points are $\eta$-grid-aligned.

**Abstract Systems.** An *abstract system* $\widehat{S}(\Sigma, \tau, \eta) = (\widehat{X}, \widehat{U}, \widehat{F})$ for a control system $\Sigma$, a time sampling parameter $\tau > 0$, and a grid parameter $\eta \in \mathbb{R}^n_{>0}$ consists of an abstract state space $\widehat{X}$, a finite abstract input space $\widehat{U} \subseteq U$, and an abstract transition function $\widehat{F} : \widehat{X} \times \widehat{U} \to 2^{\widehat{X}}$. To ensure that $\widehat{S}$ is finite, we consider a compact *region of interest* $Y = [\![\alpha, \beta]\!] \subseteq X$ with $\alpha, \beta \in \mathbb{R}^n$ s.t. $\beta - \alpha$ is an integer multiple of $\eta$. Then we define $\widehat{X} = \widehat{Y} \cup \widehat{X}'$ s.t. $\widehat{Y}$ is the *finite* set of *$\eta$-grid-aligned* cells covering $Y$ and $\widehat{X}'$ is a finite set of large unbounded cells covering the (unbounded) region $X \setminus Y$. We define $\widehat{F}$ based on the dynamics of $\Sigma$ only within $Y$. That is, for all $\widehat{x} \in \widehat{Y}$, $\widehat{x}' \in \widehat{X}$, and $u \in \widehat{U}$ we require

$$\widehat{x}' \in \widehat{F}(\widehat{x}, u) \text{ if } \exists \xi \in \cup_{x \in \widehat{x}} \mathrm{Sol}_f(x, \tau, u) \,.\, \xi(\tau) \in \widehat{x}'. \tag{2}$$

For all states in $\widehat{x} \in (\widehat{X} \setminus \widehat{Y})$ we have that $\widehat{F}(\widehat{x}, u) = \emptyset$ for all $u \in \widehat{U}$. We extend $\widehat{F}$ to sets of abstract states $\Upsilon \subseteq \widehat{X}$ by defining $\widehat{F}(\Upsilon, u) := \bigcup_{\widehat{x} \in \Upsilon} \widehat{F}(\widehat{x}, u)$.

While $\widehat{X}$ is not a partition of the state space $X$, notice that cells only overlap at the boundary and one can define a deterministic function that resolves the resulting non-determinism by consistently mapping such boundary states to a unique cell covering it. The composition of $\widehat{X}$ with this function defines a partition. To avoid notational clutter, we shall simply treat $\widehat{X}$ as a partition.

**Control Problem.** It was shown in [35], Thm. III.5 that the relation $\widehat{Q} \subseteq X \times \widehat{X}$, defined by all tuples $(x, \widehat{x}) \in \widehat{Q}$ for which $x \in \widehat{x}$, is an FRR between $\overrightarrow{S}$ and $\widehat{S}$, i.e., $\overrightarrow{S} \preccurlyeq_{\widehat{Q}} \widehat{S}$. Hence, we can apply ABCS as described in Sect. 2.1 by computing a controller $C$ for $\widehat{S}$ which can then be refined to a controller for $\overrightarrow{S}$ under the pre-conditions of Proposition 1.

More concretely, we consider safety and reachability control problems for the continuous-time system $\Sigma$, which are defined by a set of *static obstacles* $\mathsf{O} \subset X$ which should be avoided and a set of *goal states* $\mathsf{G} \subseteq X$ which should be reached, respectively. Additionally, when constructing $\widehat{S}$, we used a compact region of interest $Y \subseteq X$ to ensure *finiteness* of $\widehat{S}$ allowing to apply tools from reactive synthesis [28] to compute $C$. This implies that $C$ is only valid within $Y$. We therefore interpret $Y$ as a *global safety requirement* and synthesize a controller which keeps the system within $Y$ while implementing the specification. This interpretation leads to a safety and reach-avoid control problem, w.r.t. a safe set $R = Y \setminus \mathsf{O}$ and target set $T = \mathsf{G} \cap R$. As $R$ and $T$ can be interpreted as predicates over the state space $X$ of $\overrightarrow{S}$, this directly defines the control problems $(\overrightarrow{S}, \psi_{\text{safe}})$ and $(\overrightarrow{S}, \psi_{\text{reach}})$ via

$$\langle\!|\psi_{\text{safe}}|\!\rangle_{\overrightarrow{S}} := \left\{ \xi \in \mathcal{B}(\overrightarrow{S}) \,\middle|\, \forall k \in \mathrm{dom}(\xi) \,.\, \xi(k) \in R \right\}, \text{ and} \tag{3a}$$

$$\langle\!|\psi_{\text{reach}}|\!\rangle_{\overrightarrow{S}} := \left\{ \xi \in \mathcal{B}(\overrightarrow{S}) \,\middle|\, \left( \exists k \in \mathrm{dom}(\xi) \,.\, \begin{pmatrix} \xi(k) \in T \\ \wedge \forall k' \leq k \,.\, \xi(k') \in R \end{pmatrix} \right) \right\} \tag{3b}$$

for safety and reach-avoid control, respectively. Intuitively, a controller $C \in \mathcal{C}(\overrightarrow{S}, \psi)$ applied to $\Sigma$ is a sample-and-hold controller, which ensures that the specification holds on all closed-loop trajectories *at sampling instances.*[2]

[2] This implicitly assumes that sampling times and grid sizes are such that no "holes" occur between consecutive cells visited by a trajectory. This can be formalized by assumptions on the growth rate of $f$ in (1) which is beyond the scope of this paper.

To compute $C \in \mathcal{C}(\overrightarrow{S}, \psi)$ via ABCS as described in Sect. 2.1 we need to ensure that the pre-conditions of Proposition 1 hold. This is achieved by *under-approximating* the safe and target sets by abstract state sets

$$\widehat{R} = \{\widehat{x} \in \widehat{X} \mid \widehat{x} \subseteq R\}, \text{ and } \widehat{T} = \{\widehat{x} \in \widehat{X} \mid \widehat{x} \subseteq T\}, \tag{4}$$

and defining $\langle\!\langle \psi_{\text{safe}} \rangle\!\rangle_{\widehat{S}}$ and $\langle\!\langle \psi_{\text{reach}} \rangle\!\rangle_{\widehat{S}}$ via (3) by substituting $\overrightarrow{S}$ with $\widehat{S}$, $R$ with $\widehat{R}$ and $T$ with $\widehat{T}$. With this, it immediately follows from Proposition 1 that $C \in \mathcal{C}(\widehat{S}, \psi)$ can be refined to the controller $C \circ Q \in \mathcal{C}(\overrightarrow{S}, \psi)$.

### 2.3 Multi-layered ABCS

We now recall how ABCS can be performed over multiple abstraction layers [25]. The goal of multi-layered ABCS is to construct an abstract controller $C$ which uses coarse grid cells in as much part of the state space as possible, and only resorts to finer grid cells where the control action needs to be precise. In particular, the domain of this abstract controller $C$ must not be smaller then the domain of any controller $C'$ constructed for the finest layer, i.e., $C$ must be relatively complete w.r.t. the finest layer. In addition, $C$ should be refinable into a controller implementing $\psi$ on $\Sigma$, as in classical ABCS (see Proposition 1).

The computation of such a multi-resolution controller via established abstraction-refinement techniques (as in, e.g., [12]), requires a common transition system connecting states of different coarseness but with the same time step. To construct the latter, a FRR between any two abstraction layers must exist, which is not the case in our setting. We can therefore not compute a single multi-resolution controller $C$. We therefore synthesize a set $\mathbf{C}$ of single-layered controllers instead, each for a different coarseness and with a different domain, and refine each of those controllers separately, using the associated FRR. The resulting refined controller is a sample-and-hold controller which selects the current input value $u \in \widehat{U} \subseteq U$ and the duration $\tau_l$ for which this input should be applied to $\Sigma$. This construction is formalized in the remainder of this section.

**Multi-layered Systems.** Given a grid parameter $\underline{\eta}$, a time sampling parameter $\underline{\tau}$, and $L \in \mathbb{Z}_{>0}$, define $\eta_l = 2^{l-1}\underline{\eta}$ and $\tau_l = 2^{l-1}\underline{\tau}$. For a control system $\Sigma$ and a subset $Y \subseteq X$ with $Y = [\![\alpha, \beta]\!]$, s.t. $\beta - \alpha = k\eta_L$ for some $k \in \mathbb{Z}^n$, $\widehat{Y}_l$ is the $\eta_l$-grid-aligned cover of $Y$. This induces a sequence of time-sampled systems

$$\overrightarrow{\mathbf{S}} := \{\overrightarrow{S}_l(\Sigma, \tau_l)\}_{l \in [1;L]} \quad \text{and} \quad \widehat{\mathbf{S}} := \{\widehat{S}_l(\Sigma, \tau_l, \eta_l)\}_{l \in [1;L]}, \tag{5}$$

respectively, where $\overrightarrow{S}_l := (X, U, \overrightarrow{F}_l)$ and $\widehat{S}_l := (\widehat{X}_l, \widehat{U}, \widehat{F}_l)$. If $\Sigma$, $\tau$, and $\eta$ are clear from the context, we omit them in $\overrightarrow{S}_l$ and $\widehat{S}_l$.

Our multi-layered synthesis algorithm relies on the fact that the sequence $\widehat{\mathbf{S}}$ of abstract transition systems is monotone, formalized by the following assumption.

**Assumption 1.** *Let $\widehat{S}_l$ and $\widehat{S}_m$ be two abstract systems with $m, l \in [1; L]$, $l < m$. Then*[3] $\widehat{F}_l(\Upsilon_l) \subseteq \widehat{F}_m(\Upsilon_m)$ *if* $\Upsilon_l \subseteq \Upsilon_m$.

As the exact computation of $\cup_{x \in \widehat{x}} \mathrm{Sol}_f(x, \tau, u)$ in (2) is expensive (if not impossible), a numerical over-approximation is usually computed. Assumption 1 states that the approximation must be monotone in the granularity of the discretization. This is fulfilled by many numerical methods e.g. the ones based on decomposition functions for mixed-monotone systems [11] or on growth bounds [37]; our implementation uses the latter one.

**Induced Relations.** It trivially follows from our construction that, for all $l \in [1; L]$, we have $\overrightarrow{S}_l \preccurlyeq_{\widehat{Q}_l} \widehat{S}_l$, where $\widehat{Q}_l \subseteq X \times \widehat{X}_l$ is the FRR induced by $\widehat{X}_l$. The set of relations $\{\widehat{Q}_l\}_{l \in [1;L]}$ induces transformers $\widehat{R}_{ll'} \subseteq \widehat{X}_l \times \widehat{X}_{l'}$ for $l, l' \in [1; L]$ between abstract states of different layers such that

$$\widehat{x} \in \widehat{R}_{ll'}(\widehat{x}') \Leftrightarrow \widehat{x} \in \widehat{Q}_l(\widehat{Q}_{l'}^{-1}(\widehat{x}')). \tag{6}$$

However, the relation $\widehat{R}_{ll'}$ is generally *not* a FRR between the layers due to different time sampling parameters used in different layers (see [25], Rem. 1). This means that $\widehat{S}_{l+1}$ cannot be directly constructed from $\widehat{S}_l$, unlike in usual abstraction refinement algorithms [10,12,21].

**Multi-layered Controllers.** Given a multi-layered abstract system $\widehat{\mathbf{S}}$ and some $P \in \mathbb{N}$, a multi-layered controller is a set $\mathbf{C} = \{C^p\}_{p \in [1;P]}$ with $C^p = (D^p, \widehat{U}, G^p)$ being a single-layer controller with $G^p : D^p \to 2^{\widehat{U}}$. Then $\mathbf{C}$ is a controller for $\widehat{\mathbf{S}}$ if for all $p \in [1; P]$ there exists a unique $l_p \in [1; L]$ s.t. $C^p$ is a controller for $\widehat{S}_{l_p}$, i.e., $D^p \subseteq \widehat{X}_{l_p}$. The number $P$ may not be related to $L$; we allow multiple controllers for the same layer and no controller for some layers.

The *quantizer induced by* $\mathbf{C}$ is a map $\mathbf{Q} : X \to 2^{\widehat{\mathbf{X}}}$ with $\widehat{\mathbf{X}} = \bigcup_{l \in [1;L]} \widehat{X}_l$ s.t. for all $x \in X$ it holds that $\widehat{x} \in \mathbf{Q}(x)$ iff there exists $p \in [1; P]$ s.t. $\widehat{x} \in \widehat{Q}_{l_p}(x) \cap D^p$ and no $p' \in [1; P]$ s.t. $l_{p'} > l_p$ and $\widehat{Q}_{l_{p'}}(x) \cap D^{p'} \neq \emptyset$. In words, $\mathbf{Q}$ maps states $x \in X$ to the *coarsest* abstract state $\widehat{x}$ that is both related to $x$ and is in the domain $D^p$ of some $C^p \in \mathbf{C}$. We define $\mathbf{D} = \{\widehat{x} \in \widehat{\mathbf{X}} \mid \exists x \in X \,.\, \widehat{x} \in \mathbf{Q}(x)\}$ as the effective domain of $\mathbf{C}$ and $D = \{x \in X \mid \mathbf{Q}(x) \neq \emptyset\}$ as its projection to $X$.

**Multi-layered Closed Loops.** The abstract multi-layered *closed loop system* formed by interconnecting $\widehat{\mathbf{S}}$ and $\mathbf{C}$ in *feedback* is defined by the system $\widehat{\mathbf{S}}^{cl} = (\widehat{\mathbf{X}}, \widehat{U}, \widehat{\mathbf{F}}^{cl})$ with $\widehat{\mathbf{F}}^{cl} : \widehat{\mathbf{X}} \times \widehat{U} \to 2^{\widehat{\mathbf{X}}}$ s.t. $\widehat{x}' \in \widehat{\mathbf{F}}^{cl}(\widehat{x}, \widehat{u})$ iff (i) there exists $p \in [1; P]$ s.t. $\widehat{x} \in \mathbf{D} \cap D^p$, $\widehat{u} \in G^p(\widehat{x})$ and there exists $\widehat{x}'' \in \widehat{F}_{l_p}(\widehat{x}, \widehat{u})$ s.t. either $\widehat{x}' \in \mathbf{Q}(\widehat{Q}_{l_p}^{-1}(\widehat{x}''))$, or $\widehat{x}' = \widehat{x}''$ and $\widehat{Q}_{l_p}^{-1}(\widehat{x}'') \nsubseteq D$, or (ii) $\widehat{x} \in \widehat{X}_l$, $\widehat{Q}_l^{-1}(\widehat{x}) \nsubseteq D$ and $\widehat{x}' \in \widehat{F}_l(\widehat{x}, \widehat{u})$. This results in the time-sampled closed loop system $\overrightarrow{\mathbf{S}}^{cl} = (X, U, \overrightarrow{\mathbf{F}}^{cl})$ with $\overrightarrow{\mathbf{F}}^{cl} : X \times U \to 2^X$ s.t. $x' \in \overrightarrow{\mathbf{F}}^{cl}(x, u)$ iff (i) $x \in D$ and there exists $p \in [1; P]$ and $\widehat{x} \in \mathbf{Q}(x) \cap D^p$ s.t. $u \in G^p(\widehat{x})$ and $x' \in \overrightarrow{F}_{l_p}(x, u)$, or (ii) $x \notin D$ and $x' \in \overrightarrow{F}_l(x, u)$ for some $l \in [1; L]$.

[3] We write $\Upsilon_l \subseteq \Upsilon_m$ with $\Upsilon_l \subseteq \widehat{X}_l$, $\Upsilon_m \subseteq \widehat{X}_m$ as short for $\bigcup_{\widehat{x} \in \Upsilon_l} \widehat{x} \subseteq \bigcup_{\widehat{x} \in \Upsilon_m} \widehat{x}$.

**Multi-layered Behaviors.** Slightly abusing notation, we define the behaviors $\mathcal{B}(\overrightarrow{\mathbf{S}})$ and $\mathcal{B}(\widehat{\mathbf{S}})$ via the construction for systems $S$ in Sect. 2.1 by interpreting the sequences $\overrightarrow{\mathbf{S}}$ and $\widehat{\mathbf{S}}$ as systems $\widehat{\mathbf{S}} = (\widehat{\mathbf{X}}, \widehat{U}, \widehat{\mathbf{F}})$ and $\overrightarrow{\mathbf{S}} = (X, U, \overrightarrow{\mathbf{F}})$, s.t.

$$\widehat{\mathbf{F}}(\widehat{x}, \widehat{u}) = \bigcup_{l \in [1;L]} \widehat{R}_{ll'}(\widehat{F}_{l'}(\widehat{x}, \widehat{u})), \text{ and } \overrightarrow{\mathbf{F}}(x, u) = \bigcup_{l \in [1;L]} \overrightarrow{F}_l(x, u), \quad (7)$$

where $\widehat{x}$ is in $\widehat{X}_{l'}$. Intuitively, the resulting behavior $\mathcal{B}(\widehat{\mathbf{S}})$ contains trajectories with non-uniform state size; in every time step the system can switch to a different layer using the available transition functions $\widehat{F}_l$. For $\mathcal{B}(\overrightarrow{\mathbf{S}})$ this results in trajectories with non-uniform sampling time; in every time step a transition of any duration $\tau_l$ can be chosen, which corresponds to some $\overrightarrow{F}_l$. For the closed loops $\overrightarrow{\mathbf{S}}^{cl}$ and $\widehat{\mathbf{S}}^{cl}$ those behaviors are restricted to follow the switching pattern induced by $\mathbf{C}$, i.e., always apply the input chosen by the coarsest available controller. The resulting behaviors $\mathcal{B}(\overrightarrow{\mathbf{S}}^{cl})$ and $\mathcal{B}(\widehat{\mathbf{S}}^{cl})$ are formally defined as in Sect. 2.1 via $\overrightarrow{\mathbf{S}}^{cl}$ and $\widehat{\mathbf{S}}^{cl}$.

**Soundness of Multi-layered ABCS.** As shown in [25], the soundness property of ABCS stated in Proposition 1 transfers to the multi-layered setting.

**Proposition 2.** **([25], Cor. 1).** *Let* $\mathbf{C}$ *be a multi-layered controller for the abstract multi-layered system* $\widehat{\mathbf{S}}$ *with effective domains* $\mathbf{D} \in \widehat{\mathbf{X}}$ *and* $D \in X$ *inducing the closed loop systems* $\overrightarrow{\mathbf{S}}^{cl}$ *and* $\widehat{\mathbf{S}}^{cl}$*, respectively. Further, let* $\mathbf{C} \in \mathcal{C}(\widehat{\mathbf{S}}, \psi)$ *for a specification* $\psi$ *with associated behavior* $\langle\!\langle \psi \rangle\!\rangle_{\widehat{\mathbf{S}}} \subseteq \mathcal{B}(\widehat{\mathbf{S}})$ *and* $\langle\!\langle \psi \rangle\!\rangle_{\overrightarrow{\mathbf{S}}} \subseteq \mathcal{B}(\overrightarrow{\mathbf{S}})$*. Suppose that for all* $\xi \in \mathcal{B}(\overrightarrow{\mathbf{S}})$ *and* $\widehat{\xi} \in \mathcal{B}(\widehat{\mathbf{S}})$ *s.t. (i)* $\mathrm{dom}(\xi) = \mathrm{dom}(\widehat{\xi})$*, (ii) for all* $k \in \mathrm{dom}(\xi)$ *it holds that* $(\xi(k), \widehat{\xi}(k)) \in \mathbf{Q}$*, and (iii)* $\widehat{\xi} \in \langle\!\langle \psi \rangle\!\rangle_{\widehat{\mathbf{S}}} \Rightarrow \xi \in \langle\!\langle \psi \rangle\!\rangle_{\overrightarrow{\mathbf{S}}}$*. Then* $\mathcal{B}(\overrightarrow{\mathbf{S}}^{cl}, \mathbf{D}) \subseteq \langle\!\langle \psi \rangle\!\rangle_{\overrightarrow{\mathbf{S}}}$*, i.e., the time-sampled multi-layered closed loop* $\overrightarrow{\mathbf{S}}^{cl}$ *fulfills specification* $\psi$*.*

**Control Problem.** Consider the safety and reach-avoid control problems defined over $\Sigma$ in Sect. 2.2. As $R$ and $T$ can be interpreted as predicates over the state space $X$ of $\overrightarrow{\mathbf{S}}$, this directly defines the control problems $(\overrightarrow{\mathbf{S}}, \psi_{\mathrm{safe}})$ and $(\overrightarrow{\mathbf{S}}, \psi_{\mathrm{reach}})$ via (3) by substituting $\overrightarrow{S}$ with $\overrightarrow{\mathbf{S}}$.

To solve $(\overrightarrow{\mathbf{S}}, \psi)$ via multi-layered ABCS we need to ensure that the preconditions of Proposition 2 hold. This is achieved by *under-approximating* the safe and target sets by a set $\{\widehat{R}_l\}_{l \in [1;L]}$ and $\{\widehat{T}_l\}_{l \in [1;L]}$ defined via (4) for every $l \in [1;L]$. Then $\langle\!\langle \psi_{\mathrm{safe}} \rangle\!\rangle_{\widehat{\mathbf{S}}}$ and $\langle\!\langle \psi_{\mathrm{reach}} \rangle\!\rangle_{\widehat{\mathbf{S}}}$ can be defined via (3) by substituting $\overrightarrow{S}$ with $\widehat{\mathbf{S}}$, $R$ with $\widehat{R}_{\lambda(\xi(k))}$ and $T$ with $\widehat{T}_{\lambda(\xi(k))}$, where $\lambda(\widehat{x})$ returns the $l \in [1;L]$ to which $\widehat{x}$ belongs, i.e., for $\widehat{x} \in \widehat{X}_l$ we have $\lambda(\widehat{x}) = l$. We collect all multi-layered controllers $\mathbf{C}$ for which $\mathcal{B}(\widehat{\mathbf{S}}^{cl}, \mathbf{D}) \subseteq \langle\!\langle \psi \rangle\!\rangle_{\widehat{\mathbf{S}}}$ in $\mathcal{C}(\widehat{\mathbf{S}}, \psi)$. With this, it immediately follows from Proposition 2 that $\mathbf{C} \in \mathcal{C}(\widehat{\mathbf{S}}, \psi)$ also solves $(\overrightarrow{\mathbf{S}}, \psi)$ via the construction of the time-sampled closed loop system $\overrightarrow{\mathbf{S}}^{cl}$.

A multi-layered controller $\mathbf{C} \in \mathcal{C}(\widehat{\mathbf{S}}, \psi)$ is typically not unique; there can be many different control strategies implementing the same specification. However, the largest possible controller domain for a particular abstraction layer $l$ always exists and is unique. In this paper we will compute a *sound* controller $\mathbf{C} \in \mathcal{C}(\widehat{\mathbf{S}}, \psi)$ with a maximal domain w.r.t. the lowest layer $l = 1$. Formally, for any sound layer 1 controller $\widetilde{C} = (\widetilde{D}, U, \widetilde{G}) \in \mathcal{C}(\widehat{S}_1, \psi)$ it must hold that $\widetilde{D}$ is contained in the projection $D_1 = \widehat{Q}_1(D)$ of the effective domain of $\mathbf{C}$ to layer 1. We call such controllers $\mathbf{C}$ *complete w.r.t. layer* 1. On top of that, for faster computation we ensure that cells within its controller domain are only refined if needed.

## 3 Controller Synthesis

Our synthesis of an abstract multi-layered controller $\mathbf{C} \in \mathcal{C}(\widehat{\mathbf{S}}, \psi)$ has three main ingredients. First, we use the usual fixed-point algorithms from reactive synthesis [28] to compute the maximal set of winning states (i.e., states which can be controlled to fulfill the specification) and deduce an abstract controller (Sect. 3.1). Second, we allow switching between abstraction layers during these fixed-point computations by saving and re-loading intermediate results of fixed-point computations from and to the lowest layer (Sect. 3.2). Third, through the use of *frontiers*, we compute abstractions lazily by only computing abstract transitions in parts of the state space currently explored by the fixed-point algorithm (Sect. 3.3). We prove that frontiers always over-approximate the set of states possibly added to the winning region in the corresponding synthesis step.

### 3.1 Fixed-Point Algorithms for Single-Layered ABCS

We first recall the standard algorithms to construct a controller $C$ solving the safety and reach-avoid control problems $(\widehat{S}, \psi_{\text{safe}})$ and $(\widehat{S}, \psi_{\text{reach}})$ over the finite abstract system $\widehat{S}(\Sigma, \tau, \eta) = (\widehat{X}, \widehat{U}, \widehat{F})$. The key to this synthesis is the *controllable predecessor* operator, $\mathrm{CPre}_{\widehat{S}} : 2^{\widehat{X}} \to 2^{\widehat{X}}$, defined for a set $\Upsilon \subseteq \widehat{X}$ by

$$\mathrm{CPre}_{\widehat{S}}(\Upsilon) := \{\widehat{x} \in \widehat{X} \mid \exists \widehat{u} \in \widehat{U} \,.\, \widehat{F}(\widehat{x}, \widehat{u}) \subseteq \Upsilon\}. \tag{8}$$

$(\widehat{S}, \psi_{\text{safe}})$ and $(\widehat{S}, \psi_{\text{reach}})$ are solved by iterating this operator.

**Safety Control.** Given a safety control problem $(\widehat{S}, \psi_{\text{safe}})$ associated with $\widehat{R} \subseteq \widehat{Y}$, one iteratively computes the sets

$$W^0 = \widehat{R} \text{ and } W^{i+1} = \mathrm{CPre}_{\widehat{S}}(W^i) \cap \widehat{R} \tag{9}$$

until an iteration $N \in \mathbb{N}$ with $W^N = W^{N+1}$ is reached. From this algorithm, we can extract a safety controller $C = (D, \widehat{U}, G)$ where $D = W^N$ and

$$\widehat{u} \in G(\widehat{x}) \Rightarrow \widehat{F}(\widehat{x}, \widehat{u}) \subseteq D \tag{10}$$

for all $\widehat{x} \in D$. Note that $C \in \mathcal{C}(\widehat{S}, \psi_{\text{safe}})$.

We denote the procedure implementing this iterative computation until convergence $\mathsf{Safe}_\infty(\widehat{R}, \widehat{S})$. We also use a version of $\mathsf{Safe}$ which runs one step of (9) only. Formally, the algorithm $\mathsf{Safe}(\widehat{R}, \widehat{S})$ returns the set $W^1$ (the result of the first iteration of (9)). One can obtain $\mathsf{Safe}_\infty(\widehat{R}, \widehat{S})$ by chaining $\mathsf{Safe}$ until convergence, i.e., given $W^1$ computed by $\mathsf{Safe}(\widehat{R}, \widehat{S})$, one obtains $W^2$ from $\mathsf{Safe}(W^1, \widehat{S})$, and so on. In Sect. 3.2, we will use such chaining to switch layers after every iteration within our multi-resolution safety fixed-point.

**Reach-Avoid Control.** Given a reach-avoid control problem $(\widehat{S}, \psi_{\text{reach}})$ for $\widehat{R}, \widehat{T} \subseteq \widehat{Y}$, one iteratively computes the sets

$$W^0 = \widehat{T} \text{ and } W^{i+1} = \left(\mathrm{CPre}_{\widehat{S}}(W^i) \cap \widehat{R}\right) \cup \widehat{T} \tag{11}$$

until some iteration $N \in \mathbb{N}$ is reached where $W^N = W^{N+1}$. We extract the reachability controller $C = (D, \widehat{U}, G)$ with $D = W^N$ and

$$G(\widehat{x}) = \begin{cases} \{\widehat{u} \in \widehat{U} \mid \widehat{F}(\widehat{x}, \widehat{u}) \subseteq W^{i*}\}, & \widehat{x} \in D \setminus \widehat{T} \\ \widehat{U}, & \text{else,} \end{cases} \tag{12}$$

where $i^* = \min(\{i \mid \widehat{x} \in W^i \setminus \widehat{T}\}) - 1$.

Note that the safety-part of the specification is taken care of by only keeping those states in $\mathrm{CPre}_{\widehat{S}}$ that intersect $\widehat{R}$. So, intuitively, the fixed-point in (11) iteratively enlarges the target state set while always remaining within the safety constraint. We define the procedure implementing the iterative computation of (11) until convergence by $\mathsf{Reach}_\infty(\widehat{T}, \widehat{R}, \widehat{S})$. We will also use a version of $\mathsf{Reach}$ which runs $m$ steps of (11) for a parameter $m \in \mathbb{Z}_{>0}$. Here, we can again obtain $\mathsf{Reach}_\infty(\widehat{T}, \widehat{R}, \widehat{S})$ by chaining $\mathsf{Reach}_m$ computations, i.e., given $W^m$ computed by $\mathsf{Reach}_m(\widehat{T}, \widehat{R}, \widehat{S})$, one obtains $W^{2m}$ from $\mathsf{Reach}_m(W^m, \widehat{R}, \widehat{S})$, if no fixed-point is reached beforehand.

### 3.2 Multi-resolution Fixed-Points for Multi-layered ABCS

Next, we present a controller synthesis algorithm which computes a multi-layered abstract controller $\mathbf{C}$ solving the safety and reach-avoid control problems $(\widehat{\mathbf{S}}, \psi_{\text{safe}})$ and $(\widehat{\mathbf{S}}, \psi_{\text{reach}})$ over a sequence of $L$ abstract systems $\widehat{\mathbf{S}} := \{\widehat{S}_l\}_{l \in [1;L]}$. Here, synthesis will perform the iterative computations $\mathsf{Safe}$ and $\mathsf{Reach}$ from Sect. 3.1 at each layer, but also switch between abstraction layers during this computation. To avoid notational clutter, we write $\mathsf{Safe}(\cdot, l)$, $\mathsf{Reach}_\cdot(\cdot, \cdot, l)$ to refer to $\mathsf{Safe}(\cdot, \widehat{S}_l)$, $\mathsf{Reach}_\cdot(\cdot, \cdot, \widehat{S}_l)$ within this procedure.

The core idea that enables switching between layers during successive steps of the fixed-point iterations are the saving and re-loading of the computed winning states to and from the lowest layer $l = 1$ (indicated in green in the subsequently discussed algorithms). This projection is formalized by the operator

$$\Gamma^{\downarrow}_{ll'}(\Upsilon_{l'}) = \begin{cases} \widehat{R}_{ll'}(\Upsilon_{l'}), & l \leq l' \\ \{\hat{x} \in \widehat{X}_l \mid \widehat{R}_{l'l}(\hat{x}) \subseteq \Upsilon_{l'}\}, & l > l' \end{cases} \tag{13}$$

where $l, l' \in [1; L]$ and $\Upsilon_{l'} \subseteq \widehat{X}_{l'}$. The operation $\Gamma^{\downarrow}_{ll'}(\Upsilon_{l'}) \subseteq \widehat{X}_l$ under-approximates a set $\Upsilon_{l'} \subseteq \widehat{X}_{l'}$ with one in layer $l$.

In this section, we shall assume that each $\widehat{F}_l$ is pre-computed for all states within $\widehat{R}_l$ in every $l \in [1; L]$. In Sect. 3.3, we shall compute $\widehat{F}_l$ lazily.

**Safety Control.** We consider the computation of a multi-layered safety controller $\mathbf{C} \in \mathcal{C}(\widehat{\mathbf{S}}, \psi_{\mathsf{safe}})$ by the iterative function SafeIteration in Algorithm 1 assuming that $\widehat{\mathbf{S}}$ is pre-computed. We refer to this scenario by the wrapper function EagerSafe($\widehat{R}_1, L$), which calls the iterative algorithm SafeIteration with parameters $(\widehat{R}_1, \emptyset, L, \emptyset)$. For the moment, assume that the ComputeTransitions method in line 1 does nothing (i.e., the gray lines of Algorithm 1 are ignored in the execution).

When initialized with SafeIteration($\widehat{R}_1, \emptyset, L, \emptyset$), Algorithm 1 performs the following computations. It starts in layer $l = L$ with an outer recursion count $i = 1$ (not shown in Algorithm 1) and reduces $l$, one step at the time, until $l = 1$ is reached. Upon reaching $l = 1$, it starts over again from layer $L$ with recursion count $i + 1$ and a new safe set $\Upsilon$. In every such iteration $i$, one step of the safety fixed-point is performed for every layer and the resulting set is stored in the layer 1 map $\Upsilon \subseteq \widehat{X}_1$, whereas $\Psi \subseteq \widehat{X}_1$ keeps the knowledge of the previous iteration. If the finest layer ($l = 1$) is reached and we have $\Psi = \Upsilon$, the algorithm terminates. Otherwise $\Upsilon$ is copied to $\Psi$, $\Upsilon$ and $\mathbf{C}$ are reset to $\emptyset$ and SafeIteration starts a new iteration (see Line 10).

After SafeIteration has terminated, it returns a multi-layered controller $\mathbf{C} = \{C^l\}_{l \in [1;L]}$ (with one controller per layer) which only contains the domains of the respective controllers $C^l$ (see Line 3 in Algorithm 1). The transition functions $G^l$ are computed afterward by choosing one input $\widehat{u} \in \widehat{U}$ for every $\widehat{x} \in D^l$ s.t.

$$\widehat{u} = G^l(\widehat{x})\widehat{F}_l(\widehat{x}, \widehat{u}) \subseteq \Gamma^{\downarrow}_{l1}(\Psi). \tag{14}$$

As stated before, the main ingredient for the multi-resolution fixed-point is that states encountered for layer $l$ in iteration $i$ are saved to the lowest layer 1 (Line 4, green) and "loaded" back to the respective layer $l$ in iteration $i + 1$ (Line 2, green). This has the effect that a state $\widehat{x} \in \widehat{X}_l$ with $l > 1$, which was not contained in $W$ computed in layer $l$ and iteration $i$ via Line 2, might be included in $\Gamma^{\downarrow}_{l1}(\Psi)$ loaded in the next iteration $i+1$ when re-computing Line 2 for $l$. This happens if all states $x \in \widehat{x}$ were added to $\Upsilon$ by some layer $l' < l$ in iteration $i$.

Due to the effect described above, the map $W$ encountered in Line 2 for a particular layer $l$ throughout different iterations $i$ might not be monotonically shrinking. However, the latter is true for layer 1, which implies that EagerSafe($\widehat{R}_1, L$) is sound and complete w.r.t. layer 1 as formalized by Theorem 1.

**Algorithm 1.** SafeIteration

**Require:** $\Psi \subseteq \widehat{X}_1$, $\Upsilon \subseteq \widehat{X}_1$, $l$, $\mathbf{C}$

ComputeTransitions($\Gamma^{\downarrow}_{l1}(\Psi) \setminus \Gamma^{\downarrow}_{l1}(\Upsilon), l$)
$W \leftarrow$ Safe($\Gamma^{\downarrow}_{l1}(\Psi), l$)
$\mathbf{C} \leftarrow \mathbf{C} \cup \{C_l \leftarrow (W, \widehat{U}, \emptyset)\}$ // store the controller domain, but not moves
$\Upsilon \leftarrow \Upsilon \cup \Gamma^{\downarrow}_{1l}(W)$
**if** $l \neq 1$ **then** // go finer
  $\langle \Psi, \mathbf{C} \rangle \leftarrow$ SafeIteration($\Psi, \Upsilon, l-1, \mathbf{C}$)
  **return** $\langle \Psi, \mathbf{C} \rangle$
**else**
  **if** $\Psi \neq \Upsilon$ **then**
    $\langle \Psi, \mathbf{C} \rangle \leftarrow$ SafeIteration($\Upsilon, \emptyset, L, \emptyset$) // start new iteration
    **return** $\langle \Psi, \mathbf{C} \rangle$
  **else**
    **return** $\langle \Psi, \mathbf{C} \rangle$ // terminate
  **end if**
**end if**

**Theorem 1** ([23]). EagerSafe *is sound and complete w.r.t. layer* 1.

It is important to mention that the algorithm EagerSafe is presented only to make a smoother transition to the lazy ABCS for safety (to be presented in the next section). In practice, EagerSafe itself is of little algorithmic value as it is always slower than Safe($\cdot, \widehat{S}_1$), but produces the same result. This is because in EagerSafe, the fixed-point computation in the finest layer does not use the coarser layers' winning domain in any meaningful way. So the computation in all the layers—except in $\widehat{S}_1$—goes to waste.

**Reach-Avoid Control.** We consider the computation of an abstract multi-layered reach-avoid controller $\mathbf{C} \in \mathcal{C}(\widehat{\mathbf{S}}, \psi_{\text{reach}})$ by the iterative function ReachIteration in Algorithm 2 assuming that $\widehat{\mathbf{S}}$ is pre-computed. We refer to this scenario by the wrapper function EagerReach($\widehat{T}_1, \widehat{R}_1, L$), which calls ReachIteration with parameters ($\widehat{T}_1, \widehat{R}_1, L, \emptyset$). Assume in this section that ComputeTransitions and ExpandAbstraction$_m$ do not modify anything (i.e., the gray lines of Algorithm 2 are ignored in the execution).

The recursive procedure ReachIteration$_m$ in Algorithm 2 implements the switching protocol informally discussed in Sect. 1. Lines 1–12 implement the fixed-point computation at the coarsest layer $\widehat{S}_L$ by iterating the fixed-point over $\widehat{S}_L$ until convergence (line 3). Afterward, ReachIteration$_m$ recursively calls itself (line 9) to see if the set of winning states ($W$) can be extended by a lower abstraction layer. Lines 12–28 implement the fixed-point computations in layers $l < L$ by iterating the fixed-point over $\widehat{S}_l$ for $m$ steps (line 14) for a given fixed parameter $m > 0$. If the analysis already reaches a fixed point, then, as in the first case, the algorithm ReachIteration$_m$ recursively calls itself (line 21) to check if further states can be added in a lower layer. If no fixed-point is reached in line 14, more states could be added in the current layer by running Reach for

**Algorithm 2.** $\mathsf{ReachIteration}_m$

**Require:** $\Upsilon \subseteq \widehat{X}_1, \Psi \subseteq \widehat{X}_1$, $l$, $\mathbf{C}$
1: **if** $l = L$ **then**
2: ComputeTransitions($\Gamma^{\downarrow}_{l1}(\Psi), l$)
3: $\langle W, C \rangle \leftarrow \mathsf{Reach}_{\infty}(\Gamma^{\downarrow}_{l1}(\Upsilon), \Gamma^{\downarrow}_{l1}(\Psi), l)$
4: $\mathbf{C} \leftarrow \mathbf{C} \cup \{C\}$
5: $\Upsilon \leftarrow \Upsilon \cup \Gamma^{\downarrow}_{1l}(W)$ // save $W$ to $\Upsilon$
6: **if** $L = 1$ **then** // single-layered reachability
7: **return** $\langle \Upsilon, \mathbf{C} \rangle$
8: **else** // go finer
9: $\langle \Upsilon, \mathbf{C} \rangle \leftarrow \mathsf{ReachIteration}_m(\Upsilon, \Psi, l-1, \mathbf{C})$
10: **return** $\langle \Upsilon, \mathbf{C} \rangle$
11: **end if**
12: **else**
13: ExpandAbstraction$_m(\Upsilon, l)$
14: $\langle W, C \rangle \leftarrow \mathsf{Reach}_{m}(\Gamma^{\downarrow}_{l1}(\Upsilon), \Gamma^{\downarrow}_{l1}(\Psi), l)$
15: $\mathbf{C} \leftarrow \mathbf{C} \cup \{C\}$
16: $\Upsilon \leftarrow \Upsilon \cup \Gamma^{\downarrow}_{1l}(W)$ // save $W$ to $\Upsilon$
17: **if** Fixed-point is reached in line 14 **then**
18: **if** $l = 1$ **then** // finest layer reached
19: **return** $\langle \Upsilon, \mathbf{C} \rangle$
20: **else** // go finer
21: $\langle \Upsilon, \mathbf{C} \rangle \leftarrow \mathsf{ReachIteration}_m(\Upsilon, \Psi, l-1, \mathbf{C})$
22: **return** $\langle \Upsilon, \mathbf{C} \rangle$
23: **end if**
24: **else** // go coarser
25: $\langle \Upsilon, \mathbf{C} \rangle \leftarrow \mathsf{ReachIteration}_m(\Upsilon, \Psi, l+1, \mathbf{C})$
26: **return** $\langle \Upsilon, \mathbf{C} \rangle$
27: **end if**
28: **end if**

more then $m$ steps. However, this might not be efficient (see the example in Sect. 1). The algorithm therefore attempts to go coarser when recursively calling itself (line 25) to expand the fixed-point in a coarser layer instead. Intuitively, this is possible if states added by lower layer fixed-point computations have now "bridged" a region where precise control was needed and can now be used to enable control in coarser layers again. This also shows the intuition behind the parameter $m$. If we set it to $m = 1$, the algorithm might attempt to go coarser before this "bridging" is completed. The parameter $m$ can therefore be used as a tuning parameter to adjust the frequency of such attempts and is only needed in layers $l < L$. The algorithm terminates if a fixed-point is reached in the lowest layer (line 7 and line 9). In this case the layer 1 winning state set $\Upsilon$ and the multi-layered controller $\mathbf{C}$ is returned.

It was shown in [25] that this switching protocol ensures that $\mathsf{EagerReach}_m$ is sound and complete w.r.t. layer 1.

**Theorem 2** ([25]). $\mathsf{EagerReach}_m$ *is sound and complete w.r.t. layer* 1.

**Algorithm 3.** ComputeTransitions

**Require:** $\Upsilon \subseteq \widehat{X}_l, l$

**for** $\widehat{x} \in \Upsilon, \widehat{u} \in \widehat{U}$ **do**
  **if** $\widehat{F}_l(\widehat{x}, \widehat{u})$ is undefined **then**
    compute $\widehat{F}_l(\widehat{x}, \widehat{u})$ as in (2)
  **end if**
**end for**

**Algorithm 4.** $\mathsf{ExpandAbstraction}_m$

**Require:** $\Upsilon \subseteq \widehat{X}_1, l$

$W' \leftarrow \mathrm{Pre}^m_{\widehat{A}^L_l}(\Gamma^{\uparrow}_{L1}(\Upsilon)) \setminus \Gamma^{\downarrow}_{L1}(\Upsilon)$
$W'' \leftarrow \Gamma^{\downarrow}_{lL}(W')$
ComputeTransitions($W'' \cap \widehat{R}_l, l$)

### 3.3 Lazy Exploration Within Multi-layered ABCS

We now consider the case where the multi-layered abstractions $\widehat{\mathbf{S}}$ are computed lazily. Given the multi-resolution fixed-points discussed in the previous section, this requires tightly over-approximating the region of the state space which might be explored by Reach or Safe in the current layer, called the *frontier.* Then abstract transitions are only constructed for *frontier states* and the currently considered layer $l$ via Algorithm 3. As already discussed in Sect. 1, the computation of *frontier states* differs for safety and reachability objectives.

**Safety Control.** We now consider the *lazy* computation of a multi-layered safety controller $\mathbf{C} \in \mathcal{C}(\widehat{\mathbf{S}}, \psi_{\mathrm{safe}})$. We refer to this scenario by the wrapper function LazySafe($\widehat{R}_1, L$) which simply calls SafeIteration($\widehat{R}_1, \emptyset, L, \emptyset$).

This time, Line 1 of Algorithm 1 is used to explore transitions. The frontier cells at layer $l$ are given by $\mathcal{F}_l = \Gamma^{\downarrow}_{l1}(\Psi) \setminus \Gamma^{\downarrow}_{l1}(\Upsilon)$. The call to ComputeTransitions in Algorithm 3 updates the abstract transitions for the frontier cells. In the first iteration of SafeIteration($\widehat{R}_1, \emptyset, L, \emptyset$), we have $\Psi = \widehat{R}_1$ and $\Upsilon = \emptyset$. Thus, $\mathcal{F}_L = \Gamma^{\downarrow}_{1L}(\widehat{R}_1) = \widehat{R}_L$, and hence, for layer $L$, all transitions for states inside the safe set are pre-computed in the first iteration of Algorithm 1. In lower layers $l < L$, the frontier $\mathcal{F}_l$ defines all states which are (i) not marked unsafe by all layers in the previous iteration, i.e., are in $\Gamma^{\downarrow}_{l1}(\Psi)$, but (ii) cannot stay safe for $i$ time-steps in any layer $l' > l$, i.e., are not in $\Gamma^{\downarrow}_{l1}(\Upsilon)$. Hence, $\mathcal{F}_l$ defines a small boundary around the set $W$ computed in the previous iteration of Safe in layer $l + 1$ (see Sect. 1 for an illustrative example of this construction).

It has been shown in [23] that all states which need to be checked for safety in layer $l$ of iteration $i$ are indeed explored by this frontier construction. This implies that Theorem 1 directly transfers from EagerSafe to LazySafe.

**Theorem 3.** LazySafe *is sound and complete w.r.t. layer* 1.

**Reach-Avoid Control.** We now consider the lazy computation of a multi-layered reach-avoid controller $\mathbf{C} \in \mathcal{C}(\widehat{\mathbf{S}}, \psi_{\text{reach}})$. We refer to this scenario by the wrapper function $\mathsf{LazyReach}_m(\widehat{T}_1, \widehat{R}_1, L)$ which calls $\mathsf{ReachIteration}_m(\widehat{T}_1, \widehat{R}_1, L, \emptyset)$.

In the first iteration of $\mathsf{ReachIteration}_m$ we have the same situation as in LazySafe; given that $\Psi = \widehat{R}_1$, line 2 in Algorithm 2 pre-computes all transitions for states inside the safe set and ComputeTransitions does not perform any computations for layer $L$ in further iterations. For $l < L$ however, the situation is different. As Reach computes a smallest fixed-point, it iteratively enlarges the set $\widehat{T}_1$ (given when ReachIteration is initialized). Computing transitions for all not yet explored states in every iteration would therefore be very wasteful (see the example in Sect. 1). Therefore, $\mathsf{ExpandAbstraction}_m$ determines an over-approximation of the frontier states instead in the following manner: it computes the predecessors (not controllable predecessors!) of the already-obtained set $\Upsilon$ optimistically by (i) using (coarse) auxiliary abstractions for this computation and (ii) applying a *cooperative predecessor* operator.

This requires a set of auxiliary systems, given by

$$\widehat{\mathbf{A}} = \{\widehat{A}_l^L\}_{l=1}^L, \qquad \widehat{A}_l^L := \widehat{S}(\Sigma, \tau_l, \eta_L) = (\widehat{X}_L, \widehat{U}, \widehat{F}_l^L). \tag{15}$$

The abstract system $\widehat{A}_l^L$ induced by $\Sigma$ captures the $\tau_l$-duration transitions in the coarsest layer state space $\widehat{X}_L$. Using $\tau_l$ instead of $\tau_L$ is important, as $\tau_L$ might cause "holes" between the computed frontier and the current target $\Upsilon$ which cannot be bridged by a shorter duration control actions in layer $l$. This would render $\mathsf{LazyReach}_m$ unsound. Also note that in $\mathsf{ExpandAbstraction}_m$, we do not restrict attention to the safe set. This is because $\widehat{R}_l \supseteq \widehat{R}_L$, and when the inequality is strict then the safe states in layer $l$ which are possibly winning but are covered by an obstacle in layer $L$ (see Fig. 1) can also be explored.

For $\Upsilon \subseteq \widehat{X}_L$ and $l \in [1; L]$, we define the *cooperative predecessor* operator

$$\mathrm{Pre}_{\widehat{A}_l^L}(\Upsilon) = \{\widehat{x} \in \widehat{X}_L \mid \exists \widehat{u} \in \widehat{U} \,.\, \widehat{F}_l^L(\widehat{x}, \widehat{u}) \cap \Upsilon \neq \emptyset\}. \tag{16}$$

in analogy to the controllable predecessor operator in (8). We apply the cooperative predecessor operator $m$ times in $\mathsf{ExpandAbstraction}_m$, i.e.,

$$\begin{aligned} &\mathrm{Pre}^1_{\widehat{A}_l^L}(\Upsilon) = \mathrm{Pre}_{\widehat{A}_l^L}(\Upsilon) \text{ and} \\ &\mathrm{Pre}^{j+1}_{\widehat{A}_l^L}(\Upsilon) = \mathrm{Pre}^j_{\widehat{A}_l^L}(\Upsilon) \cup \mathrm{Pre}_{\widehat{A}_l^L}(\mathrm{Pre}^j_{\widehat{A}_l^L}(\Upsilon)). \end{aligned} \tag{17}$$

Calling $\mathsf{ExpandAbstraction}_m$ with parameters $\Upsilon \subseteq \widehat{X}_1$ and $l < L$ applies $\mathrm{Pre}^m_{\widehat{A}_l^L}$ to the over-approximation of $\Upsilon$ by abstract states in layer $L$. This over-approximation is defined as the dual operator of the under-approximation operator $\Gamma^{\downarrow}_{ll'}$:

$$\Gamma^{\uparrow}_{ll'}(\Upsilon_{l'}) := \begin{cases} \widehat{R}_{ll'}(\Upsilon_{l'}), & l \leq l' \\ \{\hat{x} \in \widehat{X}_l \mid \widehat{R}_{l'l}(\hat{x}) \cap \Upsilon_{l'} \neq \emptyset\}, & l > l' \end{cases} \tag{18}$$

where $l, l' \in [1; L]$ and $\Upsilon_{l'} \subseteq \widehat{X}_{l'}$. Finally, $m$ controls the size of the frontier set and determines the maximum progress that can be made in a single backwards synthesis run in a layer $l < L$.

It can be shown that all states which might be added to the winning state set in the current iteration are indeed explored by this frontier construction, implying that $\mathsf{LazyReach}_m(\widehat{T}_1, \widehat{R}_1, L)$ is sound and complete w.r.t. layer 1. In other words, Theorem 2 can be transfered from $\mathsf{EagerReach}_m$ to $\mathsf{LazyReach}_m$ (see the extended version [24] for the proof).

**Theorem 4.** $\mathsf{LazyReach}_m$ *is sound and complete w.r.t. layer* 1.

## 4 Experimental Evaluation

We have implemented our algorithms in the MASCOT tool and we present some brief evaluation.[4]

### 4.1 Reach-Avoid Control Problem for a Unicycle

We use a nonlinear kinematic system model commonly known as the *unicycle model*, specified as

$$\dot{x}_1 \in u_1 \cos(x_3) + W_1 \quad \dot{x}_2 \in u_1 \sin(x_3) + W_2 \quad \dot{x}_3 = u_2$$

where $x_1$ and $x_2$ are the state variables representing 2D Cartesian coordinates, $x_3$ is a state variable representing the angular displacement, $u_1$, $u_2$ are control input variables that influence the linear and angular velocities respectively, and $W_1$, $W_2$ are the perturbation bounds in the respective dimensions given by $W_1 = W_2 = [-0.05, 0.05]$. The perturbations render this deceptively simple problem computationally intensive. We run controller synthesis experiments for the unicycle inside a two dimensional space with obstacles and a designated target area, as shown in Fig. 2. We use three layers for the multi-layered algorithms $\mathsf{EagerReach}$ and $\mathsf{LazyReach}$. All experiments presented in this subsection were performed on a Intel Core i5 3.40 GHz processor.

**Algorithm Comparison.** Table 1 shows a comparison on the $\mathsf{Reach}$, $\mathsf{EagerReach}_2$, and $\mathsf{LazyReach}_2$ algorithms. The projection to the state space of the transitions constructed by $\mathsf{LazyReach}_2$ for the finest abstraction is shown in Fig. 2b. The corresponding visualization for $\mathsf{EagerReach}_2$ would show all of the uncolored space being covered by red. The savings of $\mathsf{LazyReach}_2$ over $\mathsf{EagerReach}_2$ can be mostly attributed to this difference.

[4] Available at http://mascot.mpi-sws.org/.

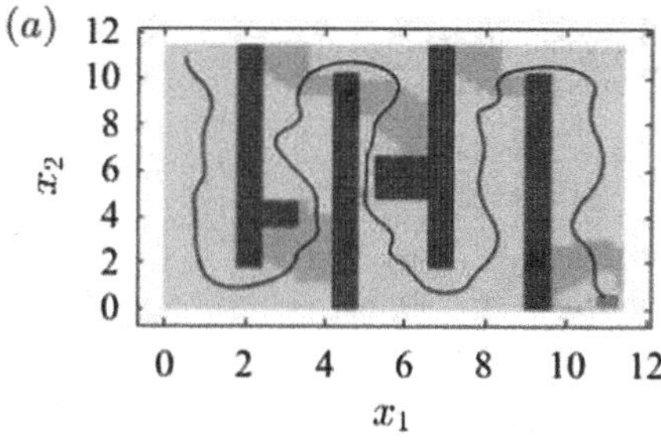


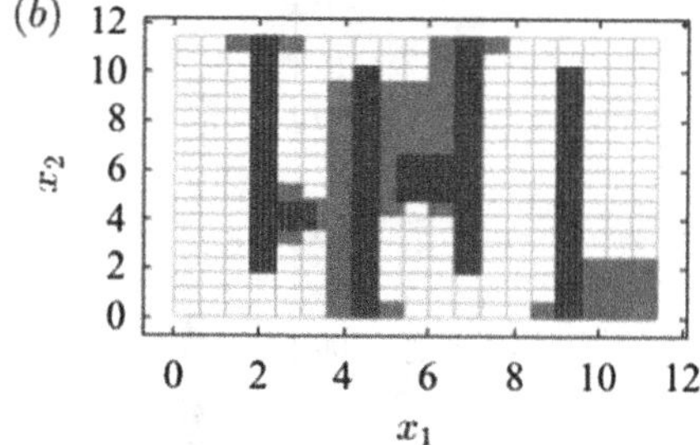


**Fig. 2.** (a) Solution of the unicycle reach-avoid problem by $\mathsf{LazyReach}_2$. (b) Cells of the finest layer ($l = 1$) for which transitions were computed during $\mathsf{LazyReach}_2$ are marked in red. For $\mathsf{EagerReach}_2$, all uncolored cells would also be red. (Color figure online)

**Table 1.** Comparison of running times (in seconds) of reachability algorithms on the perturbed unicycle system.

| | Reach | EagerReach$_2$ | LazyReach$_2$ |
|---|---|---|---|
| Abstraction | 2590 | 2628 | 588 |
| Synthesis | 818 | 73 | 21 |
| Total | 3408 (126%) | 2701 (100%) | 609 (22.5%) |

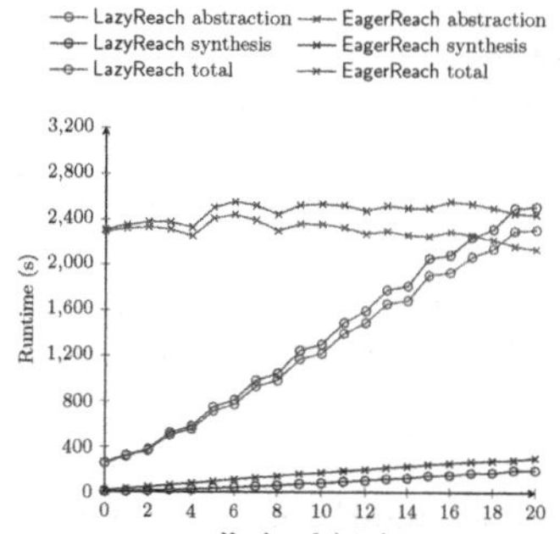


**Fig. 3.** Runtime with increasing number of obstacles

**Varying State Space Complexity.** We investigate how the lazy algorithm and the multi-layered baseline perform with respect to the structure of the state space, achieved by varying the number of identical obstacles, $o$, placed in the open area of the state space. The runtimes for $\mathsf{EagerReach}_2$ and $\mathsf{LazyReach}_2$ are plotted in Fig. 3. We observe that $\mathsf{LazyReach}_2$ runs fast when there are few obstacles by only constructing the abstraction in the finest layer for the immediate surroundings of those obstacles. By $o = 20$, $\mathsf{LazyReach}_2$ explores the entire state space in the finest layer, and its performance is slightly worse than that of $\mathsf{EagerReach}_2$ (due to additional bookkeeping). The general decreasing trend in the abstraction construction runtime for $\mathsf{EagerReach}_2$ is because transitions outgoing from obstacle states are not computed.

### 4.2 Safety Control Problem for a DC-DC Boost Converter [23]

We evaluate our safety algorithm on a benchmark DC-DC boost converter example from [17,31,37]. The system $\Sigma$ is a second order differential inclusion $\dot{X}(t) \in A_p X(t) + b + W$ with two switching modes $p \in \{1, 2\}$, where

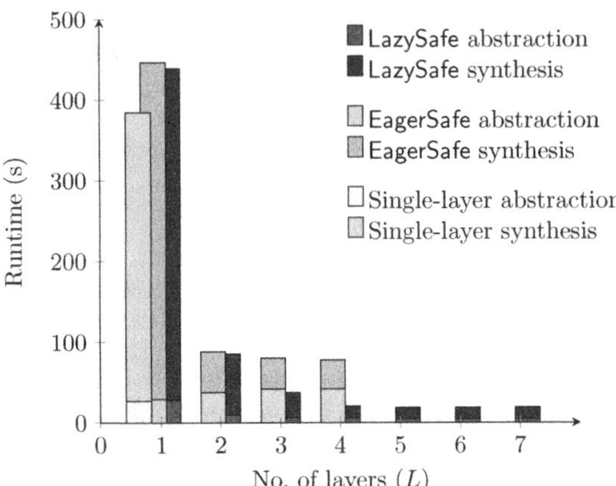


**Fig. 4.** Run-time comparison of LazySafe and EagerSafe on the DC-DC boost converter example. $L > 4$ is not used for EagerSafe since coarser layers fail to produce a non-empty winning set. The same is true for $L > 7$ in LazySafe.

$$b = \begin{bmatrix} \frac{v_s}{x_l} \\ 0 \end{bmatrix}, A_1 = \begin{bmatrix} -\frac{r_l}{x_l} & 0 \\ 0 & -\frac{1}{x_c}\frac{r_0}{r_0+r_c} \end{bmatrix}, A_2 = \begin{bmatrix} -\frac{1}{x_l}(r_l + \frac{r_0 r_c}{r_0+r_c}) & \frac{1}{5}(-\frac{1}{x_l}\frac{r_0}{r_0+r_c}) \\ 5\frac{r_0}{r_0+r_c}\frac{1}{x_c} & -\frac{1}{x_c}\frac{1}{r_0+r_c} \end{bmatrix},$$

with $r_0 = 1$, $v_s = 1$, $r_l = 0.05$, $r_c = 0.5r_l$, $x_l = 3$, $x_c = 70$ and $W = [-0.001, 0.001] \times [-0.001, 0.001]$. A physical and more detailed description of the model can be found in [17]. The safety control problem that we consider is given by $\langle \Sigma, \psi_{\text{safe}} \rangle$, where $\psi_{\text{safe}} = always([1.15, 1.55] \times [5.45, 5.85])$. We evaluate the performance of our LazySafe algorithm on this benchmark and compare it to EagerSafe and a single-layered baseline. For LazySafe and EagerSafe, we vary the number of layers used. The results are presented in Fig. 4. In the experiments, the finest layer is common, and is parameterized by $\eta_1 = [0.0005, 0.0005]$ and $\tau_1 = 0.0625$. The ratio between the grid parameters and the sampling times of the successive layers is 2.

From Fig. 4, we see that LazySafe is significantly faster than both EagerSafe (and the single-layered baseline) as $L$ increases. The single layered case ($L = 1$) takes slightly more time in both LazySafe and EagerSafe due to the extra book-keeping in the multi-layered algorithms. In Fig. 5, we visualize the domain of the constructed transitions and the synthesized controllers in each layer for LazySafe$(\cdot, 6)$. The safe set is mostly covered by cells in the two coarsest layers. This phenomenon is responsible for the computational savings over LazySafe$(\cdot, 1)$.

In contrast to the reach-avoid control problem for a unicycle, in this example, synthesis takes significantly longer time than the abstraction. To reason about this difference is difficult, because the two systems are completely incomparable, and the abstraction parameters are very different. Still we highlight two suspected reasons for this mismatch: (a) Abstraction is faster because of the lower dimension and smaller control input space of the boost converter, (b) A smaller

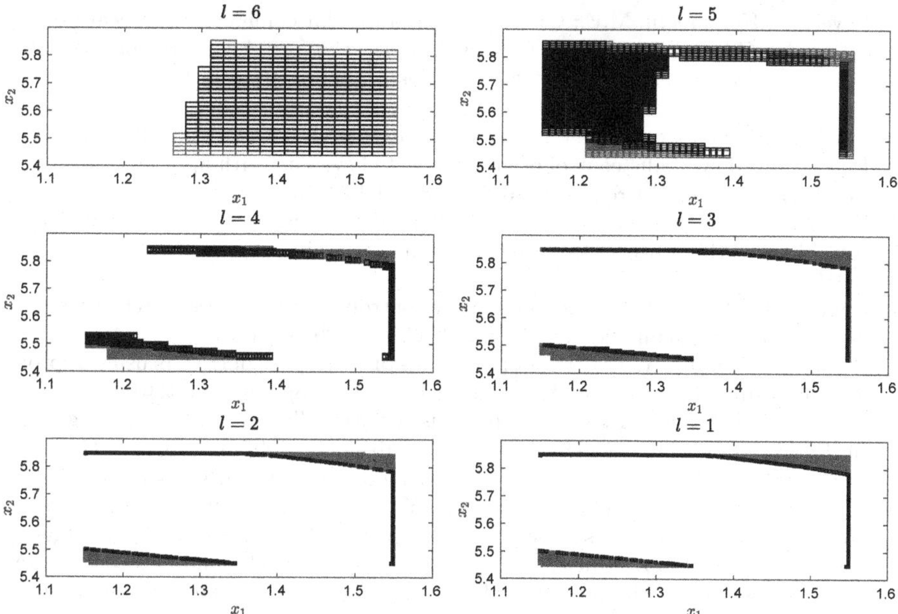


**Fig. 5.** Domain of the computed transitions (union of red and black region) and the synthesized controllers (black region) for the DC-DC boost converter example, computed by LazySafe(·, 6). (Color figure online)

sampling time (0.0625 s as compared to 0.225 s for the unicycle) in the finest layer of abstraction for the boost converter results in slower convergence of the fixed-point iteration.

## 5 Conclusion

ABCS is an exciting new development in the field of formal synthesis of cyber-physical systems. We have summarized a multi-resolution approach to ABCS. Fruitful avenues for future work include designing scalable and robust tools, and combining basic algorithmic techniques with structural heuristics or orthogonal techniques (e.g. those based on data-driven exploration).

## References


1. Ames, A.D., et al.: First steps toward formal controller synthesis for bipedal robots. In: Proceedings of the 18th International Conference on Hybrid Systems: Computation and Control, pp. 209–218. ACM (2015)
2. Gol, E.A., Lazar, M., Belta, C.: Language-guided controller synthesis for discrete-time linear systems. In: HSCC, pp. 95–104. ACM (2012)
3. Beyer, D., Henzinger, T.A., Jhala, R., Majumdar, R.: The software model checker blast. Int. J. Softw. Tools Technol. Transf. **9**(5–6), 505–525 (2007)

4. Beyer, D., Keremoglu, M.E.: CPAchecker: a tool for configurable software verification. In: Gopalakrishnan, G., Qadeer, S. (eds.) CAV 2011. LNCS, vol. 6806, pp. 184–190. Springer, Heidelberg (2011). https://doi.org/10.1007/978-3-642-22110-1_16
5. Borri, A., Dimarogonas, D.V., Johansson, K.H., Di Benedetto, M.D., Pola, G.: Decentralized symbolic control of interconnected systems with application to vehicle platooning. IFAC Proc. Vol. **46**(27), 285–292 (2013)
6. Bulancea, O.L., Nilsson, P., Ozay, N.: Nonuniform abstractions, refinement and controller synthesis with novel BDD encodings. arXiv preprint arXiv:1804.04280 (2018)
7. Cámara, J., Girard, A., Gössler, G.: Safety controller synthesis for switched systems using multi-scale symbolic models. In: CDC, pp. 520–525 (2011)
8. Cámara, J., Girard, A., Gössler, G.: Synthesis of switching controllers using approximately bisimilar multiscale abstractions. In: HSCC, pp. 191–200 (2011)
9. Cassez, F.: Efficient on-the-fly algorithms for partially observable timed games. In: Raskin, J.-F., Thiagarajan, P.S. (eds.) FORMATS 2007. LNCS, vol. 4763, pp. 5–24. Springer, Heidelberg (2007). https://doi.org/10.1007/978-3-540-75454-1_3
10. Clarke, E., Grumberg, O., Jha, S., Lu, Y., Veith, H.: Counterexample-guided abstraction refinement for symbolic model checking. J. ACM **50**(5), 752–794 (2003)
11. Coogan, S., Arcak, M.: Efficient finite abstraction of mixed monotone systems. In: Proceedings of the 18th International Conference on Hybrid Systems: Computation and Control, pp. 58–67. ACM (2015)
12. de Alfaro, L., Roy, P.: Solving games via three-valued abstraction refinement. Inf. Comput. **208**(6), 666–676 (2010)
13. Fribourg, L., Kühne, U., Soulat, R.: Constructing attractors of nonlinear dynamical systems. In: OASIcs-OpenAccess Series in Informatics, vol. 31. Schloss Dagstuhl-Leibniz-Zentrum fuer Informatik (2013)
14. Fribourg, L., Kühne, U., Soulat, R.: Finite controlled invariants for sampled switched systems. Form. Methods Syst. Des. **45**(3), 303–329 (2014)
15. Girard, A.: Towards a multiresolution approach to linear control. TAC **51**(8), 1261–1270 (2006)
16. Girard, A., Gössler, G., Mouelhi, S.: Safety controller synthesis for incrementally stable switched systems using multiscale symbolic models. TAC **61**(6), 1537–1549 (2016)
17. Girard, A., Pola, G., Tabuada, P.: Approximately bisimilar symbolic models for incrementally stable switched systems. TAC **55**(1), 116–126 (2010)
18. Gruber, F., Kim, E.S., Arcak, M.: Sparsity-aware finite abstraction. In: 2017 IEEE 56th Annual Conference on Decision and Control (CDC), pp. 2366–2371. IEEE (2017)
19. Grüne, L.: An adaptive grid scheme for the discrete Hamilton-Jacobi-Bellman equation. Numer. Math. **75**(3), 319–337 (1997)
20. Henzinger, T.A., Jhala, R., Majumdar, R.: Counterexample-guided control. In: Baeten, J.C.M., Lenstra, J.K., Parrow, J., Woeginger, G.J. (eds.) ICALP 2003. LNCS, vol. 2719, pp. 886–902. Springer, Heidelberg (2003). https://doi.org/10.1007/3-540-45061-0_69
21. Henzinger, T.A., Jhala, R., Majumdar, R., Sutre, G.: Lazy abstraction. ACM SIGPLAN Not. **37**(1), 58–70 (2002)
22. Herbreteau, F., Srivathsan, B., Walukiewicz, I.: Lazy abstractions for timed automata. In: Sharygina, N., Veith, H. (eds.) CAV 2013. LNCS, vol. 8044, pp. 990–1005. Springer, Heidelberg (2013). https://doi.org/10.1007/978-3-642-39799-8_71

23. Hsu, K., Majumdar, R., Mallik, K., Schmuck, A.-K.: Lazy abstraction-based control for safety specifications. In: 2018 IEEE Conference on Decision and Control (CDC), pp. 4902–4907. IEEE (2018)
24. Hsu, K., Majumdar, R., Mallik, K., Schmuck, A.-K.: Lazy abstraction-based controller synthesis. arXiv preprint arXiv:1804.02722 (2018)
25. Hsu, K., Majumdar, R., Mallik, K., Schmuck, A.-K.: Multi-layered abstraction-based controller synthesis for continuous-time systems. In: HSCC, pp. 120–129. ACM (2018)
26. Khaled, M., Zamani, M.: pFaces: an acceleration ecosystem for symbolic control. In: Proceedings of the 22nd ACM International Conference on Hybrid Systems: Computation and Control, pp. 252–257. ACM (2019)
27. Li, Y., Liu, J.: ROCS: a robustly complete control synthesis tool for nonlinear dynamical systems. In: HSCC, pp. 130–135. ACM (2018)
28. Maler, O., Pnueli, A., Sifakis, J.: On the synthesis of discrete controllers for timed systems. In: Mayr, E.W., Puech, C. (eds.) STACS 1995. LNCS, vol. 900, pp. 229–242. Springer, Heidelberg (1995). https://doi.org/10.1007/3-540-59042-0_76
29. Mallik, K., Schmuck, A.-K., Soudjani, S., Majumdar, R.: Compositional synthesis of finite-state abstractions. IEEE Trans. Autom. Control **64**(6), 2629–2636 (2018)
30. Mitchell, I.M.: Comparing forward and backward reachability as tools for safety analysis. In: Bemporad, A., Bicchi, A., Buttazzo, G. (eds.) HSCC 2007. LNCS, vol. 4416, pp. 428–443. Springer, Heidelberg (2007). https://doi.org/10.1007/978-3-540-71493-4_34
31. Mouelhi, S., Girard, A., Gössler, G.: CoSyMA: a tool for controller synthesis using multi-scale abstractions. In: HSCC, pp. 83–88. ACM (2013)
32. Nilsson, P., et al.: Correct-by-construction adaptive cruise control: two approaches. IEEE Trans. Contr. Sys. Techn. **24**(4), 1294–1307 (2016)
33. Nilsson, P., Ozay, N., Liu, J.: Augmented finite transition systems as abstractions for control synthesis. Discret. Event Dyn. Syst. **27**(2), 301–340 (2017)
34. Pola, G., Borri, A., Di Benedetto, M.D.: Integrated design of symbolic controllers for nonlinear systems. TAC **57**(2), 534–539 (2012)
35. Reissig, G., Weber, A., Rungger, M.: Feedback refinement relations for the synthesis of symbolic controllers. TAC **62**(4), 1781–1796 (2017)
36. Rungger, M., Stursberg, O.: On-the-fly model abstraction for controller synthesis. In: ACC, pp. 2645–2650. IEEE (2012)
37. Rungger, M., Zamani, M.: SCOTS: a tool for the synthesis of symbolic controllers. In: HSCC, pp. 99–104. ACM (2016)
38. Saoud, A., Girard, A., Fribourg, L.: Contract based design of symbolic controllers for vehicle platooning. In: HSCC, pp. 277–278. ACM (2018)
39. Tabuada, P.: Verification and Control of Hybrid Systems: A Symbolic Approach. Springer, Heidelberg (2009). https://doi.org/10.1007/978-1-4419-0224-5
40. Vizel, Y., Grumberg, O., Shoham, S.: Lazy abstraction and sat-based reachability in hardware model checking. In: FMCAD, pp. 173–181. IEEE (2012)
41. Hussien, O., Tabuada, P.: Lazy controller synthesis using three-valued abstractions for safety and reachability specifications. In: CDC 2018, pp. 3567–3572 (2018)

# Truth Assignments as Conditional Autarkies

Benjamin Kiesl[1], Marijn J. H. Heule[2], and Armin Biere[3](✉)

[1] CISPA Helmholtz Center for Information Security, Saarbrücken, Germany
[2] Computer Science Department, CMU, Pittsburgh, USA
[3] Institute for Formal Models and Verification, JKU, Linz, Austria
armin.biere@jku.at

**Abstract.** An autarky for a formula in propositional logic is a truth assignment that satisfies every clause it touches, i.e., every clause for which the autarky assigns at least one variable. In this paper, we present how conditional autarkies, a generalization of autarkies, give rise to novel preprocessing techniques for SAT solving. We show that conditional autarkies correspond to a new type of redundant clauses, termed globally-blocked clauses, and that the elimination of these clauses can simulate existing circuit-simplification techniques on the CNF level.

## 1 Introduction

Satisfiability (SAT) solvers have been successfully used for a broad spectrum of applications ranging from formal verification [1] over security [2] to classical mathematics [3,4]. This success came as a slight surprise because the translation of problem instances from application domains into propositional logic can lead to a loss of domain-specific information. However, this loss of information is often harmless since many domain-specific reasoning techniques (e.g., for Boolean circuits or number theory) can be simulated by SAT-preprocessing techniques such as blocked-clause elimination [5]. In this paper, we present further evidence of this observation by introducing a new propositional reasoning technique that simulates the removal of redundant inputs from Boolean circuits.

Our reasoning technique, which we call *globally-blocked-clause elimination*, is strongly related to the concept of *conditional autarkies* [6]—a generalization of *autarkies* [7,8]. Given a propositional formula in conjunctive normal form, an *autarky* is a truth assignment that satisfies every clause it touches, that is, it satisfies every clause of which it assigns at least one variable. For example, given the formula $(\overline{a} \vee b) \wedge (a \vee \overline{b} \vee \overline{c} \vee d) \wedge (c \vee \overline{d})$, the (partial) assignment that makes both $a$ and $b$ true is an autarky. In contrast, neither the assignment that makes only $a$ true nor the assignment that makes only $b$ true are autarkies because they touch clauses without satisfying them.

A *conditional autarky* is an assignment that can be split into two parts—the *conditional part* and the *autarky part*—such that the autarky part becomes an autarky after applying the conditional part to the formula. For example, after making $a$ true in the formula $(a \vee \overline{b} \vee \overline{c}) \wedge (\overline{a} \vee b \vee \overline{d}) \wedge (\overline{a} \vee \overline{b} \vee c) \wedge (\overline{a} \vee d)$ we obtain the formula $(b \vee \overline{d}) \wedge (\overline{b} \vee c) \wedge (d)$ for which the assignment that makes $b$ and $c$ true is an autarky. Hence, the assignment that makes $a$, $b$, and $c$ true is a


Y.-F. Chen et al. (Eds.): ATVA 2019, LNCS 11781, pp. 48–64, 2019.
https://doi.org/10.1007/978-3-030-31784-3_3

conditional autarky with conditional part $a$ although it is not an autarky. In fact, every truth assignment is a conditional autarky with an empty autarky part, but we are particularly interested in conditional autarkies with *non-empty* autarky parts. We show that such conditional autarkies help us find redundant clauses (i.e., clauses that can be removed from a formula without affecting satisfiability). More specifically, we present *globally-blocked clauses*, a novel type of redundant clauses that is strongly related to the conditional-autarky concept.

Globally-blocked clauses are a strict generalization of set-blocked clauses [9], which themselves are a strict generalization of blocked clauses [10]. This means that every set-blocked clause (and thus every blocked clause) is a globally-blocked clause but not vice versa. The elimination of blocked clauses can improve the efficiency of SAT solvers [11], first-order theorem provers [12], and solvers for quantified Boolean formulas (QBF) [13,14]. Moreover, it can simulate several reasoning techniques for Boolean circuits on the propositional level. Set-blocked clauses form the basis of the *satisfaction-driven clause learning* [6] paradigm for SAT solving, which can lead to exponential speed-ups on hard formulas compared to traditional *conflict-driven clause learning* [15].

We show how the elimination of globally-blocked clauses simulates circuit-reasoning techniques that could not be performed by SAT solvers so far. In a preprocessing step for the actual solving, our approach takes a formula and tries to find conditional autarkies with large autarky parts. It then uses the resulting conditional autarkies to identify and eliminate globally-blocked clauses from the formula, which results in a simplified formula that is easier to solve. In a more theoretic part of the paper, we present several properties of conditional autarkies and pin down their relationship with globally-blocked clauses and other existing types of redundant clauses.

The main purpose of this invited paper is to discuss the concept of globally-blocked clauses and relate it to conditional autarkies [6]. This concept was partially described in section 2.2.4 of the PhD thesis of the first author [16]. In this paper, we provide more details and also describe an algorithm for fast computation of multiple globally-blocked clauses from one arbitrary total assignment. This algorithm has also been implemented in the SAT solver CaDiCaL. The second purpose of this paper is to describe the history and applications of such notions of redundancy as well as how these are used in clausal proofs.

## 2 Preprocessing, Redundancy, and Proofs

Preprocessing (simplifying a formula before search) and inprocessing (simplifying a formula during search) [17] are crucial techniques in state-of-the-art SAT solvers. This line of research started with *bounded variable elimination*, which allows to significantly reduce the size of large industrial verification problems [18]. Bounded variable elimination removes variables from a formula—by combining the variable elimination with substitution—if this removal does not increase the size of the formula. More recently, some solvers even allow a small increase of the formula size.

Another popular approach to preprocessing and inprocessing are so-called *clause-elimination* techniques, which remove clauses from a formula without affecting satisfiability. Examples are the two particularly well-known clause-elimination techniques of *subsumed-clause elimination* [18] and *blocked-clause elimination* [11]. Blocked-clause elimination simulates many circuit simplification techniques on the CNF level and it allows the simulation of other high-level reasoning techniques, such as the elimination of redundant Pythagorean triples, which was crucial to solving the Pythagorean triples problem [19]. Several generalizations of subsumed clauses and blocked clauses have been proposed to further reduce the size of propositional formulas [20–22]. Moreover, clause-elimination techniques boost the effectiveness of variable-elimination techniques since the removal of clauses often enables further variable-elimination steps.

Although preprocessing techniques have contributed significantly to the improvement of SAT solvers in the last decade, they can also be expensive. To deal with this issue, SAT solvers have shifted their focus from preprocessing to inprocessing, meaning that only limited preprocessing is done initially and that later on the solver interleaves additional variable and clause-elimination techniques with the search process. One advantage of this is that inprocessing can simplify a formula after important clauses have been learned, allowing for further simplifications compared to preprocessing. As a matter of fact, inprocessing solvers have been dominating the SAT competitions since 2013.

As a drawback, the incorporation of inprocessing has made SAT solvers more complex and thus more prone to implementation errors and conceptual errors [17]. Various communities that use SAT solvers have therefore expressed interest in verifiable SAT solver output. For example, SAT solvers are used in industry to show the correctness of safety-critical hardware and software, or in mathematics to solve long-standing open problems. In both cases, it is crucial that a SAT solver not just returns a simple yes/no answer but instead produces verifiable output that certifies the correctness of its result—a so-called proof.

Constructing such proofs is a non-trivial issue as several inprocessing techniques cannot be expressed succinctly in the resolution proof system, which was commonly used in the past. This led to the search for stronger proof systems that are well-suited for practical SAT solving, and it turned out that clause-redundancy notions that form the theoretical foundation of clause-elimination techniques can also act as ideal building blocks for stronger proof systems. The DRAT proof system [23], which is based on the notion of *resolution asymmetric tautologies*, has since become the de-facto standard proof system in SAT solving. DRAT is now supported by all state-of-the-art SAT solvers and there exist formally-verified tools—in ACL2, Coq, and Isabelle [24,25]—that check the correctness of DRAT proofs. Such tools have not only been used for validating the unsatisfiability results of recent SAT competitions [26] but also for verifying the solutions of some long-standing math problems, including the Erdős discrepancy conjecture, the Pythagorean triples problem, and Schur number five [3,4,19].

To strengthen the DRAT proof system even further, proof systems based on stronger redundancy notions than resolution asymmetric tautologies have been proposed, leading to the *Propagation Redundancy* (PR) proof system [27]. This proof system is surprisingly strong even without the introduction of new variables, which usually is a key technique to obtaining short proofs. As has been shown, there exist short PR proofs without new variables for pigeon hole formulas, Tseitin formulas, and mutilated chessboard problems [28,29]—these problem families are notorious for admitting only resolution proofs of exponential size. Moreover, the PR proofs for these problems can be found automatically using the *satisfaction-driven clause learning* paradigm (SDCL) [6,30], which is a generalization of *conflict-driven clause learning*.

As DRAT has been shown to polynomially simulate the PR [28] proof system, it is possible to transform PR proofs into DRAT proofs and then check their correctness using a formally-verified checker, meaning that one can have high confidence in the correctness of results obtained by SDCL.

Research on preprocessing, clause redundancy, and proofs has also expanded beyond propositional logic. When solving quantified Boolean formulas, QBF generalizations of blocked-clause elimination have been used successfully [13]. Also, the QRAT proof system [31] (a generalization of DRAT) allows the succinct expression of virtually all QBF inprocessing techniques, and QRAT has given rise to various new QBF preprocessing techniques, such as the elimination of blocked literals [32] as well as of QRAT clauses and their generalizations [33,34]. The research on generalizing redundancy notions has also been extended to first-order logic [35], where especially the elimination of blocked clauses has proven to be a valuable preprocessing technique [12].

In the following, we present globally-blocked clauses, a new kind of redundant clauses that generalizes existing notions of redundancy in propositional logic.

## 3 Motivating Example

Consider a single-output circuit $F(I)$ (where $I$ is a set of inputs) that can be decomposed syntactically into $F(I) = G(J, H(K))$, where both $G$ and $H$ are single output sub-circuits, and $J$ and $K$ partition the inputs $I$. If we want to solve the satisfiability problem for $F$, i.e., the problem of deciding if there exists a set of inputs such that $F$ produces a 1 as its output (CIRCUIT-SAT), we can proceed as follows: We show that $G(J, x)$ is satisfiable, where $x$ is a new variable, and that $H(K)$ can produce both 0 and 1 as its output. In many situations, if the sub-circuit $H$ is given, the second requirement can be shown easily using random simulation. Checking satisfiability of $G$ remains to be shown, but is hopefully easier, since $G$ is smaller than $F$.

This circuit-level technique is also called "unique sensitization" in the FAN algorithm [36] and $H$ would be called a "headline". However, if we are only given a CNF encoding of $F$, previously known CNF preprocessing techniques are in general not able to perform such a simplification, whereas globally-blocked-clause elimination in essence allows to remove all clauses of the CNF encoding of $H$.

To continue the example, assume for simplicity that the top-level gate of $H$ is an AND gate (the same arguments apply to arbitrary top gates of $H$). After introducing Tseitin variables $x$ for $H$, $y$ and $z$ for the AND gate inputs, etc., the Tseitin encoding $F'$ of $F$ has the following structure

$$\begin{aligned} F'(I,S,T,x,y,z) &= G'(J,S,x) \wedge H'(K,x,y,z,T) \qquad \text{with} \\ H'(K,x,y,z,T) &= \underbrace{(\overline{x} \vee y) \wedge (\overline{x} \vee z) \wedge (x \vee \overline{y} \vee \overline{z})}_{\text{Tseitin encoding of top AND gate in } H} \wedge H''(K,y,z,T) \end{aligned}$$

where $S \cup T \cup \{x, y, z\}$ are new Tseitin variables. Note that $F'$, $G'$, $H'$ and $H''$ are in CNF. Further assume we find two assignments $\alpha$ and $\beta$ over the variables of $H'$, which both satisfy $H'$, i.e., $\alpha(H') = \beta(H') = 1$, and $\alpha(x) = 1$, $\beta(x) = 0$.

It is not that hard to find such assignments through local search or random decisions and unit propagation. Actually, one can also start with a total assignment with these properties, which will then—by our algorithms—be pruned down to range only over variables in $H'$. These assignments are conditional autarkies where the conditional part consists of the assignment to $x$ and the autarky part consists of the assignments to the other variables of $H'$.

It turns out that the first two binary clauses encoding the top AND gate of $H$ contain the negation $\overline{x}$ of the condition in $\alpha$, and the last ternary clause of the AND gate contains the negation $x$ of the condition in $\beta$. Moreover, these three clauses are satisfied by the autarky parts of $\alpha$ and $\beta$. As we are going to prove, this situation allows to deduce that the clauses are globally blocked and thus redundant. After removing the three AND gate clauses, both conditional autarkies $\alpha$ and $\beta$ become autarkies, allowing to remove $H'$ too.

Alternatively, blocked-clause elimination [11] or bounded variable elimination [18] would also remove $H'$, since after removing the clauses of the top gate of $H$ *cone-of-influence reduction* applies, which is simulated by both techniques [5]. Thus, for this example the key aspect of globally-blocked-clause elimination is that it allows to the remove the clauses of the headline gate connecting the two parts of the CNF, in fact simulating unique sensitization on the CNF level.

## 4 Preliminaries

Here, we present the background necessary for understanding the rest of the paper. We consider propositional formulas in conjunctive normal form (CNF), which are made up of variables, literals, and clauses, as defined in the following. A *literal* is either a variable $x$ (a *positive literal*) or the negation $\overline{x}$ of a variable $x$ (a *negative literal*). The *complement* $\overline{l}$ of a literal $l$ is defined as $\overline{l} = \overline{x}$ if $l = x$ and as $\overline{l} = x$ if $l = \overline{x}$. For a literal $l$, we denote the variable of $l$ by $var(l)$. A *clause* is a finite disjunction of the form $(l_1 \vee \dots \vee l_n)$ where $l_1, \dots, l_n$ are literals. A *tautology* is a clause that contains both a literal and its complement. If not stated otherwise, we assume that clauses are not tautologies. A *formula* is a finite conjunction of the form $C_1 \wedge \dots \wedge C_m$ where $C_1, \dots, C_m$ are clauses. Clauses can be viewed as sets of literals and formulas can be viewed as sets of clauses. For a set $L$ of literals and a formula $F$, we define $F_L = \{C \in F \mid C \cap L \neq \emptyset\}$. We sometimes write $F_l$ for $F_{\{l\}}$.

A *truth assignment* (or short, *assignment*) is a function from a set of variables to the truth values 1 (*true*) and 0 (*false*). An assignment is *total* with respect to a formula if it assigns a truth value to all variables occurring in the formula. If not stated otherwise, we do not require assignments to be total. We denote the domain of an assignment $\alpha$ by $var(\alpha)$. A literal $l$ is *satisfied* by an assignment $\alpha$ if $l$ is positive and $\alpha(var(l)) = 1$ or if it is negative and $\alpha(var(l)) = 0$. A literal is *falsified* by an assignment if its complement is satisfied by the assignment. An assignment *touches* a clause if it assigns a truth value to at least one of its literals. A clause is satisfied by an assignment $\alpha$ if it contains a literal that is satisfied by $\alpha$. Finally, a formula is satisfied by an assignment $\alpha$ if all its clauses are satisfied by $\alpha$. A formula is *satisfiable* if there exists an assignment that satisfies it. Two formulas are *logically equivalent* if they are satisfied by the same total assignments; they are *satisfiability-equivalent* if they are either both satisfiable or both unsatisfiable. We often view assignments as the sets of literals they satisfy and denote them as sequences of literals. For instance, given an assignment $\alpha$ that makes $x$ true and $y$ false, we would denote $\alpha$ by $x\,\overline{y}$ and write things like $x \in \alpha$.

We denote the empty clause by $\bot$ and the satisfied clause by $\top$. Given an assignment $\alpha$ and a clause $C$, we define $C\,|\,\alpha = \top$ if $\alpha$ satisfies $C$, otherwise $C\,|\,\alpha$ denotes the result of removing from $C$ all the literals falsified by $\alpha$. Moreover, for a formula $F$, we define $F\,|\,\alpha = \{C\,|\,\alpha \mid C \in F \text{ and } C\,|\,\alpha \neq \top\}$.

We consider a clause to be redundant with respect to a formula if the clause can be removed from the formula without affecting the formula's satisfiability or unsatisfiability:

**Definition 1.** *A clause $C$ is* redundant *with respect to a formula $F$ if $F$ and $F \wedge C$ are satisfiability-equivalent.*

For instance, the clause $C = (a \vee b)$ is redundant with respect to the formula $F = (\overline{a} \vee \overline{b})$ since $F$ and $F \wedge C$ are satisfiability-equivalent (although they are not logically equivalent).

## 5 Conditional Autarkies

In the following, we discuss the notions of autarkies and conditional autarkies from the literature. We then present new theoretical results for conditional autarkies and use these results to develop an algorithm that identifies particular conditional autarkies. This section provides the basis for our SAT-preprocessing approach. We start with autarkies (remember that we do not require assignments to be total) [7,8]:

**Definition 2.** *An assignment $\alpha$ is an* autarky *for a formula $F$ if $\alpha$ satisfies every clause $C \in F$ for which $var(\alpha) \cap var(C) \neq \emptyset$.*

In other words, an autarky satisfies every clause it touches.

*Example 3.* Let $F = (a \vee b \vee \overline{c}) \wedge (\overline{b} \vee c \vee d) \wedge (\overline{a} \vee \overline{d})$ and let $\alpha = bc$. Then, $\alpha$ touches only the first two clauses. Since it satisfies them, it is an autarky for $F$.

One crucial property of autarkies, which follows easily from the definition, is that they can be applied to a formula without affecting the formula's satisfiability:

**Theorem 4.** *If an assignment $\alpha$ is an autarky for a formula $F$, then $F$ and $F\,|\,\alpha$ are satisfiability-equivalent.*

Theorem 4 can be viewed as follows: If $\alpha = l_1 \dots l_n$ is an autarky for $F$, then $F$ and $F \wedge (l_1) \wedge \dots \wedge (l_n)$ are satisfiability-equivalent. This view is useful in the context of *conditional autarkies* [6]. Informally, a conditional autarky is an assignment that can be partitioned into two parts such that one part becomes an autarky after the other part has been applied to the formula:

**Definition 5.** *An assignment $\alpha_\mathsf{c} \cup \alpha_\mathsf{a}$ (with $\alpha_\mathsf{c} \cap \alpha_\mathsf{a} = \emptyset$) is a* conditional autarky *for a formula $F$ if $\alpha_\mathsf{a}$ is an autarky for $F\,|\,\alpha_\mathsf{c}$.*

We call $\alpha_\mathsf{c}$ the *conditional part* and $\alpha_\mathsf{a}$ the *autarky part* of $\alpha_\mathsf{c} \cup \alpha_\mathsf{a}$. Observe that every assignment is a conditional autarky with an empty autarky part. We are mainly interested in conditional autarkies with *non-empty* autarky parts:

*Example 6.* Consider the formula $F = (a \vee \overline{b} \vee \overline{c}) \wedge (\overline{a} \vee b \vee \overline{d}) \wedge (\overline{a} \vee \overline{b} \vee c) \wedge (\overline{a} \vee d)$ and the assignments $\alpha_\mathsf{c} = a$ and $\alpha_\mathsf{a} = bc$. The assignment $\alpha_\mathsf{c} \cup \alpha_\mathsf{a}$ is a conditional autarky for $F$ since $\alpha_\mathsf{a}$ is an autarky for $F\,|\,\alpha_\mathsf{c} = (b \vee \overline{d}) \wedge (\overline{b} \vee c) \wedge (d)$. Notice that neither $\alpha_\mathsf{a}$ alone nor $abc$ (or any subset) are autarkies for $F$.

Theorem 4 above tells us that the application of an autarky to a formula does not affect the formula's satisfiability. The following statement, which is a simple consequence of Theorem 4 and the fact that $\alpha_\mathsf{a}$ is an autarky for $F\,|\,\alpha_\mathsf{c}$, generalizes this statement for conditional autarkies:

**Corollary 7.** *Let $F$ be a formula and $\alpha_\mathsf{c} \cup \alpha_\mathsf{a}$ a conditional autarky for $F$ with conditional part $\alpha_\mathsf{c}$ and autarky part $\alpha_\mathsf{a}$. Then, $F\,|\,\alpha_\mathsf{c}$ and $F\,|\,\alpha_\mathsf{a} \cup \alpha_\mathsf{c}$ are satisfiability-equivalent.*

As for ordinary autarkies, where we can add all unit clauses $l \in \alpha$ of an autarky $\alpha$ to a formula $F$, we get a similar result for conditional autarkies:

Given a conditional autarky $c_1 \dots c_m a_1 \dots a_n$ (with conditional part $c_1 \dots c_m$) for a formula $F$, we can safely add to $F$ the clause form of the implication

$$c_1 \wedge \dots \wedge c_m \;\rightarrow\; a_1 \wedge \dots \wedge a_n.$$

This will later allow us to prove the redundancy of globally-blocked clauses:

**Theorem 8.** *Let $c_1 \dots c_m\, a_1 \dots a_n$ be a conditional autarky (with conditional part $c_1 \dots c_m$) for a formula $F$. Then, $F$ and $F \wedge \bigwedge_{1 \leq i \leq n} (\overline{c}_1 \vee \dots \vee \overline{c}_m \vee a_i)$ are satisfiability-equivalent.*

*Proof.* We have to show that the satisfiability of $F$ implies the satisfiability of $F \wedge \bigwedge_{1 \leq i \leq n}(\bar{c}_1 \vee \cdots \vee \bar{c}_m \vee a_i)$. Assume that $F$ is satisfiable and let $\tau$ be a satisfying assignment of $F$. If $\tau$ falsifies one of the literals $c_1, \ldots, c_m$, the statement trivially holds. Assume thus that $\tau$ satisfies all of $c_1, \ldots, c_m$ and define $\tau'(a_i) = 1$ for $1 \leq i \leq n$ and $\tau'(l) = \tau(l)$ for each remaining literal $l$. Since $c_1 \ldots c_m \, a_1 \ldots a_n$ is a conditional autarky for $F$ with conditional part $c_1 \ldots c_m$, we know that $a_1 \ldots a_n$ is an autarky for $F|c_1 \ldots c_m$. Hence, since $\tau$ satisfies $F$ and all of $c_1 \ldots c_m$, the clauses that were affected by making $a_1, \ldots, a_n$ true must also be satisfied by $\tau'$. We conclude that $\tau'$ satisfies $F \wedge \bigwedge_{1 \leq i \leq n}(\bar{c}_1 \vee \cdots \vee \bar{c}_m \vee a_i)$.

We already mentioned that we are interested in conditional autarkies with non-empty autarky parts. In fact, for our preprocessing approach, we try to find the smallest conditional parts (and thus the largest autarky parts) for given assignments. As we show next, the smallest conditional part of a given assignment is unique and we can find it efficiently. For this, we need the notion of the *least* conditional part of an assignment:

**Definition 9.** *Given an assignment $\alpha$ and a formula $F$, the* least conditional part *of $\alpha$ on $F$ is the assignment $\alpha_\mathsf{c}$ such that (1) $\alpha$ is a conditional autarky for $F$ with conditional part $\alpha_\mathsf{c}$ and (2) for all assignments $\alpha'_\mathsf{c}$ such that $\alpha$ is a conditional autarky for $F$ with conditional part $\alpha'_\mathsf{c}$, it holds that $\alpha_\mathsf{c} \subseteq \alpha'_\mathsf{c}$.*

The least conditional part of an assignment is unique. To see this, assume $\alpha_1$ and $\alpha_2$ are least conditional parts for $\alpha$ on a formula $F$. Then, $\alpha_1 \subseteq \alpha_2$ and $\alpha_2 \subseteq \alpha_1$ and thus $\alpha_1 = \alpha_2$.

The algorithm LeastConditionalPart in Fig. 1 computes the least conditional part of a given assignment for a formula. In a greedy fashion, the algorithm iterates over all clauses of the formula and whenever it encouters a clause that is touched but not satisfied by the given assignment, it adds all the touched literals of the clause to the conditional part.

```
LeastConditionalPart(assignment α, formula F)
1    α_c := ∅
2    for C ∈ F do
3      if α touches C without satisfying C then
4        α_c := α_c ∪ (α ∩ C̄)
5    return α_c
```

**Fig. 1.** Compute the least conditional part of an assignment.

**Theorem 10.** *Let $\alpha_\mathsf{c} = \mathsf{LeastConditionalPart}(\alpha, F)$ given a CNF formula $F$ and an assignment $\alpha$. Then, $\alpha_\mathsf{c}$ is the least conditional part of $\alpha$ on $F$.*

*Proof.* Clearly, $\alpha$ is a conditional autarky for $F$ with conditional part $\alpha_\mathsf{c}$: Whenever $\alpha$ touches a clause without satisfying it, all the touched literals are added to $\alpha_\mathsf{c}$ (in line 4). Thus a clause in $F|\alpha_\mathsf{c}$ touched by $\alpha \setminus \alpha_\mathsf{c}$ is also satisfied by it.

It remains to show that for every assignment $\alpha'_c$ such that $\alpha$ is a conditional autarky with conditional part $\alpha'_c$, it holds that $\alpha_c \subseteq \alpha'_c$. Let $l \in \alpha_c$. Then, $l$ occurs in a clause $C$ that is touched but not satisfied by $\alpha$. Now, assume that $l$ is not contained in $\alpha'_c$. It follows that $l \in \alpha \setminus \alpha'_c$. But then $\alpha \setminus \alpha'_c$ touches $C\,|\,\alpha'_c$ without satisfying it and so it is not an autarky for $F\,|\,\alpha'_c$. It follows that $\alpha_c \subseteq \alpha'_c$.

## 6 Globally-Blocked Clauses

We now have an algorithm that identifies the least conditional part of a given conditional autarky. In the following, we use this algorithm to find redundant clauses in a propositional formula. To this end, we introduce *globally-blocked clauses*—a type of redundant clauses that generalizes the existing notion of *blocked clauses* [10] (note that in our notation, the set operators have precedence over logical operators, i.e., $D \setminus \{\bar{l}\} \vee C$ means $(D \setminus \{\bar{l}\}) \vee C$):

**Definition 11.** *A clause $C$ is* blocked *by a literal $l \in C$ in a formula $F$ if for every clause $D \in F_{\bar{l}}$, the clause $D \setminus \{\bar{l}\} \vee C$ is a tautology.*

*Example 12.* Let $F = (a \vee b) \wedge (\bar{a} \vee c) \wedge (\bar{b} \vee \bar{a})$ and $C = a \vee b$. The literal $b$ blocks $C$ in $F$ since the only clause in $F_{\bar{b}}$ is the clause $D = \bar{b} \vee \bar{a}$, and $D \setminus \{\bar{b}\} \vee C = \bar{a} \vee a \vee b$ is a tautology.

Blocked clauses are redundant clauses and according to [6] are related to conditional autarkies as follows:

**Theorem 13.** *A clause $(c_1 \vee \dots \vee c_n \vee l)$ is blocked by $l$ in $F$ iff the assignment $\bar{c}_1 \dots \bar{c}_n l$ is a conditional autarky (with conditional part $\bar{c}_1 \dots \bar{c}_n$) for $F$.*

Globally-blocked clauses generalize blocked clauses by not only considering a single literal $l$, but a set $L$ of literals:

**Definition 14.** *A clause $C$ is* globally blocked *by a set $L$ of literals in a formula $F$ if $L \cap C \neq \emptyset$ and all $D \in F_{\bar{L}} \setminus F_L$, the clause $D \setminus \bar{L} \vee C$ is a tautology.*

We say a clause is globally blocked if there exists some set $L$ of literals by which the clause is globally blocked.

*Example 15.* Consider $F = (a \vee \bar{b} \vee \bar{c}) \wedge (\bar{a} \vee b \vee \bar{d}) \wedge (\bar{a} \vee \bar{b} \vee c) \wedge (\bar{a} \vee d)$ from Example 6. The clause $C = (\bar{a} \vee c)$ is globally blocked in $F$. To see this, consider the set $L = \{b, c\}$ and the formulas $F_{\bar{L}} = (a \vee \bar{b} \vee \bar{c}) \wedge (\bar{a} \vee b \vee \bar{d}) \wedge (\bar{a} \vee \bar{b} \vee c)$ and $F_L = (\bar{a} \vee b \vee \bar{d}) \wedge (\bar{a} \vee \bar{b} \vee c)$. We then have $F_{\bar{L}} \setminus F_L = (a \vee \bar{b})$. Let $D = (a \vee \bar{b} \vee \bar{c})$. Then, $D \setminus \bar{L} \vee C = (a \vee \bar{a} \vee c)$ is a tautology and so $C$ is globally blocked by $L$ in $F$. Note, $C$ is not blocked in $F$. In a similar manner $(\bar{a} \vee b)$ is globally blocked.

Remember that we showed in the previous section (Example 6) that $abc$ is a conditional autarky for $F$ with conditional part $a$ and autarky part $bc$. Now in Example 15, to demonstrate that $C$ is globally blocked, we used the literals of the autarky part as the set $L$ and we could observe that the literal $a$ of the conditional part together with its complement $\bar{a}$ caused the clause $D \setminus \bar{L} \vee C$ to be a tautology. This is a consequence of the following statement, which will help us with finding globally-blocked clauses using conditional autarkies:

**Theorem 16.** *Let $F$ be a formula, let $C$ be a clause, let $L$ be a set of literals such that $L \cap C \neq \emptyset$, and define the assignments $\alpha_c = \overline{C \setminus L}$ and $\alpha_a = L$. Then, $C$ is globally blocked by $L$ in $F$ if and only if $\alpha_c \cup \alpha_a$ is a conditional autarky (with conditional part $\alpha_c$) for $F$.*

*Proof.* For the "only if" direction, assume $C$ is globally blocked by $L$ in $F$. We show that $\alpha_a$ is an autarky for $F|\alpha_c$. Let $D|\alpha_c \in F|\alpha_c$. Then, $D$ is not satisfied by $\alpha_c$. Since $\alpha_c$ falsifies exactly the literals of $C \setminus L$, it follows that $D$ cannot contain the complement of a literal in $C \setminus L$. This implies that $C$ cannot contain the complement of a literal in $D \setminus \overline{L}$ and so $D \setminus \overline{L} \vee C$ is not a tautology. But then $D$ cannot be contained in $F_{\overline{L}} \setminus F_L$, meaning that if $D$ is touched by $\alpha_a$ (which satisfies exactly the literals of $L$), $D$ is also satisfied by $\alpha_a$. Hence, since $\alpha_a$ assigns only variables that are not assigned by $\alpha_c$, it cannot be the case that $\alpha_a$ touches $D|\alpha_c$ without satisfying it. We thus conclude that $\alpha_a$ is an autarky for $F|\alpha_c$.

For the "if" direction, assume $\alpha_c \cup \alpha_a$ is a conditional autarky for $F$ with conditional part $\alpha_c$. We show that for every clause $D \in F_{\overline{L}} \setminus F_L$, the clause $D \setminus \overline{L} \vee C$ is a tautology. Let $D \in F_{\overline{L}} \setminus F_L$. Then, $D$ is a clause that is touched but not satisfied by $\alpha_a$. Hence, $\alpha_c$ must satisfy a literal $l$ of $D$, for otherwise $D|\alpha_c$ would be touched but not satisfied by $\alpha_a$. Moreover, since $\alpha_c$ assigns no literals of $\overline{L}$, it must actually be the case that $l \in D \setminus \overline{L}$. But then, since $\alpha_c$ falsifies only literals of $C$, it follows that $\overline{l} \in C$ and so $C \vee D \setminus \overline{L}$ is a tautology. It follows that $C$ is globally blocked by $L$ in $F$.

Before we focus on finding and removing globally-blocked clauses, we have to show that they are indeed redundant:

**Theorem 17.** *If a clause $C$ is globally blocked in a formula $F$, it is redundant with respect to $F$.*

*Proof.* Assume that $C$ is globally blocked by some set $L = \{l_1, \ldots, l_n\}$ in $F$ and that $F$ is satisfiable. We show that the formula $F \wedge C$ is satisfiable. First, observe that $C$ is of the form $(c_1 \vee \ldots c_m \vee l_1 \vee \cdots \vee l_k)$ where $\{l_1, \ldots, l_k\} \subseteq L$ and $k \geq 1$. By Theorem 16, we know that the assignment $\alpha_c \cup \alpha_a$, with $\alpha_c = \overline{c}_1 \ldots \overline{c}_m$ and $\alpha_a = l_1 \ldots l_n$, is a conditional autarky (with conditional part $\alpha_c$) for $F$. Hence, by Theorem 8, $F$ and $F' = F \wedge \bigwedge_{1 \leq i \leq n} (c_1 \vee \cdots \vee c_m \vee l_i)$ are satisfiability-equivalent and so $F'$ must be satisfiable. But then, as $C$ is subsumed by each clause $(c_1 \vee \cdots \vee c_m \vee l_i)$ with $i \in 1, \ldots, k$, every satisfying assignment of $F'$ must also satisfy $F \wedge C$. It follows that $C$ is redundant with respect to $F$.

Finally, we note that globally-blocked clauses are a subclass of propagation-redundant clauses (for details, see [27]) but we omit the proof here [16]:

**Theorem 18.** *If a clause $C$ is globally blocked in a formula $F$, it is propagation-redundant with respect to $F$.*

## 7 Detecting Globally-Blocked Clauses

We have seen that globally-blocked clauses are redundant and that they correspond closely to conditional autarkies. In the next step, we use this correspondence to find globally-blocked clauses in a formula. The idea is as follows: We take an assignment (we will see later how this assignment can be obtained) and then check for all clauses whether the assignment *witnesses* that the clause is globally blocked. We start with a formal notion of a witness:

**Definition 19.** *Given a clause $C$ and a formula $F$, a conditional autarky $\alpha_{\mathsf{c}} \cup \alpha_{\mathsf{a}}$ (with conditional part $\alpha_{\mathsf{c}}$) for $F$* witnesses *that $C$ is globally blocked in $F$ if $\alpha_{\mathsf{a}} \cap C \neq \emptyset$ and $\alpha_{\mathsf{c}} \subseteq \overline{C}$.*

Suppose we have a conditional autarky $\alpha_{\mathsf{c}} \cup \alpha_{\mathsf{a}}$ with conditional part $\alpha_{\mathsf{c}}$ for $F$ and we want to use it for checking if a clause $C$ is globally blocked. We know from Theorem 16 that $C$ is globally blocked by $L = \alpha_{\mathsf{a}}$ in $F$ if $\alpha_{\mathsf{a}} \cap C \neq \emptyset$ and $\alpha_{\mathsf{c}} = \overline{C \setminus L}$. However, a closer look reveals that the requirement $\alpha_{\mathsf{c}} = \overline{C \setminus L}$ is needlessly restrictive for our purpose: Theorem 20 below implies that it suffices if $\alpha_{\mathsf{c}}$ is a subset of $\overline{C \setminus L}$ (and thus of $\overline{C}$, since $\alpha_{\mathsf{c}}$ assigns no variables of $L = \alpha_{\mathsf{a}}$) to guarantee that $C$ is globally blocked. Hence, if we have a conditional autarky which witnesses (as defined above) that $C$ is globally blocked, we can be sure that the clause is indeed globally blocked.

**Theorem 20.** *Let $F$ be a formula, $\alpha$ a conditional autarky for $F$ with autarky part $\alpha_{\mathsf{a}}$, and $\tau$ an assignment such that $\alpha \subseteq \tau$. Then, $\tau$ is a conditional autarky for $F$ with autarky part $\alpha_{\mathsf{a}}$.*

*Proof.* Let $\alpha_{\mathsf{c}} = \alpha \setminus \alpha_{\mathsf{a}}$ and $\tau_{\mathsf{c}} = \tau \setminus \alpha_{\mathsf{a}}$. We know that $\alpha_{\mathsf{a}}$ is an autarky for $F|\alpha_{\mathsf{c}}$. Since $\alpha \subseteq \tau$, it follows that $\alpha_{\mathsf{c}} \subseteq \tau_{\mathsf{c}}$. Now, let $D|\tau_{\mathsf{c}} \in F|\tau_{\mathsf{c}}$. If $D$ is not satisfied by $\tau_{\mathsf{c}}$, then it is also not satisfied by $\alpha_{\mathsf{c}}$. Thus, if $D|\tau_{\mathsf{c}}$ is touched by $\alpha_{\mathsf{a}}$, then it must be satisfied by $\alpha_{\mathsf{a}}$, for otherwise $\alpha_{\mathsf{a}}$ is not an autarky for $F|\alpha_{\mathsf{c}}$. It follows that $\alpha_{\mathsf{a}}$ is an autarky for $F|\tau_{\mathsf{c}}$.

We can now present the algorithm (Fig. 2) for finding globally-blocked clauses. The algorithm repeatedly computes the least conditional part $\alpha_{\mathsf{c}}$ of the given assignment (line 1) and then removes from $\alpha_{\mathsf{c}}$ all literals that are not in $\overline{C}$ (line 2) because of the requirement $\alpha_{\mathsf{c}} \subseteq \overline{C}$. If the algorithm finally reaches a fixpoint, meaning that $\alpha_{\mathsf{c}} \subseteq \overline{C}$, it returns whether the autarky part has a non-empty intersection with $C$ (line 3), which is necessary to guarantee that the assignment witnesses that $C$ is globally blocked.

**Theorem 21.** *Let $C$ be a clause, $F$ a formula, and $\alpha$ an assignment. Then,* $\mathsf{IsGloballyBlocked}(C, F, \alpha) = \mathsf{TRUE}$ *if and only if a subassignment of $\alpha$ witnesses that $C$ is globally blocked in $F$.*

*Proof.* In the rest of the proof, we denote by $\alpha^i$ the assignment passed to $\mathsf{IsGloballyBlocked}$ at the $i$-th recursive call (we denote the initial call as the 0-th recursive call, i.e., $\alpha^0 = \alpha$). The assignments $\alpha^i_c$ and $\alpha^i_a$ are defined accordingly.

$\mathsf{IsGloballyBlocked}$(clause $C$, formula $F$, assignment $\alpha$)

1 $\alpha_{\mathsf{c}} := \mathsf{LeastConditionalPart}(\alpha, F)$, $\alpha_{\mathsf{a}} := \alpha \setminus \alpha_{\mathsf{c}}$

2 $\alpha' := \alpha_{\mathsf{a}} \cup (\alpha_{\mathsf{c}} \cap \overline{C})$

3 **if** $(\alpha' = \alpha)$ **then return** $\alpha_{\mathsf{a}} \cap C \neq \emptyset$

4 **return** $\mathsf{IsGloballyBlocked}(C, F, \alpha')$

**Fig. 2.** Algorithm for detecting globally-blocked clauses.

For the "only if" direction, assume that $\mathsf{IsGloballyBlocked}(C, F, \alpha) = \mathsf{TRUE}$ and let $\alpha^n$ be the assignment to the last recursive call (i.e., $\alpha^n$ is the assignment for which the algorithm returns if $\alpha^n_{\mathsf{a}} \cap C \neq \emptyset$). Then, since the algorithm only modifies the initial assignment $\alpha$ by unassigning variables, $\alpha^n$ is a subassignment of $\alpha$. Now, since $\alpha^n_c = \mathsf{LeastConditionalPart}(\alpha, F)$, we know that $\alpha^n$ is a conditional autarky for $F$ with (least) conditional part $\alpha^n_c$. Moreover, all literals of $\alpha^n_c$ are contained in $\overline{C}$ due to line 2 of the algorithm. Finally, since $\alpha^n_a$ and $C$ have a non-empty intersection, $\alpha^n$ witnesses that $C$ is globally blocked in $F$.

For the "if" direction, suppose some subassignment $\tau = \tau_c \cup \tau_\alpha$ of $\alpha$ witnesses that $C$ is globally blocked in $F$. Below, we show by induction on $i$ that $\tau \subseteq \alpha^i$ and $\tau_a \subseteq \alpha^i_a$. From this, the statement follows then easily: Denote by $\alpha^n$ the assignment passed to the final recursive call (it can be easily seen that the algorithm terminates). Since $\tau_a \subseteq \alpha^n_{\mathsf{a}}$ and since $\tau_a \cap C \neq \emptyset$, it must then be the case that $\alpha_{\mathsf{a}} \cap C \neq \emptyset$. We conclude with the induction proof of the mentioned statement:

Induction start ($i = 0$): In this case, $\alpha^0 = \alpha$. By assumption $\tau \subseteq \alpha$. Thus, by Theorem 20, we know that $\tau_a$ is an autarky for $F|\alpha \setminus \tau_a$. Hence, as $\alpha_{\mathsf{c}}$ is the least conditional part of $\alpha$, it follows that $\alpha_{\mathsf{c}} \subseteq \alpha \setminus \tau_a$ and thus $\tau_a \subseteq \alpha \setminus \alpha_{\mathsf{c}} = \alpha_{\mathsf{a}}$.

Induction step ($i > 0$): We assume that $\tau \subseteq \alpha^{i-1}$ and $\tau_a \subseteq \alpha^{i-1}_a$. We first show that $\tau \subseteq \alpha^i$. The assignment $\alpha_i$ is obtained as $\alpha' = \alpha^{i-1}_a \cup \{l \mid l \in \alpha^{i-1}_c \text{ and } l \in \overline{C}\}$ in the $(i-1)$-th recursive call. Thus, since $\tau_a \subseteq \alpha^{i-1}_a$, we know that $\tau_a \subseteq \alpha_i$. Therefore, the only literals that are contained in $\alpha^i$ but not in $\alpha_{i-1}$ are literals of $\alpha^{i-1}_c$ that are not in $\overline{C}$. But such literals cannot be contained in $\tau_c$ since $\tau_c \subseteq \overline{C}$. It follows that $\tau \subseteq \alpha^i$. Hence, by Theorem 20, it follows that $\tau_a \subseteq \alpha^i_a$.

## 8 Implementation

The abstract algorithm presented in the previous section connects well to the presented theory of globally-blocked clauses, but is hard to implement efficiently. Figure 3 describes a refinement of the algorithm and further discusses implementation details which are crucial for efficiency. Without giving a detailed analysis, it is easy to see that for each candidate clause, the running time of the algorithm is similar and thus bounded by the time it would take to propagate all conditional variables obtained during the first step of the algorithm.

1. Split the assignment into a conditional part $\alpha_c$ and an autarky part $\alpha_a$ (one initial call to LeastConditionalPart in Fig. 1). Mark the resulting literals of $\alpha_c$ and save them on a *conditional stack*, gather *candidate clauses* (those with a literal that is true but not yet in the conditional part) and watch a true literal in all clauses with a true literal.
2. For each candidate clause $C$:
3. If $C$ contains no literal from $\alpha_a$, continue with next clause (goto 2).
4. Watch one literal $l_a$ of $\alpha_a$ in $C$ and mark all literals in $C$ to be part of $C$. Actually have a variable pointing to the literal $l_a$.
5. For each unprocessed literal $l_c$ on the conditional stack:
6. If $\bar{l}_c \in C$ (cheap check since literals in $C$ are marked) continue (goto 5).
7. Unassign $\bar{l}_c \in C$ and push it on an *unassigned* stack.
8. For each unassigned literal $u$ on the unassigned stack not processed yet:
9. For each clause $D$ watched by $u$ (through watches initialized in step 1):
10. Search for a replacement literal $r \in D$ which satisfies $D$. If such $r$ is found, stop watching $D$ with $u$, watch it with $r$ instead, and continue with next clause $D$ watched by $u$ (goto 9).
11. Otherwise no replacement is found.
12. If there is no literal $k \in \alpha_a$ with $\bar{k} \in D$, continue with next clause $D$ watched by $u$ (goto 9).
13. For each literal $k \in \alpha_a$ with $\bar{k} \in D$:
14. Put $k$ into the conditional part $\alpha_c$ by using another mark bit and push it onto the conditional stack.
15. If $k$ is different from the watched literal $l_a \in C$ (see step 4), continue with the next unassigned and unprocessed literal $u$ on the unassigned stack.
16. Otherwise, search for a replacement of $l_a$ in $C$.
17. If no replacement is found, $C$ is not a globally-blocked clause; continue with next candidate clause (goto 2 – thus jump out of four loops).
18. If there are no unprocessed literals, neither on the conditional nor on the unassigned stack, and we still watch a literal of $\alpha_a$ in the candidate clause $C$, then we now reached a fix-point and $C$ is globally blocked.
19. Eliminate $C$ and put the autarky part as witness (found by traversing the assignment trail) and $C$ on the extension stack for witness reconstruction.
20. Pop literals from unassigned stack and reassign them to their original value.
21. Pop literals from conditional stack pushed after initialization in step 1 and unmark their conditional bit.
22. Now we are back to the initial assignment after step 1, with the initial literals of the conditional part $\alpha_c$ marked as such and the literals of $\alpha_a$ unmarked.
23. Unmark literals marked in step 4 and continue with next clause (goto 2).

**Fig. 3.** Algorithm to extract globally-blocked clauses from a given assignment.

This variant has been implemented in C++ in CaDiCaL [37] and is available at http://fmv.jku.at/globalblocking (see "`condition.cpp`"). We experimented on SAT Competition benchmarks and also in an incremental bounded model checking setting [38]. Our algorithm in Fig. 3 does find non-trivial globally blocked clauses, but at this point we have not found an instance or application where the removal of globally-blocked clauses results in an overall improvement in running time. It thus remains to be seen whether or not the idea of removing globally-blocked clauses can be beneficial in practice.

One issue is particularly problematic: For some instances with many globally-blocked clauses, the large number of literals on the reconstruction stack requires too much memory, particularly if the autarky part—which serves as witness—contains a substantial fraction of all variables.

## 9 Conclusion

We introduced globally-blocked clauses, a new kind of redundant clauses that generalizes the existing notions of blocked clauses and set-blocked clauses. As we have shown, globally-blocked clauses correspond closely to conditional autarkies, which are special assignments that can be partitioned into two parts such that one part becomes an autarky once the other part has been applied to the formula.

Since finding globally-blocked clauses is non-trivial, we presented an algorithm that takes as input a formula and a clause together with a candidate assignment and then checks if the assignment (or a subassignment thereof) can witness that the clause is globally blocked in the formula.

Our algorithm simulates a well-known circuit preprocessing technique, known as unique sensitization, on the CNF level. Although our algorithm is conceptually simple, implementing it efficiently is far from straight-forward. We thus presented an implementation of our algorithm, which we ran on a range of formulas to evaluate its effectiveness in practice.

**Acknowledgment.** This work has been supported by the National Science Foundation under grant CCF-1618574 and by the Austrian Science Fund (FWF) under project W1255 (LogiCS) and S11409-N23 (RiSE).

We want to thank Oliver Kullmann, who explained to the second author an (as far as we know unpublished) algorithm to compute the maximal autarky of a total assignment, which is a special case of LeastConditionalPart in Fig. 1.

This work was triggered by Gianpiero Cabodi who asked the last author whether there is a CNF level version of unique sensitization as explained in Sect. 3 with potential applications in SAT-based model checking.

We would finally also like to thank the organizers of ATVA'19 for inviting the last author to present these ideas as invited talk and include this invited paper in the proceedings.

## References

1. Clarke, E.M., Biere, A., Raimi, R., Zhu, Y.: Bounded model checking using satisfiability solving. Form. Methods Syst. Des. **19**(1), 7–34 (2001)
2. Stevens, M., Bursztein, E., Karpman, P., Albertini, A., Markov, Y.: The first collision for full SHA-1. In: Katz, J., Shacham, H. (eds.) CRYPTO 2017. LNCS, vol. 10401, pp. 570–596. Springer, Cham (2017)
3. Konev, B., Lisitsa, A.: A SAT attack on the Erdős discrepancy conjecture. In: Sinz, C., Egly, U. (eds.) SAT 2014. LNCS, vol. 8561, pp. 219–226. Springer, Cham (2014)
4. Heule, M.J.H.: Schur number five. In: Proceedings of the 32nd AAAI Conference on Artificial Intelligence (AAAI 2018). AAAI Press (2018)
5. Järvisalo, M., Biere, A., Heule, M.J.H.: Simulating circuit-level simplifications on CNF. J. Autom. Reason. **49**(4), 583–619 (2012)
6. Heule, M.J.H., Kiesl, B., Seidl, M., Biere, A.: PRuning through satisfaction. In: Strichman, O., Tzoref-Brill, R. (eds.) HVC 2017. LNCS, vol. 10629, pp. 179–194. Springer, Cham (2017)
7. Monien, B., Speckenmeyer, E.: Solving satisfiability in less than $2^n$ steps. Discrete Appl. Math. **10**(3), 287–295 (1985)
8. Kleine Büning, H., Kullmann, O.: Minimal unsatisfiability and autarkies. In: Biere, A., Heule, M.J.H., van Maaren, H., Walsh, T. (eds.) Handbook of Satisfiability, pp. 399–401. IOS Press, Amsterdam (2009)
9. Kiesl, B., Seidl, M., Tompits, H., Biere, A.: Super-blocked clauses. In: Olivetti, N., Tiwari, A. (eds.) IJCAR 2016. LNCS (LNAI), vol. 9706, pp. 45–61. Springer, Cham (2016)
10. Kullmann, O.: On a generalization of extended resolution. Discrete Appl. Math. **96–97**, 149–176 (1999)
11. Järvisalo, M., Biere, A., Heule, M.J.H.: Blocked clause elimination. In: Esparza, J., Majumdar, R. (eds.) TACAS 2010. LNCS, vol. 6015, pp. 129–144. Springer, Heidelberg (2010)
12. Kiesl, B., Suda, M., Seidl, M., Tompits, H., Biere, A.: Blocked clauses in first-order logic. In: Proceedings of the 21st International Conference on Logic for Programming, Artificial Intelligence and Reasoning (LPAR-21). EPiC Series in Computing, vol. 46, pp. 31–48. EasyChair (2017)
13. Biere, A., Lonsing, F., Seidl, M.: Blocked clause elimination for QBF. In: Bjørner, N., Sofronie-Stokkermans, V. (eds.) CADE 2011. LNCS (LNAI), vol. 6803, pp. 101–115. Springer, Heidelberg (2011)
14. Lonsing, F., Bacchus, F., Biere, A., Egly, U., Seidl, M.: Enhancing search-based QBF solving by dynamic blocked clause elimination. In: Davis, M., Fehnker, A., McIver, A., Voronkov, A. (eds.) LPAR 2015. LNCS, vol. 9450, pp. 418–433. Springer, Heidelberg (2015)
15. Marques Silva, J.P., Sakallah, K.A.: GRASP: a search algorithm for propositional satisfiability. IEEE Trans. Comput. **48**(5), 506–521 (1999)
16. Kiesl, B.: Structural reasoning methods for satisfiability solving and beyond. Ph.D. thesis, TU Wien (2019)
17. Järvisalo, M., Heule, M.J.H., Biere, A.: Inprocessing rules. In: Gramlich, B., Miller, D., Sattler, U. (eds.) IJCAR 2012. LNCS (LNAI), vol. 7364, pp. 355–370. Springer, Heidelberg (2012)
18. Eén, N., Biere, A.: Effective preprocessing in SAT through variable and clause elimination. In: Bacchus, F., Walsh, T. (eds.) SAT 2005. LNCS, vol. 3569, pp. 61–75. Springer, Heidelberg (2005)

19. Heule, M.J.H., Kullmann, O., Marek, V.W.: Solving and verifying the Boolean Pythagorean Triples problem via Cube-and-Conquer. In: Creignou, N., Le Berre, D. (eds.) SAT 2016. LNCS, vol. 9710, pp. 228–245. Springer, Cham (2016)
20. Heule, M., Järvisalo, M., Biere, A.: Clause elimination procedures for CNF formulas. In: Fermüller, C.G., Voronkov, A. (eds.) LPAR 2010. LNCS, vol. 6397, pp. 357–371. Springer, Heidelberg (2010)
21. Heule, M., Järvisalo, M., Biere, A.: Covered clause elimination. In: Short papers for the 17th International Conference on Logic for Programming, Artificial intelligence, and Reasoning (LPAR-17-short). EPiC Series, vol. 13, pp. 41–46. EasyChair (2010)
22. Heule, M.J.H., Järvisalo, M., Lonsing, F., Seidl, M., Biere, A.: Clause elimination for SAT and QSAT. J. Artif. Intell. Res. **53**, 127–168 (2015)
23. Wetzler, N.D., Heule, M.J.H., Hunt Jr., W.A.: DRAT-trim: efficient checking and trimming using expressive clausal proofs. In: Sinz, C., Egly, U. (eds.) SAT 2014. LNCS, vol. 8561, pp. 422–429. Springer, Cham (2014)
24. Cruz-Filipe, L., Heule, M.J.H., Hunt Jr., W.A., Kaufmann, M., Schneider-Kamp, P.: Efficient certified RAT verification. In: de Moura, L. (ed.) CADE 2017. LNCS (LNAI), vol. 10395, pp. 220–236. Springer, Cham (2017)
25. Lammich, P.: Efficient verified (UN)SAT certificate checking. In: de Moura, L. (ed.) CADE 2017. LNCS (LNAI), vol. 10395, pp. 237–254. Springer, Cham (2017)
26. Heule, M.J.H., Järvisalo, M., Suda, M.: SAT competition 2018 (2019)
27. Heule, M.J.H., Kiesl, B., Biere, A.: Short proofs without new variables. In: de Moura, L. (ed.) CADE 2017. LNCS (LNAI), vol. 10395, pp. 130–147. Springer, Cham (2017)
28. Heule, M.J.H., Biere, A.: What a difference a variable makes. In: Beyer, D., Huisman, M. (eds.) TACAS 2018. LNCS, vol. 10806, pp. 75–92. Springer, Cham (2018)
29. Heule, M.J.H., Kiesl, B., Biere, A.: Clausal proofs of mutilated chessboards. In: Badger, J.M., Rozier, K.Y. (eds.) NFM 2019. LNCS, vol. 11460, pp. 204–210. Springer, Cham (2019)
30. Heule, M.J.H., Kiesl, B., Biere, A.: Encoding redundancy for satisfaction-driven clause learning. In: Vojnar, T., Zhang, L. (eds.) TACAS 2019. LNCS, vol. 11427, pp. 41–58. Springer, Cham (2019)
31. Heule, M.J.H., Seidl, M., Biere, A.: Solution validation and extraction for QBF preprocessing. J. Autom. Reason. **58**, 1–29 (2016)
32. Heule, M., Seidl, M., Biere, A.: Blocked literals are universal. In: Havelund, K., Holzmann, G., Joshi, R. (eds.) NFM 2015. LNCS, vol. 9058, pp. 436–442. Springer, Cham (2015)
33. Lonsing, F., Egly, U.: QRAT+: generalizing QRAT by a more powerful QBF redundancy property. In: Galmiche, D., Schulz, S., Sebastiani, R. (eds.) IJCAR 2018. LNCS (LNAI), vol. 10900, pp. 161–177. Springer, Cham (2018)
34. Lonsing, F., Egly, U.: QRATPre+: effective QBF preprocessing via strong redundancy properties. In: Janota, M., Lynce, I. (eds.) SAT 2019. LNCS, vol. 11628, pp. 203–210. Springer, Cham (2019)
35. Kiesl, B., Suda, M.: A unifying principle for clause elimination in first-order logic. In: de Moura, L. (ed.) CADE 2017. LNCS (LNAI), vol. 10395, pp. 274–290. Springer, Cham (2017)
36. Fujiwara, H.: FAN: a fanout-oriented test pattern generation algorithm. In: Proceedings of the IEEE International Symposium on Circuits and Systems (ISCAS 1985), pp. 671–674 (1985)

37. Biere, A.: CaDiCaL, Lingeling, Plingeling, Treengeling and YalSAT entering the SAT competition 2018. In: Heule, M., Järvisalo, M., Suda, M. (eds.) Proceedings of SAT Competition 2018 – Solver and Benchmark Descriptions, pp. 13–14. Volume B-2018-1 of Department of Computer Science Series of Publications B, University of Helsinki (2018)
38. Fazekas, K., Biere, A., Scholl, C.: Incremental inprocessing in SAT solving. In: Janota, M., Lynce, I. (eds.) SAT 2019. LNCS, vol. 11628, pp. 136–154. Springer, Cham (2019)

# Can We Trust Autonomous Systems? Boundaries and Risks

Joseph Sifakis(✉)

Univ. Grenoble Alpes, Verimag laboratory, Bâtiment IMAG, 700 avenue Centrale, 38401 St Martin d'Hères, France
joseph.sifakis@imag.fr

**Abstract.** Can we trust autonomous systems? This question arises urgently with the perspective of massive use of AI-enabled techniques in autonomous systems, critical systems intended to replace humans in complex organizations.

We propose a framework for tackling this question and bringing reasoned and principled answers. First, we discuss a classification of different types of knowledge according to their truthfulness and generality. We show basic differences and similarities between knowledge produced and managed by humans and computers, respectively. In particular, we discuss how differences in the system development process of knowledge affect its truthfulness.

To determine whether we can trust a system to perform a given task, we study the interplay between two main factors: (1) the degree of trustworthiness achievable by a system performing the task; and (2) the degree of criticality of the task. Simple automated systems can be trusted if their trustworthiness can match the desired degree of criticality. Nonetheless, the acceptance of autonomous systems to perform complex critical tasks will additionally depend on their ability to exhibit symbiotic behavior and allow harmonious collaboration with human operators. We discuss how objective and subjective factors determine the balance in the division of work between autonomous systems and human operators.

We conclude emphasizing that the role of autonomous systems will depend on decisions about when we can trust them and when we cannot. Making these choices wisely goes hand in hand with compliance with principles promulgated by policy-makers and regulators rooted both in ethical and technical criteria.

**Keywords:** Autonomous systems · Knowledge · Truthfulness · Trustworthiness

## 1 Introduction

Can we trust autonomous systems? This recurrent question arises quite often be-cause of their increasing importance in our everyday and future lives. Of course, we trust automated systems, as they are ubiquitous in services, devices


Y.-F. Chen et al. (Eds.): ATVA 2019, LNCS 11781, pp. 65–78, 2019.
https://doi.org/10.1007/978-3-030-31784-3_4

and appliances striving for enhanced quality of life and resource management. Nonetheless, for autonomous systems, trustworthiness becomes a major concern. They make massive use of machine learning techniques while they are highly critical as they are supposed to replace human agents in large organizations such as transport systems, smart factories, and energy production and distribution systems. Autonomous systems have already replaced to a great extent decision-making in investment markets and especially with respect to asset management (robo-advisors).

Autonomous systems significantly differ from existing automated systems in the following three key characteristics:

1. Autonomous systems deal with many different possibly conflicting goals, which is necessary for achieving adaptive behavior. This reflects the trend of transitioning from "narrow AI" or "weak AI" to "strong" or "general" AI. There is a big difference between a chess playing robot pursuing a single well-defined goal and a self-driving car that should adaptively deal with a large variety of goals including short term goals (avoiding collision and trajectory tracking) as well as longer term goals such as reaching a destination achieved by combining various intermediate maneuver goals.
2. Autonomous systems have to deal not only with a great variety of known environment configurations, but also with ones for which there is no explicit specification. This is due to the surge of cyber-physical environments: agents are sensitive to a multitude of conditions regarding the objects they need to manipulate and those that may interfere with their tasks. Another source of unpredictability is increased mobility and geographical distribution. Autonomous systems are naturally distributed which implies uncertainty on their global state and requires specific mechanisms and computational overhead to cope with it.
3. Autonomous systems are intended to accomplish complex and highly critical missions and their failure may seriously endanger their environment. It is thus desirable that in case of deviation from their normal behavior, a human operator could override their decisions and bring the system into a failsafe state. For this to be achievable, special care should be taken at design time to equip systems with adequate interaction protocols and interfaces to allow a safe transition from automated to manual regime. An alternative mode of collaboration is that the system proactively asks a human operator to take over when it diagnoses a potentially dangerous situation.

In [14] we provide an architectural characterization of the behavior of autonomous agents as the combination of five basic functions. Perception and Reflection, allow achieving situational awareness. The combination of Goal Management and Planning allows achieving adaption that depending on the perceived situation, selects relevant goals and generates corresponding action plans. A fifth function deals with the creation and handling of different types of knowledge that is essential for self-awareness and self-adaptation.

This characterization provides insight about the distinction between automated and autonomous systems. A thermostat, a lift or a flight controller are automated systems because they operate in well-defined environments that do admit a simple interpretation. They additionally pursue simple and well-defined goals and their corresponding decision process is a controller defined at design time. On the contrary, autonomous systems should exhibit self-awareness and self-adaptation for which knowledge production and management is instrumental. Although our characterization is abstract and implementation-agnostic, autonomic behavior cannot be effectively achieved without extensive use of data-based techniques and machine learning, in particular.

The use of data-based techniques in autonomous systems currently challenges our ability to provide conclusive evidence that we meet critical trustworthiness requirements. Systems engineering comes to a turning point, as traditional model-based design methodologies are not applicable to autonomous systems. Moreover, an important trend is the end-to-end development of autonomous systems based exclusively on machine learning techniques, e.g. self-driving systems providing steering angle and acceleration/deceleration from video information [3,16]. For these systems, validation is possible only by testing which cannot match the level of confidence achieved by model-based design methodologies [14].

What are the basic criteria for deciding whether a given task can be fully automated? Our analysis links truthfulness of knowledge about the behavior of a system and the resulting system trustworthiness. It comprises two steps.

The first step involves a classification of different types of knowledge according to their truthfulness and generality. We show basic differences and similarities between knowledge produced and managed by humans and machines, respectively. In particular, we note that model-based knowledge generated by algorithms can have the status of mathematical knowledge when rooted in rigorous semantics. On the contrary, data-based knowledge of neural systems is implicit empirical knowledge. It differs from scientific knowledge in that it allows prediction without understanding. We examine to what extent a principled method is applicable to machine learning techniques and highlight difficulties for achieving explainability.

The second step provides a framework allowing reasoned and comprehensive analysis of the problem whether we can trust an autonomous system for the execution of a particular task. We study the interplay between two main factors: (1) the degree of trustworthiness achievable by the system accomplishing the task; and (2) the degree of criticality of the task. In the two-dimensional space defined by these two factors, systems can be trusted when the achievable trustworthiness can match the desired degree of criticality. Otherwise, fully automated solutions are not safe enough. Nonetheless, with the advent of autonomous systems, such tasks can be jointly performed by human operators and systems, if we can achieve their harmonious and safe collaboration. We show in particular, how objective and subjective factors can influence the division of work between humans and machines.

We conclude emphasizing that the role of autonomous systems will depend on choices we make about when we trust them and when we do not. Making these choices wisely, goes hand in hand with compliance with principles rooted both in ethical and scientific criteria.

## 2 About Knowledge

### 2.1 The Truthfulness of Knowledge – A Hierarchical Classification

We consider that knowledge is truthful information which when embedded into the right network of conceptual interrelations can be used either to understand a subject matter or to solve a problem. We discuss key characteristics of knowledge and criteria that determine its truthfulness and value in use.

According to our definition, knowledge has a dual nature. It allows both situational awareness and decision-making. Thus it is crucial for perception and interpretation of the real world but also for acting on the world in order to achieve specific goals.

Knowledge can have different degrees of truthfulness and generality. It spans from factual information, to general empirical knowledge, scientific knowledge and mathematical knowledge. An important distinction is the one between empirical and non-empirical knowledge. Empirical knowledge is acquired and developed from experience. It requires thorough validation to check that it is consistent with observation and measurement. On the contrary, non-empirical knowledge is deemed independent of experience. Its truthfulness depends only on logical reasoning, while empirical knowledge is the result of (a logically arbitrary) generalization and can be falsified. It comprises in particular mathematical knowledge, theory of computing and any kind of knowledge rooted in a semantically sound framework. The Pythagorean Theorem or Gödel's theorems are "eternal" truth depending on the axioms underlying Euclidean Geometry and arithmetic, respectively.

The difference between these two types of knowledge reflects two radically different approaches for its production. One is a purely logical construction while the other concerns information extracted from observations and experimental data. Figure 1 proposes a classification allowing a comparison between types of knowledge produced and managed by machines and humans.

The most common kind of empirical knowledge is explicit knowledge about facts characterizing situations of the world at a certain time and place e.g. "the temperature in Paris today is 24 °C" or "the battle of Waterloo took place on Sunday, 18 June 1815". Factual knowledge is of limited generality but indispensable for situational awareness.

General empirical knowledge is the result of generalization and abstraction of factual knowledge. It comprises in particular, implicit empirical knowledge which involves learning and skills but not in a way that can be explained and analyzed. This is the most common knowledge humans use to walk, speak, play instruments, dance, etc. It is produced and managed by automated (non-conscious) effortless fast thinking (System 1 of thinking according to D. Kahneman's terminology [9]). When we walk, our mind solves a very hard computational problem whose explicit modeling would involve dynamic equations describing the kinetics of our bodies. Note that neural systems produce and handle implicit empirical knowledge. They learn to distinguish "cats from dogs" exactly as kids do. This type of knowledge also comprises statistical knowledge and knowledge produced using data analytics techniques.

Scientific and Technical knowledge is past empirical knowledge that has been processed and systematized through the use of models. Scientific knowledge allows understanding the physical world while technical knowledge allows building new products or processes based on scientific knowledge e.g. engineering constructions. The big difference between implicit knowledge and scientific and technical knowledge is that the letter is model-based and thus it is amenable to falsification analysis, which drastically improves confidence in its truthfulness.

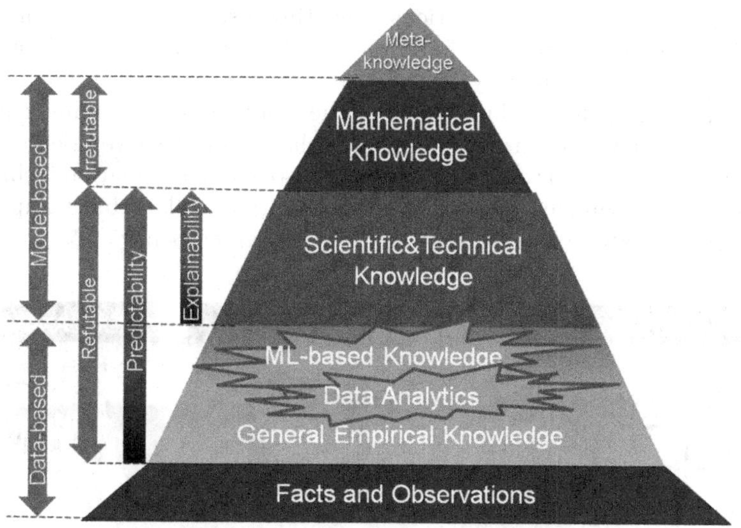


**Fig. 1.** The knowledge pyramid

As explained, non-empirical knowledge is model-based knowledge rooted in logical rules.

Finally, meta-knowledge is knowledge about how to deal with knowledge. It allows combining various kinds of knowledge for situational awareness and decision-making. It includes design methodologies, problem-solving techniques, data acquisition and analysis techniques. It also includes non-formalized knowledge related to various jobs and skills.

Note that mathematical knowledge as well as scientific and technical knowledge are model-based. Humans produce this type of knowledge by slow conscious, effort-ful procedural thinking (System 2 of thinking according to D. Kahneman's terminology [9]). Conventional computers can handle this type of knowledge, when it is adequately formalized, and produce new knowledge e.g. by executing algorithms. There is a remarkable similarity between the two types of thinking (fast and slow thinking) and the two types of computing (conventional algorithmic and neural computing). Both slow procedural thinking and ordinary computing are model-based in the sense that it is possible to produce a model explicating step-by-step the underlying computational process. On the contrary, both neural computing and fast thinking emerge as the result of some learning process that does not rely on any explicit procedural model.

## 2.2 Scientific vs. Machine-Learning Knowledge

We discuss differences in the production processes of scientific and machine learning knowledge respectively, and how these affect their corresponding degree of truthfulness.

The scientific method consists in developing knowledge that faithfully accounts for experimental observations. Scientific discovery is the result of the implicit learning mental process of an experimenter who builds a model allowing predictability and explainability.

Neural systems generate knowledge as the result of a long training process with experiential data. Their explainability is the object of active research investigating various definitions of the concept and associated explanation techniques, e.g. [6,11]. For our comparison we simply consider that explainability implies the existence of an analyzable model matching the observed behavior.

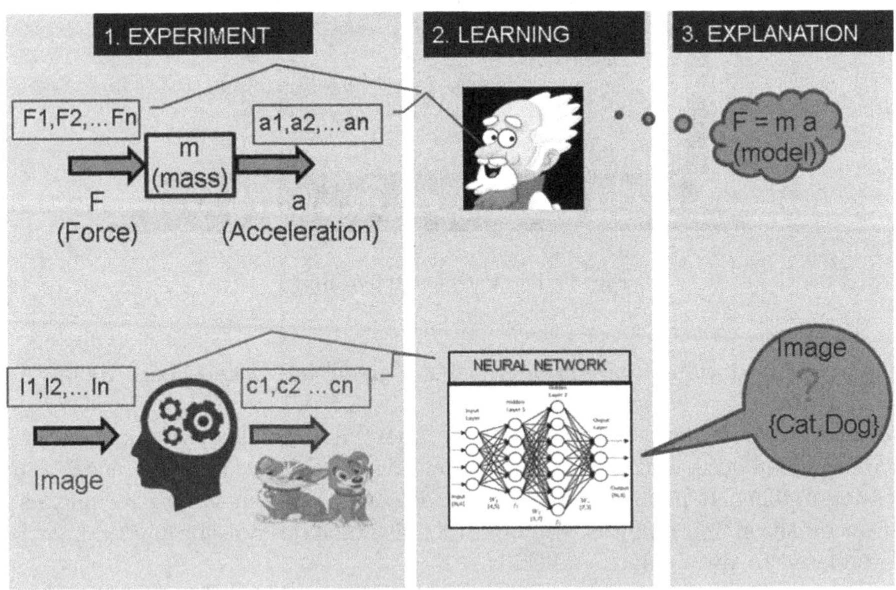


**Fig. 2.** Comparing scientific and machine learning based knowledge

Figure 2 illustrates a comparison between the scientific approach for studying a physical process (mass acceleration a by force F) and the technical approach for learning a mental process (distinguishing between images of cats and dogs). They both have a common purpose to characterize the input/output behavior of the considered processes and achieve predictability: they are able to guess the response of the process for a given input.

Scientific knowledge is empirical knowledge represented by analyzable models whose behavior can be studied and tested. In that manner, observations and experimental data take a higher value and generality. Scientific discovery is not possible without adequate models. We know that Newton has developed infinitesimal calculus so that he could formulate his laws. Our difficulty with fully understanding and predicting complex phenomena such as social, meteorological and economic, does not necessarily imply that they do not follow laws, but simply that we do not have the adequate models explaining of the observed data. Additionally, the development of scientific knowledge requires that the models can be analyzed to study their behavior and extract significant properties. So it implies some computational complexity that may limit explainability.

Similarly, the machine-learning paradigm involves an experimental step followed by a learning step applied to a neural network. It consists in adjusting weights of the network so that it computes a function fitting as closely as possible the observed behavior. The so obtained neural system allows predictability with a probability depending on the degree of training. The application of the third step to find a model explaining the network behavior, is a largely open problem, in particular for neural systems that emulate mental processes dealing with hard to formalize concepts of the natural language. Is there a rigorous model relating images to cats and dogs? Nonetheless, explainability seems feasible for specific classes of neural networks dealing with physical entities for which it is possible to characterize rigorously their I/O behavior e.g. by sets of constraints as for example in [10]).

# 3 Trustworthiness vs. Criticality

## 3.1 System Trustworthiness

Our trust in systems depends on the truthfulness of our knowledge about their components and the way they are built.

Trustworthiness characterizes system resilience to any kind of hazard including [12,15]: (a) software design and implementation errors; (b) failures of the execution infra-structure and system peripherals; (c) interaction with potential users including erroneous actions and threats; and (d) interaction with the physical environment including disturbances.

Note that trustworthiness concerns not only functional properties but also general non-functional properties including safety and security. It characterizes the whole system's computing environment. Among the possible hazards, only software design errors and defects require functional validation. The others require the analysis of a system model in interaction with its physical and human environment. Trustworthiness depends on both technical and subjective factors. Technical trustworthiness assessment is a complex task involving separate evaluation of functional correctness for a nominal behavior against a set of requirements [15]. It is followed by a risk analysis of potential issues that could affect the system safety and security. Trustworthiness is especially characterized by the probability that events with catastrophic con-sequences occur – as an example, this probability for transport category aircraft should be less than $10^{-9}$ failures per flight hour. The assessment of system trustworthiness involves three different levels of knowledge.

1. *Irrefutable evidence* that a mathematical system model meets given requirements. This is the type of knowledge obtained by analysis of system models. In that manner, we can estimate the energy consumption of a circuit model, compute a program in-variant, or show that the RTL model of a piece of hardware computes a given function.
2. *Conclusive evidence* that a system meets given requirements. This is the type of knowledge obtained as the result of a two-step process. The first step involves the construction of a mathematical model of the system and checking that the model is faithful, i.e. each true statement about the model holds for the real system. Then, the so obtained model is analyzed to get irrefutable evidence that will hold for the real system under the assumption of model faithfulness. Conclusive evidence is the most truthful knowledge one can get about real systems. It is often required by critical systems standards that explicitly recommend the use of model-based design techniques.
3. *Sufficient evidence* that a system implementation passes a test campaign. Testing allows discovering defects but cannot guarantee absence of defects, which is possible by conclusive evidence. Its efficiency can vary depending on the rigorousness of test coverage criteria. This type of experimental validation suffices only for non-critical systems.

Lack of explainability of neural systems implies that our knowledge about their behavior is restricted to sufficient evidence. On the contrary, for systems developed according to rigorous model-based approaches, the three types of knowledge are equally useful to ascertain their trustworthiness. Reasoning on system models allows irrefutable guarantees and strong predictability. Verification of system components and of the system development process brings conclusive evidence about correctness with respect to requirements. Finally system testing plays a complementary role. It brings additional sufficient evidence about the actual system implementation by exercising the code generated by a compiler from the application software and running in a given execution environment.

### 3.2 The Automation Frontier

How we decide whether a system can be trusted to perform a given task? Our decision depends on two main factors: (1) System trustworthiness; (2) Task criticality, which characterizes the severity of the impact of a failure in the fulfilment of the task.

We assume that system trustworthiness varies in the interval [0, 1]. The highest trustworthiness corresponds to systems that in all cases would behave as expected while the lowest to systems that exhibit completely random behavior.

Task criticality characterizes pure functionality provided by the system and is completely independent from implementation issues. Driving a car, operating on a patient, and nuclear plant control involve intrinsic risks that do not depend on the way these tasks are carried out and the means employed.

We similarly assume that the degree of task criticality is in the interval [0, 1]. The highest criticality corresponds to catastrophic errors with costly consequences. The lowest criticality means indifference to errors in the performance of tasks. Further-more, we assume that there is a monotonic correspondence between the achievable system trustworthiness and the required task criticality: a given trustworthiness level allows satisfaction of a corresponding criticality requirement.

Consider the two-dimensional space defined by the two quantities, system trust-worthiness and task criticality. A system for a given task is represented as a point in this space (Fig. 3).

Based on these definitions, the answer to the problem is simple: if the trustworthiness of a system realizing a given task is greater than the required degree of criticality, then the system can be trusted. Otherwise, it is not reasonable to trust the system; the task may be assigned to skilled human operators or cannot be performed by either humans or systems.

Figure 3(a) shows automated systems that are trusted because they meet this requirement. It also shows tasks assigned to humans and for which the achievable trustworthiness cannot match the required criticality level e.g. teaching. For the sake of simplicity, we assume that each trustworthiness level matches exactly the same level of criticality. In that case, the angle bisector defines the frontier of automation, which separates the space in two regions: one where machines can be trusted (below the frontier) and another where humans may be more trusted than systems for the same task. With increasing automation human-operated tasks cross the automation frontier and pass from the red to the green region.

As explained, the advent of autonomous systems will allow the automation of complex tasks that are currently entrusted to humans in large organizations. The transition to fully autonomous systems will be progressive and will be eventually completed in some distant future. Meanwhile, the challenge is how to achieve symbiotic autonomy [4] by determining the appropriate balance in the division of work machines between humans and computers. This idea illustrated in Fig. 3(b) is reflected in the concept of degree of autonomy e.g. SAE definitions for self-driving cars [1].

### 3.3 Other Factors Shaping the Automation Frontier

It is important to note that the defined ideal automation frontier can be distorted by other objective or subjective factors (Fig. 4).

One factor is the big difference in performance between machines and humans. If the task performed by the system is not critical, we may use auto-

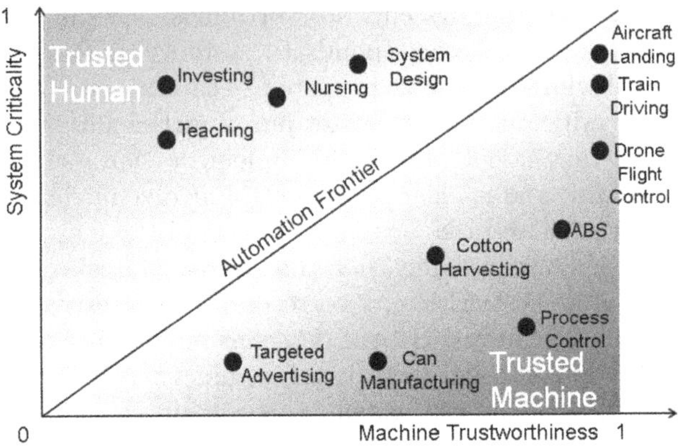


(a) The automation frontier

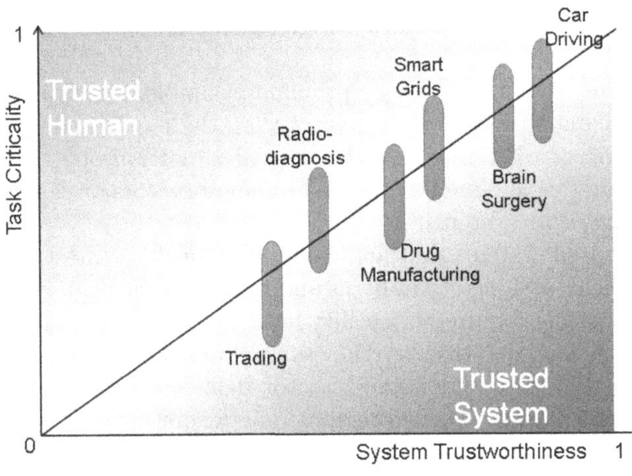


(b) Degree of automation for autonomous systems

**Fig. 3.** The automation frontier and the degree of automation (Color figure online)

mated systems above the automation frontier because the gains in performance can be substantial and compensate a relatively high failure rate. Today, we use many automated services such as internet bots that perform repetitive non critical tasks at a much higher rate than would be possible for humans.

On the contrary, for high criticality levels, people have the tendency to accept and excuse human mistakes if they understand the circumstances which shaped the wrongful or reckless behavior.

As a rule, the public opinion is more unforgiving for system failures than for human errors e.g. accidents caused by self-driving car vs. accidents caused by human drivers. This bias in favor of humans shapes the automation frontier in

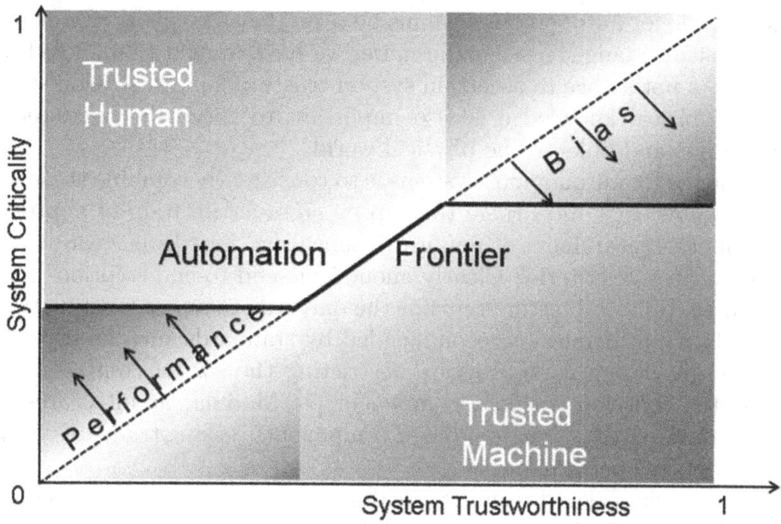


**Fig. 4.** Shaping factors of the automation frontier

the opposite manner. Even if systems may be as trustworthy as humans, their acceptance to perform highly critical tasks would always be questioned.

We have assumed that system trustworthiness and criticality are quantities rigorously and indisputably defined. We explained that conclusive evidence is achievable only when specific model-based system design methodologies are applied. Such methodologies fall short for autonomous systems due to several reasons including the non-predictability of their environment and of course, the inevitable use of data-based techniques.

Besides these considerations, it should be emphasized that trustworthiness has a subjective and social dimension. We should not ignore the role of institutions that directly or indirectly contribute to shaping public perceptions about what is true, right, safe, etc. in modern societies. It is not enough to build a system complying with the acknowledged rules of the state of the art. Care should be taken that the compliance of the construction process can be checked by independent experts [5]. Certification of critical systems should remain the prerogative of independent agencies according to well-founded standards requiring conclusive model-based evidence.

## 4 Discussion

We presented a classification of knowledge depending on its truthfulness and resulting types of evidence about system trustworthiness. This classification should not be associated with a judgment of value. Scientific knowledge is deemed more truthful than general empirical knowledge, but its development and application are limited to formal domains of discourse. Machine learning techniques are indispensable for autonomous systems because they can effectively deal with concepts of natural languages. Furthermore, we have argued that model-based knowledge does not suffice to ascertain system trustworthiness. Reasoned development of empirical knowledge is also important to check the consistency of implementations and links to the physical world.

The challenge for autonomous systems is to consistently combine these different types of knowledge and bridge the gap by cross-fertilization of approaches. How to enhance truthfulness of empirical knowledge based on rigorous qualitative or quantitative criteria? Clearly, monolithic end-to-end solutions are not amenable to analysis and testing remains the only way to assess trustworthiness. Using modularity principles as recommended by standards such as ISO 26262, allows mastering design complexity by restricting the size of components and maximizing the cohesion within a component [7]. Modular architectures could involve both data-based and model-based components seeking trade-offs between trustworthiness and performance.

Furthermore, data-based techniques can be profitably used to overcome limitations of the scientific method. One well-identified limitation comes from the cognitive complexity of the relations that our mind can apprehend: we can deal with relations of rank up to five (one predicate + four arguments) [8]. This is especially reflected in the fact that scientific theories involve a limited number of fundamental independent concepts. Einstein was considering that we are lucky that basic physical laws are simple enough ("The most incomprehensible thing about the universe is that it is comprehensible."). The impressive success of physical sciences often makes us believe that everything should be explainable in terms of formal theory, simple enough to be developed by humans. However, our current lack of holistic understanding of complex phenomena does not necessarily mean that they are not subject to laws. They may well obey to laws that we cannot discover as their complexity exceeds our cognitive capabilities. There are many examples where computers contribute to the analysis and deeper understanding of complex phenomena via the combined use of data analytics and learning techniques e.g. [13]. The challenge is to defeat cognitive complexity by achieving computer-assisted development of scientific knowledge.

The role of autonomous systems will depend on our decisions about when we trust them and when we do not. Making these choices wisely depends on two factors. The first factor is our ability to appreciate, based on well-founded criteria, whether and to what extent we can trust knowledge produced by computers. Our analysis emphasizes the importance of two inter-related concepts: truthfulness of knowledge about how a system behaves and the resulting system trustworthiness. We need new theoretical foundation and technology for the evaluation of trustworthiness of autonomous systems that integrate both model-based and data-based components. Such results could be a basis for the definition of standards for the development and use of autonomous systems (as we do for all artifacts from toasters to bridges and aircraft). The current trend for self-regulation and self-certification should be considered as a temporary stopgap rather than the definitive answer to the trustworthiness issue.

The second factor is increased social awareness and sense of political responsibility. It would be good to apply the precautionary principle that already underlies laws and regulations in European Union: when computers are part of critical-decision processes we should make sure that their judgment is safe and fair [2]. This principle should be embodied in laws and regulations governing their development and deployment.

We are on the verge of a great knowledge revolution. We should be vigilant and question the use of machine-produced knowledge allowing predictability without under-standing critical decision processes. I believe that the threat is not that computer intelligence surpasses human intelligence and that computers take power and control over human societies by hatching a plot. The real danger comes from the massive re-placement of accountable and responsible human operators in critical decision processes. Let us hope that we will not grant the power of decision to autonomous systems without rigorous and strictly grounded guarantees under the pressure of economic interests and on the grounds of an ill-understood performance benefit.

## References

1. National Highway Traffic Safety Administration, et al.: Federal automated vehicles policy: accelerating the next revolution in roadway safety. US Department of Transportation (2016)
2. Benkler, Y.: Don't let industry write the rules for AI. Nature **569**(7755), 161–161 (2019)
3. Bojarski, M., et al.: Explaining how a deep neural network trained with end-to-end learning steers a car. arXiv preprint arXiv:1704.07911 (2017)
4. Dambrot, S.M., de Kerchove, D., Flammini, F., Kinsner, W., Glenn, L.M., Saracco, R.: IEEE symbiotic autonomous systems white paper II (2018)
5. De Millo, R.A., Lipton, R.J., Perlis, A.J.: Social processes and proofs of theorems and programs. Commun. ACM **22**(5), 271–280 (1979)
6. Doran, D., Schulz, S., Besold, T.R.: What does explainable AI really mean? A new conceptualization of perspectives. arXiv preprint arXiv:1710.00794 (2017)
7. Frtunikj, J., Fürst, S.: Engineering safe machine learning for automated driving systems. In: Proceedings of the 2019 Safety-Critical Systems Symposium, pp. 115–133 (2019)
8. Halford, G.S., Baker, R., McCredden, J.E., Bain, J.D.: How many variables can humans process? Psychol. Sci. **16**(1), 70–76 (2005)
9. Kahneman, D.: Thinking, Fast and Slow. Macmillan, London (2011)
10. Katz, G., Barrett, C., Dill, D.L., Julian, K., Kochenderfer, M.J.: Reluplex: an efficient SMT solver for verifying deep neural networks. In: Majumdar, R., Kunčak, V. (eds.) CAV 2017. LNCS, vol. 10426, pp. 97–117. Springer, Cham (2017). https://doi.org/10.1007/978-3-319-63387-9_5
11. Lipton, Z.C.: The mythos of model interpretability. arXiv preprint arXiv:1606.03490 (2016)
12. Neumann, P.G.: Trustworthiness and truthfulness are essential. Commun. ACM **60**(6), 26–28 (2017)
13. Rouet-Leduc, B., Hulbert, C., Lubbers, N., Barros, K., Humphreys, C.J., Johnson, P.A.: Machine learning predicts laboratory earthquakes. Geophys. Res. Lett. **44**(18), 9276–9282 (2017)

14. Sifakis, J.: Autonomous systems-an architectural characterization. arXiv preprint arXiv:1811.10277 (2018)
15. Sifakis, J., et al.: Rigorous system design. Found. Trends® Electron. Des. Autom. **6**(4), 293–362 (2013)
16. Zeng, W., et al.: End-to-end interpretable neural motion planner. In: Proceedings of the IEEE Conference on Computer Vision and Pattern Recognition, pp. 8660–8669 (2019)

# Cyber-Physical Systems

# Teaching Stratego to Play Ball: Optimal Synthesis for Continuous Space MDPs

Manfred Jaeger[1], Peter Gjøl Jensen[1(✉)], Kim Guldstrand Larsen[1], Axel Legay[1,2], Sean Sedwards[3], and Jakob Haahr Taankvist[1]

[1] Department of Computer Science, Aalborg University, Aalborg, Denmark
pgj@cs.aau.dk
[2] Université catholique de Louvain, Ottignies-Louvain-la-Neuve, Belgium
[3] University of Waterloo, Waterloo, Canada

**Abstract.** Formal models of cyber-physical systems, such as priced timed Markov decision processes, require a state space with continuous and discrete components. The problem of controller synthesis for such systems then can be cast as finding optimal strategies for Markov decision processes over a Euclidean state space. We develop two different reinforcement learning strategies that tackle the problem of continuous state spaces via online partition refinement techniques. We provide theoretical insights into the convergence of partition refinement schemes. Our techniques are implemented in Uppaal Stratego. Experimental results show the advantages of our new techniques over previous optimization algorithms of Uppaal Stratego.

## 1 Introduction

Machine learning and artificial intelligence have become standard methods for controlling complex systems. For systems represented as priced timed Markov decision processes (PTMDP), Uppaal Stratego [6] has demonstrated that near-optimal strategies can be learned [5,11,13]. However, as we shall demonstrate in this paper, for the rich class of PTMDPs we can still improve significantly on the existing learning techniques, in terms of learning better strategies and obtaining better convergence characteristics with respect to the training data size.

In most machine learning applications one learns from real-world data that is provided in batch, or as a data stream. However, for many cyber-physical systems it is impossible to obtain sufficient data from the real-world system. On the other hand, accurate formal models of the systems may be available. We therefore base the controller synthesis on data generated from a model of the system, an approach we refer to as *in-silico* synthesis.

We extend the method of David et al. [5,6] by developing an *online* learning method based on reinforcement learning principles. Since we are dealing with


Y.-F. Chen et al. (Eds.): ATVA 2019, LNCS 11781, pp. 81–97, 2019.
https://doi.org/10.1007/978-3-030-31784-3_5

systems operating in hybrid discrete-continuous state spaces, a suitable approach to deal with continuous state spaces in a reinforcement learning setting needs to be chosen. Traditional (linear) function approximations of value functions [18] are not expressive enough to deal with the often highly non-linear, multi-modal value functions we encounter in typical cyber-physical system models. Recent developments in which neural network representations of non-linear state-value functions are learned [15] have the drawback that the learned strategy faces similar drawbacks as any neural network in terms of verification [9], and the lack of safety guarantees. While we do not directly address safety of learned strategies in this paper, we note that the simple partition-based function approximations that we will employ are not only highly flexible regarding the types of functions that can be approximated, but also closely aligned with continuous-time model-checking techniques such as *regions* and *zones*.

In order to obtain an online method whose computational efficiency does not deteriorate over time due to the accumulation of training data, we need to base our approach on fixed-size running summaries of the data, specifically online standard deviations and running means [17]. In this paper we develop two versions of our basic partition refinement approach: one based on *Q-learning* [19] and one related to *Real Time Dynamic Programming* [1,16] (RTDP). While Q-learning is a so-called model-free learning-method, RTDP is a model-centric learning-method and we will thus denote the latter *M-learning*.

To demonstrate our approach we have implemented the proposed algorithms in UPPAAL STRATEGO and investigated their performance experimentally. We also provide an Open Source C++ implementation of the algorithms.

*Related Work:* In the area of synthesis for reactive systems, David et al. [5,6] extended the work of Henriques et al. [8] to continuous space systems. In the work of Henriques et al. the problem of optimization is seen as one of classification. As we shall later demonstrate experimentally, examples exist where these algorithms do not converge towards optimal controllers.

Several abstraction and partition refinement-based methods have been applied to speed up verification of finite state MDPs [3,10,14], utilizing underlying symbolic techniques. We distinguish ourselves from this approach by considering a richer class of MDPs, while doing an empirical partition refinement online, based on statistical tests.

The partition refinement scheme we deploy can be seen as a classical regression or classification problem. As such, alternative approaches could be based on classical decision and regression trees [2]. However, these often require a batch of data samples to be kept in memory and are thus incompatible with our online scheme.

## 2 Euclidean MDP and Expected Cost

In this section we introduce our formal system model and controller synthesis objective.

**Definition 1 (($K$-Dimensional, Euclidean) Markov Decision Processes).** *A MDP is a tuple $\mathcal{M} = (\mathcal{S}, Act, s_{init}, T, \mathcal{C}, \mathcal{G})$ where:*

- $\mathcal{S} \subseteq \mathbb{R}^K$ *is a bounded and closed subset of the Euclidean space,*
- *Act is a finite set of actions,*
- $s_{init} \in \mathcal{S}$ *is the initial state,*
- $T : \mathcal{S} \times Act \to (\mathcal{S} \to \mathbb{R}_{\geq 0})$ *yields a probability density function over $\mathcal{S}$ i.e. for all $(s, \alpha) \in \mathcal{S} \times Act$ we have $\int_{t \in \mathcal{S}} T(s, \alpha)(t)dt = 1$,*
- $\mathcal{C} : \mathcal{S} \times Act \times \mathcal{S} \to \mathbb{R}$ *is a cost-function for state-action-state triples,*
- $\mathcal{G} \subseteq \mathcal{S}$ *is the set of goal states.*

A run $\pi$ of an MDP is a sequence of alternating states and actions $s_1 a_1 s_2 a_2 \cdots$ where $s_1 = s_{init}$ and $T(s_i, \alpha_i)(s_{i+1}) > 0$ for all $i > 0$. We denote the set of all runs of an MDP $\mathcal{M}$ as $\Pi_{\mathcal{M}}$, and all finite runs of $\mathcal{M}$ as $\Pi^f_{\mathcal{M}}$. We use the notation $\pi|_i$ to denote the prefix of the run up to $s_i$, i.e. $\pi|_i = s_1 a_1 s_2 a_2 \cdots a_{i-1} s_i$. We denote the length of a run $\pi = s_1 \alpha_1 s_2 \cdots s_n$ as $|\pi| = n$. We let $\epsilon$ denote the empty run and by agreement let $|\epsilon| = 0$. To define the cost of a run $\pi = s_1 a_1 s_2 a_2 \cdots \in \Pi_{\mathcal{M}}$ let $s_{i_{\min}}$ be the first state in $\pi$ which is included in $\mathcal{G}$, i.e. $i_{min} = \min_{i \in \mathbb{N}}\{s_i \in \pi \mid s_i \in \mathcal{G}\}$. Then the cost of $\pi$ up to $\mathcal{G}$ is the sum of costs until $i_{\min}$, defined as the random variable $\mathcal{C}_{\mathcal{G}}$:

$$\mathcal{C}_{\mathcal{G}}(\pi) = \sum_{s_i a_i s_{i+1} \in \pi|_{i_{\min}}} \mathcal{C}(s_i, a_i, s_{i+1}).$$

**Definition 2 (Strategy).** *A (memoryless) strategy for an MDP $\mathcal{M}$ is a function $\sigma : \mathcal{S} \to (Act \to [0, 1])$, mapping a state to a probability distribution over Act.*

Given a strategy $\sigma$, the expected costs of reaching a goal state is defined as the solution to a Volterra integral equation as follows:

**Definition 3 (Expected cost of a strategy).** *Let $\mathcal{G}$ be a set of goal-states and let $\sigma$ be a strategy. The expected cost of reaching $\mathcal{G}$ starting in a state $s$ – $\mathbb{E}^{\mathcal{M}}_{\sigma}(\mathcal{C}_{\mathcal{G}}, s)$ – is the solution to the following system of equations*[1]*:*

$$\mathbb{E}^{\mathcal{M}}_{\sigma}(\mathcal{C}_{\mathcal{G}}, s) = \sum_{a \in Act} \sigma(s)(a) \cdot \int_{t \in \mathcal{S}} T(s, a)(t) \cdot \big(\mathcal{C}(s, a, t) + \mathbb{E}^{\mathcal{M}}_{\sigma}(\mathcal{C}_{\mathcal{G}}, t)\big)dt$$

*when $s \notin \mathcal{G}$ and $\mathbb{E}^{\mathcal{M}}_{\sigma}(\mathcal{C}_{\mathcal{G}}, s) = 0$ when $s \in \mathcal{G}$.*

The problem we address in this paper is to find the strategy $\sigma$ which minimizes $\mathbb{E}^{\mathcal{M}}_{\sigma}(\mathcal{C}_{\mathcal{G}}, s_{init})$. Since analytic solutions of the integral equations of Definition 3 are usually unobtainable, we develop an approximation approach based on finite partitionings of the state space.

*Example 1.* Consider the MDP in Fig. 1, described as a stochastic priced timed game [4] over the clock $x$ and the cost-variable $C$. Here the state space $\mathcal{S}$ is given by the values of the clock $x$, i.e. $\mathcal{S} = [0, 10]$. The action set is $Act = \{a, b\}$.

[1] We shall assume that the equation system has a solution for the considered MDP and goal set under any strategy.

The goal set $\mathcal{G}$ is $(9, 10]$. In the (urgent) location $\ell_0$ the (probabilistic) choice between the actions $a$ or $b$ is made. Note that for $x > 9$, neither $a$ nor $b$ affects the state. In the case $x \leq 9$ choosing $a$ will reset $x$ (at no cost), whereas $b$ will increase the cost by 15. In both cases – now at location $\ell_1$ – the new state (i.e. the new value of the clock $x$) will be chosen uniformly from the current value of $x$ to 10. Thus, $T(x,a)(y) = \frac{1}{10}$ for all $y \in [0, 10]$, and $T(x,b)(y) = 0$ whenever $y < x$ and $T(x,b)(y) = \frac{1}{10-x}$ when $y \geq x$. Furthermore, $\mathcal{C}(x,a,y) = 2y$ for $y \in [0, 10]$, and $\mathcal{C}(x,b,y) = 2(y-x) + 15$ for $y \geq x$.

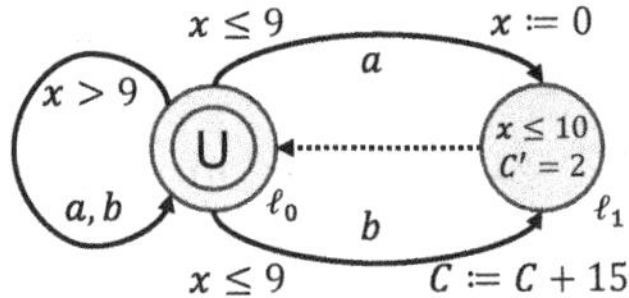


**Fig. 1.** MDP described as a stochastic priced timed game with $s_{init} = 0$.

Let $\sigma_u$ be the random strategy choosing uniformly between $a$ and $b$ for any value of $x$, i.e. $\sigma_u(x)(a) = \sigma_u(x)(b) = \frac{1}{2}$ for any $x \in [0, 10]$. Then the expected costs $\mathbb{E}_{\sigma_u}(x)$ of reaching $\mathcal{G}$ from state $x$ satisfy the following integral equation

$$\mathbb{E}_{\sigma_u}(x) = \frac{1}{2} \cdot \int_{y=0}^{10} \frac{2y + \mathbb{E}_{\sigma_u}(y)}{10} dy + \frac{1}{2} \cdot \int_{y=x}^{10} \frac{15 + 2(y-x) + \mathbb{E}_{\sigma_u}(y)}{10-x} dy$$

when $x \leq 9$ and $\mathbb{E}_{\sigma_u}(x) = 0$ when $x > 9$. Using statistical model checking [7], we find that $\mathbb{E}_{\sigma_u}(\mathcal{G}, s_{init}) \approx 81.73$. Considering the deterministic strategy $\sigma_7$ with $\sigma_7(x)(a) = 1$ for $x \leq 7$ and $\sigma_7(x)(b) = 1$ for $x > 7$, we find that $\mathbb{E}_{\sigma_7}(\mathcal{G}, s_{init}) \approx 51.91$, thus providing an improvement over the random strategy. Using the learning methods presented in the next sections, we find that the optimal strategy $\sigma^o$ has $\mathbb{E}_{\sigma^o}(\mathcal{G}, s_{init}) \approx 48.16$ and chooses $a$ when $x \leq 4.8$ and $b$ otherwise.

## 3 Approximation by Partitioning

The expected cost of a strategy is the solution to a Volterra integral equation. Such equations are notoriously hard to solve, even in the case of stochastic priced timed games, as in Example 1. In this paper we offer a solution method combining reinforcement learning with an online partition refinement scheme.

First let us formally introduce the notion of a *partition* and see how it may be used symbolically to approximate the optimal expected cost. We say that $\mathcal{A} \subseteq 2^{\mathcal{S}}$ is a partition of $\mathcal{S}$ if $\mathcal{S} = \bigcup_{\nu \in \mathcal{A}} \nu$ and for any $\nu, \nu' \in \mathcal{A}$ we have $\nu \cap \nu' = \emptyset$ whenever $\nu \neq \nu'$. We call an element $\nu$ of $\mathcal{A}$ a *region* and shall assume that each such $\nu$ is Borel measurable (e.g. a k-dimensional interval). Whenever $s \in \mathcal{S}$ we denote by $[s]_{\mathcal{A}}$ the unique region $\nu \in \mathcal{A}$ such that $s \in \nu$. For $\delta \in \mathbb{R}_{>0}$ we shall say that that $\mathcal{A}$ has granularity $\delta$ if $diam(\nu) \leq \delta$ for any region $\nu \in \mathcal{A}$. We say that a partition $\mathcal{B}$ refines a partition $\mathcal{A}$ if for any $\nu \in \mathcal{B}$ there exist $\mu \in \mathcal{A}$ with $\nu \subseteq \mu$. We write $\mathcal{A} \sqsubseteq \mathcal{B}$ in this case.

Given an MDP, a partition $\mathcal{A}$ of its state space induces an abstracting Markov Interval Decision Process (MIDP) [10,14] as follows:

**Definition 4.** *Let $\mathcal{M} = (\mathcal{S}, Act, s_{init}, T, \mathcal{C}, \mathcal{G})$ be an MDP, and let $\mathcal{A}$ be a finite partition of $\mathcal{S}$ consistent with $\mathcal{G}$*[2]*. Then $\mathcal{M}_\mathcal{A} = (\mathcal{S}_\mathcal{A}, Act, \nu_{init}, T_\mathcal{A}, \mathcal{C}_\mathcal{A}, \mathcal{G}_\mathcal{A})$ is the MIDP s.t.:*

- $\mathcal{S}_\mathcal{A} = \mathcal{A}$,
- $\nu_{init} = [s_{init}]_\mathcal{A}$ *is the initial state,*
- $\nu \in \mathcal{G}_\mathcal{A}$ *if* $\nu \subseteq \mathcal{G}$,
- $T_\mathcal{A} : \mathcal{A} \times Act \rightarrow (\mathcal{A} \rightarrow [0,1] \times [0,1])$ *is the transition-function,*
- $\mathcal{C}_\mathcal{A} : \mathcal{A} \times Act \times \mathcal{A} \rightarrow \mathbb{R} \times \mathbb{R}$ *is the transition cost-function*

*where*

$$T_\mathcal{A}(\nu, a)(\nu') = \left(\inf_{s\in\nu} \int_{\nu'} T(s,a)(t)dt,\ \sup_{s\in\nu} \int_{\nu'} T(s,a)(t)dt\right)$$

*and*

$$\mathcal{C}_\mathcal{A}(\nu, a, \nu') = \left(\inf_{s\in\nu, s'\in\nu'} \mathcal{C}(s,a,s'),\ \sup_{s\in\nu, s'\in\nu'} \mathcal{C}(s,a,s')\right)$$

For a region $\nu$ and an action $a$, let $\Delta(T_\mathcal{A}(\nu, a))$ be the set of probability functions over $\mathcal{A}$ that are consistent with $T_\mathcal{A}(\nu, a)$, i.e. if $p \in \Delta(T_\mathcal{A}(\nu, a))$ then $\sum_{\nu'\in\mathcal{A}} p(\nu') = 1$ and $p(\nu') \in T_\mathcal{A}(\nu, a)(\nu')$ for all $\nu'$.

We can now define the *lower* expected costs from partitions $\nu \in \mathcal{A}$ to $\mathcal{G}$ as the least solution to the following (finite) system of equations[3]:

$$\mathbb{E}^{\min}_{\mathcal{M},\mathcal{A}}(\mathcal{C}_\mathcal{A}, \nu) = \min_{a\in Act} \inf_{p\in\Delta(T_\mathcal{A}(\nu,a))} \sum_{\nu'\in\mathcal{A}} p(\nu') \cdot (\mathcal{C}^{\inf}_\mathcal{A}(\nu, a, \nu') + \mathbb{E}^{\min}_{\mathcal{M},\mathcal{A}}(\mathcal{C}_\mathcal{A}, \nu'))$$

when $\nu \cap \mathcal{G} = \emptyset$ and $\mathbb{E}^{\min}_{\mathcal{M},\mathcal{A}}(\mathcal{C}_\mathcal{A}, \nu) = 0$ when $\nu \subseteq \mathcal{G}$. Similarly, we can define the *upper* expected costs $\mathbb{E}^{\max}_{\mathcal{M},\mathcal{A}}(\mathcal{C}_\mathcal{A}, \nu)$ (simply replace the occurrences of inf with sup in the above equation). The following Theorem shows their importance for approximating the expected cost of the optimal strategy.

**Theorem 1.** *Let $\mathcal{M} = (\mathcal{S}, Act, s_{init}, T, \mathcal{C}, \mathcal{G})$ be an MDP and let $\mathcal{A}$ be a finite partition of $\mathcal{S}$ consistent with $\mathcal{G}$. Then for all $s \in \mathcal{S}$:*

$$\mathbb{E}^{\min}_{\mathcal{M},\mathcal{A}}(\mathcal{C}_\mathcal{A}, [s]_\mathcal{A}) \leq \inf_\sigma \mathbb{E}^\mathcal{M}_\sigma(\mathcal{C}, s) \leq \mathbb{E}^{\max}_{\mathcal{M},\mathcal{A}}(\mathcal{C}_\mathcal{A}, [s]_\mathcal{A})$$

We also note that, whenever $\mathcal{A} \sqsubseteq \mathcal{B}$, then $\mathcal{B}$ offers a (possible) better approximation than $\mathcal{A}$ in the sense that $\mathbb{E}^{\min}_{\mathcal{M},\mathcal{A}}(\mathcal{C}_\mathcal{A}, [s]_\mathcal{A}) \leq \mathbb{E}^{\min}_{\mathcal{M},\mathcal{B}}(\mathcal{C}_\mathcal{A}, [s]_\mathcal{B}) \leq \mathbb{E}^{\max}_{\mathcal{M},\mathcal{B}}(\mathcal{C}_\mathcal{A}, [s]_\mathcal{B}) \leq \mathbb{E}^{\max}_{\mathcal{M},\mathcal{B}}(\mathcal{C}_\mathcal{A}, [s]_\mathcal{A})$ for any $s \in \mathcal{S}$.

---

[2] $\mathcal{A}$ is consistent with $\mathcal{G}$ if for any $\nu \in \mathcal{A}$ either $\nu \subseteq \mathcal{G}$ of $\nu \cap \mathcal{G} = \emptyset$.

[3] Here $\mathcal{C}^{\inf}_\mathcal{A}(\nu, a, \nu') = \inf_{s\in\nu, s'\in\nu'} \mathcal{C}(s,a,s')$.

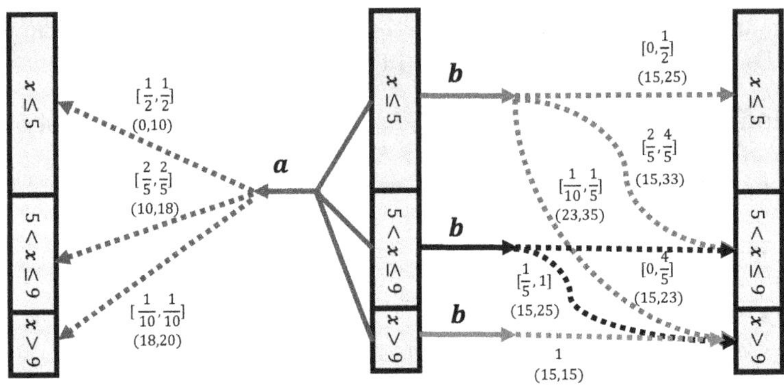


**Fig. 2.** Markov Interval Decision Process abstracting Fig. 1.

*Example 1.* Reconsider the MDP $\mathcal{M}$ from Fig. 1. Now consider the partition $\mathcal{A}$ of the state-space $[0,10]$ given by the three parts $[0,5]$, $(5,9]$ and $(9,10]$. Note that this partition is consistent with the goal set $(9,10]$. The finite-state Markov Interval Decision Process in Fig. 2 provides the abstraction $\mathcal{M}_\mathcal{A}$. From this it may be found that $\mathbb{E}^{\min}_{\mathcal{M},\mathcal{A}}(\mathcal{C}_\mathcal{A},[0,5]) = 23.6$ is obtained by the strategy $\sigma_{\min}$ with $\sigma_{\min}([0,5]) = a$ and $\sigma_{\min}((5,9]) = b$. Similarly, $\mathbb{E}^{\max}_{\mathcal{M},\mathcal{A}}(\mathcal{C}_\mathcal{A},[0,5]) = 152$ is obtained by the strategy $\sigma_{\max}$ with $\sigma_{\max}([0,5]) = \sigma_{\max}((5,9]) = b$.

A natural question to ask now is: *under which conditions may the optimal expected cost be approximated arbitrarily closely by successively refining partitions?* As we shall detail now, convergence is guaranteed for bounded horizon MDPs with continuous transition and cost functions. This class covers all the MDPs that we consider in the evaluation of our new learning algorithms.

For an MDP $\mathcal{M} = (\mathcal{S}, Act, s_{init}, T, \mathcal{C}, \mathcal{G})$ and $N \in \mathbb{N}$, we define the induced bounded horizon MDP $\mathcal{M}^N = (\mathcal{S}^N, Act, s^N_{init}, T^N, \mathcal{C}^N, \mathcal{G}^N)$, being essentially $N$ unfoldings of $\mathcal{M}$, i.e. $\mathcal{S}^N = \{0,\ldots,N\} \times \mathcal{S}$, $s^N_{init} = (0, s_{init})$, $T^N((n,s),a)((n+1,t)) = T(s,a)(t)$, $\mathcal{C}^N((n,s),\alpha,((n+1),t)) = C(s,\alpha,t)$ and $(n,s) \in \mathcal{G}^N$ if $(n = N \vee s \in \mathcal{G})$. Thus in $\mathcal{M}^N$ we will with probability 1 be in a goal state after at most $N$ steps. Note that any partition $\mathcal{A}$ of $\mathcal{S}$ may be extended to a partition $\mathcal{A}^N$ of $\mathcal{S}^N$ by $(\{i\} \times \nu) \in \mathcal{A}^N$ whenever $\nu \in \mathcal{A}$ and $i \in \{0,\ldots,N\}$.

**Theorem 2.** *Let $\mathcal{M} = (\mathcal{S}, Act, s_{init}, T, \mathcal{C}, \mathcal{G})$ be an MDP with $T$ and $\mathcal{C}$ being continuous functions. Let $\mathcal{A}_0 \sqsubseteq \mathcal{A}_1 \sqsubseteq \cdots \sqsubseteq \mathcal{A}_i \sqsubseteq \cdots$ be a refining sequence of partitions consistent with $\mathcal{G}$ and with decreasing granularity $\delta_0 \geq \delta_1 \geq \cdots \geq \delta_i \geq \cdots$ with $\lim_{i\to\infty} \delta_i = 0$. Let $\mathcal{M}^N$ be the induced bounded horizon MDP for $N \in \mathbb{N}$. Then for any $s \in \mathcal{S}$:*

$$\inf_{i\to\infty} \mathbb{E}^{\min}_{\mathcal{M}^N,\mathcal{A}_i}(\mathcal{C}^N_{\mathcal{A}_i}, [(0,s)]_{\mathcal{A}_i}) = \inf_{\sigma} \mathbb{E}^{\mathcal{M}^N}_{\sigma}(\mathcal{C}^N, (0,s)) = \inf_{i\to\infty} \mathbb{E}^{\max}_{\mathcal{M}^N,\mathcal{A}_i}(\mathcal{C}^N_{\mathcal{A}_i}, [(0,s)]_{\mathcal{A}_i})$$

*Proof Sketch:* We show by induction on $(N-n)$ that:

$$\forall\varepsilon > 0.\exists i.\forall\nu \in \mathcal{A}_i. \\ \left|\mathbb{E}^{\max}_{\mathcal{M}^N,\mathcal{A}_i}(\mathcal{C}^N_{\mathcal{A}_i}, \{N-n\}\times\nu) - \mathbb{E}^{\min}_{\mathcal{M}^N,\mathcal{A}_i}(\mathcal{C}^N_{\mathcal{A}_i}, \{N-n\}\times\nu)\right| \leq \varepsilon$$

Crucial for the induction step is uniform continuity of $T$ and $\mathcal{C}$ due to compactness of $\mathcal{S}$, i.e. $\forall\varepsilon > 0.\exists i.\forall\nu,\nu' \in \mathcal{A}_i.\forall a.\, |T_{\mathcal{A}_i}(\nu,a)(\nu')| \leq \varepsilon$. □

## 4 Algorithms

While the previous section hints that a partition refinement scheme aids in the computation of near-optimal strategies for continuous state MDPs, it assumes that minimal and maximal values of the transition and cost functions are known. It can be shown that these values, in general, are undecidable to attain for stochastic hybrid systems (which can be modeled in UPPAAL SMC). We shall therefore in the sequel rely on simulation-based learning methods, using an online partition refinement scheme.

We first present the underlying learning algorithms as if a fixed partition is given, then return to the partition refinement scheme in Sect. 4.2.

We adopt the (adaptive, online) Q- and M-learning terminology from [18] and thus see both as methods for solving the Bellman equations online, commonly called *Q-values*, while guiding the search of the state space. While Q-learning is a so-called model-free learning method, directly learning the Q-values, M-learning attempts to derive the Q-values from the approximate transition-functions and cost functions. Common for both learning-methods is the online nature of the strategy synthesis, along with an online partition refinement scheme. We only present the pseudocode of the Q-learning variants of our algorithms here due to space limitations.

### 4.1 Learning on Static Partitions

In the sequel the reader will encounter maps and partial functions as $X : 2^{\mathbb{R}^K} \hookrightarrow \dots$. We use such partial functions for brevity and one can think of them as: the region $\nu \in 2^{\mathbb{R}^K}$ is decorated with some information by the $X$ function – and $\nu$ is a specific (continuous) region of the state space. While these functions are defined as partial we implement them as maps over $2^{\mathbb{R}^K}$ in which non-updated elements have the same default value. This allows us to memorize only the (finite) number of non-default values, thus making these maps implementable.

In the sequel we let $\mathcal{A}_\alpha \subseteq 2^{\mathbb{R}^K}$ denote a partition for a given action $\alpha \in \mathit{Act}$. Notice that this differs slightly from the use of $\mathcal{A}$ in Sect. 3 where we omit the action-indexing for clarity and readability.

For both Q-learning and M-learning we shall assume the existence of the following global two modifiable functions. 1. $\mathcal{F}_\alpha : 2^{\mathbb{R}^K} \hookrightarrow \mathbb{N}_0$, for each $\alpha \in \mathit{Act}$, yielding an occurrence count for a given region, and 2. $Q : \mathit{Act} \times 2^{\mathbb{R}^K} \hookrightarrow \mathbb{R}$,

**Data:** An MDP $\mathcal{M}$, an initial state $s_{init}$, a cost-function $\mathcal{C}$, a termination criterion and a set of goal states $\mathcal{G}$

**Result:** A near-optimal, strategy $\sigma$ for the MDP $\mathcal{M}$ under the cost function $\mathcal{C}$ for the goal $\mathcal{G}$.

1 Initially let $\sigma(s)(\alpha) = \frac{1}{|Act|}$ for any $s \in \mathbb{R}^K$ and any $\alpha \in Act$<br>
2 **while** *Termination criterion is not met* **do**<br>
3     $\pi \leftarrow \epsilon$, $s \leftarrow s_{init}$<br>
4     **while** $s \notin \mathcal{G}$ **do**<br>
5         Draw $\alpha$ from $Act$ according to $\sigma(s)$<br>
6         Draw $s'$ from $\mathcal{S}$ according to $T(s, \alpha)$<br>
7         $\pi \leftarrow (\pi \circ (s, \alpha, s'))$, $s \leftarrow s'$<br>
8     **for** $i$ *from* $n$ *to* $1$ *with* $(s_1, \alpha_1, s_2) \ldots (s_n, \alpha_n, s_{n+1}) = \pi$ **do**<br>
9         Let $\alpha = \alpha_n$<br>
10         Let $\nu = \mathcal{A}_\alpha[s_n]$, $\nu' = \mathcal{A}_\alpha[s_{n+1}]$<br>
11         $\mathcal{F}_\alpha(\nu) \leftarrow \min(\mathcal{F}_\alpha(\nu) + 1, R)$<br>
12         $Q_\alpha(\nu) \leftarrow (1 - \frac{1}{\mathcal{F}_\alpha(\nu)}) \cdot Q_\alpha(\nu) + \frac{1}{\mathcal{F}_\alpha(\nu)} \cdot (\mathcal{C}(s_n, \alpha, s_{n+1}) + \min_{\alpha' \in Act} Q_{\alpha'}(\nu'))$<br>
13         $(Q, \mathcal{F}, \mathcal{A}) \leftarrow \texttt{Refine}_\texttt{Q}(Q, \mathcal{F}, \mathcal{A}, (s_n, \alpha, s_{n+1}))$<br>
14         $\sigma \leftarrow \texttt{normalize}(Q)$<br>
15 **return** $\sigma$

**Algorithm 1.** The Q-learning training algorithm.

yielding an approximation of the expected cost for a given action in a given region. By default, we let $\mathcal{F}_\alpha(\nu) = 0$ and $Q_\alpha(\nu) = 0$ for all $\nu \in 2^{\mathbb{R}^K}$ and all $\alpha \in Act$. Furthermore, we let the singleton set $\mathcal{A}_\alpha = \{\mathbb{R}^K\}$, for all $\alpha \in Act$, be the initial partition.

**Q-Learning.** Q-learning is a model-free learning method where the Q-values are derived directly from the samples [19]. For Q-learning, in addition to the globally defined functions, we introduce a learning-rate constant $R \in \mathbb{N}$. In Algorithm 1 we present the Q-learning training algorithm. After a uniform strategy $\sigma$ is created (line 1), samples are drawn from the MDP $\mathcal{M}$ in accordance with $\sigma$ (lines 3–7), backpropagated to the learning algorithm (lines 8–14) until some termination condition is met (e.g. a sample budget). Notice that we use the textbook Q-learning update function [19] on line 12, followed by our refinement-method (line 13), and a normalization of Q-values into pseudo-probabilistic weights yielding a stochastic strategy (line 14).

**M-Learning.** For M-learning (otherwise known as RTDP [16]) the aim is to produce an approximation of the transition- and cost-function of a finite-state MDP, where each state comes from $2^{\mathbb{R}^K}$. We therefore need the additional bookkeeping function $\hat{\mathcal{C}}_\alpha : 2^{\mathbb{R}^K} \times 2^{\mathbb{R}^K} \hookrightarrow \mathbb{R}$ tracking the empirically obtained cost-function. While Algorithm 1 learns the $Q$-function directly form samples, the equivalent M-learning algorithm infers the $Q$-function based on the sampled cost and frequency function.

**Determinization.** A deterministic, near-optimal strategy can be obtained from the Q-function returned by Algorithm 1 by selecting, for each state, the action with the lowest Q-value (with ties broken by a random choice).

### 4.2 Refinement Functions

We say that $\rho : 2^{\mathbb{R}^K} \hookrightarrow 2^{\mathbb{R}^K} \times 2^{\mathbb{R}^K}$ is a refinement function iff whenever $(\nu', \nu'') = \rho(\nu)$ then $\nu' \cap \nu'' = \emptyset$ and $\nu' \cup \nu'' = \nu$. For a given action $\alpha \in Act$ we consider a finite set of functions denoted by $\mathtt{R}_\alpha : 2^{\mathbb{R}^K} \hookrightarrow 2^{\mathbb{R}^K} \times 2^{\mathbb{R}^K}$.

Note that many such functions can exist, and the method puts no restraints on these, other than what is given above. In our implementation we restrict ourselves to computing refinement functions defined as single-dimensional difference constraints (as done in Fig. 2 but generalized to multiple dimensions). We thus consider partition-functions of the form $\rho(\nu) = (\{p \in \nu \mid p_i \leq b\}, \{p \in \nu \mid p_i > b\})$ for some constant $b$ and fixed dimension $0 < i \leq K$. For practical reasons our $\mathtt{R}_\alpha$-set only consists of one such refinement function for each dimension in the implementation. Also note that in a practical setting, one such refinement may contain only unreachable parts of the state space, and thus occasionally we readjust our refinement functions. We can then readjust a refinement by increasing or decreasing $b$ according to the number of samples observed in the two different sub-refinements. This adjustment is omitted from the presented pseudocode, but does however occur at each call to $\mathtt{Refine}_{\{\mathtt{Q},\mathtt{M}\}}$, and entails a reset of the statistics of the specific readjusted partition function $\rho$, implying a modification of $\mathtt{R}_\alpha$. Due to the loss of information, this operation occurs only infrequently and is guarded by statistical tests.

Observe that this continued refinement induces a sequence of MIDP abstractions, leaning on the theoretical framework presented in Sect. 3.

**Refinement Heuristics.** For each region $\nu$ in the current partition $\mathcal{A}_\alpha$ and each candidate refinement $(\nu', \nu'') = \rho(\nu)$ we maintain summary statistics of the Q-values obtained at sampled states in $\nu$, respectively $\nu'$. In the case of M-learning, we also maintain statistics on transition frequencies between pairs of regions. For the remainder of this section we focus on Q-learning. The same principles are applied in M-learning. Our summary statistics consist of triples

$$(m, v, f) \in \Xi := \mathbb{R} \times \mathbb{R} \times \mathbb{N}_0$$

representing empirical means, variances, and frequency counts[4]. Given a new data point $x \in \mathbb{R}$, the statistics are updated by the $\mathtt{US}$ update function (see the online appendix[5]), which makes use of Welford's algorithm for an online approximation of variance [20] and otherwise updates the mean and frequency appropriately.

[4] Notice that Definition 1 is only applicable to integrable transition functions, voiding most statistical assumptions, including normality. We thus merely provide heuristics.

[5] http://doi.org/10.5281/zenodo.3268381

After each update of $(m', v', f')$ or $(m'', v'', f'')$ we calculate two functions W and KS as indicators for whether the distributions of Q-values in $\nu'$ and $\nu''$ are different. The first function is inspired by the test statistic of the 2-sample t-test:

$$\mathtt{W}((m',v',f'),(m'',v'',f'')) := \frac{m'-m''}{\sqrt{f'v'+f''v''}}\sqrt{\frac{f'+f''-2}{1/f'+1/f''}}$$

The W value provides evidence for or against equality of the two means $m', m''$. In order to also take possible disparities in the variances into account, we use a second function that is modeled on the Kolmogorov-Smirnov test statistic. For this we interpret the given means $m$ and variances $v$ to be given by simple distributions with "triangular" density functions of the form

$$d(x) = \begin{cases} 0 & x < m-c \text{ or } x > m+c \\ a(x-m+c) & m-c \leq x \leq m \\ -a(m+c-x) & m \leq x \leq m+c \end{cases}$$

where $a, c$ are uniquely determined by the conditions that $d(x)$ is a probability density function with variance $v$. We then compute $\mathtt{KS}((m',v',f'),(m'',v'',f''))$ as the product of the maximal difference of the cumulative distribution functions of triangular distributions with means and variances $(m', v')$, respectively $(m'', v'')$, and a weight factor $f'f''/(f'+f'')$. We note that triangular density functions are here used for computational convenience, not because they are assumed to be a particularly accurate model for the actual distributions of Q-values.

Given three thresholds $t_l$, $t_u$ and $q$, with $t_l < t_u$, we now make a four-fold distinction for the obtained W and KS values. Abbreviating $(m', v', f') =: a$ and $(m'', v'', f'') =: b$:

$$\mathtt{DIF}_{q,t}(a,b) = \begin{cases} \dagger & \text{if } \mathtt{KS}(a,b) > q \text{ and } \mathtt{W}(a,b) > t_u \\ \triangleleft & \text{if } a.m < b.m \text{ and } \mathtt{W}(a,b) < t_l \\ \triangleright & \text{if } b.m < a.m \text{ and } \mathtt{W}(a,b) < t_l \\ \bullet & \text{otherwise} \end{cases}$$

Here the outcomes are heuristics as to whether ($\triangleleft$) $a$ has a significantly lower mean than $b$ (and vice-versa for $\triangleright$), ($\dagger$) the distributions of $a$ and $b$ significantly differ but $a$ and $b$ have similar mean, and ($\bullet$) not enough data for a verdict or $a$ and $b$ have similar distributions.

Using the outcome of $\mathtt{DIF}_{q,t}(a,b)$ directly to decide whether to refine $\nu$ to $\nu', \nu''$ can lead to a somewhat fragile behaviour, due to possible large fluctuations of sampled Q-values on the one hand, and dependencies between successive samples on the other. We therefore maintain a discounted running count $(x_\triangleleft, x_\triangleright, x_\dagger)$ of the three critical outcomes $\triangleleft, \triangleright, \dagger$, and perform a refinement when one of these counts exceeds a given threshold $\psi$.

**Data:** $\texttt{Refine}_\texttt{Q}(Q, \mathcal{F}, \mathcal{A}, (s, \alpha, s'))$
**Result:** Refined $Q$, $\mathcal{F}$ and $\mathcal{A}$-functions.

1 Let $\nu = \mathcal{A}_\alpha[s]$, $\nu' = \mathcal{A}_\alpha[s']$
2 $c \leftarrow \mathcal{C}(s, \alpha, s') + \min_{\alpha' \in Act} Q_{\alpha'}(\nu')$
3 **for** *all* $\rho \in \mathtt{R}_\alpha(\nu)$ **do**
4     Let $(\widetilde{\nu}', \widetilde{\nu}'') = \rho(\nu)$ and let $\widetilde{\nu} \in \{\widetilde{\nu}', \widetilde{\nu}''\}$ s.t. $s \in \widetilde{\nu}$
5     $(m, v, f) \leftarrow \texttt{Stats}_\alpha(\widetilde{\nu})$
6     $\texttt{Stats}_\alpha(\widetilde{\nu}) \leftarrow \texttt{US}(\texttt{Stats}_\alpha(\widetilde{\nu}), (1 - \frac{1}{f}) \cdot m + \frac{1}{f} \cdot c)$
7     $\bowtie \leftarrow \texttt{DIF}_{q,t}(\texttt{Stats}_\alpha(\widetilde{\nu}'), \texttt{Stats}_\alpha(\widetilde{\nu}''))$
8     $\texttt{LMSVal}^\rho_\alpha(\nu) \leftarrow \texttt{LMS}(\texttt{LMSVal}^\rho_\alpha(\nu), \bowtie)$
9 Let $\mathtt{R}' \leftarrow \{\rho \in \mathtt{R}_\alpha \mid \max(x_\triangleleft, x_\triangleright, x_\dagger) \geq \psi$ where $(x_\triangleleft, x_\triangleright, x_\dagger) = \texttt{LMSVal}^\rho_\alpha(\nu)\}$
10 **if** $\mathtt{R}' \neq \emptyset$ **then**
11     Pick $\rho$ randomly from $\mathtt{R}'$
12     Let $(\widetilde{\nu}', \widetilde{\nu}'') = \rho(\nu)$
13     $\mathcal{A}_\alpha \leftarrow (\mathcal{A}_\alpha \setminus \nu) \cup \{\widetilde{\nu}', \widetilde{\nu}''\}$
14     $(m', v', f') \leftarrow \texttt{Stats}_\alpha(\widetilde{\nu}')$, $(m'', v'', f'') \leftarrow \texttt{Stats}_\alpha(\widetilde{\nu}'')$
15     $Q_\alpha(\widetilde{\nu}') \leftarrow m'$, $Q_\alpha(\widetilde{\nu}'') \leftarrow m''$
16     $\mathcal{F}_\alpha(\widetilde{\nu}') \leftarrow f'$, $\mathcal{F}_\alpha(\widetilde{\nu}'') \leftarrow f''$
17 **return** $\langle Q, \mathcal{F}, \mathcal{A} \rangle$

**Algorithm 2.** Partition refinement function for Q-learning

### 4.3 Q-Learning on Partitions

We present the partition refinement function for Q-learning in Algorithm 2. The algorithm consists of two main parts, first the statistics are updated and then a (if deemed necessary) a refinement occurs. In lines 2–8 we update the statistics of candidate refinements. Lines 7 and 8 update the discounted counts $(x_\triangleleft, x_\triangleright, x_\dagger)$ using a simple procedure `LMS` (see the online appendix, footnote 5). The `LMS`-function maintains a *least mean square*-like filter over each of the three significant outcomes of the `DIF`-function, essentially smoothing out jitter.

In line 9 we identify the candidate partitions that display significantly different behaviour within their regions. If one or more candidates is deemed significant, we choose one randomly and update the partition $\mathcal{A}$, the $Q$-function and the $\mathcal{F}$-function in an appropriate manner (lines 13–16).

### 4.4 M-Learning on Partitions

While Algorithm 2, much in the spirit of Q-learning, infers the variance of a new hypothetical split in a model-free way, we here adopt an M-learning approach for the inference of variance over the Q-values obtained, which in turn are computed from the empirical cost ($\hat{\mathcal{C}}$) and transition-function (inferred from the frequency-function). As such, the variance of the Q-function for M-learning cannot be inferred from samples (as in Q-learning), but has to stem from an aggregate over the empiric cost and transition functions. This change exacerbates some types of errors compared to Q-learning (inaccuracies in aggregation) while reducing others (sensitive to wildly fluctuating Q-values in the successor states). The full pseudocode for $\texttt{Refine}_{\texttt{M}}$ is available in the online appendix (see footnote 5).

## 5 Experimental Results

To evaluate the proposed methods we conduct a series of experiments on a number of different case studies, each generated from one of four scalable models that we will shortly present in more detail. Furthermore, we provide the implementation of the presented algorithms under the LGPL license[6] as well as a library for parsing and working with the strategies[7]. We run our experiments on an AMD Opteron 6376 processor, limited to 16 GB of RAM. The models, full table of results and the version of UPPAAL STRATEGO implementing the proposed algorithms is available in an online appendix (see footnote 5).

For each instance we learn a strategy from varying numbers of samples (i.e. the training-budget). We measure time and memory consumption of learning. We evaluate the quality of a strategy by measuring the cost on a test run of 1000 samples using the determinized version of the learned strategy. Each experiment was repeated 50 times using a different initial random seed. We here report the 25% quantile and the 50% quantile (median) of the costs obtained in the test runs (Table 1).

The proposed algorithms are compared to those of David et al. [5] (shortened D-algorithms). The D-algorithms perform batch learning and therefore require a slightly different learning regime. We train the D-algorithms on 20 batches, each of $\frac{1}{20}$ of the training budget. For each batch, we allow for an extra $\frac{1}{20}$ of the training budget to be used for strategy evaluation, to avoid overfitting. This intermediate validation step gives an advantage to the D-algorithms over Q- and M-learning, which are only evaluated after training on the full budget has completed. In addition, we consider only the best-performing of the D-algorithms for each model instance and training budget combination (measured in terms of the 25% percentile).

For Q-learning we fix $R = 2$, $t_l = 0.15$, $t_u = 1.75$, $q = 0.25$, $d = 0.99$ and $\nabla = 0.02$. For M-learning we fix $t_l = 0.05$, $t_u = 1.8$, $q = 0.2$, $d = 0.99$ and $\nabla = 0.97$. These constants were settled by an initial set of experiments.

We note that all the presented case studies effectively fall in the class of switch-control systems, in which we sample only until a finite horizon, thus also residing inside the conditions of Theorem 2.

We next provide a short description of our models. **Bouncing Ball:** We model $N$ balls in the physical system displayed in Fig. 3. The goal is to keep the ball "alive" by utilizing the piston for *hitting* the ball - however, each hit comes with a cost and only has an effect if the ball is above a certain height. A sample trace can be seen in Fig. 4 of the ball under an untrained strategy (many hits, yet still a "dead" ball), and similar for a trained strategy (fewer and more significant hits). A visualization of the learned cost function can be seen in Fig. 3.

[6] http://doi.org/10.5281/zenodo.3252096.

[7] http://doi.org/10.5281/zenodo.3252098.

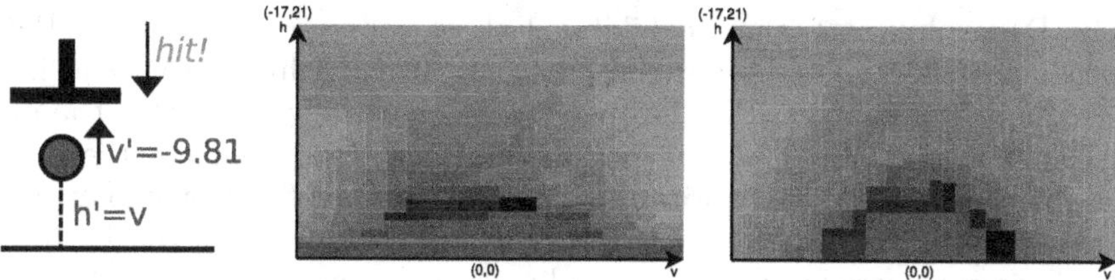


**Fig. 3.** A visualization of the BouncingBall model and the learned, colour-coded $Q$-function for *hit* and $no - hit$ action (red being more expensive and green less) in over the $h$ (height) and $v$ (velocity) state variables. (Color figure online)

The middle image is the cost of the hitting action, the rightmost image is the cost of not hitting. **Floorheating:** We slightly modify the case study of Larsen et al. [12] by replacing the outdoor temperature measurements/predictions with a simplified sinusoidal curve. **Highway Control:** We model a set of different highway scenarios for an autonomous vehicle. The goal of the controller is to avoid collisions for as long as possible (i.e. minimize the time from a crash until the time-bound of the simulation). Several environment cars are in the models, each having stochastic behaviour and reacting in a non-trivial (but intuitive) way to the proximity of other cars. A visualization can be found in the online appendix (see footnote 5). **Mixed Integer Linear Programming:** We have obtained a series of MILP programs for optimizing a switch-control system from an industrial partner. The purpose is to minimize the cost of energy utilization of a residence-unit by the use of buffers and on-demand smart-metering. We note that our methods are capable of delivering controllers which are sufficiently close to the optimal solution s.t. these are usable within the domain of our partner, often with significantly reduced computation times.

**Results.** Due to brevity we only present a representative subset of the experiments conducted in Table 1, a full set of results can be found in the online appendix (see footnote 5).

In general we observe significantly improved convergence tendencies when applying M- and Q-learning compared to D-learning.

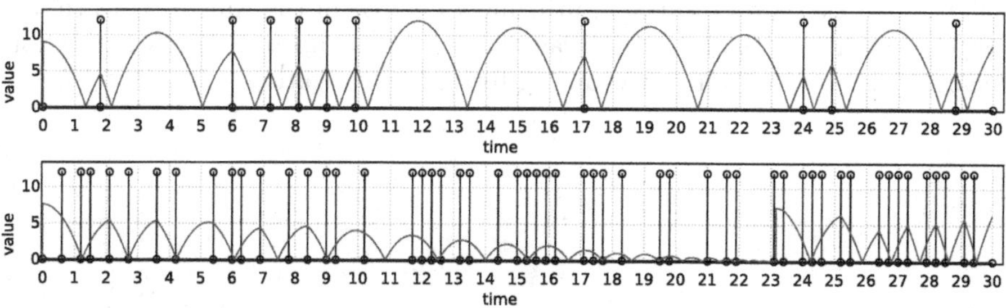


**Fig. 4.** A plot of the bouncing ball under control of a learned strategy (top) and a random strategy (bottom) with vertical lines indicating a *hit*.

The D-learning algorithms exhibit a lack of convergence (BouncingBall), or even divergence from the optimal controller (e.g. Highway-3car) which we believe can be attributed to the filtering-step [5], essentially biasing the training-samples in an optimistic direction. In the BouncingBall experiments, the lack of model refinement of the D-algorithms combined with the filtering-step explains the degrading performance with the addition of balls whereas the Highway-3car experiment degrades with the sampling-size, suggesting a higher degree of the aforementioned biased samples from filtering. These effects can, to a lesser degree, be observed in the Floorheating experiments, where the D-algorithms perform equally well to M- and Q-learning with a low sampling budget but Q- and M-learning eventually overtake the D-algorithms.

While both Q- and M-learning show similar tendencies, differences remain in the speed of convergence. In [16] the authors note a faster convergence of M-learning (in terms of sample-size) at the cost of a computational overhead, with both effects attributed to the explicit model representation and the delayed propagation of Q-values when applying Q-learning. Another benefit of M-learning is the omission of the learning rate $R$, yielding full use of historical samples. To some degree we observe a similar tendency in the MILP, FloorHeating and Highway-3car experiments (in terms of convergence), with M-learning eventually outperforming Q-learning in these experiments.

In the remaining experiments we observe the computationally simpler Q-learning being dominant. While M-learning can converge faster if the learned transition relation and the learned partitions are reasonably accurate, we hypothesize that complex cost functions impede performance due to the difficulty of learning this explicit representation. On the other hand, Q-learning trains directly on the Q-functions and can thus manage with simpler representation. This is in particular what is observed in the BouncingBall examples.

Q-learning puts higher weight on new samples given the learning-rate ($R$), implicitly forgetting old samples. When the underlying partition of the statespace changes, Q-learning will be quicker to adapt, while M-learning has to retrain parts of the approximate transition function. This works well when changes are minor but is impeding when drastic changes in the explicit representation occur.

Finally, to briefly touch upon the runtime, we observe in general that Q-learning uses roughly 50%–70% of the time of the D-algorithms, while M-learning is slightly slower than Q-learning, utilizing 70%-85% of the time of D-learning. However, we notice that the Highway-examples take up to 5 times longer for M-learning than Q-learning, warranting further investigation.

**Table 1.** Comparison of $\{M, Q, D\}$-learning in terms of expected cost of the strategy synthesized. We report the 25 percentile and the median. All experiments were repeated 50 times.

| Alg | 25% | 50% | 25% | 50% | 25% | 50% | 25% | 50% | 25% | 50% | 25% | 50% | 25% | 50% |
|---|---|---|---|---|---|---|---|---|---|---|---|---|---|---|
| Runs | 100 | | 250 | | 500 | | 1000 | | 2500 | | 5000 | | 10000 | |
| *BouncingBall-1* | | | | | | | | | | | | | | |
| M | 100 | 188 | 57 | 73 | 46 | 53 | 42 | 46 | 40 | 41 | 39 | 39 | 38 | 39 |
| Q | 61 | 75 | 47 | 71 | 44 | 49 | 41 | 47 | 40 | 42 | 40 | 41 | 39 | 40 |
| D | 317 | 354 | 5044 | 5052 | 5042 | 5050 | 78 | 100 | 70 | 88 | 68 | 104 | 66 | 160 |
| *BouncingBall-2* | | | | | | | | | | | | | | |
| M | 203 | 367 | 204 | 376 | 151 | 242 | 134 | 179 | 124 | 184 | 82 | 101 | 72 | 102 |
| Q | 152 | 236 | 117 | 189 | 112 | 153 | 94 | 134 | 95 | 114 | 76 | 86 | 69 | 76 |
| D | 361 | 4840 | 3865 | 8550 | 10096 | 10103 | 171 | 254 | 487 | 1624 | 935 | 3265 | 1244 | 6015 |
| *BouncingBall-3* | | | | | | | | | | | | | | |
| M | 392 | 1032 | 430 | 1017 | 364 | 1198 | 402 | 739 | 197 | 388 | 187 | 230 | 154 | 250 |
| Q | 257 | 362 | 204 | 283 | 142 | 242 | 181 | 345 | 120 | 166 | 114 | 136 | 106 | 128 |
| D | 377 | 10635 | 3373 | 10168 | 15136 | 15155 | 417 | 1043 | 1952 | 4144 | 1791 | 6763 | 2595 | 9283 |
| *Floorheating-1-5* | | | | | | | | | | | | | | |
| M | 394 | 419 | 381 | 391 | 366 | 380 | 327 | 341 | 283 | 289 | 272 | 276 | 264 | 267 |
| Q | 491 | 568 | 368 | 405 | 340 | 398 | 285 | 302 | 283 | 292 | 281 | 287 | 273 | 278 |
| D | 344 | 367 | 370 | 393 | 374 | 413 | 341 | 369 | 335 | 353 | 335 | 347 | 296 | 310 |
| *Floorheating-6-11* | | | | | | | | | | | | | | |
| M | 395 | 450 | 357 | 389 | 343 | 371 | 323 | 337 | 300 | 305 | 285 | 290 | 277 | 282 |
| Q | 1059 | 1394 | 614 | 767 | 450 | 553 | 387 | 457 | 296 | 307 | 288 | 298 | 284 | 287 |
| D | 487 | 527 | 496 | 520 | 495 | 530 | 438 | 468 | 419 | 437 | 383 | 415 | 355 | 384 |
| *Highway-3car* | | | | | | | | | | | | | | |
| M | 113 | 138 | 81 | 119 | 54 | 85 | 38 | 57 | 22 | 31 | 16 | 22 | 11 | 14 |
| Q | 108 | 163 | 70 | 118 | 25 | 97 | 11 | 31 | 9 | 15 | 8 | 12 | 5 | 8 |
| D | 0 | 0 | 0 | 3 | 2 | 10 | 2 | 13 | 3 | 9 | 1 | 5 | 1 | 6 |
| *Highway-4car-overtake4* | | | | | | | | | | | | | | |
| M | 131 | 156 | 134 | 147 | 106 | 123 | 96 | 107 | 49 | 69 | 18 | 28 | 8 | 12 |
| Q | 126 | 160 | 97 | 140 | 108 | 128 | 80 | 104 | 58 | 73 | 31 | 49 | 17 | 22 |
| D | 103 | 104 | 56 | 100 | 57 | 94 | 33 | 67 | 43 | 67 | 38 | 63 | 31 | 71 |
| *MILP-sfhd-4500* | | | | | | | | | | | | | | |
| M | 35 | 39 | 30 | 32 | 28 | 29 | 25 | 26 | 23 | 23 | 22 | 23 | 22 | 22 |
| Q | 228 | 243 | 82 | 205 | 37 | 47 | 32 | 34 | 29 | 30 | 28 | 28 | 26 | 26 |
| D | 38 | 40 | 36 | 40 | 37 | 40 | 36 | 39 | 35 | 38 | 33 | 37 | 32 | 35 |
| *MILP-sfhd-9500* | | | | | | | | | | | | | | |
| M | 65 | 81 | 80 | 99 | 53 | 62 | 55 | 63 | 60 | 66 | 59 | 64 | 57 | 61 |
| Q | 77 | 77 | 56 | 63 | 55 | 61 | 56 | 59 | 56 | 61 | 58 | 65 | 61 | 70 |
| D | 77 | 77 | 77 | 77 | 72 | 77 | 69 | 76 | 71 | 77 | 65 | 71 | 68 | 75 |

## 6 Conclusion

Throughout this paper we have argued for the correctness and theoretical soundness of applying Q- and M-learning on a MIDP-abstraction of a Euclidean MDP. Leaning on this theoretical argumentation, we introduced an online partition refinement adaptions of Q- and M-learning, facilitating a data-driven refinement scheme. While we leave the theoretical question of convergence open for online refinement, our experiments demonstrate convergence-like tendencies for both

Q- and M-learning. In particular, we observe that better convergence is attained with little or no additional overhead compared to the methods of [6]. In fact, for certain examples like the Bouncing Ball, we see that methods of [6] show no signs of convergence. We also observe that Q-learning seems to be computationally lighter, but with generally slower convergence compared to M-learning, supporting the claims of Strehl et al. [16].

Several directions of future work are opened by this paper, including direct comparison with Neural Network alternatives, verification of the learned strategies, feature-reductions and online partition simplification. We also think that alternate refinement heuristics could improve the performance of the methods, such as using rank-based statistical tests. More complex refinement functions and function representation could also improve the proposed methods.

**Acknowledgements.** This work is partly supported by the Innovation Fund Denmark center DiCyPS, the ERC Advanced Grant LASSO, and the JST ERATO project: HASUO Metamathematics for Systems Design (JPMJER1603).

## References

1. Barto, A.G., Bradtke, S.J., Singh, S.P.: Learning to act using real-time dynamic programming. Artif. Intell. **72**(1–2), 81–138 (1995). https://doi.org/10.1016/0004-3702(94)00011-O. ISSN 0004-3702
2. Breiman, L., Friedman, J.H., Olshen, R.A., Stone, C.J.: Classification and Regression Trees (1984)
3. D'Argenio, P.R., Jeannet, B., Jensen, H.E., Larsen, K.G.: Reduction and refinement strategies for probabilistic analysis. In: Hermanns, H., Segala, R. (eds.) PAPM-PROBMIV 2002. LNCS, vol. 2399, pp. 57–76. Springer, Heidelberg (2002). https://doi.org/10.1007/3-540-45605-8_5
4. David, A., et al.: Statistical model checking for networks of priced timed automata. In: Fahrenberg, U., Tripakis, S. (eds.) FORMATS 2011. LNCS, vol. 6919, pp. 80–96. Springer, Heidelberg (2011). https://doi.org/10.1007/978-3-642-24310-3_7
5. David, A., et al.: On time with minimal expected cost!. In: Cassez, F., Raskin, J.-F. (eds.) ATVA 2014. LNCS, vol. 8837, pp. 129–145. Springer, Cham (2014). https://doi.org/10.1007/978-3-319-11936-6_10
6. David, A., Jensen, P.G., Larsen, K.G., Mikučionis, M., Taankvist, J.H.: UPPAAL STRATEGO. In: Baier, C., Tinelli, C. (eds.) TACAS 2015. LNCS, vol. 9035, pp. 206–211. Springer, Heidelberg (2015). https://doi.org/10.1007/978-3-662-46681-0_16
7. David, A., Larsen, K.G., Legay, A., Mikucionis, M., Poulsen, D.B.: Uppaal SMC tutorial. STTT **17**(4), 397–415 (2015). https://doi.org/10.1007/s10009-014-0361-y
8. Henriques, D., Martins, J.G., Zuliani, P., Platzer, A., Clarke, E.M.: Statistical model checking for Markov decision processes. In: QEST 2012, pp. 84–93 (2012). https://doi.org/10.1109/QEST.2012.19
9. Huang, X., Kwiatkowska, M., Wang, S., Wu, M.: Safety verification of deep neural networks. In: Majumdar, R., Kunčak, V. (eds.) CAV 2017. LNCS, vol. 10426, pp. 3–29. Springer, Cham (2017). https://doi.org/10.1007/978-3-319-63387-9_1
10. Kwiatkowska, M.Z., Norman, G., Parker, D.: Game-based abstraction for Markov decision processes. In: QEST 2006, pp. 157–166. IEEE Computer Society (2006). https://doi.org/10.1109/QEST.2006.19. ISBN 0-7695-2665-9

11. Larsen, K.G., Mikučionis, M., Taankvist, J.H.: Safe and optimal adaptive cruise control. In: Meyer, R., Platzer, A., Wehrheim, H. (eds.) Correct System Design. LNCS, vol. 9360, pp. 260–277. Springer, Cham (2015). https://doi.org/10.1007/978-3-319-23506-6_17
12. Larsen, K.G., Mikučionis, M., Muñiz, M., Srba, J., Taankvist, J.H.: Online and compositional learning of controllers with application to floor heating. In: Chechik, M., Raskin, J.-F. (eds.) TACAS 2016. LNCS, vol. 9636, pp. 244–259. Springer, Heidelberg (2016). https://doi.org/10.1007/978-3-662-49674-9_14
13. Larsen, K.G., Le Coënt, A., Mikučionis, M., Taankvist, J.H.: Guaranteed control synthesis for continuous systems in UPPAAL TIGA. In: Chamberlain, R., Taha, W., Törngren, M. (eds.) CyPhy/WESE-2018. LNCS, vol. 11615, pp. 113–133. Springer, Cham (2019). https://doi.org/10.1007/978-3-030-23703-5_6. ISBN 978-3-030-23703-5
14. Lun, Y.Z., Wheatley, J., D'Innocenzo, A., Abate, A.: Approximate abstractions of Markov chains with interval decision processes. ADHS 2018, pp. 91–96 (2018). https://doi.org/10.1016/j.ifacol.2018.08.016
15. Mnih, V., et al.: Human-level control through deep reinforcement learning. Nature **518**(7540), 529 (2015)
16. Strehl, L. Li, A.L., Littman, M.L.: Incremental model-based learners with formal learning-time guarantees. CoRR (2012)
17. Sun, L., Guo, Y., Barbu, A.: A novel framework for online supervised learning with feature selection. arXiv e-prints, art. arXiv:1803.11521 (2018)
18. Sutton, R.S., Barto, A.G.: Reinforcement Learning: An Introduction. MIT Press (2018)
19. Watkins, C.J.C.H.: Learning from delayed rewards. Ph.D. thesis, King's College, Cambridge (1989)
20. Welford, B.P.: Note on a method for calculating corrected sums of squares and products. Technometrics **4**(3), 419–420 (1962). https://doi.org/10.1080/00401706.1962.10490022

# Using Symmetry Transformations in Equivariant Dynamical Systems for Their Safety Verification

Hussein Sibai(✉), Navid Mokhlesi, and Sayan Mitra

University of Illinois, Urbana, IL 61801, USA
{sibai2,navidm2,mitras}@illinois.edu

**Abstract.** In this paper, we investigate how symmetry transformations of equivariant dynamical systems can reduce the computation effort for safety verification. Symmetry transformations of equivariant systems map solutions to other solutions. We build upon this result, producing reachsets from other previously computed reachsets. We augment the standard simulation-based verification algorithm with a new procedure that attempts to verify the safety of the system starting from a new initial set of states by transforming previously computed reachsets. This new algorithm required the creation of a new cache-tree data structure for multi-resolution reachtubes. Our implementation has been tested on several benchmarks and has achieved significant improvements in verification time.

## 1 Introduction

Symmetry plays an important role in analysis of physical processes by summarizing the laws of nature independent of specific dynamics [14,25]. Symmetry related concepts have been used to explain and suppress unstable oscillations in feedback connected systems [21], show existence of passive gaits under changing ground slopes [26], and design control inputs for synchronization of neural networks [13,23].

Symmetry has also played an important role in handling the state space explosion in model checking computational processes. The idea of *symmetry reduction* is to reduce the state space by considering two global states to be equivalent (*bisimilar*), if the states are identical, including permuting the identities of participating components [3,7]. Equivalently, symmetry can reduce the number of behaviors to be explored for verification when one behavior can be seen as a permutation, or a more general transformation, of another. Symmetry reduction was incorporated in early explicit state model checkers like Mur$\phi$ [17], but translating the idea into improved performance of model checking has proven to be both fruitful and nontrivial as witnessed by the sustained attention that this area has received over the past three decades [2,19].

In this paper, we investigate how symmetry principles could benefit the analysis of cyberphysical systems (CPS). Not surprisingly, the verification problem for CPS inherits the state space explosion problem. Autonomous CPS commonly work in multi-agent environments, e.g., a car in an urban setting—where even the number of scenarios to consider explodes combinatorially with the number of agents. This has been identified as an important challenge for testing and verification [18]. The research program on data-driven verification and falsification has recently been met with some


Y.-F. Chen et al. (Eds.): ATVA 2019, LNCS 11781, pp. 98–114, 2019.
https://doi.org/10.1007/978-3-030-31784-3_6

successes [1,5,6,11]. The idea is to use simulation, together with model-based sensitivity analysis or property-specific robustness margins, to provide *coverage guarantees* or expedite the discovery of counterexamples. Software tools implementing these approaches have been used to verify embedded medical devices, automotive, and aerospace systems [1,5,9,11]. In this paper, we examine the question: how can we reduce the number of simulations needed to verify a CPS utilizing more information about the model in the form of its symmetries?

*Contributions.* The paper builds-up on the foundational results in symmetry transformations for dynamical systems [14,15,25] to provide results that allow us to compute the *reachable states* of a dynamical from a given initial set $K'$, by transforming previously computed reachable states from a *different* initial set $K$. Since the computation of reachsets from scratch is usually more expensive than applying a transformation to a set, this reduces the number of reachset computations, and therefore, the number of simulations. Secondly, we identify symmetries that can be useful for analyzing CPS including translation, linear transforms, reflections, and permutations.

Third, we present a verification algorithm symCacheTree based on transforming cached reachtubes using a given symmetry transformation $\gamma$ of the system instead of computing new ones. We augment the standard data-driven safety verification algorithm with symCacheTree to reduce the number of reachtubes that need to be computed from scratch. We do that by caching reachtubes as they are computed by the main algorithm in a tree structure representing refinements. Before any new reachtube is computed from a given refinement of the initial set, symCacheTree is asked if it can determine the safety of the system based on the cached reachtubes. It will then do a breadth-first search (BFS) over the tree to find suitable cached reachtubes that are useful under the transformation, $\gamma$. It either returns a decision on safety or says it cannot determine that. In that case, the main algorithm computes the reachtube from scratch. We prove that the symmetry assisted algorithm is sound and complete. We further generalize symCacheTree to use a set of symmetry transformations instead of one. We call the new algorithm symGrpCacheTree.

Finally, we implemented the algorithms on top of the DryVR tool [10]. We augmented DryVR with symCacheTree and symGrpCacheTree. We tested our approach on several linear and nonlinear examples with different symmetry transformations. We showed that in certain cases, by using symmetry, one can eliminate several dimensions of the system from the computation of reachtubes, which resulted in significant speedups (more than 1000$\times$ in some cases).

The paper starts with notations and definitions in Sect. 2. Examples of dynamical systems and symmetry transformations are given in Sect. 3. The main theorems of transforming reachtubes appear in Sect. 4. In Sect. 5, we present symCacheTree and symGrpCacheTree along with the key guarantees. The results of experiments are in Sect. 6 and conclusions and future directions are in Sect. 7.

## 2 Preliminaries

For any point $x \in \mathbb{R}^n$, we denote by $x_i$ the $i^{th}$ component of $x$. For any $\delta > 0$ and $x \in \mathbb{R}^n$, $B(x,\delta) \subseteq \mathbb{R}^n$ is a closed hypercube of radius $\delta$ centered at $x$. For a hyperrectangle

$S \subseteq \mathbb{R}^n$ and $\delta > 0$, $Grid(S,\delta)$, is a collection of $2\delta$-separated points along axis parallel planes such that the $\delta$-balls around these points cover $S$. Given a positive integer $N$, we denote by $[N]$ the set of integers $\{1,\ldots,N\}$. Given an operator $\gamma : \mathbb{R}^n \to \mathbb{R}^n$ and a set $X \subseteq \mathbb{R}^n$, with some abuse of notation we denote by $\gamma(X)$ the subset of $\mathbb{R}^n$ that results from applying $\gamma$ to every element on $X$. Let $D \in [N]$. We denote by the set $X \downarrow_D = \{x' : \exists x \in X, \forall\, i \in D, x_i = x'_i \text{ and } x'_i = 0, \text{otherwise}\}$. A continuous function $\beta : \mathbb{R}^+ \to \mathbb{R}^+$ is said to be a class-$\mathscr{K}$ function if it is strictly increasing and $\beta(0) = 0$.

Consider a dynamical system:

$$\dot{x} = f(x), \tag{1}$$

where $x \in \mathbb{R}^n$ is the state vector and $f : \mathbb{R}^n \to \mathbb{R}^n$ is a *Lipschitz continuous* function which guarantees existence and uniqueness of solutions [4]. The initial condition of the system is a compact set $K \subseteq \mathbb{R}^n$. A *solution* of the system is a function $\xi : \mathbb{R}^n \times \mathbb{R}^+ \to \mathbb{R}^n$ that satisfies (1) and for any initial state $x_0 \in K, \xi(x_0,0) = x_0$. For a bounded time solution $\xi$, we denote the time domain by $\xi$.dom. Given an *unsafe set* $U \subset \mathbb{R}^n$ and a time bound $T > 0$, the *bounded safety verification problem* requires us to check whether there exists an initial state $x_0 \in K$ and time $t \leq T$ such that $\xi(x_0,t) \in U$.

The standard method for solving the (bounded) safety verification problem is to compute or approximate the reachable states of the system. The set of *reachable states* of (1) between times $t_1$ and $t_2$, starting from initial set $K \subset \mathbb{R}^n$ at time $t_0 = 0$ is defined as

$$Reach(K,[t_1,t_2]) = \{x \in \mathbb{R}^n \mid \exists\, x_0 \in K,\ t \in [t_1,t_2] \text{ s.t. } \xi(x_0,t) = x\}.$$

Thus, computing (or over-approximating) $Reach(K,[0,T])$ and checking $Reach(K,[0,T]) \cap U = \emptyset$ is adequate for verifying bounded safety. Instead of $Reach(K,[t,t])$ we write $Reach(K,t)$ in short for the set of state reachable from $K$ after exactly $t$ time units.

Sometimes we find it convenient to preserve the time information of reaching states. This leads to the notion of reachtubes. Given a time bound $T > 0$, we define *reachtube* $Rtube(K,T) = \{(X_i,t_i)\}_{i=1}^{j}$ to be a sequence of time-stamped sets such that for each $i$, $X_i = Reach(K,[t_{i-1},t_i])$, $t_0 = 0$ and $t_j = T$. The concatenation of two reachtubes $\{(X_i,t_i)\}_{i=1}^{j_1} \frown \{(X_i,t_i)\}_{i=1}^{j_2}$ is defined as the sequence $\{\{(X_i,t_i)\}_{i=1}^{j_1}, \{(X_i,t_i+t_{max})\}_{i=1}^{j_2}\}$, where $t_{max}$ is the last time stamp in the first reachtube sequence.

A numerical simulation of system (1) is a reachtube with $X_0$ being a singleton state $x_0 \in K$. It is a discrete time representation of $\xi(x_0,\cdot)$. Several numerical solvers provide such representation of trajectories such as VNODE-LP[1] and CAPD Dyn-Sys library[2].

In this paper, we will find it useful to transform solutions and reachtubes using operators $\gamma : \mathbb{R}^n \to \mathbb{R}^n$ on the state space. Given a solution $\xi$ and a reachtube $Rtube(K,T)$, we define the $\gamma$-transformed solution $\gamma \cdot \xi$ and reachtube $\gamma \cdot Rtube(K,T)$ as follows:

$$\forall\, t, (\gamma \cdot \xi)(x_0,t) = \gamma(\xi(x_0,t)) \text{ and } \gamma \cdot Rtube(K,T) = \{(\gamma(X_i),t_i)\}_{i=1}^{j}.$$

Notice that this transformation does not alter the time-stamps. Given a reachtube $rt$, $rt.last$ is the pair $(X,t)$ with the maximum $t$ in $rt$.

[1] http://www.cas.mcmaster.ca/~nedialk/vnodelp/.

[2] http://capd.sourceforge.net/capdDynSys/docs/html/odes_rigorous.html.

## 2.1 Data-Driven Verification

Data-driven verification algorithms answer the bounded safety verification question using numerical simulation data, that is, sample of simulations. The key idea is to generalize an individual simulation of a trajectory $\xi(x_0,\cdot)$ to over-approximate the reachtube $Rtube(B(x_0,\delta),T)$, for some $\delta > 0$. This generalization covers a $\delta$-ball $B(x_0,\delta)$ of the initial set $K$, and several simulations can then cover all of $K$ and over-approximate $Rtube(K,T)$, which in turn could prove safety. If the over-approximations turn out to be too conservative and safety cannot be concluded, then $\delta$ has to be reduced, and more precise over-approximations of $Rtube(K,T)$ have to be computed with smaller generalization radius $\delta$ and more simulation data.

Thus far, the generalization strategy has been entirely based on computing sensitivity of the solution $\xi(x_0,t)$ to the initial condition $x_0$. The precise notion of sensitivity needed for the verification algorithm to have soundness and relative completeness is formalized as *discrepancy function* [6].

**Definition 1.** *A discrepancy function of system (1) with initial set of states* $K \subseteq \mathbb{R}^n$ *is a class-*$\mathcal{K}$ *function in the first argument* $\beta : \mathbb{R}^+ \times \mathbb{R}^+ \rightarrow \mathbb{R}^+$ *that satisfies the following conditions: (1)* $\forall\ x,x' \in K, t \geq 0$, $\|\xi(x,t) - \xi(x',t)\| \leq \beta(\|x-x'\|,t)$, *(2)* $\beta(\|\xi(x,t) - \xi(x',t)\|,t) \rightarrow 0$ *as* $\|x-x'\| \rightarrow 0$.

The first condition in Definition 1 says that $\beta$ upper-bounds the distance between two trajectories as a function of the distance between their initial states. The second condition makes the bound shrink as the initial states get closer.

Algorithms have been developed for computing this discrepancy function for linear, nonlinear, and hybrid dynamical models [5,8,11] as well as for estimating it for black-box systems [10]. The resulting software tools have been successfully applied to verify automotive, aerospace, and medical embedded systems [9,16,24].

Algorithm 1 without the boxed parts describes data-driven verification for a dynamical system (1). We refer to this algorithm as ddVer in this paper. Given the compact initial set of states $K \subseteq \mathbb{R}^n$, a time bound $T > 0$, and an unsafe set $U$, ddVer answers the safety verification question. It initializes a stack called *coverstack* with a cover of $K$. Then, it checks the safety from each element in the cover. For a given $B(x_0,\delta)$ in *coverstack*, ddVer simulates (1) from $x_0$ and bloats to compute an over-approximation of $Rtube(B(x_0,\delta),T)$. Formally, the set $sim \oplus \beta$ is a Minkowski sum. This can be computed by increasing the radius in each dimension of *sim* at a time instant $t$ by $\beta(\delta,t)$. The first condition on $\beta$ ensures that this set is indeed an over-approximation of $Rtube(B(x_0,\delta),T)$. If this over-approximation is disjoint from $U$ then it is safe and is removed from *coverstack*. If instead, the over-approximation intersects with $U$ then that is inconclusive and $B(x_0,\delta)$ is partitioned into smaller sets and added to *coverstack*. The second condition on $\beta$ ensures that this *refinement* leads to a more precise over-approximation of $Rtube(B(x_0,\delta),T)$. On the other hand, if the simulation hits $U$, that serves as a counterexample and ddVer returns Unsafe. Finally, if *coverstack* becomes empty, that implies that the algorithm reached a partition of $K$ from which all the over-approximated reachtubes are disjoint from $U$, and then ddVer returns Safe.

**Algorithm 1** ddVer safety verification algorithm

**input:** $K, T, U, \Gamma, \beta$
*coverstack* $\leftarrow$ finite cover $\cup_i B(x_i, \delta) \supseteq K$
*cachetree* $\leftarrow \emptyset$
**while** *coverstack* $\neq \emptyset$ **do**
  $B(x_0, \delta) = coverstack.pop()$
  *ans* $\leftarrow$ symGrpCacheTree $(U, \Gamma, cachetree, B(x_0, \delta))$
  **if** *ans* = Unsafe **then return:** *ans*
  **else if** *ans* = Safe **then continue**
  **else**
    *sim* $\leftarrow$simulate $\xi(x_0, \cdot)$ upto time $T$
    $rt \leftarrow sim \oplus \beta$
    *cachetree.insert(node(rt, sim))*
    **if** *sim* intersects with $U$ **then**
      **return:** Unsafe
    **else if** *rt* intersects with $U$ **then**
      Refine cover and add to the *coverstack*
**return:** Safe

## 2.2 Symmetry in Dynamical Systems

Symmetry takes a central place in analysis of dynamical systems [20]. The research line pertinent to our work develops the conditions under which one can get a solution by transforming another solution [12,20,22]. Symmetries of dynamical systems are modeled as groups of operators on the state space.

**Definition 2 (Definition 2 in** [25]**).** *Let $\Gamma$ be a group of operators acting on $\mathbb{R}^n$. We say that $\gamma \in \Gamma$ is a symmetry of (1) if for any solution, $\xi(x_0, t)$, $\gamma \cdot \xi(x_0, t)$ is also a solution. Furthermore, if $\gamma \cdot \xi = \xi$, we say that the solution $\xi$ is $\gamma$-symmetric.*

Thus, if $\gamma$ is a symmetry of (1), then new solutions can be obtained by just applying $\gamma$ to existing solutions. Herein lies the opportunity of exploiting symmetries in data-driven verification.

How can we know that $\gamma$ is a symmetry for (1)? It turns out that, a sufficient condition exists that can be checked without finding the solutions (potentially hard problem), but only by checking commutativity of $\gamma$ with the dynamic function $f$. Systems that meet this criterion are called *equivariant*.

**Definition 3 (Definition 3 in** [25]**).** *Let $\Gamma$ be a group of operators acting on $\mathbb{R}^n$. The dynamic function (vector field) $f : \mathbb{R}^n \to \mathbb{R}^n$ is said to be $\Gamma$-*equivariant *if $f(\gamma(x)) = \gamma(f(x))$, for any $\gamma \in \Gamma$ and $x \in \mathbb{R}^n$.*

The following theorem shows that for equivariant systems, solutions are symmetric.

**Theorem 1** ([14,25]). *If (1) is $\Gamma$-equivariant and $\xi$ is a solution, then so is $\gamma \cdot \xi$, $\forall \gamma \in \Gamma$.*

## 3 Symmetries in Cyber-Physical Systems

Equivariant systems are ubiquitous in nature and in relevant models of cyber-physical systems. Below are few examples of simple equivariant systems with respect to different symmetries. We start with a simple 2-dimensional linear system.

**Example 1.** Consider the circle system

$$\dot{x}_1 = -x_2, \dot{x}_2 = x_1. \tag{2}$$

where $x_1, x_2 \in \mathbb{R}$. Let $\Gamma$ be the set of matrices of the form: $B = [[a, -b], [b, a]]$ where $a, b \in \mathbb{R}$ and $B$ is not the zero matrix. Let $\circ$ be the matrix multiplication operator, then system (2) is $\Gamma$-equivariant.

**Example 2.** Lorenz attractor models the two-dimensional motion of a fluid in a container. Its dynamics are as follows:

$$\dot{x} = -px + py, \dot{y} = -xz + rx - y, \dot{z} = xy - bz. \tag{3}$$

where $p, r$, and $b$ are parameters and $x, y$ and $z \in \mathbb{R}$. Let $\Gamma$ be the group that contains $\gamma : (x, y, z) \rightarrow (-x, -y, z)$ and the identity map. Then, system (3) is $\Gamma$-equivariant[3].

**Example 3.** Third, a car model is equivariant to the group of all translations of its position. The car model is described with the following ODEs:

$$\dot{x} = v \cos\theta, \dot{y} = v \sin\theta, \dot{\phi} = u, \dot{v} = a, \dot{\theta} = \frac{v}{L}\tan(\phi). \tag{4}$$

where $u$ and $a$ can be any control signals and $x, y, v, \theta$,and $\phi \in \mathbb{R}$. We denote $r = (x, y, v, \phi, \theta) = (p, \bar{p})$, where $p = (x, y)$. Let $\Gamma$ be the set of translations of the form $\gamma : r = (p, \bar{p}) \rightarrow r' = (p + c, \bar{p})$, for all $c \in \mathbb{R}^2$. Then, system (4) is $\Gamma$-equivariant.

**Example 4.** Consider the system of two cars with states $r_1$ and $r_2$. Let $\Gamma$ be the set containing the operator $\gamma : (r_1, r_2) \rightarrow (r_2, r_1)$ and the identity operator. Moreover, assume that $u$ and $a$ are the same for both cars. Then, the system is $\Gamma$-equivariant.

**Example 5.** Let $\Gamma$ be the group generated by the set of transformations of the form $\gamma : (r_1, r_2) = ((p_1, \bar{p}_1), (p_2, \bar{p}_2)) \rightarrow (r_1', r_2') = ((p_1 + c_1, \bar{p}_1), (p_2 + c_2, \bar{p}_2))$, where $c_1$ and $c_2 \in \mathbb{R}^2$, along with the group described in Example 4. Then, the system is $\Gamma$-equivariant. Hence, it is equivariant to translations in the positions and permutation of both cars.

## 4 Symmetry for Verification

In this section, we present new results that use symmetry ideas of Sect. 2.2 towards safety verification. We show how symmetry operators can be used to get new reachtubes by transforming existing ones. This is important for data-driven verification because

[3] http://www.scholarpedia.org/article/Equivariant_dynamical_systems.

computation of new reachtubes is in general more expensive than transforming ones. We derived similar theorems for switched systems in the extended version of the paper. For convenience, we will fix a set of initial states $K \subseteq \mathbb{R}^n$, a time bound $T > 0$, a group $\Gamma$ of operators on $\mathbb{R}^n$, and an operator $\gamma \in \Gamma$ throughout this section. The following theorem formalizes transformation of reachtubes based on symmetry. It follows from Theorem 1.

**Theorem 2.** *If (1) is $\Gamma$-equivariant, then $\forall \gamma \in \Gamma$, $\gamma(Rtube(K,T)) = Rtube(\gamma(K),T)$.*

*Proof.* By Theorem 1, given any solution $\xi(x_0,\cdot)$ of system (1), where $x_0 \in K$, $\gamma(\xi(x_0,\cdot))$ is its solution starting from $\gamma(x_0)$, i.e. $\gamma(\xi(x_0,\cdot)) = \xi(\gamma(x_0),\cdot)$.

$\gamma(Rtube(K,T)) \subseteq Rtube(\gamma(K),T)$. Fix any pair $(X_i,t_i) \in Rtube(K,T)$ and fix an $x \in X_i$. Then, there exists $x_0 \in K$ such that $\xi(x_0,t) = x$ for some $t \in [t_{i-1},t_i]$. Hence, by Theorem 1, $\xi(\gamma(x_0),t) = \gamma(x)$. Therefore, $\gamma(x) \in Rtube(\gamma(K),T)$. Since $x$ is arbitrary here, $\gamma(Rtube(K,T)) \subseteq Rtube(\gamma(K),T)$.

$Rtube(\gamma(K),T) \subseteq \gamma(Rtube(K,T))$. Fix any pair $(X_i,t_i) \in Rtube(\gamma(K),T)$ and fix an $x \in X_i$. Then, there exists $x_0 \in \gamma(K)$ such that $\xi(x_0,t) = x$ for some $t \in [t_{i-1},t_i]$. Since $x_0 \in \gamma(K)$, there exists $x_0' \in K$ s.t. $\gamma(x_0') = x_0$. By Theorem 1, $\gamma(\xi(x_0',t)) = x$. Hence, $x \in \gamma(Rtube(K,T))$. Again, since $x$ is arbitrary, $Rtube(\gamma(K),T) \subseteq \gamma(Rtube(K,T))$.

Corollary 1 shows how a new reachtube from a set of initial states $K' \subseteq \mathbb{R}^n$ can be computed by $\gamma$-transforming an existing $Rtube(K,T)$.

**Corollary 1.** *If system (1) is $\Gamma$-equivariant, and $K' \subseteq \mathbb{R}^n$, then if there exists $\gamma \in \Gamma$ such that $K' \subseteq \gamma(K)$, then $Rtube(K',T) \subseteq \gamma(Rtube(K,T))$.*

**Remark 1.** Corollary 1 remains true if instead of $Rtube(K,T)$, we have a tube that over-approximates it. Moreover, Theorem 2 and Corollary 1 are also true if we replace the reachtubes with reachsets.

## 5 Verification Algorithm

In this section, we add to the ddVer procedure the symCacheTree one for caching, searching, and transforming reachtubes. The result is the new ddSymVer algorithm. symCacheTree uses symmetry to save ddVer from computing fresh reachtubes in lines 10–11 in case they can be transformed from already computed and cached reachtubes. Later we will replace symCacheTree with the more general symGrpCacheTree procedure.

The idea of symCacheTree (and symGrpCacheTree) is as follows: given a tree *cachetree* storing reachtubes as they are computed by ddVer, an initial set of states $initset_n$ that ddVer needs to compute the reachtube for, a symmetry operator $\gamma$ (or a group of them $\Gamma$) for system (1) and the unsafe set $U$, it checks if the safety of the system starting from $initset_n$ can be decided by transforming reachtubes stored in *cachetree*.

Before getting into symCacheTree and symGrpCacheTree, we note the simple additions to ddVer (shown by boxes) that lead to ddSymVer. First, *cachetree* is initialized to an empty tree (line 3). Then, symCacheTree (or symGrpCacheTree) is used for the safety check (lines 6–9) and fresh reachtube computation is performed only if the check returns inconclusive answer (lines 10–11). In the last case, fresh reachtube *rt* gets computed in line 11 and inserted as a new node in *cachetree* (line 12).

*Tree Data Structure.* Each node *node* in symCacheTree stores an initial set *initset*, a simulation *sim* of duration $T$ from the center of *initset*, and an over-approximation *rt* of $Rtube(initset, T)$. The key invariants of symCacheTree for non *Null* nodes are:

$$root.initset = K, \tag{5}$$

$$\forall\, node, node.left.initset \subseteq node.initset, \tag{6}$$

$$\forall\, node, node.right.initset \subseteq node.initset, \tag{7}$$

$$\forall\, node, node.left.initset \cap node.right.initset = \emptyset, \tag{8}$$

$$\forall\, node, node.left.initset \cup node.right.initset = node.initset. \tag{9}$$

That is, the *initset* of the root node is equal to $K$; each child's *initset* is contained in the *initset* of the parent; the disjoint union of the *initsets* of the children partition the *initset* of the parent. Hence, by property (2) of the discrepancy function $\beta$ (Definition 1) it follows that the union of the reachtubes of children is a tighter over-approximation of the reachtube of the parent, for the same initial set. Since the refinement in ddSymVer is done depth-first, symCacheTree is also constructed in the same way.

In brief, symCacheTree (symGrpCacheTree) uses symmetry to save ddVer from computing the reachtube $Rtube(initset_n, T)$ afresh in line 11 from initial set $initset_n$ in the case that safety of $Rtube(initset_n, T)$ can be inferred by transforming an existing reachtube in *cachetree*. That is, given an unsafe set $U$, a tree *cachetree* storing reachtubes (previously computed), and a symmetry operator $\gamma$ (a group of symmetries $\Gamma$) for system (1), symCacheTree (Algorithm 2) or symGrpCacheTree (Algorithm 3) checks if the safety of the system when it starts from $initset_n$ can be decided by transforming and combining the reachtubes in *cachetree*.

### 5.1 The symCacheTree Procedure

The core of the symCacheTree algorithm is to answer queries of the form: *can safety be decided from a given initial set* $initset_n$*, by transforming and combining the reachtubes in cachetree*?

They are answered by performing a *breadth first traversal (BFS)* of *cachetree*. symCacheTree first checks if the $\gamma$-transformed *initset* of *root* contains $initset_n$. If not, the transformation of the union of all *initsets* of all nodes in *cachetree* would not contain $initset_n$. In this case we cannot use Corollary 1 to get an over-approximation of $Rtube(initset_n, T)$ and symCacheTree returns SymmetryNotUseful (line 4). If the $\gamma$-transformed *initset* of the root does contain $initset_n$, we have at least one tube that over-approximates it which is $\gamma(root.rt)$ by Corollary 1. Then, the *root* is inserted to the queue *traversalQueue* that stores the nodes that need to be visited in the BFS.

Then, the algorithm proceeds similar to ddVer. There are two differences: first, it does not compute new reachtubes, it just uses the transformations of the reachtubes in *cachetree*. Second, it refines in BFS manner instead of DFS. In more detail, at each iteration, a node is dequeued from *traversalQueue*. If its transformed initial set $initset_c$ using $\gamma$ does not intersect with $initset_n$, that means that $\gamma(Rtube(initset_c, T))$ and $Rtube(initset_n, T)$ do not intersect. Hence, the node is not useful for this initial set. Also, if the transformed reachtube $\gamma(node.rt)$ does not intersects $U$, the part of $initset_n$ that is covered by $\gamma(node.initset)$ is safe and no need to refine it more. In both cases, the loop proceeds for the next node (line 10). If the transformed simulation of the node starts from $initset_n$ and hits $U$, then we have a counter example by Theorem 1. Hence, it returns Unsafe (line 12). If the transformed reachtube $\gamma(node.rt)$ intersects $U$, it cannot know if that is because of the overapproximation error, or because of a trajectory that does not start from $initset_n$ or because of one that does. Hence, it needs to refine more. Before refining, it checks if the union of the transformed *initset*s of the children of the current node covers the part of $initset_n$ that was covered by their parent. If that is NOT the case, then part of $initset_n$ cannot be covered by a node with a tighter reachtube. That is because $\gamma$ is invertible and nodes at the same level of the tree are disjoint. Hence, no node at the same level can cover the missing part. Thus, it returns Compute, asking ddVer to compute the over-approximation from scratch (line 15). Otherwise, it enqueue all the children nodes in *traversalQueue* (line 14).

If *traversalQueue* gets empty, then we have an over-approximation of the reachtube starting from $initset_n$ that does not intersect with $U$. Hence, it returns Safe (line 16).

The following two theorems show the correctness guarantees of symCacheTree. The proofs are in the extended version of the paper. Theorem 3 shows that if *cachetree* has reachtubes that can prove that the system is safe using $\gamma$, it will return Safe. If it has a simulation that can prove that the system is unsafe using $\gamma$, it will either ask ddVer to compute the reachtube from scratch or will return Unsafe. Theorem 4 shows that if symCacheTree returns Safe, then the reachtube of the system starting from $initset_n$ does not intersect $U$. Moreover, if it returns Unsafe, then there exists a trajectory that starts from $initset_n$ and intersects $U$.

**Algorithm 2.** symCacheTree

1: **input:** $U, \gamma, cachetree, initset_n$
2: $initset_c := cachetree.root.initset$
3: **if** $initset_n \not\subseteq \gamma(initset_c)$ **then**
4:     **return:** SymmetryNotUseful
5: $traversalQueue := \{cachetree.root\}$
6: **while** $traversalQueue \neq \emptyset$ **do**
7:     $node \leftarrow traversalQueue.dequeue()$
8:     $initset_c := node.initset$; $\{(R_i, t_i)_{i=0}^k\} = node.sim$
9:     **if** $\gamma(initset_c) \cap initset_n = \emptyset$ or $\gamma(node.rt) \cap U = \emptyset$ **then**
10:         continue
11:     **if** $\exists j \mid \gamma(R_j) \cap U \neq \emptyset$ and $\gamma(R_0) \in initset_n$ **then**
12:         Return Unsafe
13:     **else if** $\gamma(node.initset) \cap initset_n \subseteq \bigcup_i \gamma(node.children[i].initset)$ **then**
14:         $traversalQueue.enqueue(\{node.left, node.right\})$
15:     **else return:** Compute
16: **return:** Safe

**Theorem 3 (Completeness).** *If there exists a set of nodes S in cachetree with*

$$initset_n \subseteq \cup_{s \in S} \gamma(s.initset) \text{ and } U \cap \cup_{s \in S} \gamma(s.rt) = \emptyset,$$

symCacheTree *will return* Safe. *Also, if there exists a node s in cachetree where* $\gamma(s.sim) \cap U \neq \emptyset$ *and starts from* $initset_n$, *then* symCacheTree *will return* SymmetryNotUseful, Unsafe, *or* Compute.

**Theorem 4 (Soundness).** symCacheTree *is sound: if it returns* Safe, *then the reachtube* $Rtube(initset_n, T)$ *does not intersect* $U$ *and if it returns* Unsafe, *then there exists a trajectory starting from* $initset_n$ *that enters the unsafe set.*

In summary, symCacheTree shows that a single symmetry $\gamma$ could decrease the number of fresh reachtube computations needed for verification. Next, we revisit Example 2 to illustrate the need for multiple symmetry maps.

*Circular Orbits and Scaling Symmetry.* The linear system in Example 2 has circular orbits. Consider the initial set $K = [[21.5, 21.5], [24.5, 24.5]]$, the unsafe set $x_2 \geq 32$ after $t = 1.4$ s, and the time bound $T = 1.5$ s. Any matrix $B$ that commutes with $A$, the RHS of the differential equation, is a symmetry transformation. However, once this matrix is fixed, we do not change it as per symCacheTree. Any diagonal matrix that commutes with $A$ has equal diagonal elements. Such a matrix would scale $x_1$ and $x_2$ by the same factor. Hence, applying $B$ to any axis aligned box would either scale the box up or down on the diagonal. That means applying $B$ to $K$ wouldn't contain the upper left or bottom right partitions, but only possibly the bottom left corner. With $B = [[0.95, 0], [0, 0.95]]$, only one out of 7 reachtubes is obtained via transformation (first row of Table 1).

That is because we are using a single transform which leaves symCacheTree useless in most of the input cases. Figure 1a shows the reachtube (colored green to yellow) computed using ddVer, unsafe set (brown). Figure 1b shows the reachtube computed using ddVer and symCacheTree. The part of the reachtube that was computed using symmetry is colored between blue and violet. The other part is still between yellow and green. Only the upper left corner has been transformed instead if being computed. Next, we present symGrpCacheTree, a generalization of symCacheTree that uses a group of symmetries aiming for a bigger ratio of transformed to computed reachtubes.

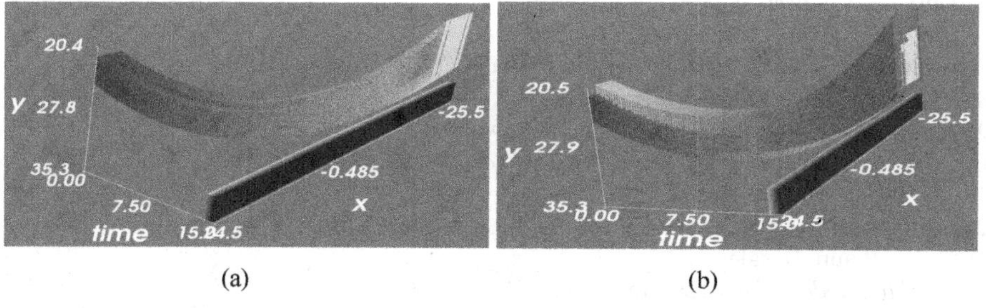


(a) (b)

**Fig. 1.** (a) Reachtube using ddVer. (b) Reachtube using ddSymVer. (Color figure online)

### 5.2 The symGrpCacheTree Procedure

Procedure symGrpCacheTree (Algorithm 3) is a generalization of symCacheTree using a group of symmetries. The symGrpCacheTree procedure still does BFS over *cachetree*, keeps track of the parts of the input initial set $initset_n$ that are not proven safe (line 11); returns Unsafe with the same logic (line 13), and return Compute in case there are parts of $initset_n$ that are not proven safe nor have refinements in *cachetree* (line 17).

The key difference from symCacheTree is that different transformations may be useful at different nodes. This leads to the possibility of multiple nodes in *cachetree*, that are not ancestors or descendants of each other, covering the same parts of $initset_n$ under different transformations. Recall that in symCacheTree, only ancestors cover the parts of $initset_n$ that are covered by their descendants since $\gamma$ is invertible. Hence, it was sufficient to not add the children of a node to *traversalQueue* to know that the part it covers, by transforming its initial set, from $initset_n$ is safe (line 10). However, it is not sufficient in symGrpCacheTree since there may be another node that cover the same part of $initset_n$ which has a transformed reachtube that intersects $U$, hence refining what already has been proven to be safe. The solution is to remove explicitly from $initset_n$ what has been proven to be safe (line 11). The resulting set may not be convex but can be stored as a set of polytopes. Moreover, it cannot return Compute when the transformed reachtube of a visited node intersects $U$ and its children initial sets do not contain the part it covers from $initset_n$ as in line 15 of symCacheTree. That is because other nodes may cover that part because of the availability of multiple symmetries. Hence, it cannot return Compute unless it traversed the whole tree and still parts of $initset_n$ could not be proven to be safe. We show that symGrpCacheTree has the same

**Algorithm 3.** symGrpCacheTree

1: **input:** U, $\Gamma$, *cachetree*, $initset_n$

2: $initset_c := cachetree.root.initset$

3: **if** $initset_n \not\subseteq \cup_{\gamma\in\Gamma}\gamma(initset_c)$ **then**

4:     **return:** SymmetryNotUseful

5: $leftstates \leftarrow initset_n$

6: $traversalQueue := \{cachetree.root\}$

7: **while** $traversalQueue \neq \emptyset$ and $leftstates \neq \emptyset$ **do**

8:     $node \leftarrow traversalQueue.dequeue()$

9:     $initset_c := node.initset$; $\{(R_i, t_i)_{i=0}^k\} = node.sim$

10:     $X = \{x : \exists\gamma\in\Gamma, x\in\gamma(initset_c)$ and $\gamma(node.rt)\cap U = \emptyset\}$

11:     $leftstates \leftarrow leftstates \setminus X$

12:     **if** $\exists\gamma\in\Gamma, j \mid \gamma(R_j)\cap U \neq \emptyset$ and $\gamma(R_0)\in leftstates$ **then**

13:         Return Unsafe

14:     **if** $len(node.children) > 0$ **then**

15:         $traversalQueue.enqueue(node.children)$

16: **if** $leftstates \neq \emptyset$ **then**

17:     **return:** Compute

18: **return:** Safe

guarantees as symCacheTree in the following two theorems with the proof being in the extended version of the paper.

**Theorem 5 (Completeness).** *If there exists a set of nodes $S$ in cachetree, where each $s \in S$ has a corresponding set of transformations $\Gamma_s \subseteq \Gamma$, such that*

$$initset_n \subseteq \cup_{s \in S, \gamma_s \in \Gamma_s} \gamma_s(s.initset) \text{ and } U \cap \cup_{s \in S, \gamma_s \in \Gamma_s} \gamma_s(s.rt) = \emptyset,$$

symCacheTree *will return* Safe. *Also, if there exists a node $s$ in cachetree and a $\gamma \in \Gamma$, where $\gamma(s.sim)$ intersects $U$ and starts from $initset_n$, then* symGrpCacheTree *will return* SymmetryNotUseful, Unsafe, *or* Compute.

**Theorem 6 (Soundness).** symGrpCacheTree *is sound: if it returns* Safe, *then the reachtube $Rtube(initset_n, T)$ does not intersect $U$ and if it returns* Unsafe, *then there exists a trajectory starting from $initset_n$ that enters the unsafe set.*

The new challenge in symGrpCacheTree is in computing the union at line 3, computing $X$ in line 10 and in the $\exists$ in line 12. These operations depend on $\Gamma$ if it is finite or infinite and on how easy is it to search over it. We revisit the arbitrary translation from Sect. 3 to show that these operations are easy to compute in some cases.

### 5.3 Revisiting Arbitrary Translations

Recall that the car model in Example 3 in Sect. 3 is equivariant to all translations in its position. In this section, we show how to apply symGrpCacheTree not just for it, but to arbitrary differential equations. Let $D$ be the set of components of the states that do not appear on the RHS of (1) and $\Gamma$ be the set of all translations of the components in $D$. To check the *if* condition at line 3, we only have to check if $initset_c$ projected to the $[n]\backslash D$ contains $initset_n$ projected to the same components. Since if it is true, $initset_c$ can be translated arbitrarily in its components in $D$ so that the union contains $initset_n$.

Given two initial sets $K$ and $K'$ and the reachtube starting from $K'$, we compute $\beta \subseteq \mathbb{R}^n$ such that $K' \downarrow_D \oplus \beta = K \downarrow_D$. Then, if $K \downarrow ([n]\backslash D) \subset K' \downarrow ([n]\backslash D)$, by Corollary 1, we can use that $\beta$ to compute an overapproximation of $Rtube(K,T)$ by computing $Rtube(K',T) \oplus \beta$. Then, let $\beta$ be such that $initset_c \downarrow_D \oplus \beta = leftstates \downarrow_D$, in line 10. We set $X$ to be equal to $initset_c \oplus \beta$ if $node.rt \oplus \beta \cap U = \emptyset$ and to $\emptyset$, otherwise. To check the $\exists$ operator in line 12, we can treat the simulation as $node.rt$ and compute $\beta$ accordingly. Then, compute $node.sim \oplus \beta$. The new condition would be then: if $R_j \oplus \beta \cap U$. Notice that we dropped $\gamma(R_0) \in leftstates$ from the condition since we know that $R_0 \in leftstates$ and $\beta$ is bloating it to the extent it is equal to $leftstates$.

*Optimized* symGrpCacheTree *for Arbitrary Translations.* The size of $K' \downarrow_D$ above does not matter, i.e. even if it is just a point, one can compute $\beta$ so that it covers $K \downarrow_D$. Hence, instead of computing $Rtube(K,T)$, we compute only $Rtube(K',T)$ and then compute $\beta$ from $K$ and $K'$ and then bloat it. This decreases the number of dimensions that the system need to refine by $|D|$. This is in contrast with what is done in symGrpCacheTree where the reachtubes are computed without changing the initial set structure. This improvement resulted in verifying models in 1s when they take an hour on DryVR as shown in Sect. 6. We call this algorithm TransOptimized and refer to it as version 2 of symGrpCacheTree when applied to arbitrary translation invariance transformations.

## 6 Experimental Evaluation

We implemented symCacheTree and symGrpCacheTree in Python 2.7 on top of DryVR[4]. DryVr implements ddVer to verify hybrid dynamical systems. We augmented it and implemented ddSymVer. In our experiments, we only consider the (non-hybrid) dynamical systems. DryVR learns discrepancy from simulations as it is designed to work with unknown dynamical models. This learning functionality is unnecessary for our experiments, as checking equivariance requires some knowledge of the model. For convenience, we use DryVR's discrepancy learning instead of deriving discrepancy functions by hand. That said, some symmetries can be checked without complete knowledge of the model. For example, we know that dynamics of vehicles do not depend on their absolute position even without knowledge of precise dynamics.

In this section, we present the experimental results on several examples using symCacheTree and symGrpCacheTree. The transformations used are linear. Two of the systems are linear and one is non-linear. The results of the experiments are shown in Table 1. The experiments were ran on a computer with specs shown in the extended version of the paper. In the reachtube plots we use the green-to-yellow colors if it was computed from scratch, the blue-to-violet colors if it was computed using symmetry transformations, and the white-to-red colors for the unsafe sets.

**Verifying Non-convex Initial Sets.** ddVer assumes that the initial set $K$ of (1) is a single hyperrectangle. However, this assumption hinders the use of some useful transformations such as permutation. For example, consider the two cars system in Example 4 moving straight and breaking with the same deceleration, i.e. $u$ is zero and $a$ is the same for both. Recall that this system is equivariant with respect to switching $r_2$ with $r_1$. The system is unsafe if the cars are too close to each other. Assume that initially $(y_1, y_2)$ belongs to $K = [[l_1, l_2], [u_1, u_2]]$. If the two intervals $[l_1, u_1]$ and $[l_2, u_2]$ do not intersect, $\gamma$ would not be useful since for any $X \subseteq K$, $\gamma(X) \cap K = \emptyset$. However, if $K = [[l_1, l_2], [u_1, u_2]] \cup [[l_1', l_2'], [u_1', u_2']]$, where $[l_1', u_1'] \cap [l_2, u_2] \neq \emptyset$ and $[l_2', u_2'] \cap [l_1, u_1] \neq \emptyset$. Then, the reachtube starting from $[l_1', u_1'] \cap [l_2, u_2]$ for the first car and $[l_2', u_2'] \cap [l_1, u_1]$ for the second one can be computed from the one starting from $[l_2', u_2'] \cap [l_1, u_1]$ for the first car and $[l_1', u_1'] \cap [l_2, u_2]$ for the second one. This can also be done for $(x_1, x_2)$ and a combination of both.

We implemented ddVer for the disjoint initial sets case as follows: We first ran ddVer to compute the reachtube of the system starting from the first hyperrectangle and cached all the computed reachtubes in the process in a *cachetree*. Then, we used that *cachetree* in ddSymVer to check the safety of the system starting from the second hyperrectangle.

**Cars and Permutation Invariance.** For the car example (Example 4), we ran ddVer on an initial set where $(x_1, y_1, x_2, y_2) \in [[0, -2.42, 0, -22.28], [2, 3.93, 0.1, -12.82]]$ and running for 5s and the unsafe set being $|y_1 - y_2| < 5$ and cached all the tubes in a *cachetree* and saved it on the hard-drive. It returned Safe. Then, we used it in

[4] https://github.com/qibolun/DryVR_0.2.

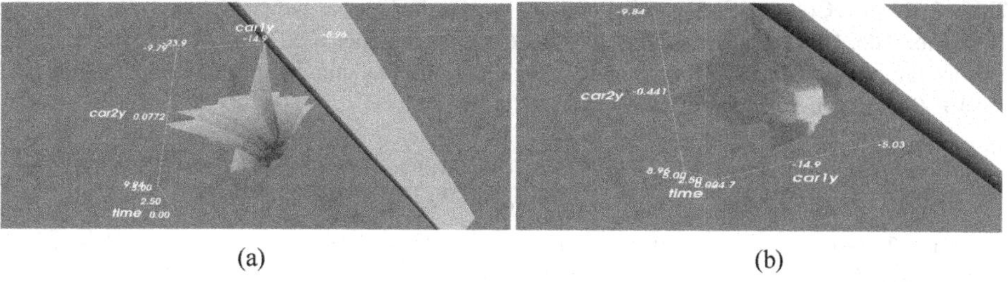


(a) (b)

**Fig. 2.** (a) Cars reachtube using ddVer. (b) Cars reachtube using ddSymVer.

symCacheTree to verify the system starting from $[[0, -22.28, 0, -2.42], [0.1, -12.82, 2, 3.93]]$. The resulting *cachetree* was around 20 GB, and traversing it while transforming the stored reachtubes takes much longer than computing the reachtube directly. We halted it manually and tried a smaller initial set: $[[0.01, -14.2, 0.01, 1.4], [0.1, -13.9, 2, 3.9]]$ using the same *cachetree* which returned Safe from the first run after 93 s; the output is shown in Figs. 2a and b. Figure 2a shows the tube when computed by ddVer and Fig. 2b when computed by ddSymVer. Figure 2b has only blue-to-violet colors since it was all computed using a symmetry transformation.

**Lorenz Attractor and Circle Revisited.** We used the disjoint initial sets verification implementation to use the symmetry transformation for the nonlinear lorenz attractor in its safety verification. Recall from Sect. 3 that its symmetry map is $(x, y, z) \to (-x, -y, z)$. So for any given initial set $K = [[l_x, l_y, l_z], [u_x, u_y, u_z]]$ and a corresponding overapproxiation of the reachtube, we automatically get an overapproximation of the reachtube with the initial set $[[-u_x, -u_y, l_z], [-l_x, -l_y, u_z]]$. We generated the *cachetree* from the initial set $[[14.9, 14.9, 35.9], [15.1, 15.1, 36.1]]$, unsafe set $x \geq 20$ and $T = 10$ s that returned Safe and used that *cachetree* in symCacheTree to verify the system starting from $[[-15.09, -15.09, 35.91], [-14.91, -14.91, 36.09]]$. The resulting statistics are in Table 1. Lorenz1 is the one corresponding to the first initial set and Lorenz2 to the for which we use permutation symmetry.

We revisit the circle example from Sect. 5 and test symCacheTree performance with the transformation being: $\gamma : (x, y) \to (-y, x)$ instead of the scaling one. Then, we compute the reachtube starting from the same initial set as before and created its *cachetree*. After that, we used ddSymVer with symCacheTree to get the one starting from $[[-24.49, 21.51], [-21.51, 24.49]]$ and running for 1.5 s. The statistics are shown in Table 1. The figures of the reachtubes are in the extended version of the paper. Again, the whole tube is blue-to-violet since it is computed fully by transforming parts of *cachetree*.

In all of the previous examples, ddVer was faster than ddSymVer since a single symmetry was used and the refinements are not large enough so that the ratio of transformed reachtubes to computed ones is large enough to account for the overhead added by the checks of symCacheTree. This can be improved by using a group of transforma-

**Table 1.** Results. Columns 3–5: number of times symCacheTree (or symGrpCacheTree) returned Compute, Safe, Unsafe, resp. Number of transformed reachtubes used in analysis (SRefs), time (seconds) to verify with DryVR+symmetry (DryVR+sym), total number reachtubes computed by DryVR (NoSRefs), time to verify with DryVR.

| Model | Transformations ($\Gamma$) | Compute | Safe | Unsafe | SRefs | DryVR+sym | NoSRefs | DryVR |
|---|---|---|---|---|---|---|---|---|
| Circle1 | $(0.95x_1, 0.95x_2)$ | 5 | 1 | 0 | 6 | 1.78 | 7 | 0.54 |
| Circle2 | $(-x_2, x_1)$ | 0 | 1 | 0 | 7 | 8.23 | 3 | 0.21 |
| Lorenz1 | $(-x, -y, z)$ | N/A | N/A | N/A | N/A | N/A | 3 | 4.67 |
| Lorenz2 | $(-x, -y, z)$ | 0 | 1 | 0 | 1 | 33.28 | 1 | 4.63 |
| bb2 | Perm. Inv. subset | 0 | 1 | 0 | 467 | 88.35 | 120 | 34.47 |
| bb (v1) | Trans. Inv. | 10 | 10 | 0 | 165 | 26.28 | 12621 | 4034.55 |
| cc (v1) | Trans. Inv. | 19 | 21 | 0 | 545 | 64.36 | N/A | OOM |
| bc (v1) | Trans. Inv. | 24 | 19 | 1 | 639 | 80.48 | 3428 | 1027.18 |
| bb (v2) | Trans. Inv. | 0 | 1 | 0 | 1 | 1.16 | 12620 | 4034.55 |
| cc (v2) | Trans. Inv. | 0 | 1 | 0 | 1 | 1.16 | N/A | OOM |
| bc (v2) | Trans. Inv. | 0 | 0 | 1 | 1 | 0.39 | 3428 | 1027 |

tions, i.e. using symGrpCacheTree, storing compressed reachtubes, and optimizing the code.

**Cars and General Translation.** Finally, we ran ddSymVer with the two versions of symGrpCacheTree for translation invariance described in Sect. 5.3 on three different scenarios of the 2-cars Example 4: both are braking (*bb*), both are at constant speed (*cc*), and one is breaking and the other at constant speed (*bc*). In all of them, the time bound is $T = 5$ s and the unsafe set is $|y_1 - y_2| < 5$. The first two cases were safe while the third was not. DryVR timed out on the *cc* case as mentioned previously in the permutation case while both versions of translation invariance algorithms were able to terminate in few seconds. The two versions of the algorithm gave the same result as DryVR while being orders of magnitude faster on the *bb* and *bc* cases. Moreover, the second version, where the initial set is a single point in the components in $D$, is an order of magnitude faster than the first version, where symGrpCacheTree is used without modifications.

## 7 Conclusions

Equivariant dynamical systems have groups of symmetry transformations that map solutions to other solutions. We use these transformations to map reachtubes to other reachtubes. Based on this, we presented algorithms (symCacheTree and symGrpCacheTree) that use symmetry transformations, to verify the safety of the equivariant system by transforming previously computed reachtubes stored in a tree structure representing refinements. We use these algorithms to augment data-driven verification algorithms to reduce the number of reachtubes need to be computed. We implemented the algorithms and tried them on several examples showing significant improvement in running times. This paper opens the doors for more investigation of the role that symmetry can help in testing, verifying, and synthesizing dynamical and hybrid systems.

**Acknowledgments.** The authors are supported by a research grant from The Boeing Company and a research grant from NSF (CPS 1739966). We would like to thank John L. Olson and Arthur S. Younger from The Boeing Company for valuable technical discussions.

## References

1. Annpureddy, Y., Liu, C., Fainekos, G., Sankaranarayanan, S.: S-TaLiRo: a tool for temporal logic falsification for hybrid systems. In: Abdulla, P.A., Leino, K.R.M. (eds.) TACAS 2011. LNCS, vol. 6605, pp. 254–257. Springer, Heidelberg (2011). https://doi.org/10.1007/978-3-642-19835-9_21
2. Antuña, L., Araiza-Illan, D., Campos, S., Eder, K.: Symmetry reduction enables model checking of more complex emergent behaviours of swarm navigation algorithms. In: Dixon, C., Tuyls, K. (eds.) TAROS 2015. LNCS (LNAI), vol. 9287, pp. 26–37. Springer, Cham (2015). https://doi.org/10.1007/978-3-319-22416-9_4
3. Clarke, E.M., Jha, S.: Symmetry and induction in model checking. In: Computer Science Today: Recent Trends and Developments, pp. 455–470 (1995)
4. Coddington, E.A., Levinson, N.: Theory of Ordinary Differential Equations. McGraw-Hill, New York (1955)
5. Donzé, A.: Breach, a toolbox for verification and parameter synthesis of hybrid systems. In: Touili, T., Cook, B., Jackson, P. (eds.) CAV 2010. LNCS, vol. 6174, pp. 167–170. Springer, Heidelberg (2010). https://doi.org/10.1007/978-3-642-14295-6_17
6. Duggirala, P.S., Mitra, S., Viswanathan, M.: Verification of annotated models from executions. In: EMSOFT (2013)
7. Emerson, E.A., Sistla, A.P.: Symmetry and model checking. In: Computer Aided Verification, 5th International Conference, CAV 1993, Elounda, Greece, Proceedings, 28 June–1 July 1993, pp. 463–478 (1993)
8. Fan, C., Mitra, S.: Bounded verification with on-the-fly discrepancy computation. In: Finkbeiner, B., Pu, G., Zhang, L. (eds.) ATVA 2015. LNCS, vol. 9364, pp. 446–463. Springer, Cham (2015). https://doi.org/10.1007/978-3-319-24953-7_32
9. Fan, C., Qi, B., Mitra, S.: Data-driven formal reasoning and their applications in safety analysis of vehicle autonomy features. IEEE Design Test **35**(3), 31–38 (2018)
10. Fan, C., Qi, B., Mitra, S., Viswanathan, M.: DryVR: data-driven verification and compositional reasoning for automotive systems. In: Majumdar, R., Kunčak, V. (eds.) CAV 2017. LNCS, vol. 10426, pp. 441–461. Springer, Cham (2017). https://doi.org/10.1007/978-3-319-63387-9_22
11. Fan, C., Qi, B., Mitra, S., Viswanathan, M., Duggirala, P.S.: Automatic reachability analysis for nonlinear hybrid models with C2E2. In: Chaudhuri, S., Farzan, A. (eds.) CAV 2016. LNCS, vol. 9779, pp. 531–538. Springer, Cham (2016). https://doi.org/10.1007/978-3-319-41528-4_29
12. Freund, P.G.O.: Introduction to Supersymmetry. Cambridge Monographs on Mathematical Physics. Cambridge University Press, Cambridge (1986)
13. Gérard, L., Slotine, J.J.: Neuronal networks and controlled symmetries, a generic framework. arXiv preprint q-bio/0612049 (2006)
14. Golubitsky, M., Stewart, I.: The Symmetry Perspective: From Equilibrium to Chaos in Phase Space and Physical Space. Progress in Mathematics, Birkhäuser Basel (2012)

15. Golubitsky, M., Stewart, I., Török, A.: Patterns of synchrony in coupled cell networks with multiple arrows. SIAM J. Appl. Dyn. Syst. **4**(1), 78–100 (2005)
16. Huang, Z., Fan, C., Mereacre, A., Mitra, S., Kwiatkowska, M.: Invariant verification of non-linear hybrid automata networks of cardiac cells. In: Biere, A., Bloem, R. (eds.) CAV 2014. LNCS, vol. 8559, pp. 373–390. Springer, Cham (2014). https://doi.org/10.1007/978-3-319-08867-9_25
17. Ip, C.N., Dill, D.L.: Better verification through symmetry. In: Proceedings of the 11th IFIP WG10.2 International Conference Sponsored by IFIP WG10.2 and in Cooperation with IEEE COMPSOC on Computer Hardware Description Languages and Their Applications, CHDL 1993, pp. 97–111. North-Holland Publishing Co., Amsterdam, The Netherlands (1993)
18. Koopman, P., Wagner, M.: Challenges in autonomous vehicle testing and validation. SAE Int. J. Transp. Saf. **4**(2016–01–0128), 15–24 (2016)
19. Kwiatkowska, M.Z., Norman, G., Parker, D.: Symmetry reduction for probabilistic model checking. In: 18th International Conference on Computer Aided Verification, CAV 2006, Seattle, WA, USA, 17–20 August 2006, Proceedings, pp. 234–248 (2006)
20. Marsden, J.E., Ratiu, T.S.: Introduction to Mechanics and Symmetry: A Basic Exposition of Classical Mechanical Systems. Springer, New York (2010). https://doi.org/10.1007/978-0-387-21792-5
21. Mehta, P.G., Hagen, G., Banaszuk, A.: Symmetry and symmetry-breaking for a wave equation with feedback. SIAM J. Appl. Dyn. Syst. **6**(3), 549–575 (2007)
22. Olver, P.J.: Applications of Lie Groups to Differential Equations. Springer, New York (1986). https://doi.org/10.1007/978-1-4684-0274-2
23. Pham, Q.C., Slotine, J.J.: Stable concurrent synchronization in dynamic system networks. Neural Netw. **20**(1), 62–77 (2007)
24. Prabhakar, P., Duggirala, P.S., Mitra, S., Viswanathan, M.: Hybrid automata-based cegar for rectangular hybrid systems. Form. Methods Syst. Des. **46**(2), 105–134 (2015)
25. Russo, G., Slotine, J.J.E.: Symmetries, stability, and control in nonlinear systems and networks. Phys. Rev. E **84**(4), 041929 (2011)
26. Spong, M.W., Bullo, F.: Controlled symmetries and passive walking. IEEE Trans. Autom. Control **50**(7), 1025–1031 (2005)

# Parametric Timed Model Checking for Guaranteeing Timed Opacity

Étienne André[1,2,3](✉) and Jun Sun[4]

[1] Université Paris 13, LIPN, CNRS, UMR 7030, 93430 Villetaneuse, France
eandre93430@lipn13.fr
[2] JFLI, CNRS, Tokyo, Japan
[3] National Institute of Informatics, Tokyo, Japan
[4] School of Information Systems, Singapore Management University, Singapore, Singapore

**Abstract.** Information leakage can have dramatic consequences on systems security. Among harmful information leaks, the timing information leakage is the ability for an attacker to deduce internal information depending on the system execution time. We address the following problem: given a timed system, synthesize the execution times for which one cannot deduce whether the system performed some secret behavior. We solve this problem in the setting of timed automata (TAs). We first provide a general solution, and then extend the problem to parametric TAs, by synthesizing internal timings making the TA secure. We study decidability, devise algorithms, and show that our method can also apply to program analysis.

## 1 Introduction

Timed systems combine concurrency and possibly hard real-time constraints. Information leakage can have dramatic consequences on the security of such systems. Among harmful information leaks, the *timing information leakage* is the ability for an attacker to deduce internal information depending on timing information. In this work, we focus on the execution time, i. e., when a system works as an almost black-box, with the ability of an attacker to mainly observe its execution time.

We address the following problem: given a timed system, a private state denoting the execution of some secret behavior and a final state denoting the completion of the execution, synthesize the execution times to the final state for which one cannot deduce whether the system has passed through the private state. We solve this problem in the setting of timed automata (TAs), which is

This work is partially supported by the ANR national research program PACS (ANR-14-CE28-0002) and by ERATO HASUO Metamathematics for Systems Design Project (No. JPMJER1603), JST.


Y.-F. Chen et al. (Eds.): ATVA 2019, LNCS 11781, pp. 115–130, 2019.
https://doi.org/10.1007/978-3-030-31784-3_7

a popular extension of finite-state automata with clocks [2]. We first prove that this problem is solvable, and we provide an algorithm, that we implement and apply to a set of benchmarks containing notably a set of Java programs known for their (absence of) timing information leakage.

Then we consider a higher-level problem by allowing (internal) timing parameters in the system, that can model uncertainty or unknown constants at early design stage. The setting becomes parametric timed automata [3], and the problem asks: given a timed system with timing parameters, a private state and a final state, synthesize the timing parameters and the execution times for which one cannot deduce whether the system has passed through the private state. Although we show that the problem is in general undecidable, we provide a decidable subclass; then we devise a general procedure not guaranteed to terminate, but that behaves well on examples from the literature.

## 2 Related Works

This work is closely related to the line of work on defining and analyzing information flow in timed automata. It is well-known (see e. g., [8,16]) that time is a potential attack vector against secure systems. That is, it is possible that a non-interferent (secure) system can become interferent (insecure) when timing constraints are added [13]. In [7], a first notion of *timed* non-interference is proposed. In [13], Gardey *et al.* define timed strong non-deterministic non-interference (SNNI) based on timed language equivalence between the automaton with hidden low-level actions and the automaton with removed low-level actions. Furthermore, they show that the problem of determining whether a timed automaton satisfies SNNI is undecidable. In contrast, timed cosimulation-based SNNI, timed bisimulation-based SNNI and timed state SNNI are decidable. In [9], the problem of checking opacity for timed automata is considered: even for the restricted class of event-recording automata, it is undecidable whether a system is opaque, i. e., whether an attacker can deduce whether some set of actions was performed, by only observing a given set of observable actions (with their timing). In [19], Vasilikos *et al.* define the security of timed automata in term of information flow using a bisimulation relation and develop an algorithm for deriving a sound constraint for satisfying the information flow property locally based on relevant transitions. In [8], Benattar *et al.* study the control synthesis problem of timed automata for SNNI. That is, given a timed automaton, they propose a method to automatically generate a (largest) sub-systems such that it is non-interferent if possible. Different from the above-mentioned work, our work considers parametric timed automata, i. e., timed systems with unknown design parameters, and focuses on synthesizing parameter valuations which guarantee information flow property. As far as we know, this is the first work on parametric model checking for timed automata for information flow property. Compared to [8], our approach is more realistic as it does not require change of program structure. Rather, our result provides guidelines on how to choose the timing parameters (e. g., how long to wait after certain program statements) for avoiding information leakage.

In [18], the authors propose a type system dealing with non-determinism and (continuous) real-time, the adequacy of which is ensured using non-interference. We share the common formalism of TA; however, we mainly focus on leakage as execution time, and we *synthesize* internal parts of the system (clock guards), in contrast to [18] where the system is fixed.

This work is related to work on mitigating information leakage through time side channel. For example, in [20], Wang *et al.* proposed to automatically generate masking code for eliminating side channel through program synthesis. In [21], Wu *et al.* proposed to eliminate time side channel through program repair. Different from the above-mentioned works, we reduce the problem of mitigating time side channel as a parametric model checking problem and solve it using parametric reachability analysis techniques.

This work is related to work on identifying information leakage through timing analysis. In [10], Chattopadhyay *et al.* applied model checking to perform cache timing analysis. In [11], Chu *et al.* performed similar analysis through symbolic execution. In [1], Abbasi *et al.* apply the NuSMV model checker to verify integrated circuits against information leakage through side channels. In [12], a tool is developed to identify time side channel through static analysis. In [22], Sung *et al.* developed a framework based on LLVM for cache timing analysis.

## 3 Preliminaries

We assume a set $\mathbb{X} = \{x_1, \dots, x_H\}$ of *clocks*, i.e., real-valued variables that evolve at the same rate. A clock valuation is $\mu : \mathbb{X} \to \mathbb{R}_{\geq 0}$. We write $\mathbf{0}$ for the clock valuation assigning 0 to all clocks. Given $d \in \mathbb{R}_{\geq 0}$, $\mu + d$ is s.t. $(\mu + d)(x) = \mu(x) + d$, for all $x \in \mathbb{X}$. Given $R \subseteq \mathbb{X}$, we define the *reset* of a valuation $\mu$, denoted by $[\mu]_R$, as follows: $[\mu]_R(x) = 0$ if $x \in R$, and $[\mu]_R(x) = \mu(x)$ otherwise.

We assume a set $\mathbb{P} = \{p_1, \dots, p_M\}$ of *parameters*. A parameter *valuation* $v$ is $v : \mathbb{P} \to \mathbb{Q}_+$. We assume $\bowtie \in \{<, \leq, =, \geq, >\}$. A guard $g$ is a constraint over $\mathbb{X} \cup \mathbb{P}$ defined by a conjunction of inequalities of the form $x \bowtie \sum_{1 \leq i \leq M} \alpha_i p_i + d$, with $p_i \in \mathbb{P}$, and $\alpha_i, d \in \mathbb{Z}$. Given $g$, we write $\mu \models v(g)$ if the expression obtained by replacing each $x$ with $\mu(x)$ and each $p$ with $v(p)$ in $g$ evaluates to true.

**Definition 1 (PTA).** *A PTA $\mathcal{A}$ is a tuple $\mathcal{A} = (\Sigma, L, \ell_0, \mathbb{X}, \mathbb{P}, I, E)$, where: (i) $\Sigma$ is a finite set of actions, (ii) $L$ is a finite set of locations, (iii) $\ell_0 \in L$ is the initial location, (iv) $\mathbb{X}$ is a finite set of clocks, (v) $\mathbb{P}$ is a finite set of parameters, (vi) $I$ is the invariant, assigning to every $\ell \in L$ a guard $I(\ell)$, (vii) $E$ is a finite set of edges $e = (\ell, g, a, R, \ell')$ where $\ell, \ell' \in L$ are the source and target locations, $a \in \Sigma$, $R \subseteq \mathbb{X}$ is a set of clocks to be reset, and $g$ is a guard.*

*Example 1.* Consider the PTA in Fig. 1 (inspired by [13, Fig. 1b]), containing one clock $x$ and two parameters $p_1$ and $p_2$. $\ell_0$ is the initial location, while $\ell_1$ is the (only) accepting location.

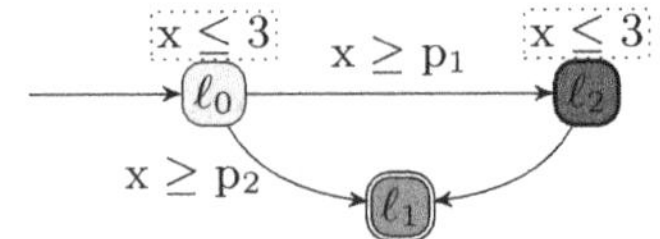


**Fig. 1.** A PTA example

Given $v$, we denote by $v(\mathcal{A})$ the non-parametric structure where all occurrences of a parameter $p_i$ have been replaced by $v(p_i)$.

The *synchronous product* (using strong broadcast, i. e., synchronization on a given set of actions) of several PTAs gives a PTA.

**Definition 2 (Semantics of a TA).** *Given a PTA $\mathcal{A} = (\Sigma, L, \ell_0, \mathbb{X}, \mathbb{P}, I, E)$, and a parameter valuation $v$, the semantics of $v(\mathcal{A})$ is given by the timed transition system (TTS) $(S, s_0, \rightarrow)$, with*

- $S = \{(\ell, \mu) \in L \times \mathbb{R}_{\geq 0}^H \mid \mu \models v(I(\ell))\}$, $s_0 = (\ell_0, \mathbf{0})$,
- $\rightarrow$ *consists of the discrete and (continuous) delay transition relations: (i) discrete transitions:* $(\ell, \mu) \overset{e}{\mapsto} (\ell', \mu')$, *if* $(\ell, \mu), (\ell', \mu') \in S$, *and there exists* $e = (\ell, g, a, R, \ell') \in E$, *such that* $\mu' = [\mu]_R$, *and* $\mu \models v(g)$. *(ii) delay transitions:* $(\ell, \mu) \overset{d}{\mapsto} (\ell, \mu + d)$, *with* $d \in \mathbb{R}_{\geq 0}$, *if* $\forall d' \in [0, d], (\ell, \mu + d') \in S$.

Moreover we write $(\ell, \mu) \overset{(e,d)}{\longrightarrow} (\ell', \mu')$ for a combination of a delay and discrete transition if $\exists \mu'' : (\ell, \mu) \overset{d}{\mapsto} (\ell, \mu'') \overset{e}{\mapsto} (\ell', \mu')$.

Given a TA $v(\mathcal{A})$ with concrete semantics $(S, s_0, \rightarrow)$, we refer to the states of $S$ as the *concrete states* of $v(\mathcal{A})$. A *run* of $v(\mathcal{A})$ is an alternating sequence of concrete states of $v(\mathcal{A})$ and pairs of edges and delays starting from the initial state $s_0$ of the form $s_0, (e_0, d_0), s_1, \cdots$ with $i = 0, 1, \ldots$, $e_i \in E$, $d_i \in \mathbb{R}_{\geq 0}$ and $s_i \overset{(e_i,d_i)}{\longrightarrow} s_{i+1}$. The *duration* of a finite run $\rho : s_0, (e_0, d_0), s_1, \cdots, s_i$ is $dur(\rho) = \sum_{0 \leq j \leq i-1} d_j$. Given $s = (\ell, \mu)$, we say that $s$ is reachable in $v(\mathcal{A})$ if $s$ appears in a run of $v(\mathcal{A})$. By extension, we say that $\ell$ is reachable. Given $\ell, \ell' \in L$ and a run $\rho$, we say that $\ell$ is reachable on the way to $\ell'$ in $\rho$ if $\rho$ is of the form $(\ell_0), (e_0, d_0), \cdots, (e_n, d_n), \cdots (e_m, d_m) \cdots$ for some $m, n \in \mathbb{N}$ such that $\ell_n = \ell$, $\ell_m = \ell'$ and $\forall 0 \leq i \leq n-1, \ell_i \neq \ell'$. Conversely, $\ell$ is unreachable on the way to $\ell'$ in $\rho$ if $\rho$ is of the form $(\ell_0), (e_0, d_0), \cdots, (e_m, d_m) \cdots$ with $\ell_m = \ell'$ and $\forall 0 \leq i \leq m-1, \ell_i \neq \ell$.

*Example 2.* Consider again the PTA $\mathcal{A}$ in Fig. 1, and let $v$ be such that $v(p_1) = 1$ and $v(p_2) = 2$. Consider the following run $\rho$ of $v(\mathcal{A})$: $(\ell_0, x = 0), (e_2, 1.4), (\ell_2, x = 1.4), (e_3, 1.3), (\ell_1, x = 2.7)$, where $e_2$ is the edge from $\ell_0$ to $\ell_2$ in Fig. 1, and $e_3$ is the edge from $\ell_2$ to $\ell_1$. We write "$x = 1.4$" instead of "$\mu$ such that $\mu(x) = 1.4$". We have $dur(\rho) = 1.4 + 1.3 = 2.7$. In addition, $\ell_2$ is reachable on the way to $\ell_1$ in $\rho$.

We will use reachability synthesis to solve the problems in Sect. 4. This procedure, called EFsynth, takes as input a PTA $\mathcal{A}$ and a set of target locations $T$,

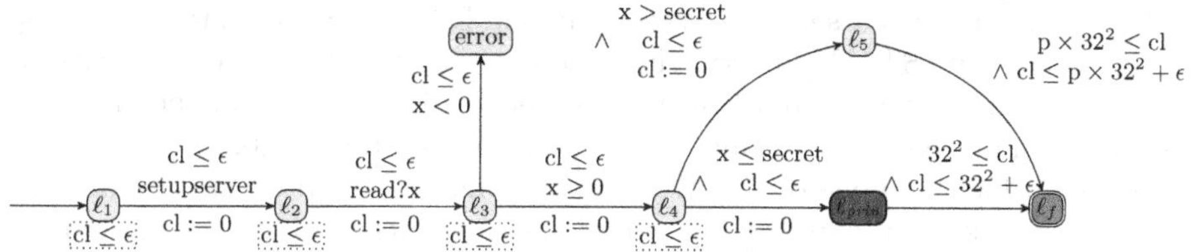


**Fig. 2.** A Java program encoded in a PTA

and attempts to synthesize all parameter valuations $v$ for which $T$ is reachable in $v(\mathcal{A})$. $\mathsf{EFsynth}(\mathcal{A}, T)$ was formalized in e. g., [15] and is a procedure that may not terminate, but that computes an exact result (sound and complete) if it terminates. EFsynth traverses the *parametric zone graph* of $\mathcal{A}$, which is a potentially infinite extension of the well-known zone graph of TAs (see, e. g., [5,15]).

*Example 3.* Consider again the PTA $\mathcal{A}$ in Fig. 1. $\mathsf{EFsynth}(\mathcal{A}, \{\ell_1\}) = p_1 \leq 3 \vee p_2 \leq 3$. Intuitively, it corresponds to all parameter constraints in the parametric zone graph associated to symbolic states with location $\ell_1$.

## 4 Timed-Opacity Problems

Let us first introduce two key concepts to define our notion of opacity. $\mathit{DReach}^{v(\mathcal{A})}_{\ell}(\ell')$ (resp. $\mathit{DReach}^{v(\mathcal{A})}_{\neg\ell}(\ell')$) is the set of the durations of the runs for which $\ell$ is reachable (resp. unreachable) on the way to $\ell'$. Formally: $\mathit{DReach}^{v(\mathcal{A})}_{\ell}(\ell') = \{d \mid \exists \rho \text{ in } v(\mathcal{A}) \text{ such that } d = \mathit{dur}(\rho) \wedge \ell \text{ is reachable on the way to } \ell' \text{ in } \rho\}$ and $\mathit{DReach}^{v(\mathcal{A})}_{\neg\ell}(\ell') = \{d \mid \exists \rho \text{ in } v(\mathcal{A}) \text{ such that } d = \mathit{dur}(\rho) \wedge \ell \text{ is unreachable on the way to } \ell' \text{ in } \rho\}$.

*Example 4.* Consider again the PTA in Fig. 1, and let $v$ be such that $v(p_1) = 1$ and $v(p_2) = 2$. We have $\mathit{DReach}^{v(\mathcal{A})}_{\ell_2}(\ell_1) = [1, 3]$ and $\mathit{DReach}^{v(\mathcal{A})}_{\neg\ell_2}(\ell_1) = [2, 3]$.

**Definition 3 (timed opacity w.r.t. $D$).** *Given a TA $v(\mathcal{A})$, a private location $\ell_{priv}$, a target location $\ell_f$ and a set of execution times $D$, we say that $v(\mathcal{A})$ is* opaque w.r.t. $\ell_{priv}$ on the way to $\ell_f$ for execution times $D$ *if* $D \subseteq \mathit{DReach}^{v(\mathcal{A})}_{\ell_{priv}}(\ell_f) \cap \mathit{DReach}^{v(\mathcal{A})}_{\neg\ell_{priv}}(\ell_f)$.

*Example 5.* Consider the PTA $\mathcal{A}$ in Fig. 2 where cl is a clock, while $\epsilon$, p are parameters. We use a sightly extended PTA syntax: read?x reads the value input on a given channel read, and assigns it to a (discrete, global) variable x. secret is a constant variable of arbitrary value. If both x and secret are finite-domain variables (e. g., bounded integers) then they can be seen as syntactic sugar for locations. Such variables are supported by most model checkers, including UPPAAL and IMITATOR.

This PTA encodes a server process from the DARPA Space/Time Analysis for Cybersecurity (STAC) library, that compares a user-input variable with a given secret and performs different actions taking different times depending on this secret. In our encoding, a single instruction takes a time in $[0, \epsilon]$, while $p$ is a (parametric) factor to one of the `sleep` instructions of the program (originally, $v(p) = 2$). For sake of simplicity, we abstract away instructions not related to time, and merge subfunctions calls.

Fix $v(\epsilon) = 1$, $v(p) = 2$. For this example, $DReach^{v(\mathcal{A})}_{\ell_{priv}}(\ell_f) = [1024, 1029]$ while $DReach^{v(\mathcal{A})}_{\neg\ell_{priv}}(\ell_f) = [2048, 2053]$. Therefore, $v(\mathcal{A})$ is opaque w.r.t. $\ell_{priv}$ on the way to $\ell_f$ for execution times $D = [1024, 1029] \cap [2048, 2053] = \emptyset$.

Now fix $v(\epsilon) = 2$, $v(p) = 1.002$. $DReach^{v(\mathcal{A})}_{\ell_{priv}}(\ell_f) = [1024, 1034]$ while $DReach^{v(\mathcal{A})}_{\neg\ell_{priv}}(\ell_f) = [1026.048, 1036.048]$. Therefore, $v(\mathcal{A})$ is opaque w.r.t. $\ell_{priv}$ on the way to $\ell_f$ for execution times $D = [1026.048, 1034]$.

We can now define the timed-opacity computation problem, which consists in computing the possible execution times ensuring opacity w.r.t. a private location. In other words, the attacker model is as follows: the attacker has only access to the computation time between the start of the program and the time it reaches a given (final) location.

**Timed-opacity Computation Problem:**
INPUT: A TA $v(\mathcal{A})$, a private location $\ell_{priv}$, a target location $\ell_f$
PROBLEM: Compute the execution times $D$ for which $v(\mathcal{A})$ is opaque w.r.t. $\ell_{priv}$ on the way to $\ell_f$ for execution times $D$

The synthesis counterpart allows for a higher-level problem by also synthesizing the internal timings guaranteeing opacity.

**Timed-opacity Synthesis Problem:**
INPUT: A PTA $\mathcal{A}$, a private location $\ell_{priv}$, a target location $\ell_f$
PROBLEM: Synthesize the parameter valuations $v$ and the execution times $D$ for which $v(\mathcal{A})$ is opaque w.r.t. $\ell_{priv}$ on the way to $\ell_f$ for execution times $D$

Note that the execution times can depend on the parameter valuations.

## 5 Timed-Opacity Computation for Timed Automata

### 5.1 Answering the Timed-Opacity Computation Problem

**Proposition 1 (timed-opacity computation).** *The timed-opacity computation problem is solvable for TAs.*

This positive result can be put in perspective with the negative result of [9], that proves that it is undecidable whether a TA (and even the more restricted subclass of event-recording automata) is opaque, in a sense that the attacker can deduce some actions, by looking at observable actions together with their timing. The difference in our setting is that only the global time is observable, which can be seen as a single action, occurring once only at the end of the computation. In other words, our attacker is less powerful than the attacker in [9].

### 5.2 Checking for Timed-Opacity

If one does not have the ability to tune the system (i. e., change internal delays, or add some `sleep()` or `Wait()` statements in the program), one may be first interested in knowing whether the system is opaque for all execution times.

**Definition 4 (timed opacity).** *Given a TA $v(\mathcal{A})$, a private location $\ell_{priv}$ and a target location $\ell_f$, we say that $v(\mathcal{A})$ is* opaque w.r.t. $\ell_{priv}$ on the way to $\ell_f$ *if $DReach^{v(\mathcal{A})}_{\ell_{priv}}(\ell_f) = DReach^{v(\mathcal{A})}_{\neg\ell_{priv}}(\ell_f)$.*

That is, a system is opaque if, for any execution time $d$, a run of duration $d$ reaches $\ell_f$ after passing by $\ell_{priv}$ iff another run of duration $d$ reaches $\ell_f$ without passing by $\ell_{priv}$.

*Remark 1.* This definition is symmetric: a system is not opaque iff an attacker can deduce $\ell_{priv}$ or $\neg\ell_{priv}$. For instance, if there is no path through $\ell_{priv}$ to $\ell_f$, but a path to $\ell_f$, a system is not opaque w.r.t. Definition 4.

As we have a procedure to compute $DReach^{v(\mathcal{A})}_{\ell_{priv}}(\ell_f)$ and $DReach^{v(\mathcal{A})}_{\neg\ell_{priv}}(\ell_f)$, (see Proposition 1), Definition 4 gives an immediate procedure to decide timed opacity. Note that, from the finiteness of the region graph, $DReach^{v(\mathcal{A})}_{\ell_{priv}}(\ell_f)$ and $DReach^{v(\mathcal{A})}_{\neg\ell_{priv}}(\ell_f)$ come in the form of a finite union of intervals, and their equality can be effectively computed.

*Example 6.* Consider again the PTA $\mathcal{A}$ in Fig. 1, and let $v$ be such that $v(p_1) = 1$ and $v(p_2) = 2$. Recall from Example 4 that $DReach^{v(\mathcal{A})}_{\ell_2}(\ell_1) = [1, 3]$ and $DReach^{v(\mathcal{A})}_{\neg\ell_2}(\ell_1) = [2, 3]$. Thus, $DReach^{v(\mathcal{A})}_{\ell_2}(\ell_1) \neq DReach^{v(\mathcal{A})}_{\neg\ell_2}(\ell_1)$ and therefore $v(\mathcal{A})$ is *not* opaque w.r.t. $\ell_2$ on the way to $\ell_1$.

Now, consider $v'$ such that $v'(p_1) = v'(p_2) = 1.5$. This time, $DReach^{v'(\mathcal{A})}_{\ell_2}(\ell_1) = DReach^{v'(\mathcal{A})}_{\neg\ell_2}(\ell_1) = [1.5, 3]$ and therefore $v'(\mathcal{A})$ is opaque w.r.t. $\ell_2$ on the way to $\ell_1$.

## 6 Decidability and Undecidability

We address here the following decision problem, that asks about the emptiness of the parameter valuations and execution times set guaranteeing timed opacity.

> **Timed-opacity Emptiness Problem:**
> INPUT: A PTA $\mathcal{A}$, a private location $\ell_{priv}$, a target location $\ell_f$
> PROBLEM: Is the set of valuations $v$ such that $v(\mathcal{A})$ is opaque w.r.t. $\ell_{priv}$ on the way to $\ell_f$ for a non-empty set of execution times empty?

Dually, we are interested in deciding whether there exists at least one parameter valuation for which $v(\mathcal{A})$ is opaque for at least some execution time.

With the rule of thumb that all non-trivial decision problems are undecidable for general PTAs [4], the following result is not surprising, and follows from the undecidability of reachability-emptiness for PTAs (Fig. 3).

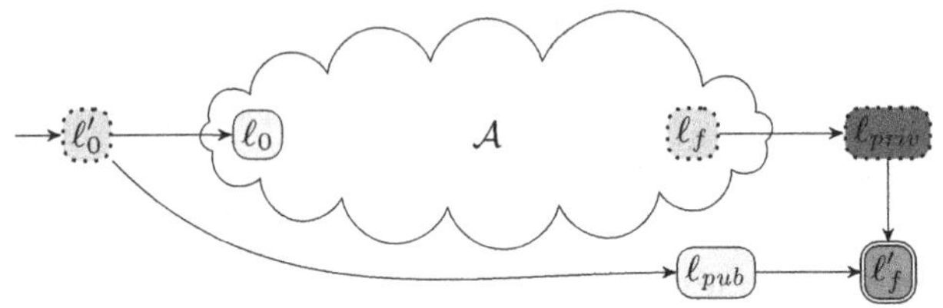


**Fig. 3.** Reduction from reachability-emptiness

**Proposition 2 (undecidability).** *The timed-opacity emptiness problem is undecidable for general PTAs.*

We now show that the timed-opacity emptiness problem is decidable for the subclass of PTAs called L/U-PTAs [14]. Despite early positive results for L/U-PTAs, more recent results mostly proved undecidable properties of L/U-PTAs [4], and therefore this positive result is welcome.

**Definition 5 (L/U-PTA).** *An* L/U-PTA *is a PTA where the set of parameters is partitioned into lower-bound parameters and upper-bound parameters, where each upper-bound (resp. lower-bound) parameter $p_i$ must be such that, for every guard or invariant constraint $x \bowtie \sum_{1 \leq i \leq M} \alpha_i p_i + d$, we have: $\alpha_i > 0$ implies $\bowtie \in \{\leq, <\}$ (resp. $\bowtie \in \{\geq, >\}$).*

*Example 7.* The PTA in Fig. 1 is an L/U-PTA with $\{p_1, p_2\}$ as lower-bound parameters, and $\emptyset$ as upper-bound parameters.

The PTA in Fig. 2 is not an L/U-PTA, because $\mathrm{p}$ is compared to $\mathrm{cl}$ both as a lower-bound (in "$\mathrm{p} \times 32^2 \leq \mathrm{cl}$") and as an upper-bound ("$\mathrm{cl} \leq \mathrm{p} \times 32^2 + \epsilon$").

**Theorem 1 (decidability).** *The timed-opacity emptiness problem is decidable for L/U-PTAs.*

*Remark 2.* The class of L/U-PTAs is known to be relatively meaningful, and many case studies from the literature fit into this class, including case studies proposed even before this class was defined in [14]. Even though the PTA in Fig. 2 does not fit in this class, it can easily be transformed into an L/U-PTA, by duplicating $\mathrm{p}$ into $\mathrm{p}^{\mathrm{l}}$ (used in lower-bound comparisons with clocks) and $\mathrm{p}^{\mathrm{u}}$ (used in upper-bound comparisons with clocks).

## 7 Parameter Synthesis for Opacity

Despite the negative theoretical result of Proposition 2, we now address the timed-opacity synthesis problem for the full class of PTAs. Our method may not terminate (due to the undecidability) but, if it does, its result is correct. Our workflow can be summarized as follows.

1. We enrich the original PTA by adding a Boolean flag $b$ and a final synchronization action;

2. We perform *self-composition* (i. e., parallel composition with a copy of itself) of this modified PTA;
3. We perform reachability-synthesis using EFsynth on $\ell_f$ with contradictory values of $b$.

We detail each operation in the following. In this section, we assume a PTA $\mathcal{A}$, a given private location $\ell_{priv}$ and a given final location $\ell_f$.

**Enriching the PTA.** We first add a Boolean flag $b$ initially set to false, and then set to true on any transition leading to $\ell_{priv}$ (in the line of the proof of Proposition 1). Therefore, $b$ = true denotes that $\ell_{priv}$ has been visited. Second, we add a synchronization action finish on any transition leading to $\ell_f$. Third, we add a new clock $x_{abs}$ (never reset) together with a new parameter $p_{abs}$, and we guard all transitions to $\ell_f$ with $x_{abs} = p_{abs}$. This will allow to measure the (parametric) execution time. Let $\mathsf{Enrich}(\mathcal{A}, \ell_{priv}, \ell_f)$ denote this procedure.

**Self-composition.** We use here the principle of *self-composition*, i. e., composing the PTA with a copy of itself. More precisely, given a PTA $\mathcal{A}' = \mathsf{Enrich}(\mathcal{A}, \ell_{priv}, \ell_f)$, we first perform an identical copy of $\mathcal{A}'$ *with distinct variables*: that is, a clock $x$ of $\mathcal{A}'$ is distinct from a clock $x$ in the copy of $\mathcal{A}'$—which can be trivially performed using variable renaming.[1] Let $\mathsf{Copy}(\mathcal{A}')$ denote this copy of $\mathcal{A}'$. We then compute $\mathcal{A}' \parallel_{\{\mathrm{finish}\}} \mathsf{Copy}(\mathcal{A}')$. That is, $\mathcal{A}'$ and $\mathsf{Copy}(\mathcal{A}')$ evolve completely independently due to the interleaving—except that they are forced to enter $\ell_f$ at the same time, thanks to the synchronization action finish.

**Synthesis.** Then, we apply reachability synthesis EFsynth (over all parameters, i. e., the "internal" timing parameters, but also the $p_{abs}$ parameter) to the following goal location: the original $\mathcal{A}'$ is in $\ell_f$ with $b$ = true while its copy $\mathsf{Copy}(\mathcal{A}')$ is in $\ell'_f$ with $b'$ = false (primed variables denote variables from the copy). Intuitively, we synthesize timing parameters and execution times such that there exists a run reaching $\ell_f$ with $b$ = true (i. e., that has visited $\ell_{priv}$) and there exists another run of same duration reaching $\ell_f$ with $b$ = false (i. e., that has not visited $\ell_{priv}$).

Let $\mathsf{SynthOp}(\mathcal{A}, \ell_{priv}, \ell_f)$ denote the entire procedure. We formalize SynthOp in Algorithm 1, where "$\ell_f \wedge b$ = true" denotes the location $\ell_f$ with $b$ = true. Also note that EFsynth is called on a set made of a single location of $\mathcal{A}' \parallel_{\{\mathrm{finish}\}} \mathsf{Copy}(\mathcal{A}')$; by definition of the synchronous product, this location is a *pair* of locations, one from $\mathcal{A}'$ (i. e., "$\ell_f \wedge b$ = true") and one from $\mathsf{Copy}(\mathcal{A}')$ (i. e., "$\ell'_f \wedge b'$ = false").

*Example 8.* Consider again the PTA $\mathcal{A}$ in Fig. 2. Fix $v(\epsilon) = 1$, $v(\mathrm{p}) = 2$. We then perform the synthesis applied to the self-composition of $\mathcal{A}'$ according to

[1] In fact, the fresh clock $x_{abs}$ and parameter $p_{abs}$ can be shared to save two variables, as $x_{abs}$ is never reset, and both PTAs enter $\ell_f$ at the same time, therefore both "copies" of $x_{abs}$ and $p_{abs}$ always share the same values.

**Algorithm 1.** $\mathsf{SynthOp}(\mathcal{A}, \ell_{priv}, \ell_f)$

**input** : A PTA $\mathcal{A}$, locations $\ell_{priv}, \ell_f$
**output** : Constraint $K$ over the parameters

$\mathcal{A}' \leftarrow \mathsf{Enrich}(\mathcal{A}, \ell_{priv}, \ell_f)$
$\mathcal{A}'' \leftarrow \mathcal{A}' \parallel_{\{finish\}} \mathsf{Copy}(\mathcal{A}')$
**return** $\mathsf{EFsynth}\Big(\mathcal{A}'', \big\{(\ell_f \wedge b = \text{true}, \ell'_f \wedge b' = \text{false})\big\}\Big)$

Algorithm 1. The result obtained with IMITATOR is: $p_{abs} = \emptyset$ (as expected from Example 5).

Now fix $v(\epsilon) = 2$, $v(p) = 1.002$. We obtain: $p_{abs} \in [1026.048, 1034]$ (again, as expected from Example 5).

Now let us keep all parameters unconstrained. The result of Algorithm 1 is the following 3-dimensional constraint: $5 \times \epsilon + 1024 \geq p_{abs} \geq 1024 \wedge 1024 \times p + 5 \times \epsilon \geq p_{abs} \geq 1024 \times p \geq 0$.

**Soundness.** We will state below that, whenever $\mathsf{SynthOp}(\mathcal{A}, \ell_{priv}, \ell_f)$ terminates, then its result is an exact (sound and complete) answer to the timed-opacity synthesis problem.

**Theorem 2 (correctness).** *Assume $\mathsf{SynthOp}(\mathcal{A}, \ell_{priv}, \ell_f)$ terminates with result $K$. Assume $v$. The following two statements are equivalent:*

1. *There exists a run of duration $v(p_{abs})$ such that $\ell_{priv}$ is reachable on the way to $\ell_f$ in $v(\mathcal{A})$ and there exists a run of duration $v(p_{abs})$ such that $\ell_{priv}$ is unreachable on the way to $\ell_f$ in $v(\mathcal{A})$.*
2. *$v \models K$.*

## 8 Experiments

We use IMITATOR [6], a tool taking as input networks of PTAs extended with several handful features such as shared global discrete variables, PTA synchronization through strong broadcast, etc. We ran experiments using IMITATOR 2.10.4 "Butter Jellyfish" on a Dell XPS 13 9360 equipped with an Intel® Core™ i7-7500U CPU @ 2.70 GHz with 8 GiB memory running Linux Mint 18.3 64 bits.[2]

### 8.1 Translating Programs into PTAs

We will consider case studies from the PTA community and from previous works focusing on privacy using (parametric) timed automata. In addition, we will be interested in analyzing programs too. In order to apply our method to the analysis of programs, we need a systematic way of translating a program (e. g.,

[2] Sources, models and results are available at doi.org/10.5281/zenodo.3251141.

a Java program) into a PTA. In general, precisely modeling the execution time of a program using models like timed automata is highly non-trivial due to complication of hardware pipelining, caching, OS scheduling, etc. The readers are referred to the rich literature in, for instance, [17]. In this work, we instead make the following simplistic assumption on execution time of a program statement and focus on solving the parameter synthesis problem. How to precisely model the execution time of programs is orthogonal and complementary to our work.

We assume that the execution time of a program statement other than `Thread.sleep(n)` is within a range $[0, \epsilon]$ where $\epsilon$ is a small integer constant (in milliseconds), whereas the execution time of statement `Thread.sleep(n)` is within a range $[n, n + \epsilon]$. In fact, we choose to keep $\epsilon$ *parametric* to be as general as possible, and to not depend on particular architectures.

Our test subject is a set of benchmark programs from the DARPA Space/-Time Analysis for Cybersecurity (STAC) program.[3] These programs are being released publicly to facilitate researchers to develop methods and tools for identifying STAC vulnerabilities in the programs.

### 8.2 A Richer Framework

The symbolic representation of variables and parameters in IMITATOR allows us to reason *symbolically* concerning variables. That is, instead of enumerating all possible (bounded) values of x and secret in Fig. 2, we turn them to parameters (i. e., unknown constants), and IMITATOR performs a symbolic reasoning. Even better, the analysis terminates for this example even when no bound is provided on these variables. This is often not possible in (non-parametric) timed automata based model checkers, that usually have to enumerate these values. Therefore, in our PTA representation of Java programs, we turn all user-input variable and secret constant variables to parameters. Other local variables are implemented using IMITATOR discrete (shared, global) variables.

### 8.3 Experiments

**Benchmarks.** As a proof of concept, we applied our method to a set of examples from the literature. The first five models come from previous works from the literature [8,13,19], also addressing non-interference or opacity in timed automata. In addition, we used two common models from the (P)TA literature, not necessarily linked to security: a toy coffee machine (`Coffee`) used as benchmark in a number of papers, and a model Fischer's mutual exclusion protocol (`Fischer-HRSV02`) [14]. In both cases, we added manually a definition of private location (the number of sugars ordered, and the identity of the process entering the critical section, respectively), and we verified whether they are opaque w.r.t. these internal behaviors.

We also applied our approach to a set of Java programs from the aforementioned STAC library. We use identifiers of the form `STAC:1:n` where `1` denotes

[3] https://github.com/Apogee-Research/STAC/.

**Table 1.** Experiments: timed opacity

| Model | | | Transf. PTA | | | Result | |
|---|---|---|---|---|---|---|---|
| Name | $\|\mathcal{A}\|$ | $\|\mathbb{X}\|$ | $\|\mathcal{A}\|$ | $\|\mathbb{X}\|$ | $\|\mathbb{P}\|$ | Time (s) | Vulnerable? |
| [19, Fig. 5] | 1 | 1 | 2 | 3 | 3 | 0.02 | (√) |
| [13, Fig. 1b] | 1 | 1 | 2 | 3 | 1 | 0.04 | (√) |
| [13, Fig. 2a] | 1 | 1 | 2 | 3 | 1 | 0.05 | (√) |
| [13, Fig. 2b] | 1 | 1 | 2 | 3 | 1 | 0.02 | (√) |
| Web privacy problem [8] | 1 | 2 | 2 | 4 | 1 | 0.07 | (√) |
| Coffee | 1 | 2 | 2 | 5 | 1 | 0.05 | × |
| Fischer-HSRV02 | 3 | 2 | 6 | 5 | 1 | 5.83 | (√) |
| STAC:1:n | | | 2 | 3 | 6 | 0.12 | (√) |
| STAC:1:v | | | 2 | 3 | 6 | 0.11 | √ |
| STAC:3:n | | | 2 | 3 | 8 | 0.72 | × |
| STAC:3:v | | | 2 | 3 | 8 | 0.74 | (√) |
| STAC:4:n | | | 2 | 3 | 8 | 6.40 | √ |
| STAC:4:v | | | 2 | 3 | 8 | 265.52 | √ |
| STAC:5:n | | | 2 | 3 | 6 | 0.24 | × |
| STAC:11A:v | | | 2 | 3 | 8 | 47.77 | (√) |
| STAC:11B:v | | | 2 | 3 | 8 | 59.35 | (√) |
| STAC:12c:v | | | 2 | 3 | 8 | 18.44 | √ |
| STAC:12e:n | | | 2 | 3 | 8 | 0.58 | √ |
| STAC:12e:v | | | 2 | 3 | 8 | 1.10 | (√) |
| STAC:14:n | | | 2 | 3 | 8 | 22.34 | (√) |

the identifier in the library, while `n` (resp. `v`) denotes non-vulnerable (resp. vulnerable). We manually translated these programs to parametric timed automata, following the method described in Sect. 8.1. We used a representative set of programs from the library; however, some of them were too complex to fit in our framework, notably when the timing leaks come from calls to external libraries (`STAC:15:v`), when dealing with complex computations such as operations on matrices (`STAC:16:v`) or when handling probabilities (`STAC:18:v`). Proposing efficient and accurate ways to represent arbitrary programs into (parametric) timed automata is orthogonal to our work, and is the object of future works.

**Timed-Opacity Computation.** First, we *verified* whether a given TA model is opaque, i. e., if for all execution times reaching a given final location, both an execution passes by a given private location and an execution does not pass by this private location. To this end, we also answer the timed-opacity computation problem, i. e., to synthesize all execution times for which the system is opaque. While this problem can be verified on the region graph (Proposition 1), we use the same framework as in Sect. 7, but without parameters in the original TA. That is, we use the Boolean flag $b$ and the parameter $p_{abs}$ to compute all possible execution times. In other words, we use a parametric analysis to solve a non-parametric problem.

We tabulate the experiments results in Table 1. We give from left to right the model name, the numbers of automata and of clocks in the original timed automaton (this information is not relevant for Java programs as the original model is not a TA), the numbers of automata, of clocks and of parameters in the transformed PTA, the computation time in seconds (for the timed-opacity computation problem), and the result. In the result column, "×" (resp. "√")

denotes that the model is opaque (resp. is not opaque), while "(√)" denotes that the model is not opaque, but could be fixed. That is, although $DReach^{v(\mathcal{A})}_{\ell_{priv}}(\ell_f) \neq DReach^{v(\mathcal{A})}_{\neg\ell_{priv}}(\ell_f)$, their intersection is non-empty and therefore, by tuning the computation time, it may be possible to make the system opaque. This will be discussed in Sect. 8.4.

Even though we are interested here in timed opacity computation (and not in synthesis), note that all models derived from Java programs feature the parameter $\epsilon$. The result is obtained by variable elimination, i. e., by existential quantification over the parameters different from $p_{abs}$. In addition, the number of parameters is increased by the parameters encoding the symbolic variables (such as x and secret in Fig. 2).

*Discussion.* Overall, our method is able to answer the timed-opacity computation problem relatively fast, exhibiting which execution times are opaque (timed-opacity computation problem), and whether *all* execution times indeed guarantee opacity (timed-opacity problem).

In many cases, while the system is not opaque, we are able to *infer* the execution times guaranteeing opacity (cells marked "(√)"). This is an advantage of our method w.r.t. methods outputting only binary answers.

We observed some mismatches in the Java programs, i. e., some programs marked n (non-vulnerable) in the library are actually vulnerable according to our method. This mainly comes from the fact that the STAC library uses some statistical analyses on the execution times, while we use an exact method. Therefore, a very small mismatch between $DReach^{v(\mathcal{A})}_{\ell_{priv}}(\ell_f)$ and $DReach^{v(\mathcal{A})}_{\neg\ell_{priv}}(\ell_f)$ will lead our algorithm to answer "not opaque", while statistical methods may not be able to differentiate this mismatch from noise. This is notably the case of `STAC:14:n` where some action lasts either 5,010,000 or 5,000,000 time units depending on some secret, which our method detects to be different, while the library does not. For `STAC:1:n`, using our data, the difference in the execution time upper bound between an execution performing some secret action and an execution not performing it is larger than 1%, which we believe is a value which is not negligible, and therefore this case study might be considered as vulnerable. For `STAC:4:n`, we used a different definition of opacity (whether the user has input the correct password, vs. information on the real password), which explains the mismatch.

Concerning the Java programs, we decided to keep the most abstract representation, by imposing that each instruction lasts for a time in $[0, \epsilon]$, with $\epsilon$ a parameter. However, fixing an identical (parametric) time $\epsilon$ for all instructions, or fixing an arbitrary time in a constant interval $[0, \epsilon]$ (for some constant $\epsilon$, e. g., 1), or even fixing an identical (constant) time $\epsilon$ (e. g., 1) for all instructions, significantly speeds up the analysis. These choices can be made for larger models.

**Timed Opacity Synthesis.** Then, we address the timed-opacity synthesis problem. In this case, we *synthesize* both the execution time and the internal

**Table 2.** Experiments: timed opacity synthesis

| Model | | | | Transf. PTA | | | Result | |
|---|---|---|---|---|---|---|---|---|
| Name | $\|\mathcal{A}\|$ | $\|\mathbb{X}\|$ | $\|\mathbb{P}\|$ | $\|\mathcal{A}\|$ | $\|\mathbb{X}\|$ | $\|\mathbb{P}\|$ | Time (s) | Constraint |
| [19, Fig. 5] | 1 | 1 | 0 | 2 | 3 | 4 | 0.02 | $K$ |
| [13, Fig. 1b] | 1 | 1 | 0 | 2 | 3 | 3 | 0.03 | $K$ |
| [13, Fig. 2] | 1 | 1 | 0 | 2 | 3 | 3 | 0.05 | $K$ |
| Web privacy problem [8] | 1 | 2 | 2 | 2 | 4 | 3 | 0.07 | $K$ |
| `Coffee` | 1 | 2 | 3 | 2 | 5 | 4 | 0.10 | $\top$ |
| `Fischer-HSRV02` | 3 | 2 | 2 | 6 | 5 | 3 | 7.53 | $K$ |
| `STAC:3:v` | | | 2 | 2 | 3 | 9 | 0.93 | $K$ |

values of the parameters for which one cannot deduce private information from the execution time.

We consider the same case studies as for timed-opacity computation; however, the Java programs feature no internal "parameter" and cannot be used here. Still, we artificially enriched one of them (`STAC:3:v`) as follows: in addition to the parametric value of $\epsilon$ and the execution time, we parameterized one of the `sleep` timers. The resulting constraint can help designers to refine this latter value to ensure opacity.

We tabulate the results in Table 2, where the columns are similar to Table 1. A difference is that the first $|\mathbb{P}|$ column denotes the number of parameters in the original model (without counting these added by our transformation). In addition, Table 2 does not contain a "vulnerable?" column as we *synthesize* the condition for which the model is non-vulnerable, and therefore the answer is non-binary. However, in the last column ("Constraint"), we make explicit whether no valuations ensure opacity ("$\bot$"), all of them ("$\top$"), or some of them ("$K$").

*Discussion.* An interesting outcome is that the computation time is comparable to the (non-parametric) timed-opacity computation, with an increase of up to 20 % only. In addition, for all case studies, we exhibit at least some valuations for which the system can be made opaque. Also note that our method always terminates for these models, and therefore the result exhibited is complete. Interestingly, `Coffee` is opaque for any valuation of the 3 internal parameters.

### 8.4 "Repairing" a Non-opaque PTA

Our method gives a result in time of a union of polyhedra over the internal timing parameters and the execution time. On the one hand, we believe tuning the internal timing parameters should be easy: for a program, an internal timing parameter can be the duration of a `sleep`, for example. On the other hand, tuning the execution time of a program may be more subtle. A solution is to enforce a minimal execution time by adding a second thread in parallel with a `Wait()` primitive to ensure a minimal execution time. Ensuring a *maximal* execution time can be achieved with an exception stopping the program after a given time; however there is a priori no guarantee that the result of the computation is correct.

## 9 Conclusion

We proposed an approach based on parametric timed model checking to not only decide whether the model of a timed system can be subject to timing information leakage, but also to *synthesize* internal timing parameters and execution times that render the system opaque. We implemented our approach in a framework based on IMITATOR, and performed experiments on case studies from the literature and from a library of Java programs. We now discuss future works.

*Theory.* We proved decidability of the timed-opacity computation problem for TAs, but we only provided an upper bound (EXPSPACE) on the complexity. It can be easily shown that this problem is at least PSPACE, but the exact complexity remains to be exhibited.

Finally, while we proved for the class of L/U-PTAs the decidability of the timed-opacity emptiness problem, i. e., the non-existence of a valuation for which the system is opaque, our result does not necessarily mean that *exact (complete) synthesis* is possible. In fact, some results for L/U-PTAs were proved to be such that the emptiness is decidable but the synthesis is intractable: that is notably the case of reachability-emptiness, which is decidable [14] while synthesis is intractable [15]. Therefore, studying the timed-opacity synthesis problem remains to be done for L/U-PTAs.

*Applications.* The translation of the STAC library required some non-trivial creativity: proposing automated translations of (possibly annotated) programs to timed automata dedicated to timing analysis is on our agenda.

**Acknowledgements.** We thank Sudipta Chattopadhyay for helpful suggestions, Jiaying Li for his help with preliminary model conversion, and a reviewer for suggesting Remark 1.

## References

1. Abbasi, I.H., Lodhi, F.K., Kamboh, A.M., Hasan, O.: Formal verification of gate-level multiple side channel parameters to detect hardware Trojans. In: Artho, C., Ölveczky, P.C. (eds.) FTSCS 2016. CCIS, vol. 694, pp. 75–92. Springer, Cham (2017). https://doi.org/10.1007/978-3-319-53946-1_5
2. Alur, R., Dill, D.L.: A theory of timed automata. TCS **126**(2), 183–235 (1994). https://doi.org/10.1016/0304-3975(94)90010-8
3. Alur, R., Henzinger, T.A., Vardi, M.Y.: Parametric real-time reasoning. In: Kosaraju, S.R., Johnson, D.S., Aggarwal, A. (eds.) STOC, pp. 592–601. ACM, New York (1993). https://doi.org/10.1145/167088.167242
4. André, É.: What's decidable about parametric timed automata? STTT **21**(2), 203–219 (2019). https://doi.org/10.1007/s10009-017-0467-0
5. André, É., Chatain, T., Encrenaz, E., Fribourg, L.: An inverse method for parametric timed automata. IJFCS **20**(5), 819–836 (2009). https://doi.org/10.1142/S0129054109006905

6. André, É., Fribourg, L., Kühne, U., Soulat, R.: IMITATOR 2.5: a tool for analyzing robustness in scheduling problems. In: Giannakopoulou, D., Méry, D. (eds.) FM 2012. LNCS, vol. 7436, pp. 33–36. Springer, Heidelberg (2012). https://doi.org/10.1007/978-3-642-32759-9_6
7. Barbuti, R., Francesco, N.D., Santone, A., Tesei, L.: A notion of non-interference for timed automata. FI **51**(1–2), 1–11 (2002)
8. Benattar, G., Cassez, F., Lime, D., Roux, O.H.: Control and synthesis of non-interferent timed systems. Int. J. Control **88**(2), 217–236 (2015). https://doi.org/10.1080/00207179.2014.944356
9. Cassez, F.: The dark side of timed opacity. In: Park, J.H., Chen, H.-H., Atiquzzaman, M., Lee, C., Kim, T., Yeo, S.-S. (eds.) ISA 2009. LNCS, vol. 5576, pp. 21–30. Springer, Heidelberg (2009). https://doi.org/10.1007/978-3-642-02617-1_3
10. Chattopadhyay, S., Roychoudhury, A.: Scalable and precise refinement of cache timing analysis via model checking. In: RTSS, pp. 193–203 (2011). https://doi.org/10.1109/RTSS.2011.25
11. Chu, D., Jaffar, J., Maghareh, R.: Precise cache timing analysis via symbolic execution. In: RTAS, pp. 293–304 (2016). https://doi.org/10.1109/RTAS.2016.7461358
12. Doychev, G., Feld, D., Köpf, B., Mauborgne, L., Reineke, J.: Cacheaudit: a tool for the static analysis of cache side channels. In: King, S.T. (ed.) USENIX Security Symposium, pp. 431–446. USENIX Association (2013)
13. Gardey, G., Mullins, J., Roux, O.H.: Non-interference control synthesis for security timed automata. ENTCS **180**(1), 35–53 (2007). https://doi.org/10.1016/j.entcs.2005.05.046
14. Hune, T., Romijn, J., Stoelinga, M., Vaandrager, F.W.: Linear parametric model checking of timed automata. JLAP **52–53**, 183–220 (2002). https://doi.org/10.1016/S1567-8326(02)00037-1
15. Jovanović, A., Lime, D., Roux, O.H.: Integer parameter synthesis for real-time systems. TSE **41**(5), 445–461 (2015). https://doi.org/10.1109/TSE.2014.2357445
16. Kocher, P.C.: Timing attacks on implementations of Diffie-Hellman, RSA, DSS, and other systems. In: Koblitz, N. (ed.) CRYPTO 1996. LNCS, vol. 1109, pp. 104–113. Springer, Heidelberg (1996). https://doi.org/10.1007/3-540-68697-5_9
17. Lv, M., Yi, W., Guan, N., Yu, G.: Combining abstract interpretation with model checking for timing analysis of multicore software. In: RTSS, pp. 339–349. IEEE Computer Society (2010). https://doi.org/10.1109/RTSS.2010.30
18. Nielson, F., Nielson, H.R., Vasilikos, P.: Information flow for timed automata. In: Aceto, L., Bacci, G., Bacci, G., Ingólfsdóttir, A., Legay, A., Mardare, R. (eds.) Models, Algorithms, Logics and Tools. LNCS, vol. 10460, pp. 3–21. Springer, Cham (2017). https://doi.org/10.1007/978-3-319-63121-9_1
19. Vasilikos, P., Nielson, F., Nielson, H.R.: Secure information release in timed automata. In: Bauer, L., Küsters, R. (eds.) POST 2018. LNCS, vol. 10804, pp. 28–52. Springer, Cham (2018). https://doi.org/10.1007/978-3-319-89722-6_2
20. Wang, C., Schaumont, P.: Security by compilation: an automated approach to comprehensive side-channel resistance. SIGLOG News **4**(2), 76–89 (2017). https://doi.org/10.1145/3090064.3090071
21. Wu, M., Guo, S., Schaumont, P., Wang, C.: Eliminating timing side-channel leaks using program repair. In: Tip, F., Bodden, E. (eds.) ISSTA, pp. 15–26. ACM (2018). https://doi.org/10.1145/3213846.3213851
22. Zhang, J., Gao, P., Song, F., Wang, C.: SCInfer: refinement-based verification of software countermeasures against side-channel attacks. In: Chockler, H., Weissenbacher, G. (eds.) CAV 2018. LNCS, vol. 10982, pp. 157–177. Springer, Cham (2018). https://doi.org/10.1007/978-3-319-96142-2_12

# Runtime Techniques

# Adaptive Online First-Order Monitoring

Joshua Schneider(✉), David Basin, Frederik Brix, Srđan Krstić(✉), and Dmitriy Traytel(✉)

Institute of Information Security,
Department of Computer Science,
ETH Zürich, Zurich, Switzerland
{joshua.schneider,srdan.krstic,
traytel}@inf.ethz.ch

**Abstract.** Online first-order monitoring is the task of detecting temporal patterns in streams of events carrying data. Considerable research has been devoted to scaling up monitoring using parallelization by partitioning events based on their data values and processing the partitions concurrently. To be effective, partitioning must account for the event stream's statistics, e.g., the relative event frequencies, and these statistics may change rapidly. We develop the first parallel online first-order monitor capable of adapting to such changes. A central problem we solve is how to manage and exchange states between the parallel executing monitors. To this end, we develop state exchange operations and prove their correctness. Moreover, we extend the implementation of the MonPoly monitoring tool with these operations, thereby supporting parallel adaptive monitoring, and show empirically that adaptation can yield up to a tenfold improvement in runtime.

## 1 Introduction

Online monitoring is a well-established runtime verification approach. System requirements are formalized as properties of an event stream that represents observations of a running system's behavior. An online monitor detects property violations in the event stream.

In practice, monitors must cope with high-volume and high-velocity event streams arising in large-scale applications. To meet these scalability demands, researchers have exploited parallel computing infrastructures [6, 11, 12, 15, 22–24], e.g., by splitting (or slicing) the event stream into smaller substreams that can be processed independently by monitors acting as black boxes. However, since monitoring is not an embarrassingly parallel task, slicing may need to duplicate events. Another performance bottleneck arises from slices with significantly more events than others. In prior work [24], we reduced duplication and distributed events evenly by leveraging insights from database research [1, 10]. We gave an algorithm that slices based on the event stream's characteristics, like the relative rates of event types or data values occurring disproportionately frequently in events. Provided the stream's characteristics are known and stable, this approach scales well.


Y.-F. Chen et al. (Eds.): ATVA 2019, LNCS 11781, pp. 133–150, 2019.
https://doi.org/10.1007/978-3-030-31784-3_8

*Example 1.* Consider a (simplified) policy for a document management system: *a document must be updated to its latest revision before being sent to a user*. The event stream contains *update* events parameterized with a document ID and *send* events parametrized with a document ID and a user ID. The above policy relates *update* and *send* events with the same document ID value and specifies that the former must precede the latter.

Let us first assume that we observe many update events to different documents. Then it makes sense to split the event stream based on a partition of the document ID values. Each parallel monitor instance (*submonitor*) would receive *send* and *update* events with document ID values from one partition. However, such a slicing strategy would not yield balanced substreams if the event stream changes to consist exclusively of send events that all have the same document ID, e.g., 955; this may occur, for example, if this is an important document sent to many users. Only one submonitor will continue receiving events. To counter this suboptimal utilization, we would like to partition the user IDs instead of the document IDs. To continue outputting correct verdicts, the state of the submonitor that was previously responsible for the document ID 955 and thus was the only one to observe its update events in the past, must be transferred to all other submonitors.

The example illustrates that a slicing strategy based on outdated stream characteristics may lead to unbalanced substreams, degrading the monitor's performance. Hence, the slicing strategy used must be changed during monitoring to adapt to the stream's changing characteristics. Furthermore, this adaptation necessitates that the submonitors exchange parts of their state and thus can no longer be treated as black boxes.

*Contribution.* In this paper, we design, prove correct, implement, and evaluate state migration functionality for a monitor for properties expressed in the monitorable fragment of metric first-order temporal logic (MFOTL) [7]. This rich specification language (Sect. 2.1) can express complex dependencies between data values coming from different events in the stream.

We significantly extend an existing stream slicing framework (Sect. 2.2) with the ability to dynamically change the slicing strategy (Sect. 3). Moreover, we develop operations to migrate the state of a simplified MFOTL monitor (Sect. 4), modeled after the state-of-the-art monitor MonPoly [7,8]. Concretely, we provide two operations that together achieve the state exchange: split for splitting a monitor's state according to a new slicing strategy and merge for combining parts of the states coming from different submonitors. These operations are conceptually straightforward. For example, split partitions the monitor's state based on the data values it stores. However, the operations' interaction with the monitor's invariants is intricate. To establish correctness, we have mechanically checked our proofs using the Isabelle proof assistant. A separate paper reports on our related formal verification of the simplified MFOTL monitor [26], which we extend here. We have also extended MonPoly with implementations of split and merge and evaluated its performance with adaptive slicing strategies (Sect. 5). Our formalization and the evaluation are available online [25].

In summary, our main contributions are: (1) the development of an abstract framework for adaptive monitoring; (2) the design of state migration operations for an MFOTL monitor; and (3) the implementation and evaluation of state migration in MonPoly. Our evaluation shows how adaptivity can substantially improve monitoring performance and enable the monitoring of high-velocity event streams.

*Related Work.* Basin et al. [6] introduce the concept of slicing for MFOTL monitors. They provide composable operators that slice both data and time and support scalable monitoring on a MapReduce infrastructure. Another data-parallel approach is parametric trace slicing [22,23], which supports only a restricted form of quantification and focuses on expressiveness, rather than on scalability or performance. Other monitors [3,5,11,12,19] decompose the specification for task-parallel execution, which limits their scalability. In prior work [24], we generalized Basin et al.'s data slicing [6] and implemented it using the Apache Flink stream processing framework [2]. The above works are limited in that they consider a single static strategy only. We develop a mechanism that lifts this restriction for first-order monitoring, making it possible to react to changes in the event streams. Note that we do not tackle the orthogonal problems of deciding *when* to change the slicing strategy and finding the *best* strategy for a given stream. The former requires a state migration mechanism already in place, while the latter requires deciding MFOTL, since for an unsatifiable formula, the best strategy is to drop all events.

Stream processing systems implement generic operations on data streams. They achieve scalability by exploiting data parallelism. The Flux operator [27] redistributes values between two parallel stages of a data stream pipeline. It adaptively changes the routing if long-term imbalances are detected. This requires state migration for downstream operators whose state must be consistent with the incoming data. Flux specifies an abstract interface to extract and implant state partitions, which our splitting and merging functions implement for a concrete monitoring operator. Megaphone [16] is a refined mechanism for state migration in Timely Dataflow [21]. Unlike other approaches, it avoids stopping the execution and excessive data duplications during migration. The mechanism is generic, hence a viable low-level streaming abstraction for our work.

Other works study adaptive controllers for distributed stream processing. The scheduler by Aniello et al. [4] continuously optimizes a task topology based on CPU load and communication traffic measurements. The granularity of tasks is much coarser than the data parallelism in our slicing approach. The DS2 controller [17] performs dynamic scaling, i.e., it selects an optimal degree of parallelism, which is orthogonal to the question of *how* to parallelize a task such as monitoring. DS2 assumes that every event can be partitioned based on a single key, which is not the case for MFOTL monitoring. In the context of complex event processing, Mayer et al. [20] optimize the assignment of overlapping temporal windows to machines. Their controller must determine the target machine at the start of each window because windows cannot be migrated in their model. A generic algorithm for deciding when to trigger adaptation is described by Kolchinsky et al. [18].

The Squall engine [28] implements various parallel join operators on data streams, including the (hash-)hypercube scheme [1]. This scheme, which we have also applied to monitoring [24], yields an optimal slicing strategy for conjunctive database queries [10]. The theta join operator by Elseidy et al. [14] can migrate its state with minimal overhead and without blocking, but only at the cost of relaxing the state's consistency. In comparison to all of these other stream processing systems, our approach supports adaptation for a much more expressive specification language (MFOTL), albeit with a larger overhead.

| | | |
|---|---|---|
| $v, i \models r(t_1, \ldots, t_n)$ if $r(v(t_1), \ldots v(t_n)) \in D_i$ | | $v, i \models \exists x.\ \varphi$ if $v[x \mapsto z], i \models \varphi$ for some $z \in \mathbb{D}$ |
| $v, i \models t_1 \approx t_2$ | if $v(t_1) = v(t_2)$ | $v, i \models \bullet_I \varphi$ if $i > 0$, $\tau_i - \tau_{i-1} \in I$, and $v, i-1 \models \varphi$ |
| $v, i \models \neg\varphi$ | if $v, i \not\models \varphi$ | $v, i \models \bigcirc_I \varphi$ if $\tau_{i+1} - \tau_i \in I$ and $v, i+1 \models \varphi$ |
| $v, i \models \varphi \vee \psi$ | if $v, i \models \varphi$ or $v, i \models \psi$ | |
| $v, i \models \varphi\, \mathsf{S}_I\, \psi$ | if $v, j \models \psi$ for some $j \leq i$, $\tau_i - \tau_j \in I$, and $v, k \models \varphi$ for all $k$ with $j < k \leq i$ | |
| $v, i \models \varphi\, \mathsf{U}_I\, \psi$ | if $v, j \models \psi$ for some $j \geq i$, $\tau_j - \tau_i \in I$, and $v, k \models \varphi$ for all $k$ with $i \leq k < j$ | |

**Fig. 1.** Semantics of MFOTL

# 2 Preliminaries

We recap the syntax and semantics of metric first-order temporal logic (MFOTL) [7] and an approach to its parallel monitoring based on slicing event streams [24].

## 2.1 Metric First-Order Temporal Logic

We fix a set of *names* $\mathbb{E}$ and for simplicity assume a single infinite *domain* $\mathbb{D}$ of values. The names $r \in \mathbb{E}$ have associated arities $\iota(r) \in \mathbb{N}$. An *event* $r(d_1, \ldots, d_{\iota(r)})$ is an element of $\mathbb{E} \times \mathbb{D}^*$. We call $1, \ldots, \iota(r)$ the *attributes* of the name $r$. We further fix an infinite set $\mathbb{V}$ of variables, such that $\mathbb{V}$, $\mathbb{D}$, and $\mathbb{E}$ are pairwise disjoint. Let $\mathbb{I}$ be the set of nonempty intervals $[a,b) := \{x \in \mathbb{N} \mid a \leq x < b\}$, where $a \in \mathbb{N}$, $b \in \mathbb{N} \cup \{\infty\}$, and $a < b$. Formulas $\varphi$ are constructed inductively, where $t_i$, $r$, $x$, and $I$ range over $\mathbb{V} \cup \mathbb{D}$, $\mathbb{E}$, $\mathbb{V}$, and $\mathbb{I}$, respectively:

$$\varphi ::= r(t_1, \ldots, t_{\iota(r)}) \mid t_1 \approx t_2 \mid \neg\varphi \mid \varphi \vee \varphi \mid \exists x.\varphi \mid \bullet_I \varphi \mid \bigcirc_I \varphi \mid \varphi\, \mathsf{S}_I\, \varphi \mid \varphi\, \mathsf{U}_I\, \varphi.$$

Along with Boolean operators, MFOTL includes the metric past and future temporal operators $\bullet$ (*previous*), $\mathsf{S}$ (*since*), $\bigcirc$ (*next*), and $\mathsf{U}$ (*until*), which may be nested freely. We define other standard Boolean and temporal operators in terms of this minimal syntax: truth $\top := \exists x.\ x \approx x$, falsehood $\bot := \neg\top$, conjunction $\varphi \wedge \psi := \neg(\neg\varphi \vee \neg\psi)$, universal quantification $\forall x.\ \varphi := \neg(\exists x.\ \neg\varphi)$, eventually $\Diamond_I \varphi := \top\, \mathsf{U}_I\, \varphi$, always $\Box_I \varphi := \neg\Diamond_I \neg\varphi$, once $\blacklozenge_I \varphi := \top\, \mathsf{S}_I\, \varphi$, and historically $\blacksquare_I \varphi := \neg\blacklozenge_I \neg\varphi$. Abusing notation, $\mathbb{V}_\varphi$ denotes the set of free variables of the formula $\varphi$. We restrict our attention to *bounded future formulas*, i.e., those in which all subformulas of the form $\bigcirc_{[a,b)}\, \alpha$ and $\alpha\, \mathsf{U}_{[a,b)}\, \beta$ satisfy $b < \infty$.

MFOTL formulas are interpreted over streams of time-stamped events. We group finite sets of events that happen concurrently (from the event source's point of view) into *databases* $\mathbb{DB} = \mathcal{P}(\mathbb{E} \times \mathbb{D}^*)$. An (*event*) *stream* $\rho$ is thus an infinite sequence $\langle \tau_i, D_i \rangle_{i \in \mathbb{N}}$ of databases $D_i \in \mathbb{DB}$ with associated time-stamps $\tau_i$. We assume discrete time-stamps, modeled as natural numbers $\tau \in \mathbb{N}$. We allow the event source to use a finer notion of time than the one used as time-stamps. In particular, databases at different indices $i \neq j$ may have the same time-stamp $\tau_i = \tau_j$. The sequence of time-stamps must be non-strictly increasing ($\forall i.\ \tau_i \leq \tau_{i+1}$) and always eventually strictly increasing ($\forall \tau.\ \exists i.\ \tau < \tau_i$).

The relation $v, i \models_\rho \varphi$ defines the satisfaction of the formula $\varphi$ for a valuation $v$ at an index $i$ with respect to the stream $\rho = \langle \tau_i, D_i \rangle_{i \in \mathbb{N}}$; see Fig. 1. Whenever $\rho$ is fixed and clear from the context, we omit the subscript on $\models$. The valuation $v$ is a mapping

$\mathbb{V} \to \mathbb{D}$, assigning domain elements to the free variables of $\varphi$. Overloading notation, $v$ is also the extension of $v$ to the domain $\mathbb{V} \cup \mathbb{D}$, setting $v(t) = t$ whenever $t \in \mathbb{D}$. We write $v[x \mapsto y]$ for the function equal to $v$, except that the argument $x$ is mapped to $y$.

An *online monitor* for a formula $\varphi$ receives time-stamped databases that incrementally extend a finite stream prefix $\pi$. It computes a stream of verdicts, i.e., the valuations and time-points that satisfy $\varphi$ given $\pi$. (Typically, one is interested in violations, but they can be obtained by monitoring the negated formula instead.) Formally, it implements a *monitor function* $\mathcal{M}_\varphi : (\mathbb{N} \times \mathbb{DB})^* \to \mathcal{P}((\mathbb{V} \to \mathbb{D}) \times \mathbb{N})$ that maps $\pi$ to the set of all verdicts output by the monitor after observing $\pi$. The monitor function must satisfy

$$\begin{aligned}
\text{Monotonicity: } & \forall \pi, \pi'.\, \pi \preceq \pi' \implies \mathcal{M}_\varphi(\pi) \subseteq \mathcal{M}_\varphi(\pi') \\
\text{Soundness: } & \forall \pi.\, \mathcal{M}_\varphi(\pi) \subseteq \{(v,i) \mid i \leq |\pi| \wedge \forall \rho \succeq \pi.\, v, i \models_\rho \varphi\} \\
\text{Completeness: } & \forall \pi, \rho, i.\, \pi \preceq \rho \wedge i \leq |\pi| \wedge (\forall \rho' \succeq \pi.\, v, i \models_{\rho'} \varphi) \implies \\
& \exists \pi' \preceq \rho.\, (v,i) \in \mathcal{M}_\varphi(\pi'),
\end{aligned}$$

where $\preceq$ denotes the prefix-of relation both between stream prefixes and between stream prefixes and infinite streams. Monotonicity prohibits the monitor from retracting its verdicts. Soundness requires it to only output satisfying valuations. Completeness forces the monitor to eventually output them. Monitor functions are not unique because we allow satisfactions to be emitted later than the point at which they become certain.

## 2.2 Slicing Framework

In prior work, we parallelized an online monitor by slicing the event stream into $N$ substreams that can be independently monitored [24]. For a fixed formula $\varphi$, their *(joint data) slicer* is parameterized by a *slicing strategy* $f : (\mathbb{V}_\varphi \to \mathbb{D}) \to (\mathcal{P}(\{1, \ldots, N\}) - \{\varnothing\})$, which specifies which of the $N$ submonitors are responsible for processing a given valuation. Thus, each submonitor indexed by $k \in \{1, \ldots, N\}$ is responsible for a subset $f[k] = \{v \mid k \in f(v)\}$ of $\varphi$'s valuations, called a *slice*. Because $f(v) \neq \varnothing$, for every valuation there is at least one slice responsible for it.

We focus on slicing strategies that consider each variable in $\mathbb{V}_\varphi$ separately. Assume that $N$ is a product $\prod_{x \in \mathbb{V}_\varphi} p_x$ of positive integers $p_x$. We say that the variable $x$ is sliced if $p_x > 1$. In this case, we must provide a partitioning function $f_x : \mathbb{D} \to \{1, \ldots, p_x\}$, e.g., a hash function. The resulting slicing strategy is $f(v) = \{q(\langle f_{x_1}(v(x_1)), \ldots, f_{x_n}(v(x_n))\rangle)\}$, where $q$ is a bijection between the Cartesian product $\prod_x \{1, \ldots, p_x\}$ and $\{1, \ldots, N\}$.

Which events must the submonitor $k$ receive? We assume that $\varphi$'s bound variables are disjoint from its free variables. Given an event $e = r(d_1, \ldots, d_n)$, matches$(\varphi, e)$ is the set of all valuations $v \in \mathbb{V}_\varphi \to \mathbb{D}$ for which there is a subformula $r(t_1, \ldots, t_n)$ in $\varphi$ where $v(t_i) = d_i$ for all $i \in \{1, \ldots, n\}$. For a database $D$ and a set of valuations $R$, called a *restriction*, we write $D \downarrow R$ for the *restricted* database $\{e \in D \mid \text{matches}(\varphi, e) \cap R \neq \varnothing\}$. The same notation restricts streams $\rho = \langle \tau_i, D_i \rangle_{i \in \mathbb{N}}$ pointwise, i.e., $\rho \downarrow R = \langle \tau_i, D_i \downarrow R \rangle_{i \in \mathbb{N}}$ (analogously for stream prefixes $\pi$). The submonitor $k$ receives the stream prefix $\pi \downarrow f[k]$.

The output of a single monitor after processing $\pi$ can be reconstructed from the submonitors' joint output: $\mathcal{M}_\varphi(\pi) = \bigcup_{k \in \{1, \ldots, N\}} (\mathcal{M}_\varphi(\pi \downarrow f[k]) \cap (f[k] \times \mathbb{N}))$. (In prior work [24], we established this fact assuming a stronger completeness property. However the weaker formulation used in this paper suffices.) The intersection with $f[k] \times \mathbb{N}$ is needed to avoid spurious verdicts for some formulas, notably those involving equality.

## 3 Adaptive Slicing

The slicing approach to scalable monitoring achieves good performance only if the events are distributed evenly and with minimal duplication [24]. Therefore, it is crucial to choose a good slicing strategy, which usually depends on the statistics of the events in the stream.

Consider the following extension of the Example 1. Documents now depend on resources, which may be modified over time. Any document $d$ sent out by the system must be based on the latest version of the resources it depends on. Events $dep(d,r)$ define dependencies between documents $d$ and resources $r$. We assume for simplicity that dependencies are never removed. An event $mod(r)$ indicates that the resource $r$ has been modified. The MFOTL formula corresponding to the negation of this policy is

$$send(d) \land (\blacklozenge dep(d,r)) \land \neg\big(\neg mod(r) \,\mathsf{S}\, (update(d) \land \blacklozenge dep(d,r))\big). \qquad (1)$$

Both variables $d$ and $r$ can be used for slicing. Some predicates do not refer to $r$ (e.g., $send(d)$), while $mod(r)$ does not refer to $d$. Therefore, any slicing strategy will result in some duplicated events. If documents are delivered much more frequently than resources are modified, it makes sense to slice only $d$. This would distribute the bulk of *send* events as much as possible, while having a negligible overhead due to duplicated *mod* events. In contrast, we should slice $r$ if modifications are much more frequent. Thus, the optimal strategy is influenced by the relative frequency of the different event types.

The optimal strategy can vary for different parts of the stream if statistics, like relative frequencies, change. Yet the existing slicing framework (Sect. 2.2) is parametrized by a fixed strategy. We propose a generalization where the strategy may change. In a setting with varying statistics, our generalization can lead to a substantially lower maximum load for the parallel monitors than what any fixed strategy can achieve. As an extreme case, consider a temporal separation between events pertaining to documents and resources in the above example. For instance, 1000 document deliveries might alternate with 1000 resource modifications. On average, both event types are equally likely. Hence, the strategy selected by the existing framework achieves a maximum load of around $1/\sqrt{N}$ for $N$ parallel monitors, e.g., 25% for $N = 16$. This strategy, based on the hypercube algorithm [1], hashes the value assigned by an event to one of the two variables into $\sqrt{N}$ buckets. Each bucket pair identifies a slice, and every event is replicated to all slices with a compatible bucket assignment. However, alternating between slicing one of the variables, according to which event is currently present, yields a maximum load of $1/N$ (6.25% for $N = 16$).

Unfortunately, adjusting the slicing strategy in the middle of a stream may result in incorrect verdicts. Monitors for temporal specifications keep state that depends on previously observed events. If the subset of events sent to a monitor instance changes, its state becomes inconsistent with respect to that subset. Continuing with the example, let there be two slices, $A$ and $B$. At time $t$, resource events are distributed by slicing

**Algorithm 1:** Adaptive monitor $\mathbf{A}(\mathbf{M}_\varphi)$

*initialization:* $i \leftarrow 0$; submonitor states $s_k \leftarrow s_\varphi^{\mathrm{init}}$ for all $k \in \{1,\ldots,N\}$
**for** every input $\langle\tau,D\rangle$ **do**
  **if** $f_{i+1} \neq f_i$ **then**
    *adaptation:*
    all submonitors $k'$ compute fragments $F_{k,k'} := \mathrm{split}(f_i[k'] \cap f_{i+1}[k], s_{k'})$ for all $k$
    all submonitors $k$ receive fragments $F_{k,k'}$ from all $k'$
    $s_k \leftarrow \mathrm{merge}(F_{k,1},\ldots,F_{k,N})$ for all $k$
  **end**
  *parallel monitoring:*
  compute slices $D_k := D \downarrow f_{i+1}[k]$ and send to $k$ for all $k$
  all submonitors $k$ perform a monitoring step $\langle X_k, s_k\rangle \leftarrow \mathbf{M}_\varphi(\langle\tau,D_k\rangle, s_k)$
  receive verdicts $X_k$ from all $k$ and output $\bigcup_k(X_k \cap (f_{i+1}[k] \times \mathbb{N}))$; $i \leftarrow i+1$
**end**

**Fig. 2.** High-level operation of the adaptive monitor

variable $r$, and in particular the event $mod(123)$ is routed to slice $A$. At time $t' > t$, the slicing strategy has changed to variable $d$. Now any delivery of a document $d$, where $d$ depends on resource 123 and is routed to slice $B$, will *not* be detected as a violation of the policy, i.e., as a satisfying valuation of the MFOTL formula (1).

There are two solutions to this problem. First, we could use the old and the new strategy in parallel, during a suitably sized interval around the adaptation point, as in temporal slicing [6]. The main drawback is that at least one of the strategies is suboptimal during the adaptation period, whose length has a lower bound that depends on the formula. Moreover, temporal slicing is ineffective if there are unbounded past temporal operators.

Second, we could instead migrate the parallel monitors' state. We shall proceed this way, taking measures to ensure the state's consistency with the updated slicing strategy. Upon strategy changes, each monitor instance first splits its state into fragments, each fragment corresponding to a slice of the new strategy. Then, the fragments of all monitors are reshuffled according to their destination slice, where they are merged. Splitting and merging must ensure that the resulting state is equivalent to one that would have been obtained if the new strategy had already been applied to the previously processed events.

Figure 2 shows the high-level control flow of our adaptive parallel monitor $\mathbf{A}(\mathbf{M}_\varphi)$. The algorithm is generic in that it wraps the actual monitor implementation $\mathbf{M}_\varphi$, which can be non-parallel. Parallelism is achieved by spawning $N$ instances of $\mathbf{M}_\varphi$ as independent submonitors. The variables $k$ and $k'$ range implicitly over the submonitors. $\mathbf{M}_\varphi$ refines the monitor function $\mathcal{M}_\varphi$ and makes its state explicit, which allows us to describe the adaptive functionality. We model $\mathbf{M}_\varphi$ as function mapping a pair consisting of a time-stamped database and the current state to a list of new verdicts and the successor state. The initial state is denoted $s_\varphi^{\mathrm{init}}$. We additionally require a *splitting function* $\mathrm{split}(R,s)$ and a *merging function* $\mathrm{merge}(s_1,s_2,\ldots)$. These are specific to the monitor implementation. The splitting function takes a restriction $R$ and a state $s$, and returns the state fragment corresponding to $R$. The associated merging function takes a nonempty, finite list of split states and combines them into a single state corresponding to the union of the restrictions.

The adaptive monitor $\mathbf{A}(\mathbf{M}_\varphi)$ is parametrized by an infinite sequence $\langle f_i \rangle_{i \in \mathbb{N}}$ of strategies. For every $i \geq 1$, $f_i$ defines the strategy for slicing the $i$-th input database. Initially, the strategy $f_0$ is used. Whenever the strategy changes between the $i$-th and the $(i+1)$-th input, i.e., $f_{i+1} \neq f_i$, adaptation occurs and each submonitor continues with a new state. Let $s_k$ be the state of submonitor $k \in \{1, \ldots, N\}$ right before adaptation. Its new state is

$$s'_k = \text{merge}(\text{split}(f_i[1] \cap f_{i+1}[k], s_1), \ldots, \text{split}(f_i[N] \cap f_{i+1}[k], s_N)).$$

We require some properties of $\mathcal{M}_\varphi$, $\mathbf{M}_\varphi$, split, and merge to show that $\mathbf{A}(\mathbf{M}_\varphi)$ has the same input–output behavior as $\mathcal{M}_\varphi$. The monitor function $\mathcal{M}_\varphi$ must be *slicable*: $\mathcal{M}_\varphi(\pi \downarrow R) \cap (R \times \mathbb{N}) = \mathcal{M}_\varphi(\pi) \cap (R \times \mathbb{N})$ for all $\pi$ and $R$. This implies that the verdicts for which a slice is responsible are detected at the exact same time points. The remaining properties are expressed in terms of a state invariant $W$. The intuitive meaning of $W(\pi, R, s)$ is that the state $s$ is consistent with prefix $\pi$ with respect to the valuations in $R$. Formally, $W$ is called a *monitoring invariant* if it satisfies the following conditions, where $\cdot$ concatenates a stream prefix and a time-stamped database:

1. $W(\varepsilon, R, s_\varphi^{\text{init}})$ for all $R$, where $\varepsilon$ denotes the empty prefix.
2. For all $\pi$, $R$, and $s$, $W(\pi, R, s)$ implies that the verdicts output by $\mathbf{M}_\varphi(\langle \tau, D \rangle, s)$ are equal to $\mathcal{M}_\varphi(\pi \cdot \langle \tau, D \rangle) - \mathcal{M}_\varphi(\pi)$ when both sets are intersected by $R \times \mathbb{N}$, and the successor state $s'$ satisfies $W(\pi \cdot \langle \tau, D \rangle, R, s')$.
3. For all $\pi$, $R_k$, $R'_k$, and $s_k$ (where $1 \leq k \leq N$), $R'_k \subseteq R_k$ and $W(\pi \downarrow R_k, R_k, s_k)$ for all $i \in \{1, \ldots, N\}$ imply $W(\pi \downarrow (\bigcup_k R'_k), \bigcup_k R'_k, \text{merge}(\text{split}(R'_1, s_1), \ldots, \text{split}(R'_N, s_N)))$.

**Lemma 1.** *The adaptive parallel monitor $\mathbf{A}(\mathbf{M}_\varphi)$ described above is functionally equivalent to $\mathcal{M}_\varphi$ if $\mathcal{M}_\varphi$ is slicable and there exists a monitoring invariant $W$.*

## 4 Monitor State Migration

The exact mechanism for state migration, which we need for adaptivity, depends on the monitor algorithm and the structure of its state. Here we provide a high-level account of a simplified version of the MonPoly algorithm with finite relations. Our presentation differs from the original description [7] by evaluating subformulas more eagerly. We also give the state an explicit representation. This allows us to define concrete splitting and merging operations. We verify the resulting adaptive monitor by proving the conditions outlined in Sect. 3.

We omit the past operators ● and S in this section and refer to our paper describing the algorithm in depth for more details [26]. Our machine-checked formalization [25] includes the algorithm for the full language with the split and merge operations.

### 4.1 Monitoring Algorithm

Like MonPoly, our simplified algorithm $\mathbf{M}_\varphi$ is restricted to a fragment of MFOTL for which all subformulas of $\varphi$ have finitely many satisfying valuations. We call a formula *monitorable* if negation is applied only to the right operand of $\wedge$ and to the left operand of $\mathsf{U}$, and $\mathbb{V}_\beta \subseteq \mathbb{V}_\alpha$ holds for all subformulas $\alpha \wedge \neg\beta$, $\mathbb{V}_\alpha = \mathbb{V}_\beta$ for subformulas $\alpha \vee \beta$, and $\mathbb{V}_\alpha \subseteq \mathbb{V}_\beta$ for subformulas $\alpha\, \mathsf{U}_I\, \beta$ and $\neg\alpha\, \mathsf{U}_I\, \beta$. Not all finitely satisfiable formulas are monitorable. In many practically relevant cases it is possible to obtain a monitorable formula that is equivalent to $\varphi$ [7]. For example, $\neg\beta \wedge \alpha$ can be rewritten to $\alpha \wedge \neg\beta$.

We present the monitor's *state* as an extension of the abstract syntax tree of the formula that it evaluates. We write a superscript after each operator to denote the state component associated with the operator. For example, $M_1 \wedge^Z M_2$ is a state corresponding to a formula $\alpha \wedge \beta$, where $M_1$ is the state for $\alpha$ (and $M_2$ for $\beta$), and $Z$ is the state component of the conjunction. In general, monitor states $M$ are constructed inductively as follows, where $\otimes \in \{\wedge, \wedge\neg, \vee\}$ and $\mathbb{U} \in \{\mathsf{U}, \neg\mathsf{U}\}$ are the monitorable operator–negation patterns.

$$M ::= r(t_1, \ldots, t_{\iota(r)}) \mid t \approx c \mid M \otimes^Z M \mid \exists x.M \mid \bigcirc_I^{(b,T)} M \mid M\, \mathbb{U}_I^{(Z,U,T)}\, M$$

The meta-variables have the following types ($X^*$ is the type of finite lists over $X$, and $\mathbf{R}$ is the type of relations, i.e., finite sets of finite tuples over $\mathbb{D}$):

$$r \in \mathbb{E},\ t_i \in \mathbb{V} \cup \mathbb{D},\ Z \in \mathbf{R}^* \times \mathbf{R}^*,\ I \in \mathbb{I},\ b \in \{\top, \bot\},\ T \in \mathbb{N}^*,\ U \in (\mathbb{N} \times \mathbf{R} \times \mathbf{R})^*.$$

The algorithm $\mathbf{M}_\varphi$ performs a bottom-up evaluation of the formula $\varphi$ for each incoming database of events. The result of evaluating a subformula $\psi$ is a list of finite relations over its free variables $\mathbb{V}_\psi$. These relations contain the valuations $v$ satisfying the subformula for increasing indices $i$, i.e., those $v$ with $v, i \models \psi$. We thus obtain the monitor's output, all $(v, i)$ with $v, i \models \varphi$, incrementally at the root $\varphi$. The evaluation of subformulas with future operators is delayed until the most recent time-stamp in the input has advanced by a sufficient lookahead, which is determined by the upper bound on the interval. Therefore, the result of evaluation is a list of relations: Several indices (or none) may be resolved at once if their lookahead has been reached (is still missing).

We choose to evaluate subformulas as much as possible with respect to the lookahead. All binary operators have a state component $Z = \langle z_1, z_2 \rangle$ that stores the results from one operand while the other is delayed. For example, if the left operand is three indices ahead, $z_1$ contains the corresponding three results and $z_2$ is empty. For temporal operators, the list $T$ stores the time-stamps of not yet evaluated indices. The flag $b$ marks whether $\bigcirc$ has been evaluated on the first index. The state component $U$ associated with a subformula $\alpha\, \mathbb{U}_I\, \beta$ is a list of triples $\langle \tau_i, R_i, R'_i \rangle$. It corresponds to a contiguous interval $i \in [n', n)$ of input indices, where $n'$ is the index of the next result to be computed for the subformula, and $n$ is the index of the next input to the monitor. The relation $R_i$ contains all valuations $v$ such that $v, k \models \alpha$ for all $k \in [i, n)$. The relation $R'_i$ contains all valuations $v$ for which there exists a $j \in [i, n)$ such that $\tau_j - \tau_i \in I$, $v, j \models \beta$, and $v, k \models \alpha$ (or $v, k \not\models \alpha$ in the negated case) for all $k \in [i, j)$. In the initial state, all lists $Z$, $T$, $U$ are empty, and $b$ is set to $\bot$.

We now describe how $\mathbf{M}_\varphi$ processes a new input $\langle \tau_n, D_n \rangle$. Evaluation of predicates and equalities is straightforward: A single relation is produced, and the state remains unchanged. For all other operators, the algorithm first evaluates and updates the substates recursively. For existential quantifiers $\exists x.M$, the recursively computed relations are projected onto $\mathbb{V}_M - \{x\}$. For the Boolean connectives in $\otimes$, the two lists of results

$r_1$, $r_2$ (which may be empty) are appended to the corresponding $z_1$, $z_2$ that were stored in the previous state, resulting in $z_1'$, $z_2'$. The first $\min\{|z_1'|,|z_2'|\}$ elements of each list are removed and combined pointwise into the result of the connective by applying standard relational operations: a natural join $\bowtie$ for $\wedge$, an antijoin $\triangleright$ for $\wedge\neg$, and a union for $\vee$. The state component $Z$ is updated to the remainder of the lists.

The state component $T$ of the temporal operators is maintained by appending $\tau_n$ and by removing a time-stamp from the front for every computed result. Evaluation of $\bigcirc_I$ discards the very first result of its operand, as indicated by $b$. Apart from this initialization, the operators forward the results, unless the corresponding time-stamp difference is not in the interval $I$. In this case, the result is replaced by the empty relation. The difference is computed using $T$. The state component $U = U_0$ of an operator $\mathbb{U}_{[a,b)}$ is updated as follows, where $z_1'$, $z_2'$, and $\ell = \min\{|z_1'|,|z_2'|\}$ are obtained as above. Let $A_k$, $B_k$, and $\tau_k'$ be the $k$-th element, $1 \le k \le \ell$, in $z_1'$, $z_2'$, and $T \cdot \tau_n$, respectively. For every $k$, $U_{k-1}$ is updated to obtain $U_k$, where $\langle \sigma_i, R_i, R_i' \rangle$ is the $i$-th tuple in $U_{k-1}$:

1. Replace every $R_i'$ by $R_i' \cup (B_k \bowtie R_i)$ (by $R_i' \cup (B_k \triangleright R_i)$ if the left operand is negated) if $\tau_k' - \sigma_i \in I$.
2. Replace every $R_i$ by $R_i \bowtie A_k$ (by $R_i \cup A_k$ if negated).
3. Append $\langle \tau_k', A_k, B_k \rangle$ if $0 \in I$. Otherwise, append $\langle \tau_k', A_k, \varnothing \rangle$.

We now consider the tuples $\langle \sigma_i, R_i, R_i' \rangle$ in $U_\ell$. Let $m$ be the largest index such that $\sigma_m + b < \tau_n$. The result of the operator is the list $\langle R_1', \ldots, R_m' \rangle$. The updated state component $U$ is $U_\ell$ without the first $m$ elements.

## 4.2 Splitting and Merging

MonPoly's state can be viewed as consisting of two parts. First, its *shape* comprises the arrangement of nodes in the abstract syntax tree, the lengths of the lists associated with the nodes, and the flags' and time-stamps' values. Second, the state has *content*, namely the relations stored in it. The key insight, which we use to define splitting and merging operations, is that the shape is independent of slicing, while the content has a direct interpretation in terms of MFOTL's semantics. We exploit the fact that the shape of the state is determined purely by the sequence of time-stamps observed by the submonitors. Note that slicing has no effect on this sequence. Therefore, the states of all submonitors at a given point in time have identical shapes. In contrast, we have $v, i \models_{\rho\downarrow R} \varphi$ iff $v, i \models_\rho \varphi$ for all $v \in R$, which is the property that allows data slicing in the first place (see the proof of [24, Prop. 1]). The inclusion of a valuation in the content associated with the submonitor for $R$ thus depends only on the full stream $\rho$ (if that valuation can be extended to some $v \in R$). We can reorganize the state's content to reflect updated restrictions $R$ by distributing valuations according to their consistency with $R$.

The splitting function for MonPoly's state is shown in Fig. 3. We use standard functional operators on lists, in particular map and zip. The splitting function is applied recursively to all parts of the state while preserving its shape. We overload it for the different state components. Only the relations in the state are affected by splitting. The operation keeps all valuations that are consistent with the restriction $R$, which we represent as a predicate function $P$ (the first argument of split). There are two reasons for

$$\text{split}(P,M) = \begin{cases} \text{split}(P,M_1) \otimes^{\text{split}(P,Z)} \text{split}(P,M_2) & \text{if } M = M_1 \otimes^Z M_2 \\ \exists x.\, \text{split}(\text{lift}(P,x),M_1) & \text{if } M = \exists x.M_1 \\ \bigcirc_I^{(b,T)} \text{split}(P,M_1) & \text{if } M = \bigcirc_I^{(b,T)} M_1 \\ \text{split}(P,M_1)\, \mathbb{U}_I^{(\text{split}(P,Z),\text{split}(P,U),T)}\, \text{split}(P,M_2) & \text{if } M = M_1 \,\mathbb{U}_I^{(Z,U,T)}\, M_2 \\ M & \text{otherwise.} \end{cases}$$

$$\text{split}(P,\langle z_1,z_2\rangle) = (\text{map}(\lambda X.\,\text{split}(P,X),z_1),\text{map}(\lambda X.\,\text{split}(P,X),z_2))$$
$$\text{split}(P,U) = \text{map}(\lambda\langle\tau,A,B\rangle.\langle\tau,\text{split}(P,A),\text{split}(P,B)\rangle,U)$$
$$\text{split}(P,X) = \{x \in X \mid P(x)\}$$

**Fig. 3.** Splitting operations for MonPoly's state

this modified representation. First, restrictions are usually infinite sets and so they cannot be passed explicitly in an implementation. Second, the finite relations stored in the monitor's state cover only a subset of the formula's free variables, possibly extended by bound variables. For example, consider the state $A(x,y) \wedge^{Z_1} (B(x)\, \mathsf{U}^{(Z_2,U,T)}\, C(x))$. The relations in the list $U$ are unary because they assign values to $x$ only. A valuation $(x \mapsto a)$ contained in such a relation is compatible with a restriction $R$ iff there exists a valuation $v \in R$ with $v(x) = a$. This generalizes in the obvious way to relations of higher arity. Thus $P$ must be true for a valuation iff it is compatible with $R$. We can always define such a $P$ in theory, but an implementation will provide a specialized function for the specific slicing strategies that it uses. The lift functional lifts a predicate function $P$ to a context with a bound variable $x$. Therefore, $\text{lift}(P,x)(v)$ is true iff $P$ is true for $v$ with $x$ removed from its domain.

The merge function $\text{merge}(s_1,s_2,\dots)$ combines the list of states by repeatedly applying a binary merge in arbitrary order. The binary merge function $\text{mrg}_2$ is shown in Fig. 4. Here, $\text{map2}(f,A,B)$ abbreviates $\text{map}(f,\text{zip}(A,B))$. We assume that the two inputs to $\text{mrg}_2$ have the same shape. Some parts of the state, like the time-stamp lists $T$, can thus be merged by simply taking the value from either state. This works because the shape is not affected by slicing, as we have argued before. Relations are merged by taking their union. This makes sense intuitively because the desired effect of $\text{mrg}_2$ and merge is to be consistent with the union of the states' restrictions.

**Theorem 1.** *There exists a slicable monitor function $\mathcal{M}_\varphi$ with a corresponding monitoring invariant for the functions $\mathbf{M}_\varphi$,* split, *and* merge *described in this section.*

We prove the existence of the invariant in our formalization [25]. Together with Lemma 1, which has also been formally verified, we obtain the correctness of the adaptive monitor.

**Corollary 1.** *The adaptive parallel monitor $\mathbf{A}(\mathbf{M}_\varphi)$ constructed from $\mathbf{M}_\varphi$,* split, *and* merge *is functionally equivalent to the monitor function $\mathcal{M}_\varphi$.*

$$\mathrm{mrg}_2(M_a,M_b) = \begin{cases} \mathrm{mrg}_2(M_{1a},M_{1b}) \otimes^{\mathrm{mrg}_2(Z_a,Z_b)} \mathrm{mrg}_2(M_{2a},M_{2b}) & \text{if } M_i = M_{1i} \otimes^{Z_i} M_{2i} \\ \exists x.\, \mathrm{mrg}_2(M_{1a},M_{1b}) & \text{if } M_i = \exists x. M_{1i} \\ \bigcirc_I^{(b_a,T_a)} \mathrm{mrg}_2(M_{1a},M_{1b}) & \text{if } M_i = \bigcirc_I^{(b_i,T_i)} M_{1i} \\ \mathrm{mrg}_2(M_{1a},M_{1b})\, \mathbb{U}_I^{(\mathrm{mrg}_2(Z_a,Z_b),\mathrm{mrg}_2(U_a,U_b),T_a)} \mathrm{mrg}_2(M_{2a},M_{2b}) & \text{if } M_i = M_{1i}\, \mathbb{U}_I^{(Z_i,U_i,T_i)} M_{2i} \\ M_a & \text{otherwise.} \end{cases}$$

$$\mathrm{mrg}_2(\langle z_{1a}, z_{2a}\rangle, \langle z_{1b}, z_{2b}\rangle) = \langle \mathrm{map2}(\cup, z_{1a}, z_{1b}), \mathrm{map2}(\cup, z_{2a}, z_{2b})\rangle$$

$$\mathrm{mrg}_2(U_a,U_b) = \mathrm{map2}(\lambda \langle \tau_a, A_a, B_a\rangle, \langle \tau_b, A_b, B_b\rangle. \langle \tau_a, A_a \cup A_b, B_a \cup B_b\rangle, U_a, U_b)$$

**Fig. 4.** Binary merging operations for MonPoly's state

## 5 Implementation and Evaluation

We have extended the MonPoly monitoring tool [8] with the state split and merge functionalities, adding about 960 lines of OCaml. The source code is available online [25]. Note that MonPoly implements optimizations that are beyond the scope of this paper. Specifically, subformula evaluation is less eager [7], with binary operators evaluating the right subformula only when the left subformula can be evaluated. MonPoly treats subformulas of the form $\Diamond_I \varphi$ and $\blacklozenge_I \varphi$ in a special way by greedily reusing intermediate computations of the (associative) union in a sliding window bounded by the interval $I$ [9]. Also, MonPoly filters out events and time points with no events when they do not influence the monitor's output [6]. Still, our implementation takes all of these optimizations into account, with the exception of the empty time-point filtering, which we leave as future work.

We have also extended our online slicing framework [24] to enable dynamic changes to the slicing strategy. The extended framework can synchronously redistribute the parallel submonitors' states. The redistribution consists of splitting the states of all submonitors and forwarding the splits to the appropriate monitors before all of them resume monitoring. The framework uses Apache Flink [2] to achieve low latency stream processing with fault tolerance. However, we directly invoke the monitors on prepared files for the purpose of this evaluation, due to Flink's limited state migration capabilities.

We have validated our approach and evaluated the performance of our implementation by answering the following research questions:

*RQ1:* Does dynamically adapting the splitting strategy improve the performance?
*RQ2:* How scalable is the adaptive monitoring with respect to the stream event rate and the degree of parallelism, i.e., the number of submonitors?
*RQ3:* How much overhead is incurred by a single adaptation?

To answer the above questions we designed a parametric testbed for measuring the performance of both non-adaptive and adaptive monitoring [25]. For $n$ adaptation steps, the testbed takes a list of $n+1$ stream statistics and creates an event stream that consists of $n+1$ parts, each conforming to the respective statistics. Given an input formula, the testbed performs two monitoring runs: a *non-adaptive run*, which uses a slicing

$$\begin{aligned}
star &= ((\blacklozenge_{[0,10\mathrm{s})} P(a,b)) \wedge Q(a,c)) \wedge \Diamond_{[0,10\mathrm{s})} R(a,d) \\
linear &= ((\blacklozenge_{[0,10\mathrm{s})} P(a,b)) \wedge Q(b,c)) \wedge \Diamond_{[0,10\mathrm{s})} R(c,d) \\
triangle &= ((\blacklozenge_{[0,10\mathrm{s})} P(a,b)) \wedge Q(b,c)) \wedge \Diamond_{[0,10\mathrm{s})} R(c,a)
\end{aligned}$$

**Fig. 5.** MFOTL formulas (after negation) used in the evaluation

strategy optimized [24] for the first part of the stream to monitor the entire stream, and an *adaptive run*, which uses stream statistics for each part of the stream to construct a sequence of optimized slicing strategies. Each part of the stream is sliced according the appropriate slicing strategy. The number of slices is equal to the degree of parallelism, which is configurable. Alternatively, we could consider the entire stream's aggregate statistics to compute a strategy for the non-adaptive run. However, we believe that our setup is more suitable for comparing the two online monitoring approaches, whereas the alternative assumes complete knowledge of the stream—a trait often associated with offline monitoring.

We fix the number of adaptations $n$ to one. Hence, we define two stream statistics for the corresponding parts of the streams. We focus our evaluation on single adaptations in order to properly isolate and measure the effects of specific changes in the stream statistics on the monitoring performance. While having multiple adaptation steps is certainly more realistic, this would not contribute to answering our research questions as the results would be harder to interpret and the space of possible stream statistics would be much larger. When monitoring a formula containing future subformulas, the monitor often needs to establish a lookahead. During this process, the monitor exhibits better performance as it performs simple updates to its state without outputting any verdicts. To prevent this behavior from effecting our measurements, we add an additional prefix to our streams as a warmup, generated with identical statistics as the stream's first part.

We monitor the three formulas shown in Fig. 5 (named *star*, *linear*, and *triangle*) over streams with different event rates and stream statistics. The different variable patterns in the formulas cover common patterns in database queries [10], which we additionally extend with temporal operators. Given a stream $\rho = \langle \tau_i, D_i \rangle_{i \in \mathbb{N}}$, its *event rate* at time $\tau$ is the total number of events in one time unit, i.e., $|\{e \in D_i \mid \tau = \tau_i\}|$. *Stream statistics* consist of *relative relation rates* (i.e., the fraction of events in a time unit with a certain name) and *heavy hitter values* (i.e., event attribute values that occur frequently).

We implemented a stream generator that takes a random seed and stream statistics, and synthesizes a random stream that conforms to the supplied statistics. Specifically, it produces streams containing events with the names $P, Q$, and $R$. The event rate and the rate of verdicts is configurable. Each of the three events has two integer attributes. The generator can also synthesize streams with configurable relative relation rates and force some event attribute values to be heavy hitters. Attribute values are sampled with two possible distribution types. Infrequent values are drawn from the uniform distribution over the set $\{0, 1, \ldots, 10^9 - 1\}$. Heavy hitter values are drawn from a Zipf distribution that can be defined per variable. Its probability mass function is $p(x) = (x-s)^{-z} / \sum_{n=1}^{10^9} n^{-z}$ for $x \in \{s+1, s+2, \ldots, s+10^9\}$, i.e., the larger the exponent $z > 0$ is, the fewer values in the variable valuation have a large relative frequency.

| | stream statistics for part 2 | description | event rate for formula *star* | *linear* | *triangle* |
|---|---|---|---|---|---|
| S1 | $r_P = 0.01, r_Q = r_R = 0.495$ | reduce relation rate for *P* | 2500 | 1300 | 1300 |
| S2 | $r_P = r_Q = 0.495, r_R = 0.01$ | reduce relation rate for *R* | 2500 | 1300 | 1300 |
| S3 | $r_P = r_Q = 0.01, r_R = 0.98$ | reduce relation rates for *P* and *Q* | 2500 | 1300 | 1300 |
| S4 | $d_a$ = Zipf, $z_a = 10$, $s_a = 1000$ | add a single heavy hitter value | 75 | 1300 | 1300 |
| S5 | default | remove a single heavy hitter value | 75 | 1300 | 1300 |
| S6 | $d_a$ = Zipf, $z_a = 10$, $s_a = 2000$ | change the heavy hitter value | 75 | 1300 | 1300 |
| S7 | $d_a$ = Zipf, $z_a = 2$, $s_a = 1000$ | add more heavy hitter values | 75 | 1300 | 1300 |
| S8 | $d_c$ = Zipf, $z_c = 10$, $s_c = 1000$ | change the heavy hitter variable | 75 | 400 | 700 |
| S9 | $d_a = d_c$ = Zipf, $z_a = z_c = 10$, $s_a = s_c = 1000$ | add more heavy hitter variables | 75 | 700 | 700 |

**Fig. 6.** Stream statistics used in our experiments (omitted parameters have default values)

The parameter $s$ is the start value, which can also be configured to control the specific heavy hitter values. We call variables with heavy hitter values *heavy hitter variables*. To prevent excessive monitor output, all Zipf-distributed values of $R$ events are shifted (i.e., increased by $10^6$), whereas events that cause the monitor to output a verdict have their values always drawn uniformly.

Figure 6 summarizes the stream statistics (in terms of the parameters supplied to the stream generator) used in our experiments. The total time span of each stream across all parts is 1000 s. The parameters $r_P, r_Q$, and $r_R$ are the relative relation rates for relations $P, Q$, and $R$, respectively, each with the default value $1/3$. The parameters $d_a$, $d_b$, and $d_c$ are the distribution types for values occurring in valuations of the variables $a$, $b$, and $c$ respectively. Values are distributed uniformly by default. For a Zipf-distributed variable $x$, $z_x$ and $s_x$ define its Zipf exponent and the starting value. We distinguish between nine representative changes in the stream statistics, labelled S1–S9 in the leftmost column in Fig. 6. For S1–S4, all parameters assume default values in the streams' first part. For S5–S9, the first part is generated using the default parameters, except that $d_a =$ Zipf, $z_a = 10$, $s_a = 1000$. The second column shows the parameters for the second part. The third column describes the change informally. Such changes of the stream statistics can have a large impact on a monitor's performance. For example, the monitoring time can differ in orders of magnitude between the two stream parts generated by S4. This is due to the size of the intermediate results that the monitor computes for the subformulas. Their size can grow significantly if a heavy hitter is added (consider the satisfying valuations of $(\blacklozenge_{[0,10s)} P(a,b)) \wedge Q(a,c)$ when $a$ is a heavy hitter variable). To overcome this problem, we have chosen the event rates such that it takes at most 25 s to monitor each slice. We searched and sampled monitoring times for event rates between 10 and 6000 events per second. The chosen event rates are summarized in the last three columns of Fig. 6.

We measured the execution time for monitoring each slice of each stream part and each run, as well as the time to split and merge states during the adaptive run. Each run is repeated three times and the measurements are averaged. Our experiments were executed on a machine with an Intel Core i5-7200U CPU running at 2.5 GHz, with 8 GB RAM. We monitored all slices sequentially, such that only one thread was active at any time.

Figure 7 summarizes the results of our evaluation using the parameters from Fig. 6. We compare the execution times between the two types of monitoring runs (non-

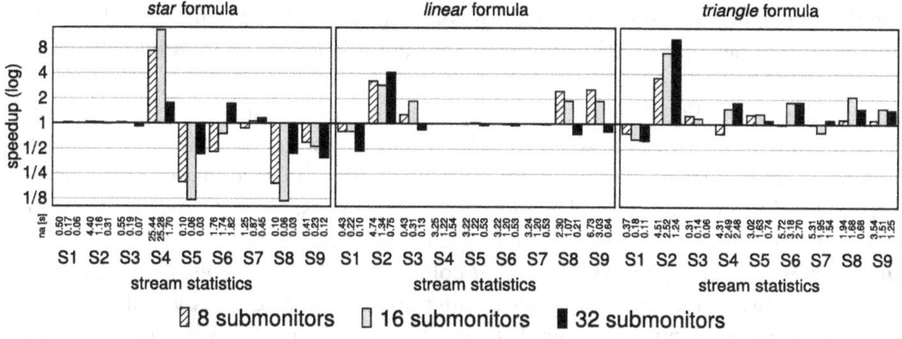


**Fig. 7.** Observed speedup (the ratio of the non-adaptive and the corresponding adaptive monitoring times) for different stream statistics, number of submonitors, and formulas

| event | *star* formula | | | | *linear* formula | | | | *triangle* formula | | | |
|---|---|---|---|---|---|---|---|---|---|---|---|---|
| rate | na [s] | ad [s] | na/ad | ohd | na [s] | ad [s] | na/ad | ohd | na [s] | ad [s] | na/ad | ohd |
| 1000 | 0.75 | 0.72 | **1.04** | 1.5% | 2.86 | 0.89 | **3.22** | 5.4% | 2.77 | 0.73 | **3.78** | 6.3% |
| 2000 | 2.82 | 2.79 | **1.01** | 2.1% | 11.05 | 3.38 | **3.27** | 3.9% | 10.63 | 2.83 | **3.76** | 2.2% |
| 4000 | 10.80 | 10.85 | 0.99 | 1.9% | 44.80 | 14.04 | **3.19** | 1.8% | 41.97 | 11.13 | **3.77** | 2.0% |
| 6000 | 24.23 | 24.39 | 0.99 | 1.0% | 111.90 | 30.75 | **3.64** | 1.1% | 94.83 | 26.45 | **3.59** | 1.5% |

**Fig. 8.** Observed **speedup** or slowdown (na/ad) and overhead (ohd) for different event rates and formulas when monitoring streams with statistics S2 using 8 submonitors

adaptive and adaptive) on the last part (part 2) of the event stream, where the slicing strategies differ. We consider the maximum time across all slices for each run. The bars show the observed speedup, i.e., the ratio of the time taken by the non-adaptive and the corresponding adaptive monitoring run. The non-adaptive time in seconds is given below each bar. To answer RQ1, note that monitoring the *star* formula does not benefit from the adaptation in most cases. This is due to its particular structure: The common variable $a$ is the most efficient choice for slicing, independently of the relation rates (S1–S3). However, if any of $a$'s valuations becomes a heavy hitter, the slices are no longer balanced and adaptivity helps (S4). In our non-adaptive runs with S4, the increased monitoring time when using 8 and 16 submonitors is due to a single slice accidentally receiving both the heavy hitter value and its shifted counterpart for $R$ events. If a heavy hitter value is removed (S5, S6, S8), all slices in the adaptive run are monitored efficiently except for one that receives the first part's state associated with the heavy hitter. As this information is still relevant up to 10 s after the statistics change (due to the temporal subformulas' intervals), the corresponding monitor has a significantly larger workload, which causes the slowdown. This could be avoided by taking the formula's intervals into account to delay the adaptation by an appropriate amount of time.

In general, adaptation helps when monitoring the *linear* and *triangle* formulas. We obtained the largest consistent speedups for S2 (between 3.5 and 10.3 times for *triangle*). Here, the reduction of the slices' event rates due to the adaptation is reflected by the reduced execution time. Adapting to heavy hitters is often beneficial for those formulas, too. The slowdown observed for some numbers of submonitors is due to the impossibility to decompose these numbers into optimal factors, e.g., 8 into an integer square root [24].

Regarding RQ2, Fig. 8 shows that higher event rates increase the benefit of adaptation if the stream statistics allow for a better strategy to be used in the first place. The columns *na* and *ad* show the maximum monitoring time (in seconds) of part 2 across all slices for the non-adaptive and adaptive monitoring runs, respectively. The measurement in the *ad* column includes the time taken to split and merge the state. The *na/ad* column shows the speedup, while the *ohd* column shows the overhead. The overhead is the ratio between the time spent performing non-monitoring tasks and the adaptive monitoring time, each summed over all slices. Non-monitoring tasks include state splitting and merging, as well as the time the submonitors would need to wait before all state fragments are available to be merged. Since we monitor the slices sequentially in our experiments, we estimate the wait time as the time difference until the last submonitor has finished splitting its state. The adaptation overhead ranges from 1% to 6% in our experiments with S2, and it decreases with the event rate (RQ3). However, the overhead can be as large as 700% in some of the other experiments from Fig. 7 (*star* formula, S5 and S8). This is generally the result of imbalanced substreams. Thus, some submonitors in a parallel implementation would be forced to wait, for which we account in the overhead calculation.

## 6 Conclusion

We have laid the foundations of adaptive online monitoring by demonstrating how to implement the core functionality required: the state exchange between the parallel monitors. The state exchange consists of two operations, split and merge, which we prove to interact correctly with a simplified MFOTL monitor. We also implement them in a realistic monitor and demonstrate empirically that adapting to changing statistics is beneficial.

As ongoing work, we are extending our operations to support MonPoly's empty time-point filtering, which significantly improves performance, especially in combination with slicing. Because the monitors for the different slices may skip events at different time-points, their state structures may diverge, which complicates merging.

We have also performed initial experiments using our adaptive version of MonPoly within our Apache Flink-based parallel monitor [24]. While this setup works in principle, its performance is suboptimal, due to limitations of Flink. For example, Flink only allows exchanging parts of the state by sending all states to all monitors and only then performing the split operations locally. This incurs a large latency, and another stream-processing framework might be better suited for our needs. Timely Dataflow [21], with its recent extension to low-latency state migrations [16] is a promising candidate.

Finally, important questions that we have not studied in this paper are how to collect the necessary statistics and at which points to trigger adaptivity. While classic sketching algorithms [13] offer partial answers to the first question, answering the second one requires a realistic cost model to precisely calculate when adaptivity pays off.

**Acknowledgment.** Christian Fania helped us implement and evaluate our adaptive monitoring framework. The anonymous reviewers gave numerous helpful comments on earlier drafts of this paper. Joshua Schneider is supported by the US Air Force grant "Monitoring at Any Cost" (FA9550-17-1-0306). Srđan Krstić is supported by the Swiss National Science Foundation grant "Big Data Monitoring" (167162).

## References

1. Afrati, F.N., Ullman, J.D.: Optimizing multiway joins in a map-reduce environment. IEEE Trans. Knowl. Data Eng. **23**(9), 1282–1298 (2011)
2. Alexandrov, A., et al.: The Stratosphere platform for big data analytics. VLDB J. **23**(6), 939–964 (2014)
3. Alur, R., Mamouras, K., Stanford, C.: Modular quantitative monitoring. PACMPL **3**(POPL), 50:1–50:31 (2019)
4. Aniello, L., Baldoni, R., Querzoni, L.: Adaptive online scheduling in Storm. In: DEBS 2013, pp. 207–218. ACM (2013)
5. Barre, B., Klein, M., Soucy-Boivin, M., Ollivier, P.-A., Hallé, S.: MapReduce for parallel trace validation of LTL properties. In: Qadeer, S., Tasiran, S. (eds.) RV 2012. LNCS, vol. 7687, pp. 184–198. Springer, Heidelberg (2013). https://doi.org/10.1007/978-3-642-35632-2_20
6. Basin, D., Caronni, G., Ereth, S., Harvan, M., Klaedtke, F., Mantel, H.: Scalable offline monitoring of temporal specifications. Form. Methods Syst. Des. **49**(1–2), 75–108 (2016)
7. Basin, D., Klaedtke, F., Müller, S., Zălinescu, E.: Monitoring metric first-order temporal properties. J. ACM **62**(2), 15:1–15:45 (2015)
8. Basin, D., Klaedtke, F., Zălinescu, E.: The MonPoly monitoring tool. In: Reger, G., Havelund, K. (eds.) RV-CuBES 2017. Kalpa Publications in Computing, vol. 3, pp. 19–28. EasyChair (2017)
9. Basin, D., Klaedtke, F., Zălinescu, E.: Greedily computing associative aggregations on sliding windows. Inf. Process. Lett. **115**(2), 186–192 (2015)
10. Beame, P., Koutris, P., Suciu, D.: Communication steps for parallel query processing. J. ACM **64**(6), 40:1–40:58 (2017)
11. Bersani, M.M., Bianculli, D., Ghezzi, C., Krstić, S., Pietro, P.S.: Efficient large-scale trace checking using MapReduce. In: Dillon, L.K., Visser, W., Williams, L. (eds.) ICSE 2016. pp. 888–898. ACM (2016)
12. Bianculli, D., Ghezzi, C., Krstić, S.: Trace checking of metric temporal logic with aggregating modalities using MapReduce. In: Giannakopoulou, D., Salaün, G. (eds.) SEFM 2014. LNCS, vol. 8702, pp. 144–158. Springer, Cham (2014). https://doi.org/10.1007/978-3-319-10431-7_11
13. Cormode, G., Garofalakis, M.N., Haas, P.J., Jermaine, C.: Synopses for massive data: samples, histograms, wavelets, sketches. Found. Trends Databases **4**(1–3), 1–294 (2012)
14. Elseidy, M., Elguindy, A., Vitorovic, A., Koch, C.: Scalable and adaptive online joins. PVLDB **7**(6), 441–452 (2014)
15. Hallé, S., Soucy-Boivin, M.: MapReduce for parallel trace validation of LTL properties. J. Cloud Comput. **4**(1), 8 (2015)
16. Hoffmann, M., Lattuada, A., McSherry, F., Kalavri, V., Liagouris, J., Roscoe, T.: Megaphone: latency-conscious state migration for distributed streaming dataflows. PVLDB **12**(9), 1002–1015 (2019)

17. Kalavri, V., Liagouris, J., Hoffmann, M., Dimitrova, D.C., Forshaw, M., Roscoe, T.: Three steps is all you need: fast, accurate, automatic scaling decisions for distributed streaming dataflows. In: Arpaci-Dusseau, A.C., Voelker, G. (eds.) OSDI 2018, pp. 783–798. USENIX Association (2018)
18. Kolchinsky, I., Schuster, A.: Efficient adaptive detection of complex event patterns. PVLDB **11**(11), 1346–1359 (2018)
19. Mamouras, K., Raghothaman, M., Alur, R., Ives, Z.G., Khanna, S.: StreamQRE: modular specification and efficient evaluation of quantitative queries over streaming data. In: Cohen, A., Vechev, M.T. (eds.) PLDI 2017, pp. 693–708. ACM (2017)
20. Mayer, R., Tariq, M.A., Rothermel, K.: Minimizing communication overhead in window-based parallel complex event processing. In: DEBS 2017, pp. 54–65. ACM (2017)
21. Murray, D.G., McSherry, F., Isaacs, R., Isard, M., Barham, P., Abadi, M.: Naiad: a timely dataflow system. In: Kaminsky, M., Dahlin, M. (eds.) SOSP 2013, pp. 439–455. ACM (2013)
22. Reger, G., Rydeheard, D.: From first-order temporal logic to parametric trace slicing. In: Bartocci, E., Majumdar, R. (eds.) RV 2015. LNCS, vol. 9333, pp. 216–232. Springer, Cham (2015). https://doi.org/10.1007/978-3-319-23820-3_14
23. Roşu, G., Chen, F.: Semantics and algorithms for parametric monitoring. Log. Methods Comput. Sci. **8**(1:9), 1–47 (2012)
24. Schneider, J., Basin, D., Brix, F., Krstić, S., Traytel, D.: Scalable online first-order monitoring. In: Colombo, C., Leucker, M. (eds.) RV 2018. LNCS, vol. 11237, pp. 353–371. Springer, Cham (2018). https://doi.org/10.1007/978-3-030-03769-7_20
25. Schneider, J., Basin, D., Brix, F., Krstić, S., Traytel, D.: Artifact associated with this paper (2019). https://bitbucket.org/jshs/monpoly/downloads/aom_atva2019.zip
26. Schneider, J., Basin, D., Krstić, S., Traytel, D.: A formally verified monitor for metric first-order temporal logic. In: Finkbeiner, B., Mariani, L. (eds.) RV 2019. LNCS, Springer (2019, to appear). http://people.inf.ethz.ch/trayteld/papers/rv19-verimon/verimon.pdf
27. Shah, M.A., Hellerstein, J.M., Chandrasekaran, S., Franklin, M.J.: Flux: an adaptive partitioning operator for continuous query systems. In: Dayal, U., Ramamritham, K., Vijayaraman, T.M. (eds.) ICDE 2003, pp. 25–36. IEEE (2003)
28. Vitorovic, A., et al.: Squall: Scalable real-time analytics. PVLDB **9**(13), 1553–1556 (2016)

# Multi-head Monitoring of Metric Temporal Logic

Martin Raszyk(✉), David Basin, Srđan Krstić, and Dmitriy Traytel(✉)

Institute of Information Security,
Department of Computer Science, ETH Zürich,
Zurich, Switzerland
{martin.raszyk,traytel}@inf.ethz.ch

**Abstract.** We present a novel approach to the offline monitoring of specifications expressed in metric temporal logic (MTL). Our monitoring algorithm exploits multiple one-way reading heads that traverse a trace sequentially. We present both theoretical and practical results that show this substantially improves upon the state-of-the-art. In particular, our algorithm is the first offline monitoring algorithm for MTL with past and bounded-future temporal operators that is almost trace-length independent and outputs a trace of Boolean verdicts denoting the monitored formula's satisfaction at every position in the input trace. In addition, our algorithm's worst-case space complexity is linear in the formula size, while previous algorithms were exponential. Moreover, we compare our implementation of the algorithm with another almost trace-length independent tool that outputs non-standard verdicts to achieve this space complexity. Our tool used less memory and runs significantly faster, for example yielding a 10-fold improvement on average on random formulas, while producing better output.

## 1 Introduction

Monitoring (or runtime verification) is the process of verifying system properties by analyzing system events against a specification formalizing which event sequences constitute the intended system behavior. Monitoring algorithms (or monitors) can be classified based on how they interact with the monitored system [11]. A core distinction is *when* the events are monitored. *Online monitors* process events at runtime, as they occur during system execution. Whereas *offline monitors* process them after the system has stopped running. Offline monitors are often seen as special cases of their online counterparts. Indeed, most monitoring algorithms are created independently of whether they will be used online or offline: they process one event at a time, in order of appearance.

There is however an important distinction between the two classes of monitors. Online monitors sequentially analyze a potentially unbounded stream of events and, due to the nature of streams, each event can be read only once. If an event is needed for subsequent analysis, an online monitor must keep it in


Y.-F. Chen et al. (Eds.): ATVA 2019, LNCS 11781, pp. 151–170, 2019.
https://doi.org/10.1007/978-3-030-31784-3_9

memory. An online monitor's computation can be viewed as reading the stream with a single one-way reading head that moves forward only, updating the monitor's state, and producing output. Offline monitors, in contrast, analyze finite sequences of events, called traces, typically stored in files. An offline monitor is thus equipped with a reading head without movement constraints. Indeed, offline monitors may, effectively, have multiple heads (corresponding to indices in the trace) that read from multiple locations simultaneously. We note though that there are good reasons to process events in order, even in offline monitoring. First, the raw performance of sequential reads outperforms random access reads due to prefetching and other low-level file system and hardware specifics [15]. Second, we can delete parts of the trace processed by all reading heads and append new events at the end, and thus, effectively emulate online monitoring. Hence, we will exploit the multiple heads, not the ability to read in both directions.

Our thesis in this paper is that by exploiting multiple (but finitely many) one-way reading heads that traverse a trace in order (Sect. 3), offline monitoring differs from, and improves upon, online monitoring. The ability to read each input multiple (but finitely many) times allows us to obtain strictly better complexity results. We establish this result for monitoring specifications expressed in metric temporal logic (MTL) [19] (Sect. 2). Moreover, we obtain the first offline almost trace-length independent [3] monitoring algorithm for MTL with past and bounded-future that outputs a trace of Boolean verdicts denoting the formula's satisfaction at every position in the input trace. Here, "almost" denotes a logarithmic dependence of the monitor's space complexity on the trace's length, stemming from the need to store the length in binary representation.

Our main contributions are: (i) a multi-head monitoring algorithm for MTL (Sect. 4); (ii) its correctness and complexity analysis (Sect. 5); and (iii) an implementation (available at [20]) and evaluation (Sect. 6). Both our complexity analysis and evaluation show significant improvements over the state-of-the-art.

*Related Work.* An MTL formula's satisfaction is defined (Sect. 2) with respect to a position in a trace, which is an infinite word. A monitor takes as input a finite prefix of this trace. Monitoring is sometimes understood as the task of computing a *single Boolean verdict* denoting whether the formula is satisfied at the first position in the trace. For such monitors, there exist trace-length independent algorithms [8, 13, 17, 24]. These are algorithms whose space complexity is independent of the length of the finite prefix. This property is highly desirable because it distinguishes the monitors that can handle large traces from those that cannot. In contrast, we consider monitors that output *entire traces* of Boolean verdicts. That is, rather than outputting that a trace violates a formula, the monitor outputs every position where such a violation occurs. This output provides more insight into why and when the property was violated. There are trace-length independent algorithms for past-only LTL based on dynamic programming [16] and Thati and Roşu's interval-shifting [24] allows one to extend these results to past-only MTL.

$(\rho, i) \models p$ iff $p \in \Gamma_i$
$(\rho, i) \models \neg\varphi$ iff $(\rho, i) \not\models \varphi$
$(\rho, i) \models \varphi_1 \vee \varphi_2$ iff $(\rho, i) \models \varphi_1$ or $(\rho, i) \models \varphi_2$
$(\rho, i) \models \bullet_I \varphi$ iff $i > 0$ and $\tau_i - \tau_{i-1} \in I$ and $(\rho, i-1) \models \varphi$
$(\rho, i) \models \bigcirc_I \varphi$ iff $\tau_{i+1} - \tau_i \in I$ and $(\rho, i+1) \models \varphi$
$(\rho, i) \models \varphi_1 \mathsf{S}_I \varphi_2$ iff $(\rho, j) \models \varphi_2$ for some $j \leq i$ with $\tau_i - \tau_j \in I$ and $(\rho, k) \models \varphi_1$ for all $j < k \leq i$
$(\rho, i) \models \varphi_1 \mathsf{U}_J \varphi_2$ iff $(\rho, j) \models \varphi_2$ for some $j \geq i$ with $\tau_j - \tau_i \in J$ and $(\rho, k) \models \varphi_1$ for all $i \leq k < j$

**Fig. 1.** Semantics of an MTL formula for a stream $\rho = \langle(\tau_i, \Gamma_i)\rangle_{i \in \mathbb{N}}$ and a time-point $i$

Roşu and Havelund [22] develop a dual trace-length independent dynamic programming offline monitor for future-only LTL that traverses the trace backwards. Their idea is generalized by Sanchez [23], who proposes to alternate forward and backward traversals in the context of stream runtime verification [9,12,14], pioneered by Lola [10]. He claims to obtain trace-length independence for well-formed Lola specifications, which can express LTL with past and future. However, his complexity analysis appears to gloss over intermediate streams, which are as large as the input trace and store the results of backward passes to be reused in later forward passes. For LTL, this corresponds to assuming that verdicts for subformulas are available to evaluate a temporal formula, e.g., an until formula, without counting the memory used to store this information.

Basin et al. [2] develop almost trace-length independent algorithms for MTL (in fact, *almost event-rate independent*, which is a stronger property that is desirable for online monitoring) with past and future temporal operators. To achieve almost trace-length independence, they mix non-standard equivalence verdicts with standard Boolean ones. Equivalences can be resolved to Boolean verdicts but this (trace-length dependent) task is offloaded to the monitor's user. Our algorithm outputs standard Boolean verdicts and is almost trace-length independent. Moreover, their algorithm's space complexity is doubly exponential in the formula size, whereas ours is linear (Sect. 5.2).

In an independent line of work, we show how multiple reading heads can be leveraged to eliminate non-determinism from functional finite-state transducers [21].

## 2 Metric Temporal Logic

We recap the discrete-time point-based semantics of metric temporal logic (MTL) and refer to Basin et al. [6] for a comprehensive comparison with other semantics.

Let $\mathbb{T} = \mathbb{N}$ be the set of time-stamps, $\mathbb{I}_{\mathit{fin}}$ the set of non-empty finite intervals over $\mathbb{T}$, and $\mathbb{I}_\infty$ the set of infinite intervals over $\mathbb{T}$. We write elements of $\mathbb{I}_{\mathit{fin}}$ as $[l, r]$, where $l, r \in \mathbb{T}$, $l \leq r$, and $[l, r] = \{x \in \mathbb{T} \mid l \leq x \leq r\}$. Similarly, elements of $\mathbb{I}_\infty$ are written $[l, \infty]$ and denote $\{x \in \mathbb{T} \mid l \leq x\}$. Let $\mathbb{I} = \mathbb{I}_{\mathit{fin}} \cup \mathbb{I}_\infty$ be the set of all (non-empty) intervals over $\mathbb{T}$.

MTL formulas over a finite set of atomic predicates $P \neq \varnothing$ are defined inductively:

$$\varphi = p \mid \neg\varphi \mid \varphi_1 \vee \varphi_2 \mid \bullet_I \varphi \mid \bigcirc_I \varphi \mid \varphi_1 \mathsf{S}_I \varphi_2 \mid \varphi_1 \mathsf{U}_J \varphi_2,$$

where $p \in P$, $I \in \mathbb{I}$, and $J \in \mathbb{I}_{fin}$. This minimal syntax includes Boolean operators and the temporal operators (*previous*) $\bullet_I$, (*since*) $\mathsf{S}_I$, (*next*) $\bigcirc_I$, and (*until*) $\mathsf{U}_J$. We employ the usual syntactic sugar for additional Boolean constants and operators $true = p \vee \neg p$, $false = \neg true$, $\varphi \wedge \psi = \neg(\neg\varphi \vee \neg\psi)$, and temporal operators (*once*) $\blacklozenge_I\varphi = true\ \mathsf{S}_I\ \varphi$, (*historically*) $\blacksquare_I\varphi = \neg\blacklozenge_I\neg\varphi$, (*eventually*) $\Diamond_J\varphi = true\ \mathsf{U}_J\ \varphi$, and (*always*) $\Box_J\varphi = \neg\Diamond_J\neg\varphi$.

MTL formulas are interpreted over *streams*, which are infinite sequences of events. An event has the form $(\tau_i, \Gamma_i)$, where the time-stamp $\tau_i \in \mathbb{T}$ is a non-negative integer and $\Gamma_i \subseteq P$ is a subset of atomic predicates. We denote the set of events by $\mathbb{E} = \mathbb{T} \times 2^P$. We further assume that the sequence of time-stamps $\langle\tau_i\rangle_{i\in\mathbb{N}}$ is monotonically (non-strictly) increasing, i.e., $\tau_i \leq \tau_{i+1}$, for all $i \in \mathbb{N}$, and *unbounded*, i.e., for every $\tau \in \mathbb{T}$, there is an index (time-point) $i \in \mathbb{N}$ such that $\tau_i \geq \tau$. A finite prefix $\rho_{\leq i} = \rho_0 \ldots \rho_i$ of an event stream $\rho$ is called a *trace*. Figure 1 shows the standard semantics of MTL formulas.

We define $reach([l, r]) = r$ if $r < \infty$, and $reach([l, r]) = l - 1$ otherwise. For the $\mathsf{S}_I$ operator (and analogously for the $\mathsf{U}_J$ operator), $reach(I)$ is the maximum value $\tau_i - \tau_j$ (see Fig. 1) that our monitor stores during its evaluation. We define the set $\mathsf{SF}(\varphi)$ of all formula $\varphi$'s subformulas as usual (including $\varphi$) and the *size* $|\varphi| = |\mathsf{SF}(\varphi)|$. We define the formula $\varphi$'s *temporal size* $\|\varphi\|$ to be the sum of $|\varphi|$ and $reach(I)$ for all intervals $I$ in $\varphi$.

## 3 Multi-head Monitoring

The computation of an online monitor on an infinite event stream can be viewed as reading the stream with a *single* head moving forwards only (i.e., a *one-way* reading head), updating the monitor's state, and optionally producing an output, i.e., some verdicts. A multi-head monitor extends an online monitor with *multiple* one-way reading heads.

**Definition 1.** *A* multi-head monitor *is a tuple $M = (P, V, \kappa, Q, q_0, \delta)$, where $P$ is a non-empty finite set of atomic predicates, $V$ is a verdict alphabet, $\kappa \in \mathbb{N}$ is the number of one-way (reading) heads, $Q$ is a set of states, $q_0 \in Q$ is an initial state, and $\delta : Q \times \mathbb{E}^\kappa \to Q \times \{0, 1\}^\kappa \times (V \cup \{\bot\})$ is a step function that maps a state and the events read by the heads to a new state, offsets that indicate which heads to advance, and an optional verdict.*

This computational model in principle allows for an infinite set of states, which may seem unreasonable in practice. Rather than a priori restricting the model, we provide a space bound for our multi-head monitoring algorithm in Sect. 5 (Theorem 3).

The *configuration* of a multi-head monitor $M$ consists of the current state and the reading heads' positions. Formally, the set of configurations is $\mathbb{C} = Q \times \mathbb{N}^\kappa$.

Let $\rho[\overline{p}] \in \mathbb{E}^\kappa$ denote the events read from the stream $\rho$ by the heads positioned at $\overline{p} \in \mathbb{N}^\kappa$. The *computation* on a stream $\rho$ is an infinite sequence of configurations $\langle(q_i, \overline{p}^i)\rangle_{i\in\mathbb{N}}$ that starts with the initial configuration $(q_0, \overline{0})$ and in which any two consecutive configurations $(q_i, \overline{p}^i)$, $(q_{i+1}, \overline{p}^{i+1})$ satisfy $\delta(q_i, \rho[\overline{p}^i]) = (q_{i+1}, \overline{p}^{i+1} - \overline{p}^i, v_i')$, for some $v_i' \in V \cup \{\bot\}$. Finally, the *output* of a computation on a stream is the concatenation of the verdicts $v_i' \neq \bot$, i.e., a (potentially empty) sequence $\langle v_i\rangle_{i<n}$, with $v_i \in V$ and $n \in \mathbb{N} \cup \{\infty\}$.

For the remainder of this paper, let $V = \mathbb{T} \times \mathbb{B}$ be the verdict alphabet, that is, a verdict $v = (t, b)$ is a Boolean value $b \in \mathbb{B} = \{\mathsf{tt}, \mathsf{ff}\}$ time-stamped by $t \in \mathbb{T}$. Note that, with this choice of $V$, the step function returns at most one time-stamped Boolean verdict at a time, which simplifies the algorithm's presentation and complexity analysis.

An output $\langle(t_k, b_k)\rangle_{k<n}$ of a computation on a stream $\rho$ is *sound* with respect to an MTL formula $\Phi$ if and only if the time-stamps $t_k$ correspond to the time-stamps on the prefix $\rho_{<n}$ and the Boolean values $b_k$ reflect the formula's semantics at the time-points $k$. Formally, the output $\langle(t_k, b_k)\rangle_{k<n}$ of the computation on a stream $\rho = \langle(\tau_i, \Gamma_i)\rangle_{i\in\mathbb{N}}$ is sound if and only if the following predicate $\mathsf{SOUND}_\Phi(\rho, \langle(t_k, b_k)\rangle_{k<n})$ holds:

$$\mathsf{SOUND}_\Phi(\rho, \langle(t_k, b_k)\rangle_{k<n}) \equiv \forall k.\ k < n \rightarrow (\tau_k = t_k \wedge ((\rho, k) \models \Phi \Longleftrightarrow b_k)).$$

In the subsequent text, we use $[m]_0$ for the set $\{0, \ldots, m\}$, and $[m]$ for the set $\{1, \ldots, m\}$.

## 4 Multi-head Monitoring of Metric Temporal Logic

We structure our multi-head monitor for a given formula $\Phi$ into two procedures. The first, recursive procedure follows $\Phi$'s structure (Sect. 4.1). In doing so, it recursively runs a separate multi-head monitor instance for each direct subformula of $\Phi$. The procedure may invoke the step function of an instance multiple times until a verdict is produced. This may be necessary when future subformulas are monitored. The verdicts already produced by other instances are cached. Once every instance has produced a verdict, the second procedure is invoked. It combines the verdicts for $\Phi$'s direct subformulas into a verdict for $\Phi$ based on the semantics of $\Phi$'s top-level operator (Sect. 4.2).

In general, a monitor running many multi-head (sub)monitors is itself a multi-head monitor, inheriting reading heads from its submonitors. All such reading heads can move independently and asynchronously. In our monitor, the number of reading heads for a formula $\Phi$ equals the number of atomic subformulas in $\Phi$.

*Example 1.* Consider the formula $\Phi = (a\ \mathsf{S}_{[0,4]}\ b) \vee (a\ \mathsf{U}_{[0,4]}\ b)$, which has four atomic subformulas corresponding to two occurrences of each of $a$ and $b$. Figure 2 shows the monitor's structure as well as a snapshot of the four reading heads' positions while monitoring a trace. The reading heads are depicted as the gray triangles. In the current snapshot, the monitor for $\Phi$ has just produced a verdict

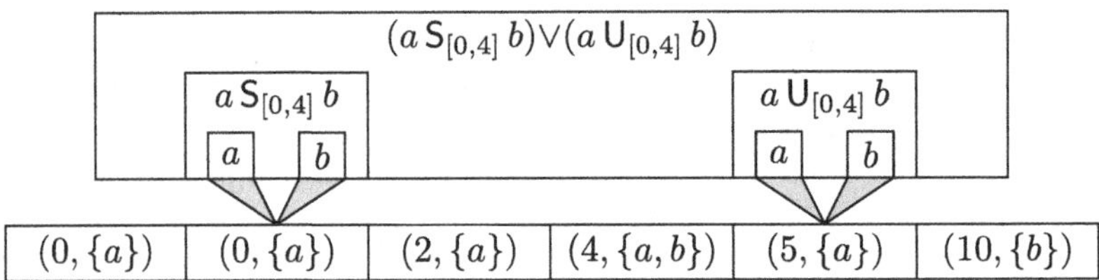


**Fig. 2.** Multi-head monitor's structure

for the first position. To do so, it needed the two corresponding verdicts for its two direct subformulas $a\ \mathsf{S}_{[0,4]}\ b$ and $a\ \mathsf{U}_{[0,4]}\ b$. The submonitor for $a\ \mathsf{S}_{[0,4]}\ b$ could deliver the verdict after reading the first position (and then advancing its heads to the second position). In contrast, the submonitor for $a\ \mathsf{U}_{[0,4]}\ b$ could only produce a verdict for the first position in this trace after reading the fourth position (and then advancing its heads to the fifth position).

### 4.1 First Procedure: Recursively Running the Multi-head Monitors

To formally construct our multi-head monitor for an MTL formula $\Phi$ over a finite set of atomic predicates $P^{\Phi}$, we perform a case distinction on the structure of $\Phi$.

*Atomic Predicate.* Let $\Phi = p$, where $p \in P^{\Phi}$. The monitor checks whether $p$ is included in an event. For this, a single reading head suffices and no state is needed. Formally, $\kappa^{\Phi} = 1$, $Q^{\Phi} = \{\bot\}$, and $q_0^{\Phi} = \bot$. The step function is $\delta^{\Phi}(\bot, (\tau, \Gamma)) = (\bot, 1, (\tau, p \in \Gamma))$.

*Recursive Formula.* Let the top-level operator of $\Phi$ be $\mathsf{op}$, where $\mathsf{op} \in \{\neg/1, \vee/2, \bullet_I/1, \bigcirc_I/1, \mathsf{S}_I/2, \mathsf{U}_J/2\}$ and the number next to an operator $\mathsf{op}$ denotes its arity $\eta(\mathsf{op})$. For $i \in [\eta(\mathsf{op})]$, let $\varphi_i$ be a direct subformula of $\Phi$ and $M^{\varphi_i} = (P^{\varphi_i}, V, \kappa^{\varphi_i}, Q^{\varphi_i}, q_0^{\varphi_i}, \delta^{\varphi_i})$ be its multi-head monitor, which we construct recursively.

At this point, we abstract the operator evaluation procedure (Sect. 4.2). Specifically, we assume that each operator $\mathsf{op}$ comes with a set of states $C^{\mathsf{op}}$, an initial state $c_0^{\mathsf{op}}$, and a step function $s^{\mathsf{op}} : C^{\mathsf{op}} \times \mathbb{T} \times \mathbb{B}^{\eta(\mathsf{op})} \to C^{\mathsf{op}} \times V^*$. The step function is applied to a state, a time-stamp, and a tuple of Boolean values coming from the recursive invocations of the submonitors. It returns the new state and a list of verdicts.

Evaluating the operator $\mathsf{op}$ does not require any reading heads. Thus the number of heads $\kappa^{\Phi}$ of $M^{\Phi}$ is the sum of the numbers of heads $\kappa^{\varphi_i}$ of $M^{\varphi_i}$ for all $\Phi$'s direct subformulas $\varphi_i$. In particular, for each $M^{\varphi_i}$, there is a subset of $M^{\Phi}$'s heads belonging to $M^{\varphi_i}$.

Figure 3 shows our multi-head monitor $M^{\Phi}$ for the formula $\Phi$. Its state, $(qs, bs, c^{\mathsf{op}}, vs)$, stores a tuple $qs$ whose $i$-th component is a submonitor's state

$\delta^{\Phi} : Q^{\Phi} \times \mathbb{E}^{\kappa^{\Phi}} \to Q^{\Phi} \times \{0,1\}^{\kappa^{\Phi}} \times (V \cup \{\bot\})$
1 $\delta^{\Phi}((qs, bs, c^{\mathsf{op}}, vs), es) =$ **match** $vs$ **do**
2 **case** $v \cdot vs' \Rightarrow$ **return** $((qs, bs, c^{\mathsf{op}}, vs'), \bar{0}, v)$
3 **case** $\varepsilon \Rightarrow$
4 let $i$ be the smallest index such that $bs[i] = \bot$
5 let $es^i$ be the events from $es$ read by heads belonging to $M^{\varphi_i}$
6 $(q^{\varphi_i}, ms^i, v) := \delta^{\varphi_i}(q^{\varphi_i}, es^i)$
7 **match** $v$ **do**
8 **case** $(\tau, b) \Rightarrow bs[i] := b$
9 **if** $i = \eta(\mathsf{op})$ **then** $(c^{\mathsf{op}}, vs) := s^{\mathsf{op}}(c^{\mathsf{op}}, \tau, bs)$
10 $bs := \overline{\bot}$ **fi**
11 **case** $\bot \Rightarrow$ **od**
12 let $ms$ extend offsets $ms^i$ (from $M^{\varphi_i}$) with zero offsets (from $M^{\varphi_j}$, $j \neq i$)
13 **return** $((qs, bs, c^{\mathsf{op}}, vs), ms, \bot)$ **od**

**Fig. 3.** Recursive monitor

$q^{\varphi_i}$ and a tuple $bs$ of optional Boolean values that cache the latest unprocessed verdict produced by $M^{\varphi_i}$. Moreover, the state of $M^{\Phi}$ stores a state $c^{\mathsf{op}}$ for evaluating the operator $\mathsf{op}$ as well as a list $vs$ of time-stamped Boolean verdicts produced by evaluating the operator $\mathsf{op}$, but not yet output. As long as $vs$ is non-empty, the monitor outputs verdicts from it (line 2). Otherwise, the monitor repeatedly triggers its submonitors to produce a verdict (lines 3–13). Note that a submonitor does not need to produce a verdict upon each evaluation of its step function (line 7). Once $M^{\Phi}$ knows the Boolean verdicts for all subformulas, it can apply the operator-specific computation (line 9), which may return some new verdicts $vs$ for $\Phi$. Afterwards, it resets $bs$ to eventually continue the subformulas' evaluation.

The initial state of $M^{\Phi}$ consists of a tuple $qs$, whose $i$-th component is $q_0^{\varphi_i}$, a tuple $bs$ consisting of $\bot$, the initial state $c_0^{\mathsf{op}}$ for evaluating the operator $\mathsf{op}$, and an empty list $\varepsilon$ of time-stamped Boolean verdicts.

### 4.2 Second Procedure: Evaluating a Top-Level Operator

We describe how to evaluate each individual MTL operator by defining its set of states $C^{\mathsf{op}}$, initial state $c_0^{\mathsf{op}}$, and the step function $s^{\mathsf{op}} : C^{\mathsf{op}} \times \mathbb{T} \times \mathbb{B}^{\eta(\mathsf{op})} \to C^{\mathsf{op}} \times V^*$.

*Negation and Disjunction.* For Boolean operators $\mathsf{op} \in \{\neg, \vee\}$, no state is needed and the step function simply combines its Boolean inputs. We have $C^{\mathsf{op}} = \{\bot\}$, $c_0^{\mathsf{op}} = \bot$, and

$$s^{\neg}(\bot, \tau, b) = (\bot, (\tau, \neg b)),$$
$$s^{\vee}(\bot, \tau, b_1, b_2) = (\bot, (\tau, b_1 \vee b_2)).$$

*Previous and Next.* For $\mathsf{op} = \bullet_I$, the state stores the time-stamped Boolean value, denoting the operator's subformula's satisfaction at a previous time-point, if the current time-point is not the initial time-point. The state for $\mathsf{op} = \bigcirc_I$ is the same, only that no Boolean value is stored. More formally, $C^{\bullet_I} = (\mathbb{T} \times \mathbb{B}) \cup \{\bot\}$ and $C^{\bigcirc_I} = \mathbb{T} \cup \{\bot\}$. The initial state is $c_0^{\mathsf{op}} = \bot$ in both cases. For $\bullet_I$, the step function propagates the stored Boolean value to its output if the time-stamp constraints given by $I$ are satisfied. For $\bigcirc_I$, the step function also checks the constraints. If the check passes, it outputs the given Boolean input denoting the satisfaction of the operator's subformula at the current time-point as the verdict for the previous time-point (whose time-stamp is stored in $c^{\bigcirc_I}$). The initial state must be treated specially in both cases. Formally, the step function is defined as follows:

$$s^{\bullet_I}(c, \tau, b) = \begin{cases} ((\tau, b), (\tau, b' \wedge (\tau - \tau' \in I))) & \text{if } c = (\tau', b'), \\ ((\tau, b), (\tau, \mathsf{ff})) & \text{if } c = \bot, \end{cases}$$

$$s^{\bigcirc_I}(c, \tau, b) = \begin{cases} (\tau, (\tau', b \wedge (\tau - \tau' \in I))) & \text{if } c = \tau', \\ (\tau, \varepsilon) & \text{if } c = \bot. \end{cases}$$

*Since and Until.* These temporal operators are more complex. For the since operator, the state keeps a history of *satisfaction witnesses* that correspond to the time-points $j$ in the MTL semantics of the since operator for the operator's satisfaction at the current time-point $i$ (Fig. 1). For the until operator, the state keeps a history of *satisfaction candidates* that correspond to the time-points $i$, for which a future time-point could become the time-point $j$ in the MTL semantics of the until operator (Fig. 1). Instead of storing the time-points explicitly, we represent them by a list of zeros interleaved with (positive) time-stamp differences between the successive time-points. For example, consider the case where the monitor for the since operator has processed the following eight time-points $j$ with the time-stamps $\tau_j$ and the corresponding Boolean values $b_1^j$ and $b_2^j$.

| $j$ | 0 | 1 | 2 | 3 | 4 | 5 | 6 | 7 |
|---|---|---|---|---|---|---|---|---|
| $\tau_j$ | 4 | 8 | 10 | 10 | 11 | 11 | 11 | 14 |
| $b_1^j$ | tt | tt | tt | tt | tt | tt | tt | tt |
| $b_2^j$ | tt | ff | tt | tt | tt | ff | ff | ff |

The satisfaction witnesses here are the time-points 0, 2, 3, 4, marked in gray above. Our history represents them with the list [0, 4, 2, 0, 0, 1, 0, 3], where every zero corresponds to a satisfaction witness and the other numbers show only the *non-zero* time-stamp differences between the successive time-points. Note that the history can be obtained from the list of all time-stamp differences [4, 2, 0, 1, 0, 0, 3] by dropping all zero time-stamp differences [4, 2, 1, 3] and then inserting a zero for each satisfaction witness at the corresponding position [0, 4, 2, 0, 0, 1, 0, 3]. Crucially for our space complexity analysis, we store such lists using a *run-length encoding*, where we compress subsequences $\tau, \ldots, \tau$ to the pair $(\tau, n)$, where $n$ is length of the subsequence. We use a shorthand notation for run-length encoded lists, e.g. writing $0420^2103$ for the above list.

The state stores also the time-stamp (and, for the since operator, the Boolean value, too, similarly to $\bullet_I$) at a previous time-point, if the current time-point

```
s^S[l,r] : C^S[l,r] × 𝕋 × 𝔹² → C^S[l,r] × V*
1  s^S[l,r]((v, ts), τ, b1, b2) = match v do
2    case (τ',b) ⇒ β := b
3                  if τ' < τ ∧ ts ≠ ε then
4                     ts := ts · (τ − τ') fi
5    case ⊥ ⇒ β := ff od
6    (_, ts) := SPLIT(ts, λs. s ≤ r)
7    if ¬b1 then ts := ε
8                β := ff fi
9    if b2 then ts := ts · 0 fi
10   if r < ∞ then
11     β := (ts ≠ ε ∧ SUM(ts) ≥ l)
12   else
13     (ds, ts) := SPLIT(ts, λs. s < l)
14     if ds ≠ ε then β := tt fi fi
15   return (((τ, β), ts), (τ, β))
```

```
s^U[l,r] : C^U[l,r] × 𝕋 × 𝔹² → C^U[l,r] × V*
1  s^U[l,r]((t, ts), τ, b1, b2) = match t do
2    case τ' ⇒ if τ' < τ ∧ ts ≠ ε then
3                 ts := ts · (τ − τ') fi
4    case ⊥ ⇒ od
5    vs := ε
6    (ds, ts) := SPLIT(ts, λs. s ≤ r)
7    vs := vs · RES(ds, τ − SUM(ts), ff)
8    ts := ts · 0
9    if b2 then
10     (ds, ts) := SPLIT(ts, λs. s < l)
11     vs := vs · RES(ds, τ − SUM(ts), tt) fi
12   if ¬b1 then
13     vs := vs · RES(ts, τ, ff)
14     ts := ε fi
15   return ((τ, ts), vs)
```

**Fig. 4.** Step functions for $\mathsf{S}_{[l,r]}$ and $\mathsf{U}_{[l,r]}$

is not the initial time-point. Formally, $C^{\mathsf{S}_I} = ((\mathbb{T} \times \mathbb{B}) \cup \{\bot\}) \times \mathbb{T}^*$ and $C^{\mathsf{U}_J} = (\mathbb{T} \cup \{\bot\}) \times \mathbb{T}^*$. The initial state is $c_0^{\mathsf{op}} = (\bot, \varepsilon)$ for both operators.

To define the step functions, we first define the following operations on the lists of time-stamp differences. $\mathsf{SUM}(ts)$ is the sum of all time-stamp differences in the list $ts$. For a predicate $\pi$ on $\mathbb{T}$, $\mathsf{SPLIT}(ts, \pi) = (ts_1, ts_2)$ partitions the list $ts$ into two lists $ts_1$ and $ts_2$, such that the list $ts_1$ is as short as possible and the list $ts_2$ is either empty or starts with a zero and its sum $\mathsf{SUM}(ts_2)$ satisfies the predicate $\pi$.

Formally, we evaluate the since and until operators on a stream $\sigma = \langle(\tau_i, \overline{b}_1^i, \overline{b}_2^i)\rangle_{i \in \mathbb{N}}$, where $\overline{b}_1$ and $\overline{b}_2$ are the streams of Boolean values incrementally received by the operator's step function. After processing the time-point $i$, each time-point $j \leq i$ satisfying

$$\begin{aligned} &\tau_i - \tau_j \leq reach([l,r]) \land \overline{b}_2^j \land \forall k.\ \left(j < k \leq i \Longrightarrow \overline{b}_1^k\right) && \text{if } \mathsf{op} = \mathsf{S}_{[l,r]}, \\ &\tau_i - \tau_j \leq reach([l,r]) \land \forall k.\ \left(j \leq k \leq i \Longrightarrow \overline{b}_1^k \land \left(\overline{b}_2^k \Longrightarrow \tau_k - \tau_j < l\right)\right) && \text{if } \mathsf{op} = \mathsf{U}_{[l,r]}, \end{aligned}$$

corresponds to a unique suffix $0 \cdot ts'$ of the list $ts$ in the operator $\mathsf{op}$'s state satisfying $\mathsf{SUM}(ts') = \tau_i - \tau_j$. In particular, $ts$ satisfies $\mathsf{SUM}(ts) \leq reach([l,r])$.

Figure 4 shows the definitions of the step functions. For the $\mathsf{S}_I$ operator, we proceed in four main steps. (1) We compute the current time-stamp difference and add it to the history (lines 3–4). (2) We drop the time-stamp differences that fall out of the interval $I$ from the history (line 6). (3) We use the Boolean values denoting the subformula's satisfaction at the current point to update the history, starting with the since operator's first (left) subformula (lines 7–9). If the

| Trace | $\varphi_1 = a\,\mathsf{S}_{[0,4]}\,b$ $c^{\mathsf{S}_{[0,4]}}$ | Verdicts | $\varphi_2 = a\,\mathsf{U}_{[0,4]}\,b$ $c^{\mathsf{U}_{[0,4]}}$ | Verdicts |
|---|---|---|---|---|
| | $(\bot,\varepsilon)$ | | $(\bot,\varepsilon)$ | |
| $(0,\{a\})$ | $((0,\mathrm{ff}),\varepsilon)$ | $(0,\mathrm{ff})$ | $(0,0)$ | $\varepsilon$ |
| $(0,\{a\})$ | $((0,\mathrm{ff}),\varepsilon)$ | $(0,\mathrm{ff})$ | $(0,0^2)$ | $\varepsilon$ |
| $(2,\{a\})$ | $((2,\mathrm{ff}),\varepsilon)$ | $(2,\mathrm{ff})$ | $(2,0^2 20)$ | $\varepsilon$ |
| $(4,\{a,b\})$ | $((4,\mathrm{tt}),0)$ | $(4,\mathrm{tt})$ | $(4,\varepsilon)$ | $(0,\mathrm{tt})(0,\mathrm{tt})(2,\mathrm{tt})(4,\mathrm{tt})$ |
| $(5,\{a\})$ | $((5,\mathrm{tt}),01)$ | $(5,\mathrm{tt})$ | $(5,0)$ | $\varepsilon$ |
| $(10,\{b\})$ | $((10,\mathrm{tt}),0)$ | $(10,\mathrm{tt})$ | $(10,\varepsilon)$ | $(5,\mathrm{ff})(10,\mathrm{tt})$ |

**Fig. 5.** Example operator evaluation for the formulas $a\ \mathsf{S}_{[0,4]}\ b$ (left) and $a\ \mathsf{U}_{[0,4]}\ b$ (right).

first subformula is not satisfied, all previous satisfaction witnesses of the since operator stored in the history are invalidated and must be dropped (line 7). If the second subformula is satisfied, we add a new satisfaction witness (line 9). (4) The output of the operator is in each step a single Boolean verdict denoting whether there is a satisfaction witness starting in the interval $I$ (lines 2, 5, and 10–14; the latter distinguish between finite and infinite intervals). For the $\mathsf{U}_J$ operator, steps (1) (lines 2–3), (2) (line 6), and (3) (lines 9–14) are similar, except that the subformulas are checked in the reverse order starting from the until operator's second (right) subformula. The main difference is the way the until operator's evaluation resolves the satisfaction candidates to Boolean verdicts (lines 7, 11, and 13). This resolution uses the auxiliary function $\mathsf{RES}(ds, \tau, b)$ that maps every suffix $0 \cdot ds'$ of the list $ds$ to a time-stamped Boolean value $(\tau - \mathsf{SUM}(ds'), b)$. We omit its straightforward definition. Note that one step of the $\mathsf{U}_J$ operator's evaluation can produce several verdicts.

*Example 1.* We continue Example 1 from this section's start by considering a monitor for the formula $\Phi = (a\ \mathsf{S}_{[0,4]}\ b) \vee (a\ \mathsf{U}_{[0,4]}\ b)$. Figure 5 describes the monitor's execution steps on the trace from Fig. 2. The trace is shown in column 1. A state $q^{\Phi}$ of the monitor consists of a pair of states $q^{\varphi_1}$ and $q^{\varphi_2}$ for its two submonitors for $\varphi_1 = a\ \mathsf{S}_{[0,4]}\ b$ and $\varphi_2 = a\ \mathsf{U}_{[0,4]}\ b$, a pair of optional Boolean values that cache the latest unprocessed verdict produced by the two submonitors, the state $\bot$ for $\Phi$'s top-level operator $\vee$, and a list of time-stamped Boolean verdicts produced by evaluating the operator $\vee$.

The state $q^{\varphi_1}$ consists of a pair $(\bot,\bot)$ of submonitor states for atomic predicates $a$ and $b$, a pair of optional Boolean values that cache the latest unprocessed verdict produced by the two submonitors, a state $c^{\mathsf{S}_{[0,4]}}$ for the top-level operator of $\varphi_1$ (column 2) and a list of time-stamped Boolean verdicts produced by evaluating the operator $\mathsf{S}_{[0,4]}$ (column 3), to be output. The length of this list is at most one since the step function $s^{\mathsf{S}_{[0,4]}}$ never produces more than one verdict at a time.

A state $q^{\varphi_2}$ has a similar structure to a state $q^{\varphi_1}$. We show $c^{\mathsf{U}_{[0,4]}}$ for the top-level operator of $\varphi_2$ in column 4. Note that the length of the list of time-stamped Boolean verdicts produced by evaluating the operator $\mathsf{U}_{[0,4]}$ may be arbitrary (column 5).

The since operator's step function produces a single verdict after each time-point and keeps the last time-stamped Boolean verdict as the first component of the operator state $c^{\mathsf{S}_{[0,4]}}$. The second component of $c^{\mathsf{S}_{[0,4]}}$ is the run-length encoded list of satisfaction witnesses. Since none of the first three time-points contains an atomic predicate $b$, the list of satisfaction witnesses is empty. The fourth time-point is a satisfaction witness, which is represented by a zero in the list of satisfaction witnesses. The fifth time-point is not a satisfaction witness, but the time-stamp difference to the previous time-point is appended to the list of satisfaction witnesses. At the last time-point, the fourth time-point falls out of the interval $[0, 4]$ of the since operator and is removed from the list of satisfaction witnesses, which becomes empty. The last time-point is a new satisfaction witness itself; hence there is a zero in the list of satisfaction witnesses.

The until operator's step function may produce no verdict or multiple verdicts after a time-point. The first three time-points do not contain the atomic predicate $b$ and thus become satisfaction candidates. Each of them corresponds to a zero in the run-length encoded list of satisfaction candidates, which is the state's second component. (The first component is the time-stamp from the previously read time-point.) Since the time-stamp difference between the second and third time-stamp is nonzero, it is prepended before the last zero corresponding to the third satisfaction candidate. The fourth time-point contains an atomic predicate $b$, which resolves all satisfaction candidates, including the current time-point, to $\mathsf{tt}$ (as none of them falls out of the until operator's interval). After the fourth time-point, there are no satisfaction candidates. The fifth time-point is a new satisfaction candidate. The time-stamp difference between the last two time-points makes the fifth time-point fall out of the interval associated with the until operator and it is thus resolved to $\mathsf{ff}$. Since the last time-point contains the atomic predicate $b$, it is immediately resolved to $\mathsf{tt}$, and the list of satisfaction candidates becomes empty.

The monitor for the formula $\Phi = \varphi_1 \vee \varphi_2$ can only produce a verdict for the first time-point once it obtains the corresponding verdicts for its two sub-formulas. The submonitor for $\varphi_1$ outputs the verdict for the first time-point immediately after processing it (column 3). In contrast, the submonitor for $\varphi_2$ only outputs the verdict for the first time-point after processing the fourth time-point (column 5). After the verdict for the first time-point has been output, the remaining three verdicts returned by the operator step function for $\varphi_2$ are stored in the state $q^{\varphi_2}$. At this point, the reading heads are at the positions shown in Fig. 2. The operator step function of $\varphi_1$ is then invoked at the second, third, and fourth time-point, making the reading heads of the submonitor for $\varphi_1$ catch up with the ones of the submonitor for $\varphi_2$. The three verdicts stored in the state $q^{\varphi_2}$ are combined with the new ones obtained from the submonitor for $\varphi_1$. At the fifth time-point, the operator step function for $\varphi_2$ is invoked again without outputting any verdicts. After its next invocation, it outputs two verdicts for the last two time-points, which are then again similarly stored in $\varphi_2$ until the submonitor for $\varphi_1$ catches up.

# 5 Correctness and Complexity Analysis

We reverse the order compared to the previous section: We first prove the correctness of operator evaluation and then the recursive monitor's correctness. Afterwards we precisely bound the space complexity of representing the multi-head monitor's state.

## 5.1 Correctness of Operator Evaluation

To prove the correctness of MTL operator evaluation, we first formulate an invariant $\mathcal{I}(\mathsf{op}, \sigma_{\leq i}, c^{\mathsf{op}}, o^{\mathsf{op}})$ on the state $c^{\mathsf{op}}$ and output $o^{\mathsf{op}} \in V^*$ produced by evaluating an operator $\mathsf{op}$ that holds after applying the step function $s^{\mathsf{op}}$ on the finite stream prefix $\sigma_{\leq i} = \langle(\tau_k, \overline{b}_1^k, \ldots, \overline{b}_{\eta(\mathsf{op})}^k)\rangle_{k \leq i}$, which stores the Boolean values $\overline{b}_1^k, \ldots, \overline{b}_{\eta(\mathsf{op})}^k$ passed to $\mathsf{op}$ on the $k$-th invocation of its step function, starting from the initial state $c_0^{\mathsf{op}}$.

We first define an auxiliary predicate $\mathsf{SOUND}_{\mathsf{op}}(\sigma_{\leq i}, o^{\mathsf{op}})$ that asserts the soundness of MTL operator evaluation. Assuming that the Boolean values from $\sigma_{\leq i}$ denote the verdicts of a formula's $\Phi$ direct subformulas, the operator has to produce the verdicts for $\Phi$:

$$\begin{aligned}&\mathsf{SOUND}_{\mathsf{op}}(\langle(\hat{\tau}_k, \overline{\hat{b}}^k)\rangle_{k \leq i}, \langle(t_k, b_k)\rangle_{k<n}) \equiv \forall \rho\ \Phi\ \varphi_1\ \ldots\ \varphi_{\eta(\mathsf{op})}.\\ &\quad \Phi = \mathsf{op}(\varphi_1, \ldots, \varphi_{\eta(\mathsf{op})}) \wedge (\forall j \in [\eta(\mathsf{op})].\ \mathsf{SOUND}_{\varphi_j}(\rho, \langle(\hat{\tau}_k, \overline{\hat{b}}_j^k)\rangle_{k<i+1})) \Longrightarrow\\ &\quad \mathsf{SOUND}_{\Phi}(\rho, \langle(t_k, b_k)\rangle_{k<n}).\end{aligned}$$

For an empty stream prefix, the invariant asserts that the state is the initial state and no output has been produced: $\mathcal{I}(\mathsf{op}, \varepsilon, c^{\mathsf{op}}, o^{\mathsf{op}}) \equiv c^{\mathsf{op}} = c_0^{\mathsf{op}} \wedge o^{\mathsf{op}} = \varepsilon$.

*Negation and Disjunction.* For $\mathsf{op} \in \{\neg, \vee\}$, the invariant asserts that sound output (second conjunct) has been produced for all time-points (from 0) up to $i$ (first conjunct):

$$\mathcal{I}(\mathsf{op}, \sigma_{\leq i}, c^{\mathsf{op}}, o^{\mathsf{op}}) \equiv |o^{\mathsf{op}}| = i + 1 \wedge \mathsf{SOUND}_{\mathsf{op}}(\sigma_{\leq i}, o^{\mathsf{op}}).$$

*Previous and Next.* For $\mathsf{op} \in \{\bullet_I, \bigcirc_I\}$, the invariant asserts that sound output has been produced for all time-points up to $i$, or $i - 1$, respectively, and that the state stores the time-stamp (and, for the $\bullet_I$ operator, also the Boolean value) from $\sigma_{\leq i}$ at $i$.

$$\begin{aligned}\mathcal{I}(\bullet_I, \sigma_{\leq i}, (t^{\mathsf{op}}, b^{\mathsf{op}}), o^{\mathsf{op}}) &\equiv |o^{\mathsf{op}}| = i + 1 \wedge (\tau_i, \overline{b}_1^i) = (t^{\mathsf{op}}, b^{\mathsf{op}}) \wedge \mathsf{SOUND}_{\mathsf{op}}(\sigma_{\leq i}, o^{\mathsf{op}})\\ \mathcal{I}(\bigcirc_I, \sigma_{\leq i}, t^{\mathsf{op}}, o^{\mathsf{op}}) &\equiv |o^{\mathsf{op}}| = i \wedge \tau_i = t^{\mathsf{op}} \wedge \mathsf{SOUND}_{\mathsf{op}}(\sigma_{\leq i}, o^{\mathsf{op}})\end{aligned}$$

In the following, let $I = [l, r]$. For the since and until operators, we use an auxiliary function $\mathsf{CSUF}$ that counts the number of suffixes of a list starting with a zero and having a fixed sum:

$$\mathsf{CSUF}(ts, \Delta) = |\{ts' \mid \exists w.\ ts = w \cdot 0 \cdot ts' \wedge \mathsf{SUM}(ts') = \Delta\}|.$$

*Since.* The invariant for the since operator $\mathsf{op} = \mathsf{S}_I$ asserts that (i) sound output has been produced for all time-points up to $i$, (ii) the state stores the verdict at the time-point $i$, and (iii) the list stored in the state contains all satisfaction witnesses (Sect. 4):

$$\mathcal{I}(\mathsf{S}_I, \sigma_{\leq i}, (v^{\mathsf{op}}, ts), o^{\mathsf{op}}) \equiv |o^{\mathsf{op}}| = i + 1 \wedge o_i^{\mathsf{op}} = v^{\mathsf{op}} \wedge \mathsf{SUM}(ts) \leq reach(I) \wedge \\ \forall \Delta \in [reach(I)]_0.\ \mathsf{WITS}(\sigma_{\leq i}, \Delta) = \mathsf{CSUF}(ts, \Delta) \wedge \mathsf{SOUND}_{\mathsf{op}}(\sigma_{\leq i}, o^{\mathsf{op}}),$$

where the auxiliary function $\mathsf{WITS}$ counts the satisfaction witnesses:

$$\mathsf{WITS}(\sigma_{\leq i}, \Delta) = |\{j \in [i]_0 \mid \tau_i - \tau_j = \Delta \wedge \overline{b}_2^j \wedge \forall k.\ j < k \leq i \Longrightarrow \overline{b}_1^k\}|.$$

*Until.* The invariant for the until operator $\mathsf{op} = \mathsf{U}_J$ is similar to the one for the since operator, but asserts that sound output has been produced for all time-points that do not have a corresponding suffix starting with a zero in the stored list $ts$:

$$\mathcal{I}(\mathsf{U}_J, \sigma_{\leq i}, (t^{\mathsf{op}}, ts), o^{\mathsf{op}}) \equiv |o^{\mathsf{op}}| = i + 1 - \textstyle\sum_{\Delta=0}^{r} \mathsf{CSUF}(ts, \Delta) \wedge \tau_i = t^{\mathsf{op}} \wedge \\ \mathsf{SUM}(ts) \leq r \wedge \forall \Delta \in [r]_0.\ \mathsf{CANDS}(\sigma_{\leq i}, \Delta) = \mathsf{CSUF}(ts, \Delta) \wedge \mathsf{SOUND}_{\mathsf{op}}(\sigma_{\leq i}, o^{\mathsf{op}}),$$

where the auxiliary function $\mathsf{CANDS}$ counts the satisfaction candidates (Sect. 4):

$$\mathsf{CANDS}(\sigma_{\leq i}, \Delta) = |\{j \in [i]_0 \mid \tau_i - \tau_j = \Delta \wedge \forall k \in \{j, \ldots, i\}.\ \overline{b}_1^k \wedge (\overline{b}_2^k \Longrightarrow \tau_k - \tau_j < l)\}|.$$

We now establish that the $\mathcal{I}$ is indeed an inductive invariant.

**Lemma 1.** *Let* $\mathsf{op}$ *be an MTL operator and* $\sigma = \langle(\tau_i, \overline{b}_1^i, \ldots, \overline{b}_{\eta(\mathsf{op})}^i)\rangle_{i \in \mathbb{N}}$. *Let* $c_0^{\mathsf{op}}$ *be the initial state for evaluating* $\mathsf{op}$ *as defined in Sect. 4. Let* $(c_{i+1}^{\mathsf{op}}, o_i^{\mathsf{op}}) = s^{\mathsf{op}}(c_i^{\mathsf{op}}, \tau_i, \overline{b}^i)$, *for all* $i \in \mathbb{N}$. *Then* $\mathcal{I}(\mathsf{op}, \sigma_{\leq 0}, c_1^{\mathsf{op}}, o_0^{\mathsf{op}})$ *holds. Moreover, for any* $i \geq 0$,

$$\mathcal{I}(\mathsf{op}, \sigma_{\leq i}, c_{i+1}^{\mathsf{op}}, o_{\leq i}^{\mathsf{op}}) \Longrightarrow \mathcal{I}(\mathsf{op}, \sigma_{\leq i+1}, c_{i+2}^{\mathsf{op}}, o_{\leq i+1}^{\mathsf{op}}).$$

**Theorem 1.** *Let* $\mathsf{op}$ *be an MTL operator,* $\sigma = \langle(\tau_i, \overline{b}_1^i, \ldots, \overline{b}_{\eta(\mathsf{op})}^i)\rangle_{i \in \mathbb{N}}$ *be a stream with unbounded time-stamps, and* $i$ *be a time-point. Then there exists a time-point* $j$ *such that, using the notation of Lemma 1,* $|o_{\leq j}^{\mathsf{op}}| > i$ *and* $\mathsf{SOUND}_{\mathsf{op}}(\sigma_{\leq j}, o_{\leq j}^{\mathsf{op}})$.

### 5.2 Correctness and Space Complexity of the Multi-head Monitor

To prove the correctness of the multi-head monitor for an MTL formula $\Phi$ over its atomic predicates $P^{\Phi}$, we formulate an invariant $\mathcal{I}(\Phi, \rho, q^{\Phi}, \overline{p}, o^{\Phi})$ on the state $q^{\Phi}$ and the produced output $o^{\Phi}$ that holds after applying the step function $\delta^{\Phi}$ on the stream $\rho$ starting from the initial state $q_0^{\Phi}$ with the reading heads positioned at $\overline{p}$.

*Atomic Predicate.* Let $\Phi = p \in P^{\Phi}$. The invariant asserts that sound output has been produced for the first $\overline{p}_1$ time-points: $\mathcal{I}(\Phi, \rho, q^{\Phi}, \overline{p}, o^{\Phi}) \equiv |o^{\Phi}| = \overline{p}_1 \wedge \mathsf{SOUND}_{\Phi}(\rho, o^{\Phi})$.

*Recursive Formula.* Let $\Phi = \mathsf{op}(\varphi_1, \ldots, \varphi_{\eta(\mathsf{op})})$ and $M^\Phi$ be its multi-head monitor. The invariant asserts that (i) the states of $M^\Phi$ for all the subformulas and the state of evaluating the operator op are obtained when the outputs of all the multi-head monitors for the subformulas are used to construct a trace for evaluating the operator op, and (ii) the list of time-stamped Boolean values stored in $M^\Phi$'s state contains exactly the values that have been output by the operator op, except those that have already been output by $M^\Phi$.

$$\begin{aligned}&\mathcal{I}(\Phi, \rho, (\langle q^{\varphi_i}\rangle_{i=1}^{\eta(\mathsf{op})}, \langle \beta_i\rangle_{i=1}^{\eta(\mathsf{op})}, c^{\mathsf{op}}, vs), \overline{p}^1 \cdots \overline{p}^{\eta(\mathsf{op})}, o^\Phi) \equiv \\ &\quad (\Phi = \mathsf{op}(\varphi_1, \ldots, \varphi_{\eta(\mathsf{op})}) \wedge \textstyle\bigwedge_{i=1}^{\eta(\mathsf{op})} |\overline{p}^i| = \kappa^{\varphi_i}) \implies \exists n > 0.\ \exists \langle (\tau_k, \overline{b}^k)\rangle_{k<n}.\ \forall i \in [\eta(\mathsf{op})]. \\ &\quad (\beta_i \neq \bot \implies \beta_i = \overline{b}_i^{n-1} \wedge \mathcal{I}(\varphi_i, \rho, q^{\varphi_i}, \overline{p}^i, \langle (\tau_k, \overline{b}^k)\rangle_{k<n})) \wedge \\ &\quad (\beta_i = \bot \implies \mathcal{I}(\varphi_i, \rho, q^{\varphi_i}, \overline{p}^i, \langle (\tau_k, \overline{b}^k)\rangle_{k<n-1})) \wedge \\ &\quad \exists i \in [\eta(\mathsf{op})].\ \beta_i = \bot \wedge \mathcal{I}(\mathsf{op}, \langle (\tau_k, \overline{b}^k)\rangle_{k<n-1}, c^{\mathsf{op}}, o^\Phi \cdot vs)\end{aligned}$$

**Lemma 2.** *Let $\Phi$ be any MTL formula and $M^\Phi = (P^\Phi, V, \kappa^\Phi, Q^\Phi, q_0^\Phi, \delta^\Phi)$ be a multi-head monitor for $\Phi$ as defined in Sect. 4. Let $\rho$ be a stream. Let $\langle (q_i^\Phi, \overline{p}^i)\rangle_{i\in\mathbb{N}}$ be the computation of $M^\Phi$ on the stream $\rho$. Moreover, let $\langle o_i^\Phi\rangle_{i\in\mathbb{N}}$ be the output of $M^\Phi$. Then $\mathcal{I}(\Phi, \rho, q_1^\Phi, \overline{p}^1, o_0^\Phi)$ holds. Moreover, for any $i \geq 0$,*

$$\mathcal{I}(\Phi, \rho, q_{i+1}^\Phi, \overline{p}^{i+1}, o_{\leq i}^\Phi) \implies \mathcal{I}(\Phi, \rho, q_{i+2}^\Phi, \overline{p}^{i+2}, o_{\leq i+1}^\Phi).$$

**Theorem 2.** *Let $\Phi$ be any MTL formula and $\rho$ a fixed stream. Let $i$ be an arbitrary time-point. Then there exists some $n$ such that, using the notation of Lemma 2, $o_{\leq n}^\Phi = \langle (t_k, b_k)\rangle_{k<l}$ with $l > i$ and $\mathsf{SOUND}_\Phi(\rho, o_{\leq n}^\Phi)$.*

Finally, we bound the space complexity of storing a state of a multi-head monitor. Our analysis relies on all lists in the monitor's state being run-length-encoded.

**Theorem 3.** *Let $\Phi$ be a formula and $M^\Phi = (P^\Phi, V, \kappa^\Phi, Q^\Phi, q_0^\Phi, \delta^\Phi)$ be a multi-head monitor for $\Phi$ as defined in Sect. 4. Let $\rho$ be an arbitrary stream. Let $\langle (q_i^\Phi, \overline{p}^i)\rangle_{i\in\mathbb{N}}$ be the computation of $M^\Phi$ on the stream $\rho$. Then $q_i^\Phi$ can be represented as a string over the alphabet $\{(;);,;\mathsf{ff};\mathsf{tt};\bot;\varepsilon;0;1\}$ of length at most $32 \cdot \|\Phi\| \cdot (2 + \log_2 i + \log_2 \tau_i)$.*

For a trace $\sigma_{\leq i}$, our monitor thus requires $\mathcal{O}(\|\Phi\| \cdot \log(i \cdot \tau_i))$ space, i.e., the space requirement grows logarithmically with the trace length and the observed time-stamps. The dependence on the trace length might possibly be avoided by using *sensing* reading heads [18], i.e., by allowing the computational model to determine if any two reading heads are currently at the same position. The dependence on the observed time-stamps could also be avoided by computing bounded (by the largest constant occurring in an interval) time-stamp differences. This should be possible to achieve with a bounded number of additional reading heads. We leave these potential improvements as future work.

## 6 Implementation and Evaluation

We have implemented the multi-head monitor in a tool called HYDRA [20], consisting of roughly 1000 lines of C++ code. Our implementation mirrors the overall structure of the multi-head monitor presented here and consists of C++ classes for monitoring atomic predicates and formulas with various top-level operators (Sect. 4.1), which also implement the evaluation of the top-level operator (Sect. 4.2). HYDRA implements some optimizations that are omitted in the presentation for the sake of simplicity. Most importantly, all reads are implemented imperatively, which allows the multi-head monitor's step function to always return a verdict (as opposed to an optional verdict as in Sect. 4.1). Finally, all lists are encoded using run-length encoding (Sect. 5.2).

We empirically validate our space complexity analysis and demonstrate HYDRA's superior time complexity by answering the following four research questions:

RQ1: *How does* HYDRA *scale with respect to the trace length?*
RQ2: *How does* HYDRA *scale with respect to the (temporal) size of the formula?*
RQ3: *How does* HYDRA *perform on inputs that trigger worst-case space complexity for online monitors?*
RQ4: *How does* HYDRA *perform compared to the state-of-the-art monitoring tools?*

To answer the above questions, we perform four experiments measuring HYDRA's average-case and worst-case time and space usage. Our analysis also includes the state-of-the-art monitors AERIAL [7] and MONPOLY [4,5]. We use AERIAL's SAFA mode in the average-case experiments, and its EXPR mode in the worst-case experiments, as this choice exhibits the best performance for AERIAL. We remark that MONPOLY is an online monitor producing Boolean verdicts for all positions in the trace and its space complexity can thus only be bounded by a linear function in the trace length [4], i.e., it is not trace-length independent.

The average-case traces are produced by a pseudorandom trace generator for a predefined event rate *er* [3]. Each trace contains events with 100 different time-stamps. The time-stamp differences are distributed uniformly in $[\Delta]$, for a predefined $\Delta$; in our experiments, we use $\Delta = 4$. The atomic predicates are generated as follows: (i) independently with probability $1 - \frac{1}{\Delta \cdot er}$, an atomic predicate $p_0, \ldots, p_3$ is included; (ii) independently with probability $\frac{1}{2}$, an atomic predicate $p_4, \ldots, p_{15}$ is included.

The average-case formulas are produced by a pseudorandom formula generator for a predefined size and maximum interval bounds. A formula $\Phi$ of size $s > 0$ is generated as follows: (i) if $s = 1$, then $\Phi = p$, for an atomic predicate $p \in \{p_0, \ldots, p_{15}\}$ chosen uniformly at random; (ii) if $s = 2$, a top-level unary operator $\mathsf{op}$ is selected uniformly at random; (iii) if $s \geq 3$, a top-level operator $\mathsf{op}$ is selected as follows: with probability $\frac{1}{2}$, the until operator is chosen, otherwise, the top-level operator $\mathsf{op}$ is chosen uniformly at random among the five remaining operators. If the top-level operator $\mathsf{op}$ has an interval, then the interval is generated as follows: (i) with probability $\frac{1}{4}$, the interval $[0, 0]$ is chosen;

| Experiment | Formula size | Family size | Trace length | Scaling factor |
|---|---|---|---|---|
| 1 | 25 | 10 | 20 000–200 000 | 1 |
| 2 | 2–50 | 10 | 50 000 | 1 |
| 3 | 25 | 10 | 50 000 | 1–10 |

**Fig. 6.** Summary of the experimental setup.

(ii) with probability $\frac{1}{4}$, an interval $[0, r]$ is chosen with $r$ distributed uniformly in $[\Delta]$, or $[\Delta] \cup \{\infty\}$, for a predefined $\Delta$ (in our experiments, we use $\Delta = 16$); (iii) with probability $\frac{1}{2}$, an interval $[l, r]$ is chosen with $l \in [\Delta]$ and $r \in \{l, \ldots, \Delta\}$, or $r \in \{l, \ldots, \Delta\} \cup \{\infty\}$, distributed uniformly at random. Finally, if the top-level operator $\mathsf{op}$ is a unary operator, a pseudorandom subformula $\varphi$ of size $s - 1$ is generated recursively, and if $\mathsf{op}$ is a binary operator, two pseudorandom subformulas of sizes $s_1, s - 1 - s_1$ are generated recursively, where $s_1 \in [s - 2]$ is chosen uniformly at random.

The first three experiments measure the average-case behavior of the tools. The first experiment assesses the impact of increasing the trace length on a family of pseudorandom formulas of a fixed size. The second experiment assesses the impact of increasing the formula size on a trace of fixed length. The third experiment assesses the impact of scaling the intervals of pseudorandom formulas and time-stamps of pseudorandom traces by a constant factor. The first three experiments are summarized in Fig. 6.

To answer RQ3, we conduct a fourth experiment where we consider a family of formulas $\langle \Phi_n \rangle_{n \in \mathbb{N}}$ that exhibits the worst-case space complexity for online monitoring when restricted to produce a *single* Boolean verdict for the first time-point. The formula $\Phi_n$ is defined over the set of atomic predicates $P^{\Phi_n} = \{e, p_1, \ldots, p_n\}$:

$$\Phi_n = \bigcirc_{[1,1]}(\neg e \; \mathsf{U}_{[0,0]} \; (\neg e \wedge \textstyle\bigwedge_{i=1}^{n}(p_i \Rightarrow \Box_{[0,0]}(e \Rightarrow p_i)) \wedge \textstyle\bigwedge_{i=1}^{n}(\neg p_i \Rightarrow \Box_{[0,0]}(e \Rightarrow \neg p_i)))) \,.$$

The family of traces for some fixed $n \in \mathbb{N}$ on which the space complexity of online monitoring for $\Phi_n$ becomes at least $2^n$ bits looks as follows: the first event is an empty event with a time-stamp $\tau_0$, then for each subset $X \in \mathcal{X} \subseteq 2^{P^{\Phi_n} \setminus \{e\}}$ of atomic predicates without $e$, we include an event with the atomic predicates $X$ and a time-stamp $\tau_0 + 1$. Next, for some $X \subseteq P^{\Phi_n}$, we include an event with the atomic predicates $X \cup \{e\}$ and a time-stamp $\tau_0 + 1$. Finally, we include an empty event with a time-stamp $\tau_0 + 3$, so that the trace uniquely determines the Boolean verdict for the first time-point.

Intuitively, for an online monitor to decide if $\Phi_n$ is satisfied at the first time-point of a trace from the family of traces, it must remember the exact subset $\mathcal{X}$ to check if the set $X$ of atomic predicates, which eventually appear with the atomic predicate $e$, belongs to $\mathcal{X}$. As there are $2^{2^n}$ different sets $\mathcal{X}$, we derive a lower bound of $2^n$ bits to store $\mathcal{X}$.

We remark that the top-level next operator in the formula $\Phi_n$ is used to make the formula trivially false on the worst-case traces described above at all time-points but the first one (recall that all analyzed monitors produce a stream of

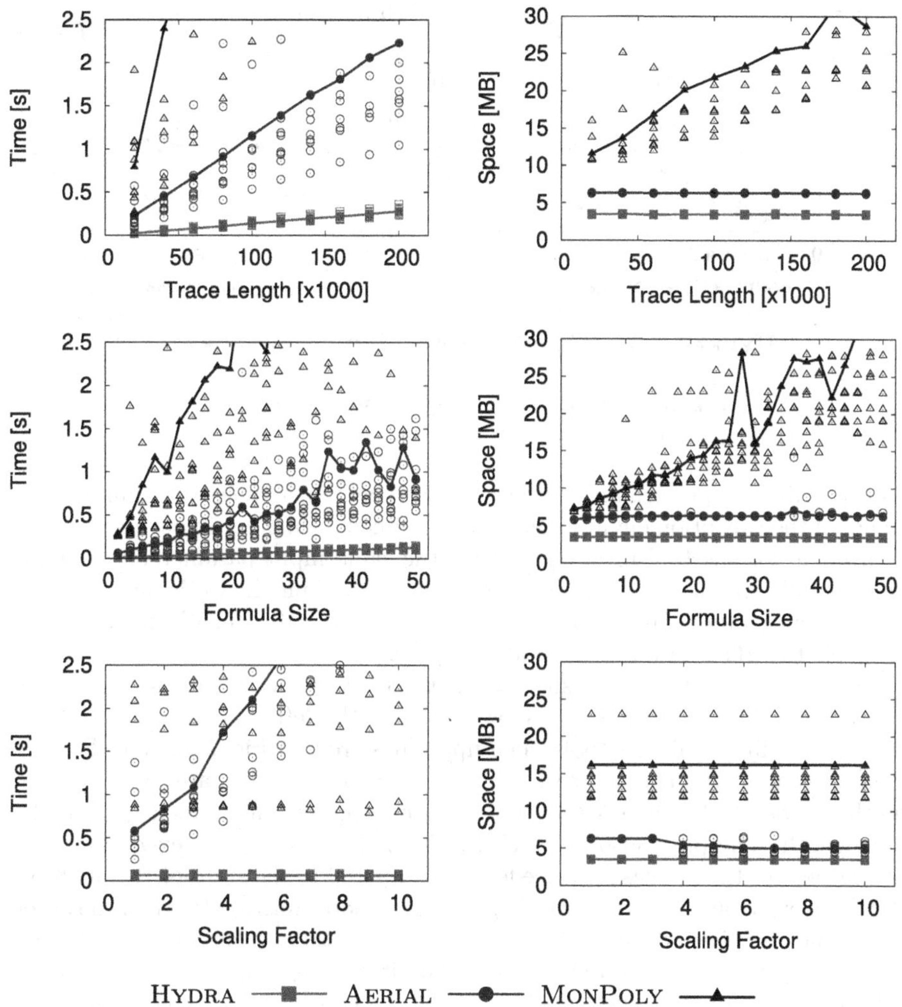


**Fig. 7.** Evaluation results for average-case behavior

Boolean verdicts at each position in the trace). In particular, monitoring $\Phi_n$ on a worst-case trace described above does not achieve the upper bound of $O(2^{2^n+n})$ on AERIAL's space complexity [7].

To benchmark the time complexity in the worst-case experiment, we use traces of fixed length obtained by repeating a worst-case trace for some fixed $n \in \mathbb{N}$ with an increasing base time-stamp $\tau_0$.

We run our experiments on an Intel Core i7-8550U, 1.80GHz computer with 32 GB RAM. We measure the tools' total execution time and maximal memory usage with the Unix time command. Having thoroughly tested the tools' outputs separately, we discard any output during the experiments to exclude the impact

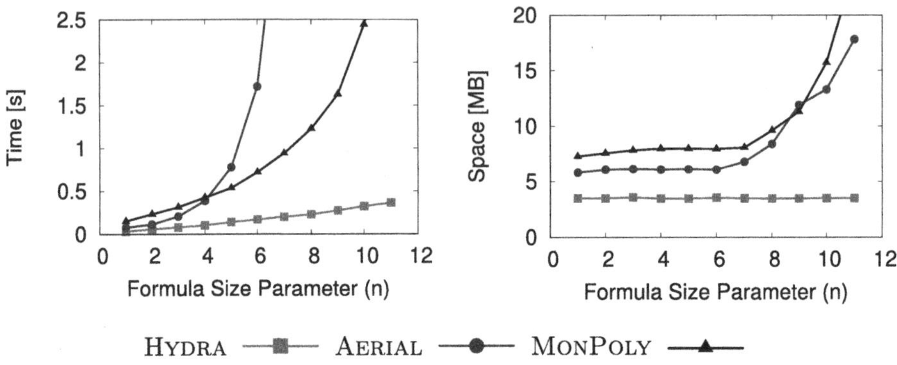


**Fig. 8.** Evaluation results for worst-case behavior

of disk writes on performance. Each run is repeated 5 times to minimize the impact of the execution environment. Each unfilled data point in our plots shows the average for the tool invocations with the same input parameters. We omit the negligible standard deviations. Each filled data point shows the average over a collection of a tool's data points with the same $x$-coordinate. We include trend lines over the filled data points in all our plots.

Figures 7 and 8 show the results of our three average-case and the worst-case experiments. The plots in Fig. 7 show time (on the left) and memory (on the right) scalability of all the tools. The uppermost row in Fig. 7 answers RQ1; it confirms that in the average case both HYDRA and AERIAL are almost trace-length independent, while MONPOLY's space usage increases linearly with the trace length. The plots also show HYDRA's modest increase in execution time with respect to the increasing trace length compared to the state-of-the-art tools (RQ4). Overall, our tool treats random formulas more consistently than the other tools, which is reflected by the trend lines which fit the measurements very well. The other four plots in Fig. 7 show the scalability of the tools with respect to formula size and temporal size (RQ2). Only MONPOLY's memory usage is impacted by these parameters and HYDRA outperforms all the tools. Finally, Fig. 8 confirms our analytical findings from Sect. 5 and shows that, in practice, when monitoring the family of formulas $\langle \Phi_n \rangle_{n \in \mathbb{N}}$, HYDRA's worst-case space complexity is asymptotically better than any state-of-the-art online monitoring tool.

## 7 Conclusion

We proposed multi-head monitoring as a novel approach to analyzing traces. A multi-head monitor reads an input trace simultaneously at multiple positions and its reading heads move asynchronously. Following this paradigm, we designed a monitor for metric temporal logic that outputs a stream of Boolean verdicts. Our monitor is sound and complete and it substantially improves upon all previous algorithms with this output format. We implemented our algorithm in a prototype tool, HYDRA, and demonstrated that it reliably outperforms other monitors, including those that produce less intelligible output.

Multi-head monitoring fills a middle-ground between offline and online monitoring. It requires the input trace to be stored on a disk, as usual in offline monitoring. However, as its reading heads move only in one direction, this allows us to (1) delete the parts of the trace that was processed by all reading heads, and (2) add new events at the end of the trace, mimicking online monitoring.

As future work, we would like to further reduce our monitors' space complexity and achieve true trace-length independence, without the theoretically annoying (albeit practically harmless) logarithmic dependence. Our preliminary results suggest that this can be achieved at the expense of using exponentially many reading heads, instead of linearly many as used in this paper. We also plan to extend our results beyond MTL, e.g., to timed regular expressions [1] or prove the impossibility of this extension.

**Acknowledgments.** We thank the anonymous reviewers for their valuable suggestions on earlier drafts of this paper, which helped us to improve the presentation. This research is supported by the Swiss National Science Foundation grant "Big Data Monitoring" (167162).

## References

1. Asarin, E., Caspi, P., Maler, O.: Timed regular expressions. J. ACM **49**(2), 172–206 (2002)
2. Basin, D., Bhatt, B.N., Krstić, S., Traytel, D.: Almost event-rate independent monitoring. Formal Methods Syst. Des. 1–30 (2019). https://doi.org/10.1007/s10703-018-00328-3
3. Basin, D., Bhatt, B.N., Traytel, D.: Almost event-rate independent monitoring of metric temporal logic. In: Legay, A., Margaria, T. (eds.) TACAS 2017. LNCS, vol. 10206, pp. 94–112. Springer, Heidelberg (2017). https://doi.org/10.1007/978-3-662-54580-5_6
4. Basin, D., Klaedtke, F., Müller, S., Zălinescu, E.: Monitoring metric first-order temporal properties. J. ACM **62**(2), 15 (2015)
5. Basin, D., Klaedtke, F., Zălinescu, E.: The MonPoly monitoring tool. In: Reger, G., Havelund, K. (eds.) RV-CuBES 2017. Kalpa Publications in Computing, vol. 3, pp. 19–28. EasyChair (2017)
6. Basin, D., Klaedtke, F., Zălinescu, E.: Algorithms for monitoring real-time properties. Acta Inf. **55**(4), 309–338 (2018)
7. Basin, D., Krstić, S., Traytel, D.: AERIAL: almost event-rate independent algorithms for monitoring metric regular properties. In: Reger, G., Havelund, K. (eds.) RV-CuBES 2017. Kalpa Publications in Computing, vol. 3, pp. 29–36. EasyChair (2017)
8. Bauer, A., Leucker, M., Schallhart, C.: Runtime verification for LTL and TLTL. ACM Trans. Softw. Eng. Methodol. **20**(4), 14:1–14:64 (2011)
9. Convent, L., Hungerecker, S., Leucker, M., Scheffel, T., Schmitz, M., Thoma, D.: TeSSLa: temporal stream-based specification language. In: Massoni, T., Mousavi, M.R. (eds.) SBMF 2018. LNCS, vol. 11254, pp. 144–162. Springer, Cham (2018). https://doi.org/10.1007/978-3-030-03044-5_10

10. D'Angelo, B., et al.: LOLA: runtime monitoring of synchronous systems. In: TIME 2005, pp. 166–174. IEEE Computer Society (2005)
11. Falcone, Y., Krstić, S., Reger, G., Traytel, D.: A taxonomy for classifying runtime verification tools. In: Colombo, C., Leucker, M. (eds.) RV 2018. LNCS, vol. 11237, pp. 241–262. Springer, Cham (2018). https://doi.org/10.1007/978-3-030-03769-7_14
12. Faymonville, P., Finkbeiner, B., Schwenger, M., Torfah, H.: Real-time stream-based monitoring. CoRR abs/1711.03829 (2017)
13. Finkbeiner, B., Sipma, H.: Checking finite traces using alternating automata. Formal Methods Syst. Des. **24**(2), 101–127 (2004)
14. Gorostiaga, F., Sánchez, C.: Striver: stream runtime verification for real-time event-streams. In: Colombo, C., Leucker, M. (eds.) RV 2018. LNCS, vol. 11237, pp. 282–298. Springer, Cham (2018). https://doi.org/10.1007/978-3-030-03769-7_16
15. Gray, J., Shenoy, P.J.: Rules of thumb in data engineering. In: Lomet, D.B., Weikum, G. (eds.) ICDE 2000, pp. 3–10. IEEE Computer Society (2000)
16. Havelund, K., Roşu, G.: Synthesizing monitors for safety properties. In: Katoen, J.-P., Stevens, P. (eds.) TACAS 2002. LNCS, vol. 2280, pp. 342–356. Springer, Heidelberg (2002). https://doi.org/10.1007/3-540-46002-0_24
17. Ho, H.-M., Ouaknine, J., Worrell, J.: Online monitoring of metric temporal logic. In: Bonakdarpour, B., Smolka, S.A. (eds.) RV 2014. LNCS, vol. 8734, pp. 178–192. Springer, Cham (2014). https://doi.org/10.1007/978-3-319-11164-3_15
18. Ibarra, O.H.: A note on semilinear sets and bounded-reversal multihead pushdown automata. Inf. Process. Lett. **3**(1), 25–28 (1974)
19. Koymans, R.: Specifying real-time properties with metric temporal logic. Real-Time Syst. **2**(4), 255–299 (1990)
20. Raszyk, M., Basin, D., Krstić, S., Traytel, D.: HYDRA. https://bitbucket.org/krle/hydra (2019)
21. Raszyk, M., Basin, D., Traytel, D.: From nondeterministic to multi-head deterministic finite-state transducers. In: Baier, C., Chatzigiannakis, I., Flocchini, P., Leonardi, S. (eds.) ICALP 2019, LIPIcs, vol. 132, pp. 127:1–127:14. Schloss Dagstuhl-Leibniz-Zentrum fuer Informatik (2019)
22. Roşu, G., Havelund, K.: Rewriting-based techniques for runtime verification. Autom. Softw. Eng. **12**(2), 151–197 (2005)
23. Sánchez, C.: Online and offline stream runtime verification of synchronous systems. In: Colombo, C., Leucker, M. (eds.) RV 2018. LNCS, vol. 11237, pp. 138–163. Springer, Cham (2018). https://doi.org/10.1007/978-3-030-03769-7_9
24. Thati, P., Roşu, G.: Monitoring algorithms for metric temporal logic specifications. Electr. Notes Theor. Comput. Sci. **113**, 145–162 (2005)

# An Efficient Algorithm for Computing Causal Trace Sets in Causality Checking

Martin Kölbl(✉) and Stefan Leue(✉)

University of Konstanz, Konstanz, Germany
{martin.koelbl,stefan.leue}@uni-konstanz.de

**Abstract.** Causality Checking [LL13a] has been proposed as a finite state space exploration technique which computes ordered sequences of events that are considered to cause the violation of a reachability property. A crucial point in the implementation of Causality Checking is the computation and storage of all minimal counterexamples found during state space exploration. We refer to the set of all minimal counterexamples as a causal trace set. However, the Duplicate State Prefix Matching (DSPM) Algorithm that is currently used in Causality Checking only under-approximates the causal trace set. As we argue, without the approximation the DSPM algorithm is inefficient. We propose the, to the best of our knowledge, first efficient algorithm that precisely computes a causal trace set, avoiding approximation, called Causal Trace Backward Search (CTBS). We compare the DSPM and CTBS algorithms with respect to their worst case complexities, and by applying them to several case studies.

## 1 Introduction

Causality Checking [LL13a] has been proposed as a finite state space exploration technique which computes sets of minimal ordered sequences of events that are considered to be causal for the violation of a reachability property. The notion of causality used in Causality Checking is an adaptation of the counterfactual causal analysis proposed in the seminal work by Halpern and Pearl on actual causation [HP05,Hal15] to a trace-based model of computation. The sets are referred to as causality classes and are computed in an automated fashion. The union of all causality classes, corresponding to their logical disjunction, is referred to as an actual cause. A causal trace is minimal when none of its non-contiguous subtraces leads to a property violation.

Causality Checking has been implemented in the SpinCause tool [LL14], which computes actual causes for SPIN [Hol04] models. More comprehensively, the QuantUM tool [LL11] implements Causality Checking in order to compute causes for the reachability of hazardous system states in SysML [Obj17] models. QuantUM represents actual causes as formulae in event order logic [LL13b] and visualizes them in the form of Fault Trees [VGRH02], which can then be used as


Y.-F. Chen et al. (Eds.): ATVA 2019, LNCS 11781, pp. 171–186, 2019.
https://doi.org/10.1007/978-3-030-31784-3_10

evidence in safety cases for safety-critical systems. We illustrate the application of QuantUM to safety analyses for automotive autonomous driving architectures in [KL18].

In this paper we restrict ourselves to considering hazards that can be detected by reachability analysis on the state space defined by the model that is being considered. When the state space exploration during Causality Checking, typically implemented using a depth-first (DFS) or breadth-first search (BFS), reaches a hazardous state, a trace leading into this state, called a counterexample, will be generated. In implementations of Causality Checking, the state space traversal is usually implemented using a modified model checking algorithm. The modifications concern the fact that we need to explore all executions of the model, including property violating counterexamples and non-violating executions, in order to implement the counterfactual-style actual cause conditions in Causality Checking.

Pivotal for the performance of Causality Checking is the computation and storage of all minimal counterexamples found during state space exploration. Existing implementations of Causality Checking use a prefix tree data structure to store system executions as well as a parallelization of the search in order to improve performance. A crucial aspect in this regard is how the state space exploration deals with the situation in which a state $s$ is visited that has been visited before during the search. $s$ is then referred to as a duplicate state. Both a BFS and a DFS would not further explore a duplicate state, since doing so would lead to an exponential time penalty. However, when performing Causality Checking all executions need to be explored, irrespective of whether they contain a state which, due to the search strategy employed, happens to be a duplicate state. As a consequence, during the exploration of the system executions it is necessary to concatenate the prefixes leading from the initial system state into a duplicate state with all possible suffixes starting with the duplicate state. This should be done efficiently, in particular by behaving benevolently on practical examples in the face of a potential exponential time and space penalty.

For performance reasons the algorithm that is implemented in SpinCause and QuantUM, which we refer to as Duplicate State Prefix Matching (DSPM) and which is documented in [Lei15], under-approximates the computation of the execution suffixes beginning in duplicate states since it cannot guarantee that all of them will be considered. It is the objective of this paper to propose an algorithm that deals with duplicates precisely, without relying on an approximation, and which is nonetheless efficient. The algorithm that we propose, which we refer to as Causal Trace Backward Search (CTBS), performs an efficient exploration and analysis of all counterexamples found during the state space exploration. It works on-the-fly and returns preliminary results at any point during the computation. While DSPM generates valuable approximations for realistic models, as we shall see, it is incomplete for Causality Checking, whereas CTBS is complete.

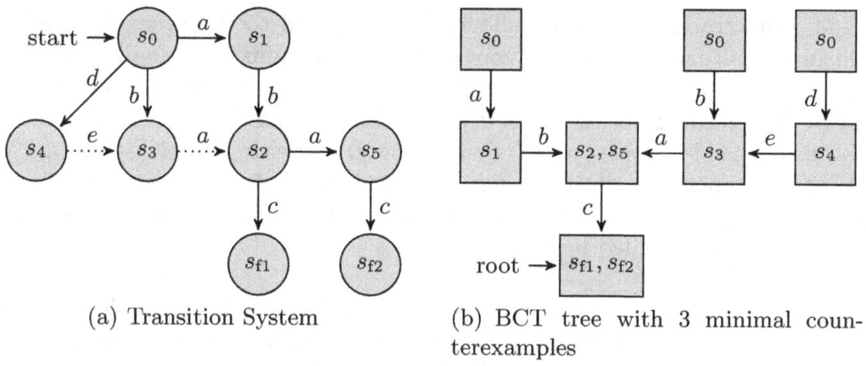


(a) Transition System

(b) BCT tree with 3 minimal counterexamples

**Fig. 1.** Running example

*A Motivating Example.* Consider the transition system depicted in Fig. 1(a). Causality Checking conceptually works on transition systems, which can be automatically derived from higher-level modeling languages, such as SysML. Assume that states $s_{f1}$ and $s_{f2}$ violate a uniquely defined reachability property $\varphi$, corresponding to the occurrence of a hazard in the underlying domain model. We henceforth refer to these states as failure states. In effect, in the context of Causality Checking, reaching a failure state corresponds to the effect for which we compute the actual causes.

The action traces *abc*, *bac* and *deac* are minimal counterexamples for the violation of $\phi$. They are minimal since they do not contain a non-contiguous subtrace that also is a counterexample of $\varphi$. In this sense, *abac* is a non-minimal counterexample, since it contains *abc* as a non-contiguous subtrace. We refer to the set of all minimal counterexamples as causal trace set. The causality classes defined in Causality Checking will be constructed from the causal trace set by grouping all traces that contain the same set of actions into one such class. In the example, the traces *abc* and *bac* form one causality class.

A standard DFS or BFS, modified to compute all traces, would not return the trace *bac* in case it had previously explored the trace *abc*, since state $s_2$ would then be a duplicate state. We, hence, need to ensure that a state space exploration concatenates all trace prefixes starting in the initial state and leading into any duplicate state with all trace suffixes that start in the respective duplicate state. In the example this means that the prefix *ba*, for instance, needs to be concatenated with the suffixes *c* and *ac*. Notice that the resulting trace *baac* will not be included in the causal trace set since it is not a minimal counterexample.

As we shall see, the DSPM algorithm under-approximates this concatenation step by not considering all suffixes starting in a duplicate state, in particular when a prefix trace leads into a duplicate state while traversing another duplicate state. Assume DSPM to explore *abc*, *b* and then *de*, which leads to duplicate state $s_3$. At this point, no suffixes starting in $s_3$ can be added since none exist. Assume *ba* to be explored next, leading to a second duplicate state

$s_2$. The suffix traces $c$ and $ac$ would be concatenated to the prefix $ba$. DSPM would in this situation disregard concatenating the suffixes of duplicate states via which $s_2$ can be reached, such as $s_3$, and therefore returns an incomplete result by disregarding, for instance, $deac$. Notice that this incompleteness would not occur in case $bac$ was explored first, followed by $de$. In this situation DSPM would correctly perform all concatenations of prefixes and suffixes at all duplicate states. The algorithm CTBS that we propose in this paper completely handles all concatenations entailed by duplicate states.

*Related Work.* There are only few papers available that address the computation of all minimal counterexamples for reachability properties required to compute causality classes [LL14, Lei15, BHK+15]. As we argue above, the algorithm described in [LL14, Lei15] only computes an approximation. The algorithm in [BHK+15] is also approximative since it is based on bounded model checking. We propose an algorithm that can in principle compute complete causality classes. Note that minimal traces in a causality class are different from minimal length paths in graphs, which is why the vast literature on shortest path searches on graphs [ES12] and the computation of minimal length counterexamples [AL10, HKD09, SB05, HK06] is not directly applicable to our problem.

*Structure of the Paper.* We discuss the foundations of our work in Sect. 2. In Sect. 3, we present the algorithm proposed in [Lei15] to compute a causal trace set, propose a new algorithm and compare the computational complexity of both algorithms. We qualitatively and quantitatively compare the algorithms by several case studies in Sect. 4. In Sect. 5, we draw conclusions and suggest future developments.

## 2 Preliminaries

Causality Checking uses a modified state space exploration algorithm to traverse the state space of a transition system.

**Definition 1 (Transition System (TS)**[BK+08]**).** *A transition system is a tuple* $(S, Act, \rightarrow, I, AP, L)$ *where* $S$ *is a finite set of states,* $Act$ *is a finite set of actions,* $\rightarrow \subseteq S \times Act \times S$ *is a transition relation,* $I \subseteq S$ *is a set of initial states,* $AP$ *is a set of atomic propositions, and* $L : S \rightarrow 2^{AP}$ *is a labeling function.*

The standard state space exploration strategies used in depth-first-search (DFS) or breath-first-search (BFS) are modified for the purpose of Causality Checking in two fundamental ways. First, the state space exploration continues after a first property violating state is found. Second, when reaching a duplicate state, a concatenation operation as explained above needs to be performed.

An *execution* $\rho$ of an $TS$ is a possibly infinite alternating sequence $s_0 a_0 s_1 a_1 \ldots$ of states and actions that starts in the initial state and any triple $(s_i, a_i, s_{i+1})$, called a transition, is an element in $\rightarrow$. During state space exploration a state $s$ may be visited twice. We then call $s$ a *duplicate state.* A finite execution $s_0 a_0 s_1 \ldots s_{n-1} a_{n-1} s_n$ of a $TS$ where the last state $s_n$ is a duplicate state is called a *duplicate execution.* A finite execution $\sigma = s_0 a_0 s_1 \dots s_{n-1} a_{n-1} s_n$ where $s_n \not\models \varphi$, for an invariant property $\varphi$, is called a *counterexample.* We then write $\sigma \not\models \varphi$. An *action trace* $a_0 a_1 \dots$ is a sequence of actions. In the following, we refer to an action trace simply as a trace.

A trace $\sigma' = a'_0 \dots a'_n$ contains another trace $\sigma = a_0 \dots a_m$ when $\sigma$ is a non-contiguous subtrace of $\sigma'$, written as $\sigma \sqsubseteq \sigma'$. Formally, $\sigma \sqsubseteq \sigma'$ holds iff the word $a'_0 \dots a'_n$ is contained in the language obtained from the regular expression $\Sigma^* a_0 \Sigma^* a_1 \Sigma^* \dots \Sigma^* a_m \Sigma^*$, where $\Sigma = \{a'_0 \dots a'_n\}$. We write $\sigma \sqsubset \sigma'$ iff $\sigma \sqsubseteq \sigma'$ and $\sigma \neq \sigma'$. Let $\eta = s_0 a_0 \dots a_m s_{m+1}$ and $\eta' = s'_0 a'_0 \dots a'_n s'_{n+1}$ executions from which traces $\sigma$ and $\sigma'$, respectively, have been derived by projection. We say $\eta'$ contains $\eta$ iff $\sigma \sqsubseteq \sigma'$. The $\sqsubseteq$ relation is transitive.

For space efficiency reasons, traces are stored using a prefix tree [Fre60] data structure. For any tree, the path of some vertex is defined as a backwards sequence of edges that leads from the considered vertex to the root vertex $r$. Note that the path of any vertex is unique. A trace of a path is the projection of the respective path on the set of actions. A path $p$ contains another path $p'$ iff the trace of $p$ contains the trace of $p'$.

## 3 Algorithms for Computing a Causal Trace Set

*Definition of Causal Trace Set.* The definition of the causal trace set relies on two essential properties of the traces included in the set. First, every counterexample needs to be represented by an element of the Causal Trace Set (completeness), and second, the causal trace set contains only traces corresponding to minimal counterexamples.

**Definition 2 (Causal Trace Set).** *Assume a TS $T$ and a safety property $\varphi$. Let $\sigma$ and $\sigma'$ be traces in $T$. A causal trace set is a subset $\Psi$ of the traces of $T$ that satisfies following conditions:*

- *TC1 (completeness): For every $\sigma'$ that satisfies $\sigma' \not\models \varphi$ there exists a $\sigma$ such that $\sigma \in \Psi$ and $\sigma \sqsubseteq \sigma'$.*
- *TC2 (minimality): $\Psi$ is minimal, that is to say, no $\sigma \in \Psi$ is a true subtrace of $\sigma' \in \Psi$.*

*We call a trace in $\Psi$ a causal trace.*

*Duplicate State Prefix Matching Algorithm (DSPM).* We now discuss the DSPM algorithm in more detail. When the state space exploration encounters a counterexample or a duplicate execution, it hands the execution over to the DSPM algorithm. The DSPM algorithm compares new with existing counterexamples and only stores minimal ones. Duplicate executions are stored in a list until the state space exploration terminates. They are then concatenated with previously stored minimal counterexamples which contain the respective duplicate state. The DSPM pseudo code can be found in [Lei15].

As discussed above, DSPM computes a potentially incomplete causal trace set when it is possible to reach a duplicate state via another duplicate state.

This is due to the fact that the duplicate processing happens only after all counterexamples have been computed. The order of processing of duplicates depends on the search order used by the state space exploration algorithm. As explained above, the order of encountering duplicate states and their processing may lead to an incompleteness in the discovery of causal traces. It is not obvious whether there is an ordering that would avoid this incompleteness. In particular, ordering the processing of duplicate states according to the length of the trace needed to reach them will not solve the problem, as we found out.

*Causal Trace Backward Search Algorithm (CTBS).* The CTBS algorithm computes minimal counterexamples using a *Backwards Causal Trace* (BCT) tree data structure. Consider the example BCT tree depicted in Fig. 1(b) which is derived from the transition system in Fig. 1(a). CTBS is interleaved with the state space exploration algorithm. When the state space exploration encounters an execution corresponding to a counterexample, to reaching a non-property violating trace ending in a terminal state or to reaching a duplicate state, the corresponding execution will be handed over to CTBS. CTBS maintains the BCT tree data structure, which is implemented as a prefix tree. The edges of the BCT are labeled with actions. The root vertex of this tree is labeled with all failure states of the system, in the example with the states $s_{f1}$ and $s_{f2}$. The non-root vertices are labeled with a set of states. These states are equivalent in the sense that one can reach one of the failure states from them via an identical trace. The trace is defined by the sequence of action labels along the edges of the BCT tree that are encountered on the path from the considered vertex to the root vertex. As an example, the vertex labeled $s_2, s_5$ implies that from states $s_2$ and $s_5$ a failure state can be reached via a trace $c$. Notice that such traces correspond to suffixes of counterexamples. When a suffix contains an initial state, then it represents a causal trace. As an example consider the trace $abc$ leading from the leaf vertex $s_0$ to the root vertex.

The CTBS algorithm is designed to satisfy two major requirements: (1) It needs to ensure that all traces in the system are completely analyzed, independently of the search order during the state space exploration. (2) The algorithm should be efficient wrt. both space and time, in particular by storing only minimal counterexamples and by ignoring non-minimal counterexamples.

CTBS computes traces as follows. Assume the BCT tree to be labeled by all failure states. When CTBS receives an execution, it will first split the execution into the transition triples $(s_i, a_i, s_{i+1})$ that it is built of. In the sequel we will refer to $s_{i+1}$ as the target state of that transition. For each of these transition triples we ensure that there is a child vertex labeled by $s_{i+1}$ for a father vertex labeled $s_i$ in the BCT tree. If the child vertex does not exist, it will be added to the tree. The edge leading to this child will be labeled with $a_i$. If the child vertex exists, but the edge to the child is labeled by some $a_j \neq a_i$, then a new child node labeled $s_{i+1}$ will be added and the edge leading to this note will be labeled with $a_i$.

In order to ensure efficiency, the algorithm exploits the observation that for each state $s$ in a minimal counterexample, there is no shorter trace to reach a failure state from $s$ than the suffix of the trace corresponding to the counterexample that starts in $s$. This implies that all non-minimal suffixes can be removed from the BCT tree, as expressed by the prune rules *PR1* and *PR2*. To illustrate this point, assume that a given BCT tree contains a path *bac* and that the state space exploration hands the trace *abac* over to CTBS. Assume further that *abac* will be split into transition triples and integrated into the BCT tree. Since *bac* is contained in *abac*, the vertex that stores *abac* and the complete subtree that hangs off it will be pruned from the BCT tree.

*PR1.* The CTBS algorithm deletes a vertex when the trace of the vertex contains a shorter counterexample.

Lemma 1 shows that the trace of a vertex deleted by prune rule PR1 is not a suffix of a minimal counterexample.

**Lemma 1.** *A suffix that contains a shorter initial trace is not a suffix of a minimal counterexample.*

*Proof.* Assume a trace $t$ and a shorter initial trace $t'$ that satisfies $t' \sqsubset t$, and an arbitrary minimal counterexample $t_c$ with suffix $t$. $t$ being a suffix of $t_c$ implies that $t \sqsubseteq t_c$. $t \sqsubseteq t_c$ and the assumption $t' \sqsubset t$ interrelate transitively, which yields $t' \sqsubset t_c$. $t'$ is a counterexample since it is initial. As consequence, any counterexample $t_c$ is not minimal since $t'$ is minimal. □

A second prune rule removes a state label from a vertex when another vertex labeled with this state has a shorter trace to reach a failure state. Assume a vertex labeled with $s_2$ to be in the BCT tree of Fig. 1(b) from which the root vertex can be reached via trace $ac$. The BCT tree contains a vertex labeled $s_2s_5$ which has a trace $c$. The trace of vertex $s_2$ contains the trace of vertex $s_2s_5$. As a consequence, prune rule PR2 removes the state label $s_2$ from the respective vertex and thereby removes the longer suffix $ac$ from the BCT tree.

*PR2.* The algorithm CTBS removes a state $s$ from a vertex $v$ whenever the trace $t_v$ of $v$ contains the trace of another vertex $v'$ labeled with $s$.

Lemma 2 shows that a counterexample with a suffix that is equivalent to the trace of the vertex $v$ in *PR2* cannot be minimal.

**Lemma 2.** *Any counterexample with a suffix starting in a state $s$ in vertex $v$ is not minimal when another vertex $v'$ with state $s$ exists and the traces $t_v$ contains trace $t_{v'}$.*

*Proof.* Assume two different vertices $v$ and $v'$ with state $s$ and with traces $t_v$ and $t_{v'}$ that satisfy $t_{v'} \sqsubseteq t_v$, and an arbitrary counterexample $c$ with suffix $t_{v'}$. The counterexample $c$ is not minimal since we can construct a shorter counterexample than $c$. Notice that $t_v \neq t_{v'}$ otherwise $v = v'$. We split $c$ in state $s$ in a prefix $s_0a_0 \ldots s$ and the suffix $t_v = s \ldots s_f$, prepend the prefix to the suffix $t_{v'} = s \ldots s_{f'}$ and result with a counterexample $c' = s_0a_0 \ldots s \ldots s_{f'}$. The assumption $t_{v'} \sqsubseteq t_v$ with $t_v \neq t_{v'}$ results in $t_{v'} \sqsubset t_v$. $c' \sqsubset c$ holds because the prefixes of $c$ and $c'$ before state $s$ are equivalent by construction and for the suffixes $t_{v'} \sqsubset t_v$ holds. Thus, $c'$ is shorter than $c$ and $c$ is not minimal. □

The pseudo code of the CTBS algorithm is shown in Listing 1.1. The algorithm uses four data structures: The vertex **root** is the root vertex of the prefix tree, a state **initial** stores the initial state of the TS, a map **v_map** returns vertices that contain a certain state, and a map **t_map** returns a list of transitions with a certain state as the target state.

```
1  Vertex root; State initial;
2  Map<State, Set<Vertex>> v_map;
3  Map<State, Set<Transition>> t_map;
4
5  function addExecution(Exection e)
6     IF e.hasBad()
7         //add property violating states to root
8         root.addState(e.lastState());
9     initial = e.firstState();
10    //iterate execution transitions
11    FOR Transition t in e
12        t_map.get(t.s2).add(t);
13        addTransition(t.s1, t.act, t.s2);
14
15 function addTransition(s1, act, s2)
16    //get all vertices with state s2
17    FOR Vertex v2 in v_map(s2)
18       //get father vertex reachable by label act
19       Vertex v1 = v2.getFather(act)
20       //ensure restriction PR1 and PR2
21       IF causalPathShorter(v1) || otherShorter(v1, s1)
22          continue;
23       v1.add(s1);
24       checkOtherLonger(v1, s1); //enforce PR2
25       IF s1 == initial
26          checkAllPaths(v1);     //enforce PR1
27          return;
28       FOR Transition t' in t_map.get(s1)
29          addTransition(t'.s1, t'.act, t'.s2);
```

**Listing 1.1.** Sketch of Backward Causal Trace Search Algorithm

The algorithm calls the function **addExecution** iteratively for a counterexample or a duplicate execution. If the function is called with a counterexample, the last state of the execution violates the property and this state is added to the root (lines 6–8). For counterexamples and duplicate executions, the algorithm saves the initial state which is the same state for all executions of a TS in variable **initial** (line 9).

The algorithm adds the transitions belonging to an execution to the **t_map** and calls, for every transition $t = (s_1, a, s_2)$, the function **addTransition** (line 11–13). This function checks for every vertex $v_2$ with state $s_2$ (line 17) whether a vertex $v_1$ with state $s_1$ and edge $(v_1, a, v)$ (line 19) does satisfy one of the prune rules PR1 and PR2 (line 21), and in this case continues with the next vertex (line 22). Otherwise, both prune rules are not satisfied, $s_1$ is part of a new minimal suffix and the state $s_1$ is added to $v_1$ (line 23). The algorithm then checks whether any other path of a vertex with state $s_1$ now contains the path of $v_1$ (line 24) and removes $s_1$ from such a vertex. If $s_1$ is an initial state, then a causal trace is found and all other paths in the tree are checked to determine whether they contain the new causal trace (line 26). The transitions of a prefix that reaches state $s_1$ can already be contained in the transition list **t_map** and need again to be added to the BCT tree. Therefore, the function calls itself recursively for all transitions $t'$ with $s_1$ as a target state (line 28–29). In order to ensure a clear presentation, we removed several optimization from the pseudo code. Most importantly, in order to optimize performance **addExecution** calls **addTransition** only for transitions not yet in **t_map**. Furthermore, if $v_1$ in the function **addTransition** already contains the state $s_1$, than this vertex is ignored and the recursion is not called.

*Correctness of the CTBS Algorithm.* First, it should be noted that CTBS delivers a sound BCT tree since every trace in the computed BCT tree corresponds to an execution of the TS that we consider. The CTBS algorithm is correct iff the set of traces that the BCT tree represents is a causal trace set, in other words, if this set satisfies conditions TC1 and TC2 from Definition 2.

**Lemma 3.** *The set of traces represented by the BCT tree computed by the CTBS algorithm satisfies condition TC1 of Definition 2.*

*Proof.* Assume a set $\Psi$ of traces computed by the CTBS algorithm for a set of executions that is returned by a state space exploration algorithm for a TS $S$, and a counterexample $t$ that does not contain any trace in $\Psi$. By the construction of $\Psi$, all traces in $\Psi$ are contained in a BCT tree $PT$. Obviously, $t$ is not a trace of the tree, otherwise, $t$ itself is in $\Psi$. $t$ is not a trace in the BCT tree in two cases.

1. $t$ was never added as a trace to $PT$. This means that there is in the sequence of transitions that corresponds to trace $t$ at least one transition $(s_i, a_i, s_{i+1})$ so that $s_i$ is not a target state of any other transition in $PT$. This means that this transition was never handed over by the state space exploration algorithm. A state space exploration algorithm explores the full state space of an $S$ and every transition of $S$ is contained in at least one execution. Since $t$ contains a transition that is not contained in $S$, $t$ is not a trace of $S$. This contradicts the assumption that $t$ is a counterexample of $S$.
2. $t$ was deleted by a prune rule because $t$ contains a shorter counterexample $t'$. In that case, $t'$ is a trace in $\Psi$. Otherwise, $t'$ is also deleted because of an even shorter counterexample that is contained in $PT$.

Either $t$ does not exist or contains a counterexample in $PT$. Both cases contradict the assumption that a counterexample $t$ exists that contains no trace in $\Psi$. □

Notice that this completeness result also holds for the CTBS algorithm when it is used with a BFS algorithm for the state space exploration. Assume that the completeness does not hold. Then there would be a counterexample of length shorter than the current search depth that contains an unexplored transition, which means that the corresponding trace is not included in the BCT tree $PT$. This, however, contradicts the property of a BFS that all states up to the current search depth have been explored. This property is beneficial in case we need to bound the search depth in causality checking for very large models since it ensures that the causal traces up to the current search depth form a causal trace set, which implies completeness up to the search depth reached.

**Lemma 4.** *The set of traces in the BCT tree computed by the CTBS algorithm contains only minimal counterexamples.*

*Proof.* Assume a BCT tree $PT$ computed by the CTBS algorithm for a TS $S$, and a vertex with an initial state $s_0$ and a non-minimal trace $t$ contained in $PT$. $t$ is a non-minimal trace if another counterexample $t'$ exists in $S$ with $t' \sqsubset t$. There are two cases where $t'$ can exist. In the first case, $t'$ is not contained in $PT$ and this case violates Lemma 3. In the second case, $t'$ is contained in $PT$. In this case a vertex $v$ with the initial state $s_0$ exists for $t$. Also, for $t$ a corresponding vertex $v'$ exists. One of the vertices already contains $s_0$ and with adding $s_0$ to the other vertex, the corresponding traces $t$ and $t'$ are compared by prune rule PR1 when determining whether the vertices of $t$ or $t'$ can be removed. This leads to two cases. If $v$ already contains $s_0$, then $s_0$ is removed from $v$. Otherwise, if $v'$ already contains $s_0$, then $s_0$ is not added to $v$. In both cases, $v$ does not contain $s_0$. This contradicts the assumption that $t$ is an initial trace. □

The correctness of CBTS follows from Lemmas 3 and 4.

*Complexity Considerations.* The *worst-case size of the causal trace set* is bounded by the number of traces in a TS, since all traces can be minimal traces. A minimal trace can be an arbitrary sequence of actions from the action set *Act*, where the corresponding execution of the TS contains any state at most once. Traces generated by loops in the TS do not need to be considered in the complexity analysis, as can easily be seen. Assume a minimal trace that reaches a state twice, then the subtrace between reaching the state for the first and the second time corresponds to a loop in the TS. A trace not including this loop is shorter and reaches the same end state as the trace that contains the loop, which means that the trace including the loop cannot be minimal. In the worst case, the number of traces in a TS is $|Act|^{n-1}$, where $|Act|$ is the number of actions and $n$ is the number of states in the TS.

The *worst case complexity of the DSPM algorithm* was shown in [Lei15] to be in $\mathcal{O}(|t|^2)$ where $|t|$ is the number of all traces in an TS. The complexity is driven by the comparison of every trace in $t$ with all causal traces, which in the worst case can be all traces.

The *worst case complexity of the CTBS algorithm* is also dominated by the number of trace comparisons. The algorithm processes iteratively the set of transitions $E$ of a TS. The number of transitions $|E|$ is at most $|t|$ in the worst case in which all traces $t$ consist of a single transition. A transition can only be added once to a trace in the BCT tree. Otherwise the trace would not be minimal since it would contain the target state of the transition twice. In the worst case a transition is added to all traces in the BCT tree. When adding a state to a vertex, the prune rules need to compare the trace of this vertex in the worst case twice with all other traces. We conclude that the CTBS algorithm has a worst case complexity of $|E| \cdot |t| \cdot 2 \cdot |t| \in \mathcal{O}(|t|^3)$.

In conclusion, under worst case complexity considerations, DSPM scales better than CTBS. The approximation performed by the DSPM algorithm does not affect the worst case runtime since the trace set $t$ consists of all traces, including the traces not analyzed by DSPM.

The worst case complexity of computing a causal trace set depends on the number of all traces that need to be computed, which as shown above can be exponential. However, for realistic models not all traces are minimal, and hence not causal. This means that there is significant potential in removing non-causal traces. The DSPM algorithm always analyzes complete counterexamples. In contrast, due to the prune rules the CTBS algorithm compares and prunes suffixes before a complete counterexample is analyzed. This is the essential performance advantage of the CTBS algorithm over DSPM, as will become obvious during the experimental evaluation.

## 4 Case Study and Experimental Evaluation

We now compare the DSPM and CTSB algorithms by analyzing several models of different size taken from [Lei15]. We implemented four variants of the considered algorithms:

(1) the CTBS algorithm based on BFS state space exploration,
(2) the CTBS algorithm based on DFS state space exploration,
(3) a modified version of the DSPM algorithm, and
(4) to obtain a baseline, an algorithm that ignores all duplicate states, i.e., behaves like a standard BFS when encountering a duplicate state.

These implementations are integrated in the `QuantUM` tool and use a modified version the model checker SpinJa [dJR10] for the state space exploration. We modified the above described DSPM algorithm in order to address its insufficiencies with respect to treating multiple duplicates encountered during state space exploration. This is accomplished by computing all minimal counterexamples by repeatedly iterating through all duplicate states stored in a list maintained by DSPM until no new counterexample is generated.

All analyses were performed on a computer with a E5-2697 CPU (2.7GHz), 785GB of RAM and a 64 bit Linux operating system. The analysis algorithms were mapped to two threads: one thread performed the state space exploration and another executed the algorithm for the causal trace set computation. The state space exploration was based on a BFS as long as nothing else is stated. A timeout for the experiments was set to two hours.

**Table 1.** Experimental results for CTBS algorithm (variant 1).

| Model | States | Transitions | Depth | #Causal | #Class | $Time_{Last}$ | $Time_R$ | Memory |
|---|---|---|---|---|---|---|---|---|
| Railroad crossing | 143 | 373 | 37 | 62 | 4 | <00:01 | 00:04 | 51 MB |
| Airbag | 3456 | 14257 | 35 | 484 | 5 | <00:01 | 07:09 | 62 MB |
| Odometer | 4032 | 19624 | 55 | 13 | 3 | <00:01 | 00:09 | 70 MB |
| FFU Star | 207052 | 964695 | 37/61 | 458 | 16 | <00:01 | timeout | 545 MB |
| FFU ECU | 235765 | 90775575 | 31/61 | 509 | 19 | <00:01 | timeout | 896 MB |
| ASR ch1 | 680897 | 3745635 | 37/61 | 67200 | 2 | 02:00:05 | timeout | 3747 MB |
| ASR Reduced | 14222115 | 45997298 | 39/61 | 76428 | 2 | 01:45:58 | timeout | 91814 MB |

Table 1 shows the results of the CTBS algorithm. The input model is characterized by the number of states that were explored, the number of transitions traversed and the maximal search depth. For the larger models `FFU Star`, `FFU ECU`, `ASR ch1` and `ASR Reduced` we limited the search depth to 60. In case of a timeout, the current search depth reached by the CTBS algorithm is given in column *Depth*. For all of the four larger models, the search depth limit was reached when the timeout occurred. We indicate time values using the format (hours:minutes:seconds). The column $\#Causal$ gives the size of the causal trace set that was computed, $\#Class$ gives the number of causal classes that were detected, and $Time_{Last}$ indicates the period of time after starting the experiment when the last causal trace was found. The computation time consumed by the analysis is given in the $Time_R$ column, and the consumed memory in the column *Memory*. Table 2 shows some experimental results for the algorithm variants (4), (3) and (2).

In order to compare the algorithm variants qualitatively, we analyzed the railroad crossing example taken from [Lei15] with the CTBS variant (1) using the QuantUM tool. We obtained the fault tree depicted in Fig. 2. The fault tree has four subtrees that represent the causality classes `Class 0` ... `Class 3`. A class is created by all causal traces with the same set of actions. The number of causal traces that a class contains is depicted next to the class name, for instance, `Class 0` contains 20 causal traces. These causal traces lead to a partial order representing 20 different linear orderings of the 5 class events in `Class 0`. Notice that the type of fault tree that we use is a dynamic fault tree, which means that the order of the occurrence of events on one of its and-branches is assumed to be linear from the top to the bottom. In effect, Causality Checking computes a partial order of these events that cannot be directly depicted in a fault tree. To describe these partial order constraints we use event order logic, and we omit these ordering constraints here.

*Quantitative Result Interpretation.* The algorithm variant (4) defines a base line for the quantitative performance of the other algorithm variants when analyzing the different models. The highest analysis time with this algorithm is observed for the model `ASR Reduced` with a value of 57:57. The algorithm variants (1), (2) and

**Table 2.** Experimental results for the algorithm variants (4), (3) and (2).

| Model | Ignore duplicate traces | | | mod. DSPM algorithm | | | CTBS with DFS | | |
|---|---|---|---|---|---|---|---|---|---|
| | #Causal | #Class | $Time_R$ | #Causal | #Class | $Time_R$ | #Causal | #Class | $Time_R$ |
| Railroad crossing | 2 | 2 | 00:04 | 48 | 4 | timeout | 62 | 3 | 00:04 |
| Airbag | 5 | 5 | 00:09 | 62 | 7 | timeout | 484 | 5 | 39:46 |
| Odometer | 3 | 3 | 00:07 | 6 | 3 | timeout | 13 | 3 | 00:08 |
| FFU Star | 16 | 16 | 00:47 | 110 | 41 | timeout | 4768 | 289 | timeout |
| FFU ECU | 19 | 19 | 00:29 | 149 | 7 | timeout | 2 | 2 | timeout |
| ASR ch1 | 2 | 2 | 01:50 | 31 | 2 | timeout | 9607 | 20 | timeout |
| ASR Reduced | 3 | 3 | 57:57 | 27 | 3 | timeout | 34972 | 7 | timeout |

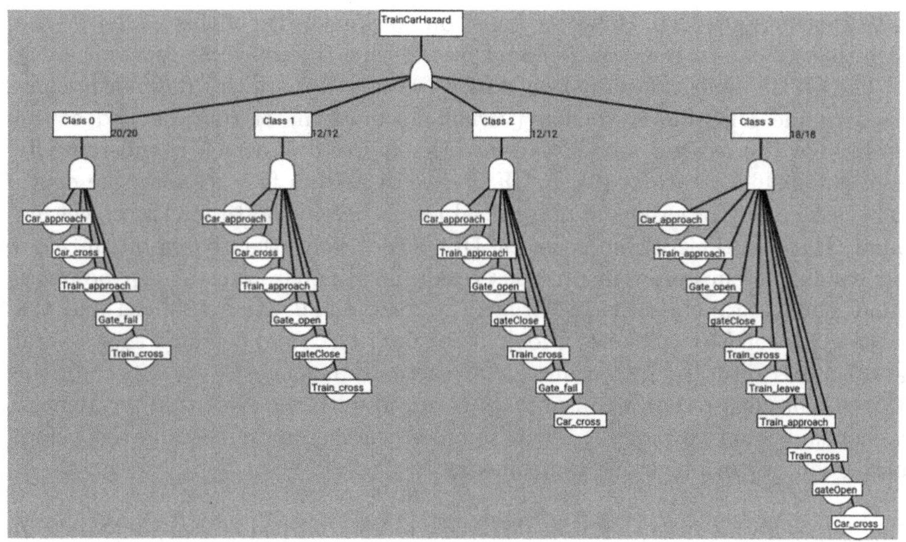


**Fig. 2.** Fault tree for railroad crossing using CTBS variant (1)

(3) have a much higher computation time demand. As opposed to the baseline, these algorithms experienced a timeout for the models `FFU Star`, `FFU ECU`, `ASR ch1` and `ASR Reduced`. We can conclude that the penalty for processing duplicate states completely is a significant increase in computation time. Algorithm variant (3), which corresponds to the approximating DSPM algorithm, experiences a timeout for all models, whereas CTBS in both variants (1) and (2) is able to analyze some models without timeout. This points to a performance advantage of CTBS over DPSM.

More generally, the advantage of CTBS over DPSM in terms of its performance on practical models can be argued as follows. First, the CTBS can return preliminary results. In particular, a causal trace set can be constructed when using a BFS state space exploration even when the computation aborts for instance due to a timeout. The analysis of the model `FFU Star` guarantees that all causal traces up to depth 37 when the timeout occurs are found, and that traces that were found up to that depth are actually causal. The same holds true for the analysis of model `FFU ECU` at depth 31, for the model `ASR ch1` at depth 37 and for the model `ASR Reduced` at depth 39. Notice that since we return causal trace sets in these situations, the results are complete and no causal traces up to the analysis depth that was reached are missing. Second, causal traces are minimal and, as a consequence, found early during the analysis. For several models the last causal trace was detected in less than 1 s, as can be gleaned from the data in column $Time_{Last}$. The remainder of the computation time is spent by the algorithm to ensure that the causal trace set contains all causal traces. For instance, for the `Airbag` model, the computation of this guarantee takes another 7 min and 9 s. For the models `FFU ECU` and `FFU Star` the checking of this guarantee timeouts after 2 h. However, based on our knowledge of this model we can state that all causal traces were found by the time the timeout occurred.

The CTBS algorithm based on a BFS (variant 1) performs differently compared to the DFS based version (variant 2) in terms of runtime and causal results. For the `Airbag` model, variant (1) requires 7:09 which is substantially less than 39:46 for variant (2). A DFS based algorithm first searches the depth and checks many orderings of non causal traces before shorter causal traces are found. The CTBS algorithm based on DFS scales worse than based on BFS and this result goes in line with previous results in [LL13a]. Variant (2), however, found more causal classes than variant (1), for the `FFU Star`, `ASR ch1` and `ASR reduced` model. We had a closer look at the fault trees and detected that several causal traces returned by variant (2) are actually not causal. As expected, the DFS cannot ensure that a causal trace is causal until the algorithm terminates. We conclude that variant (2) is not sound when the analysis is aborted before completion, for instance due to a timeout.

*Qualitative Result Interpretation.* We refer to the railroad crossing example to illustrate some qualitative differences between variant (1) and variant (4), the algorithm defining the baseline in terms of quantitative performance. In the railroad crossing model, a train can approach the crossing (Train_approach), enter the crossing (Train_cross) and finally leave the crossing. Whenever a train is approaching, the gate should close (gateClose) and will open when the train has left the crossing. Additionally, it is possible that the gate fails (Gate_fail). The car approaches the crossing (Car_approach) and enters the crossing (Car_cross) when the gate is open, and finally leaves the crossing. The fault tree computed for the railroad crossing example by variant (4) is missing the causality classes labeled `Class 2` and `Class 3`, which were on the other hand computed by variant (1), see the fault tree in Fig. 2. The events of `Class 0` are a subset of the events in `Class 2`, but the action Gate_fail happens after the action Train_cross. The events of `Class 1` are contained in `Class 3` but the action Car_approach happens after the action gateClose. When Gate_fail happens before Car_approach, the gate stays open. When Gate_fail happens after Car_approach then the gate falsely opens itself. From `Class 1` we can infer that an accident happens because the car is not leaving the crossing. From `Class 3` computed by CTBS in variant (1) we conclude that an accident can additionally happen because the train is not leaving the crossing. This exemplifies that CTBS in variant (1) can compute more information regarding the cause of an event in the system than the baseline algorithm variant (4). This is due to the completeness of variant (1) as opposed to the incompleteness of variant (4).

## 5 Conclusion

In this paper we have addressed the complete computation of causal trace sets in Causality Checking. The complete computation of the causal trace sets is essential in the analysis of safety-critical systems in order to ensure that all causal factors will be identified by the analysis. The CTBS algorithm that we propose addresses the problem of a complete and sound construction of traces that belong to this set when the state space traversal encounters multiple duplicate states during the search. We contrast the CTBS algorithm with the DSPM algorithm, which is the current basis for implementations of Causality Checking. The variant of DSPM originally implemented in QuantUM only performs an incomplete under-approximative handling of the construction of traces when encountering duplicate states. In contrast, CTBS handles the encounter of duplicate states properly and completely and manages to establish complete causal sets. In particular, CTBS outperforms a variant of DSPM modified to accomplish a naive correction of the under-approximation.

Further research addresses the application of the algorithmic scheme underlying CTBS to other applications where all executions of a state space need to be explored exhaustively. Furthermore, we will investigate the computation of causal trace sets using symbolic state space exploration techniques.

## References


[AL10] Aljazzar, H., Leue, S.: Directed explicit state-space search in the generation of counterexamples for stochastic model checking. IEEE Trans. Softw. Eng. **36**(1), 37–60 (2010)

[BHK+15] Beer, A., Heidinger, S., Kühne, U., Leitner-Fischer, F., Leue, S.: Symbolic causality checking using bounded model checking. In: Fischer, B., Geldenhuys, J. (eds.) SPIN 2015. LNCS, vol. 9232, pp. 203–221. Springer, Cham (2015). https://doi.org/10.1007/978-3-319-23404-5_14

[BK+08] Baier, C., Katoen, J.-P., et al.: Principles of Model Checking. MIT Press (2008)

[dJR10] de Jonge, M., Ruys, T.C.: The SpinJa model checker. In: van de Pol, J., Weber, M. (eds.) SPIN 2010. LNCS, vol. 6349, pp. 124–128. Springer, Heidelberg (2010). https://doi.org/10.1007/978-3-642-16164-3_9

[ES12] Edelkamp, S., Schrödl, S.: Heuristic Search - Theory and Applications. Academic Press (2012)

[Fre60] Fredkin, E.: Trie memory. Commun. ACM **3**(9), 490–499 (1960)

[Hal15] Halpern, J.Y.: A modification of the Halpern-Pearl definition of causality. In: IJCAI, pp. 3022–3033. AAAI Press (2015)

[HK06] Hansen, H., Kervinen, A.: Minimal counterexamples in o(n log n) memory and o($n^2$) time. In: ACSD, pp. 133–142. IEEE Computer Society (2006)

[HKD09] Han, T., Katoen, J.-P., Damman, B.: Counterexample generation in probabilistic model checking. IEEE Trans. Softw. Eng. **35**(2), 241–257 (2009)

[Hol04] Holzmann, G.J.: The SPIN Model Checker - Primer and Reference Manual. Addison-Wesley (2004)

[HP05] Halpern, J.Y., Pearl, J.: Causes and explanations: a structural-model approach Part I: causes. Br. J. Phil. Sci. **56**(4), 843–887 (2005)

[KL18] Kölbl, M., Leue, S.: Automated functional safety analysis of automated driving systems. In: Howar, F., Barnat, J. (eds.) FMICS 2018. LNCS, vol. 11119, pp. 35–51. Springer, Cham (2018). https://doi.org/10.1007/978-3-030-00244-2_3

[Lei15] Leitner-Fischer, F.: Causality checking of safety-critical software and systems. Ph.D. thesis, University of Konstanz, Germany (2015)

[LL11] Leitner-Fischer, F., Leue, S.: Quantum: quantitative safety analysis of UML models. In: QAPL, volume 57 of EPTCS, pp. 16–30 (2011)

[LL13a] Leitner-Fischer, F., Leue, S.: Causality checking for complex system models. In: Giacobazzi, R., Berdine, J., Mastroeni, I. (eds.) VMCAI 2013. LNCS, vol. 7737, pp. 248–267. Springer, Heidelberg (2013). https://doi.org/10.1007/978-3-642-35873-9_16

[LL13b] Leitner-Fischer, F., Leue, S.: Probabilistic fault tree synthesis using causality computation. IJCCBS **4**(2), 119–143 (2013)

[LL14] Leitner-Fischer, F., Leue, S.: SpinCause: a tool for causality checking. In: SPIN, pp. 117–120. ACM (2014)

[Obj17] Object Management Group: OMG Systems Modeling Language, Specification 1.5 (2017). http://www.omg.org/spec/SysML

[SB05] Schuppan, V., Biere, A.: Shortest counterexamples for symbolic model checking of LTL with past. In: Halbwachs, N., Zuck, L.D. (eds.) TACAS 2005. LNCS, vol. 3440, pp. 493–509. Springer, Heidelberg (2005). https://doi.org/10.1007/978-3-540-31980-1_32

[VGRH02] Vesely, W.E., Goldberg, F.F., Roberts, N.H., Haasl, D.F.: Fault Tree Handbook (2002)

# Testing

# Conditional Testing

## Off-the-Shelf Combination of Test-Case Generators

Dirk Beyer and Thomas Lemberger

LMU Munich, Munich, Germany

**Abstract.** There are several powerful automatic testers available, each with different strengths and weaknesses. To immediately benefit from different strengths of different tools, we need to investigate ways for quick and easy combination of techniques. Until now, research has mostly investigated integrated combinations, which require extra implementation effort. We propose the concept of *conditional testing* and a set of combination techniques that do not require implementation effort: Different testers can be taken 'off the shelf' and combined in a way that they *cooperatively* solve the problem of test-case generation for a given input program and coverage criterion. This way, the latest advances in test-case generation can be combined without delay. Conditional testing passes the test goals that a first tester has covered to the next tester, so that the next tester does not need to repeat work (as in combinations without information passing) but can focus on the remaining test goals. Our combinations do not require changes to the implementation of a tester, because we leverage a testability transformation (i.e., we reduce the input program to those parts that are relevant to the remaining test goals). To evaluate conditional testing and our proposed combination techniques, we (1) implemented the generic conditional tester CondTest, including the required transformations, and (2) ran experiments on a large amount of benchmark tasks; the obtained results are promising.

**Keywords:** Software testing · Test-case generation · Conditional model checking · Cooperative verification · Software verification · Program analysis · Test coverage

## 1 Introduction

Tool competitions in software verification and testing [1,2,26,34] have shown that there is no tool that is superior, but that different tools and approaches have different strengths. Therefore, we need to combine different tools and approaches. Integrated combination approaches [8,15,19,22] have shown their potential, but those combinations require additional implementation work.

The goal of this paper is to provide a generic framework that enables combinations of tools for test-case generation without the need to change the tools: We show how to take a set of testers 'off the shelf' and combine them on the

Supported in part by DFG grant BE 1761/7-1.



Y.-F. Chen et al. (Eds.): ATVA 2019, LNCS 11781, pp. 189–208, 2019.
https://doi.org/10.1007/978-3-030-31784-3_11

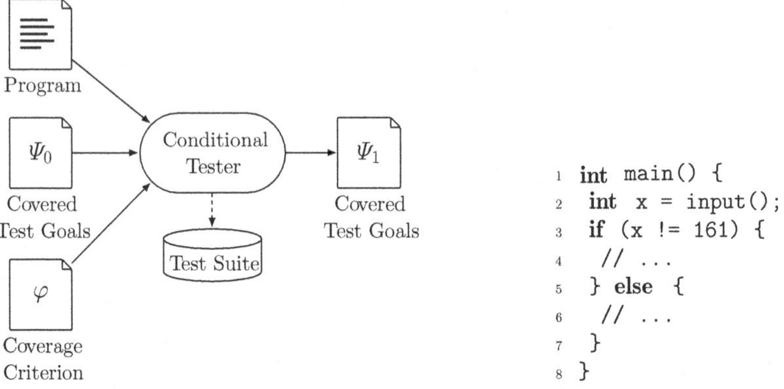


**Fig. 1.** Conditional testing

**Fig. 2.** Program under test

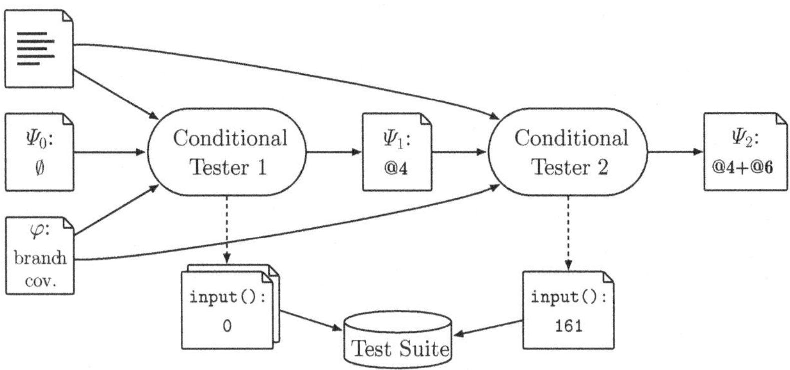


**Fig. 3.** Example usage of conditional testers

binary level. In other words, any tester can be taken as a black box, wrapped into a new meta tester (conditional tester) by a fully automated construction, and the new tester uses interfaces that make it possible to combine it with others (for an overview of combination techniques for software verification see [12]). There are several successful testers for C programs already; nine of them participated in the competition on software testing [2] and adhere to standard exchange formats for their input and output.

*Conditional testing* applies the idea of conditional model checking [7] to testing, as illustrated in Fig. 1. A *conditional tester* gets as input a program under test, a coverage criterion $\varphi$ (e.g., 'branch coverage'), and a condition $\Psi_0$ that describes a set of test goals that are already covered by existing tests. With this information, a conditional tester creates (1) a test suite that tries to cover as many test goals of $[\![\varphi]\!] \setminus \Psi_0$ as possible, and (2) a new condition $\Psi_1$ of test goals that have been covered. For a coverage criterion $\varphi$, we use $[\![\varphi]\!]$ to denote the test goals that are needed to fulfill $\varphi$. The condition $\Psi_1$ covers the test goals described by condition $\Psi_0$ and the test goals newly covered by the created test suite. With this interface for information passing, conditional testers can be combined to focus on different or remaining test goals.

Figure 2 shows a small program that we use to illustrate conditional testing. The program gets an arbitrary integer as input and stores it in program variable `x`. The program then checks whether `x` is un-equal to value 161. If it is, the if-branch is entered and some more code (`// ...`) is executed. Otherwise, the else-branch is entered. The coverage criterion of branch coverage defines two test goals for this program: (1) cover line 4 (denoted by @4 in FQL [25]), and (2) cover line 6 (@6). A test suite that covers both test goals would contain at least two test cases: One with input 161, and one with any other input. A randomized tester can quickly generate a test case with an input different from 161, because the number of possible values is very high and thus very probable to be fulfilled by a random test case. In contrast, it is difficult for a randomized tester to create a test case with input 161.

Let us consider the combination of a fast, but shallow randomized tester (Conditional Tester 1 in Fig. 3) with a tester that is slower, but uses an exhaustive reasoning technique (Conditional Tester 2), to obtain a test suite that covers all branches: Given the program under test, the coverage criterion $\varphi =$ COVER EDGES(@DECISIONEDGE) (branch coverage in FQL syntax), and the empty condition $\Psi_0 = \emptyset$ (i.e., no test goal covered yet), we run the conditional, random tester for a short amount of time. Assume it creates several different test cases, including one with input value 0. The created test cases cover line 4, but do not cover line 6. Thus, the conditional tester returns $\Psi_1 =$ **@4** for the now covered test goal. A second conditional tester, for example based on symbolic execution, then gets the same program and coverage criterion, but condition $\Psi_1$. The conditional tester focuses on the remaining test goal of covering line 6 and creates a test case with input 161. Now, all test goals are covered and $\Psi_2 =$ **@4+@6** describes both test goals.

Conditional testing does not prescribe a certain format or language to be used for specifying coverage criteria and conditions. The competition on software testing [2] uses FQL [24,25] as test-specification language, and we use FQL in the example above to describe the condition, i.e., the already-covered test goals. FQL is a versatile language for defining various test criteria, allows to define explicit sets of test goals by enumerating single locations, but it also supports to specify full program paths as test goals, as well as value constraints on variables at certain program locations, and of course standard coverage criteria such as branch coverage are provided. For the first version of our tool implementation CondTest, we started with a simpler way to denote test goals.

Since existing testers do not accept conditions, we propose a testability transformation called `reducer` that uses the coverage criterion and the condition to transform the program under test into a *residual program* that is restricted to those parts of the program that are needed to generate test cases for the remaining test goals. This residual program is then given to an off-the-shelf tester (instead of the original program under test), such that the tester is forced to generate test cases for the remaining test goals. The resulting test suite is given to an `extractor` that extracts the test goals that are covered in the original program, and computes the new condition. This process of transforming off-the-shelf testers into conditional testers can be split into three independent components: `reducer`, `tester`, and `extractor`. All three components are defined through their type and soundness-requirements, and many different implementations are possible.

To show the potential of our approach, we implemented examples for `reducer` and `extractor`. We use the common formats and infrastructure of the International Competition on Software Testing (Test-Comp) [2] to allow plug-and-play transformation of existing software testers (for example, CoVeriTest, CPA/Tiger, Klee) into conditional testers.

In addition, we contribute a construction based on conditional testing that turns an existing, formal software verifier into a conditional tester, such that existing verifiers and existing testers can be combined as well. Formal verifiers can be specialized for finding a counterexample to a certain specification, e.g., an assertion violation or a program location of interest. Verifiers have been able to create test cases from such counterexamples for over a decade [3,39] and can thus be used for directed generation of test cases for hard-to-reach test goals. Our generic conditional tester can use all verifiers (31 tools in 2019) of the International Competition on Software Verification (SV-COMP) [1]. It uses the standard violation-witness exchange-format [4] and transforms created witnesses into executable tests [5]. To feed test goals to verifiers, we provide a tailored transformation that inserts function calls at test goals and defines the specification such that the verifier shall prove unreachability of such a function call. Since most verifiers stop their analysis after finding one counterexample (i.e., creating a single test case), we repeatedly apply conditional testing with the same verifier to obtain a full test suite.

**Related Work.** We base our work on conditional model checking [7], which is a general concept for information exchange between different model checkers through the use of *conditions*. The conditions are used to instruct the next conditional model checker which parts of the state space it does not need to verify because the previous model checker had successfully verified those parts of the state space already. To transform any off-the-shelf model checker into a conditional model checker, program reduction [9,18] was proposed and successfully applied. We apply this general idea to testing and call it conditional testing. The conditions of conditional testing describe parts of the program that do not need to be tested, in terms of test goals. Similar to the reducer for conditional model checking [9] (which cuts off program paths that are already verified), we developed a reducer that cuts off program paths whose test goals are already covered. Further transformation techniques that reduce programs to only contain program paths that may be relevant for analysis include program slicing [18,38] and program trimming [20].

Other works that allow combinations of different testing techniques exists; they are either limited to specific test-case-generation techniques [8,28,30,31,36,40] or require changes of the existing implementations [8,31]. In contrast, conditional testing is completely technique-agnostic and works with existing testers 'off the shelf', that is, without changing the existing testers. Some techniques of test-suite augmentation [27,37] can be used to iteratively generate test suites with one arbitrary tester, and one specific second technique that reuses the test suite generated by the first tester. These approaches are subsumed by conditional testing as special cases. Further combination approaches of tools for verification and testing include the Electronic Tools Integration platform (ETI) [29,35], and the Evidential Tool Bus (ETB) [17,32]. Conditional model checking was also applied to combine program analysis and testing [13,16,18].

**Contributions.** This article describes the following contributions:

1. We introduce the concept of *conditional testing* (Fig. 1), which enables quick and simple combinations of conditional testers with information passing. This provides the interface to combine existing testers.
2. We present a construction of conditional testers from *off-the-shelf test-case generators*, based on program reduction and test-goal extraction (Sect. 3).
3. We present several possible combinations for conditional testers (Sect. 4).
4. Using some of these combinations, we present a construction of testers from *off-the-shelf software verifiers*, based on conditional testing (Sect. 5).
5. We have implemented the generic conditional tester CondTest, which contains all components that are necessary for the above-mentioned constructions and combinations (`https://doi.org/10.5281/zenodo.3352401`).
6. We show the potential of conditional testing for software via a thorough experimental evaluation on the large Test-Comp benchmark set, consisting of 1 720 benchmark tasks (Sect. 6).

## 2 Background

In the following, we remind the reader of some notions that are necessary to instantiate the concept of conditional testing to software. A *test vector* $\bar{v} = \langle v_0, \ldots, v_n \rangle$ is a sequence of program inputs $v_i$ with $0 \leq i \leq n$. A test vector describes a test case over the program inputs, in the order that they are passed to the program under test. A *test suite* $\{\bar{v}_0, \ldots, \bar{v}_l\}$ is a set of test vectors $\bar{v}_i$ with $0 \leq i \leq l$. We store and exchange test suites in the Test-Comp test format [2]. All Test-Comp participants can write a generated test suite in this format, which stores a test suite in a test-suite directory with several files in XML format: (1) one metadata file that contains metadata about the created test suite, and (2) one additional file for each test vector. Each test-vector file lists the test values of that test case.

We represent programs as *control-flow automata* (CFA) [6]. A CFA is an automaton $P = (L, l_0, E)$ with a set $L$ of states, initial state $l_0$, and a set $E = L \times \mathit{Ops} \times L$ of edges, with set $\mathit{Ops}$ of all possible program operations. The set $L$ of states represents the program locations, the initial state $l_0$ represents the entry point of the program, and each control-flow edge $(l, \mathit{op}, l') \in E$ represents a program transfer where the control flows from program location $l$ to program location $l'$ and program operation $\mathit{op}$ is executed. An operation is either an *assignment*, an *assumption*, or a `nop`. An assignment $x := \mathit{exp}$ assigns the value of expression $\mathit{exp}$ to program variable $x$, where $\mathit{exp}$ is a either a constant or an

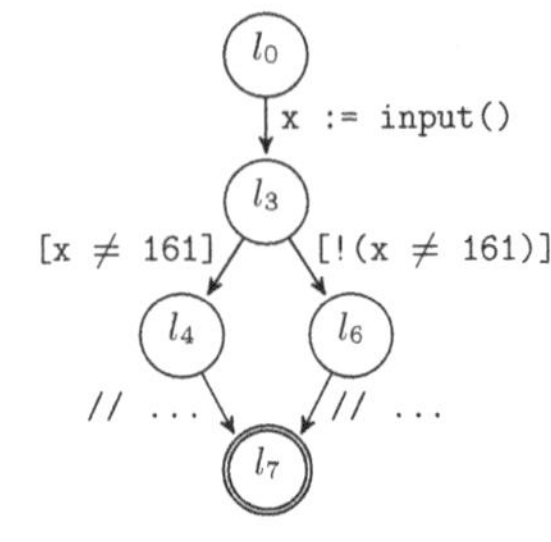


**Fig. 4.** CFA representation of the program in Fig. 2

arithmetic expression over constants and program variables. An assumption $[p]$ only transfers control from $l$ to $l'$ if $p$ is true, where $p$ is a boolean expression over constants and program variables. A `nop` is a program operation with no effect on the program's data state. A `nop` may have an arbitrary text label. Figure 4 shows a CFA representation of the program from our introductory example (Fig. 2). A *program path* $\pi = \langle l_0 \xrightarrow{op_0} l_1 \xrightarrow{op_1} \dots l_{n-1} \xrightarrow{op_{n-1}} l_n \rangle$ is a sequence of program locations that are sequentially connected through CFA edges $(l_i, op_i, l_{i+1}) \in E$. We write $\pi \in [\![P]\!]$ if $\pi$ is a program path of program $P$. The execution of a test vector $\bar{v}$ on a CFA $P$ results in a single, deterministic program path $\langle l_0 \xrightarrow{op_0} \dots \xrightarrow{op_{n-1}} l_n \rangle$, beginning at the program entry $l_0$. A test vector *covers* a test goal $g$ if its execution results in a program path that reaches $g$.

A *violation witness* [4] is a non-deterministic, finite-state automaton that describes a set of program paths from which at least one reaches a specification violation. From each violation witness, at least one test vector can be extracted [5] that follows a program path described by the witness.

A testability transformation [23] is a transformation $\mathcal{P} \times \mathcal{G} \rightarrow \mathcal{P} \times \mathcal{G}$ over the set $\mathcal{P}$ of programs and the set $\mathcal{G}$ of test-goal descriptions. A testability transformation $\tau$ transforms a given program $P$ and given test goals $G$ such that, for $\tau(P, G) = (P', G')$, the following holds: if a test-suite $S$ covers all test goals $G'$ on $P'$, test suite $S$ covers all test goals $G$ on $P$. The reducer presented in the following section will be based on a testability transformation that only transforms the program and keeps the test goals unchanged.

## 3 Construction of Conditional Testers from Existing Testers

Figure 5 shows how a conditional tester can be created from an off-the-shelf tester. A conditional software tester gets as input a program under test $P$, a coverage criterion $\varphi$, and a condition $\Psi_0$ (that describes already covered test goals). First, the set $G = [\![\varphi]\!] \setminus \Psi_0$ of remaining test goals that shall be covered is computed. Then, a program reducer `reducer` takes $G$ and $P$, and creates a residual program that contains the program behavior relevant for creating test cases that cover test goals in $G$ and that omits other program behavior. This residual program and coverage criterion $\varphi$ are then given to a (classic, existing)

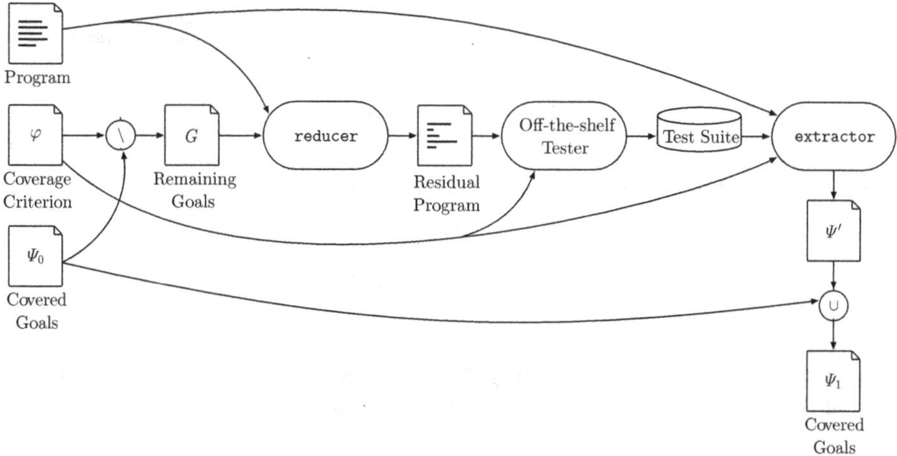


**Fig. 5.** Conditional tester $\texttt{tester}^{\text{cond}}$

tester, which creates new test cases based on them. Once the tester stops, the original program $P$, the coverage criterion $\varphi$, and the created test suite are given to a test-goal extractor `extractor`, which computes all test goals $\Psi'$ in $P$ that are described by $\varphi$ and that the test suite covers. Then, the newly covered goals $\Psi'$ are combined with $\Psi_0$ to get the full set $\Psi_1 = \Psi_0 \cup \Psi'$ of now covered test goals.

In the following, we will show requirements on the components `reducer` and `extractor`. We consider programs in their CFA representation. For ease of presentation, we assume that all program variables and constants are integers, and we only consider intra-procedural analysis here, i.e., programs with a single procedure. Our approach can be naturally extended to other data types and inter-procedural analysis. We represent test goals as CFA edges and describe conditions as sets of test goals.[1]

### 3.1 Program Reduction

A program reducer is a testability transformation $\texttt{reducer}_G : P \rightarrow P'$ that transforms, for a given set $G$ of test goals, a program $P$ to a program $P'$ that is $G$-coverage-equivalent to $P$. Two programs $P$ and $P'$ are *$G$-coverage-equivalent* if the two executions of $P$ and $P'$ on a test vector $\bar{v}$ cover the same subset $G_{\bar{v}} \subseteq G$ of test goals. Compared to traditional testability transformation [23], the set $G$ of test goals is not changed by `reducer` (we write $\texttt{reducer}_G : P \rightarrow P'$ as abbreviation for $\texttt{reducer} : P \times G \rightarrow P' \times G$). This allows us to run testers and generated test cases on the same coverage criterion, and no mapping between test goals is necessary. We require a program reducer to be *sound* and *complete.* Soundness is the basic requirement for testability transformations [23]. We also require completeness to ensure that test-case generation on the reduced program does not miss any test goal that is reachable in the original program.

[1] All coverage criteria that are based on code reachability can be reduced to reachability of CFA edges through testability transformations [23,33].

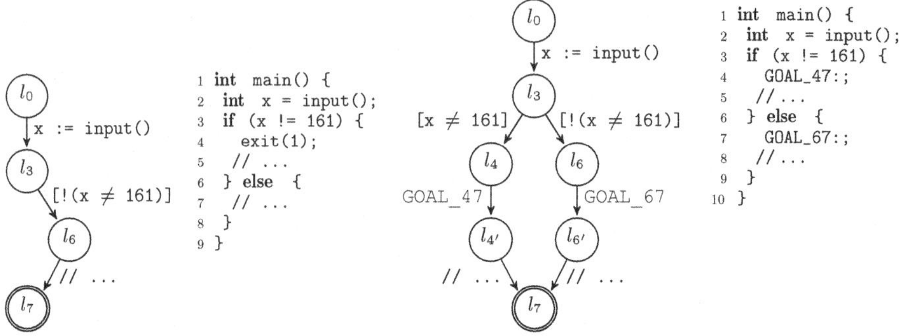


**Fig. 6.** Residual program for test goal $(l_6, /\!/ \ldots, l_7)$

**Fig. 7.** Program instrumented by Alg. 1 for test-goal extraction

*Soundness.* Given a program $P$ and a set $G$ of test goals, the reducer $\texttt{reducer}_G$ is *sound* if the following holds: if a test vector $\bar{v}$ on program $P' = \texttt{reducer}_G(P)$ covers a test goal $g \in G$, then $\bar{v}$ on program $P$ covers $g$.

*Completeness.* Given a program $P$ and a set $G$ of test goals, the reducer $\texttt{reducer}_G$ is *complete* if the following holds: if a test vector $\bar{v}$ on program $P$ covers a test goal $g \in G$, then $\bar{v}$ on program $P' = \texttt{reducer}_G(P)$ covers $g$.

**Identity Reducer.** The program reducer $\texttt{reducer}^{\texttt{id}}$ is the identity, i.e., it returns a given program without any modification.

**Pruning Reducer.** The program reducer $\texttt{reducer}^{\texttt{prune}}$ is based on syntactic reachability. Given a CFA $P = (L, l_0, E)$ and a set $G \subseteq E$ of test goals, $\texttt{reducer}^{\texttt{prune}}$ computes a new CFA $P' = (L', l_0, E')$ that only contains program locations and their corresponding edges from which a test goal is reachable. Formally, $L' = \{l \in L \mid \exists (l_g, op_g, l'_g) \in G : \langle \ldots \xrightarrow{op} l \xrightarrow{op'} \ldots l_g \xrightarrow{op_g} l'_g \rangle \in [\![P]\!]\}$ and $E' = \{(l, op, l') \in E \mid l, l' \in L'\}$.

Figure 6 shows the result of $\texttt{reducer}^{\texttt{prune}}_{\{(l_6, /\!/ \ldots, l_7)\}}(P)$ for our example program (Fig. 4), as CFA and translated to C code. Because the left branch with condition $x \neq 161$ can never reach test goal $(l_6, /\!/ \ldots, l_7)$, it is removed from the CFA. C code can not express single assumption edges, so we translate the CFA by placing an `exit`-call after the first assumption that is not part of the CFA (line 4).

**Proposition 1.** *Program reducer $\texttt{reducer}^{\texttt{prune}}$ is sound.*

*Proof.* Given a program $P = (L, l_0, E)$ and a set $G \subseteq E$ of test goals, if a program path $\langle l_0 \xrightarrow{op} \ldots l_g \xrightarrow{op_g} l'_g \rangle$ with $(l_g, op_g, l'_g) \in G$ exists in program $P' = \texttt{reducer}^{\texttt{prune}}_G(P)$, then the same program path must exist in the original program $P$, by construction. So if the execution of a test vector $\bar{v}$ on $P'$ results in program path $\langle l_0 \xrightarrow{op} \ldots l_g \xrightarrow{op_g} l'_g \ldots \rangle$, then its execution on $P$ will result in the same program path, and thus also reach test goal $(l_g, op_g, l'_g)$.

**Proposition 2.** *Program reducer* $\texttt{reducer}^{prune}$ *is complete.*

*Proof.* Given a program $P = (L, l_0, E)$ and a set $G \subseteq E$ of test goals, if a program path $\langle l_0 \xrightarrow{op} \ldots l_g \xrightarrow{op_g} l'_g\rangle$ with $(l_g, op_g, l'_g) \in G$ exists in program $P$, then the same program path must exist in the reduced program $P' = \texttt{reducer}^{\text{prune}}_G(P)$, by construction. So if the execution of a test vector $\bar{v}$ on $P$ results in program path $\langle l_0 \xrightarrow{op} \ldots l_g \xrightarrow{op_g} l'_g \ldots\rangle$, then its execution on $P'$ will result in the same program path, and thus also reach test goal $(l_g, op_g, l'_g)$.

**Annotating Reducer.** Program reducer $\texttt{reducer}^{\text{annot}}$ is based on program annotations. Given a CFA $P = (L, l_0, E)$ and a set $G \subseteq E$ of test goals, $\texttt{reducer}^{\text{annot}}$ computes (analogous to adding labels, Algorithm 1) a new CFA $P' = (L', l_0, E')$ that contains a call to custom method `VERIFIER_error` before each test goal. Method `VERIFIER_error` is defined as an empty method, i.e., it has no effect on the program state, but it can be used to guide supporting testers. Since $\texttt{reducer}^{\text{annot}}$ does not change program behavior, it is a sound and complete program reducer.

### 3.2 Test-Goal Extraction

A test-goal extractor `extractor` takes as input a program $P$, a coverage criterion $\varphi$, and a test suite, and returns as output a set $\Psi$ of test goals that are covered by the test suite. We require a test-goal extractor to be *sound* and *complete*.

*Soundness.* Given a program $P$, a coverage criterion $\varphi$, and a test suite $S$ that covers a set $G \subseteq [\![\varphi]\!]$ of test goals, then a test-goal extractor `extractor` is *sound*, if the set $\Psi = \texttt{extractor}(P, \varphi, S)$ only contains test goals that are covered by $S$, i.e., $\Psi \subseteq G$.

*Completeness.* Given a program $P$, a coverage criterion $\varphi$, and a test suite $S$ that covers a set $G \subseteq [\![\varphi]\!]$ of test goals, then a test-goal extractor `extractor` is *complete*, if the set $\Psi = \texttt{extractor}(P, \varphi, S)$ contains all test goals that are covered by $S$, i.e., $\Psi \supseteq G$.

**Test-Goal Extraction Based on Test Execution.** Test-goal extractor $\texttt{extractor}^{\text{exec}}$ computes covered test goals through execution. For a program $P$, a coverage criterion $\varphi$, and a test suite $S$, it executes each test vector $\bar{v}_i \in S$ on program $P$ and records the CFA edges of the resulting program path $\pi_i = \langle l_0 \xrightarrow{op} \ldots \xrightarrow{op_{n-1}} l_n\rangle$. From these, it computes the set of test goals covered by $S$, i.e., $\Psi = \bigcup_{\pi_i} \{(l, op, l') \in \pi_i\}$.

To be able to easily identify test goals in real C code, we perform a testability transformation that adds, for each test goal $g \in [\![\varphi]\!]$, a `nop` with label `GOAL_i_j`. Test-goal extraction for branch coverage consists of four steps: (1) Computing the set of test goals (*test-goal computation*), (2) adding, for each test goal, a label to the original program that identifies that test goal in the code (*testability transformation*), (3) executing the test suite on that transformed program (*test execution*), and (4) checking which labels are covered by the test suite (*coverage measurement*).

**Algorithm 1.** Testability Transformation: *addLabels*($P$, $G$)

**Input:** CFA $P = (L, l_0, E)$, test goals $G \subseteq E$
**Output:** CFA $(L', l_0, E')$ with test-goal labels
**Variables:** Sets $waitlist, visited \subseteq L$

$L', E' = \{\}$
$waitlist, visited = \{l_0\}$
**while** $waitlist \neq \emptyset$ **do**
  choose $l_i$ from $waitlist$; remove $l_i$ from $waitlist$
  **for** $(l_i, op, l_j) \in E$ **do**
    $L' = L' \cup \{l_i, l_j\}$
    **if** $(l_i, op, l_j) \in G$ **then**
      $L' = L' \cup \{l_i'\}$
      $E' = E' \cup \{(l_i, \texttt{GOAL\_i\_j}, l_i'), (l_i', op, l_j)\}$
    **else**
      $E' = E' \cup \{(l_i, op, l_j) \in E\}$
    **if** $l_j \notin visited$ **then**
      $waitlist = waitlist \cup \{l_j\}$
      $visited = visited \cup \{l_j\}$
**return** $(L', l_0, E')$

*(1) Test-Goal Computation.* As an example, we use the coverage criterion of branch coverage. For branch coverage and a CFA $(L, l_0, E)$, we use as test goals the set of all edges that are preceded by assume edges, i.e., $[\![\varphi]\!] = \{(l, \cdot, \cdot) \in E \mid \exists(\cdot, op, l) \in E : op \text{ is assume operation}\}$.

*(2) Testability Transformation.* We first translate a given program in real C code to a CFA $P$. Algorithm 1 takes this CFA $P$ and creates a semantically equivalent CFA with additional edges for program labels. For $P = (L, l_0, E)$, the new CFA $P' = (L', l_0, E')$ is computed as follows: Initially, the sets $L'$ and $E'$ are empty. A waitlist is initialized with the initial program location $l_0$. As long as the waitlist is not empty, a program location $l_i$ is selected and removed from the waitlist and each outgoing edge $(l_i, op, l_j) \in E$ is considered. First, $l_i$ and $l_j$ are added to $L'$.

Then, if $(l_i, op, l_j)$ is a test goal, a new program label `GOAL_i_j` is introduced just before $op$ as follows: A new program location $l_i'$ is added to $L'$, and the two edges ($l_i$, `GOAL_i_j`, $l_i'$) and $(l_i', op, l_j)$ are added to $E'$.

If the edge $(l_i, op, l_j)$ is not a test goal, it is added to $E'$ without modifications. After this, if $l_j$ was not encountered before, it is added to the waitlist and the set of visited nodes. As soon as the waitlist is empty, all locations of the original CFA have been traversed and the new CFA $(L', l_0, E')$ is returned. This transformation traverses each program location only once and thus scales well. At the end, we translate the transformed CFA back into C code.

Figure 7 shows the result of *addLabels*($P, G$) for our example program $P$ (Fig. 4) and branch coverage, i.e., $G = \{(l_4, // \ \ldots, l_7), (l_6, // \ \ldots, l_7)\}$. The figure shows the resulting CFA and the translation to C code.

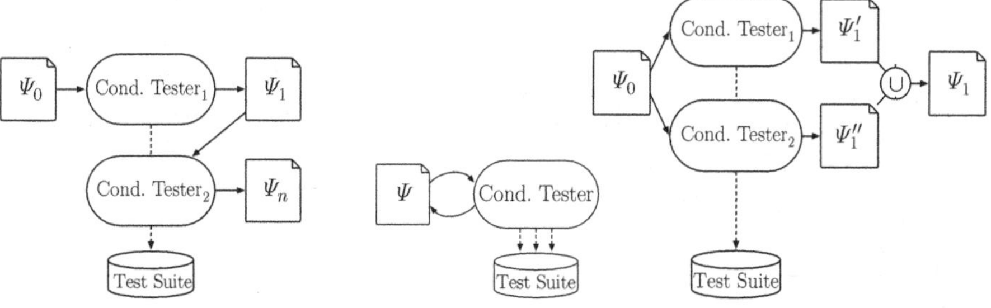


**Fig. 8.** $\texttt{tester}^{\texttt{seq}}$ **Fig. 9.** $\texttt{tester}^{\text{cyc}}$ **Fig. 10.** $\texttt{tester}^{\text{par}}$

*(3) Test Execution.* We execute all test cases of the given test suite on the transformed program as follows: We generate a test harness that reads test values from the standard input and provides the test values to the C program. We compile this test harness with the transformed program and feed each test vector to the harness in individual executions.

*(4) Coverage Measurement.* We use GCov to obtain a coverage report that lists for each line[2] of the transformed C program whether it was covered by the test suite. From this report, $\texttt{extractor}^{\texttt{exec}}$ extracts the program labels of test goals that are covered, and returns the corresponding test goals.

Since $\texttt{extractor}^{\texttt{exec}}$ is based on concrete execution of the test suite on a semantically equivalent program, the method is assumed to be both sound and complete.

## 4 Combinations of Conditional Testers

Conditional testing enables versatile combinations of testers. We have already seen a sequential combination in the introduction (Fig. 3), but it is also possible to combine conditional testers in other ways, such as in cycles, in general portfolios (i.e., also parallel), with strategy selection, or for compositional reasoning. In the following, we will present different possible combinations of conditional testers to show the potential of conditional software testing. Note that all of these combinations are themselves conditional testers, so they can be combined with each other in any way. From now on, we will omit the program under test and the coverage criterion in figures, to have simpler diagrams.

**Sequential Tester.** A sequential tester $\texttt{tester}^{\texttt{seq}}(T_1, T_2)$ (Fig. 8) consists of two component testers $T_1$ and $T_2$ that are executed sequentially to generate test cases. Several sequential testers can be used to sequentially combine an arbitrary number of testers. For simplicity, we write $\texttt{tester}^{\texttt{seq}}(T_1, T_2, T_3)$ for $\texttt{tester}^{\texttt{seq}}(T_1, \texttt{tester}^{\texttt{seq}}(T_2, T_3))$. Each tester provides the covered test goals

2 Since the transformed program is generated such that each operation is written on an own line in the output code, a line uniquely identifies a test-goal label.

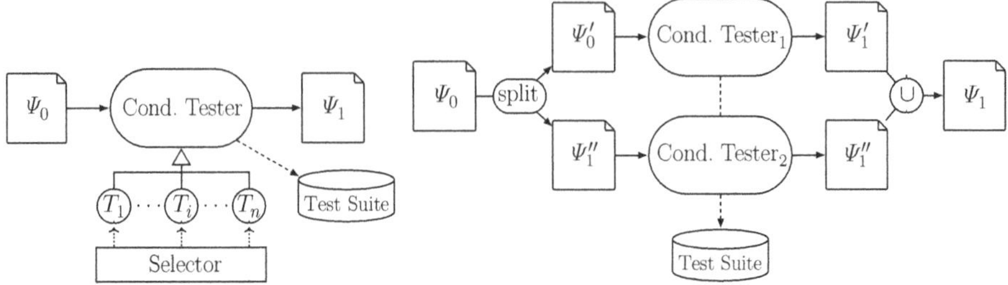


**Fig. 11.** $\texttt{tester}^{\texttt{select}}$

**Fig. 12.** $\texttt{tester}^{\texttt{comp}}$

after its run, and the set of remaining test goals will decrease. This can be used to combine strengths of different testers without further knowledge about them; testers can either get a certain time limit each, or stop early if they encounter a program feature they don't support.

**Cyclic Tester.** A cyclic tester $\texttt{tester}^{\texttt{cyc}}(T)$ (Fig. 9) iteratively calls a conditional tester $T$ with the increasing set $\Psi$ of covered test goals. This can be used, for example, to restart a tester after a certain limit is reached (e.g., memory consumption or size of path constraints in symbolic execution). In combination with $\texttt{tester}^{\texttt{seq}}$, this can also be used to cycle through a sequence of testers (round-robin principle).

**Parallel Tester.** A parallel tester $\texttt{tester}^{\texttt{par}}(T_1, T_2)$ (Fig. 10) runs testers $T_1$ and $T_2$ in parallel on the same inputs. Each tester produces its own set $\Psi_1', \Psi_1''$ of covered test goals, and their union $\Psi_1' \cup \Psi_1'' = \Psi_1$ is the final set of covered test goals. Several parallel testers can be used to combine an arbitrary number of testers, similar to $\texttt{tester}^{\texttt{seq}}$. In contrast to $\texttt{tester}^{\texttt{seq}}$, there is no information exchange between testers $T_1$ and $T_2$, so they may do redundant work.

**Strategy-Selection Tester.** A strategy-selection tester $\texttt{tester}^{\texttt{select}}(T_1, \ldots, T_n)$ (Fig. 11) uses a selector function to select to which of testers $T_1, \ldots, T_n$ the task of test-case generation is delegated. The selector function can be an arbitrary function that returns one of $T_1$ to $T_n$, e.g., a random selection, or based on a selection model that selects the most suited tester based on features of the program under test.

**Compositional Tester.** A compositional tester $\texttt{tester}^{\texttt{comp}}(T_1, T_2)$ (Fig. 12) first splits the condition $\Psi_0$ into two sets $\Psi_0'$ and $\Psi_0''$, so that $\Psi_0 = \Psi_0' \cup \Psi_0''$. Then, tester $T_1$ gets as input the first set $\Psi_0'$, and tester $T_2$ gets as input the second set $\Psi_0''$. Both testers work on the original program $P$ and original coverage criterion $\varphi$, but due to $\Psi_0'$ and $\Psi_0''$, the first tester only works on test goals $[\![\varphi]\!] \setminus \Psi_0'$, and the second tester only works on $[\![\varphi]\!] \setminus \Psi_0''$. They produce individual sets $\Psi_1'$ and $\Psi_1''$ of covered test goals. These are then merged into the final set $\Psi_1 = \Psi_1' \cup \Psi_1''$ of now covered test goals. More than two testers can be combined compositionally through nested combinations. With $\texttt{tester}^{\texttt{comp}}$, work can be split (decomposition principle), for example for parallelization or to let each tester solve the test goals it is most suited for.

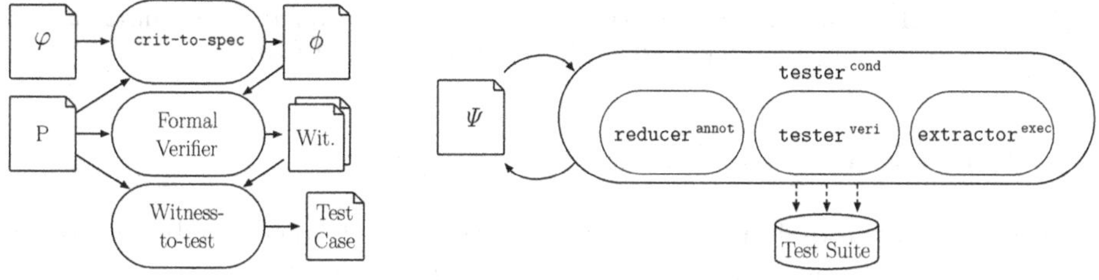


**Fig. 13.** $\texttt{tester}^{\texttt{veri}}$

**Fig. 14.** $\texttt{tester}^{\texttt{cyc}}_{\texttt{veri}}$

# 5 Construction of Conditional Testers from Existing Verifiers

It has long been possible to use formal verification of reachability properties to generate tests [3]. Compared to testers, many formal verification techniques specialize on finding single program paths to specific program states or program locations of interest; this makes them suitable for hard-to-reach test goals [10]. Figure 13 shows the (non-conditional) tester $\texttt{tester}^{\texttt{veri}}(V)$ that is based on a formal verifier $V$: First, function `crit-to-spec` transforms the coverage criterion $\varphi$, based on program $P$, to a safety specification $\phi$ which is constructed such that $P$ violates $\phi$ if $P$ covers a test goal from $[\![\varphi]\!]$. Then, $\phi$ and $P$ are given to formal verifier $V$, which checks whether $P$ satisfies $\phi$. The verifier outputs one or more violation witnesses if test goals are reachable. From these violation witnesses, test cases are created by witness-to-test [5].

We use the established formats for input programs and specifications for the reachability category of SV-COMP[3] to get access to a large catalog of tools for formal verification. There are two adaptations necessary for using SV-COMP verifiers: (1) they are only required to support the property "no call to method `__VERIFIER_error` is reachable", and may not support more general reachability properties, and (2) they are only required to output a single violation witness, and thus will always lead to a test suite that only consists of one test case.

We solve both issues in the following way: We let `crit-to-spec` always return the specification that no call to `__VERIFIER_error` is reachable. We then take $\texttt{tester}^{\texttt{veri}}$ and construct from it a conditional tester based on $\texttt{tester}^{\texttt{cond}}$ with program reducer $\texttt{reducer}^{\texttt{annot}}$ and test-goal extractor $\texttt{extractor}^{\texttt{exec}}$. At this point, we have a conditional tester that uses a formal verifier to always produce a test suite with a single test case, and that returns the set of test goals covered by that test case. To produce a full test suite for all test goals, we use a cyclic tester $\texttt{tester}^{\texttt{cyc}}(\texttt{tester}^{\texttt{cond}}(\texttt{tester}^{\texttt{veri}}(V)))$ (Fig. 14). After each test-case generation run, the newly created test case is used by $\texttt{extractor}^{\texttt{exec}}$ to update the covered test goals. Then, $\texttt{reducer}^{\texttt{annot}}$ will insert calls to `__VERIFIER_error` for the remaining test goals, and $\texttt{tester}^{\texttt{veri}}(V)$ will create a new test case that covers at least one of the remaining test goals. We use $\texttt{tester}^{\texttt{cyc}}_{\texttt{veri}}(V)$ to denote a verifier-based tester that is constructed from formal verifier $V$.

[3] `https://sv-comp.sosy-lab.org/2019/rules.php`

Through the use of any of the previously mentioned combinations, a tester $\texttt{tester}^{\texttt{cyc}}_{\texttt{veri}}$ can be combined with other conditional testers.

## 6 Evaluation

We evaluate our tool implementation CondTest and some combinations of testers using conditional testing along the following claims:

**C1** Conditional software testing with $\texttt{extractor}^{\texttt{exec}}$ and $\texttt{reducer}^{\texttt{prune}}$ does not significantly impact the performance of individual testers.
**C2** Sequential combinations of different testers without information exchange can improve the coverage of generated test suites, compared to single testers.
**C3** Sequential combinations of different testers with conditional software testing can improve the coverage of generated test suites, compared to sequential combinations without information exchange.
**C4** Sequential combinations of traditional testers and verifier-based testers can improve the coverage of generated test suites.

### 6.1 Setup

**Implementation.** We implemented a generic conditional software tester (CondTest) according to Fig. 5, including the operators $\texttt{reducer}^{\texttt{id}}$, $\texttt{reducer}^{\texttt{prune}}$, $\texttt{reducer}^{\texttt{annot}}$, and $\texttt{extractor}^{\texttt{exec}}$. CondTest can be instantiated as $\texttt{tester}^{\texttt{cond}}$, $\texttt{tester}^{\texttt{seq}}$, and $\texttt{tester}^{\texttt{cyc}}_{\texttt{veri}}$, is able to create test suites for C programs that adhere to the Test-Comp rules [2], and is available under the open-source license Apache 2.0. We use CondTest in version `2.0`[4]. CondTest uses the BenchExec tool-info modules[5] and benchmark definitions of Test-Comp[6] and SV-COMP[7] for plug-and-play integration of testers and formal verifiers. Formal verifiers are turned into testers by wrapping them each in their own instance of CondTest (configuration $\texttt{tester}^{\texttt{cyc}}_{\texttt{veri}}$).

**Tools.** We consider the best three testers of Test-Comp '19 whose licenses allow evaluation and publication of results: Klee [14], CoVeriTest [8], and CPA/Tiger[8]. We use all three tools in their respective versions of Test-Comp '19. In addition, we select the best formal verifier for reaching program locations of interest in testable programs according to a previous study [10], i.e., Esbmc-kind [21]. We use Esbmc-kind in its SV-COMP '19 version. To measure the coverage of test suites, we use GCov `7.3.0`. To ensure reproducible results, we use the benchmarking toolkit BenchExec `1.20` [11].

---

[4] `https://gitlab.com/sosy-lab/software/conditional-testing/tree/v2.0`
[5] `https://github.com/sosy-lab/benchexec/tree/2.0/benchexec/tools`
[6] `https://gitlab.com/sosy-lab/test-comp/bench-defs/tree/testcomp19/benchmark-defs`
[7] `https://github.com/sosy-lab/sv-comp/tree/svcomp19/benchmark-defs`
[8] `https://www.es.tu-darmstadt.de/testcomp19/`

**Environment.** We perform our experiments on a cluster of 168 machines, each with 33 GB of memory and an Intel Xeon E3-1230 v5 CPU, with 3.4 GHz and 8 processing units (with hyper-threading). We use Ubuntu 18.04 with Linux kernel 4.4 as operating system. We limit each benchmark run to 4 processing units and a time limit of 900 s. Each run of CondTest is limited to 15.5 GB. Each individual test-case generation run (e.g., execution of CPA/Tiger) is limited to 15 GB, both for native execution and as part of CondTest. This way, each test-case generation run has the same amount of memory for both native execution and execution within CondTest. Extractor `extractor`$^{\texttt{exec}}$ uses a time limit of 3 s for each test execution, to prevent hangups in case of incomplete or non-terminating tests. To measure the achieved coverage of the complete final test suites, we execute test cases with a memory limit of 7 GB, 2 processing units, and a time limit of 3 h for each generated test suite. At this time limit, no timeouts occurred during coverage measurement.

**Reproducibility and Benchmark Tasks.** We use all 1 720 test tasks of the *Cover-Branches* category of the Test-Comp '19 benchmark. All of our experimental data are available online[9] and through a replication package.[10]

### 6.2 Results

**C1: No Significant Overhead in CondTest.** Figure 15 shows the branch coverage per task achieved by the test suites created by CoVeriTest, CPA/Tiger, and Klee, respectively, in their original Test-Comp configurations (x-axis), and as conditional testers `tester`$^{\texttt{cond}}$ (y-axis) inside CondTest with `reducer`$^{\texttt{prune}}$ and `extractor`$^{\texttt{exec}}$ (`reducer`$^{\texttt{prune}}$ does not really prune anything because of the full set of test goals, but parses the program, runs the pruning algorithm, and writes out the transformed C program; the idea is to find out whether this process is efficient and does not negatively impact the overall process). The CPU-time limit for each test-case generation was set to 900 s (the CPU time consumed by `reducer`$^{\texttt{prune}}$ is included in the measured CPU time, and thus, implicitly subtracted from the CPU-time available for the tester). Since `extractor`$^{\texttt{exec}}$ only runs after the tester, it has no influence on the time limit in a configuration with a single tester. For points on the diagonal, the same coverage was achieved by the original tester and its integration in `tester`$^{\texttt{cond}}$; points above the diagonal represent tasks for which `tester`$^{\texttt{cond}}$ achieved a higher coverage, and the points below the diagonal represent tasks for which `tester`$^{\texttt{cond}}$ achieved a lower coverage. For CoVeriTest, the coverage for a few tasks are a bit worse when run with CondTest (just below the diagonal). This is because CondTest uses a different, more strict technique to enforce the memory limit than the benchmarking tool BenchExec, due to technical reasons. For CPA/Tiger, outliers on the left (vertical stack of points) are due to crashes from memory exhaustion. CPA/Tiger operates close to the memory limit for many tasks. Because of this, small variations in

---

9 `https://www.sosy-lab.org/research/conditional-testing/`

10 `https://doi.org/10.5281/zenodo.3352401`

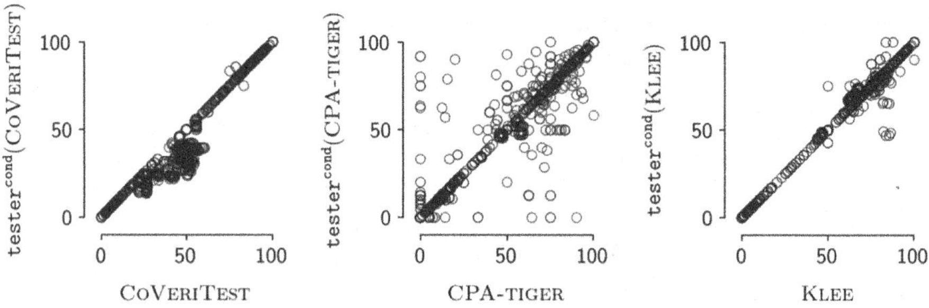


**Fig. 15.** Branch coverage of test suites created by original tools vs. their integration in tester$^{cond}$ (in percent)

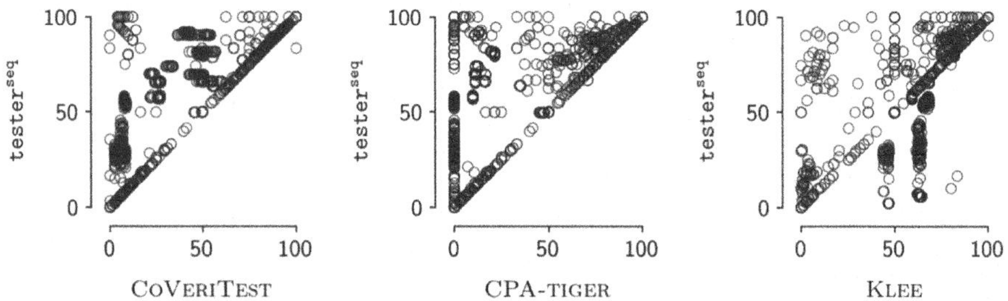


**Fig. 16.** Branch coverage of test suites created by original tools vs. their sequential combinations with reducer$^{id}$, i.e., without information exchange (in percent)

memory usage can lead to crashes. In our experiments, for most of these tasks it was random whether CPA/Tiger stayed closely below the memory limit, or exceeded it and crashed. Thus, the issue is not related to CondTest, but results from memory exhaustion of the native tester. Besides these issues, it is visible that for all three testers, no significant differences in branch coverage exist. This suggests that using tester$^{cond}$ with the proposed operators reducer$^{prune}$ and extractor$^{exec}$ does not lead to a significant negative impact on the performance just by using the conditional-testing construction.

**C2: Combinations Can Improve Coverage.** Figure 16 shows the branch coverage per task achieved by the test suites created by CoVeriTest, CPA/Tiger, and Klee, respectively, in their original Test-Comp configurations with 900 s CPU-time limit (x-axis), and the coverage per task achieved by the test suites created by CondTest (y-axis) with the sequential combination tester$^{seq}$(tester$^{cond}$(CPA/Tiger)$_{300}$, tester$^{cond}$(CoVeriTest)$_{300}$, tester$^{cond}$(Klee)$_{300}$) and the reducer reducer$^{id}$, i.e., without information exchange between the three testers. Each single conditional tester (i.e., tester$^{cond}$ based on CPA/Tiger, CoVeriTest, and Klee) was stopped after 300 s each, and each full test-case generation tester$^{seq}$ run was stopped after a total of 900 s (the CPU time consumed by CondTest for, e.g., process management, is included in the measured CPU time, and thus, implicitly subtracted from the CPU-time available for the last tester, tester$^{cond}$(Klee)).

**Table 1.** Coverage of test suites generated without information reuse (`reducer`$^{id}$) and with information reuse through `reducer`$^{prune}$

| Task | branch coverage | | |
|---|---|---|---|
| | id | → | prune |
| mod3.c.v+sep-reducer | 75.0 | + 5.00 | 80.0 |
| Problem07_label35 | 52.0 | + 2.00 | 54.0 |
| Problem07_label37 | 54.2 | + 1.97 | 56.2 |
| Problem04_label35 | 79.5 | + 1.79 | 81.3 |
| Problem06_label02 | 57.0 | + 1.70 | 58.7 |
| Problem06_label27 | 57.5 | + 1.09 | 58.6 |
| Problem04_label02 | 80.2 | + 1.06 | 81.3 |
| Problem06_label18 | 57.5 | + 1.05 | 58.6 |
| Problem04_label16 | 79.1 | + 1.01 | 80.1 |
| Problem04_label34 | 80.2 | + 0.99 | 81.2 |

**Table 2.** Coverage of test suites generated without (`prune`) and with (`vb`) support of ESBMC-KIND

| Task | branch coverage | | |
|---|---|---|---|
| | prune | → | vb |
| Problem08_label30 | 5.72 | + 56.2 | 62.0 |
| Problem08_label32 | 5.72 | + 56.1 | 61.9 |
| Problem08_label06 | 5.72 | + 56.1 | 61.8 |
| Problem08_label35 | 5.72 | + 56.0 | 61.7 |
| Problem08_label00 | 5.72 | + 55.9 | 61.6 |
| Problem08_label11 | 5.72 | + 55.8 | 61.5 |
| Problem08_label19 | 5.72 | + 55.7 | 61.5 |
| Problem08_label29 | 5.67 | + 55.7 | 61.4 |
| Problem08_label22 | 5.72 | + 55.7 | 61.5 |
| Problem08_label56 | 5.72 | + 55.7 | 61.5 |

The scatter plots in Fig. 16 show that the branch coverage of the test suites created by the sequential combination is significantly higher for a significant amount of benchmark tasks. This shows that the used testers (with CPU time limit of 300 s) can complement each other well, and that combinations can perform better than a single tester running for a longer time on its own (900 s CPU time limit).

**C3: Condition Passing Can Further Improve Coverage.** To show that conditional software testing can lead to generated test suites with improved coverage, we compare the branch coverage of the test suites generated by CONDTEST with `tester`$^{seq}$(`tester`$^{cond}$(CPA/TIGER)$_{300}$, `tester`$^{cond}$(COVERITEST)$_{300}$, `tester`$^{cond}$(KLEE)$_{300}$), and the two reducers `reducer`$^{id}$, i.e., without information exchange, and `reducer`$^{prune}$, i.e., with program reduction based on syntactic reachability. Table 1 shows a comparison of the branch coverage of test suites generated by both techniques on a selection of benchmark tasks (programs with complicated branching), rounded to three digits. It shows that information exchange can lead to generated test suites with improved branch coverage, adding up to 5 % branch coverage.

**C4: Verifiers as Test-Generators Can Improve Coverage.** To show that verifier-based testers can generate test suites with improved coverage compared to combinations of traditional testers, we compare the branch coverage of the test suites generated by CONDTEST with `tester`$^{seq}$(`tester`$^{cond}$(CPA/TIGER)$_{300}$, `tester`$^{cond}$(COVERITEST)$_{300}$, `tester`$^{cond}$(KLEE)$_{300}$) (called `prune`) and the test suites generated by CONDTEST with `tester`$^{seq}$(`tester`$^{cond}$(CPA/TIGER)$_{200}$, `tester`$^{cond}$(COVERITEST)$_{200}$, `tester`$^{cond}$(KLEE)$_{200}$, `tester`$^{cyc}_{veri}$(ESBMC)$_{300}$) (called `vb`). Both `prune` and `vb` use `reducer`$^{prune}$ and `extractor`$^{exec}$. For `prune`, each individual tester is stopped after 300 s. For `vb`, CPA/TIGER, COVERITEST, and KLEE are each stopped after 200 s, and ESBMC runs for 300 s. The total time of each run of CONDTEST is 900 s (i.e., the CPU time required by `reducer`$^{prune}$ and `extractor`$^{exec}$ is implicitly subtracted from the CPU time available for the last tester, i.e., KLEE in `prune` and ESBMC in `vb`).

Table 2 shows a comparison of the branch coverage of test suites generated by `prune` and `vb`, respectively, on a selection of benchmark tasks (programs with complicated branching). It shows that for some tasks, the use of ESBMC as directed tester can greatly improve branch coverage compared to combinations of only traditional testers, creating test suites that achieve up to 56 % additional branch coverage.

## 7 Conclusion

We have presented the concept of *conditional testing* and the tool implementation CONDTEST, a versatile and modular framework for constructing cooperative combinations of testers based on conditional testing. First, we defined a construction of a conditional tester from a given *existing tester*, based on the components `reducer` and `extractor`. Second, we defined a set of *generic combinations* that are now all possible using conditional testing. Third, we defined a construction of a conditional tester from a given *existing verifier*, based on the outlined combination opportunities. All our concepts are implemented in an adjustable framework, and we showed the potential of some new combinations through an experimental evaluation.

There are many powerful techniques for automatic test-case generation. Our goal is to construct even more powerful combinations by leveraging *cooperation*, and we hope that our construction techniques based on *conditional testing* help also other researchers and engineers to construct powerful tool combinations, without changing the implementation of the existing tools. This contributes to optimally use the techniques that we have to further improve the quality of software.

## References


1. Beyer, D.: Automatic verification of C and Java programs: SV-COMP 2019. In: Proc. TACAS, Part 3, LNCS, vol. 11429, pp. 133–155. Springer (2019). https://doi.org/10.1007/978-3-030-17502-3_9
2. Beyer, D.: Competition on software testing (Test-Comp). In: Proc. TACAS, Part 3, LNCS, vol. 11429, pp. 167–175. Springer (2019). https://doi.org/10.1007/978-3-030-17502-3_11
3. Beyer, D., Chlipala, A.J., Henzinger, T.A., Jhala, R., Majumdar, R.: Generating tests from counterexamples. In: Proc. ICSE, pp. 326–335. IEEE (2004). https://doi.org/10.1109/ICSE.2004.1317455
4. Beyer, D., Dangl, M., Dietsch, D., Heizmann, M., Stahlbauer, A.: Witness validation and stepwise testification across software verifiers. In: Proc. FSE, pp. 721–733. ACM (2015). https://doi.org/10.1145/2786805.2786867
5. Beyer, D., Dangl, M., Lemberger, T., Tautschnig, M.: Tests from witnesses: Execution-based validation of verification results. In: Proc. TAP, LNCS, vol. 10889, pp. 3–23. Springer (2018). https://doi.org/10.1007/978-3-319-92994-1_1
6. Beyer, D., Gulwani, S., Schmidt, D.: Combining model checking and data-flow analysis. In: Handbook on Model Checking, pp. 493–540. Springer (2018). https://doi.org/10.1007/978-3-319-10575-8_16
7. Beyer, D., Henzinger, T.A., Keremoglu, M.E., Wendler, P.: Conditional model checking: A technique to pass information between verifiers. In: Proc. FSE. ACM (2012). https://doi.org/10.1145/2393596.2393664

8. Beyer, D., Jakobs, M.C.: CoVeriTest: Cooperative verifier-based testing. In: Proc. FASE, LNCS, vol. 11424, pp. 389–408. Springer (2019). https://doi.org/10.1007/978-3-030-16722-6_23
9. Beyer, D., Jakobs, M.C., Lemberger, T., Wehrheim, H.: Reducer-based construction of conditional verifiers. In: Proc. ICSE, pp. 1182–1193. ACM (2018). https://doi.org/10.1145/3180155.3180259
10. Beyer, D., Lemberger, T.: Software verification: Testing vs. model checking. In: Proc. HVC, LNCS, vol. 10629, pp. 99–114. Springer (2017). https://doi.org/10.1007/978-3-319-70389-3_7
11. Beyer, D., Löwe, S., Wendler, P.: Reliable benchmarking: Requirements and solutions. Int. J. Softw. Tools Technol. Transfer **21**(1), 1–29 (2019). https://doi.org/10.1007/s10009-017-0469-y
12. Beyer, D., Wehrheim, H.: Verification artifacts in cooperative verification: Survey and unifying component framework. arXiv/CoRR 1905(08505) May 2019. https://arxiv.org/abs/1905.08505
13. Böhme, M., Oliveira, B.C.d.S., Roychoudhury, A.: Partition-based regression verification. In: Proc. ICSE, pp. 302–311. IEEE (2013). https://doi.org/10.1109/ICSE.2013.6606576
14. Cadar, C., Dunbar, D., Engler, D.R.: KLEE: Unassisted and automatic generation of high-coverage tests for complex systems programs. In: Proc. OSDI, pp. 209–224. USENIX Association (2008)
15. Chowdhury, A.B., Medicherla, R.K., Venkatesh, R.: VeriFuzz: Program-aware fuzzing (competition contribution). In: Proc. TACAS, Part 3, LNCS, vol. 11429, pp. 244–249. Springer (2019). https://doi.org/10.1007/978-3-030-17502-3_22
16. Christakis, M., Müller, P., Wüstholz, V.: Collaborative verification and testing with explicit assumptions. In: Proc. FM, LNCS, vol. 7436, pp. 132–146. Springer (2012). https://doi.org/10.1007/978-3-642-32759-9_13
17. Cruanes, S., Hamon, G., Owre, S., Shankar, N.: Tool integration with the Evidential Tool Bus. In: Proc. VMCAI, LNCS, vol. 7737, pp. 275–294. Springer (2013). https://doi.org/10.1007/978-3-642-35873-9_18
18. Czech, M., Jakobs, M., Wehrheim, H.: Just test what you cannot verify! In: Proc. FASE, LNCS, vol. 9033, pp. 100–114. Springer (2015). https://doi.org/10.1007/978-3-662-46675-9_7
19. Daca, P., Gupta, A., Henzinger, T.A.: Abstraction-driven concolic testing. In: Proc. VMCAI, LNCS, vol. 9583, pp. 328–347. Springer (2016). https://doi.org/10.1007/978-3-662-49122-5_16
20. Ferles, K., Wüstholz, V., Christakis, M., Dillig, I.: Failure-directed program trimming. In: Proc. ESEC/FSE, pp. 174–185. ACM (2017). https://doi.org/10.1145/3106237.3106249
21. Gadelha, M.Y.R., Monteiro, F.R., Cordeiro, L.C., Nicole, D.A.: ESBMC v6.0: Verifying C programs using k-induction and invariant inference (competition contribution). In: Proc. TACAS, Part 3, LNCS, vol. 11429, pp. 209–213. Springer (2019). https://doi.org/10.1007/978-3-030-17502-3_15
22. Gulavani, B.S., Henzinger, T.A., Kannan, Y., Nori, A.V., Rajamani, S.K.: SYNERGY: A new algorithm for property checking. In: Proc. FSE, pp. 117–127. ACM (2006). https://doi.org/10.1145/1181775.1181790
23. Harman, M., Hu, L., Hierons, R.M., Wegener, J., Sthamer, H., Baresel, A., Roper, M.: Testability transformation. IEEE Trans. Softw. Eng. **30**(1), 3–16 (2004). https://doi.org/10.1109/TSE.2004.1265732

24. Holzer, A., Schallhart, C., Tautschnig, M., Veith, H.: Query-driven program testing. In: Proc. VMCAI, LNCS, vol. 5403, pp. 151–166. Springer (2009). https://doi.org/10.1007/978-3-540-93900-9_15
25. Holzer, A., Schallhart, C., Tautschnig, M., Veith, H.: How did you specify your test suite. In: Proc. ASE, pp. 407–416. ACM (2010). https://doi.org/10.1145/1858996.1859084
26. Howar, F., Isberner, M., Merten, M., Steffen, B., Beyer, D., Păsăreanu, C.S.: Rigorous examination of reactive systems. The RERS challenges 2012 and 2013. Int. J. Softw. Tools Technol. Transfer **16**(5), 457–464 (2014). https://doi.org/10.1007/s10009-014-0337-y
27. Kim, Y., Xu, Z., Kim, M., Cohen, M.B., Rothermel, G.: Hybrid directed test suite augmentation: An interleaving framework. In: Proc. ICST, pp. 263–272. IEEE (2014). https://doi.org/10.1109/ICST.2014.39
28. Majumdar, R., Sen, K.: Hybrid concolic testing. In: Proc. ICSE, pp. 416–426. IEEE (2007). https://doi.org/10.1109/ICSE.2007.41
29. Margaria, T., Nagel, R., Steffen, B.: jETI: A tool for remote tool integration. In: Proc. TACAS, LNCS, vol. 3440, pp. 557–562. Springer (2005). https://doi.org/10.1007/978-3-540-31980-1_38
30. Noller, Y., Kersten, R., Pasareanu, C.S.: Badger: Complexity analysis with fuzzing and symbolic execution. In: Proc. ISSTA, pp. 322–332. ACM (2018). https://doi.org/10.1145/3213846.3213868
31. Qiu, R., Khurshid, S., Pasareanu, C.S., Wen, J., Yang, G.: Using test ranges to improve symbolic execution. In: Proc. NFM, LNCS, vol. 10811, pp. 416–434. Springer (2018). https://doi.org/10.1007/978-3-319-77935-5_28
32. Rushby, J.M.: An Evidential Tool Bus. In: Proc. ICFEM, LNCS, vol. 3785, p. 36. Springer (2005). https://doi.org/10.1007/11576280_3
33. Schneider, F.B.: Enforceable security policies. ACM Trans. Inf. Syst. Secur. **3**(1), 30–50 (2000). https://doi.org/10.1145/353323.353382
34. Song, J., Alves-Foss, J.: The DARPA cyber grand challenge: A competitor's perspective, part 2. IEEE Secur. Priv. **14**(1), 76–81 (2016). https://doi.org/10.1109/MSP.2016.14
35. Steffen, B., Margaria, T., Braun, V.: The Electronic Tool Integration platform: Concepts and design. STTT **1**(1–2), 9–30 (1997). https://doi.org/10.1007/s100090050003
36. Stephens, N., Grosen, J., Salls, C., Dutcher, A., Wang, R., Corbetta, J., Shoshitaishvili, Y., Kruegel, C., Vigna, G.: Driller: Augmenting fuzzing through selective symbolic execution. In: Proc. NDSS. Internet Society (2016). https://doi.org/10.14722/ndss.2016.23368
37. Taneja, K., Xie, T., Tillmann, N., de Halleux, J.: eXpress: Guided path exploration for efficient regression test generation. In: Proc. ISSTA, pp. 1–11. ACM (2011). https://doi.org/10.1145/2001420.2001422
38. Tip, F.: A survey of program slicing techniques. J. Program. Lang. **3**, 121–189 (1995)
39. Visser, W., Păsăreanu, C.S., Khurshid, S.: Test input generation with Java PathFinder. In: Proc. ISSTA, pp. 97–107. ACM (2004). https://doi.org/10.1145/1007512.1007526
40. Zhu, Z., Jiao, L., Xu, X.: Combining search-based testing and dynamic symbolic execution by evolvability metric. In: Proc. ICSME, pp. 59–68. IEEE (2018). https://doi.org/10.1109/ICSME.2018.00015

# Enhancing Symbolic Execution of Heap-Based Programs with Separation Logic for Test Input Generation


Long H. Pham[1(✉)], Quang Loc Le[2], Quoc-Sang Phan[3], Jun Sun[4], and Shengchao Qin[2]

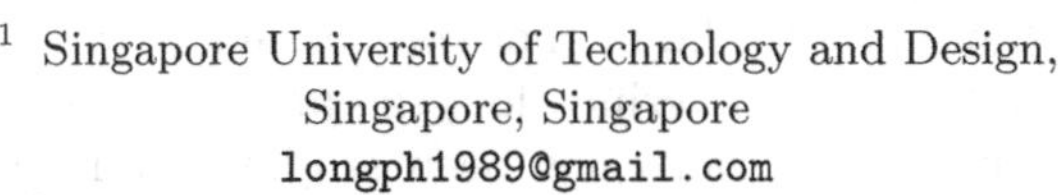

[1] Singapore University of Technology and Design, Singapore, Singapore
longph1989@gmail.com

[2] School of Computing & Digital Technologies, Teesside University, Middlesbrough, UK

[3] Synopsys, Inc., Mountain View, USA

[4] Singapore Management University, Singapore, Singapore



**Abstract.** Symbolic execution is a well established method for test input generation. Despite of having achieved tremendous success over numerical domains, existing symbolic execution techniques for heap-based programs are limited due to the lack of a succinct and precise description for symbolic values over unbounded heaps. In this work, we present a new symbolic execution method for heap-based programs based on separation logic. The essence of our proposal is context-sensitive lazy initialization, a novel approach for efficient test input generation. Our approach differs from existing approaches in two ways. Firstly, our approach is based on separation logic, which allows us to precisely capture preconditions of heap-based programs so that we avoid generating invalid test inputs. Secondly, we generate only fully initialized test inputs, which are more useful in practice compared to those partially initialized test inputs generated by the state-of-the-art tools. We have implemented our approach as a tool, called Java StarFinder, and evaluated it on a set of programs with complex heap inputs. The results show that our approach significantly reduces the number of invalid test inputs and improves the test coverage.


## 1 Introduction

Symbolic execution [22] is getting momentum thanks to its capability of discovering deep bugs. It is increasingly used not only in academic settings but also in industry, such as in Microsoft, NASA, IBM and Fujitsu [11]. Despite having achieved tremendous success, symbolic execution has limited impact on testing programs with inputs in the form of complex heap-based data structures (a.k.a. *heap-based* programs). The dominant approach to symbolic execution of



Y.-F. Chen et al. (Eds.): ATVA 2019, LNCS 11781, pp. 209–227, 2019.
https://doi.org/10.1007/978-3-030-31784-3_12

heap-based programs is lazy initialization [21], which postpones the initialization of reference variables and fields until they are accessed. However, lazy initialization makes no assumption on the shapes of the input data structures, and explicitly enumerates all possible heap objects that may bind to the inputs. This approach has the following fundamental limitations. Firstly, due to the lack of a succinct and precise description of the shapes of the input data structures, they often generate a large number of invalid test inputs. Secondly, due to the enumeration of all possible heap objects that may bind to the inputs, they often worsen the path explosion problem of symbolic execution. Lastly, due to lazy initialization, the generated test inputs may be partially initialized (if some fields are never accessed) and need to be further concretized.

In the context of logic-based verification, the problem of specifying and reasoning about heap-based programs has been studied for nearly five decades. The dominant approaches are based on separation logic [20,32]. The strength of separation logic lies in its separating conjunction operator $*$, which splits the heap into disjoint regions or *heaplets*. This enables *local reasoning*, i.e., specification and reasoning are kept confined within heaplets, independent of the rest of the heap. This is in contrast to *global reasoning*, i.e., the specification describes properties of the global heap, which "suffers from either limited applicability or extreme complexity, and scales poorly to programs of even moderate size" [32].

Surprisingly, there has been limited effort on using separation logic to enhance symbolic execution for test input generation. In this work, we start filling this gap. Firstly, we propose a novel method for symbolic execution of heap-based programs based on separation logic. In particular, we adopt a logic that combines separation logic with existentially quantified variables, inductive predicates and arithmetic which allows us to encode path conditions effectively in heap-based programs. Secondly, we enhance our method with *context-sensitive* lazy initialization, i.e., we use preconditions written in separation logic to guide the search, and only explore the states that are reachable when the inputs satisfy the preconditions. As a result, all generated test inputs are valid.

In summary, we make the following main contributions.

1. We develop a symbolic execution engine for heap-based programs based on separation logic.
2. For efficiency, we present context-sensitive lazy initialization with a *least fixed point* analysis to generate valid test inputs during symbolic execution.
3. We have implemented the proposed approach as a tool, called Java StarFinder[1], built on top of Symbolic PathFinder [31], to generate test inputs for Java bytecode.
4. We have evaluated our tool on a set of Java programs including complex and mutable data structures. All generated test inputs are valid and we achieve 98.98% branch coverage on average.

The rest of this paper is organized as follows. Section 2 presents some background and illustrates our proposal via an example. Section 3 describes the syntax of our core language and its operational semantics. Our first contribution, a

[1] https://github.com/star-finder/jpf-star.

```
node add(node x, node y) {
  node dummyHead = new node(0, null); node z = dummyHead;
  while (x != null) {
    z.next = new node(x.val + y.val, null);
    x = x.next;  y = y.next;  z = z.next;
  }
  return dummyHead.next;
}
```

**Fig. 1.** Adding two numbers represented by linked lists

symbolic execution engine based on separation logic, is presented in Sect. 4. Our second contribution, the context-sensitive lazy initialization, is shown in Sect. 5. We present our implementation and evaluation in Sect. 6. Section 7 presents related work. Finally, we conclude and discuss future works in Sect. 8.

## 2 Motivation and Illustration

In the following, we illustrate how our approach works with an example. Consider a program that represents a big non-negative integer in the form of a singly linked list, i.e., each node of the lists contains a single digit of the number. Suppose we want to generate test inputs for the method `add` shown in Fig. 1, which computes the sum of two numbers in this representation.

This method is designed to take two parameters `x` and `y` satisfying the following preconditions: (1) all the digits of `x` and `y` are less than 5, and thus there is no carry; (2) `x` and `y` have the same number of digits. Condition (1) is a simple numerical constraint which can be handled by existing symbolic execution engines. We thus leave it out of the discussion for the sake of simplicity. To capture condition (2), we define an inductive predicate `pre` based on our fragment of separation logic as follows.

$$\begin{aligned}\mathtt{pred}\ \mathtt{pre}(a,b) \equiv\ & (\mathtt{emp} \wedge a = \mathtt{null} \wedge b = \mathtt{null})\\ & \vee\ (\exists n_1, n_2.\ a{\mapsto}\mathtt{node}(\_, n_1) * b{\mapsto}\mathtt{node}(\_, n_2) * \mathtt{pre}(n_1, n_2))\end{aligned}$$

Predicate `emp` means the heap is empty; predicate $a{\mapsto}\mathtt{node}(\_, n_1)$ states $a$ points to an allocated object; and $*$ is the separating conjunction operator in separation logic. The data type `node` corresponds to the class `node` in the program, which has two instance fields: `val` containing the digit, and `next` referencing to another `node` object. The wildcard "_" is used to indicate a "don't care" value.

Intuitively, a linked list is recursively defined as a head points-to predicate with its next field pointing to a sublist. In the base case of the definition, the heap is empty, and both parameters $a$ and $b$ are `null`. In the recursive case, $a{\mapsto}\mathtt{node}(\_, n_1)$ signifies that $a$ points to an allocated object composed of a certain value (represented by "_") and its `next` field $n_1$. Similarly, $b$ points to an allocated object with its `next` field $n_2$. Furthermore, $n_1$ and $n_2$, i.e., the sublists of $a$ and $b$ respectively, satisfy `pre` as well.

In this definition, the separating conjunction operator $*$ splits the global heap into three heaplets. The first two heaplets contain the `node` objects referenced respectively by $a$ and $b$, and the third one contains the sublists. This separation enforces that $a$ and $b$ refer to two distinct objects and their sublists are disjoint too. Since $a$ and $b$ must be either both `null` or both not `null`, and likewise for the objects in their sublists, $a$ and $b$ have the same length.

To generate test inputs, we perform symbolic execution of method `add(x, y)` with precondition `pre(x, y)`. In the proposed symbolic execution, path conditions are formulae in the fragment of separation logic with inductive predicates and arithmetic. Reference variables are initialized by values obtained from a procedure, called `enum`. Initially, `x` and `y` are initialized to symbolic (stack) values $X$ and $Y$ respectively, and the path condition $\Delta$ is initialized to $\texttt{pre}(X, Y)$. When variable `x` is first accessed at line 3, our engine, through procedure `enum`, examines precondition $\texttt{pre}(X, Y)$[2] for possible heap values for `x`. Procedure `enum` gets possible values through the least fixed point analysis with procedure `LFP`. Procedure `LFP` unfolds predicate `pre` until the set of values reaches a fixed point. In this example, procedure `LFP` only needs to unfold predicate `pre` once and reach the fixed point with two formulae corresponding to two disjuncts in the definition of predicate `pre`. Then the engine substitutes the predicate $\texttt{pre}(X, Y)$ in the $\Delta$ by these two formulae (with $\alpha$-renaming, i.e., substitutions of formal/actual parameters and of bound variables to avoid name collisions) to obtain two non-deterministic choices, and symbolic execution case splits. It first explores the path corresponding to the base case and hence the constraint over $X$ and $Y$ in $\Delta$ becomes $X = \texttt{null} \wedge Y = \texttt{null}$. We use the constraint solver $\texttt{S2SAT}_{\texttt{SL}}$ [24,26,35] to check that $\Delta$ is satisfiable. There is no further case splitting in this path, and we have a test input where `x` and `y` are both `null`.

After exploring the base case, our symbolic executor explores the path corresponding to the recursive case. The updated path condition $\Delta$ over $X$ and $Y$ is:

$$\exists n_1, n_2.\ X{\mapsto}\texttt{node}(\_, n_1) * Y{\mapsto}\texttt{node}(\_, n_2) * \texttt{pre}(n_1, n_2)$$

Executing the body of the loop, at line 5, `x.next` is dereferenced; hence $n_1$ is accessed. Since $n_1$ is constrained by `pre`, our engine again tries two possible values for $n_1$. For the base case, the path condition $\Delta$ over $X$, $Y$, $n_1$ and $n_2$ is:

$$\exists n_1, n_2.\ X{\mapsto}\texttt{node}(\_, n_1) * Y{\mapsto}\texttt{node}(\_, n_2) \wedge n_1 = \texttt{null} \wedge n_2 = \texttt{null}$$

Then, $n_2$ is accessed via `y.next`. Since it has been assigned to `null` already, there is no case splitting. $n_1 = \texttt{null}$ violates the looping condition so symbolic execution finishes exploring the path and backtracks. We obtain a test input where `x` and `y` both have one digit. Likewise, we generate test inputs where `x` and `y` both have two digits, three digits and so on. Note that we put a bound on the number of unfolding for loops.

---

[2] In all path conditions in this example we only show the constraints over those variables which are relevant to the inputs `x` and `y`; the constraints over local variables `z` and `dummyHead` are separated from `x`, `y` and thus are omitted for simplicity.

$$[\text{CONST}]\frac{}{h, s \vdash k \Downarrow k} \quad [\text{VAR}]\frac{}{h, s \vdash v \Downarrow s(v)} \quad [\text{NULL}]\frac{}{h, s \vdash \texttt{null} \Downarrow \texttt{null}}$$

$$[\text{UNOP}]\frac{h, s \vdash e_1 \Downarrow k_1 \quad k' = op_u\, k_1}{h, s \vdash op_u\, e_1 \Downarrow k'} \quad [\text{BINOP}]\frac{h, s \vdash e_1 \Downarrow k_1 \quad h, s \vdash e_2 \Downarrow k_2 \quad k' = k_1\, op_b\, k_2}{h, s \vdash e_1\, op_b\, e_2 \Downarrow k'}$$

$$[\text{LOAD}]\frac{h, s \vdash v \Downarrow k_1 \quad r = h(k_1) \quad k_2 = r(\texttt{Type}(v), f_i)}{h, s \vdash v.f_i \Downarrow k_2} \quad [\text{FREE}]\frac{l = s(v) \quad h' = h \setminus \{l \mapsto \_\} \quad \iota = \Sigma(pc+1)}{\langle \Sigma, h, s, pc, \texttt{free}\ v \rangle \rightsquigarrow \langle \Sigma, h', s, pc+1, \iota \rangle}$$

$$[\text{ASSIGN}]\frac{h, s \vdash e \Downarrow k \quad s' = s[v \leftarrow k] \quad \iota = \Sigma(pc+1)}{\langle \Sigma, h, s, pc, v := e \rangle \rightsquigarrow \langle \Sigma, h, s', pc+1, \iota \rangle}$$

$$[\text{NEW}]\frac{\begin{array}{c}\texttt{fresh-map}\ r' \quad r'(c, f_i) = s(v_i)\ \forall i \in \{1..n\} \quad \texttt{fresh}\ l' \\ h' = h[l' \leftarrow r'] \quad s' = s[v \leftarrow l'] \quad \iota = \Sigma(pc+1)\end{array}}{\langle \Sigma, h, s, pc, v := \texttt{new}\ c(v_1, \ldots, v_n) \rangle \rightsquigarrow \langle \Sigma, h', s', pc+1, \iota \rangle}$$

$$[\text{STORE}]\frac{\begin{array}{c}h, s \vdash v \Downarrow k_1 \quad h, s \vdash e \Downarrow k_2 \quad r = h(k_1) \\ r' = r[(\texttt{Type}(v), f_i) \leftarrow k_2] \quad h' = h[k_1 \leftarrow r'] \quad \iota = \Sigma(pc+1)\end{array}}{\langle \Sigma, h, s, pc, v.f_i := e \rangle \rightsquigarrow \langle \Sigma, h', s, pc+1, \iota \rangle}$$

$$[\text{GOTO}]\frac{h, s \vdash e \Downarrow k \quad \iota = \Sigma(k)}{\langle \Sigma, h, s, pc, \texttt{goto}\ e \rangle \rightsquigarrow \langle \Sigma, h, s, k, \iota \rangle} \quad [\text{ASSERT}]\frac{h, s \vdash e \Downarrow \texttt{true} \quad \iota = \Sigma(pc+1)}{\langle \Sigma, h, s, pc, \texttt{assert}(e) \rangle \rightsquigarrow \langle \Sigma, h, s, pc+1, \iota \rangle}$$

$$[\text{TCOND}]\frac{h, s \vdash e_0 \Downarrow \texttt{true} \quad h, s \vdash e_1 \Downarrow k_1 \quad \iota = \Sigma(k_1)}{\langle \Sigma, h, s, pc, \texttt{if}\ e_0\ \texttt{then goto}\ e_1\ \texttt{else goto}\ e_2 \rangle \rightsquigarrow \langle \Sigma, h, s, k_1, \iota \rangle}$$

$$[\text{FCOND}]\frac{h, s \vdash e_0 \Downarrow \texttt{false} \quad h, s \vdash e_2 \Downarrow k_2 \quad \iota = \Sigma(k_2)}{\langle \Sigma, h, s, pc, \texttt{if}\ e_0\ \texttt{then goto}\ e_1\ \texttt{else goto}\ e_2 \rangle \rightsquigarrow \langle \Sigma, h, s, k_2, \iota \rangle}$$

**Fig. 2.** Operational semantics of the core language

$$\begin{aligned}
\mathit{datat} &::= \texttt{data}\ c\ \{\mathit{field};^*\ \} \\
\mathit{field} &::= t\ v \qquad t ::= c \mid \tau \qquad \tau ::= \texttt{bool} \mid \texttt{int} \\
\mathit{prog} &::= \mathit{stmt};^* \\
\mathit{stmt} &::= v := e \mid v.f_i := e \mid \texttt{goto}\ e \mid \texttt{assert}\ e \\
&\quad \mid \texttt{if}\ e_0\ \texttt{then goto}\ e_1\ \texttt{else goto}\ e_2 \\
&\quad \mid v := \texttt{new}\ c(v_1, .., v_n) \mid \texttt{free}\ v \\
e &::= k \mid v \mid v.f_i \mid e_1\ op_b\ e_2 \mid op_u\ e_1 \mid \texttt{null}
\end{aligned}$$

**Fig. 3.** A core intermediate language

In contrast to ours which always generates valid test inputs, the existing lazy approaches [9,10,36] would generate invalid test inputs such as (i) x and y have different number of digits; or (ii) x and y are aliasing; or (iii) x (or y) is a cyclic linked list.

## 3 A Core Language

In [34], Schwartz *et al.* described the algorithm of symbolic execution as an extension to the run-time semantics of a general language. The language, called SimpIL, is simple but "powerful enough to express typical languages as varied as Java and assembly code" [34]. In this work, we use a similar presentation to describe our new symbolic execution engine. This section introduces our core language, which is an extension of SimpIL with operations on heap memory. Note that our implementation is for Java bytecode, and our approach extends to other languages.

*Syntax.* The syntax of the language is defined in Fig. 3. A program in our core language consists of multiple data structures and statements. The primitive types include boolean and integer; statements consist of assignment, memory store, goto, assertion, conditional goto, memory allocation, and memory deallocation; expressions are side-effect free and consist of typical non-heap expressions and memory load. We use $\mathtt{op_b}$ to represent typical binary operators, e.g., addition, subtraction. Similarly, $\mathtt{op_u}$ is used to represent typical unary operators, e.g., logical negation. $k$ represents either a boolean or integer constant. The expressions used together with `goto` should not contain variables. For the sake of simplicity, we assume the programs are in the form of static single assignments and are well-typed in the standard way. We note that the language can be extended to handle method calls.

*Operational Semantics.* The *concrete* execution configuration of a program defined by the syntax shown in Fig. 3 is a tuple of five components $\langle \Sigma, h, s, pc, \iota \rangle$. $\Sigma$ is the list of program statements; $h$ is the current memory state (i.e., the heap); $s$ records the current value of program variables (i.e., the stack); $pc$ is the program counter; and $\iota$ is the current statement. Among these, $\Sigma$, $h$ and $s$ are mapping functions: $\Sigma$ maps a number to a statement; $h$ maps a memory location to its content; $s$ maps a variable to its value.

The concrete heap $h$ of type *Heaps* assumes a fixed finite collection *Node*, a fixed finite collection *Fields*, a disjoint set *Loc* of locations (i.e., heap addresses), a set of non-address values *Val*, such that $\mathtt{null} \in \mathit{Val}$ and $\mathit{Val} \cap \mathit{Loc} = \emptyset$. We define *Heaps* as:

$$\mathit{Heaps} \stackrel{\text{def}}{=} \mathit{Loc} \rightharpoonup_{fin} (\mathit{Node} \rightarrow \mathit{Fields} \rightarrow \mathit{Val} \cup \mathit{Loc})$$

Further, a concrete stack $s$ is of type *Stacks*, defined as follows:

$$\mathit{Stacks} \stackrel{\text{def}}{=} \mathit{Var} \rightarrow \mathit{Val} \cup \mathit{Loc}$$

is a mapping from a variable to a value or a memory address. We use $[x \leftarrow k]$ to denote updating a variable $x$ with value $k$ for mapping functions; for example, $s[x \leftarrow 13]$ denotes a new stack that is the same as stack $s$ except that it maps variable $x$ to the value 13. The operational semantics of our language is shown in Fig. 2. The rules are of the following form:

$$\frac{\text{computation}}{\langle \text{current state} \rangle \leadsto \langle \text{end state} \rangle}$$

The computation in a rule is read from the top to the bottom, the left to the right, and are applied based on syntactic pattern-matching. Given a statement, our engine finds a rule to execute the computation on the top and returns the end state in the case of success. If no rule matches (e.g., accessing a dangling pointer), the execution halts. In these rules, `fresh` is used as an overloading function to return a new variable/address. Similarly, `fresh−map` returns a new mapping and `Type` returns the type of a variable.

$$
\begin{array}{lcl}
\Phi & ::= & \Delta \mid \Phi_1 \vee \Phi_2 \\
\Delta & ::= & \exists \bar{v}.\ (\kappa \wedge \alpha \wedge \phi) \\
\kappa & ::= & \mathtt{emp} \mid v{\mapsto}c(f_i{:}v_i) \mid P(\bar{v}) \mid \kappa_1 * \kappa_2 \\
\alpha & ::= & \mathtt{true} \mid v_1{=}v_2 \mid v{=}\mathtt{null} \mid \neg\alpha \mid \alpha_1 \wedge \alpha_2 \\
\phi & ::= & \mathtt{true} \mid a_1{=}a_2 \mid a_1{\leq}a_2 \mid \neg\phi \mid \phi_1 \wedge \phi_2 \\
a & ::= & k \mid v \mid k{\times}a \mid a_1{+}a_2 \mid -a \\
\mathit{Pred} & ::= & \mathtt{pred}\ P_1(\bar{v}_1) \equiv \Phi_1; ...; \mathtt{pred}\ P_N(\bar{v}_N) \equiv \Phi_n
\end{array}
$$

**Fig. 4.** Syntax of separation logic

For the evaluation of expressions, we use $h, s \vdash e \Downarrow k$ to denote the evaluation of expression $e$ to a value $k$ in the current context $h$ and $s$. The application of these rules is also based on pattern-matching similar to the application of the statements above.

For example, rule [NEW] describes the operational semantics of the command that allocates dynamic heaps. Firstly, it creates a new mapping $r'$ to relate fields of the new object to their stack values. Next, it generates a new heap entry at the fresh address $l'$. Lastly, it updates the stack value of the variable with the heap address.

## 4 Symbolic Execution

This section presents details on symbolic execution using a separation logic-based language to encode path conditions in heap-based programs.

*Separation Logic.* We use separation logic [20,32] to capture symbolic heaps and expressions. Separation logic, an extension of Hoare logic, is a state-of-the-art assertion language designed for reasoning about heap-based programs. It provides concise and precise notations for reasoning about the heap. In particular, it supports the separating conjunction operator $*$ that splits the global heap into disjoint sub-heap regions, each of which can be analysed independently. Combined with inductive predicates, separation logic has been shown to capture semantics of unbounded heaps, loops and recursive procedures naturally and succinctly [24,26,35].

In the following, we define the separation logic formulae used in this work to encode path conditions of heap-based programs. A separation logic formula is defined by the syntax presented in Fig. 4. We assume that $c \in \mathit{Node}$ is a heap node; $f_i \in \mathit{Fields}$ is a field; and $v, v_i$ represent variables. We notice that each kind of heap nodes $c$ corresponds to a data structure declared by the user using the keyword `data` in our core language. We write $\bar{v}$ to denote a sequence of variables. A separation logic formula is denoted as $\Phi$, which can be either a symbolic heap $\Delta$ or a disjunction of them. A symbolic heap $\Delta$ is an existentially quantified conjunction of some spatial formulae $\kappa$, some pointer (dis)equalities $\alpha$, and some formulae in arithmetic $\phi$ [16]. All free variables in $\Delta$, denoted by function $FV(\Delta)$, are either program variables or implicitly universally quantified

$$[\text{S-CONST}]\frac{}{\Delta, s \vdash k \Downarrow k} \quad [\text{S-VAR}]\frac{}{\Delta, s \vdash v \Downarrow s(v)} \quad [\text{S-NULL}]\frac{}{\Delta, s \vdash \texttt{null} \Downarrow \texttt{null}}$$

$$[\text{S-UNOP}]\frac{\Delta, s \vdash e_1 \Downarrow \pi_1}{\Delta, s \vdash op_u\ e_1 \Downarrow op_u\ \pi_1} \quad [\text{S-BINOP}]\frac{\Delta, s \vdash e_1 \Downarrow \pi_1 \quad \Delta, s \vdash e_2 \Downarrow \pi_2}{\Delta, s \vdash e_1\ op_b\ e_2 \Downarrow \pi_1\ op_b\ \pi_2}$$

$$[\text{S-LOAD}]\frac{l \mapsto c(v_1, ..., v_i, ..., v_n) \in \Delta \quad \Delta, s \vdash v \Downarrow l \quad \Delta, s \vdash v_i \Downarrow \pi_i}{\Delta, s \vdash v.f_i \Downarrow \pi_i}$$

$$[\text{S-FREE}]\frac{\Delta, s \vdash v \Downarrow l \qquad \iota = \Sigma(pc+1)}{\langle \Sigma, \exists \bar{w}.\ l \mapsto c(...) * \Delta, s, pc, \texttt{free}\ v \rangle \rightsquigarrow \langle \Sigma, \exists \bar{w}.\ \Delta, s, pc+1, \iota \rangle}$$

$$[\text{S-ASSIGN}]\frac{\Delta, s \vdash e \Downarrow \pi \quad s' = s[v \leftarrow \pi] \quad \iota = \Sigma(pc+1)}{\langle \Sigma, \Delta, s, pc, v := e \rangle \rightsquigarrow \langle \Sigma, \Delta, s', pc+1, \iota \rangle}$$

$$[\text{S-NEW}]\frac{\texttt{fresh}\ l' \quad \Delta' \equiv \Delta * l' \mapsto c(v_1, ..., v_n) \quad s' = s[v \leftarrow l'] \quad \iota = \Sigma(pc+1)}{\langle \Sigma, \Delta, s, pc, v\ =\ \texttt{new}\ c(v_1, ..., v_n) \rangle \rightsquigarrow \langle \Sigma, \Delta', s', pc+1, \iota \rangle}$$

$$[\text{S-STORE}]\frac{\begin{array}{c} l \mapsto c(v_1, ..., v_i, ..., v_n) \in \Delta \quad \Delta, s \vdash v \Downarrow l \\ \Delta, s \vdash e \Downarrow \pi \quad s' = s[v_i \leftarrow \pi] \quad \iota = \Sigma(pc+1) \end{array}}{\langle \Sigma, \Delta, s, pc, v.f_i = e \rangle \rightsquigarrow \langle \Sigma, \Delta, s', pc+1, \iota \rangle}$$

$$[\text{S-GOTO}]\frac{\Delta, s \vdash e \Downarrow k \quad \iota = \Sigma(k)}{\langle \Sigma, \Delta, s, pc, \texttt{goto}\ e \rangle \rightsquigarrow \langle \Sigma, \Delta, s, k, \iota \rangle} \quad [\text{S-ASSERT}]\frac{\Delta, s \vdash e \Downarrow \pi \quad \Delta' \equiv \Delta \wedge \pi \quad \iota = \Sigma(pc+1)}{\langle \Sigma, \Delta, s, pc, \texttt{assert}(e) \rangle \rightsquigarrow \langle \Sigma, \Delta', s, pc+1, \iota \rangle}$$

$$[\text{S-TCOND}]\frac{\Delta, s \vdash e_0 \Downarrow \pi_0 \quad \Delta, s \vdash e_1 \Downarrow k_1 \quad \Delta' \equiv \Delta \wedge \pi_0 \quad \iota = \Sigma(k_1)}{\langle \Sigma, \Delta, s, pc, \texttt{if}\ e_0\ \texttt{then goto}\ e_1\ \texttt{else goto}\ e_2 \rangle \rightsquigarrow \langle \Sigma, \Delta', s, k_1, \iota \rangle}$$

$$[\text{S-FCOND}]\frac{\Delta, s \vdash e_0 \Downarrow \pi_0 \quad \Delta, s \vdash e_2 \Downarrow k_2 \quad \Delta' \equiv \Delta \wedge \neg\pi_0 \quad \iota = \Sigma(k_2)}{\langle \Sigma, \Delta, s, pc, \texttt{if}\ e_0\ \texttt{then goto}\ e_1\ \texttt{else goto}\ e_2 \rangle \rightsquigarrow \langle \Sigma, \Delta', s, k_2, \iota \rangle}$$

**Fig. 5.** Symbolic operational execution rules

at the outermost level. The spatial formula $\kappa$ may be a separating conjunction ($*$) of `emp` predicate, points-to predicates $v \mapsto c(f_i{:}v_i)$, and predicate applications $P(\bar{v})$. Whenever possible, we discard $f_i$ of the points-to predicate and use its short form as $v \mapsto c(\bar{v})$. Note that $v_1 \neq v_2$ and $v \neq \texttt{null}$ are short forms for $\neg(v_1 = v_2)$ and $\neg(v = \texttt{null})$ respectively. Each inductive predicate is defined by a disjunction $\Phi$ using the keyword `pred`. In each disjunct, we require that variables which are not formal parameters must be existentially quantified. We use $\Delta[v_1/v_2]$ for a substitution of all occurrences of $v_2$ in $\Delta$ to $v_1$.

*Symbolic Execution.* Recall that the concrete execution configuration is a 5-tuple. The *symbolic* execution configuration is also a tuple of five components: $\langle \Sigma, \Delta, s, pc, \iota \rangle$ where $\Delta$ is a path condition in the form of a separation logic formula defined above and $s$ is used to map every variable to a symbolic value[3]. The rest of the components are similar to those of the concrete execution configuration, except that symbolic values of variables are captured in $\Delta$ and $s$. We use $\pi$ (and $\pi_i$) to denote symbolic values. Memory allocations are symbolically captured in the path condition $\Delta$. A symbolic execution configuration $\langle \Sigma, \Delta, s, pc, \iota \rangle$ is *infeasible* if $\Delta$ is unsatisfiable. Otherwise, it is *feasible*.

All operational symbolic execution rules over our language are shown in Fig. 5. In these rules, similar to Fig. 2 we use function `fresh` to return a fresh

[3] We use the same symbol $s$ as in concrete setting. From the context, it should be clear as to whether we are referring to symbolic stack or concrete stack.

variable. We illustrate the execution through rule [S−NEW]. This rule allocates a new object of type $c$ and assigns to variable $v$. Firstly, it generates a fresh symbolic address $l'$ and updates the stack to map $v$ to this address. Secondly, it creates new symbolic heap for $l'$ by separately conjoining the current path condition with a new points-to predicate $l' \mapsto c(v_1, ..., v_n)$. Lastly, it loads the next statement using the program counter. Note that we assume all variables $v_1, ..., v_n$ used in memory allocation are distinct and each variable $v_i$ is only used to create at most one new object.

Rule [S−FREE] symbolically de-allocates the heaps. To capture the deallocated heaps for test input generation, we keep track the corresponding points-to predicates by storing them in a "garbage" formula. At the end of execution, those predicates are plugged into the current path condition before being used to generate the test input.

## 5 Lazy Test Input Generation

In this section, we present the test input generation based on the symbolic execution engine we depicted in the previous sections. The inputs of our method are a program `prog` in the language we defined in Sect. 3 and a precondition $\Delta_{pre}$ in the form of a separation logic formula defined in Sect. 4. The output is a set of fully initialized test inputs that satisfy the precondition and often achieve high test coverage. Our method is based on lazy initialization. The main difference between our method and previous approaches based on lazy initialization is that we generate values of reference variables and fields in a context-sensitive manner.

Our symbolic execution engine starts with the configuration: $\langle \Sigma, \Delta_{pre}\sigma, s_0, pc_0, \iota_0 \rangle$ where $\sigma$ is a substitution of input variables to their corresponding symbolic values, $s_0$ is an initial mapping of input variables to symbolic values, $pc_0$ and $\iota_0$ denote the first value of the program counter and the first statement respectively. The engine systematically derives the strongest postcondition of every program path (with a bound on the number of loop unfolding), by applying the symbolic operational execution rules (i.e., shown in Fig. 5). After obtaining the strongest post-state, our engine invokes $\texttt{S2SAT}_{\texttt{SL}}$ to check whether or not the resultant symbolic heap is satisfiable, and generate a model if it is. The model is then transformed into a test input.

*Context-Sensitive Lazy Initialization.* Recall that lazy initialization [21] leaves a reference variable or field uninitialized until it is first accessed and then enumerates all possible valuations of the variable or field. For instance, as shown in Fig. 5, a reference variable or field can be accessed in the rules [S−VAR], [S−LOAD], [S−STORE], or [S−FREE]. The problem is that many valuations obtained through enumeration are invalid (i.e., violating the precondition). Thus, in this work, we propose context-sensitive enumeration. When a reference variable or field with symbolic value $v$ is accessed during symbolic execution, procedure $\texttt{enum}(v, \Delta, s)$ is invoked to non-deterministically initialize $v$ with values derived from the symbolic execution context, i.e., $\Delta$ and $s$. For each value of the set, the symbolic

**Algorithm 1.** Procedure LFP

$SV_i \leftarrow \{P_i(\bar{t}_i)\}$ ; $A_i \leftarrow$ **false** ; /* i ∈ {1..N} */
**while** true **do**
  $SV'_i \leftarrow \{\}$ ; /* i ∈ {1..N} */
  **foreach** $i \in \{1..N\}$ **do**
    **foreach** $\Delta_j \in SV_i$ **do**
      $SV'_i \leftarrow SV'_i \cup \texttt{unfold}(\Delta_j)$ ;
    $A'_i \leftarrow \bigvee\{\exists\bar{w}.\ \texttt{abs}(\Pi(\kappa \wedge \alpha, \bar{t}_i), \bar{t}_i) \mid (\exists\bar{w}.\ \kappa \wedge \alpha \wedge \phi) \in SV'_i\}$ ;
  **if** $\forall i \in \{1..N\}.\ A'_i \Rightarrow A_i$ **then**
    **return** $\bar{SV}$ ; /* fixed point */
  **else**
    $SV_i \leftarrow SV'_i$ ; $A_i \leftarrow A'_i$ ; /* i ∈ {1..N} */

execution engine creates a new branch for exploration. Procedure $\texttt{enum}(v, \Delta, s)$ works based on the following three scenarios.

1. If $\Delta$ implies that $v$ has previously been initialized to either `null` (i.e., $\Delta \Rightarrow v = \texttt{null}$) or a points-to predicate (i.e., $\Delta \Rightarrow v{\mapsto}\_$), initializing it again is not necessary.
2. If $v$ is uninitialized and there does not exist a predicate $P_i(\bar{v}_i)$ in $\Delta$ such that $\Delta \Rightarrow v \in \bar{v}_i$ (i.e., $v$ is not constrained by the context), $v$ is initialized to `null`, to a new points-to predicate with uninitialized fields, or to a points-to predicate in $\Delta$.
3. If $v$ is uninitialized and there exists some predicates $P_i(\bar{v}_i)$ in $\Delta$ such that $\Delta \Rightarrow v \in \bar{v}_i$ (i.e., $v$ is constrained by the context), we substitute $P_i$ by $SV_i$ to instantiate $v$ where $SV_i$ is a set of possible values of $v$ which are consistent with the context $\Delta$, and computed in advance by using the least fixed point analysis (as shown below).

*Least Fixed Point Analysis.* This fixed point analysis is made use in the third case above. We assume that there are $N$ predicate definitions $P_1(\bar{t}_1)$, ..., $P_N(\bar{t}_N)$ ($\mathcal{P}$ for short). We then use the procedure LFP to compute $SV_1$, ..., $SV_N$ ($\bar{SV}$ for short) according to each predicate. Each $SV_i$ stores all possible contexts (in the form of separation logic formulae) for $\bar{t}_i$ that could be derived from $P_i(\bar{t}_i)$. After having all $\bar{SV}$, in scenario 3 mentioned above, we substitute $P_i(\bar{v}_i)$ with $SV_i[\bar{v}_i/\bar{t}_i]$ to get all possible values for $v$. Because of the substitution, new variables may be introduced in $\Delta$, we update $s$ accordingly by using the variables' names as their symbolic values. Note that we only compute $\bar{SV}$ once before running the symbolic execution engine.

The details of LFP are shown in Algorithm 1. LFP takes the set of predicate definitions $\mathcal{P}$ as input. It outputs the set of symbolic heap formulae $\bar{SV}$ of all predicates. In this algorithm, each $A_i$, a disjunctive base formula (i.e., a formula without any occurrence of inductive predicates), captures the abstraction of all formulae in accordance with $SV_i$. In intuition, LFP iteratively explores each $SV_i$ (initialized with $\{P_i(\bar{t}_i)\}$ at line 1) into a set of disjoint, complete and "smaller" contexts. At the same time, it computes an abstraction $A_i$ over heap allocations and (dis)equality constraints over $\bar{t}_i$. If the fixed point (at lines 8–9) is achieved i.e., the complete set of base formulas of every predicate has been explored, LFP stops. Otherwise, it moves to the next iteration.

In particular, for the first task LFP enumerates all possible symbolic heap locations which $\bar{t}_i$ can be assigned to. The enumeration is performed through the function $\texttt{unfold}(\Delta_j)$ (at line 6), which replaces every occurrence of inductive predicates in $\Delta_j$ by their corresponding definitions with $\alpha$-renaming. As a result, each disjunct in $SV_i$ captures a new context. For the second task, after the new contexts have been derived, at line 7, LFP computes an abstraction on the set of symbolic values which every parameters $\bar{t}_i$ can be assigned to. This abstraction is critical for the termination of the algorithm and is computed by two functions. Intuitively, these two functions compute constraints on parameters of each inductive predicate. The first function $\texttt{abs}(\kappa \wedge \alpha, \bar{t}_i)$ captures the reference values of $\bar{t}_i$, while the second function $\Pi(\kappa \wedge \alpha, \bar{t}_i)$ captures (dis)equality constraints on $\bar{t}_i$. Note that because we only want to capture heap allocations and (dis)equality constraints over $\bar{t}_i$, LFP does not consider arithmetic constraints when it computes the abstraction.

In particular, the function abs is defined as $\texttt{abs}(\texttt{emp} \wedge \alpha, \bar{v}) = \texttt{emp} \wedge \alpha$. Otherwise,

$$\texttt{abs}(v{\mapsto}c(\bar{w}) * \kappa_1 \wedge \alpha, \bar{v}) = \begin{cases} v{\mapsto}c(\bar{w}) * \texttt{abs}(\kappa_1 \wedge \alpha, \bar{v}) & \text{if } v{\in}\bar{v} \\ \texttt{abs}(\kappa_1 \wedge \alpha, \bar{v}) & \text{otherwise} \end{cases}$$

$$\texttt{abs}(P(\bar{w}) * \kappa_1 \wedge \alpha, \bar{v}) = \begin{cases} \texttt{false} & \text{if } \bar{w} \cap \bar{v} \neq \emptyset \\ \texttt{abs}(\kappa_1 \wedge \alpha, \bar{v}) & \text{otherwise} \end{cases}$$

In principle, this function retains all heap nodes allocated by variables in $\bar{v}$, maps inductive predicates with arguments in $\bar{v}$ to false, and discards other constraints in $\kappa$.

The function $\Pi(\kappa \wedge \alpha, \bar{v})$ eliminates (dis)equality constraints in $\kappa \wedge \alpha$ on all variables which are not in $\bar{v}$. In particular, $\Pi(\kappa \wedge \texttt{true}, \bar{v}) = \kappa \wedge \texttt{true}$, $\Pi(\kappa \wedge \texttt{false}, \bar{v}) = \texttt{false}$, and $\Pi(\kappa \wedge v_1 \neq v_1 \wedge \alpha_1, \bar{v}) = \texttt{false}$. Otherwise,

$$\Pi(\kappa \wedge v_1 = e \wedge \alpha_1, \bar{v}) = \begin{cases} \Pi(\kappa \wedge \alpha_1[\texttt{null}/v_1], \bar{v}) & \text{if } e = \texttt{null} \wedge v_1 \notin \bar{v} \\ \Pi((\kappa \wedge \alpha_1)[v_2/v_1], \bar{v}) & \text{if } e = v_2 \wedge v_1 \notin \bar{v} \\ \Pi((\kappa \wedge \alpha_1)[v_1/v_2], \bar{v}) & \text{if } e = v_2 \wedge v_2 \notin \bar{v} \wedge v_1 \in \bar{v} \\ \Pi(\kappa \wedge \alpha_1, \bar{v}) \wedge v_1 = e & \text{otherwise} \end{cases}$$

$$\Pi(\kappa \wedge v_1 \neq e \wedge \alpha_1, \bar{v}) = \begin{cases} \Pi(\kappa \wedge \alpha_1, \bar{v}) \wedge v_1 \neq e & \text{if } e = \texttt{null} \wedge v_1 \in \bar{v} \vee e = v_2 \wedge v_1 \in \bar{v} \wedge v_2 \in \bar{v} \\ \Pi(\kappa \wedge \alpha_1, \bar{v}) & \text{otherwise} \end{cases}$$

An equality $v_1 = v_2$ is retained if both $v_1$ and $v_2$ are in $\bar{v}$. Otherwise, it is eliminated and one of the variables must be eliminated via a substitution. A disequality $v_1 \neq v_2$ is retained if both $v_1$ and $v_2$ are in $\bar{v}$. Otherwise, it is eliminated. Similarly, $v_1 = \texttt{null}$ and $v_1 \neq \texttt{null}$ are retained if $v_1$ is in $\bar{v}$. After applying the above two functions, formulae may contain redundant variables in $\exists \bar{w}$, which may be eliminated.

*Correctness.* Correctness of the proposed enumeration method follows the correctness of the procedure LFP. We argue that LFP is sound (i.e., all generated values are correct), terminating, and complete (i.e., all possible heap and (dis)equality constraints between reference parameters in each predicate are captured at fixed point).

**Theorem 1 (Soundness).** *If $\Delta_j \in SV_i$ and $h, s \models \Delta_j$ then $h, s \models P_i(\bar{t}_i)$.*

*Proof.* The soundness of LFP follows the correctness of the unfolding, i.e., $\Delta_j$ is derived through the unfolding of $P_i(\bar{t}_i)$ and $P_i(\bar{t}_i) \equiv \bigvee\{\Delta_j \mid \Delta_j \in SV_i\}$. Hence, $\Delta_j$ is an under-approximated formula of $P_i(\bar{t}_i)$.

**Theorem 2 (Termination).** *Suppose $M$ be the maximal arity among the inductive predicates $P_i(\bar{t}_i)$, $i \in \{1..N\}$. Then* LFP *runs in $\mathcal{O}(N2^{M^2+M})$.*

*Proof.* The complexity of LFP relies on the number of disjuncts computed by two functions $\texttt{abs}(\kappa \wedge \alpha, \bar{t}_i)$ and $\Pi(\kappa \wedge \alpha, \bar{t}_i)$. It comes from the following three sub-components.

- As the maximal arity of $\bar{t}_i$ is $M$, the number of (dis)equalities among these variables is $\mathcal{O}(M^2)$. The number of its subsets is $\mathcal{O}(2^{M^2})$.
- Furthermore, the maximum number of points-to predicates is $M$. Hence, the number of its subsets is $\mathcal{O}(2^M)$.
- There are $N$ predicate definitions in the system.

Hence, the implication at line 8 in Algorithm 1 holds in a finite number of iterations.

**Theorem 3 (Completeness).** *If $h, s \models P_i(\bar{t}_i)$ then $\exists \Delta_j \in SV_i$ s.t. $h, s \models \Delta_j$. Moreover, $SV_i$ captures all possible heap and (dis)equality constraints between reference variables in $\bar{t}_i$.*

*Proof.* The first part follows the correctness of the unfolding. For the second part, notice that at least one of $A_1, ..., A_N$ gets weaker via each iteration until all of them reach fixed point. Each $A_i$ is derived from its according $SV_i$ by two functions $\texttt{abs}(\kappa \wedge \alpha, \bar{t}_i)$ and $\Pi(\kappa \wedge \alpha, \bar{t}_i)$, which captures all heap and (dis)equality constraints between $\bar{t}_i$.

*Example 1.* We demonstrate the computation of $SV$ for predicate $\texttt{pre}(a, b)$ in Sect. 2. The computation is summarized in Fig. 6 where $i$ is the number of the iteration.

Since $A^2 \Rightarrow A^1$, LFP stops after two iterations and produces $SV^1$ as the set of new contexts for this example. After that, the engine substitutes $SV^1$ into $\Delta$ to obtain the two corresponding symbolic heaps.

| $i$ | $SV^i$ | $A^i$ |
|---|---|---|
| 0 | $\texttt{pre}(a, b)$ | $\texttt{false}$ |
| 1 | $\texttt{emp} \land a{=}\texttt{null} \land b{=}\texttt{null}$<br>$\lor \exists n_1, n_2 .\ a \mapsto \texttt{node}(\_, n_1) * b \mapsto \texttt{node}(\_, n_2) * \texttt{pre}(n_1, n_2)$ | $\texttt{emp} \land a{=}\texttt{null} \land b{=}\texttt{null}$<br>$\lor \exists n_1, n_2 .\ a \mapsto \texttt{node}(\_, n_1) * b \mapsto \texttt{node}(\_, n_2)$ |
| 2 | $\texttt{emp} \land a{=}\texttt{null} \land b{=}\texttt{null}$<br>$\lor \exists n_1, n_2 .\ a \mapsto \texttt{node}(\_, n_1) * b \mapsto \texttt{node}(\_, n_2) \land n_1{=}\texttt{null} \land n_2{=}\texttt{null}$<br>$\lor \exists n_1, n_2, n_3, n_4 .\ a \mapsto \texttt{node}(\_, n_1) * b \mapsto \texttt{node}(\_, n_2) *$<br>$n_1 \mapsto \texttt{node}(\_, n_3) * n_2 \mapsto \texttt{node}(\_, n_4) * \texttt{pre}(n_3, n_4)$ | $\texttt{emp} \land a{=}\texttt{null} \land b{=}\texttt{null}$<br>$\lor \exists n_1, n_2 .\ a \mapsto \texttt{node}(\_, n_1) * b \mapsto \texttt{node}(\_, n_2)$<br>$\lor \exists n_1, n_2 .\ a \mapsto \texttt{node}(\_, n_1) * b \mapsto \texttt{node}(\_, n_2)$ |

**Fig. 6.** LFP for the motivating example

**Table 1.** Experimental results

| Program | JSF | | | | JBSE | | | | BBE | | | |
|---|---|---|---|---|---|---|---|---|---|---|---|---|
| | #Tests | Cov.(%) | #Calls | T(s) | #Tests | Cov.(%) | NCov.(%) | T(s) | #Tests | Cov.(%) | NCov.(%) | T(s) |
| DLL | 74/74 | **100** | 325 | 49 | 121/5146 | 56 | 100 | 206 | 0/35 | 0 | 21 | 21 |
| AVL | 69/69 | **100** | 623 | 400 | 76/295 | **100** | 100 | 48 | 17/117 | 70 | 89 | 69 |
| RBT | 314/314 | **100** | 2070 | 2256 | 137/291 | 87 | 91 | 38 | 14/380 | 26 | 53 | 333 |
| SUSHI | 7/7 | **100** | 30 | 5 | 0/900 | 0 | 100 | 24 | 2/27 | 25 | 25 | 8 |
| TSAFE | 5/5 | **24** | 13 | 3 | 0/32 | 0 | 5 | 10 | 0/1 | 0 | 0 | 1 |
| Gantt | 21/21 | **100** | 140 | 25 | 17/887 | 55 | 90 | 24 | 0/6 | 0 | 5 | 2 |
| SLL | 26/26 | **100** | 55 | 11 | - | - | - | - | 16/50 | 66 | 71 | 19 |
| Stack | 18/18 | **100** | 31 | 7 | - | - | - | - | 11/14 | 84 | 84 | 6 |
| BST | 182/182 | **100** | 698 | 241 | - | - | - | - | 19/260 | 69 | 86 | 131 |
| AAT | 103/103 | **100** | 1179 | 1981 | - | - | - | - | 3/166 | 6 | 43 | 111 |
| Tll | 3/3 | **100** | 11 | 2 | - | - | - | - | 1/4 | 38 | 50 | 2 |

## 6 Implementation and Evaluation

We have implemented our approach described in previous sections into a tool, called Java StarFinder (JSF), consisting of 11569 lines of Java code. The architecture of JSF was briefly described in our previous work [30]. In the following, we evaluate JSF in order to answer three research questions (RQ). All experiments are conducted on a laptop with 2.20 GHz Intel Core i7 and 16 GB RAM.

Our experimental subjects include *Singly Linked List* (SLL), *Doubly Linked List* (DLL), *Stack*, *Binary Search Tree* (BST), and *Red Black Tree* (RBT) from SIR [4]; *AVL Tree* (AVL) and *AA Tree* (AAT) from Sierum/Kiasan [5], the motivation example, *TSAFE* project, and *Gantt* project used in SUSHI [8] and a data structure called *Tll* [23]. Since JSF is yet to support string, array, and object oriented features such as inheritance and polymorphism, we exclude data structures and methods which rely on these features, i.e., *Disjoint Set* in Sierum/Kiasan and *Google Closure* in SUSHI. Supporting these features is left for future work. In total, our experimental subjects include a total of 74 methods, whose lines of code range from dozens to more than one thousand.

*RQ1: Can JSF Reduce Invalid Test Inputs?* To answer this question, we need to check whether a generated test input is valid or not. In the benchmark programs which we collect, six data structures contain *repOK* methods which are designed to check if the input is valid or not, i.e., *Stack*, *DLL*, *BST*, *RBT*, *AVL*, and *AAT*. In addition, the motivation example in SUSHI is based on *DLL* and thus we use the method *repOK* of *DLL* to validate its test inputs. We write the *repOK* methods manually for the remaining test subjects. For *SLL* and *Tll*, we write their *repOK* methods based on their standard definition. For *TSAFE* and *Gantt*, we write their *repOK* methods after reading the source code, i.e., the *repOK* encodes the condition required to avoid *RuntimeException* such as *NullPointerException*.

For each generated test input, we check its validity by passing it as arguments to the corresponding *repOK* method [36]. If *repOK* returns `true`, the test input is deemed valid. As a baseline, we compare JSF with JBSE [10], which implements the HEX approach [9], and the black box enumeration (BBE) approach documented in [36]. We do not compare with the white box enumeration approach [36] as it requires user-provided *conservative repOK* methods, which are missing in these benchmarks. Note that conservative *repOK* methods are different from *repOK* methods, and writing those methods is highly nontrivial. We do not compare our approach with SUSHI because SUSHI generates test cases in form of sequence of method calls whereas we generate test cases in form of input data structures. SUSHI and our approach are thus complementary to each other. To run JBSE, we need invariants written in HEX. We manage to find invariants for *DLL*, *RBT*, *AVL*, *TSAFE*, and *Gantt* from [6], and thus we are able to run JBSE on these subjects. It is not clear to us how to write HEX invariants for other data structures or if HEX is expressive enough to describe them.

The experimental results are shown in Table 1, where the first column show the name of test subjects, and the last three columns show the results of JSF, JBSE, and BBE respectively. Columns #Tests show the results in form of the number of valid test inputs over the number of generated test inputs. Note that because JBSE generate partial initialized test inputs, we add an additional call to *repOK* method after the method under test to concretize their test inputs. The results show that, as expected, every test input generated by JSF is valid. In comparison, JBSE generates 4.65% valid test inputs and BBE generates 7.83% valid test inputs. From the results, we conclude that JSF is effective in generating valid test inputs.

*RQ2: Can JSF Generate Test Inputs That Achieve High Code Coverage?* To answer this question, we use JaCoCo [2] to measure the branch coverage of test inputs generated by the tools. The results are shown in the columns titled Cov.(%) and NCov.(%) in Table 1. The columns NCov.(%) show the coverage of all generated test inputs, the columns Cov.(%) show the coverage of test inputs that satisfy *repOK* methods. As all test inputs generated by JSF satisfy *repOK* methods, the result of JSF has only one column Cov.(%).

For 73/74 methods (including auxiliary methods), JSF can achieve 100% branch coverage (excluding infeasible branches). The only exception is method *TS_R_3* in the *TSAFE* project. It is because this method invokes native methods and handling native methods is beyond the capability of JSF at the moment. In general, JSF achieves 98.98% coverage on average. In comparison, when considering all test inputs, JBSE achieves 95.59% coverage on average and BBE achieves 54.66% coverage on average. Since many of these test inputs are invalid, these coverage are inflated. When considering only test inputs that satisfy *repOK* method, JBSE is only able to achieve 68.54% coverage on average and BBE achieves 37.85% coverage on average. From these results, we conclude that JSF can generate test inputs with high branch coverage for the methods under test.

*RQ3: Is JSF Sufficiently Efficient?* To answer this question, we measure the time spent to generate test inputs for each method. The results are shown in the columns titled T(s) in Table 1. From the results, JBSE and BBE are clearly faster than JSF. That is, JBSE and BBE takes average 8.75 and 9.50 s respectively to handle each method, whereas JSF's time ranges from 1 s to half an hour, with an average of 67.29 s per method. We also report the number of solver calls used by JSF. In average, JSF needs 70 calls per method. The main reason JSF is slower than JBSE and BBE is JSF has to solve harder path conditions with inductive predicates. However, the efficiency of JBSE and BBE comes with the tradeoff of excessive number of invalid test inputs as discussed above, whereas JSF only generates valid test inputs. From these results, we conclude that JSF is slower than JBSE and BBE, but still sufficiently efficient to provide higher quality results.

## 7 Related Work

This work is based on *generalized symbolic execution* (GSE) [21], which is the state-of-the-art way for the symbolic execution [22] of heap-based programs. At the heart of GSE is the lazy initialization algorithm which executes programs on inputs with reference variables and fields being *uninitialized.* When a reference variable or field is first accessed, lazy initialization enumerates all possible heap objects that it can: (i) be `null`, (ii) point to a new object with all reference fields being uninitialized, or (iii) point to any previously initialized object of the same type. This explicit enumeration quickly leads to path explosion in any non-trivial program, and existing approaches to addressing this problem can be roughly grouped into two categories:

- *State merging* approaches group together the choices of lazy initialization. For instance, the work in [14,15] represented the choices (ii) and (iii) with a variable, while the work in [19] captured all choices (i), (ii) and (iii) in a symbolic heap using guarded value set. Those work cannot avoid path explosion, but delay it to later stage [14,15], or delegate the burden to an SMT solver [19].
- *State pruning* approaches [9,33,36] truly mitigate the path explosion problem by using a precondition to describe *some properties* of the input. After explicitly enumerating all possible choices, i.e. both valid and invalid paths, these approaches will prune the invalid paths that violate the precondition.

A principle difference between our work and the aforementioned approaches is that we use separation logic, which is expressive enough to *define* arbitrary unbounded data structures. Consequently, we are able to construct valid choices from the definition, without explicit enumeration of invalid paths, and without false positives. We discuss some notable state pruning approaches in the following.

**repOK.** As GSE with lazy initialization results in partially initialized structures containing both concrete and symbolic values, the work in [36] propose to use a particular kind of *repOK*, called *conservative* or *hybrid repOK*, that returns `true` when running into parts of the structure that are still symbolic. This, of course, leads to false positives.

**JML.** The BLISS approach in [33] used both hybrid *repOK* and JML [27] together as preconditions. The JML precondition is used to precompute relational bounds on the interpretation of class fields. It is translated into a SAT problem by the TACO tool [17]. As pointed out in [18], this translation introduces duplication, which undermines the benefit of eliminating invalid structures when the size is big. BLISS uses symmetry breaking and refine bounds to mitigate this problem.

**HEX.** Braione *et al.* [9] introduced Heap EXploration Logic (HEX) as a specification language to constrain heap inputs. However, the language is not expressive enough to describe many common data structures, and users have to provide additional methods, called *triggers* [3], to check the properties that cannot be written in HEX. Moreover, HEX does not support numerical constraints, and it represents unbounded data structures using regular operators (using $(\pi)^+$ operator). Therefore, it is unable to capture the non-regular data structures, e.g., singly-linked lists which have $2^n$ nodes ($n \geq 0$). Finally, it is unclear how the HEX solver discharges an unbounded heap formula with regular operators.

**Separation Logic.** Our work is also related to research on Smallfoot symbolic execution [7] and its following work, e.g. [13,28]. Those work are not based on lazy initialization, and it is not clear how they can be used for test input generation. As far as we know, our work is the first to explore the use of separation logic for testing and there is only one more testing tool based on separation logic, which is a concolic execution engine named CSF [29].

## 8 Conclusion and Future Work

We present a symbolic execution framework for heap-based programs using separation logic. Our novelty is the proposed context-sensitive lazy initialization for test input generation. The experimental results show that our approach significantly reduces the number of invalid test inputs and improves the test coverage. For future work, we might combine JSF with bi-abduction and frame inference tools (i.e., Infer [1,12], S2 [23,25]) to both verify safety and generate test inputs to locate/confirm real bugs in heap-based programs. Finally, we are actively investigating the use of JSF tool for automatic program repair, a preliminary results were reported in [37].

**Acknowledgments.** This research is supported by the project 19-C220-SMU-001. The first author is also partially supported by the Google Summer of Code 2017 program.

## References

1. Facebook Infer. https://fbinfer.com/
2. JaCoCo. https://www.eclemma.org/jacoco/
3. JBSE. https://github.com/pietrobraione/jbse
4. SIR. http://sir.unl.edu/portal/index.php
5. Sireum. https://code.google.com/archive/p/sireum/downloads
6. SUSHI Experiments. https://github.com/pietrobraione/sushi-experiments
7. Berdine, J., Calcagno, C., O'Hearn, P.W.: Symbolic execution with separation logic. In: Yi, K. (ed.) APLAS 2005. LNCS, vol. 3780, pp. 52–68. Springer, Heidelberg (2005). https://doi.org/10.1007/11575467_5
8. Braione, P., Denaro, G., Mattavelli, A., Pezzè, M.: Combining symbolic execution and search-based testing for programs with complex heap inputs. In: Bultan, T., Sen, K. (eds.) ISSTA 2017, pp. 90–101. ACM (2017). https://doi.org/10.1145/3092703.3092715
9. Braione, P., Denaro, G., Pezzè, M.: Symbolic execution of programs with heap inputs. In: Nitto, E.D., Harman, M., Heymans, P. (eds.) FSE 2015, pp. 602–613. ACM (2015). https://doi.org/10.1145/2786805.2786842
10. Braione, P., Denaro, G., Pezzè, M.: JBSE: a symbolic executor for Java programs with complex heap inputs. In: Zimmermann, T., Cleland-Huang, J., Su, Z. (eds.) FSE 2016, pp. 1018–1022. ACM (2016). https://doi.org/10.1145/2950290.2983940
11. Cadar, C., et al.: Symbolic execution for software testing in practice: preliminary assessment. In: Taylor, R.N., Gall, H.C., Medvidovic, N. (eds.) ICSE 2011, pp. 1066–1071. ACM (2011). https://doi.org/10.1145/1985793.1985995
12. Calcagno, C., Distefano, D., O'Hearn, P.W., Yang, H.: Compositional shape analysis by means of bi-abduction. JACM **58**(6), 26:1–26:66 (2011). https://doi.org/10.1145/2049697.2049700
13. Chin, W.N., David, C., Nguyen, H.H., Qin, S.: Automated verification of shape, size and bag properties via user-defined predicates in separation logic. Sci. Comput. Program. **77**(9), 1006–1036 (2012). https://doi.org/10.1016/j.scico.2010.07.004
14. Deng, X., Lee, J., Robby: Bogor/Kiasan: a K-bounded symbolic execution for checking strong heap properties of open systems. In: ASE 2006, pp. 157–166. IEEE Computer Society (2006). https://doi.org/10.1109/ASE.2006.26
15. Deng, X., Robby, Hatcliff, J.: Towards a case-optimal symbolic execution algorithm for analyzing strong properties of object-oriented programs. In: SEFM 2007. IEEE Computer Society (2007). https://doi.org/10.1109/SEFM.2007.43
16. Enderton, H.B.: A Mathematical Introduction to Logic, 2nd Edn. pp. 67–181. Academic Press (2001). https://doi.org/10.1016/B978-0-08-049646-7.50008-4
17. Galeotti, J.P., Rosner, N., López Pombo, C.G., Frias, M.F.: Analysis of invariants for efficient bounded verification. In: Tonella, P., Orso, A. (eds.) ISSTA 2010, pp. 25–36. ACM (2010). https://doi.org/10.1145/1831708.1831712
18. Geldenhuys, J., Aguirre, N., Frias, M.F., Visser, W.: Bounded lazy initialization. In: Brat, G., Rungta, N., Venet, A. (eds.) NFM 2013. LNCS, vol. 7871, pp. 229–243. Springer, Heidelberg (2013). https://doi.org/10.1007/978-3-642-38088-4_16

19. Hillery, B., Mercer, E., Rungta, N., Person, S.: Exact heap summaries for symbolic execution. In: Jobstmann, B., Leino, K.R.M. (eds.) VMCAI 2016. LNCS, vol. 9583, pp. 206–225. Springer, Heidelberg (2016). https://doi.org/10.1007/978-3-662-49122-5_10
20. Ishtiaq, S.S., O'Hearn, P.W.: BI as an assertion language for mutable data structures. In: Hankin, C., Schmidt, D. (eds.) POPL 2001, pp. 14–26. ACM (2001). https://doi.org/10.1145/360204.375719
21. Khurshid, S., Păsăreanu, C.S., Visser, W.: Generalized symbolic execution for model checking and testing. In: Garavel, H., Hatcliff, J. (eds.) TACAS 2003. LNCS, vol. 2619, pp. 553–568. Springer, Heidelberg (2003). https://doi.org/10.1007/3-540-36577-X_40
22. King, J.C.: Symbolic execution and program testing. Commun. ACM **19**(7), 385–394 (1976). https://doi.org/10.1145/360248.360252
23. Le, Q.L., Gherghina, C., Qin, S., Chin, W.-N.: Shape analysis via second-order bi-abduction. In: Biere, A., Bloem, R. (eds.) CAV 2014. LNCS, vol. 8559, pp. 52–68. Springer, Cham (2014). https://doi.org/10.1007/978-3-319-08867-9_4
24. Le, Q.L., Sun, J., Chin, W.-N.: Satisfiability modulo heap-based programs. In: Chaudhuri, S., Farzan, A. (eds.) CAV 2016. LNCS, vol. 9779, pp. 382–404. Springer, Cham (2016). https://doi.org/10.1007/978-3-319-41528-4_21
25. Le, Q.L., Sun, J., Qin, S.: Frame inference for inductive entailment proofs in separation logic. In: Beyer, D., Huisman, M. (eds.) TACAS 2018. LNCS, vol. 10805, pp. 41–60. Springer, Cham (2018). https://doi.org/10.1007/978-3-319-89960-2_3
26. Le, Q.L., Tatsuta, M., Sun, J., Chin, W.-N.: A decidable fragment in separation logic with inductive predicates and arithmetic. In: Majumdar, R., Kunčak, V. (eds.) CAV 2017. LNCS, vol. 10427, pp. 495–517. Springer, Cham (2017). https://doi.org/10.1007/978-3-319-63390-9_26
27. Leavens, G.T., Baker, A.L., Ruby, C.: JML: a notation for detailed design. In: Kilov, H., Rumpe, B., Simmonds, I. (eds.) Behavioral Specifications of Businesses and Systems, vol. 523, pp. 175–188. Springer, Heidelberg (1999). https://doi.org/10.1007/978-1-4615-5229-1_12
28. Müller, P., Schwerhoff, M., Summers, A.J.: Automatic verification of iterated separating conjunctions using symbolic execution. In: Chaudhuri, S., Farzan, A. (eds.) CAV 2016. LNCS, vol. 9779, pp. 405–425. Springer, Cham (2016). https://doi.org/10.1007/978-3-319-41528-4_22
29. Pham, L.H., Le, Q.L., Phan, Q.S., Sun, J.: Concolic testing heap-manipulating programs. In: FM 2019 (2019, to appear)
30. Pham, L.H., Le, Q.L., Phan, Q.S., Sun, J., Qin, S.: Testing heap-based programs with Java StarFinder. In: Chaudron, M., Crnkovic, I., Chechik, M., Harman, M. (eds.) ICSE 2018, pp. 268–269. ACM (2018). https://doi.org/10.1145/3183440.3194964
31. Păsăreanu, C.S., Visser, W., Bushnell, D., Geldenhuys, J., Mehlitz, P., Rungta, N.: Symbolic PathFinder: integrating symbolic execution with model checking for Java bytecode analysis. Autom. Softw. Eng. **20**(3), 391–425 (2013). https://doi.org/10.1007/s10515-013-0122-2
32. Reynolds, J.: Separation logic: a logic for shared mutable data structures. In: LICS 2002, pp. 55–74. IEEE Computer Society (2002). https://doi.org/10.1109/LICS.2002.1029817
33. Rosner, N., Geldenhuys, J., Aguirre, N., Visser, W., Frias, M.F.: BLISS: improved symbolic execution by bounded lazy initialization with SAT support. IEEE Trans. Softw. Eng. **41**(7), 639–660 (2015). https://doi.org/10.1109/TSE.2015.2389225

34. Schwartz, E.J., Avgerinos, T., Brumley, D.: All you ever wanted to know about dynamic taint analysis and forward symbolic execution (but Might Have Been Afraid to Ask). In: S&P 2010, pp. 317–331. IEEE Computer Society (2010). https://doi.org/10.1109/SP.2010.26
35. Tatsuta, M., Le, Q.L., Chin, W.-N.: Decision procedure for separation logic with inductive definitions and presburger arithmetic. In: Igarashi, A. (ed.) APLAS 2016. LNCS, vol. 10017, pp. 423–443. Springer, Cham (2016). https://doi.org/10.1007/978-3-319-47958-3_22
36. Visser, W., Păsăreanu, C.S., Khurshid, S.: Test input generation with Java PathFinder. In: Avrunin, G.S., Rothermel, G. (eds.) ISSTA 2004, pp. 97–107. ACM (2004). https://doi.org/10.1145/1007512.1007526
37. Zheng, G., Le, Q.L., Nguyen, T., Phan, Q.S.: Automatic data structure repair using separation logic. In: JPF 2018 (2018)

# BUBEN: Automated Library Abstractions Enabling Scalable Bug Detection for Large Programs with I/O and Complex Environment

Pavel Parízek(✉)

Faculty of Mathematics and Physics, Department of Distributed and Dependable Systems, Charles University, Prague, Czechia
parizek@d3s.mff.cuni.cz

**Abstract.** An important goal of software engineering research is to create methods for efficient verification and detecting bugs. In this context, we focus on two challenges: (1) scalability to large and realistic software systems and (2) tools unable to directly analyze programs that perform I/O operations and interact with their environment. The common sources of problems with scalability include the huge number of thread interleavings and usage of large libraries. Programs written in managed languages, such as Java, cannot be directly analyzed by many verification tools due to insufficient support for native library methods. Both issues affect especially path-sensitive verification techniques.

We present the BUBEN system that automatically generates abstractions of complex software systems written in Java. The whole process has three phases: (1) dynamic analysis that records under-approximate information about behavior of native methods and library methods that perform I/O, (2) static analysis that computes over-approximate summaries of side effects of library methods, and (3) program code transformation that replaces calls of native methods and creates abstractions of library methods. Software systems abstracted in this way can be analyzed, e.g. for the presence of bugs, without the risk of a tool failure caused by unsupported libraries and more efficiently too. We evaluated BUBEN on several programs from popular benchmark suites, including DaCapo.

## 1 Introduction

An important goal of software engineering research is to develop techniques and tools for verification and detecting bugs in software. Out of the many associated challenges, we focus on these two: (1) scalability to realistic software systems that typically include many large libraries and (2) tools unable to directly analyze programs that perform I/O operations (including data storage, GUI and networking) and whose behavior depends on interaction with their environment.


Y.-F. Chen et al. (Eds.): ATVA 2019, LNCS 11781, pp. 228–245, 2019.
https://doi.org/10.1007/978-3-030-31784-3_13

The problems with scalability of verification and bug finding have several causes. For example, one cause is the huge number of thread interleavings that have to be analyzed even for rather small multithreaded programs. Another cause is the usage of large libraries, which greatly increases the total amount of code that a verification tool has to process and the time needed to analyze individual execution paths. Typical realistic programs involve many calls of library methods. However, in practice, developers are usually looking just for bugs in application programs that are relatively small when compared to all the libraries. Therefore, most library methods included with a program can be assumed correct, and many of them do not actually influence the program control flow and visible behavior—for these reasons, execution of such library methods does not have to be checked. In the case of managed languages such as Java, some library methods even involve native code, which is usually not handled well by the respective verification tools.

The presence of native library methods is, in fact, the main reason why many state-of-the-art verification tools cannot be directly used to analyze programs that access files, communicate over network, or involve GUI—where *directly* means without prior substantial modifications of the program code. We say that such programs *manipulate and interact with external entities* (e.g., with files and human users). For example, Java Pathfinder (JPF) [16], a popular verification framework, when run standalone it crashes on many realistic programs due to insufficient support for libraries that perform I/O via native methods.

Both challenges, that means (1) limited scalability to programs using large libraries and (2) inability to analyze programs that manipulate with external entities through I/O operations, affect especially path-sensitive verification techniques based on state space traversal, which aim to analyze every possible execution trace separately. Authors of verification tools usually focus on algorithmic improvements, neglecting the hard and tedious work needed to handle real-world programs that use many libraries and interact with external entities. For example, manually creating models (stubs) of the respective methods and abstractions of the environment is certainly not a practical option in general.

We present the BUBEN system that automatically creates abstractions of libraries in order to enable analysis of realistic programs with tools like Java Pathfinder. For an input large program, BUBEN computes abstractions of library methods called from within the application code and then generates an abstract variant of the program by the means of several code transformations. The abstract program does not contain any calls to library methods that are either native, perform I/O, or interact with external entities—thus avoiding calls of library methods that cause problems to verification tools. A particular tool (e.g., Java Pathfinder) can be then successfully run on the abstracted program without the risk of a failure due to missing support for library methods. In addition, usage of library abstractions generated by BUBEN helps to improve the performance and scalability of verification, because the total amount of code and possible behaviors to be analyzed is much lower. Even though we described the challenges that BUBEN addresses mostly on the specific case of Java Pathfinder, it can be used also together with other program analysis and verification tools quite easily. Only minor customizations of BUBEN are needed in order to support a new tool—for example, the user has to define the name of the tool's API procedure that performs a non-deterministic choice.

The key characteristic of the whole process involving BUBEN is nearly full automation. A user only has to provide a configuration file, which specifies the set of library methods and command line arguments.

In the rest of this paper, first we provide an overview of BUBEN, and then we present specific details in the following sections.

**Overview.** When generating abstractions, BUBEN distinguishes between library methods and the application classes. Only the library methods (and their calls) are to be abstracted. The set of library methods is then split further into two parts, where the first part contains native methods and library methods that manipulate with external entities (I/O), and the second part contains all other library methods. Each part is processed in a different way.

For the given input program, BUBEN creates its abstracted variant that consists of the original application code and generated abstractions of library methods. The whole process has the following three steps:

1. Dynamic analysis records information about side effects and outputs of library methods in the first group (native, I/O).
2. For every other library method, a summary of its possible side effects is computed using a static analysis.
3. Several code transformations are performed in order to create an abstract variant of the input original program.

We have to use dynamic analysis mainly because the side effects and outputs of native methods, respectively library methods that perform I/O, cannot be determined statically. In order to compute a summary of a given library method (step 2), BUBEN actually performs *symbolic interpretation* that is based on a linear traversal of method's code. Note that the dynamic analysis must run before the static analysis, since data collected by the dynamic analysis are used by the procedure for computing method summaries. For example, when the static analysis inspects the code of a method $m$, it needs to have information about possible side effects for its callees (even if they are native) in order to create a proper summary of $m$.

An important property of the computed summaries is that they approximate the original behavior of library methods. More specifically, BUBEN uses dynamic analysis to record under-approximate summaries for methods processed in the first step (native, I/O), while for all other library methods it computes over-approximate summaries of their externally visible behavior (side effects) with the help of static analysis.

The intentionally unsound dynamic summaries do not limit the practical usefulness of BUBEN, because it does not need sound summaries of library methods. It is even not possible to compute a sound general summary for a library method that performs I/O. More details are given in Sects. 2 and 3.

Generated abstractions of library methods have the form of code that reflects the results of static and dynamic analysis (approximate method summaries). Program code transformations (step 3) replace the calls and original implementations of library methods with the respective abstractions. We designed our transformations in a way that preserves mutual exclusion of accesses to individual object fields and array elements by different threads. This was necessary to avoid introducing spurious concurrency errors into the abstracted program. Again, we provide more details in Sect. 4.

The BUBEN system is not optimized towards any specific kind of properties and bugs—nevertheless, we had in mind especially fast detection of concurrency errors with tools like Java Pathfinder as our motivation. On the other hand, any bug finding approach that involves BUBEN would not be sound (i.e., errors could be missed) as a consequence of the under-approximate summaries of native and I/O library methods produced in the step 1 of the whole process. This is, however, not really a big issue with respect to our primary target use case—scalable detection of bugs within the application code.

**Contribution.** The main research contribution of this paper includes:

- The whole BUBEN system that combines dynamic analysis, static analysis (method summaries), and program code transformations in a specific way for the purpose of generating abstractions of large real-world programs, which can be subsequently analyzed using tools such as Java Pathfinder.
- Specific approach to dynamic recording of possible side effects and return values of library methods that is based on runtime interpretation of program code and inspection of program state (Sect. 2).
- Static analysis procedure for computing method summaries that is based on symbolic interpretation (linear traversal) of method's code (Sect. 3).
- Implementation of the BUBEN system for Java bytecode programs, and experimental evaluation on six programs selected from the DaCapo [3] and pjbench[1] suites. Results of our experiments show that while standalone Java Pathfinder crashes on all six benchmarks, usage of BUBEN helps to avoid the failures caused by insufficient support for libraries and enables JPF to find bugs in 4 programs out of 6.

The rest of this paper contains a section for each step of the whole process, followed by experimental evaluation, presentation of an example usage scenario, and discussion of related work.

## 2 Dynamic Recording

We apply dynamic analysis on a run of the input program to record a *dynamic summary* of each library method that is either native, performs I/O, or manipulates with external entities. A dynamic summary represents an under-approximation of the method's side effects that could be observed at runtime.

[1] https://bitbucket.org/psl-lab/pjbench.

It is a structure with four items: (1) a set of possible return values, (2) a set of updated object fields together with a set of possible new values for each field, (3) a set of updated array elements, again together with a set of possible new values for each element, and (4) a set of newly allocated objects.

Unlike most of the existing frameworks for dynamic analysis, including RoadRunner [7] and DiSL [9], which are based on code instrumentation, our approach involves runtime interception of program execution and inspection of dynamic states. In the rest of this section, we explain generally relevant technical aspects of the dynamic analysis and construction of the under-approximate dynamic summary. Figure 1 shows the key components of the analysis.

The following steps are performed when a call of a library method $m$ subject to analysis (the sets *nativeMths* and *libextMths* in Fig. 1) is reached.

1. Program execution is intercepted just at the entry to $m$.
2. Then, our analysis temporarily saves relevant parts of the program state at the time of entry to $m$—in particular, the content of arrays given as parameters of the method call.
3. Execution of the library method $m$ is resumed.
4. Dynamic analysis intercepts the program execution again just at the exit (return) from the method $m$.
5. Next, the analysis temporarily saves the content of relevant arrays at the time of method exit.
6. All outcomes and side effects of the method's execution are recorded into the dynamic summary for $m$ by handlers of respective events—this includes the return value (line 13), updates of object fields (line 23) and array elements (line 36), and newly allocated objects (line 27).

Our analysis does not record values of method call parameters in the dynamic summary, because the parameter values are not needed to generate abstractions (see details in Sect. 4). The content of arrays given as parameters is saved temporarily just for the purpose of creating a list of array elements updated by the method, which is then recorded in the summary.

Updated array elements are identified through the search for differences between two snapshots of a given array—its old content at the method entry (variable *oldArray* at line 32) and new content at the method exit (variable *curArray* at line 33). These snapshots of array content are saved in the respective handlers (lines 5–8 and 14–17), and then corresponding array elements are compared pair-wise. For performance reasons, as the fast track path we use hash values to find out whether the array was modified at all by the method. We are aware that collisions of hash values may occur, but dynamic summaries capture under-approximations of the sets of possible side effects anyway.

Possible new values of object fields and array elements are saved as symbolic expressions—constant values, access paths, or arithmetic expressions. An access path is a local variable name followed by a sequence of field names.

From the perspective of usage in BUBEN, a very important aspect of the dynamic analysis is that it has to record only updates to object fields and arrays either defined within application classes or visible from them. Accesses to other variables can be safely ignored, such as those internal to libraries. This is practically realized by tracking just updates to objects given as call arguments to library methods or returned from them.

```
INPUT : nativeMths, libextMths

procedure onMethodEntry( mth, args )
  for arg ∈ args do
    if arg.isArray then
      saveArrayContentAtEntry( mth, arg )
      computeArrayHashAtEntry( mth, arg )
      markTrackedArray( mth, arg )
    end if
  end for

procedure onMethodExit( mth, res )
  recordCallReturnValue( res )
  if res.isArray then markTrackedArray( mth, res )
  for arr ∈ trackedArrays( mth ) do
    saveArrayContentAtExit( mth, arr )
    computeArrayHashAtExit( mth, arr )
  end for
  recordArrayDifferences( mth )

procedure onFieldWrite( loc, field, newVal )
  if isMethodArgType( loc.method, field.class ) then
    recordFieldUpdate( loc.method, field, newVal )
  end if

procedure onNewObject( loc, obj )
  recordNewObjectAlloc( loc.method, obj )

procedure recordArrayDifferences( mth )
  for arr ∈ trackedArrays( mth ) do
    if hashAtEntry( arr ) == hashAtExit( arr ) continue
    oldArray = getArrayContentAtEntry( mth, arr )
    curArray = getArrayContentAtExit( mth, arr )
    for i ∈ 0...length( curArray )−1 do
      if oldArray( i ) != curArray( i ) then
        recordArrayUpdate( mth, arr, i, curArray( i ) )
      end if
    end for
  end for
```

**Fig. 1.** Dynamic analysis that records side-effects of library methods

**Implementation.** Here we describe selected technical details that affect the performance and practical applicability of the dynamic analysis.

We have implemented the dynamic analysis on top of the JPDA framework[2] that is a part of the Java platform. In particular, we have used two components of JPDA—the JVM TI monitoring interface and the JDI front-end API.

JDPA provides all the necessary information about runtime program behavior and states through its API, including call arguments at method entry and return values at method exit, and it supports tracking of calls to native methods. Moreover, JPDA allows to inspect heap data structures, dynamic call stack, and runtime values of program variables (object fields, array elements)—something that is not easily achievable probably in all the dynamic analysis frameworks based on code instrumentation (e.g., RoadRunner [7] or DiSL [9]).

Based on our preliminary experiments, we have also found that the performance overhead of a dynamic analysis based on JVM TI (with respect to normal program execution) is much smaller if we separated tracking of method entry (invoke) events from method exit (return) events—namely, such that all method entry events are tracked in one run of the dynamic analysis, while all the method exit events are tracked in another distinct run. This optimization helps to achieve at least practical running times in our scenario.

In order to keep also the size of dynamic summaries within practical limits, so they can be applied during the program transformation step, we had to put an upper bound on the number of recorded possible distinct return values from a library method. This is motivated especially by certain system library methods, such as System.getCurrentTimeMillis, that are invoked many times during the run of a program and return a different value on each occasion. We set the value of the upper bound to 256 for our experiments; however, it is configurable.

## 3 Static Computation of Method Summaries

We use static analysis to compute over-approximate summaries of possible side effects for the remaining library methods, which do not perform I/O and do not interact with any external entities. In this section, first we define the content of method summaries, and then we present our algorithm for computing them.

**Summaries.** We designed summaries that capture just externally-visible side effects of the library methods' execution that may influence runtime behavior of the application part of the whole program. This includes all the changes of a runtime program state that may occur during execution of a given library method, and that may be visible in the scope of application code.

Therefore, here we define a *static method summary* as a data structure that contains the following items:

- A list of all object fields possibly updated in the method.
- A list of all possibly updated static fields.
- A list of all array elements updated in the method.
- For each updated field and array element, a list of possible new values.

[2] https://docs.oracle.com/javase/8/docs/technotes/guides/jpda/index.html.

- A boolean flag saying whether the method may return a value corresponding to its arguments, and indexes of the respective arguments.
- A set of all objects newly allocated in the method, including arrays.
- A boolean flag saying whether the method may return a new object.
- A set of all possible return values.
- A list of fields and array elements updated outside of any code region that is protected by a lock or through another mechanism of thread synchronization.

Data are stored as symbolic access paths, respectively symbolic expressions (constants, variable names, new objects, arithmetic). A *symbolic access path* begins with a local variable name and then contains any valid mixture of field names and indexed accesses to array elements (such as `o.f.a[i].g`). Only those symbolic expressions that involve local variables other than method arguments cannot be recorded in summaries, because they are not visible in the application code.

The static summary of a library method $m$ captures also the results and side effects for all methods called within the scope of $m$.

**Algorithm for Computing Summaries.** Our static analysis-based approach combines (1) a fixpoint worklist algorithm over the list of all reachable methods with (2) linear symbolic interpretation of the code of every method.

However, as a prerequisite of the main algorithm, it is necessary to compute the set of may-aliased access paths for each local variable that may appear on the left-hand-side of some assignment. We use the aliasing information to properly handle code such as **void** `myproc(Obj o) { v = o; v.f.g = 2; }` where the field update is effectively performed also upon the parameter `o`. The procedure for computing the sets of possibly aliased expressions repeatedly processes the list of assignment statements, until it reaches a fixed point.

Our approach for computing static method summaries was inspired by Naeem and Lhotak [11]. At the start of a run of the main algorithm, the worklist is filled with all library methods reachable in the call graph. In each iteration, the algorithm removes a method $m$ from the head of the worklist and performs intra-procedural analysis of $m$ (see below), which collects the necessary information about side effects of $m$ and updates its summary. When the summary of $m$ changes, all the callers of $m$ that belong to the set of library methods are added into the worklist, because their summaries depend on $m$ and have to be recomputed. The algorithm terminates when the worklist is empty, at which occasion the summary of each method captures all its results and side effects.

Summaries of individual methods are generated by *symbolic interpretation* that is based on linear code traversal. We do not have to use a full-fledged static analysis that involves fixpoint computation over the method's control-flow graph and SSA IR. Our symbolic interpretation of the code of a library method is an intra-procedural control-flow-sensitive analysis that recognizes all side effects of the method, together with other information that make up its summary. By the term *control-flow-sensitive*, we mean that our analysis distinguishes among control-flow branches within the method's code, but does not process each control-flow path separately. In this respect, our notion of control-flow-sensitivity is a weaker form of path-sensitivity. The analysis traverses the sequence of instructions just once in a linear fashion, i.e. it performs only a single linear pass through the code of a given method.

```
1  for insn ∈ mth.instructions do
2     setActiveControlFlowBranch()
3     if insn.type == condBranch then
4        if insn.jumpTarget > insn.index then
5           startNewControlFlowBranch(insn.jumpTarget)
6        end if
7     end if
8     if insn.type == goto then
9        if insn.jumpTarget > insn.index then
10          startNewControlFlowBranch(insn.jumpTarget)
11          suspendCurrentBranch()
12       end if
13    end if
14    if insn.type == getfield then
15       obj = removeExprFromStack()
16       addExprToStack(obj + "." + insn.fieldName)
17    end if
18    if insn.type == arraystore then
19       newValue = removeExprFromStack()
20       indexExpr = removeExprFromStack()
21       arrayObj = removeExprFromStack()
22       recordArrayUpdate(arrayObj, indexExpr, newValue)
23    end if
24    ...
25 end for
```

**Fig. 2.** Key aspects of symbolic interpretation with control-flow sensitivity

Figure 2 illustrates the key aspects of our symbolic analysis—specifically, how it processes control-flow branches and selected instructions. During its run, our symbolic interpretation algorithm maintains a stack of expressions that is used to store instruction operands and results. Handlers for individual instructions manipulate with the stack. For illustration, in Fig. 2 we show handlers for the getfield and arraystore instructions (lines 14–17 and 18–23, respectively).

When the analysis processes a method $m$, it propagates available summaries of other methods called from within $m$ (transitively) into the summary of $m$ to reflect their side effects and outcomes. At each call site, data about formal parameters of the callee (including `this`) are associated with the actual arguments. Existing dynamic summaries are used for the calls of native methods inside $m$. In the case of library methods that manipulate with external entities, our algorithm uses the results of dynamic analysis to initialize their summaries and refines them later during the run of static analysis. The set of possible return values from $m$ is computed through a backward traversal of def-use chains and nested method calls that starts at the explicit return statements. If a possible new value of an updated field, respectively updated array element, is a symbolic expression that refers to the return value of another method $m'$ called inside $m$, then it is expanded with actual return values captured in the summary of $m'$.

Now we describe the approach for processing of control-flow branches. At every moment during the run of our symbolic interpretation, one control-flow branch is marked as active. The active control flow branch is changed if needed just before processing of an instruction (line 2)—e.g., when the current instruction is the target of a forward jump. Upon reaching of a conditional branch (jump) instruction, the interpreter creates a new branch and schedules the branch to be active at the jump's target location (line 5). Execution of the current active branch then continues at the next instruction. Goto instructions are processed in a slightly different way. The interpreter creates a new control-flow branch and makes it active at the target location of a jump also in this case. However, the currently active branch is then suspended until the instruction corresponding to the jump target is reached (line 11). Another branch will then become active, i.e. its execution will resume, at the next instruction in a sequence, which must be a target location of another jump from elsewhere in the method. Our approach ensures that, for every instruction that may be a jump target, the symbolic interpreter distinguishes between all the possible symbolic stack contents at the instruction. Note also that our interpreter can safely ignore backward jumps, because they do not start new control-flow branches.

Like in the case of the dynamic analysis (Sect. 2), our algorithm for computing static summaries records just updates to object fields and arrays defined either in the application classes or visible from them. This is again realized by tracking only updates to method call arguments. Information about variables internal to library methods are not used for constructing abstractions (Sect. 4).

**Implementation.** We implemented the algorithm for computing static method summaries on top of the WALA library[3]. A very important aspect of our implementation is the usage of fast but imprecise approach to call graph construction (0-CFA), which finishes quickly even for large software systems. BUBEN does not need a precise call graph when generating summaries of library methods. In order to compensate for the imprecision of alias analysis, our symbolic interpreter considers as possible new values of updated fields and array elements only the symbolic expressions whose prefix is the source value of some assignment statement within the method. We apply this optimization also on the set of possible return values. This greatly improves the precision of method summaries.

## 4 Program Code Transformations

We already said that BUBEN creates an abstraction of the given program by the means of code transformations. An input for this procedure consists of (1) the original program code and (2) method summaries computed either by the

[3] T.J. Watson Libraries for Analysis (http://wala.sourceforge.net/).

dynamic analysis or static analysis. Method summaries contain all the information needed to generate abstractions of the respective library methods.

BUBEN performs especially two kinds of program code transformations:

- Replacing the calls of native methods and library methods that perform I/O or manipulate with external entities.
- Creating new abstract implementations (bodies) of all other library methods.

We want to emphasize that the only parts of application code affected by these transformations are the calls of library methods.

An abstraction of a library method is generated by a procedure that follows the template in Fig. 3. It specifies how the data captured by a method summary are translated into actual code, i.e. how the abstraction looks like.

```
summ = retrieveMethodSummary(mth)

generateBeginAtomic()

for (o.f, vals) ∈ summ.updatedObjectFields do
   if o.f ∈ summ.unsynchFieldAccesses continue
   v = generateNondetChoiceOverSet(vals)
   generateFieldUpdate(o, f, v)
end for

for (a[i], vals) ∈ summ.updatedArrayElements do
   if a[i] ∈ summ.unsynchArrayAccesses continue
   v = generateNondetChoiceOverSet(vals)
   generateArrayUpdate(a, i, v)
end for

generateEndAtomic()

for o.f ∈ summ.unsynchFieldAccess do ...
for a[i] ∈ summ.unsynchArrayAccesses do ...

c = generateNondetIntChoice(0, summ.returnValues.size)
generateLoadExpression(summ.returnValues[c])
```

**Fig. 3.** Template for method abstraction

The same template is used by the module for program code transformation both (1) to replace calls of library methods and (2) to create their new implementations. Only low-level adjustments have to be made in each case to ensure the abstraction seamlessly fits into the existing code around the target location. For example, when replacing a call of some library method, it is also necessary to generate code that removes original method call arguments from the stack.

When generating the abstract variant of the body of a library method, the first step is to remove the whole original control-flow structure. New statements defined by the template can then be inserted in any order, because there are no dependencies between them. Our transformation procedure does not strive to preserve the order of statements that corresponds to the original method body, for two reasons: (1) method summaries do not capture the order of statements anyway; (2) in the main use case for BUBEN, verification tools will receive only the transformed program as input (with the new order of statements in abstracted methods), without any reference to the original program.

Our template supports both (i) updates to fields, respectively array elements, that are protected by some kind of thread synchronization in the original program, and (ii) updates to the other fields and array elements (lines 19–20). Protected updates are enclosed within a single atomic block (lines 3 and 17). Besides that, no special processing of multithreading-related code is needed. Calls of library methods that control threads and synchronization (such as Thread.start and Object.wait) are not affected by code transformations in any way. In general, transformations preserve concurrency-related behavior, including concurrent accesses to shared variables, and therefore also possible concurrency bugs.

**Implementation.** We used the ASM bytecode manipulation framework for Java[4] to implement all the program code transformations. Generated abstractions call the API for non-deterministic choice provided by a target verification tool (e.g., Java Pathfinder).

## 5 Evaluation

We evaluated the implementation of BUBEN on multiple large Java programs taken from popular benchmark suites, including DaCapo [3] and pjbench that is available at the url https://bitbucket.org/psl-lab/pjbench.

The list of programs from DaCapo contains batik, lusearch, pmd, and sunflow. We used the smallest available configuration for each of them, and in some cases (e.g., sunflow) we set the number of threads to 2—all that with the goal of reducing the running time of dynamic analysis, because it needs to observe just few executions of each library method in order to create an under-approximation that is useful as input for program code transformations. In addition, we picked the jspider benchmark from the pjbench suite and the SPECjbb2005 benchmark.

We decided to choose these specific programs because of their size, high degree of concurrency, and usage of many libraries. Program size was the relevant criterion especially in the case of DaCapo, because tools like Java Pathfinder do not yet scale to really large programs that are included within the DaCapo suite (e.g., Tomcat and Eclipse). On the other hand, most other programs in the pjbench suite (besides jspider) are quite small.

Source code of the BUBEN system, together with small examples, scripts, and configuration files needed to run all experiments, is available at https://github.com/d3sformal/buben.

[4] http://asm.ow2.io/.

We organized our evaluation around the goal of answering the following research questions related to practical usefulness of BUBEN:

**(Q1)** Does the process of generating abstractions preserves interesting behaviors of the original input program and bugs present in its source code?
**(Q2)** Whether the generated abstract program can be successfully analyzed by verification tools such as Java Pathfinder?
**(Q3)** How much time it takes Java Pathfinder to analyze the abstracted program and to find real bugs in the application code?

**Table 1.** Running time of BUBEN

| | Init (CG) | Dynamic analysis | Computing summaries | Program transform |
|---|---|---|---|---|
| batik | 15 s | 1285 s | 3 s | 17 s |
| lusearch | 9 s | 13665 s | 4 s | 10 s |
| pmd | 9 s | 2396 s | 1 s | 9 s |
| sunflow | 12 s | 11695 s | 1 s | 9 s |
| jspider | 9 s | 94 s | 1 s | 13 s |
| specjbb | 6 s | 40680 s | 1 s | 5 s |

Our answer to the first question is positive based on the way BUBEN creates abstract programs. Since just library methods and their calls are replaced with corresponding abstractions, other parts of the application code are not affected by the respective transformations, and therefore interesting behaviors of the program at the application level (including bugs) are preserved by construction. The remaining questions 2 and 3 have to be answered empirically.

Table 1 shows the running times of the main components of BUBEN. For each program, we measure the running times of initialization (which includes call graph construction), dynamic analysis, static computation of method summaries (that includes alias analysis), and program code transformations.

Data presented in Table 1 indicate that our approach is practically feasible. However, individual steps of the whole process still have to be optimized—especially the dynamic analysis, which run over 11 h in the case of SPECjbb2005.

We also run Java Pathfinder (JPF) [16] on each generated abstract program to see whether JPF can analyze it successfully and find some bugs. For that, we had to extend the implementation and configuration of BUBEN to accommodate three special features of JPF: (1) use of a custom Java virtual machine, JPF VM, (2) hand-written models (stubs) for selected classes from the Java standard library, and (3) hand-written plain Java models for selected native methods.

Some of the models for native methods used by JPF implement key aspects of the JPF VM functionality, and therefore we tweaked BUBEN to preserve calls of the respective native methods—including, for example, most of native methods defined in the class java.lang.Thread. The variant of BUBEN tailored for JPF also automatically generates simple models for those native methods, which are invoked from within standard Java library classes but for which the hand-written models do not yet exist in the JPF distribution, in order to avoid crashes of JPF. It is necessary because modifications of classes from the standard Java library cannot be saved persistently, meaning in particular that replacing the calls of native methods by code transformations described in Sect. 4 is not applicable in the case of such classes. Finally, we manually configured BUBEN to generate abstractions also for some application methods that perform lot of I/O-related actions or load classes explicitly via reflection.

The results of applying JPF both on the original programs and transformed programs (abstractions created by BUBEN) are presented in Table 2. We provide the descriptions of reported crashes and bugs, together with execution times.

**Table 2.** Experiments with JPF

| | Original input program | | Transformed abstract program (BUBEN) | |
|---|---|---|---|---|
| | Result description | Time | Result description | Time |
| batik | crashed: exception inside libraries | 1 s | found bug: unhandled null pointer exception | 1 s |
| lusearch | crashed: exception in file I/O | 1 s | found bug: unhandled null pointer exception + deadlock | 1 s |
| pmd | crashed: incomplete stubs for libraries | 1 s | found bug: uncaught file-not-found exception | 1 s |
| sunflow | crashed: exception inside libraries | 1 s | did not report any error: run out of memory (12 GB) | (764 s) |
| jspider | crashed: incomplete stubs for libraries | 1 s | found bug: unhandled null pointer exception | 1 s |
| specjbb | crashed: incomplete stubs for libraries | 1 s | did not report any error: run out of memory (12 GB) | (3073 s) |

The left part of Table 2 shows that JPF crashed for all the original programs, and thus failed (i) to verify their application code and (ii) to find at least some bugs in them. For three programs, JPF crashed due to incomplete stubs of library methods and classes. In the other cases, JPF reported an uncaught exception thrown deep within libraries responsible, e.g., for GUI or file I/O.

The right part of Table 2 shows that, with abstractions generated using BUBEN, JPF could successfully analyze all six programs and even find bugs in four of them (batik, lusearch, pmd, jspider) very quickly. Unhandled null pointer exceptions in the case of batik, lusearch, and jspider were caused by missing checks for null references in the application code, while the uncaught file-not-found exception reported for pmd is related to a file actually present within the software package. By manual inspection of the source code, we checked that these particular bugs (detected in abstractions) exist also in the original programs.

Overall, results for the programs that we used in our experimental evaluation, presented in both tables, indicate that BUBEN is useful. It can generate abstractions of realistic large programs, which are amenable to verification and search for bugs by tools like JPF. Scalability of verification could be further improved by marking additional classes and methods as libraries in the user configuration.

## 6 Example Use Case

We illustrate the usage of BUBEN in more detail on the jspider program that we used also in our evaluation. JPF crashes when run on the original version of jspider, which is the main reason why one might consider to use BUBEN.

First, the user must define the configuration of BUBEN, similar to our example in Fig. 4. It specifies the main class (entry point) of the program, command-line arguments, Java packages that represent libraries, and Java packages containing methods that manipulate with external entities (files, network).

```
mainclass = net.javacoding.jspider.JSpiderTool
runtimeargs = download, www.google.com, index.html
libmethods = org.apache.commons.logging, junit, org.apache.log4j, \
        org.apache.commons.collections, org.apache.log, org.apache.velocity
appclasses = org.javacoding.jspider
externmethods = java.io, java.net, java.nio, javax.mail, javax.jms, jdk.net
```

**Fig. 4.** Example configuration of BUBEN for jspider

As the second step, the user executes BUBEN to generate abstraction of each library method in the call graph. Figure 5 shows both the original code (at the top) and transformed code (bottom) of the method warn from the class org.apache.log4j.Category. We picked this method because its code is quite short and therefore suitable for illustration purposes. Deeply nested within the call of forcedLog at line 5 (original variant) is a synchronized access to the field LogRecord._seqCount that is captured by a static summary of the method warn. Abstracted variant contains the field access inside an atomic block. The Verify class is a part of the JPF API.

The last step is to run JPF on the abstracted program in order to find bugs.

```
// original
public void warn(Object message) {
  if (repository.isDisabled(Level.WARN_INT)) return;
  if (Level.WARN.isGreaterOrEqual(getEffectiveLevel())) {
    forcedLog(FQCN, Level.WARN, message);
  }
}

// transformed
public void warn(Object message) {
  Verify.beginAtomic();
  int c = Verify.getInt(0,0);
  if (c == 0) LogRecord._seqCount += 1;
  Verify.endAtomic();
}
```

**Fig. 5.** Library method Category.warn: original (top) and transformed code (bottom)

## 7 Related Work

Lot of existing work is related to BUBEN and its components. In particular, we know about (1) few approaches with similar goals as the whole BUBEN system and (2) several techniques closely related to static and dynamic analysis performed by BUBEN during its run. We characterize the related approaches and techniques briefly in this section, and compare them with our solution.

Tkachuk and Dwyer [14] proposed an approach based on an idea similar to ours. It creates a model of environment for each component of a given system in order to enable its modular verification. Environment models correspond to sets of method summaries, which are computed by an intra-procedural flow-sensitive and context-sensitive side effect analysis. The main difference between this approach [14] and BUBEN is that the former captures just updates of the target component's state in order to create a minimal valid abstract environment, while the analyses performed by BUBEN collect all visible side effects of library methods. Other differences include (1) usage of dynamic analysis within BUBEN, which enables creating summaries for library methods that perform I/O, (2) better support for concurrency, such as tracking fields accessed by multiple threads, and (3) experimental evaluation on large programs.

State-of-the-art program verification frameworks handle libraries and I/O in different ways. For example, KLEE [4] uses a symbolic file system where effects of read and write operations are captured by constraints. Java Pathfinder contains manually created stubs for I/O library methods (but only the most often used are supported). Ceccarello and Tkachuk [5] improved the situation by developing a tool for automated construction of abstract property-specific models of library methods, which can be used only together with Java Pathfinder. The tool is based on two key ideas: (1) use of program code slicing that removes accesses to every field not relevant with respect to a given property, and (2) abstraction of read accesses to irrelevant fields by random values or default values of the respective data types. On the contrary, BUBEN automatically generates abstractions of library methods based on dynamic and static summaries that are computed by the corresponding analyses.

Many static analysis-based techniques for computing method summaries were proposed recently [1,6,10–13,15]. Each technique in this group computes some information about possible behavior and side effects of library methods, but none of them is directly applicable in our case—especially because none generates summaries that contain all the information that BUBEN needs, including new values of updated object fields and array elements.

For example, the analysis proposed by Cherem and Rugina [6] computes just the following information: a set of object fields updated by each method (up to a given bound on the length of field access chains), which fields of objects given as method call arguments may become aliased, and whether a returned value may be aliased with some argument or with a field of some argument.

The technique of Matosevic and Abdelrahman [10] computes method summaries that involve symbolic access paths (especially to object fields). It also uses pointer analysis to determine aliasing between method call arguments. The main difference from BUBEN is that, in our approach, we do not need to track heap locations and their possible aliasing.

In general, there is a large space of static analyses that compute summaries of some kind, where each technique is tailored for a particular use case.

One can also use slicing [2,8] to create a simplified version of an input program for the purpose of efficient and scalable verification. Nevertheless, program slicing is done with respect to some property, and takes into account dependencies between statements and threads. BUBEN completely replaces the original code of library methods in a general property-independent manner.

**Acknowledgments.** We would like to thank Ondřej Lhoták for all his suggestions regarding the paper content and presentation. This work was partially supported by the Czech Science Foundation project 18-17403S.

## References

1. Artzi, S., Kiezun, A., Glasser, D., Ernst, M.: Combined static and dynamic mutability analysis. In: Proceedings of ASE 2007. ACM (2007)
2. Binkley, D., Gallagher, K.B.: Program slicing. In: Advances in Computers, vol. 43 (1996)
3. Blackburn, S.M., et al.: The DaCapo benchmarks: Java benchmarking development and analysis. In: Proceedings of OOPSLA 2006. ACM (2006)
4. Cadar, C., Dunbar, D., Engler, D.R.: KLEE: unassisted and automatic generation of high-coverage tests for complex systems programs. In: Proceedings of OSDI 2008. USENIX (2008)
5. Ceccarello, M., Tkachuk, O.: Automated generation of model classes for Java PathFinder. In: Proceedings of Java Pathfinder Workshop 2013, ACM SIGSOFT Software Engineering Notes, vol. 39, no. 1 (2014)

6. Cherem, S., Rugina, R.: A practical escape and effect analysis for building lightweight method summaries. In: Krishnamurthi, S., Odersky, M. (eds.) CC 2007. LNCS, vol. 4420, pp. 172–186. Springer, Heidelberg (2007). https://doi.org/10.1007/978-3-540-71229-9_12
7. Flanagan, C., Freund, S.N.: The RoadRunner dynamic analysis framework for concurrent programs. In: Proceedings of PASTE 2010. ACM (2010)
8. Giffhorn, D., Hammer, C.: Precise slicing of concurrent programs. Autom. Softw. Eng. **16**(2), 197 (2009)
9. Marek, L., Villazon, A., Zheng, Y., Ansaloni, D., Binder, W., Qi, Z.: DiSL: a domain-specific language for bytecode instrumentation. In: Proceedings of AOSD 2012. ACM (2012)
10. Matosevic, I., Abdelrahman, T.S.: Efficient bottom-up heap analysis for symbolic path-based data access summaries. In: Proceedings of CGO 2012. ACM (2012)
11. Naeem, N.A., Lhoták, O.: Faster alias set analysis using summaries. In: Knoop, J. (ed.) CC 2011. LNCS, vol. 6601, pp. 82–103. Springer, Heidelberg (2011). https://doi.org/10.1007/978-3-642-19861-8_6
12. Rountev, A., Sharp, M., Xu, G.: IDE dataflow analysis in the presence of large object-oriented libraries. In: Hendren, L. (ed.) CC 2008. LNCS, vol. 4959, pp. 53–68. Springer, Heidelberg (2008). https://doi.org/10.1007/978-3-540-78791-4_4
13. Sălcianu, A., Rinard, M.: Purity and side effect analysis for Java programs. In: Cousot, R. (ed.) VMCAI 2005. LNCS, vol. 3385, pp. 199–215. Springer, Heidelberg (2005). https://doi.org/10.1007/978-3-540-30579-8_14
14. Tkachuk, O., Dwyer, M.: Adapting side effect analysis for modular program model checking. In: Proceedings of ESEC/FSE 2003. ACM (2003)
15. Yorsh, G., Yahav, E., Chandra, S.: Generating precise and concise procedure summaries. In: Proceedings of POPL 2008. ACM (2008)
16. Java Pathfinder verification framework (JPF). https://github.com/javapathfinder/jpf-core/wiki

# KLUZZER: Whitebox Fuzzing on Top of LLVM

Hoang M. Le(✉)

Group of Computer Architecture, University of Bremen, 28359 Bremen, Germany
hle@uni-bremen.de

**Abstract.** Whitebox fuzzing (a.k.a. concolic testing) has been shown to be an effective bug finding technique on its own as well as in combination with coverage-guided greybox fuzzing. However, there is currently a lack of whitebox fuzzers operating above the binary code level. We present KLUZZER, a whitebox fuzzer targeting LLVM bitcode, and thus can be easily combined with the widely deployed LLVM's coverage-guided greybox fuzzer LibFuzzer. Experimental evaluation on a set of benchmarks shows encouraging results.

## 1 Background and Motivation

Software bugs are inevitable. Especially, software developed in low-level languages like C/C++ is very error-prone. Consequently, massive effort has been put into research and development of automatic bug finding techniques and tools, with particular focus on C/C++ software. In the last few years, *coverage-guided greybox fuzzing* (CGF), pioneered by AFL [17], has risen to prominence as a mean of detecting security-related bugs (e.g. buffer overflow, use-after-free, etc.). The key efficiency of CGF lies in its ability to discover different execution paths at nearly native speed. The basic idea behind this efficiency is surprisingly simple. CGF adds lightweight instrumentation to the *program unter test* (PUT) to measure code coverage of each executed input. This coverage information is then used to guide the process of creating new inputs by (randomly) mutating existing ones (e.g. by favoring mutation of inputs whose execution discovered new coverage). Many CGF tools, most notably AFL and LibFuzzer [2], have been developed since. Recently, Google has lauched OSS-Fuzz, a continuous testing service for open-source software. OSS-Fuzz has been using AFL and LibFuzzer to uncover thousands of bugs in widely used critical open-source projects [13].

Despite its success in practice, CGF has major difficulty with discovering execution paths that involve complex branch conditions such as comparison with magic values or checksum validation. Getting past such complex checks is a known strength of *whitebox fuzzing* [10], which is also referred to as *concolic testing* or *dynamic symbolic execution* (DSE). By executing the PUT symbolically along the execution path induced by a given *seed* (i.e. concrete input), a whitebox fuzzer collects symbolic constraints at each taken conditional branch to create a path condition $\mathcal{PC}$. By negating the constraints associated with each


Y.-F. Chen et al. (Eds.): ATVA 2019, LNCS 11781, pp. 246–252, 2019.
https://doi.org/10.1007/978-3-030-31784-3_14

specific branch in $\mathcal{PC}$ and invoking an SMT solver (e.g. STP [9] or Z3 [7]) to solve the resulting path condition, inputs exploring new paths can be systematically generated. The main disadvantage here is that both creating path conditions and SMT solving can be very time-consuming.

Hybrid fuzzing, the promising idea of combining CGF with whitebox fuzzing, has attracted increasing research interest. The simplest form is to apply DSE for a given time limit first to generate a set of initial inputs, which gives CGF a good starting point. KleeFL [8] and SAFL [15] implemented this idea. State-of-the-art advanced hybrid fuzzing uses CGF as the main search algorithm and only employs whitebox fuzzing selectively on CGF-generated inputs based on a path priotization scheme (as in DigFuzz [18]) or when CGF struggles to make progress (as in Driller [14]). On a side note to complete the picture, another line of research proposes hybrid fuzzers that build and solve path conditions in an approximate manner (e.g. [5,16]), trading precision for speed. Both DigFuzz and Driller use the popular open-source DSE tool Angr [1] which operates on binary code. This is indispensable when the source code is not available. However, for use cases such as OSS-Fuzz, working above the binary code level can be much more efficient, because it is much easier to leverage static analysis as well as high-level information and structures such as types, functions, variables and objects, that are not available in binary code.

The foremost major hurdle in building an advanced hybrid fuzzer above the binary code level is the scarcity of suitable whitebox fuzzers. In fact, most state-of-the-art tools work on binary code only (open-source: S2E [6], FuzzBall [12], closed-source: SAGE [10], Mayhem [4], just to name a few), with the one exception of KLEE [3] that uses the LLVM *Intermediate Representation* (IR a.k.a. bitcode), which is very close to the source code level. However, KLEE has several shortcomings for advanced hybrid fuzzing (discussed in the next section) and is only suited for generation of initial inputs, as employed by KleeFL and SAFL.

To fill this gap, this paper introduces KLUZZER, a new whitebox fuzzer for LLVM. KLUZZER is built on the KLEE infrastructure and provides several significant enhancements that makes KLUZZER ready to use in advanced hybrid fuzzing. Having these functionalities implemented in an actively maintained and robust open-source framework such as KLEE will facilitate further research in hybrid and whitebox fuzzing. Furthermore, the use of LLVM IR opens the door to leverage other program analysis techniques available within the LLVM compiler infrastructure.

## 2 Enabling Whitebox Fuzzing for LLVM

Our overarching goal is to build an advanced hybrid fuzzer with KLUZZER being the whitebox fuzzing component. For this purpose, the most natural choice of CGF component is LibFuzzer, which is also part of the LLVM infrastructure and has been used extensively by OSS-Fuzz. In the following, we describe the main features of KLUZZER and how they address the shortcomings of KLEE to achieve our goal.

```
int LLVMFuzzerTestOneInput(const
  uint8_t *Data, size_t Size) {
  if (Size < 4)
    return 0;
  uint32_t *z = (uint32_t*) Data;
  FuzzMe(*z);
}
```

```
void FuzzMe(uint32_t z) {
  void* p = malloc((z & 0xFF) + 1);
  ...
  if (z == 0xBADCODED) free(p);
  tmp = p[0]; // bug
  ...
}
```

**Fig. 1.** Example of LibFuzzer fuzz target

**Support for LibFuzzer Fuzz Target.** LibFuzzer is designed to perform CGF on C/C++ libraries. Before fuzzing, a harness function, also called fuzz target, LLVMFuzzerTestOneInput(**const uint8_t**∗ Data, **size_t** Size) must be implemented. This function accepts an byte array, converts it into an appropriate format to feed to some API functions of the library under test. An example is shown in Fig. 1, which has a hard-to-trigger use-after-free bug guarded by a magic number comparison. The library and the fuzz target are then compiled together and linked with LibFuzzer (which provides the *main()* function) to produce a final binary. During compilation, LLVM's CoverageSanitizer instruments the library code to enable edge coverage measurement by inserting the callback __sanitizer_cov_trace_pc_guard (**uint32_t** ∗guard) on every edge. The binary is executed to perform CGF by mutating the byte array, executing the fuzz target and observing edge coverage changes.

To enable whitebox fuzzing on LibFuzzer fuzz targets, KLUZZER requires some minor modifications of the build process. Instead of linking with LibFuzzer, KLUZZER provides its own *main()* function, which marks the byte array as symbolic before calling the fuzz target, and default implementation for the coverage callbacks. Instead of the LLVM frontend compiler Clang, KLUZZER uses the wrapper *whole-program-llvm*[1] to produce LLVM bitcode from the final binary. KLUZZER interprets a binary file directly as a byte array seed and also outputs binary files when it discovers new edge. This enables KLUZZER and LibFuzzer to use the same set of inputs and to share fuzzing progress. KLEE, while also applicable on the produced bitcode, only accepts and produces its own KTest file format. Furthermore, KLEE does not understand the coverage callbacks.

**Offline Symbolic Execution.** KLEE applies online symbolic execution. At each conditional branch, KLEE formulates constraints and invokes an SMT solver to check the feasibility of both directions. If both directions are feasible, KLEE duplicates the current symbolic execution state (i.e. forking) to explore both. Thus, multiple paths can be explored simultaneously. However, keeping all execution states is very memory-consuming, even with the clever copy-on-write technique employed by KLEE. For large software with long execution paths, KLEE exhausts the memory limit very fast causing it to drop states and miss paths. Offline symbolic execution, implemented by e.g. SAGE, does not need

[1] https://github.com/travitch/whole-program-llvm.

to keep execution states. Instead, only a concrete input (much smaller memory footprint) is needed to reconstruct the path and its constraints. The drawback here is that each execution starts at the beginning and thus, a large number of instructions must be re-executed.

A lot of our effort went into augmenting KLEE with the offline symbolic execution mode. Essentially, at each conditional branch, KLUZZER just follows the direction satisfied by the concrete input it has, delaying the feasibility check of the other direction to a later stage. As KLEE has a very complex codebase, the complexity of this change should not be underestimated. In offline symbolic execution mode, KLUZZER can run over a much longer period of time without reaching the memory cap in comparison with KLEE for the same fuzz target. KLUZZER also implements a simple optimization to reduce the number of re-executed instructions. It creates a checkpoint before executing *LLVMFuzzerTestOneInput*. Every subsequent execution then starts from this checkpoint, avoids re-executing initialization code (mostly from KLEE's implementation of uClibc). More advanced combination of online and offline symbolic execution (see [4]) can be attempted in the next step.

**Generational Search.** This search heuristic, first proposed by SAGE [10], is optimized for deep execution traces to maximize code coverage and the number of new inputs generated from each expensive symbolic execution. It works as follows. First, an input is selected from a set of initial inputs. After executing this input symbolically, all branch conditions along the path are negated one-by-one and each resulting path condition is solved to generate a new input. All children inputs generated from the initial input are called a *generation*. Then, all children inputs are scored by executing them concretely and counting the number of uncovered basic blocks discovered by each child. The input with the best score (which is not necessarily from the last generation) is then selected to create the next generation. KLUZZER implemented a variant of generational search. The scoring algorithm of KLUZZER also considers and gives more weight to the number of new edges and edge hit count. Currently, concrete execution of inputs for scoring is performed by interpreting LLVM instructions. This will be boosted significantly (to near native speed) after a full integration with LibFuzzer. One more potential advantage of generational search over the default randomized, control flow graph based search of KLEE, is that it lends itself very well to incremental SMT solving.

**Precise Execution Seeding.** For a given seed, an whitebox fuzzer must precisely reconstruct the induced execution path and its constraints. In many cases, KLEE is unable to do this due to its concretization strategy. Concretization, i.e. replacing a symbolic value with a concrete value, is essential for symbolic execution of real-world programs when it is difficult to formulate and solve constraints efficiently. Some examples include memory allocation with symbolic size, floating-point operations, external function calls, etc. In such case, KLEE picks a concrete value by solving the constraints up to this point of execution. This value can be different from the value in the given seed, causing path divergence.

This issue can be illustrated using the example from Fig. 1. Calling *malloc* with a symbolic size causes KLEE (and also KLUZZER) to concretize the first byte of the input byte array. Now, even given a seed with the first 'correct' byte (0xED), KLEE still concretizes the first byte to another value (0) and thus cannot satisfy the subsequent comparison. KLUZZER, on the other hand, keeps the first byte and subsequently successfully modifies the seed to match the magic number and finds the use-after-free bug.

This issue is fixed in Zesti [11], also an extension of KLEE. However, Zesti is based on LLVM 2.9, which is very old and not supported anymore. Moreover, Zesti uses online symbolic execution and a fundamentally different search heuristic.

## 3 Experimental Evaluation

We evaluate KLUZZER on three real-world benchmarks *boringssl*, *llvm-libcxxabi* and *sqlite* from the Google's *fuzzer-test-suite*[2], which has been extracted from OSS-Fuzz. These benchmarks are chosen solely because they have no dependencies on other open-source libraries and thus, easier to build LLVM bitcode for the fuzz targets. KLUZZER is based on a version of KLEE that is very close to the latest release KLEE 2.0. Thus, KLUZZER can also use the recommended version of LLVM 6.0 and STP 2.3.3 as the underlying SMT solver. All experiments are performed on an 8-core Intel Core i7-7700 @ 3.60 GHz machine with 32 GB RAM running Fedora 28.

We measure the edge coverage achieved by KLUZZER and KLEE on the benchmarks. Due to the imprecision of execution seeding in KLEE, we do not use any seed but start the exploration from scratch for both tools. For KLUZZER, that means starting with a random input. Recommended running options for KLEE are used. We fix the time limit, the memory limit and the size of the symbolic byte array to 3 h, 4 GB and 20 bytes, respectively.

Please note that the main purpose of the evaluation is not to compare performance of KLUZZER and KLEE but to demonstrate a working implementation. Large-scale evaluation and experiments with hybrid fuzzing using KLUZZER and LibFuzzer are ongoing work. Nevertheless, the results shown in Table 1 are encouraging. Column *#Edge* and *#Path* show the number of different edges and paths, respectively, that KLEE and KLUZZER can reach under the given resource limit. At the task that KLEE is supposed to be more efficient, KLUZZER can explore more paths and find more edges in 2 out of 3 benchmarks (*boringssl* and *llvm-libcxxabi*).

**Availability.** Instructions to reproduce the evaluation as well as a virtual machine with pre-compiled binaries can be found at http://unihb.eu/kluzzer.

[2] https://github.com/google/fuzzer-test-suite.

**Table 1.** Comparison of edge coverage achieved by KLEE and KLUZZER

| Benchmark | KLEE | | KLUZZER | |
|---|---|---|---|---|
| | #Edge | #Path | #Edge | #Path |
| boringssl-2016-02-12 | 498 | 110112 | 529 | 316559 |
| llvm-libcxxabi-2017-01-27 | 1303 | 81677 | 1491 | 261523 |
| sqlite-2016-11-14 | 893 | 23855 | 857 | 21883 |

**Acknowledgment.** This work was supported by the Central Research Development Fund of the University of Bremen.

## References

1. Angr - a powerful and user-friendly binary analysis platform. https://github.com/angr/angr
2. LibFuzzer - a library for coverage-guided fuzz testing. https://llvm.org/docs/LibFuzzer.html
3. Cadar, C., Dunbar, D., Engler, D.R.: KLEE: unassisted and automatic generation of high-coverage tests for complex systems programs. In: USENIX OSDI, pp. 209–224 (2008)
4. Cha, S.K., Avgerinos, T., Rebert, A., Brumley, D.: Unleashing mayhem on binary code. In: IEEE Symposium on Security and Privacy, pp. 380–394 (2012)
5. Chen, P., Chen, H.: Angora: efficient fuzzing by principled search. In: IEEE Symposium on Security and Privacy, pp. 711–725 (2018)
6. Chipounov, V., Kuznetsov, V., Candea, G.: S2E: a platform for in-vivo multi-path analysis of software systems. In: ASPLOS, pp. 265–278 (2011)
7. de Moura, L., Bjørner, N.: Z3: an efficient SMT solver. In: Ramakrishnan, C.R., Rehof, J. (eds.) TACAS 2008. LNCS, vol. 4963, pp. 337–340. Springer, Heidelberg (2008). https://doi.org/10.1007/978-3-540-78800-3_24
8. Fietkau, J., Shastry, B.: KleeFL - seeding fuzzers with symbolic execution. In: USENIX Security (Poster presentation) (2017)
9. Ganesh, V., Dill, D.L.: A decision procedure for bit-vectors and arrays. In: Damm, W., Hermanns, H. (eds.) CAV 2007. LNCS, vol. 4590, pp. 519–531. Springer, Heidelberg (2007). https://doi.org/10.1007/978-3-540-73368-3_52
10. Godefroid, P., Levin, M.Y., Molnar, D.A.: Automated whitebox fuzz testing. In: NDSS (2008)
11. Marinescu, P.D., Cadar, C.: Make test-zesti: a symbolic execution solution for improving regression testing. In: ICSE, pp. 716–726 (2012)
12. Martignoni, L., McCamant, S., Poosankam, P., Song, D., Maniatis, P.: Path-exploration lifting: hi-fi tests for lo-fi emulators. In: ASPLOS, pp. 337–348 (2012)
13. Ruhstaller, M., Chang, O.: A new chapter for OSS-Fuzz. https://security.googleblog.com/2018/11/a-new-chapter-for-oss-fuzz.html
14. Stephens, N., et al.: Driller: augmenting fuzzing through selective symbolic execution. In: NDSS (2016)
15. Wang, M., et al.: SAFL: increasing and accelerating testing coverage with symbolic execution and guided fuzzing. In: ICSE, pp. 61–64 (2018)

16. Yun, I., Lee, S., Xu, M., Jang, Y., Kim, T.: QSYM : a practical concolic execution engine tailored for hybrid fuzzing. In: USENIX Security, pp. 745–761 (2018)
17. Zalewski, M.: American fuzzy lop (AFL) white paper. http://lcamtuf.coredump.cx/afl/technical_details.txt
18. Zhao, L., Duan, Y., Yin, H., Xuan, J.: Send hardest problems my way: probabilistic path prioritization for hybrid fuzzing. In: NDSS (2019)

# Program Analysis

# Automatic Generation of Moment-Based Invariants for Prob-Solvable Loops

Ezio Bartocci[1], Laura Kovács[1,2(✉)], and Miroslav Stankovič[1]

[1] TU Wien, Vienna, Austria
laura.kovacs@tuwien.ac.at
[2] Chalmers, Gothenburg, Sweden

**Abstract.** One of the main challenges in the analysis of probabilistic programs is to compute invariant properties that summarise loop behaviours. Automation of invariant generation is still at its infancy and most of the times targets only expected values of the program variables, which is insufficient to recover the full probabilistic program behaviour. We present a method to automatically generate *moment-based invariants* of a subclass of probabilistic programs, called Prob-solvable loops, with polynomial assignments over random variables and parametrised distributions. We combine methods from symbolic summation and statistics to derive invariants as valid properties over higher-order moments, such as expected values or variances, of program variables. We successfully evaluated our work on several examples where full automation for computing higher-order moments and invariants over program variables was not yet possible.

## 1 Introduction

Probabilistic programs (PPs), originally employed in cryptographic/privacy protocols and randomised algorithms, are now gaining momentum due to the several emerging applications in the areas of machine learning and AI [12].

One of the main problems that arise from introducing randomness into the program is that we can no longer view variables as single values; we must think about them as distributions. Existing approaches, see e.g. [5,19,27] usually take into consideration only expected values, or upper and lower bounds over program variables. As argued by [29], such information is however insufficient to characterize the full value distributions of variables; (co-)variances and other higher-order moments of variables are also needed. Computing such moments is however challenging, if possible at all – see [17] for an insight on the hardness of analyzing expected values and (co-)variances of PPs. We illustrate the

This research was supported by the Austrian Science Fund (FWF) under grants S11405-N23, S11409-N23 (RiSE/SHiNE), the ERC Starting Grant 2014 SYMCAR 639270, the Wallenberg Academy Fellowship 2014 TheProSE and the Austrian FWF project W1255-N23.


Y.-F. Chen et al. (Eds.): ATVA 2019, LNCS 11781, pp. 255–276, 2019.
https://doi.org/10.1007/978-3-030-31784-3_15

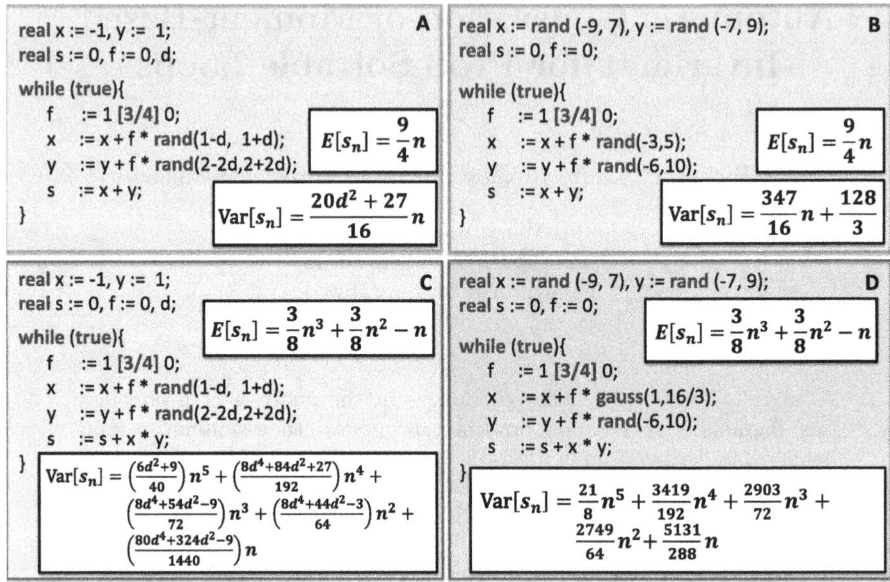


**Fig. 1.** Examples of four Prob-solvable loops. `f := 1[3/4]0` is a statement that assigns to `f` the value 1 with probability $\frac{3}{4}$ and the value 0 with probability $1 - \frac{3}{4} = \frac{1}{4}$. The function **rand**(a, b) samples a random number from a uniform distribution with support in the real interval $[a, b]$ and the function **gauss**$(\mu, \sigma^2)$ samples a random number from a normal distribution with mean $\mu$ and variance $\sigma^2$. For each loop, we provide the moment-based invariants for the first ($E[]$) and second moments ($Var[]$) of $s$ computed using our approach, where $n$ denotes the loop counter.

importance of computing higher-order moments beyond expected values, by considering for example the PPs of Fig. 1(A) and (B): the expected value of variable $s$ at each loop iteration is the same in both PPs, while the variance of the value distribution of $s$ differs in general (a similar behaviour is also exploited by Fig. 1(C)–(D)). Thus, Fig. 1(A) and (B) do not have the same invariants over higher-order moments; yet, current approaches would fail identifying such differences and only compute expected values of variables.

One of the main challenges in analysing PPs and computing their higher-order moments comes with the presence of loops and the burden of computing so-called *quantitative invariants* [19]. Quantitative invariants are properties that are true before and after each loop iteration. Weakest pre-expectations [19,27] can be used to compute quantitative invariants. This approach, supported for example in Prinsys [13], consists in annotating a loop with a template invariant and then solve constraints over the unknown coefficients of the template. Other methods [2,24] use martingales that are expressions over program variables whose expectations remain invariant. The aforementioned approaches are however not fully automatic since they require user guidance for providing templates and hints. In addition, they are limited to invariants over only expected values: with the exception of [24], they do not compute higher-order moments describing the distribution generated by the PP (see Sect. 6 for more details).

In this paper we introduce a *fully automated approach* to compute invariant properties over *higher-order moments* of so-called *Prob-solvable loops*, to stand for *probabilistic P-solvable loops*. Prob-solvable loops are PPs that extend the imperative P-solvable loops described in [23] with probabilistic assignments over random variables and parametrised distributions. As such, variable updates are expressed by random polynomial, and not only affine, updates (see Sect. 3). Each program in Fig. 1 is Prob-solvable; moreover, Fig. 1(C)–(D) involve nonlinear updates over $s$.

Our work uses statistical properties to eliminate probabilistic choices and turn random updates into recurrence relations over higher-order moments of program variables. We show that higher-order moments of Prob-solvable loops can be described by C-finite recurrences (Theorem 1). We further solve such recurrences to derive *moment-based invariants* of Prob-solvable loops (Sect. 4). A moment-based invariant is a property that holds at arbitrary loop iterations (hence, invariants), expressing closed form solutions of higher-order moments of program variables. To the best of our knowledge, no other method is able to derive higher-order moments of PPs with infinite loops in a fully automated way – for example, the work in [11] provides the exact probabilistic inference only for PPs with bounded loops. Our work hence allows to replace, for example, the required human guidance of [13,25] for Prob-solvable loops. We also support PPs with parametrised distributions (e.g., in Fig. 1(A)): instead of taking concrete instances of a given parametrised distribution, we automatically infer invariants of the entire class of PPs characterised by the considered parametrised distribution.

Our approach is both sound and terminating: given a Prob-solvable loops and an integer $k \geq 1$, we automatically infer the moment-based invariants over the $k$th moments of our input loop (see Sect. 4). Unlike the approach of [23] for deriving polynomial invariants of non-probabilistic (P-solvable) loops, our work only computes closed form expressions over higher-order moments and does not employ Gröbner basis computation to eliminate loop counters from the derived closed forms. As such, our moment-based invariants are not restrictive to polynomial properties but are linear combinations of polynomial expressions and exponential sequences over the loop counter. Moreover, Prob-solvable are more expressive than P-solvable loops as they are not restricted to deterministic updates but allow random assignments over variables.

**Contributions.** Our main contributions are: (1) we introduce the class of Prob-solvable loops with probabilistic assignments over random variables and distributions (Sect. 3); (2) we show that Prob-solvable loops can be modelled as C-finite recurrences over higher-order moments of variables (Theorem 1); (3) we provide a fully automated approach that derives moment-based invariants over arbitrary higher-order moments of Prob-solvable loops (Algorithm 1); (4) we implemented our work as an extension of the `Aligator` package [15] and evaluated over several challenging PPs (Sect. 5).

## 2 Preliminaries

We recall basic mathematical properties about recurrences and higher-order moments of variable values – for more details see [22, 26]. Throughout this paper, let $\mathbb{N}, \mathbb{Z}, \mathbb{R}$ denote the set of natural, integer and real numbers. We reserve capital letters to denote abstract random variables, e.g. $X, Y, \ldots$, and use small letters to denote program variables, e.g. $x, y, \ldots$, all possibly with indices.

### 2.1 C-Finite Recurrences

While sequences and recurrences are defined over arbitrary fields of characteristic zero, in our work we only focus over sequences/recurrences over $\mathbb{R}$.

**Definition 1 (Sequence).** *A univariate* sequence *in* $\mathbb{R}$ *is a function* $f : \mathbb{Z} \to \mathbb{R}$. *A* recurrence *for a sequence* $f(n)$ *is*

$$f(n+r) = R(f(n), f(n+1), \ldots, f(n+r-1), n), \qquad \text{with } n \in \mathbb{N},$$

*for some function* $R : \mathbb{R}^{r+1} \to \mathbb{R}$, *where* $r \in \mathbb{N}$ *is called the* order *of the recurrence.*

For simplicity, we denote by $f(n)$ both the recurrence of $f(n)$ as well as the recurrence equation $f(n) = 0$. When solving the recurrence $f(n)$, one is interested in computing a *closed form* solution of $f(n)$, expressing the value of $f(n)$ as a function of $n$ for any $n \in \mathbb{N}$. In our work we only consider the class of *linear recurrences with constant coefficients*, also called *C-finite recurrences*.

**Definition 2 (C-finite recurrences).** *A* C-finite recurrence $f(n)$ *satisfies the linear homogeneous recurrence with constant coefficients:*

$$f(n+r) = a_0 f(n) + a_1 f(n+1) + \ldots + a_{r-1} f(n+r-1), \qquad \text{with } r, n \in \mathbb{N}, \quad (1)$$

*where* $r$ *is the* order *of the recurrence, and* $a_0, \ldots, a_{r-1} \in \mathbb{R}$ *are constants with* $a_0 \neq 0$.

An example of a C-finite recurrence is the recurrence of Fibonacci numbers satisfying the recurrence $f(n+2) = f(n+1) + f(n)$, with initial values $f(0) = 0$ and $f(1) = 1$. Unlike arbitrary recurrences, closed forms of C-finite recurrences $f(n)$ always exist [22] and are defined as:

$$f(n) = P_1(n)\theta_1^n + \cdots + P_s(n)\theta_s^n, \quad (2)$$

where $\theta_1, \ldots, \theta_s \in \mathbb{R}$ are the distinct roots of the characteristic polynomial of $f(n)$ and $P_i(n)$ are polynomials in $n$. Closed forms of C-finite recurrences are called *C-finite expressions*. We note that, while the C-finite recurrence (1) is homogeneous, inhomogeneous C-finite recurrences can always be translated into homogeneous ones, as the inhomogeneous part of a C-finite recurrence is a C-finite expression.

In our work, we focus on the analysis of Prob-solvable loops and consider loop variables $x$ as sequences $x(n)$, where $n \in \mathbb{N}$ denotes the loop iteration counter. Thus, $x(n)$ gives the value of the program variable $x$ at iteration $n$.

### 2.2 Expected Values and Moments of Random Variables

Here we introduce the relevant notions from statistics that our work relies upon.

**Definition 3 (Probability space).** *A* probability space *is a triple* $(\Omega, F, P)$ *consisting of a sample space* $\Omega$ *denoting the set of outcomes, where* $\Omega \neq \emptyset$, *a* $\sigma$*-algebra* $F$ *with* $F \subset 2^{\Omega}$, *denoting a set of events, a probability measure* $P : F \to [0, 1]$ *s.t.* $P(\Omega) = 1$.

We now define random variables and their higher-order moments.

**Definition 4 (Random variable).** *A* random variable $X : \Omega \to \mathbb{R}$ *is a measurable function from a set* $\Omega$ *of possible outcomes to* $\mathbb{R}$.

In the context of our Prob-solvable loops, for each loop variable $x$, we consider elements of its corresponding sequence $x(n)$ to be random variables. When working with a random variable $X$, one is in general interested in expected values and other moments of $X$.

**Definition 5 (Expected value).** *An* expected value of a random variable $X$ *defined on a probability space* $(\Omega, F, P)$ *is the Lebesgue integral:* $E[X] = \int_{\Omega} X \cdot dP$. *In the special case* when $\Omega$ is discrete, *that is the outcomes are* $X_1, \ldots X_N$ *with corresponding probabilities* $p_1, \ldots p_N$, *we have* $E[X] = \sum_{i=1}^{N} X_i \cdot p_i$. *The expected value of* $X$ *is often also referred to as the* mean *or* $\mu$ *of* $X$.

For program variables $x$ of Prob-solvable loops, our work computes the expected values of the corresponding sequences $x(n)$ but also higher-order and mixed moments.

**Definition 6 (Higher-Order Moments).** *Let* $X$ *be a random variable,* $c \in \mathbb{R}$ *and* $k \in \mathbb{N}$. *We write* $Mom_k[c, X]$ *to denote the* $k$*th* moment about $c$ of $X$, *which is defined as:*

$$Mom_k[c, X] = E[(X - c)^k] \tag{3}$$

*whenever this exists.*

All random distributions we consider in this paper have finite (existing) moments. In the rest of this section we also assume the moments exist and are finite. In our work we will be almost solely interested in moments about 0 (called *raw moments*) and about the mean $E[X]$ (called *central moments*). We note though that we can move to moments of $X$ with different centers using Proposition 1.

**Proposition 1 (Transformation of center).** *Let* $X$ *be a random variable,* $c, d \in \mathbb{R}$ *and* $k \in \mathbb{N}$. *The* $k$th moment about $d$ of $X$, *can be calculated from moments about* $c$ *of* $X$ *by:* $E\left[(X - d)^k\right] = \sum_{i=0}^{k} \binom{k}{i} E\left[(X - c)^i\right] (c - d)^{k-i}$.

Similarly to higher-order moments, we also consider *mixed moments*, that is $E[X \cdot Y]$, where $X$ and $Y$ are random variables. For arbitrary random variables $X$ and $Y$, we have the following basic properties about their expected values and other moments:

- $E[c] = c$ for a constant $c \in \mathbb{R}$,
- expected value is linear, $E[X + Y] = E[X] + E[Y]$ and $E[c \cdot X] = c \cdot E[X]$,
- expected value is not multiplicative, in general $E[X \cdot Y] \neq E[X] \cdot E[Y]$
- expected value is multiplicative for independent random variables.

As a consequence of the above, expected values of monomials over arbitrary random variables, e.g. $E[X \cdot Y^2]$, cannot be in general further simplified.

The moments of a random variable $X$ with bounded support fully characterise its value distribution. While computing all moments of $X$ is generally very hard, knowing only a few moments of $X$ gives useful information about its value distributions. The most common moments are variance, covariance, skewness, as defined below.

**Definition 7 (Common moments).** Variance *measures how spread the distribution is and is defined as the second central moment:* $Var[X] = Mom_2[E[X], X]$.

Covariance *is a mixed moment measuring variability of two distributions and is defined as:* $Cov[X, Y] = E[(X - E[X]) \cdot (Y - E[Y])]$.

Skewness *measures asymmetry of the distribution and is defined as the normalised third central moment:* $Skew[X] = \frac{Mom_3[E[X], X]}{(Var[X])^{3/2}}$.

Basic results about variance and covariance state: $Cov[X, X] = Var[X]$, $Var[X] = E[X^2] - (E[X]^2)$, and $Cov[X, Y] = E[X \cdot Y] - E[X] \cdot E[Y]$.

**Definition 8 (Moment-Generating Function (MGF)).** *A moment generating function of a random variable $X$ is given by:*

$$M_X(t) = E[e^{tX}], \quad \textit{with } t \in \mathbb{R} \tag{4}$$

*whenever this expectation exists.*

Moment-generating functions, as the name suggests, can be used to compute higher-order moments of a random variable $X$. If we take the $k$th derivative of the moment-generating function of $X$, evaluated at 0, we get the $k$th moment about 0 of $X$, that is $Mom_k[0, X]$[1]. For many standard distributions, including Bernoulli, uniform and normal distributions, the moment-generating function exists and gives us a way to compute the moments for random variables drawing from these distributions. Thanks to these properties, we can use common distributions in our Prob-solvable programs.

[1] due to the series expansion $e^{tX} = 1 + tE[X] + \frac{t^2 E[X^2]}{2!} + \frac{t^3 E[X^3]}{3!} + \ldots$ and derivative w.r.t. $t$.

## 3 Programming Model: Prob-Solvable Programs

We now introduce our programming model of *Prob-solvable programs*, to stand for *probabilistic P-solvable programs.* P-solvable programs [23] are non-deterministic loops whose behaviour can be expressed by a system of C-finite recurrences over program variables. Prob-solvable programs build upon P-solvable programs by also allowing probabilistic assignments over random variables and distributions.

**Prob-Solvable Loops.** Let $m \in \mathbb{N}$ and $x_1, \ldots, x_m$ denote real-valued program variables. We define Prob-solvable loops with $x_1, \ldots, x_m$ variables as programs of the form:

$$I; \texttt{while(true)}\{U\}, \qquad \text{where:} \tag{5}$$

- $I$ is a sequence of initial assignments over $x_1, \ldots, x_m$. That is, $I$ is an assignments sequence $x_1 := c_1; x_2 := c_2; \ldots, x_m := c_m$, with $c_i \in \mathbb{R}$ representing a number drawn from a known distribution[2] - in particular, $c_i$ can be a real constant.
- $U$ is the loop body and is a sequence of $m$ random updates, each of the form:

$$x_i := a_i x_i + P_i(x_1, \ldots, x_{i-1}) \; [p_i] \; b_i x_i + Q_i(x_1, \ldots, x_{i-1}), \tag{6}$$

  or, in case of a deterministic assignment,

$$x_i := a_i x_i + P_i(x_1, \ldots, x_{i-1}), \tag{7}$$

  where $a_i, b_i \in \mathbb{R}$ are constants and $P_i, Q_i \in \mathbb{R}[x_1, \ldots, x_{i-1}]$ are polynomials over program variables $x_1, \ldots, x_{i-1}$. Further, $p_i \in [0, 1]$ in (6) is the probability of updating $x_i$ to $a_i x_i + P_i(x_1, \ldots, x_{i-1})$, whereas the probability to update $x_i$ to $b_i x_i + Q_i(x_1, \ldots, x_{i-1})$ in (6) is $1 - p_i$.

The coefficients $a_i$, $b_i$ and the coefficients of $P_i$ and $Q_i$ in the variable assignments (6)-(7) of Prob-solvable loops can be drawn from a random distribution as long as the moments of this distribution are known and are independent from program variables $x_1, \ldots, x_m$. Hence, the variable updates of Prob-solvable loop can involve coefficients drawn from Bernoulli, uniform, normal, and other distributions. Moreover, Prob-solvable support parametrised distributions, for example one may have the random distribution $\texttt{rand}(\texttt{d}_1, \texttt{d}_2)$ with arbitrary $d_1, d_2 \in \mathbb{R}$ symbolic constants. Similarly, rather than only considering concrete numeric values of $p_i$, the probabilities $p_i$ in the probabilistic updates (6) of Prob-solvable loops can also be symbolic constants. Notice that our current model assumes 'true' loop condition. We will see later that it allows us to compute invariants for any loop with set number of iterations. In the future we plan to extend the model to work with more general loop conditions.

---

[2] a known distribution is a distribution with known and computable moments.

*Example 1.* The programs in Fig. 1 are Prob-solvable, using uniform distributions given by `rand()`. Figure 1(D) also uses a normal distribution given by `gauss()`. Note that while the random distributions of Fig. 1(B, D) are defined in terms of concrete constants, Fig. 1(A, C) have a parametrised random distribution, defined in terms of $d \in \mathbb{R}$.

**Prob-Solvable Loops and Moment-Based Recurrences.** Let us now consider a Prob-solvable program with $n \in \mathbb{N}$ denoting the loop iteration counter. We show that variable updates of Prob-solvable programs yield special recurrences in $n$, called *moment-based recurrences.* For this, we consider program variables $x_1, \ldots, x_m$ as sequences $x_1(n), \ldots, x_m(n)$ allowing us to precisely describe relations between values of $x_i$ at different loop iterations. Using this notation, probabilistic updates (6) over $x_i$ turn $x_i(n)$ into a random variable, yielding the relation (similarly, for deterministic updates (7)):

$$x_i(n+1) = a_i x_i(n) + P_i(x_1(n), \ldots, x_{i-1}(n))\,[p_i]\,b_i x_i(n) + Q_i(x_1(n), \ldots, x_{i-1}(n)).$$

The relation above could be treated as a recurrence equation over random variables $x_i(n)$ provided the probabilistic behaviour depending on $p_i$ is encoded (as an extension) into a recurrence equation. To analyse such probabilistic updates of Prob-solvable loops, for each random variable $x_i(n)$ we consider their expected values $E[x_i(n)]$ and create new recurrence variables from expected values of monomials over original program variables (e.g. a new variable $E[x_i \cdot x_j]$). We refer to these new recurrence variables as *E-variables.* We note that any program variable yields an E-variable, but not every E-variable corresponds to one single program variable as E-variables are expected values of monomials over program variables. We now formulate recurrence equations over E-variables rather than over program variables, yielding *moment-based recurrences.*

**Definition 9 (Moment-Based Recurrences).** *Let $x(n)$ be a sequence of random variables. A* moment-based recurrence *for $x$ is a recurrence over E-variable $E[x]$:*

$$E[x(n+r)] = R(E[x(n)], E[x(n+1)], \ldots, E[x(n+r-1)], n) \quad (n \in \mathbb{N}),$$

*for some function $R : \mathbb{R}^{r+1} \to \mathbb{R}$, where $r \in \mathbb{N}$ is the* order *of the moment-based recurrence.*

Similarly to [27], note that variable updates $x_i := f_1(x_i)\ [p_i]\ f_2(x_i)$ yield the relation:

$$\begin{aligned} E[x_i(n+1)] &= E\big[p_i \cdot f_1(x_i(n)) + (1-p_i) \cdot f_2(x_i(n))\big] \\ &= p_i \cdot E\big[f_1(x_i(n))\big] + (1-p_i) \cdot E\big[f_2(x_i(n))\big] \end{aligned} \tag{8}$$

Thanks to this relation, probabilistic updates (6) are rewritten into the moment-based recurrence equation:

$$\begin{aligned} E[x_i(n+1)] = p_i \cdot E\big[&a_i x_i(n) + P_i(x_1(n), \ldots, x_{i-1}(n))\big] \\ +(1-p_i) \cdot E\big[&b_i x_i(n) + Q_i(x_1(n), \ldots, x_{i-1}(n))\big]. \end{aligned} \tag{9}$$

In particular, we have $E[x_i(n+1)] = p_i \cdot E[a_i x_i(n) + P_i(x_1(n), \ldots, x_{i-1}(n))]$ for the deterministic assignments of (7) (that is, $p_i = 1$ in (7)).

By using properties of expected values of expressions $expr_1, expr_2$ over random variables, we obtain the following simplification rules:

$$\begin{array}{ll} E[expr_1 + expr_2] & \to E[expr_1] + E[expr_2] \\ E[expr_1 \cdot expr_2] & \to E[expr_1] \cdot E[expr_2], \text{ if } expr_1, expr_2 \text{ are independent} \\ E[c \cdot expr_1] & \to c \cdot E[expr_1] \\ E[c] & \to c \\ E[\mathcal{D} \cdot expr_1] & \to E[\mathcal{D}] \cdot E[expr_1] \end{array} \tag{10}$$

where $c \in \mathbb{R}$ is a constant and $\mathcal{D}$ is a known independent distribution.

*Example 2.* The moment-based recurrences of the Prob-solvable loop of Fig. 1(A) are:

$$\begin{cases} E[f(n+1)] = \frac{3}{4}E[1] + \frac{1}{4}E[0] \\ E[x(n+1)] = E\big[x(n) + f(n+1) \cdot rand(1-d, 1+d)\big] \\ E[y(n+1)] = E\big[y(n) + f(n+1) \cdot rand(2-2d, 2+2d)\big] \\ E[s(n+1)] = E\big[x(n+1) + y(n+1)\big] \end{cases}$$

By using the simplification rules (10) on the above recurrences, we obtain the following simplified moment-based recurrences of Fig. 1(A):

$$\begin{cases} E[f(n+1)] = \frac{3}{4} \\ E[x(n+1)] = E[x(n)] + E[f(n+1)] \cdot E[rand(1-d, 1+d)] \\ E[y(n+1)] = E[y(n)] + E[f(n+1)] \cdot E[rand(2-2d, 2+2d)] \\ E[s(n+1)] = E[x(n+1)] + E[y(n+1)] \end{cases} \tag{11}$$

In Sect. 4 we show that Prob-solvable loops can further be rewritten into a system of C-finite recurrences over E-variables.

**Prob-Solvable Loops and Mutually Dependent Updates.** Consider PP loops with mutually dependent affine updates:

$$x_i := \sum_{k=1}^{m} a_{i,k} x_k \; + c_i \; [p_i] \; \sum_{k=1}^{m} b_{i,k} x_k \; + d_i, \tag{12}$$

where $a_{i,k}, b_{i,k}, c_i, d_i \in \mathbb{R}$ are constants. While such assignments are not directly captured by updates (6) of Prob-solvable loops, this is not a restriction of our work. Variable updates given by (12) yield mutually dependent C-finite recurrences over E-variables. Using methods from [22], this coupled system of C-finite recurrences can be rewritten into an equivalent system of independent C-finite recurrences over E-variables, yielding an independent system of moment-based recurrences over which our invariant generation algorithm from Sect. 4 can be applied. Hence probabilistic loops with affine updates are special cases of Prob-solvable loops.

**Multi-path Prob-Solvable Loops.** While (5) defines Prob-solvable programs as single-path loops, the following class of multi-path loops can naturally be modeled by Prob-solvable programs:

$$I;\texttt{while(true)}\{\texttt{if } t \texttt{ then } U_1 \texttt{ else } U_2\}, \qquad \text{where:} \tag{13}$$

$I$ is as in (5), $t$ is a boolean-valued random variable, and $U_1$ and $U_2$ are respectively sequences of deterministic updates $x_i := a_i x_i + P_i(x_1, \dots, x_{i-1})$ and $x_i := b_i x_i + Q_i(x_1, \dots, x_{i-1})$ as in (7). PPs (13) can be rewritten to equivalent Prob-solvable loops, as follows. A pair of updates $x := u_1[p]v_1$ from $U_1$ and $x := u_2[p]v_2$ from $U_2$ is rewritten by the following sequence of updates:

$$\begin{aligned} &f := 1[p]0;\\ &g := 1[p]0;\\ &x := t(u_1 f + v_1(1-f)) + (1-t)(u_2 g + v_2(1-g)) \end{aligned} \tag{14}$$

with $f, g$ fresh program variables. The resulting program is Prob-solvable and we can thus compute moment-based invariants of multi-path loops as in (13). The programs Coupon, Random_Walk_2D of Table 1 are Prob-solvable loops corresponding to such multi-path loops. Notice that the last term in (14) grows exponentially in terms of branch degree. This is similar to the *weakest pre-expectation* reasoning approach [19,27].

## 4 Moment-Based Invariants of Prob-solvable Loops

Thanks to probabilistic updates, the values of program variables of Prob-solvable loops after a specific number of loop iterations are not a priori determined. The value distributions $x_i(n)$ of program variables $x_i$ are therefore random variables. When analysing Prob-solvable loops, and in general probabilistic programs, one is therefore required to capture relevant properties over expected values and higher moments of the variables in order to precisely summarise the value distribution of program variables.

**Moment-Based Invariants.** We are interested in automatically generating so-called *moment-based invariants* of Prob-solvable loops. Moment-based invariants are properties over expected values and higher moments of program variables such that these properties hold at arbitrary loop iterations (and hence are invariants).

**Automated Generation of Moment-Based Invariants of Prob-Solvable Loops.** Our method for generating moment-based invariants of Prob-solvable loops is summarized in Algorithm 1. Algorithm 1 takes as input a Prob-solvable loop $\mathcal{P}$ and a natural number $k \geq 1$ and returns *moment-based invariants over the kth moments* of the program variables $\{x_1, \dots, x_m\}$. We denote by $n$ the loop counter of $\mathcal{P}$.

**Algorithm 1.** Moment-Based Invariants of Prob-solvable Loops

**Input:** Prob-solvable loop $\mathcal{P}$ as defined in (5), with variables $\{x_1, \ldots, x_m\}$, and $k \geq 1$
**Output:** Set $MI$ of Moment-based invariants of $\mathcal{P}$ over the $k$th moments of $\{x_1, \ldots, x_m\}$
**Assumptions:** $n \in \mathbb{N}$ is the loop counter of $\mathcal{P}$

1: Extract the moment-based recurrence relations of $\mathcal{P}$, for $i = 1, \ldots, m$:

$$E[x_i(n+1)] = p_i \cdot E\big[a_i x_i(n) + P_i(x_1(n), \ldots, x_{i-1}(n))\big] \\ +(1-p_i) \cdot E\big[b_i x_i(n) + Q_i(x_1(n), \ldots, x_{i-1}(n))\big].$$

2: $MBRecs = \{E[x_i(n+1)] \mid i = 1, \ldots, m\}$ ▷ initial set of moment-based recurrences
3: $S := \{x_1^k, \ldots, x_m^k\}$ ▷ initial set of monomials of E-variables as $Mom_k[0, x_i(n)] = E[x_i(n)^k]$
4: **while** $S \neq \emptyset$ **do**
5: $M := \prod_{i=1}^m x_i^{\alpha_i}$, where and $M \in S$ $\alpha_i \in \mathbb{N}$
6: $S := S \setminus \{M\}$
7: $M' = M[x_i^{\alpha_i} \leftarrow upd_i]$, for each $i = m, \ldots, 1$ ▷ replace each $x_i^{\alpha_i}$ in $M$ with $upd_i$

where $upd_i$ denotes:
$p_i \cdot \big(a_i x_i + P_i(x_1, \ldots, x_{i-1})\big)^{\alpha_i} + (1-p_i) \cdot \big(b_i x_i + Q_i(x_1, \ldots, x_{i-1})\big)^{\alpha_i}$

8: Rewrite $M'$ as $M' = \sum N_j$ for monomials $N_j$ over $x_1, \ldots, x_m$
9: Simplify the moment-based recurrence $E[M(n+1)] = E[\sum N_j]$ using the rules (10) ▷ $M(n+1)$ denotes $\prod_{i=1}^m x_i(n+1)^{\alpha_i}$
10: $MBRecs = MBRecs \cup \{E[M(n+1)]\}$ ▷ add $E[M(n+1)]$ to the set of moment-based recurrences
11: **for** each monomial $N_j$ in $M$ **do**
12: **if** $E[N_j] \notin MBRecs$ **then** ▷ there is no moment-based recurrence for $N_j$
13: $S = S \cup \{N_j\}$ ▷ add $N_j$ to $S$
14: **end while**
15: Solve the system of moment-based recurrences $MBRecs$
16: $MI = \{E[x_i(n)^k] - CF_i(k, n) = 0 \mid i = 1, \ldots m\}$ ▷ $CF_i(k, n)$ is the closed form solution of $E[x_i^k]$
17: **return** the set $MI$ of moment based invariants of $\mathcal{P}$ for the $k$th moments of $x_1, \ldots, x_m$

**Theorem 1.** *Higher-order moments of variables in Prob-solvable loops can be modeled by C-finite recurrences over E-variables.*

*Proof.* We want to show that $E[x_i^{\alpha_i}]$ can be expressed using recurrence equations. The idea is to express $x_i^{\alpha_i}(n+1)$ in terms of the value of $x_i$ at the $n$-th iteration. Value of $x_i(n+1)$ is $a_i x_i(n) + P_i(x_1(n+1), \ldots, x_{i-1}(n+1)$ with probability $p_i$ and $b_i x_i(n) + Q_i(x_1(n+1), \ldots, x_{i-1}(n+1)$ with probability $(1-p_i)$. From here we can derive that $E[x_i^{\alpha_i}(n+1)] = E[p_i \cdot \big(a_i x_i + P_i(x_1, \ldots, x_{i-1})\big)^{\alpha_i} + (1-p_i) \cdot \big(b_i x_i + Q_i(x_1, \ldots, x_{i-1})\big)^{\alpha_i}]$. For arbitrary monomial $M = \prod x_i^{\alpha_i}(n+1)$ we can express $E[M]$ by substituting each $x_i^{\alpha_i}(n+1)$ as above. This process is captured by line 7 of Algorithm 1. The new equations can be further simplified using properties of expected values and the simplification rules (10) to give recurrence equations over E-variables.

We now describe Algorithm 1. Our algorithm first rewrites $\mathcal{P}$ into a set $MBRecs$ of moment-based recurrences, as described in Sect. 3. That is, program variables $x_i$ are turned into random variables $x_i(n)$ and variable updates over $x_i$ become moment-based recurrences over E-variables by using the relation of (8) (lines 1–2) of Algorithm 1).

The algorithm next proceeds with computing the moment-based recurrences of the $k$th moments of $x_1, \ldots, x_m$. Recall that the $k$th moment of $x_i$ is given by:

$$Mom_k[0, x_i(n)] = E[x_i(n)^k].$$

Hence, the set $S$ of monomials yielding E-variables for which moment-based recurrences need to be solved is initialized to $\{x_1^k, \ldots, x_m^k\}$ (line 3 of Algorithm 1). Note that by considering the resulting E-variables $E[x_i^k]$ and solving the moment-based recurrences of $E[x_i^k]$, we derive closed forms of the $k$th moments of $\{x_1, \ldots, x_m\}$ (line 16 of Algorithm 1). To this end, Algorithm 1 recursively computes the moment-based recurrences of every E-variable arising from the moment-based recurrences of $E[x_i^k]$ (lines 4–14 of Algorithm 1), thus ultimately computing closed forms for $E[x_i^k]$. One can then use transformations described in Proposition 1 to compute closed forms for other moments, such as variance and covariance. In more detail,

- for each monomial $M = \prod x_j^{\alpha_j}$ from $S$, we substitute $x_i^{\alpha_i}$ in $M$ by its probabilistic behaviour. That is, the update of $x_i$ in the Prob-solvable loop $\mathcal{P}$ is rewritten, according to (8), into the sum of its two probabilistic updates, weighted by their respective probabilities (lines 5–7 of Algorithm 1). Rewriting in line 7 of Algorithm 1 represents the most non-trivial step in our algorithm, combining non-deterministic nature of our program with polynomial properties. The resulting polynomial $M'$ from $M$ is then reordered to be expressed as a sum of new monomials $N_j$ (line 8 of Algorithm 1); such a sum always exists as $M'$ involves only addition and multiplication over $x_1, \ldots, x_m$ (recall that $P_i$ and $Q_i$ are polynomials over $x_1, \ldots, x_m$).
- By applying the simplification rules(10) of E-variables over the moment-based recurrence of $E[\sum N_j]$, the recurrence of $E[M(n+1)]$ is obtained and added to the set $MBRecs$. Here, $M(n+1)$ denotes $\prod_{i=1}^m x_i(n+1)^{\alpha_i}$. As the recurrence of $E[M(n+1)]$ depends on $E[N_j]$, moment-based recurrences of $E[N_j]$ need also be computed and hence $S$ is enlarged by $N_j$ (lines 9–13 of Algorithm 1).

As a result, the set $MBRecs$ of moment-based recurrences of E-variables corresponding to $S$ are obtained. These recurrences are C-finite expressions over E-variables (see correctness argument of Theorem 3) and hence their closed form solutions exist. In particular, the closed forms $CF_i(k, n)$ of $E[x_i(n)^k]$ is derived, turning $E[x_i(n)^k] - CF_i(k, n) = 0$ into a inductive property that holds at arbitrary loop iterations and is hence a moment-based invariant of $\mathcal{P}$ over the $k$th moment of $x_i$ (line 16 of Algorithm 1).

**Theorem 2 (Soundness).** *Consider a Prob-solvable loop $\mathcal{P}$ with program variables $x_1, \ldots, x_m$ and let $k$ be a non-negative integer with $k \geq 1$. Algorithm 1 generates moment-based invariants of $\mathcal{P}$ over the $k$th moments of $x_1, \ldots, x_m$.*

Note when $k = 1$, Algorithm 1 computes the moment-based invariants as invariant relations over the closed form solutions of expected values of $x_1, \ldots, x_m$. In this case, our moment-based invariants are quantitative invariants as in [19].

*Example 3.* We illustrate Algorithm 1 for computing the second moments (i.e. $k = 2$) of the Prob-solvable loop of Fig. 1(A).

Our algorithm initializes $MBRecs = \{E[f(n+1)], E[x(n+1)], E[y(n+1)], E[s(n+1)]\}$ and $S = \{f^2, x^2, y^2, s^2\}$.

We next (arbitrarily) choose $M$ to be the monomial $f^2$ from $S$. Thus, $S = \{x^2, y^2, s^2\}$. Using the probabilistic update of $f$, we replace $f^2$ by $\frac{3}{4} \cdot 1^2 + (1 - \frac{3}{4}) \cdot 0^2$, that is by $\frac{3}{4}$. As a result, $MBRecs = MBRecs \cup \{E[f(n+1)^2] = \frac{3}{4}\}$ and $S$ remains unchanged.

We next choose $M$ to be $x^2$ and set $S = \{y^2, s^2\}$. We replace $x^2$ by its randomised behaviour, yielding $E[M(n+1)] = E[x(n+1)^2] = E[\big(x(n) + f(n+1) \cdot \texttt{rand}(1-\texttt{d}, 1+\texttt{d})\big)^2]$. By the simplification rules (10) over E-variables, we obtain:

$$E[x(n+1)^2] = E[x(n)^2] + 2 \cdot E[x(n)] \cdot E[f(n+1)] + E[f(n+1)^2] \cdot \frac{1}{3}(d^2 + 3), \quad (15)$$

as $f(n+1)$ is independent from $x(n)$ and $E[\texttt{rand}(1-\texttt{d}, 1+\texttt{d})^2] = \frac{1}{3}(d^2+3)$. We add the recurrence (15) to $MBRecs$ and keep $S$ unchanged as the E-variables $E[x(n)], E[f(n+1)], E[f(n+1)^2]$ have their recurrences already in $MBRecs$.

We next set $M$ to $y^2$ and change $S = \{s^2\}$. Similarly to $E[x(n+1)^2]$, we get:

$$E[y(n+1)^2] = E[y(n)^2] + 4 \cdot E[y(n)] \cdot E[f(n+1)] + E[f(n+1)^2] \cdot \frac{4}{3}(d^2 + 3), \quad (16)$$

by using that $f(n+1)$ is independent from $y(n)$ and $E[\texttt{rand}(2-2\texttt{d}, 2+2\texttt{d})^2] = \frac{4}{3}(d^2+3)$. We add the recurrence (16) to $MBRecs$ and keep $S$ unchanged. We set $M$ to $s^2$, yielding $S = \emptyset$. We extend $MBRecs$ with the recurrence:

$$E[s(n+1)^2] = E[\big(x(n+1) + y(n+1)\big)^2] = E[x(n+1)^2] + 2E[(xy)(n+1)] + E[y(n+1)^2]$$

and add $xy$ to $S$. We therefore consider $M$ to be $xy$ and set $S = \emptyset$. We obtain:

$$E[(xy)(n+1)] = E[(xy)(n)] + 2 \cdot E[x(n)] \cdot E[f(n+1) + E[y(n)] \cdot E[f(n+1)] + 2 \cdot E[f(n+1)^2],$$

by using that $E[\texttt{rand}(1-\texttt{d}, 1+\texttt{d})] = 1$ and $E[\texttt{rand}(2-2\texttt{d}, 2+2\texttt{d})] = 2$. We add the recurrence of $E[(xy)(n+1)]$ to $MBRecs$ and keep $S = \emptyset$.

As a result, we proceed to solve the moment-based recurrences of $MBRecs$. We focus first on the recurrences over expected values:

$$\begin{aligned}
E[f(n+1)] &= \tfrac{3}{4} \\
E[x(n+1)] &= E[x(n)] + E[f(n+1) \cdot \texttt{rand}(1-\texttt{d}, 1+\texttt{d})] &&= E[x(n)] + \tfrac{3}{4} \\
E[y(n+1)] &= E[y(n)] + E[f(n+1) \cdot \texttt{rand}(2-2\texttt{d}, 2+2\texttt{d})] &&= E[x(n)] + 2 \cdot \tfrac{3}{4} \\
E[s(n+1)] &= E[x(n+1)] + E[y(n+1)]
\end{aligned}$$

Note that the above recurrences are C-finite recurrences over E-variables. For computing closed forms, we respectively substitute $E[f(n+1)$ by its closed form in $E[y(n+1)]$ and $E[x(n+1)]$, yielding closed forms for $E[y(n+1)]$ and $E[x(n+1)]$, and hence for $E[s(n+1)]$. By also using the initial values of Fig. 1, we derive the closed forms:

$$\begin{aligned} E[f(n)] &= \tfrac{3}{4} & E[s(n)] &= \tfrac{9}{4}n \\ E[x(n)] &= \tfrac{3}{4}n - 1 & E[y(n)] &= \tfrac{3}{2}n + 1 \end{aligned}$$

We next similarly derive the closed forms for higher-order and mixed moments:

$$\begin{aligned} E[f(n)^2] &= \tfrac{3}{4} & E[s(n)^2] &= \tfrac{81}{16}n^2 + \tfrac{20d^2+27}{16}n \\ E[x(n)^2] &= \tfrac{9}{16}n^2 + \tfrac{4d^2--21}{16}n + 1 & E[y(n)^2] &= \tfrac{9}{4}n^2 + \tfrac{4d^2+15}{4}n + 1 \\ E[(xy)(n)] &= \tfrac{9}{8}n^2 - \tfrac{3}{8}n - 1 \end{aligned}$$

yielding hence the moment-based invariants over the second moments of variables of Fig. 1. Using Proposition 1 and Definition 7, we derive the variance of $s(n)$ as $Var(s(n)) = \frac{20d^2+27}{16}n$. □

Let us finally note that the termination of Algorithm 1 depends on whether for every monomial $M$ (from the set $S$, line 4 of Algorithm 1) the moment-based recurrence equation over the corresponding E-variable $E[M(n+1)]$ can be computed as a C-finite recurrence over E-variables. We prove this using transfinite induction over monomials and properties of inhomogeneous C-finite recurrences.

**Theorem 3 (Termination).** *For any non-negative integer $k$ with $k \geq 1$ and any Prob-solvable loop $\mathcal{P}$ with program variables $x_1, \ldots, x_m$, Algorithm 1 terminates. Moreover, Algorithm 1 terminates in at most $\mathcal{O}(k^m \cdot d_m^{m-1} \cdot d_{m-1}^{m-2} \cdots \cdot d_2^1)$ steps, where $d_i = max\{deg(P_i), deg(Q_i), 1\}$ with $deg(P_i), deg(Q_i)$ denoting the degree of polynomials $P_i$ and $Q_i$ of the variable updates* (6).

*Proof.* We associate every monomial with an ordinal number as follows:

$$x_k^{\alpha_k} \cdot x_{k-1}^{\alpha_{k-1}} \ldots x_1^{\alpha_1} \xrightarrow{\sigma} \omega^k \cdot \alpha_k + \omega^{k-1} \cdot \alpha_{k-1} \cdots + \alpha_1,$$

and order monomials $M, N$ such that $M > N$ if $\sigma(M) > \sigma(N)$. Algorithm 1 terminates if for every monomial $M$ (from the set $S$, line 4 of Algorithm 1) the moment-based recurrence equation over the corresponding E-variable $E[M(n+1)]$ can be computed as a C-finite recurrence over E-variables. We will show that this is indeed the case by transfinite induction over monomials.

Let $M = \prod_{k=1}^{K} x_k^{\alpha_k}$ be a monomial and assume that every smaller monomial has a closed form solution in form of a C-finite expression. Let

$$x_i^{\alpha_i} := \left(c_i x_i + P_i(x_1, \cdots x_{i-1})\right)^{\alpha_i} \tag{17}$$

be the updates of our variables after removing the probabilistic choice, as in line 5 of Algotithm 1. Then the recurrence for $M$ is:

$$E[M(n+1)] = E\Big[\prod_{i=1}^{K}\Big(p_i \cdot \big(a_i x_i + P_i(x_1, \dots x_{i-1})\big)^{\alpha_i}$$

$$+ (1-p_i)\cdot\big(b_i x_i + Q_i(x_1, \dots x_{i-1})\big)^{\alpha_i}\Big)(n)\Big]$$

$$= E[M(n)] + \sum_{j=1}^{J} b_j \cdot E\big[N_j(n)\big] \tag{18}$$

for some $J$, constants $b_i$ and monomials $N_1, \dots, N_J$ all different than $M$. By Lemma 1, we have an inhomogeneous C-finite recurrence relation $E[M(n+1)] = E[M(n)]+\gamma$, for some C-finite expression $\gamma$. Hence, the closed form of $E[M(n+1)]$ exists and is a C-finite expression. □

We finally prove our auxiliary lemma, used in the above proof of Theorem 3.

**Lemma 1.** *In the recurrence* (18) *over E-variables, we have* $M > N_j$ *for all* $j \leq J$.

*Proof.* Let $M = \prod_{k=1}^{K} x_k^{\alpha_k}$ and have $N_j = \prod_{k=1}^{K} x_k^{\beta_k}$ coming from

$$\prod_{i=1}^{K}\big(c_i x_i + P_i(x_1, \cdots x_{i-1})\big)^{\alpha_i}. \tag{19}$$

Assume $M \leq N_j$, i.e. $\omega^K \cdot \alpha_K + \cdots + \alpha_1 \leq \omega^K \cdot \beta_K + \cdots + \beta_1$, so we have $\alpha_K \leq \beta_K$. Note that in (19) $x_K$ only appears in factor $c_K x_K + P_K(x_1, \dots x_{K-1})$. Considering the multiplicity, we get at most $\alpha_K$th power of $x_K$, hence $\alpha_K \geq \beta_K$. Thus $\alpha_K = \beta_K$. So for $M \leq N_j$ we need $N_j$ from $(c_K x_K)^{\alpha_K} \cdot \prod_{i=1}^{K-1}(c_i x_i + P_i(x_1, \cdots x_{i-1}))^{\alpha_i}$.

Proceeding similarly for $x_{K-1}, x_{K-2}, \dots$, we get that for each $k \leq K$ we have $\alpha_k = \beta_k$, which contradicts the assumption, thus $M > N_j$ as needed.

Regarding the termination time of Algorithm 1, let us look at what monomials can possibly be added to $S$. Let $M = \prod x_i^{\alpha_i} \in S$. Based on the above reasoning, it is clear that in case $i = m$ we have $\alpha_m \leq k$. For any $i < m$ the maximum value of $\alpha_i$ is $\alpha_{i+1} \cdot d_{i+1}$. Therefore, we have $\alpha_i \leq k \cdot \prod_{j=i+1}^{m} d_j$. Thus, we can count all possible monomials and hence derived the upper bound on the time complexity of Algorithm 1 as the product of theses upper bounds. That is, the upper bound on the time complexity of Algorithm 1 is given by $k^m \cdot d_m^{m-1} \cdot d_{m-1}^{m-2} \cdots \cdot d_2^1$. □

## 5 Implementation and Experiments

We implemented our work in the Julia language, using `Aligator`[15] for handling and solving recurrences. We evaluated our work on several challenging probabilistic programs with parametrised distributions, symbolic probabilities and/or both discrete and continuous random variables. All our experiments were run on MacBook Pro 2017 with 2.3 GHz Intel Core i5 and 8GB RAM. Our implementation and benchmarks are available at: `github.com/miroslav21/aligator`.

**Benchmarks.** We evaluated our work on 13 probabilistic programs, as follows. We used 7 programs from works [5,7,9,19,24] on invariant generation. These examples are given in lines 1–7 of Table 1; we note though that BINOMIAL ("$p$") represents our generalisation of a binomial distribution example taken from [7,9,19] to a probabilistic program with parametrised probability $p$. We further crafted 6 examples of our own, illustrating the distinctive features of our work. These examples are listed in lines 8–13 of Table 1: lines 8–11 correspond to the examples of Fig. 1; line 12 of Table 1 shows a variation of Fig. 1, with a parametrized distribution $p$; line 13 corresponds to a non-linear Prob-solvable loop computing squares. All our benchmarks are available at the aforementioned url.

**Experimental Results with Moment-Based Invariants.** Results of our evaluation are presented in Table 1. While Algorithm 1 can compute invariants over arbitrary $k$th higher-order moments, due to lack of space and readability, Table 1 lists only our moment-based invariants up to the third moment (i.e. $k \leq 3$), that is for expected values, second- and third-order moments. The first column of Table 1 lists the benchmark name, whereas the second column gives the degree of the moments (i.e. $k = 1, 2, 3$) for which we compute invariants. The third column reports the timings (in seconds) our implementation needed to derive invariants. The last column shows our moment-based invariants; for readability, we decided to omit intermediary invariants (up to 30 for some programs) and only show the most relevant invariants.

We could not perform a fair practical comparison with other existing methods: to the best of our knowledge, existing works, such as [2,13,19,24], require user guidance/templates/hints. Further, most of the existing techniques do not support symbolic probabilities and/or parametrised distributions - which are, for example, required in the analysis of programs STUTTERINGA, STUTTERINGC, STUTTERINGP of Table 1. We also note that examples COUPON, STUTTERINGC, STUTTERINGP involve non-linear probabilistic updates hindering automation in existing methods, while such updates can naturally be encoded as moment-based recurrences in our framework. We finally note that while second-order moments are computed only by [24], but with the help of user-provided templates, no existing approaches compute moments for $k \geq 3$. Our experiments show that inferring third-order moments are in general not expensive. Yet, for examples STUTTERINGA, STUTTERINGC, STUTTERINGP with parametrized distributions/probabilities more computation time is needed. This increase in time comes from handling more complex symbolic expressions due to the non-linear updates and parametrized distributions, and from non-optimal recurrence solving.

**Table 1.** Moment-based invariants of Prob-solvable loops, where $n$ is the loop counter.

| Program | Moment | Runtime ($s$) | Computed Moment-Based Invariants |
|---|---|---|---|
| COUPON [24] | 1 | 0.37 | $E[c(n)] = (2^n - 1)/(2^n)$ |
| | 2 | 0.40 | $E[c^2(n)] = (2^n - 1)/(2^n)$ |
| | 3 | 0.34 | $E[c^2(n)] = (2^n - 1)/(2^n)$ |
| COUPON4 [24] | 1 | 0.90 | $E[c(n)] = (4^n - 3^3)/(4^n)$ |
| | 2 | 1.1 | $E[c^2(n)] = (4^n - 3^3)/(4^n)$ |
| | 3 | 1.3 | $E[c^3(n)] = (4^n - 3^3)/(4^n)$ |
| RANDOM_WALK_1D_CTS [24] | 1 | 0.12 | $E[x(n)] = n/5$ |
| | 2 | 0.45 | $E[x^2(n)] = n^2/25 + 22n/75$ |
| | 3 | 1.00 | $E[x^3(n)] = n^3/125 + n^2 22/125 - n21/250$ |
| SUM_RND_SERIES [7] | 1 | 0.31 | $E[x(n)] = n^2/4 + n/4$ |
| | 2 | 2.89 | $E[x^2(n)] = n^4/16 + 5n^3/24 + 3n^2/16 + n/24$ |
| | 3 | 17.7 | $E[x^3(n)] = n^6/64 + 7n^5/64 + 13n^4/64 + 9n^3/64 + n^2/32$ |
| PRODUCT_DEP_VAR [7] | 1 | 0.65 | $E[p(n)] = n^2/4 - n/4$ |
| | 2 | 6.27 | $E[p(n)] = n^4/16 - n^3/8 + 3n^2/16 - n/8$ |
| | 3 | 37.5 | $E[p^3(n)] = n^6/64 - 3n^5/64 + 9n^4/64 - 21n^3/64 + 15n^2/32 - n/4$ |
| RANDOM_WALK_2D [5, 24] | 1 | 0.07 | $E[x(n)] = 0$ |
| | 2 | 0.26 | $E[x^2(n)] = n/2$ |
| | 3 | 0.49 | $E[x^3(n)] = 0$ |
| BINOMIAL("$p$") [7,9,19] | 1 | 0.17 | $E[x(n)] = np$ |
| | 2 | 0.47 | $E[x^2(n)] = n^2p^2 + np(1-p)$ |
| | 3 | 1.6 | $E[x^3(n)] = n^3p^3 - 3n^2p^3 + 3n^2p^2 + 2np^3 - 3np^2 + np$ |
| STUTTERINGA – FIG. 1(A) | 1 | 0.44 | $E[s(n)] = 9n/4$ |
| | 2 | 2.2 | $E[s^2(n)] = 81n^2/16 + (20d^2 + 27)/16n$ |
| | 3 | 8.48 | $E[s^3(n)] = 81d^2n^2/16 + 63d^2n/16 + 729n^3/64 + 9n^2(4d^2 - 9)/32 + 9n^2(4d^2 + 9)/16 + 567n^2/64 + 3n(-6d^2 - 21)/8 + 3n(6d^2 - 12)/16 + 243n/32$ |
| STUTTERINGB – FIG. 1(B) | 1 | 0.49 | $E[s(n)] = 9n/4$ |
| | 2 | 2.03 | $E[s^2(n)] = 81n^2/16 + 347/16n + 128/3$ |
| | 3 | 7.43 | $E[s^3(n)] = 729n^3/64 + 9369n^2/64 + 1359n/32 =$ |
| STUTTERINGC – FIG. 1(C) | 1 | 1.8 | $E[s(n)] = 3n^3/8 + 3n^2/8 - n$ |
| | 2 | 72.5 | $E[s^2(n)] = 9n^6/64 + 3n^5(8d^2 + 27)/160 + n^4(8d^4 + 84d^2 - 90)/192 + n^3(32d^4 + 216d^2 - 252)/288 + n^2(8d^4 + 44d^2 + 61)/64 + n(80d^4 + 324d^2 - 9)/1440$ |
| | 3 | 2144 | $E[s^3(n)] = 27n^9/512 + 27n^8(16d^2 + 39)/2560 + 3n^7(824d^4 + 6444d^2 + 1242)/17920 + n^6(1900d^4 + 3996d^2 - 4365)/2560 + n^5(2004d^4 + 1704d^2 - 54)/2560 + n^4(-1900d^4 - 7056d^2 + 13446)/7680 + n^3(-6948d^4 - 12708d^2 - 6969)/7680 + n^2(-1900d^4 - 3114d^2 - 315)/3840 + n(-108d^4 - 603d^2 + 288)/6720$ |

*(continued)*

**Table 1.** (*continued*)

| Program | Moment | Runtime (*s*) | Computed Moment-Based Invariants |
|---|---|---|---|
| StutteringD – Fig. 1(D) | 1 | 1.92 | $E[s(n)] = 3n^3/8 + 3n^2/8 - n$ |
| | 2 | 46.3 | $E[s^2(n)] = 9n^6/64 + 93n^5/32 + 1651n^4/96 + 2849n^3/72 + 2813n^2/64 + 5131n/288$ |
| | 3 | 2076 | $E[s^3(n)] = 27n^9/512 + 1593n^8/512 + 94587n^7/1792 + 545971n^6/2560 + 270117n^5/1280 - 58585n^4/768 - 132599n^3/512 - 536539n^2/3840 - 771n/140$ |
| StutteringP | 1 | 0.28 | $E[s(n)] = 3np$ |
| | 2 | 1.68 | $E[s^2(n)] = 11n^2p^2 + 3np(-2p+1) + np(-p-1) + 4np(-p+2) - 1$ |
| | 3 | 6.05 | $E[s^3(n)] = 27n_1^3p^3 - 3n_1^2p^3 + 3n_1^2p^2 (-6p+3) + 12n_1^2p^2(-3p+3) + 12n_1^2p^2 (-2p+3) + 3n_1p(4p^2 - 3p + 3) + 3n_1p (8p^2 - 12p + 9) + n_1p(p^2 - 3p(-p-1) - 3p + 2)/2 + 2n_1p(2p^2 - 6p(-p+2) - 6p + 13) + 6$ |
| Square | 1 | 0.38 | $E[y(n)] = n^2 + n$ |
| | 2 | 2.46 | $E[y^2(n)] = n^4 + 6 * n^3 + 3 * n^2 - 2 * n$ |
| | 3 | 8.70 | $E[y^3(n)] = n^6 + 15 * n^5 + 45 * n^4 - 15 * n^3 - 30 * n^2 + 16 * n$ |

## 6 Related Work

Despite the impressive advancements [14,16,21], probabilistic model checking [1] tools [8,20,25] are in general not able to handle programs with unbounded and real variables. Model checking algorithms suffer from the state explosion problem and their performance in terms of time and memory consumption degrades as the number of reachable states to be considered increases. Furthermore, probabilistic model checking tools have no support for invariant generation. Our approach, based on symbolic summation over probabilistic expressions, can instead analyse probabilistic programs with a potentially infinite number of reachable states.

In [27], one of the first deductive frameworks to reason about probabilistic programs was proposed by annotating probabilistic programs with real-valued expressions over the expected values of program variables. Of particular interest are the annotations as *quantitative invariants*, summarising loop behaviors. The setting of [27] considers probabilistic programs where the stochastic inputs are restricted to discrete distributions with finite support and can deal also with demonic non-deterministic choice. Although our approach does not yet support demonic non-determinism, we are not restricted to discrete input distributions as long as we know their moments (e.g., the Gaussian distribution is characterised only by two moments: the mean and the variance). Moreover, our work is not restricted to quantitative invariants as invariants over expected values of program variables. Rather, we generate moment-based invariants that precisely capture invariant properties of higher-order and mixed moments of program variables.

Katoen et al. provided in [19] the first semi-automatic and complete method synthesising the linear quantitative invariants defined in [27]. The work of [19], implemented in PRINSYS [13], consists in annotating a loop with a linear template invariants and uses a constraint solver to find the parameters for which the template yields an invariant. The works [7,9] synthesize non-linear quantitative invariants.

In [3] the authors consider PPs with loops where the assignments in each loop iteration is statistically independent and identically distributed. This restriction is powerful enough to encode Bayesian networks in PPs and to obtain automatically a closed-form expression over the expected values of the program variables. Although the expression in the loop-guard can be more complex than in our setting, our approach can handle also assignments that depend on previous iterations.

The work in [11] proposes the PSI tool, a symbolic analysis system for exact inference in probabilistic programs with both continuous and discrete random variables. PSI can compute succinct symbolic representations of the joint posterior distribution represented by a given PP. However, the tool supports the analysis only of PP with specified number of loop interations, while our approach can handle arbitrary number of loop iterations and also infinite loops.

Another related line of research is given in [2], where martingales are used to compute invariants of probabilistic programs. The martingales generated by [2] however heavily depend on the user-provided hints and hence less generic hints yield less expressive/precise invariants. Moreover, of [2] mainly focuses on invariants over expected values and it remains unclear which extensions of martingales need to be considered to compute higher-order moments. The work of [24] addresses such generalizations of martingales for computing higher-order moments of program variables, with the overall goal of approximating runtimes of randomized programs. The approach in [24] is however again restricted to user-provided templates. Unlike the works of [2,7,9,13,19,24], our work does not rely on a priori given templates/hints, but computes the most precise invariant expression over higher-order or mixed moments of program variables. To do so, we use symbolic summation to compute closed forms of higher-order moments. In addition, Prob-solvable loops support parametrized distributions and symbolic probabilities, which is not the case of [2,24].

There are two orthogonal problems related to quantitative invariants generation: program termination [10,28] and worst-case execution [4,6,18]. The first is to assess whether a probabilistic program terminates with probability 1 or if the expected time of termination is bounded. In principle, one can use our approach to solve this class of problems for Prob-solvable loops, but this is not the focus of this paper. The second class of problems is related to finding bounds over the expected values. In [4] the authors consider bounds also over higher-order moments for a specific class of probabilistic programs with probabilistic affine assignments. This approach can handle also nonlinear terms using interval arithmetic and fresh variables, at the price to produce very conservative bounds. On the contrary our approach supports natively probabilistic polynomial assignments (in the form of Prob-solvable loops) and provides a precise symbolic expression over higher-order moments.

## 7 Conclusion

We introduced a novel approach for automatically generating *moment-based invariants* of a subclass of probabilistic programs (PPs), called Prob-solvable loops, with polynomial assignments over random variables and parametrised distributions. We combine methods from symbolic summation and statistics to derive invariants over higher-order moments, such as expected values or variances, of program variables. To the best of our knowledge, our approach is the first fully automated method computing higher-order moments of PPs with infinite loops and polynomial assignments over random variables and parametrised distributions. Extending our approach to a richer class of PPs, in particular by supporting nested loops and demonic non-determinism, is an interesting line for future work.

**Acknowledgements.** We would like to thank Joost-Pieter Katoen for his constructive feedback on a preliminary version of the manuscript.

## References

1. Baier, C., Katoen, J.P.: Principles of Model Checking. The MIT Press, Cambridge (2008)
2. Barthe, G., Espitau, T., Ferrer Fioriti, L.M., Hsu, J.: Synthesizing probabilistic invariants via Doob's decomposition. In: Chaudhuri, S., Farzan, A. (eds.) CAV 2016. LNCS, vol. 9779, pp. 43–61. Springer, Cham (2016). https://doi.org/10.1007/978-3-319-41528-4_3
3. Batz, K., Kaminski, B.L., Katoen, J.-P., Matheja, C.: How long, O Bayesian network, will I sample thee? In: Ahmed, A. (ed.) ESOP 2018. LNCS, vol. 10801, pp. 186–213. Springer, Cham (2018). https://doi.org/10.1007/978-3-319-89884-1_7
4. Bouissou, O., Goubault, E., Putot, S., Chakarov, A., Sankaranarayanan, S.: Uncertainty propagation using probabilistic affine forms and concentration of measure inequalities. In: Chechik, M., Raskin, J.-F. (eds.) TACAS 2016. LNCS, vol. 9636, pp. 225–243. Springer, Heidelberg (2016). https://doi.org/10.1007/978-3-662-49674-9_13
5. Chakarov, A., Sankaranarayanan, S.: Expectation invariants for probabilistic program loops as fixed points. In: Müller-Olm, M., Seidl, H. (eds.) SAS 2014. LNCS, vol. 8723, pp. 85–100. Springer, Cham (2014). https://doi.org/10.1007/978-3-319-10936-7_6
6. Chatterjee, K., Fu, H., Goharshady, A.K., Goharshady, E.K.: Polynomial invariant generation for non-deterministic recursive programs. In: PLDI (2019, to appear)
7. Chen, Y.-F., Hong, C.-D., Wang, B.-Y., Zhang, L.: Counterexample-guided polynomial loop invariant generation by lagrange interpolation. In: Kroening, D., Păsăreanu, C.S. (eds.) CAV 2015. LNCS, vol. 9206, pp. 658–674. Springer, Cham (2015). https://doi.org/10.1007/978-3-319-21690-4_44

8. Dehnert, C., Junges, S., Katoen, J.-P., Volk, M.: A storm is coming: a modern probabilistic model checker. In: Majumdar, R., Kunčak, V. (eds.) CAV 2017. LNCS, vol. 10427, pp. 592–600. Springer, Cham (2017). https://doi.org/10.1007/978-3-319-63390-9_31
9. Feng, Y., Zhang, L., Jansen, D.N., Zhan, N., Xia, B.: Finding polynomial loop invariants for probabilistic programs. In: D'Souza, D., Narayan Kumar, K. (eds.) ATVA 2017. LNCS, vol. 10482, pp. 400–416. Springer, Cham (2017). https://doi.org/10.1007/978-3-319-68167-2_26
10. Fu, H., Chatterjee, K.: Termination of nondeterministic probabilistic programs. In: Enea, C., Piskac, R. (eds.) VMCAI 2019. LNCS, vol. 11388, pp. 468–490. Springer, Cham (2019). https://doi.org/10.1007/978-3-030-11245-5_22
11. Gehr, T., Misailovic, S., Vechev, M.: PSI: exact symbolic inference for probabilistic programs. In: Chaudhuri, S., Farzan, A. (eds.) CAV 2016. LNCS, vol. 9779, pp. 62–83. Springer, Cham (2016). https://doi.org/10.1007/978-3-319-41528-4_4
12. Ghahramani, Z.: Probabilistic machine learning and artificial intelligence. Nature **521**(7553), 452–459 (2015)
13. Gretz, F., Katoen, J.-P., McIver, A.: Prinsys—on a quest for probabilistic loop invariants. In: Joshi, K., Siegle, M., Stoelinga, M., D'Argenio, P.R. (eds.) QEST 2013. LNCS, vol. 8054, pp. 193–208. Springer, Heidelberg (2013). https://doi.org/10.1007/978-3-642-40196-1_17
14. Hermanns, H., Wachter, B., Zhang, L.: Probabilistic CEGAR. In: Gupta, A., Malik, S. (eds.) CAV 2008. LNCS, vol. 5123, pp. 162–175. Springer, Heidelberg (2008). https://doi.org/10.1007/978-3-540-70545-1_16
15. Humenberger, A., Jaroschek, M., Kovács, L.: Aligator.jl – a Julia package for loop invariant generation. In: Rabe, F., Farmer, W.M., Passmore, G.O., Youssef, A. (eds.) CICM 2018. LNCS (LNAI), vol. 11006, pp. 111–117. Springer, Cham (2018). https://doi.org/10.1007/978-3-319-96812-4_10
16. Jansen, N., Dehnert, C., Kaminski, B.L., Katoen, J.-P., Westhofen, L.: Bounded model checking for probabilistic programs. In: Artho, C., Legay, A., Peled, D. (eds.) ATVA 2016. LNCS, vol. 9938, pp. 68–85. Springer, Cham (2016). https://doi.org/10.1007/978-3-319-46520-3_5
17. Kaminski, B.L., Katoen, J., Matheja, C.: On the hardness of analyzing probabilistic programs. Acta Inf. **56**(3), 255–285 (2019)
18. Karp, R.M.: Probabilistic recurrence relations. J. ACM **41**(6), 1136–1150 (1994)
19. Katoen, J.-P., McIver, A.K., Meinicke, L.A., Morgan, C.C.: Linear-invariant generation for probabilistic programs: automated support for proof-based methods. In: Cousot, R., Martel, M. (eds.) SAS 2010. LNCS, vol. 6337, pp. 390–406. Springer, Heidelberg (2010). https://doi.org/10.1007/978-3-642-15769-1_24
20. Katoen, J.P., Zapreev, I.S., Hahn, E.M., Hermanns, H., Jansen, D.N.: The ins and outs of the probabilistic model checker MRMC. Perform. Eval. **68**(2), 90–104 (2011)
21. Kattenbelt, M., Kwiatkowska, M.Z., Norman, G., Parker, D.: A game-based abstraction-refinement framework for Markov decision processes. Formal Methods Syst. Des. **36**(3), 246–280 (2010)
22. Kauers, M., Paule, P.: The Concrete Tetrahedron - Symbolic Sums, Recurrence Equations, Generating Functions, Asymptotic Estimates. Texts & Monographs in Symbolic Computation. Springer, Heidelberg (2011)
23. Kovács, L.: Reasoning algebraically about P-solvable loops. In: Ramakrishnan, C.R., Rehof, J. (eds.) TACAS 2008. LNCS, vol. 4963, pp. 249–264. Springer, Heidelberg (2008). https://doi.org/10.1007/978-3-540-78800-3_18

24. Kura, S., Urabe, N., Hasuo, I.: Tail probabilities for randomized program runtimes via martingales for higher moments. In: Vojnar, T., Zhang, L. (eds.) TACAS 2019. LNCS, vol. 11428, pp. 135–153. Springer, Cham (2019). https://doi.org/10.1007/978-3-030-17465-1_8
25. Kwiatkowska, M., Norman, G., Parker, D.: PRISM 4.0: verification of probabilistic real-time systems. In: Gopalakrishnan, G., Qadeer, S. (eds.) CAV 2011. LNCS, vol. 6806, pp. 585–591. Springer, Heidelberg (2011). https://doi.org/10.1007/978-3-642-22110-1_47
26. Lin, G.L.: Characterizations of Distributions via Moments. Indian Statistical Institute (1992)
27. McIver, A., Morgan, C.: Abstraction, Refinement and Proof for Probabilistic Systems. Monographs in Computer Science. Springer, Heidelberg (2005)
28. McIver, A., Morgan, C., Kaminski, B.L., Katoen, J.P.: A new proof rule for almost-sure termination. PACMPL **2**(POPL), 33:1–33:28 (2018)
29. Novi Inverardi, P.L., Tagliani, A.: Discrete distributions from moment generating function. Appl. Math. Comput. **182**(1), 200–209 (2006)

# Chain-Free String Constraints

Parosh Aziz Abdulla[1], Mohamed Faouzi Atig[1], Bui Phi Diep[1(✉)], Lukáš Holík[2], and Petr Janků[2]

[1] Uppsala University, Uppsala, Sweden
{parosh,mohamed_faouzi.atig,bui.phi-diep}@it.uu.se
[2] Brno University of Technology, Brno, Czech Republic
{holik,ijanku}@fit.vutbr.cz

**Abstract.** We address the satisfiability problem for string constraints that combine relational constraints represented by transducers, word equations, and string length constraints. This problem is undecidable in general. Therefore, we propose a new decidable fragment of string constraints, called weakly chaining string constraints, for which we show that the satisfiability problem is decidable. This fragment pushes the borders of decidability of string constraints by generalising the existing straight-line as well as the acyclic fragment of the string logic. We have developed a prototype implementation of our new decision procedure, and integrated it into in an existing framework that uses CEGAR with under-approximation of string constraints based on flattening. Our experimental results show the competitiveness and accuracy of the new framework.

**Keywords:** String constraints · Satisfiability modulo theories · Program verification

## 1 Introduction

The recent years have seen many works dedicated to extensions of SMT solvers with new background theories that can lead to efficient analysis of programs with high-level data types. A data type that has attracted a lot of attention is *string* (for instance [2,4,7,9,10,14,16–18,20,33,37,38]). Strings are present in almost all programming and scripting languages. String solvers can be extremely useful in applications such as verification of string-manipulating programs [4] and analysis of security vulnerabilities of scripting languages (e.g., [20,29,30,37]). The wide range of the commonly used primitives for manipulating strings in such languages requires string solvers to handle an expressive class of string logics. The most important features that a string solver have to model are *concatenation* (which is used to express assignments in programs), *transduction* (which can be used to model sanitisation and replacement operations), and *string length* (which is used to constraint lengths of strings).

This work has been supported by the Czech Science Foundation (project No. 19-24397S), the IT4Innovations Excellence in Science (project No. LQ1602), and the FIT BUT internal projects FIT-S-17-4014 and FEKT/FIT-J-19-5906.


Y.-F. Chen et al. (Eds.): ATVA 2019, LNCS 11781, pp. 277–293, 2019.
https://doi.org/10.1007/978-3-030-31784-3_16

It is well known that the satisfiability problem for the full class of string constraints with concatenation, transduction, and length constraints is undecidable in general [10, 23] even for a simple formula of the form $\mathcal{T}(x,x)$ where $\mathcal{T}$ is a rational transducer and $x$ is a string variable. However, this theoretical barrier did not prevent the development of numerous efficient solvers such as Z3-str3 [7], Z3-str2 [38], CVC4 [18], S3P [33, 34], and TRAU [2,3]. These tools implement semi-algorithms to handle a large variety of string constraints, but do not provide completeness guarantees. Another direction of research is to find meaningful and expressive subclasses of string logics for which the satisfiability problem is decidable. Such classes include the acyclic fragment of Norn [5], the solved form fragment [13], and also the straight-line fragment [9,14,20].

In this paper, we propose an approach which is a mixture of the two above research directions, namely finding decidable fragments and making use of it to develop efficient semi-algorithms. To that aim, we define the class of *chain-free* formulas which strictly subsumes the acyclic fragment of Norn [5] as well as the straight-line fragment of [9,14,20], and thus extends the known border of decidability for string constraints. The extension is of a practical relevance. A straight-line constraint models a path through a string program in the single static assignment form, but as soon as the program compares two initialised string variables, the string constraint falls out of the fragment. The acyclic restriction of Norn on the other hand does not include transducer constraints and does not allow multiple occurrences of a variable in a single string constraint (e.g. an equation of the form $xy = zz$). Our chain-free fragment is liberal enough to accommodate constraints that share both these forbidden features (including $xy = zz$).

The following pseudo-PHP code (a variation of a code at [35]) that prompts a user to change his password is an example of a program that generates a chain-free constraint that is neither straight-line nor acyclic according to [4,20].

```
$old=$database->real_escape_string($oldIn);
$new=$database->real_escape_string($newIn);
$pass=$database->query("SELECT password FROM users WHERE userID=".$user);
if($pass == $old)
   if($new != $old)
      $query = "UPDATE users SET password=".$new." WHERE userID=".$user;
      $database->query($query);
```

The user inputs the old password `oldIn` and the new password `newIn`, both are sanitized and assigned to `old` and `new`, respectively. The old sanitized password is compared with the value `pass` from the database, to authenticate the user, and then also with the new sanitized password, to ensure that a different password was chosen, and finally saved in the database. The sanitization is present to prevent SQL injection. To ensure that the sanitization works, we wish to verify that the SQL query `query` is safe, that is, it does not belong to a regular language *Bad* of dangerous inputs. This safety condition is expressed by the constraint

$$\texttt{new} = \mathcal{T}(\texttt{newIn}) \wedge \texttt{old} = \mathcal{T}(\texttt{oldIn}) \wedge \texttt{pass} = \texttt{old} \wedge \texttt{new} \neq \texttt{old} \\ \wedge \texttt{query} = u.\texttt{new}.v.\texttt{user} \wedge \texttt{query} \in \mathit{Bad}$$

The sanitization on lines 1 and 2 is modeled by the transducer $\mathcal{T}$, and $u$ and $v$ are the constant strings from line 7. The constraints fall out from the straight-line due to the test `new` $\neq$ `old`. The main idea behind the chain-free fragment is to associate to the set of relational constraints a *splitting graph* where each node corresponds to an occurrence of a variable in the relational constraints of the formula (as shown in Fig. 1). An edge from an occurrence of $x$ to an occurrence of $y$ means that the source occurrence of $x$ appears in a relational constraint which has in the opposite side an occurrence of $y$ different from the target occurrence of $y$. The chain-free fragment prohibits loops in the graph, that we call *chains*, such as those shown in red in Fig. 1.

Then, we identify the so called *weakly chaining* fragment which strictly extends the chain-free fragment by allowing *benign* chains. Benign chains relate relational constraints where each left side contains only one variable, the constraints are all *length preserving*, and all the nodes of the cycles appear exclusively on the left or exclusively on the right sides of the involved relational constraints (as is the case in Fig. 1). Weakly chaining constraints may in practice arise from the checking that an encoding followed a decoding function is indeed the identity, i.e., satisfiability of constraints of the form $\mathcal{T}_{\text{enc}}(\mathcal{T}_{\text{dec}}(x)) = x$, discussed e.g. in [15]. For instance, in situations similar to the example above, one might like to verify that the sanitization of a password followed by the application of a function supposed to invert the sanitization gives the original password.

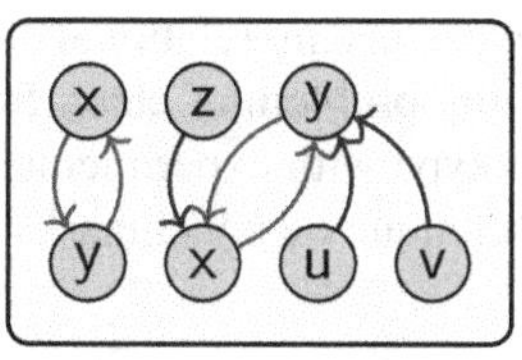


**Fig. 1.** The splitting graph of $x = z \cdot y \wedge y = x \cdot u \cdot v$. (Color figure online)

Our decision procedure for the weakly chaining formulas proceeds in several steps. The formula is transformed to an equisatisfiable chain-free formula, and then to an equisatisfiable concatenation free formula in which the relational constraints are of the form $\mathcal{T}(x, y)$ where $x$ and $y$ are two string variables and $\mathcal{T}$ is a transducer/relational constraint. Finally, we provide a decision procedure of a chain and concatenation-free formulae. The algorithm is based on two techniques. First, we show that the chain-free conjunction over relational constraints can be turned into a single equivalent transducer constraint (in a similar manner as in [6]). Second, consistency of the resulting transducer constraint with the input length constraints is checked via the computation of the Parikh image of the transducer.

To demonstrate the usefulness of our approach, we have implemented our decision procedure in SLOTH [14], and then integrated it in the open-source solver TRAU [2,3]. TRAU is a string solver which is based on a Counter-Example Guided Abstraction Refinement (CEGAR) framework which contains both an under- and an over-approximation module. These two modules interact together in order to automatically make these approximations more precise. We have implemented our decision procedure inside the over-approximation module which takes as an input a constraint and checks if it belongs to the weakly chaining fragment. If it is the case, then we use our decision procedure outlined above. Otherwise, we start by choosing a minimal set of occurrences of variables $x$ that needs to be replaced by fresh ones such that the resulting constraint falls in our decidable fragment. We compare our prototype implementation against four other state-of-the-art string solvers, namely Ostrich [10], Z3-str3 [7], CVC4 [18,19], and TRAU [1]. For our comparison with Z3-str3, we use the version that is part of Z3

4.8.4. Our experimental results show the competitiveness as as well as accuracy of the framework compared to the solver TRAU [2,3]. Furthermore, the experimental results show the competitiveness and generality of our method compared to the existing techniques. In summary, our main contributions are: (1) a new decidable fragment of string constraints, called chain-free, which strictly generalises the existing straight-line as well as the acyclic fragment [4,20] and precisely characterises the decidability limitations of general relational/transducer constraints combined with concatenation, (2) a relaxation of the chain-free fragment, called weakly chaining, which allows special chains with length preserving relational constraints, (3) a decision procedures for checking the satisfiability problem of chain-free as well as weakly chaining string constraints, and (4) a prototype with experimental results that demonstrate the efficiency and generality of our technique on benchmarks from the literature as well as on new benchmarks.

## 2 Preliminaries

*Sets and Strings.* We use $\mathbb{N}$, $\mathbb{Z}$ to denote the sets of natural numbers and integers, respectively. A finite set $\Sigma$ of *letters* is an *alphabet*, a sequence of symbols $a_1 \cdots a_n$ from $\Sigma$ is a *word* or a *string* over $\Sigma$, with its *length n* denoted by $|w|$, $\varepsilon$ is the *empty word* with $|\varepsilon| = 0$, it is a neutral element with respect to string concatenation $\circ$, and $\Sigma^*$ is the set of all words over $\Sigma$ including $\varepsilon$.

*Logic.* Given a predicate formula, an occurrence of a predicate is *positive* if it is under an even number of negations. A formula is in *disjunctive normal form* (DNF) if it is a disjunction of *clauses* that are themselves conjunctions of (negated) predicates. We write $\Psi[x/t]$ to denote the formula obtained by substituting in the formula $\Psi$ each occurrence of the variable $x$ by the term $t$.

*(Multi-tape)-Automata and Transducers.* A *Finite Automaton* (FA) over an alphabet $\Sigma$ is a tuple $\mathcal{A} = \langle Q, \Delta, I, F \rangle$, where $Q$ is a finite set of *states*, $\Delta \subseteq Q \times \Sigma_\varepsilon \times Q$ with $\Sigma_\varepsilon = \Sigma \cup \{\varepsilon\}$ is a set of *transitions*, and $I \subseteq Q$ (resp. $F \subseteq Q$) are the *initial* (resp. *accepting*) states. $\mathcal{A}$ accepts a word $w$ iff there is a sequence $q_0 a_1 q_1 a_2 \cdots a_n q_n$ such that $(q_{i-1}, a_i, q_i) \in \Delta$ for all $1 \le i \le n$, $q_0 \in I$, $q_n \in F$, and $w = a_1 \circ \cdots \circ a_n$. The *language* of $\mathcal{A}$, denoted $\mathcal{L}(\mathcal{A})$, is the set all accepted words.

Given $n \in \mathbb{N}$, a *n-tape automaton* $\mathcal{T}$ is an automaton over the alphabet $(\Sigma_\varepsilon)^n$. It *recognizes* the relation $\mathcal{R}(\mathcal{T}) \subseteq (\Sigma^*)^n$ that contains vectors of words $(w_1, w_2, \ldots, w_n)$ for which there is $(a_{(1,1)}, a_{(2,1)}, \ldots, a_{(n,1)}) \cdots (a_{(1,m)}, a_{(2,m)}, \ldots, a_{(n,m)}) \in \mathcal{L}(\mathcal{T})$ with $w_i = a_{(i,1)} \circ \cdots \circ a_{(i,m)}$ for all $i \in \{1, \ldots, n\}$. A $n$-tape automaton $\mathcal{T}$ is said to be *length-preserving* if its transition relation $\Delta \subseteq Q \times \Sigma^n \times Q$. A *transducer* is a 2-tape automaton.

Let us recall some well-know facts about the class of multi-tape automata. First, the class of $n$-tape automata is closed under union but not under complementation nor intersection. However, the class of *length-preserving* multi-tape automata is closed under intersection. Multi-tape automata are closed under composition. Let $\mathcal{T}$ and $\mathcal{T}'$ be two multi-tape automata of dimension $n$ and $m$, respectively, and let $i \in \{1, \ldots, n\}$ and $j \in \{1, \ldots, m\}$ be two indices. Then, it is possible to construct a $(n+m-1)$-tape automaton $\mathcal{T} \wedge_{(i,j)} \mathcal{T}'$ which accepts the set of words $(w_1, \ldots, w_n, u_1, \ldots, u_{j-1}, u_{j+1}, \ldots, u_m)$ if and only if $(w_1,\ldots,w_n) \in \mathcal{R}(\mathcal{T})$ and $(u_1,\ldots,u_{j-1},w_i,u_{j+1},\ldots,u_m) \in \mathcal{R}(\mathcal{T}')$. Furthermore, we can show that multi-tape automata are closed under permutations: Given a permutation $\sigma : \{1,\ldots,n\} \to \{1,\ldots,n\}$ and a $n$-tape automaton $\mathcal{T}$, it is possible to construct a $n$-tape automaton $\sigma(\mathcal{T})$ such that $\mathcal{R}(\sigma(\mathcal{T})) = \{(w_{\sigma(1)},\ldots,w_{\sigma(n)}) \mid (w_1,w_2,\ldots,w_n) \in \mathcal{R}(\mathcal{T})\}$. Finally, given a $n$-tape automaton $\mathcal{T}$ and a natural number $k \geq n$, we can construct a $k$-tape automaton s. t. $(w_1,\ldots,w_k) \in \mathcal{R}(\mathcal{T}')$ if and only if $(w_1,\ldots,w_n) \in \mathcal{R}(\mathcal{T})$.

## 3 String Constraints

The syntax of a string formula $\Psi$ over an alphabet $\Sigma$ and a set of variables $\mathbb{X}$ is given in Fig. 2. It is a Boolean combination of memberships, relational, and arithmetic constraints over string terms $t_{str}$ (i.e., concatenations of variables in $\mathbb{X}$). *Membership constraints* denote membership in the language of a finite-state automaton $\mathcal{A}$ over $\Sigma$. *Relational constraints* denote either an equality of string terms, which we normally write as $t = t'$ instead of $=(t,t')$, or that the terms are related by a relation recognised by a transducer $\mathcal{T}$. (Observe that the equality relations can be also expressed using length preserving transducers.) Finally, arithmetic terms $t_{ar}$ are linear functions over term lengths and integers, and arithmetic constraints are inequalities of arithmetic terms. String formulae allow using negation with one restriction, namely, constraints that are *not invertible* must have only positive occurrences. General transducers are not invertible, it is not possible to negate them. Regular membership, length preserving relations (including equality), and length constraints are invertible.

$$
\begin{aligned}
\Psi &::= \varphi \mid \Psi \wedge \Psi \mid \Psi \vee \Psi \mid \neg\Psi \\
\varphi &::= \mathcal{A}(t_{str}) \mid R(t_{str}, t_{str}) \mid t_{ar} \geq t_{ar} \\
R &::= \mathcal{T} \mid = \\
t_{str} &::= \varepsilon \mid x \mid t_{str} \circ t_{str} \\
t_{ar} &::= k \mid |t_{str}| \mid t_{ar} + t_{ar}
\end{aligned}
$$

**Fig. 2.** Syntax of string formulae

To simplify presentation, we do not consider *mixed* string terms $t_{str}$ that contain, besides variables of $\mathbb{X}$, also symbols of $\Sigma$. This is without loss of generality because a mixed term can be encoded as a conjunction of the pure term over $\mathbb{X}$ obtained by replacing every occurrence of a letter $a \in \Sigma$ by a fresh variable $x$ and the regular membership constraints $\mathcal{A}_a(x)$ with $\mathcal{L}(\mathcal{A}_a) = \{a\}$. Observe also that membership and equality constraints may be expressed using transducers.

**Semantics.** We describe the semantics of our logic using a mapping $\eta$, called *interpretation*, that assigns to each string variable in $\mathbb{X}$ a word in $\Sigma^*$. Extended to string terms by $\eta(t_{s_1} \circ t_{s_2}) = \eta(t_{s_1}) \circ \eta(t_{s_2})$. Extended to arithmetic terms by $\eta(|t_s|) = |\eta(t_s)|$, $\eta(k) = k$ and $\eta(t_i + t_i') = \eta(t_i) + \eta(t_i')$. Extended to atomic constraints, $\eta$ returns a truth value:

$$
\begin{aligned}
\eta(\mathcal{A}(t_{str})) = \top \quad &\text{iff} \quad \eta(t_{str}) \in \mathcal{L}(\mathcal{A}) \\
\eta(R(t_{str}, t'_{str})) = \top \quad &\text{iff} \quad (\eta(t_{str}), \eta(t'_{str})) \in \mathcal{R}(R) \\
\eta(t_{i_1} \leq t_{i_2}) = \top \quad &\text{iff} \quad \eta(t_{i_1}) \leq \eta(t_{i_2})
\end{aligned}
$$

Given two interpretations $\eta_1$ and $\eta_2$ over two disjoint sets of string variables $\mathbb{X}_1$ and $\mathbb{X}_2$, respectively. We use $\eta_1 \cup \eta_2$ to denote the interpretation over $\mathbb{X}_1 \cup \mathbb{X}_2$ such that $(\eta_1 \cup \eta_2)(x) = \eta_1(x)$ if $x \in \mathbb{X}_1$ and $(\eta_1 \cup \eta_2)(x) = \eta_2(x)$ if $x \in \mathbb{X}_2$.

The truth value of a Boolean combination of formulae under $\eta$ is defined as usual. If $\eta(\Psi) = \top$ then $\eta$ is a *solution* of $\Psi$, written $\eta \models \Psi$. The formula $\Psi$ is *satisfiable* iff it has a solution, otherwise it is *unsatisfiable*.

A relational constraint is said to be *left-sided* if and only if it is on the form $R(x, t_{str})$ where $x \in \mathbb{X}$ is a string variable and $t_{str}$ is a string term. Any string formula can be transformed into a formula where all the relational constraints are left-sided by replacing any relational constraint of the form $R(t_{str}, t'_{str})$ by $R(x, t'_{str}) \wedge x = t$ where $x$ is fresh.

A formula $\Psi$ is said to be *concatenation free* if and only if for every relational constraint $R(t_{str}, t'_{str})$, the string terms $t_{str}$ and $t'_{str}$ appearing in the parameters of any relational constraints in $\Psi$ are variables (i.e., $t_{str}, t'_{str} \in \mathbb{X}$).

## 4 Chain Free and Weakly Chaining Fragment

It is well known that the satisfiability problem for the class of string constraint formulas is undecidable in general [10,23]. This problem is undecidable already for a single transducer constraint of the form $\mathcal{T}(x,x)$ (by a simple reduction from the Post-Correspondence Problem). In the following, we define a subclass called *weakly chaining fragment* for which we prove that the satisfiability problem is decidable.

**Splitting Graph.** Let $\Psi ::= \bigwedge_{j=1}^{m} \varphi_j$ be a conjunction of relational string constraints with $\varphi_j ::= R_j(t_{2j-1}, t_{2j}), 1 \leq j \leq m$ where for each $i : 1 \leq i \leq 2m$, $t_i$ is a concatenation of variables $x_i^1 \circ \cdots \circ x_i^{n_i}$. We define the set of *positions* of $\Psi$ as $P = \{(i,j) \mid 1 \leq j \leq 2m \wedge 1 \leq i \leq n_j\}$. The *splitting graph* of $\Psi$ is then the graph $G_\Psi = (P, E, \mathtt{var}, \mathtt{con})$ where the positions in $P$ are its nodes, and the mapping $\mathtt{var} : P \to \mathbb{X}$ labels each position $(i,j)$ with the variable $x_j^i$ appearing at that position. We say that $(i, 2j-1)$ (resp. $(i, 2j)$) is the $i$th *left* (resp. *right*) positions of the $j$th constraint, and that $R_j$ is the predicate of these positions. Any pair of a left and a right position of the same constraint are called *opposing*. The set of edges $E$ then consists of edges $(p, p')$ between positions for which there is an intermediate position $p''$ (different from $p'$) that is opposing to $p$ and is labeled by the same variable as $p'$ ($\mathtt{var}(p'') = \mathtt{var}(p')$). Finally, the labelling $\mathtt{con}$ of edges assigns to $(p, p')$ the constraint of $p$, that is, $\mathtt{con}(p, p') = R_j$ where $p$ is a position of the $j$th constraint. An example of a splitting graph is on Fig. 1.

**Chains.** A *chain*[1] in the graph is a sequence of the form $(p_0, p_1), (p_1, p_2), \ldots, (p_n, p_0)$ of edges in $E$. A chain is *benign* if (1) all the relational constraints corresponding to the edges $\mathtt{con}(p_0, p_1), \mathtt{con}(p_1, p_2), \ldots, \mathtt{con}(p_n, p_0)$ are left sided and and all the string relations involved in these constraints are length preserving, and (2) the sequence of positions $p_0, p_1, \ldots, p_n$ consists of left positions only, or from right positions only. Observe that if there is a benign chain that uses only right positions then there exists also a benign chain that uses only left positions. The graph is *chain-free* if it has no chains, and it is *weakly chaining* if all its chains are benign. A formula is *chain-free* (resp. *weakly chaining*) if the splitting graph of every clause in its DNF is chain-free (resp. weakly chaining). Benign chains are on Fig. 1 shown in red.

[1] We use chains instead of cycles in order to avoid confusion between our decidable fragment and the ones that exist in literatures.

In the following sections, we will show decision procedures for the chain-free and weakly chaining fragments. Particularly, we will show how a weakly chaining formula can be transformed to a chain-free formula by elimination of benign cycles, how then concatenation can be eliminated from a chain-free formula, and finally how to decide a concatenation free-formula.

**Undecidability of Chaining Formulae.** Before presenting the decision procedures for weakly chaining formulae, we finish the current section by stating that the chain-free fragment is indeed the limit of decidability of general transducer constraints, in the following sense: We say that two conjunctive string formulae have the same *relation-concatenation skeleton* if one can be obtained from the other by removing membership and length constraints and replacing a constraint of the form $R(t,t')$ by another constraint of the form $R'(t,t')$. A *skeleton class* is then an equivalence class of string formulae that have the same relation-concatenation skeleton.

**Lemma 1.** *The satisfiability problem is undecidable for every given* skeleton class.

The proof of the above lemma can be done through a reduction from undecidability of general transducer constraints of the form $\mathcal{T}(x,x)$. Together with decidability of chain-free formulae, discussed in Sects. 6 and 7, the lemma implies that the satisfiability problem for a skeleton class is decidable *if and only if* its splitting graph is chain-free. In other words, chain-freeness is the most precise criterion of decidability of string formulae based on relation-concatenation skeletons (that is, a criterion independent of the particular values of relational, membership, and length constraints).

## 5 Weakly Chaining to Chain-Free

In the following, we show that, given a weakly chaining formula, we can transform it to an equisatisfiable chain-free formula.

**Theorem 1.** *A weakly chaining formula can be transformed to an equisatisfiable chain-free formula.*

The rest of this section is devoted to the proof of Theorem 1 (which also provides an algorithm how to transform any weakly chaining formula into an equisatisfiable chain-free formula). In the following, we assume w.l.o.g. that the given weakly-chaining formula $\Psi$ is conjunctive. The proof is done by induction on the number $\mathbf{B}$ of relational constraints that are labelling the set of benign chains in the splitting graph of $\Psi$.

*Base Case (*$\mathbf{B}=0$*).* Since there is no benign chain in $G_\Psi$, Theorem 1 holds.

*Induction Case (*$\mathbf{B}>0$*).* In the following, we will show how to remove one benign chain (and its set of labelling relational constraints) in the case where the splitting graph of $\Psi$ does not contain nested chains. If nested chains are present, then the proof follows the same main ideas, but the reasoning is generalised from one benign chain to strongly connected components. Let $\rho=(p_0,p_1),(p_1,p_2),\ldots,(p_n,p_0)$ be a benign chain in the splitting graph $G_\Psi$. For every $i \in \{0,\ldots,n\}$, let $R_i(x_i,t_i)$ be the length preserving relational constraint to which the position $p_i$ belongs. We assume w.l.o.g.[2] that all the positions $p_0, p_1, \ldots, p_n$ are left positions. Since $\rho$ is a benign chain, we have that the variable $x_i$ is appearing in the string term $t_{(i+n)mod(n+1)}$ for all $i \in \{0,\ldots,n\}$. Furthermore, we can use the fact that the relational constraints are length preserving to deduce that the variables $x_0, x_1, \ldots, x_n$ have the same length. This implies also that, for every $i \in \{0,1,\ldots,n\}$, the string term $t_i'$ that is constructed by removing from $t_i$ one occurrence of $x_{(i+1)mod(n+1)}$ is equivalent to the empty word. Therefore, the relational constraint $R_i(x_i,t_i)$ can be rewritten as $R_i(x_i, x_{(i+1)mod(n+1)})$ for all $i \in \{0,1,\ldots,n\}$.

Let $x_{i_1}, x_{i_2}, \ldots, x_{i_k}$ be the maximal subsequence of pairwise distinct variables in $x_0, x_1, \ldots, x_n$. Let index be a mapping that associates to each index $\ell \in \{0,\ldots,n\}$ the index $j \in \{1,\ldots,k\}$ such that $x_\ell = x_{i_j}$. We can transform the transducer $R_i$, with $i \in \{0,\ldots,n\}$, to a length preserving $k$-tape automaton $A_i$ such that a word $(w_1, w_2, \ldots, w_k)$ is accepted by $A_i$ if and only if $(w_{\mathtt{index}(i)}, w_{\mathtt{index}((i+1)mod(n+1))})$ is accepted by $R_i$. Let then $A$ be the $k$-tape automaton resulting from the intersection of $A_0, \ldots, A_n$. Observe that $A$ is also length-preserving. Furthermore, we have that $(w_1, w_2, \ldots, w_k)$ is accepted by $A$ if and only if $(w_{\mathtt{index}(i)}, w_{\mathtt{index}((i+1)mod(n+1))})$ is accepted by $R_i$ for all $i \in \{0,\ldots,n\}$ (i.e., the automaton $A$ characterizes all possible solutions of $\bigwedge_{i=0}^n R_i(x_i, x_{(i+1)mod(n+1)})$). Ideally, we would like to replace the $\bigwedge_{i=0}^n R_i(x_i, x_{(i+n)mod(n+1)})$ by $A(x_{i_1}, x_{i_2}, \ldots, x_{i_k})$, however, our syntax forbids such $k$-ary relation. To overcome this problem, we first extend our alphabet $\Sigma$ by all the letters in $\Sigma^k$ and then we replace $\bigwedge_{i=0}^n R_i(x_i, x_{(i+1)mod(n+1)})$ by $\varphi := A(x) \wedge \bigwedge_{j=1}^k \pi_j(x_{i_j}, x)$ where $x$ is a fresh variable and for every $j \in \{1,\ldots,k\}$, $\pi_j$ is the length preserving transducer that accepts all pairs of the form $(w_j, (w_1, w_2, \ldots, w_k))$. Finally, let $\Psi'$ be the formula obtained from $\Psi$ by replacing the subformula $\bigwedge_{i=0}^n R_i(x_i,t_i)$ in $\Psi$ by $\varphi \wedge |t_i'| = 0$ (remember that the string term $t_i'$ is $t_i$ from which we have removed one occurrence of the variable $x_{(i+1)mod(n+1)}$). It is easy to see that $\Psi'$ is satisfiable iff $\Psi$ is also satisfiable. Furthermore, the number of relational constraints that are labelling the set of benign chains in the splitting graph of $\Psi'$ is strictly less than $\mathbf{B}$ (since $\pi_j$ can not be used to label any benign chain in $\Psi'$).

## 6 Chain-Free to Concatenation Free

In the following, we show that we can reduce the satisfiability problem for a chain free formula to the satisfiability problem of a concatenation free formula. To that aim, we describe an algorithm that eliminates concatenation from relational constraints by iterating simple splitting steps. When it terminates, it returns a formula over constraints that are concatenation free. The algorithm can be applied if the string constraints in the formula *allow splitting*, and it is guaranteed to terminate if the formula is *chain-free*. We will explain these two notions below together with the description of the algorithm.

[2] This is possible since if there is benign chain that uses only right positions then there exists also a benign chain that uses only left positions.

**Splitting.** The *split* of a relational constraint $\varphi ::= R(x \circ t, y \circ t')$ with $t, t' \neq \varepsilon$ is the formula $\Phi_L \vee \Phi_R$ where

$$\Phi_L ::= \bigvee_{i=1}^{n} R_i(x_1, y) \wedge R'_i(x_2 \circ t, t') \; [x/x_1 \circ x_2]$$
$$\Phi_R ::= \bigvee_{j=1}^{m} R_j(x, y_1) \wedge R'_j(t, y_2 \circ t') \; [y/y_1 \circ y_2]$$

$m, n \in \mathbb{N}$, $x_1, x_2, y_1, y_2$ are fresh variables, and $\eta \models \varphi$ if and only if there is an assignment $\eta' : \{x_1, x_2, y_1, y_2\} \rightarrow \Sigma^*$ such that $\eta \cup \eta' \models (\Phi_L \wedge x = x_1 \circ x_2) \vee (\Phi_R \wedge y = y_1 \circ y_2)$. The formula $\Phi_L$ is called the *left split* and $\Phi_R$ is called the *right split* of $\varphi$. In case $t' = \varepsilon$, the split is defined in the same way but with $\Phi_L$ left out, and if $t = \varepsilon$, then $\Phi_R$ is left out. If both $t$ and $t'$ equal $\varepsilon$, then $\varphi$ is concatenation free and does not have a split. A simple example is the equation $xy = zz$ with the split $(x_1 = z \wedge x_2 y = z) \vee (x = z_1 \wedge y = z_2 z_1 z_2)$. A class of relational constraints $C$ *allows splitting* if for every constraint in $C$ that is not concatenation free, it is possible to compute a split that belongs to $C$. Equalities as well as transducer constraints allow splitting. A left split of an equality $x \circ t = y \circ t'$ is $x_1 = y \wedge x_2 \circ t = t'$. A left split of a transducer constraint $\mathcal{T}(x \circ t, y \circ t')$ is the formula

$$\bigvee_{q \in Q} \mathcal{T}_q(x_1, y) \wedge {}_q\mathcal{T}(x_2 \circ t, t')$$

where $Q$ is the set of states of $\mathcal{T}$, and ${}_q\mathcal{T}$ and $\mathcal{T}_q$ are the $\mathcal{T}$ with the original set of initial and final states, respectively, replaced by $\{q\}$ (this is the automata splitting technique of [4] extended to transducers in [20]). The right splits are analogous.

**Splitting Algorithm.** A *splitting algorithm* for eliminating concatenation iterates *splitting steps* on a formula in DNF. A *splitting step* can be applied to one of the clauses if it can be written in the form $\Upsilon ::= \varphi \wedge \Psi$ where $\varphi ::= R(x \circ t, y \circ t')$. It then replaces the clause by a DNF of the disjunction

$$(\Phi_L \wedge \Psi[x/x_1 \circ x_2] \wedge |x| = |x_1| + |x_2|) \vee (\Phi_R \wedge \Psi[y/y_1 \circ y_2] \wedge |y| = |y_1| + |y_2|)$$

where $\Phi_L$ and $\Phi_R$ are the left and the right split, respectively, of $\varphi$. The left or the right disjunct is omitted if $t' = \varepsilon$ or $t = \varepsilon$, respectively. The splitting step is not applied when both $t$ and $t'$ equal $\varepsilon$, i.e. $\varphi$ is concatenation free. In order to ensure termination, the algorithm applies splitting steps under the following regimen consisting of two phases.

In Phase 1, the algorithm maintains each clause $\Upsilon$ of a DNF of the string formula annotated with a *reminder*, a sub-graph $H_\Upsilon$ of its splitting graph $G_\Upsilon$. The reminders restrict the choice of splitting steps so that a splitting step can be applied to a clause $\Upsilon = \varphi \wedge \Psi$ only if $\varphi$ is a *root constraint* in $H_\Upsilon$, meaning that all positions at one of the sides of $\varphi$ are root nodes of $H_\Upsilon$. The reminder graphs are assigned to clauses as follows. The algorithm is initialised with $H_\Upsilon ::= G_\Upsilon$ for each clause $\Upsilon$. After taking a splitting step, the reminder graph of each new clause $\Upsilon'$ is a sub-graph $H_{\Upsilon'}$ of its splitting graph $G_{\Upsilon'}$. Particularly, $H_{\Upsilon'}$ contains only those constraints of $\Upsilon'$ (their positions that is) that are non-concatenation-free successors of the constraints of $\Upsilon$ that appear in $H_\Upsilon$. The newly created concatenation free constraints do not propagate to $H_{\Upsilon'}$. Here, by saying that a constraint $\varphi'$ of $\Upsilon'$ is a *successor* of a constraint $\varphi$ of $\Upsilon$ means that either $\varphi' = \varphi[x/x_1 \circ x_2]$ or $\varphi' = \varphi[y/y_1 \circ y_2]$, or that they are the constraints explicitly mentioned in the definition of left or right split. Phase 1 terminates when the reminder graphs of all clauses are empty.

Phase 2 then performs splitting steps in any order until all constraints are concatenation free.

**Theorem 2.** *When run on a chain-free formula, the splitting algorithm terminates with an equisatisfiable chain and concatenation-free formula.*

Hereafter, we provide a brief overview of the proof of Theorem 2. The main difficulty with proving termination of splitting is the substitution of variables involved in the left and right split. The left split makes a step towards concatenation freeness by removing one concatenation operator $\circ$ from the clause, since the terms $x \circ t$ and $y \circ t'$ are replaced by $x_1$, $y$, $t'$, and $x_2 \circ t$. However, the substitution of $x$ by $x_1 \circ x_2$ in the reminder of the clause introduces as many new concatenations as there are occurrences of $x$ other than the one explicit in the definition of the left split (and similarly for the right split). Therefore, to guarantee termination of splitting, we must limit the effect of substitution by enforcing chain-freeness.

Why chain-freeness is the right property here may be intuitively explained as follows. The splitting graph of a clause is in fact a map of how chains of substitutions may increase the number of concatenations in the clause. Consider an edge in the splitting graph from a position $p$ to a position $p'$. By definition, there is an intermediate position $p''$ opposite $p$ and carrying the same variable as $p'$. This means that when splitting decreases the number of concatenations on the side of $p$ by one (the label of $p$ may be $y$ referred to in the left split), the substitution of the label of $p''$ (this would be $x$ in the left split) would cause that the position $p'$ also labeled by $x$ is replaced by the concatenation $x_1 \circ x_2$. Moreover, since the length of the side of $p'$ is now larger, it is possible to perform more splitting steps that follow edges starting at the side of $p'$ and increase numbers of $\circ$ at positions reachable from $p'$ and consequently also further along the path in the splitting graph starting at $(p, p')$. Hence the intuitive meaning of the edge is that decreasing the number of $\circ$ at the side of $p$ might increase the number of $\circ$ at the side of $p'$. Chain-freeness now guarantees that it can happen only finitely many times that decreasing the number of $\circ$ at the side of a position $p$ can through a sequence of splitting steps lead to increasing this number.

## 7 Satisfiability of Chain and Concatenation-Free Formula

In this section, we explain a decision procedure of a chain and concatenation-free formula. The algorithm is essentially a combination of two standard techniques. First, concatenation and chain-free conjunction over relational constraints is a formula in the "acyclic fragment" of [6] that can be turned into a single equivalent transducer constraint (an approach used also in e.g. [14]). Second, consistency of the resulting transducer with the input length constraints may be checked via computation of the Parikh image of the transducer.

We will now describe the two steps in a more detail. For simplicity, we will assume only transducer and length constraints. This is without loss of generality because the other types of constraints can be encoded to transducers.

**Transducer Constraints.** A conjunction of transducer constraints may be decided through computing an equisatisfiable multi-tape transducer constraint and checking emptiness of its language. The transducer constraint is computed by synchronizing pairs of constraints in the conjunction. That is, synchronization of two transducer constraints $\mathcal{T}_1(x_1,\ldots,x_n)$ and $\mathcal{T}_2(y_1,\ldots,y_m)$ is possible if they share at most one variable (essentially the standard automata product construction where the two transducers synchronise on the common variable). The result of their synchronization is then a constraint $\mathcal{T}_1 \wedge_{(i,j)} \mathcal{T}_2(x_1,\ldots,x_n,y_1\ldots y_{j-1},y_{j+1},\ldots,y_m)$ where $y_j$ is the common variable equal to $x_i$ for some $1 \leq i \leq n$ or a constraint $\mathcal{T}_1 \wedge \mathcal{T}_2(x_1,\ldots,x_n,y_1,\ldots,y_m)$ if there is no common variable. The $\mathcal{T}_1 \wedge \mathcal{T}_2$ is a lose version of $\wedge_{(i,j)}$ that does not synchronise the two transition relations (see e.g. [14,20] for details on implementation of a similar construction). Since the original constraint is chain and concatenation-free, two constraints may share at most one variable. This property is an invariant under synchronization steps, hence they may be preformed in any order until only single constraint remains. Termination of this procedure is immediate because every step decreases the number of constraints.

**Length Constraints.** A formula of the form $\Psi_r \wedge \Psi_l$ where $\Psi_r$ is a conjunction of relational constraints and $\Psi_l$ is a conjunction of length constraints may be decided through replacing $\Psi_r$ by a Presburger formula $\Psi_r'$ over length constraints that captures the length constraints implied by $\Psi_r$. That is, an assignment $\nu : \{|x| \mid x \in \mathbb{X}\} \to \mathbb{N}$ is a solution of $\Psi_r'$ if and only if there is a solution $\eta$ of $\Psi_r$ such that $|\eta(x)| = \nu(|x|)$ for all $x \in \mathbb{X}$. The conjunction $\Psi_r' \wedge \Psi_l$ is then an existential Presburger formula equisatisfiable to the original conjunction, solvable by an of-the-shelf SMT solver.

Construction of $\Psi_r'$ is based on computation of the Parikh image of the synchronised constraint $\mathcal{T}(x_1,\ldots,x_n)$ equivalent to $\Psi_r$. Since $\mathcal{T}$ is a standard finite automaton over the alphabet of $n$-tuples $\Sigma_\varepsilon^n$, its Parikh image can be computed in the form of a semi-linear set represented as an existential Presburger formula $\Psi_{\text{Parikh}}$ by a standard automata construction (see e.g. [32]). The formula captures the relationship between the numbers of occurrences of letters of $\Sigma_\varepsilon^n$ in words of $\mathcal{L}(\mathcal{T})$. Particularly, the numbers of letter occurrences are represented by the *Parikh variables* $\mathbb{P} = \{\#\alpha \mid \alpha \in \Sigma_\varepsilon^n\}$ and it holds that The formula$\nu \models \Psi_{\text{Parikh}}$ iff there is a word $w \in \mathcal{L}(\mathcal{T})$ such that for all $\alpha \in \Sigma_\varepsilon^n$, $\alpha$ appears $\nu(\#\alpha)$ times in $w$.

The formula $\Psi_r'$ is then extracted from $\Psi_{\text{Parikh}}$ as follows. Let $\mathbb{A} = \{\#a_i \mid a \in \Sigma, 1 \leq i \leq n\}$ be a set of *auxiliary variables* expressing how many times the letter $a \in \Sigma$ appears on the $i$th position of a symbol from $\Sigma_\varepsilon^n$ in a word from $\mathcal{L}(\mathcal{T})$. Let $\alpha[i]$ denotes the $i$th component of the tuple $\alpha \in \Sigma_\varepsilon^n$. We construct the formula $\Phi$ that uses variables $\mathbb{A}$ to describe the relation between values of $|x_1|,\ldots,|x_n|$ and variables of $\mathbb{P}$:

$$\Phi := \bigwedge\nolimits_{i=1}^{n} \left(|x_i| = \sum\nolimits_{a\in\Sigma} \#a_i \wedge \bigwedge\nolimits_{a\in\Sigma} \left(\#a_i = \sum\nolimits_{\alpha\in\Sigma_\varepsilon^n \text{ s.t. } \alpha[i]=a} \#\alpha\right)\right)$$

We the obtain $\Psi_r'$ by eliminating the quantifiers from $\exists\mathbb{P}\exists\mathbb{A} : \Phi \wedge \Psi_{\text{Parikh}}$.

## 8 Experimental Results

We have implemented our decision procedure in SLOTH [14] and then used it in the over-approximation module of the string solver TRAU+, which is an extension of TRAU[3]. TRAU+ is as an open source string solver and used Z3 [11] as the SMT solver to handle generated arithmetic constraints. TRAU+ is based on a Counter-Example

**Table 1.** Results of running solvers over Chain-Free, two sets of the SLOG, and four sets of PyEx suite.

| | | Ostrich | Z3-str3 | CVC4 | TRAU | TRAU+ |
|---|---|---|---|---|---|---|
| **Chain-Free** (26) | sat | 0 | - | - | - | **5** |
| | unsat | 0 | - | - | - | **14** |
| | timeout | 6 | - | - | - | 7 |
| | error/unknown | 20 | - | - | - | 0 |
| **ReplaceAll** (120) | sat | **106** | - | - | 26 | 105 |
| | unsat | **14** | - | - | 4 | **14** |
| | timeout | 0 | - | - | 0 | 1 |
| | error/unknown | 0 | - | - | 90 | 0 |
| **Replace** (3392) | sat | 1250 | 298 | 1278 | 1174 | **1287** |
| | unsat | 2022 | 2075 | 2079 | 2080 | **2081** |
| | timeout | 3 | 903 | 9 | 24 | 23 |
| | error/unknown | 117 | 116 | 26 | 114 | 1 |
| **PyEx-td** (5569) | sat | 36 | 839 | 4178 | 4244 | **4245** |
| | unsat | 299 | 1477 | 1281 | 1287 | **1287** |
| | timeout | 0 | 3027 | 105 | 35 | 35 |
| | error/unknown | 5234 | 226 | 5 | 3 | 2 |
| **PyEx-z3** (8414) | sat | 35 | 1211 | 5617 | 6680 | **6681** |
| | unsat | 466 | **1870** | 1346 | 1357 | 1357 |
| | timeout | 0 | 4760 | 1449 | 374 | 374 |
| | error/unknown | 7913 | 573 | 2 | 3 | 2 |
| **PyEx-zz** (11438) | sat | 38 | 2840 | **9817** | 8966 | 8967 |
| | unsat | 141 | 1974 | **1202** | 1192 | 1193 |
| | timeout | 0 | 5988 | 416 | 1277 | 1276 |
| | error/unknown | 11259 | 636 | 3 | 3 | 2 |
| **Total** (28959) | solved | 4407 | 12730 | 26798 | 27010 | **27236** |
| | unsolved | 24552 | 16229 | 2161 | 1949 | **1723** |

Guided Abstraction Refinement (CEGAR) framework which contains both an under- and an over-approximation module. These two modules interact together in order to automatically make these approximations more precise. The extension of SLOTH in the over-approximation module of TRAU+ takes as an input a constraint and checks if it belongs to the weakly-chaining fragment. If it is the case, then we use our decision procedure outlined above. Otherwise, we start by choosing a minimal set of occurrences of variables $x$ that needs to be replaced by fresh ones such that the resulting constraint falls in our decidable fragment.

We compare TRAU+ performance against the performance of four other state-of-the-art string solvers, namely Ostrich [10], Z3-str3 [7], CVC4 1.6 [18,19], and TRAU [1]. For our comparison with Z3-str3, we use the version that is part of Z3 4.8.4. The goal of our experiments is twofold:

- TRAU+ handles transducer constraints in an efficient manner TRAU+ can handle more cases than TRAUsince the new over-approximation of TRAU+ supports more and new transducer constraints that the one of TRAU.
- TRAU+ performs either better or as well as existing tools on transducer-less benchmarks.

We carry experiments on suites that draw from the real world applications with diverse characteristics. The first suite is our new suite Chain-Free. Chain-Free is obtained from variations of various PHP code, including the introductory example. The second suite is SLOG [36] that is derived from the security analysis of real web applications. The suite was generated by Ostrich group. The last suite is PyEx [27] that is derived from PyEx - a symbolic executor designed to assist Python developers to achieve high coverage testing. The suite was generated by CVC4 group on 4 popular Python packages: `httplib2`, `pip`, `pymongo`, and `requests`. The summary of experimenting Chain-Free, SLOG, and PyEx is given in Table 1. All experiments were performed on an Intel Core i7 2.7 Ghz with 16 GB of RAM. The time limit is 30s for each test which is widely used in the evaluation of other string solvers. Additionally, we use 2700 s for Chain-Free suite - much larger than usual as its constraints are difficult. Rows with heading "sat"("unsat") indicate the number of times the solver returned satisfiable (unsatisfiable). Rows with heading "timeout" indicate the number of times the solver exceeded the time limit. Rows with heading "error/unknown" indicate the number of times the solver either crashed or returned unknown.

Chain-Free suite consists of 26 challenging chain-free tests, 6 of them being also straight-line. The tests contain Concatenation, ReplaceAll, and general transducers constraints encoding various JavaScript and PHP functions such as htmlescape, escapeString. Since Z3-str3, CVC4, and TRAU do not support the language of general transducers, we skip performing experiments on those tools in the suite. Ostrich returns 6 times "timeout" for straight-line tests, and times 20 "unknown" for the rest. TRAU+ handles well most cases, and gets "timeout" for only 7 tests.

SLOG suite consists of 3512 tests which contain transducer constraints such as Replace and ReplaceAll. Since Z3-str3 and CVC4 do not support the ReplaceAll function, we skip doing experiments on those tools in the ReplaceAll set. In both sets, the result shows that TRAU+ clearly improved TRAU. In particular, TRAU+ can handle most cases where TRAU returns either "unknown" and "timeout". TRAU+ has also better performance than other solvers.

PyEx suite consists of 25421 tests which contain diverse string constraints such as IndexOf, CharAt, SubString, Concatenation. TRAU and CVC4 have similar performance on the suite. While TRAU is better on PyEx-dt and PyEx-z3 sets (3 less error/unknown results, roughly 1000 less timeouts), CVC4 is better on PyEx-zz set (about 800 less timeouts). CVC4 and TRAU clearly have an edge over Z3-str3 in all aspects. Comparing with Ostrich on this benchmark is problematic because it mostly fails due to unsupported syntactic features. TRAU+ is better than TRAU on all three benchmark sets. This shows that our proposed procedure is efficient in solving not only transducer examples, but also in transducer-less examples.

To summarise our experimental results, we can see that:

- TRAU+ handles more transducer examples in an efficient manner. This is illustrated by the Chain-Free and Slog suites. The experiment results on these benchmarks show that TRAU+ outperforms TRAU. Many tests on which TRAU returns "unknown" are now successfully handled by TRAU+ .
- TRAU+ performs as well as existing tools on transducer-less benchmarks and in fact sometimes TRAU+ outperforms them. This is illustrated by the PyEx suite. In fact, this benchmark is handled very well by TRAU, but nevertheless, as evident from the table, our tool is doing better than TRAU. In fact, As TRAU+ out-performs TRAU in some examples in the PyEx suite. In those examples, TRAU returned "unknown' while TRAU+ returned "unsat". This means that the new over-approximation not only improves TRAU in transducer benchmarks, but it also improves TRAU in transducer-less examples. Furthermore, observe that the PyEx suite has only around 4000 "unsat" cases out of 25k cases.

## 9 Related Work

Already in 1946, Quine [26] showed that the first order theory of string equations is undecidable. An important line of work has been to identify subclasses for which decidability can be achieved. The pioneering work by Makanin [21] proposed a decision procedure for quantifier-free word equations, i.e., Boolean combinations of equalities and disequalities, where the variables may denote words of arbitrary lengths. The decidability and complexity of different subclasses have been considered by several works, e.g. [12,13,22,24,25,28,31]. Generalizations of the work of Makanin by adding new types of constraints have been difficult to achieve. For instance, the satisfiability of word equations combined with length constraints of the form $|x| = |y|$ is open [8]. Recently, regular and especially relational transducers constraints were identified as a strongly desirable feature of string languages especially in the context software analysis with an emphasis on security. Adding these to the mix leads immediately to undecidability [23] and hence numerous decidable fragments were proposed [4,6,9,10,20]. From these, the straight line fragment of [20] is the most general decidable combination of concatenation and transducers. It is however incomparable to the acyclic fragment of [4] (which does not have transducers but could be extended with them in a straightforward manner). Some works add also other syntactic features, such as [9,10], but the limit of decidable combinations of the core string features—transducers/regular constraints, length constraints, and concatenation stays at [20] and [4]. The weakly chaining decidable fragment present in this paper significantly generalises both these fragments in a practically relevant direction.

The strong practical motivation in string solving led to a rise of a number of SMT solvers that do not always provide completeness guarantees but concentrate on solving practical problem instances, through applying a variety of calculi and algorithms. A number of tools handle string constraints by means of *length-based under-approximation* and translation to bit-vectors [17,29,30], assuming a fixed upper bound on the length of the possible solutions. Our method on the other hand allows to analyse constraints without a length limit and with completeness guarantees. More recently, also *DPLL(T)-based* string solvers lift the restriction of strings of bounded length; this generation of solvers includes Z3-str3 [7], Z3-str2 [38], CVC4 [18], S3P [33,34], Norn [5], Trau [3], Sloth [14], and Ostrich [10]. DPLL(T)-based solvers handle a variety of string constraints, including word equations, regular expression membership, length constraints, and (more rarely) regular/rational relations; the solvers are not complete for the full combination of those constraints though, and often only decide a (more or less well-defined) fragment of the individual constraints. Equality constraints are normally handled by means of splitting into simpler sub-cases, in combination with powerful techniques for Boolean reasoning to curb the resulting exponential search space. Our implementation is combining strong completeness guarantees of [14] extended to handle the fragment proposed in this paper with an efficient approximation techniques of [3] and its performance on existing benchmarks compares favourably with the most efficient of the above tools.

A further direction is *automata-based* solvers for analyzing string-manipulated programs. Stranger [37] soundly over-approximates string constraints using regular languages, and outperforms DPLL(T)-based solvers when checking single execution traces, according to some evaluations [16]. It has recently also been observed [14,36] that automata-based algorithms can be combined with model checking algorithms, in particular IC3/PDR, for more efficient checking of the emptiness for automata. However, many kinds of constraints, including length constraints and word equations, cannot be handled by automata-based solvers in a complete manner.

## References


1. Abdulla, P.A., et al.: Trau String Solver. https://github.com/diepbp/FAT
2. Abdulla, P.A., et al.: Flatten and conquer: a framework for efficient analysis of string constraints. In: PLDI. ACM (2017)
3. Abdulla, P.A., et al.: Trau: SMT solver for string constraints. In: FMCAD. IEEE (2018)
4. Abdulla, P.A., et al.: String constraints for verification. In: Biere, A., Bloem, R. (eds.) CAV 2014. LNCS, vol. 8559, pp. 150–166. Springer, Cham (2014). https://doi.org/10.1007/978-3-319-08867-9_10
5. Abdulla, P.A., et al.: Norn: an SMT solver for string constraints. In: Kroening, D., Păsăreanu, C.S. (eds.) CAV 2015. LNCS, vol. 9206, pp. 462–469. Springer, Cham (2015). https://doi.org/10.1007/978-3-319-21690-4_29
6. Barceló, P., Figueira, D., Libkin, L.: Graph logics with rational relations. Logical Methods Comput. Sci. **9**(3) (2013). https://doi.org/10.2168/LMCS-9(3:1)2013
7. Berzish, M., Zheng, Y., Ganesh, V.: Z3str3: a string solver with theory-aware branching. CoRR abs/1704.07935 (2017)
8. Büchi, J.R., Senger, S.: Definability in the existential theory of concatenation and undecidable extensions of this theory. Z. Math. Logik Grundlagen Math. **34**(4) (1988)
9. Chen, T., Chen, Y., Hague, M., Lin, A.W., Wu, Z.: What is decidable about string constraints with the replace all function. Proc. ACM Program. Lang. **2**(POPL) (2018). https://doi.org/10.1145/3158091
10. Chen, T., Hague, M., Lin, A.W., Rümmer, P., Wu, Z.: Decision procedures for path feasibility of string-manipulating programs with complex operations. Proc. ACM Program. Lang. **3**(POPL) (2019). https://doi.org/10.1145/3290362

11. de Moura, L., Bjørner, N.: Z3: an efficient SMT solver. In: Ramakrishnan, C.R., Rehof, J. (eds.) TACAS 2008. LNCS, vol. 4963, pp. 337–340. Springer, Heidelberg (2008). https://doi.org/10.1007/978-3-540-78800-3_24
12. Ganesh, V., Berzish, M.: Undecidability of a theory of strings, linear arithmetic over length, and string-number conversion. CoRR abs/1605.09442 (2016)
13. Ganesh, V., Minnes, M., Solar-Lezama, A., Rinard, M.: Word equations with length constraints: what's decidable? In: Biere, A., Nahir, A., Vos, T. (eds.) HVC 2012. LNCS, vol. 7857, pp. 209–226. Springer, Heidelberg (2013). https://doi.org/10.1007/978-3-642-39611-3_21
14. Holík, L., Janku, P., Lin, A.W., Rümmer, P., Vojnar, T.: String constraints with concatenation and transducers solved efficiently. PACMPL **2**(POPL) (2018). https://doi.org/10.1145/3158092
15. Hu, Q., D'Antoni, L.: Automatic program inversion using symbolic transducers. In: SIGPLAN Notices, vol. 52, no. 6, June 2017
16. Kausler, S., Sherman, E.: Evaluation of string constraint solvers in the context of symbolic execution. In: ASE 2014. ACM (2014)
17. Kiezun, A., Ganesh, V., Guo, P.J., Hooimeijer, P., Ernst, M.D.: HAMPI: a solver for string constraints. In: ISTA 2009. ACM (2009)
18. Liang, T., Reynolds, A., Tinelli, C., Barrett, C., Deters, M.: A DPLL($T$) theory solver for a theory of strings and regular expressions. In: Biere, A., Bloem, R. (eds.) CAV 2014. LNCS, vol. 8559, pp. 646–662. Springer, Cham (2014). https://doi.org/10.1007/978-3-319-08867-9_43
19. Liang, T., Reynolds, A., Tinelli, C., Barrett, C., Deters, M.: CVC4 (2016). http://cvc4.cs.nyu.edu/papers/CAV2014-strings/
20. Lin, A.W., Barceló, P.: String solving with word equations and transducers: towards a logic for analysing mutation XSS. In: POPL 2016. ACM (2016)
21. Makanin, G.: The problem of solvability of equations in a free semigroup. Math. USSR-Sbornik **32**(2) (1977)
22. Matiyasevich, Y.: Computation paradigms in light of Hilbert's tenth problem. In: Cooper, S.B., Löwe, B., Sorbi, A. (eds.) New Computational Paradigms, pp. 59–85. Springer, New York (2008). https://doi.org/10.1007/978-0-387-68546-5_4
23. Morvan, C.: On rational graphs. In: Tiuryn, J. (ed.) FoSSaCS 2000. LNCS, vol. 1784, pp. 252–266. Springer, Heidelberg (2000). https://doi.org/10.1007/3-540-46432-8_17
24. Plandowski, W.: Satisfiability of word equations with constants is in PSPACE. J. ACM **51**(3) (2004)
25. Plandowski, W.: An efficient algorithm for solving word equations. In: STOC 2006. ACM (2006)
26. Quine, W.V.: Concatenation as a basis for arithmetic. J. Symb. Log. **11**(4) (1946)
27. Reynolds, A., Woo, M., Barrett, C., Brumley, D., Liang, T., Tinelli, C.: Scaling up DPLL(T) string solvers using context-dependent simplification. In: Majumdar, R., Kunčak, V. (eds.) CAV 2017. LNCS, vol. 10427, pp. 453–474. Springer, Cham (2017). https://doi.org/10.1007/978-3-319-63390-9_24
28. Robson, J.M., Diekert, V.: On quadratic word equations. In: Meinel, C., Tison, S. (eds.) STACS 1999. LNCS, vol. 1563, pp. 217–226. Springer, Heidelberg (1999). https://doi.org/10.1007/3-540-49116-3_20
29. Saxena, P., Akhawe, D., Hanna, S., Mao, F., McCamant, S., Song, D.: A symbolic execution framework for JavaScript. In: IEEE Symposium on Security and Privacy. IEEE (2010)
30. Saxena, P., Hanna, S., Poosankam, P., Song, D.: FLAX: systematic discovery of client-side validation vulnerabilities in rich web applications. In: NDSS. The Internet Society (2010)

31. Schulz, K.U.: Makanin's algorithm for word equations-two improvements and a generalization. In: Schulz, K.U. (ed.) IWWERT 1990. LNCS, vol. 572, pp. 85–150. Springer, Heidelberg (1992). https://doi.org/10.1007/3-540-55124-7_4
32. Seidl, H., Schwentick, T., Muscholl, A., Habermehl, P.: Counting in trees for free. In: Díaz, J., Karhumäki, J., Lepistö, A., Sannella, D. (eds.) ICALP 2004. LNCS, vol. 3142, pp. 1136–1149. Springer, Heidelberg (2004). https://doi.org/10.1007/978-3-540-27836-8_94
33. Trinh, M.T., Chu, D.H., Jaffar, J.: S3: a symbolic string solver for vulnerability detection in web applications. In: CCS 2014. ACM (2014)
34. Trinh, M.-T., Chu, D.-H., Jaffar, J.: Progressive reasoning over recursively-defined strings. In: Chaudhuri, S., Farzan, A. (eds.) CAV 2016. LNCS, vol. 9779, pp. 218–240. Springer, Cham (2016). https://doi.org/10.1007/978-3-319-41528-4_12
35. TwistIt.tech: PHP tutorials (2019). https://www.makephpsites.com/php-tutorials/user-management-tools/changing-passwords.php. Accessed 29 Apr 2019
36. Wang, H.-E., Tsai, T.-L., Lin, C.-H., Yu, F., Jiang, J.-H.R.: String analysis via automata manipulation with logic circuit representation. In: Chaudhuri, S., Farzan, A. (eds.) CAV 2016. LNCS, vol. 9779, pp. 241–260. Springer, Cham (2016). https://doi.org/10.1007/978-3-319-41528-4_13
37. Yu, F., Alkhalaf, M., Bultan, T.: Stranger: an automata-based string analysis tool for PHP. In: Esparza, J., Majumdar, R. (eds.) TACAS 2010. LNCS, vol. 6015, pp. 154–157. Springer, Heidelberg (2010). https://doi.org/10.1007/978-3-642-12002-2_13
38. Zheng, Y., Zhang, X., Ganesh, V.: Z3-str: a Z3-based string solver for web application analysis. In: ESEC/FSE 2013. ACM (2013)

# Synthesizing Efficient Low-Precision Kernels

Anastasia Izycheva[1(✉)], Eva Darulova[2], and Helmut Seidl[1]

[1] Fakultät für Informatik, TU München, Münich, Germany
{izycheva,seidl}@in.tum.de
[2] MPI-SWS, Saarland Informatics Campus, Saarbrücken, Germany
eva@mpi-sws.org

**Abstract.** In this paper, we present a *fully automated* approach for synthesizing fast numerical kernels with *guaranteed* error bounds. The kernels we target contain elementary functions such as sine and logarithm, which are widely used in scientific computing, embedded as well as machine-learning programs. However, standard library implementations of these functions are often overly accurate and therefore unnecessarily expensive. Our approach trades superfluous accuracy against performance by approximating elementary function calls by polynomials and by implementing arithmetic operations in low-precision fixed-point arithmetic. Our algorithm soundly distributes and guarantees an overall error budget specified by the user. The evaluation on benchmarks from different domains shows significant performance improvements of 2.23× on average compared to state-of-the-art implementations of such kernel functions.

**Keywords:** Synthesis · Approximation · Finite precision · Elementary functions

## 1 Introduction

Automated program synthesis promises to simplify and speed up common programming tasks: the programmer only needs to write a specification of what should be computed and a synthesis tool automatically generates an implementation, whose correctness is guaranteed by construction. Today's techniques generate programs over algebraic data structures [24], APIs [19], string manipulation [22], probabilistic programs [39], linear arithmetic computations [25], etc.

Many of these synthesis techniques explicitly or implicitly generate programs optimized for a particular metric. For instance, enumerative techniques often choose the program of smallest size which satisfies the specification [3], or use an explicit static cost model to prune inefficient programs [32].

An additional way to improve the efficiency of a program is to introduce approximations. We can leverage the fact that many applications are tolerant


Y.-F. Chen et al. (Eds.): ATVA 2019, LNCS 11781, pp. 294–313, 2019.
https://doi.org/10.1007/978-3-030-31784-3_17

to a certain amount of error or noise and thus need not compute their results exactly, but only as accurately as necessary [46]. Approximations introduce a tradeoff between accuracy and efficiency, which is in general challenging to navigate. In order to determine whether a particular approximation is suitable, we need to be able to verify the overall program accuracy. Furthermore, the space of possible approximations is in general prohibitively large, making manual program optimizations tedious, error prone, and inefficient.

Most of today's synthesis techniques consider only exact specifications, and are thus unsuitable to generate programs which are only correct up to some error bound [3,19,22,24,25,32,39]. Furthermore, most techniques do not explicitly optimize for efficiency of the generated program. A few approaches exist which do generate approximate programs, but which check correctness via testing on a few sample inputs and thus cannot provide accuracy guarantees [18,42].

We propose a fully automated synthesis approach for the domain of numerical kernels, which approximates both arithmetic operations as well as elementary functions, and which provides sound end-to-end accuracy guarantees. The user specifies an ideal, real-valued program together with a maximum error bound. Our technique generates an efficient finite-precision implementation with polynomial approximations of elementary functions.

The numerical kernels we handle cover widely used applications in various domains: for instance, embedded control to compute rotations of robotic components, scientific computing simulations to determine the state of a periodic event, and machine learning models with sigmoid activation functions. By default, programmers today implement the elementary functions in these kernels using library implementations. While these are convenient and optimized, they usually provide only a limited set of accuracies, e.g. single and double floating-point precision, severely limiting optimization opportunities.

We furthermore target fixed-point arithmetic implementations, which allow arbitrary bit-widths for individual operations and thus provide high flexibility in the accuracy-efficiency tradeoff space when executed on accelerators such as FPGAs. Compared to an implementation in floating-point arithmetic, this choice, however, increases the search space significantly and thus makes code synthesis more challenging.

In this paper, we present our synthesis algorithm, which distributes the overall error budget provided by the user among different operations in the kernel, and soundly takes care of the error propagation as well as finite-precision roundoff errors. To generate approximations, our algorithm extends and combines an existing polynomial approximation technique [27] and roundoff error analysis [14].

We implemented our algorithm and evaluate it on several embedded, scientific computing and machine learning kernels. Compared to implementations using default library functions, our synthesized programs on average need 2.23$\times$ less machine cycles to execute.

*Contributions.* To summarize, this paper presents: (a) the first sound and automated synthesis algorithm for efficient numerical kernels with both arithmetic and elementary function approximations, (b) an experimental evaluation using existing and several new benchmarks, (c) a prototype implementation of the synthesis algorithm, which we release as open-source: https://github.com/malyzajko/daisy/tree/approx.

## 2 Background

**Fixed-Point Arithmetic.** Floating-point arithmetic [23] is a common and convenient choice to implement an approximation of real numbers on today's discrete computers. However, floating-point units usually support only a limited set of precisions (e.g. 16, 32, and 64 bit), and the exponent always occupies a fixed number of bits. For applications which operate over limited ranges, many of these bits remain unused, effectively wasting resources such as energy or time.

Fixed-point arithmetic allows a programmer to implement a computation in purely integer arithmetic (i.e. without special hardware) and with exactly as many bits for the exponent and precision as are actually needed. On an accelerator such as an FPGA, fixed-point arithmetic thus provides a resource-efficient implementation.

To compile a fixed-point arithmetic program (e.g. with a high-level synthesis tool such as Xilinx' Vivado [45]), the programmer has to select suitable fixed-point *formats* for a program's inputs and operations. A fixed-point format specifies at least the total wordlength $W$ and the number of integer bits $I$. The latter have to be chosen such that no overflow can occur. The remaining $F = W - I$ bits are used to represent the fractional part of a number and determine the accuracy of the computation. A larger $F$ makes the computation more accurate, but also more costly. Choosing a suitable tradeoff is challenging to do manually (a) due to the large number of format options—we can choose different and arbitrary wordlengths for individual operations—and (b) due to the need to verify the overall accuracy of the computation.

As part of the fixed-point format, usually one can also choose the rounding mode and the overflow behaviour. In this work, we consider the default truncation as the rounding mode. We also leave the overflow mode to default (wrap around), but note that our analysis guarantees that no overflow can occur.

*Elementary Functions.* For both floating-point and fixed-point arithmetic, elementary functions are supported via library functions. Here, we focus on the implementation and specification provided and used by Xilinx Vivado, which we use in our experiments and which is widely used in industry. We note, however, that our approach is not tied to a particular choice of fixed-point compiler.

Xilinx Vivado supports 32 bit fixed-point implementations for sine and cosine, and 8 or 16 bit versions of the exponential function. The compiler further supports automated conversion to floating-point arithmetic, such that floating-point implementations of elementary function calls can be used within fixed-point arithmetic programs. These are provided for precisions 16, 32, and 64 bit. Thus, while some support for elementary functions is provided, it is only available for a small variety of precisions, effectively limiting optimization options.

**Fixed-Point Roundoff Error Analysis and Precision Assignment.** Current static analysis tools [11,14,15,17,21] provide automated dataflow analyses which compute finite-precision roundoff errors w.r.t. to a real-valued semantics using the interval [35] and affine [20] arithmetic abstract domains. These analyses are applicable to both floating-point as well as fixed-point arithmetic, whereas other tools use a different, global optimization-based approach and only support floating-point arithmetic [33,36,44]. Several of these tools can analyze programs with elementary function calls, but always assume library implementations. Reasoning about loops and conditionals is always reduced to reasoning about straight-line code, e.g. through loop unrolling [11], special loop invariants [15,21,36], or path-by-path analysis of conditionals [15,36]. In this work we thus focus on the core issue and consider straight-line programs only.

Because of the nature of fixed-point arithmetic, the error specification is fundamentally absolute: the fixed-point format for each operation is fixed at compile time, thus the worst-case error is the same no matter what the magnitude of the value actually is at runtime. In this work we thus consider absolute errors.

Several tools perform mixed-precision tuning [9,10,16], which assigns different precisions to individual operations. Due to the large number of possible precision assignments, the search for such an assignment is necessarily incomplete. These approaches only consider arithmetic operations, i.e. no elementary functions, and only Daisy [16] supports fixed-point arithmetic.

**Polynomial Approximation in Metalibm.** Polynomials are a common choice for approximating complex functions. The approximation accuracy largely depends on the degree of the polynomial, larger degrees incurring a higher execution cost. Given an elementary function, an input domain and a target error which the approximation has to satisfy, the recent tool Metalibm [27] selects a suitable degree fully automatically. It employs Remez' algorithm [37], which guarantees the best possible polynomial approximation. It additionally performs domain splitting [26], which allows different polynomials and degrees to be used on different parts of the input domain, and supports a number of further features such as generation of tables for table lookup and range reduction.

Metalibm currently generates double floating-point C implementations which can outperform highly optimized library implementations [8]. It can be applied to individual or compound elementary functions as long as they are univariate (Remez' algorithm only supports univariate functions), though it usually times out after several hours on more complex compound functions. To summarize, Metalibm generates efficient individual floating-point approximations, but cannot be applied to entire programs and it does not support fixed-point arithmetic.

## 3 Our Synthesis Algorithm

In this section, we present our approach for synthesizing approximate programs with error guarantees for straight-line input programs with elementary function calls. We do not consider loops or branches, but note that our approach can

```
def xu1(x1: Real, x2: Real): Real = {
  require(0.01 <= x1 && x1 <= 0.75 && 0.01 <= x2 && x2 <= 1.5)
   2 * sin(x1) + 0.8 * cos(2 * x1) + 7 * sin(x2) - x1
} ensuring(res => res +/- 4.24e-06)
```

**Fig. 1.** Example input program with elementary function calls

be combined with previous techniques which reduce reasoning about loops and conditionals to straight-line code [11,15,21,36].[1]

To illustrate our approach, Fig. 1 shows an example synthesis specification of a program, which is taken from the benchmark set of the CORPIN project [1]. It consists of: a program with three elementary function calls `sin(x1)`, `cos(2*x1)` and `sin(x2)`, input ranges for variables in the `require` clause, and the maximum tolerated absolute error for the program in the `ensuring` clause: 4.24e−6.

Given this specification, our goal is to automatically synthesize a program which approximates the expensive elementary function calls and implements the arithmetic operations in a suitable fixed-point precision, while respecting the specified error bound.

The specified maximum tolerated error for the program can be seen as a budget, which has to be distributed between all the different sources of errors in the program, namely the elementary function approximations as well as the finite-precision arithmetic. Note that the approximation polynomials themselves have to be implemented in fixed-point arithmetic as well. In our example we thus need to assign a roundoff error budget to the four multiplications, two additions and one subtraction of the top-level program, as well as to the yet unknown polynomial approximations of `sin(x1)`, `cos(2*x1)` and `sin(x2)`.

Thus, in order to synthesize an approximate program which satisfies the specified error bound, we need to:

1. distribute the error budget, specified for the whole program, between arithmetic operations in the top-level function, potentially multiple elementary function calls, and the finite-precision implementation of the polynomials,
2. find a (piecewise-) polynomial approximation for every elementary function which stays within limits of the assigned approximation error budget, and
3. assign a finite precision to each arithmetic operation of the top-level function, as well as the polynomial approximations.

Each of the above challenges involves finding a solution in a large search space, and the search is furthermore complicated by the fact that individual errors interact in nonlinear and discrete ways. Every error introduced at one

[1] These techniques are applied to underlying roundoff error analysis, and our approach can be combined with any sound roundoff error analysis. Therefore, the application domain for our technique is only limited by what a roundoff error analysis can handle. For programs with discrete decisions – like machine-learning classifiers – the effect of the approximations on decision errors can be obtained experimentally, or to a limited extent via static analysis [31].

```
Input: 𝕊 - all variables, arithmetic operations and elementary function calls;
s_ef - elementary function calls; ε_g - global error budget
```

1. $\forall s \in \mathbb{S}$ assign precision $p_s$ wrt. cost of $s$ and $\epsilon_g$
2. Based on $p_s$ assign local budget $\epsilon_i$ to all $s_{ef}$
3. $\forall s_{ef}$ and $k.0 \leq k \leq 5$ REPEAT:
   - Split $\epsilon_i$ into $\epsilon_{i\_approx}$ and $\epsilon_{i\_fp}$, for $k = 0$ $\epsilon_{i\_approx} = \epsilon_{i\_fp}$, $k \geq 1$: $\epsilon_{i\_fp} = \epsilon_{i\_fp} \circ \delta$, where $\delta = \epsilon_i/2^{k+1}, \circ \in \{+, -\}$
   - Call Metalibm to generate a polynomial approximation wrt. $\epsilon_{i\_approx}$
   - Generate a finite-precision implementation, such that $e_{fp} \leq \epsilon_{i\_fp}$
   - Compute cost $c_k$ of the obtained finite-precision implementation $i_k$
   - Consider following cases:
     - $c_k > c_{k-1}$: if $k = 1$ choose the opposite $\circ \in \{+, -\}$, else RETURN $i_{k-1}$
     - $c_k = c_{k-1}$: if $k = 1$ REPEAT, else RETURN $i_k$
     - $c_k < c_{k-1}$: if $k < 5$ REPEAT, else RETURN $i_k$

**Fig. 2.** High-level synthesis algorithm

point in the program gets propagated through the remaining part of the computation, in the course of which it may be magnified, or diminished.

Because we are explicitly aiming to synthesize a more efficient program, we furthermore have to keep in mind the accuracy-efficiency trade off. If we assign a significant portion of the error budget to elementary function calls, we might need to use a higher, and thus more expensive, precision for the rest of the operations in order to satisfy the error budget for the whole program. Thus, performance gained by approximation might be negated by the need for high finite precision. This is a multiple-objective optimization task, which is known to be difficult in general.

Previous work provides only partial solutions to some of these challenges, which furthermore only exist in isolation. While Metalibm generates polynomial solutions with guaranteed bounds, it requires the user to provide range bounds and target errors *at the call site* and thus does not consider the full program and error propagation. Additionally, Metalibm only generates double-precision floating-point implementations. The tool Daisy can assign uniform or mixed fixed-point precisions to arithmetic computations, but does not consider elementary function calls or their approximations.

### 3.1 High-Level Algorithm

In this paper, we provide a complete solution for the above mentioned challenges and propose an overall algorithm which takes into account the interactions between different errors and synthesizes efficient numerical kernels, which are guaranteed to be accurate up to a specified total error bound.[2]

[2] We optimize for running time, but our algorithm is also applicable to other objectives such as energy, with an appropriate cost function. We note that running time often correlates with energy.

We distinguish two error budgets. The *global* budget covers errors of elementary function calls and roundoffs of arithmetic operations in the original program. The *local* budget covers the approximation error of individual elementary function calls and roundoff errors introduced by their polynomial approximations.

Figure 2 shows our high-level algorithm. The algorithm operates top-down. It first distributes the global error budget (Subsect. 3.2), which assigns local error budgets to individual elementary function calls. The local budget is distributed itself in a feedback loop between approximation and implementation errors (Subsect. 3.3). The approximation error, as well as other information obtained using static analysis is used to call Metalibm to generate polynomial approximations (Subsect. 3.4). Finally, the implementation error budget is used to assign fixed-point precisions to the approximation polynomials (Subsect. 3.5). We discuss alternatives to this top-down approach in Subsect. 3.6.

### 3.2 Distributing the Global Error Budget

Given the global error budget $\epsilon_g$ we first distribute it to local budgets for each arithmetic operation, variable and elementary function call, taking into account error propagation. Our *key observation* for this distribution is that the accuracy of the elementary function calls is unlikely to be very different from the other arithmetic operations, otherwise the errors they introduce would dominate the overall error. Based on this observation, we *treat the approximation errors introduced by elementary functions as a kind of roundoff error* of a given finite precision. With this assumption, we can leverage a precision assignment algorithm to distribute the global error budget.

In particular, we use the two assignment strategies implemented in the tool Daisy, which provide a uniform- or mixed-precision assignment. They assign a fixed-point precision to every arithmetic operation and elementary function call. For elementary functions, we interpret the associated roundoff error with this fixed-point format as the local error budget.

Daisy's uniform precision assignment performs a linear search and selects the smallest uniform precision which satisfies the provided overall error bound. Mixed-precision tuning is more involved, as it introduces cast operations which incur a certain cost. Unlike uniform precision assignment, mixed-precision tuning thus requires a cost function to choose between efficient programs. However, at this point, we do not know the actual implementation of the elementary function approximations. Furthermore, the performance of fixed-precision implementations on an accelerator depends on the compilation algorithm, which is a highly complex, and generally unknown function (e.g. the commercial Xilinx Vivado compiler). Thus the cost function has to *estimate* the cost of elementary function calls and arithmetic operations as well as possible.

We extend Daisy's mixed-precision tuning to be parametric in the cost function, which allows us to explore different options. We consider three cost functions: (1) an area-based [28] one used by Daisy previously, (2) one obtained with machine learning, and (3) an equally weighted combination of (1) and (2)[3].

For (2), we learned a multi-layer perceptron regressor [2] from random precision assignments on a set of benchmarks, for which we obtained actual performance data by compiling them to an FPGA with Xilinx Vivado. We furthermore extended both the area-based and the machine learned cost function so that elementary function calls incur twice the cost of arithmetic operations. The factor 2 has been found empirically; it confirms our intuition that the error introduced by the elementary function call is comparable to errors of arithmetic operations.

We have empirically determined that the weighted combination (i.e. option 3) works best in general. We have also observed that whether uniform or mixed precision is best is highly application specific. Thus, our algorithm tries both a uniform and a mixed-precision assignment with a weighted cost function and returns the better result. For our running example, uniform precision assignment performs best overall and assigns precision `Fixed(26)` to `sin(x1)`, `cos(2*x1)` and `sin(x2)`. From this, we obtain local error budgets $\epsilon_0 = \epsilon_1 = \epsilon_2 = 5.96e{-}8$.

### 3.3 Distributing the Local Error Budget

Once a local error budget $\epsilon_i$ is assigned to each individual elementary function call, we have to decide how much of $\epsilon_i$ will be spent on the approximation $\epsilon_{i\_approx}$ and how much on the finite-precision implementation of the approximation polynomial $\epsilon_{i\_fp}$.

To find an optimal split between the two local budgets we use a refinement loop. We start with an equal split, i.e. $\epsilon_{i\_approx} = \epsilon_{i\_fp} = 0.5\epsilon_i$, synthesize a polynomial approximation respecting $\epsilon_{i\_approx}$ and assign finite precision such that $\epsilon_{i\_fp}$ is satisfied (see sections below). We then estimate a cost $c_0$ of the obtained implementation using a cost function.

Then, our algorithm increases $\epsilon_{i\_fp}$ by $\delta = \epsilon_i/2^{k+1}$, where $k$ is the number of steps taken in one direction, and decreases $\epsilon_{i\_approx}$ respectively. We repeat synthesis of a polynomial and finite-precision assignment for the new values of $\epsilon_{i\_fp}$ and $\epsilon_{i\_approx}$ and compute the updated cost $c_k$. The obtained cost $c_k$ is used to determine the fitness of the local error budget distribution. We accept an implementation found at the step $k-1$ if $c_k > c_{k-1} \wedge k > 1$. In case the cost increases at the very first step, we change the direction of the search, i.e. decrease $\epsilon_{i\_fp}$, reset $k$ to 0 and repeat the refinement. If the cost has not changed $c_k = c_{k-1}$ at the beginning of the search ($k = 1$), we make one more refinement iteration, for $k > 1$ the $k$-th implementation is accepted. If after the $k$-th step we have $c_k < c_{k-1}$, this indicates that the performance of the implementation at the step $k$ has improved. We then repeat the refinement until the $(k-1)$-step implementation has been accepted. To ensure termination we set the maximum number of steps to $k = 5$.

The quality of refinement depends on how accurately a cost function reflects the actual compiler behavior, i.e. how well it can predict the circuit that will

[3] All cost functions are available in the source code in *repo*/opt/CostFunctions.scala.

be implemented. Our approach is parametric in the cost function, which allows flexibility in optimization for different objectives and hardware. Similarly to global budget distribution with mixed-precision tuning, we evaluated an area-based, machine-learned and a combined cost function, and found that an equally weighted combination of the area-based and machine-learned cost function had best performance overall.

For our running example, the refinement loop needed two iterations for `sin(x1)`, meaning that the optimal distribution found was $\epsilon_{0\_fp} = 3\epsilon_{0\_approx}$. The corresponding values are: $\epsilon_{0\_fp}$ =4.47e−8 and $\epsilon_{0\_approx}$= 1.49e−8. For `cos(2*x1)` and `sin(x2)` the initial equal split already had a minimum cost, i.e. $\epsilon_{i\_fp} = \epsilon_{i\_approx} =$ 2.98e−8 for $i \in \{1, 2\}$.

### 3.4 Synthesizing the Approximation Polynomial

For finding a polynomial approximation of each individual elementary function we leverage the tool Metalibm. To generate an approximation, we need to specify the folllowing parameters: (a) the elementary function $f(x)$ to be approximated, (b) the domain $x \in I$, on which $f(x)$ will be approximated, (c) the assigned local approximation error budget $\epsilon_{i\_approx}$, and (d) the maximum polynomial degree. Note that domain $I$ is not the input domain specified by the user, but the local input domain of the function's parameter $x$. This domain should be computed as tightly as possible, as this may allow Metalibm to use polynomials of smaller degree or less internal domain subdivisions. In general, determining these domains is challenging to do manually. Our algorithm uses static analysis of ranges and finite-precision errors using interval and affine arithmetic to compute this information fully automatically. Whenever a program contains the same elementary function call several times, we check whether we have already synthesized an approximation for a given range and assigned local error budget $\epsilon_i$. In this case, we reuse already generated approximation.

We have empirically found a suitable value for the maximum polynomial degree to be 7, although Metalibm does not necessarily generate polynomials of degree 7. If possible, it will choose a smaller degree. Limiting the polynomial degree influences the number of domain subdivisions, and thus one looks for a good tradeoff between a reasonable number of subdivisions and polynomial degrees. We leave the remaining parameters of Metalibm to their default values.

Metalibm generates the approximation as code optimized for double floating-point precision. Therefore, most of the implemented optimizations for range reduction, expression decomposition and meta-splitting are not applicable to fixed-point implementations.

Our implementation thus extracts only the generated piece-wise polynomial from the generated C code, and adds it to our top-level program as a separate function. The elementary function call is then replaced by the call to the generated function.

We currently do not support automated range reduction; for some of our benchmarks we have reduced ranges manually during preprocessing. In general, many programs implemented in fixed-point arithmetic will not need auto-

```
def cos_0_02to1_5_err2_9802322387695312em08(x: Real): Real = {
  require((0.02 <= x) && (x <= 1.5))
    if ((x < 1.165)) {
      c0 + (c1 + (c2 + (c4 + (c6 + (c7 + c8*x)* x)* x*x)* x)* x)* x*x
  } else {
    let t = (x - 1.33) in
       b0 + (b1 + (b2 + (b3 + (b4 + b5*t)* t)* t)* t)* t
  }
} ensuring (res => res +/- 2.9802322387695312e-08) // finite-precision budget
```

**Fig. 3.** Approximation polynomial parsed from Metalibm output.

matic range reduction, as many kernels have by design limited ranges. For other cases, adding the automatic range reduction is only an engineering task, since we already handle all necessary operations and have the ranges computed by Daisy.

Figure 3 shows the extracted polynomial approximating `cos(2*x1)` over the input domain $[0.02, 1.5]$ with an approximation target error of 2.98e−8 for our running example.

### 3.5 Assigning Finite Precision

Once the approximation polynomial has been generated, our algorithm assigns a finite precision to the generated polynomials. The goal is to find an assignment that satisfies the local roundoff error budget $\epsilon_{i\_fp}$, but uses as coarse precision as possible for performance reasons. The generated polynomials contain branching, but the branches are always at the top-level. For this simple structure there are no discontinuity errors, i.e. errors due to diverging control-flow between the finite-precision and real-valued execution, so that we can safely handle each branch separately.

For assigning the lowest possible finite precision to obtained polynomials, such that their roundoff error $e_{fp}$ satisfies $\epsilon_{i\_fp}$, we again leverage the uniform or mixed-precision assignment of Daisy. Finally, we re-run the roundoff error analysis on the whole program, where elementary function errors are replaced by the sum of $e_{fp}$ and $e_{approx}$. This error is potentially smaller than the originally allocated local error budget, as Metalibm or the precision assignment usually cannot exhaust the budget due to complex, discrete constraints. That is, our tool in the end reports the actually achieved error of the final implementation.

### 3.6 Alternative Algorithm Designs

Alternatively to the proposed error distribution strategy, we could have designed our algorithm bottom-up: first assign local error budgets for both approximation and roundoff errors for elementary function calls, generate their approximations, then distribute what is left of the global error budget between other operations and variables. Or, we could first assign an approximation error budget to each elementary function call, generate approximations, then use the rest of the global

**Table 1.** Running time in machine cycles of baseline and synthesized programs, and error budgets together with the achieved accuracy

| Target errors | Small | | | | Large | | | |
|---|---|---|---|---|---|---|---|---|
| Benchmark | Baseline | Approx | Target | Actual | Baseline | Approx | Target | Actual |
| axisRot.X | 52–60 | **24** | 1.49e−10 | 7.52e−11 | 30–34 | **14** | 1.49e−6 | 5.5e−7 |
| axisRot.Y | 52–60 | **24** | 1.49e−10 | 7.52e−11 | 30–34 | **14** | 1.49e−6 | 5.5e−7 |
| fwdk2jX | 97–113 | **23** | 8.39e−11 | 2.98e−11 | 30–34 | **24** | 8.39e−7 | 2.41e−7 |
| fwdk2jY | 94–110 | **22** | 4.89e−11 | 1.49e−11 | 30–34 | **12** | 4.89e−7 | 1.06e−7 |
| xu1 | 97–113 | **43** | 1.89e−10 | 2.47e−10 | 53–61 | **14** | 1.89e−6 | 1.93e−6 |
| xu2 | 96–112 | **44** | 1.88e−10 | 2.3e−10 | 54–62 | **13** | 1.88e−6 | 1.86e−6 |
| rodriguesRot | 52–60 | **25** | 1.70e−8 | 1.11e−8 | 31–35 | **14** | 1.70e−4 | 9.07e−5 |
| sinxx10 | 52–60 | **28** | 2.51e−9 | 1.61e−9 | 31–35 | **15** | 2.51e−5 | 1.26e−5 |
| pendulum1 | 33–37 | **27** | 4.79e−11 | 3.74e−11 | 32–36 | **16** | 4.79e−7 | 3.06e−7 |
| pendulum2 | 53–61 | **26** | 1.07e−10 | 8.11e−11 | 32–36 | **15** | 1.07e−6 | 6.64e−7 |
| pred.Gaus | 84 | 119–125 | 4.15e−7 | 4.07e−7 | 58 | 77 | 4.15e−3 | 4.08e−3 |
| pred.SVC | 22 | 20–28 | 1.46e−6 | 1.47e−7 | 21 | 21 | 1.46e−2 | 6.82e−4 |
| pred.MLPLog | 195 | **191** | 2.15e−6 | 4.14e−10 | 143 | **126** | 2.15e−2 | 7.21e−7 |

error budget to assign finite-precisions to the entire generated program at once. We note that for these alternatives it is unclear how to distribute the initial error budgets. Crucial information becomes available only later so backtracking would likely be necessary, which may be costly. In the top-down approach, we still have to distribute the global error budget in the first step, but we do so on the top-level program, without it being prohibitively large.

## 4 Experimental Evaluation

We implemented our algorithm on top of the tools Daisy and Metalibm and evaluate it on several benchmarks from scientific computing, embedded and machine learning domains. We evaluate our approach on a commonly used FPGA board (Xylinx Zync 7000 with 10 ns clock period), but note that our technique is not specific to any particular hardware and believe that our results qualitatively carry over. Synthesis has been performed on a MacBook Pro with an 3.1 GHz Intel Core i5 processor and 16 GB RAM, macOS Mojave 10.14.

Our set of benchmarks contains programs with up to 5 elementary function calls in straight-line code (all benchmarks are provided in the appendix). The number of elementary function calls for each benchmark is shown in Table 2. The benchmarks *predictGaussianNB*, *predictSVC* and *predictMLPLogistic* are machine learning classifiers generated by the python scikit-learn library on the standard Iris data set. The benchmarks *forwardk2j** are taken from the Axbench approximate computing benchmark suite [47] and compute a forward kinetics expression. We have created the benchmarks *axisRotation**, *rodriguesRotation*, which rotate coordinate axes and a vector respectively. The *pendulum** benchmarks come from the Rosa project for analysis of finite-precision code [15]. Finally, benchmarks *xu** and *sinxx10* are from the CORPIN project [1].

**Table 2.** Size of the generated polynomials and the running times for program synthesis

| Benchmark | # elem. fnc calls | Small errors | | Large errors | |
|---|---|---|---|---|---|
| | | Time | # arith. ops | Time | # arith. ops |
| axisRot.X | 2 | 3 m 13.26 s | 142 | 41.54 s | 48 |
| axisRot.Y | 2 | 3 m 1.61 s | 142 | 40.66 s | 48 |
| fwdk2jX | 2 | 5 m 56.5 s | 222 | 1 m 35.33 s | 102 |
| fwdk2jY | 2 | 1 m 29.16 s | 71 | 24.75 s | 24 |
| xu1 | 3 | 3 m 50.24 s | 168 | 50.97 s | 61 |
| xu2 | 3 | 6 m 56.96 s | 212 | 1 m 31.22 s | 73 |
| rodriguesRot | 2 | 2 m 40.15 s | 126 | 30.73 s | 45 |
| sinxx10 | 1 | 1 m 38.28 s | 71 | 25.8 s | 24 |
| pendulum1 | 1 | 2 m 18.36 s | 71 | 27.64 s | 22 |
| pendulum2 | 1 | 1 m 43.24 s | 71 | 23.98 s | 24 |
| pred.Gaus | 5 | 1 h 45 m 27.7 s | 708 | 4 m 26.231 s | 255 |
| pred.SVC | 1 | 21 m 33.35 s | 247 | 1 m 51.62 s | 95 |
| pred.MLPLog | 1 | 3 h 19 m 48.57 s | 399 | 57 m 29.185 s | 170 |

We perform all experiments for two different sets of target errors—small and large. To obtain these error bounds, we first run roundoff analysis on the benchmarks with uniform fixed-point precision with 32 bits. Small and large target errors are by two orders of magnitude smaller, resp. larger than these computed roundoff errors. Both target errors are reported in Table 1.

For performance measurements we compile our generated programs using Xilinx Vivado HLS v.2019.1, which reports the minimum and maximum number of machine cycles of the compiled design, and thus provides an exact performance measurement. We do not measure actual running time as such a measurement is necessarily noisy.

The baseline programs against which we compare correspond to the programs a user can implement with today's state of the art: by running Daisy on the input program without approximations to assign a uniform precision to all operations and then by compiling the generated code using Xilinx' elementary function library. The compiled programs can use either the fixed-point or the floating-point versions of library functions. For our baseline, we evaluate all valid versions (those which satisfy the overall error bound), and use the smallest number of cycles obtained.

**Performance Improvements.** Table 1 compares the running time in terms of machine cycles of programs synthesized by our approach (columns 3 and 7) with the baseline implementation (columns 2 and 6) for small and large target errors. A pair '52–60' denotes minimum and maximum cycles; whenever these values coincide, we show only one number.

We report the number of cycles for the fastest approximated program, obtained by distributing the global error budget using either uniform or mixed-precision assignment.

For all benchmarks, except *predictGaussianNB*, we observe a significant performance improvement when elementary function calls are replaced with piecewise polynomial approximations. Our synthesized approximate programs run on average 2.23× faster than the baseline, and up to 4.64× (4.46×) faster for small (large) target errors respectively.

For 10 out of 13 of the benchmarks the largest speedup was achieved when using uniform precision assignment for both top-level program and polynomial approximations. For three *predict** benchmarks the best performance has been achieved using mixed-precision tuning. We believe that mixed-precision can be improved further by using a more accurate cost function. Disabling the refinement loop produced slower programs for 3 benchmarks and did not change results for the rest. We observed the largest speedup when using a combination of the area-based and the machine-learned cost functions.

We noticed that on the benchmark *predictGaussianNB* the baseline programs run faster than the synthesized ones. We suspect the reason is that *predictGaussianNB* repeatedly calls the `log` function on slightly different, but largely overlapping, domains. Our implementation generates a different polynomial for each call, when in this scenario reusing the code seems to be beneficial. We leave the detection of such cases to future work. We noticed that the largest improvements are observed for benchmarks with `sin, cos`, whereas for the `exp` function in the *predictMLPLogistic* improvements are smaller, and for *predictSVC*, our approach cannot improve the running time. We suspect this effect is due to an efficient implementation of `exp` in the Xilinx math library.

**Accuracy Comparison.** In Table 1 we also show the target errors (columns 4 and 8), as well as the errors of the best synthesized approximated programs (columns 5 and 9), for both the small and large error setting. We observe that not all of the available error budget is used up by our synthesized programs. This is to be expected, as the space of precisions is not continuous, and a precision even 1 bit less precise may just not be enough to satisfy the target error. Small error budgets are used up more than large ones: for small error budgets the average usage is 62.33%, while for the large budget it is only 41.12%. The coarser a finite precision gets, the greater becomes the difference between roundoff errors computed for two neighboring precisions.

**Size of Generated Approximations.** Table 2 shows the number of elementary functions and the size of the generated polynomials (sum over all elementary functions) per benchmark (for the setting with the largest performance improvement, as reported in Table 1). Factors that influence the reported total size are: *(a)* the number of elementary function calls with distinct input ranges and local error budgets, because we generate an approximation for each of them; *(b)* the local error budget and thus approximation error budget, which influences the size of each polynomial inversely, the smaller the error budget, the larger the polynomial satisfying this budget needs to be. The largest total size of generated polynomials is 708. (We note that this size exceeds the sizes of benchmarks usually used in the area of sound roundoff error verification and optimization by an order of magnitude.)

**Running Times.** Table 2 shows the synthesis times of our implementation. As expected, synthesis of programs with small target errors is significantly slower than with large ones, but still reasonable as synthesis needs to be run only once. Smaller target errors usually require polynomial approximations with larger degrees and result in larger programs. Additionally, to satisfy smaller round-off error bounds, finite-precision tuning has to consider higher precisions, thus searching a larger space for a suitable precision assignment.

## 5 Related Work

*Program Synthesis.* Program synthesis [6] aims to automatically generate programs from (possibly declarative) specifications, and has had considerable success to generate programs from a variety of domains [4,12,19,22,24,32,38,39]. However, the vast majority of these techniques require that the generated program satisfies the user-given specification exactly. Furthermore, most approaches do not explicitly optimize for a non-correctness metric.

A branch of program synthesis – automated repair – allows to modify parts of a program to satisfy given criteria. The tool AutoRNP [48] repairs numerical programs by detecting an input subdomain that triggers high floating-point errors and replacing the matematical function by its piece-wise quadratic approximation on this subdomain. Opposite to our approach, AutoRNP aims to increase accuracy while introducing time overhead for repaired programs.

The Metasketches framework [7] searches for an optimal program with smallest cost according to a cost function. It has been used for synthesizing polynomial approximations, however, the accuracy of the generated programs is only verified based on a small set of test inputs, and thus without accuracy guarantees. In contrast, Metalibm's polynomial approximation algorithm is guaranteed to find the best polynomial approximation, and our entire approach guarantees end-to-end accuracy.

*Approximate Computing.* Our approach trades acceptable accuracy loss for resource savings. This idea has been recently pursued extensively under the name of approximate computing [46]. Techniques in this domain span all layers of the computing stack from approximate hardware [29] to software-based approximations such as skipping loop iterations [43] or removing synchronization [41]. Most related to our work from this domain is another recent combination of Daisy and Metalibm [13]. However, it only considers floating-point arithmetic and, unlike our tool, does not optimize obtained approximations. Another approximate computing tool Chisel [34] optimizes arithmetic programs by selecting which operations can be run on approximate hardware. Its error analysis is a slightly simplified version of ours in this work. While Chisel considers also probabilistic specifications, it only optimizes arithmetic operations.

Other work allows programmers to specify several versions of a program with different accuracy-efficiency tradeoffs, and let a specialized compiler autotune a program to a particular environment [5]. While this approach handles programs of larger size than ours, it requires the library writer to provide the different versions, together with accuracy specifications. It furthermore ensures accuracy by testing, i.e. does not provide guarantees.

Approximations can be particularly efficient when run on custom hardware, such as neural processing units, for which one can learn an approximate program which mimics the original imperative one [18]. Verification is again performed only on a limited set of test inputs. STOKE is an autotuner which operates on low-level machine code, and has also been applied to generate approximate floating-point programs [42]. Its scalability is limited as it considers low-level code, and furthermore it also cannot guarantee accuracy.

Finally, approximations are naturally also applied manually, e.g. for obtaining efficient, low-resource heartbeat classifiers [40]. In particular, this work has approximated an exponential function by a piece-wise linear function, but due to the manual process without accuracy guarantees.

*Numerical Program Analysis.* We reviewed roundoff error analysis tools in Sect. 2; they all assume fixed library implementations and do not optimize for efficiency. Library functions themselves have been also verified for accuracy [30]. Mixed-precision tuning approaches do optimize programs, but are only applicable in a relatively restricted space where one floating-point precision is not enough. Our presented work leverages the much larger tradeoff space of fixed-point arithmetic *and* elementary function approximations, and achieves significantly larger performance savings.

## 6 Conclusion

We have presented a fully automated synthesis approach for generating efficient numerical kernels for accelerator hardware by approximating elementary function calls as well as individual arithmetic operations, while guaranteeing user-provided error bounds for the entire program. Our technique relies on an existing static analysis to verify the end-to-end accuracy of introduced approximations. The strength of the approach comes as a result of our key intuition that the approximation errors should not be vastly different from arithmetic errors, and our experiments confirmed this intuition. To navigate the large search space of possible approximations, we present a novel error distribution algorithm and extend existing search techniques for assigning finite precisions, as well as a synthesis technique which guarantees to generate the best polynomial approximation. In a suitable combination, these techniques allow us to generate programs which are significantly more efficient than current default implementations.

## A Benchmarks

All benchmarks are provided below. Error specification given in the ensuring clause corresponds to the small error, the larger errors are given in comments.

```
def axisRotationX(x: Real, y: Real, theta: Real): Real = {
  require(-2 <= x && x <= 2 && -2 <= y && y <= 2 && 0.01 <= theta && theta <= 1.5)
  x * cos(theta) + y * sin(theta)
} ensuring (res => res +/- 1.49e-10) // 1.49e-06

def axisRotationY(x: Real, y: Real, theta: Real): Real = {
  require(-2 <= x && x <= 2 && -2 <= y && y <= 2 && 0.01 <= theta && theta <= 1.5)
  -x * sin(theta) + y * cos(theta)
} ensuring (res => res +/- 1.49e-10) // 1.49e-06

def forwardk2jX(theta1: Real, theta2: Real): Real = {
  require(0.01 <= theta1 && theta1 <= 1.5 && 0.01 <= theta2 && theta2 <= 1.5)
  val l1: Real = 0.5
  val l2: Real = 0.5

  l1 * cos(theta1) + l2 * cos(theta1 + theta2)
} ensuring (res => res +/- 8.39e-11) // 8.39e-07

def forwardk2jY(theta1: Real, theta2: Real): Real = {
  require(0.01 <= theta1 && theta1 <= 1.5 && 0.01 <= theta2 && theta2 <= 1.5)
  val l1: Real = 0.5
  val l2: Real = 0.5

  l1 * sin(theta1) + l2 * sin((theta1 + theta2) / 2)
} ensuring (res => res +/- 4.89e-11) //4.89e-07

def rodriguesRotation(v1: Real, v2: Real, v3: Real,
     k1: Real, k2: Real, k3: Real, theta: Real): Real = {
  require(-2 <= v1 && v1 <= 2 && -2 <= v2 && v2 <= 2 &&
   -2 <= v3 && v3 <= 2 && -5 <= k1 && k1 <= 5 && -5 <= k2 &&
   k2 <= 5 && -5 <= k3 && k3 <= 5 && 0 <= theta && theta <= 1.5)

  val t1 = cos(theta)
  v1 * t1 + (k2 * v3 - k3 * v2) * sin(theta) +
            k1 * (k1 * v1 + k2 * v2 + k3 * v3) * (1 - t1)
} ensuring (res => res +/- 1.7e-08) // 1.7e-04


def sinxx10(x: Real): Real = {
  require(0.01 <= x && x <= 1.5)
  val t1 = sin(x)
  (3 * x * x * x - 5 * x + 2) * t1 * t1 + (x * x * x + 5 * x) * t1 - 2*x*x - x - 2
} ensuring(res => res +/- 2.51e-09) // 2.51e-05


def xu1(x1: Real, x2: Real): Real = {
  require(0.01 <= x1 && x1 <= 0.75 && 0.01 <= x2 && x2 <= 1.5)
  2 * sin(x1) + 0.8 * cos(2 * x1) + 7 * sin(x2) - x1
} ensuring(res => res +/- 4.24e-10) // 4.24e-06
```

```
def xu2(x1: Real, x2: Real): Real = {
  require(0.01 <= x1 && x1 <= 1.5 && 0.01 <= x2 && x2 <= 0.5)
  1.4 * sin(3 * x2) + 3.1 * cos(2 * x2) - x2 + 4 * sin(2 * x1)
} ensuring(res => res +/- 5.8e-10) // 5.8e-06

 def pendulum1(t: Real, w: Real): Real = {
  require(0.01 <= t && t <= 1.6 && -5 <= w && w <= 5)
  val h: Real = 0.01
  val L: Real = 2.0
  val m: Real = 1.5
  val g: Real = 9.80665
  val k1w = -g/L * sin(t)
  val k2t = w + h/2*k1w
  val tNew = t + h*k2t
  tNew
} ensuring(res => res +/- 4.79e-11) // 4.79e-07

def pendulum2(t: Real, w: Real): Real = {
  require(0.05 <= t && t <= 1.5 && -5 <= w && w <= 5)
  val h: Real = 0.01
  val L: Real = 2.0
  val m: Real = 1.5
  val g: Real = 9.80665
  val k1t = w
  val k2w = -g/L * sin(t + h/2*k1t)
  val wNew = w + h*k2w
  wNew
} ensuring(res => res +/- 1.07e-10) // 1.07e-06

// Gaussian Naive Bayes classifier
def predictGaussianNB(f0: Real, f1: Real, f2: Real, f3: Real, sigma0: Real,
  sigma1: Real, sigma2: Real, sigma3: Real, theta0: Real, theta1: Real,
  theta2: Real, theta3: Real, prior: Real): Real = {
  require(0.12 <= sigma0 && sigma0 <= 0.40 && 0.09 <= sigma1 && sigma1 <= 0.15 &&
    0.02 <= sigma2 && sigma2 <= 0.30 && 0.01 <= sigma3 && sigma3 <= 0.08 &&
    5.0 <= theta0 && theta0 <= 6.6 && 2.7 <= theta1 && theta1 <= 3.5 &&
    1.4 <= theta2 && theta2 <= 5.6 && 0.2 <= theta3 && theta3 <= 2.1 &&
    0.25 <= prior && prior <= 0.5 && 4.0 <= f0 && f0 <= 8.0 &&
    2.0 <= f1 && f1 <= 4.5 && 1.0 <= f2 && f2 <= 7.0 && 0.0 <= f3 && f3 <= 2.5)

  val pi: Real = 3.141
  val sum = log(2.0 * pi * sigma0) + log(2.0 * pi * sigma1) +
               log(2.0 * pi * sigma2) + log(2.0 * pi * sigma3)
  val nij = -0.5 * sum
  val sum2 = (f0 - theta0) * (f0 - theta0) / sigma0 +
    (f1 - theta1) * (f1 - theta1) / sigma1 +
    (f2 - theta2) * (f2 - theta2) / sigma2 +
    (f3 - theta3) * (f3 - theta3) / sigma3

  -0.5 * sum - 0.5 * sum2 + log(prior)
} ensuring (res => res +/- 4.15e-07) // 4.15e-03
```

```
// C-Support Vector Classification with rbf kernel
def predictSVC(f0: Real, f1: Real, f2: Real, f3: Real, vectors0: Real,
  vectors1: Real, vectors2: Real, vectors3: Real, coefficient: Real,
  intercept: Real, factor: Real): Real = {
  require(4.0 <= f0 && f0 <= 7.0 && 2.0 <= f1 && f1 <= 4.5 &&
    1.0 <= f2 && f2 <= 6.0 && 0.0 <= f3 && f3 <= 2.5 &&
    4.5 <= vectors0 && vectors0 <= 5.9 && 2.2 <= vectors1 && vectors1 <= 4.4 &&
    1.3 <= vectors2 && vectors2 <= 4.9 && 0.2 <= vectors3 && vectors3 <= 2.3 &&
    -0.12 <= intercept && intercept <= 0.06 && -1 <= coefficient && coefficient <= 1.0 &&
    5 <= factor && factor <= 50)

  val gamma: Real = 0.1
  val k = (vectors0 - f0) * (vectors0 - f0) + (vectors1 - f1) * (vectors1 - f1) +
                  (vectors2 - f2) * (vectors2 - f2) + (vectors3 - f3) * (vectors3 - f3)
  val kernel = exp(gamma * k)

  factor * coefficient * kernel + intercept
} ensuring (res => res +/- 1.46e-06) // 1.46e-02

// Multi-layer Perceptron with logistic activation function
def predictMLPLogistic(f0: Real, f1: Real, f2: Real, f3: Real, weights_0_0: Real,
  weights_0_1: Real, weights_0_2: Real, weights_0_3: Real, weights_1_0: Real,
  weights_1_1: Real, weights_1_2: Real, bias_0: Real, bias_1: Real): Real = {

  require(4.0 <= f0 && f0 <= 8.0 && 2.0 <= f1 && f1 <= 4.5 &&
    1.0 <= f2 && f2 <= 7.0 && 0.0 <= f3 && f3 <= 2.5 &&
    -0.3 <= weights_0_0 && weights_0_0 <= 0.3 && -0.5 <= weights_0_1 && weights_0_1 <= 0.0 &&
    -0.2 <= weights_0_2 && weights_0_2 <= 0.1 && 0.1 <= weights_0_3 && weights_0_3 <= 0.3 &&
    -0.4 <= weights_1_0 && weights_1_0 <= 0.8 && -0.3 <= weights_1_1 && weights_1_1 <= 0.3 &&
    0.0 <= weights_1_2 && weights_1_2 <= 0.4 &&
    0.0 <= bias_0 && bias_0 <= 0.5 && -0.4 <= bias_1 && bias_1 <= 0.5)

  val n1 = f0 * weights_0_0 + f1 * weights_0_1 + f2 * weights_0_2 + f3 * weights_0_3 + bias_0
  val hidden = 1.0 / (1.0 + exp(-n1))

  val n2 = hidden * weights_1_0 + hidden * weights_1_1 + hidden * weights_1_2 + bias_1
  1.0 / (1.0 + exp(-n2))

} ensuring (res => res +/- 2.15e-06) // 2.15e-02
```

## References


1. Project CORPIN. https://www-sop.inria.fr/corpin/logiciels/ALIAS/Benches/
2. Python sklearn - multi-layer perceptron regressor (2019). https://scikit-learn.org/stable/modules/generated/sklearn.neural_network.MLPRegressor.html
3. Alur, R., et al.: Syntax-guided synthesis. In: FMCAD, pp. 1–8. IEEE (2013)
4. Alur, R., Radhakrishna, A., Udupa, A.: Scaling enumerative program synthesis via divide and conquer. In: Legay, A., Margaria, T. (eds.) TACAS 2017. LNCS, vol. 10205, pp. 319–336. Springer, Heidelberg (2017). https://doi.org/10.1007/978-3-662-54577-5_18
5. Ansel, J., Wong, Y.L., Chan, C., Olszewski, M., Edelman, A., Amarasinghe, S.: Language and compiler support for auto-tuning variable-accuracy algorithms. In: CGO (2011)
6. Bodik, R., Jobstmann, B.: Algorithmic program synthesis: introduction. STTT **15**(5), 397–411 (2013)

7. Bornholt, J., Torlak, E., Grossman, D., Ceze, L.: Optimizing Synthesis with Metasketches. In: POPL (2016)
8. Brunie, N., De Dinechin, F., Kupriianova, O., Lauter, C.: Code generators for mathematical functions. In: ARITH (2015)
9. Chiang, W.F., Baranowski, M., Briggs, I., Solovyev, A., Gopalakrishnan, G., Rakamarić, Z.: Rigorous floating-point mixed-precision tuning. In: POPL (2017)
10. Damouche, N., Martel, M.: Mixed precision tuning with salsa. In: PECCS, pp. 185–194. SciTePress (2018)
11. Damouche, N., Martel, M., Chapoutot, A.: Improving the numerical accuracy of programs by automatic transformation. STTT **19**(4), 427–448 (2017)
12. D'Antoni, L., Samanta, R., Singh, R.: QLOSE: program repair with quantitative objectives. In: Chaudhuri, S., Farzan, A. (eds.) CAV 2016. LNCS, vol. 9780, pp. 383–401. Springer, Cham (2016). https://doi.org/10.1007/978-3-319-41540-6_21
13. Darulova, E., Volkova, A.: Sound approximation of programs with elementary functions. In: Dillig, I., Tasiran, S. (eds.) CAV 2019. LNCS, vol. 11562, pp. 174–183. Springer, Cham (2019). https://doi.org/10.1007/978-3-030-25543-5_11
14. Darulova, E., Izycheva, A., Nasir, F., Ritter, F., Becker, H., Bastian, R.: Daisy - framework for analysis and optimization of numerical programs (tool paper). In: Beyer, D., Huisman, M. (eds.) TACAS 2018. LNCS, vol. 10805, pp. 270–287. Springer, Cham (2018). https://doi.org/10.1007/978-3-319-89960-2_15
15. Darulova, E., Kuncak, V.: Towards a compiler for reals. TOPLAS **39**(2), 8 (2017)
16. Darulova, E., Sharma, S., Horn, E.: Sound mixed-precision optimization with rewriting. In: ICCPS (2018)
17. De Dinechin, F., Lauter, C.Q., Melquiond, G.: Assisted verification of elementary functions using Gappa. In: ACM Symposium on Applied Computing (2006)
18. Esmaeilzadeh, H., Sampson, A., Ceze, L., Burger, D.: Neural acceleration for general-purpose approximate programs. In: MICRO (2012)
19. Feng, Y., Martins, R., Wang, Y., Dillig, I., Reps, T.W.: Component-based synthesis for complex APIs. In: POPL (2017)
20. de Figueiredo, L.H., Stolfi, J.: Affine arithmetic: concepts and applications. Numer. Algorithms **37**(1–4), 147–158 (2004)
21. Goubault, E., Putot, S.: Static analysis of finite precision computations. In: Jhala, R., Schmidt, D. (eds.) VMCAI 2011. LNCS, vol. 6538, pp. 232–247. Springer, Heidelberg (2011). https://doi.org/10.1007/978-3-642-18275-4_17
22. Gulwani, S.: Automating string processing in spreadsheets using input-output examples. In: POPL (2011)
23. IEEE: IEEE Standard for Floating-Point Arithmetic. IEEE Std 754–2008 (2008)
24. Kneuss, E., Kuraj, I., Kuncak, V., Suter, P.: Synthesis modulo recursive functions. In: OOPSLA (2013)
25. Kuncak, V., Mayer, M., Piskac, R., Suter, P.: Complete functional synthesis. In: PLDI (2010)
26. Kupriianova, O., Lauter, C.: A domain splitting algorithm for the mathematical functions code generator. In: Asilomar (2014)
27. Kupriianova, O., Lauter, C.: Metalibm: a mathematical functions code generator. In: Hong, H., Yap, C. (eds.) ICMS 2014. LNCS, vol. 8592, pp. 713–717. Springer, Heidelberg (2014). https://doi.org/10.1007/978-3-662-44199-2_106
28. Lee, D.U., Gaffar, A.A., Cheung, R.C., Mencer, O., Luk, W., Constantinides, G.A.: Accuracy-guaranteed bit-width optimization. TCAD **25**(10), 1990–2000 (2006)
29. Lee, S., John, L.K., Gerstlauer, A.: High-level synthesis of approximate hardware under joint precision and voltage scaling. In: DATE, pp. 187–192 (2017)

30. Lee, W., Sharma, R., Aiken, A.: On automatically proving the correctness of math.h implementations. Proc. ACM Program. Lang. **2**(POPL), 47 (2018)
31. Lohar, D., Darulova, E., Putot, S., Goubault, E.: Discrete choice in the presence of numerical uncertainties. IEEE TCAD **37**, 2381–2392 (2018)
32. Loncaric, C., Torlak, E., Ernst, M.D.: Fast synthesis of fast collections. ACM SIGPLAN Not. **51**(6), 355–368 (2016)
33. Magron, V., Constantinides, G., Donaldson, A.: Certified roundoff error bounds using semidefinite programming. ACM Trans. Math. Softw. **43**(4), 34 (2017)
34. Misailovic, S., Carbin, M., Achour, S., Qi, Z., Rinard, M.C.: Chisel: reliability- and accuracy-aware optimization of approximate computational kernels. In: OOPSLA (2014)
35. Moore, R.: Interval Analysis. Prentice-Hall, Upper Saddle River (1966)
36. Moscato, M., Titolo, L., Dutle, A., Muñoz, C.A.: Automatic estimation of verified floating-point round-off errors via static analysis. In: Tonetta, S., Schoitsch, E., Bitsch, F. (eds.) SAFECOMP 2017. LNCS, vol. 10488, pp. 213–229. Springer, Cham (2017). https://doi.org/10.1007/978-3-319-66266-4_14
37. Briesbarre, N., Chevillard, S.: Efficient polynomial l-approximations. In: ARITH (2007)
38. Neider, D., Saha, S., Madhusudan, P.: Compositional synthesis of piece-wise functions by learning classifiers. ACM Trans. Comput. Logic **19**(2), 10:1–10:23 (2018)
39. Nori, A.V., Ozair, S., Rajamani, S.K., Vijaykeerthy, D.: Efficient synthesis of probabilistic programs. In: PLDI. ACM (2015)
40. Braojos, R., Ansaloni, G., Atienza, D.: A methodology for embedded classification of heartbeats using random projections. In: DATE. EPFL (2013)
41. Renganarayana, L., Srinivasan, V., Nair, R., Prener, D.: Programming with relaxed synchronization. In: RACES, pp. 41–50 (2012)
42. Schkufza, E., Sharma, R., Aiken, A.: Stochastic optimization of floating-point programs with tunable precision. In: PLDI (2014)
43. Sidiroglou-Douskos, S., Misailovic, S., Hoffmann, H., Rinard, M.: Managing performance vs. accuracy trade-offs with loop perforation. In: ESEC/FSE (2011)
44. Solovyev, A., Jacobsen, C., Rakamaric, Z., Gopalakrishnan, G.: Rigorous estimation of floating-point round-off errors with symbolic taylor expansions. In: FM (2015)
45. Xilinx: Vivado design suite (2018). https://www.xilinx.com/products/design-tools/vivado.html
46. Xu, Q., Mytkowicz, T., Kim, N.S.: Approximate computing: a survey. IEEE Des. Test **33**(1), 8–22 (2016)
47. Yazdanbakhsh, A., Mahajan, D., Esmaeilzadeh, H., Lotfi-Kamran, P.: AxBench: a multiplatform benchmark suite for approximate computing. IEEE Des. Test **34**(2), 60–68 (2017)
48. Yi, X., Chen, L., Mao, X., Ji, T.: Efficient automated repair of high floating-point errors in numerical libraries. In: POPL (2019)

# Automata

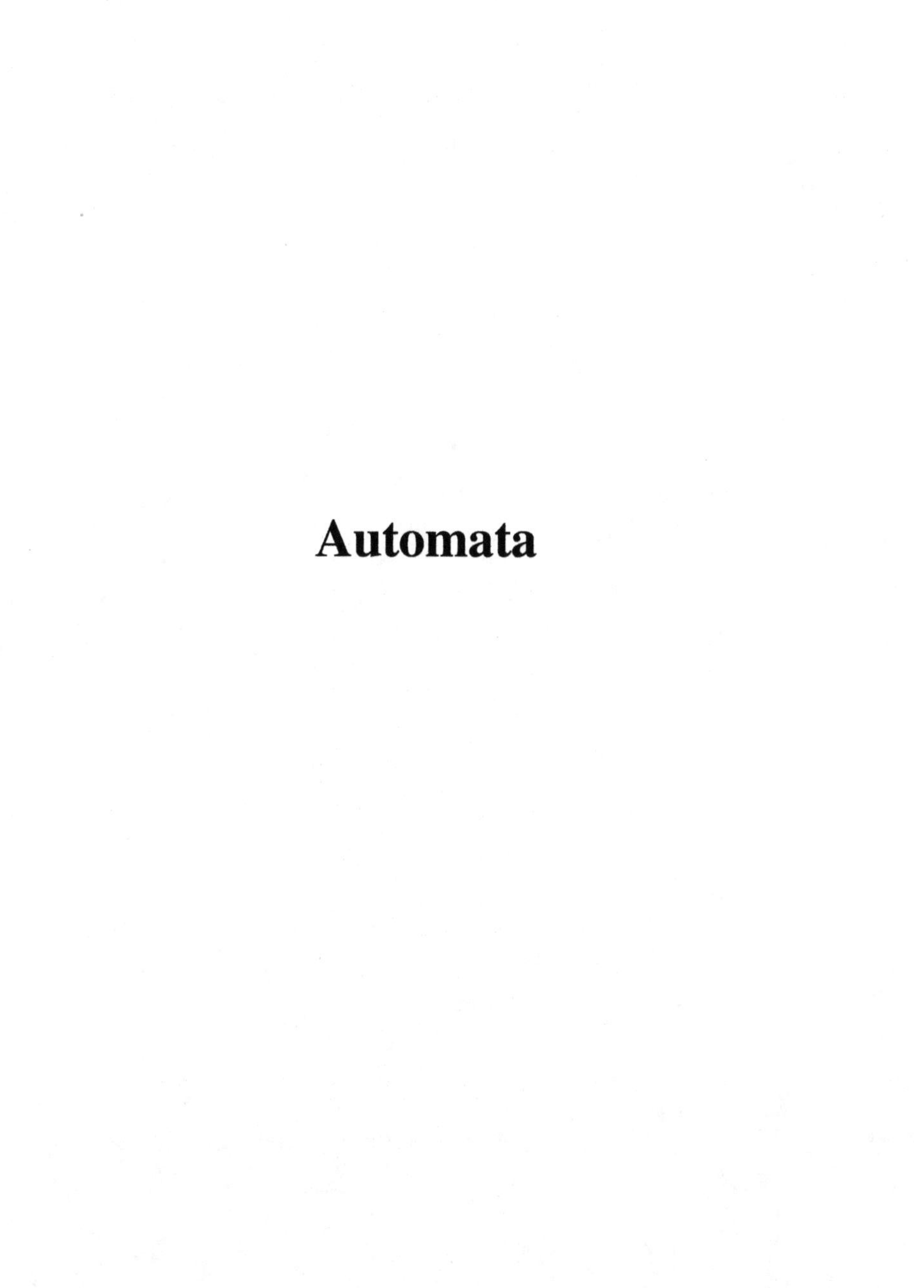

# New Optimizations and Heuristics for Determinization of Büchi Automata

Christof Löding(✉) and Anton Pirogov(✉)

RWTH Aachen University, Templergraben 55, 52062 Aachen, Germany
{loeding,pirogov}@cs.rwth-aachen.de

**Abstract.** In this work, we present multiple new optimizations and heuristics for the determinization of Büchi automata that exploit a number of semantic and structural properties, most of which may be applied together with any determinization procedure. We built a prototype implementation where all the presented heuristics can be freely combined and evaluated them, comparing our implementation with the state-of-the-art tool `spot` on multiple data sets with different characteristics. Our results show that the proposed optimizations and heuristics can in some cases significantly decrease the size of the resulting deterministic automaton.

**Keywords:** Büchi · Parity · Automata · Determinization · Heuristics

## 1 Introduction

Nondeterministic Büchi automata (NBA) [4] are a well-established formalism for the representation of properties of non-terminating executions of finite state programs, and arise often as a low-level representation obtained by translation of some formula describing the desired behaviour in a logic like e.g. LTL [32]. In the field of model checking, Büchi automata are an important tool in verification algorithms for finite state systems (see, e.g., [2]). In order to capture the full class of regular $\omega$-languages, Büchi automata need to be nondeterministic. In some applications, however, the algorithms require the property to be represented by a deterministic automaton. For example, in probabilistic model checking, the natural product of an automaton with a Markov chain requires the automaton to be deterministic in order to produce again a Markov chain. Therefore, many algorithms in this setting need deterministic automata as input (see, e.g., [2, Section 10.3]). Another example is the problem of synthesis of finite state systems from $\omega$-regular specifications, where the specification can be translated into a game over a finite graph based on a deterministic parity automaton [26,39].

For this reason, the determinization of Büchi automata is a well-researched problem. In order to obtain a deterministic automaton model that is as expressive

A. Pirogov—This work is supported by the German research council (DFG) Research Training Group 2236 UnRAVeL.


Y.-F. Chen et al. (Eds.): ATVA 2019, LNCS 11781, pp. 317–333, 2019.
https://doi.org/10.1007/978-3-030-31784-3_18

as nondeterministic Büchi automata, one needs to use a more expressive acceptance condition such as Muller, Rabin, Streett, or parity conditions (see, e.g., [37,40]). The first determinization construction by McNaughton [25] resulted in doubly-exponential Muller automata, whereas the first asymptotically optimal construction was presented by Safra [34], which yields Rabin automata with $2^{\mathcal{O}(n \log n)}$ states. Since then, modifications of Safra's construction have been proposed in order to improve the constants in the exponent of the state complexity [31,35], resulting in a construction for which tight lower bounds exist [6,35]. In particular, Piterman was the first to present a direct construction of a deterministic parity automaton (DPA) [31], which is described in a slightly different way in [35]. Another variant of Safra's construction is presented in [33].

While the Safra construction (and its variants) is the most famous determinization construction for Büchi automata, there is another approach which can be derived from a translation of alternating tree automata into nondeterministic ones by Muller and Schupp [30]. Determinization constructions for Büchi automata based on the ideas of Muller and Schupp have been described in [12,13,18]. The two types of constructions, Safra and Muller/Schupp, are unified in [24].

While in theory, constructions with tight upper and lower bounds have been achieved, there is a lot of room for optimizations when implementing determinization constructions. A first implementation of Safra's construction in the version of [31] is `ltl2dstar`, presented in [19]. While `ltl2dstar` already implements some optimizations and heuristics in order to reduce the size of the output automaton, the resulting automata are still quite large, even for small input Büchi automata. The current state-of-the-art tool for determinization of Büchi automata is part of the library `spot` [8], which implements the variant of Safra's construction presented in [33]. Furthermore, `spot` also implements more optimizations to reduce the size of the output automata.

The contribution of this paper is the identification of new heuristics for reducing the size of DPA produced by determinization from Büchi automata and a simple framework for their implementation. More specifically, our contributions can roughly be described as follows:

- We present a modularized version of the construction in [24] which enables the integration of SCC-based heuristics.
- By exploiting properties of the used construction, we make stronger use of language inclusions between states of the given NBA (e.g. obtained by simulation), permitting to use inclusions between states in the same SCC.
- We treat specific types of SCCs in the NBA in a special way, namely those without accepting states, those with only accepting states, and those with a deterministic transition relation.
- The construction from [24] leaves some freedom in the choice of successor states. Our implementation admits different options for this successor choice, in particular those leading to the constructions of Safra and of Muller/Schupp. Furthermore, we have an optimization that exploits this freedom of successor selection by checking whether admissible successor states have already been constructed before adding a new state.

- We make use of language equivalences of states in the constructed DPA in order to remove some SCCs of the resulting DPA. These language equivalences are derived during construction time from the powerset automaton for the given NBA.
- We propose to use known minimization techniques as post processing, which to the best of our knowledge, have not yet been used in this context. We first minimize the number of priorities of the DPA using an algorithm from [5], and then reduce the size of the resulting DPA by Hopcroft's algorithm [16], treating it as a finite automaton that outputs the priorities.
- We have evaluated the combination of different heuristics on different types of data-sets (randomly generated NBAs, NBAs constructed from random LTL formulas, NBAs generated from some families of LTL formulas taken from the literature, and NBAs obtained from specifications of the competition SYNT-COMP [17]), and compared the size of the resulting automata with the ones produced by `spot`.

This work is organized as follows. After some preliminaries in Sect. 2, we sketch the general construction on which we based our implementation in Sect. 3, and then describe our optimizations and heuristics in Sect. 4. In Sect. 5 we present our experiments and in Sect. 6 we conclude.

## 2 Preliminaries

First we briefly review basic definitions concerning $\omega$-automata and $\omega$-languages. If $\Sigma$ is a finite alphabet, then $\Sigma^\omega$ is the set of all infinite *words* $w = w_0 w_1 \ldots$ with $w_i \in \Sigma$. For $w \in \Sigma^\omega$ we denote by $w(i)$ the $i$-th symbol $w_i$. For convenience, we write $[n]$ for the set of natural numbers $\{1, \ldots, n\}$. A *Büchi automaton* $\mathcal{A}$ is a tuple $(Q, \Sigma, \Delta, Q_0, F)$, where $Q$ is a finite set of states, $\Sigma$ a finite alphabet, $\Delta \subseteq Q \times \Sigma \times Q$ is the transition relation and $Q_0, F \subseteq Q$ are the sets of initial and final states, respectively. When $Q$ is understood and $X \subseteq Q$, then $\overline{X} := Q \setminus X$. We write $\Delta(p, a) := \{q \in Q \mid (p, a, q) \in \Delta\}$ to denote the set of *successors* of $p \in Q$ on symbol $a \in \Sigma$, and $\Delta(P, a)$ for $\bigcup_{p \in P} \Delta(p, a)$. A *run* of an automaton on a word $w \in \Sigma^\omega$ is an infinite sequence of states $q_0, q_1, \ldots$ starting in some $q_0 \in Q_0$ such that $(q_i, w(i), q_{i+1}) \in \Delta$ for all $i \geq 0$. As usual, an automaton is *deterministic* if $|Q_0| = 1$ and $|\Delta(p, a)| \leq 1$ for all $p \in Q, a \in \Sigma$, and *non-deterministic* otherwise. In this work, we assume Büchi automata to be non-deterministic and refer to them as NBA. A *(transition-based) deterministic parity automaton* (DPA) is a deterministic automaton $(Q, \Sigma, \Delta, Q_0, c)$ where instead of $F \subseteq Q$ there is a *priority function* $c : \Delta \to \mathbb{N}$ assigning a natural number to each transition.

A run of an NBA is *accepting* if it contains infinitely many accepting states. A run of a DPA is accepting if the smallest priority of transitions along the run which appears infinitely often is even. An automaton $\mathcal{A}$ *accepts* $w \in \Sigma^\omega$ if there exists an accepting run on $w$, and the language $L(\mathcal{A}) \subseteq \Sigma^\omega$ *recognized* by $\mathcal{A}$ is the set of all accepted words. If $P$ is a set of states of an automaton, we write $L(P)$ for the language accepted by this automaton with initial state set $P$. For sets consisting of one state $q$, we write $L(q)$ instead of $L(\{q\})$. We sometimes refer to states of a DPA that is obtained by a determinization construction as *macrostates* to distinguish them from the states of the underlying Büchi automaton.

We write $p \xrightarrow{x} q$ if there exists a path from $p$ to $q$ labelled by $x \in \Sigma^+$ and $p \to q$ if there exists some $x$ such that $p \xrightarrow{x} q$. The *strongly connected component (SCC)* of $p \in Q$ is $\mathsf{scc}(p) := \{q \in Q \mid p = q \text{ or } p \to q \text{ and } q \to p\}$. The set $\mathsf{SCCs}(\mathcal{A}) := \{\mathsf{scc}(q) \mid q \in Q\}$ is the set of all SCCs and partitions $Q$. A component $C \in \mathsf{SCCs}(\mathcal{A})$ is *trivial* if $C = \{q\}$ for some $q \in Q$ and $q \not\to q$. $C$ is *bottom* if $p \to q$ implies $q \in C$ for all $p \in C$ and $q \in Q$. In a Büchi automaton, $C$ is *rejecting* if it is trivial or contains no accepting states, and *accepting* if it is not trivial and all cycles inside $C$ contain an accepting state. If an SCC is neither accepting or rejecting, it is *mixed.* Notice that rejecting and accepting components are often called *inherently weak* in the literature (e.g. [3]). Finally, $C$ is *deterministic* if $|\Delta(p,a) \cap C| \leq 1$ for all $p \in C$ and $a \in \Sigma$. An NBA is *limit-deterministic,* if all its non-rejecting SCCs are deterministic and cannot reach non-deterministic SCCs again.

## 3 Construction

For our prototype implementation, we applied new optimizations and heuristics to an adaptation of a recent generalized determinization construction from NBA to DPA that was presented in [24]. This construction unifies the constructions of Safra and of Muller and Schupp, and also introduces new degrees of freedom, which we exploit in one of our heuristics (see Sect. 4.2).

Let $\mathcal{A} = (Q, \Sigma, \Delta, Q_0, F)$ be the NBA to be determinized. The macrostates $(\alpha, t)$ in the deterministic automaton (called *ranked slices*) are tuples of disjoint non-empty sets $t := (S_1, S_2, \ldots, S_n)$ equipped with a bijection $\alpha : [n] \to [n]$ that assigns to each set $S_i$ the rank $\alpha(i)$. These ranks are used to define the priorities of the transitions. When reading symbol $a \in \Sigma$ in macrostate $(\alpha, t)$, the successor $(\alpha', t')$ is obtained by applying the successive operations $\mathsf{step}$, $\mathsf{prune}$, $\mathsf{merge}$ and $\mathsf{normalize}$. An overview of the complete transition is sketched in Fig. 1 and we refer to [24] for more details.

$(\alpha, t = (S_1, \ldots, S_n))$
$\mathsf{step} \downarrow$ separate acc./non-acc. successors, only keep leftmost occurrences
$(\hat{\alpha}, \hat{t} = (\hat{S}_1, \ldots, \hat{S}_{2n}))$
$\mathsf{prune} \downarrow$ remove empty sets, obtain good and bad signals (sets $G, R$)
$(\tilde{\alpha}, \tilde{t} = (\tilde{S}_1, \ldots, \tilde{S}_{\tilde{n}}))$
$\mathsf{merge} \downarrow$ merge adjacent sets, depending on $G, R$ from $\mathsf{prune}$ *(optional, nondet.)*
$(\check{\alpha}, \check{t} = (\check{S}_1, \ldots, \check{S}_{n'}))$
$\mathsf{normalize} \downarrow$ reassign ranks in order-preserving way
$(\alpha', t' = \check{t})$

**Fig. 1.** Sketch of some transition $(\alpha, t) \xrightarrow{a \in \Sigma} (\alpha', t')$ of the determinization construction. The nondeterminism in the optional $\mathsf{merge}$ operation enables the simulation of different constructions and provides freedom for optimizations.

### 3.1 A Modular Variant of the Construction

We present a generalization of the construction above which offers a clean framework to implement our heuristics, specifically the heuristics that exploit the SCC structure of the Büchi automaton. This variant of the construction runs multiple interacting instances of the construction above in parallel, where each instance is essentially a ranked slice as above, but manages only an SCC of the Büchi automaton (or a union of SCCs). A macrostate in this modular construction consists of not one, but (in general) multiple tuples with a global ranking function (see illustration in Fig. 2). Furthermore, for some heuristics it is not needed to have a rank assigned to certain states of the Büchi automaton. We therefore additionally store a separate "buffer set" in each macrostate with no assigned rank where such Büchi states can be placed in. The states in the buffer set are not used to track an accepting run directly, but they may reach successors later that should be managed inside of a tuple.

$$(\{q_1, q_3\}^5, \{q_2\}^3) \mid (\{q_4\}^1, \{q_6\}^6, \{q_5\}^4) \mid (\{q_7, q_8, q_9\}^2) \mid\mid \{q_{10}\}$$

**Fig. 2.** Illustration of some macrostate of the modularized determinization procedure. In this example, assume that the underlying automaton has components with the states $q_1, q_2, q_3$ and $q_4, q_5, q_6$ and $q_7, \ldots, q_{10}$, respectively. The superscripts denote the global rank of the corresponding set. State $q_{10}$ is currently not considered to track accepting runs, so it is stored in the separated buffer set and has no assigned rank. The vertical bars separate the different components from each other.

To ensure the correct interaction of the tuples, the ranks assigned to sets must be unique in the whole macrostate. Apart from this difference, the construction above is applied to each tuple individually. Whenever a transition in the Büchi automaton moves from an SCC $C_1$ to a different SCC $C_2$, and the same state is not also reached by some transition inside of $C_2$, then the resulting state is added in a new right-most set in the tuple responsible for SCC $C_2$. The rank of this new set is the least important (i.e., largest in the tuple) one.

The correctness of this modular approach essentially follows from the fact that each accepting run eventually stays in the same SCC of the Büchi automaton forever, i.e., the states along this run eventually stay in the same tuple forever and are managed by the construction above without interference.

## 4 Optimizations and Heuristics

In the following, we describe the optimizations and heuristics we suggest to consider during determinization of Büchi automata.

### 4.1 Using Known Language Inclusions of Büchi states

We are aware of only two rather simple optimizations that are exploiting known language inclusion relations between states of the Büchi automaton—a "true-loop" optimization from `ltl2dstar` [19] that syntactically identifies NBA states that can be treated as accepting sinks, and an optimization used in `spot` [8] that is restricted to pairs of states from different SCCs of the NBA, which we refer to as "external" language inclusions. In general, it is nontrivial to use the language inclusions between pairs of states in the same SCC of the NBA, because both of them can occur infinitely often in the same run.

However, there is a possibility to use the language inclusion relation more generally within the same SCC in a safe manner by exploiting properties of the determinization construction from [24]. The result is what we call the "internal" language inclusion optimization, which works for the original non-modular version of the construction, which uses a single ranked tuple $(\alpha, t)$ per macrostate, as follows. Let $Q_t := \bigcup_{i=1}^{n} S_i$ for $t = (S_1, \dots, S_n)$ and let the function $\mathsf{idx}_t : Q_t \to [n]$ map each state $q \in Q_t$ to the tuple index $i$ such that $q \in S_i$.

**Theorem 1.** *Let $p, q \in Q$ with $L(p) \subseteq L(q)$ and let $(\alpha, t)$ be a macrostate of the determinization construction such that $p, q \in Q_t$. If $q$ is to the left of $p$ (i.e. $\mathsf{idx}_t(q) < \mathsf{idx}_t(p)$), then $p$ may be omitted from the macrostate without changing the language of the determinized automaton.*

Since the internal or external language inclusion optimization change the structure of the macrostates, the overall structure of the constructed DPA might change significantly. For this reason, there is no guarantee that this technique cannot increase the number of states in some cases. In our experiments we found no instance where this is the case, i.e., in practice they only decrease the number of states.

### 4.2 Using Properties of SCCs in the NBA

In the following, we describe some heuristics to simplify the treatment of SCCs in the NBA that are rejecting, accepting, or deterministic. Earlier, we described how the determinization construction can be performed in a modular way. The following heuristics can be implemented very cleanly in that framework, but in principle could also be used with other constructions.

*Rejecting SCCs:* It is known that one can keep states from rejecting NBA SCCs separate from the determinization construction, as no accepting run can visit them infinitely often. This can be realized in our modular construction by keeping states of rejecting SCCs outside of the determinization tuples in the buffer set. A related optimization is already implemented in `spot` as a modification of the construction from [33].

*Accepting SCCs:* For accepting SCCs, it is sufficient to check that at least one run eventually stays in the same SCC forever. For this, an adaptation of the Miyano-Hayashi construction [28] (often called "breakpoint"-construction) can be used, which requires to manage only two different sets—a track set and a background set. In a transition, the track set is updated to all successors of the current track set that are in an accepting SCC. The background set contains all other states from accepting SCCs that are reached in this transition. This pair of sets has one rank assigned by the global ranking function. As long as the track set is non-empty, the rank signals a good event. If the track set becomes empty in a transition, then the rank signals a bad event, the background set becomes the new track set, and a new rank is assigned that is larger than all the ranks that survived the last transition. It is not very difficult to see that this construction correctly detects runs of the NBA that remain inside an accepting SCC.

This heuristic is realized in our modular construction by delaying the movement of states into the corresponding component tuple until a "breakpoint" happens, thereby ensuring that the tuple responsible for all accepting components always contains at most one non-empty set. If the two heuristics for rejecting and accepting SCCs are used, and the input NBA is a weak automaton (in which all SCCs are either rejecting or accepting), then one obtains the pure breakpoint construction, which is used, e.g., in [3] to determinize weak automata. The overall state complexity is then reduced from $2^{\mathcal{O}(n \log n)}$ to $3^n$.

*Deterministic SCCs:* If an SCC has both accepting and rejecting states, but is deterministic, a run never branches into multiple runs as long as the successors stay in the same component. Hence, the number of different runs can only decrease or stay the same. This excludes the possibility that an accepting state is visited infinitely often by different runs, but not by a single infinite run. Therefore, whenever a set of states in a deterministic SCC is reached from some other SCC, it suffices to add the states to the tuple which is responsible for this SCC with a new rank, but in the following steps there is no need to refine this set, i.e. separate accepting from non-accepting states, as this is only required for filtering out infinite non-accepting runs. For a good event to be signalled by such a component in the construction, it suffices that a set just contains an accepting state. If this set eventually never becomes empty and infinitely often contains accepting states, clearly at least one of the finitely many runs evolving in this set must visit accepting states infinitely often. Applying this heuristic on limit-deterministic NBA simplifies the determinization procedure to a variant of the construction described in [9], because then the importance ordering given by ranks coincides with the tuple index ordering, effectively mimicking the tuples as used in [9].

It should be pointed out that all these SCC-based heuristics can in fact increase the number of states for specific instances, even though they restrict the state space in general and therefore must be applied with greater care.

### 4.3 Smart Successor Selection

The determinization construction in [24] permits, in general, multiple valid successor macrostates because of the freedom in the merge operation. Determinization in practice usually works by starting in some initial state and fully exploring the state space which is reachable using the transitions prescribed by some construction. A natural optimization to be derived from the non-determinism of merge is to check for each transition whether a permissible successor state has already been constructed. In this case, just a new edge is added, and a new state is constructed only if no viable existing successor could be found.

The question is then how to find such a state as efficiently as possible. A naive approach would be to check for every already visited state whether it satisfies the constraints on the shape of a successor for the current transition. This would incur a blow-up in the running time that is quadratic in the size of the output automaton, which can be very large in general. A better approach is to structure the set of already visited states in a reasonable way that accelerates this search. We achieve this by managing a trie where each node corresponds to a macrostate. Each trie node is labelled by a set $S \subseteq Q$ of states of the NBA and can be marked to denote whether the corresponding macrostate already exists in the DPA. There exists a simple bijection that maps each ranked slice into a sequence of sets (without ranks) which uniquely determines a node in the trie. The resulting sequence of sets $S_1, S_2, \ldots, S_n$ is the "word" over the alphabet $2^Q$ which is inserted into the trie if the corresponding macrostate is added to the DPA (the sequence $S_1, S_2, \ldots, S_n$ is different from the tuple in the ranked slice).

When constructing a successor state, we first apply the operations step and prune. From that, we obtain the minimal active rank $k$. Under the constraints of the construction sketched in Sect. 3, the merge operation can now merge sets with rank at least $k$ which in turn means that the sets with rank smaller than $k$ do not change during merge. This sequence of sets of rank smaller than $k$ determines a trie node such that all possible successors that can be constructed by merge are below this node.

Only a simple check must be performed on remaining candidate macrostates that are found in the trie, and all required steps can be carried out efficiently using bit-set operations, so that the overall slowdown incurred by this optimized successor selection is very moderate.

This optimization only prevents new redundant states from being constructed, thus the resulting automaton can never become larger than without this optimization enabled. However, in combination with other heuristics, like the post-processing described in Sect. 4.5, it might also have a negative effect.

### 4.4 The Benefits of the Powerset Structure

It is a well-known fact that language equivalent states of a deterministic or non-deterministic $\omega$-automaton cannot be merged, in general, without changing the accepted language. However, if the two states are in different SCCs, it is possible to remove one of them. The aim of the heuristic that we describe next, is to exploit this fact during construction of the DPA. Formally, we rely on the following proposition, which we consider folklore.

**Proposition 1.** *Let $s, s'$ be states of a DPA. If $L(s) = L(s')$ and $s \not\rightarrow s'$, then all incoming edges of $s'$ can be redirected to $s$ without changing the recognized language (and $s'$ can be removed, since it becomes unreachable).*

This implies that the whole SCC containing such a state $s'$ can be removed because the language equivalence holds for all the successor states of $s$ and $s'$ as well, due to the deterministic transitions.

In order to use this insight in the determinization construction, we need to detect language equivalences of states of the DPA at construction time. We do this by using the *powerset structure* $\mathsf{PS}(\mathcal{A})$ of the given NBA $\mathcal{A}$, which is the transition system with nodes from $2^Q$ obtained by using the NFA powerset construction on the Büchi automaton, with $Q_0$ as initial state and a deterministic transition function $\delta^{\mathsf{PS}(\mathcal{A})}(P, a) := \Delta(P, a)$. Our optimization is based on the following simple observation.

**Proposition 2.** *Let $\mathcal{B}$ be a DPA that is equivalent to the NBA $\mathcal{A}$. Let $u$ be a finite word such that in $\mathcal{B}$ the state $s$ is reached via $u$, and in $\mathsf{PS}(\mathcal{A})$ the set $P$ is reached via $u$. Then $\mathcal{B}$ accepts from $s$ the same language as $\mathcal{A}$ accepts from $P$.*

This implies that states of the DPA that can be reached simultaneously with the same set $P$ in $\mathsf{PS}(\mathcal{A})$ are language equivalent. In combination with Proposition 1, we obtain that a DPA equivalent to $\mathcal{A}$ only needs one SCC per SCC in $\mathsf{PS}(\mathcal{A})$.

**Corollary 1.** *Let $\mathcal{A}$ be an NBA and $\mathsf{PS}(\mathcal{A})$ its powerset structure. Then there exists a DPA $\mathcal{B}$ recognizing the same language such that for each SCC of $\mathsf{PS}(\mathcal{A})$ there is at most one SCC in $\mathcal{B}$.*

Based on this observation, we separately construct for each SCC $C$ of $\mathsf{PS}(\mathcal{A})$ one SCC of the DPA, as explained in the following. The construction picks some node $S \in C$ (which is a set of NBA states), and starts the determinization procedure using $S$ as initial states. Furthermore, it tracks for each macrostate $s$ also the corresponding node $P_s$ in $C$. On each transition, the successor macrostate for the DPA is only constructed, if the corresponding transition in $\mathsf{PS}(\mathcal{A})$ stays in $C$.

This construction gives us a DPA $\mathcal{B}_C$ that can be partial in the case of non-bottom SCCs $C$ of $\mathsf{PS}(\mathcal{A})$, with "holes" for transitions that exit $C$. Note that $\mathcal{B}_C$ might consist of several SCCs itself. Based on Propositions 1 and 2, we only need to keep one bottom SCC of $\mathcal{B}_C$.

In order to complete the missing transitions, consider such a transition leading outside of $C$ to some $P'$ in an SCC $C'$ of $\mathsf{PS}(\mathcal{A})$. We assume that we have already done the determinization for $C'$ (starting at the bottom SCCs of $\mathsf{PS}(\mathcal{A})$ and then going backwards), so there already exists a macrostate that corresponds to $P'$, and we can let the transition of the DPA point to that macrostate. This idea is illustrated in Fig. 3.

Putting this into practice and keeping only bottom SCCs of the partial DPAs that have the smallest size, is what we call the "topological" optimization. While this still requires the exploration of all macrostates that are reached by the determinization of a single SCC in $\mathsf{PS}(A)$, many of those may be removed afterwards.

Alternatively, one could explore in a depth-first fashion and greedily just keep the first completed bottom SCC, effectively trading an even smaller automaton size for possibly faster computation.

Notice that this optimization is generic and can be used with any determinization construction based on state exploration.

It can be easily implemented in such a way that the resulting automaton will have at most the same size as without this optimization, by picking appropriate initial states for the construction of the partial DPAs $\mathcal{B}_C$ (i.e. picking initial states that would also be reached by the unoptimized construction anyway).

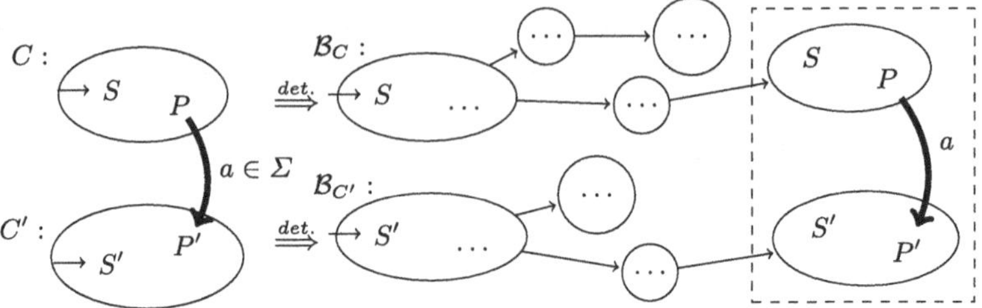


**Fig. 3.** Abstract sketch of the determinization guided by SCCs of $\mathsf{PS}(\mathcal{A})$. The two powerset SCCs $C$ and $C'$ were determinized starting with the sets $S$ and $S'$, respectively. The states in the constructed partial DPAs $\mathcal{B}_C$ and $\mathcal{B}_{C'}$ are depicted by the sets from $\mathsf{PS}(\mathcal{A})$ to which they are language-equivalent. It suffices to keep just one bottom SCC of each partial DPA (e.g. in the dotted rectangle) and connect them by exploiting the known language equivalences to introduce missing edges (e.g. the depicted bold edge).

### 4.5 State Reduction Using Mealy Minimization

A simple but powerful optimization that to our knowledge has not been considered yet, consists of first minimizing the number of priorities of the DPA (which can be done efficiently using a simple algorithm from [5]) and then applying the classical minimization algorithm by Hopcroft [16], by interpreting the DPA as a Mealy machine that outputs priorities. Since the minimization as Mealy machine preserves the priority sequence for each input, this clearly does not change the language of the DPA.

We believe that the effectiveness is due to the determinization procedure often returning automata with an unnecessarily large number of different priorities. Thus, the new priority function may assign edges with initially distinct priorities the same new priority. Thereby, paths with initially different priority sequences might become equivalent, ultimately leading to more states that can be merged. Because this is a pure post-processing step, it can be integrated easily into any determinization tool-chain.

## 5 Experiments and Discussion

Our quantitative experiments[1] involved different sets of Büchi automata that can be roughly grouped into two categories—automata obtained from LTL formulas and arbitrary automata. Most sets were generated and/or processed using tools included with `spot` [8] (version 2.6.3). All sets were filtered to exclude already deterministic Büchi automata. Furthermore, we filtered the sets to include only automata that are determinizable by `spot` (via `autfilt -D -P --high`) in reasonable time (between 1–30 min, depending on the size of the corresponding test set). This was also our benchmark for comparison. We explicitly compare

[1] Our prototype can be obtained at https://github.com/apirogov/nbautils.

only the size of the resulting automata and do not aim for competitive performance. However, most heuristics we proposed are computationally cheap, being essentially simple modifications of the successor calculation.

All LTL formulas were transformed to state-based Büchi automata using `ltl2tgba -B`. As we are evaluating only the impact of the heuristics during the transformation from Büchi to parity automata, the method to transform LTL formulas to Büchi automata does not matter. For the same reason, we do not compare with tools like `Rabinizer` [21] that bypass Büchi automata and Safra-style constructions. We are also aware of the fact that `spot` might have been able to produce smaller automata from LTL when using the usually smaller transition-based automata as input. As all our heuristics and optimizations in principle would work on those as well, we believe that this does not matter for our evaluation.

We used `autcross` to obtain statistics about different combinations of our heuristics as well as to ensure correctness of the generated automata. The test sets that we used were the following:

**raut:** 1662 random automata generated by `randaut` with 5–20 states (9 on average), mostly in one SCC.
**rautms:** 2112 random automata with 10–30 states (13 on average) generated by `randaut`, but filtered to have more than one SCC, specifically having at least one rejecting and at least one accepting component.
**rltl:** 11798 automata of various size (8 states on average) from random LTL formulas generated by `randltl`.
**gltl:** 68 automata from various parametrized LTL formula families generated by `genltl` that yield nondeterministic automata [7,14,15,22,23,29,36].
**scomp:** 113 automata from LTL formulas extracted from the TLSF-benchmarks directory of the SYNTCOMP [17] benchmark repository.

To reduce the exponential number of possible combinations of different heuristics and algorithm variants to a manageable amount, we fixed an order in which to add optimizations additionally to the previous configuration. We tested this sequence of cumulatively enabled optimizations for the three successor construction strategies proposed in the description of the generalized determinization algorithm [24], which correspond to the Muller-Schupp construction (abbreviated M.-S.), Safra's construction and the maximally collapsing merge rule (abbreviated Max.). The following list explains the used parameter combinations. In the tables, the optimization listed in a column is enabled *in addition* to the ones used in all previous columns.

**def:** only trimming of the automaton and the known true-loop optimization [19]
**+T:** topological optimization (Sect. 4.4)
**+E:** known external language inclusion [8] (Sect. 4.1)
**+I:** internal language inclusion (Sect. 4.1)
**+M:** priority minimization and state reduction (Sect. 4.5)
**+S:** smart successor selection using tries (Sect. 4.3)
**+A:** breakpoint construction for accepting SCCs (Sect. 4.2)

**+W:** optimization for both, accepting and rejecting SCCs (Sect. 4.2)
**+D:** optimization for deterministic SCCs (Sect. 4.2)

The results for our main benchmark test sets are shown in Table 1.

**Table 1.** Results of the quantitative experiments. The numbers show the fraction of the sum of states obtained by the indicated configuration of our implementation, compared to the sum of states of the automata obtained by `spot`. On the SYNTCOMP set we did not evaluate the least optimized configurations, as some optimizations were necessary to obtain results in acceptable time.

| | $\Sigma$ `spot` | mode | def | +T | +E | +I | +M | +S | +W | +D |
|---|---|---|---|---|---|---|---|---|---|---|
| | | M.-S | 2.42 | 2.31 | 2.31 | 2.31 | 1.33 | 1.07 | 1.07 | 1.07 |
| **raut** | 334523 | Safra | 1.14 | 1.00 | 1.00 | 1.00 | **0.80** | 0.82 | 0.82 | 0.82 |
| | | Max | 1.21 | 1.07 | 1.06 | 1.06 | 0.84 | 0.83 | 0.83 | 0.83 |
| | | M.-S | 1.28 | 1.21 | 0.92 | 0.92 | 0.77 | 0.70 | 0.68 | 0.68 |
| **rautms** | 286967 | Safra | 0.70 | 0.70 | 0.68 | 0.68 | 0.62 | 0.61 | **0.60** | 0.60 |
| | | Max | 0.73 | 0.72 | 0.71 | 0.71 | 0.64 | 0.62 | 0.61 | 0.61 |
| | | M.-S | 3.63 | 2.05 | 1.42 | 1.33 | **0.84** | 0.93 | 0.94 | 0.90 |
| **rltl** | 174251 | Safra | 4.15 | 2.67 | 1.76 | 1.61 | 0.93 | 0.96 | 0.97 | 0.92 |
| | | Max | 3.94 | 2.47 | 1.79 | 1.65 | 0.98 | 0.99 | 1.01 | 0.93 |
| | | M.-S | 3.12 | 1.98 | 1.97 | 1.87 | 1.18 | 1.08 | 1.07 | 1.00 |
| **gltl** | 3658 | Safra | 2.77 | 1.93 | 1.92 | 1.84 | 1.18 | 1.07 | 1.06 | 0.995 |
| | | Max | 2.39 | 1.71 | 1.70 | 1.62 | 1.00 | 1.05 | 1.05 | **0.994** |
| | | M.-S | | | 1.84 | 1.59 | 0.97 | 0.77 | 0.85 | 0.74 |
| **scomp** | 14502 | Safra | | | 1.92 | 1.58 | 0.98 | 0.72 | 0.78 | **0.69** |
| | | Max | | | 1.62 | 1.22 | 0.73 | 0.74 | 0.85 | 0.70 |

Our results show that for each test set there is a configuration of our prototype that, on average, produces automata that are not larger than the ones produced by `spot`. In many cases, the best configuration produces automata with up to 40% less states.

Unfortunately, the effect of the post-processing step with the priority minimization and state reduction (**+M**) is not robust even under minor variations of the automaton. This is, e.g., witnessed by the test set **rltl**, for which the state reduction without the smart successor selection yields better results. As only states that agree on all priority sequences of runs going through them can be merged by Hopcroft's algorithm, slight variations that lead to "symmetry breaking" may already render states non-mergeable. This optimization is more costly than the others, because equivalent states must be computed in the resulting automaton. But we believe that this is one of the most generally useful optimizations which is worth the additional computation time, as it quite consistently reduces the number of states by approximately 20–40%.

The smart selection of successors (**+S**) is the only proposed optimization which is "stateful", in the sense that it depends on the already constructed part of the automaton, which in turn depends on other enabled optimizations. In all but one test sets, this optimization was especially helpful in reducing states when using the Muller-Schupp successors. Interestingly, it was most successful in the Safra-based construction for the SYNTCOMP test set, where this optimization alone was responsible for an additional state reduction of 26%. The topological optimization (**+T**) yields a mild state reduction on random automata and significant reduction of up to 36% in the LTL-based test sets.

The application of the optimization that exploits language inclusion relations inside of a single SCC (**+I**) seems to have no visible effect on random automata, but was responsible for a decent additional state reduction of 6–8% for any variant of the construction in the LTL-based test sets. In our prototype we used only a simple direct simulation [10] for the optimizations. We are optimistic that using more involved simulations [11] to under-approximate language inclusion, e.g. fair simulation, would lead to even better results.

The heuristics for accepting and rejecting SCCs of the NBA (**+W**), while sometimes helpful, in other cases lead to an increase of the number of states. The separate handling of deterministic components, which is enabled in addition to all other optimizations, shows a positive effect mainly in the LTL-based automata test sets.

We now give some further examples that illustrate the potential effect of some of the heuristics. We start with the effect of our state reduction when determinizing the family of automata introduced by Michel in [27] (see also [38]) and which was used as a benchmark in [1]. A deterministic automaton recognizing the same language must have at least $n!$ states and is usually much larger in practice. While in [1] the Muller-Schupp construction performed significantly worse than Safra's construction, we were surprised to see that using the Muller-Schupp update in our own experiments, the Hopcroft minimization is able to drastically reduce the size of the automaton, producing much smaller automata than any other construction variant we tried (see Table 2).

**Table 2.** Results for Michel's automata family (input NBA have $n+1$ states for all $n$). The table demonstrates the surprising efficiency of the Muller-Schupp construction with subsequent state reduction.

| $n$ | spot | mode | def+TEI | +M | $n$ | spot | mode | def+TEI | +M |
|---|---|---|---|---|---|---|---|---|---|
| 2 | 18 | M.-S. | 19 | **17** | 4 | 2284 | M.-S. | 2725 | **457** |
| | | Safra | 18 | 18 | | | Safra | 2202 | 2106 |
| | | Max. | 18 | 18 | | | Max. | 2094 | 2094 |
| 3 | 145 | M.-S. | 166 | **82** | 5 | 60109 | M.-S. | 72616 | **2936** |
| | | Safra | 142 | 142 | | | Safra | 57714 | 57714 |
| | | Max. | 142 | 142 | | | Max. | 51094 | 51094 |

The heuristics for handling rejecting/accepting (**+W**) and deterministic (**+D**) SCCs of the NBA were enabled in addition to all other heuristics in the experiments shown in Table 1, and thus only had a small or even negative effect. In the following we give some examples showing that these heuristics indeed can have a strong positive effect. The deterministic SCC optimization is very useful for determinization of automata obtained from formulas $\varphi_{GH}(n) := \bigwedge_{i=1}^{n} \mathsf{GF}a_i \vee \mathsf{FG}a_{i+1}$ from [15]. An example where the heuristic which applies the breakpoint-style construction to accepting SCCs is very helpful is the family of formulas $\varphi_{MS}(n) := \bigvee_{i=0}^{n} \mathsf{FG}(\neg^i a \vee \mathsf{X}^i b)$ from [29], where the bottom SCCs of the automata are increasingly complex accepting SCCs (see Table 3).

**Table 3.** Results for some instances of the $\varphi_{GH}(n)$ and $\varphi_{MS}(n)$ formulas, with and without usage of suitable heuristics. Number of states obtained by `spot` is provided as reference in the tables. In case of $\varphi_{GH}$ formulas, `spot` profits significantly from the stutter-invariance optimization [20], which we do not utilize.

| | | M.-S. | | Safra | | max. | |
|---|---|---|---|---|---|---|---|
| Formula | `spot` | def.+TEI | +D | def.+TEI | +D | def.+TEI | +D |
| $\varphi_{GH}(2)$ | 18 | 30 | 32 | 29 | 32 | 28 | 32 |
| $\varphi_{GH}(3)$ | 108 | 385 | 255 | 327 | 255 | 381 | 266 |
| $\varphi_{GH}(4)$ | 2143 | 15206 | 5612 | 10922 | 5612 | 12394 | 5036 |
| Formula | `spot` | def.+TEI | +A | def.+TEI | +A | def.+TEI | +A |
| $\varphi_{MS}(2)$ | 21 | 40 | 16 | 40 | 16 | 36 | 16 |
| $\varphi_{MS}(3)$ | 170 | 371 | 46 | 371 | 46 | 155 | 46 |
| $\varphi_{MS}(4)$ | 1816 | 4933 | 132 | 4933 | 132 | 620 | 132 |
| $\varphi_{MS}(5)$ | 22196 | 67173 | 358 | 67173 | 358 | 2419 | 358 |

In summary, we noticed that the positive effects of the heuristics become stronger with growing size of the input automaton. This is not surprising, as for e.g. the SCC heuristics to have a positive effect, the automaton needs to be sufficiently complex. Unfortunately, larger input automata are not suitable for a thorough quantitative analysis in reasonable time. We are convinced, that for sufficiently large automata, even the heuristics that may appear not very effective in the presented benchmarks would have a stronger positive effect on average.

Our results also show that every proposed choice of the merge operation in the unified determinization construction seems to be superior in some cases. The Muller-Schupp update was the best choice on the random LTL test set, while the maximal collapse update was superior on the test set with the parametrized LTL formulas. Even though the unoptimized Muller-Schupp update usually seems to perform worst, combining it with some optimizations makes it a viable choice. The maximal collapsing update seems to perform comparably with the Safra update, but appears to be slightly worse in most cases, whereas the well-known Safra update seems to be a good middle ground.

## 6 Conclusion

We presented a number of new heuristic optimizations for the determinization of Büchi automata, and evaluated them in a prototype implementation using different test sets of automata, ranging from randomly generated automata to automata constructed from specifications from the competition SYNTCOMP. Our results show that these heuristics can significantly reduce the number of states in comparison with the base construction, and also in comparison with the current state-of-the-art tool `spot` for determinization of NBAs.

In future work, we want to study in more depth the effect of the heuristic based on language inclusions, by using stronger tools for identifying language inclusions between states of the Büchi automaton (currently we are only using direct simulation). We also see further potential in the smart successor selection, which could be used for redirecting transitions in the constructed automaton in order to reduce its size.

## References

1. Althoff, C.S., Thomas, W., Wallmeier, N.: Observations on determinization of Büchi automata. In: Farré, J., Litovsky, I., Schmitz, S. (eds.) CIAA 2005. LNCS, vol. 3845, pp. 262–272. Springer, Heidelberg (2006). https://doi.org/10.1007/11605157_22
2. Baier, C., Katoen, J.P.: Principles of Model Checking. MIT Press, Cambridge (2008)
3. Boigelot, B., Jodogne, S., Wolper, P.: On the use of weak automata for deciding linear arithmetic with integer and real variables. In: Goré, R., Leitsch, A., Nipkow, T. (eds.) IJCAR 2001. LNCS, vol. 2083, pp. 611–625. Springer, Heidelberg (2001). https://doi.org/10.1007/3-540-45744-5_50
4. Büchi, J.R.: On a decision method in restricted second order arithmetic. In: Studies in Logic and the Foundations of Mathematics, vol. 44, pp. 1–11. Elsevier (1966)
5. Carton, O., Maceiras, R.: Computing the Rabin index of a parity automaton. RAIRO-Theoret. Inform. Appl. **33**(6), 495–505 (1999)
6. Colcombet, T., Zdanowski, K.: A tight lower bound for determinization of transition labeled Büchi automata. In: Albers, S., Marchetti-Spaccamela, A., Matias, Y., Nikoletseas, S., Thomas, W. (eds.) ICALP 2009. LNCS, vol. 5556, pp. 151–162. Springer, Heidelberg (2009). https://doi.org/10.1007/978-3-642-02930-1_13
7. Duret-Lutz, A.: Manipulating LTL formulas using spot 1.0. In: Van Hung, D., Ogawa, M. (eds.) ATVA 2013. LNCS, vol. 8172, pp. 442–445. Springer, Cham (2013). https://doi.org/10.1007/978-3-319-02444-8_31
8. Duret-Lutz, A., Lewkowicz, A., Fauchille, A., Michaud, T., Renault, É., Xu, L.: Spot 2.0 — a framework for LTL and $\omega$-automata manipulation. In: Artho, C., Legay, A., Peled, D. (eds.) ATVA 2016. LNCS, vol. 9938, pp. 122–129. Springer, Cham (2016). https://doi.org/10.1007/978-3-319-46520-3_8
9. Esparza, J., Křetínský, J., Raskin, J.-F., Sickert, S.: From LTL and limit-deterministic Büchi automata to deterministic parity automata. In: Legay, A., Margaria, T. (eds.) TACAS 2017. LNCS, vol. 10205, pp. 426–442. Springer, Heidelberg (2017). https://doi.org/10.1007/978-3-662-54577-5_25

10. Etessami, K., Holzmann, G.J.: Optimizing Büchi automata. In: Palamidessi, C. (ed.) CONCUR 2000. LNCS, vol. 1877, pp. 153–168. Springer, Heidelberg (2000). https://doi.org/10.1007/3-540-44618-4_13
11. Etessami, K., Wilke, T., Schuller, R.A.: Fair simulation relations, parity games, and state space reduction for Büchi automata. SIAM J. Comput. **34**(5), 1159–1175 (2005)
12. Fisman, D., Lustig, Y.: A modular approach for Büchi determinization. In: CONCUR 2015. LIPIcs (2015)
13. Fogarty, S., Kupferman, O., Vardi, M.Y., Wilke, T.: Profile trees for Büchi word automata, with application to determinization. Inf. Comput. **245**, 136–151 (2015)
14. Gastin, P., Oddoux, D.: Fast LTL to Büchi automata translation. In: Berry, G., Comon, H., Finkel, A. (eds.) CAV 2001. LNCS, vol. 2102, pp. 53–65. Springer, Heidelberg (2001). https://doi.org/10.1007/3-540-44585-4_6
15. Geldenhuys, J., Hansen, H.: Larger automata and less work for LTL model checking. In: Valmari, A. (ed.) SPIN 2006. LNCS, vol. 3925, pp. 53–70. Springer, Heidelberg (2006). https://doi.org/10.1007/11691617_4
16. Hopcroft, J.: An n log n algorithm for minimizing states in a finite automaton. In: Theory of Machines and Computations, pp. 189–196. Elsevier (1971)
17. Jacobs, S., et al.: The 4th reactive synthesis competition (syntcomp 2017): benchmarks, participants & results. arXiv preprint arXiv:1711.11439 (2017)
18. Kähler, D., Wilke, T.: Complementation, disambiguation, and determinization of Büchi automata unified. In: Aceto, L., Damgård, I., Goldberg, L.A., Halldórsson, M.M., Ingólfsdóttir, A., Walukiewicz, I. (eds.) ICALP 2008. LNCS, vol. 5125, pp. 724–735. Springer, Heidelberg (2008). https://doi.org/10.1007/978-3-540-70575-8_59
19. Klein, J.: Linear time logic and deterministic omega-automata. Diploma thesis, University of Bonn (2005)
20. Klein, J., Baier, C.: On-the-fly stuttering in the construction of deterministic $\omega$-automata. In: Holub, J., Žd'árek, J. (eds.) CIAA 2007. LNCS, vol. 4783, pp. 51–61. Springer, Heidelberg (2007). https://doi.org/10.1007/978-3-540-76336-9_7
21. Křetínský, J., Meggendorfer, T., Sickert, S., Ziegler, C.: Rabinizer 4: from LTL to your favourite deterministic automaton. In: Chockler, H., Weissenbacher, G. (eds.) CAV 2018. LNCS, vol. 10981, pp. 567–577. Springer, Cham (2018). https://doi.org/10.1007/978-3-319-96145-3_30
22. Kupferman, O., Rosenberg, A.: The blow-up in translating LTL to deterministic automata. In: van der Meyden, R., Smaus, J.-G. (eds.) MoChArt 2010. LNCS (LNAI), vol. 6572, pp. 85–94. Springer, Heidelberg (2011). https://doi.org/10.1007/978-3-642-20674-0_6
23. Kupferman, O., Vardi, M.Y.: From linear time to branching time. TOCL **6**, 273–294 (2005)
24. Löding, C., Pirogov, A.: Determinization of Büchi automata: unifying the approaches of Safra and Muller-Schupp. ICALP 2019 https://arxiv.org/abs/1902.02139
25. McNaughton, R.: Testing and generating infinite sequences by a finite automaton. Inf. Control **9**(5), 521–530 (1966)
26. Meyer, P.J., Sickert, S., Luttenberger, M.: Strix: explicit reactive synthesis strikes back!. In: Chockler, H., Weissenbacher, G. (eds.) CAV 2018. LNCS, vol. 10981, pp. 578–586. Springer, Cham (2018). https://doi.org/10.1007/978-3-319-96145-3_31
27. Michel, M.: Complementation is more difficult with automata on infinite words. Manuscript, CNET, Paris (1988)

28. Miyano, S., Hayashi, T.: Alternating finite automata on $\omega$-words. Theoret. Comput. Sci. **32**(3), 321–330 (1984)
29. Müller, D., Sickert, S.: LTL to deterministic Emerson-Lei automata. In: GandALF 2017
30. Muller, D.E., Schupp, P.E.: Simulating alternating tree automata by nondeterministic automata: new results and new proofs of the theorems of Rabin, McNaughton and Safra. Theoret. Comput. Sci. **141**(1–2), 69–107 (1995)
31. Piterman, N.: From nondeterministic Büchi and Streett automata to deterministic parity automata. In: LICS 2006. IEEE (2006)
32. Pnueli, A.: The temporal logic of programs. In: 1977 18th Annual Symposium on Foundations of Computer Science, pp. 46–57. IEEE (1977)
33. Redziejowski, R.R.: An improved construction of deterministic omega-automaton using derivatives. Fundamenta Informaticae **119**(3–4), 393–406 (2012)
34. Safra, S.: On the complexity of omega-automata. In: 1988 29th Annual Symposium on Foundations of Computer Science, pp. 319–327. IEEE (1988)
35. Schewe, S.: Tighter bounds for the determinisation of Büchi automata. In: de Alfaro, L. (ed.) FoSSaCS 2009. LNCS, vol. 5504, pp. 167–181. Springer, Heidelberg (2009). https://doi.org/10.1007/978-3-642-00596-1_13
36. Tabakov, D., Vardi, M.Y.: Optimized temporal monitors for systemC. In: Barringer, H., et al. (eds.) RV 2010. LNCS, vol. 6418, pp. 436–451. Springer, Heidelberg (2010). https://doi.org/10.1007/978-3-642-16612-9_33
37. Thomas, W.: Automata on infinite objects. In: Handbook of Theoretical Computer Science, vol. B, pp. 133–192. Elsevier Science Publishers, Amsterdam (1990)
38. Thomas, W.: Languages, automata, and logic. In: Rozenberg, G., Salomaa, A. (eds.) Handbook of Formal Languages, pp. 389–455. Springer, Heidelberg (1997). https://doi.org/10.1007/978-3-642-59126-6_7
39. Thomas, W.: Church's problem and a tour through automata theory. In: Avron, A., Dershowitz, N., Rabinovich, A. (eds.) Pillars of Computer Science. LNCS, vol. 4800, pp. 635–655. Springer, Heidelberg (2008). https://doi.org/10.1007/978-3-540-78127-1_35
40. Vardi, M.Y., Wilke, T.: Automata: from logics to algorithms. In: Logic and Automata - History and Perspectives, Texts in Logic and Games, vol. 2, pp. 629–724. Amsterdam University Press (2007)

# Approximate Automata for Omega-Regular Languages

Rayna Dimitrova[1], Bernd Finkbeiner[2], and Hazem Torfah[2(✉)]

[1] University of Leicester, Leicester, UK
[2] Saarland University, Saarbrücken, Germany
torfah@react.uni-saarland.de

**Abstract.** Automata over infinite words, also known as $\omega$-automata, play a key role in the verification and synthesis of reactive systems. The spectrum of $\omega$-automata is defined by two characteristics: the *acceptance condition* (e.g. Büchi or parity) and the *determinism* (e.g., deterministic or nondeterministic) of an automaton. These characteristics play a crucial role in applications of automata theory. For example, certain acceptance conditions can be handled more efficiently than others by dedicated tools and algorithms. Furthermore, some applications, such as synthesis and probabilistic model checking, require that properties are represented as some type of deterministic $\omega$-automata. However, properties cannot always be represented by automata with the desired acceptance condition and determinism.

In this paper we study the problem of approximating linear-time properties by automata in a given class. Our approximation is based on preserving the language up to a user-defined precision given in terms of the size of the finite lasso representation of infinite executions that are preserved. We study the state complexity of different types of approximating automata, and provide constructions for the approximation within different automata classes, for example, for approximating a given automaton by one with a simpler acceptance condition.

## 1 Introduction

The specification of linear-time properties is a key ingredient of all typical frameworks for the verification and synthesis of reactive systems. The application of both automata-theoretic and symbolic algorithms requires that specifications are translated to some kind of $\omega$-automata. Depending on the considered problem, or on the applied methods and tools, there are often constraints on the type of the resulting automaton, that is, on its acceptance condition, and on whether it is deterministic or not. For example, while for model checking of non-stochastic

This work was partially supported by the German Research Foundation (DFG) as part of the Collaborative Research Center "Methods and Tools for Understanding and Controlling Privacy" (CRC 1223) and the Collaborative Research Center "Foundations of Perspicuous Software Systems" (TRR 248, 389792660), and by the European Research Council (ERC) Grant OSARES (No. 683300).


Y.-F. Chen et al. (Eds.): ATVA 2019, LNCS 11781, pp. 334–349, 2019.
https://doi.org/10.1007/978-3-030-31784-3_19

systems it suffices to consider nondeterministic Büchi automata, synthesis and probabilistic model checking require deterministic automata (e.g., deterministic parity automata). Furthermore, it is often the case that efficient specialized methods and tools exist for specific classes of automata i.e., specific acceptance conditions. For instance, efficient synthesis algorithms exist for the class GR(1) of linear-time temporal logic specifications [2], which defines properties that are expressible as deterministic parity automata with three colors.

Finding an equivalent automaton with a simpler acceptance condition is not always possible. The canonical example is the property defined by the linear-time temporal logic (LTL) formula $\Diamond\Box p$, for which no deterministic Büchi automaton exists. A more interesting example is given by the LTL formula $\varphi = (\Box\Diamond p \rightarrow \Box\Diamond q) \wedge (\Box\Diamond r \rightarrow \Box\Diamond s)$, which requires that if the proposition $p$ holds infinitely often then the proposition $q$ should hold infinitely often as well, and the same for the propositions $r$ and $s$. Requirements of this form occur often in the synthesis of reactive systems, but the formula $\varphi$ cannot be represented by a deterministic parity automaton with three colors, and cannot be transformed to a formula in the efficient class of GR(1) specifications. Moreover, automata with simpler acceptance conditions can often be larger in size than automata with more general acceptance conditions. For instance, there are languages for which deterministic Streett automata are exponentially smaller than nondeterministic Büchi automata [17].

Motivated by this, we study the problem of approximating linear-time properties (respectively $\omega$-automata) by automata in a given class (respectively automata from a given subclass). The choice of language approximation is inspired by applications in bounded model checking [5] and bounded synthesis [9]. These methods are based on the observation that for finite-state systems, it suffices to consider lasso-shaped executions of bounded size. Our approximation exploits the same idea for the construction and transformation of automata. Furthermore, equivalent $\omega$-regular languages share the same set ultimately-periodic words [4], and thus lasso-shaped words of bounded size provide an approximation to this set of words, one that improves when considering larger bounds on the size of lassos.

Given an $\omega$-language $L$ and a bound $n \in \mathbb{N}$, we consider the language $L_n$ of the ultimately-periodic words in $L$ representable in the form $u \cdot v^\omega$, and where $|u \cdot v| \leq n$. That is, the language $L_n \subseteq L$ consists of the words in $L$ representable as *lassos of length $n$ or smaller*. We are then interested in approximations of $L$ that are precise with respect to the language $L_n$, termed *$n$-lasso-precise approximations.*

We study the properties of $n$-lasso-precise approximations across the three dimensions of the complexity of the automata for such languages: size, acceptance condition, and determinism. More precisely, we establish worst case bounds, in terms of $n$, on the size of automata for $n$-lasso-precise approximations. We also show that we can approximate a parity automaton with $m$ colors by one with $m' < m$ colors, with at most polynomial increase in the size of the automaton. For example, considering the formula $\varphi$ above, if we underapproximate the language of $\varphi$ with a language that is precise with respect to the set of words representable by lassos of length $n$ for a fixed $n$, we can represent the resulting language by a safety automaton (a parity automaton with one color). Furthermore, if, for example, $n = 2$ the resulting automaton has 4 states, while the minimal deterministic parity automaton for the language of $\varphi$ has 95 states and 10 colors. We also study the approximation of nondeterministic by deterministic automata, and show that the worst-case exponential blow-up in the size is unavoidable for $n$-lasso-precise approximations.

As another example, consider the property described by the LTL formula $(\Diamond\Box p) \wedge (\Box\Diamond q)$, where $p$ and $q$ are some atomic propositions. This is a conjunction of a stability property and a liveness property, which is also not expressible in the fragment GR(1). We can approximate this property by an $n$-lasso-precise deterministic Büchi automaton, enabling the application of efficient synthesis tools. Most importantly, unlike existing approaches, our method is not limited to approximating liveness properties by safety properties, which benefits the precision of the approximation.

The paper is structured as follows. In Sect. 2 we start with a short background on linear-time properties and $\omega$-automata. In Sect. 3 we introduce the notion of $n$-lasso-precise approximation of linear-time temporal properties, and present all relevant automata constructions for these approximations. Here, we establish property-independent upper and lower bounds on the size of $\omega$-automata for $n$-lasso-precise approximations, and study the overhead in terms of size incurred when approximating an automaton by one with a simpler acceptance condition. In Sect. 4 we show that the problem of computing lasso-precise automata of bounded size for properties given as LTL formulas is in $\Sigma_2^P$. In Sect. 5 we conclude our results with a discussion on our approach and its potential for the development of new verification and synthesis algorithms.

**Related Work.** Our definition of bounded lasso-precise approximation is motivated by bounded model checking [5], bounded synthesis [9], synthesis for bounded environments [6], and synthesis of approximate implementations [15]. We extend these ideas of focusing on small counterexamples, small implementations, or bounded-state environments, respectively, to the realm of specifications.

The structural complexity of $\omega$–automata has been studied in [3,14], where the acceptance conditions of deterministic automata are related to their complexity. Here, on the other hand, we study complexity questions in the context of language approximations.

There is a rich body of work on the minimization of Büchi automata. Typical approaches, such as [8,12,21] are based on merging states according to simulation and bisimulation relations. In [7] the authors propose a SAT-solver based minimization method. All these approaches consider language equivalence, while in this paper we study language approximation.

Reducing the size of automata by language approximation has been studied in the context of languages over finite words. The approach in [10] fixes a bound in the number of the states of a deterministic finite automaton for a safety language, and computes an automaton within that bound that approximates the original language. In addition to the fact that their method applies to languages over finite words, the key difference to our work is that while their goal is to optimize precision within a state budget, we approximate automata with ones with simpler acceptance conditions that guarantees a desired precision. In descriptive complexity, there is a related notion to our $n$-lasso precision, which is the notion of the automaticity [20] of a language which is the size of the minimal automaton that is precise for that language on words of length up to a given bound $n$. As automaticity is defined for finite-word languages, $n$-lasso precision can be seen as lifting these ideas to $\omega$-languages.

The approximation of $\omega$-regular properties by ones with simpler acceptance conditions has not been, to the best of our knowledge, systematically studied so far. Standard approaches, such as [1,19], approximate liveness and other temporal properties via safety properties. In contrast, our approximation allows us to approximate temporal properties with other temporal properties that are not necessarily safety.

## 2 Preliminaries

*Linear-Time Properties and Lassos.* A *linear-time property* $\varphi$ over an alphabet $\Sigma$ is a set of infinite words $\varphi \subseteq \Sigma^\omega$. Elements of $\varphi$ are called *models* of $\varphi$. A *lasso of length* $n$ over an alphabet $\Sigma$ is a pair $(u, v)$ of finite words $u \in \Sigma^*$ and $v \in \Sigma^+$ with $|u \cdot v| = n$ that induces the ultimately-periodic word $u \cdot v^\omega$. We call $u \cdot v$ the *base* of the lasso or ultimately-periodic word, and $n$ the *length of the lasso.* The set $Bases(\varphi, n)$ is the set of bases of lassos of length $n$ that induce words that are models of $\varphi$.

For a bound $n \in \mathbb{N}$, we define the language $L_n(\varphi) = \{\sigma \in \Sigma^\omega \mid \exists u \cdot v \in Bases(\varphi, n).\ \sigma = u \cdot v^\omega\}$ as the language of models of $\varphi$ that can be represented by lassos of length $n$. We call the elements of $L_n(\varphi)$ the *n-models* of $\varphi$.

If a finite word $w \in \Sigma^*$ is a prefix of a word $\sigma \in \Sigma^* \cup \Sigma^\omega$, we write $w \preceq \sigma$. For a language $L \subseteq \Sigma^* \cup \Sigma^\omega$, we define $Prefix(L) = \{w \in \Sigma^* \mid \exists \sigma \in L : w \preceq \sigma\}$ as the set of all finite words that are prefixes of words in the language $L$. For a word $w = \alpha_1\alpha_2 \ldots \alpha_n \in \Sigma^*$ we define $w(i) = \alpha_i$ for each $i \in \{1, \ldots, n\}$.

*Automata Over Infinite Words.* A *nondeterministic parity automaton* over an alphabet $\Sigma$ is a tuple $\mathcal{A} = (Q, Q_0, \delta, \mu)$, where $Q$ denotes a finite set of states, $Q_0 \subseteq Q$ denotes a set of initial states, $\delta : Q \times \Sigma \to \mathcal{P}(Q)$ denotes a transition function that maps a state and an input letter to a set of states, and $\mu : Q \to C \subset \mathbb{N}$ is a coloring function with a finite set of colors $C$.

A *run* of $\mathcal{A} = (Q, Q_0, \delta, \mu)$ on an infinite word $\sigma = \alpha_1\alpha_2 \cdots \in \Sigma^\omega$ is an infinite sequence $\rho = q_0q_1q_2 \ldots \in Q^\omega$ of states such that $q_0 \in Q_0$, and for every $i \in \mathbb{N}$ it holds that $q_{i+1} \in \delta(q_i, \alpha_{i+1})$. A run $\rho = q_0q_1q_2 \ldots$ is *accepting* if it satisfies the *parity condition*, which requires that the highest number occurring infinitely often in the sequence $\mu(q_0)\mu(q_1)\mu(q_2) \cdots \in C^\omega$ is even. An infinite word $\sigma$ is *accepted* by an automaton $\mathcal{A}$ if there exists an accepting run of $\mathcal{A}$ on $\sigma$. The set of infinite words accepted by an automaton $\mathcal{A}$ is called its *language* $L(\mathcal{A})$.

We say that a run $\rho$ *has size* $n \in \mathbb{N}$ if $\rho$ is an ultimately-periodic run and $n$ is the smallest natural number such that $\rho = \rho_1 \cdot (\rho_2)^\omega$ and $|\rho_1 \cdot \rho_2| = n$.

An automaton is *deterministic* if $|Q_0| = 1$, and for all states $q$ and input letters $\alpha$, $|\delta(q, \alpha)| \leq 1$. For a deterministic automaton we will see $\delta$ as a partial function $\delta : Q \times \Sigma \rightarrow Q$. We use the notation $\delta(q, \alpha) = \emptyset$ to denote that state $q$ has no successor for the letter $\alpha$. We define the size $|\mathcal{A}|$ of an automaton $\mathcal{A}$ to be the number of its states, i.e., $|\mathcal{A}| = |Q|$.

A parity automaton is called a *Büchi automaton* if and only if the image of $\mu$ is contained in $\{1, 2\}$, and a *safety* automaton if the image of $\mu$ is $\{0\}$. Büchi automata are denoted by $(Q, Q_0, \delta, F)$, where $F \subseteq Q$ denotes the states with the higher color. Safety automata are denoted by $(Q, Q_0, \delta)$. A run of a Büchi automaton is thus accepting, if it contains infinitely many visits to $F$. For safety automata, every infinite run is accepting.

We define an *automaton type* to indicate whether the automaton is deterministic or nondeteministic, and its acceptance condition. We abbreviate deterministic as D and nondeterministic as N. For the acceptance conditions we use the abbreviations P (parity) and B (Büchi). Thus, for example, DPA stands for deterministic parity automaton, while NBA stands for Nondeterministic Büchi automaton.

## 3 Lasso-Precise Approximations of Linear-Time Properties

We begin this section with a formal definition of the approximation of linear-time properties discussed in the introduction. More precisely, we introduce the notion of *lasso-precise under-* and *overapproximation* of a linear-time property $\varphi$ for a given bound $n \in \mathbb{N}$, in which we underapproximate (overapproximate) $\varphi$ with a linear-time property that has the same $n$-models as $\varphi$. That is, the approximation is precise for $n$-models.

### 3.1 Lasso-Precise Approximations

**Definition 1 (Lasso-precise Underapproximation).** *For a bound $n \in \mathbb{N}$, we say that a linear-time property $\varphi'$ is an $n$-lasso-precise underapproximation of a linear-time property $\varphi$, denoted $\varphi' \subseteq_n \varphi$, if $\varphi' \subseteq \varphi$ and $L_n(\varphi') = L_n(\varphi)$.*

**Definition 2 (Lasso-precise Overapproximation).** *For a bound $n \in \mathbb{N}$, we say that a linear-time property $\varphi'$ is an $n$-lasso-precise overapproximation of a linear-time property $\varphi$, denoted $\varphi' \supseteq_n \varphi$, if $\varphi' \supseteq \varphi$ and $L_n(\varphi') = L_n(\varphi)$.*

In the rest of the paper we focus on underapproximations. All the results extend easily to lasso-precise overapproximations. In fact, if we have also the complement language of $\varphi$, an $n$-lasso-precise overapproximation of a property $\varphi$ can be computed by computing an $n$-lasso-precise underapproximation of the complement of $\varphi$.

In the next sections we show how to construct automata for $n$-lasso-precise approximations of linear-time properties. For a property $\varphi$ the automata will recognize the language $L_n(\varphi)$. This language includes also all words in $\varphi$ that are representable by a lasso of size $n' \leq n$, a fact that we establish with the next lemma.

**Lemma 1.** *For any linear-time property $\varphi$ and bounds $n, n' \in \mathbb{N}$, we have that $L_n(\varphi) \subseteq L_{n'}(\varphi)$, if $n \leq n'$.*

*Proof.* Every lasso of length $n$ can be unrolled to a lasso of length $n'$ by unrolling the loop $n' - n$ times. □

### 3.2 The Size of Lasso-Precise Automata for Linear-Time Properties

Since for any $\varphi$ the language $L_n(\varphi)$ is a safety language, we can always construct a deterministic safety automaton that is $n$-lasso-precise. In the following we provide a construction which yields a deterministic safety automaton for a language $L_n(\varphi)$, and establish a lower bound on the size of an automaton for $L_n(\varphi)$.

**Theorem 1 (Safety automata for $n$-lasso-precise approximations).** *For every linear-time property $\varphi$ over an alphabet $\Sigma$ and a bound $n \in \mathbb{N}$, there is a deterministic safety automaton $\mathcal{A}$ of size $O(|\Sigma|^n \cdot 2^{n \log n})$, such that $L(\mathcal{A}) \subseteq_n \varphi$.*

*Idea and Construction.* The automaton $\mathcal{A}$ accepts a word in two phases. The states used in the first phase are of the form $w \cdot \#^{m-1} \in (\Sigma \cup \{\#\})^n$, where $w$ is the portion of the prefix of length $n$ of the input word that has been read so far. In this phase, the automaton reads the prefix of length $n$ and stores it in the automaton state. Once the whole prefix is read, it checks whether the prefix of length $n$ is in $Bases(\varphi, n)$. If this is the case, then it transitions to the second phase, and checks if the word being read is an $n$-lasso, with this base.

The states in the second phase are of the form $(w, (t_1, \ldots, t_n)) \in \Sigma^n \times \{-, 1, \ldots, n\}^n$, where $w \in \Sigma^n$ is the prefix read in the first phase, and $(t_1, \ldots, t_n)$ are indices of letters in $w$, whose role is explained below. To check that the word is an $n$-lasso, the automaton has to check if for some $\ell \in \{1, \ldots, n\}$ the input word is of the form $w(1) \ldots w(\ell - 1)(w(\ell) \ldots w(n))^\omega$, that is, there is an $\ell$ which is a loop start position. To this end, the automaton tracks the possible loop start positions, starting with all positions, and for each new letter $\alpha$ it eliminates those positions that are not compatible with $\alpha$. More precisely, if the automaton reads a letter $\alpha$ in state $(w, (t_1, \ldots, t_n))$, it uses each $t_i$ to check whether the loop can start in position $i$ of $w$. Intuitively, $t_i$ is a position in $w$ that points to the letter that has to be read next in order for $i$ to still be a possible loop start position. If the next letter $\alpha$ is not the same as $w(t_i)$, then $i$ cannot be a loop start position, and $t_i$ is eliminated by replacing it by $-$. Otherwise, $t_i$ is incremented, or set back to the loop start $i$ if the end of $w$ is reached. A run of $\mathcal{A}$ is accepting if it never reaches a state $(w, (-, \dots, -))$, that is, a state in which each position is no longer a possible start of a loop.

Formally, the states of the automaton are given by $\mathcal{A} = (Q, \{q_0\}, \delta)$ where:

- $Q = Q_1 \cup Q_2$, where $Q_1 = (\Sigma \cup \{\#\})^n$ and $Q_2 = \Sigma^n \times \{-, 1, \dots, n\}^n$
- In the initial state no letter has been read: $q_0 = \#^n$.
- The transition relation $\delta$ is defined as follows.
  - In the first phase if we are at a state $q = w \cdot \#^m$ for some $1 < m \leq n$ and $w \in \Sigma^{n-m}$, then
$$\delta(q, \alpha) = w \cdot \alpha \cdot \#^{m-1}$$
  - In the transition between the first and the second phase, which happens once the prefix of length $n$ has been read, and when we are at a state $q = w \cdot \#$ for some $w \in \Sigma^{n-1}$ the transition is given by
$$\delta(q, \alpha) = (w \cdot \alpha, (t_1, \dots, t_n))$$
where
$$t_i = \begin{cases} i & w(1) \dots (w(i) \dots w(n))^\omega \in \varphi \\ - & \text{otherwise} \end{cases}$$
Note that determining the successor state in this case requires checking if a given word is in $\varphi$. Initially, only loop start positions $i$ for which $w(1) \dots (w(i) \dots w(n))^\omega \in \varphi$ are allowed, so the second phase starts with state $(w, (t_1, \dots, t_n))$, in which each pointer $t_i$ points to the start of the corresponding loop if $w(1) \dots (w(i) \dots w(n))^\omega \in \varphi$, and is set to $-$ otherwise.
  - In the second phase, for a state $q = (w, (t_1, \dots, t_n))$ with $w \in \Sigma^n$ and where there exists $i \leq n$ with $t_i \neq -$, the transition for such a state is given by
$$\delta(q, \alpha) = (w, (t'_1, \dots, t'_n))$$
where
$$t'_i = \begin{cases} - & t_i = - \\ & \text{or } w(t_i) \neq \alpha \\ t_i + 1 & t_i < n \ \wedge \ w(t_i) = \alpha \\ i & t_i = n \ \wedge \ w(t_i) = \alpha \end{cases}$$
Here we track valid loop start position as follows. If $\alpha \neq w(t_i)$, then the loop start $i$ is eliminated by replacing $t_i$ by $-$. Otherwise, we move the pointer one step to the right by incrementing $t_i$. In case $t_i$ is equal to $n$, i.e., at the end of the lasso, $t_i$ is reset to the corresponding loop start position $i$.
  - If only $-$ remain in the tuple $(t_1, \dots, t_n)$, the automaton rejects
$$\delta((w, (-, \dots, -)), \alpha) = \emptyset$$
for any $w \in \Sigma^n$.

The number of states in $Q_1$ is $(|\Sigma|+1)^n$, and for $Q_2$ it is $|\Sigma|^n \cdot (n+1)^n$. □

The number of states of the deterministic safety automaton defined above is exponential in the parameter $n$ on the length of the lassos for which the approximation should be precise. In the next theorem we exhibit a family of linear-time properties for which this exponent is unavoidable, that is, the minimal $n$-lasso-precise NPA has size exponential in $n$.

**Theorem 2.** *There is a family of linear-time properties $\varphi_n$ for $n \in \mathbb{N}$ over an alphabet $\Sigma$, such that, every parity automaton that is $n$-lasso-precise for $\varphi_n$ has at least $|\Sigma|^n$ states.*

*Proof.* Let $\Sigma$ be an alphabet. We define $\varphi_n = \{\sigma^\omega \mid \sigma \in \Sigma^n\}$ for $n \in \mathbb{N}$. We show that the family $\varphi_n$ of linear-time properties has the required properties.

Fix $n \in \mathbb{N}$, and consider the language $\varphi_n$. By definition of $\varphi_n$, every lasso-precise automaton for $\varphi_n$ for the bound $n$ is in fact an automaton for $\varphi_n$. Let $\mathcal{A} = (Q, Q_0, \delta, \mu)$ be a nondeterministic parity automaton for $\varphi_n$. For each $\sigma^\omega \in \varphi_n$ there exists at least one accepting run $\rho = q_0 q_1 q_2, \ldots$ of $\mathcal{A}$ on $\sigma^\omega$. We denote with $q(\rho, n)$ the state $q_n$ that appears at the position indexed $n$ of a run $\rho$. Let us define the set

$$Q_n = \{q(\rho, n) \mid \exists \sigma^\omega \in \varphi_n : \rho \text{ is an accepting run of } \mathcal{A} \text{ on } \sigma^\omega\}.$$

That is, $Q_n$ consists of the states that appear at position $n$ on some accepting run on some word from $\varphi_n$. We will show that $|Q_n| \geq |\Sigma|^n$.

Assume that this does not hold, that is, $|Q_n| < |\Sigma|^n$. Since $|\varphi_n| = |\Sigma|^n$, this implies that there exist $\sigma_1, \sigma_2 \in \Sigma^n$, such that $\sigma_1 \neq \sigma_2$ and there exists accepting runs $\rho_1$ and $\rho_2$ of $\mathcal{A}$ on $\sigma_1^\omega$ and $\sigma_2^\omega$ respectively, such that $q(\rho_1, n) = q(\rho_2, n)$. That is, since we assumed that the number of states in $Q_n$ is smaller than the number of words in $\varphi_n$, there must be two different words who have accepting runs visiting the same state at position $n$. We now construct a run $\rho_{1,2}$ that follows $\rho_1$ for the first $n$ steps, ending in state $q(\rho_1, n)$, and from there on follows $\rho_2$. It is easy to see that $\rho_{1,2}$ is a run on the word $\sigma_1 \cdot \sigma_2^\omega$. It is accepting, since $\rho_2$ is accepting. This is a contradiction, since $\sigma_1 \cdot \sigma_2^\omega \notin L(\mathcal{A})$ as $\sigma_1 \neq \sigma_2$.

Thus, we have shown that $|Q| \geq |Q_n| \geq |\Sigma|^n$. Since $\mathcal{A}$ was an arbitrary NPA for $\varphi_n$, this implies that the minimal NPA for $\varphi_n$ has at least $|\Sigma|^n$ states. □

In the theorems above we established an upper and a lower bound on the size of automata for $n$-lasso-precise approximations. These bounds are independent of the way the original language is represented. If a language $L$ is given as an $\omega$-automaton, this automaton is clearly an automaton for the most precise $n$-lasso-precise underapproximation of $L$. In practice, however, we might be interested in finding a smaller/minimal automaton of the same type for an $n$-lasso-precise approximation of $L$. Note that the minimal $n$-lasso-precise automaton of the same type will never be larger than the given automaton.

### 3.3 Lasso-Precise Approximations with Simpler Acceptance Conditions

We now turn to establishing the upper bounds for approximating Büchi automata with safety automata, and, more generally, approximating parity automata with parity automata with fewer colors. More precisely, we present constructions for approximating linear-time properties with automata with certain acceptance conditions and show that the size of the constructed automaton is polynomial in the size of an automaton for the original property.

**Theorem 3 (Approximating Büchi automata by safety automata).** *For every (deterministic or nondeterministic) Büchi automaton* $\mathcal{A} = (Q, Q_0, \delta, F)$ *and a bound* $n \in \mathbb{N}$*, there is a (deterministic or nondeterministic, respectively) safety automaton* $\mathcal{A}'$ *with* $n \cdot |Q \setminus F|^2 + |F|$ *states, such that,* $L(\mathcal{A}') \subseteq_n L(\mathcal{A})$*.*

*Idea and Construction.* We construct a safety automaton $\mathcal{A}'$ using the following idea: If an ultimately-periodic word $\sigma = u \cdot v^\omega$ with $|u \cdot v| = n$ is accepted by a Büchi automaton $\mathcal{A} = (Q, Q_0, \delta, F)$, then $\mathcal{A}$ has a run for $\sigma$, where it takes no more than $n \cdot |Q \setminus F|$ steps to observe a state in $F$, and, furthermore $F$ is visited at least once every $n \cdot |Q \setminus F|$ steps. In the automaton $\mathcal{A}'$, we keep track of the number of steps without seeing an accepting state, and reset the counter every time we visit one. If the counter exceeds $n \cdot |Q \setminus F|$, then $\mathcal{A}'$ rejects.

Formally, we define $\mathcal{A}' = (Q', Q'_0, \delta')$ as follows:

- $Q' = ((Q \setminus F) \times \{1, \ldots, n \cdot |Q \setminus F|\}) \cup (F \times \{0\})$
- $Q'_0 = (Q_0 \cap F) \times \{0\} \cup (Q_0 \setminus F) \times \{1\}$
- For the transition relation we distinguish two cases. For $c < n \cdot |Q \setminus F|$

$$\delta((q,c),\alpha) = \{(q',d) \mid q' \in \delta(q,\alpha),\ d = 0 \text{ if } q' \in F,\ d = c+1 \text{ if } q' \notin F\}$$

otherwise $\delta((q,c),\alpha) = \emptyset$.

Note that, if the given Büchi automaton is deterministic, then our construction also produces a deterministic safety automaton. □

Theorems 1 and 3 provide safety automata of different sizes: the safety automaton obtained by Theorem 1 is exponential in the bound, the safety automaton obtained by Theorem 3 is linear in the bound. The reason for this difference is that the size of the automaton constructed according to Theorem 1 is independent of the linear-time property, whereas the size of the automaton constructed according to Theorem 3 is for a specific linear-time property (given as a Büchi automaton, whose size enters as a quadratic factor). The following theorem shows that a further reduction, below the linear number of states in the bound, is impossible.

**Theorem 4.** *There is a linear-time property* $\varphi$*, such that, for every bound* $n \in \mathbb{N}$*, every safety* $n$*-lasso-precise automaton for* $\varphi$ *has at least* $n$ *states.*

*Proof.* Let $\Sigma = \{0, 1\}$. We define $\varphi$ as the language over $\Sigma$ that consists of all words where the letter 1 occurs infinitely often. Let $\mathcal{A} = (Q, Q_0, \delta)$ be a safety $n$-lasso-precise automaton for $\varphi$. We consider the set $Q' \subseteq Q$ of states on the first $n$ positions of an accepting run of the word $(0^{n-1}1)^\omega$. We show that $|Q'| = n$ and, therefore, $|Q| \geq n$.

Assume that this does not hold, i.e., $|Q'| < n$; then some state $q$ must appear on two different positions among the first $n$ positions of the run. By repeating the part of the run between the two occurrences of $q$ infinitely often, we obtain an accepting run for the word $0^\omega$, which contradicts our assumption that $\mathcal{A}$ is $n$-lasso-precise for $\varphi$. □

With a construction similar to Theorem 3, we can approximate a parity automaton with $m + 1$ colors by a parity automaton with $m$ colors.

**Theorem 5 (Approximating parity automata by parity automata with one color less).** *For every deterministic parity automaton* $\mathcal{A} = (Q, Q_0, \delta, \mu)$ *with* $m + 1$ *colors and a bound* $n \in \mathbb{N}$, *there is a deterministic parity automaton* $\mathcal{A}'$ *with* $m$ *colors and* $n \cdot |Q \setminus F|^2 + |F|$ *states, where* $F$ *is the set of states with highest color, such that* $L(\mathcal{A}') \subseteq_n L(\mathcal{A})$.

By iteratively applying Theorem 5, we can approximate any parity automaton with $m$ colors by a corresponding parity automaton with $m' < m$ colors. This, however, will incur a blow-up in the size of the automaton that is exponential in the number $m$ of colors. We now provide a direct construction, which is polynomial both in $m$ and in the size of $\mathcal{A}$.

**Theorem 6 (Approximating parity automata by parity automata with fewer colors).** *For every deterministic parity automaton* $\mathcal{A} = (Q, Q_0, \delta, \mu)$ *with* $m$ *colors, a bound* $n \in \mathbb{N}$ *and* $0 < m' < m$, *there is a deterministic parity automaton* $\mathcal{A}'$ *with* $m'$ *colors and* $(n \cdot |Q| + 1) \cdot |Q| \cdot (m - m' + 2)$ *states such that* $L(\mathcal{A}') \subseteq_n \mathcal{L}(\mathcal{A})$.

*Idea and Construction.* Our automaton construction is based on the following idea. An ultimately-periodic word in $L(\mathcal{A})$ representable by a lasso of length $n$ has an ultimately-periodic run in $\mathcal{A}$ of size at most $n \cdot |Q|$. The ultimately-periodic run is accepting if the highest color occurring in its period is even. For a given ultimately-periodic word with lasso of length $n$, our constructed automaton $\mathcal{A}'$ checks whether this word has an ultimately-periodic accepting run of size $n \cdot |Q|$ in $\mathcal{A}$. Adapting the same idea as in Theorem 3, we check whether the colors we wish to eliminate appear within $n \cdot |Q|$ steps. We reject words with runs where these colors appear with distances larger than $n \cdot |Q|$. On the other runs we use the acceptance condition of the remaining colors.

Let $\mathcal{A} = (Q, Q_0, \delta, \mu)$ where $\mu : Q \to \{0, \dots, m-1\}$. We construct the parity automaton $\mathcal{A}' = (Q', Q'_0, \delta', \mu')$ with $\mu' : Q \to \{0, \dots, m'-1\}$ and where:

$$Q' = (Q \times \{0, \dots, n \cdot |Q|\}) \cup (Q \times \{0, \dots, n \cdot |Q|\} \times \{-1, m', \dots, m-1\})$$

and

$$Q'_0 = \{(q, 0) \mid q \in Q_0\}.$$

The transition relation and coloring function are given as follows. In contrast to Theorem 3 we now need to first check which is the highest color that appears in the period of the run. This check is done respecting the following cases.

$$\text{Case (1): } \delta'((q,c),\alpha) = \{(q', c+1) \mid q' \in \delta(q,\alpha)\} \quad \text{if } c < n \cdot |Q| - 1$$

As we are only interested in the highest color that appears in the period of the run, case (1) makes sure that we reach this period by skipping the first $n \cdot |Q|$ steps, i.e., we simply follow the transition relation of $\mathcal{A}$ and increase the counter (denoted by $c$).

$$\begin{aligned}\text{Case (2): } \delta'((q,c),\alpha) =& \{(q', 0, \mu(q')) \mid q' \in \delta(q,\alpha), \mu(q') \geq m'\} \cup \\ & \{(q', 0, -1) \mid q' \in \delta(q,\alpha),\ \mu(q') < m'\} \quad \text{if } c = n \cdot |Q| - 1\end{aligned}$$

In Case (2) is the transition to the second phase, once we have skipped the first $n \cdot |Q|$ states. From here on we save the highest color seen that is larger than $m' - 1$.

$$\begin{aligned}\text{Case (3): } \delta'((q,c,h),\alpha) =& \{(q', 0, \mu(q')) \mid q' \in \delta(q,\alpha), \mu(q') > h, \mu(q') \geq m'\} \cup \\ & \{(q', 0, h) \mid q' \in \delta(q,\alpha),\ \mu(q') = h\} \cup \\ & \{(q', c+1, h) \mid q' \in \delta(q,\alpha),\ \mu(q') < h \vee \mu(q') < m'\} \\ & \text{if } c \leq n \cdot |Q| - 1\end{aligned}$$

In case (3) we track the highest color $h$ seen so far. If $h$ is higher than $m' - 1$ we save this color and check how long it takes for this color to reappear. In case it appears in less that $n \cdot |Q|$ steps ($\mu(q') = h$) we reset the counter for this color. If a higher color is observed ($\mu(q') > h$), $h$ is replaced by the color and the counter is reset.

$$\begin{aligned}\text{Case (4): } \delta'((q,c,h),\alpha) =& \{(q', c, h) \mid q' \in \delta(q,\alpha),\ \mu(q') < m'\} \\ & \text{if } c = n \cdot |Q| \text{ and } h = -1\end{aligned}$$

In the case where the counter exceeds $n \cdot |Q|$ for some saved color, the automaton rejects, but only if colors higher than $m'$ were observed along the way. Otherwise, the automaton $\mathcal{A}'$ accepts as $\mathcal{A}$ with the non-eliminated colors. The coloring function is defined as follows

$$\mu'(\tilde{q}) = \begin{cases} 0 & \tilde{q} = (q, c) \\ 1 & \tilde{q} = (q, c, h),\ 0 \leq c < n \cdot |Q|, h \text{ is odd} \\ 0 & \tilde{q} = (q, c, h),\ 0 \leq c < n \cdot |Q|, h \text{ is even} \\ \mu(q) & \tilde{q} = (q, c, -1),\ c = n \cdot |Q| \end{cases}$$

□

With this, we conclude the study of the approximation of linear-time properties represented by $\omega$-automata with lasso-precise automata with simpler acceptance conditions preserving their determinism. In the next subsection, we turn to the approximation of nondeterministic automata with lasso-precise deterministic automata.

### 3.4 Lasso-Precise Deterministic Approximations

We now study lasso-precise approximations from the point of view of the determinism of the automata representing $\omega$-regular languages. The complexity of determinizing $\omega$-automata, in particular the construction of deterministic parity automata, has been studied extensively (cf. [18]). The size of the deterministic automaton that recognizes the same language as the given nondeterministic automaton is, in the worst case, exponential in the number of states of the given automaton. By contrast, the size of the deterministic safety automaton provided by Theorem 1 is independent of the given language and exponential only in the bound. For small bounds, Theorem 1 thus provides a deterministic lasso-precise approximation with a small number of states. The following theorem shows that, for large bounds, it is not, in general, possible to produce small deterministic lasso-precise approximations. If the bound is as large as the number of states of the given nondeterministic automaton, then the deterministic lasso-precise approximation has, in the worst case, an exponential number of states.

**Theorem 7.** *For every $k \in \mathbb{N}$ there exists a nondeterministic parity automaton $\mathcal{A}$ with $O(k)$ states, such that, for every bound $n \geq |\mathcal{A}|$, the minimal deterministic parity automaton $\mathcal{A}'$ with $L(\mathcal{A}') \subseteq_n L(\mathcal{A})$ has at least $2^k$ states.*

*Proof.* Let $\Sigma = \{0, 1, 2\}$, and consider the language

$$\Omega = \{\{0,1\}^i \cdot 1 \cdot \{0,1\}^{(k-1)} \cdot 2 \cdot 1^\omega \mid i < k\}.$$

That is, $\Omega$ consists of the infinite words over $\{0, 1, 2\}$ in which the letter 2 appears exactly once, and the letter exactly $k$ positions prior to that is a 1, preceded by at most $k - 1$ letters.

We can construct a nondeterministic parity automaton $\mathcal{A} = (Q, Q_0, \delta, \mu)$ for $\Omega$ with $2k + 1$ states as follows. We let $Q = \{0, 1\} \times \{1, \ldots, k\} \cup \{q_a\}$ and $Q_0 = \{(0, 1)\}$. The function $\mu$ is such that $\mu(q_a) = 0$, and $\mu(q) = 1$ for all $q \neq q_a$. We define the transition relation $\delta$ such that $\delta(q_a, 1) = \{q_a\}$ and $\delta(q_a, \alpha) = \emptyset$ if $\alpha \in \{0, 2\}$ and

$$\delta((b,i),\alpha) = \begin{cases} \{(0,i+1)\} & \text{if } b = 0, i < k, \alpha = 0, \\ \{(0,i+1),(1,1)\} & \text{if } b = 0, i < k, \alpha = 1, \\ \{(1,1)\} & \text{if } b = 0, i = k, \alpha = 1, \\ \{(1,i+1)\} & \text{if } b = 1, i < k, \alpha \neq 2 \\ \{q_a\} & \text{if } b = 1, i = k, \alpha = 2. \end{cases}$$

Let $n \in \mathbb{N}$ be a bound such that $n \geq 2k+1$, and let $\mathcal{A}'$ be a DPA such that $L(\mathcal{A}') \subseteq_n L(\mathcal{A})$. By the definition of $\Omega$ and the fact that $n \geq 2k+1$ we have that $L(\mathcal{A}') = \Omega$. We will show that $\mathcal{A}'$ has at least $2^k$ states.

Suppose that $|\mathcal{A}'| < 2^k$. This means that there exist two different words $\sigma_1, \sigma_2 \in \{0,1\}^k$ such that $\mathcal{A}'$ ends up in the same state when run on $\sigma_1 = \alpha_{1,1} \ldots \alpha_{1,k}$ and when run on $\sigma_2 = \alpha_{2,1} \ldots \alpha_{2,k}$. Since $\sigma_1$ and $\sigma_2$ are different, there must exist an $i$ such that $\alpha_{1,i} \neq \alpha_{2,i}$. W.l.o.g., suppose that $\alpha_{1,i} = 1$ and $\alpha_{2,i} = 0$. Let $\sigma = 1^{i-1} \cdot 2 \cdot 1^\omega$. Consider the words $\sigma_1 \cdot \sigma$ and $\sigma_2 \cdot \sigma$. In $\sigma_1 \cdot \sigma$, the letter appearing $k$ positions before the letter 2 is 1, and in $\sigma_2 \cdot \sigma$ this letter is 0. Thus, by the definition of $\Omega$ and $\mathcal{A}'$ we have that $\sigma_1 \cdot \sigma$ must be accepted by $\mathcal{A}'$, and $\sigma_2 \cdot \sigma$ must be rejected, which is a contradiction with the fact that $\mathcal{A}'$ is deterministic and the assumption that $\sigma_1$ and $\sigma_2$ lead to the same state.

Since $\mathcal{A}'$ is an arbitrary deterministic parity automaton such that $L(\mathcal{A}') \subseteq_n L(\mathcal{A})$, we conclude that the minimal such automaton has at least $2^k$ states. □

## 4 Automata with Bounded Size

In many cases, one is interested in constructing an automaton of minimal size for a given language. In this section, we solve the problem of computing $n$-lasso-precise automata of *bounded size*. By iteratively increasing the bound on the size of the automaton, this approach can be used to construct minimal automata.

Here we consider languages given as LTL formulas [16]. LTL formulas are a common starting point for many verification and synthesis approaches. Rather than going through an intermediate precise automaton, here we propose a symbolic approach that directly yields an automaton whose language is $n$-lasso-precise approximation for the LTL formula.

**Theorem 8.** *For a linear-time property $\varphi$ given as an LTL formula over AP, and given bounds $n$, $k$ and $m$, deciding whether there exists a deterministic parity automaton $\mathcal{A}$ of size $k$ and number of colors $m$, such that, $L(\mathcal{A}) \subseteq_n \varphi$ is in $\Sigma_2^P$.*

*Proof.* We show that the problem can be encoded by a quantified Boolean formula with one quantifier alternation (2-QBF) of size polynomial in the length of the LTL formula $\varphi$, and the bounds $k, n$ and $m$. Deciding quantified Boolean formulas in the 2-QBF fragment is in $\Sigma_2^P$ [13].

*Construction.*

$$\exists\{\delta_{s,\alpha,s'} \mid s, s' \in Q, \alpha \in 2^{AP}\}.$$
$$\exists\{\mu_{s,c} \mid s \in Q, 0 \leq c < m\}$$
$$\forall\{a_j \mid a \in AP, 0 \leq j < \max\{k,n\}\}.$$
$$\forall\{l_j \mid 0 \leq j < \max\{k,n\}\}$$
$$\forall\{s_j \mid s \in Q, 0 \leq j < n \cdot k\}.$$
$$\forall\{r_j \mid 0 \leq j < n \cdot k\}$$
$$\phi_{\mathrm{DPA}}^{k,m} \wedge (\phi_{\mathrm{loop}} \rightarrow \phi_{\mathcal{A}\subseteq\varphi} \wedge \phi_{=_n})$$

where

- $\phi_{\mathcal{A}\subseteq\varphi} \equiv \phi_{k\text{-accrun}} \wedge \phi_{\text{match(k)}} \rightarrow \phi_{\in L_k(\varphi)}$
- $\phi_{=_n} \equiv \phi_{\in L_n(\varphi)} \wedge \phi_{\text{match}(n\cdot k)} \rightarrow \phi_{\in L_n(\mathcal{A})}$

The formula encodes the existence of a deterministic parity automaton $\mathcal{A} = (Q, q_0, \delta, \mu)$ with $L(\mathcal{A}) \subseteq_n \varphi$. The transition relation of the automaton is encoded in the variables $\delta_{s,\alpha,s'}$ that define whether the automaton has a transition from state $s \in Q$ to state $s' \in Q$ with a letter $\alpha \in 2^{AP}$. Additional variables $\mu_{s,c}$ define the coloring of the states of the guessed automaton. A variable $\mu_{s,c}$ is true if a state $s$ has color $c$. Using the constraint $\phi_{\text{DPA}}^{k,m}$ we force a deterministic transition relation for the automaton and make sure that each state has exactly one color.

The relation $\subseteq_n$ is encoded in the formula $\phi_{\text{loop}} \rightarrow \phi_{\mathcal{A}\subseteq\varphi} \wedge \phi_{=_n}$. To check whether $\mathcal{A} \subseteq_n \varphi$ we need to check that: (1) $\mathcal{A}$ is a strengthening of $\varphi$, i.e., $\mathcal{A} \subseteq \varphi$, and (2) $\mathcal{A}$ is precise up to ultimately-periodic words of size $n$, i.e., $L_n(A) = L_n(\varphi)$. The strengthening is encoded in the constraint $\phi_{\mathcal{A}\subseteq\varphi} \equiv \phi_{k\text{-accrun}} \wedge \phi_{\text{match(k)}} \rightarrow \phi_{\in L_k(\varphi)}$. To check whether $\mathcal{A}$ is a strengthening of $\varphi$ we need to check that all accepting ultimately-periodic runs of size $k$ of $\mathcal{A}$ induce ultimately-periodic words of size $k$ that satisfy $\varphi$. This is encoded in the formulas $\phi_{k\text{-accrun}}$, $\phi_{\text{match(k)}}$ and $\phi_{\in L_k(\varphi)}$. The formula $\phi_{\text{match(k)}}$ encodes an ultimately-periodic run in $\mathcal{A}$ of size $k$ using the variables $s_j$ for $0 \leq j < k$ which determine which state of the automaton is at each position in the run and variables $r_j$ which determine the loop of the run. The formula $\phi_{k\text{-accrun}}$ checks whether this run is accepting by checking the highest color in the period of the run. If both formulas are satisfied then it remains to check whether the induced run satisfies $\varphi$, which is done using the constraint $\phi_{\in L_k(\varphi)}$. The constraint resembles the encoding given in [5] for solving the bounded model checking problem. It is defined over the variables $a_j$, where $a \in AP$ and $0 \leq j < k$ and the variables $l_j$ for $0 \leq j < k$. A variable $a_j$ is true if the transition at position $j$ in the run that satisfies $\phi_{k\text{-accrun}}$ and $\phi_{\text{match(k)}}$ represents a letter where $a$ is true and if $\varphi$ allows $a$ to be true at that position. Variables $l_j$ define the position of the loop of the ultimately-periodic word induced by the run.

If $\mathcal{A}$ satisfies the strengthening condition it remains to check whether $\mathcal{A}$ accepts all ultimately-periodic words of size $n$ that satisfy $\varphi$. This condition is encoded in the constraint $\phi_{=_n} \equiv \phi_{\in L_n(\varphi)} \wedge \phi_{\text{match}(n\cdot k)} \rightarrow \phi_{\in L_n(\mathcal{A})}$. If an ultimately-periodic word of size $n$ encoded by the variables $a_j$ for $0 \leq j < n$ and loop variables $l_j$ satisfies $\varphi$ (checked by the formula $\phi_{\in L_n(\varphi)}$), then we match this ultimately-periodic word to its run in $\mathcal{A}$ (using the formula $\phi_{\text{match}(n\cdot k)}$). Notice that we have to match the word to a run in $\mathcal{A}$ of size $n \cdot k$ as words of length $n$ might induce runs of size $n \cdot k$. If the latter formulas are satisfied it remains to check whether the run in the automaton is accepting.

Finally, the formula $\phi_{\text{loop}}$ asserts that only one loop is allowed at a time. All formulas are of size polynomial in $k$, $n$, $m$ and $\varphi$. □

The construction above can also be used for computing nondeterministic automata by changing the constraints on the transition relation of the automaton.

## 5 Discussion

The key idea behind algorithmic methods like bounded model checking [5] and bounded synthesis [9] is that, for finite-state systems, it suffices to consider lasso-shaped executions of bounded size. The notion of $n$-lasso-precise approximation, introduced in this paper, exploits the same observation for the construction and transformation of automata.

The new constructions for $n$-lasso-precise underapproximations have attractive properties. Theorem 1 shows that it is possible to approximate a given language with a deterministic safety automaton whose size is exponential in the bound, but independent of the given language. For small bounds, any language can thus be effectively approximated by a deterministic safety automaton. Theorem 6 shows that reducing the number of colors of a parity automaton incurs at most a polynomial increase in the number of states of the original automaton.

The results indicate significant potential for new verification and synthesis algorithms that work with $n$-lasso-precise approximations instead of precise automata. A key novelty is that our constructions allow us to approximate a given temporal property with a property of a simpler type without necessarily reducing all the way to safety. For example, we can approximate a given temporal property with a parity automaton with three colors, for which efficient synthesis algorithms exist [2].

The constructions of the paper allow us to directly construct automata for the approximations. An interesting topic for future work is to complement these constructions with fast techniques that reduce the number of states of an automaton without necessarily producing a minimal automaton. Similar techniques, which, however, guarantee full language equivalence rather than $n$-lasso precision, are commonly used in the translation of LTL formulas to Büchi automata (cf. [11]).

## References

1. Biere, A., Artho, C., Schuppan, V.: Liveness checking as safety checking. Electron. Notes Theoret. Comput. Sci. **66**(2), 160–177 (2002)
2. Bloem, R., Jobstmann, B., Piterman, N., Pnueli, A., Sa'ar, Y.: Synthesis of reactive (1) designs. J. Comput. Syst. Sci. **78**(3), 911–938 (2012). In Commemoration of Amir Pnueli
3. Boker, U.: Why these automata types? In: Barthe, G., Sutcliffe, G., Veanes, M. (eds.) 22nd International Conference on Logic for Programming, Artificial Intelligence and Reasoning, LPAR-22. EPiC Series in Computing, vol. 57, pp. 143–163. EasyChair (2018)
4. Calbrix, H., Nivat, M., Podelski, A.: Ultimately periodic words of rational $\omega$-languages. In: Brookes, S., Main, M., Melton, A., Mislove, M., Schmidt, D. (eds.) MFPS 1993. LNCS, vol. 802, pp. 554–566. Springer, Heidelberg (1994). https://doi.org/10.1007/3-540-58027-1_27

5. Clarke, E., Biere, A., Raimi, R., Zhu, Y.: Bounded model checking using satisfiability solving. Formal Methods Syst. Des. **19**(1), 7–34 (2001)
6. Dimitrova, R., Finkbeiner, B., Torfah, H.: Synthesizing approximate implementations for unrealizable specifications. In: Dillig, I., Tasiran, S. (eds.) CAV 2019. LNCS, vol. 11561, pp. 241–258. Springer, Cham (2019). https://doi.org/10.1007/978-3-030-25540-4_13
7. Ehlers, R., Finkbeiner, B.: On the virtue of patience: minimizing Büchi automata. In: van de Pol, J., Weber, M. (eds.) SPIN 2010. LNCS, vol. 6349, pp. 129–145. Springer, Heidelberg (2010). https://doi.org/10.1007/978-3-642-16164-3_10
8. Etessami, K., Holzmann, G.J.: Optimizing Büchi automata. In: Palamidessi, C. (ed.) CONCUR 2000. LNCS, vol. 1877, pp. 153–168. Springer, Heidelberg (2000). https://doi.org/10.1007/3-540-44618-4_13
9. Finkbeiner, B., Schewe, S.: Bounded synthesis. Int. J. Softw. Tools Technol. Transfer **15**(5–6), 519–539 (2013)
10. Gange, G., Ganty, P., Stuckey, P.J.: Fixing the state budget: approximation of regular languages with small DFAs. In: D'Souza, D., Narayan Kumar, K. (eds.) ATVA 2017. LNCS, vol. 10482, pp. 67–83. Springer, Cham (2017). https://doi.org/10.1007/978-3-319-68167-2_5
11. Gastin, P., Oddoux, D.: Fast LTL to Büchi automata translation. In: Berry, G., Comon, H., Finkel, A. (eds.) CAV 2001. LNCS, vol. 2102, pp. 53–65. Springer, Heidelberg (2001). https://doi.org/10.1007/3-540-44585-4_6
12. Giannakopoulou, D., Lerda, F.: From states to transitions: improving translation of LTL formulae to Büchi automata. In: Peled, D.A., Vardi, M.Y. (eds.) FORTE 2002. LNCS, vol. 2529, pp. 308–326. Springer, Heidelberg (2002). https://doi.org/10.1007/3-540-36135-9_20
13. Büning, H.K., Bubeck, U.: Theory of quantified Boolean formulas. In: Biere, A., Heule, M., van Maaren, H., Walsh, T. (eds.) Handbook of Satisfiability, Volume 185 of Frontiers in Artificial Intelligence and Applications, pp. 735–760. IOS Press, Amsterdam (2009)
14. Krishnan, S.C., Puri, A., Brayton, R.K.: Structural complexity of $\omega$-automata. In: Mayr, E.W., Puech, C. (eds.) STACS 1995. LNCS, vol. 900, pp. 143–156. Springer, Heidelberg (1995). https://doi.org/10.1007/3-540-59042-0_69
15. Kupferman, O., Lustig, Y., Vardi, M.Y., Yannakakis, M.: Temporal synthesis for bounded systems and environments. In: 28th International Symposium on Theoretical Aspects of Computer Science, STACS 2011, Dortmund, Germany, 10–12 March 2011, pp. 615–626 (2011)
16. Pnueli, A.: The temporal logic of programs. In: the 18th Annual Symposium on Foundations of Computer Science, SFCS 1977, Washington, DC, USA. IEEE Computer Society (1977)
17. Safra, S.: Complexity of automata on infinite objects. Ph.D. thesis, Weizmann Institute of Science, Rehovot, Israel, March 1989
18. Schewe, S., Varghese, T.: Determinising parity automata. In: Csuhaj-Varjú, E., Dietzfelbinger, M., Ésik, Z. (eds.) MFCS 2014. LNCS, vol. 8634, pp. 486–498. Springer, Heidelberg (2014). https://doi.org/10.1007/978-3-662-44522-8_41
19. Schuppan, V., Biere, A.: Efficient reduction of finite state model checking to reachability analysis. STTT **5**(2–3), 185–204 (2004)
20. Shallit, J., Breitbart, Y.: Automaticity I: properties of a measure of descriptional complexity. J. Comput. Syst. Sci. **53**(1), 10–25 (1996)
21. Somenzi, F., Bloem, R.: Efficient Büchi automata from LTL formulae. In: Emerson, E.A., Sistla, A.P. (eds.) CAV 2000. LNCS, vol. 1855, pp. 248–263. Springer, Heidelberg (2000). https://doi.org/10.1007/10722167_21

# DEQ: Equivalence Checker for Deterministic Register Automata

A. S. Murawski[1(✉)], S. J. Ramsay[2], and N. Tzevelekos[3]

[1] University of Oxford, Oxford, UK
andrzej.murawski@cs.ox.ac.uk
[2] University of Bristol, Bristol, UK
[3] Queen Mary University of London, London, UK

**Abstract.** Register automata are one of the most studied automata models over infinite alphabets with applications in learning, systems modelling and program verification. We present an equivalence checker for deterministic register automata, called DEQ, based on a recent polynomial-time algorithm that employs group-theoretic techniques to achieve succinct representations of the search space. We compare the performance of our tool to other available implementations, notably in the learning library RALib and nominal frameworks LOIS and NLambda.

## 1 Introduction

Register automata [8,16] are one of the simplest models of computation over infinite alphabets. They operate on an infinite domain of data by storing data values in a finite number of registers, where the values are available for future comparisons or updates. The automata can recognise when a data value does not appear in any of the registers or has not been seen so far at all [21].

Recent years have seen a surge of interest in models over infinite alphabets due to their ability to account for computational scenarios with unbounded data. For instance, XML query languages [18] need to compare attribute values that originate from infinite domains. In program verification there is need for abstractions of computations over infinite datatypes [6,8] and unbounded resources, such as Java objects [13] or ML references [15]. More broadly, they have been advocated as a convenient formalism for systems modelling, which fuelled interest in extending learning algorithms to the setting [1,3,5,12,17].

This paper presents DEQ, a tool for verifying language equivalence of deterministic register automata (the nondeterministic case is undecidable [16]). As many of the above-mentioned applications rely on equivalence checking, several implementations are available online for comparison. We compare the performance of our tool to the equivalence routine from RALib [4] (a library for active learning of register automata), and two others, programmed in the LOIS [10] and NLambda [9] frameworks. The equivalence-testing routine coded in NLambda has recently been used as part of an automata learning framework [12].


Y.-F. Chen et al. (Eds.): ATVA 2019, LNCS 11781, pp. 350–356, 2019.
https://doi.org/10.1007/978-3-030-31784-3_20

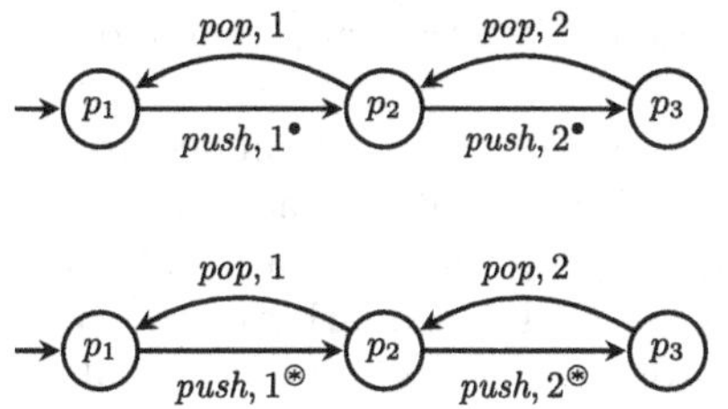


**Fig. 1.** Two size-2 "fresh" stacks.

```
R = R_init; Δ = {u_0};
while (Δ is not empty) do
  u = Δ.get();
  if u ∉ Gen(R)
    if u fails 1-step test return NO;
    Δ.add(succ-set(u));
    R = R updated with u;
return YES
```

**Fig. 2.** Algorithm in outline.

Our experiments show that DEQ compares favourably to its competitors. At the theoretical level, this is thanks to being based on the first polynomial-time algorithm [14] for the problem. The algorithm improves upon the "naive" algorithm that would expand a register automaton to a finite-state automaton over a sufficiently large finite alphabet, often incurring an exponential blow-up. Ours is also the only tool that can handle global freshness, i.e. the recognition/generation of values that have not been seen thus far during the course of computation. This is an important feature in the context of programming languages that makes it possible to model object creation faithfully.

**Register Automata.** Let $\mathcal{D}$ be an infinite set (alphabet). Its elements will be called *data values*. Register automata are a simple model for modelling languages and behaviours over such an alphabet. They operate over finitely many states and, in addition, are equipped with a finite number of *registers*, where they can store elements of $\mathcal{D}$. Each automaton transition can refer to the registers by requiring e.g. that the data value from a specific register be part of the transition's label or, alternatively, that the label feature a *fresh* data value: either not *currently* in the registers, or globally fresh (never seen before), which could then be stored in one of the registers. Formally, transition labels are pairs $(t,d)$, where $t$ is a tag drawn from a finite alphabet and $d \in \mathcal{D}$. We write $q \xrightarrow{t,i} q'$ to specify transitions labelled with $(t,d)$ where $t$ is a tag and $d$ is the data value currently stored in register $i$. Similarly, $q \xrightarrow{t,i^\bullet} q'$ describes transitions labelled with $(t,d)$, where $d \in \mathcal{D}$ is currently *not* stored in any registers. Once the transition fires, $d$ will be stored in register $i$. In contrast, $q \xrightarrow{t,i^\circledast} q'$ captures transitions with labels $(t,d)$, where $d$ ranges over all elements of $\mathcal{D}$ that have not yet been encountered by the automaton ($d$ is "globally fresh").

Consider the automaton at the top of Fig. 1, which simulates a bounded "fresh" stack of size 2. By the latter we mean that the simulated stack can store up to two 2 distinct data values. The automaton starts from state $p_1$, with all its registers empty (erased). It can make a transition labelled with $(push, d_1)$, for any data value $d_1$, store it in register 1, and go to state $p_2$. From there, it can either pop the data value already stored in register 1 and go back to $p_1$ (also erasing the register), or push another data value by making a transition $(push, d_2)$, for any data value $d_2 \neq d_1$, and go to state $p_2$. From there, it can pop the data value already stored in register 2 (and erase that register) and go to $p_1$, and so on.

The other automaton in Fig. 1 (bottom) also simulates a 2-bounded fresh stack, but it does so using globally fresh transitions. That is, each $(push, d)$ transition made by the automaton is going to have a data value $d$ that is different from all data values used before. We can thus see that bisimilarity of the two automata will fail after one pop: the upper automaton will erase a data value from its registers and, consequently, will be able to push the same data value again later. The automaton below, though, will always be pushing globally fresh data values. In other words, the following trace $(push, d_1)\,(pop, d_1)\,(push, d_1)$ is permitted by the upper automaton, but not by the lower one.

**Implementation.** We have developed a command-line tool for deciding language equivalence of this class of automata, implemented in Haskell[1]. The two input automata (DRA) are specified using an XML file format (parsed using the *xml-conduit* library [20]). Strictly speaking, the algorithm presented in [14] decides whether two states within the same automaton are bisimilar. Hence, our implementation first transforms the input (an instance of the language equivalence problem for two DRA) into an instance of the bisimilarity problem, by constructing the disjoint union of the two automata.

Our algorithm exploits the observation that (in the deterministic setting) language equivalence and bisimilarity are related, and it attempts to build a bisimulation relation incrementally. To avoid exponential blow-ups, we rely on symbolic representations based on (partial) permutations, which capture matches between register content in various configurations. The outline of the algorithm is presented in Fig. 2.

The algorithm is similar in flavour to the classic Hopcroft-Karp algorithm for DFA [7], which maintains *sets of pairs of states*. In contrast, we work with four-tuples $(q_1, \sigma, q_2, h)$, where $q_1, q_2$ are states, $\sigma$ is a partial permutation and $h$ is a parameter related to the number of registers. DEQ represents partial permutations using an implementation of immutable integer maps that is based on big endian patricia trees [11]. Most operations complete in amortized time $O(\mathsf{min}(n, W))$, where $W$ is the number of bits of an integer. This is important because manipulating partial permutations through insertion and deletion is at the core of the innermost loop (line 7).

Starting from a four-tuple $u_0$, which represents the input equivalence problem, our implementation uses a queue $\Delta$ (initialised to $\{u_0\}$). This is used to store the four-tuples that still need to be scrutinised to establish the original equivalence. Since the total number of possible four-tuples is exponential in the number of registers (because one component is a partial permutation over the register indexes), the algorithm prescribes a sophisticated compact representation called a generating system. The generating system $\mathcal{R}$ represents the set of four-tuples that have already been analysed (its initial value $\mathcal{R}_{init}$ contains four-tuples with identical states and identity permutations).

[1] The tool and its source are available at http://github.com/stersay/deq.

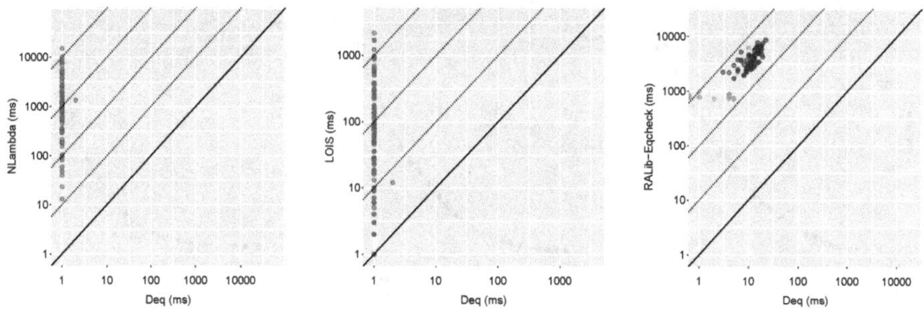


**Fig. 3.** Tool comparison. (Color figure online)

Each iteration of the loop considers a four-tuple $u$ taken from the queue (line 3): first we check if it is already generated by the generating system accumulated so far (line 4). Querying the generating system for membership requires deciding if a permutation belongs to a permutation group generated by $\mathcal{R}$. For this purpose, DEQ uses an implementation of the celebrated Schreier-Sims polynomial time group membership algorithm [19] provided by the HaskellForMaths library [2].

If the four-tuple is already generated we move on to the next iteration. Otherwise we check if the configurations represented by $u$ can withstand a one-step attack in the corresponding bisimulation game (line 5). If $u$ fails single-step testing, the algorithm can immediately terminate and return NO. If $u$ passes the tests, the algorithm generates a set $\mathsf{succ\text{-}set}(u)$ consisting of "successor four-tuples" that are added to $\Delta$ for future verification (line 6). In this case, the generating system is extended to represent $u$ as well (line 7). For efficiency reasons, DEQ fuses these two parts of the algorithm together. A collection of successors is computed by looping over all outgoing transitions relevant to $u$, and failing if any cannot be constructed. In what follows we refer to this as the inner loop of the algorithm. The successor four-tuples are then added to the queue and the generating system $\mathcal{R}$ is extended so that it generates $u$.

**Case Studies.** In theory the worst-case performance of the algorithm is dominated by the complexity of permutation group membership testing, which is $O(n^5)$ for a straightforward implementation of the Schreier-Sims algorithm. In the following series of case studies we examine the performance of our implementation outside of the worst case, in particular where the group structure is quite simple.

All the experiments were carried out on an Ubuntu 16.04 virtual machine, running on a Windows 10 host equipped with an Intel Core i7-8650U CPU at 1.9 GHz and 8GB of RAM. Z3 4.4.1 and OpenJDK 1.8.0_191 are used for the purposes of running the tools LOIS and RALib-EqCheck (see below).

*Stack Data Structure (stacks).* In this case study, we describe two families of automata simulating finite stacks, indexed by the stack size. Similar families

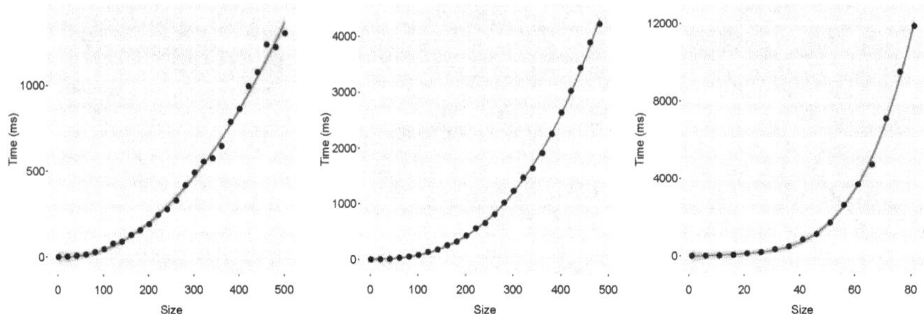


**Fig. 4.** Tool scaling (stacks, glolo, cpt).

have been considered within the nominal automata learning framework of [12]. In both families of machines, the registers under their natural order are used in order to store the elements of a stack, but one family "pushes" data into the registers from right to left and the other from left to right (so the machines are nevertheless equivalent).

By considering the plot of running time against stack size in Fig. 4 (left), we conclude that any overhead due to the group membership algorithm is insignificant when the groups are easy to describe (as growth remains roughly quadratic in $n$).

*Global Simulating Local Freshness (glolo).* In this case study we maintain a relatively simple group structure in the generating system, but introduce globally fresh transitions. Due to the use of global freshness, no other tools will process this example. In this study we consider pairs of machines which first read and store exactly $r$ globally fresh names. Next, one machine reads a locally fresh name, whilst the other reads a globally fresh name, but because all of the history of the computation is stored in registers, local and global freshness coincide, and the configurations are bisimilar. Associated run times are plotted in Fig. 4 (middle). It can be seen that the management of the history that is required by supporting global freshness adds a linear factor: the curve displayed is a cubic polynomial, fit using R's *lm* algorithm.

*Partial Permutations Represented Compactly (cpt).* Here we consider a family of instances in which the collection of partial permutations occurring in constructed bisimulations is large.

In the pairs of automata of this study, all $r$ registers are initially populated over the course of the first $r$ states, but the order in which they are populated may differ. Afterwards, the machines may store a fresh letter in any register or read from any register, and return to the same state. Due to these possibilities, the correspondence between these states in the two machines can become complex. However, since all transitions are available to both automata, they will nevertheless be bisimilar, and hence accept the same language. Running times are plotted in Fig. 4 (right); the curve displayed is a fourth-degree polynomial.

*Tool Comparison.* We can encode the stacks family of examples using the frameworks of LOIS [10] and NLambda [9], and directly as a set of inputs to RALib-EqCheck[2] [4]. However, these other tools can only handle instances of relatively small size. This is not surprising, since they support classes of automata that are much more general. In contrast, the polynomial time algorithm implemented by DEQ is highly specialised to a specific subclass. Hence, we have restricted our comparison to stacks of size at most 15. The scatter plots in Fig. 3 show the running times of the three implementations compared on all possible pairs of stack sizes[3]. We can encode the cpt family of examples also as inputs to RALib-EqCheck; the results of comparing the two tools on this family (up to size 5) is shown in light blue in the right-most plot of Fig. 3. The results show quite clearly that DEQ can determine (in)equivalence several orders of magnitude faster than the other tools.

**Acknowledgment.** Research funded by EPSRC (EP/J019577/1, EP/P004172/1).

## References

1. Aarts, F., Fiterau-Brostean, P., Kuppens, H., Vaandrager, F.: Learning register automata with fresh value generation. In: Leucker, M., Rueda, C., Valencia, F.D. (eds.) ICTAC 2015. LNCS, vol. 9399, pp. 165–183. Springer, Cham (2015). https://doi.org/10.1007/978-3-319-25150-9_11
2. Amos, D.: http://hackage.haskell.org/package/HaskellForMaths
3. Bollig, B., Habermehl, P., Leucker, M., Monmege, B.: A robust class of data languages and an application to learning. LMCS **10**(4), (2014)
4. Cassel, S., Howar, F., Jonsson, B.: RALib: a LearnLib extension for inferring EFSMs. In: Proceedings of DIFTS (2015)
5. Cassel, S., Howar, F., Jonsson, B., Steffen, B.: Active learning for extended finite state machines. Formal Asp. Comput. **28**(2), 233–263 (2016)
6. Grigore, R., Distefano, D., Petersen, R.L., Tzevelekos, N.: Runtime verification based on register automata. In: Piterman, N., Smolka, S.A. (eds.) TACAS 2013. LNCS, vol. 7795, pp. 260–276. Springer, Heidelberg (2013). https://doi.org/10.1007/978-3-642-36742-7_19
7. Hopcroft, J.E., Karp, R.M.: A linear algorithm for testing equivalence of finite automata. Technical Report 114, Cornell University (1971)
8. Kaminski, M., Francez, N.: Finite-memory automata. TCS **134**(2), 329–363 (1994)
9. Klin, B., Szynwelski, M.: SMT solving for functional programming over infinite structures. In: Proceedings of MSFP, EPTCS 207, pp. 57–75, 2016
10. Kopczyński, E., Toruńczyk, S.: LOIS. In: Proceedings of POPL, pp. 586–598 (2017)
11. http://hackage.haskell.org/package/containers

[2] We used an unreleased implementation of the equivalence checking algorithm that was kindly communicated to us by F. Howar.

[3] The encoding used for the comparison with RALib-EqCheck was slightly modified to reflect certain structural constraints imposed by that tool. This alternative encoding is larger and hence runtimes are not comparable with the other two experiments. Note that the timing data for RALib-EqCheck contains JVM start-up time.

12. Moerman, J., Sammartino, M., Silva, A., Klin, B., Szynwelski, M.: Learning nominal automata. In: Proceedings of POPL, pp. 613–625 (2017)
13. Murawski, A.S., Ramsay, S.J., Tzevelekos, N.: A contextual equivalence checker for IMJ*. In: Finkbeiner, B., Pu, G., Zhang, L. (eds.) ATVA 2015. LNCS, vol. 9364, pp. 234–240. Springer, Cham (2015). https://doi.org/10.1007/978-3-319-24953-7_19
14. Murawski, A.S., Ramsay, S.J., Tzevelekos, N.: Polynomial-time equivalence testing for deterministic fresh-register automata. In: Proceedings of MFCS, pp. 72:1–72:14 (2018)
15. Murawski, A.S., Tzevelekos, N.: Algorithmic nominal game semantics. In: Barthe, G. (ed.) ESOP 2011. LNCS, vol. 6602, pp. 419–438. Springer, Heidelberg (2011). https://doi.org/10.1007/978-3-642-19718-5_22
16. Neven, F., Schwentick, T., Vianu, V.: Finite state machines for strings over infinite alphabets. ACM Trans. Comput. Log. **5**(3), 403–435 (2004)
17. Sakamoto, H.: Studies on the Learnability of Formal Languages via Queries. PhD thesis, Kyushu University (1998)
18. Schwentick, T.: Automata for XML. J. Comput. Syst. Sci. **73**(3), 289–315 (2007)
19. Sims, C.C.: Computational methods in the study of permutation groups. In: Computational Problems in Abstract Algebra, pp. 169–183. Pergamon, Oxford (1970)
20. Snoyman, M., Breitkreuz, A.: http://hackage.haskell.org/package/xml-conduit
21. Tzevelekos, N.: Fresh-register automata. In: Proceedings of POPL, pp. 295–306 (2011)

# `ltl3tela`: LTL to Small Deterministic or Nondeterministic Emerson-Lei Automata

Juraj Major[1], František Blahoudek[2], Jan Strejček[1(✉)], Miriama Sasaráková[1], and Tatiana Zbončáková[1]

[1] Masaryk University, Brno, Czech Republic
{major,strejcek}@fi.muni.cz
[2] University of Mons, Mons, Belgium
xblahoud@fi.muni.cz

**Abstract.** The paper presents a new tool `ltl3tela` translating LTL to deterministic or nondeterministic transition-based Emerson-Lei automata (TELA). Emerson-Lei automata use generic acceptance formulae with basic terms corresponding to Büchi and co-Büchi acceptance. The tool combines algorithms of Spot library, a new translation of LTL to TELA via alternating automata, a pattern-based automata reduction method, and few other heuristics. Experimental evaluation shows that `ltl3tela` can produce deterministic automata that are, on average, noticeably smaller than deterministic TELA produced by state-of-the-art translators Delag, Rabinizer 4, and Spot. For nondeterministic automata, the improvement over Spot is smaller, but still measurable.

## 1 Introduction

Translation of LTL formulae into equivalent automata over infinite words is an important part of many methods for model checking, control synthesis, monitoring, vacuity checking etc. Different applications require different types of automata, which are specified by restrictions on automata structure or acceptance condition. Two most popular structures are deterministic and nondeterministic. While nondeterministic automata have been traditionally considered with Büchi, deterministic automata have typically used Rabin, Streett, or parity acceptance as deterministic Büchi automata are strictly less expressive.

With rising number of practical automata applications, we can see a clear shift towards more complex acceptance conditions which allow to construct and manipulate automata with less states and often lead to performance improvements. This trend started slowly with generalized Büchi and generalized Rabin acceptance and accelerates after introduction of the Hanoi Omega-Automata Format [3]. The format reinvented a generic acceptance condition originally considered by Emerson and Lei in 1980s [8], which can uniformly present all the mentioned conditions.

J. Major and J. Strejček have been supported by Czech Science Foundation, grant GA19-24397S. F. Blahoudek has been supported by F.R.S.-FNRS under Grant n° F.4520.18 (ManySynth).


Y.-F. Chen et al. (Eds.): ATVA 2019, LNCS 11781, pp. 357–365, 2019.
https://doi.org/10.1007/978-3-030-31784-3_21

Recently, first tools that aim to take advantage of Emerson-Lei (EL) acceptance in order to produce smaller automata appeared. In particular, the tool Delag [12] translates LTL to deterministic EL automata and Spot [7] can produce deterministic or nondeterministic EL automata for LTL since version 2.6. The development of tools producing small EL automata creates a demand for efficient algorithms that directly process these automata (without previous transformation to any simpler automata type). Fresh results of this kind are algorithms for checking emptiness of EL automata and for probabilistic model checking under properties specified by deterministic EL automata [4].

We present a tool `ltl3tela` that combines algorithms of Spot with a novel LTL to EL-automata translation, pattern-based automata reduction method, and some other techniques in order to translate LTL to deterministic or nondeterministic *transition-based Emerson-Lei automata (TELA)* with low number of states. The overall translation algorithm is explained in Sect. 2 together with precise definition of TELA and brief description of individual translation components. Section 3 discusses implementation and basic usage of the tool, and Sect. 4 compares `ltl3tela` with state-of-the-art tools translating LTL to deterministic or nondeterministic automata using random formulae and formulae collected from the literature.

## 2 Translation Algorithm

### Transition-Based Emerson-Lei Automata (TELA)

A *nondeterministic TELA* $\mathcal{A}$ is a tuple $\mathcal{A} = (Q, \Sigma, M, \delta, q_I, \varphi)$, where $Q$ is a finite set of *states*, $\Sigma$ is a finite *alphabet*, $M$ is a finite set of *acceptance marks*, $\delta \subseteq Q \times 2^{\Sigma} \times 2^{M} \times Q$ is a set of *edges*, $q_I \in Q$ is the *initial state*, and $\varphi$ is the acceptance formula built by the following grammar with $m$ ranging over $M$.

$$\varphi \ ::= \ \mathsf{t} \mid \mathsf{f} \mid \mathsf{Inf}(m) \mid \mathsf{Fin}(m) \mid (\varphi \wedge \varphi) \mid (\varphi \vee \varphi)$$

A *run* $\rho$ is an infinite sequence of consecutive edges starting in the state $q_I$. Every run satisfies $\mathsf{t}$ (true) and does not satisfy $\mathsf{f}$ (false). A run satisfies $\mathsf{Inf}(m)$ if $m$ is present on infinitely many edges of $\rho$, and only satisfies $\mathsf{Fin}(m)$ otherwise. A run is *accepting* if it satisfies $\varphi$. Automaton $\mathcal{A}$ is *complete* if for each $q \in Q$ and $a \in \Sigma$ there is at least one edge $(q, A, M', q') \in \delta$ such that $a \in A$. Finally, $\mathcal{A}$ is *deterministic* if for each $q \in Q$ and $a \in \Sigma$ there is at most one edge $(q, A, M', q') \in \delta$ such that $a \in A$. We emphasize that the term *nondeterministic* is not the opposite of *deterministic*, but a deterministic automaton is a special case of a nondeterministic one.

### Translation Components

The most important novel component of `ltl3tela` is an LTL to nondeterministic TELA translation via *self-loop alternating automata (SLAA)* [11]. It builds upon the ideas of `ltl2ba` [9] and `ltl3ba` [1], which translate LTL to *transition-based generalized Büchi automaton (TGBA)* via very weak alternating co-Büchi automata. Our new translation uses alternating automata with similar structure, but with more complex acceptance conditions and acceptance marks on transitions (in particular, SLAA are not weak any more). Such alternating automata are often smaller and allow us to produce smaller nondeterministic automata. We refer to this translation as `ltl3slaa3tela`.

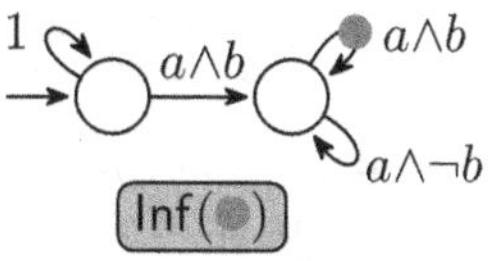

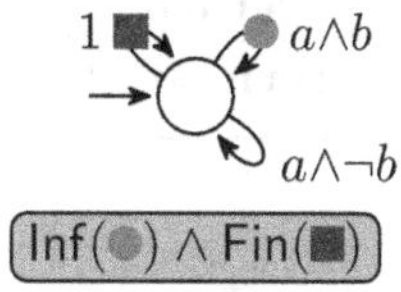

Another new concept is a pattern-based reduction applicable to TGBA [15]. Intuitively, the procedure looks for automata subgraphs corresponding to certain patterns. Each pattern includes states that can be merged into one state for the price of a more complicated acceptance condition containing a subformula $\mathsf{Fin}(m)$, where $m$ is a fresh acceptance mark. Hence, this pattern-based reduction method transforms TGBA into TELA. On the right, you can see a TGBA for the formula $\mathsf{F}\mathsf{G}a \wedge \mathsf{G}\mathsf{F}b$ (top) and the corresponding automaton after pattern-based reduction (bottom).



Further, we use a lot of functionality offered by the Spot library, in particular:

- LTL formulae parsing and preprocessing
- LTL to nondeterministic TELA translation performed by `ltl2tgba -G`
- LTL to deterministic TELA translation performed by `ltl2tgba -DG`
- automata determinization based on the algorithm of Redziejowski [13],
- automata reduction procedure based on SCC pruning [14], minimization of WDBA [5], and simulation-based reductions [14],
- functions for the synchronous product of two automata and specialized functions creating potentially smaller product if one of the automata is *suspendable* [2].

We also define the functions *min* and *trans* used later in the algorithm. The function *min* selects the minimal automaton out of a given sequence $\mathcal{A}_1, \ldots, \mathcal{A}_n$. More precisely, to each automaton $\mathcal{A}_i = (Q, \Sigma, M, \delta, q_I, \varphi)$ it assigns the tuple $(|Q|, d, |M|, |\delta|, i)$ with $d$ being 1 for deterministic automata and 2 otherwise, and returns the automaton with the lexicographically minimal tuple.

The function $trans(\psi, t)$ aims to get the best automaton for $\psi$ using the translator $t$. More precisely, it translates both $\psi$ and $\neg\psi$ using $t$, simplifies both automata using Spot's reduction procedure and the pattern-based reduction (if applicable), resulting in $\mathcal{A}_\psi$ and $\mathcal{A}_{\neg\psi}$. If $\mathcal{A}_{\neg\psi}$ is deterministic, the function complements it (makes it complete and dualizes the acceptance condition by swapping $\mathsf{Inf}$ for $\mathsf{Fin}$, $\mathtt{t}$ for $\mathtt{f}$, and $\wedge$ for $\vee$) into $\mathcal{A}'_\psi$, and returns $min(\mathcal{A}_\psi, \mathcal{A}'_\psi)$. If $\mathcal{A}_{\neg\psi}$ is not deterministic, $trans(\psi, t)$ simply returns $\mathcal{A}_\psi$.

## The Algorithm

Our translation of LTL into nondeterministic TELA follows the idea introduced by Delag (and followed also by `ltl2tgba` with the `-G` option): we split the input

**Algorithm 1.** `ltl3tela` translation of LTL for nondeterministic TELA

preprocess $\varphi$ to contain only Boolean operators $\wedge, \vee, \neg$ and $\neg$ not before $\wedge, \vee$
$\mathcal{A} \leftarrow min(trans(\varphi, \texttt{ltl3slaa3tela}), trans(\varphi, \texttt{ltl2tgba -G}), transRec(\varphi))$

**function** *transRec*($\varphi$)
  **if** $\varphi$ *is a conjunction* **then**
    let $\varphi = \varphi_1 \wedge \ldots \wedge \varphi_n \wedge \psi_1 \wedge \ldots \wedge \psi_m$ where $\psi_i$ are suspendable
    **foreach** $\rho \in \{\varphi_1, \ldots, \varphi_n, \psi_1, \ldots, \psi_m\}$ **do** $\mathcal{A}_\rho \leftarrow transRec(\rho)$
    **return** $(\ldots((\mathcal{A}_{\varphi_1} \hat{\otimes} \ldots \hat{\otimes} \mathcal{A}_{\varphi_n}) \hat{\otimes}_s \mathcal{A}_{\psi_1}) \hat{\otimes}_s \ldots) \hat{\otimes}_s \mathcal{A}_{\psi_m}$
  **if** $\varphi$ *is a disjunction* **then**
    let $\varphi = \varphi_1 \vee \ldots \vee \varphi_n \vee \psi_1 \vee \ldots \vee \psi_m$ where $\psi_i$ are suspendable
    **foreach** $\rho \in \{\varphi_1, \ldots, \varphi_n, \psi_1, \ldots, \psi_m\}$ **do** $\mathcal{A}_\rho \leftarrow transRec(\rho)$
    **return** $(\ldots((\mathcal{A}_{\varphi_1} \check{\otimes} \ldots \check{\otimes} \mathcal{A}_{\varphi_n}) \check{\otimes}_s \mathcal{A}_{\psi_1}) \check{\otimes}_s \ldots) \check{\otimes}_s \mathcal{A}_{\psi_m}$
  **return** $min(trans(\varphi, \texttt{ltl3slaa3tela}), trans(\varphi, \texttt{ltl2tgba -G}))$

formula recursively into temporal subformulae, translate each subformula independently, and merge the automata for subformulae using synchronous products. This allows us to use different translations where appropriate for the subformulae. Our take on the approach is described by Algorithm 1 where we use product operations $\check{\otimes}, \hat{\otimes}$ for automata union and intersection, respectively, and their optimized versions $\check{\otimes}_s, \hat{\otimes}_s$ when the right argument is a suspendable automaton. Each product operation applies Spot's automata reduction procedure and the pattern-based reduction (if applicable) before returning the product. At the end, we compare the resulting automaton with the automata produced directly for the input formula and return the minimal one.

The translation of LTL to deterministic TELA works in the same way with only two changes. First, instead of `ltl2tgba -G` we always call `ltl2tgba -DG`. Second, the function *trans* calls the Spot's automata reduction procedure with the request to produce a deterministic TELA. Hence, if `ltl3slaa3tela` produces an automaton that is not deterministic, it is determinized by Spot.

## 3 Implementation

The tool `ltl3tela` is written in C++14 and requires only the Spot library [7] version 2.6 or higher for compilation. The tool is available at https://github.com/jurajmajor/ltl3tela under the GNU GPL 3.0 license. The default mode takes an LTL formula $\varphi$ as input, runs Algorithm 1 to produce a nondeterministic TELA for $\varphi$, and output it in the Hanoi Omega-Automata (HOA) format [3]. Deterministic automata are produced by `ltl3tela -D1`. The tool can also produce self-loop alternating automata. See the documentation for more details.

## 4 Experimental Evaluation

We compare `ltl3tela` to state-of-the-art LTL to deterministic TELA translators `ltl2tgba -DG`, Delag, and Rabinizer 4, which produces *transition-based generalized Rabin automata (TGRA)*. For the nondeterministic case, we compare `ltl3tela` to `ltl2tgba -G` and two LTL to TGBA translators `ltl2tgba` and `ltl3ba`. For references and version numbers of all the tools see Table 1.

**Table 1.** References and versions of compared LTL to automata translators

| Tool name | Version | Homepage |
|---|---|---|
| Delag [12], Rabinizer 4 [10] | Owl 18.06 | owl.model.in.tum.de |
| `ltl2tgba` [7] | Spot 2.7.4 | spot.lrde.epita.fr |
| `ltl3ba` [1] | 1.1.3 | sourceforge.net/projects/ltl3ba |
| `ltl3tela` | 2.0.0 | github.com/jurajmajor/ltl3tela |

We use two sets of LTL formulae for the comparison:

**random** contains 1000 random formulae generated with `randltl`[1] such that there are no duplicates and formulae equivalent to *true* or *false*,

**literature** contains 397 formulae from the literature provided by `genltl` (for each formula pattern, we consider instances with parameter values $1, \ldots, 5$).

Each translator has been executed on each formula using the tool `ltlcross` with 60 s time limit. The experiments ran on a laptop with Intel® Core™ i7-8550U, 16 GB of RAM, and Debian 9.9. Table 2 presents the cumulative numbers of states, edges, and acceptance marks for each translator and set of formulae. While all translators finished successfully on random formulae, we encountered

**Table 2.** Sums of states, edges, and marks of automata produced by individual translators for considered formula sets, the number of timeouts (TO) and parse errors (PE)

| | | Random | | | Literature | | | | |
|---|---|---|---|---|---|---|---|---|---|
| | Tool | States | Edges | Acc | States | Edges | Acc | TO | PE |
| Det. | `ltl3tela-D1` | 5934 | 18520 | 1268 | 2536 | 10641 | 454 | 39 | 0 |
| | `ltl2tgba-DG` | 6799 | 24131 | 1575 | 3905 | 26643 | 652 | 20 | 0 |
| | Delag | 7176 | 71672 | 3089 | 8661 | 2209807 | 1196 | 11 | 10 |
| | Rabinizer4 | 7581 | 31099 | 2786 | 2969 | 12358 | 1133 | 12 | 8 |
| Nondet. | `ltl3tela` | 5109 | 12481 | 1135 | 2378 | 20718 | 544 | 28 | 0 |
| | `ltl2tgba-G` | 5391 | 13144 | 1041 | 2398 | 20555 | 642 | 12 | 0 |
| | `ltl2tgba` | 5413 | 13059 | 1034 | 2651 | 8721 | 502 | 11 | 0 |
| | `ltl3ba-H2` | 6103 | 15636 | 1616 | 4654 | 21180 | 822 | 4 | 0 |

[1] We use the tools `randltl`, `genltl`, and `ltlcross` [6] from the Spot library 2.7.4.

**Table 3.** Formulae from the literature (described by the corresponding `genltl` options) that are not covered by the accumulated results in Table 2 (Nondet.) due to some timeout (TO), and sizes of nondeterministic automata for these formulae

| Formula (as `genltl` option) | `ltl3tela` | `ltl2tgba -G` | `ltl2tgba` | `ltl3ba -H2` |
|---:|:---:|---:|---:|---:|
| `--gh-r=5` | TO | 1 | 14 | 244 |
| `--hkrss-patterns=45` | TO | 12 | 12 | 12 |
| `--kr-n=2` | TO | TO | 25 | 25 |
| `--kr-n=3` | TO | TO | 58 | 58 |
| `--kr-n=4` | TO | TO | TO | 131 |
| `--kr-n=5` | TO | TO | TO | TO |
| `--kr-nlogn=2` | TO | TO | 43 | 44 |
| `--kr-nlogn=3` | TO | TO | TO | TO |
| `--kr-nlogn=4` | TO | TO | TO | TO |
| `--kr-nlogn=5` | TO | TO | TO | TO |
| `--kv-psi=2` | TO | 19 | 19 | 29 |
| `--kv-psi=3` | TO | 39 | 39 | 73 |
| `--kv-psi=4` | TO | TO | TO | 177 |
| `--kv-psi=5` | TO | TO | TO | 417 |
| `--ms-phi-h=5` | TO | 32 | 64 | 64 |
| `--rv-counter-carry=5` | TO | 160 | 160 | 160 |
| `--rv-counter-carry-linear=5` | TO | 160 | 160 | 160 |
| `--sejk-f=4,1` | TO | 13 | 13 | 64 |
| `--sejk-f=4,2` | TO | 14 | 14 | 112 |
| `--sejk-f=4,3` | TO | 15 | 15 | 192 |
| `--sejk-f=4,4` | TO | 16 | 16 | 336 |
| `--sejk-f=4,5` | TO | 17 | 17 | 608 |
| `--sejk-f=5,1` | TO | 15 | 15 | 128 |
| `--sejk-f=5,2` | TO | 16 | 16 | 224 |
| `--sejk-f=5,3` | TO | 17 | 17 | 384 |
| `--sejk-f=5,4` | TO | TO | TO | 672 |
| `--sejk-f=5,5` | TO | TO | TO | 1216 |
| `--sejk-k=4` | 1 | 1 | TO | 82 |
| `--sejk-k=5` | TO | 1 | TO | 244 |

some timeouts and *parse errors* (`ltlcross` cannot parse automata with more than 32 acceptance marks) on formulae from the literature and thus we had to remove some formulae from the cumulative numbers in Table 2. We have complete results (no timeout or parse error) on 353 formulae for deterministic automata and on 368 formulae for nondeterministic automata. The lists of excluded formulae are in Tables 3 and 4.

The results show that `ltl3tela` is the slowest one, which is not surprising as it internally translates every formula several times. However, it produces significantly smaller deterministic automata (in sum) comparing the other tools. The differences are less dramatic for nondeterministic automata. Detailed analysis of the results shows that `ltl3tela -D1` is always better (in the sense of function

**Table 4.** Formulae from the literature (described by the corresponding `genltl` options) that are not covered by the accumulated results in Table 2 (Det.) due to some timeout (TO) or parse error (PE), and sizes of deterministic automata for these formulae

| Formula (as `genltl` option) | `ltl3tela -D1` | `ltl2tgba -DG` | Delag | Rabinizer 4 |
|---:|---:|---:|---:|---:|
| `--gf-equiv=4` | 1 | 1 | 1 | PE |
| `--gf-equiv=5` | TO | 1 | 1 | PE |
| `--gh-r=5` | 1 | 1 | 1 | PE |
| `--hkrss-patterns=45` | TO | 12 | 12 | 12 |
| `--kr-n=2` | TO | TO | 183 | 141 |
| `--kr-n=3` | TO | TO | 6937 | TO |
| `--kr-n=4` | TO | TO | TO | TO |
| `--kr-n=5` | TO | TO | TO | TO |
| `--kr-nlogn=2` | TO | TO | 288 | TO |
| `--kr-nlogn=3` | TO | TO | TO | TO |
| `--kr-nlogn=4` | TO | TO | TO | TO |
| `--kr-nlogn=5` | TO | TO | TO | TO |
| `--kv-psi=2` | TO | 106 | TO | 115 |
| `--kv-psi=3` | TO | 3057 | TO | TO |
| `--kv-psi=4` | TO | TO | TO | TO |
| `--kv-psi=5` | TO | TO | TO | TO |
| `--ms-phi-h=5` | TO | 32 | 32 | 420 |
| `--ms-phi-r=4` | TO | 1 | 1 | 1 |
| `--ms-phi-r=5` | 1 | 1 | 1 | TO |
| `--ms-phi-s=4` | TO | 1 | 1 | PE |
| `--ms-phi-s=5` | 1 | 1 | 1 | TO |
| `--rv-counter-carry=5` | TO | 160 | 160 | 160 |
| `--rv-counter-carry-linear=5` | TO | 160 | 163 | 163 |
| `--sejk-f=3,1` | TO | 2781 | 3 | 3 |
| `--sejk-f=3,2` | TO | 2782 | 4 | 4 |
| `--sejk-f=3,3` | TO | 2783 | 5 | 5 |
| `--sejk-f=3,4` | TO | 2784 | 6 | 6 |
| `--sejk-f=3,5` | TO | 2785 | 7 | 7 |
| `--sejk-f=4,1` | TO | TO | PE | 3 |
| `--sejk-f=4,2` | TO | TO | PE | 4 |
| `--sejk-f=4,3` | TO | TO | PE | 5 |
| `--sejk-f=4,4` | TO | TO | PE | 6 |
| `--sejk-f=4,5` | TO | TO | PE | 7 |
| `--sejk-f=5,1` | TO | TO | PE | 3 |
| `--sejk-f=5,2` | TO | TO | PE | 4 |
| `--sejk-f=5,3` | TO | TO | PE | 5 |
| `--sejk-f=5,4` | TO | TO | PE | 6 |
| `--sejk-f=5,5` | TO | TO | PE | 7 |
| `--sejk-j=4` | TO | 1 | 1 | PE |
| `--sejk-j=5` | TO | 1 | 1 | PE |
| `--sejk-k=4` | TO | 1 | 1 | PE |
| `--sejk-k=5` | TO | 1 | 1 | PE |
| `--tv-uu=4` | 28 | 51 | TO | 52 |
| `--tv-uu=5` | TO | 298 | TO | 199 |

*min*) than `ltl2tgba -DG`. There is no such other case. A surprising result is the significantly low number of acceptance marks for `ltl3tela -D1`.

All considered formulae, measured results, scripts generating the formulae, Jupyter notebooks that run experiments and process them, and some more tables can be found at: https://github.com/jurajmajor/ltl3tela/blob/master/ATVA19.md

## 5 Conclusion

We presented the tool `ltl3tela` that combines some new ideas with functionality of Spot in order to translate LTL to small deterministic or nondeterministic automata with Emerson-Lei acceptance condition. Experiments indicated that our tool produces (on average) the smallest automata compared to state-of-the-art translators. In particular, we produced deterministic automata with the least number of states, edges, and acceptance marks compared to other translators.

## References


1. Babiak, T., Křetínský, M., Řehák, V., Strejček, J.: LTL to Büchi automata translation: fast and more deterministic. In: Flanagan, C., König, B. (eds.) TACAS 2012. LNCS, vol. 7214, pp. 95–109. Springer, Heidelberg (2012). https://doi.org/10.1007/978-3-642-28756-5_8
2. Babiak, T., Badie, T., Duret-Lutz, A., Křetínský, M., Strejček, J.: Compositional approach to suspension and other improvements to LTL translation. In: Bartocci, E., Ramakrishnan, C.R. (eds.) SPIN 2013. LNCS, vol. 7976, pp. 81–98. Springer, Heidelberg (2013). https://doi.org/10.1007/978-3-642-39176-7_6
3. Babiak, T., et al.: The Hanoi omega-automata format. In: Kroening, D., Păsăreanu, C.S. (eds.) CAV 2015. LNCS, vol. 9206, pp. 479–486. Springer, Cham (2015). https://doi.org/10.1007/978-3-319-21690-4_31
4. Baier, C., Blahoudek, F., Duret-Lutz, A., Klein, J., Müller, D., Strejček, J.: Generic emptiness check for fun and profit. In: Proceedings of ATVA 2019 (2019, to appear)
5. Dax, C., Eisinger, J., Klaedtke, F.: Mechanizing the powerset construction for restricted classes of $\omega$-automata. In: Namjoshi, K.S., Yoneda, T., Higashino, T., Okamura, Y. (eds.) ATVA 2007. LNCS, vol. 4762, pp. 223–236. Springer, Heidelberg (2007). https://doi.org/10.1007/978-3-540-75596-8_17
6. Duret-Lutz, A.: Manipulating LTL formulas using Spot 1.0. In: Van Hung, D., Ogawa, M. (eds.) ATVA 2013. LNCS, vol. 8172, pp. 442–445. Springer, Cham (2013). https://doi.org/10.1007/978-3-319-02444-8_31
7. Duret-Lutz, A., Lewkowicz, A., Fauchille, A., Michaud, T., Renault, É., Xu, L.: Spot 2.0—a framework for LTL and $\omega$-automata manipulation. In: Artho, C., Legay, A., Peled, D. (eds.) ATVA 2016. LNCS, vol. 9938, pp. 122–129. Springer, Cham (2016). https://doi.org/10.1007/978-3-319-46520-3_8
8. Emerson, E.A., Lei, C.-L.: Modalities for model checking: branching time logic strikes back. Sci. Comput. Program. **8**(3), 275–306 (1987)
9. Gastin, P., Oddoux, D.: Fast LTL to Büchi automata translation. In: Berry, G., Comon, H., Finkel, A. (eds.) CAV 2001. LNCS, vol. 2102, pp. 53–65. Springer, Heidelberg (2001). https://doi.org/10.1007/3-540-44585-4_6

10. Křetínský, J., Meggendorfer, T., Sickert, S., Ziegler, C.: Rabinizer 4: from LTL to your favourite deterministic automaton. In: Chockler, H., Weissenbacher, G. (eds.) CAV 2018. LNCS, vol. 10981, pp. 567–577. Springer, Cham (2018). https://doi.org/10.1007/978-3-319-96145-3_30
11. Major, J.: Translation of LTL into nondeterministic automata with generic acceptance condition. Master's thesis, Masaryk University, Brno (2017)
12. Müller, D., Sickert, S.: LTL to deterministic Emerson-Lei automata. In: Proceedings Eighth International Symposium on Games, Automata, Logics and Formal Verification (GandALF). EPTCS, vol. 256, pp. 180–194 (2017). http://arxiv.org/abs/1709.02102
13. Redziejowski, R.R.: An improved construction of deterministic omega-automaton using derivatives. Fundam. Inf. **119**(3–4), 393–406 (2012)
14. Somenzi, F., Bloem, R.: Efficient Büchi automata from LTL formulae. In: Emerson, E.A., Sistla, A.P. (eds.) CAV 2000. LNCS, vol. 1855, pp. 248–263. Springer, Heidelberg (2000). https://doi.org/10.1007/10722167_21
15. Zbončáková, T.: Redukce omega-automatů s využitím Emerson-Lei akceptační podmínky. Bachelor's thesis, Masaryk University, Brno (2018)

# Synthesis

# Efficient Trace Encodings of Bounded Synthesis for Asynchronous Distributed Systems

Jesko Hecking-Harbusch(✉) and Niklas O. Metzger

Saarland University, Saarbrücken, Germany
{hecking-harbusch,metzger}@react.uni-saarland.de

**Abstract.** The manual implementation of distributed systems is an error-prone task because of the asynchronous interplay of components and the environment. Bounded synthesis automatically generates an implementation for the specification of the distributed system if one exists. So far, bounded synthesis for distributed systems does not utilize their asynchronous nature. Instead, concurrent behavior of components is encoded by all interleavings and only then checked against the specification. We close this gap by identifying true concurrency in synthesis of asynchronous distributed systems represented as Petri games. This defines when several interleavings can be subsumed by one true concurrent trace. Thereby, fewer and shorter verification problems have to be solved in each iteration of the bounded synthesis algorithm. For Petri games, experimental results show that our implementation using true concurrency outperforms the implementation based on checking all interleavings.

## 1 Introduction

One ambitious goal in computer science is the automatic generation of programs. For a given specification, a *synthesis algorithm* either generates a program satisfying the specification or determines that no such program exists. Nowadays, most synthesis tools deploy a game-theoretic view on the problem [2,4,6,23]. The synthesis of *distributed systems* [30] can be represented by a team of system players and a team of environment players playing against each other. Each system player acts on individual information and requires a local strategy, which in combination with the strategies of the other system players satisfies an objective against the decisions of the team of environment players. The environment players can cooperate to prevent the satisfaction of the objective by the system players. In the *synchronous* setting where all players progress at the same rate, the synthesis problem for distributed systems is undecidable [12,31].

This work was supported by the German Research Foundation (DFG) Grant Petri Games (392735815) and the Collaborative Research Center "Foundations of Perspicuous Software Systems" (TRR 248, 389792660), and by the European Research Council (ERC) Grant OSARES (683300).


Y.-F. Chen et al. (Eds.): ATVA 2019, LNCS 11781, pp. 369–386, 2019.
https://doi.org/10.1007/978-3-030-31784-3_22

*Petri games* represent *asynchronous* behavior in the synthesis of distributed systems where processes can progress at individual rates between synchronizations. Furthermore, the players of the team of system players have *causal memory*, i.e., a system player can base decisions on its local past and the local past of all other players up to their last synchronization. The synthesis problem for Petri games is decidable if for a maximum of one for the number of system players or the number of environment players [10,11]. If the restrictions on the team size cannot be met, *bounded synthesis* [13] is applied to incrementally increase the memory of possible system strategies until a winning one is found.

Each iteration of the bounded synthesis algorithm for Petri games [7] checks the existence of a winning system strategy with bounded memory by simulating the resulting Petri game. This simulation is represented as all *interleavings* of fired transitions allowed by possible system strategies. For two independent decisions, it makes no difference whether one decision or the other is scheduled first. It suffices to only check one scheduling where both decisions happen *true concurrently*. The true concurrent scheduling not only considers fewer schedulings but also shorter ones. Furthermore, the true concurrent scheduling enables us to refine the detection of loops in bounded synthesis. This results in a considerable speed-up of the verification part of bounded synthesis for Petri games.

To identify true concurrency, we introduce *environment strategies* for Petri games which explicitly represent the decisions of environment players. Environment strategies restrict a given system strategy and try to reach markings which prove the system strategy to *not* be winning. We present how the explicit environment decisions of environment strategies allow the firing of maximal sets of true concurrent transitions while preserving the applicability to bounded synthesis. This requires some *stalling* options for the environment. For bounded synthesis, we encode the assumptions on system and environment strategies as well as the winning objective of Petri games as *quantified Boolean formula* (QBF). We compare the implementations of the *sequential encoding* based on all interleavings and our new *true concurrent encoding* on an extended set of benchmarks[1]. Our experimental results show that the true concurrent encoding outperforms the sequential encoding by a considerable margin.

The key contributions of this paper are the following:

- We develop the theoretical foundation of *true concurrency* of components in synthesis for asynchronous distributed systems by representing environment decisions explicitly in *environment strategies* of Petri games.
- We prove that environment strategies *preserve existence of winning system strategies* and encode them as QBFs for bounded synthesis for Petri games.
- We *implement* the true concurrent encoding and show considerable improvements against the sequential encoding on an extended benchmark set.

The paper is structured as follows: In Sect. 2, we give an intuitive introduction to Petri games and the benefits of true concurrent scheduling for bounded synthesis for Petri games. Section 3 recalls the required background on Petri nets, Petri

[1] The sequential and the concurrent encoding can be tested online as part of the ADAM toolkit [9]: https://www.react.uni-saarland.de/tools/online/ADAM/.

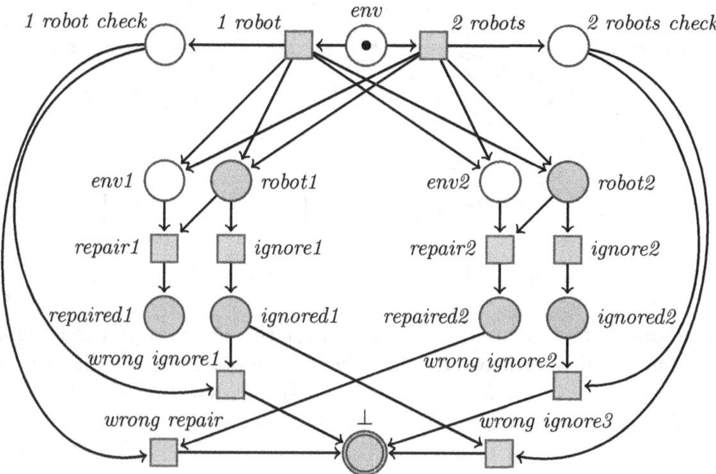


**Fig. 1.** This Petri game specifies a production line where two robots can repair a product. The product either requires repair by only one or by both robots.

games, and bounded synthesis. In Sect. 4, we introduce environment strategies and prove that they preserve the existence of winning strategies. Section 5 gives the true concurrent encoding formally as QBF. Section 6 surveys experimental results for the implementation of the true concurrent encoding.

## 2 Example of Bounded Synthesis for Petri Games

Figure 1 illustrates how Petri games represent the synthesis problem of asynchronous distributed systems and how true concurrency simplifies bounded synthesis for Petri games. This Petri game specifies a production line for repairing a product. The different possible requirements for repair are modeled as choices of the environment. The product can either require repair by a single robot or by both robots concurrently. These robots are represented by system players and have to collectively meet the requirement of the product.

Petri games are based on an underlying Petri net and distribute the places into two disjoint sets for the team of environment players and for the team of system players. White places belong to the environment and represent the product and its requirements for repair. Gray places belong to the system and represent the robots of the production line. The players are represented as tokens and their team is determined by the type of the place they are residing in. Initially, there is one token in the place *env* representing an environment player. Transitions define the flow of tokens through the Petri game as in Petri nets. When all places before a transition contain a token, then this transition is enabled. Firing an enabled transition consumes the tokens in all places before the transition and produces tokens in all places after it. The firing of enabled transition 1_*robot*

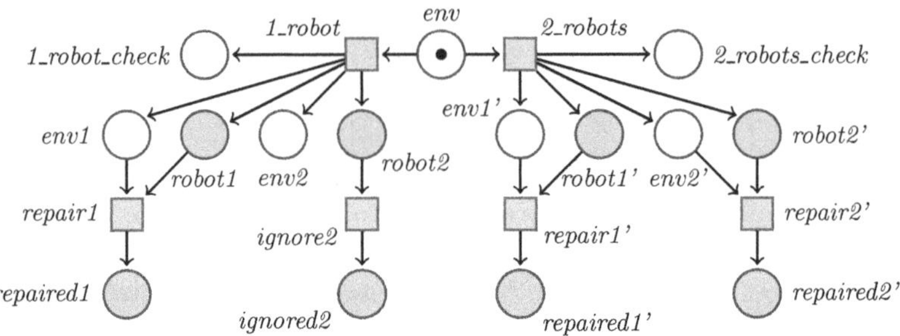


**Fig. 2.** A winning system strategy is presented for the Petri game from Fig. 1, which specifies a production line with two robots. The system players make different decisions depending on the choice of the environment. Transitions which cannot be enabled and unreachable places are removed.

results in a consumption of the token in *env* and the production of tokens in places 1*_robot_check*, *env1*, *robot1*, *env2*, and *robot2*. By this transition, both robots are started and it is required that only the first one repairs a part of the product.

The winning objective of the game is represented by the bad place $\bot$. The team of system players has to avoid reaching this place for all choices of the environment. Based on its causal past, a system player can decide which outgoing transitions to fire. For example, the system place *robot2* can either be reached via transition 1*_robot* or via 2*_robots* and then the player can decide in both cases independently between transitions *repair2* and *ignore2*. Deciding independently is necessary because if the environment has chosen 1*_robot*, no repair by the second robot is allowed whereas if the environment has chosen 2*_robots*, repair by the second robot is required. The winning system strategy is presented in Fig. 2 where primed places and transitions result from different causal pasts. The outgoing transitions *ignore2* of place *robot2* and *repair2'* of *robot2'* represent the necessary different decisions of the system. Notice that the bad place is not reachable based on the decisions in the winning system strategy.

Bounded synthesis for Petri games uses quantified Boolean formulas (QBFs) to decide the existence of a winning system strategy for a given memory bound. The decisions at system places are represented explicitly as existentially quantified variables which are tested to be avoiding bad places for subsequent distributions of tokens until the game either terminates or reaches a loop. The memory bound implies the length of these sequences. The sequential encoding tests all possible interleavings of transitions, e.g., in our example, first the environment makes a decision between 1*_robot* and 2*_robots* and then two interleavings are tested depending on the ordering of the decisions of both system players. Our new concurrent flow semantics identifies such situations and replaces them with one true concurrent step for the decisions of both robots. Thereby, we reduce the number of considered traces from four interleavings of length three to two true concurrent traces of length two to verify the winning system strategy of Fig. 2.

# 3 Background

We introduce the necessary background on Petri nets [32], Petri games [11], and the sequential encoding of bounded synthesis for Petri games [7]. Notice that we limit ourselves to 1-*bounded (safe)* Petri nets for simpler notation.

## 3.1 Petri Nets

A (1-bounded) *Petri net* $\mathcal{N} = (\mathcal{P}, \mathcal{T}, \mathcal{F}, In)$ consists of a set of *places* $\mathcal{P}$, a set of *transitions* $\mathcal{T}$, a *flow relation* $\mathcal{F} \subseteq (\mathcal{P} \times \mathcal{T}) \cup (\mathcal{T} \times \mathcal{P})$, and an *initial marking* $In \subseteq \mathcal{P}$. The flow relation defines the *arcs* from places to transitions ($\mathcal{P} \times \mathcal{T}$) and from transitions to places ($\mathcal{T} \times \mathcal{P}$). The state of a Petri game is represented by a *marking* $M \subseteq \mathcal{P}$ which positions one *token* each in all places $p \in M$. The elements of $\mathcal{P} \cup \mathcal{T}$ are considered as *nodes*. We define the *preset* (and *postset*) of a node $x$ from Petri net $\mathcal{N}$ as $pre^{\mathcal{N}}(x) = \{y \in \mathcal{P} \cup \mathcal{T} \mid (y, x) \in \mathcal{F}\}$ (and $post^{\mathcal{N}}(x) = \{y \in \mathcal{P} \cup \mathcal{T} \mid (x, y) \in \mathcal{F}\}$). The preset and postset of transitions are non-empty and finite. We use decorated names like $\mathcal{N}^b$ to also decorate the net's components. We abbreviate $pre^{\mathcal{N}^b}(x)$ and $post^{\mathcal{N}^b}(x)$ by $pre^b(x)$ and $post^b(x)$. A transition $t$ is *enabled* at a marking $M$ if $pre^{\mathcal{N}}(t) \subseteq M$ holds (denoted by $M[t\rangle$). An enabled transition $t$ can be *fired* from a marking $M$ resulting in the successor marking $M' = (M \setminus pre^{\mathcal{N}}(t)) \cup post^{\mathcal{N}}(t)$ (denoted by $M[t\rangle M'$). We define the set of *reachable markings* of a Petri net $\mathcal{R}(\mathcal{N}) = \{M \subseteq \mathcal{P} \mid \exists t_1, ..., t_n \in \mathcal{T} : \exists M_1, ..., M_n \subseteq \mathcal{P} : In[t_1\rangle M_1 ... [t_n\rangle M_n = M\}$. Two nodes $x, y$ are *in conflict* (denoted by $x \sharp y$) if there exists a place $p \in \mathcal{P} \setminus \{x, y\}$ from which $x$ and $y$ can be reached, exiting $p$ by different transitions.

## 3.2 (Bounded) Unfoldings and Subprocesses

The *unfolding* $\beta_U = (\mathcal{N}^U, \lambda^U)$ of a Petri net $\mathcal{N}$ explicitly represents the *causal pasts* of all places by eliminating all joins of places in the Petri net and separating these places into appropriate copies. Therefore, a loop in a Petri net results in an infinite unfolding. The homomorphism $\lambda^U : \mathcal{P}^U \cup \mathcal{T}^U \rightarrow \mathcal{P} \cup \mathcal{T}$ gives for nodes in the unfolding the corresponding original nodes. For bounded synthesis, we consider *bounded unfoldings* $\beta_U^b = (\mathcal{N}^b, \lambda^b)$, where the memory bound $b$ defines how many causal pasts per place can be represented as separate copies. Thereby, loops are only finitely often unfolded. A net-theoretic *subprocess* of a Petri net or an unfolding (denoted by $\sqsubseteq$) is defined by removing a set of transitions and all following places and transitions that cannot be reached anymore.

## 3.3 Petri Games

A *Petri game* $\mathcal{G} = (\mathcal{P}_S, \mathcal{P}_E, \mathcal{T}, \mathcal{F}, In, \mathcal{B})$ [11] with $\mathcal{B} \subseteq \mathcal{P}_S \cup \mathcal{P}_E$ has an underlying Petri net $\mathcal{N} = (\mathcal{P}, \mathcal{T}, \mathcal{F}, In)$ with $\mathcal{P} = \mathcal{P}_S \uplus \mathcal{P}_E$. The sets $\mathcal{P}_S$, $\mathcal{P}_E$, and $\mathcal{B}$ define the *system places*, the *environment places*, and the *bad places*. Unfoldings translate from Petri nets to Petri games by keeping the classification of places as system, environment, and bad places. A *system strategy* for $\mathcal{G}$ is a subprocess $\sigma = (\mathcal{N}^\sigma, \lambda^\sigma)$ of the unfolding $\beta_U = (\mathcal{N}^U, \lambda^U)$ of $\mathcal{G}$ where system places can remove outgoing transitions such that the following requirements hold:

(S1) *Determinism*:
$\forall M \in \mathcal{R}(\mathcal{N}^\sigma) : \forall p \in M \cap \mathcal{P}_S^\sigma : \exists^{\leq 1} t \in \mathcal{T}^\sigma : p \in pre^\sigma(t) \wedge pre^\sigma(t) \subseteq M$

(S2) *System refusal*: $\forall t \in \mathcal{T}^U : t \notin \mathcal{T}^\sigma \wedge pre^\sigma(t) \subseteq \mathcal{P}^\sigma \implies (\exists p \in pre^\sigma(t) \cap \mathcal{P}_S^\sigma : \forall t' \in post^U(p) : \lambda^U(t) = \lambda^U(t') \implies t' \notin \mathcal{T}^\sigma)$

(S3) *Deadlock-avoidance*:
$\forall M \in \mathcal{R}(\mathcal{N}^\sigma) : \exists t_U \in \mathcal{T}^U : pre^U(t_U) \subseteq M \implies \exists t_\sigma \in \mathcal{T}^\sigma : pre^\sigma(t_\sigma) \subseteq M.$

*Determinism* requires each system player to have at most one transition enabled for all reachable markings. *System refusal* requires that the removal of a transition from the unfolding is based on a system place deleting all outgoing copies of that transition. This enforces that system players base their decisions only on their causal past. *Deadlock-avoidance* requires the system strategy to enable at least one transition for each reachable marking as long as one transition is enabled in the unfolding. A system strategy is *winning* for the winning condition *safety* if no bad place can be reached in the system strategy, i.e., $\forall M \in \mathcal{R}(\mathcal{N}^\sigma) : \lambda^\sigma[M] \cap \mathcal{B} = \emptyset$. The synthesis problem for Petri games with safety as winning objective is EXPTIME-complete if we limit the number of system players or the number of environment players to one [10, 11].

### 3.4 Sequential Encoding of Bounded Synthesis for Petri Games

The bounded synthesis algorithm [7] takes a Petri game and increases the memory bound $b$ until a winning system strategy is found (or runs forever). The finite bounded unfolding $\beta_U^b = (\mathcal{N}^b, \lambda^b)$ is used to encode the existence of a winning system strategy (as variables $\mathcal{S}^b$) for all sequences of markings (as variables $\mathcal{M}_n$) up to the maximal simulation length $n \leq 2^{|\mathcal{P}^b|} + 1$ as QBF. In the encoding, concurrent transitions are represented by all possible interleavings as between two markings only a single transition is fired. For readability, we abbreviate $pre^{\mathcal{N}^b}(x)$ by ${}^\bullet x$ and $post^{\mathcal{N}^b}(x)$ by $x^\bullet$. The QBF has the form $\exists \mathcal{S}^b : \forall \mathcal{M}_n : \phi_n$ where $\mathcal{S}^b \overset{def.}{=} \{(p, \lambda^b(t)) \mid p \in \mathcal{P}_S^b \wedge t \in p^\bullet\}$ and $\mathcal{M}_n \overset{def.}{=} \{(p, i) \mid p \in \mathcal{P}^b \wedge 1 \leq i \leq n\}$.

The system strategy $\mathcal{S}^b$ consists of Boolean variables representing the system's choice for each pair of system place in the bounded unfolding and outgoing transition of the corresponding system place in the original game. This encoding ensures that each system strategy satisfies *system refusal* (S2) because neither pure environment transitions can be disabled nor can transitions be differentiated due to the bounded unfolding. The marking sequence $\mathcal{M}_n$ contains Boolean variables for each pair of place in the bounded unfolding and number $1 \leq i \leq n$ to encode in which of the $n$ subsequent markings this place is contained.

The matrix $\phi_n$ of the QBF $\exists \mathcal{S}^b : \forall \mathcal{M}_n : \phi_n$ is defined as follows:

$$\phi_n \overset{def.}{=} \bigwedge_{1 \leq i < n} \left( sequence_i \implies win_i \right) \wedge \left( sequence_n \implies win_n \wedge loop \right)$$

$$sequence_i \stackrel{def.}{=} initial \land seqflow_1 \land seqflow_2 \land \cdots \land seqflow_{i-1}$$

$$initial \stackrel{def.}{=} \bigwedge_{p \in In^b} (p,1) \land \bigwedge_{p \in \mathscr{P}^b \setminus In^b} \neg(p,1)$$

$$seqflow_i \stackrel{def.}{=} \bigvee_{t \in \mathscr{T}^b} \Bigg( \bigwedge_{p \in {}^\bullet t} (p,i) \land \bigwedge_{p \in {}^\bullet t \cap \mathscr{P}^b_S} (p, \lambda^b(t)) \land \bigwedge_{p \in t^\bullet} (p, i+1) \land \bigwedge_{p \in {}^\bullet t \setminus t^\bullet} \neg(p, i+1) \land \bigwedge_{p \in \mathscr{P}^b \setminus ({}^\bullet t \cup t^\bullet)} ((p,i) \iff (p,i+1)) \Bigg)$$

For each simulation point $1 \leq i \leq n$, it is tested whether the variables in $\mathcal{M}_n$ represent a correct $sequence_i$ of markings up to $i$ corresponding to a play in the bounded unfolding. If this is the case then $win_i$ tests whether the marking at $i$ fulfills the requirements to be winning. If $i = n$, i.e., the limit on the simulation is reached, it is additionally tested that a *loop* occurred. A correct *sequence* of markings starts from the *initial* marking followed by the *sequential flow* of $i-1$ enabled and by the system strategy allowed transitions. The *sequential flow* of a transition from time point $i$ requires all places in its preset to contain a token and the system strategy of system places in its preset to allow the transition. Then, at $i+1$, the places of its postset are set to true, places in its preset but not its postset are set to false, and all other places retain their truth value.

$$win_i \stackrel{def.}{=} nobadplace_i \land deterministic_i \land \big(deadlock_i \implies terminating_i\big)$$

$$nobadplace_i \stackrel{def.}{=} \bigwedge_{p \in \mathscr{B}^b} \neg(p,i)$$

$$deterministic_i \stackrel{def.}{=} \bigwedge_{\substack{t_1,t_2 \in \mathscr{T}, t_1 \neq t_2, \\ {}^\bullet t_1 \cap {}^\bullet t_2 \cap \mathscr{P}^b_S \neq \emptyset}} \Bigg( \bigvee_{p \in {}^\bullet t_1 \cup {}^\bullet t_2} \neg(p,i) \lor \bigvee_{\substack{p_1 \in {}^\bullet t_1 \cap \mathscr{P}^b_S, \\ p_2 \in {}^\bullet t_2 \cap \mathscr{P}^b_S}} \neg(p_1, \lambda^b(t_1)) \lor \neg(p_2, \lambda^b(t_2)) \Bigg)$$

$$deadlock_i \stackrel{def.}{=} \bigwedge_{t \in \mathscr{T}^b} \Bigg( \bigvee_{p \in {}^\bullet t} \neg(p,i) \lor \bigvee_{p \in {}^\bullet t \cap \mathscr{P}^b_S} \neg(p, \lambda^b(t)) \Bigg)$$

$$terminating_i \stackrel{def.}{=} \bigwedge_{t \in \mathscr{T}^b} \Bigg( \bigvee_{p \in {}^\bullet t} \neg(p,i) \Bigg)$$

$$loop \stackrel{def.}{=} \bigvee_{1 \leq i_1 < i_2 \leq n} \Bigg( \bigwedge_{p \in \mathscr{P}^b} ((p,i_1) \iff (p,i_2)) \Bigg)$$

If $sequence_i$ is fulfilled then $win_i$ tests whether the last marking fulfills the requirements to be winning at $i$. If $i = n$, i.e., the limit on the simulation is reached, it is additionally tested that a *loop* occurred. The play is winning if *no bad place* is reached, the system makes only *deterministic* decisions (S1), and each *deadlock* is caused by *termination* (S3). A deadlock occurs when no transition is enabled including the choices of the system strategy $\mathcal{S}^b$. Meanwhile, termination occurs when no transition is enabled independently of the system strategy. Therefore, $deadlock_i \implies terminating_i$ ensures that the system does not prevent the reaching of bad places by stopping to fire transitions, but deadlocks are only allowed when the entire game terminates. A *loop* in a Petri game occurs when the same marking is repeated at two different simulation points. As the system strategy has to be deterministic, its behavior repeats infinitely often in the loop such that the system strategy is also winning in an infinite play.

## 4 True Concurrency in Petri Games

In this section, we define true concurrency in Petri games. Therefore, we first formalize *environment strategies* to explicitly represent environment decisions in response to a given system strategy. This enables us to define the *true concurrent flow semantics* for Petri games, which enforces that transitions are fired as early and as parallel as possible. We prove that this semantics agrees with the interleaving semantics on the existence of a winning strategy for the system.

### 4.1 Environment Strategy

System strategies represent the system's restrictions of enabled transitions but purely environmental transitions remain uncontrollable. Therefore, a system strategy can result in different fired transitions. We introduce *environment strategies* to explicitly represent decisions of environment players and to obtain a unique sequence of fired transitions up to reordering of independent transitions.

An *environment strategy* $\gamma = (\mathcal{N}^\gamma, \lambda^\gamma)$ is a subprocess of a system strategy $\sigma = (\mathcal{N}^\sigma, \lambda^\sigma)$ (which, in turn, is a subprocess of the unfolding $\beta_U = (\mathcal{N}^U, \lambda^U)$ of the given Petri game $\mathcal{G}$) where environment places can remove outgoing transitions such that the following three requirements hold:

(E1) *Explicit choice*: $\forall p \in \mathcal{P}_E^\gamma : \exists^{\leq 1} t \in \mathcal{T}^\gamma : p \in pre^\gamma(t)$
(E2) *Environment refusal*: $\forall t \in \mathcal{T}^\sigma : t \notin \mathcal{T}^\gamma \wedge pre^\sigma(t) \subseteq \mathcal{P}^\gamma \Rightarrow pre^\sigma(t) \cap \mathcal{P}_E^\gamma \neq \emptyset$
(E3) *Progress*:
$$\forall M \in \mathcal{R}(\mathcal{N}^\gamma) : \exists t_\sigma \in \mathcal{T}^\sigma : pre^\sigma(t_\sigma) \subseteq M \Rightarrow \exists t_\gamma \in \mathcal{T}^\gamma : pre^\gamma(t_\gamma) \subseteq M.$$

*Explicit choice* requires each environment player to choose at most one of its outgoing transitions. *Environment refusal* enforces environment strategies to only remove transitions with at least one environment place in their preset. *Progress* requires the environment strategy to enable at least one transition for each reachable marking as long as a transition is enabled in the system strategy. Environment strategies resolve the remaining conflicts of a Petri game:

**Theorem 1.** *An environment strategy $\gamma$ leads to a unique sequence of fired transitions up to reordering of independent transitions* ($\forall p \in \mathcal{P}^\gamma : |post^\gamma(p)| \leq 1$).

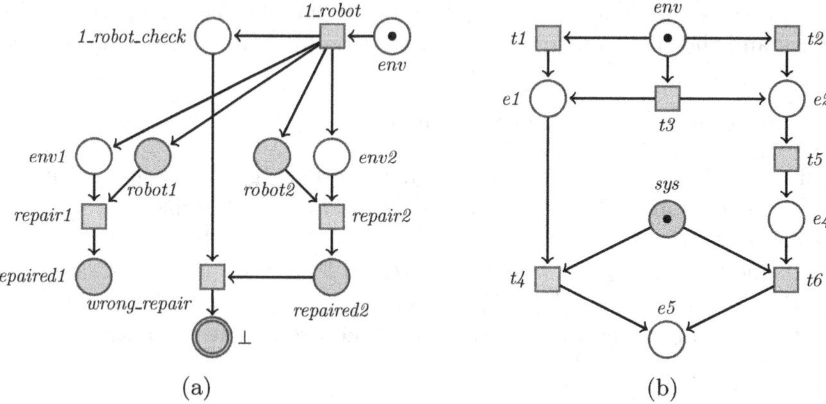


**Fig. 3.** Two strategies are depicted for the Petri game specifying a production line from Fig. 1: a winning environment strategy for a system strategy (a) and a winning system strategy with more than one outgoing transition at place *sys* (b).

*Proof.* A system strategy $\sigma$ satisfies for all system places $p \in \mathscr{P}_S^\sigma$ either the condition $|post^\sigma(p)| \leq 1$ or the non-determinism in the choice of the successor transition is resolved by the environment strategy $\gamma$. Since the environment strategy explicitly chooses at most one outgoing transition in each environment place, $\forall p \in \mathscr{P}_S^\gamma : |post^\gamma(p)| \leq 1$ is satisfied. For all environment places $p \in \mathscr{P}_E^\gamma$, the condition $|post^\gamma(p)| \leq 1$ is satisfied by the definition of environment strategies. Since $\mathscr{P}_S^\gamma \cup \mathscr{P}_E^\gamma = \mathscr{P}^\gamma$ holds, $\mathscr{N}^\gamma$ has a unique sequence of fired transitions up to reordering of independent transitions. □

The requirements for environment strategies are similar to the ones for system strategies: (E1) does not iterate over reachable markings in comparison to (S1) to require unique decisions by environment players, (E2) allows differentiation of transitions due to the unfolding in comparison to (S2), again, to enable unique decision, and (E3) is (S3) lifted directly to environment strategies.

$\gamma \sqsubseteq_E \sigma$ denotes an environment strategy $\gamma$ as subprocess of a system strategy $\sigma$ subject to (E1) to (E3). $\sigma \sqsubseteq_S \beta_U$ denotes a system strategy $\sigma$ as a subprocess of the unfolding $\beta_U$ subject to (S1) to (S3). An environment strategy $\gamma$ is *winning* (and a *counterexample* to the system strategy $\sigma$ being winning) if it reaches a bad place. We define a system strategy to be *winning* against all its environment strategies: a system strategy $\sigma$ is winning if no bad places are reached for all environment strategies, i.e., $\forall \gamma \sqsubseteq_E \sigma : \forall M \in \mathscr{R}(\mathscr{N}^\gamma) : \lambda^\gamma[M] \cap \mathscr{B} = \emptyset$.

Figure 3a shows a winning environment strategy for a system strategy of our running example with the bad place $\bot$. By the initial decision for 1_*robot* by the environment strategy, the right side of the system strategy becomes unreachable. The system chooses the transitions *repair1* and *repair2* in response to 1_*robot* by the environment strategy. By choosing 1_*robot*, the second robot should have ignored the product. The system strategy has to enable *wrong_repair* to avoid a deadlock and the environment strategy agress on firing it to reach the bad place.

### 4.2 True Concurrent Flow Semantics

We define the *true concurrent flow semantics* for Petri games by firing a maximal set of enabled, conflict-free transitions in every step. For the marking $M$ and the set of enabled, conflict-free transitions $T = \{t_1, \dots, t_n\}$, the successor marking $M'$ is defined by $M[T\rangle M'$, where $pre^{\mathcal{N}}(t_1) \uplus \dots \uplus pre^{\mathcal{N}}(t_n) \subseteq M$ and $M' = (M \setminus (pre^{\mathcal{N}}(t_1) \uplus \dots \uplus pre^{\mathcal{N}}(t_n))) \uplus post^{\mathcal{N}}(t_1) \uplus \dots \uplus post^{\mathcal{N}}(t_n)$. The set of reachable markings according to the true concurrent flow semantics is defined by

$$\begin{aligned}\mathcal{R}^{tc}(\mathcal{N}) = \{M \subseteq \mathcal{P} \mid \exists \text{ maximal } T_1, \dots, T_n \subseteq \mathcal{T} : \exists M_1, \dots, M_n \subseteq \mathcal{P} :\\ In[T_1\rangle M_1[T_2\rangle \dots [T_n\rangle M_n = M\} \qquad \text{where } |T_1|, \dots, |T_n| > 0\end{aligned}$$

We denote the set of reachable markings in the sequential flow semantics by $\mathcal{R}^{seq}(\mathcal{N}) = \mathcal{R}(\mathcal{N})$. Firing all enabled transitions in the true concurrent flow semantics at once yields a unique sequence of markings and therefore a unique sequence of sets of fired transitions. This brings us to the following theorem:

**Theorem 2.** *There exists a winning system strategy of a Petri game under the sequential flow semantics iff there exists a winning system strategy of a Petri game under the true concurrent flow semantics.*

*Proof.* We show that (1) $\exists \sigma \sqsubseteq_S \beta_U : \forall M \in \mathcal{R}^{seq}(\mathcal{N}^\sigma) : \lambda^\sigma[M] \cap \mathcal{B} = \emptyset \iff \exists \sigma \sqsubseteq_S \beta_U : \forall \gamma \sqsubseteq_E \sigma : \forall M \in \mathcal{R}^{seq}(\mathcal{N}^\gamma) : \lambda^\gamma[M] \cap \mathcal{B} = \emptyset$ and that (2) $\exists \sigma \sqsubseteq_S \beta_U : \forall \gamma \sqsubseteq_E \sigma : \forall M \in \mathcal{R}^{seq}(\mathcal{N}^\gamma) : \lambda^\gamma[M] \cap \mathcal{B} = \emptyset \iff \exists \sigma \sqsubseteq_S \beta_U : \forall \gamma \sqsubseteq_E \sigma : \forall M \in \mathcal{R}^{tc}(\mathcal{N}^\gamma) : \lambda^\gamma[M] \cap \mathcal{B} = \emptyset$. Since (1) is based on the sequential flow, every sequence of markings in $\mathcal{R}^{seq}(\mathcal{N}^\sigma)$ can be produced with an environment strategy choosing exactly the transitions of the sequence and vice versa. For (2), we show that the environment wins on the same nets by reaching a bad place: either $\exists \gamma \sqsubseteq_E \sigma : \exists M \in \mathcal{R}^{seq}(\mathcal{N}^\gamma) : \lambda^\gamma[M] \cap \mathcal{B} \neq \emptyset$ holds or not. As each environment strategy results in a unique sequence of fired transitions (up to reordering of independent transitions), the sets of reachable places in the reachable markings $\mathcal{R}^{seq}(\mathcal{N}^\gamma)$ and $\mathcal{R}^{tc}(\mathcal{N}^\gamma)$ are the same. □

## 5 True Concurrent Encoding of Bounded Synthesis

We show how the requirements (E1) to (E3) on environment strategies and the true concurrent flow semantics can be encoded as QBF. We introduce *stalling* of transitions to let environment players find non-determinism in a system strategy. Furthermore, we present how the true concurrent flow semantics can be used to detect loops earlier in the encoding of bounded synthesis for Petri games.

### 5.1 Stalling of Transitions to Find Non-determinism

To use the true concurrent flow semantics in bounded synthesis for Petri games, we ensure that all possible system strategies fulfill the assumptions (S1) to (S3) and do not reach any bad place. The determinism requirement can be violated when the sequential flow encoding is simply replaced by the true concurrent flow encoding as markings may be skipped by firing transitions as early as possible.

Figure 3b shows a Petri game without bad places. It is not winning for the system, as *t4* and *t6* have to be enabled (deadlock-avoidance) and there is a marking where both transitions are enabled (non-determinism). This contradicts *determinism* (S1) but in the true concurrent flow semantics, *t4* will always be fired before *t6* such that the marking with non-determinism of the system is never reached. To check the requirements for system strategies in the true concurrent encoding, environment players can *stall* transitions with at least one system place in their preset globally to catch up with the system. The requirement *determinism* (S1) can only be violated at system places. In Fig. 3b, the environment strategy needs to stall the firing of $t4$ until $t5$ is fired to prove that a potential system strategy enabling both transitions is non-deterministic.

### 5.2 Encoding True Concurrency as QBF

We extend the sequential encoding of bounded synthesis for Petri games [7,8] to environment strategies with stalling and the true concurrent flow semantics. The strategy of the environment is translated into additional universally quantified variables. The QBF-formula is $\exists \mathcal{S}^b : \forall \mathcal{M}_n : \forall \mathcal{E}^b : \phi_n$ with $\mathcal{E}^b$ as the union of variables for each environment choice in the firing of transitions and variables for transitions with at least one system place in their preset to stall their progress. This encoding preserves the requirement of *environment refusal* (E2):

$$\mathcal{E}^b \overset{def.}{=} \{(p,t,i) \mid p \in \mathscr{P}_E^b \wedge t \in p^\bullet \wedge 1 \leq i < n\} \cup \{(t) \mid t \in \mathscr{T}^b \wedge {}^\bullet t \cap \mathscr{P}_S^b \neq \emptyset\}$$

Bounded unfoldings may contain loops. The variables for the environment are different for every simulation point, such that decisions of revisited environment places do not depend on previous visits. By contrast, a global decision independent of the simulation points suffices for stalling. The case when variable $(t)$ is set to false results in the stalling of transition $t$. In the following, not mentioned formulas are as they are in the sequential encoding. We apply the requirement *explicit choice* (E1) of the environment strategy to $\phi_n$ and encode it in *choice*:

$$\phi_n \overset{def.}{=} \mathit{choice} \implies \bigwedge_{1 \leq i < n} \left( \mathit{seq}_i \implies \mathit{win}_i \right) \wedge \left( \mathit{seq}_n \implies \mathit{win}_n \wedge \mathit{loop} \right)$$

$$\mathit{choice} \overset{def.}{=} \bigwedge_{p \in \mathscr{P}_E^b, 1 \leq i < n} \left( \bigvee_{t \in p^\bullet} \left( (p,t,i) \wedge \bigwedge_{t' \in p^\bullet \setminus \{t\}} \neg (p,t',i) \right) \right)$$

$$seq_i \overset{def.}{=} initial \wedge tcflow_1 \wedge tcflow_2 \wedge \cdots \wedge tcflow_{i-1}$$

Each environment place has to choose exactly one outgoing transition which results in the firing of at most one outgoing transitions per environment place, because the other places in the preset of the transition also have to decide for the transition. This encoding furthermore ensures *progress* (E3). We substitute the sequential flow $seqflow_i$ by the true concurrent flow $tcflow_i$, which enforces the firing of all enabled and not stalled transitions and maintains all other tokens.

$$\begin{aligned}
tcflow_i &\overset{def.}{=} fireenabled_i \wedge updateplaces_i \\
fireenabled_i &\overset{def.}{=} \bigwedge_{t \in \mathcal{T}^b} \left( enabled_{i,t} \implies \bigwedge_{p \in {}^\bullet t \setminus t^\bullet} \neg(p, i+1) \wedge \bigwedge_{p \in t^\bullet} (p, i+1) \right) \\
updateplaces_i &\overset{def.}{=} \bigwedge_{p \in \mathcal{P}^b} \left( \bigwedge_{t \in {}^\bullet p \cup p^\bullet} \neg enabled_{i,t} \implies ((p, i) \iff (p, i+1)) \right) \\
enabled_{i,t} &\overset{def.}{=} \bigwedge_{p \in {}^\bullet t} (p, i) \wedge \bigwedge_{p \in \mathcal{P}^b_S \cap {}^\bullet t} (p, \lambda^b(t)) \wedge \bigwedge_{p \in \mathcal{P}^b_E \cap {}^\bullet t} (p, t, i) \wedge (t)
\end{aligned}$$

$enabled_{i,t}$ requires tokens in all places in the preset of the transition, both the system and the environment strategy to allow the transition for corresponding places in the preset of the transition, and that stalling allows the transition.

$win_i$ remains unchanged. Therefore, environment strategies and stalling only affect the flow of tokens but not the check that reached markings are winning.

### 5.3 Shorter Loops via Strongly Connected Components

Environment strategies allow us to define the true concurrent flow semantics which allows us to detect loops earlier by searching for them in *strongly connected components* (SCCs) [22]. The definition of SCCs can be directly lifted to Petri games by including an additional set with all places that are not in any other SCC. With SCCs, we find loops in independent parts of the Petri game as early as possible. We encode that a loop no longer only occurs at the repetition of a global marking but also when all $SCCs \subseteq 2^{\mathcal{P}^b}$ repeat their marking, respectively:

$$loop \overset{def.}{=} \bigwedge_{scc \in SCCs} \left( \bigvee_{1 \le i_1 < i_2 \le n} \left( \bigwedge_{p \in scc} ((p, i_1) \iff (p, i_2)) \right) \right)$$

## 6 Experimental Results

We compare the sequential encoding [7] with our new true concurrent encoding from Sect. 5 on five benchmark families. At first, we describe the asynchronous and distributed nature of these benchmark families stemming from alarm systems, routing, robotics, and communication protocols. Afterwards, we outline the technical details of our comparison framework and state our observations and explanations concerning the observed times for finding winning strategies.

### 6.1 Benchmark Families

Table 1 refers to the following scalable benchmark families where Collision Avoidance, Disjoint Routing, and Production Line are new benchmark families:

- **AS:** *Alarm System* [8]. *Parameters:* $m$ locations. There are $m$ secured locations and a burglar can intrude one of them. The local alarm system of each location can communicate with all other local alarm systems. The local alarm systems should indicate the position of an intrusion and should not issue unsubstantiated warnings of an intrusion.
- **CA:** *Collision Avoidance. Parameters:* $m$ robots. A subset of $m$ robots is initialized to drive on individual paths of increasing length with several goal states. They should avoid collisions and drive forever on the chosen route.
- **DR:** *Disjoint Routing. Parameters:* $m$ packets. In a software-defined network, $m$ packets should be routed disjointly between an ingress and an egress switch where the network allows $m$ disjoint paths between the two switches.
- **PL:** *Production Line. Parameters:* $m$ robots. The $m$ independent robots are able to repair or ignore $m$ features of a product. Depending on the product, some features need to be repaired while others must not be repaired.
- **DW:** *Document Workflow* [9]. *Parameters:* $m$ workers. A document circulates between $m$ workers with the environment choosing the first worker. It is required that all workers unanimously endorse or reject the document.

### 6.2 Comparison Framework

As both the sequential and the true concurrent encoding result in a 2-QBF not in conjunctive normal form, we use the QBF solver QuAbS [19,33]. The results from Table 1 were obtained on an Intel i7-2700K CPU with 3.50 GHz and 32 GB RAM and are the average over five runs. For each benchmark family (column *Ben.*), we report on the attempted parameters of the benchmark (*Par.*), the necessary model checking iterations (*Iter.*) of bounded synthesis, and on the runtime for finding a winning system strategy. A timeout of 30 min is used. We prepared an artifact to replicate our experimental results [18].

### 6.3 Observation

The true concurrent encoding shows considerable improvements over the sequential encoding on the presented benchmark set: It solves more instances and has mostly faster solving times as shown in Table 1. The improvements are based on fewer model checking iterations of the bounded synthesis algorithm witnessed by the *Iter.* column. The lower iteration count and runtime are indicated in bold.

**Table 1.** Benchmarking results on our Petri game *benchmark families* for increasing *parameters*. For the *sequential* and the *true concurrent* encoding, the needed model checking *iterations* with accumulated *runtime in seconds* are reported.

| *Ben.* | *Par.* | *Sequential* | | *True Concurrent* | |
|---|---|---|---|---|---|
| | | *Iter.* | *Runtime in sec.* | *Iter.* | *Runtime in sec.* |
| AS | 2 | 7 | 13.26 | **6** | **11.15** |
| | 3 | - | Timeout | - | Timeout |
| CA | 2 | 8 | 7.27 | **5** | **6.25** |
| | 3 | - | Timeout | **6** | **14.21** |
| | 4 | - | Timeout | **7** | **346.23** |
| | 5 | - | Timeout | - | Timeout |
| DR | 2 | 8 | 6.16 | **7** | **6.05** |
| | 3 | 11 | 11.03 | **9** | **10.07** |
| | 4 | 14 | 69.50 | **11** | **65.31** |
| | 5 | - | Timeout | - | Timeout |
| PL | 1 | **4** | **5.59** | **4** | **5.59** |
| | 2 | 5 | 6.08 | **4** | **5.85** |
| | 3 | 6 | 8.51 | **4** | **6.95** |
| | 4 | 7 | 20.99 | **4** | **12.54** |
| | 5 | 8 | 87.33 | **4** | **41.95** |
| | 6 | - | Timeout | **4** | **742.36** |
| | 7 | - | Timeout | - | Timeout |
| DW | 1 | 8 | 5.90 | **7** | **5.79** |
| | 2 | 10 | 6.58 | **9** | **6.44** |
| | 3 | 12 | 7.90 | **11** | **7.80** |
| | 4 | 14 | 11.45 | **13** | **11.22** |
| | 5 | 16 | **16.59** | **15** | 19.82 |
| | ... | ... | ... | ... | ... |
| | 10 | 26 | **716.61** | **25** | 823.94 |
| | 11 | **28** | **1304.14** | - | Timeout |
| | 12 | - | Timeout | - | Timeout |

We can make the following observations concerning the specific benchmark families: The complex communication structure of Alarm System prevents larger examples to be synthesized because the alarm system observing the intrusion has to broadcast the information to all other alarm systems. Similarly, Collision Avoidance has a complex pairwise communication structure which can be better synthesized by the true concurrent encoding. The simpler communication structure of Production Line allows constant bounds for the true concurrent encoding compared to linearly increasing bounds for the sequential encoding.

The communication structure of Disjoint Routing lays between complex and simple such that the true concurrent encoding enables a smaller linear increase in the bound. The true concurrent encoding therefore can solve larger examples even though the bounded unfolding grows with the number of considered players for both encodings. The possibilities for communication of information are less open in the benchmark families DR and PL whereas they are completely open in the benchmark family AS and CA. In Document Workflow, the communication structure is fixed to a specific pairwise ring between neighboring clerks. However, this prevents almost all true concurrency between them. The difference in bound of one is caused by the concurrent test that all workers have seen the document and that the decisions of workers have been unanimously.

## 7 Related Work

The *control problem of asynchronous automata* is an alternative approach to the synthesis of distributed asynchronous systems with causal memory. The modeling with asynchronous automata does not allow the spawning and termination of players. Also, it does not explicitly represent environment processes. Instead, every process can have uncontrollable behavior. The decidability of the control problem of asynchronous automata is open in general [28]. There are some decidability results for the control problem of asynchronous automata for restrictions on the dependencies of actions [15] or on the synchronization behavior [25,26]. Decidability has also been obtained for acyclic communication structures [16,29]. The class of *Decomposable games* [17] proposes a new proof technique to unify and extend these results. Recently, an exponential gap between the control problem of asynchronous automata and Petri games has been identified [1].

There is a broad theory and several implementations for model checking of distributed systems: For Petri nets as representation of distributed systems, it often suffices to only consider finite prefixes of the unfolding [3,5,24]. It is most interesting whether these results can be lifted to Petri games and causal past. Partial order reduction and true concurrency have been studied thoroughly to speed up the model checking of finite distributed systems [14,20,21,27]. The systems we synthesize are especially powerful as both the system and the environment can run infinitely and non-determinism of the environment is represented.

## 8 Conclusion

We presented how to utilize concurrency in bounded synthesis for asynchronous distributed systems by firing as many true concurrent transitions as possible in our new true concurrent encoding. The previous sequential encoding enumerated all interleavings. For the true concurrent encoding, we represent the decisions of the environment players explicitly as environment strategies for Petri games and showed that this enables us to fire all enabled transitions as early as possible while maintaining the existence of winning system strategies. The experimental results show that our tool implementation of the true concurrent encoding outperforms the sequential encoding on all benchmark families by a considerable margin. Even in the rare case of benchmark families without true concurrent transitions, the true concurrent encoding slightly outperforms the sequential encoding despite resulting in larger QBFs.

For future work, we want to apply environment strategies and true concurrency in ADAM to improve synthesis for a bounded number of system players and one environment players. Furthermore, we plan to extend the bounded synthesis encoding further. On the one hand, we want to identify disconnected parts of the Petri game, solve them in isolation, and compose them back together. On the other hand, we plan to extend the expressivity of considered winning conditions. Local liveness conditions of places to reach should be straightforward whereas global winning conditions in the form of markings to reach or avoid could prove difficult for the true concurrent encoding as certain interleavings may be skipped. Therefore, we believe that local winning conditions on the progress of individual tokens could be a good middle ground between the current local winning conditions of bad places and global winning conditions.

## References


1. Beutner, R., Finkbeiner, B., Hecking-Harbusch, J.: Translating asynchronous games for distributed synthesis. In: CONCUR 2019, pp. 26:1–26:16 (2019). https://doi.org/10.4230/LIPIcs.CONCUR.2019.26
2. Bohy, A., Bruyère, V., Filiot, E., Jin, N., Raskin, J.-F.: Acacia+, a tool for LTL synthesis. In: Madhusudan, P., Seshia, S.A. (eds.) CAV 2012. LNCS, vol. 7358, pp. 652–657. Springer, Heidelberg (2012). https://doi.org/10.1007/978-3-642-31424-7_45
3. Bonet, B., Haslum, P., Khomenko, V., Thiébaux, S., Vogler, W.: Recent advances in unfolding technique. Theor. Comput. Sci. **551**, 84–101 (2014)
4. Ehlers, R.: Unbeast: symbolic bounded synthesis. In: Abdulla, P.A., Leino, K.R.M. (eds.) TACAS 2011. LNCS, vol. 6605, pp. 272–275. Springer, Heidelberg (2011). https://doi.org/10.1007/978-3-642-19835-9_25
5. Esparza, J., Heljanko, K.: Unfoldings - A Partial-Order Approach to Model Checking. Springer, Heidelberg (2008). https://doi.org/10.1007/978-3-540-77426-6
6. Faymonville, P., Finkbeiner, B., Rabe, M.N., Tentrup, L.: Encodings of bounded synthesis. In: Legay, A., Margaria, T. (eds.) TACAS 2017. LNCS, vol. 10205, pp. 354–370. Springer, Heidelberg (2017). https://doi.org/10.1007/978-3-662-54577-5_20
7. Finkbeiner, B.: Bounded synthesis for Petri games. In: Meyer, R., Platzer, A., Wehrheim, H. (eds.) Correct System Design. LNCS, vol. 9360, pp. 223–237. Springer, Cham (2015). https://doi.org/10.1007/978-3-319-23506-6_15
8. Finkbeiner, B., Gieseking, M., Hecking-Harbusch, J., Olderog, E.: Symbolic vs. bounded synthesis for Petri games. In: SYNT 2017, pp. 23–43 (2017)
9. Finkbeiner, B., Gieseking, M., Olderog, E.-R.: ADAM: causality-based synthesis of distributed systems. In: Kroening, D., Păsăreanu, C.S. (eds.) CAV 2015. LNCS, vol. 9206, pp. 433–439. Springer, Cham (2015). https://doi.org/10.1007/978-3-319-21690-4_25

10. Finkbeiner, B., Gölz, P.: Synthesis in distributed environments. In: FSTTCS 2017, pp. 28:1–28:14 (2017)
11. Finkbeiner, B., Olderog, E.: Petri games: synthesis of distributed systems with causal memory. Inf. Comput. **253**, 181–203 (2017)
12. Finkbeiner, B., Schewe, S.: Uniform distributed synthesis. In: LICS 2005, pp. 321–330 (2005)
13. Finkbeiner, B., Schewe, S.: Bounded synthesis. STTT **15**(5–6), 519–539 (2013)
14. Flanagan, C., Godefroid, P.: Dynamic partial-order reduction for model checking software. In: POPL 2005, pp. 110–121 (2005)
15. Gastin, P., Lerman, B., Zeitoun, M.: Distributed games with causal memory are decidable for series-parallel systems. In: Lodaya, K., Mahajan, M. (eds.) FSTTCS 2004. LNCS, vol. 3328, pp. 275–286. Springer, Heidelberg (2004). https://doi.org/10.1007/978-3-540-30538-5_23
16. Genest, B., Gimbert, H., Muscholl, A., Walukiewicz, I.: Asynchronous games over tree architectures. In: Fomin, F.V., Freivalds, R., Kwiatkowska, M., Peleg, D. (eds.) ICALP 2013. LNCS, vol. 7966, pp. 275–286. Springer, Heidelberg (2013). https://doi.org/10.1007/978-3-642-39212-2_26
17. Gimbert, H.: On the control of asynchronous automata. In: FSTTCS 2017, pp. 30:1–30:15 (2017)
18. Hecking-Harbusch, J., Metzger, N.O.: BoundedAdam – efficient trace encodings for bounded synthesis of Petri games (2019). https://doi.org/10.6084/m9.figshare.8313215
19. Hecking-Harbusch, J., Tentrup, L.: Solving QBF by abstraction. In: GandALF 2018, pp. 88–102 (2018)
20. Heljanko, K.: Using logic programs with stable model semantics to solve deadlock and reachability problems for 1-safe Petri nets. Fundam. Inf. **37**(3), 247–268 (1999)
21. Heljanko, K.: Combining symbolic and partial order methods for model checking 1-safe Petri nets. Ph.D. thesis, Aalto University, Helsinki, Finland (2002)
22. Jensen, K.: Coloured Petri Nets: Basic Concepts, Analysis Methods and Practical Use, vol. 2. Springer, Heidelberg (2013)
23. Jobstmann, B., Galler, S., Weiglhofer, M., Bloem, R.: Anzu: a tool for property synthesis. In: Damm, W., Hermanns, H. (eds.) CAV 2007. LNCS, vol. 4590, pp. 258–262. Springer, Heidelberg (2007). https://doi.org/10.1007/978-3-540-73368-3_29
24. Khomenko, V., Koutny, M., Vogler, W.: Canonical prefixes of Petri net unfoldings. Acta Inf. **40**(2), 95–118 (2003)
25. Madhusudan, P., Thiagarajan, P.S.: A decidable class of asynchronous distributed controllers. In: Brim, L., Křetínský, M., Kučera, A., Jančar, P. (eds.) CONCUR 2002. LNCS, vol. 2421, pp. 145–160. Springer, Heidelberg (2002). https://doi.org/10.1007/3-540-45694-5_11
26. Madhusudan, P., Thiagarajan, P.S., Yang, S.: The MSO theory of connectedly communicating processes. In: Sarukkai, S., Sen, S. (eds.) FSTTCS 2005. LNCS, vol. 3821, pp. 201–212. Springer, Heidelberg (2005). https://doi.org/10.1007/11590156_16
27. Meulen, J.V., Pecheur, C.: Combining partial order reduction with bounded model checking. In: CPA 2009, pp. 29–48 (2009)
28. Muscholl, A.: Automated synthesis of distributed controllers. In: Halldórsson, M.M., Iwama, K., Kobayashi, N., Speckmann, B. (eds.) ICALP 2015. LNCS, vol. 9135, pp. 11–27. Springer, Heidelberg (2015). https://doi.org/10.1007/978-3-662-47666-6_2

29. Muscholl, A., Walukiewicz, I.: Distributed synthesis for acyclic architectures. In: FSTTCS 2014, pp. 639–651 (2014)
30. Pnueli, A., Rosner, R.: On the synthesis of an asynchronous reactive module. In: Ausiello, G., Dezani-Ciancaglini, M., Della Rocca, S.R. (eds.) ICALP 1989. LNCS, vol. 372, pp. 652–671. Springer, Heidelberg (1989). https://doi.org/10.1007/BFb0035790
31. Pnueli, A., Rosner, R.: Distributed reactive systems are hard to synthesize. In: FOCS 1990, pp. 746–757 (1990)
32. Reisig, W.: Petri Nets: An Introduction. Springer, Heidelberg (1985). https://doi.org/10.1007/978-3-642-69968-9
33. Tentrup, L.: Non-prenex QBF solving using abstraction. In: Creignou, N., Le Berre, D. (eds.) SAT 2016. LNCS, vol. 9710, pp. 393–401. Springer, Cham (2016). https://doi.org/10.1007/978-3-319-40970-2_24

# Reactive Synthesis of Graphical User Interface Glue Code

Rüdiger Ehlers[1(✉)] and Keerthi Adabala[2]

[1] Clausthal University of Technology, Clausthal-Zellerfeld, Germany
ruediger.ehlers@tu-clausthal.de
[2] University of Bremen, Bremen, Germany
adabala@uni-bremen.de

**Abstract.** We present an approach to synthesize *glue code* for graphical user interfaces. Such code starts computation and I/O threads in response to user interface events and changes the state of the interface according to the interaction scheme envisioned by the UI designer.

Our approach integrates several ideas that work best in combination. For instance, by translating all specification parts to universal very-weak (UVW) automata and building a game from them, we obtain a natural order over the positions in the game that enables us to prune the game graph substantially while constructing it. Furthermore, we present an approach to compute *kind* strategies that constrain the environment as little as possible and hence make the UIs as responsive as possible. The use of UVWs gives rise to a simple formalization of this idea.

We apply our approach to a case study with an Android (cell phone) application and show experimentally that previous reactive synthesis tools are unable to synthesize controllers for this application.

## 1 Introduction

The large number of ways in which a user of a program can interact with its graphical user interface (GUI) makes writing code for such interfaces highly difficult. Events in user interfaces trigger computation or I/O threads that can run concurrently while the user interface needs to remain responsive and to service requests that are unconnected to the computation or I/O taking place in the background. Unsurprisingly, user interface *glue code* that reacts to events, changes the state of the user interface, and triggers computation or I/O is difficult and tedious to write and thus susceptible to bugs.

User interfaces often go through several iterations of user testing before they are finalized. While programs for designing the graphical appearance of user interfaces exist, how the system to be developed behaves in response to events is still normally implemented manually, which leaves the implementation burden for every iteration to the UI designer and the user experience (UX) engineer, which makes experimenting with different interaction styles difficult.

This work was supported by the German Science Foundation (DFG) under Grant No. 322591867.


Y.-F. Chen et al. (Eds.): ATVA 2019, LNCS 11781, pp. 387–403, 2019.
https://doi.org/10.1007/978-3-030-31784-3_23

Automatically *synthesizing* GUI code from user interface interaction specifications has the potential to solve this problem. It is a special case of *reactive synthesis*, where a system that continuously interacts with its environment is computed that satisfies its specification for all possible input sequences. The specification is typically given in some form of temporal logic, such as *linear temporal logic* (LTL). Despite the provably high computational complexity of this problem for most specification logics, practical reactive synthesis has seen a substantial improvement in the last few years, with tools such as *Strix* [15] winning the *2018 Reactive Synthesis Competition* for LTL specifications.

Unfortunately, classical reactive synthesis frameworks are not well-applicable to synthesize GUI glue code:

1. In synthesis from LTL, the system is assumed to read input bit values and set output bit values in every time step. There is no fixed time step in user interfaces – rather, the controller can respond to *events* by executing a sequence of *actions*. These cannot happen in parallel, and there can also be a *last* event after which the system and the controller stall.
2. Specifications for user interfaces are normally huge, requiring a very high scalability of the synthesis approach, which traditional approaches for synthesis from LTL specifications do not provide.
3. Synthesis approaches that trade the full expressivity of LTL against improved efficiency, such as *Generalized Reactivity(1) Synthesis* [7], cannot deal with specifications parts that describe chains of events, which are common in user interface specifications.
4. The application-specific quality metrics for user interface glue code, such as starting computation as quickly as possible and enabling UI elements such as buttons whenever possible (but only then) cannot be accurately captured by traditional quality metrics in reactive synthesis, such as maximizing pay-offs in games [4].

Nevertheless, GUI glue code is an application that is quite a natural fit for reactive synthesis: there is a clear notion of state in user interfaces, the lower bound on the complexity of all interesting problems for LTL induced by the inclusion of propositional logic does not apply (as events cannot happen in parallel in GUIs), and the rapid prototyping cycles during UI/UX design provide a clear motivation for employing synthesis technology.

In this paper, we present an approach to perform reactive synthesis of user interface glue code. We carefully selected and devised components for a synthesis approach that in combination avoid the four drawbacks of classical synthesis algorithms stated above and hence enable the synthesis of GUI glue code. Our approach builds on the following ideas:

- Rather than assuming an execution in fixed timesteps, we use an interaction semantics in which the GUI controller can react to every input event with arbitrary long but finite sequences of output actions.
- We use an LTL fragment that can easily be translated to *universal very weak* automata as specification language [1].

- We reuse the main ideas of the efficient *Generalized Reactivity(1) Synthesis* approach to solve the *synthesis games* built from environment assumptions and system guarantees in this LTL fragment.
- Contrary to how Generalized Reactivity(1) Synthesis was used with binary decision diagrams (BDD) in earlier works, we perform explicit-state game solving, where only those game positions are explored that form the *anti-chain* of incomparable best-case reactions by the system.
- After solving the game, we constrain the strategy to play action sequences that restrict the environment as little as possible, hence making the UIs as responsive as possible.

These design decisions work together in concert. For instance, the use of universal very-weak automata enables us to define a natural order over the obligations of the system player on the further play of the game. This allows the system player to chose its action sequences in a way that all successor positions are optimal with respect to this order, which minimizes the explicit-state size of the game graph. We show that in this way, the synthesis problem for GUI glue code becomes much more tractable than with earlier synthesis approaches. At the same time, the supported specification class is powerful enough to capture user interface interaction rules.

We present the overall methodology in this paper and highlight the insights that led to the choice of its components. We apply our methodology to a case study for a *cost splitting* application for Google Android cell phones on which we demonstrate the scalability of our synthesis approach.

### 1.1 Related Work

Reactive synthesis is an classical topic in the formal methods literature. While the identification of the problem as doubly exponential-time complete for logics such as linear temporal logic (LTL) [16] implied that the problem is intractable in theory, more recently, optimizations that try to make use of the structure of specifications of interest in practice have emerged. Of particular interest in this context is the *Generalized Reactivity(1) Synthesis* approach [7], which trades the full expressivity of LTL against a reduction of the synthesis complexity. The approach, abbreviated as *GR(1) synthesis*, has been shown to be expressive enough for many applications in robotics [13] and device driver synthesis [17]. Just like it is the case for GR(1) synthesis, the approach we present in this paper lies at a *sweet spot* between expressivity and efficiency for interesting application domains.

We focus on the domain of user interfaces. Experience shows that getting them correct is difficult [14], which suggests that more formal approaches to developing user interface code may be useful. Model-driven engineering of user interfaces helps to mitigate this problem [12] and builds on iterative refinement of the model. With the present work, we aim for a less disruptive approach to change the way GUI glue code is engineered. We only require the UI/UX designers to specify the behavior in a form of temporal logic, without the need to model any other representation of the interaction or perform any form of refinement, hence allowing for very quick revision cycles of the interaction scheme.

While classical reactive synthesis uses environment and system propositions to model the interaction of a system with its environment, GUIs communicate with their environments via *events*, of which only one can happen at a time. Synthesis of event-based systems has been considered previously [8], but incorporating the idea that the system can react with a sequence of actions to input events, as it is the case in GUIs and exploited in our synthesis algorithm to simplify the synthesis problem, appears to be novel.

When synthesizing an implementation, there is normally an infinite number of candidate implementations to choose from. In such a case, implementations that do not prevent the environment from fulfilling the assumptions made about it in the specification are commonly preferred [6,8]. Furthermore, if a specification comes with a *cost metric* for performing actions, we may be interested in cost-optimal controllers (see, e.g., [4]). In contrast, the *kindness* definition for GUI glue code given in Sect. 6 is a domain-specific optimization objective that builds on the representation of the specification using very-weak automata.

## 2 Running Example: `SplitExpenses`

We consider a *cost splitting* application for Android cell phones. With the application, an (informal) team can split its running costs. Team members paying for expenses can add their expenses to a list. The application then gives an overview of who owes how much money to make the split fair. The application uses a server to synchronize the data, and it supports being a member of multiple teams. The application has several views of which one is visible at every point in time:

- Account/team selection
- New team/account
- Overview of who owes how much money
- List of expenses
- Administrator's panel for removing unjustified expense items
- Adding an expense
- Recording reimbursements within the group
- Expenses not yet confirmed by the current user
- List of actions not yet executed due to a missing internet connection.

A new group is started by an administrator, who forwards team login codes to other team members. If a user does not have an internet connection, changes performed by the user are not dropped, but rather executed when the connection is restored. So offline use is possible with delayed synchronization. The application has three threads for creating a new team, receiving team data from the server, and submitting changes to the server.

The overall specification for the GUI glue code consists of 118 individual properties (expressed in an LTL fragment that permits an efficient translation to universal very-weak automata [1]). There are, in addition, 8 properties that express assumptions about the environment, such as that all threads eventually terminate and that disabled buttons cannot be clicked by the user.

## 3 Preliminaries

*Basics:* Given a finite set $X$, the set of finite words over $X$ is denoted as $X^*$, while the set of infinite words is denoted as $X^\omega$.

*Linear Temporal Logic (LTL):* Let $\mathsf{AP}$ be a finite set of *atomic propositions*. An LTL formula describes a specification over infinite *traces* with trace elements in $2^{\mathsf{AP}}$. Syntactically, LTL formulas are built using the following grammar:

$$\psi ::= p \mid \neg\psi \mid \psi \vee \psi' \mid \psi \wedge \psi' \mid \mathsf{X}\psi \mid \mathsf{G}\psi \mid \mathsf{F}\psi \mid \psi\,\mathcal{U}\,\psi' \mid \psi\,\mathcal{R}\,\psi' \mid \psi\,\mathcal{W}\,\psi'$$

An LTL formula holds at a position in a trace or not. By default, the first element of the trace is looked at. A formal semantics of LTL can be found in [3].

*Automata over Infinite Words:* Let $\Sigma$ be a finite alphabet. An $\omega$-automaton $\mathcal{A} = (Q, \Sigma, Q_0, \delta, F)$ over $\Sigma$ is a tuple consisting of a set of states $Q$, the set of initial states $Q_0$, the transition relation $\delta \subseteq Q \times \Sigma \times Q$, and the set of *final states* $F$. An infinite word $w = w_0 w_1 \ldots \in \Sigma^\omega$ induces an infinite run $\pi = \pi_0 \pi_1 \ldots \in Q^\omega$ in $\mathcal{A}$ if we have $\pi_0 \in Q_0$ and for every $i \in \mathbb{N}$, we have $(\pi_i, w_i, \pi_{i+1}) \in \delta$. Finite runs are defined similarly, where we require that they cannot be further extended. Automata reject or accept words $w$ depending on which runs $w$ induces. The set of words accepted by an automaton is called its *language*. A *universal co-Büchi automaton* accepts all words for which no infinite run exists that visits states in $F$ infinitely often, i.e., for which there are infinitely many $i \in \mathbb{N}$ with $\pi_i \in F$. We also call $F$ the set of *rejecting states* in this paper. We will only be concerned with a subclass of these automata here, which are called *universal very-weak* (or *one-weak*) automata. These are universal co-Büchi automata for which every loop is a self-loop. This requirement can be formalized by stating that there should exist a *leveling* function $l : Q \to \mathbb{N}$ such that for every $(q, x, q') \in \delta$, we have $l(q') \geq l(q)$. For many (but not all) LTL formulas, there exists a universal very-weak (UVW) automaton whose language is the set of traces that satisfies the LTL formula. Pointers to the literature discussing this topic are given in [1]. We say that a UVW state $q$ is left along all runs for the last character of a word $w_0 \ldots w_n$ if $(q, w_n, q) \notin \delta$ or there is no run that is in state $q$ after the prefix word $w_0 \ldots w_{n-1}$.

## 4 An Execution Semantics for GUI Glue Code

Traditional temporal logics either use a *real-time semantics* in which the passing of time can be reasoned about (such as in *Metric Time Logic* [2]), or assume a discrete-time semantics with regular steps in the execution of a system (such as

LTL). For synthesizing GUI glue code, neither of these choices is satisfactory. User interfaces should normally be *patient* and give the user time to react, so that the concrete timing of the interaction with a user should not matter. Given that even for simple real-time temporal logics such as *Metric Interval Time Logic*, the reactive synthesis problem is undecidable [9], real-time logics appear to be an unsuitable choice. Linear temporal logic (LTL) synthesis on the other hand has been conceptualized for settings with evenly distributed time steps, for which the abstraction that a system runs infinitely long is reasonable, and for which in every step of the system's execution, all input and output propositions of a system have values. This is also not the case for GUIs, as all events such as clicking a button and starting a computation thread are ordered, so that no two events can happen at the same time. The assumption that the system always runs infinitely long is also unreasonable: GUI code always eventually returns control to the operating system (OS) and then only *wakes up* if and when an external event happens. If a user is finished with a user interface, it may never wake up again and hence good GUI glue code must perform actions such as saving settings to flash memory *eagerly* to avoid not being able to satisfy its specification. Finally, the strict temporal alternation between input and output that is common in current reactive synthesis approaches is also not suitable, as a GUI controller can perform arbitrary many actions before giving control back to the operating system, which is a precondition for the next user interaction event (such as a button press) to occur. None of these differences to previous synthesis approaches prevent conflicts with the use of LTL as specification logic if we define a suitable execution semantics for GUI glue code, however, as we show in this section.

We formalize the interaction between the GUI code and its environment by defining a set of *environment events* $\Sigma^{\mathcal{I}}$ that model events not under the control of the GUI glue code to be synthesized and *controller actions* $\Sigma^{\mathcal{O}}$ that the said glue code can trigger. We assume that the controller can only react to events from $\Sigma^{\mathcal{I}}$ with arbitrarily long sequences of actions. Hence, a controller to be synthesized has the form $f : (\Sigma^{\mathcal{I}})^* \rightarrow (\Sigma^{\mathcal{O}})^*$, where providing the *history* of past input events to $f$ yields the reaction to the *last* such event. To simplify specifying the desired properties of GUI glue code, we define a designated initialization event $init \in \Sigma^{\mathcal{I}}$ that the controller can always assume to get first when the application starts. Likewise, we define a designated "done" action $done \in \Sigma^{\mathcal{O}}$ that signals that a controller yields control back to the operating system and that always has to be exactly the last action in every sequence returned by $f$. Thus, the value of $f(w)$ for some $w \in (\Sigma^{\mathcal{I}})^*$ needs to be defined for words $w$ that start with *init*, and $f(w)$ ends with *done* in this case.

Let $w^I = w_0^I w_1^I \ldots$ be a sequence of input events. We say that $w^I$ induces a system trace $w = w_0^I f(w_0^I) w_1^I f(w_0^I w_1^I) w_2^I f(w_0^I w_1^I w_2^I) \ldots$. We define that $w$ satisfies some LTL specification $\psi$ if the word $w'$ that results from translating each letter $x$ in $w$ to the letter $\{x\} \in 2^{\Sigma^{\mathcal{I}} \cup \Sigma^{\mathcal{O}}}$ satisfies $\psi$. If $w^I$ is finite, the word $w$ eventually ends, and we append an infinite number of repetitions of $\emptyset$ (the empty set) to $\psi$ before interpreting the LTL formula.

*Example 1.* To motivate these definitions, let us look at a fragment of the expense split application specification. Specifications to be fulfilled by GUI glue code often contain assumptions made about the environment and the guarantees that the controller must fulfill. Let us consider that the guarantees contain the following specification part:

$$\psi_g = \mathsf{G}(\mathit{newTeamButton.click} \rightarrow (\neg \mathit{done}\, \mathcal{U}\, \mathit{regTeam.start}) \\ \wedge (\neg \mathit{regTeam.terminate}\, \mathcal{U}\, (\mathit{regTeam.terminate} \wedge (\neg \mathit{done}\, \mathcal{U}\, \mathit{updateTeamList}))))$$

This guarantee states that whenever the GUI button for starting a new team is clicked, then a thread for registering a new team is started before the controller hands back control to the operating system. Registering a new team requires communication with a server, and a GUI should not be blocked until an answer from the server is received. This implies the need to offload the communication task to a separate thread. Furthermore, the specification states that when the thread eventually terminates afterwards, some instantaneous action *updateTeamList* is to be executed before control is given back to the operating system. Both this action and starting the thread lead to user-written back-end code being executed. The *updateTeamList* action is fast enough so that executing it in the context of the GUI does not lead to it blocking, and GUI frameworks such as the one used for Android applications even require such updates to be performed from the GUI (main) thread.

On its own, the specification is unrealizable, because the *regTeam* thread may never terminate. This can be fixed by adding the assumption to the specification that whenever the thread for registering a new team is started, it eventually terminates:

$$\psi_a = \mathsf{G}(\mathit{threadA.start} \rightarrow \mathsf{F}\mathit{threadA.terminates})$$

The specification used for synthesizing the glue code is then $\psi_a \rightarrow \psi_g$.

Figure 1 shows two trace parts of traces satisfying the specification. In the left example, the system correctly starts the team registration thread when the corresponding button is clicked. Eventually, the thread terminates (with no other GUI event happening in this example), and the controller chooses action *updateTeamList* as response, as specified.

The right trace shows an example for a finite trace. After starting the thread and giving back control to the OS by choosing action *done*, the GUI glue code never gets control back. This means that the trace is filled with $\emptyset$ to interpret the specification $\psi_a \rightarrow \psi_g$. Since $\psi_a$ is violated on this trace, this means that the trace also fulfills the specification $\psi_a \rightarrow \psi_g$. Note that this is important as otherwise no controller would exist for this specification as the termination of a manually written thread is outside of the control of the synthesized GUI controller.

## 5 GR(1) Games for Event-Based Specifications

Given an environment event set $\Sigma^{\mathcal{I}}$, a controller action set $\Sigma^{\mathcal{O}}$, an environment assumption formula $\psi^A$ in LTL, and a system guarantee LTL formula $\psi^G$, the

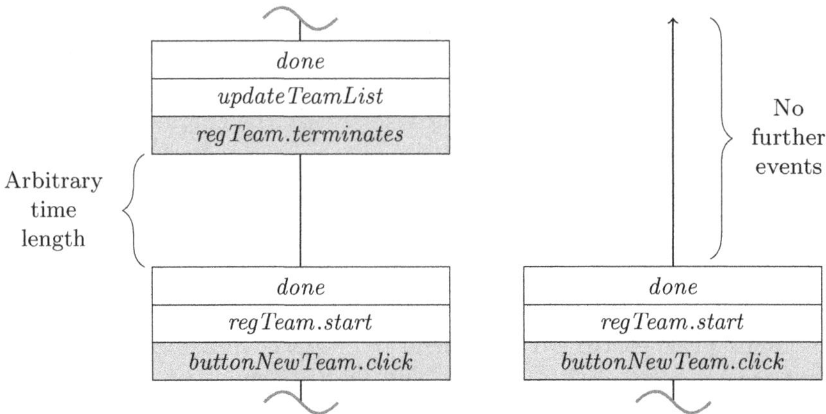


**Fig. 1.** Two trace parts of a controller satisfying the specification from Example 1. Time progresses from the bottom to the top.

GUI controller synthesis problem is to check if there exists a controller function $f : (\Sigma^{\mathcal{I}})^* \rightarrow (\Sigma^{\mathcal{O}})^*$ such that all traces induced by the controller (using the semantics from the previous section) satisfy the specification $\psi^A \rightarrow \psi^G$.

Controller synthesis is commonly conceptually reduced to solving a game between an environment player and a system player. The environment player has the role of choosing the uncontrollable input, and the system player wins the game if and only if it can always react in a way such that the *play* satisfies the specification for which the game was built. A play is built from following the edges of the game according to the events and actions that the two players choose. A play is in some position at every point in time, and the positions encode the *obligations* of the system player for the remainder of the play. Readers who want to learn more about game-based synthesis are referred to [5] and for conciseness, we assume familiarity with its basic ideas in the following.

### 5.1 Game Definitions

For the approach in this paper, we build games from assumptions and guarantees that are both representable as universal very-weak automata (UVWs). We identified a fragment of LTL that can be efficiently translated into this form in earlier work [1], so that we can assume that UVWs for the assumptions and guarantees in a specification are given. The following game construction captures the main ideas of Generalized Reactivity(1) synthesis [7], but is adapted to the case of having UVW specifications:

**Definition 1.** *Let* $\mathcal{A}^A = (Q^A, \Sigma, Q_0^A, \delta^A, F^A)$ *be a UVW representing* $\psi^A$ *and* $\mathcal{A}^G = (Q^G, \Sigma, Q_0^G, \delta^G, F^G)$ *be a UVW representing* $\psi^G$*. We define the* synthesis game *induced by* $\mathcal{A}^A$ *and* $\mathcal{A}^G$ *as a tuple* $\mathcal{G} = (V, \Sigma^I, \Sigma^O, E, v_0)$ *with the finite set of positions* $V = 2^{Q^A} \times 2^{Q^G}$*, the input and output players' action* *sets* $\Sigma^I$ *and* $\Sigma^O$*, the initial position* $v_0 = (Q_0^A, Q_0^G) \in V$*, and the set of edges* $E \subseteq Q \times \Sigma^I \times \Sigma^O \times 2^{F^A} \times 2^{F^G} \times Q'$*, which consists of all elements* $((v^A, v^G), x^I, x_0^O \ldots x_n^O, L^A, L^G, (v'^A, v'^G))$ *for which we have:*

$$
\begin{aligned}
& x_n^O = done \\
\wedge\ & \exists Q'_0 \ldots Q'_{n+2} \subseteq Q^A. \\
& \quad Q'_0 = v^A, Q'_{n+2} = v'^A, Q'_1 = \{q' \in Q^A \mid \exists q \in Q'_0, (q, x^I, q') \in \delta^A\}, \\
& \quad \forall i \in \{0, \ldots, n\}.\ Q'_{i+2} = \{q' \in Q^A \mid \exists q \in Q'_{i+1}.(q, x_i^O, q') \in \delta^A\}, \\
& \quad L^A = \{q \in F^A \mid \exists i \in \{0, \ldots, n+2\}.q \notin Q'_i \vee (q, x^I, q) \notin \delta^A\} \\
& \quad\quad \cup \{q \in F^A \mid \exists i \in \{0, \ldots, n\}.(q, x_i^O, q) \notin \delta^A\} \\
\wedge\ & \exists Q'_0 \ldots Q'_{n+2} \subseteq Q^G. \\
& \quad Q'_0 = v^G, Q'_{n+2} = v'^G, Q'_1 = \{q' \in Q^G \mid \exists q \in Q'_0, (q, x^I, q') \in \delta^G\}, \\
& \quad \forall i \in \{0, \ldots, n\}.\ Q'_{i+2} = \{q' \in Q^G \mid \exists q \in Q'_{i+1}.(q, x_i^O, q') \in \delta^G\} \\
& \quad L^G = \{q \in F^G \mid \exists i \in \{0, \ldots, n+2\}.q \notin Q'_i \vee (q, x^I, q) \notin \delta^G\} \\
& \quad\quad \cup \{q \in F^G \mid \exists i \in \{0, \ldots, n\}.(q, x_i^O, q) \notin \delta^G\}
\end{aligned}
$$

The edge set definition requires some explanation. An edge $((v^A, v^G), x^I, x_0^O \ldots x_n^O, L^A, L^G, (v'^A, v'^G))$ denotes that if from position $(v^A, v^G)$, the environment player chooses input action $x^I$ and the system player chooses action sequence $x_0^O \ldots x_n^O$, then the next position in a play is $(v'^A, v'^G)$. The additional components $L^A$ and $L^G$ denote the rejecting UVW automaton states that are *left* along such an edge.

The definition of a synthesis game is carefully crafted for the case that the specification from which the game is built comes in the form of assumption and guarantee UVWs, and hence deviates from the definitions found in other works. We chose to keep the strict alternation between the environment and system players' choices, which required that the system player chooses sequences of actions from $\Sigma^O$ rather than single actions. Keeping the strict alternation greatly simplifies the presentation of the optimizations for game solving defined later in this paper. For the same reason, we also encoded the usual winning condition in GR(1) synthesis into the edges rather than separately (which is explained below). Finally, we do not have explicitly *owned* vertices for the two players. This is only a minor difference in case of strict alternation between the players and ensures that the controller definition from the previous section fits exactly the strategy definition for games given below.

More formally, we say that a sequence $\pi = \pi_0\pi_1 \ldots \in V^\omega$ is a *play* in the game if there exist corresponding decision sequences $\rho^{env} = \rho_0^{env}\rho_1^{env} \ldots \in (\Sigma^I)^\omega$ and $\rho^{sys} = \rho_0^{sys}\rho_1^{sys} \ldots \in ((\Sigma^O)^*)^\omega$ for the two players such that $\pi_0 = v_0$ and for every $i \in \mathbb{N}$, there is some suitable edge $(\pi_i, \rho_i^{env}, \rho_i^{sys}, L_i^A, L_i^G, \pi_{i+1})$ in the edge set of the game. We say that the play is *winning* if either:

- there exists some state $q \in F^A$ that appears in only finitely many sets $L_i^A$ (for $i \in \mathbb{N}$), or

- for all states $q \in F^G$, there exist infinitely many sets $L_i^G$ (for $i \in \mathbb{N}$) with $q \in L_i^G$.

Note that the edges are defined in a way such that the positions $(v^A, v^G)$ track in which states runs of the automata $\mathcal{A}^A$ and $\mathcal{A}^G$ can be after reading a prefix of the *interleaved* decision sequence $\tilde{\rho} = \rho_0^{env} \rho_0^{sys} \rho_1^{env} \rho_1^{sys} \ldots$. Furthermore, the sets $L_i^A$ and $L_i^G$ keep track of which rejecting states *every* run needs to leave (if it is in that state) when reading a part of $\tilde{\rho}$. If and only if some rejecting state occurs only finitely often in $\{L_i^A\}_{i \in \mathbb{N}}$, this means that some run of $\mathcal{A}^A$ gets stuck in a rejecting state when reading $\tilde{\rho}$. Likewise, if and only if some rejecting state occurs only finitely often in $\{L_i^G\}_{i \in \mathbb{N}}$, this means that some run of $\mathcal{A}^G$ gets stuck in a rejecting state when reading $\tilde{\rho}$. Hence, the winning condition of the game implements the requirement that if the interleaved decision sequence satisfies $\psi^A$, then it also needs to satisfy $\psi^G$ for the system player to win the game. This observation enables us to frame the problem of finding a controller function $f$ for a user interface as defined in the previous section as the problem of finding a *winning strategy* $f$ for the system player in $\mathcal{G}$.

If there is a winning strategy in such a game, then there is also a finite-state one. This follows from the fact that the winning condition type is the same as in GR(1) game structures [7], so that the result that a strategy that is *positional per goal* suffices for GR(1) games carries over to our game definition. In our case, this means that the next choice of the strategy only depends on (1) the current position in the game, (2) the last input chosen by the environment player, and (3) the current *goal* of the system, which in our case is the state in $F^G$ that is to be left next. By letting the controller cycle though all such goals, concatenating the sub-strategies for each goal leads to a correct finite-state controller implementation.

How to solve such games is described in [7]. We use a variation of the algorithm presented in [10] as it permits the definition of goal transitions rather than goal states. This is important to be able to define leaving a rejecting state of the guarantee automaton as a goal.

## 5.2 Pruning the Game

The game specified in Definition 1 has an infinite number of edges since the system player can choose sequences of actions rather than individual actions. Not all such decision sequences make sense, however. We want to prune the game before actually *solving* it, i.e., determining whether the system player has a winning strategy and computing such a strategy.

We prune the game based on the following observation:

**Lemma 1.** *Let $f$ be a winning strategy for some game $\mathcal{G}$ built according to Definition 1 and let $\rho_0^{env} \ldots \rho_{m-1}^{env}$ be some finite sequence of actions chosen by the environment.*

*(1) By Definition 1, there is exactly one edge $((v^A, v^G), x^I, x_0^O \ldots x_n^O, L^A, L^G, (v'^A, v'^G))$ with $x^I = \rho_{m-1}^{env}$ and $x_n^O = f(\rho_0^{env} \ldots \rho_{m-1}^{env})$ that can be taken at the nth step of the play.*

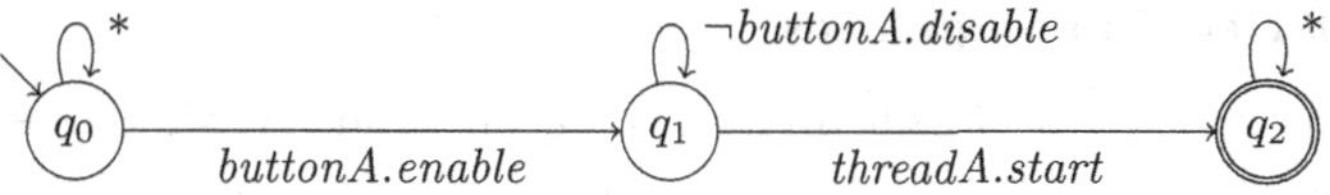


**Fig. 2.** Example guarantee UVW part for the example from Sect. 5.2.

*(2) If there is another edge* $((v^A, v^G), x^I, \hat{x}_0^O \ldots \hat{x}_m^O, \hat{L}^A, \hat{L}^G, (\hat{v}'^A, \hat{v}'^G))$ *such that* $\hat{L}^A \subseteq L^A$, $\hat{L}^G \supseteq L^G$, $\hat{v}'^A \supseteq v'^A$, *and* $\hat{v}'^G \subseteq v'^G$, *then the strategy that results from modifying* $f$ *to return* $\hat{x}_0^O \ldots \hat{x}_m^O$ *instead of* $x_0^O \ldots x_m^O$ *for* $\rho_0^{env} \ldots \rho_{m-1}^{env}$ *is still winning.*

*Proof.* The first claim follows directly from the definition of the game. The second claim follows from the fact that whether a strategy is winning depends on the labels of the positions visited along a play - if a state set $v^G$ is replaced by a subset of $v^G$, then a suffix strategy is still winning as the states along the $v^G$ components of the positions along of the play will then also be subsets, and hence the system player is less restricted in the possible moves (without being unable to satisfy the winning condition). The same holds for $v^A$, but in the reverse direction, as a superset of states in a $v^A$ component means that the environment is more restricted without violating its assumptions. Similar arguments can be made about the $L^A$ and $L^G$ components. □

The incorporation of the $L^A$ and $L^G$ components into the argument ensures that the claim also holds if infinitely many strategy choices are replaced. This enables us to prune the game during its construction: we only need to enumerate edges that are not *dominated* by other edges. We say that an edge is dominated by another edge if the criterion from the preceding lemma can be applied to make a winning strategy never take that edge. Since there are only finitely many different sets $v^A$, $v^G$, $L^A$, and $L^G$, this makes the game graph finite. This idea can be made mathematically precise by defining a partial order over the positions and to then only explore the *anti-chain* of best-case states (for the system). Anti-chains over game positions have also been used in earlier works on reactive synthesis from full linear temporal logic [11].

We observed that anti-chains based game pruning greatly reduces the sizes of the games built from GUI specifications. As a trivial example, consider the case that $\psi^G$ has a conjunct that requires the system to not start a certain thread while a certain button is enabled. Figure 2 shows a part of the corresponding UVW. If there is no reason to enable a button (meaning that enabling it does not change any other state in $F^G$ or $F^A$ to be left or a state in $v^A$ or $v^G$ to be reached) from some position $(v^A, v^G)$, then the pruned game graph will simply not contain an edge from $(v^A, v^G)$ along which the button is enabled, as this would cause state $q_1$ to become part of the $v^G$ component, which is avoidable and hence is a dominated move.

### 5.3 Short Decision Sequences

Specifications for graphical user interfaces reason about events triggered by the user and the change of the interface's state. There are many combinations of actions that do not usually make sense, such as the controller disabling and enabling a button in the same step. When building a game according to Definition 1 and the anti-chains based pruning approach described above, we typically do not want the game edges to include such sequences.

We can avoid them by performing a *breadth-first search* of the feasible controller response sequences while enumerating all edges from a position in a game. If there are multiple ways to get to the same combination of successor position and *leaving state label* $(L^A, L^G)$, the resulting edge will have one of the possible shortest such sequences.

For instance, this approach prevents the action sequence *buttonA.disable*; *buttonA.enable* from being a edge label from a position $(v^A, \{q0, q1\})$ in a game built using the UVW part from Fig. 2 as the only guarantee automaton. Since the successor guarantee automaton state set (for some arbitrary input event) is the same set for both the sequences *buttonA.disable*; *buttonA.enable* and *buttonA.enable* with the same set of rejecting states left along the game edge, only the shorter sequence has a chance to be found in the resulting game (assuming that none of the actions affected the assumption automaton).

## 6 Kind Strategies

Good GUI controllers are *responsive* by enabling GUI elements whenever they can be enabled. While the UI designer could be required to specify exactly in which situations a GUI element should be enabled, this defeats the purpose of synthesis to enable designers to quickly prototype systems. It thus makes sense to integrate this requirement into the synthesis process itself.

The anti-chains based pruning approach from the previous section makes unresponsive controllers particularly likely to be found. For instance, if there is a button that can be disabled or enabled, and there is an assumption that states that the button cannot be clicked if it is not enabled, then there is an incentive for the system to disable the button, as in this case, the resulting successor position in the game is labelled by the additional assumption automaton state that checks this condition. This happens even if the button does not need to be disabled.

We solve this problem by defining a notion of a *kind* strategy that makes use of the fact that assumptions are encoded in UVW form and hence the situation-dependent obligations of the environment can be compared. A kind strategy make *kind* choices, which we define as follows:

**Definition 2.** *Let* $(v^A, v^G)$ *be a position in a game* $\mathcal{G}$, $x^I \in \Sigma^{\mathcal{I}}$ *be an environment action, and* $x^{O,1}$ *and* $x^{O,2}$ *be two output sequences from* $(\Sigma^{\mathcal{O}})^*$. *We say that* $x^{O,1}$ *is* kinder *than* $x^{O,2}$ *if for the corresponding successor positions* $(v^{A,1}, v^{G,1})$ *and* $(v^{A,2}, v^{G,2})$ *reached by an edge for* $(x^I, x^{O,1})$ *and* $(x^I, x^{O,2})$, *respectively, we have that* $v^{A,1} \subseteq v^{A,2}$.

Note that the kindest strategy choices are typically *not* part of a game pruned according to the definition from the previous section, as successor states with smaller assumption automaton sets $v^A$ are filtered out by the algorithm. Yet, the definition captures that the controller should perform actions that restrict the environment as little as possible, as witnessed by the assumption automaton being in fewer states.

To marry these two concepts, we developed an iterative approach that combines anti-chain based game pruning with the search for kind moves in a synthesized strategy. Whenever a winning strategy is found, we iterate over the reachable positions in the game and for every input event replace the edges for the input event by edges that are strictly kinder than the one selected in the previous strategy (or by multiple ones if different ones are selected for different next goals of the system). Among the strictly kinder ones, we still perform pruning as described in Sect. 5.2 to keep the game small. Whenever the game becomes losing for the system after this change, our algorithm undoes the change. Otherwise, the changed game is kept. When the process completes for all positions reachable by the last strategy computed, this last strategy is the final kindest strategy found.

Note that this process can increase the number of positions in the game. It also requires many game solving iterations. We picked it because of its simplicity – if there is a strategy that is as kind as possible in every step and still satisfies the specification, the approach finds such a strategy. If kindness in every step conflicts with the system making progress towards leaving rejecting states, the system player does not win any more when trying to remove the last unkind edge useful for satisfying the specification. In this case, the edge removal is undone. The approach naturally avoids the problem that optimal strategies could become infinite-state, as it is the case when integrating quantitative objectives such as mean-payoff into a game in which the players have obligations to fulfil infinitely often [4, p. 150].

## 7 Case Study

We modelled the scenario from Sect. 2 using specification parts in the fragment of LTL that is easy to translate to UVWs [1]. All in all, our specification consists of 8 assumption LTL formulas and 118 guarantee LTL formulas.

When writing the specification, we made active use of the fact that we assume that the computed implementations use the shortest decision sequences as defined in Sect. 5.3 and that the strategy is *kind* as defined in Sect. 6. For instance, the guarantee parts

$$\mathsf{G}(\mathit{MenuItemOfflineActions} \rightarrow \neg \mathit{done}\,\mathcal{U}\,\mathit{PanelExpensesToApprove.hide})$$
$$\mathsf{G}(\mathit{MenuItemOfflineActions} \rightarrow \neg \mathit{done}\,\mathcal{U}\,\mathit{PanelOfflineActions.show})$$

enforce that when the offline actions menu item is selected from the main menu of the application, the view (panel) for the expenses to approve are hidden, and the

**Table 1.** Results for the expense splitting example application. Time-outs (after two hours) are listed as "t/o", all other times are given in seconds (on an Intel i5 Processor with 1, 6 GHz clock rate and 6 GB RAM available).

| Specification | | Translation to UVWs | | Game solving (not kind) | | | Game solving (kind) | | | Slugs | Strix |
|---|---|---|---|---|---|---|---|---|---|---|---|
| Rev. | # Properties | Time | # states | Time | Size strat. | Size st. flat | Time | Size strat. | Size st. flat | Time | Time |
| 1 | 8 | 0.04 | 10 | 0.00 | 2 | 16 | 0.00 | 2 | 16 | 0.16 | 3.30 |
| 2 | 21 | 0.43 | 20 | 0.00 | 4 | 88 | 0.00 | 6 | 108 | 675.52 | 8.64 |
| 3 | 57 | 2.05 | 32 | 0.25 | 4 | 246 | 2.28 | 14 | 565 | t/o | t/o |
| 4 | 105 | 5.77 | 41 | 18.44 | 6 | 537 | 45.45 | 15 | 1044 | t/o | t/o |
| 5 | 124 | 10.41 | 44 | 182.87 | 6 | 630 | 389.14 | 15 | 1245 | t/o | t/o |
| 6 | 115 | 7.21 | 44 | 102.84 | 6 | 618 | 215.32 | 15 | 1215 | t/o | t/o |
| 7 | 135 | 12.0 | 47 | 589.04 | 6 | 711 | 1020.28 | 15 | 1413 | t/o | t/o |
| 8 | 134 | 10.76 | 46 | 186.28 | 6 | 675 | 283.00 | 15 | 1413 | t/o | t/o |
| 9 | 131 | 12.37 | 45 | 106.03 | 6 | 660 | 198.62 | 15 | 1392 | t/o | t/o |
| 10 | 127 | 11.35 | 45 | 60.39 | 6 | 660 | 267.90 | 48 | 3676 | t/o | t/o |
| 11 | 127 | 10.6 | 47 | 60.31 | 8 | 876 | 268.68 | 64 | 5129 | t/o | t/o |
| 12 | 126 | 13.49 | 50 | 483.67 | 48 | 3756 | 916.39 | 138 | 10074 | t/o | t/o |

offline actions view should be shown. There is no specification part that prevents the controller from hiding the latter view again immediately afterwards. But it is also not necessary, as that would lead to unnecessarily long decision sequences, and hence cannot be part of the strategy. Similarly, the specification does not have guarantees that require the system to enable buttons in certain situations - whenever there is an assumption that a disabled button cannot be clicked, a kind strategy enables it whenever possible.

To validate our approach, we implemented the ideas presented in this paper in an explicit-state game solving tool written in `C++` and developed a prototype tool that analyzes a GUI layout of an Android application to enumerate the possible events, to build a game from the specification together with the event list, and to translate a computed strategy to synthesized GUI glue code in the programming language Java that can be compiled into the Android application. Both tools can be found at https://github.com/tuc-es/guisynth together with the expense splitting application.

To test the effectiveness of the approach presented in this paper, we also implemented translator scripts that encode the synthesis problem into generalized reactivity(1) specifications and into the standard LTL format used for the SYNTCOMP competition. In both cases, we binary-encoded the events and actions to reduce the number of atomic propositions. The resulting specifications are quite complex as for comparability, the execution semantics from Sect. 4 also needed to be encoded. For the translation to GR(1), doing so would lead to specifications outside of the supported fragment; to mitigate this issue, we restricted all controller decision sequences to be of length at most 16, which is the longest sequences that we found our game solver to produce for the case study.

We use the resulting specifications for the GR(1) and full LTL synthesis tools `Slugs` and [10] `Strix` [15], where the latter won the full LTL synthesis competition SyntComp in 2018. For fairness, we must note that neither Strix nor Slugs are especially designed for the shape of GUI specifications, while our approach was especially crafted for the execution semantics described in Sect. 4.

Table 1 shows computation times and strategy sizes for kind and unkind strategies for several versions of our specification which represent its evolution during the writing process of the case study. Computation times for Slugs and Strix on the translated specifications are given as well, where it needs to be noted that these tools do not compute kind strategies.

It can be observed that the computed strategies are quite small. Since in our strategy definition, the system can output multiple actions at the same step, we also give the sizes of *flattened* finite-state machines from the strategies in which this is not the case. It can be observed that such a representation increases the number of states substantially.

## 8 Conclusion

In this paper, we presented a framework for the synthesis of graphical user interface glue code. Synthesizing such code allows rapid iteration cycles, and we did a first step towards even more scalable synthesis algorithms that are useful for establishing GUI glue code synthesis in industry. Our solution was carefully designed to make use of the particular properties of the application domain – thanks to the special execution semantics of GUI glue code, the system can perform multiple actions in a row, which keeps the game graph small when building the game only with best-case responses by the system. This enables explicit-state game solving and helps with the definition of *kind* strategies that represent responsive GUI controllers.

This work is only the first step, though. Our case study shows that the approach is already applicable, but will reach its scalability limit for more complex specifications. There are many opportunities for improvement, though. We did not perform incremental building of the game yet, as it was not necessary - the solving time is dominated by the time needed to find the edges in the game graph. Enumerating the anti-chain of best case responses requires to consider many action sequences by the system player – we believe that there is potential to optimize the search for best-case responses substantially.

In our framework, we separated control and data considerations completely to obtain a decidable synthesis problem. We also assumed that there can be at most one copy of a type of a thread at the same time. The reason is that employing finite-state games does not enable encoding the number of threads of a type running. Extending synthesis by this capability can easily lead to undecidability, and in many applications, it is easy to write threads to collect work and perform it sequentially, which removes the need to have more than one thread of a type running at the same time.

Performing more case studies to collect specifications to drive the scalability of synthesis from UI specifications forward is subject of future work. Furthermore, UI and user experience (UX) designers may benefit from more application-oriented specification languages for UI code rather than LTL. We will explore how such specification languages can look like while still permitting an efficient translation to UVWs.

## References

1. Adabala, K., Ehlers, R.: A fragment of linear temporal logic for universal very weak automata. In: Lahiri, S.K., Wang, C. (eds.) ATVA 2018. LNCS, vol. 11138, pp. 335–351. Springer, Cham (2018). https://doi.org/10.1007/978-3-030-01090-4_20
2. Alur, R., Henzinger, T.A.: Logics and models of real time: a survey. In: de Bakker, J.W., Huizing, C., de Roever, W.P., Rozenberg, G. (eds.) REX 1991. LNCS, vol. 600, pp. 74–106. Springer, Heidelberg (1992). https://doi.org/10.1007/BFb0031988
3. Baier, C., Katoen, J.: Principles of Model Checking. MIT Press, Cambridge (2008)
4. Bloem, R., Chatterjee, K., Henzinger, T.A., Jobstmann, B.: Better quality in synthesis through quantitative objectives. In: Bouajjani, A., Maler, O. (eds.) CAV 2009. LNCS, vol. 5643, pp. 140–156. Springer, Heidelberg (2009). https://doi.org/10.1007/978-3-642-02658-4_14
5. Bloem, R., Chatterjee, K., Jobstmann, B.: Graph games and reactive synthesis. In: Clarke, E., Henzinger, T., Veith, H., Bloem, R. (eds.) Handbook of Model Checking, pp. 921–962. Springer, Cham (2018). https://doi.org/10.1007/978-3-319-10575-8_27
6. Bloem, R., Ehlers, R., Könighofer, R.: Cooperative reactive synthesis. In: Finkbeiner, B., Pu, G., Zhang, L. (eds.) ATVA 2015. LNCS, vol. 9364, pp. 394–410. Springer, Cham (2015). https://doi.org/10.1007/978-3-319-24953-7_29
7. Bloem, R., Jobstmann, B., Piterman, N., Pnueli, A., Sa'ar, Y.: Synthesis of reactive(1) designs. J. Comput. Syst. Sci. **78**(3), 911–938 (2012)
8. D'Ippolito, N., Braberman, V.A., Piterman, N., Uchitel, S.: Synthesizing nonanomalous event-based controllers for liveness goals. ACM Trans. Softw. Eng. Methodol. **22**(1), 9:1–9:36 (2013)
9. Doyen, L., Geeraerts, G., Raskin, J.-F., Reichert, J.: Realizability of real-time logics. In: Ouaknine, J., Vaandrager, F.W. (eds.) FORMATS 2009. LNCS, vol. 5813, pp. 133–148. Springer, Heidelberg (2009). https://doi.org/10.1007/978-3-642-04368-0_12
10. Ehlers, R., Raman, V.: `Slugs`: extensible GR(1) synthesis. In: Chaudhuri, S., Farzan, A. (eds.) CAV 2016. LNCS, vol. 9780, pp. 333–339. Springer, Cham (2016). https://doi.org/10.1007/978-3-319-41540-6_18
11. Filiot, E., Jin, N., Raskin, J.: Exploiting structure in LTL synthesis. STTT **15**(5–6), 541–561 (2013)
12. Hussmann, H., Meixner, G., Zuehlke, D. (eds.): Model-Driven Development of Advanced User Interfaces, Studies in Computational Intelligence, vol. 340. Springer, Heidelberg (2011). https://doi.org/10.1007/978-3-642-14562-9
13. Kress-Gazit, H., Lahijanian, M., Raman, V.: Synthesis for robots: guarantees and feedback for robot behavior. Ann. Rev. Control Robot. Auton. Syst. **1**, 211–236 (2018)
14. Masci, P., Zhang, Y., Jones, P., Curzon, P., Thimbleby, H.: Formal verification of medical device user interfaces using PVS. In: Gnesi, S., Rensink, A. (eds.) FASE 2014. LNCS, vol. 8411, pp. 200–214. Springer, Heidelberg (2014). https://doi.org/10.1007/978-3-642-54804-8_14
15. Meyer, P.J., Sickert, S., Luttenberger, M.: Strix: explicit reactive synthesis strikes back!. In: Chockler, H., Weissenbacher, G. (eds.) CAV 2018. LNCS, vol. 10981, pp. 578–586. Springer, Cham (2018). https://doi.org/10.1007/978-3-319-96145-3_31

16. Pnueli, A., Rosner, R.: On the synthesis of an asynchronous reactive module. In: Ausiello, G., Dezani-Ciancaglini, M., Della Rocca, S.R. (eds.) ICALP 1989. LNCS, vol. 372, pp. 652–671. Springer, Heidelberg (1989). https://doi.org/10.1007/BFb0035790
17. Ryzhyk, L., et al.: User-guided device driver synthesis. In: OSDI, pp. 661–676 (2014)

# Semantic Labelling and Learning for Parity Game Solving in LTL Synthesis

Jan Křetínský, Alexander Manta, and Tobias Meggendorfer(✉)

Technical University of Munich, Munich, Germany
{jan.kretinsky,alexander.manta,tobias.meggendorfer}@in.tum.de

**Abstract.** We propose "semantic labelling" as a novel ingredient for solving games in the context of LTL synthesis. It exploits recent advances in the automata-based approach, yielding more information for each state of the generated parity game than the game graph can capture. We utilize this extra information to improve standard approaches as follows. (i) Compared to strategy improvement (SI) with random initial strategy, a more informed initialization often yields a winning strategy directly without any computation. (ii) This initialization makes SI also yield smaller solutions. (iii) While Q-learning on the game graph turns out not too efficient, Q-learning with the semantic information becomes competitive to SI. Since already the simplest heuristics achieve significant improvements the experimental results demonstrate the utility of semantic labelling. This extra information opens the door to more advanced learning approaches both for initialization and improvement of strategies.

## 1 Introduction

*Reactive synthesis* is a classical problem to find a strategy that given a stream of inputs gradually produces a stream of outputs so that a given specification over the inputs and outputs is satisfied. In LTL synthesis the specification is given as a formula of *linear temporal logic (LTL)*. The classical solution technique is the *automata-theoretic approach* [31] that transforms the specification into an automaton. The partitioning of atomic propositions into inputs and outputs then yields a game over this automaton. Subsequently, the game is solved and the winning strategy in the game induces a winning strategy for the original problem. The standard type of automaton to be used in this context is the *deterministic parity automaton (DPA)* since (i) determinism ensures we obtain a well-defined game and (ii) the parity condition yields a *parity game*, which can be solved reasonably cheaply in practice [8,26,33] with good tool support [9,30].

While solving large games still takes significant resources, the bottleneck of this procedure is already the construction of the game. Indeed, after transforming the LTL formula into a non-deterministic automaton [31] this automaton is

This research was funded in part by the Czech Science Foundation grant No. P202/12/G061, and the German Research Foundation (DFG) projects KR 4890/1-1 "Verified Model Checkers" and KR 4890/2-1 "Statistical Unbounded Verification".


Y.-F. Chen et al. (Eds.): ATVA 2019, LNCS 11781, pp. 404–422, 2019.
https://doi.org/10.1007/978-3-030-31784-3_24

determinized using *Safra's construction* [25] or its improvements [23,27]. This is notoriously known to be practically inefficient [17] despite some tool support [15]. As a result, other approaches for the synthesis problem have been suggested that avoid Safra's determinization, see the related work below. However, recent translators, e.g. [4,16], yield significantly smaller automata to the extent that the traditional parity-game approach, e.g. [20,21], becomes competitive [1,10]. Apart from the smaller sizes of automata, one of their decisive advancements is the ability to generate the automaton on the fly and terminate as soon as a winning strategy is found, possibly way earlier than the whole automaton is constructed.

Yet these approaches suffer from several inefficiencies. In order to tackle them let us observe their roots. Firstly, despite the relative efficiency, solving the parity game can still take significant time. Either the whole game is solved, e.g. using Zielonka's algorithm [33] as in [21], or growing on-the-fly explored parts are repetitively solved, e.g. using strategy improvement as in [20]. In both cases, large parts of the state space are processed and the overall effort is still significant since the strategy improvement is executed many times during the process. Secondly, in the case with on-the-fly exploration, it is not clear in which direction the game should be explored. In the graph game, the available extra information is only the priorities and computing their attractors is a global computation defeating the purpose of on-the-fly exploration.

In this paper, we suggest a framework for a theoretically fundamental improvement of solving parity games that arise from LTL synthesis and we instantiate it with the first simple heuristics. The experimental results confirm the potential of this approach. The main idea is to exploit, to our best knowledge for the first time, the *semantics* of the vertices of the game.

Where does the semantics come from? Since the original specification is translated to an automaton, its states have a strong correspondence to the monitored property. However, Safra's determinization and the subsequent latest appearance record for obtaining a DPA leaves us with permutation over Safra's trees over sets of LTL formulae, whose semantics is extremely hard to decipher. In contrast, the new approach of [5,16] yields a description of each state in terms of a single formula to be satisfied and a list of formulae describing progress of satisfying each sub-goal. This clearer structure allows us to exploit the meaning of available successors and to choose the most promising one in the sense of satisfying the goal of each player. This addresses issue of exploration guidance. The other issue of updating the whole or whole explored part of the state space can be addressed using reinforcement learning [29]. Since the degree how promising a vertex is can be quantified, we can use it as a reward, together with the priorities, in Q-learning. This way we update only the most promising parts of the state space.

*Our contribution* is the following:

- We introduce a semantics-based framework for heuristics for parity games in LTL synthesis and instantiate it as follows.

- We utilize the semantic labelling of vertices to get a better initial strategy for the parity game, often yielding (i) an optimal solution directly and (ii) a smaller one.
- We show how reinforcement learning can be applied to parity games and accelerated by the semantic labelling.
- We demonstrate the potential of this approach experimentally on formulae from the SYNTCOMP competition [10] as well as random formulae, opening a door for learning-based approaches to automata-based LTL synthesis.

**Related Work**
Firstly, one can reduce the synthesis problem to emptiness of nondeterministic Büchi tree automata [18]; it has been implemented with considerable success in [11]. The second approach is to use heuristic to improve Safra's determinization procedure [14,15]. The third approach is to consider fragments of LTL. For instance, the generalized reactivity(1) fragment of LTL (called GR(1)) was introduced in [24] and a cubic time symbolic representation of an equivalent automaton was presented. The approach has been implemented in the ANZU tool [12]. Another approach, prominent in competitions like SYNTCOMP [10], is bounded synthesis [28], as implemented by, e.g., BoSy [7] and PARTY [13]. The tool Acacia+ [2] uses symbolic incremental algorithms based on antichains.

Besides, there are learning approaches that utilize some information on the state space. However, this is typically not the information on the property currently to be satisfied, e.g. [22] uses automata learning, but only for safety properties and not focusing on the property itself. Further, [3] takes the property into account, but only as its respective automaton. It tries to decrease the distance to the accepting vertex, which can be very different from making the property easier to satisfy. Moreover, it is not designed for games, although the alternating distance might address this drawback. More importantly, it is not suited for partial models as we need to construct the whole automaton, which is the bottleneck for complex properties.

## 2 Preliminaries

In this section, we give some basic background knowledge and establish fundamental notation. Due to space constraints, we touch only briefly on several topics and encourage the reader to refer to the mentioned literature.

*Basic Notation.* We use $\mathbb{N}$ to denote the set of non-negative integers. Given a propositional formula $\phi$ over a set of propositions $\mathsf{AP}$, we use $\text{sat}(\phi) = \{v \in 2^{\mathsf{AP}} \mid v \models \phi\}$ to denote the set of all satisfying assignments. The constants `tt` and `ff` denote *true* and *false*, respectively.

### 2.1 Synthesis and Games

The synthesis problem in its general form asks whether a system can be controlled in a way such that it satisfies a given specification under any (possible) environment. Moreover, one often is interested in obtaining a witness to this query, i.e. some *controller* or *strategy* which specifies the system's actions. For example, one might ask whether a robot can be steered over difficult terrain such that it arrives at a particular target location.

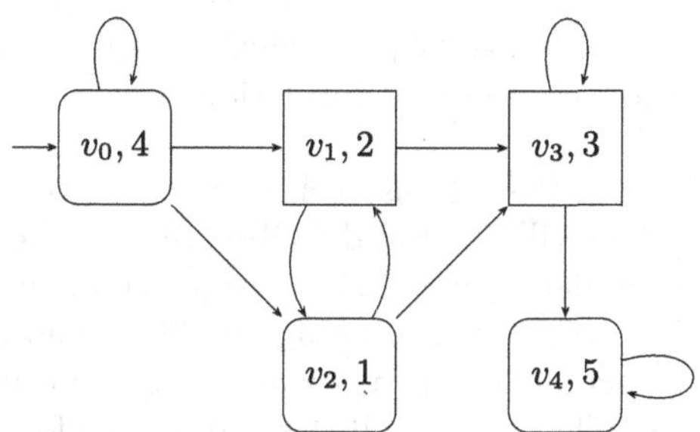


**Fig. 1.** An example (parity) game. Rounded rectangles belong to the system player and normal rectangles to the environment player. The vertices are additionally labelled with their priorities. For readability, we omit the requirement of alternation.

*Graph games* are a standard formalism used in synthesis. A game, denoted by $\mathcal{G} = ((V, E), v_0, P, \textsc{Win})$, consists of a digraph $(V, E)$, a *starting vertex* $v_0 \in V$, a *player mapping* $P$, and a *winning condition* $\textsc{Win}$, described later. Each vertex belongs to one of the two players 0 (called *system*) and 1 (called *environment*), specified by the mapping $P : V \to \{0, 1\}$. In other words, the set of vertices is partitioned into player 0's vertices $V_0$ and player 1's vertices $V_1$; $V = V_0 \mathbin{\dot{\cup}} V_1$. See Fig. 1 for an example of such a game. For ease of notation, we write $vE := \{(v, u) \in E \mid u \in V\}$ to denote all outgoing edges of some vertex $v$ and define $E_i := \{(u, v) \in E \mid u \in V_i\}$ the set of all edges "controlled" by player $i$.

To play the game, a token is placed in the initial vertex $v_0$. Then, the player owning the token's current vertex moves the token along an outgoing edge of the current vertex. This is repeated infinitely, giving rise to an infinite sequence of vertices containing the token $\rho = v_0 v_1 v_2 \cdots \in V^\omega$, called a *play*. The set of all possible plays is denoted by $\mathfrak{P}$.

For simplicity, we assume in the following that all games are *alternating*, i.e. the successors of a vertex belong to a different player than the vertex itself.

*Winning conditions* are a mapping from plays to the winning player $\textsc{Win} : \mathfrak{P} \to \{0, 1\}$. Numerous kinds of winning conditions have been studied. In this work, we consider the following three:

**Safety** is defined by a set of vertices $T$ to be avoided. The system player loses iff one of the vertices in the given set is visited.

**Co-Safety** (or *reachability*) is, as the name suggests, dual to safety. Here, the system player wins iff one of the given vertices is visited at least once. Observe that this exactly corresponds to a safety objective for the environment player.

**Parity** is based on a *priority assignment* for each vertex $\mathfrak{p} : V \to \mathbb{N}$. The system player wins iff the *maximum* of all infinitely often occurring priorities is *odd.*[1] Formally, we define $\inf(\rho) = \{p \mid \forall j. \exists k \geq j. \mathfrak{p}(\rho_k) = p\}$ and system wins a play $\rho$ iff $\max \inf(\rho)$ is odd. We refer to odd priorities as *good* (for the system player) and to even priorities as *bad* (for the system player).

Note that both safety and co-safety are special cases of the parity condition, with a straightforward linear time transformation.

*Strategies* are mappings $\sigma_i : V_i \to E$, assigning to each of the player's vertices an edge along which the token will be moved.[2] Observe that once both players fix a strategy, the game is fully determined and a unique run is induced. This means that given a game with a particular winning condition and a strategy for each player, we can decide which of the players wins the game using these strategies. A strategy of a player is called *winning* if the player wins for *any* strategy of the opponent. Thus, we can rephrase the synthesis question to "Is there a winning strategy for the system player?".

For example, consider again the game depicted in Fig. 1. Fixing the strategies $\sigma_0 = \{v_0 \mapsto (v_0, v_2), v_2 \mapsto (v_2, v_3), v_4 \mapsto (v_4, v_4)\}$ and $\sigma_1 = \{v_1 \mapsto (v_1, v_2), v_3 \mapsto (v_3, v_3)\}$ induces the play $v_0 v_2 v_3 v_3 \cdots$. The set of infinitely often seen priorities equals $\{3\}$, hence the system player wins with these strategies. Moreover, the strategy $\sigma_0$ is winning, since the play always ends up in either $v_3$ or $v_4$.

*Strategy Improvement* (or *strategy iteration*) is the most prominent way of solving parity games, i.e. answering the above question. In recent times, it received significant attention due to both theoretical and practical advances. We explain the approach only very briefly, since its details are not important for this work.

In essence, strategy improvement works as follows. First, arbitrary initial strategies are picked for both players. Then, the algorithm checks whether one of the current strategies is winning. If yes, this strategy is returned. Otherwise, the algorithm tries to improve one of the strategies by changing its choices in some vertices. If an improvement is not possible, there exists no winning strategy for the respective player. Otherwise, the process is repeated with the new strategy.

It is known that this algorithm converges to the correct result in finite time for any initial strategy. This gives us a straightforward way of optimization, namely the choice of the initial strategy. Intuitively, a heuristic which often comes up with a "good" strategy may improve the runtime significantly over arbitrary or random choice, since then only a few improvement steps are necessary.

Throughout this work, we refer to a reference implementation of SI, denoted `SI`, e.g., when running SI with a particular initial strategy. In our implementation, we used the algorithm of [32], but other variants could be substituted.

---

1 Instead of the maximum, one could also decide based on the minimum; similarly instead of "odd", "even" sometimes is considered winning for the system.

2 Strategies may be significantly more complex, e.g., by using memory. Since "positional" strategies are sufficient for all properties we consider, we intentionally omit the general definition in the interest of space.

## 2.2 Linear Temporal Logic

*Linear Temporal Logic* (LTL) is a standard logics used in verification and synthesis to specify the desired behaviour of a system. The logic is given by the syntax

$$\phi ::= \mathtt{ff} \mid a \mid \neg\phi \mid \phi \wedge \phi \mid \mathbf{X}\,\phi \mid \phi\,\mathbf{U}\,\phi,$$

where $a \in \mathsf{AP}$ is an *atomic proposition*, inducing the *alphabet* $\Sigma = 2^{\mathsf{AP}}$. LTL formulae are interpreted over infinite sequences $w \in \Sigma^\omega$ called $\omega$-words. Intuitively, a word $w = w_0 w_1 \cdots \in \Sigma^\omega$ satisfies the *next* $\mathbf{X}\,\phi$ iff $\phi$ is satisfied in the next step. The *until* operator $\phi\,\mathbf{U}\,\psi$ is satisfied iff $\phi$ holds until $\psi$ is satisfied. Apart from the mentioned operators, we also consider *finally* $\mathbf{F}\,\phi := \mathtt{tt}\,\mathbf{U}\,\phi$ and *globally* $\mathbf{G}\,\phi := \neg\,\mathbf{F}\,\neg\phi$, which require that $\phi$ holds at least once or always, respectively.

Given an LTL formula $\phi$, the set of its *sub-formulae* is denoted by $\mathrm{sub}(\phi)$. The *top-level temporal operators* $\mathrm{top}(\phi)$ are all temporal operators not nested inside other temporal operators. For example, the formula $\phi = \mathbf{G}((\mathbf{F}\,a) \wedge b) \wedge \mathbf{F}\,b$ has sub-formulae $\mathrm{sub}(\phi) = \{a, b, \mathbf{F}\,a, (\mathbf{F}\,a) \wedge b, \mathbf{G}((\mathbf{F}\,a) \wedge b), \mathbf{F}\,b, \phi\}$ and top-level operators $\mathrm{top}(\phi) = \{\mathbf{G}((\mathbf{F}\,a) \wedge b), \mathbf{F}\,b\}$.

*LTL Synthesis* is an instance of the general synthesis problem. Here, the specification to be satisfied by the system is given in form of an LTL formula. Due to recent advances [16,20], the *automata-based approach* [31] to LTL synthesis received significant attention. Essentially, the given LTL formula is translated into an $\omega$-automaton, which in turn is transformed into a parity game. By solving the resulting game, we obtain a solution to the original synthesis question.

Technically, the game is obtained by "splitting". To this end, the set of atomic propositions is split into system- and environment-controlled propositions. Then, the players' actions correspond to choosing which of their propositions to enable. Once both players chose their propositions' values, the automaton moves to the next vertex according to the chosen valuation. See, e.g., [20], for more detail.

*Semantic translations* from LTL to automata are the key ingredient to our new approach. These translations not only produce a parity game, but also provide a semantic labelling of the game's vertices. In particular, using the approach introduced in [5] and implemented in [16], we obtain for each vertex a list of LTL formulae, roughly corresponding to (sub-)goals which still have to be (possibly repetitively) fulfilled. Due to space constraints, we describe the ideas of these constructions only briefly in Sect. 3.1. This labelling is not easily derived from the structure of the game graph and provides additional information not accessible to conventional, general-purpose parity game solvers. The primary goal of this paper is to show that this additional information can be exploited for a significant increase in performance.

## 2.3 Q-Learning

Q-Learning is a well known, simple yet versatile *reinforcement learning* technique [29]. It usually is applied in machine learning to find performant strategies for (stochastic) systems. The technique roughly works as follows. Each edge $(u, v)$ has a *Q-value* $Q(u, v)$, indicating the *quality* assigned to the respective edge. This value is initialized according to some heuristic and then repeatedly updated through *learning episodes*. Each episode consists of sampling a path through the system, following the maximal Q-value. In order to encourage exploration, randomization is added to this choice. While sampling, the learning agent receives rewards based on his choices. The Q-value of the respective edge is then updated with the obtained reward and the Q-value of it's successor.[3] To smoothen the learning process, the propagated value is weighted by a *learning rate* $\alpha$. Together, the update essentially is computed by $Q(v, u) \leftarrow (1 - \alpha) \cdot Q(v, u) + \alpha \cdot (\mathcal{R}(v, u) + Q(u))$ where $v$ and $u$ are the current and next vertex, respectively, $\mathcal{R}(v, u)$ is the obtained reward, and $Q(u) = \max_{(u,u') \in E} Q(u, u')$ is the Q-value of the successor vertex $u$.

## 3 Our Contributions

In this section, we explain the central ideas of our contributions. First, we highlight the peculiarities of the mentioned labelling function. Then, we introduce the concept of *trueness*, which we directly use to augment strategy improvement. Finally, we explain our adaptation of Q-learning to parity games and how we derive a semantic reward signal from the labelling, using trueness.

### 3.1 Input Details

We assume that we are given a parity game, where each vertex is labelled by a structured list of LTL formulae. The labelling corresponds to the remaining goals to be achieved by the system player (or violated by the environment player). More precisely, the labelling consists of one *master formula* and potentially several *monitors*. The master formula tracks the "overall progress" and all finitely achievable parts of the formula. In particular, the master formula `tt` corresponds to the formula being satisfied by the prefix, analogously `ff` corresponds to a falsified formula. The system player automatically wins if a vertex labelled with `tt` is reached and, similarly, loses on a `ff` vertex. In the special case of reachability or safety specifications, the labelling actually only consists of the master formula.

For more complex specifications, the labelling also exhibits a more intricate structure. Intuitively, there is one monitor for each sub-formula which needs to be satisfied infinitely often (liveness conditions) or may only be violated finitely often (safety conditions). Each monitor tracks a list of formulae which have to be fulfilled in order to satisfy its overall goal. The monitors are ordered according to an appearance-record style construction. "Failing" monitors emit a bad priority and are moved at the beginning of the list, succeeding monitors instead emit a

[3] The exact details of this update vary between different instantiations of Q-learning. For example, a discount factor may be included.

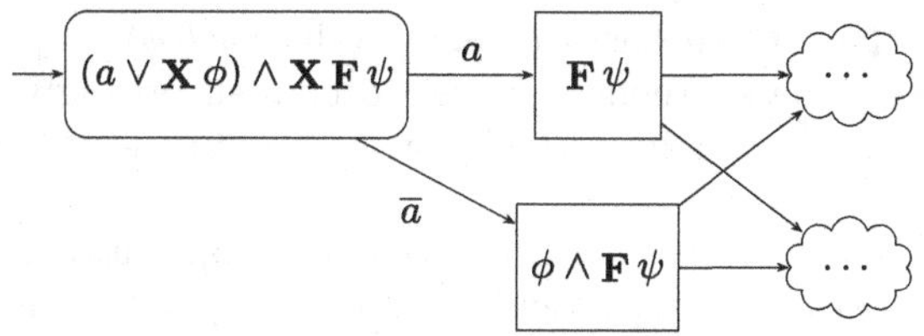


**Fig. 2.** An example showing the application of trueness initialization. For readability, we only show the vertex labels. $\phi$ and $\psi$ are some non-trivial LTL formulae.

good priority. Both priorities are based on the respective monitor's position in the list. Intuitively, for a fixed word $\omega$, all monitors which only fail finitely often eventually are ranked higher than all the monitors which fail infinitely often. Thus, if such a non-failing monitor emits a good priority, it overrules all of the failing monitors' bad priorities.

Consider, for example, the formula $\mathbf{F}\,\mathbf{G}\,a$, meaning "eventually, $a$ appears every step". Here, there is no ultimate `tt` or `ff` vertex, since this formula cannot be satisfied or violated by any finite prefix. The construction gives us $\mathbf{F}\,\mathbf{G}\,a$ as master formula and $\mathbf{G}\,a$ as a monitored goal. Whenever we see a $\neg a$, this monitor would fail, emit a bad priority, and move to the front of the list. Dually, for every $a$, it emits a good priority.

The details of this construction are described in [6]. It is implemented in the tool `Rabinizer` [16] which we use for our constructions. An online demo thereof is located at https://owl.model.in.tum.de/try/. A simplified example can be found in Fig. 3 later on.

### 3.2 (Co-)Safety Games

Recall that for these games, the labelling we obtain is a single LTL formula per vertex. The system player wants to reach the `tt` vertex and avoid the `ff` vertex. Consequently, the system player naturally is interested in taking "trueness-maximizing" edges, analogously the environment player wants to move away from `tt`. This simple observation directly leads us to the concept of *trueness*.

**Trueness** of an LTL formula $t : \text{LTL} \to [0, 1]$ intuitively denotes how "close" a given formula is to being satisfied. We compute this value by treating the formula as purely propositional, i.e. each temporal operator is considered to be a fresh variable. Formally, given an LTL formula $\phi$, we interpret it as a propositional formula over $\Sigma = 2^{\mathsf{AP} \cup \mathsf{top}(\phi)}$. For this formula, we then determine and scale the ratio of satisfying assignments, i.e. $t(\phi) := |\text{sat}(\phi)|/|\Sigma|$. This value can be computed efficiently by representing the formula as *binary decision diagram (BDD)*, as implemented in `Rabinizer`. Even for formulae with several hundred syntax elements the trueness is computed virtually instantaneously.

At first, this notion may seem rather unintuitive, since the temporal aspect of a formula is not necessarily reflected by the trueness value. For example, the formula $\phi = \mathbf{G}\, a \wedge \mathbf{G}\, \neg a$ has a trueness value of $t(\phi) = \frac{1}{4}$, but actually is unsatisfiable. Nevertheless, trueness proves to be a surprisingly good initialization heuristic, which we explain in the following and further demonstrate in our evaluation.

One particular reason for its performance in our application is due to the way the labelling is constructed. In particular, temporal operators are "unfolded" as an essential step of the construction. For example, the formula $\mathbf{G}\, a$ is unfolded to $a \wedge \mathbf{G}\, a$ while $\mathbf{F}\, a$ yields $a \vee \mathbf{F}\, a$ and $a \,\mathbf{U}\, b$ gives $b \vee (a \wedge (a \,\mathbf{U}\, b))$. The unfolded variants are semantically equivalent to the original formula, but provide us with a one-step propositional "approximation" of the temporal operators. The above $\phi$ then is unfolded to $\phi \equiv (a \wedge \mathbf{G}\, a) \wedge (\neg a \wedge \mathbf{G}\, \neg a) \equiv \mathtt{ff}$.

**Initializing Strategies Based on Trueness** can be achieved as follows. Fix some game $\mathcal{G}$ with a (co-)safety objective and labelling function $L : V \to \mathrm{LTL}$. The strategies $\sigma_0$ and $\sigma_1$ are called *trueness-optimal* if they satisfy

$$\sigma_0(v_0) \in \arg\max_{(v_0,u)\in E} t(L(u)) \qquad\qquad \sigma_1(v_1) \in \arg\min_{(v_1,u)\in E} t(L(u))$$

for all vertices $v_0 \in V_0$ and $v_1 \in V_1$, respectively. Observe that, since we assumed the game to be alternating, all $u$ vertices in the above equations belong to the respective opponent.

This immediately yields our first semantic algorithm $\mathtt{SI}_{sem}$, which runs $\mathtt{SI}$ initialized with trueness optimal strategies.

For a small example, consider the simplified part of a game depicted in Fig. 2. Here, the system player can choose whether or not to play $a$ in the initial vertex. The successors' trueness value, namely $t(\mathbf{F}\, \psi) = \frac{1}{2}$ and $t(\phi \wedge \mathbf{F}\, \psi) \leq \frac{1}{4}$ (for a non-trivial $\phi$), suggest the natural choice of $a$, leading to $\mathbf{F}\, \psi$. Intuitively, $\mathbf{F}\, \psi$ is "easier" to satisfy than $\phi \wedge \mathbf{F}\, \psi$. Observe that without the labelling and its trueness value this choice would not be as obvious, since the impact of this decision may only become visible much later in the game. Quite surprisingly, this initialization solves a *majority* of randomly generated games *instantly* without the need for any further improvements step, as shown in the experimental evaluation.

### 3.3 Parity Games

To apply our ideas to parity games, there are several hurdles to overcome. Recall that the labelling we obtain for these games has a non-trivial structure, compared to the singleton labelling in the special cases. Hence, we cannot use the trueness value directly. Rather, we need a more intricate way of deriving meaning from the labelling. Because of its simplicity, we decided to use Q-learning. Recall that Q-learning usually works with a single agent, interested in maximizing the obtained reward. In our case, we instead have two antagonistic agents and we need to adapt the Q-learning framework to this setting. Furthermore, there are some technical peculiarities when we want to incorporate priorities and the labelling.

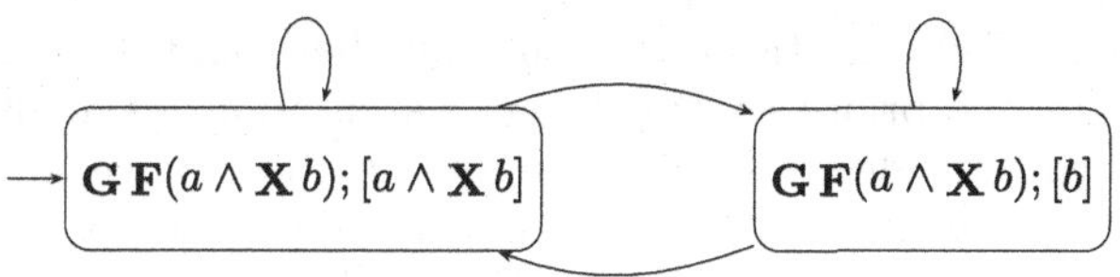


**Fig. 3.** A simplified example for a monitor labelling as produced by `Rabinizer`. The first formula represents the master formula, while the second one corresponds to the only monitor's formula.

*Remark 1.* We again stress that our main goal is to show the usefulness of the so far unexploited semantic labelling. In particular, the exact approach to extracting rewards or even the fact that we use Q-learning is of secondary importance for our research goal. Using more advanced techniques, e.g., extract reward from the formula using neural networks, is left for future work.

**Basic Concepts.** For all variants, our Q-values lie between $-1$, corresponding to a presumably guaranteed loss for the system player, and $+1$, analogously corresponding to a win. As usual in Q-learning, we repeatedly sample paths and update vertex values. But, since the two players are antagonistic, we don't always pick a maximizing action while sampling. Instead, we choose a successor with maximal Q-value in system vertices and a minimal one in environment vertices. Once we encounter a vertex for a second time and consequently would enter a loop, we stop the sampling.

In the following we present three variants of Q-learning. The first, agnostic variant obtains rewards only based on whether an episode is winning or losing. This approach is widely applicable, since basically no domain knowledge is necessary. Not surprisingly, it also is not too efficient. We then present a first adaption, which additionally incorporates priorities. This variant is tailored towards parity games, but does not employ any semantic information provided by the labelling. Our experiments show that it outperforms the first variant, but only by a slim margin. Finally, we present our semantic approach, which on top also considers the labelling, employing the trueness function in several ways. In our experiments, this significantly outperforms the first two ideas and, on some datasets, even beats strategy improvement by a large factor. Note that each variant also incorporates the reward signals of the previous approaches.

**Rewards Based on Winning Paths** are binary, yielding $+1$ for winning and $-1$ for losing. In our case, this means that when we stop sampling after entering a loop, we determine whether the loop is winning or losing and propagate the value accordingly. We initialize the Q-values with 0, since there is no a-priori information available. The resulting Q-learning variant is denoted by $\texttt{QL}_{win}$.

**Priority Rewards** are the first step to a more intricate reward signal. Here, the agent additionally obtains intermediate rewards based on the priority of the edge. Recall that these priorities are natural numbers, and the system player is interested in large, odd priorities. Dually, large even priorities should be avoided.

There are two difficulties associated with this idea. Since we assumed our Q-values to lie between $-1$ and $+1$, we need to rescale the priorities into this domain. Furthermore, we need to rescale them such that larger priorities significantly "overrule" smaller ones, reflecting the nature of the parity objective. For example, obtaining ten 5 priorities in a row is irrelevant if afterwards one 6 is encountered.

We approach this problem by rescaling the priorities as follows. Let $p_i$ be the priorities occurring in the given game, sorted in ascending order. We first compute the absolute frequency of each priority as $f(p_i) = |\{s \mid \mathfrak{p}(s) = p_i\}|$, i.e. the number of vertices in the whole game labelled with priority $p_i$. Then, we define the scaled priorities $\overline{p}_i$ by $\overline{p}_0 = p_0$, $\overline{p}_i = 2 \cdot f(p_{i-1}) \cdot \overline{p}_{i-1} + 1$. Observe that $\overline{p}_i$ is larger than the sum of all $\overline{p}_j$ with $j < i$ occurring in the game. Finally, we re-normalize $\overline{p}_i$ into the $[-1, +1]$ domain by $r_i := (-1)^{p_i+1}\overline{p}_i(1+\sum_j \overline{p}_j \cdot f(p_j))^{-1}$ Even priorities are mapped to the negative domain, as the system player wants to avoid them. As before, we initialize the Q-values with 0.

We denote this Q-learning variant by $\texttt{QL}_{pri}$. Note that this approach is applicable to general parity games. In our case, it indirectly uses the labelling, since the priorities of the game are directly derived from the labelling and correspond to progress in the monitors.

**Semantic Rewards** are our idea for exploiting the information provided by the vertex labelling, denoted by $\texttt{QL}_{sem}$. Firstly, we describe how we assign the initial Q-values. Recall that we cannot apply the trueness value to the whole labelling, since in general it comprises several different LTL formulae corresponding to different goals. Nevertheless, we can still easily exploit the master formula to obtain a sensible value. In particular, we initialize the Q-value of each action based on the trueness of the master formula in the successor vertex. This directly generalizes the approach of the special case of (co-)safety, where the labelling consists only of the master formula.

Now, we introduce our ideas for deriving the reward signal from the labelling. Recall that apart from the master formula we have several monitor formulae, corresponding to goals which we have to fulfil repeatedly. We present a motivating example in Fig. 3. There, we show a (simplified) labelling produced for the formula $\psi = \mathbf{G}\,\mathbf{F}(a \wedge \mathbf{X}\, b)$. In order to satisfy $\psi$, we repeatedly need to play $a$ and then in the next step $b$. The master formula is the same in both vertices, hence we need to analyse the monitors instead. Intuitively, playing $a$ seems to be the more natural choice in the initial vertex, since $b$ is easier to satisfy than $a \wedge \mathbf{X}\, b$. Hence, our main idea is to also apply trueness analysis to the monitor labels.

Consequently, the system player should be interested not only in the ad-hoc reward obtained by following good priorities, but also in "progressing" other monitors. To this end, we also give a reward proportional to the change in trueness for all monitors which are ranked higher than the current priority as follows.

Let $e = (u, v)$ be an edge in some game $\mathcal{G}$ with priority assignment $\mathfrak{p}$ and labelling $L$. By taking this edge, each monitor updates its monitored formulae. In particular, some monitor may fail or succeed due to this transition. Let $m_e$ be the index of the highest-ranked of such failing or succeeding monitors in the labelling of vertex $u$. If there is no such monitor, let $m_e = -1$. Then, all monitors ranked higher than $m_e$ made some progress, but did not fail or succeed. Nevertheless, the system player is interested in succeeding at least one of those monitors and let none of them fail. Hence, we incentivise the system player to take actions which additionally bring monitors closer to succeeding or at least do not worsen their state. As basis for this approximation, we again use the trueness value. Note that we still use the winning and priority based rewards, hence the "progress" of the monitor at $m_e$ is already incorporated.

Each monitor is a list of formulae which all have to be fulfilled repeatedly. Since we want all of these goals to be satisfied, we first take the minimum trueness value for all formulae tracked by a particular monitor. Furthermore, since the progress of all monitors ranked lower than $m_e$ is irrelevant due to the success or fail event of $m_e$, we ignore them. Together, we are left with one value for each monitor ranked higher than $m_e$. To aggregate these values, we pick the maximal one, letting the learner focus on improving a single monitor instead of slowly progressing all of them. The overall "progress" reward thus is given by

$$\mathsf{progress} = \max_{m > m_e} \left( \min_{\phi \in L(v)_m} t(\phi) - \min_{\phi \in L(u)_m} t(\phi) \right),$$

where $L(v)_m$ are the formulae tracked by monitor $m$ in vertex $v$.

Note that this is only one of many possible choices. Since we are only interested in showing the general applicability of our idea, we simply picked the best heuristic out of several hand-crafted definitions of $\mathsf{progress}$.

## 4 Experimental Evaluation

In this section, we evaluate the presented techniques to show their potential. We show how initializing strategy improvement using semantic information leads to significant improvements of the algorithm. We evaluate our Q-learning variants on several data sets, both real-world and randomly generated. We compare it to strategy improvement, showing our semantic variant to be competitive on several models. Further data, left out due to space constraints, can be found in [19].

### 4.1 Setup

The experiments have been carried out on consumer-grade hardware, a laptop with a $2 \times 2$, 9 GHz Intel Core i5 and 8 GB RAM. We investigate several algorithms and models, which we briefly explain in the following.

**Algorithms.** In our evaluation, we investigate the following algorithms:

- SI: A reference SI implementation with random initial strategy.
- $\mathtt{SI}_{sem}$: SI with semantic initialization.
- $\mathtt{QL}_{win}$: Q-learning with only win/loss as reward signal.
- $\mathtt{QL}_{pri}$: Q-learning with priority-based rewards.
- $\mathtt{QL}_{sem}$: Q-learning with semantic rewards.

**Table 1.** Percentage of games solved in the starting vertex by the initial strategy and the size of the final solutions. "Near" refers to the Near(Co-)Safety dataset. To obtain more deterministic results, we used additional semantic information obtained from the monitors for tie-breaking in $\mathtt{SI}_{sem}$, where applicable.

| | Immediately solved games | | | Solution size | | |
|---|---|---|---|---|---|---|
| | (Co-)Safety | Near | Parity | (Co-)Safety | Near | Parity |
| SI | 32% | 11% | 10% | 7% | 13% | 8% |
| $\mathtt{SI}_{sem}$ | 65% | 67% | 56% | 7% | 13% | 9% |

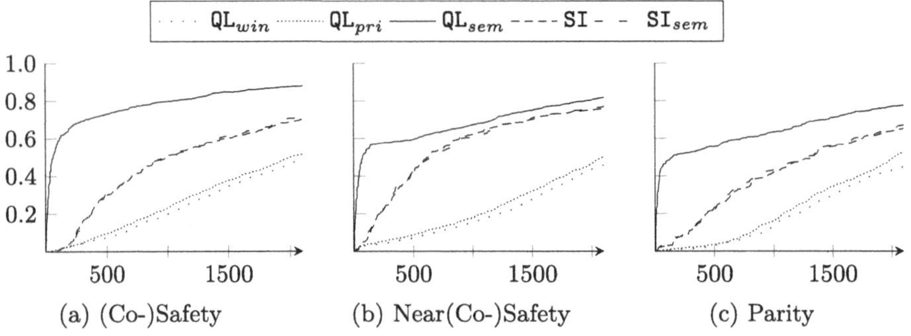


(a) (Co-)Safety (b) Near(Co-)Safety (c) Parity

**Fig. 4.** Detailed analysis of all considered methods on randomly generated games. We show the percentage of games solved within the given number of steps.

While running the Q-learning variants, we repeatedly check whether the current strategy is winning in the starting vertex in order to determine when to stop the learning. We do not use any information gained by this check during the learning process itself.

**Metrics.** First, we count the *number of evaluation steps* until convergence for each algorithm. Since our implementation is only a prototype, we consider time to be less relevant, and use this metric instead to approximate the time needed

**Table 2.** Summary of our evaluation on the real-world data set of SYNTCOMP and several sets of randomly generated formulae. We show the geometric average of the number of evaluation steps on the respective data set. "Unrealizable" are all models in the SYNTCOMP data set which are not realizable. Out of the `QL` variants, we only include the average solution size for $\texttt{QL}_{sem}$, since the solution sizes of all our `QL` methods are essentially equal.

| Class (#models) | Avg. Eval. Steps | | | | | Avg. Solution Size | | |
|---|---|---|---|---|---|---|---|---|
| | $\texttt{QL}_{win}$ | $\texttt{QL}_{pri}$ | $\texttt{QL}_{sem}$ | `SI` | $\texttt{SI}_{sem}$ | $\texttt{QL}_{sem}$ | `SI` | $\texttt{SI}_{sem}$ |
| `amba` (13) | 11540 | 9765 | 1271 | 1119 | 1089 | 78% | 73% | 46% |
| `lily` (23) | 2179 | 2052 | 168 | 639 | 580 | 21% | 21% | 27% |
| `ltl2dpa` (22) | 4909 | 3490 | 3944 | 561 | 552 | 44% | 36% | 18% |
| Unrealizable (53) | 1141 | 1223 | 101 | 951 | 762 | 3% | 4% | 5% |
| Overall (206) | 3142 | 2664 | 1004 | 631 | 531 | 22% | 26% | 14% |
| (Co-)Safety | 2177 | 1993 | 103 | 1094 | 1060 | 7% | 7% | 7% |
| Near(Co-)Safety | 2243 | 1922 | 151 | 682 | 673 | 12% | 13% | 12% |
| Parity | 2869 | 2141 | 174 | 1294 | 1157 | 7% | 8% | 9% |

by an efficient implementation of each variant. For Q-learning, this equates to the number of vertices visited in all learning episodes; for SI we count the number of iterations times the size of the game, to allow for a fair comparison, giving a slight advantage to SI to be on the safe side. See the below remark for further details.

Second, we investigate the *size of the solution*, i.e. the number of vertices reachable under the identified winning strategy. The size of a solution is a good estimate for its quality. For example, a smaller solution means that its implementation requires less memory, since decisions need to be stored for fewer states. We give the solution size as a fraction of the overall size of the respective game.

As both methods involve randomization – Q-learning during sampling, SI in its initialization – we ran our methods five times on each model. We chose a timeout of 60 s for each run to allow for a reasonably fast evaluation. Since timeouts are difficult to properly incorporate into averages, we chose to ignore the few timeouts that occurred, usually less than 5%. See [19] for details.

*Remark 2.* Q-learning and SI evaluate the strategy in vastly different ways. Q-learning picks the currently best action whenever it visits a particular vertex, potentially switching back and forth between two similar actions. In contrast, strategy improvement repeatedly evaluates the current strategy on the whole game, simultaneously changing choices in all vertices which allow for improvement. Intuitively, Q-learning evaluates fewer, important vertices more often, while the evaluations of SI are spread over the whole game. The evaluation of a strategy in SI is costly, since the whole game is considered, while Q-learning simply compares and updates the current Q-values along a single path.

**Models.** We investigate both randomly generated and real-world games.

The random formulae are generated using Spot's [4] `randltl`. We selected three classes of random formulae:

- (Co-)Safety: Pure safety or co-safety formulae
- Near(Co-)Safety: Formulae which mostly consist of either safety or co-safety elements, but contain a few sub-formulae of the other type.
- Parity: Fully random formulae.

We investigate the special case of "Near(Co-)Safety" formulae separately, since a lot of real-world specifications often comprise mostly safety and only a few other conditions. This dataset is supposed to imitate this asymmetry.

In order to generate these formulae, we parametrize `randltl` with priorities on the syntax elements. For the "Parity" dataset, we used the default priorities. For the other two, we used the priorities listed in [19]. Furthermore, to obtain a reasonable test-set, we filter the generated formulae as follows. First, we remove all formulae where the translation to a parity game using `Rabinizer` takes more than 5 GB of memory or more than 30 s, as this would lead to disproportionately large games. Then, we also remove games which have more than 10,000 nodes. We generated 100 such formulae per class.

We also use several real-world formulae from the SYNTCOMP 2017 competition [10]. The specifications are given in the *TLSF* format, which `Rabinizer` can translate to LTL and then to parity games. Again, we filter out games with more than 10,000 nodes, leading to a total of 195 models.

## 4.2 Results

In Table 1, we present our analysis of the trueness initialization on random formulae. In particular, we compare $\mathtt{SI}$ and $\mathtt{SI}_{sem}$ with respect to how many games are solved by the initial strategy and the average solution size after the algorithm has converged. In order to evaluate the initialization in $\mathtt{SI}_{sem}$, we additionally break ties using the monitor labelling, taking the edge with the largest progress among those optimal w.r.t. the trueness of the master formula. Our presented semantic initialization heuristic immediately identifies a winning strategy for more than half of the cases, while a randomly chosen strategy is only winning with roughly 10% probability. In particular, even in the more complex case of parity games, the trueness of the master formula proves to be a very good initialization heuristic. The solution sizes do not differ significantly on these models, since the solutions usually are rather simple for such randomly generated formulas. We highlight that for random initialization, there only is a negligible difference between the "Near(Co-)Safety" and "Parity" dataset, while our semantic approach works significantly better on the former set.

*Remark 3.* The performance of our initialization heuristic suggests interesting applications. For example, one could use this new initialization heuristic to explore and solve extremely large games. Observe that the game can be generated on the fly. Hence, when we initially follow trueness-optimal edges, we may immediately identify a solution while only constructing a small fraction of the game.

Figure 4 shows an evaluation of all our methods on the randomly generated formulae in terms of evaluation steps. The use of priorities consistently improves the performance of QL, but only by a small amount. On the other hand, the use of semantic information vastly improves the performance of QL, outperforming even strategy improvement quite significantly. Moreover, the difference between SI and $\mathtt{SI}_{sem}$ is negligible. This is due to strategy improvement running until *global* convergence, hence the algorithm spends effort in some unsolved regions of the game, even if the current strategy is already deciding optimally in most vertices.

Inspired by these results on random games, we applied our algorithms to real-world problems. The results are summarized in Table 2. In our experiments, we considered a large part of the SYNTCOMP set. We additionally hand-picked some classes of formulae to discuss several observations about the semantic rewards.

The naive $\mathtt{QL}_{win}$ method is severely underperforming compared to other methods, as expected. Moreover, $\mathtt{QL}_{sem}$ often outperforms both other QL variants.

The solution identified by the Q-learning methods often is larger than the one found by $\mathtt{SI}_{sem}$. We conjecture that this is due to Q-learning's bias towards exploration – we did not incentivise the learner to yield small solutions. The solution size practically is constant between the different QL methods, suggesting that these larger solutions are due to Q-learning itself. Nevertheless, the solution size is comparable to the one of SI. Moreover, we highlight that $\mathtt{SI}_{sem}$'s solutions are significantly smaller than the one identified by SI, although the number of steps until convergence is essentially equal. This suggests that our trueness initialization indeed identifies good initial strategies for such real-world games.

Another interesting observation is that our semantic approaches perform significantly better on unrealizable formulae, although these two cases theoretically are dual to each other. We strongly conjecture that this is due to a bias in the data set. Usually, unrealizable formulae are obtained by injecting small, local faults into an otherwise realizable formula. These local faults are easy to find for our trueness/Q-learning approach. This conjecture is strongly supported by the extremely small solutions found by all approaches.

The lily class seems to be of a similar structure, exhibiting fast convergence rates and small solutions. On the ltl2dpa class, our semantic approach performs rather poorly compared to the priority based variant. This class comprises unusually intricate temporal patterns. We conjecture that a more fine-tuned reward signal may improve performance especially on such models.

## 5 Conclusion

We have presented the first step towards exploiting semantic labelling in LTL synthesis via the concept of trueness and the subsequent Q-learning. By interpreting the labelling provided by semantic translations, the Q-learning agent can plan ahead instead of only seeing the next vertex. Our first experimental evaluation already shows the potential of this idea.

*Future work* includes several points of optimization. Firstly, we want to provide a performant implementation of the on-the-fly exploration. Once this is done, an in-depth performance comparison to state-of-the-art tools like `Strix` is desirable. Furthermore, we can employ the semantic information to guide the exploration within these on-the-fly tools, as discussed in Remark 3.

Another interesting point is a more sophisticated definition of trueness. Recall that our concept of trueness does not consider temporal aspects of the formula, yet it underpins all of our labelling-based approaches. A different heuristic could yield significant improvements here. Furthermore, one could use more complex learning methods instead of Q-learning. These methods may among other things be able to re-use experience gained while solving a single game.

Finally, we plan on combining our learning methods with strategy iteration. For example, the Q-learning agent can derive a good, but potentially not optimal strategy, and strategy iteration then solves the game with a few adjustments.

## References


1. The reactive synthesis competition: SYNTCOMP 2018 results (2018). http://www.syntcomp.org/syntcomp-2018-results/
2. Bohy, A., Bruyère, V., Filiot, E., Jin, N., Raskin, J.-F.: Acacia+, a tool for LTL synthesis. In: Madhusudan, P., Seshia, S.A. (eds.) CAV 2012. LNCS, vol. 7358, pp. 652–657. Springer, Heidelberg (2012). https://doi.org/10.1007/978-3-642-31424-7_45
3. Ding, X.C., Lazar, M., Belta, C.: LTL receding horizon control for finite deterministic systems. Automatica **50**(2), 399–408 (2014)
4. Duret-Lutz, A., Lewkowicz, A., Fauchille, A., Michaud, T., Renault, É., Xu, L.: Spot 2.0—a framework for LTL and $\omega$-automata manipulation. In: Artho, C., Legay, A., Peled, D. (eds.) ATVA 2016. LNCS, vol. 9938, pp. 122–129. Springer, Cham (2016). https://doi.org/10.1007/978-3-319-46520-3_8
5. Esparza, J., Křetínský, J.: From LTL to deterministic automata: a safraless compositional approach. In: Biere, A., Bloem, R. (eds.) CAV 2014. LNCS, vol. 8559, pp. 192–208. Springer, Cham (2014). https://doi.org/10.1007/978-3-319-08867-9_13
6. Esparza, J., Křetínský, J., Raskin, J.-F., Sickert, S.: From LTL and limit-deterministic Büchi automata to deterministic parity automata. In: Legay, A., Margaria, T. (eds.) TACAS 2017. LNCS, vol. 10205, pp. 426–442. Springer, Heidelberg (2017). https://doi.org/10.1007/978-3-662-54577-5_25
7. Faymonville, P., Finkbeiner, B., Tentrup, L.: BoSy: an experimentation framework for bounded synthesis. In: Majumdar, R., Kunčak, V. (eds.) CAV 2017. LNCS, vol. 10427, pp. 325–332. Springer, Cham (2017). https://doi.org/10.1007/978-3-319-63390-9_17
8. Fearnley, J.: Efficient parallel strategy improvement for parity games. In: Majumdar, R., Kunčak, V. (eds.) CAV 2017. LNCS, vol. 10427, pp. 137–154. Springer, Cham (2017). https://doi.org/10.1007/978-3-319-63390-9_8

9. Friedmann, O., Lange, M.: Solving parity games in practice. In: Liu, Z., Ravn, A.P. (eds.) ATVA 2009. LNCS, vol. 5799, pp. 182–196. Springer, Heidelberg (2009). https://doi.org/10.1007/978-3-642-04761-9_15
10. Jacobs, S., et al.: The 4th reactive synthesis competition (SYNTCOMP 2017): Benchmarks, participants and results. In: SYNT@CAV (2017)
11. Jobstmann, B., Bloem, R.: Optimizations for LTL synthesis. In: FMCAD (2006)
12. Jobstmann, B., Galler, S., Weiglhofer, M., Bloem, R.: Anzu: a tool for property synthesis. In: Damm, W., Hermanns, H. (eds.) CAV 2007. LNCS, vol. 4590, pp. 258–262. Springer, Heidelberg (2007). https://doi.org/10.1007/978-3-540-73368-3_29
13. Khalimov, A., Jacobs, S., Bloem, R.: PARTY parameterized synthesis of token rings. In: Sharygina, N., Veith, H. (eds.) CAV 2013. LNCS, vol. 8044, pp. 928–933. Springer, Heidelberg (2013). https://doi.org/10.1007/978-3-642-39799-8_66
14. Klein, J., Baier, C.: Experiments with deterministic $\omega$-automata for formulas of linear temporal logic. Theor. Comput. Sci. **363**(2), 180–195 (2006)
15. Klein, J., Christel, B.: On-the-fly stuttering in the construction of deterministic $\omega$-Automata. In: Holub, J., Žd'árek, J. (eds.) CIAA 2007. LNCS, vol. 4783, pp. 51–61. Springer, Heidelberg (2007). https://doi.org/10.1007/978-3-540-76336-9_7
16. Křetínský, J., Meggendorfer, T., Sickert, S., Ziegler, C.: Rabinizer 4: from LTL to your favourite deterministic automaton. In: Chockler, H., Weissenbacher, G. (eds.) CAV 2018. LNCS, vol. 10981, pp. 567–577. Springer, Cham (2018). https://doi.org/10.1007/978-3-319-96145-3_30
17. Kupferman, O.: Recent challenges and ideas in temporal synthesis. In: Bieliková, M., Friedrich, G., Gottlob, G., Katzenbeisser, S., Turán, G. (eds.) SOFSEM 2012. LNCS, vol. 7147, pp. 88–98. Springer, Heidelberg (2012). https://doi.org/10.1007/978-3-642-27660-6_8
18. Kupferman, O., Vardi, M.Y.: Safraless decision procedures. In: FOCS (2005)
19. Křetínský, J., Manta, A., Meggendorfer, T.: Semantic Labelling and Learning for Parity Game Solving in LTL Synthesis. arXiv e-prints, July 2019
20. Meyer, P.J., Sickert, S., Luttenberger, M.: Strix: explicit reactive synthesis strikes back! In: Chockler, H., Weissenbacher, G. (eds.) CAV 2018. LNCS, vol. 10981, pp. 578–586. Springer, Cham (2018). https://doi.org/10.1007/978-3-319-96145-3_31
21. Michaud, T., Colange, M.: Reactive synthesis from LTL specification with Spot. In: Proceedings of the 7th Workshop on Synthesis, SYNT@CAV 2018 (2018)
22. Neider, D., Topcu, U.: An automaton learning approach to solving safety games over infinite graphs. In: Chechik, M., Raskin, J.-F. (eds.) TACAS 2016. LNCS, vol. 9636, pp. 204–221. Springer, Heidelberg (2016). https://doi.org/10.1007/978-3-662-49674-9_12
23. Piterman, N.: From nondeterministic Büchi and Streett automata to deterministic parity automata. In: LICS (2006)
24. Piterman, N., Pnueli, A., Sa'ar, Y.: Synthesis of reactive(1) designs. In: VMCAI (2006)
25. Safra, S.: On the complexity of $\omega$-automata. In: FOCS (1988)
26. Schewe, S.: Solving parity games in big steps. In: Arvind, V., Prasad, S. (eds.) FSTTCS 2007. LNCS, vol. 4855, pp. 449–460. Springer, Heidelberg (2007). https://doi.org/10.1007/978-3-540-77050-3_37
27. Schewe, S.: Tighter bounds for the determinisation of Büchi automata. In: de Alfaro, L. (ed.) FoSSaCS 2009. LNCS, vol. 5504, pp. 167–181. Springer, Heidelberg (2009). https://doi.org/10.1007/978-3-642-00596-1_13

28. Schewe, S., Finkbeiner, B.: Bounded synthesis. In: Namjoshi, K.S., Yoneda, T., Higashino, T., Okamura, Y. (eds.) ATVA 2007. LNCS, vol. 4762, pp. 474–488. Springer, Heidelberg (2007). https://doi.org/10.1007/978-3-540-75596-8_33
29. Sutton, R.S., Barto, A.G.: Reinforcement Learning: An Introduction (2018)
30. Dijk, T.: Oink: an implementation and evaluation of modern parity game solvers. In: Beyer, D., Huisman, M. (eds.) TACAS 2018. LNCS, vol. 10805, pp. 291–308. Springer, Cham (2018). https://doi.org/10.1007/978-3-319-89960-2_16
31. Vardi, M.Y., Wolper, P.: An automata-theoretic approach to automatic program verification (preliminary report). In: LICS (1986)
32. Vöge, J., Jurdziński, M.: A discrete strategy improvement algorithm for solving parity games. In: Emerson, E.A., Sistla, A.P. (eds.) CAV 2000. LNCS, vol. 1855, pp. 202–215. Springer, Heidelberg (2000). https://doi.org/10.1007/10722167_18
33. Zielonka, W.: Infinite games on finitely coloured graphs with applications to automata on infinite trees. Theor. Comput. Sci. **200**(1–2), 135–183 (1998)

# Program Repair for Hyperproperties

Borzoo Bonakdarpour[1(✉)] and Bernd Finkbeiner[2]

[1] Iowa State University, Ames, USA
borzoo@iastate.edu
[2] Saarland University, Saarbrücken, Germany
finkbeiner@cs.uni-saarland.de

**Abstract.** We study the repair problem for hyperproperties specified in the temporal logic HyperLTL. Hyperproperties are system properties that relate multiple computation traces. This class of properties includes information flow policies like noninterference and observational determinism. The repair problem is to find, for a given Kripke structure, a substructure that satisfies a given specification. We show that the repair problem is decidable for HyperLTL specifications and finite-state Kripke structures. We provide a detailed complexity analysis for different fragments of HyperLTL and different system types: tree-shaped, acyclic, and general Kripke structures.

## 1 Introduction

*Information-flow security* is concerned with the detection of unwanted flows of information from a set of variables deemed as secrets to another set of variables that are publicly observable. Information-flow security is foundational for some of the pillars of cybersecurity such as confidentiality, secrecy, and privacy. Information-flow properties belong to the class of hyperproperties [12], which generalize trace properties to sets of sets of traces. Trace properties are usually insufficient, because information-flow properties relate multiple executions. This also means that classic trace-based specification languages such as linear-time temporal logic (LTL) cannot be used directly to specify information-flow properties. HyperLTL [11] is an extension of LTL with trace variables and quantifiers. HyperLTL can express information-flow properties by simultaneously referring to multiple traces. For example, *noninterference* [28] between a secret input $h$ and a public output $o$ can be specified in HyperLTL by stating that, for all pairs of traces $\pi$ and $\pi'$, if the input is the same for all input variables $I$ except $h$, then the output $o$ must be the same at all times:

$$\forall\pi.\forall\pi'.\ \square\big(\bigwedge_{i\in I\setminus\{h\}} i_\pi = i_{\pi'}\big) \ \Rightarrow\ \square(o_\pi = o_{\pi'})$$

Another prominent example is *generalized noninterference* (GNI) [36], which can be expressed as the following HyperLTL formula:

$$\forall\pi.\forall\pi'.\exists\pi''.\ \square(h_\pi = h_{\pi''})\ \wedge\ \square(o_{\pi'} = o_{\pi''})$$


Y.-F. Chen et al. (Eds.): ATVA 2019, LNCS 11781, pp. 423–441, 2019.
https://doi.org/10.1007/978-3-030-31784-3_25

The existential quantifier is needed to allow for nondeterminism. Generalized noninterference permits nondeterminism in the low-observable behavior, but stipulates that low-security outputs may not be altered by the injection of high-security inputs.

There has been a lot of recent progress in automatically *verifying* [14,23–25] and *monitoring* [2,8,9,21,22,29,39] HyperLTL specifications. The automatic *construction* of systems that satisfy a given set of information-flow properties is still, however, in its infancy. So far, the only known approach is bounded synthesis [14,19], which searches for an implementation up to a given bound on the number of states. While there has been some success in applying bounded synthesis to systems like the dining cryptographers [10], this approach does not yet scale to larger systems. The general synthesis problem (without the bound on the number of states) becomes undecidable as soon as the HyperLTL formula contains two universal quantifiers [19]. A less complex type of synthesis is *program repair*, where, given a model $\mathcal{K}$ and a property $\varphi$, the goal is to construct a model $\mathcal{K}'$, such that (1) any execution of $\mathcal{K}'$ is also an execution of $\mathcal{K}$, and (2) $\mathcal{K}'$ satisfies $\varphi$. A useful application of program repair is *program sketching*, where the developer provides a program with "holes" that are filled in by the synthesis algorithm [38]. Filling a hole in a program sketch is a repair step that eliminates nondeterminism. While such a repair is guaranteed to preserve trace properties, it is well known that this is not the case in the context of information-flow security policies [30]. In fact, this problem has not yet been studied in the context of hyperproperties.

In this paper, we study the problem of automated program repair of finite-state systems with respect to HyperLTL specifications. We provide a detailed analysis of the complexity of the repair problem for different shapes of the structure: we are interested in *general*, *acyclic*, and *tree-shaped* Kripke structures. The need for investigating the repair problem for tree-shaped and acyclic graphs stems from two reasons. First, many trace logs that can be used as a basis for example-based synthesis [4] and repair are in the form of a simple linear collection of the traces seen so far. Or, for space efficiency, the traces are organized by common prefixes and assembled into a tree-shaped Kripke structure, or by common prefixes as well as suffixes assembled into an acyclic Kripke structure. The second reason is that tree-shaped and acyclic Kripke structures often occur as the natural representation of the state space of a protocol. For example, certain security protocols, such as authentication and session-based protocols (e.g., TLS, SSL, SIP) go through a finite sequence of *phases*, resulting in an acyclic Kripke structure.

Table 1 summarizes the contributions of this paper. It shows our results on the complexity of automated program repair with respect to different fragments of HyperLTL. The complexities are in the size of the Kripke structure. This *system complexity* is the most relevant complexity in practice, because the system tends to be much larger than the specification. Our results show that the shape of the Kripke structure plays a crucial role in the complexity of the repair problem:

**Table 1.** Complexity of the HyperLTL repair problem in the size of the Kripke structure, where $k$ is the number of quantifier alternations in the formula.

<table>
<tr><th>HyperLTL fragment</th><th>Tree</th><th colspan="2">Acyclic</th><th colspan="2">General</th></tr>
<tr><td>$E^*$</td><td rowspan="4">L-complete (Theorem 1)</td><td rowspan="3" colspan="2">NL-complete (Theorems 5 and 6)</td><td colspan="2">NL-complete (Theorem 8)</td></tr>
<tr><td>$A^*$</td><td colspan="2">NP-complete (Theorem 9)</td></tr>
<tr><td>$EA^*$</td><td rowspan="2">PSPACE</td><td rowspan="5">(Theorem 10)</td></tr>
<tr><td>$E^*A^*$</td><td>$\Sigma_2^p$</td><td rowspan="5">(Theorem 7)</td></tr>
<tr><td>$AE^*$</td><td>P-complete (Theorem 2)</td><td rowspan="2">$\Sigma_2^p$-complete</td><td rowspan="2">PSPACE-complete</td></tr>
<tr><td>$A^*E^*$</td><td rowspan="4">NP-complete (Corollary 1)</td></tr>
<tr><td>$(E^*A^*)^k$</td><td>$\Sigma_k^p$-complete</td><td rowspan="2">$(k-1)$-EXPSPACE-complete</td></tr>
<tr><td>$(A^*E^*)^k$</td><td>$\Sigma_{k+1}^p$-complete</td></tr>
<tr><td>$(A^*E^*)^*$</td><td colspan="2">PSPACE (Corollary 2)</td><td colspan="2">NONELEMENTARY (Corollary 3)</td></tr>
</table>

- **Trees.** For trees, the complexity in the size of the Kripke structure does not go beyond NP. The problem for the alternation-free fragment and the fragment with one quantifier alternation where the leading quantifier is existential is L-complete. The problem for the fragment with one quantifier alternation where the leading quantifier is universal is P-complete. The problem is NP-complete for full HyperLTL.
- **Acyclic graphs.** For acyclic Kripke structures, the complexity is NL-complete for the alternation-free fragment and the fragment with one quantifier alternation where the leading quantifier is existential. The complexity is in the level of the polynomial hierarchy that corresponds to the number of quantifier alternations.
- **General graphs.** For general Kripke structures, the complexity is NL-complete for the existential fragment and NP-complete for the universal fragment. The complexity is PSPACE-complete for the fragment with one quantifier alternation and $(k-1)$-EXPSPACE-complete in the number $k$ of quantifier alternations.

We believe that the results of this paper provide the fundamental understanding of the repair problem for secure information flow and pave the way for further research on developing efficient and scalable techniques.

*Organization* The remainder of this paper is organized as follows. In Sect. 2, we review Kripke structures and HyperLTL. We present a detailed motivating example in Sect. 3. The formal statement of our repair problem is in Sect. 4. Section 5 presents our results on the complexity of repair for HyperLTL in the size of tree-shaped Kripke structures. Sections 6 and 7 present the results on the complexity of repair in acyclic and general graphs, respectively. We discuss related work in Sect. 8. We conclude with a discussion of future work in Sect. 9. Detailed proofs are available in the full version of this paper.

## 2 Preliminaries

### 2.1 Kripke Structures

Let $\mathsf{AP}$ be a finite set of *atomic propositions* and $\Sigma = 2^{\mathsf{AP}}$ be the *alphabet*. A *letter* is an element of $\Sigma$. A *trace* $t \in \Sigma^\omega$ over alphabet $\Sigma$ is an infinite sequence of letters: $t = t(0)t(1)t(2)\dots$

**Definition 1.** *A* Kripke structure *is a tuple* $\mathcal{K} = \langle S, s_{init}, \delta, L\rangle$, *where*

- $S$ *is a finite set of* states*;*
- $s_{init} \in S$ *is the* initial state*;*
- $\delta \subseteq S \times S$ *is a* transition relation, *and*
- $L : S \to \Sigma$ *is a* labeling function *on the states of* $\mathcal{K}$.

*We require that for each* $s \in S$, *there exists* $s' \in S$, *such that* $(s, s') \in \delta$.

Figure 1 shows an example Kripke structure where $L(s_{init}) = \{a\}, L(s_3) = \{b\}$, etc. The *size* of the Kripke structure is the number of its states. The directed graph $\mathcal{F} = \langle S, \delta\rangle$ is called the *Kripke frame* of the Kripke structure $\mathcal{K}$. A *loop* in $\mathcal{F}$ is a finite sequence $s_0 s_1 \cdots s_n$, such that $(s_i, s_{i+1}) \in \delta$, for all $0 \le i < n$, and $(s_n, s_0) \in \delta$. We call a Kripke frame *acyclic*, if the only loops are self-loops on otherwise terminal states, i.e., on states that have no other outgoing transition. See Fig. 1 for an example. Since Definition 1 does not allow terminal states, we only consider acyclic Kripke structures with such added self-loops.

We call a Kripke frame *tree-shaped*, or, in short, a *tree*, if every state $s$ has a unique state $s'$ with $(s', s) \in \delta$, except for the root node, which has no predecessor, and the leaf nodes, which, again because of Definition 1, additionally have a self-loop but no other outgoing transitions.

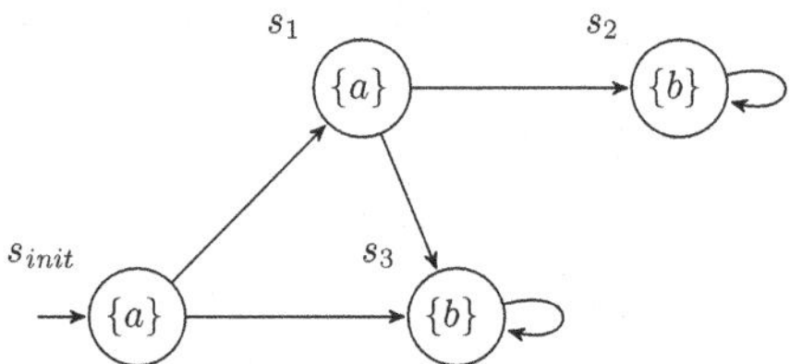

**Fig. 1.** An acyclic Kripke structure.

A *path* of a Kripke structure is an infinite sequence of states $s(0)s(1)\cdots \in S^\omega$, such that:

- $s(0) = s_{init}$, and
- $(s(i), s(i+1)) \in \delta$, for all $i \ge 0$.

A trace of a Kripke structure is a trace $t(0)t(1)t(2)\cdots \in \Sigma^\omega$, such that there exists a path $s(0)s(1)\cdots \in S^\omega$ with $t(i) = L(s(i))$ for all $i \ge 0$. We denote by $\mathsf{Traces}(\mathcal{K}, s)$ the set of all traces of $\mathcal{K}$ with paths that start in state $s \in S$.

In some cases, the system at hand is given as a tree-shaped or acyclic Kripke structure. Examples include session-based security protocols and space-efficient execution logs, because trees allow us to organize the traces according to common prefixes and acyclic graphs according to both common prefixes and common suffixes.

### 2.2 The Temporal Logic HyperLTL

HyperLTL [11] is an extension of linear-time temporal logic (LTL) for hyperproperties. The syntax of HyperLTL formulas is defined inductively by the following grammar:

$$\varphi ::= \exists\pi.\varphi \mid \forall\pi.\varphi \mid \phi$$
$$\phi ::= \mathsf{true} \mid a_\pi \mid \neg\phi \mid \phi \vee \phi \mid \phi\ \mathcal{U}\ \phi \mid \bigcirc\phi$$

where $a \in \mathsf{AP}$ is an atomic proposition and $\pi$ is a trace variable from an infinite supply of variables $\mathcal{V}$. The Boolean connectives $\neg$ and $\vee$ have the usual meaning, $\mathcal{U}$ is the temporal *until* operator and $\bigcirc$ is the temporal *next* operator. We also consider the usual derived Boolean connectives, such as $\wedge$, $\Rightarrow$, and $\Leftrightarrow$, and the derived temporal operators *eventually* $\Diamond\varphi \equiv \mathsf{true}\,\mathcal{U}\,\varphi$ and *globally* $\Box\varphi \equiv \neg\Diamond\neg\varphi$. The quantified formulas $\exists\pi$ and $\forall\pi$ are read as 'along some trace $\pi$' and 'along all traces $\pi$', respectively.

The semantics of HyperLTL is defined with respect to a trace assignment, a partial mapping $\Pi\colon \mathcal{V} \to \Sigma^\omega$. The assignment with empty domain is denoted by $\Pi_\emptyset$. Given a trace assignment $\Pi$, a trace variable $\pi$, and a concrete trace $t \in \Sigma^\omega$, we denote by $\Pi[\pi \to t]$ the assignment that coincides with $\Pi$ everywhere but at $\pi$, which is mapped to trace $t$. Furthermore, $\Pi[j,\infty]$ denotes the assignment mapping each trace $\pi$ in $\Pi$'s domain to $\Pi(\pi)(j)\Pi(\pi)(j+1)\Pi(\pi)(j+2)\cdots$. The satisfaction of a HyperLTL formula $\varphi$ over a trace assignment $\Pi$ and a set of traces $T \subseteq \Sigma^\omega$, denoted by $T, \Pi \models \varphi$, is defined as follows:

$$
\begin{array}{lll}
T,\Pi \models a_\pi & \text{iff} & a \in \Pi(\pi)(0),\\
T,\Pi \models \neg\psi & \text{iff} & T,\Pi \not\models \psi,\\
T,\Pi \models \psi_1 \vee \psi_2 & \text{iff} & T,\Pi \models \psi_1 \text{ or } T,\Pi \models \psi_2,\\
T,\Pi \models \bigcirc\psi & \text{iff} & T,\Pi[1,\infty] \models \psi,\\
T,\Pi \models \psi_1\,\mathcal{U}\,\psi_2 & \text{iff} & \exists i \geq 0 : T,\Pi[i,\infty] \models \psi_2 \ \wedge\ \forall j \in [0,i) : T,\Pi[j,\infty] \models \psi_1,\\
T,\Pi \models \exists\pi.\ \psi & \text{iff} & \exists t \in T : T,\Pi[\pi \to t] \models \psi,\\
T,\Pi \models \forall\pi.\ \psi & \text{iff} & \forall t \in T : T,\Pi[\pi \to t] \models \psi.
\end{array}
$$

We say that a set $T$ of traces satisfies a sentence $\varphi$, denoted by $T \models \phi$, if $T, \Pi_\emptyset \models \varphi$. If the set $T$ is generated by a Kripke structure $\mathcal{K}$, we write $\mathcal{K} \models \varphi$.

## 3 Motivating Example

A real-life example that demonstrates the importance of the problem under investigation in this paper is the information leak in the EDAS Conference Management System[1], first reported in [2]. The system manages the review process

[1] http://www.edas.info.

```
void Output(){
  bool ntf = GetNotificationStatus();
  bool dec = GetDecision();
  bool ses = getSession();

  string status =
    if (ntf)
    then if (dec)
         then "Accept"
         else "Reject"
    else "Pending";

  string session =
    if (?)
    then "Yes"
    else "No"

  Print(status, session);
}
```

**Fig. 2.** Program sketch for a conference management system.

for papers submitted to conferences. Throughout this process, authors can check on the status of their papers, but should not learn whether or not the paper has been accepted until official notifications are sent out. The system is correctly programmed to show status "Pending" before notification time and "Accept" or "Reject" afterwards. The leak (which has since then been fixed) occurred through another status display, which indicates whether or not the paper has been scheduled for presentation in a session of the conference. Since only accepted papers get scheduled to sessions, this allowed the authors to infer the status of their paper.

The problem is shown in Table 2. The first two rows show the output in the web interface for the authors regarding two papers submitted to a conference after their notification, where the first paper is accepted while the second is rejected. The last two rows show two other papers where the status is pending. The internal decisions on notification (`ntf`), acceptance (`dec`), and session (`ses`), shown in the table with a gray background, are not part of the observable output and are added for the reader's convenience. However, by comparing the rows for the two pending papers, the authors can observe that the Session column values are not the same. Thus, they can still deduce that the first paper is rejected and the second paper is accepted.

**Table 2.** Output with leak.

| | Internal Decisions | | | **Output** | |
|---|---|---|---|---|---|
| **Paper** | `ntf` | `dec` | `ses` | **Status** | **Session** |
| *foo1* | true | true | true | Accept | Yes |
| *bar1* | true | false | false | Reject | No |
| *foo2* | false | false | false | Pending | No |
| *bar2* | false | true | true | Pending | Yes |

**Table 3.** Output without leak.

| | Internal Decisions | | | **Output** | |
|---|---|---|---|---|---|
| **Paper** | `ntf` | `dec` | `ses` | **Status** | **Session** |
| *foo1* | true | true | true | Accept | Yes |
| *bar1* | true | false | false | Reject | No |
| *foo2* | false | false | false | Pending | No |
| *bar2* | false | true | true | Pending | No |

The information leak in the EDAS system has previously been addressed by adding a monitor that detects such leaks [2,6]. Here, we instead eliminate the leak constructively. We use *program sketching* [38] to automatically generate the code of our conference manager system. A program *sketch* expresses the high-level structure of an implementation, but leaves "holes" in place of the low-level details. In our approach, the holes in a sketch are interpreted as nondeterministic choices. The repair eliminates nondeterministic choices in such a way that the specification becomes satisfied.

Figure 2 shows a simple sketch for the EDAS example. The hole in the sketch (line 14) is indicated by the question mark in the `if` statement. The replacement for the hole determines how the the value of the `session` output in the the web interface for the authors is computed. We wish to repair the sketch so that whenever two computations both result in `status` = `"Pending"`, the value of `session` is also the same. This requirement is expressed by the following HyperLTL formula:

$$\varphi = \forall \pi . \forall \pi' . \Box \Big( \big( (\texttt{status} = \texttt{"Pending"})_{\pi} \wedge (\texttt{status} = \texttt{"Pending"})_{\pi'} \big) \Rightarrow (\texttt{session}_{\pi} \Leftrightarrow \texttt{session}_{\pi'}) \Big)$$

In this example, an *incorrect* repair would be to replace the hole in line 14 with `ses`, which would result in the output of Table 2. A *correct* repair would be to replace the hole with the Boolean condition `ntf` $\wedge$ `ses`, which would result in the output of Table 3.

In the rest of the paper, we formally define the repair problem and study its complexity for different fragments of HyperLTL.

## 4 Problem Statement

The *repair problem* is the following decision problem. Let $\mathcal{K} = \langle S, s_{init}, \delta, L \rangle$ be a Kripke structure and $\varphi$ be a closed HyperLTL formula. Does there exist a Kripke structure $\mathcal{K}' = \langle S', s'_{init}, \delta', L' \rangle$ such that:

- $S' = S$,
- $s'_{init} = s_{init}$,
- $\delta' \subseteq \delta$,
- $L' = L$, and
- $\mathcal{K}' \models \varphi$?

In other words, the goal of the repair problem is to identify a Kripke structure $\mathcal{K}'$, whose set of traces is a subset of the traces of $\mathcal{K}$ that satisfies $\varphi$. Note that since the witness to the decision problem is a Kripke structure, following Definition 1, it is implicitly implied that in $\mathcal{K}'$, for every state $s \in S'$, there exists a state $s'$ such that $(s, s') \in \delta'$. In other words, the repair does not create a *deadlock* state.

We use the following notation to distinguish the different variations of the problem:

$$\textsf{PR[Fragment, Frame Type]},$$

where

- PR is the *program repair* decision problem as described above;
- Fragment is one of the following for $\varphi$:
  - We use regular expressions to denote the order and pattern of repetition of quantifiers. For example, $\mathsf{E}^*\mathsf{A}^*$-HyperLTL denotes the fragment, where an arbitrary (possibly zero) number of existential quantifiers is followed by an arbitrary (possibly zero) number of universal quantifiers. Also, $\mathsf{AE}^+$-HyperLTL means a lead universal quantifier followed by one or more existential quantifiers. $\mathsf{E}^{\leq 1}\mathsf{A}^*$-HyperLTL denotes the fragment, where zero or one existential quantifier is followed by an arbitrary number of universal quantifiers.
  - $(\mathsf{EA})k$-HyperLTL, for $k \geq 0$, denotes the fragment with $k$ alternations and a lead existential quantifier, where $k = 0$ means an alternation-free formula with only existential quantifiers;
  - $(\mathsf{AE})k$-HyperLTL, for $k \geq 0$, denotes the fragment with $k$ alternations and a lead universal quantifier, where $k = 0$ means an alternation-free formula with only universal quantifiers,
  - HyperLTL is the full logic HyperLTL, and
- Frame Type is either tree, acyclic, or general.

## 5 Complexity of Repair for Tree-Shaped Graphs

In this section, we analyze the complexity of the program repair problem for trees. This section is organized based on the rows in Table 1. We consider the following three HyperLTL fragments: (1) $\mathsf{E}^*\mathsf{A}^*$, (2) $\mathsf{AE}^*$, and (3) the full logic.

### 5.1 The $\mathsf{E}^*\mathsf{A}^*$ Fragment

Our first result is that the repair problem for tree-shaped Kripke structures can be solved in logarithmic time in the size of the Kripke structure for the fragment with only one quantifier alternation where the leading quantifier is existential. This fragment is the least expensive to deal with in tree-shaped Kripke structures and, interestingly, the complexity is the same as for the model checking problem [6].

**Theorem 1.** PR[$\mathsf{E}^*\mathsf{A}^*$-HyperLTL, tree] *is L-complete in the size of the Kripke structure.*

*Proof.* We note that the number of traces in a tree is bounded by the number of states, i.e., the size of the Kripke structure. The repair algorithm enumerates all possible assignments for the existential trace quantifiers, using, for each existential trace variable, a counter up to the number of traces, which requires only a logarithmic number of bits in size of the Kripke structure. For each such assignment to the existential quantifiers, the algorithm steps through the assignments to the universal quantifiers, which again requires only a logarithmic number of bits in size of the Kripke structure. We consider only assignments with traces that have also been assigned to a existential quantifier. For each assignment of the trace variables, we verify the formula, which can be done in logarithmic space [6]. If the verification is affirmative for all assignments to the universal variables, then the repair consisting of the the traces assigned to the existential variables satisfies the formula.

In order to show completeness, we prove that the repair problem for the existential fragment is L-hard. The L-hardness for PR[E*-HyperLTL, tree] and PR[A*-HyperLTL, tree] follows from the L-hardness of ORD [16]. ORD is the graph-reachability problem for directed line graphs. Graph reachability from $s$ to $t$ can be checked with with the repair problems for $\exists\pi.\ \Diamond(s_\pi \wedge \Diamond t_\pi)$ or $\forall\pi.\ \Diamond(s_\pi \wedge \Diamond t_\pi)$. □

### 5.2 The AE* Fragment

We now consider formulas with one quantifier alternation where the leading quantifier is universal. The type of leading quantifier has a significant impact on the complexity of the repair problem: the complexity jumps from L-completeness to P-completeness, although the model checking complexity for this fragment remains L-complete [6].

**Theorem 2.** PR[AE*-HyperLTL, tree] *is P-complete in the size of the Kripke structure.*

*Proof Sketch.* Membership to P can be shown by the following algorithm. For $\varphi = \forall\pi_1.\exists\pi_2.\ \psi$, we begin by marking all the leaves. Then, in several rounds, we go through all marked leaves $v_1$ and instantiate $\pi_1$ with the trace leading to $v_1$. We then again go through all marked leaves $v_2$ and instantiate $\pi_2$ with the trace leading to $v_2$, and check $\psi$ on the pair of traces. If the check is successful for some instantiation of $\pi_2$, we leave $v_1$ marked, otherwise we remove the mark. When no more marks can be removed, we eliminate all branches of the tree that are not marked. For additional existential quantifiers, the number of rounds will increase linearly.

For the lower bound, we reduce the *Horn satisfiability* problem, which is P-hard, to the repair problem for AE* formulas. We first transform the given Horn formula to one that every clause consists of two negative and one positive literals. We map this Horn formula to a tree-shaped Kripke structure and a constant-size HyperLTL formula. For example, formula $(\neg x_1 \vee \neg x_2 \vee f) \wedge (\neg x_3 \vee \neg f \vee x_4) \wedge (\neg x_2 \vee \neg x_2 \vee x_4) \wedge (\neg x_1 \vee \neg x_1 \vee \bot)$ is mapped to the Kripke structure in Fig. 3.

The Kripke structure includes one branch for each clause of the given Horn formula, where the length of each branch is in logarithmic order of the number of variables in the Horn formula. We use atomic propositions $neg_1$ and $neg_2$ to indicate negative literals and $pos$ for the positive literal. We also include propositions $c$ and $h$ to mark each clause with a bitsequence. That is, for each clause $\{\neg x_{n_1} \vee \neg x_{n_2} \vee x_p\}$, we label states of its branch by atomic proposition $neg_1$ according to the bitsequence of $x_{n_1}$, atomic proposition $neg_2$ according to the bitsequence of $x_{n_2}$, and atomic proposition $pos$ according to the bitsequence

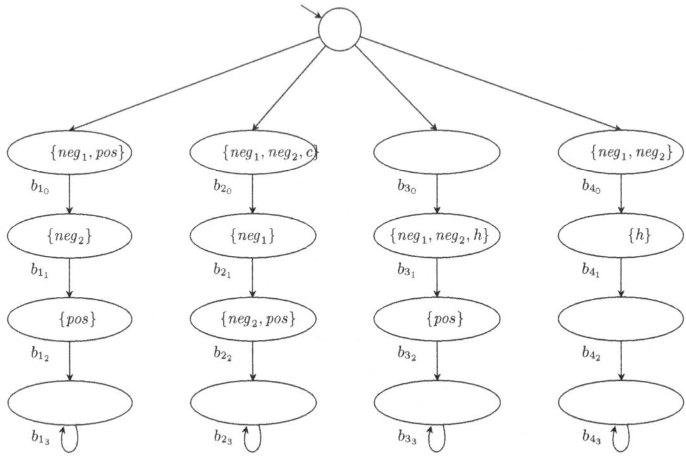


**Fig. 3.** The Kripke structure of the Horn formula.

of $x_p$. We reserve values 0 and $|X| - 1$ for $\bot$ and $\bot$, respectively, where $X$ is the set of variables of the Horn formula. Finally, we use the atomic proposition $c$ to assign to each clause a number (represented as the bitsequence of valuations of $c$, starting with the lowest-valued bit; the position after the highest-level bit is marked by the occurrence of atomic proposition $h$, which does not appear anywhere else).

The HyperLTL formula enforces that (1) $\top$ is assigned to true, (2) $\bot$ is assigned to false, (3) all clauses are satisfied, and (4) if a positive literal $l$ appears on some clause in the repaired Kripke structure, then all clauses with $l$ must be preserved by the repair. $\square$

### 5.3 The Full Logic

We now turn to full HyperLTL. We first show that the repair problem is in NP.

**Theorem 3.** PR[HyperLTL, tree] *is in NP in the size of the Kripke structure.*

*Proof.* We nondeterministically guess a solution $\mathcal{K}'$ to the repair problem. Since determining whether or not $\mathcal{K}' \models \varphi$ can be solved in logarithmic space [6], the repair problem is in NP. $\square$

For the lower bound, the intuition is that an additional leading universal quantifier allows us to encode full Boolean satisfiability, instead of just Horn satisfiability as in the previous section. Interestingly, the model checking problem remains L-complete for this fragment [6].

**Theorem 4.** PR[AAE-HyperLTL, tree] *is NP-hard in the size of the Kripke structure.*

*Proof sketch.* We map an instance of the 3SAT problem to a Kripke structure and a HyperLTL formula. Figure 4 shows an example, where each clause in 3SAT is mapped to a distinct branch and each literal in the clause is mapped to a distinct sub-branch. We label positive and negative literals by *pos* and *neg*, respectively. Also, propositions $c$ and $h$ are used to mark the clauses with bitsequences in the same fashion as in the construction of proof of Theorem 2. The HyperLTL formula $\varphi_{\mathsf{map}}$ ensures that (1) at least one literal in each clause is true, (2) a literal is not assigned to two values, and (3) all clauses are preserved during repair:

$$\varphi_{\mathsf{map}} = \forall \pi_1.\forall \pi_2.\exists \pi_3.\left[\square\left(\neg pos_{\pi_1} \vee \neg neg_{\pi_2}\right)\right] \wedge$$

$$\bigcirc\left[\left((c_{\pi_2} \wedge \neg c_{\pi_3})\ \mathcal{U}\ (\neg c_{\pi_2} \wedge c_{\pi_3} \wedge \bigcirc((c_{\pi_2} \leftrightarrow c_{\pi_3}) \mathcal{U}\, h_{\pi_2}))\right) \vee (c_{\pi_2} \wedge \neg c_{\pi_3})\ \mathcal{U}\ h_{\pi_2}\right]$$

The answer to the 3SAT problem is affirmative if and only if a repair exists for the mapped Kripke structure with respect to formula $\varphi_{\mathsf{map}}$. □

**Corollary 1.** *The following are* NP-complete *in the size of the Kripke structure:* PR[A*E*HyperLTL, tree], PR[(EA)$^k$-HyperLTL, tree], PR[(AE)$^k$-HyperLTL, tree], *and* PR[HyperLTL, tree].

# 6 Complexity of Repair for Acyclic Graphs

We now turn to acyclic graphs. Acyclic Kripke structures are of practical interest, because certain security protocols, in particular authentication algorithms, often consist of sequences of phases with no repetitions or loops. We develop our results first for the alternation-free fragment, then for formulas with quantifier alternation.

## 6.1 The Alternation-Free Fragment

We start with the existential fragment. The complexity of the repair problem for this fragment is interestingly the same as the model checking problem.

**Theorem 5.** PR[E*-HyperLTL, acyclic] *is* NL-*complete in the size of the Kripke structure.*

*Proof.* For existential formulas, the repair problem is equivalent to the model checking problem. A given Kripke structure satisfies the formula iff it has a repair. If the formula is satisfied, the repair is simply the original Kripke structure. Since the model checking problem for existential formulas over acyclic graphs is NL-complete [6, Theorem 2], the same holds for the repair problem. □

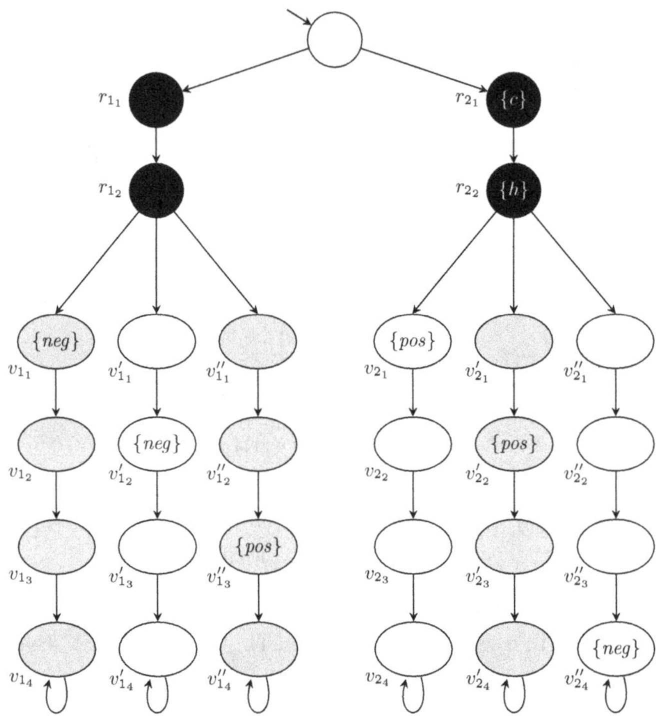


**Fig. 4.** The Kripke structure for the 3SAT formula $(\neg x_1 \vee \neg x_2 \vee x_3) \wedge (x_1 \vee x_2 \vee \neg x_4)$. The truth assignment $x_1 = \mathsf{true}$, $x_2 = \mathsf{false}$, $x_3 = \mathsf{false}$, $x_4 = \mathsf{false}$ renders the tree with white branches, i.e., the grey branches are removed during repair.

We now switch to the universal fragment.

**Theorem 6.** PR[A*-HyperLTL, acyclic] *and* PR[EA*-HyperLTL, acyclic] *is* NL-*complete in the size of the Kripke structure.*

*Proof.* To solve the repair problem of a HyperLTL formula $\varphi = \exists\pi.\ \forall\pi_1.\ \forall\pi_2 \ldots \forall\pi_m.\ \psi(\pi, \pi_1, \pi_2, \ldots, \pi_m)$ with at most one existential quantifier, which appears as the first quantifier, it suffices to find a single trace $\pi$ that satisfies $\psi(\pi, \pi, \ldots, \pi)$: suppose there exists a repair that satisfies $\varphi$ and that has more than one path, then any repair that only preserves one of these paths also satisfies the universal formula $\varphi$. For the upper bound, we nondeterministically guess a path for the trace $\pi$ and remove all other paths. Since the length of the path is bounded by the size of the acyclic Kripke structure, we can guess the path using logarithmically many bits for a counter measuring the length of the path.

NL-hardness of PR[A*-HyperLTL, acyclic] follows from the NL-hardness of the graph-reachability problem for ordered graphs [34]. Ordered graphs are acyclic graphs with a vertex numbering that is a topological sorting of the vertices. We express graph reachability from vertex $s$ to vertex $t$ as the repair problem of the universal formula $\forall\pi.\ \Diamond(s_\pi \wedge \Diamond t_\pi)$. $\square$

### 6.2 Formulas with Quantifier Alternation

Next, we consider formulas where the number of quantifier alternations is bounded by a constant $k$. We show that changing the frame structure from trees to acyclic graphs results in a significant increase in complexity (see Table 1). The complexity of the repair problem is similar to the model checking problem, with the repair problem being one level higher in the polynomial hierarchy (cf. [6]).

**Theorem 7.** *For* $k \geq 2$, PR[(EA)$k$-HyperLTL, acyclic] *is* $\Sigma^{\mathsf{P}}_{\mathsf{k}}$*-complete in the size of the Kripke structure. For* $k \geq 1$, PR[(AE)$k$-HyperLTL, acyclic] *is* $\Sigma^{\mathsf{P}}_{\mathsf{k+1}}$*-complete in the size of the Kripke structure.*

*Proof Sketch.* For the upper bound, suppose that the first quantifier is existential. Since the Kripke structure is acyclic, the length of the traces is bounded by the number of states. We can thus nondeterministically guess the repair and the existentially quantified traces in polynomial time, and then verify the correctness of the guess by model checking the remaining formula, which has $k-1$ quantifier alternations and begins with a universal quantifier. The verification can be done in $\Pi^{\mathsf{P}}_{\mathsf{k-1}}$ [6, Theorem 3]. Hence, the repair problem is in $\Sigma^{\mathsf{P}}_{\mathsf{k}}$. Analogously, if the first quantifier is universal, the model checking problem in $\Pi^{\mathsf{P}}_{\mathsf{k}}$ and the repair problem in $\Sigma^{\mathsf{P}}_{\mathsf{k+1}}$.

We establish the lower bound via a reduction from the *quantified Boolean formula* (QBF) satisfiability problem [27]. The Kripke structure (see Fig. 5) contains a path for each clause, and a separate structure that consists of a sequence of diamond-shaped graphs, one for each variable. A path through the diamonds selects a truth value for each variable, by going right or left, respectively, at the branching point.

In our reduction, the quantifiers in the QBF instance are translated to trace quantifiers (one per alternation depth), resulting in a HyperLTL formula with $k$ quantifier alternations and a leading existential quantifier. Note that, the outermost existential quantifiers are not translated to a quantifier, but instead resolved by the repair. For this reason, it suffices to build a HyperLTL formula with one less quantifier alternation than the original QBF instance. Also, in our mapping, we must make sure that the clauses and the diamonds for all variables except the outermost existential variables are not removed during the repair. Similar to the proof of Theorem 4, we add a counter to the clauses and add a constraint to the HyperLTL formula that ensures that all counter values are still present in the repair; for the diamonds of the variables, the valuations themselves form such a counter, and we add a constraint that ensures that all valuations for the variables (except for the outermost existential variables) are still present in the repair. □

Finally, Theorem 7 implies that the repair problem for acyclic Kripke structures and HyperLTL formulas with an arbitrary number of quantifiers is in PSPACE.

**Corollary 2.** PR[HyperLTL, acyclic] *is in PSPACE in the size of the Kripke structure.*

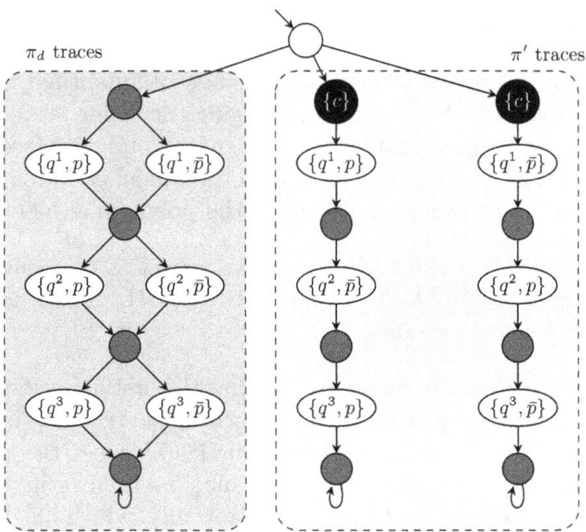


**Fig. 5.** Kripke structure for the formula $y = \exists x_1.\forall x_2.\exists x_3.(x_1 \vee \neg x_2 \vee x_3) \wedge (\neg x_1 \vee x_2 \vee \neg x_3)$.

## 7 Complexity of Repair for General Graphs

In this section, we investigate the complexity of the repair problem for general graphs. We again begin with the alternation-free fragment and then continue with formulas with quantifier alternation.

### 7.1 The Alternation-Free Fragment

We start with the existential fragment. Similar to the case of acyclic graphs, the repair problem can be solved with a model checking algorithm.

**Theorem 8.** PR[E*-HyperLTL, general] *is NL-complete in the size of the Kripke structure.*

*Proof.* Analogously to the proof of Theorem 5, we note that, for existential formulas, the repair problem is equivalent to the model checking problem. A given Kripke structure satisfies the formula if and only if it has a repair. If the formula is satisfied, the repair is simply the original Kripke structure. Since the model checking problem for existential formulas for general graphs is NL-complete [25], the same holds for the repair problem. □

Unlike the case of acyclic graphs, the repair problem for the universal fragment is more expensive, although the model checking problem is NL-complete [6].

**Theorem 9.** PR[A$^+$-HyperLTL, general] *is NP-complete in the size of the Kripke structure.*

*Proof.* For membership in NP, we nondeterministically guess a solution to the repair problem, and verify the correctness of the universally quantified HyperLTL formula against the solution in polynomial time in the size of the Kripke structure. NP-hardness follows from the NP-hardness of the repair problem for LTL [5].

### 7.2 Formulas with Quantifier Alternation

Next, we consider formulas where the number of quantifier alternations is bounded by a constant $k$. We show that changing the frame structure from acyclic to general graphs again results in a significant increase in complexity (see Table 1).

**Theorem 10.** PR[$\mathsf{E}^*\mathsf{A}^*$-HyperLTL, general] *is in PSPACE in the size of the Kripke structure.* PR[$\mathsf{A}^*\mathsf{E}^*$-HyperLTL, general] *is PSPACE-complete in the size of the Kripke structure. For $k \geq 2$,* PR[$(\mathsf{EA})^k$-HyperLTL, general] *and* PR[$(\mathsf{AE})^k$-HyperLTL, general] *are $(k-1)$-EXPSPACE-complete in the size of the Kripke structure.*

*Proof Idea.* The claimed complexities are those of the model checking problem [37]. We prove that the repair problem has the same complexity as the model checking problem. To show the upper bound of PR[$\mathsf{A}^*\mathsf{E}^*$-HyperLTL, general], we enumerate, in PSPACE, all possible repairs, and then verify against the HyperLTL formula.

For the lower bounds, we modify the Kripke structure and the HyperLTL formula such that the only possible repair is the unchanged Kripke structure. After the modification, the repair problem thus has the same result as the model checking problem. The idea of the modification is to assign numbers to the successors of each state. We add extra states such that the traces that originate from these states correspond to all possible number sequences. Finally, the HyperLTL formula states that for each such number sequence there exists a corresponding trace in the original Kripke structure. □

Finally, Theorem 10 implies that the repair problem for general Kripke structures and HyperLTL formulas with an arbitrary number of quantifiers is in NONELEMENTARY.

**Corollary 3.** PR[HyperLTL, general] *is NONELEMENTARY in the size of the Kripke structure.*

## 8 Related Work

There has been a lot of recent progress in automatically *verifying* [14,23–25] and *monitoring* [2,8,9,21,22,29,39] HyperLTL specifications. HyperLTL is also supported by a growing set of tools, including the model checker MCHyper [14,25], the satisfiability checkers EAHyper [20] and MGHyper [18], and the runtime monitoring tool RVHyper [21].

Directly related to the repair problem studied in this paper are the satisfiability and synthesis problems. The *satisfiability* problem for HyperLTL was shown to be decidable for the $\exists^*\forall^*$ fragment and for any fragment that includes a $\forall\exists$ quantifier alternation [17]. The hierarchy of hyperlogics beyond HyperLTL has been studied in [13].

The *synthesis* problem was shown to be undecidable in general, and decidable for the $\exists^*$ and $\exists^*\forall$ fragments. While the synthesis problem becomes, in general, undecidable as soon as there are two universal quantifiers, there is a special class of universal specifications, called the linear $\forall^*$-fragment, which is still decidable [19]. The linear $\forall^*$-fragment corresponds to the decidable *distributed synthesis* problems [26]. The *bounded synthesis* problem considers only systems up to a given bound on the number of states. Bounded synthesis from hyperproperties is studied in [14,19]. Bounded synthesis has been successfully applied to small examples such as the dining cryptographers [10].

The problem of model checking hyperproperties for tree-shaped and acyclic graphs was studied in [6]. Earlier, a similar study of the impact of structural restrictions on the complexity of the model checking problem has also been carried out for LTL [33].

For LTL, the complexity of the repair problem was studied independently in [5,15,32] and subsequently in [7] for distributed programs. The repair problem is also related to *supervisory control*, where, for a given plant, a supervisor is constructed that selects an appropriate subset of the plant's controllable actions to ensure that the resulting behavior is safe [31,35,40].

## 9 Conclusion and Future Work

In this paper, we have developed a detailed classification of the complexity of the repair problem for hyperproperties expressed in HyperLTL. We considered general, acyclic, and tree-shaped Kripke structures. We showed that for trees, the complexity of the repair problem in the size of the Kripke structure does not go beyond NP. The problem is complete for L, P, and NP for fragments with only one quantifier alternation, depending upon the outermost quantifiers. For acyclic Kripke structures, the complexity is in PSPACE (in the level of the polynomial hierarchy that corresponds to the number of quantifier alternations). The problem is NL-complete for the alternation-free fragment. For general graphs, the problem is NONELEMENTARY for an arbitrary number of quantifier alternations. For a bounded number $k$ of alternations, the problem is $(k-1)$-EXPSPACE-complete. These results highlight a crucial insight to the repair problem compared to the corresponding model checking problem [6]. With the notable exception of trees, where the complexity of repair is NP-complete, compared to the L-completeness of model checking, the complexities of repair and model checking are largely aligned. This is mainly due to the fact that computing a repair can be done by identifying a candidate substructure, which is comparatively inexpensive, and then verifying its correctness.

The work in this paper opens many new avenues for further research. An immediate question left unanswered in this paper is the lower bound complexity for the $\exists^*\forall^*$ fragment in acyclic and general graphs. It would be interesting to see if the differences we observed for HyperLTL carry over to other hyperlogics (cf. [1,11,13,24]). One could extend the results of this paper to the reactive setting, where the program interacts with the environment. And, finally, the ideas of this paper might help to extend popular synthesis techniques for general (infinite-state) programs, such as program sketching [38] and syntax-guided synthesis [3], to hyperproperties.

**Acknowledgments.** We would like to thank Sandeep Kulkrani, Reza Hajisheykhi (Michigan State University), and Shreya Agrawal (Google). The repair problem was originally inspired through our interaction with them. This work is sponsored in part by NSF SaTC Award 1813388. It was also supported by the German Research Foundation (DFG) as part of the Collaborative Research Center "Methods and Tools for Understanding and Controlling Privacy" (CRC 1223) and the Collaborative Research Center "Foundations of Perspicuous Software Systems" (TRR 248, 389792660), and by the European Research Council (ERC) Grant OSARES (No. 683300).

## References

1. Ábrahám, E., Bonakdarpour, B.: HyperPCTL: a temporal logic for probabilistic hyperproperties. In: McIver, A., Horvath, A. (eds.) QEST 2018. LNCS, vol. 11024, pp. 20–35. Springer, Cham (2018). https://doi.org/10.1007/978-3-319-99154-2_2
2. Agrawal, S., Bonakdarpour, B.: Runtime verification of $k$-safety hyperproperties in HyperLTL. In: Proceedings of the IEEE 29th Computer Security Foundations (CSF), pp. 239–252 (2016)
3. Alur, R., et al.: Syntax-guided synthesis. In: Formal Methods in Computer-Aided Design (FMCAD), pp.1–8 (2013)
4. Alur, R., Tripakis, S.: Automatic synthesis of distributed protocols. SIGACT News **48**(1), 55–90 (2017)
5. Bonakdarpour, B., Ebnenasir, A., Kulkarni, S.S.: Complexity results in revising UNITY programs. ACM Trans. Auton. Adapt. Syst. (TAAS) **4**(1), 1–28 (2009)
6. Bonakdarpour, B., Finkbeiner, B.: The complexity of monitoring hyperproperties. In: Proceedings of the IEEE 31th Computer Security Foundations (CSF), pp. 162–174 (2018)
7. Bonakdarpour, B., Kulkarni, S.S.: Masking faults while providing bounded-time phased recovery. In: Cuellar, J., Maibaum, T., Sere, K. (eds.) FM 2008. LNCS, vol. 5014, pp. 374–389. Springer, Heidelberg (2008). https://doi.org/10.1007/978-3-540-68237-0_26
8. Bonakdarpour, B., Sanchez, C., Schneider, G.: Monitoring hyperproperties by combining static analysis and runtime verification. In: Margaria, T., Steffen, B. (eds.) ISoLA 2018. LNCS, vol. 11245, pp. 8–27. Springer, Cham (2018). https://doi.org/10.1007/978-3-030-03421-4_2
9. Brett, N., Siddique, U., Bonakdarpour, B.: Rewriting-based runtime verification for alternation-free HyperLTL. In: Legay, A., Margaria, T. (eds.) TACAS 2017. LNCS, vol. 10206, pp. 77–93. Springer, Heidelberg (2017). https://doi.org/10.1007/978-3-662-54580-5_5
10. Chaum, D.: Security without identification: transaction systems to make big brother obsolete. Commun. ACM **28**(10), 1030–1044 (1985)

11. Clarkson, M.R., Finkbeiner, B., Koleini, M., Micinski, K.K., Rabe, M.N., Sánchez, C.: Temporal logics for hyperproperties. In: Abadi, M., Kremer, S. (eds.) POST 2014. LNCS, vol. 8414, pp. 265–284. Springer, Heidelberg (2014). https://doi.org/10.1007/978-3-642-54792-8_15
12. Clarkson, M.R., Schneider, F.B.: Hyperproperties. J. Comput. Secur. **18**(6), 1157–1210 (2010)
13. Coenen, N., Finkbeiner, B., Hahn, C., Hofmann, J.: The hierarchy of hyperlogics. In: 34th Annual ACM/IEEE Symposium on Logic in Computer Science (LICS) (2019)
14. Coenen, N., Finkbeiner, B., Sánchez, C., Tentrup, L.: Verifying hyperliveness. In: Dillig, I., Tasiran, S. (eds.) CAV 2019. LNCS, vol. 11561, pp. 121–139. Springer, Cham (2019). https://doi.org/10.1007/978-3-030-25540-4_7
15. Ebnenasir, A., Kulkarni, S.S., Bonakdarpour, B.: Revising UNITY programs: possibilities and limitations. In: Anderson, J.H., Prencipe, G., Wattenhofer, R. (eds.) OPODIS 2005. LNCS, vol. 3974, pp. 275–290. Springer, Heidelberg (2006). https://doi.org/10.1007/11795490_22
16. Etessami, K.: Counting quantifiers, successor relations, and logarithmic space. J. Comput. Syst. Sci. **54**(3), 400–411 (1997)
17. Finkbeiner, B., Hahn, C.: Deciding hyperproperties. In: Proceedings of the 27th International Conference on Concurrency Theory (CONCUR), pp. 13:1–13:14 (2016)
18. Finkbeiner, B., Hahn, C., Hans, T.: MGHyper: checking satisfiability of HyperLTL formulas beyond the $\exists^*\forall^*$ fragment. In: Lahiri, S.K., Wang, C. (eds.) ATVA 2018. LNCS, vol. 11138, pp. 521–527. Springer, Cham (2018). https://doi.org/10.1007/978-3-030-01090-4_31
19. Finkbeiner, B., Hahn, C., Lukert, P., Stenger, M., Tentrup, L.: Synthesizing reactive systems from hyperproperties. In: Chockler, H., Weissenbacher, G. (eds.) CAV 2018. LNCS, vol. 10981, pp. 289–306. Springer, Cham (2018). https://doi.org/10.1007/978-3-319-96145-3_16
20. Finkbeiner, B., Hahn, C., Stenger, M.: EAHyper: satisfiability, implication, and equivalence checking of hyperproperties. In: Majumdar, R., Kunčak, V. (eds.) CAV 2017. LNCS, vol. 10427, pp. 564–570. Springer, Cham (2017). https://doi.org/10.1007/978-3-319-63390-9_29
21. Finkbeiner, B., Hahn, C., Stenger, M., Tentrup, L.: RVHyper: a runtime verification tool for temporal hyperproperties. In: Beyer, D., Huisman, M. (eds.) TACAS 2018. LNCS, vol. 10806, pp. 194–200. Springer, Cham (2018). https://doi.org/10.1007/978-3-319-89963-3_11
22. Finkbeiner, B., Hahn, C., Stenger, M., Tentrup, L.: Monitoring hyperproperties. Formal Methods Syst. Des.(2019)
23. Finkbeiner, B., Hahn, C., Torfah, H.: Model Checking quantitative hyperproperties. In: Chockler, H., Weissenbacher, G. (eds.) CAV 2018. LNCS, vol. 10981, pp. 144–163. Springer, Cham (2018). https://doi.org/10.1007/978-3-319-96145-3_8
24. Finkbeiner, B., Müller, C., Seidl, H., Zalinescu, E.: Verifying security policies in multi-agent workflows with loops. In: Proceedings of the 15th ACM Conference on Computer and Communications Security (CCS), pp. 633–645 (2017)
25. Finkbeiner, B., Rabe, M.N., Sánchez, C.: Algorithms for model checking HyperLTL and HyperCTL$^*$. In: Kroening, D., Păsăreanu, C.S. (eds.) CAV 2015. LNCS, vol. 9206, pp. 30–48. Springer, Cham (2015). https://doi.org/10.1007/978-3-319-21690-4_3
26. Finkbeiner, B., Schewe, S.: Uniform distributed synthesis. In: Proceedings of LICS, pp. 321–330. IEEE Computer Society (2005)

27. Garey, M.R., Johnson, D.S.: Computers and Intractability: A Guide to the Theory of NP-Completeness. W. H. Freeman, New York (1979)
28. Goguen, J.A., Meseguer, J.: Security policies and security models. In: Proceedings of the IEEE Symposium on Security and Privacy (S & P), pp. 11–20 (1982)
29. Hahn, C., Stenger, M., Tentrup, L.: Constraint-based monitoring of hyperproperties. In: Vojnar, T., Zhang, L. (eds.) TACAS 2019. LNCS, vol. 11428, pp. 115–131. Springer, Cham (2019). https://doi.org/10.1007/978-3-030-17465-1_7
30. Jacob, J.: On the derivation of secure components. In: Proceedings of the IEEE Symposium on Security and Privacy (S & P), pp. 242–247 (1989)
31. Jiang, S., Kumar, R.: Supervisory control of discrete event systems with CTL* temporal logic specifications. SIAM J. Control Optim. **44**(6), 2079–2103 (2006)
32. Jobstmann, B., Griesmayer, A., Bloem, R.: Program repair as a game. In: Etessami, K., Rajamani, S.K. (eds.) CAV 2005. LNCS, vol. 3576, pp. 226–238. Springer, Heidelberg (2005). https://doi.org/10.1007/11513988_23
33. Kuhtz, L., Finkbeiner, B.: Weak Kripke structures and LTL. In: Katoen, J.-P., König, B. (eds.) CONCUR 2011. LNCS, vol. 6901, pp. 419–433. Springer, Heidelberg (2011). https://doi.org/10.1007/978-3-642-23217-6_28
34. Lengauer, T., Wagner, K.W.: The correlation between the complexities of the non-hierarchical and hierarchical versions of graph problems. J. Comput. Syst. Sci. **44**(1), 63–93 (1992)
35. Lin, F.: Analysis and synthesis of discrete event systems using temporal logic. In: Proceedings of the 1991 IEEE International Symposium on Intelligent Control, pp. 140–145, (August 1991)
36. McCullough, D.: Noninterference and the composability of security properties. In: Proceedings IEEE Symposium on Security and Privacy, pp. 177–186, (April 1988)
37. Rabe, M.N.: A Temporal Logic Approach to Information-flow Control. PhD thesis, Saarland University (2016)
38. Solar-Lezama, A.: Program sketching. J. Softw. Tool Technol. Transfer STTT **15**(5–6), 475–495 (2013). https://doi.org/10.1007/s10009-012-0249-7
39. Stucki, S., Sánchez, C., Schneider, G., Bonakdarpour, B.: Graybox monitoring of hyperproperties. In: Proceedings of the 23rd International Symposium on Formal Methods (FM) (2019). To appear
40. Thistle, J.G., Wonham, W.M.: Control problems in a temporal logic framework. Int. J. Control **44**(4), 943–976 (1986)

# Stochastic Systems

# Generic Emptiness Check for Fun and Profit

Christel Baier[1], František Blahoudek[2], Alexandre Duret-Lutz[3(✉)], Joachim Klein[1], David Müller[1], and Jan Strejček[4]

[1] Technische Universität Dresden, Dresden, Germany
{christel.baier,joachim.klein,david.mueller2}@tu-dresden.de
[2] University of Mons, Mons, Belgium
xblahoud@fi.muni.cz
[3] LRDE, EPITA, Le Kremlin-Bicêtre, France
adl@lrde.epita.fr
[4] Masaryk University, Brno, Czech Republic
strejcek@fi.muni.cz

**Abstract.** We present a new algorithm for checking the emptiness of $\omega$-automata with an Emerson-Lei acceptance condition (i.e., a positive Boolean formula over sets of states or transitions that must be visited infinitely or finitely often). The algorithm can also solve the model checking problem of probabilistic positiveness of MDP under a property given as a deterministic Emerson-Lei automaton. Although both these problems are known to be NP-complete and our algorithm is exponential in general, it runs in polynomial time for simpler acceptance conditions like generalized Rabin, Streett, or parity. In fact, the algorithm provides a unifying view on emptiness checks for these simpler automata classes. We have implemented the algorithm in Spot and PRISM and our experiments show improved performance over previous solutions.

## 1 Let's Play

Consider the graph in Fig. 1. Can you find a cycle satisfying the condition $\big((\mathsf{Fin}(⓿)\wedge\mathsf{Inf}(❶))\vee(\mathsf{Fin}(❷)\wedge\mathsf{Inf}(❸))\big)\wedge(\mathsf{Fin}(❹)\vee\mathsf{Inf}(❺))\wedge(\mathsf{Fin}(❻)\vee\mathsf{Inf}(❼))$, where $\mathsf{Fin}(ⓘ)$ is satisfied iff the mark ⓘ is not on the cycle and $\mathsf{Inf}(ⓘ)$ is satisfied iff the mark ⓘ is on the cycle? Such a cycle exists.[1]

In this paper we introduce an algorithm deciding whether a given graph contains a cycle satisfying a given condition, we show that this algorithm generalizes some known algorithms dedicated to simpler subclasses of conditions, and we discuss other related work (Sect. 3). Further, we present two implemented applications that motivated the algorithm. First, we show that the algorithm

[1] As this problem can be understood by the average Sudoku player, more instances can be found at https://adl.github.io/genem-exp/examples/ either to practice the algorithm by hand, or as an entertaining prophylaxis of Alzheimer's disease.


Y.-F. Chen et al. (Eds.): ATVA 2019, LNCS 11781, pp. 445–461, 2019.
https://doi.org/10.1007/978-3-030-31784-3_26

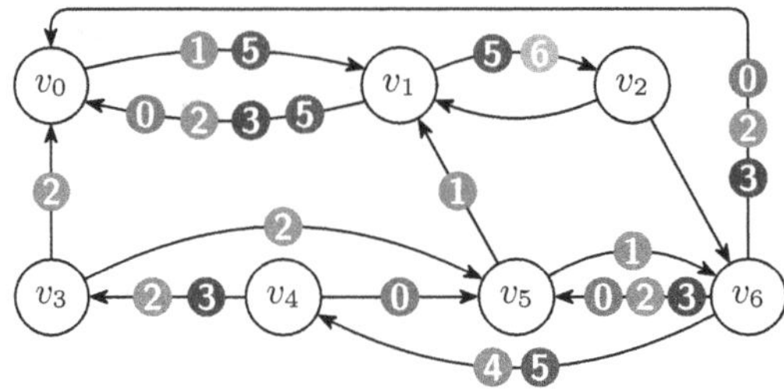


**Fig. 1.** Find a cycle satisfying the condition given in the text.

decides whether a given $\omega$-automaton with an Emerson-Lei acceptance condition represents an empty language (Sect. 4). Second, we show that the algorithm can be used in probabilistic model checking (Sect. 5). In both cases, experimental results indicate significant improvements over previous solutions.

## 2 Preliminaries

*Marked graph.* Intuitively, a *marked graph* $G$ is a graph with edges marked by non-negative integers. We denote the set of all non-negative integers as $\mathbb{N}_0$ and we call its elements *marks*. Formally, $G$ is a tuple $G = (V, E)$ of a finite set of *vertices* and a finite set of *edges* $E \subsetneq V \times 2^{\mathbb{N}_0} \times V$ where the set of *marks* $M$ is finite for each edge $(v_1, M, v_2)$. The set of all marked graphs is denoted by $\mathbf{G}$.

A *cycle* is a sequence of consecutive edges that starts and ends in the same vertex, i.e., $(v, M_0, v_1)(v_1, M_1, v_2)\dots(v_n, M_n, v)$. The union $M_0 \cup M_1 \cup \dots \cup M_n$ is the set of marks that *are on the cycle*. The marked graph $S = (V', E')$ is a *strongly connected component (SCC)* of $G = (V, E)$ if $V' \subseteq V$, $E' \subseteq E \cap (V' \times 2^{\mathbb{N}_0} \times V')$, and for each pair of distinct vertices $v, v' \in V'$ there is a sequence of consecutive edges from $E'$ that connects $v$ with $v'$. An SCC $S$ is *maximal*, if there is no other SCC $(V'', E'')$ of $G$ such that $V' \subseteq V''$ and $E' \subsetneq E''$. Further, $S$ is *non-trivial* if $E' \neq \emptyset$. Each non-trivial SCC has at least one cycle.

*Acceptance condition.* An *acceptance condition* over $\mathbb{N}_0$ is every formula $\varphi$ built by the following grammar where $m$ ranges over $\mathbb{N}_0$, and $\mathsf{t}$ and $\mathsf{f}$ stand for *true* and *false*, respectively. The set of all acceptance formulas is denoted by $\mathcal{C}$.

$$\varphi \ ::= \ \mathsf{t} \mid \mathsf{f} \mid \mathsf{Inf}(m) \mid \mathsf{Fin}(m) \mid (\varphi \wedge \varphi) \mid (\varphi \vee \varphi)$$

The concept of acceptance conditions comes from the theory of $\omega$-automata (automata that read infinite words) and the grammar above is inspired by the definition introduced by the Hanoi Omega-Automata Format [2]. Table 1 presents the shape of formulas for some traditional $\omega$-automata acceptance conditions. Note that marks can appear more than once in those formulas; for instance $(\mathsf{Fin}(0) \wedge \mathsf{Inf}(1)) \vee (\mathsf{Fin}(1) \wedge \mathsf{Inf}(0))$ is a Rabin acceptance formula.

**Table 1.** Shape of acceptance formulas corresponding to classical names. Here $m, m_0, m_1, \dots$ correspond some acceptance marks, and $J_i$ are sets of natural numbers.

| | |
|---|---|
| Büchi | $\mathsf{Inf}(m)$ |
| generalized Büchi | $\bigwedge_i \mathsf{Inf}(m_i)$ |
| Fin-less [4] | any positive formula of $\mathsf{Inf}(\dots)$ |
| co-Büchi | $\mathsf{Fin}(m)$ |
| generalized co-Büchi | $\bigvee_i \mathsf{Fin}(m_i)$ |
| Rabin | $\bigvee_i (\mathsf{Fin}(m_{2i}) \wedge \mathsf{Inf}(m_{2i+1}))$ |
| generalized Rabin [27] | $\bigvee_i \left(\mathsf{Fin}(m_i) \wedge \bigwedge_{j \in J_i} \mathsf{Inf}(m_j)\right)$ |
| Streett | $\bigwedge_i (\mathsf{Inf}(m_{2i}) \vee \mathsf{Fin}(m_{2i+1}))$ |
| parity (min even) | $\mathsf{Inf}(m_0) \vee (\mathsf{Fin}(m_1) \wedge (\mathsf{Inf}(m_2) \vee (\mathsf{Fin}(m_3) \wedge \dots)))$ |
| hyper-Rabin [5] | $\bigvee_i \bigwedge_{j \in J_i} (\mathsf{Fin}(m_{2j}) \vee \mathsf{Inf}(m_{2j+1}))$ |
| Emerson-Lei [19] | any positive formula of $\mathsf{Fin}(\dots)$ and $\mathsf{Inf}(\dots)$ |

Acceptance formulas are interpreted over sets of marks. We write $M \models \varphi$ if $M$ *satisfies* $\varphi$ with the relation $\models$ defined as follows.

$$\begin{array}{lll} M \models \mathsf{t} & M \models \mathsf{Inf}(m) \text{ iff } m \in M & M \models \varphi_1 \wedge \varphi_2 \text{ iff } M \models \varphi_1 \text{ and } M \models \varphi_2 \\ M \not\models \mathsf{f} & M \models \mathsf{Fin}(m) \text{ iff } m \notin M & M \models \varphi_1 \vee \varphi_2 \text{ iff } M \models \varphi_1 \text{ or } M \models \varphi_2 \end{array}$$

The following trivial simplifications, propagating f and t, are assumed to occur every time a formula is built or modified.

$$\begin{array}{llll} \mathsf{t} \vee \varphi = \mathsf{t} & \mathsf{f} \vee \varphi = \varphi & \mathsf{t} \wedge \varphi = \varphi & \mathsf{f} \wedge \varphi = \mathsf{f} \\ \varphi \vee \mathsf{t} = \mathsf{t} & \varphi \vee \mathsf{f} = \varphi & \varphi \wedge \mathsf{t} = \varphi & \varphi \wedge \mathsf{f} = \mathsf{f} \end{array} \quad (1)$$

The notation $\varphi[a \leftarrow b]$ means that all occurrences of the subformula $a$ are replaced by $b$ in $\varphi$. For instance, if $\varphi_1 = (\mathsf{Fin}(0) \wedge \mathsf{Inf}(1)) \vee (\mathsf{Fin}(2) \wedge \mathsf{Inf}(3))$, then we have $\varphi_1[\mathsf{Inf}(1) \leftarrow \mathsf{f}] = \mathsf{Fin}(2) \wedge \mathsf{Inf}(3)$. We can also quantify the substitution over sets of marks. For example, $\varphi_1[\forall m \in \{0,1\} : \mathsf{Inf}(m) \leftarrow \mathsf{f}]$ yields $\mathsf{Fin}(2) \wedge \mathsf{Inf}(3)$ again while $\varphi_1[\forall m \in \{1,3\} : \mathsf{Inf}(m) \leftarrow \mathsf{f}] = \mathsf{f}$.

To distinguish from f and t in formula notation, we use $\mathbb{B} = \{\bot, \top\}$ to denote the set of Boolean constants in descriptions of algorithms.

The reason we do not express acceptance conditions over sets of transitions (like $\mathsf{Inf}(\mathcal{T})$), but use marks as indirection, is so that a condition may be specified even for a graph that is not fully known (e.g., constructed on-the-fly).

## 3 Algorithm

Algorithm 1 decides whether a given graph $G \in \mathbf{G}$ contains no cycle satisfying a given condition $\varphi \in \mathcal{C}$. Its main function is called IS_EMPTY, as a graph containing no such cycle can be seen as *empty* with respect to $\varphi$.

**Algorithm 1** **Input:** a graph $G \in \mathbf{G}$ and a condition $\varphi \in \mathcal{C}$
**Output:** IS_EMPTY$(G, \varphi)$ returns $\bot$ if $G$ contains a cycle satisfying $\varphi$, otherwise it returns $\top$

```
1  IS_EMPTY(G ∈ G, φ ∈ C) → B:
2      foreach non-trivial S ∈ SCCS_OF(G) do
3          if ¬IS_SCC_EMPTY(S, φ) then return ⊥
4      return ⊤
5
6  IS_SCC_EMPTY(S ∈ G, φ ∈ C) → B:
7      (M_occur, M_every) ⟵ MARKS_OF(S)
8      φ ⟵ φ[∀m ∉ M_occur : Inf(m) ← f, Fin(m) ← t]
9      φ ⟵ φ[∀m ∈ M_every : Inf(m) ← t, Fin(m) ← f]
10     if φ = t then return ⊥
11     if φ = f then return ⊤
12     if φ[∀m ∈ M_occur : Inf(m) ← t] = t then return ⊥
13     // Every minimal model of φ contains some Fin(m) such that m ∈ M_occur
14     // We assume that φ has the form φ = ⋁_{j∈J} φ_j where φ_j are not disjunctions
15     foreach disjunct φ_j of φ do
16         if φ_j = ⋀_{m∈M'} Fin(m) ∧ φ' then
17             if ¬IS_EMPTY(REMOVE(S, M'), φ') then return ⊥
18         else
19             pick some m such that Fin(m) occurs in φ_j
20             if ¬IS_EMPTY(REMOVE(S, {m}), φ_j[Fin(m) ← t]) then return ⊥
21             if ¬IS_SCC_EMPTY(S, φ_j[Fin(m) ← f]) then return ⊥
22     return ⊤
```

Each cycle in a graph $G$ lies completely in some non-trivial SCC. Hence, the function IS_EMPTY$(G, \varphi)$ decomposes the graph $G$ into maximal SCCs using SCCS_OF$(G)$ and runs IS_SCC_EMPTY$(S, \varphi)$ for each non-trivial maximal SCC $S$. The graph is empty if and only if all its maximal SCCs are empty.

The function IS_SCC_EMPTY$(S, \varphi)$ gets a non-trivial SCC. It first calls the function MARKS_OF$(S)$ that returns the set $M_{\text{occur}}$ of the marks that occurs on some edges in $S$ and the set $M_{\text{every}}$ of the marks that occurs on all edges in $S$. Formally, if $E$ is the set of edges in $S$, then $M_{\text{occur}} = \bigcup_{(v,M,v')\in E} M$ and $M_{\text{every}} = \bigcap_{(v,M,v')\in E} M$.

This information is used to simplify $\varphi$ on lines 8 and 9. For each mark $m$ not occurring in $S$, we replace $\mathsf{Fin}(m)$ in $\varphi$ by $\mathsf{t}$ and $\mathsf{Inf}(m)$ by $\mathsf{f}$ as all cycles in $S$ satisfy $\mathsf{Fin}(m)$ and do not satisfy $\mathsf{Inf}(m)$. Similarly, for each mark $m$ appearing on all edges of $S$, we replace $\mathsf{Fin}(m)$ in $\varphi$ by $\mathsf{f}$ and $\mathsf{Inf}(m)$ by $\mathsf{t}$ as all cycles in $S$ satisfy $\mathsf{Inf}(m)$ and do not satisfy $\mathsf{Fin}(m)$. If the simplified formula $\varphi$ is equivalent to $\mathsf{t}$, then it is satisfied by all cycles of $S$ and thus we return $\bot$ as the considered SCC is nonempty. Analogously, if the current $\varphi$ is equivalent to $\mathsf{f}$, then no cycle can satisfy it and thus we return $\top$ as the SCC is empty.

Since $S$ is an SCC, there exists a cycle going through all its edges and visiting all marks in $M_{\mathrm{occur}}$. Line 12 checks whether $\varphi$ can be satisfied by such a cycle and returns $\bot$ if it is the case. If this check fails, we know that every cycle potentially satisfying the formula has to satisfy some $\mathsf{Fin}(m)$ subformula.

In the rest of the algorithm, we see $\varphi$ as a disjunction $\varphi = \bigvee_{j \in J} \varphi_j$, where $\varphi_j$ are not disjunctions. If $\varphi$ is not a disjunction, we see the whole formula as a single disjunct. The SCC is empty with respect to $\varphi$ if and only if it is empty with respect to each disjunct $\varphi_j$. Hence, the algorithm processes these disjuncts one by one and if the SCC is not empty with respect to some disjunct, we immediately return $\bot$.

The previous part of the algorithm implies that each disjunct $\varphi_j$ can be satisfied only by a cycle satisfying some subformulas $\mathsf{Fin}(m)$. We can easily detect some of these subformulas if $\varphi_j$ has the from $\varphi_j = \bigwedge_{m \in M'} \mathsf{Fin}(m) \ \wedge \ \varphi'$. Note that we see the formulas $\varphi_j = \bigwedge_{m \in M'} \mathsf{Fin}(m)$ and $\varphi_j = \mathsf{Fin}(m)$ as special cases of the conjunction and $\varphi'$ stands for $\mathsf{t}$ in these cases. In practice, we consider the set $M'$ on line 16 to be maximal in the sense that $\varphi'$ is not a conjunction with another conjunct of the form $\mathsf{Fin}(m)$. When $M'$ is identified, we remove all edges containing some marks of $M'$ from $S$ as these edges cannot be part of any cycle satisfying $\varphi_j$. The removal is done by the function REMOVE that takes a graph and a set of marks and returns the graph without all edges that contain some mark of the set. After this removal, we call IS_EMPTY to check whether the graph after the removal is empty with respect to $\varphi'$.

Finally, if $\varphi_j$ is not of the form $\bigwedge_{m \in M'} \mathsf{Fin}(m) \ \wedge \ \varphi'$, line 19 nondeterministically chooses a subformula of the form $\mathsf{Fin}(m)$. Line 20 looks whether there is a cycle satisfying $\varphi_j$ and containing no $m$ mark (i.e., automatically satisfying $\mathsf{Fin}(m)$). If there is such a cycle, we return $\bot$ as $S$ is not empty. Otherwise, line 21 checks whether there exists a cycle satisfying $\varphi_j$ independently on $\mathsf{Fin}(m)$. More precisely, we replace $\mathsf{Fin}(m)$ in $\varphi_j$ by $\mathsf{f}$ and check emptiness of $S$ against the resulting condition. As this step does not remove any edges of $S$, we can use the function IS_SCC_EMPTY to check the emptiness.

### 3.1 Solving the Puzzle from the Second Page

We illustrate how the Algorithm 1 works by running it step-by-step on the puzzle from the second page. In figures, we use gray boxes to enclose maximal SCCs. The red $S$ or $S_i$ next to each box is the name of this SCC used in the description. Trivial SCCs are indicated by a dashed border

To solve the puzzle, we call IS_EMPTY$(G, \varphi)$ where $G$ is the marked graph of Fig. 1 and $\varphi$ is the corresponding condition. The function SCCS_OF$(G)$ on line 2 identifies one maximal SCC $S$ which is the whole $G$, see Fig. 2(a). As $S$ is non-trivial, we call IS_SCC_EMPTY$(S, \varphi)$. Lines 7–9 detect that ❼ does not occur in $S$ (❼ $\notin M_{\mathrm{occur}}$) and thus $\varphi$ becomes $\varphi[\mathsf{Inf}(❼) \leftarrow \mathsf{f}]$ denoted by $\varphi_1$.

$$\varphi_1 = \Big( (\mathsf{Fin}(⓿) \wedge \mathsf{Inf}(❶)) \vee (\mathsf{Fin}(❷) \wedge \mathsf{Inf}(❸)) \Big) \wedge (\mathsf{Fin}(❹) \vee \mathsf{Inf}(❺)) \wedge \mathsf{Fin}(❻)$$

As $\varphi_1$ is neither $\mathsf{t}$ nor $\mathsf{f}$, and it cannot be satisfied only by satisfaction of $\mathsf{Inf}(m)$ subformulas, the tests on lines 10–12 fail.

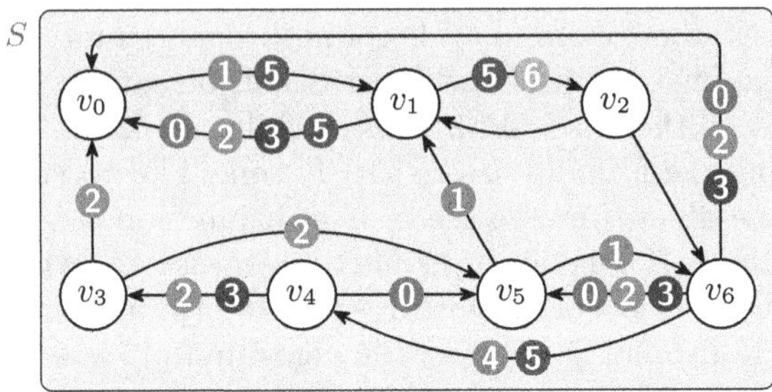


(a) Graph $G$ from Fig. 1, with one maximal SCC $S$.

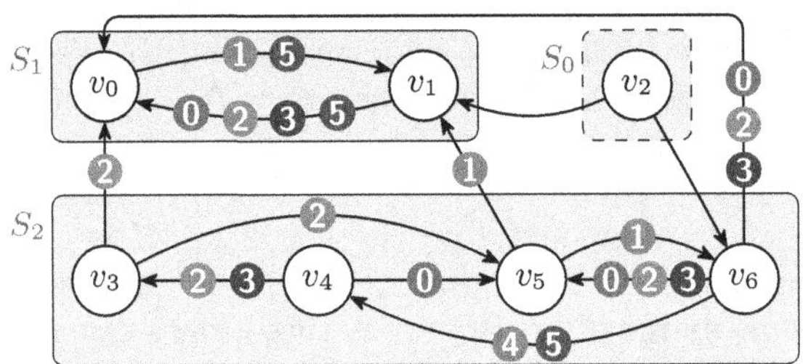


(b) Decomposition of $G_1 = \text{REMOVE}(S, \{\text{⑥}\})$ into maximal SCCs.

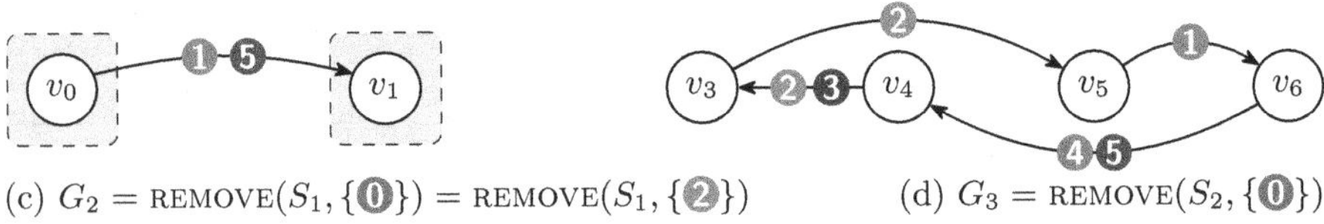


(c) $G_2 = \text{REMOVE}(S_1, \{\text{⓪}\}) = \text{REMOVE}(S_1, \{\text{②}\})$ (d) $G_3 = \text{REMOVE}(S_2, \{\text{⓪}\})$

**Fig. 2.** Intermediate automata encountered while checking the emptiness of $G$.

Further, $\varphi_1$ is a conjunction and thus the **foreach** loop on line 15 treats $\varphi_1$ as a single disjunct. As $\varphi_1$ matches the condition on line 16 for $M' = \{\text{⑥}\}$, we remove all edges marked with ⑥ from the graph and consider $\mathsf{Fin}(\text{⑥})$ as satisfied. Now we call $\text{IS\_EMPTY}(G_1, \varphi_2)$ on graph $G_1$ depicted in Fig. 2(b) with condition $\varphi_2$.

$$\varphi_2 = \Big(\big(\mathsf{Fin}(\text{⓪}) \wedge \mathsf{Inf}(\text{①})\big) \vee \big(\mathsf{Fin}(\text{②}) \wedge \mathsf{Inf}(\text{③})\big)\Big) \wedge \big(\mathsf{Fin}(\text{④}) \vee \mathsf{Inf}(\text{⑤})\big)$$

The function $\text{SCCs\_OF}(G_1)$ returns three maximal SCCs indicated in Fig. 2(b), where only $S_1$ and $S_2$ are non-trivial. Let us assume that the **foreach** loop on line 2 processes $S_1$ first and calls $\text{IS\_SCC\_EMPTY}(S_1, \varphi_2)$.

We can see that ④ does not occur in $S_1$ and the condition is thus transformed into $\varphi_3 = \varphi_2[\mathsf{Fin}(\text{④}) \leftarrow \mathsf{t}]$ on line 8.

$$\varphi_3 = \big(\mathsf{Fin}(\text{⓪}) \wedge \mathsf{Inf}(\text{①})\big) \vee \big(\mathsf{Fin}(\text{②}) \wedge \mathsf{Inf}(\text{③})\big)$$

The two disjuncts of $\varphi_3$ are checked independently in the **foreach** loop on line 15. Assume that the loop first considers the left disjunct and then the right one.

1. The disjunct $\varphi_j = \mathsf{Fin}(⓿) \wedge \mathsf{Inf}(❶)$ is matched by line 16 and thus we call IS_EMPTY$(G_2, \varphi_j)$, where $G_2$ is $S_1$ without edges marked with ⓿. You can find $G_2$ in Fig. 2(c) which also reveals that there is no non-trivial SCC in $G_5$. Therefore, IS_SCC_EMPTY$(G_2, \varphi_j)$ immediately returns $\top$.
2. For the second disjunct $\mathsf{Fin}(❷) \wedge \mathsf{Inf}(❸)$, the computation follows the same scenario as $S_1$ without edges marked with ❷ is precisely the same graph $G_2$.

Overall, IS_SCC_EMPTY$(S_1, \varphi_2)$ returns $\top$ which corresponds to the fact that $S_1$ is empty with respect to $\varphi_2$.

The **foreach** loop on line 2 now processes the second non-trivial SCC $S_2$ and calls IS_SCC_EMPTY$(S_2, \varphi_2)$. In this case, lines 7–9 have no effect on $\varphi_2$ as all marks of the condition occur in $S_2$, but none of them occurs on every edge. The tests on lines 10–12 have no effect as well. Condition $\varphi_2$ is a conjunction and thus the **foreach** loop on line 15 treats it as a single disjunct. As $\varphi_2$ does not match the pattern on line 16, we reach line 19 and select some $\mathsf{Fin}(m)$ subformula of $\varphi_2$. Assume that we pick mark ⓿ to be removed from the condition. Hence, we remove all edges marked with ⓿ from $S_2$ and call IS_EMPTY$(G_3, \varphi_4)$, where $G_3$ is $S_2$ after the removal and $\varphi_4$ stands for $\varphi_4 = \varphi_2[\mathsf{Fin}(⓿) \leftarrow \mathsf{t}]$.

$$\varphi_4 = \Big(\mathsf{Inf}(❶) \vee (\mathsf{Fin}(❷) \wedge \mathsf{Inf}(❸))\Big) \wedge (\mathsf{Fin}(❹) \vee \mathsf{Inf}(❺))$$

The graph $G_3$ can be seen in Fig. 2(d). As $G_3$ is a single maximal non-trivial SCC, we can proceed to IS_SCC_EMPTY$(G_3, \varphi_4)$. Lines 7–9 do not modify the condition, but the test on line 12 finally succeeds because $\varphi_4[\mathsf{Inf}(❶) \leftarrow \mathsf{t}, \mathsf{Inf}(❸) \leftarrow \mathsf{t}, \mathsf{Inf}(❺) \leftarrow \mathsf{t}] = \mathsf{t}$. Hence, $G_3$ is not empty with respect to $\varphi_4$. The cycle satisfying $\varphi_4$ can be easily seen in Fig. 2(d). The value $\bot$ is returned and propagated all the way back to IS_EMPTY$(G, \varphi)$. This corresponds to the fact that $G$ is nonempty with respect to $\varphi$.

### 3.2 Correctness, Complexity, and Related Work

**Theorem 1.** *Algorithm 1 always terminates, and it returns $\bot$ if and only if $G$ contains a cycle satisfying $\varphi$. Furthermore, its time complexity satisfies the upper bounds given in Table 2.*

It should be noted that lines 9–10 are not necessary for correctness, and that only the lines shown in Table 2 are needed to handle the listed acceptance types. Restricting Algorithm 1 to the specified ranges of lines also give the algorithm a behavior and complexity *comparable* to known algorithms for the subclass (as indicated in the last column), even if the actual implementation differ.

While the emptiness check for graphs with Emerson-Lei acceptance is known to be NP-complete [19, Thm. 4.7], our main goal was to write a *simple* algorithm that covers the full spectrum of Emerson-Lei acceptance formulas while

**Table 2.** Complexity of Algorithm 1 for various types of acceptance formulas. $|V|$ and $|E|$ are the number of vertices and edges in the graph, $n$ is the number of acceptance marks, $|\varphi|$ is the size of the formula, and $f$ is the number of marks $m_i$ that appears as $\mathsf{Fin}(m_i)$ in $\varphi$. We assume $|V| \leq |E|$, and that all marks between 0 and $n-1$ occur in $\varphi$ (maybe multiple times, hence $f \leq n \leq |\varphi|$). We also show the subset of lines necessary to handle the given acceptance (when line 15 is missing, it is assumed that $\varphi_j = \varphi$).

| Acceptance type | Complexity | Range of lines needed | Similar to |
|---|---|---|---|
| Büchi | $\mathcal{O}(\|E\|)$ | 1–8, 11–12 | [22] |
| generalized Büchi | $\mathcal{O}(n \cdot \|E\| + \|\varphi\| \cdot \|V\|)$ | 1–8, 11–12 | [11,37] |
| Fin-less | $\mathcal{O}(n \cdot \|E\| + \|\varphi\| \cdot \|V\|)$ | 1–8, 11–12 | |
| Rabin | $\mathcal{O}(n \cdot \|\varphi\| \cdot \|E\|)$ | 1–8, 11–17, 22 | |
| generalized Rabin | $\mathcal{O}(n \cdot \|\varphi\| \cdot \|E\|)$ | 1–8, 11–17, 22 | [4,8] |
| Streett | $\mathcal{O}(f \cdot (n \cdot \|E\| + \|\varphi\| \cdot \|V\|))$ | 1–8, 11–12, 16–17, 22 | [17,19,32] |
| parity | $\mathcal{O}(f \cdot (n \cdot \|E\| + \|\varphi\| \cdot \|V\|))$ | 1–8, 11–12, 16–17, 22 | |
| hyper-Rabin | $\mathcal{O}(\|\varphi\| \cdot (n \cdot \|E\| + \|\varphi\| \cdot \|V\|))$ | 1–8, 11–17, 22 | [19] |
| Emerson-Lei | $\mathcal{O}(2^f \cdot n \cdot \|\varphi\| \cdot \|E\|)$ | 1–8, 11–12, 19–22 | |

retaining polynomial complexity for commonly used subclasses. Emerson and Lei [19, Sec. 4.2–4.3] give an algorithm for the emptiness-check for Streett and hyper-Rabin conditions that behaves exactly like ours on these classes. They argue that at the cost of an extra $\mathcal{O}(2^{|\varphi|})$ factor, any acceptance conditions can be converted into hyper-Rabin by first converting it to disjunctive normal form (DNF), and then inserting some unsatisfiable Inf and Fin terms to match the hyper-Rabin form. Our algorithm tries to avoid this blind DNF transformation by first reducing the acceptance condition to the marks used in the SCC, and by only "distributing" Fin marks (via the recursive calls of lines 20–21).

Better algorithms exist for some of these subclasses [5, Table 2]. However, the proposed algorithm can be implemented to work on a graph $G$ that is not known explicitly, but on which forward successors can be computed on-the-fly, as usually done in the model checking community. In this context, the SCC decomposition algorithm may need to store all vertices of $G$, but the entire algorithm can be run without storing the edges of $G$, saving a lot of memory. For instance one faster emptiness check for Streett [9] requires the full graph to be available, with knowledge of the predecessors of each state.

## 4 Application 1: Emptiness Check for $\omega$-Automata

This section discuses the proposed algorithm in the context of $\omega$-automata, namely how it solves the emptiness check for *transition-based Emerson-Lei automata (TELA)* and several use cases for it. A TELA $\mathcal{A}$ over an *alphabet* $\Sigma$ can be seen as a marked graph where vertices are called states, one state $\iota$ is the *initial* state, and each edge (called *transition*) carries in addition to marks also a *label* $\ell \in \Sigma$; transitions are thus quadruples of the form $(s_1, \ell, M, s_2)$. The *language* of $\mathcal{A}$ is the set $L(\mathcal{A}) \subseteq \Sigma^\omega$ of infinite words $w$ such that there exists an infinite sequence of consecutive transitions starting in $\iota$ whose composition of labels is equal to $w$ and the set of marks that appear infinitely often in the sequence, satisfies the acceptance condition of the automaton.

Many algorithms for $\omega$-automata need to decide whether $L(\mathcal{A})$ is empty or not. This can be reduced to locating a reachable cycle whose set of marks satisfies the acceptance condition. To decide emptiness of $L(\mathcal{A})$, we can safely ignore transition labels, thus Algorithm 1 solves our problem.

The $\omega$-automata with Emerson-Lei acceptance[2] were introduced more than 30 years ago. However, tools supporting acceptance conditions more complex than generalized Büchi were rare in the past. In recent years, we could see a blossoming of tools producing $\omega$-automata with various acceptance conditions (Streett, Rabin, parity, generalized Rabin, and even Emerson-Lei) [1,8,18,20, 21,25–27,29,30,35]. The need for interaction between tools producing and consuming $\omega$-automata with various acceptance conditions has led to the introduction of the Hanoi Omega-Automata Format [2], where acceptance conditions are expressed using formulas as in Sect. 2. The existence of this format and tools supporting this format had a boosting impact on the research community.

Spot [18] is one such tool: it supports TELA and aims to offer useful $\omega$-automata algorithms that work on any acceptance formula when possible.

### 4.1 Use Cases in Spot

TELA emptiness check is useful in Spot on several places. Here are four:

- Spot's ltlcross tool is used to cross-compare the automata produced by various tools translating LTL to TELA automata and to test these tools. Initially, it only supported generalized Büchi automata [15, Sec. 3.2], but was extended to support arbitrary acceptance formulas. To detect buggy automata, `ltlcross` checks emptiness of automata products.[3]
- Deciding whether a TELA $\mathcal{A}$ is *stutter-invariant* also boils down to the emptiness check of the intersection of some modified version of $\mathcal{A}$ with its complement. Michaud and Duret-Lutz [33] describes this algorithm for generalized Büchi acceptance, but they apply (and are implemented) for TELA with arbitrary acceptance formula.
- Deciding whether a TELA $\mathcal{A}$ describes an *obligation property* also requires intersection of some modified version of $\mathcal{A}$ with its complement. Dax et al. [13] describes this algorithm for state-based Büchi acceptance, but Spot's implementation works for TELA with arbitrary acceptance formula.

[2] The original definition was *state-based*, which means that marks were on states and not transitions. As $\omega$-automata with state-based acceptance can be easily converted to transition-based acceptance without changing the transition structure, we focus on transition-based $\omega$-automata only.

[3] In fact, Fig. 1 comes from a product of a Rabin and a Streett automaton.

- Deciding whether an SCC is *inherently weak* (does not mix accepting and rejecting cycles) can be done with two emptiness checks: one with the original acceptance formula, and one with the complementary acceptance formula. If one of these emptiness checks is successful, the SCC is inherently weak.

### 4.2 Previous and New Emptiness Check Implementations

Algorithm 1 has been implemented in Spot and released in version 2.8. The implementation has the following additional optimizations:

- The enumeration of SCCs of $G$, on line 2 is done by a Dijsktra-based algorithm [14] that also records the sets $M_{occur}$ and $M_{every}$ for each SCC. As a consequence, the tests of lines 10–12 can be moved into this SCC enumeration algorithm, and that algorithm can be configured to stop as soon at it find an SCC for which line 12 (or 10) would return $\bot$. If one such SCC is found, the loop of line 2–3 is not even executed, avoiding some useless recursions into SCC using more complex conditions.
- The REMOVE function is not implemented as a function that returns a new automaton. Instead, the SCC enumeration algorithm accepts a set of marks that define which transitions should be disallowed in SCCs (this is implemented by keeping the destination of marked transitions in a set of secondary SCC roots, as in the *Fstate* of Bloemen et al. [4]). Doing so ensure that the algorithm can run in place, without making any copy of the automaton.
- Finally, the top-most call to IS_EMPTY first checks if the acceptance condition has the form $\bigwedge_{m\in M'} \mathsf{Fin}(m) \ \wedge\ \varphi'$. If yes, $M'$ is passed to the initial SCC enumeration algorithm and the relevant transitions are disallowed from start.

Before Algorithm 1 was implemented, Spot only had emptiness-check algorithms for generalized Büchi acceptance [12,37], and those were easily extended to deal with Fin-less acceptance. Basically, such an algorithm just has to enumerate the SCCs of the automaton, and check whether the set of marks occurring in some SCC satisfies the acceptance formula.

To perform emptiness checks of a TELA $\mathcal{A}$ using some Fin in its acceptance formula, old versions of Spot would first convert $\mathcal{A}$ into some Fin-less TELA $\mathcal{B}$, and then check the emptiness of $\mathcal{B}$. Spot employs four techniques for Fin-removal:

- The generic case is discussed by Bloemen et al. [4, Prop. 1] and Duret-Lutz [16, Sec. 4.5]. Essentially, a disjunctive normal form (DNF) of the acceptance condition $\varphi$ is computed as an irredundant sum-of-product [34] for a BDD representing $\varphi$ ($v_1$ encodes $\mathsf{Inf}(1)$ and $\bar{v}_1$ encodes $\mathsf{Fin}(1)$). $\mathcal{B}$ is obtained by cloning $\mathcal{A}$ once for each clause of the DNF. A clone for a clause ignores transitions with marks appearing in the Fin terms of the clause.
- A special construction similar to the DBA-realizability algorithm of Krishnan et al. [28] is used when the input is a Rabin automaton. It helps to avoid cloning some SCCs of $\mathcal{A}$ for some clauses in the previous approach.
- A Streett automaton with $k$ clauses and $|V|$ states is transformed into a generalized Büchi automaton with $k$ marks and $|V| \cdot (2^k + 1)$ states.
- Weak automata are converted into Büchi automata with identical graph.

One obvious disadvantage of going through this Fin-removal procedure is that it completely generates the automaton $\mathcal{B}$ before it can be checked for emptiness. This is usually wasting time in case the automaton is nonempty. It is also wasting space compared to Algorithm 1 which can be implemented in place without making any automaton copy (in Spot, the REMOVE function is implemented by recursively propagating a list of marks to filter in the SCC enumeration code). Finally, the first step of the Fin-removal procedure in the general case is to rewrite the acceptance formula into DNF, without any consideration for the actual automaton. Although this exponential cost is still present in Algorithm 1 (via the recursive calls of lines 20–21), the algorithm tries its best to avoid this costs by using information from the automaton to reduce the acceptance condition, by detecting acceptance conditions that can be solved linearly (lines 15–16), and in the worst case by using an exponential factor of $\mathcal{O}\left(2^f\right)$ instead of $\mathcal{O}\left(2^{|\varphi|}\right)$. (Recall that $f$ is the number of distinct Fin marks in $\varphi$.)

We report on a benchmark that shows how Algorithm 1 improved the runtime of TELA emptiness checks in Spot compared to the previous approach with the Fin-removal procedure.

We prepared 5 data sets containing a mix of empty and non-empty automata:

**random** Contains 100 000-state automata with Random acceptance conditions. Each acceptance condition uses 20 acceptance marks, and those marks occur exactly once (either as Fin or as Inf). These automata are generated using Spot's `randaut` tool configured to have a low density of transitions (to get some empty automata) and with at least one successor per state.

**random-rep** Has similar automata, except that each of the 20 acceptance marks may occur multiple times (possibly in both Fin and Inf terms).

**Rabin** Contains random 10 000-states Rabin automata with 32 marks used without repetition.

**Streett** Contains Streett automata generated from random LTL formulas as follows. First we consider only LTL formulas that are neither persistence nor recurrence properties. For some LTL formula $\psi$ and its negation, we use `ltl2dstar` 0.5.4 [24] to generate two Streett automata $A_\psi$, and $A_{\neg\psi}$. Then, if the product $P = A_\psi \otimes A_{\neg\psi}$ has more than 1000 states, we include $P$ in the dataset (this will be an empty automaton), and we also include the larger of $A_\psi$ or $A_{\neg\psi}$ (both are non-empty due to our selection of $\psi$).

**parity-like** Also contains generated automata of the form $P = A_\psi \otimes A_{\neg\psi}$, but now $A_\psi$ and $A_{\neg\psi}$ are deterministic parity min-odd automata generated by Spot's `ltl2tgba -P D` command. In this case, the product has not exactly parity acceptance formulae; it is rather a conjunction of parity acceptance. However the subset of Algorithm 1 needed to handle parity or Streett can also handle conjunction of parity. Again, for each product $P$, we also add the larger of $A_\psi$ and $A_{\neg\psi}$ to the dataset, to include some non-empty automata.

Table 3 shows the average runtime of the new version of the emptiness check (called `is_empty`) compared to the previous implementation based on Fin-removal (`old_is_empty`). Figure 3 shows a scatter plot of the same experi-

**Table 3.** Average runtime (in milliseconds) of the old and current implementations of the generic emptiness checks of Spot, over 5 different datasets with $n$ automata that can be empty or non-empty. Since arithmetic means (amean) are biased towards larger automata, geometric means (gmean) are also provided.

| | non-empty | | | | | empty | | | | |
|---|---|---|---|---|---|---|---|---|---|---|
| | | `old_is_empty` | | `is_empty` | | | `old_is_empty` | | `is_empty` | |
| | $n$ | amean | gmean | amean | gmean | $n$ | amean | gmean | amean | gmean |
| random | 44 | 1105.6 | 390.1 | 3.311 | 0.326 | 6 | 678.8 | 364.7 | 20.032 | 15.938 |
| random-rep | 43 | 254.2 | 186.3 | 2.980 | 0.306 | 7 | 91.1 | 57.1 | 18.732 | 16.595 |
| Rabin | 9 | 26.7 | 26.7 | 1.208 | 0.356 | 41 | 11.6 | 11.6 | 10.195 | 10.194 |
| Streett | 50 | 1.0 | 0.2 | 0.002 | 0.001 | 50 | 14.3 | 3.2 | 11.616 | 0.926 |
| parity-like | 50 | 1124.4 | 6.4 | 0.003 | 0.002 | 50 | 809.7 | 28.9 | 1.272 | 0.485 |
| (all) | 196 | 592.3 | 14.6 | 1.454 | 0.021 | 154 | 301.2 | 12.6 | 8.530 | 1.811 |

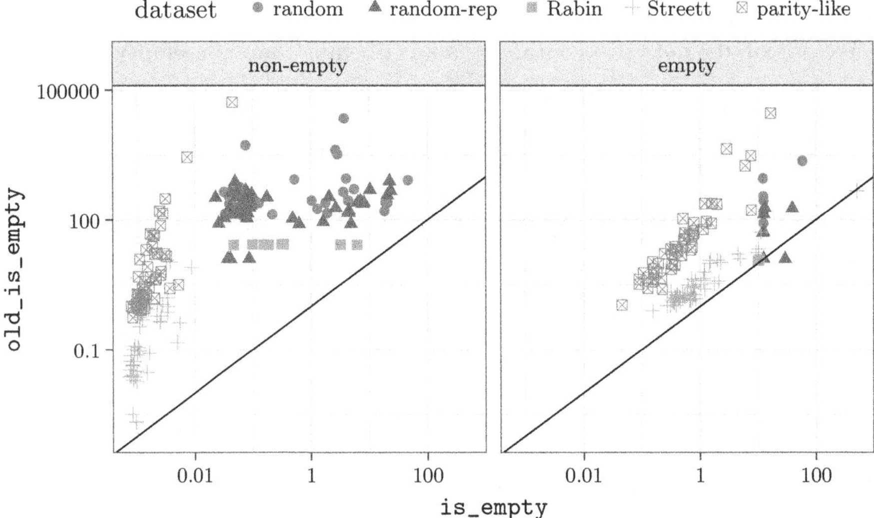


**Fig. 3.** Runtime comparison (in milliseconds) of the old and current implementations of the generic emptiness checks of Spot, over 5 different datasets.

ment. All measurements were done on an Intel Core i7-6820HQ CPU (2.70 GHz) running Linux, using a development version of Spot.[4]

We should start by commenting the results on empty Rabin automata. On those automata, the amount of work needed in `old_is_empty` to create the equivalent Fin-less automaton is similar to the amount of work performed by the new `is_empty`. The minor improvement is due to the fact that `is_empty` creates no new automaton. For empty Streett automata with $k$ clauses, the Fin-removal

[4] See https://adl.github.io/genem-exp/bench-app1/ to reproduce.

procedure has to generate a generalized Büchi automaton that is $2^k$ time larger, and `old_is_empty` pays this price. For empty automata with random and parity acceptance, `old_is_empty` is also slower due to the fact that it has to convert the acceptance formula to DNF upfront, and then process many disjuncts.

There is actually one case from the random-rep dataset where the conversion to DNF saves the day for `old_is_empty`: that point is visible below the diagonal on the right of Fig. 3. This case correspond to an automaton whose random acceptance condition is actually equivalent to false. Since our DNF conversion works by encoding the acceptance formula into a BDD, equivalence to false or true are often quickly detected. However outside of such random acceptance condition, unsatisfiable conditions are very rarely seen.

For the non-empty cases, the impressive improvement are easily explained by the fact that `old_is_empty` constructs an equivalent Fin-less automaton before starting to actually check it for emptiness, while `is_empty` will abort as soon as it finds an accepting SCC.

## 5 Application 2: Probabilistic Model Checking

Now we turn to the second application of our algorithm, *probabilistic model checking (PMC)* against $\omega$-regular path properties. Here, we are given a model incorporating stochastic behavior, such as a *discrete time Markov chain (DTMC)*, or stochastic and non-deterministic behavior, such as a *Markov decision process (MDP)*. We are then interested in computing the maximal or minimal probabilities of an $\omega$-regular path property, typically given as an LTL formula. For an overview of these topics, we refer to Baier and Katoen [3].

The standard approach for PMC against LTL [38] relies on the construction of a deterministic automaton for the formula, a product construction with the model, a subsequent analysis of so-called *bottom strongly connected components (BSCC)* in DTMCs and *maximal end-components (MEC)* in MDPs, yielding parts of the product model where the acceptance condition of the automaton holds with probability 1 (for DTMCs) or where the non-determinism in the model can be resolved such that it holds with probability 1 (for MDPs). Subsequently, a standard PMC reachability computation yields the desired probabilities. In the case of DTMCs, determining whether a BSCC, i.e., an SCC with no outgoing edges, satisfies an Emerson-Lei acceptance condition with probability 1 is easily decidable in polynomial time.

For MDP, the step of finding end components that almost surely accept an Emerson-Lei acceptance condition is more involved. Here, we are in a situation similar to finding an accepting cycle, with end-components (strongly connected subgraphs that are closed under probabilistic branching) taking the role of SCCs. The computation of maximal end-components can be done in $\mathcal{O}\left(|E| \cdot \min\left(\sqrt{|E|}, |V|\right)\right)$ if represented explicitly [6,7] and $\mathcal{O}\left(|V| \cdot \sqrt{|E|}\right)$ if represented symbolically [10]. We adapt Algorithm 1 by dealing with the graph of the product-MDP, replacing the SCC decomposition in line 2 with the computation of MECs.

**Table 4.** Model checking times for the mutual exclusion protocol with four participants. The model contains 27600 states. $t^{\mathrm{EL}}_{\mathrm{MEC}}$ denotes the time for the MEC analysis using Algorithm 1, whereas $t^{\mathrm{Rabin}}_{\mathrm{MEC}}$ denotes the time for the MEC analysis using the standard (generalized) Rabin algorithm as implemented in PRISM. $n$ stands for the number of acceptance marks occurring in the deterministic automaton. All times are measured in seconds and '–' means time-out.

| | Emerson-Lei | | generalized Rabin | | | Rabin | | |
|---|---|---|---|---|---|---|---|---|
| Property | $t^{\mathrm{EL}}_{\mathrm{MEC}}$ | $n$ | $t^{\mathrm{Rabin}}_{\mathrm{MEC}}$ | $t^{\mathrm{EL}}_{\mathrm{MEC}}$ | $n$ | $t^{\mathrm{Rabin}}_{\mathrm{MEC}}$ | $t^{\mathrm{EL}}_{\mathrm{MEC}}$ | $n$ |
| $\mathrm{Pr}^{\min}(\psi_3)$ | 109.8 | 4 | 130.7 | 121.1 | 4 | – | – | 14 |
| $\mathrm{Pr}^{\max}(\psi_4)$ | 0.4 | 3 | 234.3 | 0.7 | 6 | – | 585.9 | 8 |
| $\mathrm{Pr}^{\max}(\psi_6)$ | 0.4 | 3 | 100.1 | 0.6 | 5 | – | 855.1 | 6 |
| $\mathrm{Pr}^{\min}(\psi_8)$ | 0.6 | 4 | 251.9 | 119.0 | 6 | 1.6 | 0.6 | 6 |
| $\mathrm{Pr}^{\max}(\psi_9)$ | – | 4 | – | – | 12 | – | – | – |
| $\mathrm{Pr}^{\min}(\psi_{10})$ | 107.0 | 6 | 355.3 | 127.3 | 10 | 54.9 | 9.6 | 6 |

We have implemented this adapted algorithm as an extension to PRISM 4.4 and report here on the benchmark. This extension will be integrated in an official future PRISM version.

As PRISM itself generates deterministic Rabin automata from LTL formulas, we rely on Spot 2.7.4 for producing deterministic Emerson-Lei automata (columns "Emerson-Lei" in Table 4). We use state-based acceptance as PRISM does not support transition-based acceptance. For comparison, we consider the standard implementations in PRISM using the internal generation of deterministic Rabin automata via the algorithms of `ltl2dstar` [24] (columns "Rabin") and using deterministic generalized Rabin automata obtained from Rabinizer 4 [30] (columns "generalized Rabin"). The computation was carried out with the explicit engine of PRISM on a computer with two Intel E5-2680 8-core CPUs at 2.70 GHz with 384 GB of RAM running Linux and a time-out of 30 min and 10 GB memory limit.[5]

As the benchmark model and LTL formulas, we focus here on the mutual exclusion protocol [36], which is provided as an MDP by the PRISM benchmark suite [31]. The LTL formulas we check are described by Hahn et al. [23, Table 2]. We removed 2 formulas equivalent to $\mathtt{t}$.

Table 4 shows the running times of the MEC analysis. Algorithm 1 shows a good behavior in general. If we focus on the two first columns Emerson-Lei and Generalized Rabin, the time used in our Emerson-Lei check is always smaller than time in the original generalized Rabin check. In particular line 12 of Algorithm 1 turns out to be beneficial, as it allows determine early if the MEC is accepting. Also, the columns $n$ show that the number of acceptance marks is typically small (in this benchmark always 14 at most). In the last line of Table 4, $t^{\mathrm{EL}}_{\mathrm{MEC}}$ is much smaller for the Rabin automaton than for the Emerson-Lei automaton due to the more complicated acceptance condition of the latter.

[5] See https://adl.github.io/genem-exp/bench-app2/ to reproduce.

## 6 Conclusion

We presented a simple and efficient algorithm deciding emptiness of automata over infinite words with transition-based Emerson-Lei acceptance condition. The algorithm subsumes several known algorithms for automata classes with simpler acceptance conditions and keeps polynomial time complexity for these automata classes. We have also suggested an application of the algorithm in probabilistic model checking of MDPs. The algorithm has been implemented in Spot and PRISM and experimental evaluation shows improved performance of these tools.

The algorithm can be further improved in several directions. In particular, the running time of the current algorithm is influenced by some nondeterministic choices (lines 2, 15, and 19). We plan to replace these choices by heuristics. Another research goal is a parallel version of the algorithm.

**Acknowledgement.** This research was partially supported by the DFG through the DFG-project BA-1679/11-1, the DFG-project BA-1679/12-1, the Collaborative Research Centers CRC 912 (HAEC) and CRC 248 (DFG grant 389792660 as part of TRR 248), the Cluster of Excellence EXC 2050/1 (CeTI, project ID 390696704, as part of Germany's Excellence Strategy), the Research Training Groups QuantLA (GRK 1763), by F.R.S.-FNRS through the grant F.4520.18 (ManySynth), and by the Czech Science Foundation through the grant GA19-24397S.

## References

1. Babiak, T., Blahoudek, F., Křetínský, M., Strejček, J.: Effective translation of LTL to deterministic Rabin automata: beyond the (F,G)-fragment. In: Van Hung, D., Ogawa, M. (eds.) ATVA 2013. LNCS, vol. 8172, pp. 24–39. Springer, Cham (2013). https://doi.org/10.1007/978-3-319-02444-8_4
2. Babiak, T., et al.: The Hanoi Omega-Automata Format. In: Kroening, D., Păsăreanu, C.S. (eds.) CAV 2015. LNCS, vol. 9206, pp. 479–486. Springer, Cham (2015). https://doi.org/10.1007/978-3-319-21690-4_31. http://adl.github.io/hoaf/
3. Baier, C., Katoen, J.-P.: Principles of Model Checking. MIT Press, Cambridge (2008)
4. Bloemen, V., Duret-Lutz, A., van de Pol, J.: Model checking with generalized Rabin and Fin-less automata. Int. J. Softw. Tools Technol. Transf. **21**(3), 307–324 (2019)
5. Boker, U.: Why these automata types? In: LPAR 2018 of EPiC Series in Computing, vol. 57, pp. 143–163. EasyChair (2018)
6. Chatterjee, K., Henzinger, M.: Faster and dynamic algorithms for maximal end-component decomposition and related graph problems in probabilistic verification. In: SODA 2011, pp. 1318–1336. SIAM (2011)
7. Chatterjee, K., Henzinger, M.: Efficient and dynamic algorithms for alternating Büchi games and maximal end-component decomposition. J. ACM **61**(3), 15 (2014)
8. Chatterjee, K., Gaiser, A., Křetínský, J.: Automata with generalized Rabin pairs for probabilistic model checking and LTL synthesis. In: Sharygina, N., Veith, H. (eds.) CAV 2013. LNCS, vol. 8044, pp. 559–575. Springer, Heidelberg (2013). https://doi.org/10.1007/978-3-642-39799-8_37

9. Chatterjee, K., Henzinger, M., Loitzenbauer, V.: Improved algorithms for parity and Streett objectives. Log. Methods Comput. Sci. **13**(3) (2017)
10. Chatterjee, K., Henzinger, M., Loitzenbauer, V., Oraee, S., Toman, V.: Symbolic algorithms for graphs and Markov decision processes with fairness objectives. In: Chockler, H., Weissenbacher, G. (eds.) CAV 2018. LNCS, vol. 10982, pp. 178–197. Springer, Cham (2018). https://doi.org/10.1007/978-3-319-96142-2_13
11. Couvreur, J.-M.: On-the-fly verification of linear temporal logic. In: Wing, J.M., Woodcock, J., Davies, J. (eds.) FM 1999. LNCS, vol. 1708, pp. 253–271. Springer, Heidelberg (1999). https://doi.org/10.1007/3-540-48119-2_16
12. Couvreur, J.-M., Duret-Lutz, A., Poitrenaud, D.: On-the-fly emptiness checks for generalized Büchi automata. In: Godefroid, P. (ed.) SPIN 2005. LNCS, vol. 3639, pp. 169–184. Springer, Heidelberg (2005). https://doi.org/10.1007/11537328_15
13. Dax, C., Eisinger, J., Klaedtke, F.: Mechanizing the powerset construction for restricted classes of $\omega$-automata. In: Namjoshi, K.S., Yoneda, T., Higashino, T., Okamura, Y. (eds.) ATVA 2007. LNCS, vol. 4762, pp. 223–236. Springer, Heidelberg (2007). https://doi.org/10.1007/978-3-540-75596-8_17
14. Dijkstra, E.W.: Finding the maximal strong components in a directed graph. In: A Discipline of Programming, chapter 25, pp. 192–200. Prentice-Hall (1976)
15. Duret-Lutz, A.: Manipulating LTL formulas using spot 1.0. In: Van Hung, D., Ogawa, M. (eds.) ATVA 2013. LNCS, vol. 8172, pp. 442–445. Springer, Cham (2013). https://doi.org/10.1007/978-3-319-02444-8_31
16. Duret-Lutz, A.: Contributions to LTL and $\omega$-Automata for Model Checking. Habilitation thesis, Université Pierre et Marie Curie (Paris 6), (February 2017)
17. Duret-Lutz, A., Poitrenaud, D., Couvreur, J.-M.: On-the-fly emptiness check of transition-based Streett automata. In: Liu, Z., Ravn, A.P. (eds.) ATVA 2009. LNCS, vol. 5799, pp. 213–227. Springer, Heidelberg (2009). https://doi.org/10.1007/978-3-642-04761-9_17
18. Duret-Lutz, A., Kordon, F., Poitrenaud, D., Renault, E.: Heuristics for checking liveness properties with partial order reductions. In: Artho, C., Legay, A., Peled, D. (eds.) ATVA 2016. LNCS, vol. 9938, pp. 340–356. Springer, Cham (2016). https://doi.org/10.1007/978-3-319-46520-3_22
19. Emerson, E.A., Lei, C.-L.: Modalities for model checking: branching time logic strikes back. Sci. Comput. Prog. **8**(3), 275–306 (1987)
20. Esparza, J., Křetínský, J., Raskin, J., Sickert, S.: From LTL and limit-deterministic Büchi automata to deterministic parity automata. In: TACAS'17, LNCS 10205, pp. 426–442 (2017)
21. J. Esparza, J. Křetínský, and S. Sickert. One theorem to rule them all: A unified translation of LTL into $\omega$-automata. In LICS'18, pp. 384–393. ACM, 2018
22. Geldenhuys, J., Valmari, A.: Tarjan's algorithm makes on-the-fly LTL verification more efficient. In: Jensen, K., Podelski, A. (eds.) TACAS 2004. LNCS, vol. 2988, pp. 205–219. Springer, Heidelberg (2004). https://doi.org/10.1007/978-3-540-24730-2_18
23. Hahn, E.M., Li, G., Schewe, S., Turrini, A., Zhang, L.: Lazy probabilistic model checking without determinisation. In CONCUR 2015, vol. 42 of LIPIcs, pp. 354–367. Schloss Dagstuhl - Leibniz-Zentrum fuer Informatik (2015)
24. Klein, J., Baier, C.: Experiments with deterministic $\omega$-automata for formulas of linear temporal logic. Theor. Comput. Sci. **363**(2), 182–195 (2006)
25. Klein, J., Baier, C.: On-the-fly stuttering in the construction of deterministic $\omega$-Automata. In: Holub, J., Žďárek, J. (eds.) CIAA 2007. LNCS, vol. 4783, pp. 51–61. Springer, Heidelberg (2007). https://doi.org/10.1007/978-3-540-76336-9_7

26. Komárková, Z., Křetínský, J.: Rabinizer 3: Safraless translation of LTL to small deterministic automata. In: Cassez, F., Raskin, J.-F. (eds.) ATVA 2014. LNCS, vol. 8837, pp. 235–241. Springer, Cham (2014). https://doi.org/10.1007/978-3-319-11936-6_17
27. Křetínský, J., Esparza, J.: Deterministic automata for the (F,G)-fragment of LTL. In: Madhusudan, P., Seshia, S.A. (eds.) CAV 2012. LNCS, vol. 7358, pp. 7–22. Springer, Heidelberg (2012). https://doi.org/10.1007/978-3-642-31424-7_7
28. Krishnan, S.C., Puri, A., Brayton, R.K.: Deterministic $\omega$ automata vis-a-vis deterministic Buchi automata. In: Du, D.-Z., Zhang, X.-S. (eds.) ISAAC 1994. LNCS, vol. 834, pp. 378–386. Springer, Heidelberg (1994). https://doi.org/10.1007/3-540-58325-4_202
29. Křetínský, J., Garza, R.L.: Rabinizer 2: small deterministic automata for LTL$\setminus$GU. In: Van Hung, D., Ogawa, M. (eds.) ATVA 2013. LNCS, vol. 8172, pp. 446–450. Springer, Cham (2013). https://doi.org/10.1007/978-3-319-02444-8_32
30. Křetínský, J., Meggendorfer, T., Sickert, S., Ziegler, C.: Rabinizer 4: from LTL to your favourite deterministic automaton. In: Chockler, H., Weissenbacher, G. (eds.) CAV 2018. LNCS, vol. 10981, pp. 567–577. Springer, Cham (2018). https://doi.org/10.1007/978-3-319-96145-3_30
31. Kwiatkowska, M.Z., Norman, G., Parker, D.: The PRISM benchmark suite. In: QEST 2012, pp. 203–204. IEEE Computer Society (2012)
32. Liu, Y., Sun, J., Dong, J.S.: Scalable multi-core model checking fairness enhanced systems. In: Breitman, K., Cavalcanti, A. (eds.) ICFEM 2009. LNCS, vol. 5885, pp. 426–445. Springer, Heidelberg (2009). https://doi.org/10.1007/978-3-642-10373-5_22
33. Michaud, T., Duret-Lutz, A.: Practical stutter-invariance checks for $\omega$-regular languages. In: Fischer, B., Geldenhuys, J. (eds.) SPIN 2015. LNCS, vol. 9232, pp. 84–101. Springer, Cham (2015). https://doi.org/10.1007/978-3-319-23404-5_7
34. Minato, S.: Fast generation of irredundant sum-of-products forms from binary decision diagrams. In: SASIMI 1992, pp. 64–73 (1992)
35. Müller, D., Sickert, S.: LTL to deterministic Emerson-Lei automata. In: GandALF 2017, vol. 256 of EPTCS, pp. 180–194 (2017)
36. Pnueli, A., Zuck, L.D.: Verification of multiprocess probabilistic protocols. Distrib. Comput. **1**(1), 53–72 (1986)
37. Renault, E., Duret-Lutz, A., Kordon, F., Poitrenaud, D.: Three SCC-Based emptiness checks for generalized Büchi automata. In: McMillan, K., Middeldorp, A., Voronkov, A. (eds.) LPAR 2013. LNCS, vol. 8312, pp. 668–682. Springer, Heidelberg (2013). https://doi.org/10.1007/978-3-642-45221-5_44
38. Vardi, M.Y.: Automatic verification of probabilistic concurrent finite-state programs. In: FOCS 1985, pp. 327–338. IEEE Computer Society (1985)

# Deciding Fast Termination for Probabilistic VASS with Nondeterminism

Tomáš Brázdil[1], Krishnendu Chatterjee[2], Antonín Kučera[1], Petr Novotný[1], and Dominik Velan[1](✉)

[1] Faculty of Informatics, Masaryk University, Brno, Czech Republic
{xbrazdil,tony,petr.novotny,xvelan1}@fi.muni.cz
[2] IST Austria, Klosterneuburg, Austria
krishnendu.chatterjee@ist.ac.at

**Abstract.** A probabilistic vector addition system with states (pVASS) is a finite state Markov process augmented with non-negative integer counters that can be incremented or decremented during each state transition, blocking any behaviour that would cause a counter to decrease below zero. The pVASS can be used as abstractions of probabilistic programs with many decidable properties. The use of pVASS as abstractions requires the presence of nondeterminism in the model. In this paper, we develop techniques for checking fast termination of pVASS with nondeterminism. That is, for every initial configuration of size $n$, we consider the worst expected number of transitions needed to reach a configuration with some counter negative (the expected termination time). We show that the problem whether the asymptotic expected termination time is linear is decidable in polynomial time for a certain natural class of pVASS with nondeterminism. Furthermore, we show the following dichotomy: if the asymptotic expected termination time is not linear, then it is at least quadratic, i.e., in $\Omega(n^2)$.

**Keywords:** Angelic and demonic nondeterminism · Termination time · Probabilistic VASS

## 1 Introduction

**Probabilistic Programs and VASS.** Probabilistic systems play an important role in various areas of computing such as machine learning [26], network protocol design [25], robotics [45], privacy and security [5], and many others. For this reason, verification of probabilistic systems receives a considerable attention of the verification community. As in the classical (non-probabilistic) setting,

Tomáš Brázdil and Antonín Kučera are supported by the Czech Science Foundation Grant No. 18-11193S. Krishnendu Chatterjee is supported by the Austrian Science Fund (FWF) NFN Grants S11407-N23 (RiSE/SHiNE). Petr Novotný and Dominik Velan are supported by the Czech Science Foundation Grant No. GJ19-15134Y. The work is also supported by the COST Action CA 16228 GAMENET.


Y.-F. Chen et al. (Eds.): ATVA 2019, LNCS 11781, pp. 462–478, 2019.
https://doi.org/10.1007/978-3-030-31784-3_27

in probabilistic verification one typically constructs a suitable abstract model over-approximating the real behaviour of the system. In the past, the verification research was focused mostly on finite-state probabilistic models [4] as well as some special infinite-state classes, such as probabilistic one-counter [11] or pushdown automata [21,24]. However, the recent proliferation of general, Turing-complete *probabilistic programming languages* (PPLs) necessitates the use of more complex models, that can encompass multiple potentially unbounded numerical variables.

In the classical setting, one of the standard formalisms used for program abstraction are *vector addition systems with states (VASS)* [32]. Intuitively, a VASS is a finite directed graph where every edge is assigned a vector of integer counter updates of a fixed dimension $d$. A *configuration* $p\mathbf{v}$ is specified by a current state $p$ and a vector of current counter values $\mathbf{v}$. The computation proceeds by moving along the edges in the graph and performing the respective updates on the counters. Since VASS themselves are not Turing-complete, they have many decidable properties, and they have been successfully used as program abstractions in termination and complexity analysis [44] as well as for reasoning about parallel programs [23,32] and parameterized systems [2,6]. Applying such an abstraction to a probabilistic program yields a *probabilistic VASS (pVASS)*, which allows for a *probabilistic choice* of a transition in some states. Moreover, during the abstraction, certain complex programming constructs such as `if-then-else` branching are replaced with *nondeterministic choice*. To ensure that the abstraction over-approximates the possible behaviour, we typically interpret the nondeterminism as *demonic*, i.e., the choice is resolved by adversarial environment. However, in certain settings it makes sense to consider *angelic nondeterminism*, to be resolved by a yet-to-be-designed controller (e.g., a scheduling mechanism in a queuing system).

**Termination Complexity.** One of the fundamental problems in program analysis is to evaluate a given program's runtime. In the classical setting, this problem emerges in various flavours, ranging from worst-case execution time-analysis [13,47] in real-time systems to obtaining bounds on the number of execution steps [27], analysing asymptotic [16], or amortized complexity [28]. VASS-based abstractions were successfully used in the latter scenario [44].

Recently, several approaches to reason about the expected runtime of probabilistic programs were developed [31,40]. The analysis is much more demanding than in the classical case. For instance, deciding whether the expected runtime is finite is harder (i.e. higher in the arithmetic hierarchy) than deciding whether a probabilistic program terminates with probability one [30]. Additional obstacle is the inherent *non-compositionality* of expected runtimes. The work [31] gives an example of two programs, $P_1$, and $P_2$, which both consist of a single loop (i.e. they have a strongly connected control flow graph) and whose expected runtime is *linear* in the magnitude of initial variable valuations; but running $P_2$ after $P_1$ yields the program $P_1; P_2$ whose expected runtime is *infinite*.

These intricacies spawn fundamental questions about probabilistic models, which we aim to address: *Is there a sufficiently powerful probabilistic formalism where a fast (i.e., linear-time) termination from an arbitrary initial configuration is decidable? Can the decision procedure proceed by analysing individual strongly-connected components and composing the results? Can we provide a lower bound on the expected runtime in the case that it is not linear?* These questions were previously considered in the non-probabilistic setting, namely in the domain of VASS [10]. In this paper, we investigate them in the probabilistic context.

**Our Setting.** We show that the above questions can be answered affirmatively in the domain in pVASS with nondeterminism, which are Markov decision processes over VASS where the nondeterministic choice is resolved either demonically (i.e. the nondeterminism tries to prolong the computation) or angelically. We consider a basic variant of VASS termination: the *zero termination*, where the computation stops when some counter becomes negative. The *termination complexity* of a given pVASS is a function $\mathcal{L}\colon \mathbb{N} \to \mathbb{N} \cup \{\infty\}$ assigning to every $n$ the maximal/minimal (in the demonic/angelic case) expected length of a computation initiated in a configuration of size $n$ (the size of $p\mathbf{v}$ is defined as the maximal component of $\mathbf{v}$), where the maximum/minimum is taken over all the strategies of the environment (we consider unrestricted, i.e., history-dependent and randomized, strategies).

**Our Results.** For *strongly connected* pVASS which contain either a demonic or an angelic non-determinism (but not both) we show that

1. The problem whether $\mathcal{L} \in \mathcal{O}(n)$ is decidable in *polynomial time.*
2. If $\mathcal{L} \notin \mathcal{O}(n)$, then $\mathcal{L} \in \Omega(n^2)$.
3. If $\mathcal{L} \notin \mathcal{O}(n)$, then for every $\varepsilon > 0$, the probability of all computations of length at least $n^{2-\varepsilon}$ converges to one as $n \to \infty$, (in the demonic case, this requires the environment to use appropriate strategies).

According to **2.**, $\mathcal{L} \notin \mathcal{O}(n)$ implies that $\mathcal{L}$ is "at least quadratic". However, **3.** does not follow from **2.** (a more detailed discussion is postponed to Sect. 3).

We also show that the above results hold in general VASS with angelic nondeterminism, while in the demonic setting they extend to a restricted class pVASS whose maximal end-component (MEC) decomposition yields a directed acyclic graph (DAG), in which case **1.** can be solved compositionally by analysing individual MECs. Finally, we show that in pVASS whose MEC-decomposition is not DAG-like, the demonic complexity *cannot* be decided by analysis of individual MECs, since such VASS can emulate the non-compositional example of [31].

The results build on analogous results for non-probabilistic VASS established in [10], combining them with a novel probabilistic analysis.

**Paper Organization.** After presenting preliminaries in Sect. 2, we focus on the demonic case which contains the main technical contributions. Subsection 3.1 provides an intuitive outline of our techniques. Subsection 3.2 develops the algorithm for proving linear termination complexity and shows its soundness (i.e. that a yes-answer indeed proves $\mathcal{L}_d(n) \in \mathcal{O}(n)$). Subsection 3.3 deals with the quadratic lower bound, showing the completeness of our algorithm, and Subsect. 3.4 discusses extension of the results to the angelic case. Finally, in Sect. 4

we extend the techniques to DAG-like VASS MDPs and discuss the difficulties arising in general VASS. Missing proofs are provided in the full version of the paper available at http://arxiv.org/abs/1907.11010.

**Related Work.** The termination problems (counter-termination, control-state termination) for classical VASS as well as the related problems of boundedness and coverability have been studied very intensively in the last decades, see, e.g., [7,20,22,38,42]. The complexity of the termination problem with fixed initial configuration is EXPSPACE complete [3,38,48]. The more general reachability problem is also decidable [33,35,39], but computationally hard [19,38]. The best known upper bound is Ackermannian [37] (see [43] for an overview of hyper-Ackermannian complexity hierarchies).

The problem of existence of infinite computations in VASS has been also studied in the literature. Polynomial-time algorithms have been presented in [14,46] using results of [34]. In the more general context of games played on VASS, even deciding the existence of infinite computation is coNP-complete [14,46], and various algorithmic approaches based on hyperplane-separation technique have been studied in [15,18,29].

The study on asymptotic termination complexity of non-probabilistic VASS, initiated in [10] was continued in [36], where the existence of *some* $k$ such that $\mathcal{L} \in \mathcal{O}(n^k)$ was also shown decidable in polynomial time.

Concerning expected runtime analysis, we note the work [17] which presents a sound (but incomplete) technique for obtaining near-linear asymptotic bounds on recurrence relations arising from certain types of probabilistic programs.

## 2 Preliminaries

We use $\mathbb{N}$, $\mathbb{Z}$, $\mathbb{Q}$, and $\mathbb{R}$ to denote the sets of non-negative integers, integers, rational numbers, and real numbers. Given a function $f\colon \mathbb{N} \to \mathbb{N}$, we use $\mathcal{O}(f(n))$ and $\Omega(f(n))$ to denote the sets of all $g\colon \mathbb{N} \to \mathbb{N}$ such that $g(n) \leq a \cdot f(n)$ and $g(n) \geq b \cdot f(n)$ for all sufficiently large $n \in \mathbb{N}$, where $a, b$ are some positive constants. If $h(n) \in \mathcal{O}(f(n))$ and $h(n) \in \Omega(f(n))$, we write $h(n) \in \Theta(f(n))$.

Let $A$ be a finite index set. The vectors of $\mathbb{R}^A$ are denoted by bold letters such as $\mathbf{u}, \mathbf{v}, \mathbf{z}, \ldots$. The component of $\mathbf{v}$ of index $i \in A$ is denoted by $\mathbf{v}(i)$. If the index set is of the form $A = \{1, 2, \ldots, d\}$ for some positive integer $d$, we write $\mathbb{R}^d$ instead of $\mathbb{R}^A$. For every $n \in \mathbb{N}$, we use $\mathbf{n}$ to denote the constant vector where all components are equal to $n$. The scalar product of $\mathbf{v}, \mathbf{u} \in \mathbb{R}^d$ is denoted by $\mathbf{v} \cdot \mathbf{u}$, i.e., $\mathbf{v} \cdot \mathbf{u} = \sum_{i=1}^{d} \mathbf{v}(i) \cdot \mathbf{u}(i)$. The other standard operations and relations on $\mathbb{R}$ such as $+$, $\leq$, or $<$ are extended to $\mathbb{R}^d$ in the component-wise way. In particular, $\mathbf{v} < \mathbf{u}$ if $\mathbf{v}(i) < \mathbf{u}(i)$ for every index $i$.

### 2.1 Markov Decision Processes

**Definition 1.** *Let $L$ be a set of* labels. *A* Markov decision process (MDP) *with $L$-labeled transitions is a tuple $\mathcal{A} = (Q, (Q_n, Q_p), T, P)$, where $Q \neq \emptyset$ is a finite set of* states *split into two disjoint subsets $Q_n$ and $Q_p$ of* nondeterministic *and* probabilistic *states,* $T \subseteq Q \times L \times Q$ *is a finite set of* labeled transitions *such that every* $q \in Q$ *has at least one outgoing transition, and* $P$ *is a function assigning to each* $(p, \ell, q) \in T$ *where* $p \in Q_p$ *a positive rational probability so that, for every* $p \in Q_p$, $\sum_{(p,\ell,q) \in T} P(p, \ell, q) = 1$.

A state $q$ is an *immediate successor* of a state $p$ if there is a transition $(p, \ell, q)$ for some $\ell \in L$. A *finite path* in $\mathcal{A}$ of length $n$ is a finite sequence of the form $p_0, \ell_1, p_1, \ell_2, p_2, \ldots, \ell_n, p_n$ where $n \geq 0$ and $(p_i, \ell_{i+1}, p_{i+1}) \in T$ for all $0 \leq i < n$. If $n \geq 1$ and $p_0 = p_n$, then $\pi$ is a *cycle.* An MDP is *strongly connected* if for each pair of distinct states $p, q$ there is a finite path from $p$ to $q$. An *infinite path* in $\mathcal{A}$ is an infinite sequence $p_0, \ell_1, p_1, \ell_2, p_2, \ldots$ such that $p_0, \ell_1, p_1, \ldots, \ell_n, p_n$ is a finite path for every $n \geq 0$. For a finite sequence of the form $\pi = p_0, \ell_1, p_1, \ell_2, p_2, \ldots, \ell_n, p_n$ and a finite or infinite sequence of the form $\varrho = q_0, \kappa_1, q_1, \kappa_2, \ldots$, where $\pi$ and $\varrho$ are not necessarily paths in $\mathcal{A}$, we use $\pi \odot \varrho$ to denote the *concatenated sequence* $p_0, \ell_1, \ldots, \ell_n, p_n, \kappa_1, q_1, \kappa_2, \ldots$ (we do not require $p_n = q_0$). If $\pi, \varrho$ are both paths in $\mathcal{A}$ and $p_n = q_0$, then $\pi \odot \varrho$ is also a path in $\mathcal{A}$.

A *strategy* is a function $\sigma$ assigning to every finite path $p_0, \ell_1, p_1, \ldots, \ell_n, p_n$ ending in a nondeterministic state a probability distribution over the outgoing transitions of $p_n$. A strategy is *Markovian (M)* if it depends only on the last state $p_n$, and *deterministic (D)* if it always selects some successor state with probability one. The set of all strategies is denoted by $\Sigma$ (the underlying $\mathcal{A}$ is always clearly determined by the context). Every initial state $p \in Q$ and every strategy $\sigma$ determine the probability space over infinite paths initiated in $p$ in the standard way, and we use $\mathcal{P}_p^\sigma$ to denote the associated probability measure.

## 2.2 Probabilistic VASS with Nondeterminism

**Definition 2.** *Let* $d \in \mathbb{N}$. *A* $d$-dimensional probabilistic VASS with non-determinism (VASS MDP) *is an MDP where the set of labels is* $\mathbb{Z}^d$.

Let $\mathcal{A} = (Q, (Q_n, Q_p), T, P)$ be a $d$-dimensional VASS MDP. The encoding size of $\mathcal{A}$ is denoted by $\|\mathcal{A}\|$, where the integers representing counter updates are written in binary. A *configuration* of $\mathcal{A}$ is a pair $p\mathbf{v}$, where $p \in Q$ and $\mathbf{v} \in \mathbb{Z}^d$. If some component of $\mathbf{v}$ is negative, then $p\mathbf{v}$ is *terminal.* The set of all configurations of $\mathcal{A}$ is denoted by $C(\mathcal{A})$. The *size* of $p\mathbf{v} \in C(\mathcal{A})$ is $\|p\mathbf{v}\| = \|\mathbf{v}\| = \max\{|\mathbf{v}(i)| : 1 \leq i \leq d\}$. Given $n \in \mathbb{N}$, we say that $p\mathbf{v}$ is $n$*-bounded* if $\|p\mathbf{v}\| \leq n$.

Every (finite or infinite) path $p_0, \mathbf{u}_1, p_1, \mathbf{u}_2, p_2, \ldots$ and every initial vector $\mathbf{v} \in \mathbb{Z}^d$ determine the corresponding *computation* of $\mathcal{A}$, i.e., the sequence of configurations $p_0\mathbf{v}_0, p_1\mathbf{v}_1, p_2\mathbf{v}_2, \ldots$ such that $\mathbf{v}_0 = \mathbf{v}$ and $\mathbf{v}_{i+1} = \mathbf{v}_i + \mathbf{u}_{i+1}$. For every *infinite* computation $\pi = p_0\mathbf{v}_0, p_1\mathbf{v}_1, p_2\mathbf{v}_2, \ldots$, let $\mathit{Term}(\pi)$ be the least $j$ such that $p_j\mathbf{v}_j$ is terminal. If there is no such $j$, we put $\mathit{Term}(\pi) = \infty$ .

Recall that every strategy $\sigma$ and every $p \in Q$ determine a probability space over infinite paths initiated in $p$ with probability measure $\mathcal{P}_p^\sigma$. Similarly, $\sigma$ determines the unique probability space over all *computations* initiated in a given $p\mathbf{v}$, and we use $\mathcal{P}_{p\mathbf{v}}^\sigma$ to denote the associated probability measure, and $\mathbb{E}_{p\mathbf{v}}^\sigma[\mathit{Term}]$ denotes the expected value of *Term*.

The *angelic/demonic termination complexity* of $\mathcal{A}$ are the functions $\mathcal{L}_a, \mathcal{L}_d \colon \mathbb{N} \to \mathbb{R} \cup \{\infty\}$ defined as follows, where $C_n(\mathcal{A})$ is the set of all $p\mathbf{v} \in C(\mathcal{A})$ such that $\|p\mathbf{v}\| = n$:

$$\mathcal{L}_a(n) = \max_{p\mathbf{v} \in C_n(\mathcal{A})} \inf_{\sigma \in \Sigma} \mathbb{E}^{\sigma}_{p\mathbf{v}}[Term],$$
$$\mathcal{L}_d(n) = \max_{p\mathbf{v} \in C_n(\mathcal{A})} \sup_{\sigma \in \Sigma} \mathbb{E}^{\sigma}_{p\mathbf{v}}[Term].$$

We say that the expected angelic/demonic termination time of $\mathcal{A}$ is *linear* if $\mathcal{L}_a(n) \in \mathcal{O}(n)$ and $\mathcal{L}_d(n) \in \mathcal{O}(n)$, respectively.

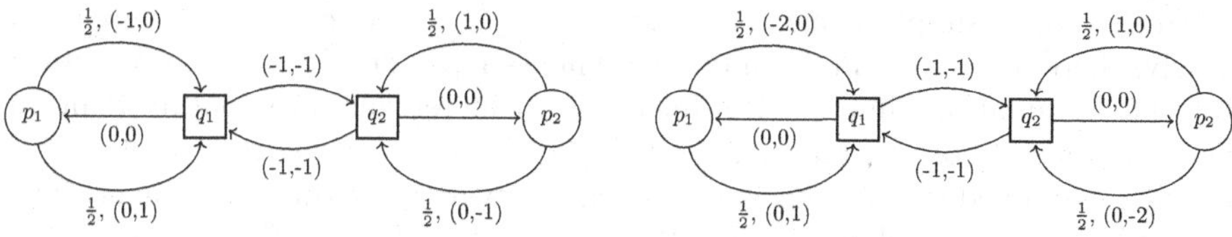


**Fig. 1.** VASS MDP $\mathcal{A}_1$ (left) and $\mathcal{A}_2$ (right). The states $p_1, p_2$ are probabilistic, and the states $q_1, q_2$ are nondeterministic.

## 3 Linearity of Demonic Termination Time

In this paper, we prove the following theorem:

**Theorem 1.** *The problem whether the expected termination time of a given strongly connected VASS MDP $\mathcal{A}$ is linear is decidable in polynomial time. If the expected termination time of $\mathcal{A}$ is* not *linear, then $\mathcal{L}_d(n) \in \Omega(n^2)$. Furthermore, for every $\varepsilon > 0$ we have that*

$$\lim_{n \to \infty} \sup_{p \in Q, \sigma \in \Sigma} \{\mathcal{P}^{\sigma}_{p\mathbf{n}}[Term \geq n^{2-\varepsilon}]\} = 1$$

The last part of Theorem 1 deserves some comments. Recall $\mathcal{L}_d(n) \in \Omega(n^2)$ if there is $b > 0$ such that $\mathcal{L}_d(n) \geq b \cdot n^2$ for all sufficiently large $n$. We prove $\mathcal{L}_d(n) \in \Omega(n^2)$ by showing the existence of $\delta, c > 0$ such that $\mathcal{P}^{\sigma}_{p\mathbf{n}}[Term \geq n^2/c] \geq \delta$ for all sufficiently large $n$, where $\sigma$ is a suitable strategy depending on $p\mathbf{n}$ (then, we can put $b = \delta/c$). Hence, $\mathcal{L}_d(n) \in \Omega(n^2)$ does *not* imply that $\sup_{\sigma \in \Sigma, p \in Q} \{\mathcal{P}^{\sigma}_{p\mathbf{n}}[Term \geq n^2/c]\}$ converges to 1 as $n \to \infty$ (for some constant $c$). The last part of Theorem 1 shows that for an arbitrarily small $\varepsilon > 0$, we have that $\sup_{\sigma \in \Sigma, p \in Q} \{\mathcal{P}^{\sigma}_{p\mathbf{n}}[Term \geq n^{2-\varepsilon}]\}$ *does* converge to 1 as $n \to \infty$. The question whether the convergence holds for $\varepsilon = 0$ remains open.

### 3.1 Outline of Techniques

The proof of Theorem 1 is non-trivial, and it is based on combining the existing techniques with new analysis invented in this paper. We use VASS MDPs $\mathcal{A}_1$ and $\mathcal{A}_2$ of Fig. 1 as running examples to illustrate our techniques.

A polynomial-time algorithm deciding asymptotic linearity of termination time for *purely non-deterministic* VASS (where the set $Q_p$ is empty) was given in [10]. Theorem 1 generalizes this result to VASS MDPs. We start by recalling the results of [10] and sketching the main ideas behind the proof of Theorem 1. These ideas are then elaborated in subsequent sections.

Consider a purely non-deterministic VASS $\mathcal{A}$ of dimension $d$. A cycle $p_0, \mathbf{u}_1, p_1, \ldots, \mathbf{u}_n, p_n$ of $\mathcal{A}$ is *simple* if all $p_1, \ldots, p_{n-1}$ are pairwise different. The total effect of a simple cycle, i.e., the sum $\sum_{i=1}^{n} \mathbf{u}_i$, is called an *increment*. Clearly, there are only finitely many increments $\mathbf{i}_1, \ldots, \mathbf{i}_k$. In [10], it was shown that the termination time of $\mathcal{A}$ is linear iff all increments are contained in an open half-space whose normal $\mathbf{w}$ is strictly positive in every component. The "if" direction is immediate, relying on a straightforward "ranking" argument. The "only if" part is more elaborate. In [10], it was shown that if the increments are *not* contained in an open half-space with positive normal, then for all sufficiently large $n$, there is a non-terminating computation initiated in $p\mathbf{n}$ whose length is at least $n^2/c$ for some constant $c$. This computation consists of simple cycles and auxiliary short paths used to "switch" from one control state to another.

Now let $\mathcal{A}$ be a VASS MDP with $d$ counters. Here, instead of simple cycles and their increments, we use the vectors of *expected counter changes per transition induced by MD strategies in their BSCCs.* More precisely, for each of the finitely many MD strategies $\sigma$ and every BSCC $\mathcal{B}$ of the finite-state Markov chain $\mathcal{A}_\sigma$ obtained by "applying" $\sigma$ to $\mathcal{A}$, we consider the unique vector $\mathbf{i}$ of expected counter changes per transition (note that $\mathbf{i}$ is the same for almost all infinite computations initiated in a state of $\mathcal{B}$). Thus, we obtain a finite set of vectors $\mathbf{i}_1, \ldots, \mathbf{i}_k$ together with the associated set of tuples $(\sigma_1, \mathcal{B}_1), \ldots, (\sigma_k, \mathcal{B}_k)$ where each $\sigma_i$ is an MD strategy and $\mathcal{B}_i$ is a BSCC of $\sigma_i$ (note that we can have $\sigma_i = \sigma_j$ for $i \neq j$ since MD strategies might have multiple BSCCs). Similarly as in [10], we check whether all $\mathbf{i}_1, \ldots, \mathbf{i}_k$ are contained in an open half-space whose normal $\mathbf{w}$ is strictly positive in every component. This is achievable in polynomial time by using the results of [8]. If such a $\mathbf{w}$ exists, we can conclude $\mathcal{L}_d(n) \in \mathcal{O}(n)$. This is because the "extremal" vectors of expected counter changes per transition are obtained by MD strategies[1], and hence the expected shift in the direction opposite to $\mathbf{w}$ per transition stays bounded away from zero even for general strategies. We than use a submartingale-based argument to show that the expected termination time is linear. This proves the first part of Theorem 1.

*Example 1.* For the VASS MDP $\mathcal{A}_2$ of Fig. 1, there are three different increments $\mathbf{i}_1 = (-1, \frac{1}{2})$, $\mathbf{i}_2 = (\frac{1}{2}, -1)$, and $\mathbf{i}_3 = (-1, -1)$. Hence, we can choose $\mathbf{w} = (1, 1)$ as a positive normal satisfying $\mathbf{i}_1 \cdot \mathbf{w} < 0$, $\mathbf{i}_2 \cdot \mathbf{w} < 0$, and $\mathbf{i}_3 \cdot \mathbf{w} < 0$. For

[1] Here we rely on well-known results about finite-state MDPs [41].

the VASS MDP $\mathcal{A}_1$ of Fig. 1, there are three different increments $\mathbf{i}_1 = (-\frac{1}{2}, \frac{1}{2})$, $\mathbf{i}_2 = (\frac{1}{2}, -\frac{1}{2})$, and $\mathbf{i}_3 = (-1, -1)$, hence no positive normal $\mathbf{w}$ satisfying $\mathbf{i}_1 \cdot \mathbf{w} < 0$ and $\mathbf{i}_2 \cdot \mathbf{w} < 0$ exists.

Now suppose there is no such $\mathbf{w}$. Recall that for *purely non-deterministic VASS*, a sufficiently long non-terminating computation initiated in $p\mathbf{n}$ consisting of simple cycles and short "switching" paths was constructed in [10]. Since $\mathbf{i}_1, \ldots, \mathbf{i}_k$ are no longer effects of simple cycles or any fixed finite executions, it is not immediately clear how to proceed and we need to use new techniques. The arguments of [10] used to construct a sufficiently long non-terminating computation are *purely geometric*, and they do not depend on the fact that increments are total effects of simple cycles. Hence, by using the same construction, we obtain a sufficiently long sequence of vectors consisting of $\mathbf{i}_1, \ldots, \mathbf{i}_k$ and some auxiliary elements representing switches between control states. We call this sequence a *scheme*, because it does not correspond to any real computation of $\mathcal{A}$ in general. When the constructed scheme is initiated in $p\mathbf{n}$, the resulting trajectory never crosses any axis. Also note that for every fixed $r \in \mathbb{N}$, we can create an extra $(r-1) \cdot n$ space between the trajectory and the axes by shifting the initial point from $p\mathbf{n}$ to $p(r \cdot \mathbf{n})$, which does not influence our asymptotic bounds. Now, we analyze what happens if the constructed scheme is *followed* from $p(r \cdot \mathbf{n})$. Here, following a vector $\mathbf{i}_j$ means to execute the transition selected by $\sigma_j$, and following a "switch" from $p$ to $q$ means to execute a strategy which eventually reaches $q$ with probability one (we use a strategy minimizing the expected number steps needed to reach $q$). Using concentration bounds of martingale theory, we show that the probability of all executions deviating from the scheme by more than $r \cdot n$ is bounded by $1 - \delta$ for some fixed $\delta > 0$ (assuming $n$ is sufficiently large), which yields the $\mathcal{L}_d(n) \in \Omega(n^2)$ lower bound of Theorem 1. The last part of Theorem 1 is proven by a more detailed analysis of the established bounds.

Let us note that the underlying martingale analysis is not immediate, since the previous work which provides the basis for this analysis (such as [11]) typically assume that the analysed strategies are memoryless in the underlying finite state space. In contrast, strategies arising of schemes are composed of multiple memoryless strategies, with the switching rules depending on the size of the initial configuration. Hence, we take a compositional approach, analysing each constituent strategy separately using known techniques and composing the results via a new approach.

### 3.2 The Algorithm

In this section we prove the first part of Theorem 1. Our analysis uses results on *multi-mean-payoff* MDPs. Recall that if $\mathcal{M}$ is an MDP with transitions labelled by elements of $\mathbb{R}^d$ (for some dimension $d$), then a *mean-payoff* of an infinite path $\pi = p_0, \mathbf{u}_1, p_1, \mathbf{u}_2, \ldots$ of $\mathcal{A}$ is $\mathrm{MP}(\pi) = \liminf_{n \to \infty} \frac{1}{n} \sum_{i=1}^{n} \mathbf{u}_i$. We say that a given vector $\mathbf{v}$ is *achievable* for $\mathcal{A}$ if there exist a strategy $\sigma$ and $p \in Q$ such that $\mathbb{E}_p^\sigma[\mathrm{MP}] \geq \mathbf{v}$. Now we recall some results on mean-payoff MDPs [8] used as tools in this section.

(a) There is a finite set $\mathcal{R}$ of vectors such that the set of all achievable vectors is precisely the set of all $\mathbf{v}$ such that $\mathbf{v} \leq \mathbf{u}$ for some $\mathbf{u} \in \mathcal{R}^*$, where $\mathcal{R}^*$ is the convex hull of $\mathcal{R}$.
(b) The problem whether a given rational $\mathbf{v}$ is achievable is decidable in polynomial time.

Furthermore, we need the following result about finite-state MDPs.

**Lemma 1.** *Let $\mathcal{M} = (Q, (Q_n, Q_p), T, P)$ be a strongly connected MDP with labels from $\mathbb{Q}$ such that*

$$\sup \{\mathbb{E}_p^\sigma[\mathrm{MP}] \mid \sigma \in \Sigma, p \in Q\} \;=\; \kappa \;<\; 0$$

*Let Dec be a function assigning to every infinite path $\pi = p_0, u_1, p_1, u_2, \ldots$ of $\mathcal{M}$ the least $m$ such that $\sum_{i=1}^{m} u_i \leq -1$. If there is no such $m$, then $Dec(\pi) = \infty$. Then there exists a constant $c$ depending only on $\mathcal{M}$ such that for every $p \in Q$ and $\sigma \in \Sigma$ we have that $\mathbb{E}_p^\sigma[Dec] \leq c$.*

Now we show how to prove the first part of Theorem 1 using the results above. Let $\mathcal{A} = (Q, (Q_n, Q_p), T, P)$ be a strongly connected VASS MDP. For each of the finitely many MD strategies $\sigma$ we can consider a finite-state Markov chain $\mathcal{A}_\sigma$ obtained from $\mathcal{A}$ by fixing in every $q \in Q_n$ the probability of transitioning to the unique successor specified by $\sigma(q)$ to 1. For each such $\mathcal{A}_\sigma$ and each its BSCC $\mathcal{B}$ we consider the unique vector $\mathbf{i}$ defined by

$$\mathbf{i} \;=\; \sum_{p \in \mathcal{B},\; p \xrightarrow{\mathbf{u}} q} \eta(p) \cdot P(p \xrightarrow{\mathbf{u}} q) \cdot \mathbf{u}$$

where $\eta$ is the invariant (stationary) distribution over the states of $\mathcal{B}$ (note that $\mathbf{i} = \mathbb{E}_p^\sigma[\mathrm{MP}]$ for every $p \in \mathcal{B}$). Thus, we obtain a finite set of *increments* $\mathbf{i}_1, \ldots, \mathbf{i}_k$ together with the associated MD strategies $\sigma_1, \ldots, \sigma_k$ and the BSCCs $\mathcal{B}_1, \ldots, \mathcal{B}_k$.

**Lemma 2.** *If there exists a vector $\mathbf{w} > \mathbf{0}$ such that $\mathbf{i}_j \cdot \mathbf{w} < 0$ for every $1 \leq j \leq k$, then there exists $\kappa < 0$ such that $\mathbf{w} \cdot \mathbb{E}_p^\sigma[\mathrm{MP}] \leq \kappa$ for every $p \in Q$ and $\sigma \in \Sigma$.*

*Proof.* Let $\kappa = \max\{\mathbf{i}_j \cdot \mathbf{w} \mid 1 \leq j \leq k\}$. Consider a $\mathbb{Q}$-labelled MDP $\mathcal{M}$ obtained from $\mathcal{A}$ by replacing each counter update vector $\mathbf{u}$ with the number $\mathbf{u} \cdot \mathbf{w}$. Note that every strategy $\sigma$ for $\mathcal{A}$ can be seen as a strategy for $\mathcal{M}$, and vice versa. For a given $\sigma \in \Sigma$, we write $\mathbb{E}_p^{\sigma,\mathcal{A}}[\mathrm{MP}]$ and $\mathbb{E}_p^{\sigma,\mathcal{M}}[\mathrm{MP}]$ to denote the expected value of MP in $\mathcal{A}$ and $\mathcal{M}$, respectively. Note that for every $\sigma \in \Sigma$ we have that $\mathbb{E}_p^{\sigma,\mathcal{M}}[\mathrm{MP}] = \mathbf{w} \cdot \mathbb{E}_p^{\sigma,\mathcal{A}}[\mathrm{MP}]$.

For every $p \in Q$, there is an optimal MD strategy $\hat{\sigma}$ maximizing the expected mean payoff in $\mathcal{M}$. Since $\mathbb{E}_p^{\hat{\sigma},\mathcal{M}}[\mathrm{MP}]$ is a convex combination of increments, we obtain $\mathbb{E}_p^{\hat{\sigma},\mathcal{M}}[\mathrm{MP}] \leq \kappa$. Now let $\sigma$ be an arbitrary strategy. Since $\mathbb{E}_p^{\sigma,\mathcal{M}}[\mathrm{MP}] \leq \mathbb{E}_p^{\hat{\sigma}}[\mathrm{MP}] \leq \kappa$, we obtain $\mathbb{E}_p^{\sigma,\mathcal{M}}[\mathrm{MP}] = \mathbf{w} \cdot \mathbb{E}_p^{\sigma,\mathcal{A}}[\mathrm{MP}] \leq \kappa$. □

A direct corollary to Lemmas 1 and 2 is the following:

**Lemma 3.** *If there exists a vector* $\mathbf{w} > \mathbf{0}$ *such that* $\mathbf{i}_j \cdot \mathbf{w} < 0$ *for every* $1 \le j \le k$, *then* $\mathcal{L}_d(n) \in \mathcal{O}(n)$ *holds for* $\mathcal{A}$.

The next lemma leads to a sound algorithm for proving of linear termination complexity.

**Lemma 4.** *The vector* $\mathbf{0}$ *is achievable for* $\mathcal{A}$ *iff there is no* $\mathbf{w} > \mathbf{0}$ *such that* $\mathbf{i}_j \cdot \mathbf{w} < 0$ *for every* $1 \le j \le k$.

*Proof.* If $\mathbf{0}$ is achievable, there exist $\sigma \in \Sigma$ and $p \in Q$ such that $\mathbb{E}_p^\sigma[\mathrm{MP}] \ge \mathbf{0}$. Suppose there is $\mathbf{w} > \mathbf{0}$ such that $\mathbf{i}_j \cdot \mathbf{w} < 0$ for every $1 \le j \le k$. By Lemma 2, $\mathbb{E}_p^\sigma[\mathrm{MP}] \cdot \mathbf{w} < 0$, which is a contradiction.

Now suppose $\mathbf{0}$ is not achievable. Consider the (convex and compact) set $\mathcal{R}^*$ of claim (a). Since $\mathbf{0}$ is not achievable, the set $\mathcal{R}^*$ has the empty intersection with the (convex) set of all vectors with non-negative components. By the hyperplane separation theorem, there exists a hyperplane with normal $\mathbf{w} > \mathbf{0}$ such that $\mathbf{v} \cdot \mathbf{w} < 0$ for all $\mathbf{v} \in \mathcal{R}^*$. Since every increment $\mathbf{i}$ is achievable, there is $\mathbf{v} \in \mathcal{R}^*$ such that $\mathbf{i} \le \mathbf{v}$. Hence, $\mathbf{i} \cdot \mathbf{w} < 0$. □

Hence, to check linear termination complexity, our algorithm simply checks whether $\mathbf{0}$ is achievable for $\mathcal{A}$. The previous lemma shows that this approach is sound. In the next subsection, we show that if there is no $\mathbf{w} > \mathbf{0}$ such that $\mathbf{i}_j \cdot \mathbf{w} < 0$ for every $1 \le j \le k$, then the expected termination time of $\mathcal{A}$ is at least quadratic. This shows that our algorithm is also complete, i.e. a decision procedure for linear termination of strongly connected demonic VASS MDPs.

### 3.3 Quadratic Lower Bound

For the rest of this section, we fix a strongly connected VASS MDP $\mathcal{A} = (Q, (Q_n, Q_p), T, P)$. Let $\mathbf{i}_1, \ldots, \mathbf{i}_k$ be the increments, and $\sigma_1, \ldots, \sigma_k$ and $\mathcal{B}_1, \ldots, \mathcal{B}_k$ the associated MD strategies and BSCCs introduced in Sect. 3.2.

Suppose that there does *not* exist a normal vector $\mathbf{w} > \mathbf{0}$ such that $\mathbf{i}_i \cdot \mathbf{w} < 0$ for every $1 \le i \le k$. By [10, Lemma 3.2][2], there exist a subset of increments $\mathbf{j}_1, \ldots, \mathbf{j}_\ell$ and positive integer coefficients $a_1, \ldots, a_\ell$ such that $\sum_{i=1}^{\ell} a_i \mathbf{j}_i \ge \mathbf{0}$. We use this subset to construct a so-called *scheme*.

**Scheme.** The definition of a scheme is parameterized by a certain function $L : \mathbb{N} \to \mathbb{N}$. This function is defined later, for now it suffices to know that $L(n) \in \Theta(n)$. For every $n \in \mathbb{N}$, we define the *scheme for* $n$, which is a concatenation of $L(n)$ identical $n$-*cycles*, where each $n$-cycle is defined as follows:

$$\underbrace{\mathbf{j}_1, \ldots, \mathbf{j}_1}_{L(n)\cdot a_1}, s_1, \underbrace{\mathbf{j}_2, \ldots, \mathbf{j}_2}_{L(n)\cdot a_2}, s_2, \quad \cdots \quad , \underbrace{\mathbf{j}_\ell, \ldots, \mathbf{j}_\ell}_{L(n)\cdot a_\ell}, s_\ell$$

[2] Technically, Lemma 3.2 in [10] assumes $\mathbf{i}_j \in \mathbb{Z}^d$ for every $1 \le j \le k$. Here, $\mathbf{i}_j \in \mathbb{Q}^d$. We can multiply all increments of by the least common multiple of all denominators and apply Lemma 3.2 afterwards.

The subsequence $\mathbf{j}_i, \ldots, \mathbf{j}_i, s_i$ of the $j$-th cycle is called the *i-th segment* of the $j$-th $n$-cycle. Since the length of each $n$-cycle is $\Theta(n)$, the length of the scheme for $n$ is $\Theta(n^2)$.

*Example 2.* Recall the VASS MDP $\mathcal{A}_1$ of Fig. 1. Here, we put $\mathbf{j}_1 = (-\frac{1}{2}, \frac{1}{2})$, $\mathbf{j}_2 = (\frac{1}{2}, -\frac{1}{2})$, and $a_1 = a_2 = 1$. So, the cycle for $n$ is

$$\underbrace{(-\tfrac{1}{2}, \tfrac{1}{2}), \ldots, (-\tfrac{1}{2}, \tfrac{1}{2})}_{L(n)}, s_1, \underbrace{(\tfrac{1}{2}, -\tfrac{1}{2}), \ldots, (\tfrac{1}{2}, -\tfrac{1}{2})}_{L(n)}, s_2$$

Note that the scheme does *not* necessarily correspond to any finite path in $\mathcal{A}$, even if the switches are disregarded. However, the scheme for $n$ determines a unique strategy $\eta_n$ for $\mathcal{A}$ defined below.

**From Schemes to Strategies.** For every $p \in Q$, we fix an MD strategy $\gamma_p$ such that for every $q \in Q$, the $\mathcal{P}_q^{\gamma_p}$ probability of visiting $p$ from $q$ is equal to one. Furthermore, we fix some state $p_i \in \mathcal{B}_i$ for every $1 \leq i \leq \ell$.

For all finite paths that are *not* initiated in $p_1$, the strategy $\eta_n$ is defined arbitrarily. Otherwise, $\eta_n$ starts by simulating the strategy $\sigma_1$ for precisely $L(n) \cdot a_1$ steps. Then, $\eta_n$ remembers the state $q_1^1$ in which the simulation of $\sigma_1$ ended, and changes to simulating $\gamma_{p_2}$ until the state $p_2$ of $\mathcal{B}_2$ is reached. After reaching $p_2$, the strategy $\eta_n$ simulates $\sigma_2$ for precisely $L(n) \cdot a_2$ steps. Then, it again remembers the final state $q_2^1$ and starts to simulate $\gamma_{p_3}$ until $p_3$ is reached, and so on, until the simulation of $\sigma_\ell$ corresponding to the $\ell$-th segment of the first $n$-cycle is completed. Then, $\eta_n$ starts to simulate the switch $s_\ell$ of the first $n$-cycle, i.e., the strategy $\gamma_{q_1^1}$. This completes the simulation of the first $n$-cycle. In general, the $j$-th $n$-cycle (for $2 \leq j \leq L(n)$) is simulated in the same way, the only difference is that every switch $s_i$ is simulated by $\gamma_{q_i^{j-1}}$ where $q_i^{j-1}$ is the state entered when terminating the simulation of $\sigma_{(i+1) \bmod \ell}$ in the $(j-1)$-th $n$-cycle. This goes on until all $n$-cycles of the scheme are simulated. After that, $\eta_n$ behaves arbitrarily.

**Lower Bound.** We now show that the family of strategies $\{\eta_n \mid n \in \mathbb{N}\}$ witnesses the quadratic complexity. First we define $L(n)$. From standard results on MDPs [41] we know that for every $p$, the expected number of steps we keep playing $\gamma_p$ before hitting $p$ is finite and dependent only on $\mathcal{A}$. Hence, there exists a constant $\xi$ depending only on $\mathcal{A}$ such that also the expected change of every counter incurred while simulating $\gamma_p$ is bounded by $\xi$. Now let $\min_{\mathcal{A}} = \min\{\mathbf{u}(i) \mid (p, \mathbf{u}, q) \in T\}$, i.e., $\min_{\mathcal{A}}$ is the minimal counter update over all transitions, and let

$$L(n) = \lfloor n \,/\, (\ell \cdot \xi - \sum_{j=1}^{\ell} a_j \cdot \min_{\mathcal{A}} + 1) \rfloor.$$

The function $L(n)$ has been chosen so that, for all sufficiently large $n$, if the scheme for $n$ is "executed" from the point $\mathbf{n}$, i.e., if we follow the vectors of the scheme, where each switch is replaced with the vector $(\xi, \ldots, \xi)$, then the resulting *trajectory* never crosses any axis (recall that $\sum_{i=1}^{\ell} a_i \mathbf{j}_i \geq \mathbf{0}$).

*Example 3.* A trajectory for the scheme of Example 2 is shown in Fig. 2. Here, $\xi = -1$, because performing every switch takes just one transition with expected change of the counters equal to $(-1, -1)$.

**Definition 3.** *Let $\pi = p_0, \mathbf{u}_1, p_1, \mathbf{u}_2, \ldots, p_j$ be a finite alternating sequence of states and vectors of $\mathbb{Q}^d$ (not necessarily a finite path in $\mathcal{A}$), and $m \in \mathbb{N}$. We say that $\pi$ is $m$-*safe *if, for every $1 \leq i \leq j$, we have that $\sum_{k=1}^{i} \mathbf{u}_k \geq -\mathbf{m}$. Furthermore, we say that an infinite sequence $\pi = p_0, \mathbf{u}_1, p_1, \mathbf{u}_2, \ldots$ is $m$* safe-until *$k$ if its prefix $p_0, \mathbf{u}_1, p_1, \mathbf{u}_2, \ldots, p_k$ is $m$-safe.*

Now consider an infinite path $\pi = q_0, \mathbf{u}_1, q_1, \mathbf{u}_2, \ldots$ in $\mathcal{A}$ initiated in $p_1$. Then almost all such $\pi$'s (w.r.t. the probability measure $\mathcal{P}_{p_1}^{\eta_n}$) can be split into a concatenation of sub-paths

$$\pi_1^1, \tau_1^1, \ldots, \pi_\ell^1, \tau_\ell^1, \pi_1^2, \tau_1^2, \ldots, \pi_\ell^2, \tau_\ell^2, \ldots \quad \ldots \pi_1^{L(n)}, \tau_1^{L(n)}, \ldots, \pi_\ell^{L(n)}, \tau_\ell^{L(n)}, \hat{\pi}$$

where $\pi_i^j$ is a path with precisely $L(n) \cdot a_i$ transitions (resulting from simulation of $\sigma_i$), $\tau_i^j$ is a *switching* path performing the switch $s_i$ of the $j$-th cycle, and $\hat{\pi}$ is the remaining infinite suffix of $\pi$. Note that for every $1 \leq i \leq \ell$, the paths $\pi_i^1, \pi_i^2, \ldots, \pi_i^{L(n)}$ can be concatenated and form a single path in $\mathcal{A}$ of length $L^2(n)$. This follows from the way of scheduling the switching strategies $\gamma_p$ in $\eta_n$. Writing $\pi = \varrho \odot \hat{\pi}$ (where $\hat{\pi}$ is the suffix of $\pi$ defined above), we denote by $SimLen(\pi)$ the length of $\varrho$. Note that $SimLen(\pi) \geq L^2(n)$ for almost all $\pi$.

We now focus on proving the following lemma:

**Lemma 5.** *For every $\delta > 0$ there exist $r, n_0 \in \mathbb{N}$ such that for all $n \geq n_0$, the $\mathcal{P}_{p_1}^{\eta_n}$ probability of all infinite paths $\pi$ initiated in $p_1$ that are $r \cdot n$-safe until $SimLen(\pi)$ is at least $1 - \delta$. Moreover, the $n_0$ is independent of $\delta$.*

The lemma guarantees that if the strategy $\eta_n$ is executed in a configuration $p_1(r \cdot \mathbf{n})$, where $n \geq n_0$, then $\mathcal{P}_{p_1(r \cdot \mathbf{n})}^{\eta_n}[Term \geq L(n)^2] \geq 1 - \delta$. This implies $\mathcal{L}(n) \in \Omega(n^2)$. Hence, it remains to prove the lemma.

**Proof of Lemma** 5. We separately bound the probabilities of "large counter deviations" while simulating the $\sigma_i$'s and the switching strategies. To this end, for every $1 \leq i \leq \ell$ let $\pi_i = p_0, \mathbf{v}_1, p_1, \mathbf{v}_2, \ldots$ be the finite path of length $L^2(n)$ obtained by concatenating all $\pi_i^1, \pi_i^2, \ldots, \pi_i^{L(n)}$. Furthermore, let $Ipath^i(\pi)$ the sequence obtained from $\pi_i$ by replacing every $\mathbf{v}_k$ with $\mathbf{v}_k - \mathbf{j}_i$. Intuitively, $Ipath^i(\pi)$ is $\pi_i$ where the transition effects are "compensated" by subtracting the expected change in the counter values per transition. We prove the following:

**Lemma 6.** *For every $\delta > 0$, there exist $c, n_0 \in \mathbb{N}$ such that for all $n \geq n_0$ it holds $\mathcal{P}_{p_1}^{\eta_n}(\{\pi \mid Ipath^i(\pi) \text{ is } c \cdot n\text{-safe}\}) \geq 1 - \delta$. Moreover, the $n_0$ does not depend on $\delta$.*

In the proof of Lemma 6, we use the martingale defined for stochastic one-counter automata in [11]. Intuitively, if $Ipath^i(\pi)$ is $n$ safe, then it must be $n$ safe in every counter. Hence, we can consider each counter one by one, abstract the other counters, and estimate the probability of being $n$ safe in each of these one-counter automata.

Similarly, we need to estimate the probability of deviating from the trajectory by performing the switches. Let $Spath(\pi)$ be the concatenation of all $\tau_i^j$ where $1 \le i \le \ell$ and $1 \le j \le L(n)$ preserving their order. We prove the following:

**Lemma 7.** *For every $\delta > 0$, there exist $c, n_0 \in \mathbb{N}$ such that for all $n \ge n_0$ it holds $\mathcal{P}_{p_1}^{\eta_n}(\{\pi \mid Spath^i(\pi) \text{ is } c{\cdot}n\text{-safe}\}) \ge 1-\delta$. Moreover, the $n_0$ does not depend on $\delta$.*

Clearly, if $Ipath^i(\pi)$ is $c_1 \cdot n$-safe for all $1 \le i \le \ell$ and $Spath(\pi)$ is $c_2 \cdot n$-safe, then $\pi$ is $(c_1 + c_2) \cdot (\ell{+}1) \cdot n$-safe until $SimLen(\pi)$. Hence, Lemma 5 is a simple consequence of Lemmas 6 and 7.

**Probability of Quadratic Behaviour.** Now we indicate how to prove the last part of Theorem 1. Directly from Lemma 5, we have that $\lim_{r\to\infty} \mathcal{P}_{p_1(r\cdot\mathbf{n})}^{\eta_n}[Term \ge L(n)^2] = 1$. However, observe that if $r$ is not a fixed constant, we cannot say that the size of the initial configuration is linear in $n$. Taking $r = n^\gamma$ for a suitable $\gamma > 0$, we may rewrite the limit in the following way: $\lim_{r\to\infty} \mathcal{P}_{p_1(r\cdot\mathbf{n})}^{\eta_n}[Term \ge L(n)^2] = \lim_{n\to\infty} \mathcal{P}_{p_1(\mathbf{n}^{1+\gamma})}^{\eta_n}[Term \ge L(n)^2] = \lim_{n\to\infty} \mathcal{P}_{p_1\mathbf{n}}^{\eta_{n^{1/(1+\gamma)}}}[Term \ge L(n^{1/(1+\gamma)})^2]$. It can be shown that $L(n^{1/(1+\gamma)})^2 > n^{2-\varepsilon}$, for every sufficiently large $n$, thus obtaining the last part of the Theorem 1.

## 3.4 Linearity of Angelic Termination Time

For angelic nondeterminism, we have a similar result as in the demonic one.

**Theorem 2.** *The problem whether the expected angelic termination time of a given strongly connected VASS MDP $\mathcal{A}$ is linear is decidable in polynomial time. If the expected angelic termination time of $\mathcal{A}$ is not linear, then $\mathcal{L}_a(n) \in \Omega(n^2)$. Furthermore, for every $\epsilon > 0$ we have that*

$$\lim_{n\to\infty} \inf_{p\in Q, \sigma\in\Sigma} \{\mathcal{P}_{p\mathbf{n}}^{\sigma}[Term \ge n^{2-\varepsilon}]\} = 1$$

*Proof (Sketch).* We analyse each counter, i.e., we consider $d$ one-dimensional VASS MDPs obtained by projecting the labelling function of $\mathcal{A}$.

If it is possible to terminate in one of these one-dimensional VASS MDPs in expected linear time, then the corresponding strategy achieves linear termination also in $\mathcal{A}$. On the other hand, if this is not possible, then every one-counter has infinite angelic termination complexity. This *does not* mean that the $\mathcal{A}$ has infinite angelic termination complexity. However, we show that there exists a constant $c > 0$ such that for sufficiently large initial configuration, the probability of runs terminating before $n^2/c$ transitions is sufficiently small for every one-counter. By union bound, the probability of runs terminating before $n^2/c$ in $\mathcal{A}$ is $1 - \delta$ for some $\delta > 0$. Thus, $\mathcal{L}_a(n) \in \Omega(n^2)$. The last part of the theorem is proved similarly to the demonic case. □

## 4 General VASS MDPs and Conclusion

We now drop the assumption that the VASS is strongly connected. Recall that an *end-component* in an MDP is a set $M$ of states that is *closed* (i.e., for $q \in Q_n \cap M$ at least one outgoing transition goes to $M$, while for $q \in Q_p \cap M$ all the outgoing transitions must end in $M$) and strongly connected. A *maximal end component (MEC)* is an EC which is not contained in any larger EC. A decomposition of an MDP into MECs can be computed in polynomial time by standard algorithms [1], and each MEC of a VASS MDP induces a strongly connected VASS sub-MDP which can be analyzed as shown in previous sections. We can construct a graph whose vertices correspond to MECs of an MDP and there is an edge from $M$ to some other $M'$ if and only if $M'$ is reachable from $M$. If the only cycles in this graph are self-loops, we say that the original MDP is *DAG-like.* MECs corresponding to "leafs" of the graph (i.e. MECs that cannot be exited) are called *bottom* MECs.

**Theorem 3.** *Theorem 1 holds also for DAG-like VASS MDPs, while Theorem 2 holds for all VASS MDPs. In particular, a DAG-like VASS MDP $\mathcal{A}$ has $\mathcal{L}_d(n) \in \mathcal{O}(n)$ if and only if each MEC of $\mathcal{A}$ induces a (strongly connected) VASS MDP in which $\mathcal{L}_d(n) \in \mathcal{O}(n)$; and $\mathcal{A}$ has $\mathcal{L}_a(n) \in \mathcal{O}(n)$ iff each bottom MEC of $\mathcal{A}$ has $\mathcal{L}_a(n) \in \mathcal{O}(n)$. Otherwise, the termination complexity of $\mathcal{A}$ is in $\Omega(n^2)$.*

*Proof (Sketch).* We sketch the proof for the demonic case where there are no self-loops in the MEC graph. Then no MEC can be re-entered once left. Moreover, there is a constant $c$ s.t. whenever we enter a MEC with a counter valuation $\mathbf{v}$, the expected time to either terminate or exit the MEC, as well as the expected size of the counter valuation at the time of termination/exiting are bounded by $c \cdot \|\mathbf{v}\|$. Hence, a straightforward induction on the number of MECs shows that the expected maximal counter value as well as the expected termination time are bounded by $c^{|Q|} \cdot n$ from any initial configuration of size $n$. Since $|Q|$ does not depend on $n$, we get the result.

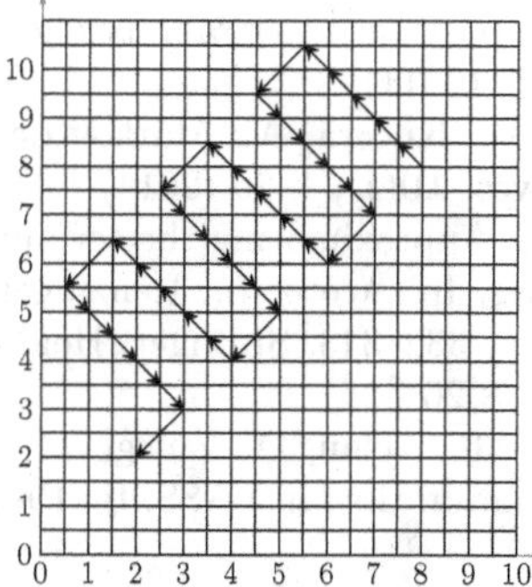

**Fig. 2.** A trajectory for the scheme of Example 2.

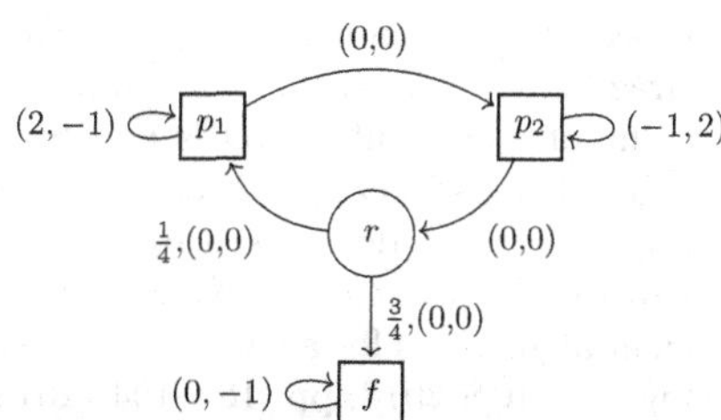


**Fig. 3.** VASS MDP with linear MECs but infinite expected termination time.

For non-DAG-like VASS MDPs, the situation gets much more complicated. Consider the MDP in Fig. 3. There are three MECs, each a singleton ($\{p_1\}$, $\{p_2\}$, $\{f\}$). Clearly all these three MECs have a linear termination complexity. Now consider the following demonic strategy starting in configuration $p_1(0, n)$: select the loop until we get the configuration $p_1(2n, 0)$; then transition to $p_2$ and play its loop until we get into $p_2(0, 4n)$; then transition to $r$ and if the randomness takes us back to $p_1$, play the loop again until we get $p_1(8n, 0)$, etc. *ad infinitum*. Clearly, the strategy eventually ends up in $f$ where it terminates. However, the expected termination time is at least $\frac{3}{4}\sum_{i=0}^{\infty}(\frac{1}{4})^i \cdot 4^{i+1} = 3\sum_{i=0}^{\infty}(\frac{4}{4})^i = \infty$.

Hence, proving the linear termination complexity in general VASS does not reduce to analysing individual MECs. Moreover, it crucially depends on the concrete probabilities in transient (non-MEC) states: in Fig. 3, the termination time would be finite (and linear) if the transition from $r$ to $f$ had probability $< \frac{1}{4}$. The transient behaviour of MDPs can be of course rather complex and it is not even clear whether the linear demonic termination complexity is even *decidable* for VASS MDPs with general structure. We see this as a very intriguing, yet complex, direction for future work.

## References

1. de Alfaro, L.: Formal verification of probabilistic systems. Phd. thesis, Stanford University, Stanford, CA, USA (1998)
2. Aminof, B., Rubin, S., Zuleger, F., Spegni, F.: Liveness of parameterized timed networks. In: Proceedings of ICALP 2015, pp. 375–387 (2015)
3. Atig, M.F., Habermehl, P.: On yen's path logic for petri nets. Int. J. Found. Comput. Sci. **22**(04), 783–799 (2011)
4. Baier, C., Katoen, J.P.: Principles of Model Checking. MIT press, Cambridge (2008)
5. Barthe, G., Gaboardi, M., Grégoire, B., Hsu, J., Strub, P.Y.: Proving differential privacy via probabilistic couplings. In: Proceedings of LICS 2016. pp. 749–758. ACM, New York (2016)
6. Bloem, R., et al.: Decidability in parameterized verification. SIGACT News **47**(2), 53–64 (2016)
7. Bozzelli, L., Ganty, P.: Complexity analysis of the backward coverability algorithm for VASS. In: Proceedings of RP 2011, pp. 96–109 (2011)
8. Brázdil, T., Brožek, V., Chatterjee, K., Forejt, V., Kučera, A.: Markov decision processes with multiple long-run average objectives. **10**(1), 1–29 (2014)
9. Brázdil, T., Brožek, V., Etessami, K., Kučera, A.: Approximating the termination value of one-counter MDPs and Stochastic games. In: Aceto, L., Henzinger, M., Sgall, J. (eds.) ICALP 2011. LNCS, vol. 6756, pp. 332–343. Springer, Heidelberg (2011). https://doi.org/10.1007/978-3-642-22012-8_26
10. Brázdil, T., Chatterjee, K., Kučera, A., Novotný, P., Velan, D., Zuleger, F.: Efficient algorithms for asymptotic bounds on termination time in VASS. In: Proceedings of LICS 2018, pp. 185–194 (2018)
11. Brázdil, T., Kiefer, S., Kučera, A.: Efficient analysis of probabilistic programs with an unbounded counter. J. ACM **61**(6) (2014)

12. Brázdil, T., Kučera, A., Novotný, P., Wojtczak, D.: Minimizing Expected termination time in one-counter Markov decision processes. In: Czumaj, A., Mehlhorn, K., Pitts, A., Wattenhofer, R. (eds.) ICALP 2012. LNCS, vol. 7392, pp. 141–152. Springer, Heidelberg (2012). https://doi.org/10.1007/978-3-642-31585-5_16
13. Cassez, F.: Timed games for computing WCET for pipelined processors with caches. In: 2011 Eleventh International Conference on Application of Concurrency to System Design, pp. 195–204, (June 2011)
14. Chatterjee, K., Doyen, L., Henzinger, T.A., Raskin, J.F.: Generalized mean-payoff and energy games. In: Proceedings of FSTTCS 2010, pp. 505–516 (2010)
15. Chatterjee, K., Velner, Y.: Hyperplane separation technique for multidimensional mean-payoff games. In: Proceedings of CONCUR 2013, pp. 500–515 (2013)
16. Chatterjee, K., Fu, H., Goharshady, A.K.: Non-polynomial worst-case analysis of recursive programs. In: Majumdar, R., Kunčak, V. (eds.) CAV 2017. LNCS, vol. 10427, pp. 41–63. Springer, Cham (2017). https://doi.org/10.1007/978-3-319-63390-9_3
17. Chatterjee, K., Fu, H., Murhekar, A.: Automated recurrence analysis for almost-linear expected-runtime bounds. In: Majumdar, R., Kunčak, V. (eds.) CAV 2017. LNCS, vol. 10426, pp. 118–139. Springer, Cham (2017). https://doi.org/10.1007/978-3-319-63387-9_6
18. Colcombet, T., Jurdzinski, M., Lazic, R., Schmitz, S.: Perfect half space games. In: Proceedings of LICS 2017, pp. 1–11 (2017)
19. Czerwinski, W., Lasota, S., Lazic, R., Leroux, J., Mazowiecki, F.: The reachability problem for petri nets is not elementary. In: Proceedings of STOC 2019, pp. 24–33 (2019)
20. Esparza, J.: Decidability and complexity of Petri net problems—an introduction. In: Reisig, W., Rozenberg, G. (eds.) ACPN 1996. LNCS, vol. 1491, pp. 374–428. Springer, Heidelberg (1998). https://doi.org/10.1007/3-540-65306-6_20
21. Esparza, J., Kučera, A., Mayr, R.: Model-checking probabilistic pushdown automata. **2**(1:2), 1–31 (2006)
22. Esparza, J., Ledesma-Garza, R., Majumdar, R., Meyer, P., Niksic, F.: An smt-based approach to coverability analysis. In: Proceedings of CAV 2014, pp. 603–619 (2014)
23. Esparza, J., Nielsen, M.: Decidability issues for petri nets - a survey. Bull. EATCS **52**, 245–262 (1994)
24. Etessami, K., Yannakakis, M.: Model checking of recursive probabilistic systems. ACM Trans. Comput. Log. **13**, 12 (2012)
25. Foster, N., Kozen, D., Mamouras, K., Reitblatt, M., Silva, A.: Probabilistic NetKAT. In: Thiemann, P. (ed.) ESOP 2016. LNCS, vol. 9632, pp. 282–309. Springer, Heidelberg (2016). https://doi.org/10.1007/978-3-662-49498-1_12
26. Ghahramani, Z.: Probabilistic machine learning and artificial intelligence. Nature **521**(7553), 452–459 (2015)
27. Gulwani, S., Mehra, K.K., Chilimbi, T.: Speed: precise and efficient static estimation of program computational complexity. In: Proceedings of POPL 2009. pp. 127–139. ACM, New York (2009)
28. Hoffmann, J., Aehlig, K., Hofmann, M.: Multivariate amortized resource analysis. ACM Trans. Prog. Lang. Syst. **34**(3), 14:1–14:62 (2012)
29. Jurdzinski, M., Lazic, R., Schmitz, S.: Fixed-dimensional energy games are in pseudo-polynomial time. In: Proceedings of ICALP 2015, pp. 260–272 (2015)
30. Kaminski, B.L., Katoen, J., Matheja, C.: On the hardness of analyzing probabilistic programs. Acta Inf. **56**(3), 255–285 (2019)

31. Kaminski, B.L., Katoen, J., Matheja, C., Olmedo, F.: Weakest precondition reasoning for expected runtimes of randomized algorithms. J. ACM **65**(5), 30:1–30:68 (2018)
32. Karp, R.M., Miller, R.E.: Parallel program schemata. J. Comput. Syst. Sci. **3**(2), 147–195 (1969)
33. Kosaraju, S.R.: Decidability of reachability in vector addition systems (preliminary version). In: Proceedings of STOC 1982, pp. 267–281. ACM (1982)
34. Kosaraju, S.R., Sullivan, G.F.: Detecting cycles in dynamic graphs in polynomial time. In: Proceedings of STOC 1988, pp. 398–406 (1988)
35. Leroux, J.: Vector addition system reachability problem: a short self-contained proof. In: Proceedings of POPL 2011, pp. 307–316 (2011)
36. Leroux, J.: Polynomial vector addition systems with states. In: Proceedings of ICALP 2018, vol. 107, pp. 134:1–134:13 (2018)
37. Leroux, J., Schmitz, S.: Reachability in vector addition systems is primitive-recursive in fixed dimension. In: Proceedings of LICS 2019 (2019)
38. Lipton, R.: The reachability problem requires exponential space. Technical Report 62 (1976)
39. Mayr, E.: An algorithm for the general Petri net reachability problem. SIAM J. Comput. **13**, 441–460 (1984)
40. Ngo, V.C., Carbonneaux, Q., Hoffmann, J.: Bounded expectations: Resource analysis for probabilistic programs. In: Proceedings of PLDI 2018, pp. 496–512. ACM, New York (2018)
41. Puterman, M.: Markov Decision Processes (1994)
42. Rackoff, C.: The covering and boundedness problems for vector addition systems. Theor. Comput. Sci. **6**, 223–231 (1978)
43. Schmitz, S.: Complexity hierarchies beyond elementary. ACM Trans. Comput. Theory **8**(1), 3:1–3:36 (2016)
44. Sinn, M., Zuleger, F., Veith, H.: A simple and scalable static analysis for bound analysis and amortized complexity analysis. In: Proccedings of CAV 2014, pp. 745–761 (2014)
45. Thrun, S., Burgard, W., Fox, D.: Probabilistic Robotics (Intelligent Robotics and Autonomous Agents). The MIT Press, Cambridge (2005)
46. Velner, Y., Chatterjee, K., Doyen, L., Henzinger, T.A., Rabinovich, A.M., Raskin, J.: The complexity of multi-mean-payoff and multi-energy games. Inf. Comput. **241**, 177–196 (2015)
47. Wilhelm, R., et al.: The worst-case execution-time problem—overview of methods and survey of tools. ACM Trans. Embed. Comput. Syst. **7**(3), 36:1–36:53 (2008)
48. Yen, H.C.: A unified approach for deciding the existence of certain petri net paths. Inf. Comput. **96**(1), 119–137 (1992)

# Are Parametric Markov Chains Monotonic?

Jip Spel(✉), Sebastian Junges, and Joost-Pieter Katoen

RWTH Aachen University, Aachen, Germany
jip.spel@cs.rwth-aachen.de

**Abstract.** This paper presents a simple algorithm to check whether reachability probabilities in parametric Markov chains are monotonic in (some of) the parameters. The idea is to construct—only using the graph structure of the Markov chain and local transition probabilities—a pre-order on the states. Our algorithm cheaply checks a sufficient condition for monotonicity. Experiments show that monotonicity in several benchmarks is automatically detected, and monotonicity can speed up parameter synthesis up to orders of magnitude faster than a symbolic baseline.

## 1 Introduction

Probabilistic model checking [3,35] takes as input a Markov model together with a specification typically given in a probabilistic extension of LTL or CTL. The key problem is computing the reachability probability to reach a set of target states. Efficient probabilistic model checkers include PRISM [36] and Storm [20]. A major practical obstacle is that transition probabilities need to be precisely given. Uncertainty about such quantities can be treated by specifying transition probabilities by intervals, as in interval Markov chains [11,32], or by parametric Markov chains [18], which allow for expressing complex parameter dependencies.

This paper considers parametric Markov chains (pMCs). Their transition probabilities are given by arithmetic expressions over real-valued parameters. A pMC represents an uncountably large family of Markov chains (MCs): each parameter value from the parameter space induces an MC. Reachability properties are easily lifted to pMCs; they are satisfied for a subset of the family of MCs, or equivalently, for a subset of the parameter values. Key problems are e.g., is there a parameter valuation such that a given specification $\varphi$ is satisfied (feasibility)?, do all parameter values within a given parameter region satisfy $\varphi$ (verification)?, which parameter values do satisfy $\varphi$ (synthesis)?, and for which parameter values is the probability of satisfying $\varphi$ maximal (optimal synthesis)? Applications of pMCs include model repair [5,12,13,24,40], strategy synthesis in AI models such as partially observable MDPs [34], and optimising randomised distributed algorithms [2]. PRISM and Storm, as well as dedicated tools including PARAM [27] and PROPhESY [19] support pMC analysis.

Supported by the DFG RTG 2236 "UnRAVeL".


Y.-F. Chen et al. (Eds.): ATVA 2019, LNCS 11781, pp. 479–496, 2019.
https://doi.org/10.1007/978-3-030-31784-3_28

Despite the significant progress in the last years in analysing pMCs [10,15,41], the scalability of algorithms severely lacks behind methods for ordinary MCs. There is little hope to overcome this gap. The feasibility problem for a reachability probability exceeding 1/2 is ETR-complete (thus NP-hard) [45]. Experiments show that symbolic computations rather than (floating-point) numeric computations have a major impact on analysis times [41].

This paper takes a different approach and focuses on *monotonicity*, in particular on (a) an algorithm to check whether pMCs are monotonic in (some of) the parameters with respect to reachability probabilities, and (b) on investigating to what extent monotonicity can be exploited to accelerate parameter synthesis. Monotonicity has an enormous potential to simplify pMC analysis; e.g., checking whether all points within a rectangle satisfy $\varphi$ reduces to checking whether a line fragment satisfies $\varphi$ when one parameter is monotonic. Thus, the verification problem for an $n + k$-dimensional hyper-rectangle reduces to checking an $n$-dimensional rectangle when the pMC at hand is monotonic in $k$ parameters. Similarly, determining a parameter instantiation that maximises the probability of $\varphi$ (optimal synthesis) simplifies considerably if all—just a single instance suffices—or some parameters are monotone. Similar problems at the heart of model repair [5,12,13,24,40] also substantially benefit from monotonicity.

Unfortunately, determining monotonicity is as hard as parameter synthesis. The key idea therefore is to construct—using the graph structure of the pMC and local transition probabilities—a pre-order on the states that is used to check a sufficient condition for monotonicity. The paper gradually develops a semi-decision algorithm, starting with acyclic pMCs, to the general setting with cycles. The algorithm uses assumptions indicating whether a state is below (or equivalent to) another one, and techniques are described to discharge these assumptions. Possible outcomes of our algorithms are: a pMC is monotonic increasing in a certain parameter for a given region, monotone decreasing, or unknown. Experiments with a prototypical implementation built on top of Storm show that monotonicity is detected automatically and scalable in several benchmarks from the literature. In addition, exploiting monotonicity in a state-of-the-art parameter synthesis can lead to speed-ups of up to an order of magnitude. (Proofs of our results can be found in [44].)

## 2 Preliminaries and Problem Statement

A *probability distribution* over a finite or countably infinite set $X$ is a function $\mu\colon X \to [0, 1] \subseteq \mathbb{R}$ with $\sum_{x \in X} \mu(x) = 1$. The set of all distributions on $X$ is denoted by $\mathit{Distr}(X)$. Let $\boldsymbol{a} \in \mathbb{R}^n$ denote $(a_1, \ldots, a_n)$, and $\boldsymbol{e}_i$ denote the vector with $e_j = 1$ if $i = j$ and $e_j = 0$ otherwise. The set of multivariate polynomials over ordered variables $\boldsymbol{x} = (x_1, \ldots, x_n)$ is denoted $\mathbb{Q}[\boldsymbol{x}]$. An *instantiation* for a finite set $V$ of real-valued variables is a function $u\colon V \to \mathbb{R}$. We typically denote $u$ as a vector $\boldsymbol{u} \in \mathbb{R}^n$ with $u_i := u(x_i)$. A polynomial $f$ can be interpreted as a function $f\colon \mathbb{R}^n \to \mathbb{R}$, where $f(\boldsymbol{u})$ is obtained by substitution i.e., $f[\boldsymbol{x} \leftarrow \boldsymbol{u}]$, where each occurrence of $x_i$ in $f$ is replaced by $u(x_i)$.

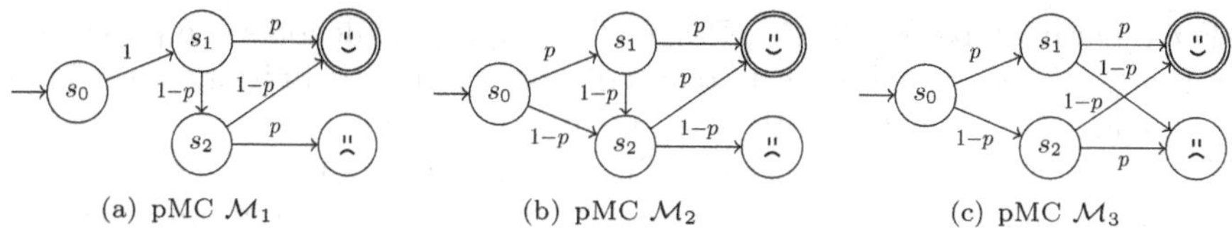


**Fig. 1.** Three simple pMCs

**Definition 1 (Multivariate monotonic function).** *A function* $f\colon \mathbb{R}^n \to \mathbb{R}$ *is* monotonic increasing in $x_i$ on set $R \subset \mathbb{R}^n$, *denoted* $f{\uparrow}^R_{x_i}$, *if*

$$f(\boldsymbol{a}) \leq f(\boldsymbol{a} + b \cdot \boldsymbol{e}_i) \qquad \forall \boldsymbol{a} \in R \; \forall b \in \mathbb{R}_{\geq 0}.$$

*A function* $f$ *is* monotone decreasing in $x_i$ on $R$, *denoted* $f{\downarrow}^R_{x_i}$, *if* $(-f){\uparrow}^R_{x_i}$. *A function* $f$ *is* monotone increasing (decreasing) on $R$, *denoted* $f{\uparrow}^R$ $(f{\downarrow}^R)$, *if* $f{\uparrow}^R_{x_i}$ $(f{\downarrow}^R_{x_i})$ *for all* $x_i \in \boldsymbol{x}$, *respectively.*

If function $f$ is continuously differentiable on the open set $R \subset \mathbb{R}^n$, then $\forall \boldsymbol{u} \in R.\ \dfrac{\partial}{\partial x_i} f(\boldsymbol{u}) \geq 0 \implies f{\uparrow}^R_{x_i}$. In particular, any $f \in \mathbb{Q}[\boldsymbol{x}]$ is continuously differentiable on $\mathbb{R}^n$.

**Definition 2 (pMC).** *A* parametric Markov Chain (pMC) *is a tuple* $\mathcal{M} = (S, s_I, T, V, \mathcal{P})$ *with a finite set* $S$ *of* states, *an* initial state $s_I \in S$, *a finite set* $T \subseteq S$ *of* target states, *a finite set* $V$ *of real-valued variables* (parameters) *and a* transition function $\mathcal{P}\colon S \times S \to \mathbb{Q}[V]$.

We define $\mathsf{succ}(s) = \{s' \in S \mid \mathcal{P}(s, s') \neq 0\}$. A pMC $\mathcal{M}$ is a *(discrete-time) Markov chain* (MC) if the transition function yields *well-defined* probability distributions, i.e., $\mathcal{P}(s, \cdot) \in \mathit{Distr}(S)$ for each $s \in S$. A state $s$ is called *parametric*, if $\mathcal{P}(s, s') \notin \mathbb{Q}$ for some $s' \in S$. Applying an *instantiation* $\boldsymbol{u}$ to a pMC $\mathcal{M}$ yields $\mathcal{M}[\boldsymbol{u}]$ by replacing each $f \in \mathbb{Q}[V]$ in $\mathcal{M}$ by $f(\boldsymbol{u})$. An instantiation $\boldsymbol{u}$ is *well-defined* (for $\mathcal{M}$) if the $\mathcal{M}[\boldsymbol{u}]$ is an MC. A well-defined instantiation $\boldsymbol{u}$ is *graph-preserving* (for $\mathcal{M}$) if the topology is preserved, that is, for all $s, s' \in S$ with $\mathcal{P}(s, s') \neq 0$ implies $\mathcal{P}(s, s')(\boldsymbol{u}) \neq 0$. A set of instantiations is called a *region*. A region $R$ is well-defined (graph-preserving) if $\forall \boldsymbol{u} \in R$, $\boldsymbol{u}$ is well-defined (graph-preserving).

*Example 1.* Figure 1 shows three pMCs, all with a single parameter $p$. Instantiation $\boldsymbol{u} = \{p \mapsto 0.4\}$ is graph-preserving for all these pMCs. Instantiation $\boldsymbol{u}' = \{p \mapsto 1\}$ is well-defined, but not graph-preserving, while $\boldsymbol{u}'' = \{p \mapsto 2\}$ is not well-defined.

*Remark 1.* Most pMCs in the literature are linear, i.e., all transition probabilities are linear. Many pMCs—including those in Fig. 1—are *simple*, i.e., $\mathcal{P}(s, s') \in \{p, 1{-}p \mid p \in V\} \cup \mathbb{Q}$ for all $s, s' \in S$. For simple pMCs, all well-defined instantiations (graph-preserving) are in $[0,1]^{|V|}$ (in $(0,1)^{|V|}$).

For a parameter-free MC $\mathcal{M}$, $\Pr^s_{\mathcal{M}}(\lozenge T) \in [0,1] \subseteq \mathbb{R}$ denotes the probability that from state $s$ the target $T$ is reached. For a formal definition, we refer to, e.g., [4, Ch. 10]. For pMC $\mathcal{M}$, $\Pr^s_{\mathcal{M}}(\lozenge T)$ is not a constant, but rather a function $\mathsf{Pr}^{s\to T}_{\mathcal{M}} : V \to [0,1]$, s.t. $\mathsf{Pr}^{s\to T}_{\mathcal{M}}(\boldsymbol{u}) = \Pr^s_{\mathcal{M}[\boldsymbol{u}]}(\lozenge T)$. We call $\mathsf{Pr}^{s\to T}_{\mathcal{M}}$ the *solution function*, and for conciseness, we typically omit $\mathcal{M}$. For two graph-preserving instantiations $\boldsymbol{u}, \boldsymbol{u}'$, we have that $\mathsf{Pr}^{s\to T}(\boldsymbol{u}) = 0$ implies $\mathsf{Pr}^{s\to T}(\boldsymbol{u}') = 0$ (analogous for $=1$). We simply write $\mathsf{Pr}^{s\to T} = 0$ (or $=1$).

*Example 2.* For the pMC in Fig. 1(a), the solution function $\mathsf{Pr}^{s\to T}$ is $p+(1-p)^2$. For the pMCs in Fig. 1(b) and (c), it is $-p^3+p^2+p$ and $p^2+(1-p)^2$, respectively.

The closed-form of $\mathsf{Pr}^{s\to T}$ on a graph-preserving region is a rational function over $V$, i.e., a fraction of two polynomials over $V$. Various methods for computing this closed form on a graph-preserving region have been proposed [18,19,22,27,30]. Such a closed-form can be exponential in the number of parameters [30], and is typically (very) large already with one or two parameters [19,27]. On a graph-preserving region, $\mathsf{Pr}^{s\to T}$ is continuously differentiable [41].

The parameter feasibility problem considered in e.g. [14,15,19,23,27,30,41] is: *Given a pMC $\mathcal{M}$, a threshold $\lambda \in [0,1]$, and a graph-preserving region $R$, is there an instantiation $\boldsymbol{u} \in R$ s.t. $\mathsf{Pr}^{s_I\to T}_{\mathcal{M}}(\boldsymbol{u}) \geq \lambda$?* This problem is square-root-sum hard [14]. For any fixed number of parameters, this problem is decidable in P [30].

*Example 3.* For the pMC in Fig. 1(a), $R = [0.4, 0.6]$, and $\lambda = 0.9$, the result to the parameter feasibility is `false`, as $\max_{\boldsymbol{u}\in R} \mathsf{Pr}^{s\to T}(\boldsymbol{u}) < 0.9$.

**Definition 3 (Monotonicity in pMCs).** *For pMC $\mathcal{M} = (S, s_I, T, V, \mathcal{P})$, parameter $p \in V$, and graph-preserving region $R$, we call $\mathcal{M}$* monotonic increasing *in $p$ on $R$, written $\mathcal{M}\!\uparrow^R_p$, if $\mathsf{Pr}^{s_I\to T}\!\uparrow^R_p$.* Monotonic decreasing, *written $\mathcal{M}\!\downarrow^R_p$, is defined analogously.*

*Example 4.* The pMC in Fig. 1(b) is monotonic in $p$ on $(0,1)$, as its derivative $-3p^2 + 2p + 1$ is strictly positive on $(0,1)$. The pMC in Fig. 1(a) is not, as witnessed by the derivative $1 - 2(1-p)$.

The above example immediately suggests a complete algorithm to decide whether $\mathcal{M}\!\uparrow^R_p$ (or analogously $\mathcal{M}\!\downarrow^R_p$): Compute the solution function, symbolically compute the derivative w.r.t. parameter $p$, and ask a solver (e.g., an SMT-solver for non-linear real arithmetic [33]) for the existence of a negative instantiation in $R$. If no such instantiation exists, then $\mathcal{M}\!\uparrow^R_p$. Observe that the size of the solution function and its derivative are in the same order of magnitude. This algorithm runs in polynomial time for any fixed number of parameters, yet the practical runtime even for medium-sized problems is unsatisfactory, due to the high costs of the symbolic operations involved. The result below motivates to look for *sufficient criteria for monotonicity that can be practically efficiently checked.*

**Theorem 1.** *pMC verification*[1] *is polynomial-time reducible to the decision problem whether a pMC is monotonic.*

[1] The complement of the parameter feasibility problem.

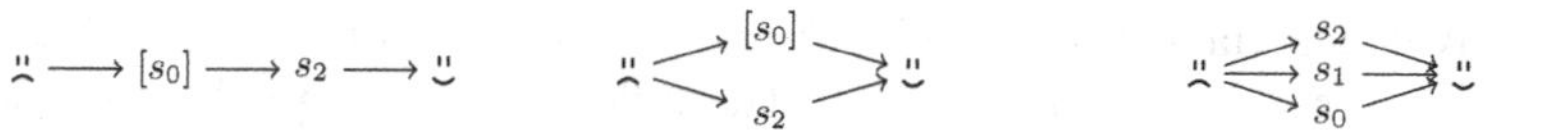

$\frown \longrightarrow [s_0] \longrightarrow s_2 \longrightarrow \smile$

(a) RO-graph for $\mathcal{M}_1$

(b) RO-graph for $\mathcal{M}_1$

(c) RO-graph for $\mathcal{M}_3$

**Fig. 2.** RO-graphs for some of the pMCs in Fig. 1

Proving *non*-monotonicity is often simpler—finding three instantiations along a line that disprove monotonicity suffices—, and less beneficial for parameter synthesis. This paper focuses on proving monotonicity rather than disproving it.

*Example 5.* The three instantiations on Fig. 1(a): $p \mapsto 0.3, 0.5, 0.9$ yield reachability probabilities: 0.79, 0.75, 0.91. Thus neither $\mathcal{M}{\uparrow}_p^R$ nor $\mathcal{M}{\downarrow}_p^R$ on $R = [0.3, 0.9]$.

**Problem Statement.** Given a pMC $\mathcal{M}$, a parameter $p$, and a region $R$, construct an *efficient* algorithm that determines either $\mathcal{M}{\uparrow}_p^R$, $\mathcal{M}{\downarrow}_p^R$, or "unknown".

In the following, let $\mathcal{M} = (S, s_I, T, V, \mathcal{P})$ be a pMC with $R$ a graph-preserving region. Let $\smile$ ($\frown$) denote all states $s \in S$ with $\mathsf{Pr}^{s \to T} = 1$ ($\mathsf{Pr}^{s \to T} = 0$). By a standard preprocessing [4], we assume a single $\smile$ and $\frown$ state. We call a parameter $p$ monotonic, if the solution function of the pMC is monotonic in $p$.

## 3 A Sufficient Criterion for Monotonicity

In this section, we combine reasoning about the underlying graph structure of a pMC and local reasoning about transition probabilities of single states to deduce a sufficient criterion for monotonicity.

**Reachability Orders**

**Definition 4 (Reachability order/RO-graph).** *An ordering relation* $\preceq_{R,T} \subseteq S \times S$ *is a* reachability order w.r.t. $T \subseteq S$ and region $R$ *if for all* $s, t \in S$*:*

$$s \preceq_{R,T} t \quad \textit{implies} \quad \forall \boldsymbol{u} \in R.\ \mathsf{Pr}^{s \to T}(\boldsymbol{u}) \leq \mathsf{Pr}^{t \to T}(\boldsymbol{u}).$$

*The order* $\preceq_{R,T}$ *is called* exhaustive *if the reverse implication holds too. The Hasse-diagram*[2] *for a reachability order is called an* RO-graph.

The relation $\preceq_{R,T}$ is a reflexive (aka: non-strict) pre-order. The exhaustive reachability order is the union of all reachability orders, and always exists. Let $\equiv_{R,T}$ denote the kernel of $\preceq_{R,T}$, i.e., $\equiv_{R,T} = \preceq_{R,T} \cap \preceq_{R,T}^{-1}$. If $\preceq_{R,T}$ is exhaustive:

$$s \equiv_{R,T} t \quad \text{iff} \quad \forall \boldsymbol{u} \in R.\ \mathsf{Pr}^{s \to T}(\boldsymbol{u}) = \mathsf{Pr}^{t \to T}(\boldsymbol{u}).$$

We often omit the subscript $R, T$ from $\preceq$ and $\equiv$ for brevity. Let $[s]$ denote the equivalence class w.r.t. $\equiv$, i.e., $[s] = \{t \in S \mid s \equiv t\}$, and $[S]$ denote the

[2] That is, $G = (S, E)$ with $E = \{(s,t) \mid s,t \in S \wedge s \preceq t \wedge (\nexists s' \in S.\ s \preceq s' \preceq t)\}$.

set of equivalence classes on $S$. We lift $\preceq$ to sets in a point-wise manner, i.e., $s \preceq X$ denotes $s \preceq x$ for all $x \in X$. In the following, we use w.l.o.g. that each reachability order $\preceq$ satisfies $\frownie \preceq S \setminus \{\frownie\}$ and $S \setminus \{\smiley\} \preceq \smiley$.

*Example 6.* Consider pMC $\mathcal{M}_1$ in Fig. 1(a) with arbitrary region $R$. Figure 2(a) shows the RO-graph of the exhaustive reachability order, with $[s_0] = \{s_0, s_1\}$. Figure 2(b) shows a non-exhaustive reachability order for $\mathcal{M}_1$. Next, consider Fig. 1(c) with region $R = (0,1)$. States $s_1$ and $s_2$ are incomparable: For $\boldsymbol{u}_1 \in R$ with $\boldsymbol{u}_1(p) < \frac{1}{2}$ : $\mathsf{Pr}^{s_1 \to T}(\boldsymbol{u}_1) < \mathsf{Pr}^{s_2 \to T}(\boldsymbol{u}_1)$, while for $\boldsymbol{u}_2 \in R$ with $\boldsymbol{u}_2(p) > \frac{1}{2}$ : $\mathsf{Pr}^{s_1 \to T}(\boldsymbol{u}_2) > \mathsf{Pr}^{s_2 \to T}(\boldsymbol{u}_2)$. Analogously, $s_0, s_1$ and $s_0, s_2$ are pairwise incomparable. Figure 2(c) depicts the corresponding exhaustive reachability order.

**Local monotonicity.** Next, we show how a local notion of monotonicity suffices to infer monotonicity.

**Definition 5 (Locally monotonic increasing).** $\mathsf{Pr}^{s \to T}$ *is* locally monotonic increasing *in parameter $p$ (at $s$) on region $R$, denoted* $\mathsf{Pr}^{s \to T}\!\uparrow_p^{\ell,R}$*, if* $\forall \boldsymbol{u} \in R$*:*

$$\left( \sum_{s' \in \mathit{succ}(s)} \left( \frac{\partial}{\partial p} \mathcal{P}(s, s') \right) \cdot \mathsf{Pr}^{s' \to T} \right) (\boldsymbol{u}) \geq 0.$$

*Locally monotonic decreasing*, denoted $\mathsf{Pr}^{s \to T}\!\downarrow_p^{\ell,R}$, is defined analogously ($\leq 0$). Thus, while global monotonicity considers the derivative of the full solution function, local monotonicity only considers the derivative of the first transition.

*Example 7.* For state $s_0$ in Fig. 1(b), we compute:

$$\left( \frac{\partial}{\partial p} p \right) \cdot \mathsf{Pr}^{s_1 \to T} + \left( \frac{\partial}{\partial p} (1-p) \right) \cdot \mathsf{Pr}^{s_2 \to T} = 1 \cdot (p + (1-p) \cdot p) - 1 \cdot p = p - p^2.$$

By checking for which instantiations this function is non-negative, we obtain that $s_0$ is locally monotonic increasing on any graph-preserving $R$. Similar computations show that $s_1$ and $s_2$ are locally monotonic increasing. In Fig. 1(c), $s_1$ is locally monotonic increasing, $s_2$ is locally monotonic decreasing, and $s_0$ is neither locally monotonic increasing nor decreasing.

Observe that non-parametric states are monotonic increasing and decreasing in any parameter. Reachability orders may induce local monotonicity:

**Lemma 1.** *Let* $\mathit{succ}(s) = \{s_1, \ldots, s_n\}$, $P(s, s_i) = f_i$ *and* $\forall j > i. s_j \preceq s_i$*. Then:*

$$\mathsf{Pr}^{s \to T}\!\uparrow_p^{\ell,R} \quad \textit{iff} \quad \exists i \in [1, \ldots, n]. \left( \forall j \leq i.\ f_j \!\uparrow_p^R \textit{ and } \forall j > i.\ f_j \!\downarrow_p^R \right).$$

**Theorem 2.**

$$\left( \forall s \in S.\, \mathsf{Pr}^{s \to T}\!\uparrow_p^{\ell,R} \right) \implies \mathsf{Pr}^{s_I \to T}\!\uparrow_p^R.$$

*Example 8.* Consider Fig. 1(b), observe that $s_2 \preceq s_1$. Applying Lemma 1 to $s_0$ with monotonic increasing $f = p$, yields that $s_0$ is locally monotonic increasing. All states are locally monotonic increasing, thus $\mathcal{M}_2$ is (globally) monotonic increasing.

**Sufficient Reachability Orders.** Above, we only regard the reachability order locally, in order to deduce (local) monotonicity. Thus, to deduce (global) monotonicity from a reachability order, it suffices to compute a subset of the exhaustive reachability order.

**Definition 6 (Sufficient reachability order).** *Reachability order* $\preceq$ *is* sufficient *for* $s \in S$ *if for all* $s_1, s_2 \in \mathsf{succ}(s)$: $(s_1 \preceq s_2 \vee s_2 \preceq s_1)$ *holds. The reachability order is* sufficient *for* $\mathcal{M}$ *if it is sufficient for all parametric states.*

A reachability order $\preceq$ is thus sufficient for $s$ if $(\mathsf{succ}(s), \preceq)$ is a total order. A sufficient reachability order does not necessarily exist.

*Example 9.* The reachability order in Fig. 2(a) is sufficient for all states. The reachability order in Fig. 2(c) is not sufficient for $s_0$.

**Corollary 1.** *Given a pMC* $\mathcal{M}$ *s.t. all states* $s \in S$ *have* $|\mathsf{succ}(s)| \leq 2$, *and only monotonic transition functions. If reachability order* $\preceq$ *is sufficient for* $s$, *then* $\mathsf{Pr}^{s \to T}$ *is locally monotonic increasing/decreasing on region* $R$ *in all parameters.*

The proof follows immediately from Definition 6 and Lemma 1. A similar statement holds for the general case with arbitrarily many successors. The reachability order $\preceq$ is called a *witness* for monotonicity of parameter $p$ on $R$ whenever either all states are locally increasing or all are locally decreasing in $p$. A sufficient $\preceq$ (for $\mathcal{M}$) does in general not imply global monotonicity of $\mathcal{M}$.

*Example 10.* While the order shown in Fig. 2(a) is sufficient for pMC $\mathcal{M}_1$ (Fig. 1(a)), $\mathcal{M}_1$ is not monotonic: state $s_1$ is locally increasing, but state $s_2$ is locally decreasing.

We call such reachability orders (with the pMC) *inconclusive* for $p$ and $R$.

## 4 Automatically Proving Monotonicity

In this section, we discuss how to automatically construct a sufficient reachability order to deduce monotonicity of (some of) the parameters in the given pMC. The following negative result motivates us to consider a heuristic approach:

**Lemma 2.** *pMC verification is polynomial-time reducible to the decision problem whether two states are ordered by the exhaustive reachability order.*

Our algorithmic approach is based on RO-graphs. We first consider how these graphs can be used to determine monotonicity (Sect. 4). The main part of this section is devoted to constructing RO-graphs. We start with a basic idea for obtaining reachability orders for acyclic pMCs (Sect. 4.1). To get *sufficient* orders, the algorithm is refined by automatically making *assumptions*, such as $s \preceq s'$ and/or $s' \preceq s$ (Sect. 4.2). We then describe how these assumptions can be discharged (Sect. 4.2), and finally extend the algorithm to treat cycles (Sect. 4.3).

**Checking Monotonicity Using a Reachability Order.** The base is to check whether the RO-graph is a witness for monotonicity. This is done as follows. Using the RO-graph, we determine global monotonicity of the pMC by checking each parametric state $s$ for local monotonicity (cf. Theorem 2). To decide whether $s$ is local monotonic, we consider the ordering of its direct successors and the derivatives of the probabilistic transition functions and apply Lemma 1.

### 4.1 Constructing Reachability Orders

Our aim is to construct a (not necessarily sufficient) reachability order from the graph structure of a pMC. Let us introduce some standard notions. For reachability order $\preceq$ and $X \subseteq S$, $\mathsf{ub}(X) = \{s \in S \mid X \preceq s\}$ and $\mathsf{lb}(X) = \{s \in S \mid s \preceq X\}$ denote the upper and lower bounds of $X$. As ☹ $\preceq S$ and $S \preceq$ ☺, these sets are non-empty. Furthermore, let $\min(X) = \{x \in X \mid \nexists x' \in X. x' \preceq x\}$, and $\max(X) = \{x \in X \mid \nexists x' \in X. x \preceq x'\}$. If $(X, \preceq)$ is a lattice, then it has a unique minimal upper bound (and maximal lower bound). Then:

**Lemma 3.** *For* $s \in S$, *either* $\mathsf{succ}(s) \subseteq [s]$ *or* $\mathsf{lb}(\mathsf{succ}(s)) \prec s \prec \mathsf{ub}(\mathsf{succ}(s))$.

The first case essentially says that if $\exists s' \in \mathsf{succ}(s)$ with $\mathsf{succ}(s) \subseteq [s']$, then also $s \in [s']$. Lemma 3 enables to construct reachability orders:

*Example 11.* Reconsider the pMC $\mathcal{M}_1$ from Fig. 1(a). Clearly ☹ $\prec$ ☺. Now consider the pMC in reverse topological order (from back to front). We start with state $s_2$. By Lemma 3, we conclude ☹ $\prec s_2 \prec$ ☺. Next, we consider $s_1$, and analogously conclude $s_2 \prec s_1 \prec$ ☺. Finally, considering $s_0$ gives $\mathsf{succ}(s_0) \subseteq [s_1]$ thus, $s_0 \in [s_1]$. The resulting (exhaustive) reachability order is given in Fig. 2(a).

This reasoning is automated by algorithm Alg. 1. It takes as input an acyclic pMC and iteratively computes a set of reachability orders, starting from the trivial order ☹ $\prec$ ☺. In fact, it computes annotated orders $(\mathcal{A}, \preceq^{\mathcal{A}})$ where $\mathcal{A}$ is a set of assumptions of the form $s \preceq s'$. At this stage, the assumptions are not relevant and not used; they become relevant in Sect. 4.2. The algorithm uses a Queue storing triples consisting of 1) annotations, 2) the order so far, and 3) the remaining states to be processed. The queue is initialised (l. 1) with no annotations, the order ☹ $\prec$ ☺, and the remaining states. In each iteration, an order is taken from the queue. If all states are processed, then the order is completed (l. 5). Otherwise, some state $s$ is selected (l. 7) to process, and after a possible extension, the queue is updated with the extended order (l. 12) The states are selected in reverse topological order. Thus, when considering state $s$, all states in $\mathsf{succ}(s)$ have been considered before. Using Lemma 3, either $s$ belongs to an already existing equivalence class (l. 9), or it can be added between some other states (l. 11) In both cases, the RO-graph of the order $\preceq$ is extended (where

**Algorithm 1.** Construction of an RO-graph

**Input:** Acyclic pMC $\mathcal{M} = (S, s_I, T, V, \mathcal{P})$
**Output:** Result = a set of annotated orders $\preceq^{\mathcal{A}}$ (represented as their RO-graph)
1: Result $\leftarrow \emptyset$, Queue $\leftarrow (\mathcal{A} : \emptyset, \prec : \{(☹, ☺)\}, S' : S \setminus \{☺, ☹\})$
2: **while** Queue not empty **do**
3: $\quad \mathcal{A}, \preceq^{\mathcal{A}}, S' \leftarrow$ Queue.pop()
4: $\quad$ **if** $S' = \emptyset$ **then**
5: $\quad\quad$ Result $\leftarrow$ Result $\cup \{(\mathcal{A}, \preceq^{\mathcal{A}})\}$.
6: $\quad$ **else**
7: $\quad\quad$ select $s \in S'$ with $s$ topologically last
8: $\quad\quad$ **if** $\exists s' \in \mathsf{succ}(s)$ s.t. $\mathsf{succ}(s) \subseteq [s']$ **then**
9: $\quad\quad\quad$ extend RO-graph($\preceq^{\mathcal{A}}$) with: $s \equiv \mathsf{succ}(s)$
10: $\quad\quad$ **else**
11: $\quad\quad\quad$ extend RO-graph($\preceq^{\mathcal{A}}$) with all:
$\quad\quad\quad s \prec^{\mathcal{A}} \min \mathsf{ub}(\mathsf{succ}(s))$ and $\max \mathsf{lb}(\mathsf{succ}(s)) \prec^{\mathcal{A}} s$
12: $\quad\quad$ Queue.push($\mathcal{A}, \preceq^{\mathcal{A}}, S' \setminus \{s\}$)
13: **return** Result

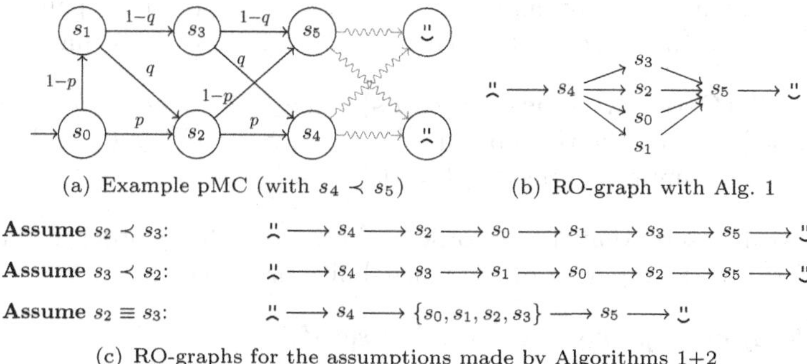


(a) Example pMC (with $s_4 \prec s_5$)

(b) RO-graph with Alg. 1

(c) RO-graphs for the assumptions made by Algorithms 1+2

**Fig. 3.** Illustrating the use of assumptions

l. 9 uses the extension of $\preceq$ to equivalence classes). As assumptions are not used, Alg. 1 in fact computes a single reachability order; it runs linear in the number of transitions.

**Lemma 4.** *Algorithm 1 returns a set with one reachability order.*

Even if there exists a sufficient reachability order for region $R$, Algorithm 1 might not find such an order, as the algorithm does not take into account $R$ at all — it is purely graph-based. Alg. 1 does obtain a sufficient reachability order if for all (parametric) states $s \in S$, $\mathsf{succ}(s)$ is totally ordered by the computed $\preceq$.

### 4.2 Making and Discharging Assumptions

Next, we aim to locally refine our RO-graph to obtain sufficient reachability orders. Therefore, we exploit the annotations (called *assumptions*) that were ignored so far. Recall from Definition 6 that a reachability order is not sufficient at a parametric state $s$, if its successors $s_1$ and $s_2$, say, are not totally ordered. We identify these situations while considering $s$ in Alg. 1. We then continue as if the ordering of $s_1$ and $s_2$ is known. By considering *all* possible orderings of $s_1$ and $s_2$, we remain sound. The fact that parametric states typically have only two direct successors (as most pMCs are simple [15,34]) limits the number of orders.

*Example 12.* Consider the pMC in Fig. 3(a). Assume that Alg. 1 yields the RO-graph in Fig. 3(b), in particular $s_4 \prec s_5$. Alg. 1 cannot order the successors of state $s_1$. But any region can be partitioned into three (potentially empty) subregions: A region with $s_2 \prec s_3$, a region with $s_2 \equiv s_3$, and a region with $s_3 \prec s_2$. We below adapt Alg. 1 such that, instead of adding $s_1$ between $s_4$ and $s_5$(l. 11), we create three copies of the reachability order. In the copy assuming $s_2 \prec s_3$ we can order $s_1$ as in Fig. 3(c). The other copies reflect $s_3 \prec s_2$ and $s_2 \equiv s_3$, respectively.

Below, we formalise and automate this. Let $\mathcal{A} = (\mathcal{A}_\prec, \mathcal{A}_\equiv)$ be a pair of sets of assumptions such that $(s,t) \in \mathcal{A}_\prec$ means $s \prec t$ while $(s,t) \in \mathcal{A}_\equiv$ means $s \equiv t$.

**Definition 7 (Order with assumptions).** *Let $\preceq$ be a reachability order, and $\mathcal{A} = (\mathcal{A}_\prec, \mathcal{A}_\equiv)$ a pair with* assumptions $\mathcal{A}_\prec, \mathcal{A}_\equiv \subseteq S \times S$. *Then $(\preceq^\mathcal{A}, \mathcal{A})$ is called an* order with assumptions *where $\preceq^\mathcal{A} = (\preceq \cup \mathcal{A}_\prec \cup \mathcal{A}_\equiv)^*$.*

The next result asserts that the pre-order $\preceq^\mathcal{A}$ is a reachability order if all assumptions conform to the ordering of the reachability probabilities.

**Lemma 5.** *If assumptions $\mathcal{A} = (\mathcal{A}_\prec, \mathcal{A}_\equiv)$ satisfy:*

$$(s,t) \in \mathcal{A}_\prec \quad \textit{implies} \quad \forall \boldsymbol{u} \in R.\ \mathsf{Pr}^{s \to T}(\boldsymbol{u}) < \mathsf{Pr}^{t \to T}(\boldsymbol{u}), \textit{ and}$$
$$(s,t) \in \mathcal{A}_\equiv \quad \textit{implies} \quad \forall \boldsymbol{u} \in R.\ \mathsf{Pr}^{s \to T}(\boldsymbol{u}) = \mathsf{Pr}^{t \to T}(\boldsymbol{u}),$$

*then $\preceq^\mathcal{A}$ is a reachability order, and we call $\mathcal{A}$* (globally) valid.

Algorithm 2 adds assumptions to the reachability order. It comes before Line 11 of Algorithm 1. If the reachability order $\preceq^\mathcal{A}$ contains two incomparable successors $s_1$ and $s_2$ of state $s$, we make three different assumptions: In particular, we assume either $s_1 \prec^\mathcal{A} s_2$, $s_2 \prec^\mathcal{A} s_1$, or $s_1 \equiv^\mathcal{A} s_2$. We then put the updated orders in the queue (without having processed state $s$). As the states $s_1, s_2$ were incomparable, the assumptions are new and do not contradict with the order so far.

The algorithm does not remove states from the queue if their successors are not totally ordered. Consequently, we have:

**Theorem 3.** *For every order with assumptions $(\preceq^\mathcal{A}, \mathcal{A})$ computed by Algorithm 1+2. Then: if $\preceq^\mathcal{A}$ is a reachability order, then it is sufficient.*

**Algorithm 2.** Assumption extension (put before l. 11 in Alg. 1).

**if** $\preceq^{\mathcal{A}}$ is not a total order for $\mathsf{succ}(s)$ **then**
  pick $s_1, s_2 \in \mathsf{succ}(s)$ s.t. neither $s_1 \preceq^{\mathcal{A}} s_2$ nor $s_2 \preceq^{\mathcal{A}} s_1$
  Queue.push($(\mathcal{A}_{\prec} \cup \{(s_1, s_2)\}, \mathcal{A}_{\equiv}), \preceq^{\mathcal{A}}$ extended with $s_1 \prec s_2, S'$)
  Queue.push($(\mathcal{A}_{\prec} \cup \{(s_2, s_1)\}, \mathcal{A}_{\equiv}), \preceq^{\mathcal{A}}$ extended with $s_1 \equiv s_2, S'$)
  Queue.push($(\mathcal{A}_{\prec}, \mathcal{A}_{\equiv} \cup \{(s_1, s_2)\}), \preceq^{\mathcal{A}}$ extended with $s_2 \prec s_1, S'$)
  **continue**

**Discharging assumptions.** Algorithm 1+2 yields a set of orders. By Theorem 3, each order $\prec^{\mathcal{A}}$ is a (proper) reachability order if the assumptions in $\mathcal{A}$ are valid.

The following result states that the assumptions can sometimes be ignored.

**Theorem 4.** *If all orders computed by Algorithm 1+2 are witnesses for a parameter to be monotonic increasing (decreasing), then the parameter is indeed monotonic increasing (decreasing).*

This can be seen as follows. Intuitively, a region $R$ is partitioned into (possibly empty) regions $R_{\mathcal{A}}$ for each possible set of assumptions $\mathcal{A}$. If on each region $R_{\mathcal{A}}$ the order $\preceq^{\mathcal{A}}$ is a witness for monotonicity (and all witnesses agree on whether the parameter is $\uparrow^R$ or $\downarrow^R$), then the parameter is monotonic on $R$.

If Theorem 4 does not apply, we establish whether or not assumptions are valid on $R$ in an on-the-fly manner, as follows: Let $(\preceq^{\mathcal{A}}, \mathcal{A})$ be the current order, and suppose we want to check whether $s_1 \prec s_2$ is a new assumption. If the outcome is $s_1 \prec s_2$, then we extend the RO-graph with $s_1 \prec s_2$, do not add this assumption, and ignore the possibilities $s_1 \equiv s_2$ and $s_2 \prec s_1$. If $s_1 \not\preceq s_2$, we do not assume $s_1 \prec s_2$ (and ignore the corresponding order). Both cases prune the number of orders. In case of an inconclusive result, $s_1 \prec s_2$ is added to $\mathcal{A}_{\prec}$.

To check whether $s_1 \prec s_2$ we describe three techniques.

*Using a local NLP.* The idea is to locally (at $s_1$ and $s_2$) consider the pMC and its characterising non-linear program (NLP) [4,5,15,19], together with the inequalities encoded by $\preceq^{\mathcal{A}}$. To refute an assumption to be globally valid, a single instantiation $\boldsymbol{u}$ refuting the assumption suffices. This suggests to let a solver prove the absence of such an instantiation $\boldsymbol{u}$ by considering a fragment of the pMC [44]. If successful, the assumption is globally valid. Otherwise, we don't know: the obtained instantiation $\boldsymbol{u}$ might be spurious.

*Using model checking.* This approach targets to cheaply disprove assumptions. We sample the parameter space at suitable points (as in e.g. [9,13]), and reduce the amount of solver runs, similar to [19]. In particular, we instantiate the pMC with instantiations $\boldsymbol{u}$ from a set $U$, and evaluate the (parameter-free) MC $\mathcal{M}[\boldsymbol{u}]$ via standard model checking. This sampling yields reachability probabilities $\mathrm{Pr}^s_{\mathcal{M}[u]}(\lozenge T)$ for every state $s$, and allows to disprove an assumption, say $s_1 \prec s_2$, by merely looking up whether $\mathrm{Pr}^{s_1}_{\mathcal{M}[u]}(\lozenge T) \geq \mathrm{Pr}^{s_2}_{\mathcal{M}[u]}(\lozenge T)$ for some $u \in U$.

*Using region checking.* Region verification procedures (e.g. parameter lifting [41]) consider a region $R$, and obtain for each state $s$ an interval $[a_s, b_s]$ s.t.

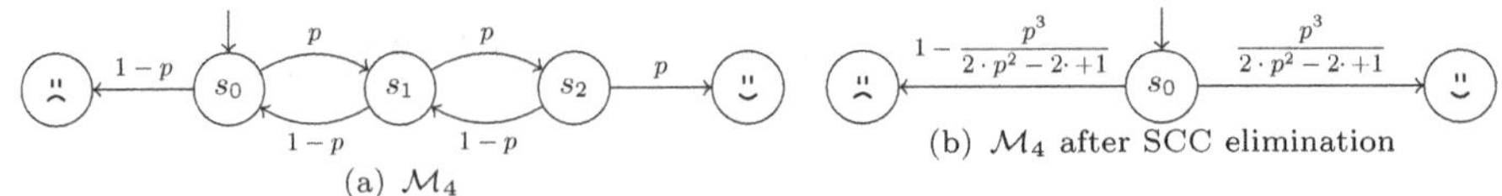


**Fig. 4.** An example pMC consisting of a single SCC

$\Pr^{s}_{\mathcal{M}[\boldsymbol{u}]}(\lozenge T) \in [a_s, b_s]$ for all $\boldsymbol{u} \in R$. Assumption $s_1 \prec s_2$ can be proven by checking $b_{s_1} \leq a_{s_2}$.

### 4.3 Treating Cycles

So far, we considered acyclic pMCs. We use two techniques to treat cycles. *SCC elimination* [31] contracts each SCC into a set of states, one for each entry state of the SCC. Figure 4(b) shows the pMC of Fig. 4(a) after SCC elimination. *Cycle-breaking.* If SCC elimination is not viable, we use an alternative. The following analogue to Lemma 3 is insightful and tailored to simple pMCs.

**Lemma 6.** *For any state $s$ with $\mathsf{succ}(s) = \{s_1, s_2\}$ the following holds: 1. if $s_1 \equiv s$, then $s_2 \equiv s$, 2. if $s_1 \prec s$, then $s \prec s_2$, 3 if $s \prec s_1$, then $s_2 \prec s$.*

This suggests to take state $s$ on a cycle and insert it into the RO-graph computed so far, which is always (trivially) possible, and then adding further states using Lemma 6. We illustrate this idea by an example.

*Example 13.* Reconsider Fig. 4(a). Lemma 3 does not give rise to extending the trivial order ☹ $\prec$ ☺. To treat the cycle, one of the states $s_0$, $s_1$ or $s_2$ is to be added. Selecting $s_0$ yields (as for any other state) ☹ $\prec s_0 \prec$ ☺. To order $s_1$ or $s_2$, Lemma 3 is (still) not applicable. Using ☹ $\prec s_0$, Lemma 6 applied to $s_1$ yields $s_0 \prec s_1$. For $s_2$, we obtain $s_1 \prec s_2$ in a similar way.

The strategy is thus to successively pick states from a cycle, insert them into the order $\preceq$ so far, and continue this procedure until all states on the cycle are covered (by either Lemma 3 or 6). The extension to Alg. 1+2 is given in . We emphasise that Theorems 3 and 4 also apply to this extension.

It remains to discuss: how to decide which states to select on a cycle? This is done heuristically. A good heuristic selects states that probably lead to cycle "breaking". The essential criteria that we empirically determined are: take cycles in SCCs that are at the front of the reverse topological ordering of SCCs, and prefer states with successors outside the SCC (as in the above example).

## 5 Experimental Evaluation

We realised a prototype of the algorithm from Sect. 4 on top of Storm (v1.3) [20] and evaluated two questions. To that end, we took *all* ten benchmarks sets

**Table 1.** Automatically inferring monotonicity

| Benchmark | Instance | A/C | $\|V\|$ | #states | #trans | Monotonic | Model building | Mon. check | Sol. func. |
|---|---|---|---|---|---|---|---|---|---|
| brp [17] | (2,16) | A | 2 | 613 | 803 | $\downarrow_{pK}$, $\downarrow_{pL}$ | <1 | <1 | <1 |
| | (10,2048) | | | 45059 | 90115 | | 6 | 1 | MO |
| | (15,4096) | | | 131075 | 262147 | | 16 | **13** | MO |
| crowds [42] | (5,6) | C | 2 | 18817 | 32677 | $\uparrow_{badC}$, $\uparrow_{pF}$ | <1 | 1 | <1 |
| | (10,6) | | | 352535 | 722015 | | 6 | 1 | <1 |
| | (20,6) | | | 10633591 | 27151191 | | 232 | 1 | <1 |
| gambler [12] | (14800,1480) | C | 1 | 16281 | 32560 | $\uparrow_p$ | <1 | 1 | **TO** |
| | (29600,2960) | | | 32561 | 65120 | | <1 | **6** | **TO** |
| | (59200,5920) | | | 65121 | 130240 | | 2 | **21** | **TO** |
| mes. auth. [21] | (3840) | A | 2 | 19201 | 30720 | $\uparrow_p$, $\uparrow_q$ | 3 | <1 | <1 |
| | (7680) | | | 38401 | 61440 | | 4 | <1 | <1 |
| | (15360) | | | 76801 | 122880 | | 4 | <1 | <1 |
| zeroconf [7] | (6400) | C | 2 | 6404 | 12805 | $\uparrow_p$, $\uparrow_q$ | <1 | <1 | **1090** |
| | (25600) | | | 25604 | 51205 | | <1 | <1 | **TO** |
| | (102400) | | | 102404 | 204805 | | 3 | **3** | **TO** |

with pMCs and non-trivial reachability properties from the PARAM website [1], and from [28], and [12]. The benchmark sets egl[37], craps[4], nand[39] and herman [29,38] are not monotonic. Their non-monotonicity can be shown by uniformly taking 100 samples on the parameter space. The benchmark haddad-monmege [25] contains only a single non-sink state after preprocessing, it is trivially monotonic. All experiments ran on a MacBook ME867LL/A. We use a 12 GB memory-out (MO), and a 4 h time-out (TO).

**Can the Algorithm Determine Monotonicity on the Benchmarks?** We consider the performance of the proposed algorithm. First and foremost, for all six benchmark sets with monotonic parameters, the algorithm automatically and without user interference determines monotonicity.

Table 1 presents details: it lists the benchmark and their instances. We then list whether the pMC is acyclic (A) or cyclic (C), the number $|V|$ of parameters, and the size of the pMC. The column *monotonic* gives the obtained results for the pMC parameters. *Model building* includes the time for construction, default preprocessing by Storm, and bisimulation minimisation. *Mon. check* shows timings for inferring monotonicity from the built model. To place these numbers in perspective, column *sol. func* shows the time to obtain the solution function from the built model by Storm (default settings, same preprocessing, based on the implementation in [19]). These times are a lower bound on the time to show monotonicity via the solution function. Timings for taking the derivative and analysing this derivative via an SMT solver are omitted (but significant).

The proposed method quickly determines monotonicity. For (only) crowds, the method applies an essential SCC elimination on the various smaller SCCs. For the available benchmarks, the method computes a single reachability order. Unsurprisingly, the method is orders of magnitude faster and scales better than obtaining monotonicity from the solution function. Naturally, our algorithm cannot establish monotonicity on all cases. The algorithm has difficulties handling subregions on non-monotonic benchmarks. Take Herman: The solution function has (up to) three local extrema [38]. On subregions, however, the graph structure easily induces inconclusive orders. A tighter integration with region verification, partially applied state elimination, or using a notion of multi-step local monotonicity (used in the proof of Theorem 2) are avenues for improvement.

**Does Monotonicity Allow for Faster Parameter Synthesis?** We consider three variants of parameter synthesis in the presence of monotonicity:

*Feasibility:* i.e., *is there an instantiation for which a specification $\varphi$ is satisfied?* becomes mostly trivial in the presence of monotonicity. For simple pMCs, a single parameter-free MC evaluation suffices, which is clearly superior to other—typically sampling-based—approaches [13,15].

*Region verification:* i.e., *do all parameter values within a region satisfy $\varphi$?* is similarly trivialised for regions given as linear polyhedra. For our benchmarks, PLA [41]—approximating region verification by MDP model checking—is very competitive. In particular, PLA does not over-approximate on locally monotonic pMCs, and needs no refinements (the reverse does not hold: even for tight bounds, one cannot infer monotonicity with PLA). Thus, whereas sampling checks a single MC, PLA checks one MDP. Typically, the MC can be checked ~20% faster.

*Parameter space partitioning:* this procedure, implemented in PROPhESY, Storm, and PARAM, *iteratively divides a region into subregions that satisfy $\varphi$ or $\neg\varphi$, respectively.* We implemented an alternative prototype based on sampling and exploiting monotonicity: therefore, region splits can be taken much more informed. We compared to Storm (using PLA). Figure 5 (log-log scale) displays cumulative model-checking runtimes to achieve a given coverage. Obtaining a coverage up to 90% is trivial. For higher coverage, our method is (on crowds and zeroconf) up to an order of magnitude faster, due to less model-checking calls. This trend is independent of the threshold. We see some room for improvement by a more sophisticated selection of samples, and by speeding up the sampling [23].

## 6 Related Work

*Monotonicity.* Monotonicity in MCs goes back to Daley [16], aiming to bound stationary probabilities of a stochastically monotone MC by another MC. These stochastic orderings $\leq_{st}$ require ordered rows in the matrix $\mathcal{P}$, and are quite different from reachability orders. MCs can be compared if $\mathcal{P}$ is monotone w.r.t. $\leq_{st}$ for all probability vectors. Such orderings have been used for multi-valued model checking of interval MCs [26], but not applied to pMCs.

*Pre-orders.* A never-worse relation (NWR) on MDP states [6,43] is similar in spirit to reachability orders: states are ordered according to their maximal reachability probabilities but without taking the probabilities into account. Dependencies between the state probabilities are thus not taken into account. Like in our setting, computing the NWR is based on the graph structure. Its usage however is quite different, reducing the size of the MDP prior to model checking.

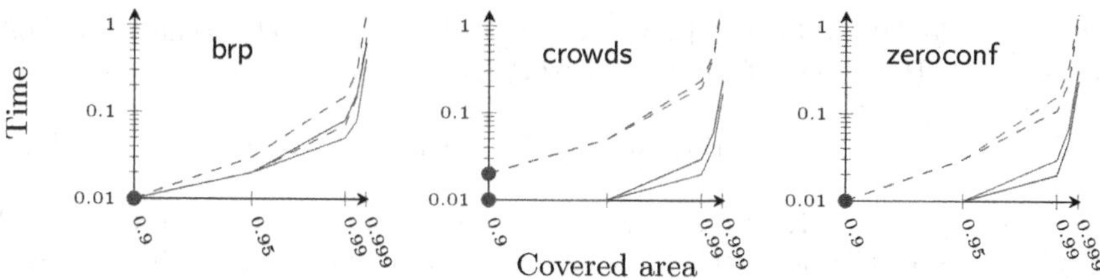


**Fig. 5.** *What coverage (x-axis) in how much time (y-axis)*? when using PLA (dotted) or Monotonicity/Sampling (solid) . The two colours indicate two different thresholds.

NWR captures most heuristics to reduce the MDP before linear programming or value iteration. The coNP-completeness [43] indicates that checking this order is simpler than our pre-order unless coETR and coNP coincide.

*Monotonicity in parameter synthesis.* Parameter lifting [41] exploits a form of local monotonicity to remove parameter dependencies in a pMC. (A similar observation for continuous-time MCs was made in [8].) The resulting monotonic pMC is replaced by an MDP that over-approximates the original pMC. No efforts are made to determine global monotonicity. Interval MCs [11,32] lack dependencies, thus all states are locally monotonic (but it remains unclear whether they are monotonically increasing or decreasing). Monotonicity also affects complexity. Hutschenreiter *et al.* [30] recently showed that the complexity of model checking (a monotone fragment of) PCTL on monotonic pMC is lower than PCTL model checking on general pMCs. They use a very restrictive sufficient criterion for a pMC to be monotonic: This includes none of the pMCs considered in this paper. Monotonicity has also been considered in the context of model repair. Pathak *et al.* [40] provide an efficient greedy approach to repair monotonic pMCs[3]. Recently, Gouberman *et al.* [24] show that particular perturbations of direct predecessors of ☺ or ☹ in a continuous-time MC are monotonic in the perturbation factor.

## 7 Conclusion and Future Work

We proposed a method that automatically infers the monotonicity of pMCs from the literature. To the best of our knowledge, our paper is the first automated procedure for determining monotonicity. Future work includes a tighter integration with parameter synthesis, and extensions to pMDPs and rewards.

## References

1. PARAM website (2019). https://depend.cs.uni-saarland.de/tools/param/
2. Aflaki, S., Volk, M., Bonakdarpour, B., Katoen, J.P., Storjohann, A.: Automated fine tuning of probabilistic self-stabilizing algorithms. In: SRDS. IEEE CS (2017)

[3] Although monotonicity is not explicitly mentioned in [40].

3. Baier, C., de Alfaro, L., Forejt, V., Kwiatkowska, M.: Model checking probabilistic systems. Handbook of Model Checking, pp. 963–999. Springer, Cham (2018). https://doi.org/10.1007/978-3-319-10575-8_28
4. Baier, C., Katoen, J.P.: Principles of Model Checking. MIT Press, Cambridge (2008)
5. Bartocci, E., Grosu, R., Katsaros, P., Ramakrishnan, C.R., Smolka, S.A.: Model repair for probabilistic systems. In: Abdulla, P.A., Leino, K.R.M. (eds.) TACAS 2011. LNCS, vol. 6605, pp. 326–340. Springer, Heidelberg (2011). https://doi.org/10.1007/978-3-642-19835-9_30
6. Bharadwaj, S., Roux, S.L., Pérez, G.A., Topcu, U.: Reduction techniques for model checking and learning in MDPs. In: IJCAI. ijcai.org (2017)
7. Bohnenkamp, H.C., van der Stok, P., Hermanns, H., Vaandrager, F.W.: Cost-optimization of the IPv4 zeroconf protocol. In: DSN. IEEE CS (2003)
8. Brim, L., Češka, M., Dražan, S., Šafránek, D.: Exploring parameter space of stochastic biochemical systems using quantitative model checking. In: Sharygina, N., Veith, H. (eds.) CAV 2013. LNCS, vol. 8044, pp. 107–123. Springer, Heidelberg (2013). https://doi.org/10.1007/978-3-642-39799-8_7
9. Calinescu, R., Ceska, M., Gerasimou, S., Kwiatkowska, M., Paoletti, N.: Efficient synthesis of robust models for stochastic systems. J. Syst. Softw. **143**, 140–158 (2018)
10. Ceska, M., Dannenberg, F., Paoletti, N., Kwiatkowska, M., Brim, L.: Precise parameter synthesis for stochastic biochemical systems. Acta Inf. **54**(6), 589–623 (2017). https://doi.org/10.1007/s00236-016-0265-2
11. Chatterjee, K., Sen, K., Henzinger, T.A.: Model-Checking $\omega$-Regular Properties of Interval Markov Chains. In: Amadio, R. (ed.) FoSSaCS 2008. LNCS, vol. 4962, pp. 302–317. Springer, Heidelberg (2008). https://doi.org/10.1007/978-3-540-78499-9_22
12. Chatzieleftheriou, G., Katsaros, P.: Abstract model repair for probabilistic systems. Inf. Comput. **259**(1), 142–160 (2018)
13. Chen, T., Hahn, E.M., Han, T., Kwiatkowska, M.Z., Qu, H., Zhang, L.: Model repair for Markov decision processes. In: TASE. IEEE (2013)
14. Chonev, V.: Reachability in augmented interval Markov chains. CoRR abs/1701.02996 (2017)
15. Cubuktepe, M., Jansen, N., Junges, S., Katoen, J.-P., Topcu, U.: Synthesis in pMDPs: a tale of 1001 parameters. In: Lahiri, S.K., Wang, C. (eds.) ATVA 2018. LNCS, vol. 11138, pp. 160–176. Springer, Cham (2018). https://doi.org/10.1007/978-3-030-01090-4_10
16. Daley, D.J.: Stochastically monotone Markov chains. Zeitschrift für Wahrscheinlichkeitstheorie und Verwandte Gebiete **10**, 305–317 (1968). https://doi.org/10.1007/BF00531852
17. D'Argenio, P.R., Jeannet, B., Jensen, H.E., Larsen, K.G.: Reachability analysis of probabilistic systems by successive refinements. In: de Alfaro, L., Gilmore, S. (eds.) PAPM-PROBMIV 2001. LNCS, vol. 2165, pp. 39–56. Springer, Heidelberg (2001). https://doi.org/10.1007/3-540-44804-7_3
18. Daws, C.: Symbolic and parametric model checking of discrete-time Markov chains. In: Liu, Z., Araki, K. (eds.) ICTAC 2004. LNCS, vol. 3407, pp. 280–294. Springer, Heidelberg (2005). https://doi.org/10.1007/978-3-540-31862-0_21
19. Dehnert, C., et al.: PROPhESY: A PRObabilistic ParamEter SYnthesis Tool. In: Kroening, D., Păsăreanu, C.S. (eds.) CAV 2015. LNCS, vol. 9206, pp. 214–231. Springer, Cham (2015). https://doi.org/10.1007/978-3-319-21690-4_13

20. Dehnert, C., Junges, S., Katoen, J.P., Volk, M.: A storm is coming: a modern probabilistic model checker. In: Majumdar, Rupak, Kunčak, Viktor (eds.) CAV 2017. LNCS, vol. 10427, pp. 592–600. Springer, Cham (2017). https://doi.org/10.1007/978-3-319-63390-9_31
21. Filieri, A., Ghezzi, C., Tamburrelli, G.: Run-time efficient probabilistic model checking. In: ICSE. ACM (2011)
22. Filieri, A., Tamburrelli, G., Ghezzi, C.: Supporting self-adaptation via quantitative verification and sensitivity analysis at run time. IEEE TSE **42**(1), 75–99 (2016)
23. Gainer, P., Hahn, E.M., Schewe, S.: Accelerated model checking of parametric Markov chains. In: Lahiri, S.K., Wang, C. (eds.) ATVA 2018. LNCS, vol. 11138, pp. 300–316. Springer, Cham (2018). https://doi.org/10.1007/978-3-030-01090-4_18
24. Gouberman, A., Siegle, M., Tati, B.: Markov chains with perturbed rates to absorption: theory and application to model repair. Perf. Eval. **130**, 32–50 (2019)
25. Haddad, S., Monmege, B.: Interval iteration algorithm for MDPs and IMDPs. Theor. Comput. Sci. **735**, 111–131 (2018)
26. Haddad, S., Pekergin, N.: Using stochastic comparison for efficient model checking of uncertain Markov chains. In: QEST. IEEE CS (2009)
27. Hahn, E.M., Hermanns, H., Zhang, L.: Probabilistic reachability for parametric Markov models. Softw. Tools Technol. Transf. **13**(1), 3–19 (2010). https://doi.org/10.1007/s10009-010-0146-x
28. Hartmanns, A., Klauck, M., Parker, D., Quatmann, T., Ruijters, E.: The quantitative verification benchmark set. In: Vojnar, T., Zhang, L. (eds.) TACAS 2019. LNCS, vol. 11427, pp. 344–350. Springer, Cham (2019). https://doi.org/10.1007/978-3-030-17462-0_20
29. Herman, T.: Probabilistic self-stabilization. Inf. Process. Lett. **35**(2), 63–67 (1990)
30. Hutschenreiter, L., Baier, C., Klein, J.: Parametric Markov chains: PCTL complexity and fraction-free Gaussian elimination. In: GandALF, EPTCS, vol. 256 (2017)
31. Jansen, N., et al.: Accelerating parametric probabilistic verification. In: Norman, G., Sanders, W. (eds.) QEST 2014. LNCS, vol. 8657, pp. 404–420. Springer, Cham (2014). https://doi.org/10.1007/978-3-319-10696-0_31
32. Jonsson, B., Larsen, K.G.: Specification and refinement of probabilistic processes. In: LICS. IEEE CS (1991)
33. Jovanovic, D., de Moura, L.: Solving non-linear arithmetic. ACM Commun. Comput. Algebra **46**(3/4) (2012)
34. Junges, S., et al.: Finite-state controllers of POMDPs using parameter synthesis. In: UAI. AUAI Press (2018)
35. Katoen, J.P.: The probabilistic model checking landscape. In: LICS. ACM (2016)
36. Kwiatkowska, M., Norman, G., Parker, D.: PRISM 4.0: verification of probabilistic real-time systems. In: Gopalakrishnan, G., Qadeer, S. (eds.) CAV 2011. LNCS, vol. 6806, pp. 585–591. Springer, Heidelberg (2011). https://doi.org/10.1007/978-3-642-22110-1_47
37. Kwiatkowska, M.Z., Norman, G., Parker, D.: The PRISM benchmark suite. In: QEST. IEEE CS (2012)
38. Kwiatkowska, M.Z., Norman, G., Parker, D.: Probabilistic verification of Herman's self-stabilisation algorithm. Formal Asp. Comput. **24**(4–6), 661–670 (2012). https://doi.org/10.1007/s00165-012-0227-6
39. Norman, G., Parker, D., Kwiatkowska, M.Z., Shukla, S.K.: Evaluating the reliability of NAND multiplexing with PRISM. IEEE Trans. CAD Integr. Circuits Syst. **24**(10), 1629–1637 (2005)

40. Pathak, S., Ábrahám, E., Jansen, N., Tacchella, A., Katoen, J.-P.: A Greedy approach for the efficient repair of Stochastic models. In: Havelund, K., Holzmann, G., Joshi, R. (eds.) NFM 2015. LNCS, vol. 9058, pp. 295–309. Springer, Cham (2015). https://doi.org/10.1007/978-3-319-17524-9_21
41. Quatmann, T., Dehnert, C., Jansen, N., Junges, S., Katoen, J.-P.: Parameter synthesis for Markov models: faster than ever. In: Artho, C., Legay, A., Peled, D. (eds.) ATVA 2016. LNCS, vol. 9938, pp. 50–67. Springer, Cham (2016). https://doi.org/10.1007/978-3-319-46520-3_4
42. Reiter, M.K., Rubin, A.D.: Crowds: anonymity for web transactions. ACM Trans. Inf. Syst. Secur. **1**(1), 66–92 (1998)
43. Le Roux, S., Pérez, G.A.: The complexity of graph-based reductions for reachability in Markov decision processes. In: Baier, C., Dal Lago, U. (eds.) FoSSaCS 2018. LNCS, vol. 10803, pp. 367–383. Springer, Cham (2018). https://doi.org/10.1007/978-3-319-89366-2_20
44. Spel, J., Junges, S., Katoen, J.P.: Are parametric Markov chains monotonic? CoRR abs/1907.08491 (2019). extended version
45. Winkler, T., Junges, S., Pérez, G.A., Katoen, J.P.: On the complexity of reachability in parametric Markov decision processes. CoRR abs/1904.01503 (2019)

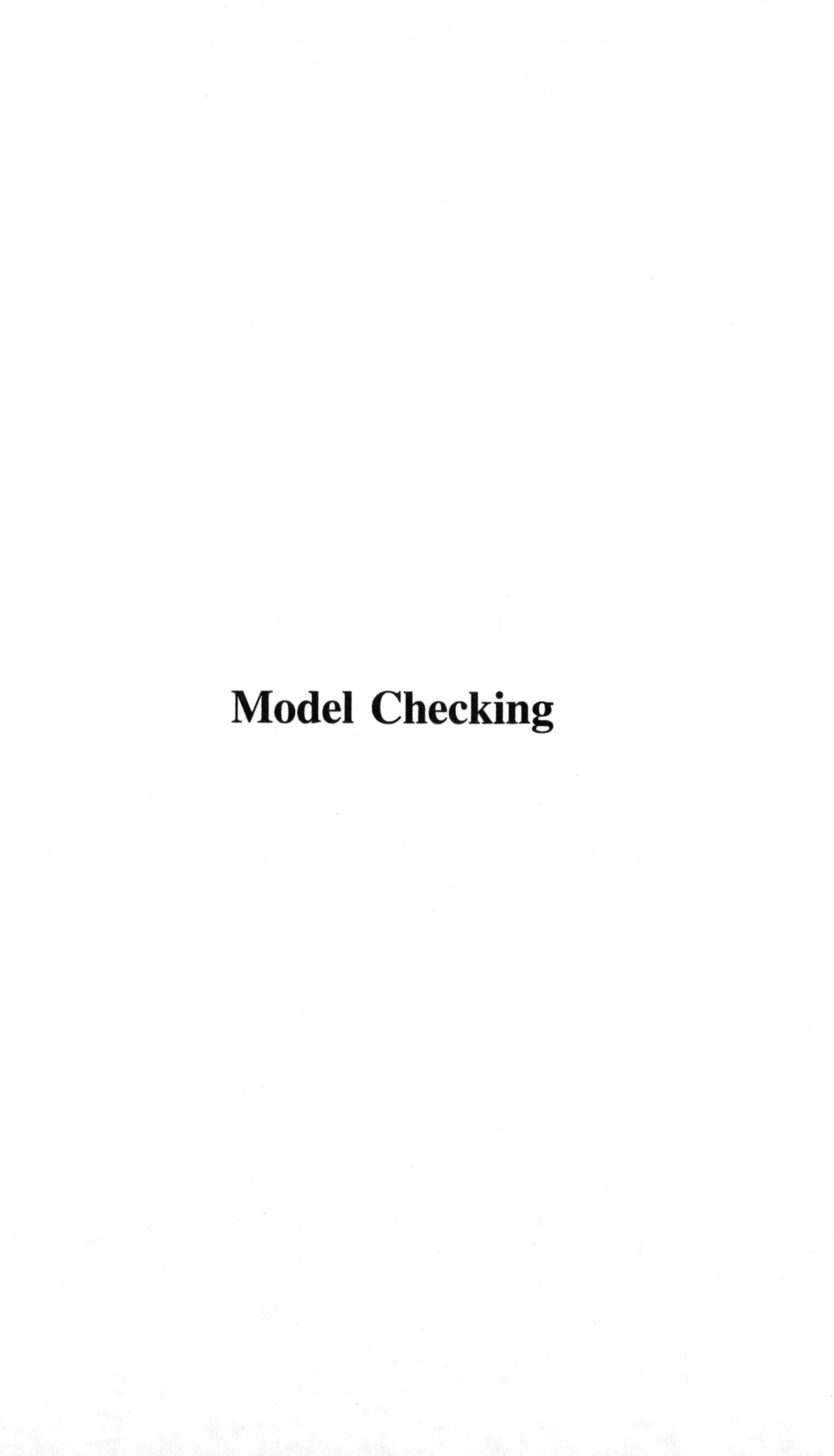

# Model Checking

# Efficient Information-Flow Verification Under Speculative Execution

Roderick Bloem[1], Swen Jacobs[2], and Yakir Vizel[3(✉)]

[1] Graz University of Technology, Graz, Austria
roderick.bloem@iaik.tugraz.at
[2] CISPA Helmholtz Center for Information Security, Saarbrücken, Germany
jacobs@cispa.saarland
[3] Technion, Haifa, Israel
yvizel@cs.technion.ac.il

**Abstract.** We study the formal verification of information-flow properties in the presence of speculative execution and side-channels. First, we present a formal model of speculative execution semantics. This model can be parameterized by the depth of speculative execution and is amenable to a range of verification techniques. Second, we introduce a novel notion of information leakage under speculation, which is parameterized by the information that is available to an attacker through side-channels. Finally, we present one verification technique that uses our formalism and can be used to detect information leaks under speculation through cache side-channels, and can decide whether these are only possible under speculative execution. We implemented an instance of this verification technique that combines taint analysis and safety model checking. We evaluated this approach on a range of examples that have been proposed as benchmarks for mitigations of the Spectre vulnerability, and show that our approach correctly identifies all information leaks.

**Keywords:** Verification · Information flow · Speculative execution · Side channels

## 1 Introduction

The Spectre attacks have shown how speculative execution in modern CPUs can lead to information leaks via side channels such as shared caches, even if the program under consideration is secure under a standard execution model [22]. Since speculative execution is an essential optimization for the performance of modern processors, the underlying vulnerability affects the vast majority of all processors in use today, and is not easy to fix without sacrificing a lot of the performance gains of recent years. The general assumption is that processors will remain vulnerable to Spectre for the foreseeable future, and therefore security can only be ensured on the software level, carefully taking into account the vulnerability of the hardware. Based on this observation, we develop a method


Y.-F. Chen et al. (Eds.): ATVA 2019, LNCS 11781, pp. 499–514, 2019.
https://doi.org/10.1007/978-3-030-31784-3_29

to detect whether a given program can potentially leak sensitive information due to the interplay of speculative execution and side-channel attacks, or prove that information-flow security properties hold despite these factors.

The Spectre vulnerability is exploited by (i) influencing the predictions that lead to the speculative execution of instructions, (ii) by feeding operands to these instructions that lead to secret data being stored or otherwise reflected in the microarchitectural state of the CPU, and (iii) observing these changes to the microarchitectural state through a side-channel. To achieve (i), the attacker can manipulate the *Pattern History Table* that predicts the choice of conditional branches [20,22], the *Branch Target Buffer* that predicts branch destination addresses [22], or the *Return Stack Buffer* that predicts return addresses [24]. To achieve points (ii) and (iii), the attacker can target different features of the microarchitecture to be observed through a side-channel, for example port contention [7] or, most commonly, caches [22].

In this paper, we provide a formal model for programs under a speculative execution semantics, and a formal notion of information-flow security that takes into account speculative execution and side-channels. Both the system model and the notion of security are designed to remain as close as possible to existing formalisms, in order to alleviate the adaptation of existing verification approaches to these new concepts. At the same time, they are sufficiently general and flexible to cover a wide range of different types of speculation and side-channels. Based on our new formalisms, we provide an algorithm that detects potential information leaks under speculative execution with cache side-channels, and demonstrate its capabilities on a benchmark set designed to test software for Spectre vulnerabilities [21].

### 1.1 An Example Problem and Our Solution

The program in Fig. 1 is a very basic example for a Spectre-style information leak.[1] Function main receives an input idx from the user. It checks whether the value of idx corresponds to an entry in array1, and if so, uses the value of array1[idx] to determine a position to read from in array2. The value of array2 at that position is then stored in a temporary variable temp.

```
int main(int argn, char* args[]) {
    int temp = 0;

    int idx = getc();
    if (idx < array1_size)
        temp = array2[array1[idx]*512];

    return 0;
}
```

**Fig. 1.** Vulnerability example

[1] It is, in fact, the basic example used in the Spectre paper [22].

Under standard execution semantics, the piece of code is harmless: since the condition on idx ensures that the access to array1 is within bounds, an attacker (that controls input idx) cannot obtain any information that is not in array1 or in the positions of array2 referenced by values in array1.

Under speculative execution, however, the command in line 6 can be executed before the condition in line 5 is evaluated. This is not a problem regarding the information available at the program level, since the value of temp will only be written into memory *after* it is determined that the speculation was correct. However, the read from array2 will load data into the cache at an address that is determined by the value in array1[idx], thus changing the microarchitectural state *during* speculation. Since the bounds check has not yet been evaluated, the access to array1 can read an arbitrary byte from memory, the value of which can leak to the attacker through a timing attack on the shared cache.

We provide a fully automatic method to detect such potential information leaks. To check whether the program above has potential information leaks under speculative execution, our implementation compiles the source code to LLVM intermediate code, which is then interpreted according to a non-standard speculative execution semantics to obtain a formal representation as a transition system. In its simplest form, the non-standard semantics allows us to ignore conditional statements, as long as we set a flag that signals that we are now operating under speculation. The resulting transition system is also equipped with a leakage model that represents the attacker's possible observations. In our example, the address of any memory access will be leaked to the attacker, modeling their capability to obtain this information through a side-channel attack. On this transition system, we then use a combination of taint analysis and safety model checking to determine whether there are information leaks, and whether they are only possible under speculative execution.

Our implementation correctly determines that there is an information leak in this example. Moreover, we support the insertion of a special stop command into the code that will halt speculative execution, as is done by insertion of serializing instructions such as LFENCE as an existing mitigation of Spectre. For the modified code with a stop added after line 5, our implementation correctly determines that no information leak is possible.

## 1.2 Contributions

The contributions of this work can be summarized as follows:

1. We provide a formal model for programs under a speculative execution semantics. Programs are modeled as transition systems, where speculation is added as an additional dimension. Moreover, the model supports *speculation barriers*, which can be used to explicitly stop speculative execution in branches that are deemed to handle sensitive information. Since this model is a very natural generalization of a standard operational semantics, it is easy to modify existing verification approaches to handle our model. Moreover, the model is based on a very general notion of speculation and is flexible with regards

to the information that is leaked to an attacker. Therefore, it covers a wide range of security vulnerabilities that are due to speculation and side-channel attacks.
2. We provide a formal notion of information-flow security under speculative execution. Like our system model, it is a natural generalization of existing formalisms, which means that existing approaches to security verification can, at least in theory, be easily adapted to reason about our new notion of security.
3. As an application of our formalisms, we present an algorithm that translates an input program into a transition system according to its speculative execution semantics, based on a leakage model for cache side-channels. The transition system is analyzed using a combination of taint analysis and safety verification that explicitly checks for operations that happen under speculation. This analysis finds potential information leaks that are due to speculation.
4. Finally, we evaluate our algorithm on a set of benchmarks that has been designed to test whether existing mitigations in compilers are effective in preventing Spectre leaks [21]. We show that it correctly detects Spectre-style information leaks in all cases, and correctly proves the absence of leaks after the manual insertion of speculation barriers.

### 1.3 Related Work

Our work is inspired by the Spectre attacks [22], which combine manipulation of speculative execution and side-channel attacks to read private data. There are several variants of the idea (summarized in [9]), and the approach we present in this paper can detect (potential) vulnerabilities of a program against Spectre variants V1 [22], V1.1 and V1.2 [20], as well as V4 [18]. Moreover, our model is sufficiently flexible to reason about leakage through a port contention side channel [7] and possibly other side channels, as long as observations that are possible through the side channel can be specified.

Several mitigations against Spectre have been proposed and partly implemented in compilers [17,25], but without any formal guarantee of security, and in some cases already demonstrated to be insufficient in general [21]. Taram et al. [30] introduced a method that introduces fences dynamically. They show that this can greatly reduce the overhead compared to static conservative fencing, but also do not give formal correctness guarantees.

There are several other variants of Spectre that rely on other features of the microarchitecture, such as branch target buffers or return stack buffers that are shared between users [22,24], or lazy context switching between users for FPU operations [29]. To support these, our model needs to be extended to a programming language with indirect jumps or return instructions, which is out of the scope of this paper.

**Formal Models for Side-Channel Attacks and Speculative Execution.** A significant number of works have considered side-channel attacks in a formal framework. One approach is to verify that a (cryptographic) program satisfies the *constant-time security* paradigm, which implies resistance against timing-based side-channel attacks. The applied reasoning methods range from deductive verification [3] and static analysis [27] to security type systems [1]. Almeida et al. [2] give a formal semantics for programs together with a flexible specification of side-channels similar to ours, and use an approach based on model-checking to verify information-flow security. While all of these approaches support verification of side-channel security in some form, none of them supports security under speculative execution, which is essential for our approach.

Correctness under speculative execution has been considered (i) at the level of the processor, i.e., aiming to verify that a given processor model with speculative execution satisfies some correctness criterion, and (ii) at the software level, based on a form of non-standard semantics of programs. Regarding (i), we note that to the best of our knowledge all of these works [16,19,23,28,32] only consider functional correctness properties (that are insufficient to express information-flow security), and also do not support side-channel leakage. One exception to the above is the framework of Arons and Pnueli [4] that allows the user to define which features of the microarchitecture can be used in the specification, in theory allowing to take side-channels into consideration. Interest in (ii) has thus far been very limited, and has also been restricted to functional correctness properties [8].

To the best of our knowledge, there are only two approaches that handle both side-channel attacks and speculative execution in a more or less formal way, both developed concurrently with our own approach. First, Wang et al. [33] have developed a static analysis to detect Spectre and Meltdown vulnerabilities. In contrast to our work, their focus has been on finding a practical solution that is specific to this class of vulnerabilities, while our main goal was to define a general model of speculative execution semantics and a corresponding notion of information-flow security that can be the basis of a wide range of solutions for the problem class. Second, Guarnieri et al. [13] have introduced a general notion of speculative non-interference, which however uses a significantly more involved model of speculative execution semantics, and results in a security notion that requires to reason about knowledge that is derivable from attacker observations. In comparison, our model and security notion are much simpler and closer to existing formalisms.

## 2 Preliminaries

We formalize the basic problem under consideration: given a program $P$, verify whether $P$ is secure against timing attacks.

**Transition Systems.** Let $X$ be a set of variables that is used to describe the program state, and $X' = \{x' \mid x \in X\}$ a copy of $X$, in the following used to represent the post-state of a transition. A *transition system* is given as a tuple $M = \langle X, \mathit{Init}(X), \mathit{Tr}(X, X')\rangle$ where $\mathit{Init}(X)$ is a (first-order) formula over $X$ representing the initial states, and $\mathit{Tr}(X, X')$ is a formula representing the transition relation.

A formula over the set of variables $X$ is called a *state formula.* A formula $\varphi(X, X')$ such that for every valuation $V$ of $X$ there is exactly one valuation $V'$ of $X'$ with $\varphi(V, V')$ is called a *state update function.* We denote by $\mathsf{unchanged}(Y)$ the state update function $\bigwedge_{x \in Y} x' = x$ for some $Y \subseteq X$. A *state* is a valuation of all variables. For a state $A$ and a variable $x \in X$, we denote by $A[x]$ the value of $x$ in $A$, and by $A[Y]$ the valuation of a set of variables $Y \subset X$. An *execution* of a transition system is a sequence of states $\pi := A_0, A_1, \ldots, A_n$, such that $A_0 \Rightarrow \mathit{Init}$ and for $1 \leq i \leq n$: $(A_{i-1}, A_i) \Rightarrow \mathit{Tr}$.

**Standard Program Semantics.** A transition system for a program can be obtained based on its operational semantics (for a fully formalized description see e.g. [2]). Programs in simple programming languages can be translated into a transition system in a straightforward way by encoding each line of the program into either a conditional or unconditional state update formula. A *conditional state update formula* is of the form

$$\tau_i := \mathsf{pc} = i \rightarrow \mathit{cond}(X) \ ? \ \varphi(X, X') : \psi(X, X'),$$

while an *unconditional state update formula* is of the form

$$\tau_i := \mathsf{pc} = i \rightarrow \varphi(X, X').$$

In both cases $i \in \mathbb{N}$ is the line of the program to be encoded, $\mathsf{pc}$ is a special program variable (the "program counter"), $\mathit{cond}(X)$ is a condition on the set of variables $X$, and $\varphi(X, X')$ and $\psi(X, X')$ are state update functions that should be executed when the condition is either true, or false, respectively. We refer to instructions as either conditional or unconditional depending on their corresponding state update formula. Moreover, the set of conditional instructions is denoted by $C \subseteq \mathbb{N}$, s.t. if $i \in C$, then $\tau_i$ is a conditional state update formula.

In addition, we consider a programming language that includes the special annotation $\mathsf{assume}(\mathit{cond}(X))$, which is encoded by

$$\tau_i := \mathsf{pc} = i \rightarrow \mathit{cond}(X) \ ? \ (\mathsf{pc}' = \mathsf{pc} + 1 \wedge \mathsf{unchanged}(X \setminus \{\mathsf{pc}\}) : \mathsf{false}.$$

This special annotation requires that at line $i$ the condition $\mathit{cond}(X)$ holds.[2] By conjoining the formulas for all lines of the program, one obtains a symbolic representation of the transition relation. Namely, $\mathit{Tr} := \bigwedge_i \tau_i$.

We will discuss in Sect. 3 how to obtain a transition system for the program under speculative semantics.

**Safety Verification.** Given a transition system $M$ and a formula $\mathit{Bad}(X)$, $M$ is *unsafe* w.r.t. *Bad* when there exists a run $\pi := A_0, A_1, \ldots, A_n$ of $M$ s.t. $A_n \Rightarrow \mathit{Bad}$. Such a run $\pi$ is called a *counterexample* (CEX). If no such $\pi$ exists, $M$ is *safe* w.r.t. *Bad*. The safety verification problem determines if $M$ is *safe* or *unsafe* w.r.t. *Bad*.

---

[2] If it does not hold, then the transition relation will evaluate to $\mathsf{false}$ for all post-states, i.e., the program halts.

### 2.1 Information Flow Analysis

Many security properties can be cast as the problem of verifying secure information flow. Namely, by proving that confidential data does not flow to non-confidential outputs (i.e. is not observable) during the execution of a system [12]. More formally, assume that $H \subset X$ is a set of *high-security* (or *secret*) variables and $L := X \setminus H$ is the set of *low-security* (or *public*) variables. Moreover, let $L = L_i \uplus L_o$, where $L_i$ are *input variables* that are controlled by the attacker, and for each *output variable* $x \in L_o$, let $O_x(X)$ be a predicate that determines when $x$ is observable. The set of output variables $L_o$ and their observation predicates $O_x$ depend on the threat model being considered.

*Example 1.* In the example from Fig. 1, we have $L_i$ = {argn, args, idx}, since these are inputs that can be chosen by the attacker. Moreover, we have $L_o = \{x\}$ for an auxiliary variable $x$ that, upon every array read a[i] is updated to the value of i, and is observable whenever it has been updated.[3] This models an attacker that uses a cache side-channel attack.

The *information flow problem* asks whether there exists a run of $M$ such that the value of variables in $H$ affects the value of a variable $x \in L_o$ in a state where $O_x(X)$ holds. Intuitively, this means that variable $x$ "leaks" secret information.

**Definition 1.** *Let $M$ be a transition system and let $H \subset X$ be a set of high-security variables and $L := X \setminus H$ a set of low-security variables with $L := L_i \uplus L_o$. $M$* leaks secret information, *denoted by $H \rightsquigarrow_M L$, iff there exists two executions $\pi^1 = A_0^1, \ldots, A_n^1$ and $\pi^2 = A_0^2, \ldots, A_n^2$ of $M$ s.t. the following formulas hold:*

$$\forall 0 \leq i \leq n, x \in L_i \cdot A_i^1[x] = A_i^2[x]$$
$$\exists 0 \leq i \leq n, x \in L_o \cdot (A_i^1 \Rightarrow O_x) \wedge (A_i^2 \Rightarrow O_x) \wedge A_i^1[x] \neq A_i^2[x]$$

When $M$ does not leak secret information, we write $H \not\rightsquigarrow_M L$. Moreover, when $M$ is clear from the context, we write $H \rightsquigarrow L$ (and respectively, $H \not\rightsquigarrow L$). Note that our definition can be instantiated to match a standard notion of non-interference that requires two executions with equal low-security values in the initial state to result in equal low-security values in the final state: assume that variables in $L_i$ are not changed during execution (otherwise generate a copy of the variable in $L_o$), and let all variables in $L_o$ only be observable in the final state.

There are two standard techniques that can be used to perform information flow analysis: *taint analysis* and *self-composition.*

**Taint Analysis.** Taint analysis instruments a program with taint variables and taint tracking code, which is used to simulate the flow of confidential data to public outputs. It operates by marking high-security variables with a "taint" and checking if this taint can propagate to low-security variables. It can be performed statically by analyzing the program's code [15,26] or symbolically when

[3] We assume that the compiler separates nested array reads into two separate reads.

described as a safety verification problem [34]. While taint analysis is efficient, it is imprecise since it over-approximates the possible leaks of the program.

**Self-composition.** In the most common use-case of safety verification, the goal is to prove a safety property that can be checked on a *single* run, such as functional correctness. Secure information flow, however, is a property that involves a comparison of two executions of the system, i.e., it is a *hyper-property* [11]. One approach to handling hyper-properties is self-composition [6], where the program $P$ is composed with one or more copies of itself. This composition results in a new program $P'$ such that a single run of $P'$ represents several runs of $P$ in parallel. By that, reasoning about hyper-properties is reduced to reasoning about properties of individual runs of the self-composed program $P'$. This allows to reason about hyper-properties using standard software model checkers [10,14]. However, in many cases, this approach does not scale to real-life programs [31].

# 3 A Formal Model for Speculative Execution

Speculative execution is an optimization technique for concurrent execution inside CPUs that reduces the idling time of a CPU by executing code *speculatively*, i.e., without knowing whether the given part of the program will actually be reached. To this end, it makes assumptions on branching conditions that may or may not turn out to be true in the future. Speculative execution is one of the cornerstones of modern out-of-order execution, and is to a large extent responsible for the dramatic performance improvement of CPUs in recent years.

We are interested in proving information-flow properties of programs that are executed in such an environment. To this end, we need a formal execution model that takes speculative execution into account. In the following, we introduce two variants of such a model and explain how to transform a given program into its formal representation.

## 3.1 Simple Speculative Execution Semantics

We explain the idea of a simple speculative execution semantics on an example.

*Example 2.* Consider the two programs that appear in Fig. 2. The program to the left (Fig. 2a) represents the standard execution semantics where the array is updated at index $i$ only if $i$ is in the range, and otherwise location 0 is updated. The program to the right (Fig. 2b), however, behaves differently. The condition that guards the array update is replaced with a non-deterministic choice, and either the `then` or `else` branch is taken. Moreover, the execution of a branch depends on both the condition and the possibility of speculative execution. This behavior is forced by the assumptions added in each branch. Note that the possibility of speculative execution is captured by a non-deterministic Boolean variable $\mathsf{spec}$.

```
int insert(int[] A, int len) {
    int v=f(), i=g();
    assume (i >= 0);
    if (i < len) {
        A[i] = v;
    } else {
        A[0] = v;
    }
    return v;
}
```

(a) Standard execution

```
int insert(int[] A, int len) {
    int v=f(), i=g();
    assume (i >= 0);
    bool spec = *;
    if (*) {
        assume(i < len ^ spec);
        A[i] = v;
    } else {
        assume(i >= len ^ spec);
        A[0] = v;
    }
    return v;
}
```

(b) Speculative execution

**Fig. 2.** Execution semantics example

**Translation to Simple Speculative Execution Semantics.** We now formalize the above example. Let $M = \langle X, \mathit{Init}, \mathit{Tr}\rangle$ be the transition system for a program $P$ according to its standard program semantics. To account for speculative execution we define a new transition system $\hat{M} = \langle X \cup \{\mathsf{spec}\}, \mathit{Init}, \hat{\mathit{Tr}}\rangle$, where $\mathsf{spec}$ is a new Boolean variable. $\mathsf{spec}$ is initialized non-deterministically and its post-state is defined by

$$\tau_i^s := \mathsf{pc} = i \rightarrow (\neg\mathsf{spec} \wedge i \in C)\ ?\ \mathsf{spec}' = * :\ \mathsf{spec}' = \mathsf{spec}.$$

Informally, this means that speculative execution can start whenever a conditional instruction executes, but then it will remain enabled for the rest of the program execution.

The effect of speculative execution is encoded by replacing every conditional instruction $\tau_i$ with:

$$\begin{aligned} \hat{\tau}_i := \mathsf{pc} = i \rightarrow * \ ?\\ (\neg\mathsf{spec} \Rightarrow (\mathit{cond}(X) \veebar \mathsf{spec}')) \wedge \varphi(X, X') :\\ (\neg\mathsf{spec} \Rightarrow (\neg\mathit{cond}(X) \veebar \mathsf{spec}')) \wedge \psi(X, X') \end{aligned}$$

where $\veebar$ represents an *exclusive or*. Note that a conjunct is added to the then and else parts of the conditional instruction. The conjunct forces the value of spec to become true when a branch is executed speculatively. Namely, the branch executes even though its condition does not hold. We emphasize that the added conjunct is guarded by the current-state value of spec. This is needed for the case of nested branches. If spec is already true when executing the conditional instruction, then the conjunct holds. Hence, if the program is already in speculative execution mode, then either branch can be taken. However, if spec is false, then the exclusive or ensures that either the guard (e.g. a condition of an if statement) for that branch holds, or the branch is executed speculatively (by forcing spec to become true), but both cannot happen simultaneously. This captures our intention of only detecting information leaks caused by misprediction.

```
int insert(int[] A, int len) {
    int v=f(), i=g();
    assume (i >= 0);

    if (i < len) {

       A[i] = v;

    } else {

       A[0] = v;

    }
    return v;
}
```

(a) Standard execution

```
int insert(int[] A, int len) {
    int v=f(), i=g();
    assume (i >= 0);
    int spec = *;
    if (*) {
       assume(i < len ^ 0 < spec < sigma);
       A[i] = v;
       if spec > 0 then spec += w();
    } else {
       assume(i >= len ^ 0 < spec < sigma);
       A[0] = v;
       if spec > 0 then spec += w();
    }
    return v;
}
```

(b) Bounded speculative execution

**Fig. 3.** Execution semantics with bound example

Unconditional instructions are kept unchanged, namely $\hat{\tau}_i := \tau_i$. The transition relation is then defined as $\hat{Tr} := (\bigwedge_i \hat{\tau}_i \wedge \tau_i^s)$.

In addition to the standard constructs of a simple language as sketched above, we assume a special command stop that acts as a barrier for stopping speculative execution. The stop command is defined by

$$\tau_i := \mathsf{pc} = i \rightarrow \neg\mathsf{spec}\ ?\ (\mathsf{pc}' = \mathsf{pc} + 1 \wedge \mathsf{unchanged}(X \setminus \{\mathsf{pc}\}) : \mathsf{false},$$

which is the same as $\mathsf{assume}(\neg\mathsf{spec})$.

### 3.2 An Architecture-Dependent Speculative Execution Semantics

In order to execute instructions speculatively, a recovery mechanism for undoing speculated instructions on miss-predicted branches or on exceptions is required. This "rollback" mechanism is implemented using a *reorder buffer* (ROB), which stores the results of instructions that are executed speculatively. When a miss-prediction is discovered, the ROB is flushed, otherwise a *commit* is performed. Note that the size of the ROB is fixed, hence it implies a bound on the number of instructions that can be executed speculatively.

In order to take this mechanism, of either rollback or commit, into account and make our analysis more precise, we introduce an advanced model where the system has a *bound* on the maximal depth of speculative execution (i.e., the number of steps that can be taken before execution under speculation is halted). We model this bound as a value $\sigma \in \mathbb{N} \cup \{\infty\}$, called the *speculative execution parameter.*

*Example 3.* The programs in Fig. 3 show the difference between standard semantics and bounded speculative execution semantics. As before, the left-hand side (Fig. 3a) represents the standard execution semantics. The right-hand side (Fig. 3b) again replaces the condition for the array update with a non-deterministic choice, but now the execution contains a condition on not only whether speculation has been enabled before, but also that the number of steps under speculation is below our bound $\sigma$. Note that the type of variable spec has changed from a Boolean to an integer. It is also important to note that spec is incremented by some value if it is enabled. The reason for this arbitrary value (represented by w() in our example) is that every instruction is translated into a different number of micro-ops. Hence, it occupies a different number of slots in the ROB.

**Translation to Architecture-Dependent Speculative Execution Semantics.** To formalize the idea, let again $M = \langle X, Init, Tr\rangle$ be a transition system for a program $P$. To model bounded speculative execution, we define a new speculative transition system $\check{M} = \langle X \cup \{\mathsf{spec}\}, Init, \check{Tr}\rangle$, where spec is a new variable of type $\mathbb{N}$. spec is initialized non-deterministically to either 0 or 1 and its post-state is defined by

$$\check{\tau}_i^s := \mathsf{pc} = i \rightarrow \mathsf{spec}' = (\mathsf{spec} > 0 \ ?\ \mathsf{spec} + w(i)\ \ : (i \in C\ ?\ \{0, w(i)\} : 0)) \\ \wedge\ \mathsf{spec}' < \sigma$$

where $\{0, w(i)\}$ is interpreted as non-deterministic choice between integers 0 and $w(i)$, and $w(i)$ represents the number of slots occupied in the ROB by instruction $i$. Informally, this means that speculative execution can start whenever a conditional instruction executes, but then it will remain enabled until we reach the speculation bound $\sigma$.

The effect of speculative execution is encoded by replacing every conditional instruction $\tau_i$ by:

$$\check{\tau}_i := \mathsf{pc} = i \rightarrow * \ ?\ (\mathsf{spec} = 0 \Rightarrow (cond(X) \veebar \mathsf{spec}' = w(i)) \wedge \varphi(X, X') \\ : (\mathsf{spec} = 0 \Rightarrow (\neg cond(X) \veebar \mathsf{spec}' = w(i)) \wedge \psi(X, X')$$

and keeping unconditional instructions unchanged, namely $\check{\tau}_i := \tau_i$. The transition relation is defined by $\check{Tr} := (\bigwedge_i \check{\tau}_i \wedge \check{\tau}_i^s)$. Similarly, we support a barrier command stop, which is in this case is defined by

$$\tau_i := \mathsf{pc} = i \rightarrow \mathsf{spec} = 0\ ?\ \ (\mathsf{pc}' = \mathsf{pc} + 1 \wedge \mathsf{unchanged}(X \setminus \{\mathsf{pc}\}) : \mathsf{false},$$

equivalent to $\mathsf{assume}(\mathsf{spec} = 0)$.

## 4 Information-Flow Security Under Speculative Execution

Our formal model for speculative execution represents the program as a transition system, which makes it amenable to many standard verification techniques. Moreover, our notion information-flow security (Definition 1) has been chosen with speculative execution in mind: since changes to the program state (in memory) based on speculative computations are only applied when it has been established that speculation was correct, the standard notion of non- interference is not affected by speculation at all. Therefore, we have to consider a notion that takes into account information about the microarchitectural state of the system that can be detected through side-channels. In the following, we generalize this notion of security to systems with speculative execution semantics.

*Example 4.* To motivate our definition, consider again the example in Fig. 1. The program receives an index idx from the user, accesses array1 at location idx, and then array2, based on the value of array1. To prevent an illegal access to array1, the access is guarded by an if statement. However, during speculative execution, the arrays may be accessed even when the condition does not hold. While this access will not change the state of the program in memory, it may alter the state of the cache, and therefore may leak sensitive information through a cache side-channel. If our attacker model includes cache side-channels, then the set of variables $L_o$ will contain a variable that is updated with every memory access a[i] to the address i, and is observable when the access happens.

Note that in order to take advantage of speculative execution, an attacker needs to be able to train the branch predictor, giving him some amount of control over speculative execution. As a conservative approximation, we assume that speculative execution is completely controlled by the attacker. Therefore, the new variable spec that indicates if speculative execution is performed in our model of speculative execution semantics should be controlled by the attacker. This very naturally leads us to the following definition of speculative information-flow:

**Definition 2.** *Let $P$ be a program, and let $\check{M}$ be the corresponding speculative transition system of $P$. Let $H, L \subset X$ be the sets of high and low security variables in $X$ with $L := L_i \uplus L_o$ and* spec $\in L_i$. *We say $\check{M}$* leaks information under speculative execution *if $H \rightsquigarrow_{\check{M}} L$.*

That is, we can reduce speculative information leaks to non-speculative information leaks by considering a model with speculative execution semantics and assuming that spec is under control of the attacker. Intuitively, if a path in $P$ that is only enabled due to speculative execution leaks private data, then we can detect this by comparing runs of that path with different values for $H$ but identical values for $L_i$, including identical speculation behavior. Note that if spec remains 0 (or false) for the whole run, then this notion of security coincides with Definition 1.

Since our notion of information-flow security under speculative execution is based on transition systems and is a natural generalization of existing notions, in theory it is not hard to extend existing approaches for verification of information flow such as self-composition or taint analysis to cover it. In practice however, the additional behaviors introduced by speculation will likely make an approach based on naive self-composition intractable. An implementation that handles non-trivial programs will require a specialized and more scalable solution.

### 4.1 Detecting Speculative Execution Leaks

We present an approach that uses the above formal model for detecting potential information leaks under speculative execution. More precisely, we are looking for

*Spectre leaks*, i.e., leaks through memory accesses that can be influenced by the user, using a cache side channel. To this end, it tries to find memory accesses a[i] such that i can be chosen or influenced by the attacker, and checks whether these accesses can happen under speculative execution. A high-level description of our approach appears in Algorithm 1.

1 $\check{M} \leftarrow$ `GetSpecTr`$(P, \sigma)$<br>
2 $I \leftarrow$ `AnalyzeInfFlow`$(\check{M})$<br>
3 **while** $I \neq \emptyset$ **do**<br>
4     pick $i \in I$<br>
5     **if** *i is memory access* **then**<br>
6         $res \leftarrow$ `CheckSpeculation`$(\check{M}, i)$<br>
7         **if** $res = \top$ **then**<br>
8             **return** possible Spectre leak<br>
9     $I \leftarrow I \setminus \{i\}$<br>
10 **return** no Spectre leaks

**Algorithm 1.** Detecting Spectre Attacks

The algorithm receives as an input a program $P$ to be analyzed, and a speculation bound $\sigma$. It then starts by creating a transition system $\check{M}$, which includes speculative execution semantics as described in Sect. 3 (line 1). Then, information flow analysis is performed to identify all instructions that may be affected by an attacker (line 2). All affected instructions are returned in $I$. This is done by tracking the effect low security variables have on high security variables. There are various ways to achieve this goal, such as *taint analysis* [26] and *self-composition* [5]. Since performing self-composition is often intractable, here we implemented a variant of the algorithm that uses taint analysis for this task.

Once $I$ is computed, the algorithm then analyzes all memory accesses in $I$. For every such memory access, a safety verification problem is generated and verified (line 6). This is achieved by adding an assertion that checks whether speculative execution is enabled at the location of the memory access (i.e. assert$(spec = 0)$). If any of these verification problems is unsafe and a counterexample is generated, then the algorithm concludes that the memory access can be executed speculatively. Moreover, this speculative execution can be manipulated by an attacker.

**Theorem 1.** *Algorithm 1 is sound.*

*Proof Idea.* If Algorithm 1 returns "no Spectre leaks" for inputs $P$ and $\sigma$, then in $\check{M}$ there is no memory access that can be influenced by the user and execute speculatively.

We emphasize that Algorithm 1 can prove the absence of Spectre-like attacks. However, it can not conclusively determine that such an attack exists. This is due to two reasons. First, identifying that a memory access can execute speculatively does not necessarily imply that it leaks secret information. Second, in the variant we implemented, we use taint analysis to compute such memory accesses that can be affected, and hence the set $I$ is an over-approximation. Making the algorithm more precise is left as an avenue for future work.

## 5 Evaluation and Conclusion

We have implemented our algorithm on top of the SeaHorn verification framework [14]. Taint analysis and the instrumentation of speculative execution semantics are implemented on top of LLVM.

For our evaluation, we used the examples from Paul Kocher's blog post [21] that have been designed to test whether existing mitigations against Spectre are sufficient to prevent information leaks. Our implementation identifies all of these examples as unsafe (possible leak due to speculative execution). In addition, we created a few SAFE examples (based on those from [21]). On these examples as well, our implementation identified the programs as SAFE.

Due to the size of these examples the runtime was small (about 1 s). We note that while these examples are only short code snippets, they cover a large range of cases in which speculation-based attacks may be possible.

To conclude, in this paper, we have introduced novel formalisms that allow us to reason about security vulnerabilities in the presence of speculative execution and side-channels, and give formal correctness guarantees by proving the absence of such vulnerabilities.

Our formalisms are designed to be as simple as possible, while still covering a wide range of Spectre-type attacks. They are also very natural generalizations of existing concepts, which makes it easy to extend existing verification algorithms to our more general setting, as demonstrated in our example algorithm based on taint analysis and safety verification.

As a future work, we aim at implementing other variants of our approach, which use our formalism and provide more precision and guarantees while remaining efficient.

**Acknowledgements.** Additional funding was provided by a generous gift from Intel. Any opinions, findings, and conclusions or recommendations expressed in this paper are those of the authors and do not necessarily reflect the views of the funding parties.

## References

1. Agat, J.: Transforming out timing leaks. In: POPL, pp. 40–53. ACM (2000). https://doi.org/10.1145/325694.325702
2. Almeida, J.B., Barbosa, M., Barthe, G., Dupressoir, F., Emmi, M.: Verifying constant-time implementations. In: USENIX Security, pp. 53–70. USENIX Association (2016). https://www.usenix.org/conference/usenixsecurity16/technical-sessions/presentation/almeida

3. Almeida, J.B., Barbosa, M., Pinto, J.S., Vieira, B.: Formal verification of side-channel countermeasures using self-composition. Sci. Comput. Program. **78**(7), 796–812 (2013). https://doi.org/10.1016/j.scico.2011.10.008
4. Arons, T., Pnueli, A.: A comparison of two verification methods for speculative instruction execution. In: Graf, S., Schwartzbach, M. (eds.) TACAS 2000. LNCS, vol. 1785, pp. 487–502. Springer, Heidelberg (2000). https://doi.org/10.1007/3-540-46419-0_33
5. Barthe, G., D'Argenio, P.R., Rezk, T.: Secure information flow by self-composition. In: Computer Security Foundations Workshop, (CSFW-17), pp. 100–114 (2004)
6. Barthe, G., D'Argenio, P.R., Rezk, T.: Secure information flow by self-composition. Math. Struct. Comput. Sci. **21**(6), 1207–1252 (2011). https://doi.org/10.1017/S0960129511000193
7. Bhattacharyya, A., et al.: Smotherspectre: exploiting speculative execution through port contention. CoRR abs/1903.01843 (2019). http://arxiv.org/abs/1903.01843
8. Boudol, G., Petri, G.: A theory of speculative computation. In: Gordon, A.D. (ed.) ESOP 2010. LNCS, vol. 6012, pp. 165–184. Springer, Heidelberg (2010). https://doi.org/10.1007/978-3-642-11957-6_10
9. Canella, C., et al.: A systematic evaluation of transient execution attacks and defenses. CoRR. https://arxiv.org/abs/1811.05441 (2018)
10. Clarke, E.M., Grumberg, O., Peled, D.A.: Model Checking. MIT Press, Cambridge (2001)
11. Clarkson, M.R., Finkbeiner, B., Koleini, M., Micinski, K.K., Rabe, M.N., Sánchez, C.: Temporal logics for hyperproperties. In: Abadi, M., Kremer, S. (eds.) POST 2014. LNCS, vol. 8414, pp. 265–284. Springer, Heidelberg (2014). https://doi.org/10.1007/978-3-642-54792-8_15
12. Denning, D.E., Denning, P.J.: Certification of programs for secure information flow. Commun. ACM **20**(7), 504–513 (1977)
13. Guarnieri, M., Köpf, B., Morales, J.F., Reineke, J., Sánchez, A.: SPECTECTOR: principled detection of speculative information flows. CoRR. http://arxiv.org/abs/1812.08639 (2018)
14. Gurfinkel, A., Kahsai, T., Komuravelli, A., Navas, J.A.: The seahorn verification framework. In: Kroening, D., Păsăreanu, C.S. (eds.) CAV 2015. LNCS, vol. 9206, pp. 343–361. Springer, Cham (2015). https://doi.org/10.1007/978-3-319-21690-4_20
15. Hammer, C., Snelting, G.: Flow-sensitive, context-sensitive, and object-sensitive information flow control based on program dependence graphs. Int. J. Inf. Secur. **8**(6), 399–422 (2009)
16. Hosabettu, R., Gopalakrishnan, G., Srivas, M.: Verifying advanced microarchitectures that support speculation and exceptions. In: Emerson, E.A., Sistla, A.P. (eds.) CAV 2000. LNCS, vol. 1855, pp. 521–537. Springer, Heidelberg (2000). https://doi.org/10.1007/10722167_39
17. Intel: White paper: intel analysis of speculative execution side channels. Tech. Rep. 336983–001, Revision 1.0. https://newsroom.intel.com/wp-content/uploads/sites/11/2018/01/Intel-Analysis-of-Speculative-Execution-Side-Channels.pdf
18. Intel: Q2 2018 speculative execution side channel update (2018). https://www.intel.com/content/www/us/en/security-center/advisory/intel-sa-00115.html. Accessed May 2019
19. Jhala, R., McMillan, K.L.: Microarchitecture verification by compositional model checking. In: Berry, G., Comon, H., Finkel, A. (eds.) CAV 2001. LNCS, vol. 2102, pp. 396–410. Springer, Heidelberg (2001). https://doi.org/10.1007/3-540-44585-4_40

20. Kiriansky, V., Waldspurger, C.: Speculative buffer overflows: attacks and defenses. CoRR. http://arxiv.org/abs/1807.03757 (2018)
21. Kocher, P.: Spectre Mitigations in Microsoft's C/C++ Compiler. https://www.paulkocher.com/doc/MicrosoftCompilerSpectreMitigation.html
22. Kocher, P., et al.: Spectre attacks: exploiting speculative execution. CoRR. http://arxiv.org/abs/1801.01203 (2018)
23. Lahiri, S.K., Bryant, R.E.: Deductive verification of advanced out-of-order microprocessors. In: Hunt, W.A., Somenzi, F. (eds.) CAV 2003. LNCS, vol. 2725, pp. 341–354. Springer, Heidelberg (2003). https://doi.org/10.1007/978-3-540-45069-6_33
24. Maisuradze, G., Rossow, C.: ret2spec: speculative execution using return stack buffers. In: CCS, pp. 2109–2122. ACM (2018). https://doi.org/10.1145/3243734.3243761
25. Pardoe, A.: Spectre mitigations in MSVC (2018). https://blogs.msdn.microsoft.com/vcblog/2018/01/15/spectre-mitigations-in-msvc/. Accessed May 2019
26. Pistoia, M., Flynn, R.J., Koved, L., Sreedhar, V.C.: Interprocedural analysis for privileged code placement and tainted variable detection. In: Black, A.P. (ed.) ECOOP 2005. LNCS, vol. 3586, pp. 362–386. Springer, Heidelberg (2005). https://doi.org/10.1007/11531142_16
27. Rodrigues, B., Pereira, F.M.Q., Aranha, D.F.: Sparse representation of implicit flows with applications to side-channel detection. In: CC, pp. 110–120. ACM (2016). https://doi.org/10.1145/2892208.2892230
28. Sawada, J., Hunt, W.A.: Processor verification with precise exceptions and speculative execution. In: Hu, A.J., Vardi, M.Y. (eds.) CAV 1998. LNCS, vol. 1427, pp. 135–146. Springer, Heidelberg (1998). https://doi.org/10.1007/BFb0028740
29. Stecklina, J., Prescher, T.: Lazyfp: leaking FPU register state using microarchitectural side-channels. CoRR. http://arxiv.org/abs/1806.07480 (2018)
30. Taram, M., Venkat, A., Tullsen, D.M.: Context-sensitive fencing: Securing speculative execution via microcode customization. In: ASPLOS, pp. 395–410. ACM (2019). https://doi.org/10.1145/3297858.3304060
31. Terauchi, T., Aiken, A.: Secure information flow as a safety problem. In: Hankin, C., Siveroni, I. (eds.) SAS 2005. LNCS, vol. 3672, pp. 352–367. Springer, Heidelberg (2005). https://doi.org/10.1007/11547662_24
32. Velev, M.N.: Formal verification of VLIW microprocessors with speculative execution. In: Emerson, E.A., Sistla, A.P. (eds.) CAV 2000. LNCS, vol. 1855, pp. 296–311. Springer, Heidelberg (2000). https://doi.org/10.1007/10722167_24
33. Wang, G., Chattopadhyay, S., Gotovchits, I., Mitra, T., Roychoudhury, A.: oo7: low-overhead defense against spectre attacks via binary analysis. CoRR. http://arxiv.org/abs/1807.05843 (2018)
34. Yang, W., Vizel, Y., Subramanyan, P., Gupta, A., Malik, S.: Lazy self-composition for security verification. In: Chockler, H., Weissenbacher, G. (eds.) CAV 2018. LNCS, vol. 10982, pp. 136–156. Springer, Cham (2018). https://doi.org/10.1007/978-3-319-96142-2_11

# Model Checking Data Flows in Concurrent Network Updates

Bernd Finkbeiner[1], Manuel Gieseking[2(✉)], Jesko Hecking-Harbusch[1], and Ernst-Rüdiger Olderog[2]

[1] Saarland University, Saarbrücken, Germany
finkbeiner@cs.uni-saarland.de, hecking-harbusch@react.uni-saarland.de
[2] University of Oldenburg, Oldenburg, Germany
{manuel.gieseking,olderog}@informatik.uni-oldenburg.de

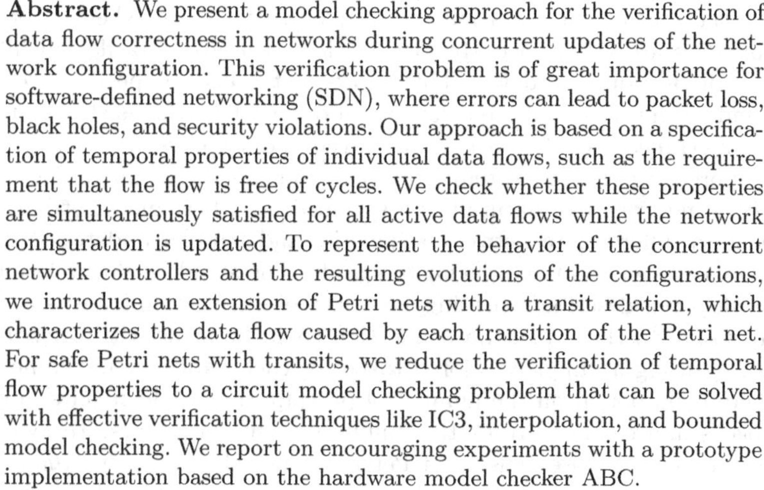

**Abstract.** We present a model checking approach for the verification of data flow correctness in networks during concurrent updates of the network configuration. This verification problem is of great importance for software-defined networking (SDN), where errors can lead to packet loss, black holes, and security violations. Our approach is based on a specification of temporal properties of individual data flows, such as the requirement that the flow is free of cycles. We check whether these properties are simultaneously satisfied for all active data flows while the network configuration is updated. To represent the behavior of the concurrent network controllers and the resulting evolutions of the configurations, we introduce an extension of Petri nets with a transit relation, which characterizes the data flow caused by each transition of the Petri net. For safe Petri nets with transits, we reduce the verification of temporal flow properties to a circuit model checking problem that can be solved with effective verification techniques like IC3, interpolation, and bounded model checking. We report on encouraging experiments with a prototype implementation based on the hardware model checker ABC.

## 1 Introduction

Software-defined networking (SDN) [7,33] is a networking technology that separates the packet forwarding process, called the *data plane*, from the routing process, called the *control plane*. Updates to the routing configuration can be initiated by a central controller and are then implemented in a distributed manner in the network. The separation of data plane and control plane makes the management of a software-defined network dramatically more efficient than a

This work was supported by the German Research Foundation (DFG) Grant Petri Games (392735815) and the Collaborative Research Center "Foundations of Perspicuous Software Systems" (TRR 248, 389792660), and by the European Research Council (ERC) Grant OSARES (683300).


Y.-F. Chen et al. (Eds.): ATVA 2019, LNCS 11781, pp. 515–533, 2019.
https://doi.org/10.1007/978-3-030-31784-3_30

traditional network. The model checking of network configurations and concurrent updates between them is a serious challenge. The distributed update process can cause issues like forwarding loops, black holes, and incoherent routing which, from the perspective of the end-user, result in performance degradation, broken connections, and security violations. Correctness of concurrent network updates has previously been addressed with restrictions like *consistent updates* [39]: every packet is guaranteed during its entire journey to either encounter the initial routing configuration or the final routing configuration, but never a mixture in the sense that some switches still apply the old routing configuration and others already apply the new routing configuration. Under these restrictions, updates to network configurations can be synthesized [12,32]. Ensuring consistent updates is slow and expensive: switches must store multiple routing tables and messages must be tagged with version numbers.

In this paper, we propose the *verification* of network configurations and concurrent updates between them. We specify desired properties of the data flows in the network, such as the absence of loops, and then automatically check, for a given initial routing configuration and a concurrent update, whether the specified properties are simultaneously satisfied for all active data flows while the routing configuration is updated. This allows us to check a specific concurrent update and to thus only impose a sequential order where this is strictly needed to avoid an erroneous configuration during the update process.

Our approach is based on temporal logic and model checking. The control plane of the network can naturally be specified as a Petri net. Petri nets are convenient to differentiate between sequential and parallel update steps. The data plane, however, is more difficult to specify. The standard flow relation of a Petri net does not describe which ingoing token of a transition transits to which outgoing token. In theory, such a connection could be made with *colored* Petri nets [22], by using a uniquely colored token for each data flow in the network. Since there is no bound on the number of packets, this would require infinitely many tokens and colors to track the infinitely many data flows. To avoid this problem, we develop an extension of Petri nets called *Petri nets with transits*, which augment standard Petri nets with a *transit relation*. This relation specifies the precise data flow between ingoing and outgoing tokens of a transition. In Petri nets with transits, a single token can carry an unbounded number of data flows.

We introduce a linear-time temporal logic called *Flow-LTL* to specify the correct data flows in Petri nets with transits. The logic expresses requirements on several separate timelines: global conditions, such as fairness, are expressed in terms of the global timeline of the system run. Requirements on individual data flows, such as that the data flow does not enter a loop, on the other hand, are expressed in terms of the timeline of that specific data flow. The next operator, for example, refers to the next step taken by the particular data flow, independently of the behavior of other, simultaneously active, data flows.

Concurrent updates of software-defined networks can be modeled as safe Petri nets with transits. We show that the model checking problem of the infinite state space of Petri nets with transits against a Flow-LTL formula can be reduced to

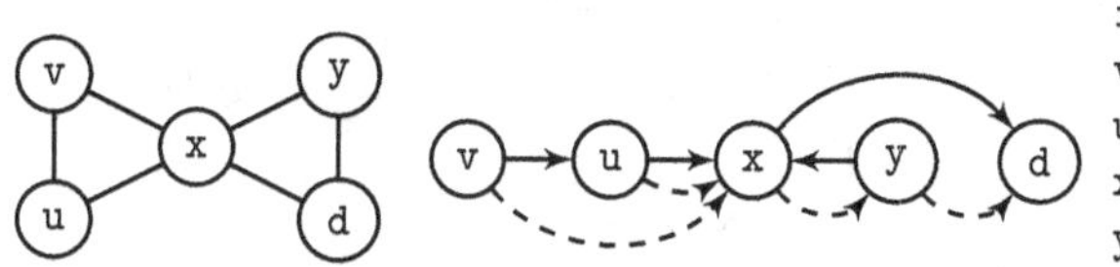


(a) Example of a network topology with five switches and six connections.

(b) Solid arrows show the forwarding rules before the update, dashed arrows the intended forwarding rules after the update.

```
ingress = {v}    ingress = {v}
v.fwd(u)              v.fwd(x)
u.fwd(x)              u.fwd(x)
x.fwd(d)              x.fwd(y)
y.fwd(x)              y.fwd(d)
egress = {d}     egress = {d}
```

(c) Network programs for the routing configurations before and after the update.

**Fig. 1.** Example (due to [19]) of an update to a software-defined network.

the LTL model checking problem for Petri nets with a finite number of tokens; and that this model checking problem can in turn be reduced to checking a hardware circuit against an LTL formula. This ultimately results in a standard verification problem, for which highly efficient tools such as ABC [2] exist.

Proofs and more detailed constructions can be found in the full paper [15].

## 2 Motivating Example

We motivate our approach with a typical network update problem taken from the literature [19]. Consider the simple network topology shown in Fig. 1a. From the global point of view, our goal is to update the network from the routing configuration shown with solid lines in Fig. 1b to the routing configuration shown with dashed lines. Such routing configurations are typically given as static NetCore [20,35] programs like the ones shown in Fig. 1c. The `ingress` and `egress` sections define where packets enter and leave the network, respectively. Expressions of the form `v.fwd(u)` define that switch `v` forwards packets to switch `u`.

It is not straightforward to see how the update from Fig. 1b can be implemented in a distributed manner. If switch `x` is updated to forward to switch `y` *before* `y` is updated to forward to switch `d`, then any data flow that reaches `x` is sent into a loop between `x` and `y`. A correct update process must thus ensure sequentiality between switch updates `upd(y.fwd(d))` and `upd(x.fwd(y))`, in this order. The only other switch with changing routing is switch `v`. This update can occur in any order. A correct concurrent update would thus work as follows:

```
(upd(y.fwd(d)) >> upd(x.fwd(y))) || upd(v.fwd(x)),
```

where `>>` and `||` denote sequential and parallel composition, respectively.

Figure 2 shows a Petri net model for the network topology and the concurrent update from the initial to the final routing configuration from Fig. 1. The right-hand side models the control plane, where, beginning in *update_start*, the update of `v` and, concurrently, the sequential update to `y` and then to `x` is initiated. Each marking of the net represents a control state of the network. Changes to the control state are thus modeled by the standard flow relation. Leaving out the control plane allows us to verify configurations of network topologies.

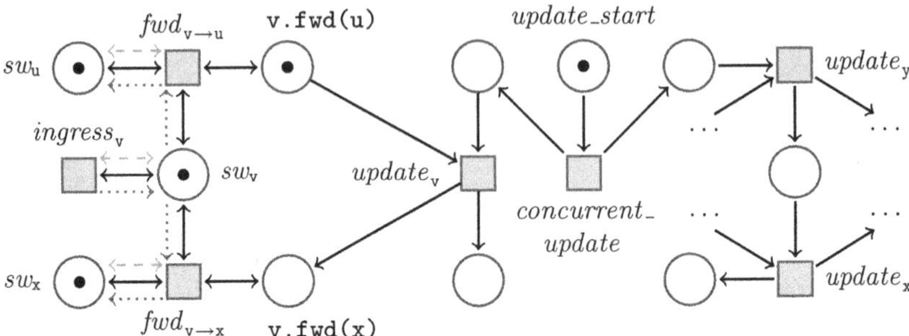


**Fig. 2.** Example Petri net with transits encoding the data plane on the left and the control plane on the right. The standard flow relation, describing the flow of tokens, is depicted by solid black arrows, the transit relation by colored arrows. Colors that occur on both ingoing and outgoing arrows of a transition define that the transition extends the data flow. If an outgoing arrow has a color that does not appear on an ingoing arrow, a new data flow is initiated.

On the left-hand side, we model the data plane by extending the Petri net with a transit relation. This new type of Petri nets will be defined formally in the next section. We only depict the update to the data flow in and from switch v. Places $sw_u$, $sw_v$, and $sw_x$ represent the switches u, v, and x, respectively. The data plane is modeled by the transit relation which indicates the extension of the data flows during each transition at the switches.

The standard flow relation is depicted by solid black arrows and the transit relation by colored arrows. If an outgoing arrow has a color that does *not* appear on an ingoing arrow, then a new data flow is initiated. In our example, data flows are initiated by transition $ingress_v$ and the (dotted) blue arrow. Colors that occur on both in-and outgoing arrows extend the data flow. In transition $fwd_{v \to u}$, the (dotted) blue arrows indicate the extension of the data flow from $sw_v$ to $sw_u$. The (dashed) green arrows between $fwd_{v \to u}$ and $sw_u$ indicate that, in addition to the incoming data flow from $sw_v$, there may be data flows that have previously reached $sw_u$ and have not yet departed from $sw_u$. These flows stay in $sw_u$.

Notice that $ingress_v$, $fwd_{v \to u}$, and $fwd_{v \to x}$ do not actually move tokens because of the double-headed arrows. None of these transitions change the control state, they only model the data flow. As the switches u, v, and x remain continuously active, their tokens in $sw_u$, $sw_v$, and $sw_x$ are never moved. By contrast, $update_v$ moves the token from `v.fwd(u)` to `v.fwd(x)`, thus disabling the data flow from $sw_v$ to $sw_u$ and enabling the data flow from $sw_v$ to $sw_x$. We specify the correctness of our update process with formulas of the temporal logic *Flow-LTL*. The formula $\mathbb{A} \Diamond \mathtt{d}$ expresses *connectivity* requiring that all data flows ($\mathbb{A}$) eventually ($\Diamond$) arrive at the egress switch d. Flow-LTL and the specification of data flow properties are discussed in more detail in Sects. 4 and 5. The general construction of the motivating example is formalized in the full paper [15].

## 3 Petri Nets with Transits

We give the formal definition of *Petri nets with transits*. We assume some basic knowledge about standard Petri nets [37]. A safe *Petri net with transits* (PNwT) is a structure $\mathcal{N} = (\mathcal{P}, \mathcal{T}, \mathcal{F}, In, \Upsilon)$, where the set of *places* $\mathcal{P}$, the set of *transitions* $\mathcal{T}$, the (*control*) *flow relation* $\mathcal{F} \subseteq (\mathcal{P} \times \mathcal{T}) \cup (\mathcal{T} \times \mathcal{P})$, and the *initial marking* $In \subseteq \mathcal{P}$ are as in *safe* Petri nets. In safe Petri nets, each reachable marking contains at most one token per place. We add the *transit relation* $\Upsilon$ of tokens for transitions to obtain Petri nets with transits. For each transition $t \in \mathcal{T}$, we postulate that $\Upsilon(t)$ is a relation of type $\Upsilon(t) \subseteq (pre^{\mathcal{N}}(t) \cup \{\rhd\}) \times post^{\mathcal{N}}(t)$, written in infix notation, where the symbol $\rhd$ denotes a *start*. $p\ \Upsilon(t)\ q$ defines that the token in place $p$ *transits* via transition $t$ to place $q$ and $\rhd\ \Upsilon(t)\ q$ defines that the token in place $q$ marks the start of a new data flow via transition $t$. The graphic representation of $\Upsilon(t)$ in Petri nets with transits uses a *color coding* as can be seen in Fig. 2. Black arrows represent the usual *control flow*. Other matching colors per transition are used to represent the transits of tokens. Transits allow us to specify which data flows are moved forward, split, and merged, which data flows are removed, and which data flows are newly created.

Data flows can be of infinite length and can be created at any point in time. Hence, the number of data flows existing in a place during an execution depends on the causal past of the place. Therefore, we recall informally the notions of unfoldings and runs [13,14] and apply them to Petri nets with transits. In the unfolding of a Petri net $\mathcal{N}$, every transition stands for the unique occurrence (instance) of a transition of $\mathcal{N}$ during an execution. To this end, every loop in $\mathcal{N}$ is unrolled and every join of transitions in a place is expanded by duplicating the place. Forward branching, however, is preserved. Formally, an *unfolding* is a branching process $\beta^U = (\mathcal{N}^U, \lambda^U)$ consisting of an occurrence net $\mathcal{N}^U$ and a homomorphism $\lambda^U$ that labels the places and transitions in $\mathcal{N}^U$ with the corresponding elements of $\mathcal{N}$. The unfolding exhibits concurrency, causality, and nondeterminism (forward branching) of the unique occurrences of the transitions in $\mathcal{N}$ during all possible executions. A *run* of $\mathcal{N}$ is a subprocess $\beta = (\mathcal{N}^R, \rho)$ of $\beta^U$, where $\forall p \in \mathcal{P}^R : |post^{\mathcal{N}^R}(p)| \leq 1$ holds, i.e., all nondeterminism has been resolved but concurrency is preserved. Thus, a run formalizes one concurrent execution of $\mathcal{N}$. We introduce the *unfolding of Petri nets with transits* by lifting the transit relation to the unfolding $\beta^U = (\mathcal{N}^U, \lambda^U)$. We define the relation $\Upsilon^U$ as follows: For any $t \in \mathcal{T}^U$, the transit relation $\Upsilon^U(t) \subseteq (pre^{\mathcal{N}^U}(t) \cup \{\rhd\}) \times post^{\mathcal{N}^U}(t)$ is defined for all $p, q \in \mathcal{P}^U$ by $p\ \Upsilon^U(t)\ q \Leftrightarrow \lambda^U(p)\ \Upsilon(\lambda^U(t))\ \lambda^U(q)$.

We use the transit relation in the unfolding to introduce (data) flow chains. A (*data*) *flow chain* in $\beta^U$ is a maximal sequence $\xi = p_0, t_0, p_1, t_1, p_2, \dots$ of places in $\mathcal{P}^U$ with connecting transitions in $\mathcal{T}^U$ such that

1. $\exists t \in \mathcal{T}^U : \rhd\ \Upsilon^U(t)\ p_0$,
2. if $\xi$ is infinite then for all $i \geq 0$ the transit relation $p_i\ \Upsilon^U(t_i)\ p_{i+1}$ holds,

3. if $\xi$ is finite, say $p_0, t_0, \ldots, t_{n-1}, p_n$ for some $n \geq 0$, then for all $i$ with $0 \leq i < n$ the transit relation $p_i \; \Upsilon^U(t_i) \; p_{i+1}$ holds, and there is no place $q \in \mathscr{P}^U$ and no transition $t \in \mathscr{T}^U$ with $p_n \; \Upsilon^U(t) \; q$.

## 4 Flow-LTL for Petri Nets with Transits

We recall LTL applied to Petri nets and define our extension *Flow-LTL* to specify the behavior of flow chains in Petri nets with transits. We fix a Petri net with transits $\mathscr{N} = (\mathscr{P}, \mathscr{T}, \mathscr{F}, In, \Upsilon)$ throughout the section.

### 4.1 Linear Temporal Logic for Petri Nets

We define $AP = \mathscr{P} \cup \mathscr{T}$ as the set of *atomic propositions*. The set LTL of *linear temporal logic* (LTL) formulas over $AP$ has the following syntax $\psi ::= true \mid a \mid \neg\psi \mid \psi_1 \wedge \psi_2 \mid \bigcirc\psi \mid \psi_1 \mathsf{U} \psi_2$, where $a \in AP$. Here, $\bigcirc$ is the *next* operator and $\mathsf{U}$ is the *until* operator. We use the abbreviated temporal operators $\Diamond$ (*eventually*) and $\Box$ (*always*) as usual. A *trace* is a mapping $\sigma : \mathbb{N} \longrightarrow 2^{AP}$. The trace $\sigma^i : \mathbb{N} \longrightarrow 2^{AP}$, defined by $\sigma^i(j) = \sigma(i+j)$ for all $j \in \mathbb{N}$, is the $i$th *suffix* of $\sigma$.

We define the traces of a Petri net based on its runs. Consider a run $\beta = (\mathscr{N}^R, \rho)$ of $\mathscr{N}$ and a finite or infinite firing sequence $\zeta = M_0[t_0\rangle M_1[t_1\rangle M_2 \cdots$ of $\mathscr{N}^R$ with $M_0 = In^R$. This sequence *covers* $\beta$ if $(\forall p \in \mathscr{P}^R \; \exists i \in \mathbb{N} : p \in M_i) \wedge (\forall t \in \mathscr{T}^R \; \exists i \in \mathbb{N} : t = t_i)$, i.e., all places and transitions in $\mathscr{N}^R$ appear in $\zeta$. Note that several firing sequences may cover $\beta$. To each firing sequence $\zeta$ covering $\beta$, we associate an infinite trace $\sigma(\zeta) : \mathbb{N} \longrightarrow 2^{AP}$. If $\zeta$ is finite, say $\zeta = M_0[t_0\rangle \cdots [t_{n-1}\rangle M_n$ for some $n \geq 0$, we define 1. $\sigma(\zeta)(i) = \rho(M_i) \cup \{\rho(t_i)\}$ for $0 \leq i < n$ and 2. $\sigma(\zeta)(j) = \rho(M_n)$ for $j \geq n$. Thus, we record for $0 \leq i < n$ (case 1) all places of the original net $\mathscr{N}$ that label the places in the marking $M_i$ in $\mathscr{N}^R$ and the transition of $\mathscr{N}$ that labels the transition $t_i$ in $\mathscr{N}^R$ outgoing from $M_i$. At the end (case 2), we *stutter* by repeating the set of places recorded in $\sigma(\zeta)(n)$ from $n$ onwards, but repeat no transition. If $\zeta$ is infinite we apply case 1 for all $i \geq 0$ as no stuttering is needed to generate an infinite trace $\sigma(\zeta)$.

We define the *semantics* of LTL on Petri nets by $\mathscr{N} \models_{\text{LTL}} \psi$ iff for all runs $\beta$ of $\mathscr{N}$ : $\beta \models_{\text{LTL}} \psi$, which means that for all firing sequences $\zeta$ covering $\beta$ : $\sigma(\zeta) \models_{\text{LTL}} \psi$, where the latter refers to the usual binary satisfaction relation $\models_{\text{LTL}}$ between traces $\sigma$ and formulas $\psi \in$ LTL defined by: $\sigma \models_{\text{LTL}} true$, $\sigma \models_{\text{LTL}} a$ iff $a \in \sigma(0)$, $\sigma \models_{\text{LTL}} \neg\psi$ iff not $\sigma \models_{\text{LTL}} \psi$, $\sigma \models_{\text{LTL}} \psi_1 \wedge \psi_2$ iff $\sigma \models_{\text{LTL}} \psi_1$ and $\sigma \models_{\text{LTL}} \psi_2$, $\sigma \models_{\text{LTL}} \bigcirc \psi$ iff $\sigma^1 \models_{\text{LTL}} \psi$, $\sigma \models_{\text{LTL}} \psi_1 \mathsf{U} \psi_2$ iff there exists a $j \geq 0$ with $\sigma^j \models_{\text{LTL}} \psi_2$ and for all $i$ with $0 \leq i < j$ the following holds: $\sigma^i \models_{\text{LTL}} \psi_1$.

### 4.2 Definition of Flow-LTL for Petri Nets with Transits

For Petri nets with transits, we wish to express requirements on several separate timelines. Based on the global timeline of the system run, global conditions like fairness and maximality can be expressed. Requirements on individual data flows, e.g., that the data flow does not enter a loop, are expressed in terms of the timeline of that specific data flow. *Flow-LTL* comprises of *run formulas* $\varphi$ specifying the usual LTL behavior on markings and *data flow formulas* $\varphi_F$ specifying properties of flow chains inside runs:

$$\varphi ::= \psi \mid \varphi_1 \wedge \varphi_2 \mid \varphi_1 \vee \varphi_2 \mid \psi \rightarrow \varphi \mid \varphi_F \quad \text{and} \quad \varphi_F ::= \mathbb{A}\ \psi$$

where formulas $\psi \in \texttt{LTL}$ may appear both inside $\varphi$ and $\varphi_F$.

To each flow chain $\xi$ in a run $\beta$, we associate an infinite *flow trace* $\sigma(\xi) : \mathbb{N} \longrightarrow 2^{AP}$. If $\xi$ is finite, say $\xi = p_0, t_0 \ldots, t_{n-1}, p_n$ for some $n \geq 0$, we define (1) $\sigma(\xi)(i) = \{\rho(p_i), \rho(t_i)\}$ for $0 \leq i < n$ and (2) $\sigma(\xi)(j) = \{\rho(p_n)\}$ for $j \geq n$.

Thus, we record for $0 \leq i < n$ (case 1) the place and the transition of the original net $\mathcal{N}$ that label the place $p_i$ in $\mathcal{N}^R$ and the transition $t_i$ in $\mathcal{N}^R$ outgoing from $p_i$. At the end (case 2), we *stutter* by repeating the place recorded in $\sigma(\xi)(n)$ infinitely often. No transition is repeated in this case.

If $\xi$ is infinite we apply case 1 for all $i \geq 0$. Here, no stuttering is needed to generate an infinite flow trace $\sigma(\xi)$ and each element of the trace consists of a place and a transition.

A Petri net with transits $\mathcal{N}$ satisfies $\varphi$, abbr. $\mathcal{N} \models \varphi$, if the following holds:

$$\begin{array}{ll}
\mathcal{N} \models \varphi & \text{iff for all runs } \beta \text{ of } \mathcal{N}: \ \beta \models \varphi \\
\beta \models \varphi & \text{iff for all firing sequences } \zeta \text{ covering } \beta: \ \beta, \sigma(\zeta) \models \varphi \\
\beta, \sigma(\zeta) \models \psi & \text{iff } \sigma(\zeta) \models_{\texttt{LTL}} \psi \\
\beta, \sigma(\zeta) \models \varphi_1 \wedge \varphi_2 & \text{iff } \beta, \sigma(\zeta) \models \varphi_1 \text{ and } \beta, \sigma(\zeta) \models \varphi_2 \\
\beta, \sigma(\zeta) \models \varphi_1 \vee \varphi_2 & \text{iff } \beta, \sigma(\zeta) \models \varphi_1 \text{ or } \beta, \sigma(\zeta) \models \varphi_2 \\
\beta, \sigma(\zeta) \models \psi \rightarrow \varphi & \text{iff } \beta, \sigma(\zeta) \models \psi \text{ implies } \beta, \sigma(\zeta) \models \varphi \\
\beta, \sigma(\zeta) \models \mathbb{A}\ \psi & \text{iff for all flow chains } \xi \text{ of } \beta: \ \sigma(\xi) \models_{\texttt{LTL}} \psi
\end{array}$$

## 5 Example Specifications

We illustrate Flow-LTL with examples from the literature on software-defined networking. Specifications on data flows like loop and drop freedom are encoded as data flow formulas. Fairness assumptions for switches are given as run formulas.

### 5.1 Data Flow Formulas

We show how properties from the literature can be encoded as data flow formulas. For a network topology, let *Sw* be the set of all switches, *Ingr* $\subseteq$ *Sw* the ingress switches, and *Egr* $\subseteq$ *Sw* the egress switches with *Ingr* $\cap$ *Egr* $= \emptyset$. The connections between switches are given by *Con* $\subseteq$ *Sw* $\times$ *Sw*.

**Loop Freedom.** Loop freedom [29] requires that a data flow visits every switch at most once. In Sect. 2, we outlined that arbitrarily ordered updates can lead

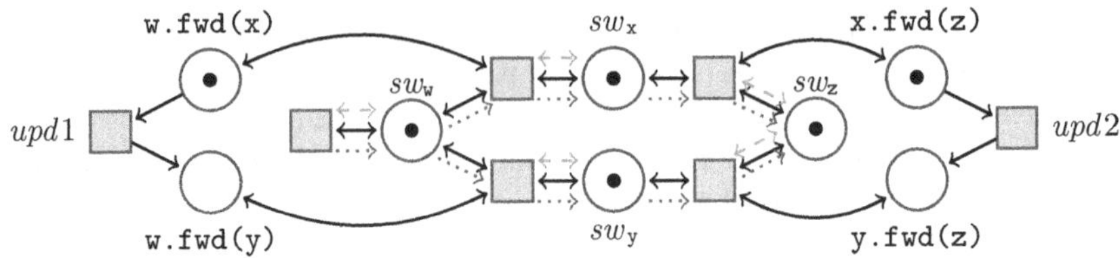


**Fig. 3.** Concurrent network update that does not preserve drop freedom.

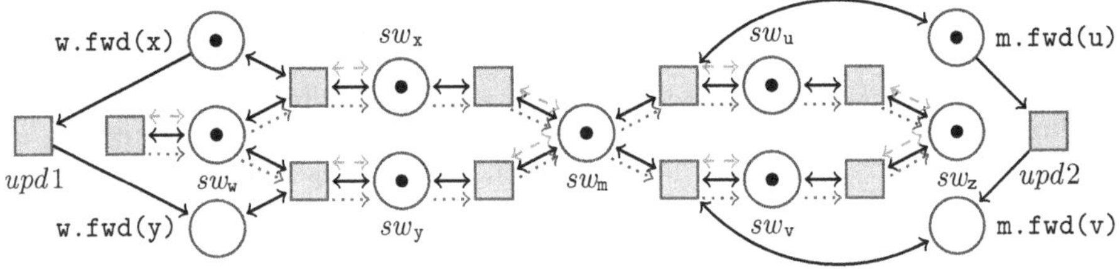


**Fig. 4.** Concurrent network update that does not preserve packet coherence.

to loops in the network. The following data flow formula expresses that each data flow is required to not visit a non-egress switch anymore after it has been forwarded and therefore left that switch (realized via the $\mathsf{U}$-operator):

$$\mathbb{A}\square(\bigwedge_{\mathsf{s}\in Sw\setminus Egr} \mathsf{s} \rightarrow (\mathsf{s}\,\mathsf{U}\,\square\neg\mathsf{s}))$$

**Drop Freedom.** Drop freedom [38] requires that no data packets are dropped. Packets are dropped by a switch if no forwarding is configured. We specify that all data flows not yet at the egress switches are extended by transitions from a set *Fwd* encoding the connections *Con* between switches (details of the encoding can be found in the full paper [15]). We obtain the following data flow formula:

$$\mathbb{A}\square(\bigwedge_{\mathsf{e}\in Egr} \neg\mathsf{e} \rightarrow \bigvee_{f\in Fwd} f)$$

*Example 1.* Figure 3 shows an example update that violates drop freedom. Packets are forwarded from switch w to switch z either via switch x or via switch y. If the forwarding of x is deactivated by firing transition *upd*2 *before* the forwarding of switch w is updated by firing *upd*1, then all packets still forwarded from w to x are dropped as no outgoing transitions from x will be enabled.

**Packet Coherence.** Packet coherence [1] requires that every data flow follows one of two paths: either the path according to the routing before the update or the path according to the routing after the update. The paths $Path_1$ and $Path_2$ are defined as the sets of switches of the forwarding route before and after the update. This results in the following data flow formula:

$$\mathbb{A}(\Box(\bigvee_{\mathtt{s}\in Path_1} \mathtt{s}) \vee \Box(\bigvee_{\mathtt{s}\in Path_2} \mathtt{s}))$$

*Example 2.* In Fig. 4, the encoding of an update to a double-diamond network topology [8] is depicted as a simple example for a packet incoherent update. Before firing the update transitions *upd*1 and *upd*2, packets are forwarded via switches x, m, and u, after the complete update, via switches y, m, and v. If m is updated by firing transition *upd*2 while packets have been forwarded to x then these packets are forwarded along the incoherent path x, m, and v.

We note that loop and drop freedom are incomparable requirements. Together, they imply that all packets reach one egress switch. Connectivity, in turn, implies drop freedom but not loop freedom, because an update can allow some loops.

### 5.2 Run Formulas

Data flow formulas require behavior on the maximal flow of packets and switches are assumed to forward packets in a fair manner. Both types of assumptions are expressed in Flow-LTL as run formulas. We typically consider implications between run formulas and data flow formulas.

**Maximality.** A run $\beta$ is *interleaving-maximal* if, whenever some transition is enabled, some transition will be taken: $\beta \models \Box(\bigvee_{t\in\mathcal{T}} pre(t) \rightarrow \bigvee_{t\in\mathcal{T}} t)$.
A run $\beta$ is *concurrency-maximal* if, when a transition $t$ is from a moment on always enabled, infinitely often a transition $t'$ (including $t$ itself) sharing a precondition with $t$ is taken: $\beta \models \bigwedge_{t\in\mathcal{T}}(\Diamond\Box\, pre(t) \rightarrow \Box\Diamond \bigvee_{p\,\in\, pre(t),\, t'\,\in\, post(p)} t')$.

**Fairness.** A run $\beta$ is *weakly fair* w.r.t. a transition $t$ if, whenever $t$ is always enabled after some point, $t$ is taken infinitely often: $\beta \models \Diamond\Box\, pre(t) \rightarrow \Box\Diamond t$.

A run $\beta$ is *strongly fair* w.r.t. $t$ if, whenever $t$ is enabled infinitely often, $t$ is taken infinitely often: $\beta \models \Box\Diamond\, pre(t) \rightarrow \Box\Diamond t$.

## 6 Model Checking Flow-LTL on Petri Nets with Transits

We solve the model checking problem of a Flow-LTL formula $\varphi$ on a Petri net with transits $\mathcal{N}$ in three steps:

1. $\mathcal{N}$ is encoded as a Petri net $\mathcal{N}^{>}$ without transits obtained by composing suitably modified copies of $\mathcal{N}$ such that each flow subformula in $\varphi$ can be checked for correctness using the corresponding copy.
2. $\varphi$ is transformed to an LTL-formula $\varphi^{>}$ which skips the uninvolved composition copies when evaluating run and flow parts, respectively.
3. $\mathcal{N}^{>}$ and $\varphi^{>}$ are encoded in a circuit and fair reachability is checked with a hardware model checker to answer if $\mathcal{N} \models \varphi$ holds.

Given a Petri net with transits $\mathcal{N} = (\mathcal{P}, \mathcal{T}, \mathcal{F}, In, \Upsilon)$ and a Flow-LTL formula $\varphi$ with subformulas $\varphi_{F_i} = \mathbb{A}\,\psi_i$, where $i = 1, \ldots, n$ for some $n \in \mathbb{N}$, we produce a Petri net $\mathcal{N}^> = (\mathcal{P}^>, \mathcal{T}^>, \mathcal{F}^>, \mathcal{F}_I^>, In^>)$ with inhibitor arcs (denoted by $\mathcal{F}_I^>$) and an LTL formula $\varphi^>$. An *inhibitor arc* is a directed arc from a place $p$ to a transition $t$, which only enables $t$ if $p$ contains no token. Graphically, those arcs are depicted as arrows equipped with a circle on their arrow tail.

### 6.1 From Petri Nets with Transits to P/T Petri Nets

We informally introduce the construction of $\mathcal{N}^>$ and Fig. 5 visualizes the process by an example. Details for this and the following constructions, as well as all proofs corresponding to Sect. 6 can be found in the full paper [15].

The *original part* of $\mathcal{N}^>$ (denoted by $\mathcal{N}_O^>$) is the original net $\mathcal{N}$ without transit relation and is used to check the run part of the formula. To $\mathcal{N}_O^>$, a *subnet* for each subformula $\mathbb{A}\,\psi_i$ of $\varphi$ is composed (denoted by $\mathcal{N}_i^>$, with places $\mathcal{P}_i^>$ and transitions $\mathcal{T}_i^>$), which serves for checking the corresponding data flow part of the formula $\varphi$. The subnet introduces the possibility to decide for the tracking of up to one specific flow chain by introducing a copy $[p]_i$ of each place $p \in \mathcal{P}$ and transitions simulating the transits. The place $[\iota]_i$ serves for starting the tracking. Each run of a subnet simulates one possible flow chain of $\mathcal{N}$, i.e., every firing sequence covering any run of $\mathcal{N}$ yields a flow chain.

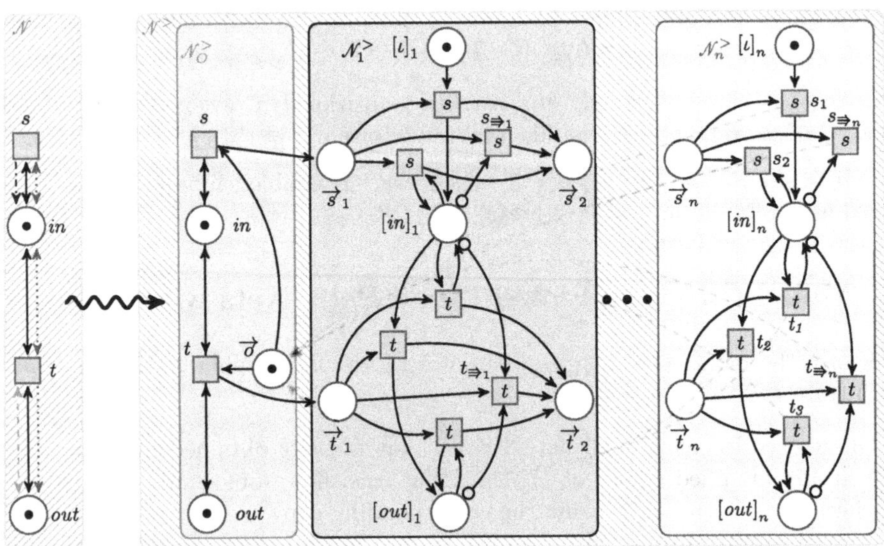


**Fig. 5.** An overview of the constructed P/T Petri net $\mathcal{N}^>$ (on the right) for an example Petri net with transits $\mathcal{N}$ (on the left) and $n$ flow subformulas $\mathbb{A}\,\psi_i$.

An *activation token* iterates sequentially through these components via places $\overrightarrow{t}$ for $t \in \mathcal{T}$. In each step, the active component has to fire exactly one transition and pass the active token to the next component. The sequence starts by $\mathcal{N}_O^>$ firing a transition $t$ and proceeds through every subnet simulating the data flows according to the transits of $t$. This implies that the subnets have to either move their data flow via a $t$-labelled transition $t'$ ($\lambda(t') = t$) or use the skipping transition $t_{\Rrightarrow_i}$ if their chain is not involved in the firing of $t$ or a newly created chain should not be considered in this run.

**Lemma 1 (Size of the Constructed Net).** *The constructed Petri net $\mathcal{N}^>$ has $\mathcal{O}(|\mathcal{N}| \cdot n)$ places and $\mathcal{O}(|\mathcal{N}|^3 \cdot n)$ transitions.*

### 6.2 From Flow-LTL Formulas to LTL Formulas

The two different kinds of timelines of $\varphi$ are encoded in the LTL formula $\varphi^>$. On the one hand, the data flow formulas $\mathbb{A}\,\psi_i$ in $\varphi$ are now checked on the corresponding subnets $\mathcal{N}_i^>$ and, on the other hand, the run formula part of $\varphi$ is checked on the original part of the net $\mathcal{N}_O^>$. In both cases, we need to ignore places and transitions from other parts of the composition. This is achieved by replacing each next operator $\bigcirc\,\phi$ and atomic proposition $t \in \mathcal{T}$ inside $\varphi$ with an until operator. Transitions which are not representing the considered timeline are called *unrelated*, others *related*. Via the until operator, all unrelated transitions can fire until a related transition is fired. This is formalized in Table 1 using the sets $O = \mathcal{T}^> \setminus \mathcal{T}$ and $O_i = (\mathcal{T}^> \setminus \mathcal{T}_i^>) \cup \{t_{\Rrightarrow_i} \in \mathcal{T}_i^> \mid t \in \mathcal{T}\}$, for the unrelated transitions of the original part and of the subnets, respectively. The related transitions of the original part are given by $\mathcal{T}$ and for the subnets by $M_i(t) = \{t' \in \mathcal{T}_i^> \setminus \{t_{\Rrightarrow_i}\} \mid \lambda(t') = t\}$ and $M_i = \mathcal{T}_i^> \setminus \{t_{\Rrightarrow_i} \in \mathcal{T}_i^> \mid t \in \mathcal{T}\}$.

**Table 1.** Row 1 considers the substitutions in the run part of $\varphi$, row 2 the substitutions in each subformula $\varphi_{F_i}$. Column 1 considers simultaneously substitutions, column 2 substitutions from the inner- to the outermost occurrence.

| $t \in \mathcal{T}$ | $\bigcirc\,\phi$ |
|---|---|
| $(\bigvee_{t' \in O} t')\,\mathsf{U}\,t$ | $((\bigvee_{t \in O} t)\,\mathsf{U}\,((\bigvee_{t' \in \mathcal{T}} t') \wedge \bigcirc\,\phi)) \vee (\square(\neg(\bigvee_{t' \in \mathcal{T}} t')) \wedge \phi)$ |
| $(\bigvee_{t_o \in O_i} t_o)\,\mathsf{U}\,(\bigvee_{t_m \in M_i(t)} t_m)$ | $((\bigvee_{t \in O_i} t)\,\mathsf{U}\,((\bigvee_{t \in M_i} t) \wedge \bigcirc\,\phi)) \vee (\square(\neg(\bigvee_{t \in M_i} t)) \wedge \phi)$ |

Additionally, every atomic proposition $p \in \mathcal{P}$ in the scope of a flow operator is simultaneously substituted with its corresponding place $[p]_i$ of the subnet. Every flow subformula $\mathbb{A}\,\psi_i$ is substituted with $\square[\iota]_i \vee ([\iota]_i\,\mathsf{U}\,\psi_i')$, where $\square[\iota]_i$ represents that no flow chain is tracked and $\psi_i'$ is the result of the substitutions of atomic propositions and next operators described before. The until operator in $[\iota]_i\,\mathsf{U}\,\psi_i'$ ensures to only check the flow subformula at the time the chain is created. Finally, restricting runs to not end in any of the subnets yields the final formula $\varphi^{>} = (\Box\Diamond\overrightarrow{o}) \rightarrow \varphi^{\mathbb{A}}$ with $\overrightarrow{o}$ being the activation place of the original part of the net and $\varphi^{\mathbb{A}}$ the result of the substitution of all flow subformulas.

**Lemma 2 (Size of the Constructed Formula).** *The size of the constructed LTL formula $\varphi^{>}$ is in $\mathcal{O}(|\mathcal{N}|^3 \cdot n \cdot |\varphi|)$.*

**Lemma 3 (Correctness of the Transformation).** *For a Petri net with transits $\mathcal{N}$ and a Flow-LTL formula $\varphi$, there exists a safe P/T Petri net $\mathcal{N}^{>}$ with inhibitor arcs and an LTL formula $\varphi^{>}$ such that $\mathcal{N} \models \varphi$ iff $\mathcal{N}^{>} \models_{\text{LTL}} \varphi^{>}$.*

### 6.3 Petri Net Model Checking with Circuits

We translate the model checking of an LTL formula $\psi$ with places and transitions as atomic propositions on a safe P/T Petri net with inhibitor arcs $\mathcal{N}$ to a model checking problem on a circuit. We define the circuit $\mathcal{C}_{\mathcal{N}}$ simulating $\mathcal{N}$ and an adapted formula $\psi'$, which can be checked by modern model checkers [2,9,18].

A *circuit* $\mathcal{C} = (\mathcal{I}, \mathcal{O}, \mathcal{L}, \mathcal{F})$ consists of boolean variables $\mathcal{I}$, $\mathcal{O}$, $\mathcal{L}$ for input, output, latches, and a boolean formula $\mathcal{F}$ over $\mathcal{I} \times \mathcal{L} \times \mathcal{O} \times \mathcal{L}$, which is deterministic in $\mathcal{I} \times \mathcal{L}$. The formula $\mathcal{F}$ can be seen as transition relation from a valuation of the input variables and the current state of the latches to the valuation of the output variables and the next state of the latches. A circuit $\mathcal{C}$ can be interpreted as a Kripke structure such that the satisfiability of a formula $\psi'$ (denoted by $\mathcal{C} \models \psi'$) can be defined by the satisfiability in the Kripke structure.

The desired circuit $\mathcal{C}_{\mathcal{N}}$ has a latch for each place $p \in \mathcal{P}$ to store the current *marking*, a latch $\mathtt{i}$ for *initializing* this marking with *In* in the first step, and a latch $\mathtt{e}$ for handling *invalid* inputs. The inputs $\mathcal{I}$ consider the firing of a transition $t \in \mathcal{T}$. The latch $\mathtt{i}$ is true in every but the first step. The latch $\mathtt{e}$ is true whenever invalid values are applied on the inputs, i.e., the firing of not enabled, or more than one transition. The marking latches are updated according to the firing of the valid transition. If currently no valid input is applied, the marking is kept from the previous step. There is an output for each place (the current marking), for each transition (the transition leading to the next marking), and for the current value of the invalid latch. We create $\psi'$ by skipping the initial step and allowing invalid inputs only at the end of a trace: $\psi' = \bigcirc(\Box(\mathtt{e} \rightarrow \Box\mathtt{e}) \rightarrow \psi)$. This allows for finite firing sequences. The concrete formula $\mathcal{F}$, the Kripke structure, and the corresponding proofs can be found in the full paper [15]. The circuit $\mathcal{C}_{\mathcal{N}}$ can be encoded as an and-inverter graph in the Aiger format [4].

**Lemma 4 (Correctness of the Circuit).** *For a safe P/T Petri net with inhibitor arcs $\mathcal{N}$ and an LTL formula $\psi$, there exists a circuit $\mathcal{C}_{\mathcal{N}}$ with $|\mathcal{P}|+2$ latches and $\mathcal{O}(|\mathcal{N}|^2)$ gates, and $\psi'$ of size $\mathcal{O}(|\psi|)$ such that $\mathcal{N} \models_{\text{LTL}} \psi$ iff $\mathcal{C}_{\mathcal{N}} \models \psi'$.*

**Theorem 1.** *A safe Petri net with transits $\mathcal{N}$ can be checked against a Flow-LTL formula $\varphi$ in single-exponential time in the size of $\mathcal{N}$ and $\varphi$.*

Checking a safe Petri net with transits against Flow-LTL has a PSPACE-hard lower bound because checking a safe Petri net against LTL is a special case of this problem and reachability of safe Petri nets is PSPACE-complete.

## 7 Implementation Details and Experimental Results

We implemented our model checking approach in a prototype tool based on the tool ADAM [16]. Our tool takes as input a Flow-LTL specification and a Petri net with transits, and carries out the transformation described in Sect. 6 to obtain an LTL formula and an Aiger circuit. We then use MCHyper [18] to combine the circuit and the LTL formula into another Aiger circuit. MCHyper is a verification tool for HyperLTL [10], which subsumes LTL. The actual model checking is carried out by the hardware model checker ABC [2]. ABC provides a toolbox of state-of-the-art verification and falsification techniques like IC3 [5]/PDR [11], interpolation (INT) [34], and bounded model checking [3] (BMC, BMC2, BMC3). We prepared an artifact to replicate our experimental results [21].

Our experimental results cover two benchmark families (SF/RP) and a case study (RU) from software-defined networking on real-world network topologies:

**Switch Failure** (SF) (*Parameter:* $n$ switches): From a sequence of $n$ switches with the ingress at the beginning and the egress at the end, a failing switch is chosen at random and removed. Then, data flows are bypassed from the predecessor to the successor of the failing switch. Every data flow reaches the egress node no matter of the update (connectivity).

**Redundant Pipeline** (RP) (*Parameters:* $n_1$ switches in pipeline one / $n_2$ switches in pipeline two / $v$ version): The *base version (B)* contains two disjoint sequences of switches from the ingress to the egress, possibly with differing length. For this and the next two versions, it is required that each data flow reaches the egress node (connectivity) and is only forwarded via the first or the second pipeline (packet coherence). *Update version (U):* Two updates are added that can concurrently remove the first node of any pipeline and return the data flows to the ingress. If both updates happen, data flows do not reach the egress. Returning the data flows violates packet coherence. *Mutex version (M):* A mutex is added to the update version such that at most one pipeline can be broken. Updates can happen sequentially such that data flows are in a cycle through the ingress. *Correct version (C):* The requirements are weakened such that each data flow only has to reach the egress when updates do not occur infinitely often.

**Routing Update** (RU) is a case study based on realistic software-defined networks. We picked 31 real-world network topologies from [26]. For each network, we choose at random an ingress switch, an egress switch, and a loop- and drop-free initial configuration between the two. For a different, random final configuration, we build a sequential update in reverse from egress to ingress. The update overlaps with the initial configuration at some point during the update or is activated from the ingress in the last step. It is checked if all packets reach the egress (T) and if all packets reach another specific switch as an egress (F).

**Table 2.** Experimental results from the benchmark families Switch Failure (SF) and Redundant Pipeline (RP), and the case study Routing Update (RU). The results are the average over five runs on an Intel i7-2700K CPU with 3.50 GHz, 32 GB RAM, and a timeout of 30 min.

| | | | PNwT | | | Translated PN | | | Circuit | | Result | | |
|---|---|---|---|---|---|---|---|---|---|---|---|---|---|
| Ben. | Par. | $\#S$ | $\|\mathcal{P}\|$ | $\|\mathcal{T}\|$ | $\|\varphi\|$ | $\|\mathcal{P}^{>}\|$ | $\|\mathcal{T}^{>}\|$ | $\|\psi'\|$ | Lat. | Gat. | Sec. | Algo. | $\models$ |
| SF | 3 | 4 | 4 | 5 | 35 | 17 | 22 | 60 | 90 | 2796 | 2.7 | IC3 | ✓ |
| | ... | ... | | | | | | | | | ... | | |
| | 9 | 10 | 10 | 11 | 95 | 35 | 46 | 138 | 186 | 8700 | 1359.9 | IC3 | ✓ |
| | 10 | 11 | 11 | 12 | 105 | 38 | 50 | 151 | 202 | 9964 | TO | - | ? |
| RP | 1/1/B | 4 | 4 | 5 | 43 | 17 | 22 | 68 | 100 | 2989 | 4.0 | IC3 | ✓ |
| | ... | ... | | | | | | | | | ... | | |
| | 4/4/B | 10 | 10 | 11 | 103 | 35 | 46 | 146 | 196 | 8893 | 646.4 | IC3 | ✓ |
| | 4/5/B | 11 | 11 | 12 | 113 | 38 | 50 | 159 | 212 | 10157 | TO | - | ? |
| | 1/1/U | 6 | 6 | 9 | 63 | 25 | 36 | 100 | 136 | 5535 | 1.6 | BMC2 | ✗ |
| | ... | ... | | | | | | | | | ... | | |
| | 5/4/U | 13 | 13 | 16 | 133 | 46 | 64 | 191 | 248 | 14523 | 945.1 | BMC3 | ✗ |
| | 5/5/U | 14 | 14 | 17 | 143 | 49 | 68 | 204 | 264 | 16127 | TO | - | ? |
| | 1/1/M | 6 | 9 | 11 | 63 | 30 | 42 | 106 | 146 | 6908 | 8.1 | BMC3 | ✗ |
| | ... | ... | | | | | | | | | ... | | |
| | 4/3/M | 11 | 14 | 16 | 113 | 45 | 62 | 171 | 226 | 13573 | 1449.6 | BMC2 | ✗ |
| | 4/4/M | 12 | 15 | 17 | 123 | 48 | 66 | 184 | 242 | 15146 | TO | - | ? |
| | 1/1/C | 6 | 9 | 11 | 70 | 30 | 42 | 113 | 151 | 7023 | 63.1 | IC3 | ✓ |
| | ... | ... | | | | | | | | | ... | | |
| | 3/3/C | 10 | 13 | 15 | 110 | 42 | 58 | 165 | 215 | 12195 | 1218.0 | IC3 | ✓ |
| | 3/4/C | 11 | 14 | 16 | 120 | 45 | 62 | 178 | 231 | 13688 | TO | - | ? |
| RU | Arpanet196912T | 4 | 14 | 10 | 117 | 31 | 39 | 154 | 188 | 7483 | 22.7 | IC3 | ✓ |
| | Arpanet196912F | 4 | 14 | 10 | 117 | 31 | 39 | 154 | 188 | 7483 | 2.0 | BMC3 | ✗ |
| | NapnetT | 6 | 23 | 17 | 199 | 48 | 64 | 254 | 292 | 15875 | 95.1 | IC3 | ✓ |
| | NapnetF | 6 | 23 | 17 | 199 | 48 | 64 | 254 | 292 | 15875 | 4.7 | BMC3 | ✗ |
| | ... | ... | | | | | | | | | ... | | |
| | NetrailT | 7 | 30 | 23 | 271 | 62 | 88 | 344 | 380 | 26101 | 145.3 | IC3 | ✓ |
| | NetrailF | 7 | 30 | 23 | 271 | 62 | 88 | 344 | 380 | 26101 | 58.3 | BMC3 | ✗ |
| | Arpanet19706T | 9 | 33 | 24 | 281 | 67 | 89 | 354 | 400 | 27619 | 507.8 | IC3 | ✓ |
| | Arpanet19706F | 9 | 33 | 24 | 281 | 67 | 89 | 354 | 400 | 27619 | 49.7 | BMC3 | ✗ |
| | NsfcnetT | 10 | 31 | 22 | 261 | 65 | 87 | 334 | 376 | 26181 | 304.8 | IC3 | ✓ |
| | NsfcnetF | 10 | 31 | 22 | 261 | 65 | 87 | 334 | 376 | 26181 | 8.4 | BMC3 | ✗ |
| | ... | ... | | | | | | | | | ... | | |
| | TwarenF | 20 | 65 | 45 | 531 | 130 | 170 | 664 | 736 | 87493 | 461.5 | BMC3 | ✗ |
| | MarnetF | 20 | 77 | 57 | 679 | 156 | 224 | 854 | 908 | 138103 | 746.1 | BMC3 | ✗ |
| | JanetlenseF | 20 | 91 | 71 | 847 | 184 | 280 | 1064 | 1104 | 203595 | 514.2 | BMC2 | ✗ |
| | HarnetF | 21 | 71 | 50 | 593 | 143 | 193 | 744 | 812 | 108415 | 919.0 | BMC3 | ✗ |
| | Belnet2009F | 21 | 71 | 50 | 597 | 145 | 199 | 754 | 816 | 113397 | 1163.3 | BMC2 | ✗ |
| | ... | ... | | | | | | | | | ... | | |
| | UranF | 24 | 56 | 38 | 449 | 106 | 133 | 552 | 618 | 57950 | 143.2 | BMC3 | ✗ |
| | KentmanFeb2008F | 26 | 82 | 56 | 669 | 167 | 223 | 844 | 920 | 142291 | 111.2 | BMC3 | ✗ |
| | Garr200212F | 27 | 86 | 59 | 703 | 174 | 232 | 884 | 964 | 153509 | 324.2 | BMC3 | ✗ |
| | IinetF | 31 | 104 | 73 | 871 | 210 | 288 | 1094 | 1176 | 227153 | 1244.5 | BMC3 | ✗ |
| | KentmanJan2011F | 38 | 117 | 79 | 943 | 236 | 312 | 1184 | 1288 | 269943 | 112.6 | BMC3 | ✗ |

**Table 3.** For the network topology Napnet and a concurrent update between two randomly generated topologies, our four standard requirements are checked.

| | | PN w. Transits | | | Translated PN | | | Circuit | | Result | | |
|---|---|---|---|---|---|---|---|---|---|---|---|---|
| Ben. | Req. | $\lvert\mathcal{P}\rvert$ | $\lvert\mathcal{T}\rvert$ | $\lvert\varphi\rvert$ | $\lvert\mathcal{P}^{>}\rvert$ | $\lvert\mathcal{T}^{>}\rvert$ | $\lvert\psi'\rvert$ | Latches | Gates | Sec. | Algo. | $\models$ |
| Napnet | Connectivity | 23 | 17 | 199 | 48 | 64 | 254 | 292 | 15875 | 95.1 | IC3 | ✓ |
| | P. coherence | 23 | 17 | 208 | 48 | 64 | 267 | 298 | 16041 | 31.9 | IC3 | ✓ |
| | Loop-free | 23 | 17 | 237 | 48 | 64 | 296 | 305 | 16289 | 52.6 | INT | ✓ |
| | Drop-free | 23 | 17 | 257 | 48 | 64 | 2288 | 325 | 30449 | 165.9 | IC3 | ✓ |

Table 2 presents our experimental results and indicates for each benchmark the model checking approach with the best performance. In the benchmarks where the specification is satisfied (✓), IC3 is the clear winner, in benchmarks where the specification is violated (✗), the best approach is bounded model checking with dynamic unrolling (BMC2/3). The results are encouraging: hardware model checking is effective for circuits constructed by our transformation with up to 400 latches and 27619 gates; falsification is possible for larger circuits with up to 1288 latches and 269943 gates. As a result, we were able to automatically verify with our prototype implementation updates for networks with topologies of up to 10 switches ($\#S$) and to falsify updates for topologies with up to 38 switches within the time bound of 30 min.

We investigated the cost of specifications drop and loop freedom compared with connectivity and packet coherence. Table 3 exemplarily shows the results for network topology *Napnet* from RU. Connectivity, packet coherence, and loop freedom have comparable runtimes due to similar formula and circuit sizes. Drop freedom is defined over transitions and, hence, expensive for our transformation.

## 8 Related Work

There is a large body of work on software-defined networks, see [28] for a good introduction. Specific solutions that were proposed for the network update problem include *consistent updates* [8,39] (cf. the introduction), *dynamic scheduling* [23], and *incremental updates* [25]. Model checking, including both explicit and SMT-based approaches, has previously been used to verify software-defined networks [1,6,30,31,36,43]. Closest to our work are models of networks as Kripke structures to use model checking for synthesis of correct network updates [12,32]. While they pursue *synthesis*, rather than verification of network updates, the approach is still based on a model checking algorithm that is called in each step of the construction of a sequence of updates. The model checking subroutine of the synthesizer assumes that each packet sees at most one switch that was updated after the packet entered the network. This restriction is implemented with explicit waits, which can afterwards often be removed by heuristics. Our model checking routine does not require this assumption. As it therefore allows for more general updates, it would be very interesting to add the new model checking algorithm into the synthesis procedure. Flow correctness also plays a role in other application areas like *access control* in physical spaces. Flow properties that are of interest in this setting, such as "from every room in the building there is a path to exit the building", have been formalized in a temporal logic [42].

There is a significant number of model checking tools (e.g., [24,40,41]) for Petri nets and an annual model checking contest [27]. In this contest, however, only LTL formulas with places as atomic propositions are checked. To the best of our knowledge, other model checking tools for Petri nets do not provide places and transitions as atomic propositions. Our encoding needs to reason about places and transitions to pose fairness conditions on the firing of transitions.

## 9 Conclusion

We have presented a model checking approach for the verification of data flow correctness in networks during concurrent updates of the network configuration. Key ingredients of the approach are Petri nets with transits, which superimpose the transit relation of data flows onto the flow relation of Petri nets, and Flow-LTL, which combines the specification of local data flows with the specification of global control. The model checking problem for Petri nets with transits and Flow-LTL specifications reduces to a circuit model checking problem. Our prototype tool implementation can verify and falsify realistic concurrent updates of software-defined networks with specifications like packet coherence.

In future work, we plan to extend this work to the synthesis of concurrent updates. Existing synthesis techniques use model checking as a subroutine to verify the correctness of the individual update steps [12,32]. We plan to study Flow-LTL specifications in the setting of Petri games [17], which describe the existence of controllers for asynchronous distributed processes. This would allow us to synthesize concurrent network updates without a central controller.

## References

1. Ball, T., et al.: Vericon: towards verifying controller programs in software-defined networks. In: Proceedings of ACM SIGPLAN Conference on Programming Language Design and Implementation, PLDI 2014, Edinburgh, United Kingdom, 9–11 June 2014, pp. 282–293 (2014). https://doi.org/10.1145/2594291.2594317
2. Berkeley Logic Synthesis and Verification Group: ABC: a system for sequential synthesis and verification, Release YMMDD. Version 1.01, Release 81030. http://www.eecs.berkeley.edu/~alanmi/abc/
3. Biere, A., Clarke, E., Raimi, R., Zhu, Y.: Verifying safety properties of a PowerPC− microprocessor using symbolic model checking without BDDs. In: Halbwachs, N., Peled, D. (eds.) CAV 1999. LNCS, vol. 1633, pp. 60–71. Springer, Heidelberg (1999). https://doi.org/10.1007/3-540-48683-6_8
4. Biere, A., Heljanko, K., Wieringa, S.: AIGER 1.9 and beyond. Tech. Rep. 11/2. Johannes Kepler University, Linz (2011)
5. Bradley, A.R.: SAT-based model checking without unrolling. In: Jhala, R., Schmidt, D. (eds.) VMCAI 2011. LNCS, vol. 6538, pp. 70–87. Springer, Heidelberg (2011). https://doi.org/10.1007/978-3-642-18275-4_7

6. Canini, M., Venzano, D., Perešíni, P., Kostić, D., Rexford, J.: A NICE way to test openflow applications. In: Proceedings of NSDI 2012, San Jose, CA, pp. 127–140 (2012). http://dl.acm.org/citation.cfm?id=2228298.2228312
7. Casado, M., Foster, N., Guha, A.: Abstractions for software-defined networks. Commun. ACM **57**(10), 86–95 (2014). https://doi.org/10.1145/2661061.2661063
8. Černý, P., Foster, N., Jagnik, N., McClurg, J.: Optimal consistent network updates in polynomial time. In: Gavoille, C., Ilcinkas, D. (eds.) DISC 2016. LNCS, vol. 9888, pp. 114–128. Springer, Heidelberg (2016). https://doi.org/10.1007/978-3-662-53426-7_9
9. Claessen, K., Eén, N., Sterin, B.: A circuit approach to LTL model checking. In: Proceedings of Formal Methods in Computer-Aided Design, FMCAD 2013, Portland, OR, USA, 20–23 October 2013, pp. 53–60 (2013). http://ieeexplore.ieee.org/document/6679391/
10. Clarkson, M.R., Finkbeiner, B., Koleini, M., Micinski, K.K., Rabe, M.N., Sánchez, C.: Temporal logics for hyperproperties. In: Abadi, M., Kremer, S. (eds.) POST 2014. LNCS, vol. 8414, pp. 265–284. Springer, Heidelberg (2014). https://doi.org/10.1007/978-3-642-54792-8_15
11. Eén, N., Mishchenko, A., Brayton, R.K.: Efficient implementation of property directed reachability. In: Proceedings of FMCAD, pp. 125–134 (2011). http://dl.acm.org/citation.cfm?id=2157675
12. El-Hassany, A., Tsankov, P., Vanbever, L., Vechev, M.: Network-wide configuration synthesis. In: Majumdar, R., Kunčak, V. (eds.) CAV 2017. LNCS, vol. 10427, pp. 261–281. Springer, Cham (2017). https://doi.org/10.1007/978-3-319-63390-9_14
13. Engelfriet, J.: Branching processes of Petri nets. Acta Informatica **28**(6), 575–591 (1991). https://doi.org/10.1007/BF01463946
14. Esparza, J., Heljanko, K.: Unfoldings - A Partial-Order Approach to Model Checking. Springer, Berlin (2008). https://doi.org/10.1007/978-3-540-77426-6
15. Finkbeiner, B., Gieseking, M., Hecking-Harbusch, J., Olderog, E.: Model checking data flows in concurrent network updates (full version). arXiv preprint. arXiv:1907.11061 (2019)
16. Finkbeiner, B., Gieseking, M., Olderog, E.-R.: ADAM: causality-based synthesis of distributed systems. In: Kroening, D., Păsăreanu, C.S. (eds.) CAV 2015. LNCS, vol. 9206, pp. 433–439. Springer, Cham (2015). https://doi.org/10.1007/978-3-319-21690-4_25
17. Finkbeiner, B., Olderog, E.: Petri games: synthesis of distributed systems with causal memory. Inf. Comput. **253**, 181–203 (2017). https://doi.org/10.1016/j.ic.2016.07.006
18. Finkbeiner, B., Rabe, M.N., Sánchez, C.: Algorithms for model checking HyperLTL and HyperCTL*. In: Kroening, D., Păsăreanu, C.S. (eds.) CAV 2015. LNCS, vol. 9206, pp. 30–48. Springer, Cham (2015). https://doi.org/10.1007/978-3-319-21690-4_3
19. Förster, K., Mahajan, R., Wattenhofer, R.: Consistent updates in software defined networks: on dependencies, loop freedom, and blackholes. In: Proceedings of IFIP Networking Conference, Networking 2016 and Workshops, Vienna, Austria, 17–19 May 2016, pp. 1–9 (2016). https://doi.org/10.1109/IFIPNetworking.2016.7497232
20. Foster, N., et al.: Frenetic: a network programming language. In: Proceeding of the 16th ACM SIGPLAN international conference on Functional Programming, ICFP 2011, Tokyo, Japan, 19–21 September 2011, pp. 279–291 (2011). https://doi.org/10.1145/2034773.2034812
21. Gieseking, M., Hecking-Harbusch, J.: AdamMC - a model checker for Petri nets with transits and flow-LTL (2019). https://doi.org/10.6084/m9.figshare.8313344

22. Jensen, K.: Coloured Petri Nets: Basic Concepts, Analysis Methods and Practical Use, vol. 1. Springer, Berlin (1992). https://doi.org/10.1007/978-3-662-03241-1
23. Jin, X., et al.: Dynamic scheduling of network updates. In: Proceedings of SIGCOMM 2014, Chicago, Illinois, USA, pp. 539–550 (2014). https://doi.org/10.1145/2619239.2626307
24. Kant, G., Laarman, A., Meijer, J., van de Pol, J., Blom, S., van Dijk, T.: LTSmin: high-performance language-independent model checking. In: Baier, C., Tinelli, C. (eds.) TACAS 2015. LNCS, vol. 9035, pp. 692–707. Springer, Heidelberg (2015). https://doi.org/10.1007/978-3-662-46681-0_61
25. Katta, N.P., Rexford, J., Walker, D.: Incremental consistent updates. In: Proceedings of HotSDN 2013, Hong Kong, China, pp. 49–54. ACM, New York (2013). https://doi.org/10.1145/2491185.2491191
26. Knight, S., Nguyen, H.X., Falkner, N., Bowden, R.A., Roughan, M.: The internet topology zoo. IEEE J. Sel. Areas Commun. **29**(9), 1765–1775 (2011). https://doi.org/10.1109/JSAC.2011.111002
27. Kordon, F., et al.: Complete Results for the 2019 Edition of the Model Checking Contest (2019)
28. Kreutz, D., Ramos, F.M.V., Veríssimo, P.J.E., Rothenberg, C.E., Azodolmolky, S., Uhlig, S.: Software-defined networking: a comprehensive survey. Proceedings of the IEEE, vol. 103, no. 1, pp. 14–76 (2015). https://doi.org/10.1109/JPROC.2014.2371999
29. Liu, H.H., Wu, X., Zhang, M., Yuan, L., Wattenhofer, R., Maltz, D.A.: zUpdate: updating data center networks with zero loss. In: Proceedings of ACM SIGCOMM 2013 Conference, SIGCOMM 2013, Hong Kong, China, 12–16 August 2013, pp. 411–422 (2013). https://doi.org/10.1145/2486001.2486005
30. Mai, H., Khurshid, A., Agarwal, R., Caesar, M., Godfrey, P.B., King, S.T.: Debugging the data plane with anteater. SIGCOMM Comput. Commun. Rev. **41**(4), 290–301 (2011). https://doi.org/10.1145/2043164.2018470
31. Majumdar, R., Tetali, S.D., Wang, Z.: Kuai: a model checker for software-defined networks. In: Proceedings of FMCAD, pp. 163–170 (2014). https://doi.org/10.1109/FMCAD.2014.6987609
32. McClurg, J., Hojjat, H., Černý, P.: Synchronization synthesis for network programs. In: Majumdar, R., Kunčak, V. (eds.) CAV 2017. LNCS, vol. 10427, pp. 301–321. Springer, Cham (2017). https://doi.org/10.1007/978-3-319-63390-9_16
33. McKeown, N., et al.: Openflow: enabling innovation in campus networks. Comput. Commun. Rev. **38**(2), 69–74 (2008). https://doi.org/10.1145/1355734.1355746
34. McMillan, K.L.: Craig interpolation and reachability analysis. In: Proceredings of Static Analysis, 10th International Symposium, SAS 2003, San Diego, CA, USA, 11–13 June 2003, p. 336 (2003). https://doi.org/10.1007/3-540-44898-5_18
35. Monsanto, C., Reich, J., Foster, N., Rexford, J., Walker, D.: Composing software defined networks. In: Proceedings of the 10th USENIX Symposium on Networked Systems Design and Implementation, NSDI 2013, Lombard, IL, USA, 2–5 April 2013, pp. 1–13 (2013). https://www.usenix.org/conference/nsdi13/technical-sessions/presentation/monsanto
36. Padon, O., Immerman, N., Karbyshev, A., Lahav, O., Sagiv, M., Shoham, S.: Decentralizing SDN policies. In: Proceedings of the 42nd Annual ACM SIGPLAN-SIGACT Symposium on Principles of Programming Languages, POPL 2015, Mumbai, India, 5–17 January 2015, pp. 663–676 (2015). https://doi.org/10.1145/2676726.2676990
37. Reisig, W.: Petri Nets: An Introduction. Springer, Berlin (1985). https://doi.org/10.1007/978-3-642-69968-9

38. Reitblatt, M., Canini, M., Guha, A., Foster, N.: Fattire: declarative fault tolerance for software-defined networks. In: Proceedings of the Second ACM SIGCOMM Workshop on Hot Topics in Software Defined Networking, HotSDN 2013, The Chinese University of Hong Kong, Hong Kong, China, 16 August 2013, pp. 109–114 (2013). https://doi.org/10.1145/2491185.2491187
39. Reitblatt, M., Foster, N., Rexford, J., Schlesinger, C., Walker, D.: Abstractions for network update. In: Proceedings of ACM SIGCOMM 2012 Conference, SIGCOMM 2012, Helsinki, Finland, 13–17 August 2012, pp. 323–334 (2012). https://doi.org/10.1145/2342356.2342427
40. Schmidt, K.: LoLA a low level analyser. In: Nielsen, M., Simpson, D. (eds.) ICATPN 2000. LNCS, vol. 1825, pp. 465–474. Springer, Heidelberg (2000). https://doi.org/10.1007/3-540-44988-4_27
41. Thierry-Mieg, Y.: Symbolic model-checking using ITS-tools. In: Baier, C., Tinelli, C. (eds.) TACAS 2015. LNCS, vol. 9035, pp. 231–237. Springer, Heidelberg (2015). https://doi.org/10.1007/978-3-662-46681-0_20
42. Tsankov, P., Dashti, M.T., Basin, D.: Access control synthesis for physical spaces. In: Proceedings of IEEE 29th Computer Security Foundations Symposium, CSF 2016, pp. 443–457 (2016). https://doi.org/10.1109/CSF.2016.38
43. Wang, A., Moarref, S., Loo, B.T., Topcu, U., Scedrov, A.: Automated synthesis of reactive controllers for software-defined networks. In: Proceedings of 21st IEEE International Conference on Network Protocols, ICNP 2013, Göttingen, Germany, 7–10 October 2013, pp. 1–6 (2013). https://doi.org/10.1109/ICNP.2013.6733666

# Performance Evaluation of the NDN Data Plane Using Statistical Model Checking

Siham Khoussi[1,2], Ayoub Nouri[1], Junxiao Shi[2], James Filliben[2], Lotfi Benmohamed[2], Abdella Battou[2], and Saddek Bensalem[1(✉)]

[1] Univ. Grenoble Alpes, CNRS, Grenoble Institute of Engineering Univ. Grenoble Alpes, VERIMAG, 38000 Grenoble, France
saddek.bensalem@univ-grenoble-alpes.fr
[2] National Institute of Standards and Technology, Gaithersburg, MD 20899, USA

**Abstract.** Named Data Networking (NDN) is an emerging internet architecture that addresses weaknesses of the Internet Protocol (IP). Since Internet users and applications have demonstrated an ever-increasing need for high speed packet forwarding, research groups have investigated different designs and implementations for fast NDN data plane forwarders and claimed they were capable of achieving high throughput rates. However, the correctness of these statements is not supported by any verification technique or formal proof. In this paper, we propose using a formal model-based approach to overcome this issue. We consider the NDN-DPDK prototype implementation of a forwarder developed at the National Institute of Standards and Technology (NIST), which leverages concurrency to enhance overall quality of service. We use our approach to improve its design and to formally demonstrate that it can achieve high throughput rates.

**Keywords:** NDN · SMC · Model-based design · Networking

## 1 Introduction

With the ever growing number of communicating devices, their intensive information usage and the increasingly critical security issues, research groups have recognized the limitations of the current Internet architecture based on the internet protocol (IP) [12]. Information-Centric Networking (ICN) is a new paradigm that transforms the Internet from a host-centric paradigm, as we know it today, to an end-to-end paradigm focusing on the content, hence more appropriate to our modern communication practices. It promises better security, mobility and scalability.

The identification of any commercial product or trade name does not imply endorsement or recommendation by the National Institute of Standards and Technology, nor is it intended to imply that the materials or equipment identified are necessarily the best available for the purpose.


Y.-F. Chen et al. (Eds.): ATVA 2019, LNCS 11781, pp. 534–550, 2019.
https://doi.org/10.1007/978-3-030-31784-3_31

Several research projects grew out of ICN. Examples include content-centric architecture, Data Oriented Network Architecture and many others [17], but one project stood out the most and was sponsored by the National Science Foundation (NSF) called Named Data Networking (NDN) [19]. NDN is gaining rapidly in popularity and has even started being advertised by major networking players [1].

IP was designed to answer a different challenge, that is of creating a communication network, where packets named only communication endpoints. The NDN project proposes to generalizes this setting, such that packets can name other objects, i.e. *"NDN changes the semantics of network services from delivering the packet to a given destination address to fetching data identified by a given name. The name in an NDN packet can name anything - an endpoint, a data chunk in a movie or a book, a command to turn on some lights, etc."* [19]. This simple change has deep implications in term of routers forwarding performance since data needs to be fetched from an initially unknown location.

Being a new concept, NDN (Sect. 2) has not undergone any formal verification work yet. The initial phase of the project was meant to come up with proof-of-concept prototypes for the proposed architecture. This has lead to a plethora of less performing implementations in terms of packets' forwarding rates (throughput). A lot of effort was then directed to optimizing NDN forwarders' performances by trying different data structures (Hash maps) and targeting different hardware (GP-GPU). Unfortunately, validation was mainly carried using pure simulation and testing techniques.

In this work, we take a step back and try to tackle the performance problem differently. We consider a model-based approach that allows for rigorous reasoning and formal verification (Sect. 3). In particular, we rely on the $\mathcal{S}$BIP framework [11,16] offering a stochastic component-based modeling formalism and Statistical Model Checking (SMC) engine. $\mathcal{S}$BIP is used along an iterative and systematic design process which consists of four phases (1) building a parameterized functional system model, which does not include performance (2) run a corresponding implementation in order to collect context information and performance measurements, characterized as probability distribution functions, (3) use these distributions to create a stochastic timed performance model and (4) use SMC to verify that the obtained model satisfies requirements of interest.

This approach is applied to verify that the NDN Data Plane Development Kit (NDN-DPDK) (an effort to develop a high performance forwarder for NDN networks at the National Institute of Standards and Technology (NIST)) can perform at high packet forwarding rates (Sect. 4). We investigate different design alternatives regarding concurrency (number of threads), system dimensioning (queues sizes) and deployment (mapping threads to multi-core). Using our approach, we were able to figure out what are the best design parameters to achieve higher performances (Sect. 5). These were taken into account by the NDN developers at NIST to enhance the ongoing design and implementation. To the best of our knowledge, this is the first work using formal methods in the context of the NDN project.

## 2 Named Data Networking

This section describes the NDN protocol and introduces the NDN-DPDK forwarder being designed and implemented at NIST.

### 2.1 Overview

NDN is a new Internet architecture different from IP. Its core design is exclusively based on naming contents rather than end points (IP addresses in the case of IP) and its routing is based on name prefix lookups [9].

The protocol supports three types of packets, namely *Interest, Data* and *Nack*. Interests are consumer requests sent to a network and Data packets are content producers replies. The Nack lets the forwarder know of the network's inability to forward Interests further. One of NDN's advantages is its ability to cache content (Data) everywhere the Data packet propagates, making the NDN router stateful. Thus, future Interests are no longer required to fetch the content from the source, instead Data could be retrieved directly from a closer node that has a cached copy.

Packets in NDN travel throughout a network as follow: first a client application sends an Interest with a name prefix that represents the requested content. Names in NDN are hierarchical (e.g., /YouTube/Alex/video1.mpg denotes a YouTube video called Video1.mpg by a Youtuber Alex). Then, this packet is forwarded by the network nodes based on its name prefix. Finally, this Interest is satisfied with Data by the original source that produced this content or by intermediate routers that cached it due to previous requests. It is also crucial to note that consecutive transmissions of Interest packets with similar name prefix might not lead to the same path each time, but could rather be forwarded along different paths each time a request is made, depending on the forwarding strategy in place. This means that the same Data could originate from different sources (producers or caches).

The NDN forwarding daemon (NFD) [3], has three different data structures: *Pending Interest Table (PIT), Content Store (CS)* and *Forwarding Interest Base (FIB)*. The packet processing, according to the NDN protocol, is as follows:

1 – For Interests, the forwarder, upon receiving an Interest, starts off by querying the CS for possible copies of the Data, if a CS match is found during this operation, the cached Data is returned downstream towards the client. Otherwise, an entry is created in the PIT with its source and destination faces (communication channels that the forwarder uses for packet forwarding) for record keeping. Using the PIT, the forwarder determines whether the Interest is looped in the network by checking a global unique number called Nonce in the Interest against existing previous PIT entries. If a duplicate nonce is found the Interest is dropped and a Nack of reason *Duplicate* is sent towards the requester. Otherwise, the FIB is queried for a possible next hop to forward the Interest towards an upstream node; if there is no FIB match, the Interest is immediately dropped and replied with a Nack of reason *No Route*.

2 – For Data, the forwarder starts off by querying the PIT. If a PIT entry is found, the Data is sent to downstream nodes listed in the PIT entry, then the PIT arms a timer to signal the deletion of this entry and a copy of the Data is immediately stored in the CS for future queries. If no record is found in the PIT, the Data is considered malicious and discarded.

## 2.2 The NDN-DPDK Forwarder

NDN-DPDK is a forwarder developed at NIST to follow the NDN protocol and to leverage concurrency. In this paper, we evaluate its capacity to achieve high throughput using Statistical Model Checking (SMC).

The NDN-DPDK forwarder's data plane has three stages: input, forwarding, and output (Fig. 1). Each stage is implemented as one or more threads pinned to CPU cores, allocated during initialization. **Input** threads receive packets from a Network Interface Card (NIC) through faces, decode them, and dispatch them to forwarding threads. The **forwarding** thread processes Interest, Data, or Nack packets according to the NDN protocol. **Output** threads send packets via faces then queue them for transmission on their respective NIC.

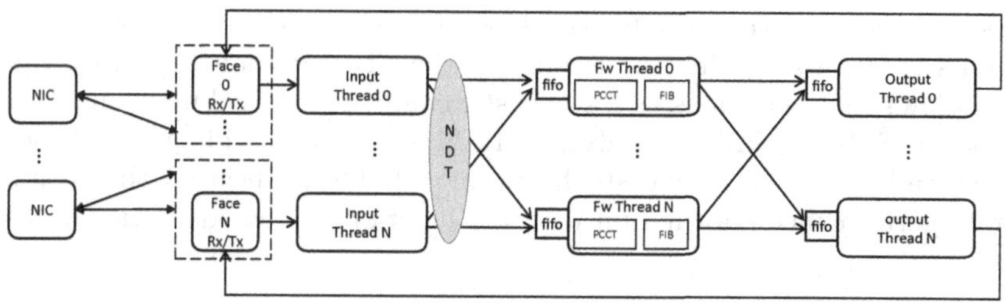


**Fig. 1.** Diagram of the NDN-DPDK forwarder

During forwarder initialization, each hardware NIC is provided with a large memory pool to place incoming packets. The input thread continuously polls the NIC to obtain bursts of 64 received packets. Then decodes, reassembles fragmented packets, and drops malformed ones. Then, it dispatches each packet to the responsible forwarding thread which is determined as follows: (a) For an Interest, the input thread computes SipHash of its first two name components and queries the last 16 bits of the hash value in the Name Dispatch Table (NDT), a 65536 entry lookup table configured by the operator, to select the forwarding thread. (b) Data and Nack carry a 1-byte field in the packet header which indicates the forwarding thread that handled the corresponding Interest. Once identified, Data (or Nack) will be dispatched to the same one.

The forwarding thread receives packets dispatched by input threads through a queue. It processes each packet according to the NDN protocol, using two data structures both implemented as hash tables: (a) The FIB records where the content might be available and which forwarding strategy is responsible for the name prefix. (b) The PIT-CS Composite Table (PCCT) records which downstream node requested a piece of content, and also serves as a content cache; it combines the PIT and CS found in a traditional NDN forwarder.

The output thread retrieves outgoing packets from forwarding threads through a queue. Packets are fragmented if necessary and queued for transmission on a NIC. The NIC driver automatically frees the memory used by packets after their transmission, making it available for newly arrived packets.

## 3 Formal Model-Based Approach

In this section, we describe the methodology used in this study which includes the underlying modeling formalism as well as the associated analysis technique.

### 3.1 Overview

Our methodology (Fig. 2) is based on a formal model. In order to evaluate a system's performance, its model must be faithful, i.e. it must reflect the real characteristics and behavior of this system. Moreover, to allow for exhaustive analyses, this model needs to be formally defined and the technique used for analysis needs to be trustworthy and scalable. Our approach adheres to these principles in two ways. First, by relying on the $\mathcal{S}$BIP formal framework (introduced below) that encompasses a stochastic component-based modeling formalism and an SMC engine for analysis [11]. Second, by providing a method for systematically building formal stochastic models for verification that combine accurate performance information with the functional behavior of the system.

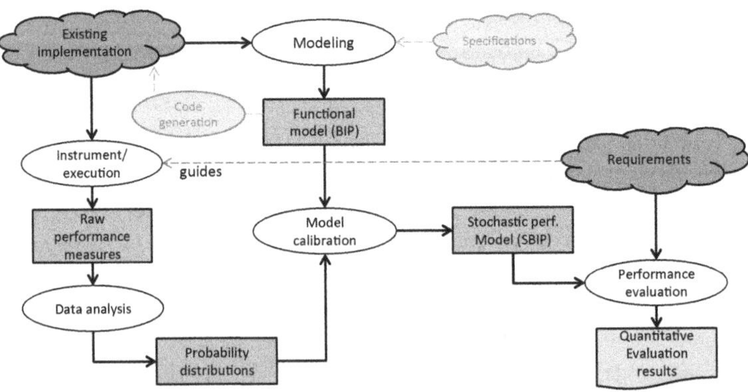


**Fig. 2.** Performance evaluation approach for NDN data plane.

This approach takes a functional system model and a set of requirements to verify. The functional model could be obtained from a high-level specification or an existing implementation (we use the latter in this paper). The system's implementation which could also be obtained by automatic code generation, is instrumented and used to collect performance measurements regarding the requirements of interest, e.g. throughput. These measurements are analyzed and characterized in the form of probability density functions with the help of statistical techniques such as sensitivity analysis and distribution fitting. The obtained probability density functions are then introduced in the functional model using a well defined calibration procedure [15]. The latter produces a stochastic timed model (when measurements concern time), which will be analyzed using the SMC engine.

Note that the considered models in this approach or workflow can be parameterized with respect to different aspects that we want to analyze and explore. Basically, the defined components types are designed to be instantiated in different context, e.g. with different probability density functions thus showing different performance behaviors. While, the model considered for analysis using SMC is a specific instance for which all the parameters are fixed, some degree of parameterization is still allowed on the verified requirements.

### 3.2 Stochastic Component-Based Modeling in BIP

BIP (Behavior, Interaction, Priority) is a highly expressive component based framework for rigorous system design [6]. It allows the construction of complex, hierarchically structured models from atomic components characterized by their behavior and their interfaces. Such components are transition systems enriched with variables. Transitions are used to move from a source to a destination location. Each time a transition is taken, component variables may be assigned new values, computed by user-defined C/C++ functions. Composition of BIP components is expressed by layered application of interactions and priorities. Interactions express synchronization constraints between actions of the composed components while priorities are used to filter among possible interactions e.g. to express scheduling policies.

The stochastic semantics of BIP were initially introduced in [14] and recently extended for real-time systems in [16]. They enable the definition of stochastic components encompassing probabilistic variables updated according to user-defined probability distributions. The underlying mathematical model behind this is a Discrete Time Markov Chain. These are modeled as classical BIP components augmented with probabilistic variables as shown in Fig. 3 and depicts a client behavior in a client-server setting where the client issues a request (**snd**) each $p$ time units. The period $p$ is set probabilistically by sampling a distribution function ($p \rhd$) given as a parameter of the model. Time is introduced by explicit **tick** transitions and waiting

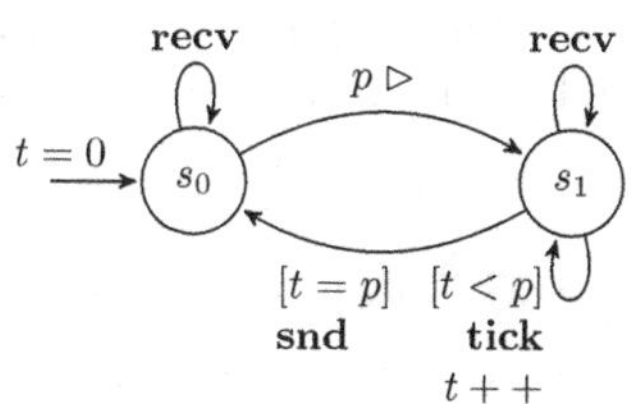


**Fig. 3.** A stochastic BIP component; client behavior issuing requests each time unit $p$.

is modeled by exclusive guards on the **tick** and **snd** transitions with respect to time (captured in this example by the variable $t$).

### 3.3 Statistical Model Checking in a Nutshell

Statistical model-checking (*SMC*) [8,18] is a formal verification method that combines simulation with statistical reasoning to provide quantitative answers on whether a stochastic system satisfies some requirements. It was successfully used in various domains such as biology [7], communication [4] and avionics [5]. It has the advantage to be applicable to models and implementations (provided that they meet specific assumptions) in addition to capturing rare events. The $\mathcal{S}$BIP SMC engine [11] implements well-known statistical algorithms for stochastic systems verification, namely, Hypothesis Testing [18], Probability Estimation [8] and Rare Events. In addition, it provides an automated parameters exploration procedure. The tools take as inputs a stochastic BIP model, a Linear-time/Metric Temporal Logic (LTL/MTL) property to check and a set of confidence parameters required by the statistical test.

## 4 NDN-DPDK Modeling

In this section we present the modeling process of the NDN-DPDK from a functional to a stochastic timed model for throughput evaluation.

### 4.1 A Parameterized Functional BIP Model

Figure 4 depicts the BIP model of the NDN-DPDK forwarder introduced in Sect. 2 which shows its architecture in terms of interacting BIP components that can easily be matched to the ones in Fig. 1. The presented model is parameterized with respect to the number of components, their mapping into specific CPU cores, FIFOs sizes, etc. Due to space limitation, we present in [10] the behaviors of all the components of the NDN-DPDK forwarder in Fig. 4. It is worth mentioning that the model is initially purely functional and untimed. Time is introduced later through the calibration procedure.

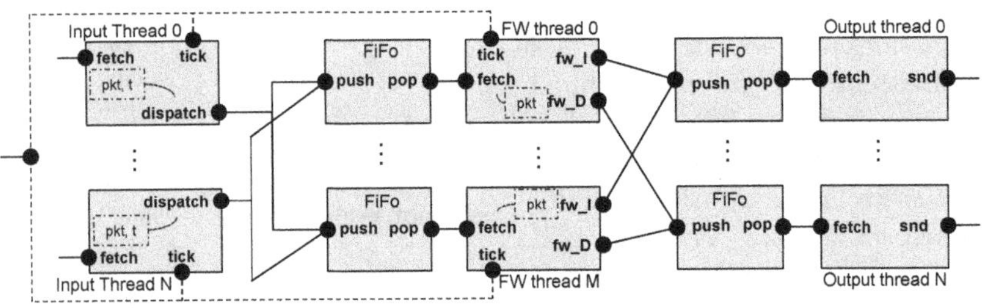


**Fig. 4.** A functional BIP model of the NDN-DPDK forwarder

### 4.2 Building the Performance Model

To build a performance model for our analysis, we consider the network topology in Fig. 5 which has a traffic generator client (consumer), a forwarder (NDN-DPDK) and a traffic generator server (producer), arranged linearly.

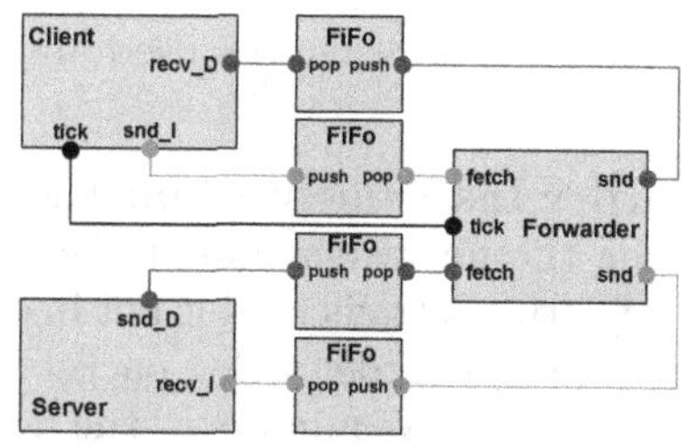


**Fig. 5.** Considered network topology (Color figure online)

The green line shows the Interest packet path from the client to the producer through the forwarder and the red line indicates the Data path towards the client. The structure of our model (Fig. 4) calls for four distribution functions to characterize performance: (a) Interest dispatching latency in input threads. (b) Data dispatching latency in input threads. (c) Interest forwarding latency in forwarding threads. (d) Data forwarding latency in forwarding threads. Notice that Nack packets are out of the scope of these experiments. We identified the following factors that can *potentially* affect the system's performance:

1. **Number of forwarding threads.** Having more forwarding threads distributes workload onto more CPU cores. The cores can compete for the shared L3 cache, and potentially increase forwarding latency of individual packets.
2. **Placement of forwarding threads onto Non Uniform Memory Access nodes (NUMA).** Input threads and their memory pools are always placed on the same NUMA node as the Ethernet adapter whereas the output threads and the forwarding threads can be moved across the two nodes. If a packet is dispatched to a forwarding thread on a different node, the forwarding latency is generally higher because memory access is crossing NUMA boundaries.
3. **Packet name length measured by the number of its components.** A longer name requires more iterations during table lookups, potentially increasing Interest forwarding latency.
4. **Data payload length.** Although the Data payloads are never copied, a higher payload length increases demand for memory bandwidth, thus potentially increasing latencies.
5. **Interest sending rate from the client.** Higher sending rate requires more memory bandwidth, thus potentially increasing latencies. It may also lead to packet loss if queues between input and forwarding threads overflow.
6. **Number of PIT entries.** Although the forwarder's PIT is a hash table that normally offers $O(1)$ lookup complexity, a large number of PIT entries inevitably leads to hash collisions, which could increase forwarding latency.
7. **Forwarding thread's queue capacity.** The queues are suspected to impact the overall throughput of the router through packet overflow and loss rates. However, it does not influence packets individual latencies.

After identifying the factors with potential influence on packet latency, we instrument the real forwarder to collect latency measurements. Then, perform statistical analysis to identify which factors are more significant. This narrows down the number of factors used and associated distribution functions.

**Forwarder Instrumentation.** Factors 1, 2, 3, 4, 5 and 7 can be controlled by adjusting the forwarder and traffic generator configuration, while factor 6 is a result of network traffic and is not in our control. To collect the measurement, we modified the forwarder to log packets latencies as well as the PIT size after each burst of packets. We minimized the extra work that input threads and forwarding threads have to perform to enable instrumentation, leaving the measurement collection to a separate logging thread or post-processing scripts. It is important to mention that this task does in fact introduce timing overhead. Therefore, the values obtained will have a bias (overestimate) that translates into additional latency but the trends observed remain valid.

We conducted the experiment on a Supermicro server equipped with two Intel E5-2680V2 processors, 512 GB DDR4 memory in two channels, and four Mellanox ConnectX-5 100 Gbit/s Ethernet adapters. The hardware resources are evenly divided into two NUMA nodes. To create the topology in Fig. 5, we connected two QSFP28 passive copper cables to connect the four Ethernet adapters and form two point-to-point links. All forwarders and traffic generator processes were allocated with separate hardware resources and could only communicate over Ethernet adapters.

In each experiment, the consumer transmitted either at sending intervals of one Interest per 700 ns or per 500 ns under 255 different name prefixes. There were 255 FIB entries registered in the NDN-DPDK forwarder at runtime (one for each name prefix used by the consumer), all of which pointed to the producer node. The producer would reply to every Interest with a Data packet of the same name. The forwarder's logging thread was configured to discard the first 67 108 864 samples (either latency trace or PIT size) during warm-up period, and then collect the next 16 777 216 samples and ignore the cool down session. Each experiment represents about 4 million Interest-Data exchanges. We repeated the experiment using different combinations of the factors in Table 1 and the following NUMA arrangements:

(P1) Client and server faces and forwarding threads are all on the same NUMA,
(P2) Client face and forwarding threads on one NUMA, server face on the other,
(P3) Client face on one NUMA, forwarding threads and server face on the other,
(P4) Client face and server face on one NUMA, forwarding threads on the other.

**Table 1.** Factors used. NUMA mapping is described below.

| Factors | Forwarding threads | Name length | Payload length | Sending intervals |
|---|---|---|---|---|
| Values | {1, 2, 3, 4, 5, 6, 7, 8} | {3, 7, 13} | {0, 300, 600, 900, 1200} | {500 ns, 700 ns} |

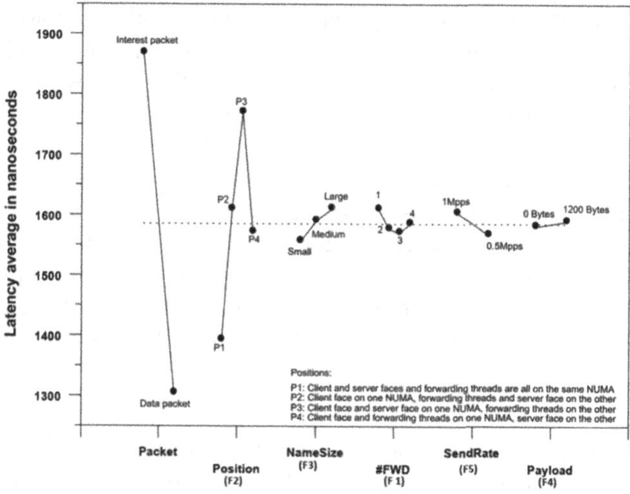


**Fig. 6.** Main effects plot for interest and data packets

In P1, packet latency is expected to be the smallest because all processes are placed on the same NUMA therefore, no inter-socket communication and no overhead are introduced. In P4, both Interests and Data packets are crossing NUMA boundaries twice since the forwarding threads are pinned to one NUMA whereas the client and the server faces, connected to the Ethernet adapters, reside on another. This is suspected to increase packet latency tremendously as opposed to P1, P2 and P3. These suspicions predict that placement P1 is the best case scenario and placement P4 is obviously the worst. However, we aim at getting more insight and confidence through quantitative formal analysis. This will provide a recommendation as to which placement is better suited based on the remaining parameters combinations.

**Model Fitting.** Before calibrating our functional BIP model with multiple distinctive probability distributions representing each combination of the factors, we choose to reduce the number of used distributions by performing a sensitivity analysis. This analysis examines the impact of several factors on the response (packet latency) and discovers the ones that are more important. In this paper, we use DataPlot [2] to produce the Main Effect Plot (Fig. 6) for factors (1) to (5).

The plot shows steeper line slopes for the packet type (packet type is not a factor. We intend to show how the NDN-DPDK forwarder processes both Interest and Data differently) as well as factors (1), (2), (3), and (5) which indicates a greater magnitude of the main effect on the latency. However, it shows almost a horizontal line for factor 4 inducing an insignificant impact on the latency. The latter is explained by the fact that the forwarder processes packet names (headers) only and doesn't read Data payloads. As for the PIT size (factor 6), it is expected to heavily increase packet latency when it is full. However, because this table's implementation is optimized for high performance and entries are continuously removed when Data packets arrive (PIT entries being satisfied), we confirmed through a correlation analysis that we can ignore this factor's impact.

Based on the analysis above, we build distribution functions for each of the factors that have greater impacts on packet latency in this study. These factors are: 1. (1) the number of forwarding threads, 2. (2) NUMA placement, 3. (3) packet name size (header), 4. (5) sending rate and, 5. (7) FIFO capacity (FIFO impacts the loss rates and not individual packet latency). We refer the reader to [10] to understand how we obtained the probability distributions for these factors.

**Model Calibration.** Calibration is a well defined model transformation that transforms functional components into stochastic timed ones [13]. In this section, we use the probability distributions obtained above to calibrate the functional BIP model of the NDN-DPDK forwarder shown in Fig. 4. Due to space limitations, we refer the reader to [10] where we describe the calibrated models of all the BIP components of the NDN-DPDK forwarder.

In the next section, we perform SMC on the calibrated model of the NDN-DPDK forwarder and explain the results.

## 5 Performance Analysis Using SMC

### 5.1 Experimental Settings

We run the SMC tests using the probability estimation algorithm (PE) with a required confidence of $\alpha = 0.1$ and a precision of $\delta = 0.1$. Each test is configured with a different combination of values for the factors previously presented. And each execution of a test with a single set of parameters generates a single trace. The property evaluated with the SMC engine is: *Estimate the probability that all the issued Interests are satisfied, i.e. a Data is obtained in return for each Interest.* The SMC result is a probability estimation $\hat{p}$ which should be interpreted as being within the confidence interval $[\hat{p} - \delta, \hat{p} + \delta]$ with probability at least $(1 - \alpha)$. In the experiments below, the shown results corresponds to $\hat{p} = 1$.

### 5.2 Analyses Results

**Queues Dimensioning.** First, we explore the impact of sizing forwarding threads queues. Each forwarding thread has an input queue. Initially, we consider a model with a single forwarding thread and vary its queue capacity with 128, 1024 or 4096 (in packets). Then set the client's sending rate to: $10^5$ packets per second (pps), $10^6$ pps or $10^7$ pps. The results are shown in Fig. 7a. The Y-axis represents the Interest satisfaction rate such that 100% (resp. 0%) indicates

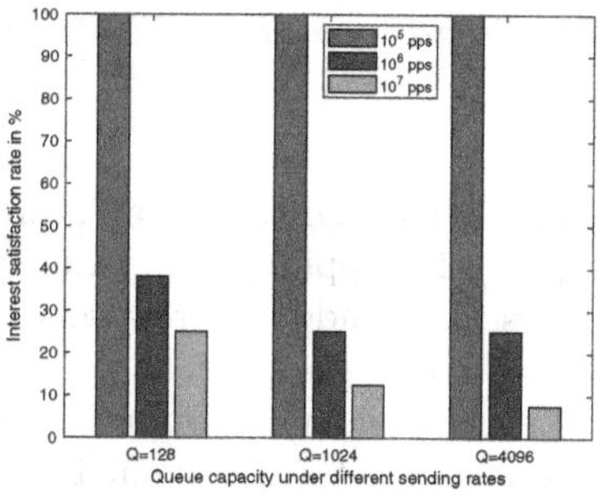


(a) One Forwarding thread with different sending rates.

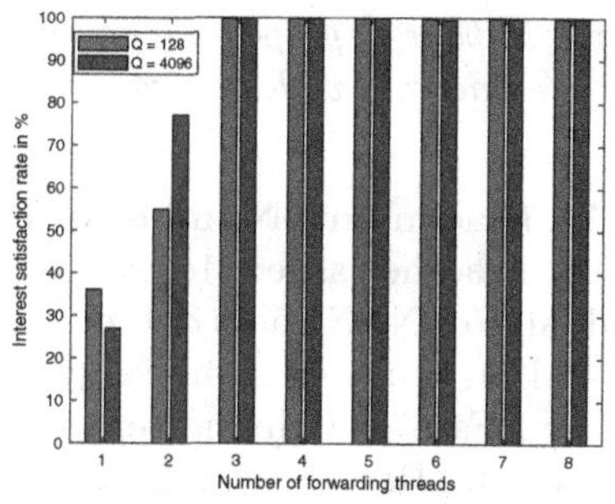


(b) Many Forwarding threads with a sending rate set to $10^6$ pps.

**Fig. 7.** Exploration results of the forwarding threads queues sizes. (Color figure online)

no loss (resp. 100% loss) and the x axis represents the queue capacity under different sending rates.

Figure 7a indicates that at $10^5$ pps (blue), the Interest satisfaction rate is 100%. This means that the forwarder (with one forwarding thread) is capable of handling all packets at this sending rate ($10^5$ pps of packet size 1500 bytes is equivalent to 1.2 Gbps), under any queue size. However, under a faster sender rate (where a single forwarder shows signs of packet loss) we unexpectedly observed a better Interest satisfaction rate with a smaller queue (Q = 128). After a thorough investigation of the real implementation, we found out that the queues don't have proper management in terms of insertion and eviction policies that would give priority to Data over Interest packets. In the absence of such policy, more Interests would be queued while Data packets would be dropped resulting in Interests not being satisfied, thus lower performance (Interest satisfaction rate). *It is thus advised for the final implementation of the NDN-DPDK forwarder, to use a queue capacity smaller than* 128 *packets when the forwarder has a single forwarding thread and packets are sent at a fast rate.*

Similarly, we explore whether this observation remains true with more forwarding threads. In order to do that, we run SMC again on eight different models each with a different number of forwarding threads (1 to 8) under a sending rate of $10^6$ pps (1 Interest per 1 us) where a loss rate was observed in Fig. 7a. Then, we experimented with two queue capacities, namely 128 and 4096 packets. The results are reported in Fig. 7b. The x Axis represents the number of forwarding threads while the y axis depicts the Interest satisfaction rate.

We observe that the queue size matters mainly in the case of a model with one and two forwarding threads. In fact, for a two threads model, a bigger queue size is preferred to maximize the performance, unlike when a single thread is used. As for the other six models, both sizes achieve almost 100% Interest satisfaction. This is due to the fact that three forwarding threads or more are capable of splitting the workload at $10^6$ pps and can pull enough packets from each queue with a minimum loss rate of 0.02%. *This result stresses that, to avoid being concerned about a proper queue size, more threads are needed for handling a faster sending rate with minimum Interest loss.*

**NUMA Placement, Number of Forwarding Threads and Packet Name Length.** Another aspect to explore, is the impact of mapping the forwarding threads and/or NDN Faces to the two NUMA nodes (0, 1) under different sending rates and for multiple name lengths where Face 0 exchanges packets with the client and Face 1 with the server. To do that, we consider the four NUMA arrangements (P1), (P2), (P3) and (P4) in Sect. 4 as well as the factors in Table 1 in the SMC analysis.

In Figs. 8, 9, 10, 11, 12 and 13, each row represents experiments with similar packet name lengths {small = 3, medium = 7, large = 13} and a queue capacity of 4096. The right-hand column indicates results for a faster sending rate of $2 * 10^6$ pps (500 ns interval) while the left-hand one shows results for a slower sending rate of $1.42 * 10^6$ pps (700 ns interval). The six figures includes four curves where each corresponds to the four NUMA arrangement options: P1 to P4.

The six Figs. 8, 9, 10, 11, 12 and 13 show that Interest satisfaction rates scale up with the increase of forwarding threads then reach a saturation plateau where

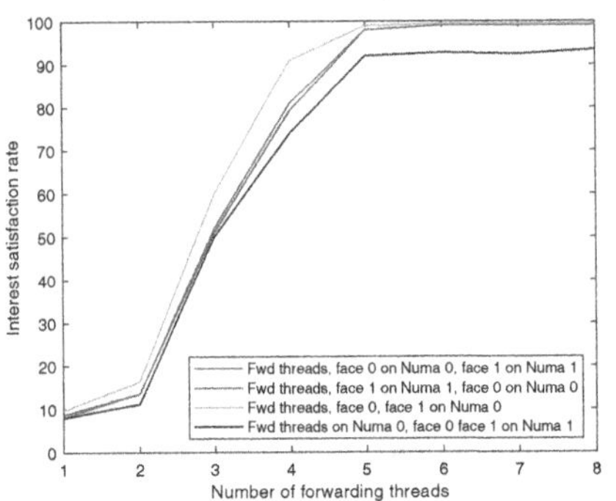


**Fig. 8.** Small names, 700 ns

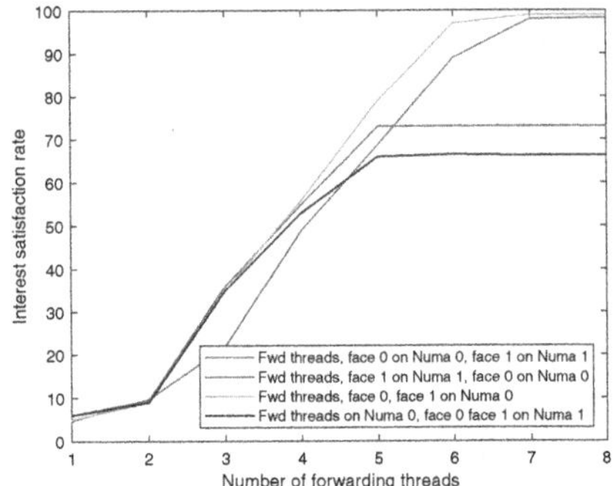


**Fig. 9.** Small names, 500 ns

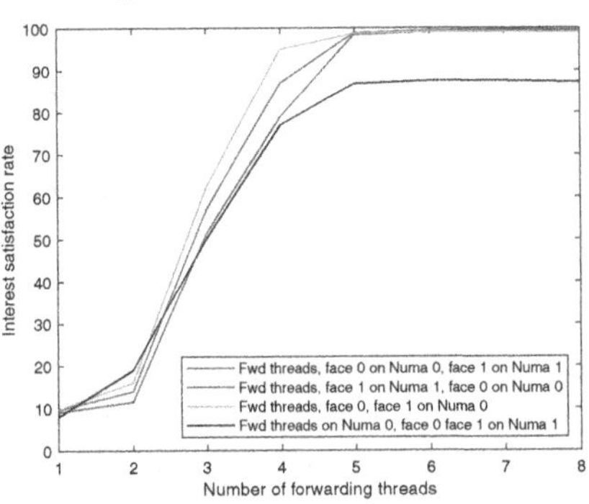


**Fig. 10.** Medium names, 700 ns

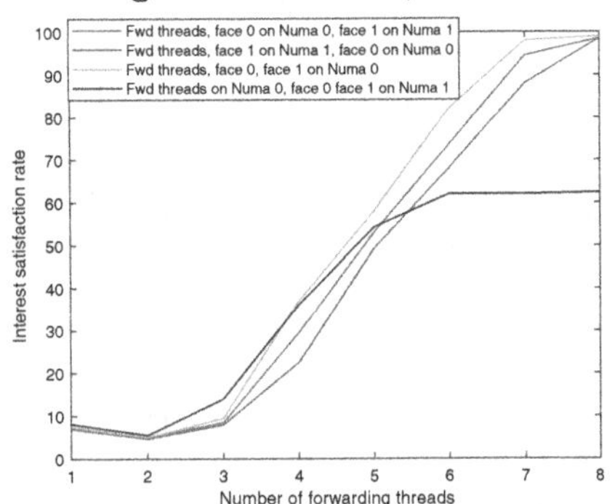


**Fig. 11.** Medium names, 500 ns

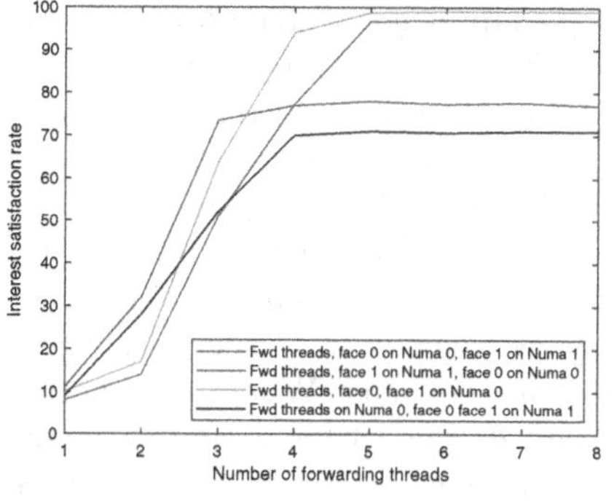


**Fig. 12.** Large names, 700 ns

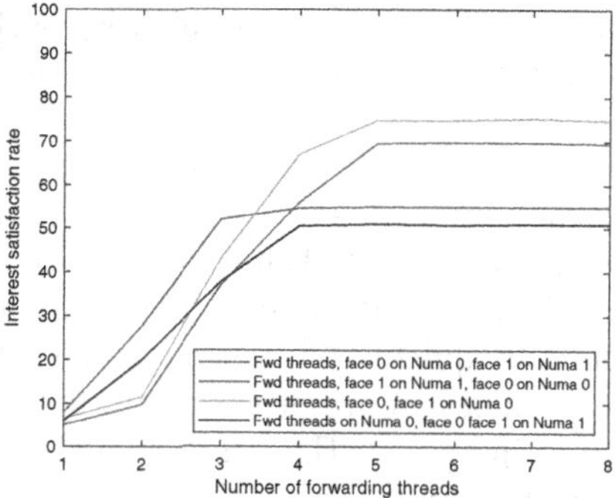


**Fig. 13.** Large names, 500 ns

adding more threads can no longer improve the performances. Furthermore, with fewer forwarding threads, the loss rate is unavoidable and exceeds 80%. This is because the sending rate is faster than the forwarding threads processing capabilities causing their FIFO queues to saturate and start dropping packets frequently. However, under a slower sending rate and packets with small, medium and large name lengths (3, 7, 13), Figs. 8, 10 and 12 show that a maximum satisfaction rate of over 90% is achievable with only five forwarding threads. Whereas when the client is generating packets faster at 2 Mpps, a saturation plateau of over 90% is reached at six threads or more for small and medium names (Figs. 9 and 11) and a plateau of slightly over 70%, with five threads, for larger names (Fig. 13). Also, Figs. 8 and 10 demonstrate that placing all processes (threads and faces) on a single NUMA (placement P1) outperforms the other three options. This observation is explained by the absence of inter-socket communication thus less timing overhead added such as in the case of the purple plot where packets are crossing NUMA boundaries twice from Face 0 to the forwarding threads then through Face 1 and back (placement P4).

Figures 9 and 11 show the impact of increasing the sending rate on packets with smaller names. In this case, it is preferred to also position all the processes on one NUMA such as the case of the yellow plot of the P1 series because NUMA boundary crossing usually downgrades the performance. In fact, the difference between no NUMA crossing and the double crossing (yellow and purple series respectively) is approximately 30% loss rate with more than five threads. The second best option P2 which is placing the forwarding threads on the NUMA receiving Interest packets with Face 0 (NUMA hosting the Ethernet adapter that receives Interests from the Client). However, when the number of threads is not in the saturation zone and the threads get overworked and start to loose packets, it is recommended to opt for placement P3. *Based on these results, we recommend that for small to medium names, to use a maximum of eight threads but no less than five arranged as in placement P1 for optimum performances under a slower or a faster sending rate.*

With a larger name however, Fig. 12 depicts an unexpected behaviour when using three threads or less. In this case, placing the forwarding threads on the same NUMA as Face 1 (which is the Ethernet adapter connected to the server and receives Data packets), surpasses the other three options. Our explanation is that since forwarding threads take longer times to process incoming packets due to their longer name and timely lookup, particularly for Interests as they are searched by names inside the two tables (PCCT and FIB) rather than a token such as the case for Data packets. Placing the forwarding threads with the Data receiving Ethernet adapter connected to Face 1, has the potential to yield better results by quickly processing packets after a quick token search especially when the workload is bigger than the threads' processing capacity. When the sending rate is increased, the same results are observed in Fig. 13 for a similar name length but with a decrease in performance. *Thus, we recommend for larger names to use NUMA arrangement P3 only when the number of forwarding threads is less than three regardless of the sending rate (not advised due to high loss rate).*

## 6 Lessons Learned and Future Work

This study shed light on a new networking technology called Named Data Networking (NDN) and its forwarding daemon. Ongoing NDN research includes the development of high-speed data plane forwarders that can operate at a hundred gigabits per second while using modern multi-processor server hardware and kernel bypass libraries. In this paper, we discussed the results of a performance evaluation effort we undertook to reach well-founded conclusions on how the NDN forwarder prototype developed by NIST (NDN-DPDK) behaves in a network in terms of achievable Interest satisfaction rate.

We conducted an extensive analysis under different factors such as the number of threads carrying tasks and function mapping to CPUs, using a model-based approach and statistical model checking. Given the wide array of design parameters involved, this effort contributes valuable insights into protocol operation and guides the choice of such parameters. The use of statistical model checking for performance analysis allowed us to discover potential sub-optimal operation and propose appropriate enhancement to the queue management solution. This has been taken into account in the ongoing NDN-DPDK forwarder implementation. Moreover, our extensive analysis provides a characterization of the achievable forwarding throughput for a given forwarder design and available hardware resources which would not have been possible to obtain, with such controllable accuracy, using traditional measurements and statistic methods. Furthermore, these results were communicated and shared with members of the NDN community in a conference throughout a poster interaction and gained attention from researchers who were interested in the methodology and its applications. In addition to that, the use of a BIP model refined at the right level of abstraction allows the generation of executable code that could be used instead of the real implementation.

It is important to note however, that our analysis depends largely on a stochastic model obtained using samples of data collected from the actual implementation of the forwarder which is suspected to have introduced timing overhead. Nevertheless, the trends observed throughout this study remain accurate and have provided valuable insight to the actual code. In the future, this analysis will be extended to answer the reverse question, namely **Given a desired throughput, what is the best hardware setup and the forwarder design to use?** Rather than the question **Given a hardware setup and a forwarder design, what is the maximum achievable throughput?** that we have investigated in this paper.

## References

1. Brown, B.: Cisco, UCLA & more launch named data networking consortium. [online] network world (2019). https://www.networkworld.com/article/2602109/ucla-cisco-more-join-forces-to-replace-tcpip.html
2. Dataplot homepage. https://www.itl.nist.gov/div898/software/dataplot/homepage.htm
3. NFD Developer's Guide. Tech. rep. http://named-data.net/techreports.html
4. Basu, A., Bensalem, S., Bozga, M., Caillaud, B., Delahaye, B., Legay, A.: Statistical abstraction and model-checking of large heterogeneous systems. In: Hatcliff, J., Zucca, E. (eds.) FMOODS/FORTE -2010. LNCS, vol. 6117, pp. 32–46. Springer, Heidelberg (2010). https://doi.org/10.1007/978-3-642-13464-7_4
5. Basu, A., Bensalem, S., Bozga, M., Delahaye, B., Legay, A., Sifakis, E.: Verification of an AFDX infrastructure using simulations and probabilities. In: Barringer, H., et al. (eds.) RV 2010. LNCS, vol. 6418, pp. 330–344. Springer, Heidelberg (2010). https://doi.org/10.1007/978-3-642-16612-9_25
6. Basu, A., Bozga, M., Sifakis, J.: Modeling heterogeneous real-time components in BIP. In: Proceedings of the Fourth IEEE International Conference on Software Engineering and Formal Methods, SEFM 2006, pp. 3–12. IEEE Computer Society, Washington (2006)
7. David, A., Larsen, K.G., Legay, A., Mikucionis, M., Poulsen, D.B., Sedwards, S.: Statistical model checking for biological systems. Int. J. Softw. Tools Technol. Transfer **17**(3), 351–367 (2015)
8. Hérault, T., Lassaigne, R., Magniette, F., Peyronnet, S.: Approximate probabilistic model checking. In: Steffen, B., Levi, G. (eds.) VMCAI 2004. LNCS, vol. 2937, pp. 73–84. Springer, Heidelberg (2004). https://doi.org/10.1007/978-3-540-24622-0_8
9. Jacobson, V., Smetters, D.K., Thornton, J.D., Plass, M.F., Briggs, N.H., Braynard, R.L.: Networking named content (2009). https://named-data.net/wp-content/uploads/Jacob.pdf
10. Khoussi, S., et al.: Performance evaluation of a NDN forwarder using statistical model checking. CoRR. http://arxiv.org/abs/1905.01607 (2019)
11. Mediouni, B.L., Nouri, A., Bozga, M., Dellabani, M., Legay, A., Bensalem, S.: $\mathcal{S}$BIP 2.0: statistical model checking stochastic real-time systems. In: Lahiri, S.K., Wang, C. (eds.) ATVA 2018. LNCS, vol. 11138, pp. 536–542. Springer, Cham (2018). https://doi.org/10.1007/978-3-030-01090-4_33
12. Named data networking project. Tech. rep., USA (October 2010). http://named-data.net/techreport/TR001ndn-proj.pdf
13. Nouri, A.: Rigorous system-level modeling and performance evaluation for embedded system design. Ph. D. thesis. Grenoble Alpes University, France (2015)
14. Nouri, A., Bensalem, S., Bozga, M., Delahaye, B., Jegourel, C., Legay, A.: Statistical model checking QoS properties of systems with SBIP. Int. J. Softw. Tools Technol. Transfer (STTT) **17**(2), 171–185 (2015)

15. Nouri, A., Bozga, M., Molnos, A., Legay, A., Bensalem, S.: ASTROLABE: a rigorous approach for system-level performance modeling and analysis. ACM Trans. Embedded Comput. Syst. **15**(2), 31:1–31:26 (2016)
16. Nouri, A., Mediouni, B.L., Bozga, M., Combaz, J., Bensalem, S., Legay, A.: Performance evaluation of stochastic real-time systems with the SBIP framework. Int. J. Crit. Comput.-Based Syst. **8**(3–4), 340–370 (2018)
17. Xylomenos, G., et al.: A survey of information-centric networking research. IEEE Commun. Surv. Tutorials **16**(2), 1024–1049 (2014)
18. Younes, H.L.S.: Verification and planning for stochastic processes with asynchronous events. Ph. D. thesis, Carnegie Mellon (2005)
19. Zhang, L., et al.: Named data networking. SIGCOMM Comput. Commun. Rev. **44**(3), 66–73 (2014)

# Author Index

Printed in the United States
by Bookmasters

Printed in the United States
By Bookmasters